WILKINSON'S
ROAD TRAFFIC
OFFENCES

AUSTRALIA

The Law Book Company Ltd.
Sydney; Melbourne; Brisbane

CANADA AND U.S.A.

The Carswell Company Ltd.
Toronto

INDIA

N.M. Tripathi Private Ltd.
Bombay

NEW ZEALAND

Sweet & Maxwell Ltd.
Wellington

WILKINSON'S
Road Traffic Offences

Eighth Edition by

P. J. HALNAN

Solicitor
Clerk to the Cambridge (County) Justices

LONDON
Oyez Publishing
1975

©
OYEZ PUBLISHING LIMITED
OYEZ HOUSE, 237 LONG LANE, LONDON, SE1 4PU
1975

ISBN 85120 238 1

First Published	.	.	.	.	*October* 1953
Second Edition	.	.	.	.	*November* 1956
Reprinted	.	.	.	.	*December* 1958
Third Edition	.	.	.	.	*October* 1960
Fourth Edition	.	.	.	.	*June* 1963
Fifth Edition	.	.	.	.	*December* 1965
Sixth Edition	.	.	.	.	*September* 1970
Seventh Edition	.	.	.	.	*February* 1973
Reprinted	.	.	.	.	*March* 1974
Eighth Edition	.	.	.	.	*November* 1975

Printed in Great Britain by Butler & Tanner Ltd
Frome and London

PREFACE

In his preface to the first edition, the late George Wilkinson stated that one of the main difficulties of those who have to concern themselves with the subject of road traffic offences is the large number of statutory provisions and (in particular) statutory regulations in which the law is to be found. As edition has succeeded edition, the truth of this statement has needed less and less emphasis. Cases on the drink/driving law continue to flow at full flood. Because of this, I was compelled largely to re-write the section on drink/driving for the last edition; for this edition I have found it necessary to devote a complete new chapter (Chapter IV) to the subject. Because of this growth of case law and of statute law, this edition is some 200 pages longer than the seventh edition.

The law is generally stated in the text as at the 1st July, 1975, but the opportunity has been taken to incorporate other parts of the Road Traffic Act, 1974, which were thought likely to be brought into force by the time of publication. Accordingly, I have included a section on vehicle owner liability (pages 584 to 593). These provisions come into force on 1st September, 1975, but unfortunately other provisions, notably those prohibiting parking on verges, footpaths and central reservations (pages 395 to 396), and some of the provisions of the Transport Act, 1968, are still not in force at the time of writing (August, 1975).

I would again like to thank correspondents for suggesting alterations or improvements. I would also like to place on record my appreciation to Mr. Geoffrey Norman for helping to read the proofs and to my Deputy, Mr. R. J. Bailey, for help in the compilation and checking of the Appendices. Any errors, however, are mine.

CAMBRIDGE   PATRICK HALNAN
AUGUST, 1975

CONTENTS

PAGE

Preface v

Table of Cases ix

Table of Statutes lvii

Table of Rules lxxxv

Abbreviations ci

Chapter I: Definitions 1

Chapter II: Procedure and Evidence 56
1. Commencing Proceedings 56
2. Venue 65
3. Limitation of Time 68
4. The Hearing 71
5. Evidence 101

Chapter III: Notices of Intended Prosecution 127

Chapter IV: Drink/Driving Offences 144

Chapter V: Other Road Traffic Offences 253
1. Causing Death and Injury by Driving .. 253
2. Dangerous and Careless Driving and Cycling .. 262
3. Traffic Signs and Police Signals 294
4. Speed Limits 316
5. Reporting Accidents 341
6. Protective Motor Cycle Helmets 349
7. Taking Conveyances 351
8. Insurance 365
9. Obstruction 383
10. Lights on Vehicles 403
11. Motor Vehicles (Construction and Use) Regulations, 1973 410
12. The Pedestrian Crossings Regulations 436

Chapter V: Other Road Traffic Offences—*continued*

		PAGE
13.	School Crossing Patrols	456
14.	Refusal to Give Information as to Driver	461
15.	Driving Licences	467
16.	Vehicle Excise Licences	485
17.	Trade Licences	519
18.	Operator's Licence for Carriage of Goods	527
19.	Records	544
20.	Drivers' Hours	555
21.	Public Service Vehicles	566
22.	Conduct on Public Service Vehicles	577
23.	Motorways	580
24.	Vehicle Owner Liability	584

Chapter VI: Penalties, Endorsement and Disqualification
594

Chapter VII: Special Reasons and Mitigating Circumstances
664

Chapter VIII: Appeals
696

Appendix I: Regulations and Orders
704

Motorways Traffic Regulations, 1959, as Amended .. 704

Traffic Signs Regulations and General Directions, 1964, as Amended .. 709

Motor Cycles (Wearing of Helmets) Regulations, 1973 .. 728

60 Miles per Hour and 50 Miles per Hour (Temporary Speed Limit) Order, 1974 .. 729

Various Trunk Roads (Prohibition of Waiting) (Clearways) Order, 1963 .. 730

Road Vehicles Lighting Regulations, 1971, as Amended 731

Road Vehicles (Use of Lights during Daytime) Regulations, 1975 .. 764

Motor Vehicles (Construction and Use) Regulations, 1973, as Amended .. 766

Appendix II: Endorsement and Sentence Codes
874

Appendix III: Suggestions for Assessing Penalties for Main Motoring Offences .. 878

Index .. 883

TABLE OF CASES

PAGE

A. *v.* Bundy (1960), 125 J.P. 89; 105 S.J. 40; 58 L.G.R. 344, D.C. 358

Abercromby *v.* Morris (1932), 147 L.T. 529; 76 S.J. 560; 48 T.L.R. 635; 96 J.P. 392; 30 L.G.R. 407; 29 Cox C.C. 553 .... 43, 508

Abraham *v.* Jutson [1963] 1 W.L.R. 658; [1963] 2 All E.R. 402; 107 S.J. 357; *revsg.* (1962), 106 S.J. 880; [1962] C.L.Y. 1883, D.C. 68

Absalom *v.* Martin [1974] R.T.R. 145; [1973] Cr.L.R. 752, D.C. 386, 387

Acerro *v.* Petroni (1815), 1 Stark. 100 125

Ackroyds Air Travel Ltd. *v.* Director of Public Prosecutions [1950] 1 All E.R. 933; 114 J.P. 251; 48 L.G.R. 398; 83 Ll.L.Rep. 431 52

Adair *v.* Craighouse Cabinet Works [1937] S.C.(J.) 89; [1937] S.L.T. 499 .... 111, 553, 562

Adair *v.* Donaldson [1935] S.C.(J.) 23; [1935] S.L.T. 76 .... 42, 412

Adair *v.* Feist [1936] S.L.T.(Sh.) 22 60

Adair *v.* Fleming [1932] S.C.(J.) 51 345

Adair *v.* M'Kenna [1951] S.L.T.(Sh.Ct.) 40 165

Adair *v.* Munn [1940] S.C.(J.) 69 665

Adams *v.* Bradley [1975] Cr.L.R. 168 678

Adams *v.* Evans [1971] 12 C.L. 339 376

Adams *v.* Valentine [1975] Cr.L.R. 238 .... 184, 189

Advocate (H.M.) *v.* Cunningham [1963] J.C. 80 270

Advocate (H.M.) *v.* Ritchie [1926] J.C. 45 269

Agnew *v.* Robertson [1956] S.L.T.(Sh.Ct.) 90; 72 Sh.Ct.Rep. 255 ... 51, 367, 495, 498

Aichroth *v.* Cottee [1954] 1 W.L.R. 1124; [1954] 2 All E.R. 856; 98 S.J. 576; 118 J.P. 499; 52 L.G.R. 494 .... 674, 687

Aitken *v.* Hamilton [1964] S.L.T. 125 575

Aitken *v.* Yarwood [1965] 1 Q.B. 327; [1964] 3 W.L.R. 64; [1964] 2 All E.R. 537; 108 S.J. 381; 128 J.P. 470; 62 L.G.R. 545 338

Albert *v.* Motor Insurers' Bureau [1972] R.T.R. 230; [1972] A.C. 301; [1971] 3 W.L.R. 291; 115 S.J. 588; [1971] 2 All E.R. 1345; [1971] 2 Ll.L. Rep. 229, H.L. 542, 576

Alderson *v.* Booth [1969] 2 Q.B. 216; [1969] 2 W.L.R. 1252; [1969] 2 All E.R. 271; 113 S.J. 268; 53 Cr.App.R. 301; *The Times*, 27th February 209

Alderton *v.* Burgon (Richard) Associates (Manpower) Ltd. [1974] R.T.R. 422; [1974] Cr.L.R. 318, D.C. 50, 530

Aldus and Another *v.* Watson [1973] Q.B. 902; [1973] 2 W.L.R. 1007; 117 S.J. 446; [1973] 2 All E.R. 1018; [1973] R.T.R. 466; [1973] Cr.L.R. 443, D.C. 74, 266, 268

Alexander *v.* Adair [1938] S.C.(J.) 28 123

Alexander *v.* Clatworthy (1969), 113 S.J. 387; [1969] Cr.L.R. 377, D.C. 178

Alexander *v.* Latter [1972] Cr.L.R. 646; R.T.R. 441 678

Allan *v.* Wiseman [1975] Cr.L.R. 37 89

Alston *v.* Nurse (1933), unreported 134

Amalgamated Roadstone Corporation Ltd. *v.* Bond [1963] 1 W.L.R. 618; [1963] 1 All E.R. 682; 107 S.J. 316; 127 J.P. 254; 61 L.G.R. 309 413

Ambrose *v.* Jamison [1967] Cr.L.R. 114 .... 673, 687

Ames *v.* MacLeod [1969] S.C. 1 (*High Court of Justiciary*) 21, 22, 25

Anderson *v.* Transport Board [1964] N.Z.L.R. 881 .... 23, 282

Anderson and Heeley Ltd. *v.* Paterson [1975] R.T.R. 248; [1975] Cr.L.R. 49; [1975] 1 All E.R. 523, D.C. 427, 497, 500

Anderson (W.R.) (Motors) Ltd. *v.* Hargreaves [1962] 1 Q.B. 425; [1962] 2 W.L.R. 349; [1962] 1 All E.R. 129; 105 S.J. 1127; 126 J.P. 100; 60 L.G.R. 139 .... 389, 390

PAGE

Andrews v. Kershaw Ltd. [1952] 1 K.B. 70; [1951] 2 All E.R. 764; 95 S.J.
698; [1951] 2 T.L.R. 867; [1951] W.N. 510; 115 J.P. 568; 49 L.G.R.
827 .... 44, 414, 419
Another v. Howard (1968), J.P.Jo.Supp., 11th June 44
Another v. Probert [1968] Cr.L.R. 564 283
Anthony v. Jenkins [1971] R.T.R. 19, D.C. 195, 210
Archer v. Blacker (1965), 109 S.J. 113 132
Archer v. Woodward [1959] Cr.L.R. 461 672
Archibald v. Keiller [1931] S.C.(J.) 34 266
Armitage v. Mountain [1957] Cr.L.R. 257 .... 495, 496, 498, 499
Armstrong v. Clark [1957] 2 Q.B. 391; [1957] 2 W.L.R. 400; [1957] 1 All
E.R. 433; 101 S.J. 208; 41 Cr.App.R. 56; 121 J.P. 193; 55 L.G.R. 118 ... 241
Armstrong v. Whitfield [1973] 2 W.L.R. 720; 117 S.J. 341; [1973] 2 All E.R.
546; 71 L.G.R. 282; [1973] Cr.L.R. 304; [1974] Q.B. 16; sub nom. Arm-
strong v. Cumberland County Council, 226 E.G. 2153, D.C. 383
Arnell v. Harris [1945] K.B. 60 268
Arnold v. Chief Constable of Kingston-upon-Hull [1969] 1 W.L.R. 1499;
[1969] 3 All E.R. 646; 113 S.J. 409; 133 J.P. 694 .... 197, 198
Arrowsmith v. Jenkins [1963] 2 Q.B. 561; [1963] 2 W.L.R. 856; [1963] 2 All
E.R. 210; 107 S.J. 215; 127 J.P. 289; 61 L.G.R. 312 388
Ashworth v. Johnson; Charlesworth v. Johnson [1959] Cr.L.R. 735 661
Askew v. Bowtell [1947] 1 All E.R. 883; 91 S.J. 249; 63 T.L.R. 316; 45
L.G.R. 476 578
Atterton v. Browne [1945] K.B. 122; 114 L.J.K.B. 68; 173 L.T. 13; 61 T.L.R.
70; 109 J.P. 25; 43 L.G.R. 13 .... 88, 89
Attorney-General v. Beynon [1970] Ch. 1; [1969] 2 W.L.R. 1447; 133 J.P.
349; 113 S.J. 468; [1969] 2 All E.R. 263 28
Attorney-General v. Brogan (1953), 87 I.L.T.R. 181 542
Attorney-General v. Downes (1959), 93 I.L.T.R. 121 379
Attorney-General v. Egan [1949] Jo.Cr.L. 207; [1948] Ir.R. 433 124
Attorney-General v. Farrel (1954), 88 I.L.T.R. 174 31
Attorney-General v. Foley (1952), 86 I.L.T.R. 30 134
Attorney-General v. Honeywill and Others [1972] 1 W.L.R. 1506; 116 S.J.
801; [1972] 3 All E.R. 641; 71 L.G.R. 81 32
Attorney-General v. Joyce (1956), 90 I.L.T.R. 47 259
Attorney-General v. Wallace [1964] I.L.T. 117 135
Attorney-General (Connor) v. Shorten (1959), 93 I.L.T.R. 168 382
Attorney-General (Croke) v. O'Sullivan (1958), 92 I.L.T.R. 21 495
Attorney-General (de Burca) v. Murtagh (1961), 95 I.L.T.R. 56 16
Attorney-General (Holland) v. Hurley [1960] Jo.Crim.L. 59 543
Attorney-General (McCloskey) v. East [1964] Jo.Crim.L. 123; 98 I.L.T.R.
33 .... 52, 367
Attorney-General (McGowan) v. Carville (1961), 95 I.L.T.R. 41 .... 123, 470
Attorney-General (O'Gara) v. Callanan (1958), 92 I.L.T.R. 74 141
Attorney-General's Reference (No. 2 of 1974) [1975] R.T.R. 142; (1974),
The Times, 21st December, C.A. 202, 203
Attorney-General's Reference (No. 1 of 1975) (1975), The Times, 25th April ... 55,
676
Attridge v. Attwood [1964] Cr.L.R. 45 422
Austin (F.) (Leyton) Ltd. v. East [1961] Cr.L.R. 119 .... 34, 412, 419, 684

Baker v. Chapman (1963), 61 L.G.R. 527; [1964] Cr.L.R. 316 .... 34, 573
Baker v. Cole [1971] 1 W.L.R. 1788n.; [1971] 3 All E.R. 680n.; [1972] R.T.R.
43n., D.C. 340, 681, 689–694
Baker v. Esau [1972] Cr.L.R. 559; [1973] R.T.R. 49, D.C. 13, 336
Baker v. Spence (1960), The Times, 27th May 282
Baker v. Sweet [1966] Cr.L.R. 51; (1965), The Guardian, 30th October ... 123, 319
Baker v. Williams (1956), 54 L.G.R. 197 .... 275, 282

PAGE

Baldwin v. Pearson (1958), 122 J.P. 321; 56 L.G.R. 229; *revsg. sub nom.* Police
v. Pearson [1957] Cr.L.R. 818; [1957] C.L.Y. 1557 .... 306, 400
Baldwin v. Worsman [1963] 1 W.L.R. 326; [1963] 2 All E.R. 8; 107 S.J. 215;
127 J.P. 321; 61 L.G.R. 279 7
Balfour Beatty & Co. Ltd. v. Grindey [1974] Cr.L.R. 120, D.C.; [1975]
R.T.R. 156 .... 47, 48, 403, 405, 412
Ballance v. Brown [1950] Cr.L.R. 384 368
Barber v. British Road Services (1964), *The Times,* 18th November 285
Barker v. Arnold [1911] 2 K.B. 120; 80 L.J.K.B. 820; 105 L.T. 112; 27 T.L.R.
374; 75 J.P. 364; 22 Cox C.C. 533 94
Barnard v. Sully (1931), 47 T.L.R. 557 120
Barnet London Borough Council v. S. & W. Transport Ltd. [1975] Cr.L.R.
171 399
Bason v. Eayrs [1958] Cr.L.R. 397 419
Bason v. Vipond, Same v. Robson [1962] 1 W.L.R. 271; [1962] 1 All E.R.
520; 106 S.J. 221; 126 J.P. 178; 61 L.G.R. 35 414
Bass v. Boynton [1960] Cr.L.R. 497; *The Times,* 4th May 28, 30
Bateman v. Evans (1964), 108 S.J. 522; [1964] Cr.L.R. 601 .... 53, 54, 653
Baxter v. Middlesex County Council [1956] Cr.L.R. 561 .... 27, 30, 114, 390
Beer v. Clench (W. H.) (1930) Ltd. [1936] 1 All E.R. 449; 154 L.T. 428; 80
S.J. 266; 52 T.L.R. 300; 100 J.P. 191; 34 L.G.R. 187; 24 Traff.Cas. 118;
30 Cox C.C. 364 .... 111, 553, 562
Beer v. Davies [1958] 2 Q.B. 187; [1958] 2 W.L.R. 920; [1958] 2 All E.R. 255;
102 S.J. 383; 122 J.P. 344; 56 L.G.R. 261; 42 Cr.App.R. 198 .... 136, 140
Beer v. Fairclough & Sons Ltd. (1937), 156 L.T. 238; 81 S.J. 180; 53 T.L.R.
345; 101 J.P. 157; 35 L.G.R. 113; 30 Cox C.C. 551; 25 Traff.Cas. 129 ... 561
Bego v. Gardner [1933] S.L.T. 110 387
Beighton v. Brown [1965] 1 W.L.R. 553; [1965] 1 All E.R. 793; 109 S.J. 295;
129 J.P. 199 .... 420, 434
Bell v. Ingham [1969] 1 Q.B. 563; [1968] 3 W.L.R. 401; [1968] 2 All E.R.
333; 112 S.J. 486 .... 605–607, 622, 655
Bensley v. Smith [1972] Cr.L.R. 239; [1972] R.T.R. 221, D.C. 272, 278, 283,
311
Beresford v. Richardson [1921] 1 K.B. 243; 90 L.J.K.B. 313; 124 L.T. 274;
37 T.L.R. 53; 85 J.P. 60; 18 L.G.R. 855; 26 Cox C.C. 673 275
Beresford v. St. Alban's Justices (1905), 22 T.L.R. 1; *sub nom. ex parte* Beres-
ford, 69 J.P.Jo. 520 .... 122, 143
Berry v. Robson (1964), 108 S.J. 259; [1964] Cr.L.R. 401 .... 117, 118
Betts v. Betts & Broderick, Betts v. Betts (1917), 33 T.L.R. 200 112
Biddle v. Johnston (1965), 109 S.J. 395; [1965] 2 Ll.L.Rep. 121 ...... 369, 372
Bingham v. Bruce [1962] 1 W.L.R. 70; [1962] 1 All E.R. 136; 105 S.J. 1086;
126 J.P. 81; 60 L.G.R. 79 .... 106, 195, 464, 465
Binks v. Department of the Environment [1975] Cr.L.R. 244 .... 7, 487
Birmingham & Midland Motor Omnibus Co. Ltd. v. Nelson [1933] 1 K.B.
188; [1932] All E.R. Rep. 351; 102 L.J.K.B. 47; 147 L.T. 435; 96 J.P.
385; 48 T.L.R. 620; 30 L.G.R. 390; 29 Cox C.C. 529, D.C. 575
Bishop v. Hosier (1962), *The Guardian,* 11th October 104, 105, 698
Blaikie v. Morrison [1957] S.C.(J.) 46; [1957] S.L.T. 290 .... 16, 505
Blakey Transport Ltd. v. Baggott [1973] Cr.L.R. 776, D.C. 90, 91
Blakey Transport Ltd. v. Casebourne [1975] Cr.L.R. 169; [1975] R.T.R.
221 548
Blayney v. Knight [1975] Cr.L.R. 237 .... 22, 352
Bloomfield v. Williams [1970] Cr.L.R. 292; (1970), *The Times,* 25th
February 502, 508
Blows v. Chapman [1947] 2 All E.R. 576; 63 T.L.R. 575; [1947] W.N. 266;
112 J.P. 8; 46 L.G.R. 13 .... 666, 682, 684
Bombay Province v. Bombay Municipal Corporation [1947] A.C. 58; [1947]
L.J.R. 380; 62 T.L.R. 643, P.C.; *revsg.* I.L.R. (Bom.) 95 31
Borders v. Swift [1957] Cr.L.R. 194 372

PAGE

Borthwick v. Vickers [1973] R.T.R. 390; [1973] Cr.L.R. 317, D.C. 120, 411

Bosley v. Long [1970] 1 W.L.R. 1411; 114 S.J. 571; [1970] 3 All E.R. 286; [1970] R.T.R. 432, D.C. 226

Boss v. Kingston [1963] 1 W.L.R. 99; [1963] 1 All E.R. 177; 106 S.J. 1053; 61 L.G.R. 109; *sub nom.* Boss and Hansford v. Kingston [1962] 2 Ll.L.Rep. 431 .... 373, 666, 683

Bottomley, *ex parte* [1909] 2 K.B. 14; 78 L.J.K.B. 547; 100 L.T. 782; 25 T.L.R. 371; 73 J.P. 246; 22 Cox C.C. 106 125

Bourlet v. Porter [1973] 1 W.L.R. 866; 117 S.J. 489; [1973] 2 All E.R. 800; [1973] R.T.R. 293; [1974] Cr.L.R. 53, H.L.; *revsg. sub nom.* R. v. Porter (1972), 117 S.J. 36; [1973] R.T.R. 116; [1973] Cr.L.R. 125; *sub nom.* R. v. Porter (Edward Charles Thomas) (1972), 57 Cr.App.R. 290, C.A. 211, 213, 226, 227

Bourne v. Norwich Crematorium Ltd. [1967] 1 W.L.R. 691; [1967] 2 All E.R. 576; 111 S.J. 256; 44 T.C. 164; [1967] T.R. 49; 46 A.T.C. 43 335

Bowyer, Philpott & Payne Ltd. v. Mather [1919] 1 K.B. 419; 88 L.J.K.B. 377; 120 L.T. 346; 83 J.P. 50; 17 L.G.R. 222 489

Boxer v. Snelling (1972), 116 S.J. 564; [1972] Cr.L.R. 441; [1972] R.T.R. 472, D.C. 4, 10

Boyce v. Absalom [1974] R.T.R. 248; [1974] Cr.L.R. 192, D.C. 468

Boyd-Gibbins v. Skinner [1951] 2 K.B. 379; [1951] 1 All E.R. 1049; [1951] 1 T.L.R. 1159; [1951] W.N. 267; 115 J.P. 360; 49 L.G.R. 713 322

Boys v. Blenkinsop, 112 S.J. 586; [1968] Cr.L.R. 513; *sub nom.* Boys v. Blenkin-sopp (1968), 118 New L.J. 613, D.C. 378

Bracegirdle v. Oxley, Bracegirdle v. Cobley [1947] K.B. 349; [1947] 1 All E.R. 126; [1947] L.J.R. 815; 176 L.T. 187; 91 S.J. 27; 63 T.L.R. 98; 111 J.P. 131; 45 L.G.R. 69 .... 275, 281, 700

Braddock v. Whittaker [1970] Cr.L.R. 112; (1969), 113 S.J. 942, D.C. 180

Bradley v. McGivern [1963] N.I. 11 .... 614, 628

Brake v. Taylor (1967), 1st June, unreported 87

Brangwynne v. Evans [1962] 1 W.L.R. 267; [1962] 1 All E.R. 446; 106 S.J. 197; 126 J.P. 173 .... 74, 265

Brazier v. Alabaster [1962] Cr.L.R. 173 307

Brend v. Wood (1946), 175 L.T. 306; 90 S.J. 381; 110 J.P. 317; 44 L.G.R. 254 .... 382, 401

Brennan v. Farrell [1969] S.C. 45; [1969] Cr.L.R. 494, High Ct. Justiciary 206

Brewer v. Metropolitan Police Commissioner [1969] 1 W.L.R. 267; [1969] 1 All E.R. 513; (1968), 112 S.J. 1022; 118 New L.J. 1196 .... 241, 666, 675

Briere v. Hailstone (1968), 112 S.J. 767; [1969] Cr.L.R. 36 322

Briggs v. Gibson's Bakery [1949] N.I. 165... 40

Bright v. Ashfold (1932), 96 J.P. 182 370

Brighty v. Pearson [1938] 4 All E.R. 127; 159 L.T. 619; 82 S.J. 910; 109 J.P. 522; 36 L.G.R. 664; 31 Cox C.C. 177 318

British Broadcasting Corporation v. Johns [1965] Ch. 32; [1964] 2 W.L.R. 1071; [1964] 1 All E.R. 923; 108 S.J. 217; [1964] R.V.R. 579; [1964] T.R. 45; 41 T.C. 471; 43 A.T.C. 38; 10 R.R.C. 239; *revsg.* [1963] R.V.R. 695; [1963] T.R. 369; 42 A.T.C. 341; 10 R.R.C. 164; [1963] R.A. 337; [1963] C.L.Y. 1750 60

British Car Auctions Ltd. v. Wright [1972] 1 W.L.R. 1519; 116 S.J. 583; [1972] 3 All E.R. 462; [1972] R.T.R. 540; [1972] Cr.L.R. 562, D.C. 424

British Road Services v. Owen (1970), 115 S.J. 267; [1971] 2 All E.R. 999; [1971] R.T.R. 372, D.C. 420

British Road Services v. Wurzal [1971] 1 W.L.R. 1508; 115 S.J. 724; [1971] 3 All E.R. 480; [1972] R.T.R. 45; *sub nom.* British Road Services and Seabourne Shipping Co. Ltd. v. Wurzal [1971] 2 Ll.L·Rep. 196, D.C. 63, 64, 411, 528

British School of Motoring v. Simms (Stafford (A.R.)) (Trading as Mini Countryman School of Motoring) and Cooper, Third Parties) [1971] 1 All E.R. 317; [1971] R.T.R. 190 .... 277, 377, 476

PAGE

Brook v. Friend [1954] Cr.L.R. 942 .... 51, 494, 495

Brooks v. Ellis [1972] 116 S.J. 509; [1972] 2 All E.R. 1204; [1972] R.T.R. 361;
[1972] Cr.L.R. 439, D.C. 234, 235

Brooks v. Jefferies [1936] 3 All E.R. 232; 80 S.J. 856; 53 T.L.R. 34 306

Brown v. Abbott (1965), 109 S.J. 437 7

Brown v. Allweather Mechanical Grouting Co. [1954] 2 Q.B. 443; [1953] 2
W.L.R. 402; [1953] 1 All E.R. 474; 97 S.J. 135; 117 J.P. 136; 51 L.G.R.
249 486

Brown v. Anderson [1965] 1 W.L.R. 528; [1965] 2 All E.R. 1; 129 J.P. 298 ... 476

Brown v. Dando (1954), 118 J.P.Jo. 319 .... 9, 13, 336

Brown v. Dougal (Henry) & Sons [1960] S.L.T. 19; [1959] S.C. (J.) 90; [1960]
Cr.L.R. 774 541

Brown v. Dyerson [1969] 1 Q.B. 45; [1968] 3 W.L.R. 615; [1968] 3 All E.R.
39; 112 S.J. 805; 132 J.P. 495; 52 Cr.App.R. 630 ... 610, 624, 629, 667, 668,
674, 694, 695

Brown v. Grange Tours Ltd. (1968), 112 S.J. 1010; [1969] Cr.L.R. 95 45

Brown v. McIndoe [1963] S.L.T. 233 429

Brown v. Roberts [1965] 1 Q.B. 1; [1963] 3 W.L.R. 75; 107 S.J. 666; [1963]
2 All E.R. 263; sub nom. Brown v. Roberts and Nicholls [1963] 1 Ll.L.Rep.
314 375

Brown & Lynn v. Western S.M.T. Co. Ltd. [1945] S.C. 41 .... 270, 287

Browne v. Central S.M.T. Co [1949] S.C. 9 285

Browning v. Phoenix Assurance Co. [1960] 2 Ll.L. Rep. 360 367

Browning v. Watson (J.W.H.) (Rochester) Ltd. [1953] 1 W.L.R. 1172; [1953]
2 All E.R. 775; 97 S.J. 591; 117 J.P. 479; 51 L.G.R. 597 ... 37, 39, 573, 576,
577

Bruce v. Odell (1939), 27 Traff.Cas. 135 51

Bryan v. Forrow [1950] 1 All E.R. 294; sub nom. Forrow v. Bryan, 94 S.J. 194;
[1950] W.N. 91; 114 J.P. 158; 48 L.G.R. 347 367

Bryant v. Marx [1932] All E.R. 518; 147 L.T. 499; 76 S.J. 577; 48 T.L.R.
624; 96 J.P. 383; 30 L.G.R. 405; 29 Cox C.C. 545 .... 27, 389

Bryant v. Morris [1972] R.T.R. 214; [1972] Cr.L.R. 115, D.C. 223, 227

Bryson v. Rogers [1956] 2 Q.B. 404; [1956] 3 W.L.R. 495; [1956] 2 All E.R.
826; 100 S.J. 569; 120 J.P. 454; 54 L.G.R. 463 334–336

Buchanan v. Motor Insurers' Bureau [1955] 1 W.L.R. 488; [1955] 1 All E.R.
607; 99 S.J. 319; 119 J.P. 227; [1954] 2 Ll.L.Rep. 519 28

Buckeridge v. Buckeridge (1962), 106 S.J. 471 112

Buckoke v. Greater London Council [1971] 1 Ch. 655; [1971] 2 W.L.R. 760;
115 S.J. 174; [1971] 2 All E.R. 254; [1971] R.T.R. 131; 69 L.G.R. 210,
C.A.; affg. [1970] 1 W.L.R. 1092; 114 S.J. 269; [1970] 2 All E.R. 193; 68
L.G.R. 543 301

Bugge v. Taylor [1941] 1 K.B. 198; 110 L.J.K.B. 710; 164 L.T. 312; 85 S.J.
82; (1940), 104 J.P. 467; 39 L.G.R. 100 .... 27, 30

Bullen v. Keay [1974] R.T.R. 559; [1974] Cr.L.R. 371, D.C. 673

Bullen v. Picking (1973), 117 S.J. 895; [1974] R.T.R. 46; [1973] Cr.L.R. 765,
D.C. 51, 493

Bulman v. Bennett [1974] R.T.R. 1; (1973), 117 S.J. 916; (1973), The Times,
28th November, D.C. 254, 345, 346

Burke v. Jobson [1972] R.T.R. 59; [1972] Cr.L.R. 187, D.C. 225

Burn v. Kernohan [1973] R.T.R. 82; [1973] Cr.L.R. 122, D.C. 223, 225

Burningham v. Lindsell [1936] 2 All E.R. 159; 80 S.J. 367 334

Burns v. Bidder [1967] 2 Q.B. 227; [1966] 3 W.L.R. 99; [1966] 3 All E.R. 29;
110 S.J. 430; 130 J.P. 342 .... 278, 301, 449, 450, 452, 459

Burns v. Currell [1963] 2 Q.B. 433; [1963] 2 W.L.R. 1106; [1963] 2 All E.R.
297; 107 S.J. 272; 127 J.P. 397; 61 L.G.R. 356 7

Burrell v. Hunter [1956] S.L.T.(Sh.) 75 275

Burrough v. Martin (1809), 2 Camp. 12 N.P. 112

Burrows v. Berry (1949), 99 L.J. 91; 113 J.P.Jo. 492 .... 5, 332

Bursey v. Barron (1971), 115 S.J. 469; [1971] R.T.R. 273, D.C. 323, 324

PAGE

Burt v. Kircaldy [1965] 1 W.L.R. 474; [1965] 1 All E.R. 741; 109 S.J. 33; 129 J.P. 190 137

Burton v. Road Transport and General Insurance Co. (1939), 63 Ll.L.Rep. 253 367

Butcher v. Catteral (1975), *The Times*, 11th June 203

Butler v. Easton (1969), 113 S.J. 906; [1970] Cr.L.R. 45; (1969), *The Times*, 23rd October; *sub nom.* Buller v. Easton, 119 New L.J. 996, D.C. 212

Butters v. J. H. Fenner & Co. (1967), *The Times*, 6th February; 117 New L.J. 213 285

Butterworth v. Shorthouse (1956), 120 J.P.Jo. 97; [1956] Cr.L.R. 341 .... 347, 417, 421

Buttwell v. Bailey [1968] 1 W.L.R. 663; (1968), 112 S.J. 381, D.C. 420

Butty v. Davey [1972] R.T.R. 75; [1972] Cr.L.R. 48, D.C. 272

Caldwell v. Hague (1914), 84 L.J.K.B. 543; 112 L.T. 502; 79 J.P. 152; 13 L.G.R. 297; 24 Cox C.C. 595 .... 471, 507

Callis v. Gunn [1964] 1 Q.B. 495; [1963] 3 W.L.R. 931; [1963] 3 All E.R. 677; 107 S.J. 831; 128 J.P. 41; 48 Cr.App.R. 36 126

Cambridgeshire and Isle of Ely County Council v. Rust [1972] 2 Q.B. 426; [1972] 3 W.L.R. 226; 116 S.J. 564; [1972] 3 All E.R. 232; 71 L.G.R. 444; [1972] Cr.L.R. 433, D.C. 388

Camp v. Horne [1965] Jo.Crim.L. 153 141

Campbell v. Adair [1945] S.C.(J.) 29; [1945] S.L.T. 135 578

Campbell v. Strangeways (1877), 3 C.P.D. 105; 47 L.J.M.C. 6; 37 L.T. 672; 42 J.P. 39 .... 471, 507, 626

Campbell v. Tormey [1969] 1 W.L.R. 189; [1969] 1 All E.R. 961; 112 S.J. 1023; 53 Cr.App.R. 99 .... 185, 209, 236

Card v. Salmon [1953] 1 Q.B. 392; [1953] 2 W.L.R. 301; [1953] 1 All E.R. 324; 97 S.J. 115; 117 J.P. 110; 51 L.G.R. 174 132

Carey v. Heath [1952] K.B. 70; [1951] 2 All E.R. 774; [1951] 2 T.L.R. 797; [1951] W.N. 513; 115 J.P. 577; 50 L.G.R. 227 .... 9, 336

Carlton v. Garrity (1963), 107 S.J. 1023; 62 L.G.R. 147; [1964] Cr.L.R. 146 683

Carmichael & Sons (Worcester) Ltd. v. Cottle [1971] Cr.L.R. 45; (1970), 114 S.J. 867; [1971] R.T.R. 11, D.C. 41, 42, 44, 45, 52, 375, 412, 508, 685

Carnegie v. Clark [1947] S.C.(J.) 74 688

Carnill v. Rowland [1953] 1 W.L.R. 380; [1953] 1 All E.R. 486; 97 S.J. 134; 117 J.P. 127; 51 L.G.R. 180; [1953] 1 Ll.L.Rep. 99 372

Carpenter v. Campbell [1953] 1 All E.R. 280; 117 J.P. 90 .... 487, 530, 573

Carpenter v. Fox [1929] 2 K.B. 458; 98 L.J.K.B. 779; 142 L.T. 234; 45 T.L.R. 571; 93 J.P. 239; 27 L.G.R. 601; 29 Cox C.C. 42 389

Carr v. Harrison (1967), 111 S.J. 57; [1967] Cr.L.R. 54; 116 New L.J. 1573; *The Times*, 18th November 141, 142

Carter v. Mace [1949] 2 All E.R. 714; 113 J.P. 527 .... 52, 537

Carter v. Richardson [1974] R.T.R. 314; [1974] Cr.L.R. 190, D.C. ... 53, 475

Cassady v. Reg. Morris Transport Ltd. [1975] Cr.L.R. 398 548

Cassady v. Ward & Smith Ltd. [1975] Cr.L.R. 399 548

Chafen v. Another, Supplement to the *Justice of the Peace and Local Government Review*, 21st March, 1970 391

Chalgray Ltd. v. Aspley (1965), 109 S.J. 394 8

Chapman v. Ingleton (1973), J.P.News. 204; 57 Cr.App.R. 476; [1973] Cr.L.R. 296, D.C. 102

Chapman v. Kirke [1948] 2 K.B. 450; [1948] 2 All E.R. 556; 92 S.J. 558; 64 T.L.R. 519; 112 J.P. 399; 46 L.G.R. 507 577

Chapman v. O'Hagan [1949] 2 All E.R. 690; 93 S.J. 694; 65 T.L.R. 657; [1949] W.N. 399; 113 J.P. 518; 47 L.G.R. 717 .... 666, 670, 671

Chapman v. Parlby (1964), 108 S.J. 35; 62 L.G.R. 150; [1964] Cr.L.R. 230 28

PAGE

Childs v. Coghlan (1968), 112 S.J. 175; [1968] Cr.L.R. 225; 118 New L.J.
182 8
Cholerton v. Copping (1906), 70 J.P. 484 94
Christie v. Leachinsky [1947] A.C. 573; [1947] L.J.R. 757; 176 L.T. 443; 63
T.L.R. 231; 111 J.P. 224; [1947] 1 All E.R. 567, H.L.; affg. sub nom.
Leachinsky v. Christie [1946] K.B. 124 .... 209, 210
Churchill v. Norris, Maidment v. Norris (1938), 158 L.T. 255; 82 S.J. 114; 31
Cox C.C. 1 .... 36, 40, 48, 111, 412
Clark v. Chalmers [1961] S.L.T. 325; [1961] S.C.(J.) 60 382
Clark v. Clark [1950] S.L.T.(Sh.) 68 164
Clark v. Dundee Town Council [1957] S.L.T. 306; [1957] S.C.(J.) 63 576
Clark v. Hunter [1956] S.L.T. 188; sub nom. Hunter v. Clark [1956] S.C.(J.)
59 .... 34, 38, 412
Clark v. Stenlake [1972] R.T.R. 276, D.C. 221
Clarke v. Cherry [1953] 1 W.L.R. 268; [1953] 1 All E.R. 267; 97 S.J. 80; 117
J.P. 86; 51 L.G.R. 160 .... 335, 544
Clarke v. Mould [1945] 2 All E.R. 551; 173 L.T. 370; 89 S.J. 370; 109 J.P.
175; 43 L.G.R. 124 141
Clarke v. National Insurance and Guarantee Corporation [1964] 1 Q.B. 199;
[1963] 3 W.L.R. 710; [1963] 3 All E.R. 375; 107 S.J. 573; [1963] 2 Ll.L.
Rep. 35, C.A.; revsg. [1963] 2 Q.B. 790; [1963] 2 W.L.R. 1396; [1963] 2
All E.R. 470; 107 S.J. 317; [1963] 1 Ll.L.Rep. 322 371
Clarke v. Winchurch [1969] 1 W.L.R. 69; [1969] 1 All E.R. 275; (1968), 112
S.J. 909 .... 284, 289
Clements v. Gill [1953] S.A.S.R. 25 348
Clifford-Turner v. Waterman [1961] 1 W.L.R. 1499; [1961] 3 All E.R. 974;
105 S.J. 932; 60 L.G.R. 52 392
Clift v. Long [1961] Cr.L.R. 121 173
Clydebank Co-operative Society Ltd. v. Binnie [1937] S.C.(J.) 17; [1937]
S.L.T. 114 .... 39, 573
Cobb v. Whorton [1971] Cr.L.R. 372; [1971] R.T.R. 392, D.C. 10, 45, 498
Cobb v. Williams [1973] R.T.R. 113; [1973] Cr.L.R. 243, D.C. 42, 47, 375
Cohen (George) 600 Group Ltd. v. Hird [1970] 1 W.L.R. 1226; 114 S.J. 552;
[1970] 2 All E.R. 650; 68 L.G.R. 781, D.C. 431
Cole v. Young [1938] 4 All E.R. 39 416
Cole Bros. v. Harrop (1915), 85 L.J.K.B. 494; 79 J.P. 519 498
Collins v. Spring [1975] Cr.L.R. 100 .... 80, 161
Collyer v. Dring [1952] 2 All E.R. 1004; 117 J.P. 22; sub nom. Practice Note
Q.B.D., D.C. (Extension of Time) 96 S.J. 784; [1952] W.N. 505 23
Commissioner of Police of the Metropolis v. Meller [1963] Cr.L.R. 856 94
Coneys v. Nicholson (1968), 112 S.J. 787; [1969] Cr.L.R. 856 236
Conn v. Westminster Motor Insurance Association Ltd. [1966] 1 Ll.L.Rep.
407; 116 New L.J. 894; revsg. [1966] 1 Ll.L.Rep. 123; 116 New L.J. 554... 371
Connelly v. Director of Public Prosecutions [1964] A.C. 1254; [1964] 2 W.L.R.
1145; [1964] 2 All E.R. 401; 108 S.J. 356; 128 J.P. 418; 48 Cr.App.R.
183; affg. sub nom. R. v. Connelly [1963] 3 W.L.R. 839; [1963] 3 All E.R.
510; 107 S.J. 793; [1963] C.L.Y. 632 93
Cook v. Atchison (1968), 112 S.J. 235; [1968] Cr.L.R. 266 .... 24, 270
Cook v. Lanyon [1972] R.T.R. 496; [1972] Cr.L.R. 570; The Times, 13th July,
D.C. 508, 514
Cook v. Plumpton (Alfred) Ltd., Cook v. Henderson (1935), 153 L.T. 462; 79
S.J. 504; 51 T.L.R. 513; 99 J.P. 308; 33 L.G.R. 363; 30 Cox C.C. 270;
24 Traff.Cas. 237 562
Cook and Another v. Briddon (1975), 119 S.J. 462 414
Cook (Siddle C.) Ltd. v. Arlidge [1962] 1 W.L.R. 203n.; 106 S.J. 154; 60
L.G.R. 121, D.C. 431, 432
Cook (Siddle C.) Ltd. v. Holden [1963] 1 Q.B. 248; [1962] 3 W.L.R. 1448;
[1962] 3 All E.R. 984; 106 S.J. 920; 127 J.P. 55; 61 L.G.R. 71 .... 18, 432
Cooke v. McCann [1974] R.T.R. 131; [1973] Cr.L.R. 522, D.C. 121

PAGE

Coombs v. Kehoe [1972] 1 W.L.R. 797; 116 S.J. 486; [1972] 2 All E.R. 55;
    [1972] R.T.R. 224; [1972] Cr.L.R. 560, D.C. 635, 673, 674
Cooper v. Hall [1968] 1 W.L.R. 360; [1968] 1 All E.R. 185; (1967), 111 S.J.
    928; 132 J.P. 152; 65 L.G.R. 271 .... 393, 394
Cooper v. Hawkins [1904] 2 K.B. 164; 73 L.J.K.B. 113; 89 L.T. 476; 19
    T.L.R. 620; 52 W.R. 233; 68 J.P. 25; 1 L.G.R. 833 .... 61, 62
Cooper v. Leeke (1968), 112 S.J. 46 55
Cooper v. Rowlands [1971] R.T.R. 291, D.C. 199, 200
Copeland v. McPherson [1970] S.L.T. 87 .... 193, 199
Corbett & Miller v. Barham [1965] 1 W.L.R. 187; [1954] Cr.L.R. 471 543
Cording v. Halse [1955] 1 Q.B. 63; [1954] 3 W.L.R. 625; [1954] 3 All E.R.
    287; 98 S.J. 769; 118 J.P. 558; 52 L.G.R. 554 .... 16, 65
Corkery v. Carpenter [1951] 1 K.B. 102; [1950] 2 All E.R. 745; 94 S.J. 488; 66
    T.L.R. (Pt. 2) 333; [1950] W.N. 442; 114 J.P. 481; 48 L.G.R. 648 ...... 9, 252
Cornish v. Ferry Masters Ltd. and Another [1975] R.T.R. 292; (1975), Law
    Society's Gazette, 12th February; [1975] Cr.L.R. 241 .... 418, 435
Corrigan v. Fox [1966] S.L.T.(Sh.) 79 660
Courteen v. Touse (1807), 1 Camp. 43 125
Cowan v. Hale [1966] N.I. 31 501
Coward v. Motor Insurers' Bureau [1963] 1 Q.B. 259; [1962] 2 W.L.R. 663;
    [1962] 1 All E.R. 531; 106 S.J. 34; [1962] 1 Ll.L.Rep. 1; affg. [1969]
    C.L.Y. 7879; [1961] 1 Ll.L.Rep. 583 .... 542, 576
Cox v. Army Council [1963] A.C. 48; [1962] 2 W.L.R. 950; [1962] 1 All E.R.
    880; 106 S.J. 305; 46 Cr.App.R. 258; affg. sub nom. R. v. Cox [1962] 2
    W.L.R. 126; [1962] 3 All E.R. 1194; 106 S.J. 17 .... 31, 61, 265
Cox v. Harrison [1968] 1 W.L.R. 1907; [1968] 3 All E.R. 811; 112 S.J. 866;
    133 J.P. 75 .... 3, 349, 476
Cox v. Sidery (1935), 24 Traff.Cas. 69 .... 35, 553
Crabtree v. McKelvie and Co. (B.M. & P.) Ltd. (1964), 62 L.G.R. 192; [1964]
    Cr.L.R. 598 432
Crampton v. Fish [1970] Cr.L.R. 235; (1969), 113 S.J. 1003, D.C. ... 53, 165, 243,
                                                                             475
Crawford v. Haughton (1971), 116 S.J. 125; [1972] 1 All E.R. 535 .... 35, 41,
                                                    42, 44, 47, 52, 375, 685
Crichton v. Burrell [1951] S.L.T. 365 .... 164, 165
Cripps v. Cooper [1936] 2 All E.R. 48 418
Cronkshaw v. Rydeheard (1969), 113 S.J. 673; [1969] Cr.L.R. 493; (1969),
    The Times, 25th June 220
Cross v. Oliver (1964), 108 S.J. 583; 62 L.G.R. 501; [1964] Cr.L.R. 723 .... 90, 323
Croston v. Vaughan [1938] 1 K.B. 540; [1937] 4 All E.R. 249; 107 L.J.K.B.
    182; 158 L.T. 221; 81 S.J. 882; 53 T.L.R. 54; 101 J.P. 11; 36 L.G.R. 1... 284
Cruickshank v. Devlin [1973] S.L.T.(Sh.Ct.) 81 192
Cunliffe v. Bleasdale (1972), 111 S.J. 746; [1973] R.T.R. 90; [1972] Cr.L.R.
    567, D.C. 226, 229
Curtis v. Geeves (1930), 143 L.T. 48; 46 T.L.R. 187; 94 J.P. 71; 28 L.G.R.
    103; 29 Cox C.C. 126 397
Custins v. Nottingham Corporation [1970] R.T.R. 365 284
Cuthbert v. Hollis [1958] S.L.T.(Sh.) 51; 74 Sh.Ct.Rep. 151 133

D. (an infant) v. Parsons [1960] 1 W.L.R. 797; [1960] 2 All E.R. 493; 104 S.J.
    605; 124 J.P. 375; 58 L.G.R. 325 .... 42, 55, 358, 374, 378
Daley v. Hargreaves [1961] 1 W.L.R. 487; [1961] 1 All E.R. 552; 105 S.J. 111;
    125 J.P. 193; 59 L.G.R. 136 .... 7, 8
Dallison v. Caffery [1965] 1 Q.B. 348; [1964] 3 W.L.R. 385; [1964] 2 All E.R.
    610; 108 S.J. 560; 128 J.P. 379; affg. (1963), The Times, 3rd July; [1963]
    C.L.Y. 2174 119
Darling v. Burton [1928] S.C.(J.) 11 16
Darnell v. Holliday [1973] R.T.R. 276; [1973] Cr.L.R. 366, D.C. 89
Darnell v. Portal [1972] R.T.R. 483; [1972] Cr.L.R. 511, D.C. 202

PAGE

Davey v. Towle [1973] R.T.R. 328; [1973] Cr.L.R. 360, D.C. 373, 379, 429

David v. Commissioner of Metropolitan Police [1962] 2 Q.B. 135; [1962] 2
W.L.R. 682; [1962] 1 All E.R. 491; 106 S.J. 113; 126 J.P. 166 698

Davidson v. Adair [1934] S.C.(J.) 37; 122 J.P.Jo.48 .... 28, 412, 421

Davies v. Griffiths [1937] 2 All E.R. 671; 157 L.T. 23; 81 S.J. 359; 53 T.L.R.
680; 101 J.P. 247; 35 L.G.R. 252; 30 Cox C.C. 595 96

Davies v. Heatley [1971] Cr.L.R. 244; [1971] R.T.R. 145, D.C. ... 311, 313, 314,
393

Davies v. Liverpool Corporation [1949] 2 All E.R. 175; 93 S.J. 373; [1949]
W.N. 268; 113 J.P. 381 579

Davies v. Warne [1973] R.T.R. 217 39

Davies, Turner & Co. Ltd. v. Brodie [1954] 1 W.L.R. 1364; [1954] 3 All E.R.
283; 98 S.J. 770; 118 J.P. 532; 52 L.G.R. 558 .... 52, 537

Davis v. Loach (1886), 51 J.P. 118 91

Davis v. Morton [1913] 2 K.B. 479; 82 L.J.K.B. 665; 108 L.T. 677; 29
T.L.R. 466; 77 J.P. 223; 23 Cox C.C. 359 91

Dawrant v. Nutt [1961] 1 W.L.R. 253; [1960] 3 All E.R. 681; 105 S.J. 129;
105 S.J. 501, 541 285

Dawson v. Winter (1932), 149 L.T. 18; 77 S.J. 29; 49 T.L.R. 128; 31 L.G.R.
298; 29 Cox C.C. 633 .... 345, 346

Day v. Harris (1953), 117 J.P. 313 135

Dean v. Wishart [1952] S.C.(J.) 9; [1952] S.L.T. 86 165

De Filippo v. De Filippo (1964), 108 S.J. 56 85

Delaroy-Hall v. Tadman, Watson v. Last, Earl v. Lloyd [1969] 2 Q.B. 208;
[1969] 2 W.L.R. 92; [1969] 1 All E.R. 25; (1968), 112 S.J. 987; The
Times, 9th November 250, 665, 670, 672, 678

Dennis v. Tame [1954] 1 W.L.R. 1338; 98 S.J. 750; 118 J.P. 358; 52 L.G.R.
329 683

Derrick v. Ryder [1972] R.T.R. 480; [1972] Cr.L.R. 710, D.C. 393

Devon County Council v. Hawkins [1967] 2 Q.B. 26; [1967] 2 W.L.R. 285;
[1967] 1 All E.R. 235; 110 S.J. 893; 65 L.G.R. 123; [1966] C.L.Y.
10608 478

Dewing v. Cummings [1971] R.T.R. 295, D.C. 701

Dickens v. Smith [1965] Cr.L.R. 312; The Times, 19th February 122

Dickson v. Atkins [1972] R.T.R. 209; [1972] Cr.L.R. 185, D.C. 178, 217

Dickson v. Brown [1959] Cr.L.R. 787; [1959] S.L.T. 207; sub nom. Brown v.
Dickson [1959] S.C.(J.) 19 419

Director of Public Prosecutions v. Carey [1970] A.C. 1072; [1969] 3 W.L.R.
1169; 113 S.J. 962; [1969] 3 All E.R. 1662, H.L.; revsg. sub nom. Webber
v. Carey [1969] 1 W.L.R. 1351; 133 J.P. 633; 113 S.J. 706; [1969] 3 All
E.R. 406; 54 Cr.App.R. 119; [1970] R.T.R. 14, D.C. ... 182, 200–204, 206,
208, 236

Director of Public Prosecutions v. Hester [1973] A.C. 296; [1972] 3 W.L.R.
910; 116 S.J. 966; [1972] 3 All E.R. 1056; 57 Cr.App.R. 212; [1973]
Cr.L.R. 43, H.L.; affg. sub nom. R. v. Hester [1972] 3 W.L.R. 719; 116 S.J.
353; [1972] 2 All E.R. 1020; 56 Cr.App.R. 534; [1972] Cr.L.R. 426, C.A. 102

Disher v. Disher [1965] P. 31; [1964] 2 W.L.R. 21; [1963] 3 All E.R. 933; 108
S.J. 37 85

Divito v. Stickings [1948] 1 All E.R. 207; [1948] L.J.R. 1079; 92 S.J. 142; 64
T.L.R. 92; 112 J.P. 166; 46 L.G.R. 151 390

Dixon v. B.R.S. (Pickfords) [1959] 1 W.L.R. 301; 123 J.P. 207; 103 S.J. 241;
[1959] 1 All E.R. 449; 57 L.G.R. 133, D.C. 4, 9, 336,432

Dixon v. Wells (1890), 25 Q.B.D. 249; 59 L.J.M.C. 116; 62 L.T. 812; 6 T.L.R.
322; 38 W.R. 606; 54 J.P. 725; 17 Cox C.C. 48 64

Dixon Bool Transport Ltd. v. Forsyth (1966), 111 S.J. 57; [1967] Cr.L.R.
52 .... 37, 560

Dobell v. Petrac [1961] V.R. 70 30

Donegani v. Ward [1969] 1 W.L.R. 1502; 133 J.P. 693; 113 S.J. 588; [1969] 3
All E.R. 636; [1969] Cr.L.R. 493, D.C. 197

PAGE

Douglas v. Wilkinson [1965] Cr.L.R. 242; [1964] S.L.T.(Sh.) 68 178
Dove (L.F.) Ltd. v. Tarvin (1964), 108 S.J. 404 .... 44, 508
Downes v. Fell (1969), 113 S.J. 387; [1969] Cr.L.R. 376 .... 284, 285
Drew v. Dingle [1934] 1 K.B. 187; 103 L.J.K.B. 97; 150 L.T. 219; 77 S.J. 799;
  50 T.L.R. 101; 98 J.P. 1; 31 L.G.R. 417; 30 Cox C.C. 53 575
Dring v. Mann (1948), 92 S.J. 272; 112 J.P. 270 89
Dryden v. Johnson [1961] Cr.L.R. 551 242
Dryden v. Surrey County Council and Stewart [1936] 2 All E.R. 535; 80 S.J.
  656 75
Drysdale v. Harrison [1972] Cr.L.R. 573, D.C.; [1973] R.T.R. 45 45
Duck v. Peacock [1949] 1 All E.R. 318; 93 S.J. 165; 65 T.L.R. 87; [1949]
  W.N. 36; 113 J.P. 135; 47 L.G.R. 271 672
Du Cros v. Lambourne [1907] 1 K.B. 40; 76 L.J.K.B. 50; 95 L.T. 782; 23
  T.L.R. 3; 70 J.P. 525; 5 L.G.R. 120; 2 Cox C.C. 311 .... 47, 55, 276
Dudley v. Holland [1965] 1 Q.B. 31; [1963] 3 W.L.R. 970; [1963] 3 All E.R.
  732; 107 S.J. 1041; 128 J.P. 51 487
Duffin v. Markham (1918), 88 L.J.K.B. 581; 119 L.T. 148; 82 J.P. 281; 16
  L.G.R. 807; 26 Cox C.C. 308 86
Duffy v. Lovegrove [1955] Jo.Crim.L. 172 143
Duncan v. Jones [1936] 1 K.B. 218; 105 L.J.K.B. 71; 154 L.T. 110; 79 S.J.
  903; 52 T.L.R. 26; 99 J.P. 399; 33 L.G.R. 491; 30 Cox C.C. 279............ 306
Dunn v. Holt (1904), 73 L.J.K.B. 341; 90 L.T. 577; 48 S.J. 299; 20 T.L.R.
  297; 68 J.P. 271; 2 L.G.R. 502; 20 Cox C.C. 625 387
Durnell v. Scott [1939] 1 All E.R. 183; 83 S.J. 196 275
Durrant v. MacLaren [1956] Cr.L.R. 632; 2 Ll.L.Rep. 70 376
Duxley v. Gilmore [1959] Cr.L.R. 632; 123 J.P.Jo. 331 .... 55, 96
Dyer v. Tulley [1894] 2 Q.B. 794; 63 L.J.M.C. 272; 43 W.R. 61; 58 J.P. 656;
  10 R. 519 488
Dyson v. Ellison [1975] 1 W.L.R. 150; (1974), 119 S.J. 66; [1975] Cr.L.R.
  48, D.C. 608

East Lothian County Council v. Lambert [1950] S.L.T.(Sh.) 41 495
East Midland Area Traffic Commissioners v. Tyler [1938] 3 All E.R. 39; 82
  S.J. 416; 36 L.G.R. 530 575
Eaton v. Cobb [1950] 1 All E.R. 1016; 114 J.P. 271; 48 L.G.R. 528 400
Eccles v. Kirke [1949] 1 All E.R. 428; 93 S.J. 119; 65 T.L.R. 133; [1949]
  W.N. 70; 113 J.P. 175; 47 L.G.R. 205 513
Edkins v. Knowles [1973] 1 Q.B. 748; [1973] 2 W.L.R. 977; 117 S.J. 395;
  [1973] 2 All E.R. 503; [1973] R.T.R. 257; 57 Cr.App.R. 751; [1973]
  Cr.L.R. 446, D.C. 187–194, 469
Edwards v. Brookes (Milk) Ltd. [1963] 1 W.L.R. 795; [1963] 3 All E.R. 62;
  107 S.J. 477; 127 J.P. 497; 61 L.G.R. 430 121
Edwards v. Bull (1956), 54 L.G.R. 338 70
Edwards v. Clarke (1951), 115 J.P.Jo. 426 273
Edwards v. Griffiths [1953] 1 W.L.R. 1199; [1953] 2 All E.R. 874; 97 S.J. 592;
  117 J.P. 514; 51 L.G.R. 549; [1953] 2 Ll.L.Rep. 269 .... 369, 639
Edwards v. Jones [1947] K.B. 659; [1947] 1 All E.R. 830; 45 L.J.R. 324; 111
  J.P. 324 .... 266, 268
Egan v. Bowler (1939), 63 Ll.L.Rep. 266 372
Eggington v. Pearl (1875), 33 L.T. 428; 40 J.P. 56 64
Elieson v. Parker (1917), 117 L.T. 276; 61 S.J. 559; 33 T.L.R. 380; 81 J.P.
  265; 15 L.G.R. 531 6
Elkington v. Kesley [1948] 2 K.B. 256; [1948] 1 All E.R. 786; [1948] L.J.R.
  1195; 92 S.J. 259; 64 T.L.R. 340; 112 J.P. 228; 46 L.G.R. 232 94
Elkins v. Cartlidge [1947] 1 All E.R. 829; 177 L.T. 519; 91 S.J. 573; 45 L.G.R.
  329 174
Elliott v. Grey [1960] 1 Q.B. 367; [1959] 3 W.L.R. 956; [1959] 3 All E.R. 733;
  103 S.J. 921; 124 J.P. 58; 57 L.G.R. 357 .... 10, 44, 45, 376, 429, 465, 517

PAGE

Ellis v. Dubowski [1921] 3 K.B. 621; 91 L.J.K.B. 89; 126 L.T. 91; 37 T.L.R.
910; 85 J.P. 230; 19 L.G.R. 641; 27 Cox C.C. 107 573
Ellis v. Nott-Bower (1896), 13 T.L.R. 35; 60 J.P. 760 .... 9, 343
Ellis v. Smith [1962] 1 W.L.R. 1468; [1962] 3 All E.R. 954; 106 S.J. 1069; 127
J.P. 51; 61 L.G.R. 64 .... 166, 390
Ellis Ltd. v. Hinds [1947] K.B. 475; [1947] 1 All E.R. 337; [1947] L.J.R. 488;
176 L.T. 425; 91 S.J. 68; 63 T.L.R. 181; 45 L.G.R. 118; 80 Ll.L.Rep.
231 .... 39, 374, 378
Ely v. Godfrey (1922), 126 L.T. 664; 86 J.P. 82; 20 L.G.R. 268; 27 Cox C.C.
191 67
Ende v. Cassidy (1964), 108 S.J. 522; [1964] Cr.L.R. 595 .... 50, 121
Entwhistle v. Woodford (1937), King's Bench Division, unreported 68
Erskine v. Hollin, 115 S.J. 207; [1971] R.T.R. 199, D.C. 192, 193
Eva (Joseph) Ltd. v. Reeves [1938] 2 K.B. 393; [1938] 2 All E.R. 115; 107
L.J.K.B. 569; 159 L.T. 1; 82 S.J. 255; 54 T.L.R. 608; 102 J.P. 261; 36
L.G.R. 425 301
Evans v. Barker [1971] R.T.R. 453, D.C. 386
Evans v. Cross [1938] 1 K.B. 694; 1 All E.R. 751; 107 L.J.K.B. 304; 159 L.T.
164; 82 S.J. 97; 54 T.L.R. 354; 102 J.P. 127; 36 L.G.R. 196; 31 Cox C.C.
118 311
Evans v. Dell [1937] 1 All E.R. 349; 156 L.T. 240; 81 S.J. 100; 53 T.L.R. 310;
101 J.P. 149; 35 L.G.R. 105; 30 Cox C.C. 558 .... 40, 573, 575
Evans v. Hassan and Matthews [1936] 2 All E.R. 107; 80 S.J. 409 572
Evans v. Lewis (1964), 108 S.J. 259; [1964] 1 Ll.L.Rep. 258; [1964] Cr.L.R.
472 373
Evans v. Walkden [1956] 1 W.L.R. 1019; [1956] 3 All E.R. 64; 100 S.J. 587;
120 J.P. 495; 54 L.G.R. 467 .... 21, 374
Exeter Corporation v. Heaman (1877), 37 L.T. 534; 42 J.P. 503 89

Farrell v. Campbell [1959] S.L.T.(Sh.) 43; (1958), 75 Sh.Ct.Rep. 24 170
Farrell v. Feighan [1961] Cr.L.R. 629; 76 Sh.Ct.Rep. 141 122
Farrell v. Nivett [1967] Cr.L.R. 425; [1967] S.L.T. 33; [1967] S.C.(J.)
1 221
Farrell v. Simpson [1959] S.L.T.(Sh.) 23; [1959] Jo.Cr.L. 349; [1959]
Jo.Cr.L. 278 319
Fearon v. Sydney [1966] 1 W.L.R. 1003; [1966] 2 All E.R. 694; 130 J.P. 329;
sub nom. Fearson v. Sydney, 110 S.J. 449 628
Fellside Transport v. Hyde (1962), unreported 414
Ferguson v. Weaving [1951] 1 K.B. 814; [1951] 1 All E.R. 412; 95 S.J. 90;
[1951] 1 T'L.R. 465; [1951] W.N. 99; 115 J.P. 142; 49 L.G.R. 339 52
Ferriby v. Sharman [1971] Cr.L.R. 288; [1971] R.T.R. 163, D.C. 181, 672
Field v. Hopkinson [1944] K.B. 42; 113 L.J.K.B. 104; 170 L.T. 56; 60 T.L.R.
75; 108 J.P. 21; 42 L.G.R. 22.. 91, 553
Fillingham v. Hall (1935), unreported 51, 552
Fisher v. Kearton (1964), 108 S.J. 258; [1964] Cr.L.R. 470 .... 42, 165, 375
Flack v. Church (1918), 87 L.J.K.B. 744; 117 L.T. 720; 34 T.L.R. 32; 82 J.P.
59; 15 L.G.R. 951; 26 Cox C.C. 110 507
Flatman v. Poole; Flatman v. Oatey [1937] 1 All E.R. 495; 25 Traff.Cas.
142 .... 51, 552
Flewitt v. Horvath (1972), 136 J.P.Jo. 164 .... 668, 674, 676
Flower Freight Co. Ltd. v. Hammond [1963] 1 Q.B. 275; [1962] 3 W.L.R.
1331; [1962] 3 All E.R. 950; 106 S.J. 919; 127 J.P. 42; 61 L.G.R.
67 .... 5, 334, 497, 504, 544
Floyd v. Bush [1953] 1 W.L.R. 242; [1953] 1 All E.R. 265; 97 S.J. 80; 117
J.P. 88; 51 L.G.R. 162; [1953] Ll.L.Rep. 64 .... 6, 23, 24, 159, 358
Forsyth v. Phillips (1964), 108 S.J. 36; [1964] Cr.L.R. 229 .... 38, 560
Foster v. Farrell [1963] Cr.L.R. 782; [1963] S.L.T. 182 .... 118, 466
Foulkes v. Baker [1975] R.T.R. 50 225

PAGE

Fox v. Dingley, Ware v. Fox. *See* Ware v. Fox, Fox v. Dingley
Franklin v. Langdown [1971] 3 All E.R. 662; [1971] R.T.R. 471, D.C. 457
Fransman v. Sexton [1965] Cr.L.R. 556; (1965), *The Guardian*, 9th July ... 38, 412
French's Dairies (Sevenoaks) Ltd. v. Davis [1973] Cr.L.R. 630, D.C. 88
Fry v. Bevan (1937), 81 S.J. 60 332
Funnell v. Johnson [1962] Cr.L.R. 488 392
Furdson v. McGovern [1954] A.L.R. 450 8

Gallacher v. H.M. Advocate [1963] S.L.T. 217 242
Galloway v. Adair [1947] S.C.(J.) 7 276
Gardner v. James [1948] 2 All E.R. 1069; 92 S.J. 732; 65 T.L.R. 36; [1948]
    W.N. 502; 113 J.P. 62; 47 L.G.R. 45 .... 683, 700
Garfield v. Maddocks [1974] Q.B. 7; [1973] 2 W.L.R. 888; 117 S.J. 145;
    [1973] 2 All E.R. 373; 57 Cr.App.R. 372; [1973] Cr.L.R. 231, D.C. ... 88,
                                                                              698
Garner v. Burr [1951] 1 K.B. 31; [1950] 2 All E.R. 683; 94 S.J. 597; 66 T.L.R.
    (Pt. 2) 768; [1950] W.N. 445; 114 J.P. 484; 49 L.G.R. 30 .... 4, 9, 497
Garrett v. Hooper [1973] R.T.R. 1; [1973] Cr.L.R. 61, D.C. 35, 47, 412
Gatland v. Metropolitan Police Commissioner [1968] 2 Q.B. 279; [1968] 2
    W.L.R. 1263; [1968] 2 All E.R. 100; 112 S.J. 336; 132 J.P. 323; 66
    L.G.R. 519 389
Gaynor v. Allen [1959] 2 Q.B. 403; [1959] 3 W.L.R. 221; [1959] 2 All E.R.
    644; 103 S.J. 677; 123 J.P. 413 268
Gelberg v. Miller [1961] 1 W.L.R. 459; [1961] 1 All E.R. 618; 105 S.J. 230;
    125 J.P. 357; *affg.* [1961] 1 W.L.R. 153; [1961] 1 All E.R. 291; 105 S.J.
    89; 125 J.P. 123 .... 387, 394, 466
Geraghty v. Morris [1939] 2 All E.R. 269; 160 L.T. 397; 83 S.J. 359; 55
    T.L.R. 599; 103 J.P. 175; 37 L.G.R. 297 660
Gerring v. Barfield (1864), 16 C.B.N.S. 579; 11 L.T. 270; 28 J.P. 615; 143
    E.R. 1261 390
Getreide-Import Gesellschaft m.b.h. v. Contimar S.A. Compania Industrial
    Commercial y Maritima [1953] 1 W.L.R. 793; [1953] 2 All E.R. 223; 97
    S.J. 434; [1953] 1 Ll.L.Rep. 572; *affg.* [1953] 1 W.L.R. 207; [1953] 1 All
    E.R. 257; 97 S.J. 66; [1952] 2 Ll.L.Rep. 551 139
Gibb v. Hill [1948] Jo.Cr.L. 185 490
Gibbons v. Kahl [1956] 1 Q.B. 59; [1955] 3 W.L.R. 596; [1955] 3 All E.R.
    345; 99 S.J. 782; 120 J.P. 1; 54 L.G.R. 35 450
Gifford v. Whittaker [1942] 1 K.B. 501; [1942] 1 All E.R. 604; 111 L.J.K.B.
    461; 166 L.T. 324; 86 S.J. 154; 58 T.L.R. 195; 106 J.P. 128; 40 L.G.R.
    146 .... 42, 47, 412, 418, 685
Gill v. Carson and Nield [1917] 2 K.B. 674; 117 L.T. 285; 81 J.P. 250; 15
    L.G.R. 567; 25 Cox C.C. 774; *sub nom.* Gill v. Carson, Nield v. Carson, 86
    L.J.K.B. 1290 .... 386, 387, 700
Gill v. Forster [1970] R.T.R 372; [1972] Cr.L.R. 45, D.C. 203
Gillespie v. Macmillan [1957] S.C.(J.) 31; [1957] S.L.T. 283; [1957] Jo.
    Crim.L. 341 319
Gleed v. Stroud [1962] Jo.Cr.L. 161 112
Glendinning v. Batty [1973] R.T.R. 405; [1973] Cr.L.R. 763, D.C. 672, 673,
                                                                              692
Glendinning v. Bell [1973] R.T.R. 52; [1973] Cr.L.R. 57, D.C. 233
Godsmark v. Knight Bros. (1960), 124 J.P.Jo. 422; (1960), *The Times*, 12th
    May 302
Goke v. Willett and Another (1973), 117 S.J. 468; [1973] R.T.R. 422, C.A. ... 286,
                                                                              288
Goldsmith v. Deakin (1933), 150 L.T. 157; 50 T.L.R. 73; 98 J.P. 4; 31
    L.G.R. 420; 30 Cox C.C. 32 .... 36, 39, 573, 575
Goldsmith v. Laver [1970] R.T.R. 162; (1970), 134 J.P.Jo. 310; [1970]
    Cr.L.R. 286, D.C. 671

PAGE

Goodbarne v. Buck [1940] 1 K.B. 771; [1940] 1 All E.R. 613; 109 L.J.K.B. 837; 162 L.T. 259; 84 S.J. 330; 56 T.L.R. 433; 66 Ll.L.Rep. 129; 31 Cox C.C. 380; *affg.* [1940] 1 K.B. 107; [1939] 4 All E.R. 107; 109 L.J.K.B. 17; 161 L.T. 348; 83 S.J. 850; 56 T.L.R. 36; 103 J.P. 393; 65 Ll.L.Rep. 27 .... 35, 38, 376
Goodley v. Kelly [1973] R.T.R. 125; [1973] Cr.L.R. 125, D.C. 211, 222
Goody v. Fletcher [1962] Cr.L.R. 324; 106 S.J. 222 142
Goosey v. Adams [1971] R.T.R. 465; [1972] Cr.L.R. 49, D.C. 423
Gordon v. Cann (1899), 68 L.J.Q.B. 434; 80 L.T. 20; 43 S.J. 225; 15 T.L.R. 165; 63 J.P. 324; 47 W.R. 269 403
Gordon v. Smith (1970), 115 S.J. 62; [1971] Cr.L.R. 173; [1971] R.T.R. 52, D.C. 673
Gosling v. Paul (1961), 125 J.P. 389; 105 S.J. 234, D.C.; [1961] Cr.L.R. 318 ... 687, 688
Gott v. Chisholm (1950), 114 J.P.Jo. 212 .... 682, 683
Gough v. Rees (1929), 142 L.T. 424; 46 T.L.R. 103; 94 J.P. 53; 28 L.G.R. 32; 29 Cox C.C. 74 .... 40, 54, 579
Gould & Co. v. Houghton [1921] 1 K.B. 509; 90 L.J.K.B. 369; 124 L.T. 566; 65 S.J. 344; 37 T.L.R. 291; 85 J.P. 93; 19 L.G.R. 85; 26 Cox C.C. 693 70
Grange Motors (Cwmbran) Ltd. v. Spencer [1969] 1 W.L.R. 53; [1969] 1 All E.R. 340; (1968), 112 S.J. 908 284
Grays v. Customs Commissioners (1884), 48 J.P. 343 65
Grays Haulage Co. Ltd. v. Arnold [1966] 1 W.L.R. 534; [1966] 1 All E.R. 896; 110 S.J. 112; 130 J.P. 908 .... 36–38, 560, 561
Greaves (G.) & Son Ltd. v. Dean [1972] R.T.R. 146 493
Green v. Burnett. *See* James & Son Ltd. v. Smee
Green v. Dunn [1953] 1 All E.R. 550 345
Grew v. Cubitt (1951), 95 S.J. 452; [1951] 2 T.L.R. 305; 49 L.G.R. 650 ... 122
Grierson v. Clark [1958] S.C.(J.) 22; [1958] S.L.T. 112 17
Griffin v. Squires [1958] 1 W.L.R. 1106; [1958] 3 All E.R. 468; 102 S.J. 828; 103 S.J. 5; 123 J.P. 40; 56 L.G.R. 442 .... 28, 30
Griffin v. Williams [1964] Cr.L.R. 60 273
Griffiths v. Studebakers Ltd. [1924] 1 K.B. 102; 93 L.J.K.B. 50; 130 L.T. 215; 68 S.J. 118; 40 T.L.R. 26; 87 J.P. 199; 21 L.G.R. 796; 27 Cox C.C. 565 .. 38, 42, 48, 468, 527
Grimble & Co. v. Preston [1914] 1 K.B. 270; 83 L.J.K.B. 347; 110 L.T. 115; 30 T.L.R. 119; 78 J.P. 72; 12 L.G.R. 382; 24 Cox C.C. 1 .... 179, 490
Groome v. Driscoll (1969), 113 S.J. 905; [1969] 3 All E.R. 1638n. 136
Gross Cash Registers Ltd. v. Vogt [1967] 2 Q.B. 77; [1966] 2 W.L.R. 470; [1965] 3 All E.R. 832; 110 S.J. 174; 130 J.P. 113; [1965] C.L.Y. 3472 ... 552
Groves v. Redbart [1975] Cr.L.R. 158 .... 113, 319
Guardian Assurance Co. v. Sutherland [1939] 2 All E.R. 246 376
Guest Scottish Carriers Ltd. v. Trend [1967] 1 W.L.R. 1371; [1967] 3 All E.R. 52; 111 S.J. 812; 131 J.P. 468 414
Gullen v. Ford; Prowse v. Clark [1975] R.T.R. 302; (1975), *Law Society's Gazette*, 5th February; [1975] Cr.L.R. 172 454
Gwennap (William) Agricultural Ltd. v. Amphlett [1957] 1 W.L.R. 910; 2 All E.R. 605; 101 S.J. 592; 121 J.P. 487; 55 L.G.R. 557 .... 5, 415, 431, 432

Haines v. Roberts [1953] 1 W.L.R. 309; [1953] 1 All E.R. 344; 97 S.J. 17; 117 J.P. 123; 51 L.G.R. 177 .... 166, 167
Hallett v. Warren (1929), 93 J.P. 225; 27 L.G.R. 773 .... 242, 276
Hamilton v. Blair and Meechan. *See* Macleod v. Penman
Hamilton v. Jones (1926), 42 T.L.R. 148 26
Hamilton v. Walker [1892] 2 Q.B. 25; 61 L.J.M.C. 134; 67 L.T. 200; 36 S.J. 505; 40 W.R. 476; 56 J.P. 583; 17 Cox C.C. 539; *sub nom.* R. v. Hamilton, 8 T.L.R. 531 77

PAGE

Hammertons Cars Ltd. *v.* Redbridge London Borough Council [1974] 1
W.L.R. 484; 118 S.J. 240; [1974] 2 All E.R. 216; [1974] Cr.L.R. 241,
D.C. 599
Hammond *v.* Hall and Ham River Ltd. [1965] A.C. 1049; [1965] 3 W.L.R.
337; [1965] 2 All E.R. 811; 109 S.J. 557; 129 J.P.488; [1965] 2 Ll.L.Rep.
115; *affg.* [1965] 1 W.L.R. 180; [1965] 1 All E.R. 108; 109 S.J. 53; 129
J.P. 107; [1964] 2 Ll.L.Rep. 549; [1964] C.L.Y. 3215 543
Hampson *v.* Powell [1970] 1 All E.R. 929, D.C. 271, 341, 344
Hampton (William) Ltd. and Another *v.* Dixon (Bryan) [1973], 22nd May,
unreported 19
Harding (An Infant) *v.* Hinchcliffe (1964), *The Times,* 8th April 285
Harding *v.* Oliver [1973] R.T.R. 497; [1973] Cr.L.R. 764, D.C. 666,
672, 678
Harding *v.* Price [1948] 1 K.B. 695; [1948] 1 All E.R. 283; [1948] L.J.R.
1624; 92 S.J. 112; 64 T.L.R. 111; 112 J.P. 189; 46 L.G.R. 142 .... 304, 305,
341, 344
Hardy *v.* Motor Insurers' Bureau [1964] 2 Q.B. 745; [1964] 3 W.L.R. 433;
[1964] 2 All E.R. 742; 108 S.J. 422; [1964] 1 Ll.L.Rep. 397 374
Hare *v.* Gocher [1962] 2 Q.B. 641; [1962] 3 W.L.R. 339; [1962] 2 All E.R.
763; 106 S.J. 531; 126 J.P. 395; 60 L.G.R. 278 69
Hargreaves *v.* Alderson [1964] 2 Q.B. 159; [1963] 2 W.L.R. 31; [1962] 3 All
E.R. 1019; 107 S.J. 15; 127 J.P. 99 .... 90, 266
Hargreaves *v.* Baldwin (1905), 93 L.J. 311; 21 T.L.R. 715; 69 J.P. 397; 3
L.G.R. 973... 275
Harman *v.* Wardrop (1971), 115 S.J. 146; [1971] R.T.R. 127; 55 Cr.App.R.
211, D.C. 163, 192
Harris *v.* Croson (1972), 117 S.J. 91; [1973] R.T.R. 57; [1973] Cr.L.R. 121,
D.C. 189
Harrison *v.* Co-operative Insurance Co. Ltd. (1968), 118 N.L.J. 910 28
Harrison *v.* Hill [1932] S.C.(J.) 13 .... 27, 29, 173
Hart *v.* Bex [1957] Cr.L.R. 622 .... 42, 48, 412, 684
Hateley *v.* Greenough [1962] Cr.L.R. 329, D.C. 464
Hawkes *v.* Hinckley (1956), 120 J.P.Jo. 642 464
Hawkins *v.* Holmes [1974] R.T.R. 436; [1974] Cr.L.R. 370, D.C. 123, 416
Hawthorn *v.* Knight. *See* MacLeod *v.* Penman
Hay *v.* Shepherd [1974] R.T.R. 64; [1974] Cr.L.R. 114, D.C. 190, 193
Hay (or Bourhill) *v.* Young [1943] A.C. 92; [1942] 2 All E.R. 396; 111
L.J.P.C. 97; 167 L.T. 261; *sub nom.* Bourhill *v.* Young, 86 S.J. 349 348
Hayes *v.* Kingsworthy Foundry Co. Ltd. [1971] Cr.L.R. 239, D.C.; [1971]
R.T.R. 286 .... 411, 492, 493
Haynes *v.* Davis [1915] 1 K.B. 332; 84 L.J.K.B. 441; 112 L.T. 417; 79 J.P.
187; 13 L.G.R. 497; 24 Cox C.C. 533 180
Haynes *v.* Swain [1974] Cr.L.R. 483, D.C.; [1975] R.T.R. 40 .... 278, 416
Heath *v.* Pearson [1957] Cr.L.R. 195 29
Hedley *v.* Sparrow [1964] N.I. 72 75
Helson *v.* Barnard [1922] S.L.T. 40 526
Henderson *v.* Bernard [1955] Cr.L.R. 715; [1955] S.L.T.(Sh.Ct.) 27 29
Henderson *v.* Gray [1927] S.C.(J.) 43 387
Henderson *v.* Jones (1955), 119 J.P. 305; 53 L.G.R. 319 273
Henderson *v.* Robson (1949), 93 S.J. 424; 113 J.P. 313; 47 L.G.R. 512 51,
494
Hennell *v.* Cuthbert [1962] Cr.L.R. 104 .... 117, 118
Henshall (John) (Quarries) Ltd. *v.* Harvey [1965] 2 Q.B. 233; [1965] 2
W.L.R. 758; [1965] 1 All E.R. 725; 109 S.J. 152 .... 36, 53,
54, 121
Hewer *v.* Cutler [1974] R.T.R. 155; [1973] Cr.L.R. 762, D.C. 33, 44, 429
Higgins *v.* Bernard [1972] 1 W.L.R. 455; 116 S.J. 179; [1972] 1 All E.R.
1037; [1972] R.T.R. 304; [1972] Cr.L.R. 242, D.C. 583
Higgins *v.* Feeney (1954), 88 I.L.T.R. 152; [1954] I.R. 45 .... 13, 371

PAGE

Hill v. Baxter [1958] 1 Q.B. 277; [1958] 2 W.L.R. 76; [1958] 1 All E.R. 193;
 102 S.J. 53; 122 J.P. 134; 56 L.G.R. 117; 42 Cr.App.R. 51 ... 24, 269, 274,
 280, 300
Hill v. Phillips (1963), 107 S.J. 890 .... 284, 289
Hill & Sons (Botley & Denmead) Ltd. v. Hampshire Chief Constable [1972]
 R.T.R. 29; [1971] Cr.L.R. 538; (1971), 115 S.J. 675 .... 34, 37, 412
Hinde v. Evans (1906), 96 L.T. 20; 70 J.P. 548; 4 L.G.R. 1152; 21 Cox C.C.
 331 389
Hinshelwood v. Auld [1926] S.C.(J.) 4 112
Hirst v. Wilson [1970] 1 W.L.R. 47; 113 S.J. 906; [1969] 3 All E.R. 1566,
 D.C. 208, 228
Hockin v. Ahlquist Brothers Ltd. [1943] 2 All E.R. 722; 60 T.L.R. 60; 107
 J.P. 217 87
Hockin v. Reed & Co. (Torquay) Ltd. (1962), 106 S.J. 198; 60 L.G.R.
 203 413
Hockin v. Weston [1972] R.T.R. 136; (1971), 115 S.J. 675; (1971), The Times,
 30th July; [1971] Cr.L.R. 541, D.C. 231, 235, 679
Hodgson v. Burn (1966), 110 S.J. 151; [1966] Cr.L.R. 226; 116 New L.J.
 501 .... 462, 464
Hoffman v. Thomas [1974] 1 W.L.R. 374; (1973), 118 S.J. 186; [1974] 2 All
 E.R. 233; [1974] R.T.R. 182; [1974] Cr.L.R. 122, D.C. 303, 309
Hogg v. Burnet [1938] S.C.(J.) 160; [1938] S.L.T. 480 .... 111, 554, 562
Hogg v. Clark [1959] S.L.T. 109; [1959] S.C. 7 114
Hogg v. Nicholson [1968] S.L.T. 265 .... 28, 29
Holder v. Walker [1964] Cr.L.R. 61 391
Holland v. Perry [1952] 2 Q.B. 923; [1952] 2 All E.R. 720; 96 S.J. 696; [1952]
 2 T.L.R. 634; [1952] W.N. 438; 116 J.P. 581; 50 L.G.R. 682 507
Holliday v. Henry [1974] R.T.R. 101; [1974] Cr.L.R. 126, D.C. ... 10, 27, 487
Hollingsworth v. Howard [1974] R.T.R. 58; [1974] Cr.L.R. 113, D.C. ... 198, 222, 224
Hollis Brothers Ltd. v. Bailey, Butwell v. Bailey [1968] 1 W.L.R. 663; (1968),
 112 S.J. 381, D.C. 420
Holroyd v. Berry [1973] R.T.R. 145; [1973] Cr.L.R. 118, D.C. 673, 692
Homewood v. Spiller (Hodder, Third Party) (1962), 106 S.J. 900; 61 L.G.R.
 29; [1963] Cr.L.R. 52 285
Homolka v. Osmond [1939] 1 All E.R. 154 70
Hopes v. Lord Advocate [1960] Cr.L.R. 566; [1960] S.L.T. 264 126
Hopgood v. Chapman [1975] Cr.L.R. 397 673
Horn v. Dobson [1933] S.C.(J.) 1 .... 9, 497
Hosein v. Edmunds (1969), 113 S.J. 759 679
Hosier v. Goodall [1962] 2 Q.B. 401; [1962] 2 W.L.R. 157; [1962] 1 All E.R.
 30; 105 S.J. 1085; 126 J.P. 52; 60 L.G.R. 500 .... 137, 138
Hougham v. Martin (1964), 108 S.J. 138; [1964] Cr.L.R. 414 273
Houghton v. Scholfield [1973] R.T.R. 239; sub nom. Houghton v. Schofield
 [1973] Cr.L.R. 126, D.C. 29, 30
Houghton v. Trafalgar Insurance Co. [1954] 1 Q.B. 247; [1953] 3 W.L.R.
 985; [1953] 2 All E.R. 1409; 97 S.J. 831; [1953] 2 Ll.L.Rep. 503 ... 371, 419
Houston v. Leslie [1958] S.L.T. 109; [1958] Cr.L.R. 477 318
Howard v. Grass Products Ltd. [1972] 1 W.L.R. 1323; 116 S.J. 786; [1972]
 3 All E.R. 530; [1972] R.T.R. 547; [1972] Cr.L.R. 572, D.C. 499
Howard v. Jones (G.T.) & Co. Ltd. [1975] R.T.R. 150; [1974] Cr.L.R.
 606, D.C. 47, 50
Howey v. Bradley (1969), 114 S.J. 37; [1970] Cr.L.R. 223, D.C. ...123, 372, 379
Howman v. Russell [1923] S.C.(J.) 32; 60 S.L.R. 363; [1923] S.L.T.
 336 .... 404, 405
Hoy v. Smith [1964] 1 W.L.R. 1377; [1964] 3 All E.R. 670; 108 S.J. 841; 129
 J.P. 33; 62 L.G.R. 661 458
Hubbard v. Messenger [1938] 1 K.B. 300; [1937] 4 All E.R. 48; 107 L.J.K.B.
 44; 157 L.T. 512; 81 S.J. 846; 54 T.L.R. 1; 101 J.P. 553; 35 L.G.R. 564;
 30 Cox C.C. 624 .... 332, 333

PAGE

Hudson v. Hornsby [1973] R.T.R. 4; [1972] Cr.L.R. 505, D.C. 163, 219
Hughes v. Hall [1960] 1 W.L.R. 733; [1960] 2 All E.R. 504; 104 S.J. 566; 124
    J.P. 411 .... 450, 453
Hughes (Claude) and Co. (Carlisle) Ltd. v. Hyde [1963] 2 Q.B. 757; [1963] 2
    W.L.R. 381; [1963] 1 All E.R. 598; 107 S.J. 115; 127 J.P. 226; 61 L.G.R.
    257 414
Humphreys v. Thompson [1970] R.T.R. 228, D.C. 236
Hunter v. Coombs [1962] 1 W.L.R. 573; [1962] 1 All E.R. 904; 106 S.J. 287;
    126 J.P. 300 .... 89, 90
Hunter v. Hammond (1964), 107 S.J. 1024; [1964] Cr.L.R. 145 391
Hunter v. Mann [1974] Q.B. 767; [1974] 2 W.L.R. 742; 118 S.J. 171; [1974]
    2 All E.R. 414; [1974] R.T.R. 338; 59 Cr.App.R. 37; [1974] Cr.L.R.
    260, D.C. 464
Hunter v. Towers [1951] 1 All E.R. 349; 95 S.J. 62; [1951] 1 T.L.R. 313;
    [1951] W.N. 95; 115 J.P. 117; 49 L.G.R. 134 .... 11, 332
Hunters the Bakers Ltd. v. Hills [1973] R.T.R. 361; [1973] Cr.L.R. 534, D.C. 526
Hurlock v. Inglis (1963), 107 S.J. 1023 285
Hutchings v. Giles [1955] Cr.L.R. 784 .... 37, 412
Hutton v. Casey (1952), 116 J.P.Jo. 223 266

Ingleton v. Dibble (1971), *The Times*, 17th November; [1972] 1 All E.R. 275,
    D.C. 206
Ingleton of Ilford Ltd. v. General Accident Fire and Life Assurance Corpora-
    tion [1967] 2 Ll.L.Rep. 179 421
Inland Revenue v. Cadwalader (1904), 7 F. (Ct. of Sess.) 146; 42 Sc.L.Rep.
    117; 12 S.L.T. 449; *sub nom*. Cooper v. Cadwalader, 5 Tax.Cas. 101 ... 63

J.R.M. (Plant) Ltd. v. Hodgson [1960] 1 Ll.L.Rep. 538; *The Times*, 21st
    May 376
Jack Motors Ltd. v. Fazackerley [1962] Cr.L.R. 486, D.C. 552
Jacob v. Garland (1973), 117 S.J. 915; [1974] R.T.R. 40; [1974] Cr.L.R.
    194, D.C. 462, 463
Jacobs v. Reed [1974] R.T.R. 81; [1973] Cr.L.R. 531, D.C. 674, 675
James v. Bowkett [1952] 2 All E.R. 320; 96 S.J. 448; [1952] 2 T.L.R. 100;
    [1952] W.N. 341; 116 J.P. 445 79
James v. Cavey [1967] 2 Q.B. 676; [1967] 2 W.L.R. 1239; [1967] 1 All E.R.
    1048; 111 S.J. 318; 131 J.P. 306; 64 L.G.R. 321 .... 298, 299, 393
James v. Davies [1953] 1 Q.B. 8; [1952] 2 All E.R. 758; 96 S.J. 729; [1952] 2
    T.L.R. 662; [1952] W.N. 480; 116 J.P. 603; 50 L.G.R. 694 496
James v. Hall (1968), 112 S.J. 642; [1968] Cr.L.R. 507; 118 New L.J. 638;
    The Times, 26th June 666, 673
James & Son Ltd. v. Smee, Green v. Burnett [1955] 1 Q.B. 78; [1954] 3
    W.L.R. 631; [1954] 3 All E.R. 273; 98 S.J. 771; 118 J.P. 536; 52 L.G.R.
    545 .... 34, 36, 37, 41, 43, 48, 412, 416, 684
Jarman v. Walsh [1936] S.A.S.R. 25 347
Jarvis v. Fuller [1974] R.T.R. 160; [1974] Cr.L.R. 116, D.C. 273, 287
Jefferson, *ex parte* (1966), *The Times*, 5th November 470
Jeffs v. Wells (1936), 100 J.P.Jo. 406 133
Jenkins v. Deane (1933), 103 L.J.K.B. 250; 150 L.T. 314; 78 S.J. 13 ... 10, 371, 419
Jesner & Sons Ltd. v. Waugh [1936] S.C.(J.) 47; [1936] S.L.T. 321 561
Jessopp v. Clarke (1908), 99 L.T. 28; 24 T.L.R. 672; 72 J.P. 358; 6 L.G.R.
    686 134
John v. Bentley (1961), 105 S.J. 406; *The Times*, 20th April 171, 172
John v. Humphreys [1955] 1 W.L.R. 325; [1955] 1 All E.R. 793; 99 S.J. 222;
    119 J.P. 309; 53 L.G.R. 321 .... 123, 379, 470, 487, 515
Johnson v. Fowler [1959] Cr.L.R. 463 .... 271, 273, 278
Johnson v. Youden [1950] 1 K.B. 544; [1950] 1 All E.R. 300; 94 S.J. 115; 66
    T.L.R. (Pt. 1) 395; [1950] W.N. 58; 114 J.P. 136; 48 L.G.R. 276 52

PAGE

Johnston v. Cruickshank [1963] S.C.(J.) 5; [1962] S.L.T. 409 ...... 11, 404, 407

Johnstone v. Dearsley [1966] C.L.Y. 10539 685

Johnstone v. Hawkins [1959] Cr.L.R. 459, 854 282

Jollye v. Dale [1960] 2 Q.B. 258; [1960] 2 W.L.R. 1027; [1960] 2 All E.R.
    369; 104 S.J. 467; 124 J.P. 333 133

Jones v. Brazil [1970] R.T.R. 449, D.C. 223

Jones v. Brooks (1968), 112 S.J. 745; 52 Cr.App.R. 614; (1968), The Times,
    26th June 163, 358

Jones v. Carter [1956] Cr.L.R. 275 .... 87, 122

Jones v. English [1951] 2 All E.R. 853; 95 S.J. 712; [1951] 2 T.L.R. 973;
    [1951] W.N. 552; 115 J.P. 609; 50 L.G.R. 111 .... 665, 667, 694

Jones v. Meatyard [1939] 1 All E.R. 140; 63 Ll.L.Rep. 4 382

Jones v. Metcalfe [1967] 1 W.L.R. 1286; [1967] 3 All E.R. 205; 111 S.J. 563;
    131 J.P. 494 .... 83, 112, 122

Jones v. Powell [1965] 2 Q.B. 216; [1965] 2 W.L.R. 683; [1965] 1 All E.R.
    674; 236 L.T. 152; 129 J.P. 187 632

Jones v. Prothero [1952] 1 All E.R. 434; 116 J.P. 141 .... 26, 348, 400

Jones v. Roberts [1973] R.T.R. 26; [1973] Cr.L.R. 123, D.C. 230

Jones v. Welsh Insurance Corporation Ltd. [1937] 4 All E.R. 149; 157 L.T.
    483; 81 S.J. 886; 54 T.L.R. 22 .... 367, 370

Jordan v. North Hampshire Plant Hire [1970] R.T.R. 212, C.A. 285

Jungnickel v. Laing (1967), 111 S.J. 19 286

Karamat v. R. [1956] A.C. 256; [1956] 2 W.L.R. 412; [1956] 1 All E.R. 415;
    100 S.J. 109; 120 J.P. 136; 40 Cr.App.R. 13 115

Kay v. Butterworth (1946), 173 L.T. 191; 89 S.J. 381; 61 T.L.R. 452; 110
    J.P. 75 .... 273, 274

Kaye v. Hougham (1964), 108 S.J. 358; 62 L.G.R. 457; [1964] Cr.L.R.
    544 392

Kayser v. London Passenger Transport Board [1950] 1 All E.R. 231; 114 J.P.
    122 448

Keeble v. Miller [1950] K.B. 601; [1950] 1 All E.R. 261; 94 S.J. 163; 66 T.L.R.
    (Pt. 1) 429; [1950] W.N. 59; 114 J.P. 143; 48 L.G.R. 235 ... 5, 16, 115, 332

Kelleher v. Christopherson (1957), 91 I.L.T.R. 191 367

Kelly v. Cornhill Insurance Co. Ltd. [1964] 1 W.L.R. 158; [1964] 1 All E.R.
    321; 108 S.J. 94; [1964] 1 Ll.L.Rep. 1; [1964] S.L.T. 81; revsg. [1963]
    C.L.Y. 3072; [1963] S.L.T. 13 .... 36, 374

Kenlin v. Gardiner [1967] 2 Q.B. 510; [1967] 2 W.L.R. 129; [1966] 3 All E.R.
    931; 110 S.J. 848; 131 J.P. 191 305

Kennett v. British Airports Authority [1975] Cr.L.R. 106 416

Kenyon v. Thorley [1973] R.T.R. 60; [1973] Cr.L.R. 119, D.C. 422, 434

Kerr v. Armstrong [1974] R.T.R. 141 672

Kerr v. McNeill [1949] N.I. 19 .... 666, 682, 684

Kerridge v. Rush [1952] 2 Ll.L.Rep. 305 371

Keyse v. Sainsbury [1971] Cr.L.R. 291; [1971] R.T.R. 218, D.C. ... 418, 419, 435

Keyte v. Dew, 114 S.J. 621; [1970] R.T.R. 481, D.C. 425

Kidd v. Kidd, Ley v. Donegani [1969] 1 Q.B. 320; [1968] 3 W.L.R. 734;
    [1968] 3 All E.R. 226; 112 S.J. 602; 132 J.P. 536; 52 Cr.App.R. 659 ... 219

Kidner v. Daniels (1910), 102 L.T. 132; 74 J.P. 127; 8 L.G.R. 159; 22 Cox
    C.C. 276 645

Kidson v. Swatridge [1957] Cr.L.R. 193 335

Kierman v. Howard (1971), 115 S.J. 350; [1971] Cr.L.R. 286; [1971] R.T.R.
    314; 69 L.G.R. 492, D.C. 394

Kierman v. Willcock [1972] R.T.R. 270; [1972] Cr.L.R. 248, D.C. ... 220, 221

Kilbride v. Lake [1962] N.Z.L.R. 590 503

Kinsey v. Herts. County Council (1972), The Times, 12th July 368, 369

Kirkland v. Cairns [1951] S.C.(J.) 61; [1951] S.L.T. 324 390

Knaggs v. Elson (1965), 109 S.J. 596 .... 28, 29

PAGE

Knight v. Baxter (1971), 115 S.J. 350; [1971] R.T.R. 270, D.C. 672

Knowler v. Rennison [1947] K.B. 488; 176 L.T. 271; 63 T.L.R. 150; 91 S.J.
85; 111 J.P. 250; sub nom. Rennison v. Knowler [1947] L.J.R. 555; 111
J.P. 171; [1947] 1 All E.R. 302 .... 665, 683

Knowles (J. M.) Ltd. v. Rand [1962] 1 W.L.R. 893; [1962] 2 All E.R. 926;
106 S.J. 513; 126 J.P. 442; 60 L.G.R. 384 .... 52, 495, 498

Knowles Transport Ltd. v. Russell [1975] R.T.R. 87 560

Kozimor v. Adey [1962] Cr.L.R. 564 452

Kuruma, Son of Kaniu v. R. [1955] A.C. 197; [1955] 2 W.L.R. 223; [1955]
1 All E.R. 236; 99 S.J. 73; 119 J.P. 157 126

Labrum v. Williamson [1947] K.B. 816; [1947] 1 All E.R. 824; [1947] L.J.R.
1362; 177 L.T. 316; 91 S.J. 560; 63 T.L.R. 488; 111 J.P. 334; 45 L.G.R.
340 681

Lambeth London Borough Council v. Saunders Transport Ltd. [1974] R.T.R.
319; [1974] Cr.L.R. 311, D.C. 399

Lambie v. Woodage. See Woodage v. Lambie

Lang v. London Transport Executive [1959] 1 W.L.R. 1168; [1959] 3 All
E.R. 609; 124 J.P. 28 284

Langley Cartage Co. v. Jenks, Adams v. Same [1937] 2 K.B. 382; [1937] 2 All
E.R. 525; 106 L.J.K.B. 559; 156 L.T. 529; 81 S.J. 399; 53 T.L.R. 654;
101 J.P. 393; 35 L.G.R. 246; 30 Cox C.C. 585 310

Langman v. Valentine [1952] 2 All E.R. 803; 96 S.J. 712; [1952] 2 T.L.R.
713; [1952] W.N. 475; 116 J.P. 576; 50 L.G.R. 685 .... 21, 374

Langridge v. Taylor [1972] R.T.R. 157 221

Langton v. Johnson [1956] 1 W.L.R. 1322; [1956] 3 All E.R. 474; 100 S.J.
802; 120 J.P. 561; 54 L.G.R. 635 416

Laurie v. Raglan Building Co. Ltd. [1942] 1 K.B. 152; [1941] 3 All E.R. 332;
111 L.J.K.B. 292; 166 L.T. 63; 86 S.J. 69 284

Law v. Stephens, 115 S.J. 369; [1971] Cr.L.R. 36; [1971] R.T.R. 358,
D.C. 230–233, 679

Law v. Thomas (1964), 108 S.J. 158; 62 L.G.R. 195 6

Lawrence v. Fisher [1947] Jo.Crim.L. 356 89

Lawrence v. Howlett [1952] 2 All E.R. 74; 96 S.J. 397; [1952] 1 T.L.R. 1476;
[1952] W.N. 308; 116 J.P. 391; 50 L.G.R. 531; [1952] 1 Ll.L.Rep.
483 .... 6, 23, 292, 358

Lawrie v. Stevenson [1968] S.L.T.(Notes) 79 178

Layton v. Shires [1960] 2 Q.B. 294; [1959] 3 W.L.R. 949; [1959] 3 All E.R.
587; 103 S.J. 856; 124 J.P. 46 .... 136, 137

Leach v. Cooper Ltd. (1950), 48 L.G.R. 526 .... 51, 552

Leach v. Evans [1952] 2 All E.R. 264; 116 J.P. 410 .... 165, 167

Leathley v. Drummond; Leathley v. Irving [1972] R.T.R. 293; [1972]
Cr.L.R. 227, D.C. 123, 372, 373, 379

Lee v. Knapp [1967] 2 Q.B. 442; [1967] 2 W.L.R. 6; [1966] 3 All E.R. 961;
110 S.J. 981; 131 J.P. 110 .... 254, 347

Lee v. Poole [1954] Cr.L.R. 942 .... 366, 367

Leggate v. Brown [1950] 2 All E.R. 564; 94 S.J. 567; 66 T.L.R. (Pt. 2) 281;
[1950] W.N. 384; 114 J.P. 454; 49 L.G.R. 27; 84 Ll.L.Rep. 395 371

Leicester v. Pearson [1952] 2 Q.B. 668; [1952] 2 All E.R. 71; 96 S.J. 397;
[1952] 1 T.L.R. 1537; [1952] W.N. 317; 116 J.P. 407; 50 L.G.R.
534 .... 305, 450, 680

Levinger v. Licenses and General Insurance Co. (1936), 54 Ll.L.Rep. 68 ... 374

Levinson v. Powell [1967] 1 W.L.R. 1472; [1967] 3 All E.R. 796; 111 S.J. 871;
132 J.P. 10 .... 334, 335, 391

Liddon v. Stringer [1967] Cr.L.R. 371; 117 New L.J. 464 283

Lines v. Hersom [1951] 2 K.B. 682; [1951] 2 All E.R. 650; [1951] 2 T.L.R.
481; [1951] W.N. 439; 115 J.P. 494; sub nom. Hersom v. Lines, 50 L.G.R.
295 664

PAGE

Lloyd v. Lee Ltd. [1951] 2 K.B. 121; [1951] 1 All E.R. 589; 95 S.J. 206; [1951] 1 T.L.R. 624; [1951] W.N. 116; 115 J.P. 189; 49 L.G.R. 353 ...... 44, 537

Lloyd v. Singleton [1953] 1 Q.B. 357; [1953] 2 W.L.R. 278; [1953] 1 All E.R. 291; 97 S.J. 98; 117 J.P. 97; 51 L.G.R. 165 .... 35, 378

Lloyd v. Young (1963), 107 S.J. 631; [1963] Cr.L.R. 703 69

Loadman v. Cragg. See Soden v. Gray

Lockie v. Lawton (1960), 124 J.P. 24; (1959), 103 S.J. 874; 57 L.G.R. 329 ... 450

London Borough of Redbridge v. Jaques [1971] 1 All E.R. 260 388

London County Council v. Hay's Wharf Cartage Co. [1953] 1 W.L.R. 677; [1953] 2 All E.R. 34; 97 S.J. 334; 117 J.P. 304; 51 L.G.R. 347 ... 16, 494, 496

London County Council v. Lee [1914] 3 K.B. 255; 83 L.J.K.B. 1373; 111 L.T. 569; 30 T.L.R. 525; 78 J.P. 396; 12 L.G.R. 733; 24 Cox C.C. 388 ... 52, 498

London Passenger Transport Board v. Sumner (1935), 154 L.T. 108; 79 S.J. 840; 52 T.L.R. 13; 99 J.P. 387; 33 L.G.R. 459 578

London Passenger Transport Board v. Upson [1949] A.C. 155; [1949] 1 All E.R. 60; [1949] L.J.R. 238; 93 S.J. 40; [1948] W.N. 492 453

Lonnkuist v. Lonnkuist (1952), 96 S.J. 135; [1952] W.N. 88 85

Lord v. Colvin (1855), 3 Drew. 222; 3 Eq.Rep. 514; 24 L.J.Ch. 517; 25 L.T.(O.S.) 42; 1 Jur.(N.S.) 298; 3 W.R. 342; 61 E.R. 888 75

Louden v. British Merchants Insurance Co. Ltd. [1961] 1 W.L.R. 798; [1961] 1 All E.R. 705; 105 S.J. 209; [1961] 1 Ll.L.Rep. 155 .... 238, 241

Lovell v. Archer, Lovell v. Duckett (1971), 115 S.J. 157; [1971] R.T.R. 237, D.C. 195

Lowe v. Stone [1948] 2 All E.R. 1076; [1949] L.J.R. 797; 93 S.J. 72; [1948] W.N. 487; 113 J.P. 59; 47 L.G.R. 127 .... 16, 505

Lowery (P.) & Sons Ltd. v. Wark [1975] R.T.R. 45 .... 40, 418

Lund v. Thompson [1959] 1 Q.B. 283; [1958] 3 W.L.R. 594; [1958] 3 All E.R. 356; 102 S.J. 811; 122 J.P. 489; 56 L.G.R. 451 140

Lyons v. Denscombe [1949] 1 All E.R. 977; 93 S.J. 389; [1949] W.N. 257; 113 J.P. 305; 47 L.G.R. 412 576

Lyons v. May [1948] 2 All E.R. 1062; 93 S.J. 59; 65 T.L.R. 51; [1948] W.N. 483; 113 J.P. 42; 47 L.G.R. 125 .... 39, 368, 377, 681

M'Arthur v. Jack [1950] S.C.(J.) 29 397

M'Boyle v. Hatton Estate Co. [1951] S.L.T.(Sh.) 101 .... 51, 498

M'Callum & Son v. Adair [1937] S.L.T. 580; [1937] S.C.(J.) 114 561

McCarthy v. British Oak Insurance Co. [1938] 3 All E.R. 1; 159 L.T. 215; 82 S.J. 568; 61 Ll.L.Rep. 194 366

M'Cowan v. Stewart [1936] S.C.(J.) 36 16

McCrone v. Riding [1938] 1 All E.R. 157; 158 L.T. 253; 82 S.J. 175; 54 T.L.R. 328; 102 J.P. 109; 36 L.G.R. 160; 30 Cox C.C. 670 270

McCrone v. J. & L. Rigby (Wigan) Ltd. (1951), 95 S.J. 712; [1951] 2 T.L.R. 911; [1951] W.N. 626; 50 L.G.R. 115 .... 8, 31, 169, 501, 514, 515

McCulloch v. Hannam [1951] 1 All E.R. 402; 95 S.J. 172; [1951] 1 T.L.R. 519; [1951] W.N. 162; 115 J.P. 141; 49 L.G.R. 568 .... 177, 539

MacDonald v. Bain [1954] S.L.T.(Sh.) 30; 70 Sh.Ct.Rep. 61 164

MacDonald v. Carmichael [1941] S.C.(J.) 27; [1941] S.L.T. 81 .... 7, 8

MacDonald v. Crawford [1952] S.L.T.(Sh.) 92; 68 Sh.Ct.Rep. 244 165

McDonald v. M'Ewen [1953] S.L.T.(Sh.) 26 174

Macdonald v. Wilmae Concrete Co. Ltd. [1954] S.L.T.(Sh.) 33; 70 Sh.Ct.Rep. 63 38

M'Fadyean v. Burton [1953] S.L.T. 301; [1954] S.C.(J.) 18 672

McGimpsey v. Carlin [1968] Jo.Crim.L. 221 662

Machin v. Ash (1950), 94 S.J. 705; [1950] W.N. 478; 49 L.G.R. 87 379

McInnes v. National Motor and Accident Insurance Union [1963] 2 Ll.L.Rep. 415; [1963] S.L.T.(Sh.Ct.) 52; 79 Sh.Ct.Rep. 148 371

McIntyre v. Coles [1966] 1 W.L.R. 831; [1966] 1 All E.R. 723; 110 S.J. 315; 130 J.P. 189 286

PAGE

Mackereth v. Madge (1968), 112 S.J. 98; 66 L.G.R. 69; [1968] Cr.L.R. 226 ... 323

McKerrell v. Robertson [1956] S.C.(J.) 50; [1956] S.L.T. 290 .... 299, 449

McKie v. Lord Advocate [1958] S.L.T. 152; [1958] Cr.L.R. 386; S.C.(J.) 24 256

Mackie v. MacLeod [1956] S.L.T. 116; [1956] S.C.(J.) 27; 106 L.J.Ch. 363 552

Mackie v. Waugh [1940] S.C.(J.) 49; [1940] S.N. 24; [1940] S.L.T. 285 ... 15, 16, 515

Mackinnon v. Peate [1936] 2 All E.R. 240; 80 S.J. 387 415

McKnight v. Davies (1973), 117 S.J. 940; [1974] R.T.R. 4; [1974] Cr.L.R. 62, D.C. 352, 356, 359

MacLean v. Cork (1968), 112 S.J. 658; [1968] Cr.L.R. 507; 118 New L.J. 638; *The Times*, 28th June 667, 668, 673

McLean v. Fearn [1954] S.L.T.(Sh.) 37 575

Maclean v. Hall [1962] S.L.T.(Sh.) 30; 77 Sh.Ct.Rep. 161 6

MacLean v. McCabe [1964] S.L.T.(Sh.) 39 8

McLennan (A. & C.) (Blairgowrie) Ltd. v. MacMillan [1964] S.L.T. 2 ... 70, 518

Macleod v. Anderson [1961] S.L.T. 297; [1961] S.C.(J.) 32 140

McLeod (or Houston) v. Buchanan [1940] 2 All E.R. 179; 84 S.J. 452; [1940] S.C.(H.L.) 17; [1940] S.L.T. 232; [1940] S.N. 20 .... 34, 35

MacLeod v. Hamilton [1965] S.L.T. 305; [1966] Cr.L.R. 342 .... 313, 393

Macleod v. Nicol [1964] Jo.Crim.L. 119; [1964] S.C.(J.) 4 178

Macleod v. Penman, Hamilton v. Blair and Meechan, Hawthorn v. Knight [1962] Cr.L.R. 332; [1962] S.C.(J.) 31; [1962] S.L.T. 69 ...... 42, 43, 44, 573, 575, 576

McLeod v. Wajkowska [1963] S.L.T.(Notes) 51 391

MacMillan v. Butter [1963] S.L.T.(Sh.) 44 498

McMillan v. Caledonian Omnibus Co. (1938), 26 Traff.Cas. 374 17

Macmillan v. Gibson [1966] S.L.T.(Sh.) 84 .... 388, 393

M'Millan v. Grant [1924] S.C.(J.) 13 489

McNeill v. Dunbar [1965] S.L.T.N. 79; [1966] Cr.L.R. 336 31

MacNeill v. Fletcher [1966] S.C.(J.) 18 .... 238, 242

McNicol v. Peters [1970] Cr.L.R. 163; [1969] S.L.T.(J.) 261 ...... 192, 227, 232

McSteen v. McCarthy [1952] N.I. 33 368

Maddox v. Storer [1963] 1 Q.B. 451; [1962] 2 W.L.R. 958; [1962] 1 All E.R. 831; 106 S.J. 372; 126 J.P. 263; 61 L.G.R. 41 ... 5, 333, 334, 497, 544, 567

Magna Plant Ltd. v. Mitchell (1966), 110 S.J. 349; [1966] Cr.L.R. 394; 116 New L.J. 780 .... 36, 37, 412

Maguire v. Crouch [1941] 1 K.B. 108; 110 L.J.K.B. 71; 164 L.T. 171; 84 S.J. 608; 57 T.L.R. 75; 104 J.P. 445; 39 L.G.R. 49; 31 Cox C.C. 441 ... 401, 421

Maher v. Prendergast [1948] Ir.R. 339 138

Manley v. Dabson, Manley v. Same [1950] 1 K.B. 100; [1949] 2 All E.R. 578; [1949] L.J.R. 1427; 93 S.J. 526; 65 T.L.R. 491; 113 J.P. 501; 48 L.G.R. 51 .... 51, 552

Markham v. Stacey [1968] 1 W.L.R. 1881; [1968] 3 All E.R. 758; 112 S.J. 866; [1969] Cr.L.R. 35 413

Marks v. Ford (1880), 45 J.P. 157 27

Marr v. Turpie [1949] Jo.Crim.L. 416 389

Marsh v. Moores [1949] 2 K.B. 208; [1949] 2 All E.R. 27; [1949] L.J.R. 1313; 93 S.J. 450; 65 T.L.R. 318; 113 J.P. 346; 47 L.G.R. 418 .... 368, 374

Marshall v. Clark [1958] S.L.T. 19 579

Marson v. Thompson [1955] Cr.L.R. 319; (1955), *The Times*, 8th March ... 281

Marston Services v. Police (1934), 98 J.P.Jo. 848 413

Martin v. Brooman (1909), 25 T.L.R. 783; 73 J.P. 484 137

Martin v. Robertson [1949] S.C.(J.) 19; [1949] S.L.T. 167 17

Martin v. White [1910] 1 K.B. 665; 79 L.J.K.B. 553; 102 L.T. 23; 26 T.L.R. 218; 74 J.P. 106; 8 L.G.R. 218; 22 Cox C.C. 236 .... 95, 121

Mawdsley v. Cox (Walter) (Transport) Ltd., Same v. Allen [1966] 1 W.L.R. 63; [1965] 3 All E.R. 728; 110 S.J. 36; 130 J.P. 62 422

PAGE

May v. Beeley [1910] 2 K.B. 722; 79 L.J.K.B. 852; 102 L.T. 326; 74 J.P. 111; 8 L.G.R. 166; 22 Cox C.C. 306 83

Maynard v. Andrews [1973] R.T.R. 398, D.C. 625

Meek v. Powell [1952] 1 K.B. 164; [1952] 1 All E.R. 347; 96 S.J. 91; [1952] 1 T.L.R. 358; [1952] W.N. 71; 116 J.P. 116; 50 L.G.R. 247 88

Melhuish v. Morris [1938] 4 All E.R. 98 318

Metropolitan Traffic Commissioner v. Alexander Thomson & Co. [1952] Jo. Crim.L. 194 543

Middleton v. Rowlett [1954] 1 W.L.R. 831; [1954] 2 All E.R. 277; 98 S.J. 373; 118 J.P. 362; 52 L.G.R. 334 .... 86, 87

Millard v. Turvey [1968] 2 Q.B. 390; [1968] 2 W.L.R. 1192; [1968] 2 All E.R. 7; 112 S.J. 235 .... 5, 334

Miller v. Howe [1969] 1 W.L.R. 1510; 133 J.P. 665; 113 S.J. 706; [1969] 3 All E.R. 451, D.C. 205

Miller v. Pill [1933] 2 K.B. 308; 102 L.J.K.B. 713; 149 L.T. 404; 77 S.J. 372; 49 T.L.R. 437; 97 J.P. 197; 31 L.G.R. 236; 29 Cox C.C. 643 576

Milliner v. Thorne [1972] Cr.L.R. 245 .... 673, 682

Miln v. Cullen [1967] S.L.T. 35; [1967] S.C.(J.) 21; [1969] Cr.L.R. 31 ... 118, 466

Milne v. McDonald [1971] S.L.T. 291, High Court of Justiciary 212

Milner v. Allen [1933] 1 K.B. 698; 102 L.J.K.B. 395; 149 L.T. 16; 77 S.J. 83; 49 T.L.R. 240; 97 J.P. 111; 31 L.G.R. 161; 29 Cox C.C. 629 ...... 142, 143

Milstead v. Sexton [1964] Cr.L.R. 474; *The Guardian*, 10th April... 10, 34, 45, 372

Mitchell v. Morrison [1938] S.C.(J.) 64 553

Mogg v. Skirton (1952), 116 J.P.Jo. 351 412

Montgomery v. Loney [1959] N.I. 171 .... 91, 174

Moody (D.H.R.) (Chemists) v. Iron Trades Mutual Insurance Co. (1970), 115 S.J. 16; [1971] R.T.R. 120; [1971] 1 Ll.L. Rep. 386; 69 L.G.R. 232 366

Moore v. Poyner [1975] R.T.R. 127; (1974), *The Times*, 2nd November, C.A. 285, 286

Moore v. Wilkinson [1969] Cr.L.R. 493, D.C. 221

Morgan v. Hertfordshire County Council (1965), 63 L.G.R. 456, C.A. 32

Morris v. The Crown Office [1970]. 2.Q.B. 114; [1970] 1 All E.R. 1079; *sub nom.* Morris v. Master of the Crown Office [1970] 2 W.L.R. 792; 114 S.J. 157, C.A. 595

Morris v. Williams (1952), 50 L.G.R. 308 .... 36, 39, 377

Morrison v. M'Cowan [1939] S.C.(J.) 45; [1939] S.L.T. 422 321

Morrison v. Sinclair [1937] S.L.T.(Sh.) 15 412

Morton v. Confer [1963] 1 W.L.R. 763; [1963] 2 All E.R. 765; 107 S.J. 417; 127 J.P. 433; 61 L.G.R. 461 169

Moscrop and Wills v. Blair (1961), 105 S.J. 950; [1962] Cr.L.R. 323, D.C. 11

Moss v. Jenkins [1975] R.T.R. 25; [1974] Cr.L.R. 715 199

Moss v. Moss [1963] 2 Q.B. 799; [1963] 3 W.L.R. 171; [1963] 2 All E.R. 829; 107 S.J. 459; 47 Cr.App.R. 222 117

Mottram v. South Lancashire Transport Co. [1942] 2 All E.R. 452; 86 S.J. 321 579

Moulder v. Judd [1974] Cr.L.R. 111 89

Moulder v. Neville [1974] R.T.R. 53; (1973), 118 S.J. 185; [1974] Cr.L.R. 126, D.C. 448, 453

Mowe v. Perraton [1952] 1 All E.R. 423; 96 S.J. 182; [1952] W.N. 96; 116 J.P. 139; 35 Cr.App.R. 194 .... 358, 359

Muir v. Lawrence [1951] S.L.T.(Sh.) 88 .... 412, 416

Muir v. Sutherland [1940] S.C.(J.) 66 670

Mumford v. Hardy [1956] 1 W.L.R. 163; [1956] 1 All E.R. 337; 100 S.J. 132; 54 L.G.R. 150; [1956] 1 Ll.L.Rep. 173 .... 369, 372, 639

Murphy v. Griffiths [1967] 1 W.L.R. 333; [1967] 1 All E.R. 424; 111 S.J. 76; [1966] C.L.Y. 10796 429

Murray v. Muir [1950] S.L.T. 41; [1949] S.C.(J.) 127 .... 238, 242

PAGE

Myers v. Director of Public Prosecutions [1965] A.C. 1001; [1964] 3 W.L.R.
145; [1964] 2 All E.R. 881; 108 S.J. 519; 128 J.P. 481; affg. sub nom. R. v.
Myers [1964] 1 All E.R. 877; 108 S.J. 221 111

N.W. Construction Co. v. Lancashire County Council (1939), unreported ... 494
Nagy v. Weston [1965] 1 W.L.R. 280; [1965] 1 All E.R. 78; 109 S.J. 215; 129
J.P. 104 .... 386, 387
Napthen v. Place [1970] Cr.L.R. 474; [1970] R.T.R. 248, D.C. ... 50, 378, 487, 506
National Coal Board v. Gamble [1959] 1 Q.B. 11; [1958] 3 W.L.R. 434;
[1958] 3 All E.R. 203; 102 S.J. 621; 122 J.P. 453; 42 Cr.App.R. 240 53
National Farmers' Union Mutual Insurance Society v. Dawson [1941] 2 K.B.
424; 111 L.J.K.B. 38; 166 L.T. 245; 70 Ll.L.Rep. 167 370
Nattrass v. Gibson (1968), 112 S.J. 866; (1968), The Times, 25th October 471,
487, 506, 507
Neal v. Bedford [1966] 1 Q.B. 505; [1965] 3 W.L.R. 1008; [1965] 3 All E.R.
250; 190 S.J. 477; 129 J.P. 534 452
Neal v. Devenish [1894] 1 Q.B. 544; 63 L.J.M.C. 78; 70 L.T. 628; 10 T.L.R.
313; 58 J.P. 246; 10 R. 578 90
Neal v. Fior [1968] 1 W.L.R. 1875; [1968] 3 All E.R. 865; 112 S.J. 948 463
Neal v. Reynolds (1966), 110 S.J. 353; [1966] Cr.L.R. 394 449
Neish v. Stevenson (1969), High Court of Justiciary, 20th February; [1970]
Cr.L.R. 161 169
Nelms v. Roe [1970] 1 W.L.R. 4; 113 S.J. 942; [1969] 3 All E.R. 1379; 54
Cr.App.R. 43; [1970] R.T.R. 45, D.C. 465, 572
Nelson v. Blackford [1936] 2 All E.R. 109 577
Nelson v. Coventry Swaging Co. (1936), 25 Traff.Cas. 68 .... 35, 553
Newberry v. Simmonds [1961] 2 Q.B. 345; [1961] 2 W.L.R. 675; [1961] 2 All
E.R. 318; 105 S.J. 324; 125 J.P. 409; 59 L.G.R. 309 .... 6, 487
Newbury v. Davis (1974), 118 S.J. 222; [1974] R.T.R. 367; [1974] Cr.L.R.
262, D.C. 39, 377
Newcastle Corporation v. Walton [1957] Cr.L.R. 479 .... 28, 30
Newell v. Cook [1936] 2 K.B. 632; [1936] 2 All E.R. 203; 105 L.J.K.B. 742;
155 L.T. 173; 80 S.J. 674; 52 T.L.R. 489; 100 J.P. 371; 34 L.G.R. 364;
30 Cox C.C. 437 40
Newman v. Overington, Harris & Ash Ltd. (1928), 93 J.P. 46; 27 L.G.R.
85 321
Newnham v. Trigg [1970] R.T.R. 107 .... 672, 675
Newsham, ex parte [1964] Cr.L.R. 57 267
Newsome v. Hayton [1974] R.T.R. 9; [1974] Cr.L.R. 112; (1973), The Times,
29th November, D.C. 189
Newstead v. Hearn (1950), 114 J.P.Jo. 690 419
Newton (G.) Ltd. v. Smith, Standerwick (W.C.) v. Smith [1962] 2 Q.B. 278;
[1962] 2 W.L.R. 926; [1962] 2 All E.R. 19; 106 S.J. 287; 126 J.P. 324; 60
L.G.R. 256 .... 91, 574
Nichol v. Leach [1972] Cr.L.R. 571; [1972] R.T.R. 476 .... 7, 10, 42, 45
Nicholas v. Penny [1950] 2 K.B. 466; sub nom. Penny v. Nicholas [1950] 2 All
E.R. 89; 94 S.J. 437; 66 T.L.R. (Pt. 1) 1122; 114 J.P. 335; 48 L.G.R.
535 .... 18, 318, 319
Nicholson v. Brown [1974] R.T.R. 177; (1974), 118 S.J. 259; [1974] Cr.L.R.
187, D.C. 665, 666, 670, 693
Nicholson v. Goddard [1954] Cr.L.R. 474 579
Nicholson v. Tapp (1972), 116 S.J. 527; [1972] 1 W.L.R. 1044; [1972] 3 All
E.R. 245; [1972] R.T.R. 313; [1972] Cr.L.R. 570, D.C. 136, 138
Norling v. Woolacott [1964] S.A.S.R. 377 347
Norman v. Magill [1972] R.T.R. 81 236
North v. Gerrish (1959), 123 J.P. 313 347
Northfield v. Pinder [1969] 2 Q.B. 7; [1969] 2 W.L.R. 50; [1968] 3 All E.R.
854; (1968), 112 S.J. 884; The Times, 30th October 168, 172

PAGE

Norton *v.* Hayward (1968), 112 S.J. 767; [1969] Cr.L.R. 36 .... 30, 31
Nottingham No. 1 Area Hospital Management Committee *v.* Owen [1958] 1
   Q.B. 50; [1957] 3 W.L.R. 707; [1957] 3 All E.R. 358; 101 S.J. 852; 122
   J.P. 5; 55 L.G.R. 550 60
Nugent *v.* Hobday [1972] Cr.L.R. 569; [1973] R.T.R. 41 220

Oakes *v.* Foster [1961] Cr.L.R. 628 .... 271, 273
Oberst *v.* Coombs (1955), 53 L.G.R. 316 56
O'Brien *v.* Trafalgar Insurance Co. (1945), 61 T.L.R. 225; 109 J.P. 107 28
Ocean Accident and Guarantee Corporation Ltd. *v.* Cole [1932] 2 K.B. 100;
   101 L.J.K.B. 362; 147 L.T. 78; 76 S.J. 378; 48 T.L.R. 392; 96 J.P. 191;
   30 L.G.R. 206; 29 Cox C.C. 464 382
O'Connell *v.* Adams [1973] R.T.R. 150; [1973] Cr.L.R. 113, D.C. 126
O'Connell *v.* Fraser (1963), 107 S.J. 95; [1963] Cr.L.R. 289 283
O'Neill *v.* Brown [1961] 1 Q.B. 420; [1961] 2 W.L.R. 224; [1961] 1 All E.R.
   571; 105 S.J. 208; 125 J.P. 225; 59 L.G.R. 198 420
O'Neill *v.* George (1969), 113 S.J. 128; 67 L.G.R. 358; (1969), *The Times,* 30th
   January 385
Original Hartlepool Collieries Co. *v.* Gibb (1877), 5 Ch.D. 713; 46 L.J.Ch.
   311; 36 L.T. 433; 41 J.P. 660; 3 Asp.M.L.C. 411 390
Orr *v.* Carmichael [1941] S.C.(J.) 27 501
Orr *v.* Strathern [1929] S.C.(J.) 30 578
Osborne *v.* Richards [1933] 1 K.B. 283; [1932] All E.R.Rep. 833; 102
   L.J.K.B. 44; 147 L.T. 419; 96 J.P. 377; 48 T.L.R. 622; 30 L.G.R. 385;
   29 Cox C.C. 524, D.C. 39, 574
Osgerby *v.* Walden (1967), 111 S.J. 259; [1967] Cr.L.R. 307 465
O'Toole *v.* Scott [1965] A.C. 939; [1965] 2 W.L.R. 1160; [1965] 2 All E.R.
   240; 109 S.J. 332 .... 73, 83
Owen *v.* Imes [1972] R.T.R. 489; [1973] Cr.L.R. 60, D.C. 623, 628, 664
Owens *v.* Minoprio [1942] 1 K.B. 193; [1942] 1 All E.R. 30; 111 L.J.K.B. 179;
   166 L.T. 134; 86 S.J. 7; 106 J.P. 53; 40 L.G.R. 27 92

Pacitti *v.* Copeland [1963] S.L.T. (Notes) 52 303
Pagett *v.* Mayo [1939] 2 K.B. 94; [1939] 2 All E.R. 362; 108 L.J.K.B. 501; 160
   L.T. 398; 83 S.J. 418; 55 T.L.R. 598; 103 J.P. 177; 37 L.G.R. 300; 31
   Cox C.C. 251 343
Palastanga *v.* Salman (1962), 106 S.J. 176; [1962] Cr.L.R. 334 .... 86, 601
Parkes *v.* Cole (1922), 127 L.T. 152; 86 J.P. 122; 20 L.G.R. 463; 27 Cox C.C.
   218 135
Parkinson *v.* Axon [1951] 2 K.B. 678; [1951] 2 All E.R. 647; 95 S.J. 641;
   [1951] W.N. 473; 115 J.P. 528 561
Parkinson *v.* Liverpool Corporation [1950] 1 All E.R. 367; 94 S.J. 161; 66
   T.L.R. (Pt. 1) 262; [1950] W.N. 43; 114 J.P. 146; 48 L.G.R. 331 284
Parson *v.* Tomlin (1956), 120 J.P. 129 .... 116, 275
Passmore *v.* Vulcan Boiler and General Insurance Co. Ltd. (1935), 154 L.T.
   258; 80 S.J. 167; 52 T.L.R. 193 366
Paterson *v.* Burnet [1939] S.C.(J.) 12 16
Paterson *v.* Ogilvy [1957] S.L.T. 354; [1957] S.C.(J.) 42 174
Patterson *v.* Helling [1960] Cr.L.R. 562 .... 487, 506
Pawley *v.* Whardall [1966] 1 Q.B. 373; [1965] 3 W.L.R. 496; [1965] 2 All
   E.R. 757; 109 S.J. 614; 129 J.P. 444 .... 50, 281, 283, 579
Payne *v.* Allcock [1932] 2 K.B. 413; 101 L.J.K.B. 775; 147 L.T. 96; 76 S.J.
   308; 48 T.L.R. 396; 96 J.P. 283; 30 L.G.R. 294; 29 Cox C.C. 475 504
Peacock *v.* R. (1858), 4 C.B.(N.S.) 264; 27 L.J.C.P. 224; 31 L.T.(O.S.) 101; 6
   W.R. 517; 22 J.P. 403; 140 E.R. 1085 699
Peak Trailer & Chassis Ltd. *v.* Jackson [1967] 1 W.L.R. 155; [1967] 1 All E.R.
   172; 110 S.J. 927; 131 J.P. 155 414

PAGE

Pearson v. Boyes [1953] 1 W.L.R. 384; [1953] 1 All E.R. 492; 97 S.J. 134; 117
J.P. 131; 51 L.G.R. 240 496
Pearson (E.) & Son (Teesside) Ltd. v. Richardson [1972] Cr.L.R. 444; [1972]
1 W.L.R. 1152; 116 S.J. 416; [1972] 3 All E.R. 277; [1972] R.T.R. 552   526
Peek v. Towle [1945] K.B. 458; [1945] 2 All E.R. 611; 114 L.J.K.B. 540; 173
L.T. 360; 61 T.L.R. 399; 109 J.P. 160; 43 L.G.R. 286 .... 343, 345
People (The) (Attorney-General) v. Carroll [1950] Ir. Jur.R. 20 129
People (The) v. Wickham [1949] Ir.R. 180 117
Percival v. Ball [1937] W.N. 106 142
Peters v. General Accident Fire and Life Assurance Corporation Ltd. [1938] 2
All E.R. 267; 158 L.T. 476; 82 S.J. 294; 54 T.L.R. 663; 36 L.G.R. 583 ... 374
Phelan v. Back [1972] 1 All E.R. 901; [1972] Cr.L.R. 104; [1972] 1 W.L.R.
273; (1971), 116 S.J. 76; 56 Cr.App.R. 257, D.C. 124
Phelon & Moore Ltd. v. Keel [1914] 3 K.B. 165; 83 L.J.K.B. 1516; 111 L.T.
214; 78 J.P. 247; 12 L.G.R. 950; 24 Cox C.C. 234 .... 44, 49
Philcox v. Carberry [1960] Cr.L.R. 563 379
Phillips v. Thomas [1974] R.T.R. 28, D.C. 424, 428
Phipps v. McCormick [1971] Cr.L.R. 540; 115 S.J. 710; [1972] R.T.R. 21,
D.C. 137, 138
Piggott v. Sims [1973] R.T.R. 15; [1972] Cr.L.R. 595, D.C. 86, 87, 124, 216
Pilbury v. Brazier [1951] 1 K.B. 340; [1950] 2 All E.R. 835; 94 S.J. 672; 66
T.L.R. (Pt. 2) 763; [1950] W.N. 464; 114 J.P. 548; 49 L.G.R. 612; 84
Ll.L.Rep. 456 681
Pilgram v. Dean [1974] 1 W.L.R. 601; 111 S.J. 149; [1974] 2 All E.R. 751;
[1974] R.T.R. 299; [1974] Cr.L.R. 194, D.C. 489, 503, 517
Pinner v. Everett [1969] 1 W.L.R. 1266; 133 J.P. 653; 113 S.J. 674; [1969] 3
All E.R. 257; [1970] R.T.R. 3, H.L.; revsg. [1969] Cr.L.R. 378 ...... 24, 182,
184–188, 195, 651
Pitcher v. Lockett (1966), 64 L.G.R. 477; [1966] Cr.L.R. 283; [1966] C.L.Y.
5559 386
Plaistow Transport Ltd. v. Graham [1966] 1 Ll.L.Rep. 639; 116 New L.J.
1033 422
Platt v. Green [1965] Cr.L.R. 311; The Guardian, 20th January 122
Police v. Bishop [1956] Cr.L.R. 569 374
Police v. O'Connor [1957] Cr.L.R. 478.. 387
Police Prosecutor v. Humphreys [1970] Cr.L.R. 234 .... 666, 680
Pollard v. Light (1950), 48 L.G.R. 447 683
Pontin v. Price (1933), 150 L.T. 177; 97 J.P. 315; 31 L.G.R. 375; 30 Cox C.C.
44 300
Poole v. Ibbotson (1949), 93 S.J. 633; 65 T.L.R. 701; 113 J.P. 466; 47 L.G.R.
661 572
Pope v. Clarke [1953] 1 W.L.R. 1060; [1953] 2 All E.R. 704; 97 S.J. 542; 117
J.P. 429; 51 L.G.R. 501; 37 Cr.App.R. 141 .... 142, 143, 300
Pope v. Minton [1954] Cr.L.R. 711 .... 54, 652
Popperwell v. Cockerton [1968] 1 W.L.R. 438; [1968] 1 All E.R. 1038; 112
S.J. 175; 132 J.P. 231 335
Porter v. Bloomer [1957] N.I. 123 498
Potter v. Gorbould [1970] 1 Q.B. 238; [1969] 3 W.L.R. 810; 133 J.P. 717; 113
S.J. 673; [1969] 3 All E.R. 828; 7 K.I.R. 349, D.C. 561
Poultry World v. Conder [1957] Cr.L.R. 803 53
Poyser and Mills Arbitration, Re [1964] 2 Q.B. 467; [1963] 2 W.L.R. 1309;
[1963] 1 All E.R. 612; sub nom. Poyser v. Mills, 107 S.J. 115.............. 133
Pratt v. Bloom [1958] Cr.L.R. 817; (1958), The Times, 21st October 282
Pratt v. Hayward [1969] 1 W.L.R. 832; [1969] 3 All E.R. 1094; 113 S.J. 369;
67 L.G.R. 445; (1969), The Times, 22nd April.................................. 391
Prescott v. Lancashire United Transport Co. [1953] 1 W.L.R. 232; [1953] 1
All E.R. 288; 97 S.J. 64; 117 J.P. 80; 51 L.G.R. 87 579
Preston v. Fennell [1951] 1 K.B. 16; [1950] 1 All E.R. 1099; 114 J.P. 308; 48
L.G.R. 479 .... 177, 539

PAGE

Price v. Humphries [1958] 2 Q.B. 353; [1958] 3 W.L.R. 304; [1958] 2 All E.R. 725; 102 S.J. 583; 122 J.P. 423 .... 57, 87, 489, 572

Price v. West London Investment Building Society Ltd. [1964] 1 W.L.R. 616; [1964] 2 All E.R. 318; 108 S.J. 276 138

Printz v. Sewell [1912] 2 K.B. 511; 81 L.J.K.B. 905; 106 L.T. 880; 28 T.L.R. 396; 76 J.P. 295; 10 L.G.R. 665; 23 Cox C.C. 23 .... 408, 513, 518

Procaj v. Johnstone (1969), 113 S.J. 1004; [1970] Cr.L.R. 110, D.C. 229

Prosser v. Richings [1936] 2 All E.R. 1627; 155 L.T. 284; 80 S.J. 794; 52 T.L.R. 677; 100 J.P. 390; 34 L.G.R. 456; 30 Cox C.C. 457 ... 17, 36, 40, 48, 412

Provincial Motor Cab Co. Ltd. v. Dunning [1909] 2 K.B. 599; 101 L.T. 231; 73 J.P. 387; 7 L.G.R. 765; 22 Cox C.C. 159; sub nom. Provincial Motor Cab Co. Ltd. v. Dunning, Kynaston's Case, 78 L.J.K.B. 822; sub nom. Provincial Motor Cab Co. Ltd. v. Dunning, Parker's Case, Same v. Same, Kynaston's Case, 25 T.L.R. 646 .... 48, 468

Prowse v. Clark [1975] Cr.L.R. 172 454

Pugh v. Knipe [1972] Cr.L.R. 247... 31, 173, 174

Pugsley v. Hunter [1973] 1 W.L.R. 578; 117 S.J. 206; [1973] 2 All E.R. 10; [1973] R.T.R. 284; [1973] Cr.L.R. 247, D.C. 172, 665, 676, 677

Pulton v. Leader [1949] 2 All E.R. 747; 94 S.J. 33; 65 T.L.R. 687; [1949] W.N. 400; 113 J.P. 537; 48 L.G.R. 146 .... 462, 463

Punshon v. Rose (1968), 113 S.J. 39; The Times, 12th December 672

Purves v. Muir [1948] S.C.(J.) 122; [1948] S.L.T. 529 29

Quelch v. Collett [1948] 1 K.B. 478; [1948] 1 All E.R. 252; [1948] L.J.R. 956; 92 S.J. 98; 64 T.L.R. 108; 112 J.P. 167; 46 L.G.R. 153 681

Quelch v. Phipps [1955] 2 Q.B.107; [1955] 2 W.L.R. 1067; [1955] 2 All E.R. 302; 99 S.J. 355; 119 J.P. 430; 53 L.G.R. 370 .... 131, 148, 196, 346

Quinn v. Scott [1965] 1 W.L.R. 1004; [1965] 2 All E.R. 588; 109 S.J. 498 ... 285

R. v. Aberdare Justices, ex parte Jones [1973] Cr.L.R. 45; (1973), J.P.News. 57, D.C. 92

R. v. Agnew (1968), 113 S.J. 58; [1969] Cr.L.R. 152 .... 665, 668, 673

R. v. Algar [1954] 1 Q.B. 279; [1953] 3 W.L.R. 1007; [1953] 2 All E.R. 1381; 97 S.J. 833; 118 J.P. 56; 37 Cr.App.R. 200 117

R. v. Allerton (1953), 117 J.P. 421; The Times, 18th June 117

R. v. Amersham Justices, ex parte Fanthorne (1964), 108 S.J. 841; [1964] Cr.L.R. 825 702

R. v. Anderson [1972] Cr.L.R. 245; (1972), The Times, 19th January ... 666, 667, 678

R. v. Andrews [1967] 1 W.L.R. 439; [1967] 1 All E.R. 170; 111 S.J. 92; 131 J.P. 210; 51 Cr.App.R. 42 77

R. v. Andrews [1973] 1 Q.B. 422; [1973] 2 W.L.R. 116; (1972), 117 S.J. 86; [1973] 1 All E.R. 857; [1973] R.T.R. 508; [1973] Cr.L.R. 117; sub nom. R. v. Andrews (Edward John) (1972), 57 Cr.App.R. 254, C.A. 263

R. v. Anthony [1965] 2 Q.B. 189; [1965] 2 W.L.R. 748; [1965] 1 All E.R. 440; 236 L.T. 122; 129 J.P. 168; 49 Cr. App.R. 104 55

R. v. Arthur [1961] Jo.Cr.L. 97 175

R. v. Ashbourne Justices, ex parte Naden (1950), 94 S.J. 148; [1950] W.N. 51; 48 L.G.R. 268 .... 74, 265, 268

R. v. Atkinson [1970] Cr.L.R. 405; sub nom. R. v. Atkinson (John Percy) (1970), 55 Cr.App.R. 1, C.A. 278, 281

R. v. Aylesbury Justices, ex parte Wisbey [1965] 1 W.L.R. 339; [1965] 1 All E.R. 602; 109 S.J. 173; 129 J.P. 175 90

R. v. Ayres (1969), 114 S.J. 16; [1970] R.T.R. 398; [1970] Cr.L.R. 114, C.A. 210

R. v. Bain [1973] R.T.R. 213, C.A. 249, 623, 624, 631, 638

R. v. Baines, 114 S.J. 669; [1970] R.T.R. 455; [1970] Cr.L.R. 590; sub nom. R. v. Baines (George John), 54 Cr.App.R. 481 .... 666, 674

                                                                          PAGE
R. v. Baldessare (1930), 144 L.T. 185; 29 Cox C.C. 193; 22 Cr.App.R.
    70 .... 123, 260, 277, 357
R. v. Baldwin (1925), 133 L.T. 191; 69 S.J. 429; 89 J.P. 116; 18 Cr.App.R.
    175; 28 Cox C.C. 17 97
R. v. Ball and Loughlin (1966), 110 S.J. 510; 50 Cr.App.R. 266; 116 New L.J.
    978 .... 257, 280
R. v. Banks [1972] R.T.R. 179; [1972] 1 W.L.R. 346; 116 S.J. 80;
    [1972] 1 All E.R. 1041; [1972] Cr.L.R. 237; sub nom. R. v. Banks
    (Jack) (1972), 56 Cr.App.R. 310, C.A. 179
R. v. Barber [1963] 3 South African L.R. 700 304
R. v. Barnett [1951] 2 K.B. 425; [1951] 1 All E.R. 917; 95 S.J. 337; [1951] 1
    T.L.R. 899; [1951] W.N. 214; 115 J.P. 305; 49 L.G.R. 401; 35 Cr.App.R.
    37 71
R. v. Bass [1953] 1 Q.B. 680; [1953] 2 W.L.R. 825; [1953] 1 All E.R. 1064; 97
    S.J. 282; 117 J.P. 246; 37 Cr.App.R. 51 112
R. v. Bates [1973] 1 W.L.R. 718; 117 S.J. 395; [1973] 2 All E.R. 509; [1973]
    R.T.R. 264; [1973] Cr.L.R. 449; sub nom. R. v. Bates (Edward John),
    57 Cr.App.R. 757, C.A. 187, 190, 196, 212, 218, 230
R. v. Beacontree Justices, R. v. Wright [1915] 3 K.B. 388; 84 L.J.K.B. 2230;
    113 L.T. 727; 31 T.L.R. 509; 79 J.P. 461; 13 L.G.R. 1094; 25 Cox C.C.
    89 66
R. v. Beattie [1946] Ir.Jur.R. 62 93
R. v. Beaumont (1964), 114 L.J. 739; [1964] Cr.L.R. 665 29
R. v. Bebbington [1969] 1 W.L.R. 1348; 133 J.P. 689; 113 S.J. 584; [1969] 3
    All E.R. 427; sub nom. R. v. Bebbington (Gordon), 53 Cr.App.R. 547,
    C.A. 703
R. v. Bedford and Sharnbrook Justices, ex parte Ward [1974] Cr.L.R. 109;
    (1973), J.P.News. 40 93
R. v. Bedwellty Justices, ex parte Munday [1970] Cr.L.R. 601, D.C. ... 76, 78, 265
R. v. Beecham [1921] 3 K.B. 464; 90 L.J.K.B. 1370; 65 S.J. 768; 37 T.L.R.
    932; 85 J.P. 276; 16 Cr.App.R. 26 97
R. v. Belfast Justices [1952] N.I. 91 265
R. v. Beresford (1952), 36 Cr.App.R. 1 258
R. v. Berkeley (Gloucestershire) Justices, ex parte Higgins (1965), 109 S.J. 77;
    [1965] Cr.L.R. 163 78
R. v. Berkshire County Council, ex parte Berkshire Lime Co. (Childrey) Ltd.
    [1953] 1 W.L.R. 1146; [1953] 2 All E.R. 779; 97 S.J. 591; 117 J.P. 505;
    51 L.G.R. 593 .... 494, 496
R. v. Bignell (1967), 111 S.J. 773; (1968), 52 Cr.App.R. 10; [1967] Cr.L.R.
    711 .... 244, 605, 635
R. v. Bilton (1964), 108 S.J. 880; [1964] Cr.L.R. 828 .... 139, 143
R. v. Birkenhead Justices, ex parte Fisher [1962] 1 W.L.R. 1410; [1962] 3 All
    E.R. 837; 106 S.J. 856; 127 J.P. 15 .... 83, 84
R. v. Bishop's Stortford Justices, ex parte Shields (1968), 113 S.J. 124; [1969]
    Cr.L.R. 201, D.C. 78, 81, 250, 630
R. v. Blaby [1894] 2 Q.B. 170; 63 L.J.M.C. 133; 70 L.T. 879; 38 S.J. 420; 10
    T.L.R. 431; 42 W.R. 511; 58 J.P. 576; 18 Cox C.C. 5; 10 R. 277 606
R. v. Blackpool Justices, ex parte Charlson [1972] 1 W.L.R. 1456; 116 S.J. 729;
    [1972] 3 All E.R 854; [1972] Cr.L.R. 641; 56 Cr.App.R.823, D.C. ... 79, 599
R. v. Blamires Transport Services Ltd., R. v. Blamire [1964] 1 Q.B. 278;
    [1963] 3 W.L.R. 496; [1963] 3 All E.R. 170; 107 S.J. 598; 127 J.P. 519;
    61 L.G.R. 594; 47 Cr.App.R. 272 .... 71, 546, 554, 562, 566
R. v. Blandford, R. v. Freestone [1955] 1 W.L.R. 331; 99 S.J. 223; [1955] 1
    All E.R. 681; 39 Cr.App.R. 51, C.C.A. 66
R. v. Blandford, Justices, ex parte G. (an infant) [1967] 1 Q.B. 82; [1966] 2
    W.L.R. 1232; [1966] 1 All E.R. 1021; 110 S.J. 465; 130 J.P. 260 .... 58, 92
R. v. Blything (Suffolk) Justices, ex parte Knight [1970] R.T.R. 218, D.C. 312
R. v. Bodmin Justices, ex parte McEwan [1947] K.B. 321; [1947] 1 All E.R.
    109; [1947] L.J.R. 338; 91 S.J. 28; 111 J.P. 47; 45 L.G.R. 74 91

PAGE

R. *v.* Boe, R. *v.* Saunders (1967), 111 S.J. 999; [1968] Cr.L.R. 171 261
R. *v.* Bogacki and Others [1973] 1 Q.B. 832; [1973] 2 W.L.R. 937; 117 S.J.
355; [1973] 2 All E.R. 864; [1973] R.T.R. 384; [1973] Cr.L.R. 385; *sub
nom.* R. *v.* Bogacki (Steven); R. *v.* Tillwach (Howard John); R. *v.* Cox
(Robert Charles), 57 Cr.App.R. 593, C.A. 25, 352, 357, 358
R. *v.* Bolkis (1932), 148 L.T. 358; 77 S.J. 13; 49 T.L.R. 128; 97 J.P. 10; 31
L.G.R. 32; 29 Cox C.C. 578; 24 Cr.App.R. 19 .... 139, 140
R. *v.* Bott [1968] 1 W.L.R. 583; [1968] 1 All E.R. 1119; 112 S.J. 170; 132 J.P.
199 82
R. *v.* Boucher (1952), 36 Cr.App.R. 152 116
R. *v.* Boulden (1957), 41 Cr.App.R. 105; *affg.* [1957] Cr.L.R. 182 396
R. *v.* Bove [1970] 1 W.L.R. 949; 114 S.J. 418; [1970] 2 All E.R. 20; *sub nom.*
R. *v.* Bove (Ettore) (1970), 54 Cr.App.R. 316, C.A. 231
R. *v.* Bow Street Magistrate, *ex parte* Palmer (1969), 113 S.J. 735; [1969]
Cr.L.R. 658, D.C. 600
R. *v.* Bowell (1974), 111 S.J. 367; [1974] R.T.R. 273; [1974] Cr.L.R. 369,
C.A. 176
R. *v.* Bowsher [1973] R.T.R. 202; [1973] Cr.L.R. 373, C.A. 627, 631, 632,
653, 658
R. *v.* Boyle (1904), 20 T.L.R. 192 82
R. *v.* Bradfield and Sonning Justices, *ex parte* Holdsworth, 115 S.J. 608; [1971]
3 All E.R. 755; [1972] R.T.R. 108, D.C. 656, 658
R. *v.* Breingan [1966] (3) S.A. 410 344
R. *v.* Brentford Justices, *ex parte* Catlin [1975] 2 All E.R. 201 .... 56, 65
R. *v.* Britton [1973] R.T.R. 502; [1973] Cr.L.R. 375, C.A. 206
R. *v.* Brogan (1975), *The Times*, 6th February 599
R. *v.* Bromley Justices, *ex parte* Church [1970] Cr.L.R. 103; [1970] Cr.L.R.
655 .... 420, 434
R. *v.* Bros, *ex parte* Hardy [1911] 1 K.B. 159; 80 L.J.K.B. 147; 103 L.T. 728; 55
S.J. 47; 27 T.L.R. 41; 74 J.P. 483; 22 Cox C.C. 352 103
R. *v.* Brown (Edward) [1975] R.T.R. 36n. 642, 643
R. *v.* Brown (John) [1974] R.T.R. 377; [1974] Cr.L.R. 670, C.A. 231
R. *v.* Brush [1968] 1 W.L.R. 1740; [1968] 3 All E.R. 467; 112 S.J. 806; 132
J.P. 579; [1969] Cr.L.R. 619; *sub nom.* R. *v.* Brush (Malcolm Neil), 52
Cr.App.R. 717 .... 214, 215
R. *v.* Bryant (1946), 110 J.P. 267; 44 L.G.R. 224 .... 112, 119, 562
R. *v.* Budd [1962] Cr.L.R. 49; (1961), *The Times*, 8th November . 24, 143, 269, 276
R. *v.* Burdett (1820), 4 B. & Ald. 95; 1 State Tr.(N.S.) 1; 106 E.R. 873;
subsequent proceedings (1821), 4 B. & Ald. 314 490
R. *v.* Burdon (1927), 20 Cr.App.R. 80 .... 242, 259
R. *v.* Burnham, Bucks., Justices, *ex parte* Ansorge [1959] 1 W.L.R. 1041; [1959]
3 All E.R. 505; 103 S.J. 920; 123 J.P. 539 .... 93, 99, 290, 353
R. *v.* Burt, *ex parte* Presburg [1960] 1 Q.B. 625; [1960] 2 W.L.R. 398; [1960] 1
All E.R. 424; 104 S.J. 148; 124 J.P. 201 600
R. *v.* Butterwasser [1948] K.B. 4; [1947] 2 All E.R. 415; 91 S.J. 586; 63
T.L.R. 463; 111 J.P. 527; 45 L.G.R. 570 97
R. *v.* Calhoun [1974] Cr.L.R. 436, C.A. 251
R. *v.* Camfield [1971] R.T.R. 449, C.A. 632
R. *v.* Campbell [1956] 2 Q.B. 432; [1956] 3 W.L.R. 219; [1956] 2 All E.R.
272; 100 S.J. 454; 120 J.P. 359; 40 Cr.App.R. 95 102
R. *v.* Cardiff Justices (1959), Queen's Bench Division, 20th January 81, 264
R. *v.* Cardiff Justices, *ex parte* Cardiff Corporation [1962] 2 Q.B. 436; [1962] 2
W.L.R. 771; 106 S.J. 113; 60 L.G.R. 176; *sub nom.* R. *v.* Cardiff City
Justices, *ex parte* Cardiff City Council [1962] 1 All E.R. 751; 126 J.P.
175 478
R. *v.* Carlson (1956), 19 W.R. 574 238
R. *v.* Carr-Briant [1943] K.B. 607; [1943] 2 All E.R. 156; 112 L.J.K.B. 581;
169 L.T. 175; 59 T.L.R. 300; 107 J.P. 167; 41 L.G.R. 183; 29 Cr.App.R.
76 .... 21, 515

                                                                          PAGE
R. v. Chadwick [1975] Cr.L.R. 105 .... 287, 416
R. v. Challoner (1964), 108 S.J. 1049; [1965] Cr.L.R. 120 261
R. v. Chambers (1939), 83 S.J. 439 77
R. v. Chapman [1969] 2 Q.B. 436; [1969] 2 W.L.R. 1004; [1969] 2 All E.R.
    321; 113 S.J. 229; 53 Cr.App.R. 336; *The Times*, 4th March 206,
                                                                              223
R. v. Chelsea Justices, *ex parte* Director of Public Prosecutions [1963] 1 W.L.R.
    1138; [1963] 3 All E.R. 657; 107 S.J. 792; 128 J.P. 18 58
R. v. Chertsey Justices, *ex parte* Edwards & Co. Ltd. (The Provision Market);
    R. v. Croydon Justices, *ex parte* Woolworth (F. W.) & Co. Ltd. [1973]
    1 W.L.R. 1545; 117 S.J. 910; [1974] 1 All E.R. 156; [1974] Cr.L.R. 41,
    D.C. 600
R. v. Chertsey Justices, *ex parte* Franks [1961] 2 Q.B. 152; [1961] 1 All E.R.
    825; 105 S.J. 181; 125 J.P. 305; 59 L.G.R. 260; 12 P. & C.R. 278 70
R. v. Chippendale [1973] R.T.R.236; [1973] Cr.L.R. 314, C.A. 215
R. v. Clark [1955] 2 Q.B. 469; [1955] 3 W.L.R. 313; [1955] 3 All E.R. 29; 99
    S.J. 527; 119 J.P. 531; 39 Cr.App.R. 120 97
R. v. Clarke (Christopher) [1969] 1 W.L.R. 1109; [1969] 2 All E.R. 1008; 113
    S.J. 428 .... 197, 205, 228, 233
R. v. Cleghorn [1938] 3 All E.R. 398; 82 S.J. 731 381
R. v. Clow [1965] 1 Q.B. 598; [1963] 3 W.L.R. 84; [1963] 2 All E.R. 216; 107
    S.J. 537; 127 J.P. 371; 47 Cr.App.R. 136 .... 91, 255, 265
R. v. Coates [1971] Cr.L.R. 370; [1971] R.T.R. 74, C.A. 203, 210
R. v. Cockermouth Justices, *ex parte* Patterson [1971] Cr.L.R. 287; [1971]
    R.T.R 216, D.C. 362, 607, 622
R. v. Coleman [1974] R.T.R. 359, C.A. 190, 191, 198
R. v. Collier, R. v. Stenning [1965] 1 W.L.R. 1470; [1965] 3 All E.R. 136; 109
    S.J. 593; 129 J.P. 531; 49 Cr.App.R. 136 118
R. v. Collins [1947] K.B. 560; [1947] 1 All E.R. 147; 91 S.J. 133; 63 T.L.R.
    90; 111 J.P. 154; 45 L.G.R. 104; 32 Cr.App.R. 27 638
R. v. Collinson (1931), 75 S.J. 491; 23 Cr.App.R. 49 174
R. v. Cook [1964] Cr.L.R. 56; (1963), 114 L.J. 59; 48 Cr.App.R. 98 ... 163, 358
R. v. Cook (Philip) [1971] Cr.L.R. 44 259
R. v. Cooper [1974] R.T.R. 489 192
R. v. Cottrell (No. 2) [1956] 1 W.L.R. 342; [1956] 1 All E.R. 751; 100 S.J.
    264; 120 J.P. 163; 54 L.G.R. 255; 40 Cr.App.R. 46 649
R. v. Courtley [1958] Jo.Crim.L. 200 255
R. v. Cowley [1971] 6 C.L. 257 400
R. v. Craske, *ex parte* Metropolitan Police Commissioner [1957] 2 Q.B. 591;
    [1957] 3 W.L.R. 308; [1957] 2 All E.R. 772; 101 S.J. 592; 121 J.P.
    502 78
R. v. Crossen [1939] N.I. 106 665
R. v. Crown Court at Lewes, *ex parte* Rogers. *See* R. v. Lewes Crown Court
R. v. Cumberland Justices, *ex parte* Hepworth (1931), 146 L.T. 5; 47 T.L.R.
    610; 95 J.P. 206; 30 L.G.R. 1; 29 Cox C.C. 374 .... 478, 479
R. v. Cummerson [1968] 2 Q.B. 534; [1968] 2 W.L.R. 1486; [1968] 2 All
    E.R. 863; 112 S.J. 424; 52 Cr.App.R. 520 .... 382, 502
R. v. Curphey [1957] Cr.L.R. 191; 41 Cr.App.R. 78 255
R. v. Curran (1975), *The Times*, 8th May 173, 235
R. v. Daly [1974] 1 W.L.R. 133; (1973), 118 S.J. 66; [1974] 1 All E.R. 290;
    sub nom. R. v. Daly (James Joseph) (1973), 58 Cr.App.R. 333; [1974]
    Cr.L.R. 263, C.A. 599
R. v. Davies [1962] 1 W.L.R. 1111; [1962] 3 All E.R. 97; 113 L.J. 580; 106
    S.J. 393; 126 J.P. 455; 46 Cr.App.R. 292; [1963] Cr.L.R. 192 241
R. v. Davis, *ex parte* Brough [1959] 1 W.L.R. 59*n*.; 103 S.J. 76 99
R. v. Davison [1972] 1 W.L.R. 1540; 116 S.J. 882; [1972] 3 All E.R. 1121;
    [1972] Cr.L.R. 786; *sub nom.* R. v. Davison (John Stuart) (1972), 57
    Cr.App.R. 113, C.A. 381
R. v. Davitt [1974] Cr.L.R. 719 251

PAGE

R. *v.* Dick-Cleland (1965), 109 S.J. 377; [1965] Cr.L.R. 440 240

R. *v.* Dolan [1969] 1 W.L.R. 1479; 133 J.P. 696; 113 S.J. 818; [1969] 3 All
E.R. 683; [1970] R.T.R. 43; *subnom.* R. *v.* Dolan (Martin), 53 Cr.App.R.
556, C.A. 214, 227, 234

R. *v.* Donelly [1975] Cr.L.R. 179; [1975] R.T.R. 243 661

R. *v.* Downey [1970] R.T.R. 257; [1970] Cr.L.R. 287, C.A. 197, 227, 232

R. *v.* Dunne, *ex parte* Sinnatt [1943] K.B. 516; [1943] 2 All E.R. 222; 112
L.J.K.B. 455; 169 L.T. 112; 107 J.P. 161; 59 T.L.R. 227 595

R. *v.* Durrant [1970] 1 W.L.R. 29; 113 S.J. 905; [1969] 3 All E.R. 1357;
[1970] R.T.R. 420*n.*; *sub nom.* R. *v.* Durrant (Leonard Arthur), 54
Cr.App.R. 24, C.A. 183

R. *v.* Edmonton Justices, *ex parte* Brooks [1960] 1 W.L.R. 697; [1960] 2 All
E.R. 475; 104 S.J. 547; 124 J.P. 409 132

R. *v.* Ellis [1947] 1 W.W.R. 717 304

R. *v.* Evans [1963] 1 Q.B. 412; [1962] 3 W.L.R. 1457; [1962] 3 All E.R. 1086;
106 S.J. 1013; 127 J.P. 49; 61 L.G.R. 32; 47 Cr.L.R. 62 ... 256, 257, 279–281

R. *v.* Evans (No. 2) [1964] 1 W.L.R. 1388; [1964] 3 All E.R. 666; 108 S.J.
880; 129 J.P. 29; 49 Cr.App.R. 10 429

R. *v.* Evans (Terence) [1974] R.T.R. 232; [1974] Cr.L.R. 315, C.A. ... 190, 193, 199

R. *v.* Fairford Justices, *ex parte* Brewster (1975), *The Times*, 22nd April 68

R. *v.* Fairhead [1975] Cr.L.R. 351 .... 598, 631

R. *v.* Fardy [1973] R.T.R. 268; [1973] Cr.L.R. 316, C.A. 193, 194

R. *v.* Fenn [1959] Jo.Crim.L. 253 119

R. *v.* Ferguson, 114 S.J. 621; [1970] Cr.L.R. 652; *sub nom.* R. *v.* Ferguson
(Frank) (1971), 54 Cr.App.R. 415, C.A. 205, 212, 230

R. *v.* Field [1965] 1 Q.B. 402 at p. 417; [1964] 3 W.L.R. 593 at p. 605; [1964]
3 All E.R. 269 at p. 279; 108 S.J. 641; 128 J.P. 578 at p. 581 466

R. *v.* Forbes [1971] Cr.L.R. 174... 215

R. *v.* Fowler [1937] 2 All E.R. 380; 157 L.T. 558; 81 S.J. 422; 53 T.L.R. 649;
101 J.P. 244; 35 L.G.R. 265; 30 Cox C.C. 643; 26 Cr.App.R. 80 638

R. *v.* Fry and Others (Justices) and Stoker, *ex parte* Masters (1898), 67 L.J.Q.B.
712; 78 L.T. 716; 42 S.J. 555; 14 T.L.R. 445; 46 W.R. 649; 62 J.P. 457;
19 Cox C.C. 135 77

R. *v.* Furness [1973] Cr.L.R. 759, C.A.. 190

R. *v.* Gaughan [1974] R.T.R. 195; [1974] Cr.L.R. 480, C.A. 189

R. *v.* Gibbs [1960] Cr.L.R. 197; 44 Cr.App.R. 77 360

R. *v.* Gilbey [1975] J.P.News. 244; [1975] Cr.L.R. 352 598

R. *v.* Godden [1971] Cr.L.R. 656; [1971] R.T.R. 462, C.A. 230

R. *v.* Godstone Justices, *ex parte* Dickson (1971), 115 S.J. 246; [1971] Cr.L.R.
602, D.C... 65, 162, 178

R. *v.* Godstone Justices, *ex parte* Secretary of State for the Environment [1974]
Cr.L.R. 110, D.C. 69, 88, 490

R. *v.* Gordon (Elliston James), 53 Cr.App.R. 614; [1970] R.T.R. 125*n.*,
C.A. 209, 210

R. *v.* Gore Justices, *ex parte* N. (an infant) [1966] 1 W.L.R. 1522; [1966] 3 All
E.R. 991; 110 S.J. 669; 131 J.P. 85 92

R. *v* Gormley [1973] R.T.R. 483; [1973] Cr.L.R. 644, C.A. 245

R. *v.* Gosney [1971] 2 Q.B. 674; [1971] 3 W.L.R. 343; 115 S.J. 608; [1971] 3
All E.R. 220; [1971] R.T.R. 321; *sub nom.* R. *v.* Gosney (Doreen Rose),
55 Cr.App.R. 502, C.A. 257, 269, 270, 278–281

R. *v.* Gould (Practice Note) [1964] 1 W.L.R. 145; [1963] 2 All E.R. 847; 127
J.P. 414; 47 Cr.App.R. 241 255

R. *v.* Gould [1965] Cr.L.R. 547; (1965), *The Times*, 3rd July; *The Guardian*,
3rd July 601

R. *v.* Gowerton Justices, *ex parte* Davies [1974] Cr.L.R. 253, D.C. 73

R. *v.* Graham [1955] Cr.L.R. 319 .... 631, 638

R. *v.* Gravesend Justices, *ex parte* Sheldon [1968] 1 W.L.R. 1699; [1968] 3 All
E.R. 466; 112 S.J. 838; Cr.L.R. 506 .... 83, 84

R. *v.* Gready [1974] R.T.R. 16; [1974] Cr.L.R. 314, C.A. 189

                                                                                        PAGE
R. *v.* Great Marlborough Street Magistrates, *ex parte* Fraser [1974] Cr.L.R. 47,
    D.C. 83
R. *v.* Green [1970] 1 All E.R. 408*n*. 225
R. *v.* Greenberg [1942] 2 All E.R. 344; 28 Cr.App.R. 160 382
R. *v.* Greenwood [1962] Cr.L.R. 639 457
R. *v.* Grimsby Borough Quarter Sessions, *ex parte* Fuller [1956] 1 Q.B. 36;
    [1955] 3 W.L.R. 563; [1955] 3 All E.R. 300; 99 S.J. 763; 119 J.P.
    560 94
R. *v.* Grundy; R. *v.* Moorhouse [1974] 1 W.L.R. 139; (1973), 118 S.J. 34;
    [1974] 1 All E.R. 292; [1974] Cr.L.R. 128, C.A. 599
R. *v.* Guest, *ex parte* Anthony [1964] 1 W.L.R. 1273; [1964] 3 All E.R. 385;
    108 S.J. 693; 128 J.P. 585 92
R. *v.* Guilfoyle [1973] 2 All E.R. 844; [1973] R.T.R. 272; [1973] Cr.L.R.
    377; *sub nom.* R. *v.* Guilfoyle (John Kenneth), 57 Cr.App.R. 549, C.A. ... 252,
                                                                              260–262, 661
R. *v.* Guttridge [1973] R.T.R. 135; [1973] Cr.L.R. 314, C.A. 147, 184, 186
R. *v.* Gwilliam [1968] 1 W.L.R. 1839; [1968] 3 All E.R. 821; 112 S.J. 825;
    133 J.P. 44; 53 Cr.App.R. 22 112
R. *v.* Hadwen [1902] 1 K.B. 882; 71 L.J.K.B. 581; 86 L.T. 601; 46 S.J. 464;
    18 T.L.R. 555; 50 W.R. 589; 66 J.P. 456; 20 Cox C.C. 206 .... 75, 77
R. *v.* Hall (1958), 43 Cr.App.R. 29 119
R. *v.* Hankey [1905] 2 K.B. 687; 74 L.J.K.B. 922; 93 L.T. 107; 21 T.L.R. 409;
    54 W.R. 80; 69 J.P. 219; 3 L.G.R. 554; 21 Cox C.C. 1; *sub nom.* R. *v.*
    Hankey, etc., Justices, *ex parte* Earl of Craven, 49 S.J. 419 464
R. *v.* Harding (1974), 118 S.J. 444; [1974] R.T.R. 325; *sub nom.* R. *v.* Harding
    (Anthony Raymond) (1974), 59 Cr.App.R. 153; [1974] Cr.L.R. 481,
    C.A. 232, 679
R. *v.* Harling [1970] R.T.R. 441; [1970] 3 All E.R. 902; (1970), 55 Cr.App.R.
    8, C.A. 196, 231, 232
R. *v.* Harnett [1955] Cr.L.R. 793 .... 164, 167
R. *v.* Hart. *See* R. *v.* Jackson
R. *v.* Haslam [1972] R.T.R. 297 .... 160, 208
R. *v.* Haverfordwest Justices, *ex parte* George (1964), 108 S.J. 199; (1964),
    The Times, 28th February 73
R. *v.* Hawarden Justices, *ex parte* Leo [1966] Cr.L.R. 220; 116 New L.J. 445;
    The Guardian, 4th February 76, 267
R. *v.* Hawkes (1931), 75 S.J. 247; 22 Cr.App.R. 172 162
R. *v.* Hazell (1965), 109 S.J. 112; [1965] Cr.L.R. 120 261
R. *v.* Hennigan (1971), 115 S.J. 268; [1971] 3 All E.R. 133; [1971] R.T.R.
    305; *sub nom.* R. *v.* Hennigan (James), 55 Cr.App.R. 262, C.A. 255
R. *v.* Herd [1973] R.T.R. 165; [1973] Cr.L.R. 315; *sub nom.* R. *v.* Herd
    (William Alan), 57 Cr.App.R. 560, C.A. 186–188
R. *v.* Hetherington [1972] Cr.L.R. 703 92
R. *v.* Higgins [1964] 3 All E.R. 714*n*. 632
R. *v.* Higgins [1973] R.T.R. 216 .... 623, 631, 638
R. *v.* Hilton [1971] 3 W.L.R. 625; 115 S.J. 565; [1971] 3 All E.R. 541; *sub
    nom.* R. *v.* Hilton (Keith), 55 Cr.App.R. 466, C.A. 75, 76
R. *v.* Hitchin Justices, *ex parte* Hilton [1974] R.T.R. 380; [1974] Cr.L.R. 319,
    D.C. 554, 566
R. *v.* Hodgon [1962] Cr.L.R. 563, C.C.A. 355
R. *v.* Holah [1973] 1 W.L.R. 127; 116 S.J. 845; [1973] 1 All E.R. 106; [1973]
    R.T.R. 74; [1973] Cr.L.R. 59; *sub nom.* R. *v.* Holah (John William Patrick)
    (1972), 57 Cr.App.R. 186, C.A. 148, 207, 208, 210,
                                                                                        228
R. *v.* Hollier [1973] R.T.R. 395; [1973] Cr.L.R. 584, C.A. 625
R. *v.* Holt [1962] Cr.L.R. 565 671
R. *v.* Horton [1974] R.T.R. 399; [1974] Cr.L.R. 721, C.A. 245
R. *v.* Howell (1938), 160 L.T. 16; 103 J.P. 9; 37 L.G.R. 8; 27 Cr.App.R.
    5 270

PAGE

R. v. Hughes (1879), 4 Q.B.D. 614; 48 L.J.M.C. 151; 40 L.T. 685; 43 J.P. 556;
14 Cox C.C. 284 .... 64, 130
R. v. Humphreys and Turner [1965] 3 All E.R. 689; 130 J.P. 45 55
R. v. Hunter (1969), 113 S.J. 161; [1969] Cr.L.R. 262 117
R. v. Hurst [1966] Cr.L.R. 683 685
R. v. Hyams [1973] 1 W.L.R. 13; 116 S.J. 886; [1972] 3 All E.R. 651;
[1973] R.T.R. 68; [1972] Cr.L.R. 645, C.A. 177, 217, 229, 230
R. v. Ipswich Justices, ex parte Robson [1971] 2 Q.B. 340; [1970] 3 W.L.R.
102; 112 S.J. 489; [1971] 2 All E.R. 1395; [1971] R.T.R. 339, D.C.... 479, 485
R. v. Jackson, R. v. Hart [1970] 1 Q.B. 647; [1969] 2 W.L.R. 1339; 133 J.P.
358; 113 S.J. 310; [1969] 2 All E.R. 453; [1970] R.T.R. 165; sub nom.
R. v. Jackson (Dennis James), R. v. Hart (Stanley), 53 Cr.App.R. 341,
C.A. 235, 671, 672, 678, 679
R. v. Jennings [1956] 1 W.L.R. 1497; [1956] 3 All E.R. 429; 100 S.J. 861; 40
Cr.App.R. 147 133
R. v. Jephcott (1966), 110 S.J. 812; [1967] Cr.L.R. 52 169
R. v. John [1974] 1 W.L.R. 624; 118 S.J. 348; [1974] R.T.R. 332; sub nom.
R. v. John (Graham) [1974] 2 All E.R. 561; 59 Cr.App.R. 75; [1974]
Cr.L.R. 670, C.A. 232, 234, 679
R. v. Johnson [1960] Cr.L.R. 430 .... 270, 282
R. v. Jones, ex parte Thomas [1921] 1 K.B. 632; 90 L.J.K.B. 543; 124 L.T. 668;
37 T.L.R. 299; 85 J.P. 112; 19 L.G.R. 354; 26 Cox C.C. 706 ...... 255, 265
R. v. Jones [1970] 3 All E.R. 815 .... 627, 638
R. v. Jones (Colin) [1974] R.T.R. 117; [1974] Cr.L.R. 671, C.A. 218, 219
R. v. Jones (E.J.M.) [1970] 1 W.L.R. 211; sub nom. R. v. Jones (Edward John
Mervyn) (1969), 113 S.J. 963; sub nom. R. v. Jones [1970] 1 All E.R. 209;
[1970] R.T.R. 56; 54 Cr.App.R. 148, C.A. 187, 191, 196, 221
R. v. Jones (Gwyn) [1969] 2 Q.B. 33; [1969] 2 W.L.R. 105; [1969] 1 All E.R.
325; 112 S.J. 984; 53 Cr.App.R. 87 79
R. v. Jones (Reginald William) [1970] 1 W.L.R. 16; 113 S.J. 962; [1970]
R.T.R. 35; 54 Cr.App.R. 63; sub nom. R. v. Jones (Reginald) [1969] 3 All
E.R. 1559, C.A. 200, 237
R. v. Jordan (1956), 40 Cr.App.R. 152 256
R. v. Kane [1965] 1 All E.R. 705; 129 J.P. 170 175
R. v. Kashyap (1971), 136 J.P.Jo. 28; [1972] R.T.R. 78; [1972] Cr.L.R. 257... 261
R. v. Kelly (Francis William) [1970] 1 W.L.R. 1050; 54 Cr.App.R. 334; sub
nom. R. v. Kelly, 114 S.J. 357; [1970] 2 All E.R. 198 .... 186, 187, 196
R. v. Kelly (H. F.) [1972] R.T.R. 447; [1972] Cr.L.R. 643, C.A. 208, 228
R. v. Kettering Justices, ex parte Patmore [1968] 1 W.L.R. 1436; [1968] 3 All
E.R. 167; 112 S.J. 656; 132 J.P. 510 78
R. v. Kitson (1955), 39 Cr.App.R. 66 21
R. v. Knight (1961), The Times, 14th June 115
R. v. Knightley [1971] 1 W.L.R. 1073; 115 S.J. 448; [1971] 2 All E.R. 1041;
[1971] R.T.R. 409; sub nom. R. v. Knightley (Alan James) (1971), 55
Cr.App.R. 390, C.A. 223–225, 228, 231, 233
R. v. Kwame [1975] R.T.R. 106 669
R. v. Lambert [1974] R.T.R. 244, C.A. 650
R. v. Lambeth Metropolitan Magistrates, ex parte Everett [1968] 1 Q.B. 446;
[1967] 3 W.L.R. 1027; [1967] 3 All E.R. 648; 111 S.J. 545; 132 J.P. 6;
51 Cr.App.R. 425 .... 645, 649, 654
R. v. Lanfear [1968] 2 Q.B. 77; [1968] 2 W.L.R. 623; [1968] 1 All E.R. 683;
112 S.J. 132; 132 J.P. 193; 52 Cr.App.R. 176 242
R. v. Lavin (1967), 51 Cr.App.R. 378; [1967] Cr.L.R. 481 244
R. v. Lawrence [1968] 1 W.L.R. 341; [1968] 1 All E.R. 579; 112 S.J. 109; 132
J.P. 173; 52 Cr.App.R. 163 .... 115, 150
R. v. Lawrence (Paul Antony) [1973] 1 W.L.R. 329; (1972), 117 S.J. 225;
[1973] 1 All E.R. 364; [1973] R.T.R. 64; (1972), 57 Cr.App.R. 285;
[1973] Cr.L.R. 242, C.A. 164, 168, 169, 171, 182, 197
R. v. Lee [1971] Cr.L.R. 177; [1971] R.T.R. 30, C.A. 638

PAGE

R. v. Leeds Justices, *ex parte* Lister (1966), 110 S.J. 92; [1966] Cr.L.R. 229 702
R. v. Leigh (1969), 113 S.J. 867; [1969] Cr.L.R. 670, C.A. 597
R. v. Lennard [1973] 1 W.L.R. 483; 111 S.J. 284; [1973] 2 All E.R. 831;
   [1973] R.T.R. 252; [1973] Cr.L.R. 312; *sub nom.* R. v. Lennard (Michael),
   57 Cr.App.R. 542, C.A. 233, 234, 679
R. v. Lewes Crown Court, *ex parte* Rogers [1974] 1 W.L.R. 196; (1973), 118
   S.J. 100; *sub nom.* R. v. Crown Court at Lewes, *ex parte* Rogers [1974]
   1 All E.R. 589; [1974] Cr.L.R. 100, D.C. 600
R. v. Lewis [1971] Cr.L.R. 414; 115 S.J. 385; *sub nom.* R. v. Lewis (Robert
   Alexander) (1971), 55. Cr.App.R. 386, C.A. 120
R. v. Liskerret Justices, *ex parte* Child [1972] R.T.R. 141 99
R. v. Llandrindod Wells Justices, *ex parte* Gibson [1968] 1 W.L.R. 598; [1968]
   2 All E.R. 20; 112 S.J. 218; 132 J.P. 282 .... 99, 630
R. v. Lobley [1974] R.T.R. 550; [1974] Cr.L.R. 373, C.A.; (1974), 59
   Cr.App.R. 63 ....261, 262, 635, 638, 661
R. v. London County Quarter Sessions, *ex parte* Rossi [1956] 1 Q.B. 682;
   [1956] 2 W.L.R. 800; 120 J.P. 239; 100 S.J. 225; [1956] 1 All E.R. 670,
   C.A. 463
R. v. Long [1960] 1 Q.B. 681; [1959] 3 W.L.R. 953; [1959] 3 All E.R. 559;
   103 S.J. 922; 124 J.P. 4; 44 Cr.App.R. 9 .... 179, 216
R. v. Lumiala (1957), 25 C.R. 361 165
R. v. Lundt-Smith [1964] 2 Q.B. 167; [1964] 2 W.L.R. 1063; [1964] 3 All
   E.R. 225; 108 S.J. 425; 128 J.P. 534; 62 L.G.R. 376 ... 268, 666, 667, 669,
                                                             674, 680
R. v. Lynn (Frederick John) (1971), 55 Cr.App.R. 423; *sub nom.* R. v. Lynn
   [1971] R.T.R. 369; [1971] Cr.L.R. 429 688
R. v. Mabley (1965), 109 S.J. 296; [1965] Cr.L.R. 377 .... 261, 293
R. v. McAllister [1974] R.T.R. 408; *sub nom.* R. v. McAllister (William
   Joseph) (1973), 59 Cr.App.R. 7; [1974] Cr.L.R. 716, C.A. ... 216, 230, 233
R. v. McBride [1962] 2 Q.B. 167; [1961] 3 W.L.R. 549; [1961] 3 All E.R. 6;
   105 S.J. 572; 125 J.P. 544; 45 Cr.App.R. 262 ...... 162, 255, 264, 274, 275
R. v. McCardle [1958] Cr.L.R. 50 .... 50, 381
R. v. McCarthy [1964] Cr.L.R. 330 261
R. v. McDonagh [1974] Q.B. 448; [1974] 2 W.L.R. 529; 118 S.J. 222; [1974]
   2 All E.R. 257; [1974] R.T.R. 372; *sub nom.* R. v. MacDonagh (Brian),
   59 Cr.App.R. 55; [1974] Cr.L.R. 317, C.A. 22, 23, 25, 26
R. v. McGall [1974] R.T.R. 216; [1974] Cr.L.R. 482, C.A. 193, 194
R. v. McGill. *See* R. v. Phipps
R. v. McKenna (1956), 40 Cr.App.R. 65 124
R. v. McKenzie [1971] 1 All E.R. 729; 55 Cr.App.R. 294 .... 163, 222
R. v. McLean (1967), 111 S.J. 925; 117 New L.J. 1243; [1968] Cr.L.R.
   108 .... 112, 122
R. v. McNulty [1965] 1 Q.B. 437; [1964] 3 W.L.R. 1168; [1964] 3 All E.R.
   713; 108 S.J. 863; 127 J.P. 12; 49 Cr.App.R. 21 632
R. v. McPherson [1973] R.T.R. 157; [1973] Cr.L.R. 457, C.A. 354
R. v. Madan [1961] 2 Q.B. 1; [1961] 2 W.L.R. 231; [1961] 1 All E.R. 588;
   105 S.J. 160; 125 J.P. 246; [1961] Cr.L.R. 253; 45 Cr.App.R. 80 60
R. v. Malden and Surbiton Justices, *ex parte* Little [1966] Cr.L.R. 387; 116
   New L.J. 837 99
R. v. Manchester Justices, *ex parte* Burke (1961), 125 J.P. 387; 105 S.J. 131..... 71
R. v. Manchester Justices, *ex parte* Gaynor [1956] 1 W.L.R. 280; [1956] 1 All
   E.R. 610; 100 S.J. 210; 54 L.G.R. 264 649
R. v. Manners-Astley [1967] 1 W.L.R. 1505; [1967] 3 All E.R. 899; 111 S.J.
   853; 132 J.P. 39; 52 Cr.App.R. 5 .... 508, 514
R. v. Maqsud Ali [1965] 2 All E.R. 464 126
R. v. Marsham, *ex parte* Pethick Lawrence [1912] 2 K.B. 362; 81 L.J.K.B. 957;
   107 L.T. 89; 28 T.L.R. 391; 76 J.P. 284; 23 Cox C.C. 77 91
R. v. Martin [1973] R.T.R. 171; [1973] Cr.L.R. 583; *sub nom.* R. v. Martin
   (Peter John) (1972), 57 Cr.App.R. 279, C.A. 187

PAGE

R. *v.* Marylebone Justices, *ex parte* Westminster (City) London Borough Council [1971] 1 W.L.R. 567; *sub nom.* R. *v.* Marylebone Justices, *ex parte* Westminster City London Borough Council, 115 S.J. 247; *sub nom.* R. *v.* Marylebone Justices, *ex parte* Westminster City Council, R. *v.* Inner London Quarter Sessions, *ex parte* Westminster City Council [1971] 1 All E.R. 1025, D.C. 74
R. *v.* Mason [1965] 2 All E.R. 308; 129 J.P. 363 .... 99, 630
R. *v.* Mathews [1975] R.T.R. 32 641
R. *v.* Mathias (1861), 2 F. & F. 570 343
R. *v.* Mayne [1973] R.T.R. 448, C.A. 210
R. *v.* Meese [1973] 1 W.L.R. 675; 111 S.J. 418; [1973] 2 All E.R. 1103; [1973] R.T.R. 400; *sub nom.* R. *v.* Meese (Kelvin Thomas), 57 Cr.App.R. 568, C.A. 623, 631, 638, 658
R. *v.* Messom [1973] R.T.R. 140; [1973] Cr.L.R. 252; *sub nom.* R. *v.* Messom (Samuel Andrew) (1972), 57 Cr.App.R. 481, C.A. 676
R. *v.* Middlesex Area Quarter Sessions, *ex parte* Bull [1972] R.T.R. 205; [1972] Cr.L.R. 189, D.C. 249, 629, 633
R. *v.* Middleton, Bromley and Bexley Justices, *ex parte* Collins [1970] 1 Q.B. 216; [1969] 3 W.L.R. 632; *sub nom.* R. *v.* Middleton Justices, *ex parte* Collins, 133 J.P. 729; 113 S.J. 816; *sub nom.* R. *v.* Middleton Justices, *ex parte* Collins, R. *v.* Bromley Justices, *ex parte* Collins, R. *v.* Bexley Justices, *ex parte* Collins [1969] 3 All E.R. 800, D.C. 650
R. *v.* Midhurst Justices, *ex parte* Thompson; R. *v.* Midhurst Justices, *ex parte* Mattesons Meats [1973] 3 W.L.R. 715; [1973] 3 All E.R. 1164; [1973] Cr.L.R. 755; *sub nom.* R. *v.* Midhurst Justices, *ex parte* Thompson, 117 S.J. 774, D.C. 85
R. *v.* Milburn [1974] R.T.R. 431; [1974] Cr.L.R. 434, C.A. 253, 260, 261
R. *v.* Miles (1890), 24 Q.B.D. 423; 59 L.J.M.C. 50; 62 L.T. 572; 6 T.L.R. 186; 38 W.R. 334; 54 J.P. 549 606
R. *v.* Millar, R. *v.* Millar (Robert) (Contractors) Ltd. [1970] 2 Q.B. 54; [1970] 2 W.L.R. 541; [1970] 1 All E.R. 577; [1970] R.T.R. 147; 54 Cr.App.R. 158, C.A.; *affg. sub nom.* R. *v.* Hart, Millar and Millar (Robert) (Contractors) Ltd. [1969] 3 All E.R. 247; *sub nom.* R. *v.* Hart, Millar, 133 J.P. 554 .... 54, 68, 257, 277, 278, 423
R. *v.* Miller [1954] 2 Q.B. 282; [1954] 2 W.L.R. 138; [1954] 2 All E.R. 529; 98 S.J. 577; 118 J.P. 340; 38 Cr.App.R. 1 348
R. *v.* Mills [1974] R.T.R. 215, C.A. 251
R. *v.* Mills, R. *v.* Rose [1962] 1 W.L.R. 1152; [1962] 3 All E.R. 298; 106 S.J. 593; 126 J.P. 506; 46 Cr.App.R. 336 .... 113, 126
R. *v.* Mitchell (1852), 6 Cox C.C. 82 113
R. *v.* Montgomery, *ex parte* Long (1910), 102, L.T. 325; 26 T.L.R. 225; 74 J.P. 110; 8 L.G.R. 234; 22 Cox C.C. 304 95
R. *v.* Moore [1954] 1 W.L.R. 893; [1954] 2 All E.R. 189; 98 S.J. 391; 118 J.P. 284; 38 Cr.App.R. 95 104
R. *v.* Moore [1968] Cr.L.R. 621; (1968), *The Times*, 20th August 79
R. *v.* Moore (Brian) [1968] 1 W.L.R. 397; *sub nom.* R. *v.* Moore [1968] 1 All E.R. 790; 112 S.J. 109; 132 J.P. 196; 52 Cr.App.R. 180 703
R. *v.* Moore [1970] Cr.L.R. 650; [1970] R.T.R. 486, C.A. 193, 215, 217, 229, 234
R. *v.* Morris [1972] 1 All E.R. 384 .... 130, 148, 196, 348
R. *v.* Mount, R. *v.* Metcalfe (1934), 78 S.J. 225; 24 Cr.App.R. 135 116
R. *v.* Mullarkey [1970] Cr.L.R. 406 672–674
R. *v.* Mullins (1848), 12 J.P. 776; 3 Cox C.C. 526 112
R. *v.* Muncaster [1974] Cr.L.R. 320, C.A. 656
R. *v.* Munning [1961] Cr.L.R. 555 21
R. *v.* Murphy [1965] N.I. 138 126
R. *v.* Najran [1973] R.T.R. 451, C.A. 234, 246, 247
R. *v.* Neal [1962] Cr.L.R. 698 242
R. *v.* Needham [1974] R.T.R. 201; [1973] Cr.L.R. 640, C.A. 189

PAGE
R. *v.* Newcastle-upon-Tyne Justices, *ex parte* Swales [1972] Cr.L.R. 111;
[1972] R.T.R. 57; (1971), 115 S.J. 949 .... 84, 92, 612
R. *v.* Newton (David) [1974] R.T.R. 451; [1974] Cr.L.R. 321, C.A. 247,
251, 665, 668, 676, 677
R. *v.* Nicholls [1972] 2 All E.R. 186; [1972] 1 W.L.R. 502; 116 S.J. 298;
[1972] Cr.L.R. 380; [1972] R.T.R. 308; *sub nom.* R. *v.* Nicholls (Gerald),
56 Cr.App.R. 382, C.A. 197, 205
R. *v.* Nisbet [1972] Q.B. 37; [1971] 3 W.L.R. 455; 115 S.J. 565; [1971] 3 All
E.R. 307; *sub nom.* R. *v.* Nisbet (Robert McPheat), 55 Cr.App.R. 490,
C.A. 79, 80
R. *v.* Nixon, R. *v.* Nixon [1968] 1 W.L.R. 577; [1968] 2 All E.R. 33; *sub nom.*
R. *v.* Nixon (1968), 112 S.J. 231; 132 J.P. 309; 52 Cr.App.R. 218 115
R. *v.* Norfolk Justices, *ex parte* D.P.P. [1950] 2 K.B. 558; 94 S.J. 436; 34
Cr.App.R. 120; 34 L.G.R. 483; *sub nom.* R. *v.* South Greenhoe Justices,
ex parte D.P.P., 66 T.L.R. (Pt. 2) 452; 114 J.P. 312; [1950] 2 All E.R. 42,
D.C. 244, 652
R. *v.* Norfolk Quarter Sessions, *ex parte* Brunson [1953] 1 Q.B. 503; [1953] 2
W.L.R. 294; [1953] 1 All E.R. 346; 97 S.J. 98; 37 Cr.App.R. 6 124
R. *v.* Norham and Islandshire Justices, *ex parte* Sunter Bros. Ltd. [1961] 1
W.L.R. 364; [1961] 1 All E.R. 455; 105 S.J. 234; 125 J.P. 181 99
R. *v.* North (1971), 115 S.J. 389; [1971] R.T.R. 366, C.A. 638
R. *v.* Northamptonshire Justices, *ex parte* Nicholson [1974] R.T.R. 97; [1973]
Cr.L.R. 762, D.C. 629
R. *v.* Nowell [1948] 1 All E.R. 794; 92 S.J. 351; 64 T.L.R. 277; 32 Cr.App.R.
173; 112 J.P. 255; 46 L.G.R. 336 242
R. *v.* Nuneaton Justices, *ex parte* Parker [1954] 1 W.L.R. 1318; [1954] 3 All
E.R. 251; 98 S.J. 751; 118 J.P. 524; 52 L.G.R. 518 265
R. *v.* Nuttall (1971), 115 S.J. 489; [1971] R.T.R. 279; [1971] Cr.L.R.
485 .... 647, 661
R. *v.* O'Boyle [1973] R.T.R. 445, C.A. 197, 205
R. *v.* Oldham Justices, *ex parte* Morrisey [1959] 1 W.L.R. 58; [1958] 3 All
E.R. 559; 103 S.J. 55; 123 J.P. 38 99
R. *v.* Oliver [1944] K.B. 68; [1943] 2 All E.R. 800; 113 L.J.K.B. 119; 170 L.T.
110; 60 T.L.R. 82; 108 J.P. 30; 42 L.G.R. 37; 29 Cr.App.R. 137 123
R. *v.* Oliver (1958), 119 C.C.C. 394 .... 304, 394
R. *v.* Orrell [1972] R.T.R. 14, C.A.; [1972] Cr. L.R. 313 179
R. *v.* O'Toole (Robert John) (1971), 55 Cr.App.R. 206, C.A. 268, 669
R. *v.* Ovenell, R. *v.* Cartwright (Walter A.) [1969] 1 Q.B. 17; [1968] 2
W.L.R. 1543; [1968] 1 All E.R. 933; 112 S.J. 502; (1968), 132 J.P. 225;
52 Cr.App.R. 167 118
R. *v.* Owen [1952] 2 Q.B. 362; [1952] 1 All E.R. 1040; 96 S.J. 281; [1952] 1
T.L.R. 1220; [1952] W.N. 217; 116 J.P. 244; 36 Cr.App.R. 16............ 124
R. *v.* Paduch (Jan) (1972), 57 Cr.App.R. 676; [1973] R.T.R. 493; [1973]
Cr.L.R. 533, C.A. 177, 217, 229
R. *v.* Palfrey, R. *v.* Sadler. *See* Sadler *v.* Metropolitan Police Commissioner
R. *v.* Parker (1895), 59 J.P. 793 259
R. *v.* Parker (1957), 122 J.P. 17; 41 Cr.App.R. 134 .... 257, 279, 282, 289, 290
R. *v.* Parsons (1972), 116 S.J. 567; [1972] Cr.L.R. 565; [1972] R.T.R. 425;
sub nom. R. *v.* Parsons (Leslie Arthur) (1972), 56 Cr.App.R. 741, C.A. 204
R. *v.* Pashley [1974] R.T.R. 149, C.A. 245, 251, 638, 654
R. *v.* Paul [1952] N.I. 61 .... 7, 166
R. *v.* Payne [1963] 1 W.L.R. 637; [1963] 1 All E.R. 848; 107 S.J. 97; 127 J.P.
230; 47 Cr.App.R. 122 .... 215, 242
R. *v.* Pearce [1961] Cr.L.R. 122 .... 352, 358
R. *v.* Pearce [1973] Cr.L.R. 321, C.A. 25, 352
R. *v.* Pearson (Donald) [1974] R.T.R. 92; [1974] Cr.L.R. 315, C.A. 198
R. *v.* Peart [1970] 2 Q.B. 672; [1970] 3 W.L.R. 63; 114 S.J. 418; [1970] 2 All
E.R. 823; *sub nom.* R. *v.* Peart (Frank) (1970), 54 Cr.App.R. 374, C.A. ... 355,
356

PAGE
R. v. Pembroke Justices, *ex parte* Perrins (1961), *The Guardian*, 26th October ... 73
R. v. Phillips [1953] 2 Q.B. 14; [1953] 2 W.L.R. 868; [1953] 1 All E.R. 968;
 97 S.J. 302; 117 J.P. 235; 37 Cr.App.R. 65 79
R. v. Phillips [1955] 1 W.L.R. 1103; [1955] 2 All E.R. 273; 99 S.J. 727; 119
 J.P. 499; 53 L.G.R. 636 .... 631, 638, 654, 687
R. v. Phipps (Owen Roger Charles), R. v. McGill (John Peter), 54 Cr.App.R.
 301; *sub nom.* R. v. Phipps, R. v. McGill [1970] R.T.R. 209; *sub nom.* R. v.
 McGill [1970] Cr.L.R. 290, C.A. 356, 359
R. v. Pico [1971] Cr.L.R. 599; [1971] R.T.R. 500, C.A. 196
R. v. Pomeroy (1935), 80 S.J. 94; 25 Cr.App.R. 147 .... 77, 162, 653
R. v. Potter [1958] 1 W.L.R. 638; [1958] 2 All E.R. 51; 102 S.J. 438; 122 J.P.
 234; 42 Cr.App.R. 168 480
R. v. Powell (1963), 113 L.J. 643; Cr.L.R. 511 175
R. v. Price [1964] 2 Q.B. 76; [1963] 3 W.L.R. 1027; [1963] 3 All E.R. 938;
 107 S.J. 933; 128 J.P. 92; 48 Cr.App.R. 65 221
R. v. Price (Kenneth) [1968] 1 W.L.R. 1853; [1968] 3 All E.R. 814; 112 S.J.
 825; 133 J.P. 47; 53 Cr.App.R. 25 .... 185, 195
R. v. Priest (1961), 35 C.R. 31 314
R. v. Pursehouse [1970] 3 All E.R. 218; (1970), 54 Cr.App.R. 478, C.A. ... 230
R. v. Quick; R. v. Paddison [1973] Q.B. 910; [1973] 3 W.L.R. 26; [1973]
 3 All E.R. 347; *sub nom.* R. v. Paddison; R. v. Quick, 117 S.J. 371; *sub nom.*
 R. v. Quick (William George Henry); R. v. Paddison (William), 57
 Cr.App.R. 722; *sub nom.* R. v. Quick [1973] Cr.L.R. 434, C.A. 269, 270
R. v. Quinn, R. v. Bloom [1962] 2 Q.B. 245; [1961] 3 W.L.R. 611; [1961] 3
 All E.R. 88; 105 S.J. 590; 125 J.P. 565 115
R. v. Reed [1975] R.T.R. 313 361
R. v. Reid (Philip) [1973] 1 W.L.R. 1283; 117 S.J. 681; [1973] 3 All E.R.
 1020; [1973] R.T.R. 536; [1973] Cr.L.R. 760; *sub nom.* R. v. Reid
 (Philip John Wilson), 57 Cr. App.R. 807, C.A. 190, 229, 230, 679
R. v. Richards (Stanley) [1975] 1 W.L.R. 131; (1974), 119 S.J. 66; [1974]
 3 All E.R. 696; [1974] R.T.R. 520; *sub nom.* R. v. Richards (Stanley
 Alexander Ernest), 59 Cr.App.R. 288, C.A. 182, 237
R. v. Richardson [1958] Cr.L.R. 480 357
R. v. Richardson [1971] 2 Q.B. 484; [1971] 2 W.L.R. 889; 115 S.J. 263;
 [1971] 2 All E.R. 773; *sub nom.* R. v. Richardson (David Ernest), 55
 Cr.App.R. 244, C.A. 113
R. v. Richardson (John) [1975] R.T.R. 173 173
R. v. Richardson, R. v. Fisher [1960] Cr.L.R. 135 274
R. v. Rimmer [1972] 1 W.L.R. 268; (1971), 116 S.J. 158; [1972] 1 All E.R.
 604; [1972] Cr.L.R. 98; *sub nom.* R. v. Rimmer (Patrick) (1971), 56
 Cr.App.R. 196, C.A. 92
R. v. Rivers [1974] R.T.R. 31; [1974] Cr.L.R. 316, C.A. 169, 170
R. v. Roberts [1964] 2 All E.R. 541; (1964), 48 Cr.App.R. 300; 108 S.J.
 383 .... 352, 357
R. v. Roberts (No. 2) [1965] 1 Q.B. 85; [1964] 3 W.L.R. 180; [1964] 2 All
 E.R. 541; 108 S.J. 383; 128 J.P. 395; 48 Cr.App.R. 296 .... 21, 25, 352
R. v. Robson; R. v. Harris [1972] 1 W.L.R. 651; 116 S.J. 313; [1972] 2 All
 E.R. 699; 56 Cr.App.R. 450; [1972] Cr.L.R. 316 .... 115, 126
R. v. Rogers [1953] 1 Q.B. 311; [1953] 2 W.L.R. 52; [1953] 1 All E.R. 206;
 97 S.J. 30; 117 J.P. 83; 36 Cr.App.R. 203 626
R. v. Rous [1965] Cr.L.R. 378 261
R. v. Rouse [1904] 1 K.B. 184; 73 L.J.K.B. 60; 89 L.T. 677; 48 S.J. 85; 20
 T.L.R. 68; 52 W.R. 236; 68 J.P. 14; 20 Cox C.C. 592 97
R. v. Rowe [1975] Cr.L.R. 245 262
R. v. Saddleworth Justices, *ex parte* Staples [1968] 1 W.L.R. 556; [1968] 1 All
 E.R. 1189; 112 S.J. 336; 132 J.P. 275 .... 369, 472, 639, 652
R. v. Sakhuja. *See* Sakhuja v. Allen
R. v. Salisbury and Amesbury Justices, *ex parte* Greatbatch [1954] 2 Q.B. 142;
 [1954] 3 W.L.R. 29; [1954] 2 All E.R. 326; 98 S.J. 392; 118 J.P. 392 78

PAGE

R. v. Sanderson [1953] 1 W.L.R. 392; [1953] 1 All E.R. 485; 97 S.J. 136; 117
J.P. 173; 37 Cr.App.R. 32 124
R. v. Saunders [1975] R.T.R. 315 361
R. v. Scales, W.L.R. (Recent Points), 7th March, 1969 117
R. v. Scammell [1967] 1 W.L.R. 1167; [1967] 3 All E.R. 97; 111 S.J. 820; 131
J.P. 462; 51 Cr.L.R. 398 256
R. v. Scott [1970] 1 Q.B. 661; [1969] 2 W.L.R. 1350n.; 133 J.P. 369; [1969] 2
All E.R. 450; [1970] R.T.R. 173; sub nom. R. v. Scott (Myra) (1968), 113
S.J. 470; sub nom. R. v. Scott (Myra June) (1968), 53 Cr.App.R. 319,
C.A. 671
R. v. Seaman (1971), 115 S.J. 741; [1971] R.T.R. 456; sub nom. R. v. Seaman
(James), 55 Cr.App.R. 569, C.A. 231, 233, 679
R. v. Seward [1970] 1 W.L.R. 323; 113 S.J. 984, C.A. 196
R. v. Sharman [1974] R.T.R. 213, C.A. 247, 251
R. v. Sharp [1968] 2 Q.B. 564; [1968] 3 W.L.R. 333; [1968] 3 All E.R. 182;
112 S.J. 602; 132 J.P. 491; sub nom. R. v. Sharp (Leonard James), 52
Cr.App.R. 607 218
R. v. Shaw (1865), 34 L.J.M.C. 169; 12 L.T. 470; 13 W.R. 692; 29 J.P. 339;
11 Jur.(N.S.) 415; 10 Cox C.C. 66 64
R. v. Shaw [1974] R.T.R. 225; [1974] Cr.L.R. 672, C.A. 27, 674
R. v. Shaw (Derek) [1974] R.T.R. 458, C.A. 178, 217
R v. Shaw (Kenneth) [1975] R.T.R. 160 .... 23, 159, 243
R. v. Shippam [1971] Cr.L.R. 434; (1971), 115 S.J. 429; [1971] R.T.R. 209,
C.A. 666, 675
R. v. Shirley [1969] 1 W.L.R. 1357; 133 J.P. 691; 113 S.J. 721; [1969] 3 All
E.R. 678n.; sub nom. R. v. Shirley (Leroy Frank), 53 Cr.App.R. 543,
C.A. 654
R. v. Short (1955), The Times, 10th December 164, 167
R. v. Sibbles [1959] Cr.L.R. 660 .... 24, 269, 274
R. v. Sixsmith, ex parte Morris [1968] 1 Q.B. 438; [1966] 3 W.L.R. 1200;
[1966] 3 All E.R. 473; 110 S.J. 606; 130 J.P. 420 ... 626, 632, 633, 659, 691
R. v. Slade [1974] R.T.R. 20; [1973] Cr.L.R. 644, C.A. 247, 250
R. v. Smith [1959] 2 Q.B. 35; [1959] 2 W.L.R. 623; [1959] 2 All E.R. 193; 103
S.J. 353; 123 J.P. 295; 43 Cr.App.R. 121 256
R. v. Smith (D. R.) [1974] Q.B. 354; [1974] 2 W.L.R. 20; (1973), 117 S.J.
938; sub nom. R. v. Smith (David Raymond) [1974] 1 All E.R. 632;
(1973), 58 Cr.App.R. 320; [1974] Cr.L.R. 101, C.A. 365
R. v. Sodo (1975), The Times, 6th May 221
R. v. South Greenhoe Justices. See R. v. Norfolk Justices
R. v. South Holderness Justices, ex parte Bonner [1964] Cr.L.R. 537; The
Guardian, 24th April 94
R. v. Southampton Justices, ex parte Atherton [1974] Cr.L.R. 108, D.C. 100
R. v. Southampton Justices, ex parte Briggs [1972] 1 W.L.R. 277; (1971), 116
S.J. 140; [1972] 1 All E.R. 573; [1972] Cr.L.R. 708, D.C. 78
R. v. Spurge [1961] 2 Q.B. 205; [1961] 3 W.L.R. 23; [1961] 2 All E.R. 688;
105 S.J. 469; 125 J.P. 502; 59 L.G.R. 323; 45 Cr.App.R. 191 .... 257, 272,
277, 278, 280, 281, 300
R. v. Stally [1960] 1 W.L.R. 79; [1959] 3 All E.R. 814; 104 S.J. 108; 124 J.P.
65; 44 Cr.App.R. 5 357
R. v. Steel (Robert Stanley) (1968), 52 Cr.App.R. 510; sub nom. R. v. Steel
[1968] Cr.L.R. 450 .... 667, 672
R. v. Stern [1967] Cr.L.R. 421 256
R. v. Stevens [1970] Cr.L.R. 158, C.A. 256, 279, 281
R. v. Stevenson, R. v. Hulse, R. v. Whitney [1971] 1 W.L.R. 1; 115 S.J. 11;
[1971] 1 All E.R. 678; sub nom. R. v. Stevenson (1971), 55 Cr.App.R. 171;
[1971] Cr.L.R. 95 126
R. v. Storey [1973] Cr.L.R. 189 293
R. v. Stratford-upon-Avon Justices, ex parte Edmonds; Edmonds v. Badham
[1973] R.T.R. 356; [1973] Cr.L.R. 241, D.C. 92

PAGE

R. *v.* Sullivan [1974] Cr.L.R. 56, C.A. 261

R. *v.* Surrey Justices, *ex parte* Witherick [1932] 1 K.B. 450; 101 L.J.K.B. 203; 146 L.T. 164; 75 S.J. 853; 48 T.L.R. 67; 95 J.P. 219; 29 L.G.R. 667; 29 Cox C.C. 414... 91, 266

R. *v.* Surrey Quarter Sessions, *ex parte* Commissioner of Metropolitan Police [1963] 1 Q.B. 990; [1962] 2 W.L.R. 1203; [1962] 1 All E.R. 825; 106 S.J. 245; 126 J.P. 269; *sub nom.* R. *v.* Brown and Taylor, *ex parte* Metropolitan Police Commissioner, 46 Cr.App.R. 218 .... 635, 697

R. *v.* Swindall (1846), 2 Car. & Kir. 230; 2 Cox C.C. 141 277

R. *v.* Tahsin (1969), 114 S.J. 56; [1970] R.T.R. 88; [1970] Cr.L.R. 160, C.A. 6, 23, 159, 175, 358

R. *v.* Talgarth Justices, *ex parte* Bithell [1973] 1 W.L.R. 1327; 117 S.J. 796; [1973] 2 All E.R. 717; [1973] R.T.R. 546; [1973] Cr.L.R. 756, D.C. ... 111, 608, 629, 631

R. *v.* Taylor (1927), 20 Cr.App.R. 71 .... 242, 276

R. *v.* Thomas [1961] Cr.L.R. 839 293

R. *v.* Thomas [1973] R.T.R. 325; [1973] Cr.L.R. 379; *sub nom.* R. *v.* Thomas (Colin), 57 Cr.App.R. 496, C.A. 247, 251

R. *v.* Thomas (Derek) [1975] R.T.R. 38 642

R. *v.* Thorpe [1972] R.T.R. 118; (1972), *The Times*, 17th January 162, 255, 256, 274

R. *v.* Thorpe (Thomas) [1974] R.T.R. 465; 59 Cr. App.R. 295, C.A. 206–208

R. *v.* Tinsley [1963] Cr.L.R. 392; [1963] Cr.L.R. 520 243

R. *v.* Togo [1966] (3) S.A. 695 345

R. *v.* Tolhurst, R. *v.* Woodhead (1962), 106 S.J. 16; [1962] Cr.L.R. 489 ... 360

R. *v.* Tottenham Justices, *ex parte* Rubens [1970] 1 W.L.R. 800; *sub nom.* R. *v.* Tottenham Justices, *ex parte* Rubens, R. *v.* Middlesex Quarter Sessions, *ex parte* Rubens [1970] 1 All E.R. 879; (1969), 54. Cr.App.R. 183, D.C. 74

R. *v.* Totton Justices [1958] Cr.L.R. 543 99

R. *v.* Tulsiani [1973] Cr.L.R. 186 211

R. *v.* Tunde-Olarinde [1967] 1 W.L.R. 911; [1967] 2 All E.R. 491; 111 S.J. 117; 131 J.P. 323; 51 Cr.App.R. 249 638

R. *v.* Tupa (Paul Michael) (1973), 58 Cr.App.R. 234; *sub nom.* R. *v.* Tupa [1974] R.T.R. 153; [1973] Cr.L.R. 58, C.A. 244, 246, 247, 251

R. *v.* Tyrer [1972] Cr.L.R. 55 261

R. *v.* Van Pelz [1943] 1 All E.R. 36 96

R. *v.* Veevers (1970), 115 S.J. 62; [1971] R.T.R. 47, C.A. 210

R. *v.* Wagner (1970), 114 S.J. 669; [1970] Cr.L.R. 535; [1970] R.T.R. 422, C.A. 205, 228

R. *v.* Wakefield Justices, *ex parte* Butterworth (1969), 114 S.J. 30; [1970] 1 All E.R. 1181; [1970] Cr.L.R. 102 .... 73, 353

R. *v.* Wall [1969] 1 W.L.R. 400; 133 J.P. 310; 113 S.J. 168; [1969] 1 All E.R. 968n.; *sub nom.* R. *v.* Wall (Harry), 53 Cr.App.R. 283, C.A. 185, 212, 236

R. *v.* Wallace [1955] N.I. 137.. 638

R. *v.* Wallace [1972] R.T.R. 9 233

R. *v.* Walsby [1972] R.T.R. 301 217

R. *v.* Walters [1972] Cr.L.R. 381 225

R. *v.* Ward [1954] Cr.L.R. 940 275

R. *v.* Ward (Ronald) (1968), 53 Cr.App.R. 23; *sub nom.* R. *v.* Ward [1969] Cr.L.R. 43, C.A. 79

R. *v.* Ward [1971] Cr.L.R. 665, C.A. 638

R. *v.* Warr (1969), 113 S.J. 287; [1969] Cr.L.R. 331; (1969), *The Times*, 18th March 196

R. *v.* Warren (1909), 25 T.L.R. 633; 73 J.P. 359; 2 Cr.App.R. 194 82

R. *v.* Waterfield [1964] 1 Q.B. 164; [1963] 3 W.L.R. 946; [1963] 3 All E.R. 659; 107 S.J. 833; 128 J.P. 48; 48 Cr.App.R. 42.................. 28, 30, 303

R. *v.* Waters (1963), 107 S.J. 275; 47 Cr.App.R. 149; [1963] Cr.L.R. 437 ..... 27, 29, 173

PAGE

R. *v.* Weir [1972] 3 All E.R. 906 210
R. *v.* Welsh [1974] R.T.R. 478, C.A. 206, 246
R. *v.* West [1964] 1 Q.B. 15; [1962] 3 W.L.R. 218; [1962] 2 All E.R. 624; 106
  S.J. 514 93
R. *v.* Weston-super Mare Justices, *ex parte* Townsend [1968] 3 All E.R. 225;
  112 S.J. 541; 132 J.P. 526 97
R. *v.* Whibley [1938] 3 All E.R. 777; 158 L.T. 527; 82 S.J. 478; 102 J.P. 326;
  36 L.G.R. 438; 26 Cr.App.R. 184 396
R. *v.* Wibberley [1966] 2 Q.B. 214; [1966] 2 W.L.R. 1; [1965] 3 All E.R. 718;
  109 S.J. 877; 130 J.P. 58; 50 Cr.App.R. 51 359
R. *v.* Wickens (1958), 112 J.P. 518; 42 Cr.App.R. 236; [1958] Cr.L.R.
  619 .... 665, 666, 670, 671
R. *v.* Wilkins (1951), 115 J.P. 443 21
R. *v.* Willis [1960] 1 W.L.R. 55; [1960] 1 All E.R. 331; 103 S.J. 1029; 124
  J.P. 111; 44 Cr.App.R. 32 120
R. *v.* Wilmot (1933), 149 L.T. 407; 77 S.J. 372; 49 T.L.R. 427; 97 J.P. 149; 31
  L.G.R. 189; 29 Cox C.C. 652; 24 Cr.App.R. 63 265
R. *v.* Wimbledon Justices, *ex parte* Derwent [1953] 1 Q.B. 380; [1953] 2
  W.L.R. 350; [1953] 1 All E.R. 390; 97 S.J. 116; 117 J.P. 113; 51 L.G.R.
  432 70
R. *v.* Withecombe [1969] 1 W.L.R. 84; [1969] 1 All E.R. 157; (1968), 112
  S.J. 949 231
R. *v.* Woking Justices, *ex parte* Johnstone [1942] 2 K.B. 248; [1942] 2 All E.R.
  179; 111 L.J.K.B. 618; 167 L.T. 255; 86 S.J. 260; 106 J.P. 232; 40 L.G.R.
  234 595
R. *v.* Worrell [1965] Cr.L.R. 561 261
R. *v.* Wright (John) [1975] R.T.R. 193 220
R. *v.* Yoxall (Andrew Thomas) (1972), 57 Cr.App.R. 263; [1973] Cr.L.R. 63,
  C.A. 246, 247, 250
Rabjohns *v.* Burgar [1972] Cr.L.R. 46; [1971] R.T.R. 234*n*., D.C. ... 85, 271, 278
Radcliffe *v.* Bartholomew [1892] 1 Q.B. 161; 61 L.J.M.C. 63; 65 L.T. 677; 36
  S.J. 53; 40 W.R. 63; 56 J.P. 262 69
Railway Executive *v.* Henson (1949), 93 S.J. 433; 65 T.L.R. 336; [1949] W.N.
  242; 113 J.P. 333; 47 L.G.R. 554 573
Ralph *v.* Hurrell (1875), 44 L.J.M.C. 145; 132 L.T. 816; 40 J.P. 119 89
Randall *v.* Motor Insurers' Bureau [1968] 1 W.L.R. 1900; [1969] 1 All E.R.
  21; 112 S.J. 883; [1968] 2 Ll.L Rep. 553 27
Randall *v.* Tarrant [1955] 1 W.L.R. 255; [1955] 1 All E.R. 600; 99 S.J.
  184 285
Rathbone *v.* Bundock [1962] 2 Q.B. 260; [1962] 2 W.L.R. 1066; [1962] 2 All
  E.R. 257; 106 S.J. 245; 126 J.P. 328; 60 L.G.R. 221 .... 106, 195, 465
Ratledge *v.* Oliver [1974] R.T.R. 394; [1974] Cr.L.R. 432, D.C. 224
Rawlinson *v.* Broadley (1969), 113 S.J. 310; 67 L.G.R. 439; 119 New L.J. 274;
  (1969), *The Times*, 14th March 385
Rayner *v.* Hampshire Chief Constable [1971] R.T.R. 15; [1970] Cr.L.R.
  703 .... 204, 207
Reay *v.* Young [1949] 1 All E.R. 1102; [1949] L.J.R. 1265; 93 S.J. 405; 65
  T.L.R. 315; [1949] W.N. 242; 113 J.P. 336; 47 L.G.R. 431 ... 666, 682, 683, 686
Record Tower Cranes Ltd. *v.* Gisbey [1969] 1 W.L.R. 148; [1969] 1 All E.R.
  418; 113 S.J. 38 .... 463, 465, 572
Redbridge London Borough Council *v.* Jaques [1970] 1 W.L.R. 1604; 114 S.J.
  847; [1971] R.T.R. 56; 69 L.G.R. 228; *sub nom.* London Borough of Red-
  bridge *v.* Jaques [1971] 1 All E.R. 260, D.C. 388
Reed *v.* Wastie and Another [1972] Cr.L.R. 221 .... 390, 582
Rees *v.* Taylor (1939), unreported, cited in Stone (1965), p. 2344 ...... 300, 304
Reeve *v.* Webb [1973] R.T.R. 130; [1973] Cr.L.R. 120; (1972), 117 S.J. 127,
  D.C. 419
Reid *v.* MacNicol [1958] S.L.T. 42 578
Reid *v.* Nixon, Dumigan *v.* Brown [1948] S.C.(J.) 68 242

PAGE

Rendell *v.* Hooper [1970] 1 W.L.R. 747; 114 S.J. 248; [1970] 2 All E.R. 72;
[1970] R.T.R. 252, D.C. 206

Rendlesham *v.* Dunne (1964), 114 L.J. 208; [1964] 1 Ll.L.Rep. 192; *The
Times*, 23rd January 368

Rennison *v.* Knowler. *See* Knowler *v.* Rennison

Renouf *v.* Franklin [1971] R.T.R. 489; [1972] Cr.L.R. 115, D.C. 423

Reynolds *v.* Austin (G.H.) & Sons Ltd. [1951] 2 K.B. 135; [1951] 1 All E.R.
606; 95 S.J. 173; [1951] 1 T.L.R. 614; [1951] W.N. 135; 115 J.P. 192; 49
L.G.R. 377 .... 43, 573

Rhind *v.* Irvine [1940] 2 W.W.R. 333 451

Richards *v.* Gardner [1974] Cr.L.R. 119, D.C. 269, 272, 278

Richley *v.* Faull [1965] 1 W.L.R. 1454; [1965] 3 All E.R. 109; 109 S.J. 937;
129 J.P. 498 284

Rigby *v.* Woodward [1957] 1 W.L.R. 250; [1957] 1 All E.R. 391; 101 S.J. 148;
121 J.P. 129; 41 Cr.App.R. 73 75

Ritchie *v.* Pirie [1972] Cr.L.R. 251; [1972] S.L.T. 2, *High Ct. of Justiciary*...181, 197

Rivers *v.* Hague (1837), cited in Phipson, *Manual of Evidence*, 7th ed.,
p. 202 125

Robb *v.* M'Kechnie [1936] S.L.T. 300; [1936] S.C.(J.) 25 371

Roberts *v.* Croxford (1969), 113 S.J. 269; 67 L.G.R. 408; [1969] Cr.L.R.
322 322

Roberts *v.* Evans and Evans. *See* Roberts *v.* Roberts

Roberts *v.* Jones (1968), 112 S.J. 884; [1969] Cr.L.R. 90 236

Roberts *v.* Morris [1965] Cr.L.R. 46 .... 121, 541

Roberts *v.* Powell (1966), 110 S.J. 113; 64 L.G.R. 173; [1966] Cr.L.R. 225;
116 New L.J. 445 385

Roberts *v.* Warne; Davis *v.* Warne [1973] R.T.R. 217; [1973] Cr.L.R. 244,
D.C. 372

Robertson *v.* Rosenberg (1951), 95 S.J. 138; [1951] 1 T.L.R. 417; [1951] W.N.
97; 115 J.P. 128; 49 L.G.R. 210 90

Robinson *v.* Secretary of State for the Environment [1973] 1 W.L.R. 1139;
117 S.J. 603; [1973] 3 All E.R. 1045; [1973] R.T.R. 511, D.C. 577

Robson *v.* Hallett [1967] 2 Q.B. 939; [1967] 3 W.L.R. 28; [1967] 2 All E.R.
407; 111 S.J. 254; 131 J.P. 333; 51 Cr.App.R. 307 398

Rodgers *v.* Ministry of Transport [1952] 1 All E.R 634; 96 S.J. 197; [1952] 1
T.L.R. 625; [1952] W.N. 136; 116 J.P. 200; 50 L.G.R. 520 390

Rogerson *v.* Edwards (1951), 95 S.J. 172; [1951] W.N. 101; 49 L.G.R.
358 .... 132, 139, 141

Rogerson *v.* Scottish Automobile and General Insurance Co. Ltd. (1931), 146
L.T. 26; 75 S.J. 724; 48 T.L.R. 17; 37 Com.Cas. 23 373

Rogerson *v.* Stephens [1950] 2 All E.R. 144; 94 S.J. 421; [1950] W.N. 284; 48
L.G.R. 644 .... 89, 372

Rooney *v.* Haughton [1970] 1 W.L.R. 550; 114 S.J. 93; [1970] 1 All E.R.
1001; [1970] R.T.R. 119, D.C. 210, 213

Roper *v.* Taylor's Central Garages (Exeter) Ltd. *See* Taylor's Central Garages
(Exeter) Ltd. *v.* Roper

Ross *v.* Hodges [1975] R.T.R. 55 217

Ross *v.* Rivenall [1959] 1 W.L.R. 713; [1959] 2 All E.R. 376; 103 S.J. 491; 123
J.P. 352 .... 123, 374, 375

Ross Hillman Ltd. *v.* Bond [1974] Q.B. 435; [1974] 2 W.L.R. 436; 118 S.J.
243; [1974] 2 All E.R. 287; [1974] R.T.R. 279; 59 Cr.App.R. 42,
D.C. 33, 34, 38, 40, 41, 412, 418

Rothes Transport Co. *v.* Hogg [1963] S.C.(J.) 1; [1962] S.L.T. 411 12

Rowland *v.* Thorpe (1970), 114 S.J. 707; [1970] 3 All E.R. 195, D.C. 231–3

Rowlands *v.* Hamilton [1971] 1 W.L.R. 647; 115 S.J. 268; [1971] 1 All E.R.
1089; [1971] R.T.R. 153; 55 Cr.App.R. 347, H.L. ...168, 181, 183, 197, 237

Rowlands *v.* Harper [1972] R.T.R. 469; [1973] Cr.L.R. 122, D.C. 180

Royal *v.* Prescott-Clarke [1966] 1 W.L.R. 788; [1966] 2 All E.R. 366; 110 S.J.
312; 130 J.P. 274 .... 86, 299, 489, 582

PAGE

Rubie v. Faulkner [1940] 1 K.B. 571; [1940] 1 All E.R. 285; 109 L.J.K.B. 241; 163 L.T. 212; 84 S.J. 257; 56 T.L.R. 303; 104 J.P. 161; 38 L.G.R. 119; 31 Cox C.C. 385 .... 53, 277, 475

Rumping v. Director of Public Prosecutions [1964] A.C. 814; [1962] 3 W.L.R. 763; [1962] 3 All E.R. 256; 106 S.J. 668; affg. sub nom. R. v. Rumping [1962] 2 All E.R. 233; 106 S.J. 330 116

Rushton v. Higgins [1972] Cr.L.R. 440 .... 216, 233

Rushton v. Martin (1952), 96 S.J. 345; [1952] W.N. 258 .... 34, 412

Ryan v. Smith [1967] 2 Q.B. 893; [1967] 2 W.L.R. 390; [1967] 1 All E.R 611; 110 S.J. 854; 131 J.P. 193 302

S. v. Grandin [1970] (2) S.A.L.R. 621, Transvaal Provisional Division; [1971] 4 C.L. 319 303

S. v. Lalla [1964] (4) S.A.L.R. 320 289

S. v. Lombard [1964] (4) S.A.L.R. 346 288

S. (an infant) by Parsons (his next friend) v. Recorder of Manchester [1970] 2 W.L.R. 21; sub nom. S. (an infant) by Parsons (his next friend) v. Manchester City Recorder, 113 S.J. 872; sub nom. S. (an infant) v. Manchester City Recorder [1969] 3 All E.R. 1230, H.L. 74, 84, 85, 92

Sadler v. Metropolitan Police Commissioner [1970] Cr.L.R. 284; The Times, 19th February, H.L.; affg. sub nom. R. v. Palfrey, R. v. Sadler [1970] 1 W.L.R. 416; 114 S.J. 92; [1970] 2 All E.R. 12; [1970] R.T.R. 127; sub nom. R. v. Palfrey (Henry), R. v. Sadler (Edward Daniel), 54 Cr.App.R. 217, C.A. 162, 215, 237, 241

Saines v. Woodhouse [1970] 1 W.L.R. 961; 114 S.J. 339; [1970] 2 All E.R. 388, D.C. 423

St. Mary Newington Vestry v. Jacobs (1871), L.R. 7 Q.B. 47 397

Sakhuja v. Allen [1973] A.C. 152; [1972] 2 W.L.R. 1116; 116 S.J. 375; [1972] 2 All E.R. 311; [1972] R.T.R. 315; 56 Cr.App.R. 464; [1972] Cr.L.R. 379, H.L.; affg. sub nom. R. v. Sakhuja [1971] R.T.R. 361, C.A. 148, 184–8, 191, 198, 234, 250

Salt v. Macknight [1947] S.C.(J.) 99; [1947] S.L.T. 327 .... 62, 369

Sanders v. Scott [1961] 2 Q.B. 326; [1961] 2 W.L.R. 864; [1961] 2 All E.R. 403; 105 S.J. 383; 125 J.P. 419; 59 L.G.R. 395 132

Sanderson (Arthur) (Great Broughton) Ltd. v. Vickers (1964), 108 S.J. 425; 62 L.G.R. 350; [1964] Cr.L.R. 474 .... 537, 544

Sandford Motor Sales v. Habgood [1962] Cr.L.R. 487 425

Sandy v. Martin [1974] R.T.R. 263; [1974] Cr.L.R. 258, D.C. 174

Sasson v. Taverner [1970] 1 W.L.R. 338; 114 S.J. 75; [1970] 1 All E.R. 215, D.C. 191

Saunders v. Johns [1965] Cr.L.R. 49 .... 83, 87, 122, 124

Saville v. Bache (1969), 113 S.J. 228; The Times, 28th February 283, 406

Saycell v. Bool [1948] 2 All E.R. 83; 92 S.J. 311; 64 T.L.R. 421; [1948] W.N. 232; 112 J.P. 341; 46 L.G.R. 447 21,170

Sayer v. Johnson [1970] R.T.R. 286; [1970] Cr.L.R. 589, D.C. 203

Scarr v. Wurzal [1951] 1 All E.R. 1014; 95 S.J. 285; [1951] 1 T.L.R. 1001; [1951] W.N. 234; 115 J.P. 338; 49 L.G.R. 634 51

Scobie v. Graham [1970] Cr.L.R. 589, D.C. 235, 678

Scott v. Baker [1969] 1 Q.B. 659; [1968] 3 W.L.R. 796; [1968] 2 All E.R. 993; 112 S.J. 425; 132 J.P. 422; 52 Cr.App.R. 566 ...... 144, 145, 183, 200, 651

Scott v. Clint (1960), The Times, 28th October 450, 680

Scott v. Dickson (1939), 83 S.J. 317 .... 15, 515

Scott v. Gutteridge Plant Hire Ltd. [1974] R.T.R. 292; [1974] Cr.L.R. 125, D.C. 526

Scott v. Jelf [1974] R.T.R. 256; [1974] Cr.L.R. 191, D.C. 640, 652, 662

Scott v. Warren (1973), 117 S.J. 916; [1974] R.T.R. 104; [1974] Cr.L.R. 117, D.C. 270, 273, 284, 287

Scottish Farmers' Dairy Co., Re (1934), 98 J.P.Jo. 848 419

PAGE

Seekings v. Clarke (1961), 105 S.J. 181; 59 L.G.R. 268 388
Seeney v. Dean [1971] Cr.L.R. 545, D.C. 526
Sellwood v. Butt (1962), 106 S.J. 835; [1962] Cr.L.R. 841 415
Selvey v. Director of Public Prosecutions [1970] A.C. 304; [1968] 2 W.L.R.
    1494; [1968] 2 All E.R. 497; 112 S.J. 461; 132 J.P. 430; 52 Cr.App.R.
    443; affg. sub nom. R. v. Selvey [1968] 1 Q.B. 706; [1967] 3 W.L.R. 1637;
    [1968] 1 All E.R. 94; 111 S.J. 924; 132 J.P. 114; [1967] C.L.Y. 741 97
Series v. Poole [1969] 1 Q.B. 676; [1968] 2 W.L.R. 261; 132 J.P. 82; 111 S.J.
    871; [1967] 3 All E.R. 849, D.C. 553
Sharples v. Blackmore [1973] R.T.R. 249; [1973] Cr.L.R. 248, D.C. 307, 313,
    314, 324
Shave v. Rosner [1954] 2 Q.B. 113; [1954] 2 W.L.R. 1057; [1954] 2 All E.R.
    280; 98 S.J. 355; 118 J.P. 364; 52 L.G.R. 337 34
Shaw v. Knill [1974] R.T.R. 142; [1973] Cr.L.R. 622, D.C. 163, 655
Shears v. Matthews [1948] 2 All E.R. 1064; 93 S.J. 103; 65 T.L.R. 194; [1948]
    W.N. 472; 113 J.P. 36; 47 L.G.R. 170 400
Shehan v. Cork Justices, quoted in Brian Harris, Criminal Jurisdiction of
    Magistrates, 2nd edition 373
Sheldon v. Jones (1969), 113 S.J. 942; [1970] Cr.L.R. 38, D.C. 165, 172
Sheldon Deliveries Ltd. v. Willis [1972] R.T.R. 217 .... 39, 377
Shenton v. Tyler [1939] Ch. 620; [1939] 1 All E.R. 827; 108 L.J.Ch. 256; 160
    L.T. 314; 83 S.J. 194; 55 T.L.R. 522 116
Sherrard v. Jacob [1965] N.I. 151 241
Sherrard v. Woods [1958] N.I. 13 648
Shield v. Crighton [1974] Cr.L.R. 605, D.C. 129, 133, 134, 143
Shimmell v. Fisher [1951] 2 All E.R. 672; 95 S.J. 625; [1951] 2 T.L.R. 753;
    [1951] W.N. 484; 115 J.P. 526; 49 L.G.R. 813; 35 Cr.App.R. 101 ...... 24, 25,
    299, 355, 356
Sidcup Building Estates Ltd. v. Sidery (1936), 24 Traff.Cas. 164 .... 38, 560
Sidery v. Evans and Peters [1938] 4 All E.R. 137; 160 L.T. 12; 82 S.J. 892; 55
    T.L.R. 54; 102 J.P. 517; 36 L.G.R. 672 577
Silke v. Whelan (1939), 73 I.L.T.R. 248 404
Simmons v. Fowler, Simmons v. Stringer (1950), 48 L.G.R. 623 .... 412, 421
Simpson v. Peat [1954] 2 Q.B. 24; [1952] 1 All E.R. 447; 96 S.J. 132; [1952]
    1 T.L.R. 469; [1952] W.N. 97; 116 J.P. 151 271
Sinclair v. Clark [1962] Cr.L.R. 777; [1962] S.C.(J.) 57; [1962] S.L.T.
    307 134
Sleith v. Godfrey (1920), 90 L.J.K.B. 193; 124 L.T. 152; 85 J.P. 46; 18
    L.G.R. 727; 26 Cox C.C. 655 388
Sly v. Randall [1916] 1 K.B. 710; 85 L.J.K.B. 1057; 114 L.T. 560; 80 J.P. 199;
    14 L.G.R. 550; 25 Cox C.C. 321 507
Smart v. Allan [1963] 1 Q.B. 291; [1962] 3 W.L.R. 1325; [1962] 3 All E.R.
    893; 106 S.J. 881; 127 J.P. 35; 60 L.G.R. 548 .... 6, 487
Smith v. Alexander and Alexander [1965] 1 Ll.L.Rep. 283 373
Smith v. All-Wheel Drive Co. Ltd. (1962), The Guardian, 12th February 562
Smith v. Baker [1972] Cr.L.R. 25; [1971] R.T.R. 350, D.C. 55, 375,
    378
Smith v. Cole (1970), 114 S.J. 887; [1971] 1 All E.R. 200n.; [1970] R.T.R.
    459, D.C. 220
Smith v. Henderson [1950] S.L.T. 182; [1950] S.C.(J.) 48 .... 669, 670
Smith v. Jenner (1968), 112 S.J. 52; [1968] Cr.L.R. 99 .... 53, 476
Smith v. North-Western Traffic Area Licensing Authority [1974] R.T.R. 236;
    [1974] Cr.L.R. 193, D.C. 416, 431, 432
Smith v. Ralph [1963] 2 Ll.L.Rep. 439 .... 373, 374
Smith of Maddiston Ltd. v. Macnab [1975] S.L.T. 86 .... 33, 38
Soden v. Gray (1862), 7 L.T. 324; sub nom. Loadman v. Cragg, 26 J.P.
    743 89
Solesbury v. Pugh [1969] 1 W.L.R. 1114; 133 J.P. 544; 113 S.J. 429; [1969] 2
    All E.R. 1171; 53 Cr.App.R. 326, D.C. 216, 232, 233

PAGE

Solomon v. Durbridge (1956), 120 J.P. 231 .... 386, 387
Sopp v. Long [1970] 1 Q.B. 518; [1969] 2 W.L.R. 587; [1969] 1 All E.R. 855;
    67 L.G.R. 389; *sub nom.* Long v. Sopp, 113 S.J. 123, C.A. 33
Sorrie v. Robertson [1944] S.C.(J.) 95 283
Spain v. Johns (1950), 48 L.G.R. 532 517
Spencer v. Silvester (1963), 107 S.J. 1024; [1964] Cr.L.R. 146 283
Spires v. Smith [1956] 1 W.L.R. 601; [1956] 2 All E.R. 277; 100 S.J. 400; 120
    J.P. 363; 54 L.G.R. 352 579
Spittle v. Thames Grit & Aggregates Ltd. [1937] 4 All E.R. 101; 107 L.J.K.B.
    200; 158 L.T. 374; 81 S.J. 902; 101 J.P. 557; 35 L.G.R. 627; 31 Cox C.C.
    6; 26 Traff.Cas. 109 543
Sprake v. Tester (1955), 53 L.G.R. 194; [1955] Cr.L.R. 509 391
Springate v. Questier [1952] 2 All E.R. 21; 116 J.P. 367 141
Squire v. Metropolitan Police Commissioner [1957] Cr.L.R. 817 282
Squires v. Botwright [1972] R.T.R. 462; [1973] Cr.L.R. 106, D.C. 469
Stamper (John) (Farms) Ltd. v. Hyde (1963), 107 S.J. 982; 62 L.G.R. 55;
    [1964] Cr.L.R. 147 414
Standen v. Robertson (1975), *The Times*, 23rd May 217
Stanton & Sons Ltd. v. Webber (1972), 116 S.J. 667, 668 .... 53, 468, 476
Starfire Diamond Rings Ltd. v. Angel (1962), 106 S.J. 452; [1962] 1 Ll.L.Rep.
    526; *revsd.* 106 S.J. 854; [1962] 2 Ll.L.Rep. 217 421
Starkey v. Hall [1936] 2 All E.R. 18; 80 S.J. 347 376
State (The) (McLoughlin) v. The President of the Circuit Court [1948] Ir.R.
    439 141
State (The) (Prendergast) v. Porter [1962] Jo.Crim.L. 217; [1961] Ir.Jur.R.
    15 163
State (The) (Sullivan) v. Robinson (1954), 88 I.L.T.R. 169 242
Staunton v. Coates (1924), 94 L.J.K.B. 95; 132 L.T. 199; 69 S.J. 126; 41
    T.L.R. 33; 88 J.P. 193; 23 L.G.R. 6; 27 Cox C.C. 663 129
Stephenson v. Johnson [1954] 1 W.L.R. 375; [1954] 1 All E.R. 369; 98 S.J.
    128; 118 J.P. 199 .... 65, 90
Stevens v. General Steam Navigation Co. [1903] 1 K.B. 890; 72 L.J.K.B.417;
    88 L.T. 542; 47 S.J. 469; 19 T.L.R. 418; 67 J.P. 415 462
Stevens v. Thornborrow [1970] 1 W.L.R. 23; 113 S.J. 961; [1969] 3 All E.R.
    1487; [1970] R.T.R. 31, D.C. 185
Stevens (A.) & Co. (Haulage) Ltd. v. Brown (1970), 115 S.J. 62; *sub nom.*
    Stevens (A.) & Co. (Haulage) Ltd. v. Brown, Brown (E.J.) v. Brown
    [1971] Cr.L.R. 103; [1971] R.T.R. 43, D.C. 11
Stevenson v. Beatson [1966] Cr.L.R. 339; [1965] S.L.T.(Sh.) 11 .... 24, 270
Stewart v. Chapman [1951] 2 K.B. 792; [1951] 2 All E.R. 613; 95 S.J. 641;
    [1951] 2 T.L.R. 640; [1951] W.N. 474; 115 J.P. 473; 49 L.G.R. 816; 35
    Cr.App.R. 102 .... 69, 136, 138
Stewart v. McFadyen (Archibald) & Sons [1958] S.L.T.(Sh.) 7; 74 Sh.Ct.Rep.
    31 543
Stone v. Bastick [1967] 1 Q.B. 74; [1965] 3 W.L.R. 1233; [1965] 3 All E.R.
    713; 109 S.J. 877; 130 J.P. 54 .... 94, 653
Stone v. Horton (1949), 113 J.P.Jo. 674 .... 44, 47,507
Stoneley v. Coleman [1974] Cr.L.R. 254, D.C. 84
Stoneley v. Richardson [1973] R.T.R. 229; [1973] Cr.L.R. 310, D.C. ... 417, 424
    428
Stowers v. Darnell [1973] R.T.R. 459; [1973] Cr.L.R. 528, D.C. 90
Strathern v. Gladstone [1937] S.C.(J.) 11; [1937] S.L.T. 62 338
Strong v. Dawtry [1961] 1 W.L.R. 841; [1961] 1 All E.R. 926; 105 S.J. 235;
    125 J.P. 378; 59 L.G.R. 241 385
Strowger v. John (1973), 118 S.J. 101; [1974] R.T.R. 124; [1974] Cr.L.R. 123,
    D.C. 503, 517
Strutt v. Clift [1911] 1 K.B. 1; 80 L.J.K.B. 114; 103 L.T. 722; 27 T.L.R. 14;
    74 J.P. 471; 8 L.G.R. 989 .... 44, 49, 507
Stubbs v. Morgan [1972] R.T.R. 459; [1972] Cr.L.R. 443, D.C. 324

PAGE
Subramaniam v. Public Prosecutor [1956] 1 W.L.R. 965; 100 S.J. 566 120
Sulston v. Hammond [1970] 1 W.L.R. 1164; 114 S.J. 533; [1970] 2 All E.R.
    830, D.C. 129, 445
Sunter Bros. Ltd. v. Arlidge [1962] 1 W.L.R. 199; [1962] 1 All E.R. 510; 106
    S.J. 154; 126 J.P. 159; 60 L.G.R. 142 .... 431, 432
Surtees v. Benewith [1954] 1 W.L.R. 1335; [1954] 3 All E.R. 261; 98 S.J. 751;
    52 L.G.R. 515 683
Swain v. Gillett [1974] R.T.R. 446; [1974] Cr.L.R. 433, D.C. 318
Sweetway Sanitary Cleansers Ltd. v. Bradley [1962] 2 Q.B. 108; [1961] 3
    W.L.R. 196; [1961] 2 All E.R. 821; 105 S.J. 444; 125 J.P. 470; 59
    L.G.R. 402 .... 335, 542
Swell v. McKechnie [1956] Cr.L.R. 423 683
Swift v. Norfolk County Council [1955] Cr.L.R. 785 478
Sykes v. Millington [1953] 1 Q.B. 770; [1953] 2 W.L.R. 973; [1953] 1 All E.R.
    1098; 97 S.J. 317; 117 J.P. 257, 51 L.G.R. 352 541

Tait v. Odhams Press Ltd. (1937), 26 Traff.Cas. 80 .... 334, 543
Talbot de Malahide (Lord) v. Cusack (1864), 12 L.T. 678 112
Tamlin v. Hannaford [1950] K.B. 18; [1949] 2 All E.R. 327; 93 S.J. 465; 65
    T.L.R. 422; revsg. (1948), 98 L.J. 660 60
Tapsell v. Maslen (1966), 110 S.J. 853; [1967] Cr.L.R. 53 .... 38, 377
Tarbox v. St. Pancras Metropolitan Borough Council [1952] 1 All E.R. 1306;
    96 S.J. 360; [1952] 1 T.L.R. 1293; [1952] W.N. 254 113
Tattersall v. Drysdale [1935] 2 K.B. 174; 104 L.J.K.B. 511; 153 L.T. 75; 79
    S.J. 418; 51 T.L.R. 405 373
Taylor v. Allon [1966] 1 Q.B. 304; [1965] 2 W.L.R. 598; [1965] 1 All E.R.
    557; 109 S.J. 78; [1965] 1 Ll.L.Rep. 155 373
Taylor v. Armand [1975] Cr.L.R. 227; [1975] R.T.R. 225 .... 113, 225, 242
Taylor v. Austin [1969] 1 W.L.R. 264; [1969] 1 All E.R. 544; (1968), 112 S.J.
    1024 .... 671, 672
Taylor v. Campbell [1956] Cr.L.R. 342 .... 139, 141
Taylor v. Emerson (1962), 106 S.J. 552; 60 L.G.R. 311 .... 381, 480, 514
Taylor v. Grey [1973] R.T.R. 281; [1974] Cr.L.R. 46, D.C. 89
Taylor v. Horn [1929] S.C.(J.) 111; [1929] S.L.T. 600 134
Taylor v. Kenyon [1952] 2 All E.R. 726; 96 S.J. 479; [1952] W.N. 478; 116
    J.P. 599 ....609, 631, 638, 653
Taylor v. Mead [1961] 1 W.L.R. 435; [1961] 1 All E.R. 626; 105 S.J. 159; 125
    J.P. 286; 59 L.G.R. 202 .... 5, 334, 495, 496, 544
Taylor v. Rajan; Fraser v. Barton [1974] Q.B. 424; [1974] 2 W.L.R. 385;
    [1974] 1 All E.R. 1087; [1974] R.T.R. 304; sub nom. Taylor v. Rajan, 118
    S.J. 135; 59 Cr.App.R. 11, 15; [1974] Cr.L.R. 188, 189, D.C. 665, 668,
                                                                             675
Taylor v. Rogers (1960), 124 J.P. 217 270
Taylor v. Saycell [1950] 2 All E.R 887; 94 S.J. 705; [1950] W.N. 479; 114
    J.P. 574; 66 T.L.R. (Pt. 2) 842 .... 380, 680, 683
Taylor v. Thompson [1956] 1 W.L.R. 167; [1956] 1 All E.R. 352; 100 S.J.
    133; 120 J.P. 124; 54 L.G.R. 144 .... 333, 495, 544
Taylor's Central Garages (Exeter) Ltd. v. Roper [1951] W.N. 383; 115 J.P.
    445; sub nom. Roper v. Taylor's Central Garages (Exeter) Ltd. [1951] 2
    T.L.R. 284 .... 74, 502
Teall v. Teall [1938] P. 250; [1938] 3 All E.R. 349; 107 L.J.P. 118; 82 S.J.
    682; 54 T.L.R. 960; 102 J.P. 428; 36 L.G.R. 574 68
Tesco Supermarkets v. Nattrass [1972] A.C. 153; [1971] 2 W.L.R. 1166;
    115 S.J. 285; [1971] 2 All E.R. 127; 69 L.G.R. 403, H.L.; revsg. [1971]
    1 Q.B. 133; [1970] 3 W.L.R. 572; 114 S.J. 664; [1970] 3 All E.R. 357;
    68 L.G.R. 722, D.C. 553
Test Valley Investments Ltd. v. Tanner [1964] Cr.L.R. 62; 15 P. & C.R.
    279 40

PAGE

Thaw v. Segar [1962] Cr.L.R. 776; [1962] S.L.T.(Sh.Ct.) 63; 78 Sh.Ct.Rep.
150 168
Thomas v. Dando [1951] 2 K.B. 620; [1951] 1 All E.R. 1010; [1951] 1 T.L.R.
1067; [1951] W.N. 264; 115 J.P. 344; 49 L.G.R. 793 .... 27, 30
Thomas v. Galloway [1935] S.C.(J.) 27 17
Thomas v. Thomas [1961] 1 W.L.R. 1; [1961] 1 All E.R. 19; 105 S.J. 17; 125
J.P. 95 173
Thompson v. Charlwood (1969), 113 S.J. 1004, D.C. 220
Thomson v. Knights [1947] K.B. 336; [1947] 1 All E.R. 112; [1947] L.J.R.
445; 176 L.T. 367; 91 S.J. 68; 63 T.L.R. 38; 111 J.P. 43; 45 L.G.R.
35 .... 91, 162
Thornton v. Mitchell [1940] 1 All E.R. 339; 162 L.T. 296; 84 S.J. 257; 56
T.L.R. 296; 104 J.P. 108; 38 L.G.R. 168 55
Thornton v. Proudlock, unreported, Queen's Bench Division, 29th May,
1952 .... 5, 494, 497
Thurrock District Council v. Pinch (L.A. & A.) Ltd. [1974] R.T.R. 269;
[1974] Cr.L.R. 425, D.C. 20, 412
Tidswell v. Llewellyn [1965] Cr.L.R. 732; The Times, 22nd October 424
Tidy v. Battman [1934] 1 K.B. 319; 103 L.J.K.B. 158; 150 L.T. 90 284
Timmins v. Perry [1970] R.T.R. 477, D.C. 194
Tolhurst v. Webster [1936] 3 All E.R 1020; 156 L.T. 111; 80 S.J. 1015; 53
T.L.R. 174; 101 J.P. 121; 35 L.G.R. 102 306
Tolley v. Giddings [1964] 2 Q.B. 354; [1964] 2 W.L.R. 471; 1 All E.R. 201;
108 S.J. 36; 128 J.P. 182; 62 L.G.R. 158; 48 Cr.App.R. 105 ...... 353, 358
Torok v. Lake [1964] N.Z.L.R. 824 452
Tremelling v. Martin [1971] R.T.R. 196, D.C. 341, 380, 469, 470
Trentham v. Rowlands [1974] R.T.R. 164; [1974] Cr.L.R. 118, D.C. 270,
285, 287, 288, 582
Trevett v. Lee [1955] 1 W.L.R. 113; [1955] 1 All E.R. 406; 99 S.J. 110 389
Tribe v. Jones (1961), 105 S.J. 931; 59 L.G.R. 582; [1961] Cr.L.R. 835 282
Trigg v. Griffin (1969), 113 S.J. 962; [1970] Cr.L.R. 44, D.C. 190, 191
Trim Joint District School Board of Management v. Kelly [1914] A.C. 667;
83 L.J.P.C. 220; 111 L.T. 305; 58 S.J. 493; 30 T.L.R. 452; 7 B.W.C.C.
274; affg. S.C. sub nom. Kelly v. Trim Joint District Board of Management,
6 B.W.C.C. 921 348
Troughton v. Manning (1905), 92 L.T. 855; 21 T.L.R. 408; 53 W.R. 493; 69
J.P. 207; 3 L.G.R. 548; 20 Cox C.C. 861; sub nom. Houghton v. Manning,
49 S.J. 446 281
Turner & Son Ltd. v. Owen [1956] 1 Q.B. 48; [1955] 3 W.L.R. 700; [1955] 3
All E.R. 565; 99 S.J. 799; 120 J.P. 15; 54 L.G.R. 69 700

Ulster Transport Authority v. Ardill [1955] N.I. 34 541
Union Cartage Co. Ltd. v. Heamon, Eggleton v. Heamon [1937] 1 All E.R.
538; 25 Traff.Cas. 137 421
Unwin v. Gayton (1949), 93 S.J. 72; 47 L.G.R. 194 416
Urey v. Lummis [1962] 1 W.L.R. 826; [1962] 2 All E.R. 463; 106 S.J. 430;
126 J.P. 346; 60 L.G.R. 358 .... 468, 475

Vanderpant v. Mayfair Hotel Co. Ltd. [1930] 1 Ch. 138; 99 L.J.Ch. 84; 142
L.T. 198; 94 J.P. 23 389
Vassall v. Harris [1964] Cr.L.R. 322 595
Vaughan v. Biggs [1960] 1 W.L.R. 621; [1960] 2 All E.R. 473; 104 S.J. 508;
124 J.P. 341; 58 L.G.R. 218 .... 70, 396
Venn v. Morgan [1949] 2 All E.R. 562; 93 S.J. 616; 65 T.L.R. 571; [1949]
W.N. 353; 113 J.P. 504; 47 L.G.R. 665 142
Vernon v. Paddon [1973] 1 W.L.R. 663; 117 S.J. 416; [1973] 3 All E.R. 302;
[1974] Cr.L.R. 51, D.C. 91, 265

PAGE

Victoria Motors (Scarborough) Ltd. v. Wurzal [1951] 2 K.B. 520; [1951] 1
    All E.R. 1016; 95 S.J. 382; [1951] 1 T.L.R. 837; [1951] W.N. 233; 115
    J.P. 333 576
Vincent v. Whitehead [1966] 1 W.L.R. 975; [1966] 1 All E.R. 917; 110 S.J.
    112; 130 J.P. 214 .... 5, 476

Waddell v. Winter (1967), 202 E.G. 1225; 65 L.G.R. 370; 18 P. & C.R.
    497 36
Walker v. Lovell [1975] R.T.R. 61; (1974), The Times, 19th December,
    D.C. 207, 208, 228
Walker v. Rountree [1963] N.I. 23 167
Walker v. Walker (Practice Note) (1966), 110 S.J. 270 85
Wall v. Walwyn [1974] R.T.R. 24; [1973] Cr.L.R. 376, D.C. 457
Wall v. Williams [1966] Cr.L.R. 50 385
Wallace v. Major [1946] K.B. 473; [1946] 2 All E.R. 87; 115 L.J.K.B. 402;
    175 L.T. 84; 90 S.J. 331; 62 T.L.R. 406; 110 J.P. 231; 44 L.G.R.
    237 .... 22, 23
Wallwork v. Giles (1969), 114 S.J. 36, D.C. 199
Wallwork v. Roland (1971), 116 S.J. 17; [1972] R.T.R. 86; sub nom. Wallwork
    v. Rowland [1972] 1 All E.R. 53, D.C. 582
Walton v. Hawkins [1973] R.T.R. 366; [1973] Cr.L.R. 187, D.C. ... 142, 300, 311
Ward v. Keene [1970] R.T.R. 177 220
Ward v. London County Council [1938] 2 All E.R. 341; 82 S.J. 274; 36
    L.G.R. 340 301
Wardell-Yerburgh v. Surrey County Council [1973] R.T.R. 462 268
Wardhaugh Ltd. v. Mace [1952] 2 All E.R. 28; 96 S.J. 396; [1952] 1 T.L.R.
    1444; [1952] W.N. 305; 116 J.P. 369; 50 L.G.R. 526 68
Ware v. Fox, Fox v. Dingley [1967] 1 W.L.R. 379; [1967] 1 All E.R. 100; 111
    S.J. 111; 131 J.P. 113; [1966] C.L.Y. 7600 91
Waters v. Eddison Steam Rolling Co. Ltd. [1914] 3 K.B. 818; 83 L.J.K.B.
    1550; 111 L.T. 805; 30 T.L.R. 587; 78 J.P. 327; 12 L.G.R. 1232 6
Watkins v. O'Shaughnessy [1939] 1 All E.R. 385; 83 S.J. 215 38
Watkinson v. Barley [1975] R.T.R. 136 202
Watmore v. Jenkins [1962] 2 Q.B. 572; [1962] 3 W.L.R. 463; [1962] 2 All
    E.R. 868; 106 S.J. 492; 126 J.P. 432; 60 L.G.R. 325 .... 24, 241, 269
Watson v. Lowe [1950] 1 All E.R. 100; 94 S.J. 15; 66 T.L.R. (Pt. 1) 169;
    [1950] W.N. 26; 114 J.P. 85; 48 L.G.R. 139 400
Watson v. Paterson (1957), 121 J.P.Jo. 336 .... 50, 120, 121, 488
Watson v. Ross [1920] 1 S.L.T. 65 388
Watt v. Smith [1942] S.C.(J.) 109; [1942] Jo.Crim.L. 293 134
Watts v. Berryman [1958] Cr.L.R. 56 472
Watts v. Carter (1959), The Times, 22nd October 282
Watts v. Carter (Note) [1971] R.T.R. 232 272
Waugh v. Mentiplay [1938] S.C.(J.) 117 554
Waugh v. Paterson [1924] S.C.(J.) 52; 61 S.L.R. 366; [1924] S.L.T. 432 ... 527
Waugh v. R. [1950] A.C. 203; 66 T.L.R. (Pt. 1) 554; [1950] W.N. 173 ... 105, 253
Weatherson v. Connop [1975] Cr.L.R. 239 677
Webb v. Eastleigh Borough Council (1957), 56 L.G.R. 124 .... 32, 114
Webb v. Leadbetter [1966] 1 W.L.R. 245; [1966] 2 All E.R. 114; 110 S.J. 90;
    130 J.P. 277 .... 87, 124
Webb v. Maidstone & District Motor Services Ltd. (1934), 78 S.J. 336 .... 39, 573
Webber v. Carey. See Director of Public Prosecutions v. Carey
Webster v. Wishart [1955] S.L.T. 243 .... 122, 277
Wells v. Woodward (1956), 54 L.G.R. 142 .... 122, 300, 303
Wells & Son Ltd. v. Sidery [1939] 4 All E.R. 54; 161 L.T. 352; 83 S.J. 891; 56
    T.L.R. 25; 103 J.P. 375 561
Welton v. Taneborne (1908), 99 L.T. 668; 24 T.L.R. 878; 72 J.P. 419; 6
    L.G.R. 891; 21 Cox C.C. 702 .... 93, 264, 314, 339

PAGE

Westminster City Council *v.* Peart (1968), 112 S.J. 543; 66 L.G.R. 561;
[1968] Cr.L.R. 504 88
Westminster Coaching Services Ltd. *v.* Piddlesden, Hackney Wick Stadium
Ltd. *v.* Piddlesden (1933), 149 L.T. 449; 49 T.L.R. 475; 97 J.P. 185; 31
L.G.R. 245; 29 Cox C.C. 660 ....466, 467, 572, 575
Wharton *v.* Taylor (1965), 109 S.J. 475 .... 471, 507
Wheatley *v.* Lodge [1971] 1 W.L.R. 29; 114 S.J. 907; [1971] 1 All E.R. 173;
[1971] R.T.R. 22, D.C. 135, 209
Whitby *v.* Stead [1975] R.T.R. 169 560
White *v.* Cubitt [1930] 1 K.B. 443; 99 L.J.K.B. 129; 142 L.T. 427; 73 S.J.
863; 46 T.L.R. 99; 94 J.P. 60; 28 L.G.R. 44; 29 Cox C.C. 80 .... 27, 174
White *v.* Trainor [1959] N.I. 147 472
Whitehead *v.* Haines [1965] 1 Q.B. 200; [1964] 3 W.L.R. 197; [1964] 2 All
E.R. 530; 108 S.J. 336; 128 J.P. 372; 62 L.G.R. 344 700
Whitehead *v.* Unwins (York) Ltd. [1962] Cr.L.R. 323 367
Whiteside *v.* Watson [1952] S.L.T. 367; [1952] S.C.(J.) 98 .... 387, 391
Whittall *v.* Kirby [1947] K.B. 194; [1946] 2 All E.R. 552; 175 L.T. 449; 90
S.J. 571; 62 T.L.R. 696; 111 J.P. 1; 123 J.P.Jo. 723 ...... 664, 667, 669, 672,
680, 683
Wilkins *v.* Day (1883), 12 Q.B.D. 110; 49 L.T. 399; 32 W.R. 123; 48 J.P. 6 ... 390
Wilkinson *v.* Barrett (1958), 122 J.P. 349 .... 9, 411
Williams *v.* Boyle (1962), 106 S.J. 939; [1963] Cr.L.R. 204 .... 31, 173
Williams *v.* Evans (1876), 1 Ex.D. 277; 35 L.T. 864; 41 J.P. 151 292
Williams *v.* Hallam (1943), 112 L.J.K.B. 353; 59 T.L.R. 287; 41 L.G.R.
165 77
Williams *v.* Jones, W.L.R., 7th March, 1969 (Recent Points) 44
Williams *v.* Jones [1972] R.T.R. 4 .... 193, 194
Williams *v.* Letheren [1919] 2 K.B. 262; 88 L.J.K.B. 944; 121 L.T. 145; 63
S.J. 535; 35 T.L.R. 378; 83 J.P. 159; 17 L.G.R. 338; 26 Cox C.C. 419 ... 180
Williams *v.* Neale [1971] Cr.L.R. 598; [1971] R.T.R. 149, D.C. 675, 676
Williams *v.* Osborne [1975] R.T.R. 181 173
Williams *v.* Russell (1933), 149 L.T. 190; 77 S.J. 198; 49 T.L.R. 315; 97 J.P.
128; 31 L.G.R. 182; 29 Cox C.C. 640 .... 101, 123, 373, 379
Williamson *v.* MacMillan [1962] S.L.T. 63 632
Williamson *v.* O'Keefe, Williamson *v.* Wilson [1947] 1 All E.R. 307; 176 L.T.
274; 63 T.L.R. 152; 111 J.P. 175; 45 L.G.R. 128 378
Wilson *v.* Bird (1962), 106 S.J. 880; [1963] Cr.L.R. 57 37
Wimperis *v.* Griffin [1973] Cr.L.R. 533, D.C. 159, 164, 237
Windle *v.* Dunning & Son Ltd. [1968] 1 W.L.R. 552; [1968] 2 All E.R. 46;
112 S.J. 196; 132 J.P. 284; 66 L.G.R. 516 .... 43, 43, 412
Wingroves C.B. *v.* Scottish Omnibuses Ltd. [1965] S.L.T.N. 55 579
Winter *v.* Morrison [1954] S.C.(J.) 7 166
Wishart *v.* Fenwick [1968] S.L.T. 263 242
Wishart *v.* MacDonald (1902), S.L.T.(Sh.Ct.) 29; 78 Sh.Ct.Rep. 3 ...... 449, 451
Witchell *v.* Abbott [1966] 1 W.L.R. 852; [1966] 2 All E.R. 657; 110 S.J. 388;
130 J.P. 297 561
Witts *v.* Williams [1974] Cr.L.R. 259, D.C. 195, 198
Wolverton Urban District Council *v.* Willis [1962] 1 W.L.R. 205; [1962] 1 All
E.R. 243; 106 S.J. 153; 126 J.P. 84; 60 L.G.R. 135 388
Wood *v.* Brown [1969] S.L.T. 297 182
Wood *v.* General Accident Fire and Life Assurance Corporation Ltd. (1949),
92 S.J. 720; 65 T.L.R. 53; [1948] W.N. 430; 82 Ll.L. Rep. 77............. 366
Woodage *v.* Jones (No. 2) [1975] R.T.R. 119 .... 163, 166, 236, 237
Woodage *v.* Lambie [1971] 1 W.L.R. 1781; 115 S.J. 588; [1971] 3 All E.R.
674; [1972] R.T.R. 37, D.C.; *revsg. sub nom.* Lambie *v.* Woodage [1972]
2 All E.R. 462, C.A. 340, 689, 690, 693, 694
Woodriffe *v.* Plowman (1962), 106 S.J. 198; 60 L.G.R. 183 .... 300, 302
Woodward *v.* Dykes (1968), 112 S.J. 787; 67 L.G.R. 168; [1968] Cr.L.R.
33 .... 477, 480

PAGE

Woodward *v.* Young (James) (Contractors) [1959] Cr.L.R. 131; [1958]
  S.L.T. 289; [1958] S.C.(J.) 28   8
Worgan (T.K.) & Son Ltd. *v.* Gloucestershire County Council, H. Lancaster
  & Co. Ltd. *v.* Same [1961] 2 Q.B. 123; [1961] 2 W.L.R. 729; [1961] 2
  All E.R. 301; 105 S.J. 403; 125 J.P. 381; 59 L.G.R. 295 .... 494, 496
Worth *v.* Brooks [1959] Cr.L.R. 855; (1959), *The Times*, 13th October ... 28, 387, 388
Wright *v.* Brobyn, 115 S.J. 310; [1971] R.T.R. 204, D.C. 204, 207
Wright *v.* Howard [1973] R.T.R. 12; [1972] Cr.L.R. 710, D.C. 299
Wright *v.* Nicholson [1970] 1 W.L.R. 142; (1969), 113 S.J. 939; [1970] 1 All
  E.R. 12; 54 Cr.App.R. 38, D.C.   88
Wright *v.* Wenlock [1972] Cr.L.R. 49; [1971] R.T.R. 228, D.C. 272
Wurzal *v.* Addison [1965] 2 Q.B. 131; [1965] 2 W.L.R. 131; [1965] 1 All E.R.
  20; 236 L.T. 24; 108 S.J. 1046; 129 J.P. 86 .... 567, 571, 576
Wurzal *v.* Dowker [1954] 1 Q.B. 52; [1953] 2 W.L.R. 1196; [1953] 2 All E.R.
  88; 97 S.J. 390; 117 J.P. 336; 51 L.G.R. 576 576
Wurzal *v.* Houghton Main Home Delivery Service Ltd., Wurzal *v.* Atkinson
  [1937] 1 K.B. 380; [1936] 3 All E.R. 311; 106 L.J.K.B. 197; 155 L.T.
  575; 80 S.J. 895; 53 T.L.R. 81; 34 L.G.R. 587; 25 Traff.Cas. 59 .... 544, 574
Wurzal *v.* Reader Bros. Ltd. and Another [1974] R.T.R. 383; [1973] Cr.L.R.
  640, D.C. 19, 412, 428
Wurzal *v.* Wilson [1965] 1 W.L.R. 285; [1965] 1 All E.R. 26; 23 L.T. 24; 109
  S.J. 179; 129 J.P. 112 .... 573, 575

Young *v.* Day (1959), 123 J.P. 317 143

TABLE OF STATUTES

[Figures in **bold type** *indicate pages where the text of an enactment is given. Entries are in alphabetical order.]*

PAGE

Administration of Justice Act, 1960 [8 & 9 Eliz. 2, c. 65]—
    s. 1 .... 698, 701
    s. 16 .... 597, 638, 639, 702
Administration of Justice Act, 1964 [c. 42]—
    ss. 2, 10 67
Administration of Justice Act, 1973 [c. 15]—
    s. 1 67
    s. 17 600
Administration of Justice (Miscellaneous Provisions) Act, 1933 [23 & 24 Geo. 5, c. 36]—
    s. 2 701
Agriculture Act, 1947 [10 & 11 Geo. 6, c. 48]—
    s. 109 (3) 550
Agriculture (Scotland) Act, 1948 [11 & 12 Geo. 6, c. 45]—
    s. 86 (3) 550
Air Force Act, 1955 [3 & 4 Eliz. 2, c. 19]—
    s. 133 61
Airports Authority Act, 1965 [c. 16]—
    s. 1 (7) 60
    s. 12 30
Armed Forces Act, 1966 [c. 45]—
    s. 25 61
Army Act, 1955 [3 & 4 Eliz. 2, c. 18]—
    s. 70 .... 61, 133, 265
    s. 133 61

Bank Holidays Act, 1871 [33 & 34 Vict. c. 17] 866
British Transport Commission Act, 1956 [4 & 5 Eliz. 2, c. lxxiv].............. 30
    s. 27 (4) 317
British Transport Commission Act, 1957 [5 & 6 Eliz. 2, c. xxxiii]—
    s. 66 727
British Transport Commission Act, 1959 [7 & 8 Eliz. 2, c. xliv]—
    s. 20 30

Children and Young Persons Act, 1933 [22 & 23 Geo. 5, c. 12] 459
    s. 15 .... 115, 116, 253, 256, 259
    s. 38 102
    s. 42 104
    s. 46 57
        (1A) 58
    s. 99 58
    Sched. 1 .... 104, 256
Children and Young Persons Act, 1963 [c. 37]—
    s. 16 (2) 95, 97
    s. 18 57
    s. 28 .... 102, 103
Children and Young Persons Act, 1969 [c. 54] 58
    s. 6 .... 57, 258
    s. 7 58
        (8) 57

PAGE

Chronically Sick and Disabled Persons Act, 1970 [c. 44]—
  s. 20 4
Civic Amenities Act, 1967 [c. 69] 7
  s. 19 70
    (1), (2) 396
  ss. 20–22 396
  s. 27 (1) 7, 396
Civil Aviation Act, 1968 [c. 61]—
  s. 1 30
Companies Act, 1948 [11 & 12 Geo. 6, c. 38]—
  s. 154 540
Consular Relations Act, 1968 [c. 18]—
  Sched., arts. 1, 43, 45 60
Coroners (Amendment) Act, 1926 [16 & 17 Geo. 5, c. 15]—
  s. 20 258
    (5) 258
Costs in Criminal Cases Act, 1973 [c. 14]—
  s. 1 599
  s. 2 599–601
    (4) 600
    (5) 600, 601
  s. 12 600
Countryside Act, 1968 [c. 41]—
  Sched. 3, para. 9 (2) (b) 32
Courts Act, 1971 [c. 23] 101, 511, 643, 644, 648, 696
  ss. 4 (5), 5 (4) 647
  s. 9 698
    (4), (5) 697, 698
  s. 10 698
  s. 13 (4) 697
Criminal Appeal Act, 1968 [c. 19]—
  ss. 1 (2), 7 702
  s. 9 .... 644, 702
  s. 10 .... 702, 703
    (3) 644, 703
  s. 11 702
    (1) 644
    (3) 650, 703
  s. 18 703
  s. 50 (1) 644, 702
  Sched. 2 104
Criminal Damage Act 1971 [c. 48] 79, 364, 365
  s. 1 (1) 364
    (2) 364, 365
  s. 10 365
Criminal Evidence Act, 1898 [61 & 62 Vict. c. 36]—
  s. 1 116
Criminal Evidence Act, 1965 [c. 20] 111
Criminal Justice Act, 1925 [15 & 16 Geo. 5, c. 86]—
  s. 13 (3) 103, 105
  s. 33 (6) 73
Criminal Justice Act, 1948 [11 & 12 Geo. 6, c. 58]—
  s. 21 626
  s. 37 697
  s. 41 114
    (5) 114
Criminal Justice Act, 1961 [9 & 10 Eliz. 2, c. 39]—
  s. 3 596
  s. 4 360

PAGE

Criminal Justice Act 1961 *continued*
 s. 4 (4) 596
 s. 7 596
 s. 12 .... 605, 635
Criminal Justice Act, 1967 [c. 80] 562
 s. 1 .... 57, 81, 82, 162
 s. 2 .... 82, 85, 102, 104, 105, 107, 162
  (2) 82
   (*d*) 82
  (3) 82
 s. 3 82
  (3) 173
 s. 6 71
 s. 8 382
 s. 9 .... 88, 99, 101–5, 107, 159
  (1) 101
 s. 10 .... 82, 120, 122, 186, 534, 653,
                668
 s. 16 (7) 517
 s. 21 669
 s. 22 697
  (1) 669
 s. 24 72
  (1) 56
  (2) 56, 98
  (3) 72
 s. 26 (2) 250, 630
  (3) 98, 99, 250, 630
 s. 28 .... 65, 66, 229
 s. 29 73
  (3) 99
 s. 36 (2) 65
 s. 41 (2) 79
 s. 44 .... 511, 527, 595
  (11) 511, 516
 s. 44–50 594
 s. 51 (1) 610
  (2) 621
 s. 56 .... 79, 360, 611, 636, 652
  (1) 636, 637
  (5) 611, 636, 637
  (6) 611, 636
 s. 62 636
  (6) 79, 611
 ss. 73 100
 Sched. 3 .... 398, 401, 402
Criminal Justice Act, 1972 [c. 71] 640
 s. 1 505
 s. 23 640
 s. 24 .... 259, 640, 647, 649, 875
 s. 41 .... 73, 85
  (1), (3) 612
  (4) 73
 s. 44 82
 s. 46 (1) 106
  (2) 105
 s. 47 365
Criminal Justice Administration Act, 1962 [10 & 11 Eliz. 2, c. 15]—
 s. 13 81

PAGE

Criminal Justice (Scotland) Act, 1949 [12, 13 & 14 Geo. 6, c. 94]—
    s. 1 .... 610, 623, 624, 628, 630
    s. 2 610
        (1) 623, 624, 628, 630
    s. 9 (1) 625
        (2) 623, 625, 628, 630
Criminal Law Act, 1967 [c. 58] 263
    s. 2 .... 253, 258, 351
        (2), (4), (5) 354
    s. 6 (3) 133, 253, 254
    s. 7 (3) 260
Criminal Law Amendment Act, 1867 [30 & 31 Vict. c. 35] 104, 105
    s. 6 103
Criminal Procedure (Attendance of Witnesses) Act, 1965 [c. 69] 101
Customs and Excise Act, 1952 [15 & 16 Geo. 6 & 1 Eliz. 2, c. 44] 489
    s. 234 .... 491, 506
    s. 281 488
    s. 283 (1) 488
        (4) 490, 697
    s. 284 489
    s. 286 (2) 507
    s. 290 (1) 488
        (2) 504, 515
    Pt. XI 486
Customs and Inland Revenue Act, 1888 [51 & 52 Vict. c. 8]—
    s. 4 497

Diplomatic Privileges Act, 1964 [c. 81]—
    Sched. 1, arts. 31, 37 59

European Communities Act, 1972 [c. 68]........................ 554, 555, 558, 570
    Sched. 4 .... 546, 550, 552

Family Law Reform Act, 1969 [c. 46]—
    s. 9 58
Finance Act, 1953 [1 & 2 Eliz. 2, c. 34]—
    s. 33 486
Finance Act, 1970 [c. 24]—
    s. 9 (3) 526
Finance Act, 1971 [c. 68]—
    s. 6 .... 493, 494
Firearms Act, 1968 [c. 27]—
    Sched. 6, Pt. II, para. 3 353
Food and Drugs Act, 1955 [4 & 5 Eliz. 2, c. 16]—
    s. 89 .... 155, 177
    s. 108 (3) 180
    s. 110 (1) 177
    s. 113 78
        (3) 350
    ss. 113–116... 350
Food and Drugs (Scotland) Act, 1956 [4 & 5 Eliz. 2, c. 30]—
    s. 27 .... 155, 177
Forgery Act, 1861 [24 & 25 Vict. c. 98]—
    s. 34 211
Forgery Act, 1913 [3 & 4 Geo. 5, c. 27]—
    s. 1 .... 381, 514

Heavy Commercial Vehicles (Controls and Regulations) Act, 1973 [c. 44]
    392, 395

PAGE

Highway Act, 1835 [5 & 6 Will. 4, c. 50]...................................... 61, 460
    s. 72 .... 397, 398
    s. 78 .... 61, 292, 306, 400, 401
Highways Act, 1959 [7 & 8 Eliz. 2, c. 25] 383, 402, 705
    ss. 11, 12, 19 705
    s. 35 .... 32, 114
    s. 121 .... 61, 62, 383, 386, 388, 390, 582
        (1) 386
    s. 127 .... 388, 390
    s. 249 330
    s. 294 26
    s. 295 395
        (1) 32
    Sched. 4 .... 580, 705
           Class I **580–81**
           Class II **581**
Highways Act, 1971 [c. 41]—
    s. 31 .... 389, 399
        (1), (3), (5), (6), (7), (11) 399
    s. 32 389
Holidays Extension Act, 1875 [38 & 39 Vict. c. 13] 866
House to House Collections Act 1939 [2 & 3 Geo. 6, c. 44] 381
Hovercraft Act, 1968 [c. 59] 3, 4

International Headquarters and Defence Organisations Act, 1964 [c. 5]—
    s. 3 58
International Organisations Act, 1968 [c. 48] 60
Interpretation Act, 1889 [52 & 53 Vict. c. 63] 438, 705
                            728–30, 736, 765, 774
    s. 26 .... 139, 463, 587, 592, 609
    s. 33 447
    s. 34 .... 67, 114
    s. 38 .... 438, 705, 728, 730, 736, 774
        (1) 59, 195, 462

Justices of the Peace Act, 1949 [12, 13 & 14 Geo. 6, c. 101]—
    s. 15 463
Justices of the Peace Act, 1968 [c. 69]—
    s. 5 (1) 69

Law of Property Act, 1925 [15 & 16 Geo. 5, c. 20]—
    s. 193 397
        (2), (4) 398
Legal Aid Act, 1974 [c. 4]—
    Pt. I 698, 701
    Pt. II 100
    s. 28 (5) 698
    s. 29 (6) 100
    s. 30 (5) 698, 701
Licensing Act, 1872 [35 & 36 Vict. c. 94]—
    s. 12 .... 144, 158, 243, 252
    s. 13 243
Licensing (Scotland) Act, 1903 [3 Edw. 7, c. 25]—
    s. 70 158
Local Government Act, 1972 [c. 70].. 67
    s. 223 83
    s. 238 402
    s. 270 363
    Scheds. 1, 4 67

PAGE

Local Government Act, 1972—*continued*
Sched. 14, para. 23 383
Sched. 19 .... 396, 397
London Government Act, 1963 [c. 33]—
s. 16 (2) 383
London Hackney Carriage Act, 1831 [1 & 2 Will. 4, c. 22]—
s. 35 30

Magistrates' Courts Act, 1952 [15 & 16 Geo. 6 & 1 Eliz. 2, c. 55]—
s. 1 (2) 66
    (b) 66
s. 2 65
    (1) 67
    (3), (4) 65
s. 3 67
    (2) 490
    (3) 67
s. 13 .... 73, 98, 353
s. 14 (3) 250, 608
s. 15 98
s. 18 .... 79, 81, 145, 160, 161, 264, 381, 502, 643, 652
    (1) 80, 161, 246, 652
    (3) 79
    (5) 80, 81, 161
s. 19 .... 65, 79, 81, 95, 98, 353, 360, 361, 643, 652
s. 25 .... 69, 80, 81, 98, 145, 160, 161, 244, 264, 381, 283, 652
    (2) 78
s. 27 .... 504, 597
s. 28 .... 79, 360, 361, 610, 636, 652
s. 29 .... 79, 246, 360, 361, 610, 636, 637, 641, 652
s. 31 .... 247, 594
s. 35 .... 47, 66, 510, 562, 613, 614
s. 37 135
s. 38 .... 163, 222
    (2) 211
s. 41 103–5
s. 55 648
Pt. III 594
s. 77 101
s. 81 .... 123, 319, 372, 373, 469, 515
Pt. V 696
s. 83 .... 601, 614
    (3) (d) 614, 696, 697
s. 84 644
    (2), (3) 696
s. 86 648
s. 87 .... 644, 699
    (2) 643
s. 90 701
s. 98 (1), (6) 71
    (7) 72
s. 99 .... 83, 630
s. 100 .... **88,** 89
    (1), (2) 88
s. 101 69
s. 103 .... 72, 101
s. 104 .... 68–70, 268
ss. 109, 110 596
ss. 116, 123 103

PAGE

Magistrates' Court Act, 1952—*continued*
  s. 125 .... 94, 95
    (b) 69
  s. 126 (5) 58
  Sched. 1 65
  Sched. 2 98
  Sched. 3 595
Magistrates' Courts Act, 1957 [5 & 6 Eliz. 2, c. 29] 99, 510, 630
    631, 690
  s. 1 .... 58, 94, 98
    (2) proviso (iii) 99, 630
    (3) 99
  s. 3 .... 94–6, 110
Manœuvres Act, 1958 [7 & 8 Eliz. 2, c. 7] 753
Mental Health Act, 1959 [7 & 8 Eliz. 2, c. 72]—
  s. 60 (2) 511, 610, 623, 624, 628, 631
  s. 67 636
Mental Health (Scotland) Act, 1960 [8 & 9 Eliz. 2, c. 61]—
  s. 55 (3) 610, 623, 624, 628, 631
Merchant Shipping Act, 1894 [57 & 58 Vict. c. 60]—
  Pt. IX 339
  s. 691 105
Metropolitan Police Act, 1839 [2 & 3 Vict. c. 47] 67
  s. 54 292
  s. 66 263
Metropolitan Public Carriage Act, 1869 [32 & 33 Vict. c. 115] 851
Mines and Quarries Act, 1954 [2 & 3 Eliz. 2, c. 70]—
  s. 163 (5) 70
Motor Car Act, 1903 [3 Edw. 7, c. 36]..................... 615, 617, 776, 808, 811
Motor Vehicles and Road Traffic Act (Northern Ireland), 1930—
  s. 6 682
    (2) 682
  Pt. II 682
Motor Vehicles (International Circulation) Act, 1952 [15 & 16 Geo. 6 & 1 Eliz. 2, c. 39] 63
Motor Vehicles (Passenger Insurance) Act, 1971 [c. 36] 1

National Health Service Act, 1946 [9 & 10 Geo. 6, c. 81]—
  Pt. II 757, 788
National Health Service (Scotland) Act, 1947 [10 & 11 Geo. 6, c. 27]—
  Pt. II 757, 788
National Parks and Access to the Countryside Act, 1949 [12, 13 & 14 Geo. 6, c. 97] 32, 114
  s. 31 (1) 383
  s. 32 (4) 32
Naval Discipline Act, 1957 [5 & 6 Eliz. 2, c. 53]—
  s. 129 (1), (2) 61
Noise Abatement Act, 1960 [8 & 9 Eliz. 2, c. 68]—
  s. 2 (1), (3) 838

Oaths Act, 1961 [9 & 10 Eliz. 2, c. 21].. 102
Offences Against the Person Act, 1861 [24 & 25 Vict. c. 100] 116
  s. 35 .... 104, 294, **258–9**, 260

Parks Regulation (Amendment) Act, 1926 [16 & 17 Geo. 5, c. 36]—
  s. 2 339
Partnership Act, 1890 [53 & 54 Vict. c. 39]—
  s. 15 122
Penalties for Drunkenness Act, 1962 [10 & 11 Eliz. 2, c. 52] 252

PAGE

Petroleum (Consolidation) Act, 1928 [18 & 19 Geo. 5, c. 32]—
    s. 23 .... 785, 831
Police Act, 1964 [c. 48] 732, 866
    s. 19 .... 199, 305
    Sched. 8 466
Police (Property) Act, 1897 [60 & 61 Vict. c. 30] 641, 643
Police (Scotland) Act, 1967 [c. 77] 732, 866
Port of London Act, 1968 [c. xxxii] 28
    s. 199 30
        (4) 316
Post Office Act, 1953 [1 & 2 Eliz. 2, c. 36]—
    s. 87 730
Post Office Act, 1969 [c. 48]—
    s. 6 (5) 60
Powers of Criminal Courts Act, 1973 [c. 62] 365, 641
    s. 1 .... 598, 599
        (3) 598
    s. 6 .... 611, 646
    s. 7 .... 301, 597, 635
    s. 8 .... 611, 646
        (6) 610
    s. 13 380
        (3) 646
    ss. 19, 20 595
    s. 21 596
    s. 22 (1) 596
        (2) 597
    s. 23 597
    s. 24 636
        (2) 611
    s. 26 597
    s. 35 .... 361, 365, 598
        (2) 361, 598
        (3) 361, 365, 599
        (4), (5) 361
    ss. 36 (1), 38 599
    s. 43 .... 640, **640–41,** 641-3
        (1) 643
        (2) 641
        (3), (4), (5) 643
    s. 44 .... 602, 629, 640, **641,** 642, 643, 647, 649, 875
        (3) 642
Prevention of Crime Act, 1953 [1 & 2 Eliz. 2, c. 14] 175
Prevention of Offences Act, 1851 [13 & 14 Vict. c. 19]—
    s. 11 263
Prison Act, 1952 [15 & 16 Geo. 6 & 1 Eliz. 2, c. 52]—
    s. 22 101
Public Bodies Corrupt Practices Act, 1889 [52 & 53 Vict. c. 69] 160
Public Health Act, 1875 [38 & 39 Vict. c. 55]—
    s. 171 383
Public Health Act, 1925 [15 & 16 Geo. 5, c. 71]—
    s. 68 .... 390, 393
    s. 74 .... 56, 292, 460
Public Health Act, 1961 [9 & 10 Eliz. 2, c. 64]—
    s. 49 398
Public Order Act, 1936 [1 Edw. 8 & 1 Geo. 6, c. 6]—
    s. 5 91
Public Service Vehicles (Arrest of Offenders) Act, 1975 [c. 53] 580

PAGE

Purchase Tax Act, 1963 [c. 9]—
  s. 23 .... 740, 775, 782
Remission of Penalties Act, 1859 [22 Vict. c. 32]—
  s. 1 703
Representation of the People Act, 1949 [12, 13 & 14 Geo. 6, c. 68]—
  s. 89 500
Restrictive Trade Practices Act, 1956 [4 & 5 Eliz. 2, c. 68]—
  s. 16 (3) 70
Roads Act, 1920 [10 & 11 Geo. 5, c. 72] 734, 771, 773, 776, 811, 816
Road Safety Act, 1967 [c. 30]......... 1, 146, 168, 210, 238, 248, 665–7, 671, 673
  Pt. I 144, 145, 235
  s. 1 .... 180, 236, 621, 670, 671, 674, 675
    (1) 6, 237, 678, 701
    (2) 678
  s. 2 .... 237, 651
    (1) 185, 651
    (4) 211
  s. 3 236
    (3) 678
  s. 4 211
  Pt. II 427
  ss. 8, 9.. 873
  s. 30 651
Roads and Bridges (Scotland) Act, 1878 [41 & 42 Vict. c. 51].................. 394
Roads Improvement Act, 1925 [15 & 16 Geo. 5, c. 68] 431
  s. 6 330
Road Traffic Acts, 1930–56 707
Road Traffic Act, 1930 [20 & 21 Geo. 5, c. 43] 62, 278, 279, 574
  s. 2 (1) (b) 5
  s. 5 (3) 707
  s. 11 (3) 667
  s. 12 142
  s. 22 347
    (4) 347
Road Traffic Act, 1934 [24 & 25 Geo. 5, c. 50]—
  s. 1 (4) 838
  s. 6 (3) 661
Road Traffic Act, 1956 [4 & 5 Eliz. 2, c. 67]................................. 681
  s. 35 704
  s. 40 574
Road Traffic Act, 1960 [8 & 9 Eliz. 2, c. 16]   1, 59, 97, 195, 248, 287, 356, 524,
                           540, 541, 544, 551, 552, 617, 730, 766
  s. 1 .... 674, 734
    (1) 248
  s. 2 262
    (2) 254, 263
    (3) 253, 263
  s. 3 263
    (2) 128
    (3) 248
  s. 6 .... 144, 146, 162, 237, 621, 670, 675, 677
    (1) 6, 248
    (2) (ii) 168
    (4) 210, 237
  s. 14 .... 296, 393, 710
  s. 16 401
  s. 18 32
  ss. 26, 34.. 392

PAGE

Road Traffic Act, 1960—*continued*
  s. 51 709
      (2) 730
  s. 64 ....411, 581, 758
      (4) 581, 735, 758
  s. 73 ....38, 111, 533, 555
  s. 77 342
      (4) 347
  s. 81 393
  Pt. II 110, 656
  s. 97 639
  s. 105 (1).. 650
  s. 106 646
      (2).. 650
  s. 110 650
      (b) 656, 657
  s. 111 (5).. 607
      (9).. 615
  Pt. III 43, 56, 153, 195, 566, 567, 570, 572, 573 577, 851
  s. 117 ....**566–7,** 570, 734, 838
      (1)... 567
  s. 118 ....**567–8,** 568, 570, 574, 734, 838
      (3).. 574, 575
          (b) 576
          (d) 571, 575
  s. 127 .... 325, 326, 567, 571–3, 575, 577
      (2) 572
      (3) 572
      (7) 577
  s. 128 (3) 430
  s. 133 577
  s. 134 ....91, 567, 571–5, 577
      (3) 574
  s. 144 467
  s. 146 ....577, 579
  s. 147 ....577, 579, 580
  s. 148 828
      (2) 580
  s. 160 570
  s. 161 ....56, 467, 572, 578
  Pt. IV 540, 851
  s. 164 (5) (a) 543
  s. 186 .... 533, 546
  Pt. V 474
  s. 201 .... 44, 45
      (1) 365
  Pt. VI 531
  s. 203 (4) 542, 576
  s. 217 .... 24, 351, 352, 356, 362, 363
  s. 224 .... 19, 726
      (3) 111
  s. 232 118
  s. 233 50
  s. 235 79
  s. 241 ....127, 276
  s. 244 550
  s. 253 ....2, 734, 735
  s. 255 736
  s. 259 ....411, 541

PAGE

Road Traffic Act, 1960—*continued*
Sched. 1, para. 2 336
        para. 14 732
Sched. 11, para. 4 667
Sched. 12 .... 566, 567, **568–70,** 572, 575
        Pt. I.. 567, 571, 572, 576
        Pt. II 567, 570–72
        para. 3 575
        para. 4 569
        para. 5 575
        Pts. III, IV 567, 569, 571, 572
        para. 9 569
        paras. 10, 12 576
Road Traffic Act, 1962 [10 & 11 E 112. 2. c. 59]   1, 110, 136, 144, 601, 617, 646,
                                                                                    650, 667
s. 2 (1) 239
s. 5 ....57, 616, 617, 667
    (1) 624
    (3) 624, 657
    (5) 624, 655, 656
s. 6 (2) 646
s. 7 .... 57, 602, 607, 640, 667
s. 18 .... 10, 11
s. 44 363
s. 110 655
Sched. 1, para. 13 728
Road Traffic Act, 1972 [c. 20]   1, 2, 4, 51, 59, 97, 107, 109, 144, 145, 248, 306,
    404, 405, 408, 410, 435, 538, 566, 615, 617, 619, 635, 639, 641, 644, 655, 664,
                                                                                    673, 678, 766
Pt. 1 60
s. 1 ....21, 95, 254–6, 258, 260–63, 294, 617, 618, 622
    (2) 258
s. 2.........104, 115, 128, 131, 133, 134, 136, 255, **262–3,** 264, 265, 267–9, 271,
                    279, 282, 290–94, 314, 364, 469, 617, 618, 622
    (1) 80, 254, 275, 283
s. 3......51, 104, 115, 128, 131, 133, 134, 142, 263, 265–8, 271, 273, 279, 284,
                    290, 291, 293, 294, 314, 469, 618
    (1), (2), (3)–(6) 430
s. 4 ....467, 472, 482, 639, 652
    (1) 472
    (4) 618
s. 5.........23, 61, 144, 146, 148–51, 153, 158, 159, 162, 163, 173, 174, 176–8,
        183, 209–13, 215, 218, 220, 231, 235–42, 247, 251, 252, 275, 348,
                                                                                    670, 673, 677
    (1) 80, 156, 158, 160, 162, 168, 182, 243–9, 252, 604, 615, 617
    (2) 80, 145, 150, 156, 160–62, 165, 166, 169–71, 243–6, 251, 618
    (3) 164, 166–70, 173
    (4) 237
    (5) 148–51, 153, 158, 164, 183, 208, 210, 236, 237, 618
ss. 5–12 130
ss. 5–13 .... 144, 150, **150–55, 158**
s. 6 ...23, 24, 61, 144, 146, 148–50, **151,** 158, 159, 162, 163, 165, 173, 176–
        178, 182, 183, 200, 204, 209, 210, 212, 214, 215, 217–21, 231, 235,
        236, 239, 247, 251, 252, 256, 274, 475, 665, 666, 670, 671, 673, 701
    (1) 23, 80, 144–6, 150, 156, 158, 160, 168, 175, 176, 182, 183, 196, 199,
        208, 213, 217, 226, 229, 230, 234, 236, 237, 243, 245–9, 252, 604,
                                                                                    615, 617, 676
    (2) 80, 144, 145, 149, 150, 156, 160, 161, 163–5, 168, 170–72, 182, 183,
                    197, 234, 237, 243–6, 251, 618

PAGE

Road Traffic Act, 1972—*continued*

s. 6 (3) 150, 164, 167, 168, 170, 172
   (4) 168, 171, 236
ss. 6–11 155
ss. 6–12 .... 183, 232
ss. 6–13 145
s. 7 ....146, **151–2,** 239, 240, 430
   (1) 153, 158, 213, 239, 240, 241
   (2) 158
   (4) 430
s. 8 .... 146, **152–3,** 155, 159, 163, 208, 210–12, 231, 236, 237, 348, 651
   (1) 24, 147–50, 158, 159, 164, 182–5, 192, 195, 197, 204, 227, 231, 234,
                                          235, 237, 468, 618, 651
     (*a*) 198, 232
     (*b*) 232
   (2) 148, 150, 153, 158, 159, 164, 168, 183, 184, 195, 197, 198, 204, 214,
                         222, 223, 225, 227, 237, 468, 618
   (3) 144, 145, 156, 159, 208, 227, 228, 243, 247
   (4) 148, 183, 200, 203–8, 210, 211, 213
   (5) 148, 183, 190, 205–8, 210, 213, 228
   (7) 153, 213, 214, 236
s. 9 ...... 146, **153–4,** 155, 158, 159, 177, 204, 208, 213, 236, 239–41, 604, 678
   (1) 155, 214, 215, 217, 226, 227, 229, 236, 239
   (2) 222, 224–6
     (*a*), (*b*) 224
   (3) 80, 144, 145, 150, 156, 158–61, 163, 164, 173, 183, 184, 196, 209,
      213, 217, 228–31, 240, 244–9, 251, 252, 604, 607, 615, 617, 618, 622
   (5) 215–17, 226, 229
     (*a*) 229
     (*b*) 230
   (6) 217
   (7) 149, 162, 214, 215, 224, 225, 234, 237
s. 10 .... **154–5,** 177, 180, 240, 241
   (1) 177, 180
     (*a*) 178
   (2) 179, 180, 216
   (3) 86, 177–80, 216
   (5) 151, 159, 217–19, 221
     (*a*) 219
   (6) 159, 220, 221
   (7) 177
s. 11 ....**155,** 163, 176, 211, 222
s. 12 ....**155,** 175, 200, 205, 222
   (1) 148, 228
   (2) 215
   (3) 207, 208, 228
   (4) 175, 178
s. 13 ....**158,** 252
s. 14 618
s. 15 461
s. 16 618
ss. 17, 18 .... 127, 129, 291–3
ss. 18–21 32
s. 19 .... 144, 156, 158, 159, 218, 220, 238, 240, 247, 252
   (2), (3), (4) 158
s. 22......129, 131, 292, 295, **295,** 296–300, 302–5, 307–12, 314–16, 393, 448,
                                           604, 618
   (1) 297
     (*a*) 296, 303, 309

PAGE

Road Traffic Act, 1972—*continued*

(2) 297–9, 309
    (a) 298
(3) 300, 309, 310
(4) 310
s.22A 2, **295–6,** 304, 309, 310
    (1) (a), (b) 309, 310
    (2) 309
    (3) 309, 310
    (4) 310
s. 23 .... 304, **304,** 305, 448
s. 24 .... 129, 131, 132, **401,** 402, 421, 618
s. 25 .... 26, 141, 254, 341, **342,** 343, 344, 347–9, 400, 681, 851
    851
    (1) 343, 347
    (2) 345, 346
    (4) 618
s. 29 .... 363, 364
s. 30 363
    (1) 363, 364
s. 32 .... 349, 350, 461
    (3) 349
s. 33 .... 78, 350
    (2), (6) 350
s. 34 .... 13, 14, 849, 850, 867
    (1) 13, 21
    (2) 13
s. 36 .... 32, **397,** 398
s. 36A 390, 395, 396, 461
    (3A), (5), (6)–(8) 395
s. 36B 390, 395, 396, 461
s. 37 .... 125, 253
    (5) 253, 286, 287, **287,** 288
Pt. II 18, 19, 60
s. 40 .... 18, 38, 40, 45, 46, 49, 383, 403, 411, 424, 873
    (5) 19, 44, 403, 410–12, 431, 433, 434, 436, 628, 631, 684, 686
        (b) 33
    (6) **19–20**
        (a), (b) 20
s. 41 (2) 417
s. 42 431
s. 43 .... 426, 427, 500, 775
s. 44 .... 33, 45, 426, 427, 429
    (2), (3) 426
s. 45 .... 427, 500, 775, 873
    (3), (4) 775
    (7) 461
s. 46 427
    (1) 427, 853
    (2), (3), (4) 427
s. 50 (5) 461
s. 53 .... 427–30, 851
    (3) 428
    (4) 461
s. 54 428
    (3), (4) 428
    (5) 461
s. 56 .... 428, 430, 549
    (1) 851

                                                              PAGE
Road Traffic Act, 1972—*continued*
    s. 56 (3) 428, 461
    s. 57 428
        (7) 20
    s. 58 428
    s. 60 ....18, 407, 424, 425
        (4) 425
    s. 60A 425
        (1), (3) 426
    ss. 61, 62 425
    s. 64 18
        (1) 19
        (2) 18, 19
        (3) 20
        (4) 17
    s. 65 12
        (3), (4) 12
    s. 66 418
        (5) 418
    s. 68 ....404, 407, 408
        (2) 406
    ss. 68–73 795
    ss. 68–77 406
    ss. 68–82 ....403, 764, 765
    s. 70 407
    s. 71 406
    s. 72 407
        (3) 407
    s. 74 ....406, 407
        (c), (d) 406
    s. 75 ....51, 406, 407
    s. 76 ....406, 407, 409
    ss. 76–79 795
    s. 77 406
        (1) (c) 407
    s. 78 407
    s. 81 .... 33, 34, 48, 49, 290, 403, 405, 410
        (2) 407
    s. 82 ....404, 765
    Pt. III 4, 60, 110, 153, 467, 605, 641, 652
    s. 84 ....471, 473, 477, 482, 609
        (1) 473, 481, 619
        (2) 468, 481
        (3), (4) 471
    s. 85 (1) 471, 480, 483
        (3) 660
    s. 87 ....471, 477, 479
        (3) (b) 478
        (5) 477, 478, 662
        (6) 477
    s. 87A 479
    s. 88 (1) (a) 604
        (2) (c) 476, 477
        (6) 619
    s. 89 476
        (2) 473
        (3) 69, 472, 473, 481
    s. 90 477–9
        (2) 479, 660

PAGE

Road Traffic Act, 1972—*continued*

s. 91 .... **290–91,** 291, 461, 605
    (1) **290–91,** 291, 619, 623
    (2) **291,** 619, 623
s. 92 .... 291, 479, 662
s. 93 .... 57, 248, 401, 402, 482, 537, 602, **616–17,** 652
    (1) 260, 622–4, 627–30, 633–5, 642, 664, 668, 696
    (2) 361, 455, 460, 629, 630, 633, 642, 689, 697
    (3) 110, 249, 251, 252, 260, 291, 294, 316, 340, 348, 362, 363, 380,
              401, 435, 455, 460, 482, 605, 611–13, 623–30, 632–5, 642, 653,
                                     655, 657, 663, 664, 668, 688–96
    (4) **248,** 249, 621, 668
    (5) 249, 252, 294, 627, 631–6, 653, 658
    (6) 252, 614, 623, 628, 631
    (7) 252, 260, 262, 291, 294, 316, 340, 349, 361, 380, 461, 456, 583,
                                     639, 647, 652, 654, 655, 660–62
s. 94 (1) 650, 696
    (2) 642, 650
    (3) 643, 644
    (3A) 645
    (4) 631, 639, 645, 649
s. 94A 642, 644
    (2) 644
    (3) 645
    (4), (5) 644
    (7) 645
s. 94B 642, 644
    (3) 645
s. 95 .... 262, 635, 641, 642, 646, 647, 649, 656, 661, 662
    (1) 649
    (4) 648, 650
    (5) 647, 661
    (6) 647
s. 96 .... 369, 472, 639
s. 98 (3) 471, 660
s. 99 (a) 70, 472, 639, 650, **650,** 651, 652, 662
    (a) 651, 653
    (b) 80, 619, 635, 639, 651, 653–5
s. 100 .... 209, 651
s. 101 .... 57, 247, 293, 294, 402, 482, 484, 537, 602, 603, **603–4,**
                         605–8, 611, 612, 614, 617, 624, 640, 645
    (1) 610–12, 642, 653
    (2) 455, 460
    (4) 472, 481, 604, 607–9, 611, 613, 641, 642
    (4A) 95, 604, 607, 613
    (6) 368, 473, 481, 609
    (7) 473, 604, 615
    (6) 368, 473, 481, 609
    (7) 473, 604, 615
    (8) 604, 607
s. 102 .... 628, 630, 664
    (1) 610, 623, 646
    (2) 621, 622, 624
s. 103 (1) 611, 625, 636, 637
    (2), (3), (4) 611
    (5) 636
s. 104 466
    (4) 613
    (5) 466, 613

PAGE

Road Traffic Act, 1972—*continued*
  s. 105 .... 642, 668, 695
       (1) 610, 612, 629
       (2) 613
       (3) 615
       (5) 606
  s. 107 617
  s. 110 .... 368, 605
  s. 111 (1) 608
       (2) 481
  Pt. IV 60, 467, 483, 549
  s. 112 .... 483, 484
  s. 114 484
       (3) 484
  ss. 114–116 484
  s. 115 (1) 484
  ss. 117, 118 485
  s. 119 461
       (2) 485
  s. 123 467
  s. 124 483
  Pt. V 153, 195, 461, 473
  s. 126 (2) 473
  s. 143 .... 33, 42, 44, 45, 47, 48, 50, 70, 369–72
                                            374–80, 461, 609, 619
       (1) **365,** 378, 379
       (2) 41, 48, 377, **378,** 682
       (3) 4, 369
         (a) 366
  s. 144 369
       (2) (d) 369
  s. 145 .... **365–6,** 381
       (2) 366
       (3) 376
       (4) 366
  s. 147 (1) 376
  s. 148 370
       (1) 370
         (a), (d) 370
       (2) 370
  s. 149 373
  s. 158 (1) 376
  s. 159 .... 183, 189, 303, 305, 314, 448
  s. 160 .... 15, 19, 430
       (3) 111
       (7) 28, 30
  s. 161 .... 305, 346, 466, 469, 470, 481, 485
       (1) 468–70
         (a), (b), (c) 469
       (2), (3) 470
       (4) 469, 470
       (5) 466
  s. 162 .... 341, 342, 346, 380, 381, 429, 466, 468–70
       (1) 55
         (a) 469
       (2) 470
       (4) 55, 381
  s. 164 (2) 263, 469
  s. 165 304

PAGE

Road Traffic Act, 1972—*continued*

s. 166	55, 341, 342, 345, 400
(1)	341
(2)	341, 470
s. 167	118, 461, 462
(2)	55, 461
s. 168	66, 118, 297, 461–7, 508
(1)	464
(2)	107, 461, 464
(a)	462
(b)	462, 464
(3)	461–3
s. 169	50, 381, 382, 480
ss. 169–171	70
ss. 169–174	461
s. 170	79, 381, 382, 480, 651
(1)	381
(6)	381, 382
s. 171	381, 382, 429
s. 173	382, 480
s. 175	352, 354, 362, 363, 461, 462, 619
s. 177	431
(2)	260
s. 178	417
s. 179	**127–8,** 129–43, 255, 268, 276, 300, 340, 401, 445
(1) (b)	129
(2)	130, 136, 268
(c)	132, 136, 137
(3)	132
(3A)	128, 130, 131, 300
(4)	137, 140
(a)	141
s. 180	**69,** 70, 379, 381, 473, 480, 550, 586, 651
s. 181	106, 107, 156, 157, 396
(3)	106
s. 182	95, 107, **108–9,** 608, 653
(2A)	95, 109, 110
s. 183	107, 156, 157, 396, 463, 466
s. 187	12, 466
(8)	60
s. 188	60, 61, 263, 297, 351, 369, 406, 467
(1)	14
(3)	467
s. 189 (4)	476
s. 190	2, 3, 14, 15, 332
(1)	2, 9, 400, 436
(1)–(10)	**2–3**
(2)	5
(b)	871
(2)–(8)	4
(4)	349
(7)	5
(9)	9, 11, 336
(10)	5
(11)	3
s. 191	**11**
s. 192 (1), (2)	4

                                                                      PAGE
Road Traffic Act, 1972—*continued*
    s. 193 8
        (1) 407
        (2) 8
    s. 194 .... 14, **15,** 332, 515
    s. 195 .... 9, 158
        (1) 258
    s. 196 .... 21, 22, 26, 31, 173, 291, 292
        (1) 59
        (2) 3
    s. 197 406
        (4) 342
    s. 198 .... 9, 254, 369, 383, 411
        (1) 255, 263
        (4) 476, 637
        (6) 129
        (7) 9
    s. 203 .... 316, 597
    Sched. 1 .... 78, 350
        para. 2 (3) 350
    Sched. 4 ...... 129, 144, 145, 173, 247, 248, 260, 292, 300, 314, 348, 363, 364,
                    380, 401, 410, 429, 433, 455, 460, 481, 484, 485, 601, 610, 617
        Pt. I 106, 107, 127, **156–7,** 158, 260, 434, 607, 618
            column 1 .... 603, 616
            column 4 434
            column 5 .... 315, 436, 616–18, 628, 629, 631, 684, 686
            column 6 .... 602–4, 684, 686
        Pt. II 260, 602–4, 607, 616, 618
        Pt. III 602–4, 607, 616, 618, **619–20,** 629
            para. 1 .... 362, 620
            para. 2 362
            para. 3 .... 362, 620
        Pt. IV, para. 1 253
            para. 2 263
            para. 3 .... 156, 157
            para. 4 ... 74, 76, 77, 93, 133, 142, 264, **266,** 267, 268, 292
            para. 5 .... 127, **128,** 133, 255
            para. 6 .... 127, **128**
            para. 7 .... 127, **128,** 133, 142, 266, 268
        Pt. V 158, 234, 618
            para. 1 .... **158,** 235
    Sched. 9 550
    Sched. 10, para. 1 110
        para. 2 646
        para. 3 .... 30, 90
        para. 5 248
        para. 7 .... 639, 655, **656,** 657, 658, 662
            (1) **656,** 659
            (2) **656**
Road Traffic Act, 1974 [c. 50] 1, 2, 95, 128, 145, 160, 245–7, 314, 315,
                    343, 348, 363, 364, 380, 381, 392, 395, 401,
                    402, 410, 455, 457, 460, 461, 470, 472, 479,
                    481, 485, 577, 579, 594, 604, 618, 651, 652
    s. 1 .... 385, 584, 587, **587–9,** 593
        (1) 591, 592
            (b) 591
        (2), (4) 585
        (5) 586
        (6) 584–7, 591, 592

PAGE

Road Traffic Act, 1974—*continued*
s. 1 (7) 585, 587, 593
   (8) 586, 591, 593
   (9) (*a*), (*b*), (*c*) 585
ss. 1–4 .... 584, 591–3
ss. 1–5 584
s. 2 .... 385, 584, 587, **589–91,** 593
   (2), (4) 585
   (5) 586
   (6) 584–7, 591, 592
   (7) 585, 587, 593
   (8) 586, 591, 593
   (9) (*a*), (*b*), (*c*) 585
s. 3 .... 586, 587, 591, 593
   (5), (7) 586
s. 4 .... **591**
   (1) 586
   (1)–(3) 591
   (2), (3) 586
   (4) 584
   (5) 96
s. 5 .... **591–2**
   (1) 584, 585
   (3), (4) 584
   (5), (6) 587
s. 6 295
s. 9 (1), (2) 403
   (4) 49, 403
s. 11 .... 424, 425
s. 12 425
s. 13 (3) 110
s. 14 30
s. 15 472
s. 20 366
s. 21 97
   (4) 420, 433, 434
ss. 22, 24 615
Sched. 1 .... 385, 586, 591, 592, **592–3**
   Pt. I 584, 588, 590
     para. 2 587
   Pt. II 585, 588, 590
Sched. 3 .... 479, 644, 645
     para. 5 (1) 469
     para. 10 (1) 95, 607
        (3) 615
        (4) 607
Sched. 5 97
Sched. 6 645
     para. 12 342
     para. 20 341
     para. 22 130
Road Traffic (Amendment) Act, 1967 [c. 70]—
s. 7 .... 434, 435, 684, 686
Road Traffic and Roads Improvement Act, 1960 [8 & 9 Eliz. 2, c. 63]—
s. 11 393
s. 21 417
Road Traffic (Disqualification) Act, 1970 [c. 23] 1, 624, 638, 654
s. 1 (1) 654, 655
   (2) 655

PAGE

Road Traffic (Disqualification) Act, 1970 [c. 23]—*continued*
   s. 2 .... 655, 657
Road Traffic (Driving Instruction) Act, 1967 [c. 79] 1, 473
Road Traffic (Driving of Motor Cycles) Act, 1960 [8 & 9 Eliz. 2, c. 69] ... 1
Road Traffic (Foreign Vehicles) Act, 1972 [c. 27] 430
   Sched. 2 430
Road Traffic Regulation Act, 1967 [c. 76] 1, 2, 4, 15, 51, 59, 97, 153, 195,
                                                 287, 295–8, 317, 321, 339, 340,
                                                     384, 838
   s. 1 .... 300, 394, 402
      (3), (3AA), (3AB), (5) 392
      (8) 298, 315, 392, 395, 402
   s. 1–8 392
   ss. 1–84 462
   s. 1A 392
   s. 6 (9) 392, 395
   s. 13 .... 338, 340, 583
      (2) 130
      (4) 130, 583, 619
   s. 15 393
   s. 17 (5) 462
   s. 18 305
   s. 20 397
   s. 21 437
   ss. 21–23 445
   s. 22 437
   s. 23 129
      (4) 447
      (5) 455, 620
      (6) 445
   s. 24 456
   s. 25 .... 61, 62, **456–7,** 458–60
      (1) 457–60
        (a) 458
      (2) 304, 460, 620
        (a), (b) 457, 458
      (4) 458
        (b), (c) 459
   s. 26 (6) 620
   ss. 26–31 363
   s. 26A (5) 620
   s. 31 (5) 462, 464
   s. 35 .... 589, 590
   ss. 35–44 384
   s. 36 589–91
      (2) 384
   s. 41 384
   s. 42 .... 21, 384, 464, 589
      (2), (3), (6), (7) 384
   ss. 52, 53 397
   s. 54 .... **296–7,** 298, 310, 311, 393
      (1) 323
      (2) 313, 323, 324
   s. 55 .... 294, 298
   s. 57 294
   s. 58 .... 295, 297, 302, 310, 315
      (1) 295
      (2) 298, 310
   s. 71 .... 317, 321, 395, 838

PAGE

Road Traffic Regulation Act, 1967—*continued*

s. 72 .... 321, 322
　　(2) 322
　　(3) 838
　　(4) 322
　　(5) 299, 582
s. 74 .... 317, 321, 395, 729
　　(1) 321
s. 75 324
　　(1) (*a*) 323
　　(3), (4) 322, 323
s. 77 .... 316, 317, 337
　　(1) (*b*) 316, 324
　　(5) 323, 324
　　　(*a*) 317
　　(7) 127, 129, 316, 318, 340, 462
　　(9) 316, 317
s. 78 317
s. 78A 127, 129, 130, 316, 317, 340, 620
　　(2) 318
　　(4) 111, 321
s. 79 .... 338, 339
s. 80 .... 93, 96, 591, 597
　　(1) (*a*)-(*c*), (*b*), (*f*) 588
　　(2) 587, 589
　　(3) 588
　　(7) 587
　　(8) 462
　　(10) 96
s. 81 460
　　(4A) 305, 315
s. 84C 298
s. 85 .... 462, 463, 465–7
s. 86 311
s. 87 .... 311, 312
s. 90 .... 107, 463
s. 97 .... 60–62, 445, 466
s. 99 .... 3, 332
　　(10) 334
s. 100 11
s. 101 4
s. 103 9
s. 104 384
　　(1) 21, 26, 31, 55
s. 106 317
Sched. 1, para. 1 334
Sched. 5 .... 317, 324, 325, **325–32,** 333, 334, 336, 337,
                                       339, 571, 816, 827, 828

　　　　para. 1 333–5
　　　　　　(1), (2), (3) 333
　　　　　　(4) (*a*) 336
　　　　　　(5) 335
　　　　para. 2 332–5
　　　　　　(1) 336
　　　　　　(3) (*a*) 336
　　　　　　　(*b*) 335
　　　　　　(4) 336

PAGE

Road Traffic Regulation Act, 1967—*continued*
        para. 3 337
        para. 13 332
        para. 14 .... 333, 335
              (1) (*b*) 335
        para. 17 .... 11, 336
        para. 24 (2) 339
        para. 25 .... 336, 337
        para. 26 336
  Sched. 8, paras. 1, 10 838
Road Transport Lighting Act, 1957 [5 & 6 Eliz. 2, c. 51]... 403, 731, 753, 755
  s. 1 .... 756, 757, 761
    (1) (*a*) 753
       (*b*) 754
    (2) 754
       (1) (*b*) 757, 759
  ss. 3, 8 (2) 754
Road Transport Lighting Act, 1967 [c. 55] 403, 405
Road Transport Lighting (Amendment) Act, 1958 [6 & 7 Eliz. 2, c. 22] ... 403

School Crossing Patrols Act, 1953 [1 & 2 Eliz. 2, c. 45]........................ 62, 63
Special Roads Act, 1949 [12, 13 & 14 Geo. 6, c. 32]—
  ss. 1, 2, 12, 15 705
  Sched. 2 .... 580, 705
        Class I **580–81**
        Class II **581**
Stage Carriages Act, 1832 [2 & 3 Will. 4, c. 120] 577, 580
  ss. 48, 103 578
Statute Law (Repeals) Act, 1969 [c. 52]—
  s. 1 138
Summary Jurisdiction Act, 1857 [20 & 21 Vict. c. 43]—
  s. 6 700
Summary Jurisdiction (Appeals) Act, 1933 [23 & 24 Geo. 5, c. 38] 696
Summary Jurisdiction (Process) Act, 1881 [44 & 45 Vict. c. 24] 72
Summary Jurisdiction (Scotland) Act, 1954 [2 & 3 Eliz. 2, c. 48]—
  ss. 15 (5), 31 (1) 604
Sunday Observance Act, 1677 [29 Cha. 2, c. 7] 138

Telegraph Act, 1878 [41 & 42 Vict. c. 76] 717, 740
Theft Act, 1968 [c. 60] 361, 362, 365, 598, 599, 620, 876
  s. 1 642
  s. 9 355
    (1), (2) 355
  s. 12 .... 24, 25, 95, 195, 209, 351, **351**, 352–7, 359–63, 399, 462, 605,
                                         607, 619, 620, 642
    (1) 351, 353–5, 357, 358, 360
    (2) 360
    (3) 354
    (4) 355
    (5) 351–3, 358
    (6) 351, 354, 355
    (7) 352
       (*b*) 360
  s. 22 353
  s. 25 .... 361, 362, 605, 619
    (3), (5) 355
  s. 29 .... 353, 361
  Sched. 2 353

PAGE

Town Police Clauses Act, 1847 [10 & 11 Vict. c. 89]................. 61, 383, 402
    s. 28 .... 56, 292, 383, 386
    s. 62 422
Trade Descriptions Act, 1968 [c. 29].................. 553, 739, 749, 752, 763, 779
Tramways Act, 1870 [33 & 34 Vict. c. 78] 580
Transport Act, 1947 [10 & 11 Geo. 6, c. 49]—
    s. 65 573
Transport Act, 1968 [c. 73]... 1, 2, 97, 555
    s. 30 567
    s. 35 (2) (b) 545
    Pt. V 27, 50, 527, 531, 540, 544, 550, 554
    s. 59 .... 527, 539
    s. 60 .... 430, 527, **528–9,** 529, 530
        (2) 528
        (4) 528
          (a) 544
    s. 61 .... **530–31**
        (1) (b), (c) 541
        (5) 531
    s. 62 (4) (b) 545
    s. 64 (2) (c) 545
    s. 65 .... 531, **531–3,** 534
        (1) 533, 534
        (5) 533
        (9) 534
        (11) 533
    s. 66 531
        (2) **531**
    s. 69 (4) (c) 546
        (6) 539
    s. 71 .... 534, **535–7,** 537, 538, 540
        (3), (4), (5) 537
        (6) 534, 538
        (9) 534
        (10) 537
    ss. 72–80 537
    s. 76 537
        (3) 537
    s. 81 .... 538, **538**
        (3), (4) 538
    s. 82 538
    s. 83 539
    s. 84 .... 539, **539**
    s. 85 .... 531, 537
    s. 91 (1) (c) 430
    s. 92 .... 534, 540, 541, 544
        (1) 27, 527, **540–41**
        (2) 50, 529, 530, 537
        (5) 527
        (6) 539
    s. 94 540
    Pt. VI 23, 27, 533, 546, 550, 555, 565
    s. 95 .... **545–6,** 555, 559, 565
        (1) 546
        (3) 23, 545, 550
    s. 96 .... 555, 556, **556–8,** 558, 559, 561–3, 566
        (1) 559, 563
        (1)–(6), (1)–(9) 545

Transport Act, 1968—*continued*

s. 96 (2) **563**

(3) 563

(c) **563**

(4) (a) 563

(b) 551, 563

(5) 563

(6) **563–4**

(7) **564–5**

(7A), (7B) 564, **564**

(8) (b) 565

(9) 559

(11) 559, 560, 566

(b) 561

(i) 560

(ii) 38, 560

(11A) 555, 558, 566

(12) 558

ss. 96–98 430

s. 97 .... 548, 549, 565

(2) (a) 551

(4), (5) 565

s. 98 .... 33, **547,** 548, 549, 553, 556, 562

(1) 545

(2) (e) 551

(4) 35, 38, 546, 553–5

(5) 554, 562

s. 99 .... 4 30, **548–50**

(1) (d), (3), (5) 550

s. 102 .... **550,** 556

(1) 546

(2), (4) 550

s. 103 .... **550–52,** 655

(1) 27, 51, 545, 559

(b) 560

(3) 23, 545

(4) 559, 561

(a) 561

(6) 547, 565

(7) 554, 566

s. 126 .... 317, 392

(7) 394

s. 127 384

s. 128 393

s. 131 597

s. 145 (4) 15

s. 149 .... 31, 63

(1) 31

s. 159 (1) 441

s. 166 (2) 552

Sched. 9 .... 533, 539–41

para. 2 (5) 545

Sched. 10 544

Sched. 11 .... 550, 552

Sched. 14 .... 300, 384, 394

Transport (London) Act, 1969 [c. 35] 842

Vagrancy Act, 1824 [5 Geo. 4, c. 83] 79, 610, 636

s. 4 354

PAGE

Vehicle and Driving Licences Act, 1969 [c. 27] 1, 476, 485, 486, 650
     s. 27 .... **108–9**
Vehicles (Excise) Act, 1949 [12, 13 & 14 Geo. 6, c. 89] ... 734, 771, 773, 816
Vehicles (Excise) Act, 1962 [10 & 11 Eliz. 2, c. 13] ... 734, 752, 771, 773, 816
     s. 7 45
     s. 12 525
Vehicles (Excise) Act, 1971 [c. 10] 1, 2, 5, 8, 10, 11, 31, 44, 46, 47, 50, 51,
                               55, 56, 68, 96, 109, 110, 184, 195, 332,
                               370, 430, 485, 486, 489, 491, 498, 508,
                               516, 592, 734, 748, 749, 752, 771, 773,
                               779, 783, 816, 819, 821, 851
     s. 1 491
       (1) 45, 487
     s. 2 486
     s. 3 501
       (2) 489
       (3) 501
     s. 4 .... 494, 500, 501
       (1) (*e*) 492
     s. 5 .... 500, 501
     s. 6 .... 500, 513
     s. 7 (1), (3), (4) 500
     s. 8 .... 10, 33, 44–6, 50, 70, 462, 486, 488, 489, 503, 506–8, 510,
                                 511, 514, 517, 520
       (1) (*b*) 506
       (2) 486, 506, 507
       (3) (*a*) 509, **509**, 518
          (*b*) 507
     ss. 8–20 486
     s. 9 .... 506, 507, 509, 510, 517, 697
       (2) 509, 510, 512, 513
         (*a*) 512
       (2)–(4) 509
       (3) 509, 511
         (*b*) 513
       (4) 512, 513
       (5) 509
     s. 10 486
     s. 11 (2) 488
     s. 12 517
       (4) 489, 502, 503, 517
       (5) 486, 503, 517
     s. 13 486
     s. 16 .... 504, 510, 519, **519–21,** 773
       (4), (5) 519
       (7) 70, 462, 486, 488, 506–8, 514, 527
       (8) 523, 525, 526
     s. 18 .... 492, 504, 505, 508, 510, 514
       (1), (2) 504
       (4) 70, 462, 486, 488, 499, 508, 511, 517
       (5) 504
       (6) 496, 505
       (7), (8) 499, 505
     s. 19 513
     s. 21 .... 492, 513
     s. 22 .... 47, 48, 408, 517, 518
       (1), (2) 513

TABLE OF STATUTES

PAGE

Vehicles (Excise) Act, 1971—*continued*
ss. 23–26, 24 486
s. 26 .... 502, 514
    (1), (2) 70, 488, 508, 514, 517
s. 27 .... 462, 463, 465, 467, 508, 517
    (1) 508
s. 28 .... 70, **488,** 490, 505, 506, 518, 527
    (2) 488
    (3) (*b*) 489
s. 29 70
s. 30 .... 505, 510
s. 31 .... 107, **108–9,** 515
s. 32 .... 463, 508
s. 33 .... 501, 502, 504, 507, 508, 514
s. 34 510
s. 35 (4) (*g*), (*h*) 11
s. 37 .... 486, 517
    (3) (*b*) 527
s. 38 .... 26, 516
    (1) 486, 492
    (2) 487, 517
    (3) 6
Sched. 1 .... 491, 520
Scheds. 1–5 491
Sched. 2 .... 491, 492, 505
    Pt. I, para. 3 492
Sched. 3 .... 427, 492–5, 501, 516, 517
    para. 2 .... 51, 581
        (1) (*b*) 494
          (*d*) 493
        (2) (*a*) 494
    para. 5 492
Sched. 4 .... 491, 492, 494–7, 500, 516
    para. 1 (1) 496
          (2) 496, 498
    para. 2 .... 496, 499
    para. 3 (*b*) 493, 494
          (*d*) 495
    para. 4 .... **499**
    para. 5 (1) 499
    para. 6 (1) 11, 498
          (2) 498
    para. 7 (2) 495
          (3) 768
          (6) 495
    para. 8 769
        (2) 779
    para. 9 .... 495, 497
        (1) 497, 499, 504
        (2) 497
    Pt. II, Table A, para. 3 497
              para. 4 499
Sched. 5 .... 491, 492, 499, 505
Sched. 6 .... 15, 16, 515, 516
    para. 2 516
    para. 3 515
        (2), (3) 516
    paras. 4, 5 516

PAGE

Vehicles (Excise) Act, 1971—*continued*
  Sched. 7 .... 485, 491, 506, 519, 527
        Pt. I 486
        Pt. II, para. 1 110
Visiting Forces Act, 1952 [15 & 16 Geo. 6 & 1 Eliz. 2, c. 67] 58, 605
  s. 3 354
  s. 4 59

TABLE OF RULES

*[Figures in **bold type** indicate pages where the text of an order or regulation is given. Entries are listed alphabetically and arranged chronologically within each group.]*

PAGE

Brakes on Pedal Cycles Regulations, 1954 [S.I. 1954 No. 966] 417
Breath Test Device (Approval) (No. 1) Order, 1968 [9th Feb.] 200
Breath Test Device (Approval) (No. 2) Order, 1968 [13th March] 200

Civil Defence Vehicles (Relief from Duty) Regulations, 1953 [S.I. 1953 No. 269] 500
Controlled Areas (Pedestrians) Regulations, 1965 [S.I. 1965 No. 545]......... 445
Coroners Rules, 1953 [S.I. 1953 No. 205]... 258
Criminal Appeal Rules, 1908 [S.R. & O. 1908 No. 227] 644
Criminal Appeal Rules, 1968 [S.I. 1968 No. 1262] 644, 703
Crown Court Rules, 1971 [S.I. 1971 No. 1292] 696
    r. 7 (3) 697
    r. 21 698

Diplomatic Privileges (Citizens of the United Kingdom and Colonies) Order, 1964 [S.I. 1964 No. 2043] 60
Drivers' Hours (Goods Vehicles) (Exemptions) Regulations, 1972 [S.I. 1972 No. 574] 559
    Sched., Pts. I, II 559
Drivers' Hours (Goods Vehicles) (Keeping of Records) Regulations, 1970 [S.I. 1970 No. 123] 545
    reg. 3 (4), (7) 545
    regs. 5 (8), 8 (1) 548
    reg. 12 (1), (2) 545
Drivers' Hours (Goods Vehicles) (Keeping of Records) (Amendment) Regulations, 1971 [S.I. 1971 No. 847] 545
Drivers' Hours (Goods Vehicles) (Modifications) Order, 1970 [S.I. 1970 No. 257].. 559
Drivers' Hours (Passenger and Goods Vehicles) (International Rules) Regulations, 1973 [S.I. 1973 No. 379] 63, 555
Drivers' Hours (Passenger and Goods Vehicles) (Keeping of Records) (International Rules) Regulations, 1973 [S.I. 1973 No. 380] 63, 555
Drivers' Hours (Passenger and Goods Vehicles) (Modifications) Order, 1971 [S.I. 1971 No. 818] 559, 563

Evidence by Certificate Rules, 1961 [S.I. 1961 No. 248] 106
    r. 3 106
Evidence by Certificate Rules, 1962 [S.I. 1962 No. 2319] 106

Fixed Penalty (Procedure) (No. 2) Regulations, 1974 [S.I. 1974 No. 1475] ... 597
Fuel Control (Modification of Enactments) (Speed Limits) Order, 1973 [S.I. 1973 No. 2051].. 316, 317, 467
Functions of Traffic Wardens Order, 1970 [S.I. 1970 No. 1958] 305, 460
    reg. 3 (3) 305
Functions of Traffic Wardens (Scotland) Order, 1962 [S.I. 1962 No. 1271] ... 306
Functions of Traffic Wardens (Scotland) Order, 1966 [S.I. 1966 No. 222] ... 306

                                                                      PAGE
Goods Vehicles (Operators' Licences) Regulations, 1969 [S.I. 1969 No. 1656] 527
    reg. 3 528
    reg. 20 531
    Sched. 1 528
    Sched. 3 531
Goods Vehicles (Operators' Licences) (Fees) Regulations, 1971 [S.I. 1971
    No. 149] 527
Goods Vehicles (Operators' Licences) (Temporary Use in Great Britain)
    Regulations, 1972 [S.I. 1972 No. 716] 528
    reg. 3 528
        (1) 528
Goods Vehicles (Operators' Licences) (Temporary Use in Great Britain)
    (Amendment) Regulations, 1972 [S.I. 1972 No. 1535] 528
Goods Vehicles (Plating and Testing) Regulations, 1968 [S.I. 1968 No. 601] 63
Goods Vehicles (Plating and Testing) Regulations, 1971 [S.I. 1971 No. 352] 19,
                                                                   427, 772
    Sched. 2 427
        para. 24 63
Goods Vehicles (Plating and Testing) (Amendment) Regulations, 1971
    [S.I. 1971 No. 2074]... 427
Goods Vehicles (Plating and Testing) (Amendment) Regulations, 1972
    [S.I. 1972 No. 195] 427
Goods Vehicles (Plating and Testing) (Amendment) (No. 2) Regulations,
    1972 [S.I. 1972 No. 806] 427
Goods Vehicles (Plating and Testing) (Amendment) Regulations, 1974
    [S.I. 1974 No. 99].. 427
Goods Vehicles (Plating and Testing) (Amendment) Regulations, 1975
    [S.I. 1975 No. 36]... 427

Heavy Goods Vehicles (Drivers' Licences) Regulations, 1969 [S.I. 1969
    No. 903]—
    regs. 3 (3), 7 485
    reg. 9 484
    reg. 10 (1) 485
    reg. 12 484
        (1) 485
    regs. 13 (2), 14 485
    reg. 25 467
    Sched. 1 484
Heavy Goods Vehicles (Drivers' Licences) Regulations, 1975 [S.I. 1975
    No. 739] 467, 483

Justices' Clerks Rules, 1970 [S.I. 1970 No. 231] 56, 69, 71, 101

Local Authorities' Traffic Orders (Procedure) (England and Wales) Regu-
    lations, 1969 [S.I. 1969 No. 463]—
    reg. 17 (1) (f) 394

Magistrates' Courts Rules, 1968 [S.I. 1968 No. 1920] 657
    r. 1 (1) 56
    r. 12 65
    r. 13 .... 82, 83
    r. 28 .... 601, 606
    r. 29 104
    r. 55 .... 216, 463
        (2) 609
    r. 58 82
    r. 59 .... 82, 120
    rr. 62–64.. 696

PAGE

Magistrates' Court Rules, 1968—*continued*
  rr. 63, 65 644
  rr. 65–68... 699
  r. 81 56
      (3) 65
  r. 82 72
      (1), (2) 135
  r. 83 65
  r. 84 .... 647–9, 657
Magistrates' Courts (Amendment) (No. 2) Rules, 1975 [S.I. 1975 No. 518]... 699
  rr. 65 (1), (2), 67 699
Motor Cycles (Protective Helmets) Regulations, 1968 [S.I. 1968 No. 844]... 350
Motor Cycles (Protective Helmets) Regulations, 1974 [S.I. 1974 No. 2000]... 350
  Sched. 350
Motor Cycles (Wearing of Helmets) Regulations, 1973 [S.I. 1973 No. 180] ... 349
  reg. 2 .... 349, **728–9**
      (1) (*a*) (i) 350
          (*b*) 349
  reg. 3 .... 349, **729**
Motor Vehicles (Authorisation of Special Types) General Order, 1969 [S.I.
  1969 No. 344] 581
  arts. 16, 17, 21 581
Motor Vehicles (Authorisation of Special Types) General Order, 1973 [S.I.
  1973 No. 1101] 14, 18, 325, 414, 430, 432
  arts. 10, 13, 14, 15, 16, 23 325
  art. 24 .... 431, 432
      (2), (3) 14
  art. 28 (2) 431
  Pt. II 430
  Pt. III.. 431
  Sched. 2 431
Motor Vehicles (Construction and Use) (Amendment) (No. 2) Regulations,
  1959 [S.I. 1959 No. 2231] 411
Motor Vehicles (Construction and Use) Regulations, 1969 [S.I. 1969 No. 321]
  731, 764
  reg. 3 (1), (2) 736
  reg. 4 (3), (6), (6A), (7), (8) 760
  reg. 110 (2) 11
  reg. 121 19
Motor Vehicles (Construction and Use) (Amendment) (No. 2) Regulations,
  1971 [S.I. 1971 No. 979] 11
Motor Vehicles (Construction and Use) Regulations, 1973 [S.I. 1973
  No. 24] 4, 9, 10, 14, 36, 40–47, 49, 54, 62, 63, 65, 325,
          332, 336, 383, 410, 426, 430, 666, 668, 684–6,
          688
  reg. 2 774
  reg. 3 ....9, 51, 410, 411, 413, 414, 424, 517, **766–74**, 801, 806
      (1) 11, 13, 492
          (*a*)–(*f*), (*a*)–(*h*) 844
      (2) 548
      (4) 416
      (5) 423
  reg. 4 .... 26, 411, 413, **774–6**
      (4), (5) 411
      (6) 63, 779
      (7) 819, 821
      (9) 59, 417
      (10), (11) 411
      (12) 9

PAGE

Motor Vehicles (Construction and Use) Regulations, 1973—*continued*

reg. 4A 840, 841, **776–7**
    (1)... 830, 834, 837, 840, 841
reg. 4B **777**
reg. 5 .... 413, **777–9**
    Table 777
reg. 6 .... **779**
reg. 7 .... **779**
    (1)... 414
Pt. II 416, 425, 433, 774–6
reg. 8 .... **780**
    (2) 776
reg. 9 .... 775, **780**
    (1)... 414
regs. 9–12 .... 774, 775
reg. 10 .... **780**
reg. 11 .... 774, **780**, 827, 857
reg. 12 .... 774, 778, **780–81**
reg. 13 .... 415, 427, 777, **781–2**, 840
    (2) 803, 808, 829, 831
       (*b*) (ii) 830
reg. 14 .... 415, 427, 777, 782
regs. 14–20 775
regs. 14–21 774
regs. 15, 16... 777, 782
reg. 17 .... 423, **782–5**
    (2) 423
reg. 18 .... 415, 427, 776, 778, **785**, 828
reg. 19 .... 777, **785–6**
reg. 20 .... 774, 776, 786
reg. 21 786
reg. 22 .... 427, **786**
regs. 22–30 775
reg. 23 .... 422, 427, 774, **786–7**
    (1) (*b*) 422
    (3)... 777
reg. 24 .... 774, **787**
reg. 25 .... **787–8**
regs. 25–27 427
reg. 26 .... **788**
reg. 27 .... 411, 424, 774, 778, **788–9**
    (1)... 837
    (2)... 424, 777
    (4) 776
    (5) 838
    (6) 837
reg. 28 .... 424, **789**
regs. 28–74 774
reg. 29 .... 777, **789–90,** 836, 869–71
    (1), (3) 836
    (5)... 837
reg. 30 .... 778, **790**
reg. 31 .... **790**
reg. 32 .... **790**
    (2), proviso (ii)... 835
reg. 33 .... **790–91,** 835
reg. 33A 775, 778, 790, **791–3**
reg. 34 .... 775, 778, **793–4,** 834
    (1) 779

PAGE

Motor Vehicles (Construction and Use) Regulations, 1973—*continued*

regs. 35, 36.. **794**
regs. 36–88 775
reg. 37 .... **794**
reg. 38 .... 11, 404, 407, 410, 413, **794–5,** 832
    (2) 831
reg. 39 .... 18, 427, **796,** 826, 853, 855, 870
    (1) 826, 827, 831
       (*a*) **796**
       (*b*) 796, 826
       (*c*) 18
    (2) 796, 819–25, 861, 863, 865, 870
reg. 40 .... 15, **796–7,** 797, 829, 855
    (1) 779
reg. 41 .... 15, **797**
    (1) 779
reg. 42 .... 797, 858
regs. 42–44 .... 774, 775
reg. 43 .... **797**
reg. 44 .... 15, 774, **797**
reg. 45 .... 774, **797–8**
reg. 46 .... 415, 781, **798**
reg. 47 .... 415, 777, 781, **798–9**
reg. 48 .... 431, 774, 775, **799**
regs. 48–51 778
reg. 49 .... 774, **799**
reg. 50 .... 415, 777, 781, **799–800**
reg. 51 .... 774, **801**
reg. 52 .... 774, 775, **801**
regs. 52–61 778
reg. 53 .... **801–2**
reg. 54 .... 415, 416, 427, 777, 781, **802–5,** 858
    (2) 781
    (4) 829
    (5) 781, 821, 829, 830, 854
    (6), (7) 829–31, 854
reg. 55 .... 774, **805**
reg. 56 .... **805**
reg. 57 .... 774, 775, **806**
reg. 58 .... 774, **806**
reg. 59 .... 415, 427, 777, 781, **806–10,** 858
    (1)–(3) 776
    (2) 781
    (4) 829
    (5) 781, 829, 830, 854
    (5)–(7) 776
    (6), (7) 829–31, 854
    (8), (9)–(11), (13)–(15) 776
reg. 60 .... 427, 774, **810**
reg. 61 .... 411, 774, 776, **810**
reg. 62 .... 415, **811,** 858
    (1), (2) 776
    (3) 829
    (4), (5), (6) 776
reg. 63 811
reg. 64 .... 427, 774, 776, **811**
reg. 65 .... 774, 775, **811**
reg. 66 .... 415, 777, **811–12**
reg. 67 .... **812**

PAGE

Motor Vehicles (Construction and Use) Regulations, 1973—*continued*
reg. 68 .... 418, 774, **812**
reg. 69 .... 774, **812–13**
reg. 70 .... 331, 415, 427, 777, **813–15**
        (2) 829
            (c) (iii) 830
        (3) 796
reg. 71 .... 774, **815**
reg. 72 .... 427, 774, 815, **815–16**
reg. 73 .... **816**
Pt. III.. 425
reg. 74 .... 18, 19, 774, 778, **816**
regs. 74–106 775
reg. 75 .... 776, **816–17**, 860
reg. 76 .... 16, **817,** 827
regs. 76–88 774
reg. 77 .... **817**
reg. 78 .... 16, **818**
regs. 78–82 18
regs. 78–89 15
reg. 79 .... 16, 17, **818–20**, 823, 854, 855, 860
        (1) (b), (c) 823, 824
reg. 79 (3) 822, 823
            (c) 870
regs. 79–88 .... 19, 827, 853
reg. 80 .... 16, **820–21,** 823, 854, 855, 860
        (3) 819
        (4) 823
        (5) 822–4
reg. 81 .... 432, **821–2,** 854
reg. 82 .... **822,** 824, 854, 855, 860
reg. 83 .... 818, **822–3,** 854, 855, 857
        (1) (a) (i), (ii) 823, 824
            (b) (i) 823–5, 861, 863, 865
            (c) (i), (ii) 824
            (d) (i) 824, 825, 861, 865
                (ii) 824
regs. 83–86 861
regs. 83–87 774
reg. 84 .... **823–4,** 854, 857, 863
        (1) (a), (b) 824
reg. 85 .... **824,** 854, 855, 863
reg. 86 .... **824–5,** 825, 857
        (2), (3), (4) 864
        (5) 826, 865
        (6) 826
reg. 87 .... **825–6,** 857
reg. 88 .... 824–6, **826,** 855
reg. 89 .... 774, **826–7**
reg. 89A **827–8**
reg. 90 .... 413, 414, 418–21, 427, **828**
        (1) 419, 420, 425, 433, 434, 610
        (2) 418, 420, 433, 434, 610
        (3) 420, 433, 434, 610
reg. 91 .... 415, 425, 774, **828–9**
reg. 92 .... **829**
reg. 93 .... 425, **829**
regs. 93–95 427

PAGE

Motor Vehicles (Construction and Use) Regulations, 1973—*continued*
reg. 94 .... 416, 425, 433, **829–31,** 858
    (1) (*c*), (*d*) 854
reg. 95 .... 419, 433, **831**
reg. 96 .... 424, **831**
reg. 97 .... 404, 410, 413, **831–2**
reg. 98 .... 424, 425, **832**
reg. 99 .... 46, 425, 427, 433, **832–3**
    (1) 423
    (*a*), (*a*)–(*f*), (*c*), (*e*), (*f*) 423
    (4) 423
reg. 100 .... 423, **833–4**
reg. 101 .... 424, 425, 427, **834**
reg. 102 .... **834**
reg. 103 .... 427, **834–5**
regs. 104, 105.. **835**
reg. 106 .... **835,** 836
    provisos (i), (ii) 836
regs. 106–108 424
reg. 107 .... **835**
reg. 108 .... **835–7**
    (2) 871
    (3) (*a*), (*b*) 869–71
reg. 109 .... 422, 836, **837**
reg. 110 .... 424, **837–8**
    (2) 776
reg. 111 .... **838–9**
regs. 112, 113.. **839**
reg. 114 .... 383, 385, 386, 388–90, 413, **839**
reg. 115 .... 402, **839–40**
reg. 116 .... 412, 421, 422, 434, **840**
reg. 117 .... 400, **400,** 401, 413, **840**
reg. 118 .... 776, **840–41**
regs. 119, 120... **841**
reg. 121 .... 3, **841**
reg. 122 .... 12, **841**
regs. 123, 124, 125 .... 12, **842**
reg. 126 .... **842**
reg. 127 .... 12, **842**
reg. 128 .... 13, **842–3,** 865–7
reg. 129... **843**
reg. 130 .... 414, 769, 770, 775, **843–4,** 869
    (1) (*g*), (*h*) 843
reg. 131 .... 11, 414, 843, 844, **844–8,** 850, 865
    (2) 865–7
    (4) 865, 867
      (*a*), (*b*) 866
    (5) 866, 867, 869
      (*a*) 867
      (*b*) 869
      (*c*), (*d*) 867
    (6) 865–7, 869
      (*a*) 867
      (*b*) 869
      (*c*), (*d*) 867
    (7) 865–7, 869
    (8) 869
    (9) 865–7
reg. 132 .... 422, 775, **848**

PAGE

Motor Vehicles (Construction and Use) Regulations, 1973—*continued*
    regs. 133, 134.. **849**
    reg. 135 .... 13, 421, **849–50**
    reg. 136 .... 12, **850**
    reg. 137 .... 426, **851**
    Pt. V 774
    reg. 138 .... 825, **852,** 861, 863, 865
    reg. 139 .... **852**
    reg. 140 .... 427, **853,** 854
    reg. 141 .... **853**
    reg. 142 .... 15, 19, 411, 428, 432, **853,** 854
    regs. 143, 144, 145 .... **854**
    reg. 146 .... 427, **855**
    Sched. 1 855
    Sched. 2 .... 18, **855–8**
        Pt. I 796, **855,** 856, 857
        Pt. II 796, **856,** 857
        Pt. III 796, **856–8**
    Sched. 3 .... 797, 858
    Sched. 4 .... 415, 802, 807, 808, 811, 829, **858–60**
        column 5 416
    Sched. 5 .... 417, 817, 860
    Sched. 6 .... 15, **860–61**
        para. 1 818
        para. 2 .... 819, 820
        para. 3 822
    Sched. 7 .... 15, 774, **861–5**
        Pt. I 823, **861–3**
        Pt. II 823, **863**
        Pt. III 824, **863–4**
        Pt. IV 824, 825, **864**
        Pt. V 825, **864**
        Pt. VI 825, **865**
    Sched. 8 .... 843, 844, **865–9**
        Pt. I 865–9
            para. 1 .... 842, 845–7
            para. 2 .... 14, 843, 845–7, 850
            para. 3 .... 846, 848
            para. 4 846–8
        Pt. II 869
    Sched. 9 .... 424, 790, 837, **869–71**
        column 1 .... 789, 836
        column 2 789
        columns 3, 4 836
    Sched. 10 .... 835, 837, **871–2**
        para. 4 836
    Sched. 11 .... 852, **873**
Motor Vehicles (Construction and Use) (Amendment) Regulations, 1973
[S.I. 1973 No. 756] 766
Motor Vehicles (Construction and Use) (Amendment) (No. 2) Regulations,
1973 [S.I. 1973 No. 1347] 766
Motor Vehicles (Construction and Use) (Amendment) (No. 3) Regulations,
1973 [S.I. 1973 No. 1706] 766
Motor Vehicles (Construction and Use) (Amendment) (No. 4) Regulations,
1973 [S.I. 1973 No. 1864] 766
Motor Vehicles (Construction and Use) (Amendment) Regulations, 1974
[S.I. 1974 No. 64]... 766
Motor Vehicles (Construction and Use) (Amendment) (No. 2) Regulations,
1974 [S.I. 1974 No. 765] 766

Motor Vehicles (Construction and Use) (Amendment) (No. 3) Regulations, 1974 [S.I. 1974 No. 973] 766

Motor Vehicles (Construction and Use) (Amendment) Regulations, 1975 [S.I. 1975 No. 186] 766

Motor Vehicles (Construction and Use) (Amendment) (No. 2) Regulations, 1975 [S.I. 1975 No. 238] 766

Motor Vehicles (Construction and Use) (Amendment) (No. 3) Regulations, 1975 [S.I. 1975 No. 641] 766

Motor Vehicles (Construction and Use) (Track Laying Vehicles) Regulations, 1955 [S.I. 1955 No. 990] 18, 411, 430
    reg. 4 59
    reg. 54A 404

Motor Vehicles (Construction and Use) (Track Laying Vehicles) (Amendment) Regulations, 1957 [S.I. 1957 No. 439] 411

Motor Vehicles (Construction and Use) (Track Laying Vehicles) (Amendment) (No. 2) Regulations, 1957 [S.I. 1957 No. 972] 411

Motor Vehicles (Construction and Use) (Track Laying Vehicles) (Amendment) Regulations, 1959 [S.I. 1959 No. 2053] 411

Motor Vehicles (Designation of Approval Marks) (No. 2) Regulations, 1964 [S.I. 1964 No. 1561] 751

Motor Vehicles (Designation of Approval Marks) Regulations, 1968 [S.I. 1968 No. 171]—
    reg. 2 (2) 739, 748, 763

Motor Vehicles (Designation of Approval Marks) (No. 2) Regulations, 1969 [S.I. 1969 No. 962]—
    reg. 2 (1) 790

Motor Vehicles (Designation of Approval Marks) (No. 2) Regulations, 1972 [S.I. 1972 No. 1303]—
    reg. 2 (3) 793

Motor Vehicles (Designation of Approval Marks) Regulations, 1975 [S.I. 1975 No. 635]—
    reg. 2 793

Motor Vehicles (Driving Licences) Regulations, 1971 [S.I. 1971 No. 451] ... 467
    reg. 6 .... 474, 477
         (1) (b) **474–5**
            (d) 476
         (2) 474
            (b), (e) 476
         (3), (4) 474
         (5) 475
    reg. 20 .... 477, 478
         (1) (h) 291
         (2) (a), (b), (c) **478**
         (2A) 478
    reg. 21 63
         (1) 480
    reg. 22 470
    reg. 23 4
    Sched. 2 474
    Sched. 3 .... 468, 471

Motor Vehicles (Driving Licences) (Amendment) Regulations, 1973 [S.I. 1973 No. 2015] 474

Motor Vehicles (Driving Licences) (Amendment) Regulations, 1975 [S.I. 1975 No. 521] 467

Motor Vehicles (International Circulation) Order, 1957 [S.I. 1957 No. 1074] 63, 851
    art. 2 .... 64, 481
         (4) 635

PAGE

Motor Vehicles (InternationalCirculation) Order, 1957—*continued*
  art. 3 481
  Sched. 3 .... 470, 480, 608, 616
Motor Vehicles (International Circulation) (Amendment) Order, 1962 [S.I.
  1962 No. 1344] 63, 64, 481
Motor Vehicles (International Circulation) (Amendment) Order, 1969 [S.I.
  1969 No. 1086] 63
Motor Vehicles (International Circulation) (Amendment) Order, 1971 (S.I.
  1971 No. 869] 63, 500
Motor Vehicles (International Circulation) Regulations, 1971 [S.I. 1971 No.
  937] 63
  reg. 5 332
Motor Vehicles (International Motor Insurance Card) Regulations, 1971
  [S.I. 1971 No. 792] 63, 369, 380, 381
  reg. 6 (1) 381
Motor Vehicles (Minimum Age for Driving) Regulations, 1963 [S.I. 1963
  No. 1015] 472
Motor Vehicles (Minimum Age for Driving) (Motor Cycles) Regulations,
  1971 [S.I. 1971 No. 1979] 472, 477, 482
Motor Vehicles (Rear Markings) Regulations, 1970 [S.I. 1970 No. 1700] ... 415,
                                                                          847, 868
  regs. 2, 4, 5 415
  Sched., Pts. I, II, III 415
Motor Vehicles (Rear Markings) (Amendment) Regulations, 1972 [S.I. 1972
  No. 842] 415
Motor Vehicles (Rear Markings) Regulations, 1975 [S.I. 1975 No. 29] 415
Motor Vehicles (Speed Limits on Motorways) Regulations, 1973 [S.I. 1973
  No. 748] 130, 336, 581
  Sched. **337**
      paras. 2, 5 337
Motor Vehicles (Speed Limits on Motorways) (Amendment) Regulations,
  1973 [S.I. 1973 No. 2058] 336–7
Motor Vehicles (Tests) (Extension) Order, 1966 [S.I. 1966 No. 973] 426
Motor Vehicles (Tests) Regulations, 1968 [S.I. 1968 No. 1714] 426
  reg. 15 (1) 429
Motor Vehicles (Tests) (Exemption) Regulations, 1969 [S.I. 1969 No. 419] 426
Motor Vehicles (Tests) (Amendment) Regulations, 1969 [S.I. 1969 No. 1171] 426
Motor Vehicles (Tests) (Amendment) Regulations, 1971 [S.I. 1971 No. 165] 426
Motor Vehicles (Tests) (Amendment) Regulations, 1972 [S.I. 1972 No. 898] 426
Motor Vehicles (Third Party Risks) Regulations, 1972 [S.I. 1972 No. 1217] 376
  regs. 5 (3), 10, 13 376
  Sched., Forms B, C 376
Motor Vehicles (Type Approval) Regulations, 1973 [S.I. 1973 No. 1199]—
  reg. 3 (1) 777
  regs. 5, 6 776
  Sched. 2 777
Motor Vehicles (Variation of Speed Limit) Regulations, 1947 [S.R. & O.
  1947 No. 2192] 338, 339
Motor Vehicles (Variation of Speed Limit) (Amendment) Regulations, 1954
  [S.I. 1954 No. 943] 59, 338, 339
Motor Vehicles (Variation of Speed Limits) Regulations, 1973 [S.I. 1973 No.
  747] 325, 333
Motorways Traffic Regulations, 1959 [S.I. 1959 No. 1147] 581, 582, 704
  reg. 2 705
  reg. 3 582
      (1) **704**
          (a) 582
      (2) **704**
      (3), (4), (5) **705**

PAGE

Motorway Traffic Regulations 1959—*continued*
reg. 4 .... 704, **705**
reg. 5 .... **705**
reg. 6 .... **705–6,** 706
reg. 7 .... 582, 706, **706**
   (1) 582
   (2) 582, 707, 708
     (*b*) 583
   (3) 707
reg. 8 .... 583, **706–7**
reg. 9 .... 582, 583, **707**
reg. 10 .... 583, **707**
reg. 11 .... 583, 707, **707**
reg. 11A 583, **707**
reg. 12 .... 582, 583, **707**
reg. 13 .... **708**
reg. 14 .... 583, 708, **708**
reg. 15 .... 583, **708–9**
   (1) (*b*), (*d*), (*e*), (*f*) 708
Motorways Traffic (England) (Amendment) Regulations, 1966 [S.I. 1966 No. 530] 704
Motorways Traffic (Scotland) Regulations, 1964 [S.I. 1964 No. 1002] 704
Motorways Traffic (Speed Limit) Regulations, 1974 [S.I. 1974 No. 502] ... 130, 337, 338, 340
Motorways Traffic (Speed Limit) (England) Regulations, 1967 [S.I. 1967 No. 1041] 130

Parking Meters (Description and Testing) (England and Wales) Order, 1957 [S.I. 1957 No. 822] 384
Parking Meters (Description and Testing) (England and Wales) Order, 1961 [S.I. 1961 No. 705] 384
   art. 2 384
Parking Meters (Description and Testing) (Scotland) Order, 1959 [S.I. 1959 No. 1348] 384
Parking Meters (Type and Design Approval) (Appointed Day) Order, 1962 [S.I. 1962 No. 947] 385
Pedestrian Crossings Regulations, 1954 [S.I. 1954 No. 370] 299, 305, 436, 452, 453
   reg. 4 .... 449, 450
"Pelican" Pedestrian Crossings Regulations and General Directions, 1969 [S.I. 1969 No. 888] 437, 445, 455
   regs. 6, 9, 11, 12 445
Public Service Vehicles and Trolley Vehicles (Carrying Capacity) Regulations, 1954 [S.I. 1954 No. 1612] 579, 580
Public Service Vehicles and Trolley Vehicles (Carrying Capacity) (Amendment) Regulations, 1958 [S.I. 1958 No. 472] 579
Public Service Vehicles and Trolley Vehicles (Carrying Capacity) (Amendment) Regulations, 1966 [S.I. 1966 No. 674] 579
Public Service Vehicles (Conduct of Drivers, Conductors and Passengers) Regulations, 1936 [S.R. & O. 1936 No. 619] 577–80
   regs. 9, 11 578
Public Service Vehicles (Conduct of Drivers, Conductors and Passengers) (Amendment) Regulations, 1946 [S.R. & O. 1946 No. 357] 578
Public Service Vehicles (Contract Carriage Records) Regulations, 1960 [S.I. 1960 No. 1503] 570
Public Service Vehicles (Equipment and Use) Regulations, 1958 [S.I. 1958 No. 926] 411
Public Service Vehicles (Equipment and Use) (Amendment) Regulations, 1966 [S.I. 1966 No. 676] 411

PAGE

Public Service Vehicles (Equipment and Use) (Amendment) Regulations,
1968 [S.I. 1968 No. 826] 411

Removal and Disposal of Vehicles (Alteration of Enactments) Order, 1967
[S.I. 1967 No. 1900] 397
Removal and Disposal of Vehicles Regulations, 1968 [S.I. 1968 No. 43] ... 397
Road Traffic (Owner Liability) Regulations, 1975 [S.I. 1975 No. 324] 584,
586, 587
   reg. 4 587
   Sched. 2 587
Road Transport (International Passenger Services) Regulations, 1973 [S.I.
1973 No. 806] 63, 570
   regs. 5 (a), (b), (c), 16 570
Road Vehicles (Excise) (Prescribed Particulars) Regulations, 1972 [S.I. 1972
No. 850] 502
Road Vehicles (Index Marks) Regulations, 1964 [S.I. 1964 No. 404] 486
Road Vehicles Lighting Regulations, 1971 [S.I. 1971 No. 694] ... 289, 290, 403,
410, 769, 817
   reg. 2 736
   reg. 3 .... 407, **731–6,** 765
   Pt. II 406
   reg. 4 .... **736–7**
   regs. 5, 6 .... **737**
   reg. 7 .... 407, 732, 736, **737**
   reg. 8 .... 736, **737–8**
      (2) 737
   reg. 9 .... 406, 737, **738,** 794, 832
   reg. 10 .... 406, **739**
   regs. 11, 12 .... **739**
   reg. 13 .... 406, **739–40**
   Pt. III 409
   reg. 14 .... **740–41**
   regs. 14–16 409
   reg. 15 .... 733, 734, **741–2,** 746
   reg. 16 .... 403, 733, 734, **742–4,** 746
   reg. 17 .... 403, 409, **744**
   reg. 18 .... 409, **744**
   reg. 19 .... 409, **744–5**
   reg. 20 .... 409, **745**
   reg. 21 .... 289, 290, 403, 409, **745–6,** 765
      (4) 765
   reg. 22 .... 403, 409, **746,** 765
      (4) 765
   Pt. IV 407
   reg. 23 .... **747,** 817
   reg. 24 .... **747–8,** 754
      (2), (5) 749
   reg. 25 .... **748–9,** 754
      (6) 747
      (8) 748
      (9) 747, 748
      (10) 747
   Pt. V 407
   regs. 26, 27, 28, 29 .... **750**
   Pt. VI 406, 407
   reg. 30 .... **750,** 751, 756
   reg. 31 .... **751**
      (3) (a) 752
   reg. 32 .... 407, **751–2**

PAGE

Road Vehicles Lighting Regulations, 1971—*continued*
reg. 33 .... 751, **752**
regs. 34, 35 .... **752**
Pt. VII 406, 407
reg. 48 735
reg. 49 .... 732, 735
reg. 57 .... **753**
regs. 57–60 .... 59, 406
reg. 58 .... 753, **753–4**
reg. 59 .... 753, **754–5**
reg. 60 .... **755**
reg. 61 .... 407, **755–6**
reg. 62 .... **756–7**
reg. 63 .... 63, 406, 407, **757**
reg. 64 .... 406, 738, 739, **757–9**
          (1) 759
               (*a*) 759
reg. 65 .... 406, 738
reg. 66 .... **759**
reg. 67 .... 406, **759–60**
reg. 68 .... **760**
reg. 69 .... 410, **760**
reg. 70 .... 410, **760–61**
          (2) (*a*) 762
               (*b*) 762
                    (iii) 762
reg. 71 .... 410, **762–3**
reg. 72 .... **763**
regs. 72–75 410
regs. 73, 74 .... **763**
reg. 75 .... **763–4**
regs. 76, 77 .... 410, **764**
Sched. 1 .... 407, 747, 756
Sched. 2 .... 406, 750, 756
Sched. 3 753
          column 2 731
Sched. 4, column 2 732
Sched. 5 .... 410, 760–62
Sched. 6 .... 763, 764
Road Vehicles Lighting (Amendment) Regulations, 1973 [S.I. 1973 No.
1006] 731
Road Vehicles Lighting (Amendment) Regulations, 1975 [S.I. 1975 No.
239] 731
Road Vehicles Lighting (Standing Vehicles) (Exemption) (General) (No. 2)
Regulations, 1972 [S.I. 1972 No. 557] 408
Road Vehicles (Registration and Licensing) Regulations, 1964 [S.I. 1964
No. 1178] 486
Road Vehicles (Registration and Licensing) Regulations, 1971 [S.I. 1971
No. 450] 486, 492, 517
regs. 3 (1), 7, 8 (2), 10–15 517
reg. 12 (1) 70, 518
          (2) (*a*), (*b*) 70
reg. 16 517
          (1) 503, 517
regs. 17–22 518
reg. 19 518
          (2) 408
          (3) 408, 518
reg. 22 13

PAGE

Road Vehicles (Registration and Licensing) Regulations, 1964
Pt. IV 518
Pt. V 504, 519, 521
regs. 28, 29, 30, 31, 32, 33 521
reg. 34 .... **521**
reg. 35 .... **521–3**
    (1) (*a*), (*b*), (2), (3) 525
    (4) (*a*) 523
        (*a*)–(*l*) 525, 526
        (*c*) 523, 526
        (*d*) 523, 525
        (*e*) 523
        (*f*) 523, 525
        (*g*) 523
        (*g*)–(*k*) 525
        (*h*), (*i*), (*l*) 523
reg. 36 .... 521, 522, **523,** 525
reg. 37 .... **532**
reg. 38 .... **523–4**
reg. 39 .... **524**
reg. 40 .... **524–5**
Pt. VI 513, 518
reg. 41 492
Pt. VII 518
reg. 45 .... 15, 518
Sched. 2 518
    Pt. II, paras. 6, 7, 8 518
Sched. 3 518
    para. 4 408
Sched. 4 .... 492, 518
Road Vehicles (Registration and Licensing) (Amendment) Regulations, 1971
[S.I. 1971 No. 1285] 486, 517
Road Vehicles (Registration and Licensing) (Amendment) Regulations, 1972
[S.I. 1972 No. 1865] 486, 517
Road Vehicles (Use of Lights during Daytime) Regulations, 1975 [S.I. 1975
No. 245] 403, 410
reg. 1 .... **764–5**
    (2) 403
reg. 2 .... **765**
    (3) 403
Rules of the Supreme Court (Revision) Order, 1965 [S.I. 1965 No. 1776]—
ord. 53 702
ords. 56, 57 699
ord. 79, r. 9 669

Special Roads (Classes of Traffic) Order, 1971 [S.I. 1971 No. 1156] 580
Special Roads (Notice of Opening) Regulations, 1962 [S.I. 1962 No. 1320]...582

Traffic Signs Regulations and General Directions, 1964 [S.I. 1964 No.
1857] 297, 298, 302, 307, 310–14, 393
reg. 3 (1) 724, 727
reg. 6 .... **709**
reg. 7 .... 297, 298, 301, 307, 308, 310–12, **710**
reg. 8 .... 313, **710,** 722
    (1) 306, 308
    (3) 313
reg. 9 .... 313, **710–11,** 718
reg. 10 .... 313, **711**
reg. 11 .... **711–12**

PAGE

Traffic Signs Regulations and General Directions, 1964—*continued*
reg. 11 (2) 306, 307
reg. 11A 308, 309, **712**
    (2) (*b*) 308
reg. 12 .... 313, 713
reg. 13 .... 313, **713**
reg. 14 .... 306, 307, 313, **713**
reg. 15 .... 308, **713–15,** 715
    (1)–(8) 714
    (1)–(9) 715
    (9) 306
regs. 15–19 300
reg. 16 .... 713, 715, **715**
reg. 17 715
reg. 18 .... 306, **715–16**
    (1)–(3) 715
    (2) 308
    (5), (6) 715
reg. 19 .... 308, 714–16
regs. 20, 21 .... **716**
reg. 22 .... **716**
    (2) 285, 311, 716
reg. 23 .... 309, 311, 312, **716–18**
    (1) 718
    (2) 710
    (3), (4) 312, 717
    (5) 312, 716
reg. 24 .... **718**
    (1) 313
reg. 25 .... **718**
    (1) 313
reg. 26 718
reg. 27 .... **718–19,** 726
regs. 27–29 310
regs. 28, 29 726
reg. 31 .... 710, 713, **720–21,** 726, 728
    (2) 721–3
    (*a*), (*b*), (*c*), (*e*), (*f*), (*g*) 302, 722
    (3) 724, 727
    (3A) 303, 309, 721, 724
regs. 31–35 301
reg. 32 .... 710, 713, **721–2,** 723, 726, 728
reg. 33 .... 710, **722–3,** 723, 726-8
    (1) 302
    (2) (*b*) 723
    (3) 722
    (*d*) 302, 722
    (4) 722
reg. 34 .... 302, **723–4**
    (1) (*b*), (*d*), (3) 301
    (4A) (*b*) 303
dirs. 5, 5A, 6 .... **725**
dir. 10 .... 306, 307, **725**
dir. 11 .... **725–6**
dir. 12 .... **726**
dirs. 18, 19, 20, 24, 25 .... **726**
dir. 32 .... **726–7**
dir. 34 .... **727–8**
dir. 36 307

PAGE

Traffic Signs Regulations and General Directions, 1964—*continued*
   dir. 37 .... 307, 314
   Sched. 1 .... 306, 710, 713, 715, 728
       Pts. I, II 711, 714, 719
       Pt. III 711, 713, 716
       Pt. IV 711
       Pt. V 711, 713, 716
   Sched. 2 .... 710, 716, 718, 728
   Sched. 3 .... 710, 721, 722
   Sched. 4 710
   Sched. 5, Pts. I–IX 713
Traffic Signs (Amendment) Regulations, 1964 [S.I. 1964 No. 2069] 297, 709
Traffic Signs General Directions, 1966 [S.I. 1966 No. 489] 297, 709
Traffic Signs (Amendment) Regulations, 1966 [S.I. 1966 No. 490] 297, 709
Traffic Signs (Amendment) Regulations, 1969 [S.I. 1969 No. 1269]. 297, 308, 709
Traffic Signs (Amendment) Regulations, 1970 [S.I. 1970 No. 468]. 297, 308, 709
Traffic Signs (Amendment) (No. 2) Regulations, 1970 [S.I. 1970 No. 1972]
   297, 709
Traffic Signs (Amendment) Regulations, 1971 [S.I. 1971 No. 2095] ... 297, 308, 309, 709
Traffic Signs (Disqualification for Offences) Regulations, 1964 [S.I. 1964
   No. 1858] 728
Traffic Signs (Disqualification for Offences) (Amendment) Regulations, 1966
   [S.I. 1966 No. 491] 728
Traffic Signs (Disqualification for Offences) Regulations, 1969 [S.I. 1969
   No. 1270] 297, 298, 315
   regs. 1, 2 .... **728**
Traffic Signs (School Crossing Patrols) Regulations, 1968 [S.I. 1968 No.
   1826] 458
Traffic Signs (Speed Limits) Regulations and General Directions, 1969 [S.I.
   1969 No. 1487] 314, 323
   reg. 4 324
      (4) 323
   reg. 6 (4) 323
   dirs. 2 (1), (2), (3), (4), 4, 9 324

Use of Invalid Carriages on Highways Regulations, 1970 [S.I. 1970 No.
   1391]—
   regs. 3–6 4
   Sched. 1 4

Value Added Tax (General) Regulations, 1972 [S.I. 1972 No. 1147]—
   regs. 44, 45 .... 740, 741, 775, 782
Various Trunk Roads (Prohibition of Waiting) (Clearways) Order, 1963
   [S.I. 1963 No. 1172] 394
   art. 2 730
   arts. 3, 4 .... **730**
   art. 5 .... **730–31**
   art. 6 .... **731**
   Sched. 1 .... 730, 731
Various Trunk Roads (Prohibition of Waiting) (Clearways) (London) Order,
   1963 [S.I. 1963 No. 1347] 394, 395
Vehicle and Driving Licences Records (Evidence) Regulations, 1970 [S.I.
   1970 No. 1997] **109–10**
Vehicles (Conditions of Use on Footpaths) Regulations, 1963 [S.I. 1963 No.
   2126] 398
Vehicles (Conditions of Use on Footpaths) (Amendment) Regulations, 1966
   [S.I. 1966 No. 864] 398

PAGE

Visiting Forces and International Headquarters (Application of Law) Order,
  1965 [S.I. 1965 No. 1536] 12, 14, 59, 369, 500, 773
  art. 8 (6) 332, 735, 753, 772

"Zebra" Pedestrian Crossings Regulations, 1971 [S.I. 1971 No. 1524] ...436, 455
  reg. 1 437
  reg. 2 .... 437, 438
  reg. 3 .... **437–8**
      (1) 447, 453
  reg. 4 .... **438,** 441, 445, 453
  reg. 5 .... **438,** 443
      (2) 448
      (3) 443, 444, 447
  reg. 6 .... **439,** 447, 453
  reg. 7 .... 439, 447
  reg. 8 .... 438, 439, **439,** 440, 445, 447, 448, 450, 453, 454
  reg. 9 .... **439,** 453
  reg. 10 .... 438, **439–40,** 454
      (a) 454
      (b) 440, 454, 455
  reg. 11 .... **440,** 455
  reg. 12 .... 438, 440, **440,** 441, 445, 453, 454
  reg. 13 440
  reg. 14 .... 440, **440,** 445, 453
  reg. 15 .... 440, **441,** 453
  Sched. 1 441
  Sched. 2 .... 438, **441–3,** 445
      Pt. I 438, 446
          para. 1 446
              (1) 453
              (2), (3) 446
          para. 2 446
          para. 4 (1), (3) 446
      Pt. II 438, 442
          para. 2 (1), (2), (4) 446
          para. 3 446
              (b) 446
  Sched. 3 .... 437–9, 446
      Pt. I **443–4,** 453
          para. 2 437
          para. 7 .... 447, 453
      Pt. II 444, 453

ABBREVIATIONS

Archbold	... ...	Archbold's "Criminal Pleading, Evidence and Practice".
Cr.L.R.	... ...	The Criminal Law Review.
E. & E. Dig.	... ...	The English and Empire Digest.
Halsbury	... ...	Halsbury's "Laws of England".
Jo.Cr.L.	... ...	The Journal of Criminal Law.
Stone ...	... ...	Stone's "Justices' Manual".

CHAPTER I

DEFINITIONS

In this book various terms are used which, unless the context otherwise requires, will generally be used in the sense given below, but it should be remembered that the meaning of some terms, notably " to permit " and " to use ", varies according to the context of the section of the particular statute in which they are used; also, definitions of the same word may vary as between the Road Traffic Act and the Vehicles (Excise) Act, 1971.

" Magistrates' Court "

" Magistrates' court " includes a juvenile court, but not the Crown Court, except in so far as the powers of the Crown Court on appeal are limited to those of a magistrates' court.

" The Act of 1972 " etc.

References to the Act of 1972 are to the Road Traffic Act, 1972, and earlier Road Traffic Acts are mentioned similarly. The Road Traffic Act, 1972, is a consolidating Act intended to make no alteration in the law. It consolidated most of the Road Traffic Act, 1960, most of the 1962 Act, the whole of the Road Safety Act, 1967, all the Road Transport Lighting Acts, together with the Road Traffic (Driving of Motor Cycles) Act, 1960, the Road Traffic (Driving Instruction) Act, 1967, the Road Traffic (Disqualification) Act, 1970, and the Motor Vehicles (Passenger Insurance) Act, 1971. It incorporated those provisions of the Vehicle and Driving Licences Act not already incorporated in the Vehicles (Excise) Act, 1971, which is sometimes referred to as the Act of 1971. The Road Traffic Regulation Act, 1967, and the Transport Act, 1968 (which are the other major enactments relating to road traffic) together with all other Acts are referred to by their full titles.

" The Act of 1974 "

The Road Traffic Act, 1974 (referred to in the text as " the Act of 1974 ") made extensive and unrelated amendments to the Road Traffic Acts, 1960 and 1972, the Road Traffic Regulation Act, 1967, and the Transport Act, 1968. The amendments effected by the Act are where in operation noted in the text and other important amendments not yet in operation and likely to be in operation within the currency of this edition are usually outlined in the text. As the Road Traffic Act, 1972, the Road Traffic Regulation Act, 1967, and the Transport Act, 1968, are all modern consolidating enactments, where the Act of 1974 enacts new provisions relating to any of these Acts it normally does so by inserting new sections. These may be detected by the use of capital letters (e.g., s. 22A of the Act of 1972 (see p. 295)).

" Motor Vehicle "

" Motor vehicle " is defined for the purposes of the Road Traffic Act and regulations made thereunder by s. 190 of the Road Traffic Act, 1972; such definition would not necessarily apply under the Vehicles (Excise) Act, 1971, but for many purposes it would be the same save that under the Vehicles (Excise) Act, 1971, it need not be intended or adapted for use on a road (see p. 487). The Vehicles (Excise) Act, 1971, uses the term " mechanically propelled vehicle ". Section 190 of the Road Traffic Act, 1972, replaces s. 253 of the Road Traffic Act, 1960, and subs. (1) defines " motor vehicle " as a mechanically propelled vehicle intended or adapted for use on roads. Section 190 reads:—

" (1) In this Act ' *motor vehicle* ' means a mechanically propelled vehicle intended or adapted for use on roads, and ' *trailer* ' means a vehicle drawn by a motor vehicle:
Provided that a side-car attached to a motor cycle shall, if it complies with such conditions as may be specified in regulations made by the Secretary of State, be regarded as forming part of the vehicle to which it is attached and not as being a trailer.
(2) In this Act ' *motor car* ' means a mechanically propelled vehicle, not being a motor cycle or an invalid carriage, which is constructed itself to carry a load or passengers and the weight of which unladen—

    (*a*) if it is constructed solely for the carriage of passengers and their effects, is adapted to carry not more than seven passengers exclusive of the driver, and is fitted with tyres of such type as may be specified in regulations made by the Secretary of State, does not exceed three tons;

    (*b*) if it is constructed or adapted for use for the conveyance of goods or burden of any description, does not exceed three tons, or three tons and a half if the vehicle carries a container or containers for holding for the purpose of its propulsion any fuel which is wholly gaseous at 60° Fahrenheit under a pressure of 30 inches of mercury or plant and materials for producing such fuel;

    (*c*) does not exceed two tons and a half in a case falling within neither of the foregoing paragraphs.

(3) In this Act ' *heavy motor car* ' means a mechanically propelled vehicle, not being a motor car, which is constructed itself to carry a load or passengers and the weight of which unladen exceeds two tons and a half.

(4) In this Act ' *motor cycle* ' means a mechanically propelled vehicle, not being an invalid carriage, with less than four wheels and the weight of which unladen does not exceed eight hundredweight.

(5) In this Act ' *invalid carriage* ' means a mechanically propelled vehicle the weight of which unladen does not exceed five hundredweight and which is specially designed and constructed, and not merely adapted, for the use of a person suffering from some physical defect or disability and is used solely by such a person."

[For the purposes of the minimum age for driving and licensing of drivers and all regulations relating thereto the weight of invalid carriages is varied to 10 cwt. Generally, see p. 4.

" (6) In this Act ' *motor tractor* ' means a mechanically propelled vehicle which is not constructed itself to carry a load, other than the following articles, that is to say, water, fuel, accumulators and other equipment used for the purpose of propulsion, loose tools and loose equipment, and the weight of which unladen does not exceed seven tons and a quarter.

(7) In this Act ' *light locomotive* ' means a mechanically propelled vehicle which is not constructed itself to carry a load, other than any of the articles aforesaid, and the weight of which unladen does not exceed eleven tons and a half but does exceed seven tons and a quarter.

(8) In this Act ' *heavy locomotive* ' means a mechanically propelled vehicle which is not constructed itself to carry a load, other than any of the articles aforesaid, and the weight of which unladen exceeds eleven tons and a half.

(9) For the purposes of this section, in a case where a motor vehicle is so constructed that a trailer may by partial super-imposition be attached to the vehicle in such a manner as to cause a substantial part of the weight of the trailer to be borne by the vehicle, that vehicle shall be deemed to be a vehicle itself constructed to carry a load.

(10) For the purposes of this section, in the case of a motor vehicle fitted with a crane, dynamo, welding plant or other special appliance or apparatus which is a permanent or essentially permanent fixture, the appliance or apparatus shall not be deemed to constitute a load or goods or burden of any description, but shall be deemed to form part of the vehicle."

Section 190 (11) gives power to vary the maximum and minimum weights.

The prescribed conditions as to sidecars are found in reg. 121 of the Motor Vehicles (Construction and Use) Regulations, 1973 (see p. 841 and *Cox* v. *Harrison* on p. 476).

The Road Traffic Regulation Act, 1967, s. 99, contains a similar definition to s. 190. Section 196 (2) of the 1972 Act provides that references in the Act to a class of vehicle or traffic shall be construed as references to a class defined by reference to any characteristics of the vehicles or to any other circumstances whatsoever.

Hover Vehicles

A hovercraft within the meaning of the Hovercraft Act, 1968,

shall be a motor vehicle, whether or not it is adapted or intended for
use on roads, but shall be treated as not being a vehicle of any of the
classes or descriptions specified in s. 190 (2) to (8) of the Act of
1972 (Road Traffic Act, 1972, s. 192 (1)). Regulations may
modify any of the provisions of the 1972 Act in relation to hovercraft (s. 192 (2)). Like provisions are in the Road Traffic Regulation Act, 1967, s. 101. A discussion of the law in relation to hovercraft, written prior to the Hovercraft Act, 1968, is in McNair,
The Law of the Air, 3rd ed., pp. 325–7.

Invalid Carriages

The raising of the weight to 10 cwt. is for the purposes of Pt. III
of the Act of 1972 and Regulations thereunder only; Pt. III relates
to driving licences and driving tests (Motor Vehicles (Driving
Licences) Regulations, 1971, reg. 23). For the purposes of other
Parts of the Road Traffic and Road Traffic Regulation Acts and
of the Motor Vehicles (Construction and Use) Regulations, an invalid carriage exceeding 5 cwt. in unladen weight is a motor
car or, if it has three or less wheels and does not exceed 8 cwt., a
motor cycle; it will also require third-party insurance, though one
of 5 cwt. or less does not (s. 143 (3)). Invalid carriages not exceeding 250 lbs. and incapable under their own power of exceeding
4 m.p.h. and complying with regs. 3 to 6 of the Use of Invalid
Carriages on Highways Regulations, 1970 (S.I. 1970 No. 1391)
shall be treated for the purposes of the Act of 1972 and the Road
Traffic Regulation Act, 1967, as not being motor vehicles (s. 20 of
the Chronically Sick and Disabled Persons Act, 1970). These invalid carriages may also use footpaths and are only required to
show the lights set out in Sched. 1 to the regulations above.

Other Vehicles

"Dual purpose vehicle", "land locomotive" and "land tractor"
are defined in the Motor Vehicles (Construction and Use) Regulations; see also p. 335 as to "dual purpose vehicle", p. 332 as to
"passenger vehicles", p. 333 as to "goods vehicle", and p. 492
as to "works truck".

Change of Use

The term "vehicle" usually means one vehicle, not two linked
together (*Dixon* v. *B.R.S.* (*Pickfords*), *Ltd.* [1959] 1 All E.R. 449).

A poultry shed can be a vehicle (see *Garner* v. *Burr*, p. 497, *post*),
and in *Boxer* v. *Snelling* [1972] R.T.R. 472 a movable stall with
tyred wheels was also held to be a "vehicle" for the purposes of the
Road Traffic Regulation Act, 1967. Where there is no statutory

definition of the word " vehicle " a court should consider in a borderline case not only the construction or nature or function of the contrivance but also the circumstances in which the contrivance is used (*ibid.*).

Note that by virtue of s. 190 (2) goods vehicles are " motor cars " so long as (in most cases) they do not exceed 3 tons in unladen weight. The distinction between heavy and light locomotives and motor tractors on the one hand, and heavy motor cars and motor cars on the other, is that the former are not constructed to carry any load; as to the meaning of " loose equipment ", see under " Weight " on p. 14. In *Thornton* v. *Proudlock* (unreported, Queen's Bench Division, 29th May, 1952) it was held that a tractor with a transport box is a vehicle " adapted for use for the conveyance of goods ". This case was apparently under the Vehicles (Excise) Act and would not necessarily apply under the Road Traffic Act. A locomotive or motor tractor permanently fitted with a crane, dynamo, etc., does not thereby become a goods vehicle (see s. 190 (10)); combine harvesters which are self-propelled would be tractors or locomotives (see *William Gwennap Agricultural, Ltd.* v. *Amphlett* [1957] 2 All E.R. 605). Other cases on the term " goods vehicle " are at pp. 334–335, 495–499.

A mini-car fitted with only one seat but designed with space for another seat which could easily be added was held to be constructed for the carriage of more than one person (*Vincent* v. *Whitehead* [1966] 1 All E.R. 917).

A motor vehicle can change from one type to another (*Keeble* v. *Miller* [1950] 1 All E.R. 261; heavy motor car converted to light locomotive); " constructed " in s. 2 (1) (*b*) of the Act of 1930 (now s. 190 (7) of the Act of 1972) means " constructed as at the time of the offence " not " originally constructed ". The vehicle here was permanently fitted with a fairground lighting plant. " Constructed " usually means " as constructed when completed " (*Millard* v. *Turvey* [1968] 2 All E.R. 7, a case on a motor vehicle chassis). An article at 121 J.P.Jo. 479 discusses conversion of vehicles from one type to another; generally it would seem that there must be a major reconstruction (*Burrows* v. *Berry* (1949), 113 J.P.Jo. 492). Where the word " adapted " is used in the Road Traffic Act disjunctively as an alternative to " constructed " it means " altered so as to make fit ", but, where it is used on its own, the context will often show that " adapted " means " fit and apt " for a purpose without alteration (*Maddox* v. *Storer* [1962] 1 All E.R. 831) as well as " altered". See further *Taylor* v. *Mead* and *Flower Freight Co., Ltd.* v. *Hammond* on pp. 496, 497, and, as to adding cattle containers, p. 16.

Meaning of " Mechanically Propelled "

The term includes not only petrol-driven and oil-driven vehicles, but also, it seems, steam-driven and electrically driven ones (see *Waters* v. *Eddison Steam Rolling Co.* (1914), 78 J.P. 327, where the term interpreted was " locomotive " and the vehicle a steam-roller, and *Elieson* v. *Parker* (1917), 81 J.P. 265, where an electrically propelled bath chair was held to be a vehicle propelled by mechanical power). Section 38 (3) of the Vehicles (Excise) Act, 1971, makes special provision as to electric vehicles. Where a pedal cycle is fitted with an auxiliary engine and the engine is connected up, it is a motor vehicle whether the engine is running or not (*Floyd* v. *Bush* [1953] 1 All E.R. 265). In *Newberry* v. *Simmonds* [1961] 2 All E.R. 318 it was held that a motor car from which the engine had been removed did not thereby cease to be a mechanically propelled vehicle if the evidence admitted the possibility that the engine might shortly be replaced and the motive power restored. Different considerations might apply if the mechanical means of propulsion had been permanently removed; it would be a question of fact and degree in which both the extent to which the power unit and transmission have been removed and the permanence of the removal are matters for consideration (*ibid.*). *Semble*, the onus of proof that a vehicle had ceased to be mechanically propelled would lie on the defence so long as it resembled an ordinary motor vehicle. In *Lawrence* v. *Howlett* [1952] 2 All E.R. 74, the cylinder, piston and connecting rod had been removed temporarily from the engine of an auto-assisted cycle; it was held that it was a pedal cycle, not a motor vehicle. This case is distinguishable from *Floyd* v. *Bush, supra*, on the ground that an auto-assisted cycle is capable of use either as a cycle or as a motor vehicle and, on the special facts, it was not only being used as a pedal cycle but was then incapable of use as a motor vehicle; and in *R.* v. *Tahsin* [1970] R.T.R. 88 a defendant pedalling a moped was held to be rightly convicted under s. 6 (1) of the Road Traffic Act, 1960, and s. 1 (1) of the Road Safety Act, 1967. *Floyd* v. *Bush* was applied and on p. 92 it was explained that the true test by Lord Goddard, C.J., in that case as to whether a vehicle is mechanically propelled is " Is the vehicle constructed so that it can be mechanically propelled? " *not* " Has it an engine which is in working order at the relevant time? " *Newberry's* case was distinguished in *Maclean* v. *Hall* (1962), 77 Sh.Ct.Rep. 161, and in *Smart* v. *Allan* [1962] 3 All E.R. 893 (vehicles without gear box, or with engine in such state that no prospect of vehicle being made mobile, held not motor vehicles), but a broken-down car which can be repaired in a matter of minutes is still a mechanically-propelled vehicle (*Law* v. *Thomas*

(1964), 62 L.G.R. 195). A car is still a motor vehicle though incapable of being started because of a flat battery (*R.* v. *Paul* [1952] N.I. 61). The test to be applied as to whether a vehicle is a mechanically propelled vehicle is whether the stage has been reached that there is no reasonable prospect of the vehicle's ever being made mobile again (*Binks* v. *Department of the Environment* [1975] Crim.L.R. 244).

For the purpose of the Civic Amenities Act, 1967, which relates to the removal of abandoned vehicles, the term " motor vehicle " includes those which are in an unfit as well as in a fit state for use on the road and a chassis or body of a motor vehicle with or without wheels and trailers in similar condition (see s. 27 (1)).

A vehicle was held to be equipped with means for reversing although the reverse gear was not usable because it had been blanked-off (*Baldwin* v. *Worsman* [1963] 2 All E.R. 8; the regulation referring to means of reversing with which this case was concerned has been revoked and the term now occurs only in respect of the Groups covered by a driving licence).

Intended or Adapted for Use on Roads

The vehicle, so far as the Road Traffic Act applies, should be intended or adapted for use on roads. The test as to whether a vehicle is intended or adapted for use on roads is an objective one. It depends neither on the owner's intention nor, unless there is evidence of regular use on roads, on its particular use at the time.

A motor go-kart was held not to be a motor vehicle where there was no evidence of regular use on the road, but it might be otherwise if there was such evidence; the test is whether a reasonable man looking at it would say that one of its uses would be a road use (*Burns* v. *Currell* [1963] 2 All E.R. 297). In *Nichol* v. *Leach* [1972] R.T.R. 476 a mini-car re-built solely for " auto cross " racing was held to have retained its original intended character even though the owner never intended it to be used on roads. *Brown* v. *Abbott* (1965), 109 S.J. 437, where the magistrates' finding that a Ford Anglia adapted for stock car racing was not a mechanically propelled vehicle intended or adapted for use on roads was upheld with reluctance by the High Court, was not cited to the court in *Nichol* v. *Leach*. It is submitted that *Nichol* v. *Leach* is the better authority as its reasoning follows that of *Burns* v. *Currell, supra,* and in particular *Daley* v. *Hargreaves, infra,* in that the intention of the owner was disregarded. A diesel dumper used solely for road construction work and not intended to be driven along the parts of the highway open to the public was held not to be a motor vehicle for insurance purposes (*MacDonald* v. *Carmichael* [1941]

S.C.(J.) 27). Where there was no evidence whether some dumpers were suitable for being driven on the road in transit or to carry material from one site to another, the High Court, following *MacDonald* v. *Carmichael, supra,* held that they were not intended or adapted for use on the road but it was said that the High Court might have found differently had there been evidence of such suitability (*Daley* v. *Hargreaves* [1961] 1 All E.R. 552). It was also said that it might be that the legislature had no particular person's intention in view—manufacturer, seller, owner or user—as to " intended " for use on the road; " intended " may mean no more than suitable or apt for use. In *Chalgray, Ltd.* v. *Aspley* (1965), 109 S.J. 394, a dumper used on a site was from time to time driven on the adjoining road for short distances; it was held that it was not a motor vehicle as there was no proof of general use on roads as opposed to occasional use. The driver's action could not make, in the absence of further evidence, a dumper into a motor vehicle; the fact that a dumper might emerge on the highway did not alone make it a motor vehicle. On the other hand, in *Childs* v. *Coghlan* (1968), 112 S.J. 175, a Euclid earth scraper which was too big to be transportable and the primary uses of which were to dig up earth on building sites and carry that earth to places away from those sites under its own power was held to be intended for use on roads; there was evidence that it could go at 45 m.p.h. It was said that a machine, albeit its primary use was not on roads, which regularly went on roads from one site to another was clearly intended to be used on roads, especially if it had to go under its own power from one site to another. The facts that a dumper could go at a fairly fast speed and that the driver had good forward vision did not make that particular dumper into a motor vehicle in *MacLean* v. *McCabe* [1964] S.L.T.(Sh.) 39; it had no horn or driving mirror. Dumpers and excavators are specially dealt with for excise licence purposes under the Vehicles (Excise) Act, 1971, but see *McCrone* v. *Rigby* (1951), 50 L.G.R. 115. An agricultural tractor can be a vehicle intended or adapted for use on roads (*Woodward* v. *Young* [1958] S.L.T. 289). So can a " Hyster " Grab fitted with an engine and rotating arms in front for picking up goods (*Furdson* v. *McGovern* [1954] A.L.R. 450; the Australian statutory definition was much the same).

Miscellaneous Vehicles

By the Road Traffic Act, 1972, s. 193, an implement for cutting grass controlled by a pedestrian and not capable of being used or adapted for any other purpose shall, for the purposes of the Act, be treated as not being a motor vehicle. By virtue of s. 193 (2) the implement must either be constructed or adapted for use only under the control of a pedestrian or, if it is constructed so that it can be controlled either by a pedestrian or someone carried on it, the implement can only be treated as not being a mechanically propelled vehicle so long as it is controlled on foot. Section 103 of the Road Traffic Regulation Act, 1967, is in like terms. Any other pedestrian-controlled motor vehicle otherwise remains a motor vehicle, unless exempt by regulations.

The term " goods vehicle " is discussed on pp. 334–335 and 495–499.

The term " articulated vehicle " is discussed on p. 10. See also s. 190 (9) on p. 3.

Trolley vehicles are within the Road Traffic Act for some purposes, but not for others (see s. 198). Very few provisions apply to tramcars (*ibid.*). In the case of both trolley vehicles and tramcars, s. 198 applies only to those operated under statutory powers, as defined in s. 198 (7), and the Road Traffic Act, 1972, applies in full to those not so operated. Trolley vehicles, trams, bicycles, horse-drawn carts and hand carts are generally vehicles and carriages within the meaning of most other Acts (see 210 L.T.News. 201) and motor vehicles are carriages within the meaning of the Highway, Town Police Clauses, Public Health and other Acts and byelaws (Road Traffic Act, 1972, s. 195). A bicycle is a vehicle (*Ellis* v. *Nott-Bower* (1896), 60 J.P. 760) and also a carriage (*Corkery* v. *Carpenter* [1950] 2 All E.R. 745).

" Trailer "

" Trailer " is defined in s. 190 (1) of the 1972 Act as a vehicle drawn by a motor vehicle. The term includes an empty poultry shed being drawn along by a tractor (*Garner* v. *Burr* [1950] 2 All E.R. 683), and a hut used as an office so drawn (*Horn* v. *Dobson* [1933] S.C.(J.)1). The Motor Vehicles (Construction and Use) Regulations, 1973, give certain exemptions for trailers forming part of an articulated vehicle or being a land implement (as defined in reg. 3 of the 1973 Regulations; see p. 768). A poultry shed is not a land implement (*Garner* v. *Burr*, *supra*). Nor does a four-wheeled vehicle being towed with two wheels in the air thereby become a two-wheeled trailer (*Carey* v. *Heath* [1951] 2 All E.R. 774). A vehicle and trailer closely coupled together do not thereby become one vehicle (*Dixon* v. *B.R.S. (Pickfords), Ltd.* [1959] 1 All E.R. 449). A mobile car jack, i.e., a long tow bar with two wheels on a short axle at right angles to the tow bar, is a trailer (*Wilkinson* v. *Barrett* (1958), 122 J.P. 349). This case is modified to some extent by reg. 4 (12) of the Motor Vehicles (Construction and Use) Regulations, 1973 (p. 776, *infra*). See also *Brown* v. *Dando*, *infra*, pp. 13 and

336. In *Jenkins* v. *Deane* (1933), 103 L.J.K.B. 250, an insurance
policy excepted use of the insured vehicle " whilst it has a trailer
attached thereto "; towing a broken-down lorry was held not to be
within the exception.   This case was not cited in the other cases
given in this paragraph.   Quarter sessions have held that a van
inhabited by a family can be a trailer (Jo.Crim.L. (1962) 21).   In
Boxer v. *Snelling* [1972] R.T.R. 472 a movable stall with wheels
was held in the circumstances of the case to be a " vehicle ".   It
was said to be a " borderline " case.   Where there is no statutory
definition of " vehicle ", a court should consider not only the construction or nature of the contrivance in a borderline case but also
the circumstances in which the contrivance is used (*ibid.*).

A motor vehicle which is being towed by another motor vehicle
both remains a motor vehicle and becomes for the time being a
trailer also (*Milstead* v. *Sexton* [1964] Crim.L.R. 474), and there is
nothing in the Vehicles (Excise) Act, 1971, to exempt a mechanically
propelled vehicle which is being towed and is for the time being
a trailer (*Cobb* v. *Whorton* [1971] R.T.R. 392).   The vehicle is
" used " for the purposes of insurance while stationary (*Elliott* v.
Grey [1959] 3 All E.R. 733).   A mechanically propelled vehicle does
not cease to be " used " on a road when it is towed by another
vehicle (*Cobb* v. *Whorton, supra; Nichol* v. *Leach* [1972] R.T.R. 476).
The use of the towed vehicle must therefore be covered by insurance,
it must be taxed, and it must comply with the Motor Vehicles
(Construction and Use) Regulations both as a motor vehicle and as
a trailer.   It would be a trailer only, however, if it had ceased to
be mechanically propelled, e.g., if it was a wreck, or if it was not
intended or adapted for use on roads, e.g., a high-powered racing
car designed for use only on a race track (but not a racing car
designed also for ordinary use or even a mini re-built for use in
" auto cross " events: see *Nichol* v. *Leach, supra*).   Even the high-
powered racing car would be liable to excise duty, however, when
on a public road, as the Vehicles (Excise) Act applies to " mechanically propelled vehicles used on public roads " without requiring
that they are intended or adapted for such use.

A car supported on roller skates so that its wheels did not touch
the road surface was held, nevertheless, to be kept " on " a road
for the purposes of s. 8 of the Vehicles (Excise) Act, 1971 (*Holliday*
v. *Henry* [1974] R.T.R. 101), nor would it appear to be on a trailer
(*ibid.*).

Articulated Vehicles

The Road Traffic Act, 1962, s. 18, settled the question whether
an articulated vehicle is one vehicle or a vehicle and a trailer in

favour of the latter view; s. 191 of the 1972 Act (which re-enacted s. 18) reads:—

"A vehicle so constructed that it can be divided into two parts both of which are vehicles and one of which is a motor vehicle shall (when not so divided) be treated for the purposes of this Act as that motor vehicle with the other part attached as a trailer."

The Road Traffic Regulation Act, 1967, s. 100, is in like terms.

The case of *Moscrop and Wills* v. *Blair* (1961), 105 S.J. 950, is thus overruled and the drawing unit of an articulated vehicle is a motor car or heavy car, according to its unladen weight without including the trailer's weight (s. 190 (9) on p. 3). For speed limit purposes, however, an articulated vehicle which falls within the definition in para. 17 of Sched. 5 to the 1967 Act is treated as one vehicle (see p. 336). So long as the drawing unit is equipped with the obligatory front and rear lights and reflectors, the trailer unit of an articulated vehicle need not carry them during daylight under reg. 38 of the Motor Vehicles (Construction and Use) Regulations, 1973, but it must display the obligatory lights and reflectors at night (*Johnston* v. *Cruikshank* [1962] S.L.T. 409).

The effect of *A. Stevens & Co. (Haulage), Ltd.* v. *Brown* [1970] Crim.L.R. 103 (which decided that in measuring the overall length of an articulated lorry with a projecting load the length of the tractor should be excluded) was reversed by the Motor Vehicles (Construction and Use) (Amendment) (No. 2) Regulations, 1971, which revoked reg. 110 (2) of the 1969 Regulations (see now reg. 131 of the 1973 regulations, p. 844).

An articulated vehicle, as defined by reg. 3 (1) of the Motor Vehicles (Construction and Use) Regulations, 1973, is a heavy motor car or motor car with a trailer so attached to the drawing vehicle that part of the trailer is superimposed upon the drawing vehicle, and when the trailer is uniformly loaded, not less than 20 per cent. of the weight of its load is borne by the drawing vehicle; if the towed vehicle is not superimposed on the drawing vehicle, there is not an "articulated vehicle" (*Hunter* v. *Towers* [1951] 1 All E.R. 349).

For the purposes of the Vehicles (Excise) Act, 1971, an articulated vehicle is deemed to be one vehicle and additional trailer duty is not chargeable (Sched. 4, para. 6 (1)). Where, however, the chasses of articulated trailers were constructed at one factory and were towed to another factory for the body work to be completed, a magistrates' court in a test case held that the manufacturer could not rely on this provision to enable him to be entitled to use a trade licence on the trailer for the purposes of s. 35 (4) (*g*) or (*h*) of the Vehicles (Excise) Act, 1971 (see p. 525). There was no appeal.

Drawing of Trailers

The Road Traffic Act, 1972, s. 65, restricts the number of trailers which can be drawn by locomotives, motor tractors, heavy motor cars and motor cars; " trailer " in s. 65 does not include a vehicle used solely for carrying water for the purposes of the drawing vehicle nor any agricultural vehicle not constructed to carry a load (s. 65 (3)). An agricultural vehicle which carries a load off, and never on, the highway is still one constructed to carry a load (*Rothes Transport Co.* v. *Hogg* [1962] S.L.T. 411).

Section 65 is prospectively repealed by the Act of 1974 but the provision repealing it has not yet (July, 1975) been brought into force.

Section 65 also does not apply to the vehicles of H.M. Forces and visiting forces (*ibid.*, s. 187, and Visiting Forces and International Headquarters (Application of Law) Order, 1965: S.I. 1965 No. 1536). Section 65 (4) gives an exemption for the drawing by another motor vehicle of broken-down heavy motor cars and motor cars to which unladen trailers are attached by partial superimposition; in other words, a broken-down articulated vehicle is treated as one trailer under s. 65, not as two, when being towed. But a complete articulated vehicle can itself tow only a water-carrier or agricultural vehicle not constructed to carry a load. A locomotive may tow three trailers. A tractor may tow one laden or two unladen trailers. A heavy motor car or motor car may tow only one trailer by virtue of s. 65 of the 1972 Act save that where one of them is a towing implement and the other is secured to that implement, two may be towed (Motor Vehicles (Construction and Use) Regulations, 1973, reg. 136). A solo motor bicycle may not draw a trailer (other than a broken-down motor cycle); a combination or other three-wheeled vehicle may draw a trailer not exceeding 254 kilos in unladen weight or 1·5 metres in width (Motor Vehicles (Construction and Use) Regulations, 1973, regs. 122 and 123; see pp. 841, 842). An invalid carriage or a straddle carrier may not tow a trailer (*ibid.*, reg. 124; see p. 842). No trailer may be used to convey passengers for hire or reward except as is allowed by the regulation (see reg. 125 on p. 842). No trailer shall be drawn by a public service vehicle (see p. 842) save that one may draw another public service vehicle in an emergency and a gas trailer (see p. 842) or a trailer approved as indicated in the regulation on behalf of the licensing authority may be drawn (reg. 127; see p. 842).

In cases under the Construction and Use Regulations affecting trailers, the regulations themselves should be carefully considered for their definitions and exemptions as to trailers. As to the meaning of "sidecar", see 115 J.P.Jo. 611. In *Brown* v. *Dando* (1954), 118 J.P.Jo. 319, a car was towing a two-wheeled caravan with the aid of a " vandolly ", a small chassis with two wheels; this was held to be a four-wheeled trailer, so that the speed-limit was that applicable to the towing of a four-wheeled trailer. In *Baker* v. *Esau* [1972] Crim.L.R. 559 the justices were held to be " plainly right " in holding that a racing car rigidly placed on a two-wheeled " ambulance trailer " so that its front wheels remained on the road together constituted one trailer, not two.

The permitted length of a combination of vehicles (towing vehicle and trailer or trailers) is indicated by reg. 128 of the 1973 Regulations (see p. 842).

The rearmost trailer must exhibit the drawing vehicle's number, with minor exceptions for works trucks and certain agricultural tractors (Road Vehicles (Registration and Licensing) Regulations, 1971, reg. 22).

A sidecar is part of the motor cycle itself, not of its equipment (*Higgins* v. *Feeney* (1954), 88 I.L.T.R. 152).

The view is advanced at 126 J.P.Jo. 247 that a motor-cyclist who allows a cyclist to hold his shoulder is drawing a trailer.

Attendants on Trailers

By the Road Traffic Act, 1972, s. 34 (1), and subject to reg. 135, *infra*, where a heavy or light locomotive (see p. 3) is drawing a trailer or trailers on a highway (the term " road " is not used), one or more persons, in addition to the two required in the driving-cab, shall be employed for the purpose of attending to the trailer or trailers at the rate of one such additional person for each trailer in excess of one; this requirement does not apply to road rollers while rolling. By s. 34 (2), and subject to reg. 135, *infra*, where any motor vehicle other than a heavy or light locomotive is drawing a trailer or trailers on a highway, one person, in addition to the driver of the vehicle, shall be carried on the vehicle or on a trailer for the purpose of attending to the trailer or trailers. Under s. 34, " trailer " does not include a vehicle used solely for carrying water for the purposes of the drawing vehicle or an agricultural vehicle not constructed to carry a load; " agricultural vehicle " is not defined but " agricultural trailer " is defined in reg. 3 (1) of the Motor Vehicles (Construction and Use) Regulations, 1973, as a trailer the property of a person engaged in agriculture which is not used on a road for the conveyance of any goods or burden other than agricultural produce or articles required for the purposes of agriculture. Further, by reg. 135 of those Regulations (see

p. 849) s. 34 does not apply to articulated vehicles; to a land loco-motive or land tractor driving a land implement or land implement conveyor, or where a land tractor is drawing an agricultural tractor; to motor cars and motor cycles drawing a two-wheeled trailer or to motor cars drawing a four-wheeled one with two close-coupled wheels on each side; to motor tractors drawing closed trailers, con-veying meat between docks, stations and markets, or drawing machines, etc., used for road maintenance, repair or cleansing, or drawing trailers used in street cleansing, refuse disposal or the re-moval of the contents of gullies or cesspools; to works trucks drawing works trailers provided each does not exceed 1525 kilos; to motor cars or heavy motor cars drawing a gas trailer; to motor vehicles drawing a trailer which has no brakes other than a parking brake, and brakes which automatically come into operation on the over-run of the trailer; to a road roller; to British Defence Department vehicles used for their purposes if drawing a trailer fitted with brakes which the driver can apply; to unsteerable broken-down vehicles; to towing implements not in use for towing; to vehicles towed away under a statutory power of removal; to locomotives propelled by the combustion of liquid fuel or electrically whether drawing a trailer or not; or to motor vehicles drawing a trailer with power assisted brakes which can be operated by the driver and are not rendered ineffective by the non-rotation of the driver's engine (where two or more such trailers are carried only one attendant is required who may be either on the drawing vehicle or a trailer). Section 34 applies to Crown vehicles (s. 188 (1)), with the exception above for Defence Department vehicles, and to vehicles of visiting forces (S.I. 1965 No. 1536). Attendants under s. 34 qualify as attendants under Sched. 8, para. 2, of the Regulations (p. 421). The Motor Vehicles (Authorisation of Special Types) Order, 1973 (p. 430), may also require attendants in certain circumstances. See art. 24 (2) and (3) as to the number of attendants required where two motor vehicles are engaged in transporting a wide load.

" Weight "

The provisions of the law relating to weight distinguish between laden and unladen weight; the distinction is relevant because there are prohibitions on the total weight which a laden vehicle may transmit to the road surface, while unladen weight is one of the criteria by which the maximum speed and the excise licence duty are computed.

The Road Traffic Act, 1972, ss. 190 and 194, and the Motor Vehicles (Construction and Use) Regulations, 1973, provide the code in relation to matters arising under the Road Traffic Act and those Regulations. The Vehicles (Excise) Act, 1971, Sched. 6, indicates the method of computing weight for the purposes of that Act, and this Schedule is much longer than s. 194 of the Road Traffic Act. This may result in a vehicle's unladen weight being computed differently under the two Acts (*Mackie* v. *Waugh* [1940] S.C.(J.) 49). The terms of Sched. 6 to the Vehicles (Excise) Act are discussed at p. 515. The Road Traffic Act, 1972, s. 190, as pointed out, *supra*, classifies motor vehicles by their unladen weight into heavy and light locomotives, motor tractors, heavy motor cars, motor cars, motor cycles and invalid carriages. The relevant Construction and Use Regulations are Nos. 40, 41, 44, 78–89, 142 and Schedules 6 and 7 (all set out in the Appendix).

The Road Traffic Act, 1972, s. 194, indicates the method of calculating unladen weight; it reads:—

" For the purposes of this Act and of the Road Traffic Regulation Act 1967, and of any other enactment relating to the use of motor vehicles or trailers on roads, the weight unladen of a vehicle or trailer shall be taken to be the weight of the vehicle or trailer inclusive of the body and all parts (the heavier being taken where alternative bodies or parts are used) which are necessary to or ordinarily used with the vehicle or trailer when working on a road, but exclusive of the weight of water, fuel or accumulators used for the purpose of the supply of power for the propulsion of the vehicle, or, as the case may be, of any vehicle by which the trailer is drawn, and of loose tools and loose equipment."

Section 194 applies for the purposes both of the Act of 1972 and of the Road Traffic Regulation Act, 1967, and also for the purposes of any enactment relating to the use of other motor vehicles or trailers on roads and as if a reference to the propulsion of the vehicle were a reference to the propulsion of any vehicle by which the trailer is drawn (Transport Act, 1968, s. 145 (4)).

By s. 160, persons authorised by highway authorities and police officers authorised on behalf of such authorities by a chief officer of police may cause vehicles and trailers to be weighed, but not unloaded. By reg. 45 of the Road Vehicles (Registration and Licensing) Regulations, 1971, licensing authorities are also given power to require proof of the unladen weight of a vehicle.

The weight of a vehicle which has been registered as being in a heavier class remains at the registered weight in the eyes of the law until it is re-registered as being in another class, though it may be used with a detachable body which, on removal, brings it in fact into that other class (*Scott* v. *Dickson* (1939), 83 S.J. 317).

Loose Equipment

" Loose equipment " does not include loose boards fitted in slots at the side of a lorry and used to enable it to carry a heavier load of coal (*Lowe* v. *Stone* [1948] 2 All E.R. 1076) nor a heavy iron block used for ballast (*London County Council* v. *Hay's Wharf Cartage Co.* [1953] 2 All E.R. 34), but does include movable shelves fitted to slide on brackets in a baker's van and used to facilitate the delivery of goods to customers (*Darling* v. *Burton* [1928] S.C.(J.) 11, approved in *Lowe* v. *Stone*, *supra*). Planks and poles to load oil drums on a vehicle fitted with a diesel lighting plant are " loose tools and equipment " (*Keeble* v. *Miller* [1950] 1 All E.R. 261). Side, tail and front boards which, when in use, were fitted inside the vehicle's sides and secured to posts let into the body were held not to be " loose equipment "; the test is the nature of the super-structure, the use to which it would be put and the character of its attachment to the vehicle, and the question is largely one of fact (*Blaikie* v. *Morrison* [1957] S.L.T. 290).

Removable Containers

A motor lorry, used to carry cattle and sheep, had superimposed on it a removable " float " or large box secured by ropes, and not adapted for use on the lorry alone as a separate body but only in conjunction with the lorry's fixed body. It was held that the float was neither an alternative body nor a part necessary to, or ordinarily used with, the lorry, and should therefore not be in-cluded in computing the unladen weight of the vehicle (*M'Cowan* v. *Stewart* [1936] S.C.(J.) 36). In *Cording* v. *Halse* [1954] 3 All E.R. 287 the Queen's Bench Division came to a like conclusion in respect of a similar vehicle; in *Mackie* v. *Waugh* [1940] S.C.(J.) 49 it was held that a container for transporting sheep, held on a lorry by its own weight and by projections fitted over the platform, removed by a block and tackle and used on the lorry three days a week, was not to be included in its unladen weight. In *Paterson* v. *Burnet* [1939] S.C.(J.) 12, however, the High Court upheld a finding that a lift-able container with roof, sides and floor, secured by bolts and rope cleats, was constructed primarily as an additional body and was not a receptacle, and distinguished *M'Cowan's* case. There is special wording in the Vehicles (Excise) Act, 1971, Sched. 6, so far as the computation of weight for excise duties is concerned, and the cases cited above are distinguishable in that context. A decision of the High Court in Eire on weight as including a con-tainer is *A.-G.* (*de Burca*) v. *Murtagh* (1961), 95 I.L.T.R. 56. The cases cited on p. 414 under " Overhang and Length " may be of some relevance.

Transmission and Ascertainment of Weight

The words " the weight transmitted to the road surface by any two wheels in line transversely " occur in regs. 76, 78, 79 and 80 of the Construction and Use Regulations, 1973 (see pp. 817–821). " Transversely " does not mean " obliquely " or " diagonally " and the wheels concerned are (for a four-wheeled vehicle) the two front or the two back wheels; the measurement is from nearside back to offside back wheel (or nearside front to offside front wheel) and not from offside front to nearside back wheel (*Thomas* v. *Galloway* [1935] S.C.(J.) 27). Regulation 79 indicates in respect of heavy motor cars and motor cars the maximum weights which may be transmitted to the road surface (*a*) by any one wheel where no other wheel is in the same line transversely, (*b*) by any two wheels in line transversely, and (*c*) by all the wheels. Breach of (*a*) or of (*b*) or of (*c*) is in itself an offence and, in a charge in respect of the weight transmitted by two wheels in line transversely, the prosecution need not also show that a forbidden weight was transmitted by all the wheels (*Martin* v. *Robertson* [1949] S.C.(J.) 19). Prosecutions under this regulation are discussed at 125 J.P.Jo. 477 on the question whether there can be offences simultaneously of excess axle weight and excess overall weight; *Martin's* case seems to be in point. Moreover it should be remembered that while the regulations prohibiting excess axle weight are designed primarily to prevent damage to the surfaces and foundations of roads, the regulations prohibiting excess overall weight are designed to ensure that a vehicle does not exceed the weight for which it is designed and constructed to carry loads and is able to pull up within the distance for which its brakes were designed.

The regulations, in limiting the weight transmitted to the road surface, make no exception with regard to the place at which, or the gradient on which, the weight was ascertained. When a weighing was done on ground which was uneven because of the camber of the road and it was considered by the magistrates that a different weight might be shown on a flat surface, it was nevertheless held by the High Court that, if the weighing on the camber showed an illegal weight, an offence had been committed under (what is now) reg. 79 (*Prosser* v. *Richings* [1936] 2 All E.R. 1627). But a weighing done with the engine still running and on an incline was held not to have been properly done (*McMillan* v. *Caledonian Omnibus Co*. (1938), 26 Traff.Cas. 374). Where in any proceedings in Scotland for a road traffic offence any question arises as to a weight of any description in relation to a goods vehicle, a certificate of, or oral evidence by an inspector of weights and measures as to, the accuracy of the weighbridge or weighing machine used shall be sufficient evidence of that fact (Road Traffic Act, 1972, s. 64 (4)); if such evidence is not produced, its lack may be fatal to the prosecution (*Grierson* v. *Clark* [1958] S.L.T. 112). This case would not

necessarily be followed in England, however, as evidence of
mechanical devices is acceptable without proof of their accuracy
if the court think fit and the excess weight shown is considerable
(*cf. Nicholas* v. *Penny* [1950] 2 All E.R. 89). In any proceedings
for an offence under Pt. II of the 1972 Act other than ss. 40 and 60
or under the Construction and Use Regulations, the date marked
on the vehicle under regulations as the date of manufacture shall be
evidence, in England, and sufficient evidence, in Scotland, that it
was manufactured on the date so marked (Road Traffic Act, 1972,
s. 64 (2)).

By reg. 74 of the Construction and Use Regulations (see p. 816),
the unladen weight must be painted on the nearside of locomotives,
motor tractors and heavy motor cars. This does not apply to
heavy motor cars not registered under the Vehicles (Excise) Acts.

The Motor Vehicles (Construction and Use) (Track Laying
Vehicles) Regulations, 1955, and the Motor Vehicles (Authorisation
of Special Types) General Order, 1973, indicate the maximum lawful weights for vehicles to which they apply. Where excess weight
may be allowed under the Special Types Order, all the conditions
as to attendants, etc., must be fulfilled; if one of them is not, an
offence arises under the appropriate regulations of the Construction
and Use Regulations (*Siddle C. Cook, Ltd.* v. *Holden* [1962] 3 All
E.R. 984).

Plated Weights

Regulation 39 of the Motor Vehicles (Construction and Use)
Regulations, 1973, requires all heavy motor cars and motor cars
first registered on or after 1st January, 1968 (not being passenger
or dual-purpose vehicles, land tractors, works trucks or pedestrian-
controlled vehicles), and every trailer manufactured on or after
that date exceeding 1020 kilos in weight unladen (with the exceptions mentioned in reg. 39 (1) (*c*) on p. 796) to be equipped with a
plate securely affixed to the vehicle in a conspicuous and readily
accessible position and containing the particulars required by Sched.
2, including maximum axle, gross and train weights for vehicles
(see p. 855). All such vehicles are still subject to the weight limits
laid down in regs. 78 to 82. No provision is made by s. 64 of the
Road Traffic Act, 1972, as to weights marked on a plate affixed
pursuant to reg. 39 being evidence of the permissible weights; possibly the plate might be deemed to be an admission at common
law by the vehicle owner as to the permitted weights, but this is
doubtful as the weights are those fixed by the manufacturer and
the owner is merely saying on the plate what the manufacturer
has said and this is hearsay. The prosecutor should seemingly

prove his case by evidence of the actual weight and type of vehicle, though the marking of the unladen weight on a locomotive, tractor or heavy motor car under reg. 74, being done by the owner, is presumably an admission by him. Where a goods vehicle has a " Ministry plate " issued under the Road Traffic Act, 1972, Pt. II, and the Goods Vehicles (Plating and Testing) Regulations, 1971 (S.I. 1971 No. 352), s. 64 (1) of the Act of 1972 says that if in proceedings for an offence under the Construction and Use Regulations under s. 40 (5) any question arises as to a weight of any description specified in a plating certificate (see *infra*) for a goods vehicle and a weight of that description is marked on the vehicle in the Ministry plate, it shall be assumed, unless the contrary is proved, that the weight marked on the vehicle is the weight so specified; by reg. 142 (see p. 853) the certified weights, which may be less than those allowed by regs. 79 to 88, must not be exceeded and so evidence that the actual weight exceeded the plated weight will suffice. It was held in *William Hampton, Ltd. and Another* v. *Bryan Dixon*, 22nd May, 1973 (unreported), that s. 40 (5) of the Act (*supra*) obviated any necessity for the prosecution to serve a notice on the defendant to produce the plating certificate. Once the prosecution have proved the weight shown on the Ministry plate on the vehicle, it is at once assumed by virtue of s. 40 (5), in the absence of evidence to the contrary, that the plating certificate shows the same figure (*ibid.*). See s. 64 (2), *supra*, as to proof of date of manufacture.

In *Wurzal* v. *Reader Bros., Ltd. and Another* [1973] Crim.L.R. 640 justices were held to be wrong in dismissing information under reg. 121 of the 1969 Construction and Use Regulations (now reg. 142 of the 1973 Regulations: see p. 853) because the traffic examiner did not produce his authority when requiring the vehicle to proceed to a weighbridge under s. 224 of the 1960 Act. It was held that production of authority was only a prerequisite of prosecutions under s. 224 of the 1960 Act (now s. 160 of the 1972 Act) and it did not prevent prosecution for an overweight vehicle under reg. 121 of the 1969 Construction and Use Regulations.

Defences to Weight Prosecutions

Section 40 (6) of the Act of 1972 reads:—

" (6) In any proceedings for an offence under subsection (5) above in which there is alleged a contravention of or failure to comply with a construction and use requirement relating to any description of weight applicable to a goods vehicle, it shall be a defence to prove either—

(*a*) that at the time when the vehicle was being used on the road it was proceeding to a weighbridge which was the nearest available one to the place where the loading of the vehicle was completed for the purpose of being weighed, or was proceeding from a weighbridge after

being weighed to the nearest point at which it was reasonably practicable to reduce the weight to the relevant limit, without causing an
obstruction on any road; or

(b) in a case where the limit of that weight was not exceeded by more
than five per cent., that that limit was not exceeded at the time
the loading of the vehicle was originally completed and that since
that time no person has made any addition to the load."

The burden of proof of establishing a defence under s. 40 (6) is
upon the defendant and the standard is that of a balance of probabilities. Thus in *Thurrock D. C.* v. *L. A. A. Pinch, Ltd.* [1974]
R.T.R. 269 a magistrates' court was held to be wrong in dismissing
charges on the ground that because they were in doubt whether
or not the vehicles were proceeding to a weighbridge to be weighed,
the defendant was entitled to the benefit of that doubt. Local
knowledge as to the location of weighbridges may be important
in cases under s. 40 (6) (a); *semble*, if the paragraph is interpreted
literally, a defendant driver who is on his way to a weighbridge
which he genuinely believes to be the nearest one but which in fact
is not will be unable to set up the defence, but there is obvious
mitigation. The weighbridge to which a driver is proceeding must
be the " nearest available " one and it is submitted that, when the
driver leaves the place of loading, he must, to avail himself of the
defence, believe that there is a weighbridge open within a reasonable
distance; a driver who starts on a long journey late in the evening,
when the weighbridges are all shut, should not be able to say in
his defence that he is on the way to the nearest available weighbridge which is perhaps 150 miles' and several hours' driving away.
If he does and it is shown that he could not reasonably have believed
that there was a weighbridge open within a reasonable distance,
on this argument he should be convicted; the standard of proof,
no doubt, on him is that of balance of probabilities. When he is
coming from the weighbridge after being weighed and found overweight, he must, to avail himself of the defence under the second
part of s. 40 (6) (a), be going to the nearest practicable unloading
point. Often, there may be no such place available, e.g., because
the yard where he loaded is shut for the evening; it is suggested
that he may not then proceed on his journey but should take the
vehicle off the highway, or, at least, stop driving until the yard
opens again or some of the excess load can be put into other vehicles.
The " 5 per cent. addition " under s. 40 (6) (b) is to deal with cases
where snow or petrol, etc., have increased the weight. By s. 57 (7)
of the 1972 Act, powers of immediately prohibiting the use on the
road of overweight vehicles are conferred; and by s. 64 (3), if
any question arises whether a weight has been reduced to the
permitted limit in proceedings under s. 57 (7), the burden of proof

is on the accused. Where the burden of proof lies on a defendant, the standard of proof is only on a balance of probabilities (*R.* v. *Carr-Briant* [1943] K.B. 607).

" Driver "

" Driver " (except for the purposes of s. 1 (causing death by dangerous driving)), where a separate person acts as steersman of a motor vehicle, includes that person as well as any other person engaged in the driving of the vehicle, and the expression " drive " shall be construed accordingly (Road Traffic Act, 1972, s. 196). A like definition is in the Road Traffic Regulation Act, 1967, s. 104 (1), except for the purposes of s. 42 thereof, which relates to parking places on highways where charges are made. By s. 34 (1) of the 1972 Act two persons shall be employed in driving or attending to a heavy or light locomotive whilst it is being driven on a highway (the term " road " is not used) but only one need be so employed where no trailer is being drawn, with exceptions (see p. 13).

There are a number of cases on whether or not a person is driving and it is not easy to reconcile the cases. In *Saycell* v. *Bool* [1948] 2 All E.R. 83 a person who sat in the driving seat, released the brake and let the vehicle run a hundred yards downhill was held to " drive " it although there was no petrol in the tank and the engine was not started. In *Ames* v. *MacLeod* [1969] S.C. 1 the Court of Session in Scotland held that a person " drove " his car which had run out of petrol when he steered it by placing his hand on the wheel while walking beside it as it coasted down a slight incline in the road. In *R.* v. *Munning* [1961] Crim.L.R. 55 a magistrates' court held that pushing a motor scooter was not driving. In *R.* v. *Roberts* (*No.* 2) [1965] 1 Q.B. 85 releasing the brake of a lorry parked on a hill and putting the vehicle in motion so that it ran down the hill was held not to be " driving ". A learner-driver, sitting in the driving seat, is a driver, although the instructor who retains simultaneous control of the car may also be a driver (*Langman* v. *Valentine* [1952] 2 All E.R. 803; see also *R.* v. *Wilkins* (1951), 115 J.P. 443, Q.S.). In *Langman's* case the instructor had his hands on the brake and steering-wheel; where a licensed person merely sat beside a young boy (who was in the driving seat) and, though able to reach the steering-wheel and footbrake, apparently did not have a hand on the wheel, he was held not to be a driver as he was not in control of the car (*Evans* v. *Walkden* [1956] 3 All E.R. 64). A passenger awoke to find the driver gone and the car moving; he steered it for 200 yards until he could safely stop. He was held to be a " driver " (*R.* v. *Kitson* (1955), 39 Cr.App.R. 66). A taxi-driver left his taxi which had automatic transmission with the

engine running.   The defendant who had no intention of driving sat
on the driver's seat.   In the course of a struggle with the taxi-driver
the defendant's foot touched the accelerator causing the taxi to drive
along the road, mount the pavement and swerve back to the offside.
The defendant was held not to be " driving " (*Blayney* v. *Knight*
[1975] Crim.L.R. 237).

It was held in *Wallace* v. *Major* [1946] 2 All E.R. 87 that the
steersman of a towed vehicle is not a driver on the ground that the
definition of " driver ", as re-enacted in s. 196 of the 1972 Act,
contemplates a steersman in charge of the same vehicle as some
other person, e.g., on a traction engine, and such a towed steersman
would not be guilty of an offence described as driving, e.g., careless
driving, driving while disqualified or driving without a licence,
although he would be guilty of " using ".   Finally, in the most
recent case, *R.* v. *MacDonagh* [1974] R.T.R. 372, it was held that
a person who pushed a car along a road with both feet on the
ground with one arm in the car to control the steering wheel was
not " driving " the car and could not be therefore convicted of
driving while disqualified.

It will be noted that the facts of *Ames* v. *MacLeod* and *R* v. *Mac-
Donagh* are virtually indistinguishable.   *R.* v. *MacDonagh* must be
taken as representing the law in England and Wales.   The conflict
between the two cases may be the reason for a court of five judges
in the latter case.   A reading of the judgment of Lord Widgery, C.J.,
in *MacDonagh* leads, it is submitted, to the following conclusions:—

(1) The primary consideration as to whether a person is " driv-
     ing " is essentially a question of fact, dependent on the
     degree and extent to which the person has control of the
     direction and movement of the vehicle.
(2) One test is whether the accused was " in a substantial sense
     controlling the movement and direction of the car " (*Ames* v.
     MacLeod).   A person cannot be said to be " driving "
     unless he satisfies this test.
(3) The fact that a person satisfies the test of control in *Ames* v.
     MacLeod is not necessarily exhaustive.   It has still to be
     considered whether the activity in question could fall within
     the ordinary meaning of the word " driving " in the English
     language.

Applying these principles it was held that the defendant in *Mac-
Donagh* was " pushing " rather than " driving ".   Similarly it was
suggested that a person pushing a broken-down motor cycle and
walking beside it could not be said to be " driving ".   On the
other hand it was suggested that it would be possible to find as a fact

that a person was driving if a motorist pushing the vehicle had one foot in the car in order to make more effective use of the controls.

The principle of *Wallace* v. *Major* that a steersman of a towed vehicle is not a " driver " must also be regarded as doubtful as a result of *MacDonagh*, where the court doubted whether a correct conclusion was reached on the facts in that case. It is submitted that whether a steersman can be said to drive a towed vehicle depends on the extent and degree to which he controls the movement and direction of the towed vehicle. If, for example, the vehicle is towed by a rigid towbar and the brakes of the towed vehicle are inoperative, it might well be said that that person is only " steering "; using the ordinary meaning of the word, it would be difficult to say that he was " driving ". On the other hand, if the vehicle is towed by a rope or chain, with the person in charge of the towed vehicle having to be prepared to use his brakes, surely that person may well be said to be " driving " and not merely " steering "?

In *R.* v. *Shaw* (*Kenneth*) [1975] R.T.R. 160, a conviction under s. 6 (1) of the Act of 1972 was set aside when the recorder did not leave to the jury the question of whether the steersman of a towed vehicle was " driving ".

Pedalling an auto-assisted cycle without starting the engine is "driving away " (*Floyd* v. *Bush* [1953] 1 All E.R. 265; *R.* v. *Tahsin*, on p. 6, where a defendant pedalling a moped with the engine out of action was held to be driving within the meaning of ss. 5 and 6 of the Act of 1972; see also *Lawrence* v. *Howlett* on p. 6). Driving a towing vehicle in such a way that the towed one snakes dangerously about the road can be dangerous driving (*Anderson* v. *Transport Board* [1964] N.Z.L.R. 881).

In Pt. VI of the Transport Act, 1968, which relates to drivers' hours, s. 95 (3) refers to " employee-drivers " and " owner-drivers " and s. 103 (3) declares that references to a person driving a vehicle are references to his being at the driving controls of the vehicle for the purpose of controlling its movement, whether it is in motion or stationary with its engine running.

A young girl entered a motor car parked in a private forecourt off the road, intending to drive it round the forecourt only and not to go on the road. Through her inexperience she engaged reverse gear and the car went on to the road. On being charged with careless driving and with uninsured use, she contended that she was not driving " on the road " inasmuch as she was on it involuntarily and also that she was not using the car on the road. Her conviction on both charges was upheld by the Queen's Bench Division (*Collyer* v. *Dring*, 22nd January, 1953).

" Driving or Attempting to Drive "

It should be noted that the relevant words in s. 8 (1) of the 1972 Act as to the person from whom a constable may lawfully require a breath test with a view to a subsequent prosecution under s. 6 of the Act for driving with excess blood-alcohol are " driving or attempting to drive ". The words " the driver " or " actual driving " do not appear in the provisions of the Act relating to the offence and the words cited should be interpreted in accordance with *Pinner* v. *Everett* and the other cases cited on p. 184, where their meaning is discussed.

Automatism

The person sitting in the driving seat when the car is in motion is deemed to be the driver and the onus is on him to show that he was incapable of controlling the car by reason of having an epileptic fit or being in a coma or being knocked unconscious by a stone or being under attack by a swarm of bees; unless he can show that he was temporarily incapable through some such circumstances, he is responsible as the driver (*Hill* v. *Baxter* [1958] 1 All E.R. 193). Automatism connotes in law no wider concept than involuntary movement of a person's body or limbs (*Watmore* v. *Jenkins* [1962] 2 All E.R. 868). There must be evidence to raise a reasonable doubt whether the driver's bodily movements which turned his car hither and thither and kept it moving at a fairly steady speed were wholly uncontrolled and uninitiated by any function of conscious will (*ibid.*). That was a case of dangerous driving where the defendant, a diabetic, was in a state of confusion through his illness but, as he had driven for five miles in that state, a conviction was directed. As to the burden of proof where a defence of automatism is raised or suggested, see also *R.* v. *Budd* on p. 269, *Stevenson* v. *Beatson* and *Cook* v. *Atchison* on p. 270 and *R.* v. *Sibbles* on p. 269 as to a driver who knows that he is subject to dizzy spells.

Taking and Driving Away

" Driving away " under s. 271 of the 1960 Act (now replaced in England and Wales by s. 12 of the Theft Act), means causing the vehicle to move from the place where it is standing; where one man held the steering wheel and two others pushed, without the engine being started, all were held to be driving away (*Shimmell* v. *Fisher* [1951] 2 All E.R. 672). Pedalling an auto-assisted cycle without starting the engine was " driving away " under s. 217 (*Floyd* v. *Bush* [1953] 1 All E.R. 265). Releasing a vehicle's brake at the top of an incline and then quitting it, so that it runs downhill unattended, is not taking and driving it away under s. 217; there cannot be driving unless the defendant is in the driving seat or in control of the steering wheel and also has something to do with the propulsion of the vehicle (*R.* v. *Roberts* [1964] 2 All E.R. 541). The offence under s. 12 of the Theft Act, 1968, is now " takes " and the words " and driving away " are omitted. It was held in *R.* v. *Bogacki and Others* [1973] R.T.R. 384 that " taking " should not be equated with " using "; the word " takes " requires not only an unauthorised taking of possession or control of the vehicle but also some movement of the vehicle however small. Thus taking control of a bus and unsuccessfully trying to start the engine so that the bus did not move could not justify a conviction for " taking " the bus contrary to s. 12, only for attempting to do so (*ibid.*). However, the conveyance does not have to be moved in its own element for an offence to be committed. *P* was convicted of " taking " a rubber dinghy by putting it on a road trailer and driving the trailer away (*R.* v. *Pearce* [1973] Crim.L.R. 321).

Pushing as Driving

Proceedings are sometimes brought against persons who have been disqualified from driving or have no driving licence when they have been caught pushing a car or motor cycle, with the engine not running, or against persons pushing a car with someone else at the steering-wheel. In the former case the defendant would be " driving " if he was in the driving seat or otherwise in control of the steering and had something to do with the propulsion, e.g., if he was engaged in a common design with his friends who were pushing, if not actually pushing himself (*R.* v. *Roberts* [1964] 2 All E.R. 541). If neither he nor his accomplices had any control over the steering, they would not appear to be driving. In the other case (the accomplices pushing from behind or at the side but with no personal control of the steering), it is submitted that they would be aiding and abetting the one in control of the steering, if they were all engaged in a common design, and could therefore properly be charged (*Shimmell* v. *Fisher* [1951] 2 All E.R. 672). These cases suggest that pushing motor vehicles with control of the steering would be " driving ", although sometimes the facts would point also to an attempt to drive; in almost all cases it would be " using " by those engaged in the common design whether there was " driving " or not. The position has now been clarified by the decision of *R.* v. *MacDonagh* [1974] R.T.R. 373. The primary test of whether a person drives (see p. 22) is one of fact whether the person is substantially controlling the movement and direction of the vehilce (see *Ames* v. *MacLeod* on p. 21), but even if the activity of the person satisfies this test, it is not necessarily exhaustive.

It has still to be considered whether the activity in question can fall within the ordinary meaning of the word " driving " in the English language. Thus a person who pushed a car with two feet on the ground and one arm in the car on the steering wheel could not be said to be " driving ", he was " pushing " (*R.* v. *MacDonagh, supra*). It was also said that it mattered not how the vehicle was propelled, whether it was moving under its own power, driven by the force of gravity or even pushed by others but there must be a distinction between " pushing " and " driving ". It was said a person pushing a broken-down motor cycle could not be said to be " driving " even though he is in full control of its steering and possibly brakes. It was observed that cases such as these are near the borderline: if for example the defendant in *R.* v. *MacDonagh* also had had one foot in the car to control the brakes he might well be properly convicted.

For the purpose of reporting accidents under s. 25 of the 1972 Act, " driver " means the person who takes the vehicle on the road, and he remains the driver whilst in the car, although he may have stopped the car and engine (*Jones* v. *Prothero* [1952] 1 All E.R. 434). In *Hamilton* v. *Jones* (1926), 42 T.L.R. 148, a demand for production of a driving licence made several hours after the accused had been seen driving was held to have been made to " the driver ".

The term " rides " is discussed on p. 292.

" Road "

" Road " means any highway and any other road to which the public has access and includes bridges over which a road passes (Road Traffic Act, 1972, s. 196; Road Traffic Regulation Act, 1967, s. 104 (1)). Public bridges are highways so far as the right of passage is concerned (Halsbury, 3rd ed., vol. 19, p. 13). The Highways Act, 1959, s. 294, includes bridges and tunnels over or through which a highway passes as a part of the highway for the purposes of that Act. The Vehicles (Excise) Act, 1971, affects vehicles on " public roads " (i.e., those repairable at the public expense; see s. 38) and certain of the Construction and Use Regulations only apply to vehicles on highways (see the Regulations, reg. 4, *infra*, p. 774). The term " highway " is discussed in Jowett's Dictionary of English Law, and it is narrower than " road " under the Road Traffic Acts. There should be some evidence of permanent dedication to the public; the maxim is " once a highway, always a highway " and that would not apply to some of the ways held to be " roads " in the cases cited below.

" Road " has the same meaning under Pts. V and VI of the Transport Act, 1968 (see ss. 92 (1) and 103 (1)) as it has under the 1972 Act.

Generally it may be said to be a matter of fact and degree whether it is a " road " or " public place ", the burden of proof in both cases being usually on the prosecution.

In *Randall* v. *Motor Insurers' Bureau* [1969] 1 All E.R. 21, a vehicle was deemed on a road when it was partly on the road and partly on private land and in *Holliday* v. *Henry* [1974] R.T.R. 101, a vehicle was held to be " on " a road when, because a roller skate was interposed between each wheel and the surface of the road, it could not be said to be in actual physical contact with the road.

Public Access

The definition in the Road Traffic Act shows that the class of road intended is wider than the class of public roads to which the public has access in virtue of a positive right belonging to the public, and flowing either from statute or prescriptive user. A forecourt of an hotel was private property and the public had no access as of right but there was no obstruction of any kind separating the forecourt from High Street, Sutton, and members of the public had in fact used the forecourt not only to reach the hotel but also as a short cut from High Street to another street. On occasions vehicles had been along it. The forecourt was held to be a road (*Bugge* v. *Taylor* (1940), 104 J.P. 467). Applying *Harrison* v. *Hill, infra*, and *R.* v. *Waters* on p. 173, it was held to be a matter of fact and degree as to whether the public generally have access (*R.* v. *Shaw* [1974] R.T.R.225) (lane on council estate frequently used by pedestrians as a short cut between two public roads found to be a road to which the public have access). The footway as well as the carriageway is included in the definition of " road " in the Road Traffic Act (*Bryant* v. *Marx* (1932), 96 J.P. 383). But a place is not necessarily a road, even if it is not separated by a wall or rail from the highway, and the forecourt of a shop not separated from the street pavement but used only by the customers and not habitually used by the public was held not to be a road (*Thomas* v. *Dando* [1951] 1 All E.R. 1010). Contrast *White* v. *Cubitt* (1930), 94 J.P. 60, p. 174, *infra*, as to " public place ". In *Baxter* v. *Middlesex County Council* [1956] Crim.L.R. 561, a forecourt was held on the facts not to be part of the highway. Normally, a right of way extends to the whole space between the fences, and a grass verge between the pavement and the fence was held to be part of a road in *Worth* v. *Brooks* [1959] Crim. L.R.855. In *A.-G.* v. *Beynon* [1969] 2 All E.R. 263, it was held that the mere fact that a road ran between fences or hedges did not give rise by itself to a presumption. It was first necessary to decide whether the fences were put up by reference to the highway or for some other reason. If it would appear that the fences were put up with reference to the highway a rebuttable presumption of law then arose that the highway extended to the whole space between the fences and was not confined to such part as had been made up. A cul-de-sac can be a road (*Bass* v. *Boynton* [1960] Crim. L.R. 497). Nor does it matter if the road is not made up (*ibid.*). In *Griffin* v. *Squires* [1958] 3 All E.R. 468 on the facts a car park was held not to be a road, but a conviction was upheld where a jury, on a proper direction, had found a market place to be a road (*R.* v. *Waterfield* (1964), 48 Cr.App.R. 42, is the only report on this point). A road led from the public highway to a Government depôt and had a solid white line half-way across it from about half-way along. It was held that the part between the highway and the white line was a road, there being no obstacle or prohibition, express or implied, to any member of the public till he reached the white line, and the road being available to the public (*Chapman* v. *Parlby* (1964), 62 L.G.R. 150). A road in the docks, to which the general public do not have access either by right or tolerance of the docks authority, is not a road under the Road Traffic Acts (*Buchanan* v. *Motor Insurers' Bureau* [1955] 1 All E.R. 607, but see now the Port of London Act, 1968, *infra*, and s. 160 (7) of the 1972 Act (p. 30) which includes within the definition of road any " harbour " for the purposes of that section). A road inside a factory, which only passholders could enter through gates guarded by the police, is not a road to which the public has access (*O'Brien* v. *Trafalgar Insurance Co.* (1945), 109 J.P. 107). In *Harrison* v. *Co-operative Insurance Co., Ltd.* (1968), 118 N.L.J. 910, a road inside factory premises was used by the public to gain access to a weighbridge and to avoid congested highways; a " private road " sign had been removed some time previously. It was held to be a road to which the public had access. A quayside where the public were free to walk or motor and where there was no notice or hindrance to stop them was held to be a road in *Newcastle Corporation* v. *Walton* [1957] Crim.L.R. 479.

In Scotland, the private drive leading to a house has been held to be a road (*Davidson* v. *Adair* [1934] S.C. (J.) 37), but this case will not be followed in England (*Knaggs* v. *Elson* (1965), 109 S.J. 596) and it was doubted in *Hogg* v. *Nicholson* [1968] S.L.T., at p. 268. So has a road leading off the public road to a farm-house; this road had no gate and was maintained by the farmer, who sometimes turned away people using it, but at other times people with no business at the farm used it (*Harrison* v. *Hill* [1932] S.C.(J.) 13). In *Hogg* v. *Nicholson, supra*, a road, marked " private road " on an estate served a few houses but was used by police cars, visitors and delivery vans; a sub-post-office to which people on the estate and from a village a mile away had access as of right was on the road. It was held to be a road to which the public had access; " private " notices are thus not conclusive. *Harrison* v. *Hill* was distinguished in *R.* v. *Beaumont* [1964] Crim.L.R. 665, where an occupation road led to a farm, to a site for 200–250 caravans on that farm, and to a river where anglers went by leave of the farmer, and was also used by picnickers. At the entrance there was an ever-open gate, a 10 m.p.h. speed limit sign and two " Tresspassers will be prosecuted " signs. It was held that there was no evidence that the general public used the road and the fact that a large number of persons in a particular class of people used it did not make it a road. In *Knaggs* v. *Elson, supra*, a cul-de-sac led to thirty-six houses; there was no gate but there were notices reading " Private Property—No Parking ". There was evidence that a motorist not living there had turned his car round there, but this was held to be insufficient to show that the cul-de-sac was a road used by the public in general. If only a restricted class of the public is admitted, it is not a road; if only a restricted class is excluded, it would be a road (*cf. R.* v. *Waters* on p. 173). The test as to what " access " is was said by Lord Sands in *Harrison's* case (*ibid.*, p. 17) to be: " any road may be regarded as a road to which the public have access upon which members of the public are to be found who have not obtained access either by overcoming a physical obstruction or in defiance of prohibition express or implied." This test was approved and applied by the Divisional Court in *Houghton* v. *Scholfield* [1973] R.T.R. 239, where a justices' finding that a cul-de-sac behind some shops was part of a road was upheld because the public had been found there and there was no physical obstruction or prohibition express or implied.

Car Parks and Forecourts

There must be a mode of communication which can be described in ordinary speech as a road and the mere possibility of vehicular access is not enough; one must first find a road and then ask if it is a road to which the public has access (*Purves* v. *Muir* [1948] S.C.(J.) 122). A courtyard leading off a highway to serve private premises was held not to be a road (*Henderson* v. *Bernard* [1955] S.L.T.(Sh.) 27) and in *Heath* v. *Pearson* [1957] Crim.L.R. 195 a yard serving several houses was held on the facts not to be a road. A drive-in theatre can be a highway " open to or used by the public " (*Dobell* v. *Petrac* [1961] V.R. 70 (Aus.)). A cul-de-sac may be a road (*Bass* v. *Boynton* [1960] Crim.L.R. 497): a justices' finding that a cul-de-sac behind some shops adjoining a road leading to a multi-storey car park was part of a road was upheld in *Houghton* v. *Scholfield* [1973] R.T.R. 239; but in *Griffin* v. *Squires* [1958] 3 All E.R. 468 a car park was held not to be one; the fact that the public have access to it does not of itself make a place a road (*ibid.*). Streatfield, J., said that no one in the ordinary acceptance of the word " road " would think of a car park as a road. Contrast *R.* v. *Waterfield* on p. 28: market place as a " road ". See also *Bugge* v. *Taylor*, *Thomas* v. *Dando* and *Baxter* v. *Middlesex County Council* (all *supra*) as to forecourts and *Newcastle Corporation* v. *Walton* (*supra*) as to a quayside. The fact that an area is private land does not prevent it from being part of a road (*Norton* v. *Hayward* (1968), 112 S.J. 767).

Dock, Airfield and Crown Roads

The Port of London Act, 1968, s. 199, applied a number of sections of the Road Traffic Acts to roads within the jurisdiction of the Port of London Authority, and the British Transport Commission Act, 1956, as extended by s. 20 of the like Act of 1959, likewise applied a number of sections of the same Acts within dock or harbour premises of the Commission. " Dock road " is defined in both Acts as any road, pier, wharf, quay, bridge, work or land so situate. The Airports Authority Act, 1965, s. 12, applied the enactments relating to road traffic, including the lighting and parking of vehicles, and statutory instruments made thereunder, to roads within aerodromes owned or managed by that authority. Any road or place within an aerodrome in the Metropolitan Police District is deemed to be a street or place under s. 35 of the London Hackney Carriage Act, 1831. Section 1 of the Civil Aviation Act, 1968, applied all enactments relating to road traffic, including lighting and parking, to roads on airport authority and local authority airports subject to any modifications made by order of the Secretary of State in respect of a particular airport road. By virtue of para. 3 of Sched. 10 to the 1972 Act the references to the former Road Traffic Acts, etc., in the Acts cited shall be deemed to refer to the corresponding provision in the Road Traffic Act, 1972. Section 160 (7) of the Act of 1972 (inserted by s. 14 of the Act of 1974) which relates to the weighing of motor vehicles (see p. 15) defines a road for the purpose of that section as including any land forming part of a harbour or adjacent to a harbour and occupied wholly or partly for the purpose of harbour operations. A Crown road is defined in s. 149 of the Transport Act, 1968, as a "road, other than a highway, to which the public has access by permission granted by the appropriate Crown authority, or otherwise by or on behalf of the Crown." Generally, therefore, a Crown road would come within the definition of " road " within the meaning of the Road Traffic Act, 1972, s. 196, and the Road Traffic Regulation Act, 1967, s. 104 (1) (see p. 26). Section 149 (1) of the Transport Act, 1968, enables the road traffic enactments to be applied by order to Crown roads. The purpose of the section, it is understood, is to enable provisions to be applied to particular Crown roads which, because they might affect the status of the Crown road, could not otherwise be made. It is, therefore, submitted that statutory provisions which apply on roads generally and relate to vehicles and persons and which do not affect the interests of the Crown adversely will apply on Crown roads as they do elsewhere. Thus, it is submitted, a member of the public charged for example with dangerous or careless driving or a drink/driving offence cannot escape liability because the offence took place on a Crown road. A statute will necessarily bind the Crown if it is apparent that the Act would be wholly frustrated unless the Crown were bound (*Province of Bombay* v. *Bombay Corporation* [1947] A.C. at p. 63). As to the application of road traffic legislation to vehicles and persons in the service of the Crown, see p. 60.

Other Roads

A highway remains a highway though temporarily roped off (*McCrone* v. *Rigby* (1952), 50 L.G.R. 115; *Norton* v. *Hayward, supra*).

The Concise Oxford Dictionary defines " road " as a line of communication for use of foot passengers and vehicles. The term " road " can include a road to which the public of a foreign country have access in relation to proceedings against a serviceman for committing a civil offence outside Great Britain (*Cox* v. *Army Council* [1962] 1 All E.R. 880). The onus is on the prosecution to prove that a road is one within the Act (*Williams* v. *Boyle* (1962), 106 S.J. 939), and also to prove that it is a " public place " (*Pugh* v. *Knipe* [1972] Crim.L.R. 247). The meaning of " public road " in the Vehicles (Excise) Act is discussed at 120 J.P.Jo. 54. A lay-by was held part of a public road for this purpose though not maintained by the highway authority as such (*McNeill* v. *Dunbar* [1965] S.L.T.N. 79). The detailed definitions of " road " and " public place " in an Irish statute were considered in *A.-G.* v. *Farrel* (1954), 88 I.L.T.R. 174, a case on a road in hospital grounds. A footpath and a bridleway (defined *infra*) would not normally be roads under the Road Traffic Act save as indicated *infra*. The reference in s. 18 of the Road Traffic Act, 1960 (now s. 36 of the 1972 Act), to " any road being a footpath or bridleway " is not overlooked but it is submitted that it does not make a place unsuited for vehicles into a road, especially as s. 18 is not a definition section.

Any court before determining whether a way has been dedicated as a highway shall take into consideration any map, plan, local history or other document tendered in evidence, attaching such weight thereto as it thinks proper (Highways Act, 1959, s. 35). Such maps are not evidence of the boundaries of the highway (*Webb* v. *Eastleigh Borough Council* (1957), 56 L.G.R. 124). If a road is shown on a " definitive map " prepared under the Country-side Act, 1968, Sched. 3, as a " byway open to all traffic " that is conclusive evidence that it is a public right of way for vehicular and all other kinds of traffic (Sched. 3, para. 9 (2) (*b*)). This statutory presumption should be contrasted with s. 32 (4) of the National Parks and Access to the Countryside Act, 1949, which states that " a footpath ", " bridleway " or a " road used as a public path " shown on a " definitive map " prepared under that Act is conclusive evidence as to the existence of these public rights of way (*Morgan* v. *Hertfordshire County Council* (1965), 63 L.G.R. 456), but this presumption only relates to these rights of way and is without prejudice to any question whether the public had any right of way other than these rights. Thus in *A.-G.* v. *Honeywill and Others* [1972] 3 All E.R. 641 the fact that a right of way was shown only as a footpath on a definitive map prepared under the National Parks and Access to the Countryside Act, 1949, did not prevent the court holding that in fact and in law the public had a right of passage with vehicles also along the particular right of way in question.

A bridleway, i.e., a highway over which the public have a right of way on foot or horseback or leading a horse or driving animals but no other right of way (Highways Act, 1959, s. 295 (1)) is a road for the purposes of offences of dangerous, careless, and drunken cycling and carrying two persons on a bicycle (Road Traffic Act, 1972, ss. 18 to 21).

" To Cause "; " To Permit "; " To Use "

Generally

" One may obtain some help from cases in which the construction of similar words in other statutes has had to be considered, but particular care must be taken " (*per* Edmund Davies, L.J., in

Sopp v. *Long* [1970] 1 Q.B. 518, at p. 524). The truth of this dictum is particularly apparent when one has to consider the meaning of the phrases "To cause", "To permit" and "To use". Not only has one to construe words in the context of the statute in which they appear but one may have to consider the mischief which the statutory provision is aimed at preventing (see for example *Hewer* v. *Cutler* [1974] R.T.R. 155, at p. 159, where it was doubted whether the word " use " in s. 44 of the Act of 1972, which prohibits motor vehicles being used without test certificates, meant the same as " use " in s. 143 of the same Act, which prohibits the use of vehicles without the user being insured, even though both s. 44 and s. 143 are in virtually identical language and in the same statute) (see also pp. 426 and 375).

It will be seen that where the statutory provisions create three separate offences by reason of the words " using ", " causing " or " permitting to be used " appearing in juxtaposition, as for example in s. 40 (5) (*b*) of the Act of 1972 (contravention of construction and use regulations) and ss. 44 (test certificates) and 143 (third party insurance) of the same Act, the words are construed differently where all three phrases do not appear together, e.g., " uses or keeps " in s. 8 of the Vehicles (Excise) Act, 1971 (see p. 487), " causes or permits " in s. 81 of the Act of 1972 (lighting of vehicles: see p. 405), and " causes to be kept " in s. 98 of the Transport Act, 1968 (driver's records: see p. 546). Where these three phrases are used in juxtaposition, " to cause " or " to permit " generally require the prosecution to prove *mens rea*, while the words " to use " will create an offence of absolute liability. Both the employer and the employee driver may be convicted of " using " the contravening vehicle if it is used on the employer's business. Where the prosecution are in doubt as to whether a corporate defendant should be charged with " causing " or " permitting " on the one hand or " using " on the other, the prosecution should lay charges in the alternative (*Ross Hillman, Ltd.* v. *Bond* [1974] R.T.R., at p. 285 and p. 290). Similarly as to Scotland see *Smith of Maddiston, Ltd.* v. *Macnab* on p. 38.

" To Cause "

The leading case on the meaning of " to cause ", where it appears in statutory provisions relating to road traffic offences, is now, it is submitted, *Ross Hillman, Ltd.* v. *Bond* [1974] R.T.R. 279, where most of the cases cited in the 7th Edition of this book were reviewed. The defendant company was summoned for " causing " one of its vehicles to be used on a road with excess rear axle weight contrary to s. 40 (5) (*b*) of the Act of 1972. Those responsible for

the direction of the company's affairs did not know of the overloading of the vehicle.   Following *James & Son, Ltd.* v. *Smee* [1955]
1 Q.B. 78, it was held that where the statute makes it an offence
to " cause " or " permit " a contravening vehicle to be used on a
road as well as the offence of actually " using " the vehicle, the
words " cause " or " permit " require proof of *mens rea* on the part
of the defendant and in the case of a corporate defendant, following *Hill & Sons (Botley & Denmead), Ltd.* v. *Hampshire Chief
Constable* [1972] R.T.R. 29, such guilty knowledge must be knowledge
of someone exercising a directing mind over the company's affairs.
Clark v. *Hunter* [1956] S.L.T. 188 where a partner was convicted
of causing a vehicle to be used with, unknown to him, a defective
handbrake was disapproved and it was also pointed out in *Ross
Hillman* that *F. Austin (Leyton), Ltd.* v. *East* [1961] Crim.L.R. 119
should not be cited as authority that a company could be convicted of unlawfully causing a motor vehicle to be used in a dangerous condition without proof of *mens rea* as the point in issue was
never argued in that case.

   " To cause " involves some express or positive mandate from
the person " causing " to the other person, or some authority from
the former to the latter, arising in the circumstances of the case
(*McLeod* v. *Buchanan* [1940] 2 All E.R. 179, at p. 187).   The general
manager of five depôts, at each of which there is a vehicle superintendent, is not guilty of causing a vehicle to be on a road in a
dangerous condition where he has no knowledge that it is on the
road (*Rushton* v. *Martin* [1952] W.N. 258).   In *Shave* v. *Rosner* [1954]
2 All E.R. 280 a van was left at a garage for repairs but the garage
staff negligently failed to tighten hub nuts on a wheel.   The owner
of the van then drove the van on the road with the wheel in this
defective condition.   It was held that the garage proprietor was
not guilty of causing the van to be used in a defective condition,
as the term " cause " involves some degree of control and direction;
once he had delivered the van to its owner, he ceased to have control
and dominion over it and had done nothing which was the active
cause of the owner driving it on the road.   The owner of a vehicle
causes it to be used when he drives it himself as well as when it is
driven by another person on his orders (*Baker* v. *Chapman* (1963),
61 L.G.R. 527).   Towing a motor vehicle is causing it to be
used (*Milstead* v. *Sexton* [1964] Crim.L.R. 474).

   Where, however, the statute makes it an offence only to " cause
or permit " the contravention, without the use of the word " use ",
an offence of absolute liability without proof of *mens rea* may be
created.   Thus s. 81 of the Act of 1972 (causing a vehicle to be
used in contravention of the requirements as to the lighting of

vehicles) has long been held to constitute an absolute offence (see p. 405). Where the statute requires an employer or other person " to cause " something to be done, it may be also held that an absolute offence without proof of *mens rea* is created. An employer whose driver keeps incorrect records is guilty of failing to cause correct records to be kept, though he had no chance of correcting the entries (*Cox* v. *Sidery* (1935), 24 Traff.Cas. 69). An employer whose driver enters his records in advance is guilty of failing to cause current records to be kept (*Nelson* v. *Coventry Swaging Co.* (1936), 25 Traff.Cas. 68). These cases are now modified by s. 98 (4) of the Transport Act, 1968, which allows a defence to an employer charged with failing to cause records to be kept where he can prove he gave proper instructions to the driver and took reasonable steps to secure his instructions were carried out.

Where the owner of a vehicle is not the employer of the driver as, for example, where the owner hires out a defective vehicle, the owner cannot be said to be " using " the vehicle; in such a case, however, the owner may be charged with " causing " or " permitting " and may be convicted on proof of *mens rea*: see *Crawford* v. *Haughton* on p. 46. Similarly, where a vehicle is owned by a partnership, a partner who is not the driver cannot be convicted of using (see *Garrett* v. *Hooper* on p. 47), but on proof of *mens rea* he may be convicted, it is submitted, of "causing" or " permitting " the unlawful use. If uncertain as to whether to charge " causing " or " permitting " on the one hand or " using " on the other, prosecutors may prefer alternative charges.

" To Permit " (see also general note on pp. 32, 33)

" To permit " is a vaguer term than " to cause ". It may denote an express permission, general or particular, as distinguished from a mandate. The other person is not told to use the vehicle in a particular way, but he is told that he may do so if he desires. The word also includes cases in which permission is merely inferred. If the other person is given the control of the vehicle, permission may be inferred if the vehicle is left at the other person's disposal in such circumstances as to carry with it a reasonable implication of a discretion or liberty to use it in the manner in which it was used (*McLeod* v. *Buchanan* [1940] 2 All E.R. 179, at p. 187). The statement in *Goodbarne* v. *Buck* [1940] 1 All E.R. 613, at p. 616, that the only person who can permit the use of a car, in that he can forbid another person to use it, is the owner, is incorrect; any person who has control on the owner's behalf, e.g., a chauffeur or a manager of a company, can permit its use (*Lloyd* v. *Singleton* [1953]

1 All E.R. 291; *Morris* v. *Williams* (1952), 50 L.G.R. 308). Permission is not necessarily revoked by the grantor's death (*Kelly* v. *Cornhill Insurance Co.* [1964] 1 All E.R. 321, H.L.). " Permitting " means getting someone else to do something and it is wrong to charge a man with permitting himself to do something (*Waddell* v. *Winter* (1967), 202 E.G. 1225: a planning case).

A leading case on " permitting " is *James* v. *Smee* [1954] 3 All E.R. 273. A vehicle belonging to a company had been sent on the road by the company in good condition but, while away from the control of any of the responsible officers of the company, the brakes became defective through the negligence of the vehicle's crew (also company employees) in coupling up the trailer. It was held that the company was not guilty of " permitting " the use of the vehicle with defective brakes contrary to the Construction and Use Regulations, as there was no evidence of any permission *by a responsible officer*, and that the position would be the same whether the owner was a company or an individual. It must be proved that some person for whose criminal act the owner is responsible permitted it, said the court, but this statement, it seems, does not extend to every servant (*cf. John Henshall (Quarries), Ltd.* v. *Harvey* [1965] 1 All E.R. 725, where a company was held not guilty of aiding and abetting where the illegal action had been done by a minor servant). Knowledge to constitute permitting can include shutting one's eyes (*semble*, in the case of a company, the eyes of responsible officers) to the obvious or allowing a servant to do something in circumstances where a contravention is likely, not caring whether it takes place or not (*James* v. *Smee*, at p. 278). *Goldsmith* v. *Deakin*, *Prosser* v. *Richings* and *Churchill* v. *Norris* (all *infra*) were all cited in support of the latter view by the court. In *Grays Haulage Co., Ltd.* v. *Arnold* [1966] 1 All E.R. 896, it was said that the essence of permitting the commission of an offence is knowledge and, where there was no question of actual knowledge in the defendants, knowledge could not be imputed to them in the absence of *prima facie* evidence from which it could be said that they had shut their eyes to the obvious or had allowed something to go on not caring whether an offence was committed or not. Even where there has been recklessness in a member of the staff in allowing a vehicle to go on the road in a defective condition, the employing company may not be liable even though it has handed over responsibility to that person; the company is not criminally liable in the absence of knowledge of the facts constituting the offence for the failure of a servant to whom it has delegated a task, for the servant is not " the brains of the company " and his knowledge cannot be imputed to a director (*Magna Plant, Ltd.* v. *Mitchell* (1966), 110 S.J. 349). This case together with *James* v. *Smee* and *Grays Haulage Co., Ltd.* v. *Arnold, supra*, were all considered in *Hill & Sons (Botley & Denmead), Ltd.* v. *Hampshire Chief Constable* [1972] R.T.R. 29. The defendant company was convicted of permitting one of its haulage vehicles to be used with inefficient brakes. Quarter sessions upheld the conviction on the grounds that the managing director was reckless in not ensuring that the vehicle was lubricated more frequently than once every four weeks and also in not ensuring that the four-weekly lubrications were properly carried out. The company's conviction was set aside on the grounds that there was nothing to justify quarter sessions' finding that a four-week interval for lubrication was reckless, nor was it reckless (although it might be negligent) for the managing director not to check up on the foreman fitter, a man of long experience, who was responsible for overseeing the lubrication. Lord Widgery, C.J., expressly affirmed *Magna Plant, Ltd.* v. *Mitchell* in that it requires one to look at the minds of those officers of the company who can be described as its " brains " rather than " hands " and that if an employee of the company is shown to be reckless it is not sufficient to impute knowledge of that recklessness unless that person is one who can be fairly described as the " brains " of the company. It seems that, to make a company liable for permitting, a member of the directing staff should generally know what is happening but it is submitted that a company may still be liable for permitting if it has delegated, through its directors, duties relating to vehicle-maintenance, etc., to a subordinate employee, whom it knows to be unskilled and uninstructed in those duties, e.g., allowing a junior typist to say if a lorry shall go on the road. In such a case could not it be said that " the brains " of the company were reckless in so doing? In *Dixon Bool Transport, Ltd.* v. *Forsyth* [1967] Crim.L.R. 52, a conviction for permitting was upheld where the company knew that its drivers had been breaking the law by driving for excessive periods and had not taken steps to remedy this or to acquaint them with the law. *Browning* v. *Watson* [1953] 2 All E.R. 775 is distinguishable. There a company was guilty of permitting a breach of the law on a motor-coach in the charge of a driver because the company failed to take adequate precautions by instructing its staff by other means to see that the law was not broken. The decision in *Hutchings* v. *Giles* [1955] Crim.L.R. 784 is not correctly reported; the prosecution need not prove actual knowledge and it may suffice if constructive knowledge is shown, e.g., shutting one's eyes to the obvious (*Wilson* v. *Bird* (1962), 106 S.J. 880, where there was evidence of actual knowledge). Knowledge is an essential element in permitting and knowledge is not imputed by

mere negligence but by something more, such as recklessly sending
out a car not caring what would happen (*Fransman* v. *Sexton* [1965]
Crim.L.R. 556).   In that case the defendant owner had previously
hired his car to a mechanical engineer who told him, on returning it,
that the brakes had been tested and were operating efficiently.
In fact they were not and it was held that in those circumstances
the owner was not negligent in failing to take the only steps which
would have revealed the defects.

An employer charged with permitting his driver to drive for an
excessive period contrary to the Road Traffic Act, 1960, s. 73,
may be guilty, although the driver may have had orders from him
not to drive for a longer period than the law allows (*Sidcup Building
Estates* v. *Sidery* (1936), 24 Traff.Cas. 164; *Forsyth* v. *Phillips* (1964),
108 S.J. 36; see *Grays Haulage Co.* v. *Arnold* [1966] 1 All E.R., at
p. 898, letter H).   In the first two cases the defendant had left to
his staff, or his wife, the duty of collecting from the drivers their log
books which showed that they had been driving excessive hours and
had thus shut his eyes, through his responsible officers, to their
breaches of the law.   Compare *Griffiths* v. *Studebakers* (1924), 87
J.P. 199, p. 42, *infra*, where the master was convicted of using,
though the driver had disobeyed his orders.   Section 96 (11) (ii)
and s. 98 (4) of the Transport Act, 1968, provide special statutory
defences for employers and others charged with breaches of the law
relating to drivers' hours and keeping records (see pp. 558, 547).

In *Macdonald* v. *Wilmae Concrete Co.* [1954] S.L.T.(Sh.) 33, a
company was held not guilty of causing and permitting use with
defective brakes when no responsible official knew of the defect.

Following *Ross Hillman*, *supra*, the Scottish High Court of Justiciary
overruled *Clark* v. *Hunter* [1956] S.L.T. 188 and held that knowledge
was essential for a company to be convicted of " causing " or " permitting " the use of a vehicle contrary to s.40 of the Act of 1972
(*Smith of Maddiston, Ltd.* v. *Macnab* [1975] S.L.T. 86).   Again, where
auctioneers had sold a car and, unknown to them, their servants had
given a bogus cover note to the buyer, who then drove the car uninsured, the auctioneers did not cause or permit such use by him
(*Watkins* v. *O'Shaughnessy* [1939] 1 All E.R. 385).   Assistance in a
fraud on an insurance company by the car owner does not necessarily
render the aider liable for permitting uninsured use (*Goodbarne* v.
Buck [1940] 1 All E.R. 613).

In some contexts, e.g., permitting a vehicle to be used without
third-party insurance, the statute imposes an absolute prohibition
without proof of *mens rea* and it suffices to convict the defendant if
he is shown to have permitted use, irrespective of whether he knew if
the vehicle was insured or not (*Tapsell* v. *Maslen* [1967] Crim.L.R.

53, following *Lyons* v. *May* [1948] 2 All E.R. 1062; *Morris* v. *Williams, supra,* on p. 36). These cases were not cited to or apparently considered by the Divisional Court in *Davies* v. *Warne* [1973] R.T.R. 217 where nevertheless a conviction of permitting the use of an uninsured vehicle was upheld where both the user and permitter genuinely and reasonably believed that the user's use of the vehicle was covered by insurance. A person who permits another to use his vehicle on the express condition that the user first insures the vehicle, cannot be convicted of the offence of permitting because he has not permitted the vehicle to be used while uninsured; permission given subject to a condition which was unfulfilled is no permission (*Newbury* v. *Davis* [1974] R.T.R. 367). In *Sheldon Deliveries, Ltd.* v. *Willis* [1972] R.T.R. 217 a delivery car firm were held not to have permitted the uninsured use of a car when their delivery driver, contrary to his express instructions, used it on a Sunday and without trade plates; although the judgments infer that the delivery car firm should not be convicted because knowledge of the fact that the vehicle was uninsured could not be imputed to the company, it was pointed out in *Newbury* v. *Davis,* at p. 371, that the true *ratio decidendi* in *Sheldon's* case was lack of knowledge that the vehicle was to be used on the journey in question. Knowledge that a vehicle is used in contravention of the statute is a different matter from knowledge that a vehicle is to be used. This latter kind of knowledge is an essential ingredient of permission (*ibid.*) but on construing exceptions clauses in policies relating to circumstances occurring " to the knowledge of the assured ", the latter must be shown to have actual knowledge (*Ellis* v. *Hinds* [1947] 1 All E.R. 337).

The court ought to look at the object of the statute and see whether the principal might be held responsible for the conduct of his agent, though himself unaware of the statute being infringed. If the principal in effect hires out his coach, putting his servant in charge of it and at least leaving it to chance whether it would be used as a stage carriage or not, he permits it to be used as a stage carriage without a licence (*Goldsmith* v. *Deakin* (1933), 98 J.P. 4; *Clydebank Co-operative Society* v. *Binnie* [1937] S.C.(J.) 17); *a fortiori* where he has been warned that it may be so used (*Osborne* v. *Richards* (1933), 96 J.P. 377; *Webb* v. *Maidstone, etc., Services* (1934), 78 S.J. 336). *Browning* v. *Watson, supra,* on p. 37, is in accord with these cases as, there, no adequate precautions in instructing the staff or in seeing that the law was obeyed had been taken. But where the owner has no reason to know that his vehicle may be used without the necessary licence, or there are no circumstances which ought either to have aroused his suspicion or

put him on his guard, he is not guilty of permitting use without a
licence for express carriages (*Newell* v. *Cook* [1936] 2 All E.R. 203).
Nor is he guilty of permitting use as a stage carriage if he does not
know that such use is proposed and does not deliberately refrain
from making inquiries or shut his eyes to the obvious (*Evans* v.
Dell [1937] 1 All E.R. 349). An owner may be liable for permitting
overcrowding on a bus when he has appointed a young and inexperienced conductor and has given him no instructions (*cf. Gough*
v. *Rees* (1929), 94 J.P. 53), provided that the regulations justify
the use of the word " permit " in the context.

It was held that employers who put their driver in a position to
receive a load and accept it (*semble*, through him) permit the
vehicle to transmit an excessive weight to the road by consequence
of such load contrary to the Construction and Use Regulations
(*Prosser* v. *Richings* (1936), 100 J.P. 390). A driver had instructions
not to carry excessive weight and to get his loads weighed at the
first opportunity. His employers sent him to pick up a load and,
when he finished loading it, the weighbridges were shut and he
misjudged the weight by eye. The employers, who had no benefit
from the excess, were convicted of permitting excessive weight on
the road contrary to the above regulations, as the fact that the loading finished so late and that they had told him to get his loads
weighed showed that they took the risk of his driving sometimes
with excessive loads (*Churchill* v. *Norris* (1938), 158 L.T. 255). It
is submitted that this case and *Prosser* v. *Richings* (*supra*) should no
longer be followed in view of *Ross Hillman, Ltd.* v. *Bond* [1974]
R.T.R. 279 (see p. 33), where the defendant company could not
be convicted of " causing " its vehicle to be used with excess
axle weight because the prosecution were unable to prove guilty
knowledge on the part of any officer responsible for directing the
company's business. It was said that such *mens rea* was a necessary
ingredient both of the offence of " causing " and of " permitting ".
Ross Hillman was followed and applied in *P. Lowery & Sons Ltd.* v.
Wark [1975] R.T.R. 45 where a conviction (under s. 40) of the
defendant company for " permitting " their vehicle to be used
with a dangerously insecure load was set aside where there was
no proof of *mens rea* on behalf of a person controlling the company.

A corporation can permit an offence for which disqualification is
a punishment though not disqualifiable itself (*Briggs* v. *Gibson's
Bakery* [1948] N.I. 165). While a person may be guilty of permitting if he fails to take proper steps to prevent something, he
is not guilty if he merely fails to take unreasonable steps to prevent it
(*Test Valley Investments, Ltd.* v. *Tanner* [1964] Crim.L.R. 62, a case
under another Act).

The following propositions as to what constitutes " permitting " are submitted:—

(1) The context of the statutory provisions requires examination together with the mischief at which the prohibition is aimed. This may result in stricter liability under some statutory provisions than others, e.g., for insurance offences.

(2) A distinction should normally be drawn between knowledge of the use of the vehicle and knowledge of the unlawfulness of its use. Knowledge of the former kind is an essential ingredient of permitting, knowledge of the latter kind may or may not be an essential ingredient.

(3) Normally, such knowledge of the unlawfulness of the vehicle's use is required such as " permitting to be used ": in contradistinction " using " imports *mens rea*. *Aliter* in the case of insurance offences.

(4) Where such *mens rea* is an essential element of the offence of permitting, a limited company cannot be convicted unless the *mens rea* can be imputed to the " brains " rather than " hands " of the company.

(5) Such *mens rea* can consist not only of actual knowledge but also of constructive knowledge in the sense that he wilfully shuts his eyes to the obvious or deliberately refrains from making proper inquiry. Possibly, a failure on the part of an employee can be " permitting " on the part of the employer if it can be shown that the employer left duties to the employee without adequate supervision and in the knowledge that the employee would be employed on work for which he was unskilled.

(6) A prosecutor who is uncertain of being able to prove *mens rea* may prefer alternative charges of " causing " or " permitting " or " using ". The last generally does not require proof of *mens rea* (see *infra* and *Green* v. *Burnett* and *Ross Hillman, Ltd.* v. *Bond, supra*), but only the employer or employee driver can be convicted and the former may be appropriate for owners who are not the driver's employers (see *Carmichael & Sons, Ltd.* v. *Cottle* on p. 45 and *Crawford* v. *Haughton* on p. 46).

" To Use " (see also general note on pp. 32–33).

Many charges are brought for offences of " using " a motor vehicle without third-party insurance or in breach of the Construction and Use Regulations. The term in such cases usually imports absolute liability (unless there is some special statutory defence such as that given by s. 143 (2) of the Road Traffic Act, 1972, for employees using their master's vehicle in ignorance of the lack of insurance cover) and those responsible for the use of the vehicle can be prosecuted, e.g., the driver and his employer, if the journey was made on the employer's business. An employer may thus find himself charged with an offence of which he himself was quite ignorant and which may have been committed hundreds of miles from his office. It was said in *Hart* v. *Bex* [1957] Crim.L.R. 622, however, where a defect in a braking system (a case of absolute liability) arose unexpectedly and suddenly and the driver was not under a duty to inspect the brakes, that the police should refrain from prosecuting him and, if he was charged, he should be given an absolute discharge. This advice from the High Court, it is submitted, should be considered by all prosecutors and defending advocates in cases where the driver or the owner of the vehicle appears to be morally guiltless and has not been guilty of negligence in relation to the causes of the defect or in carrying on after it has developed.

A person does not use a motor vehicle under s. 143 (insurance) of the 1972 Act unless there is an element of controlling, managing and operating the vehicle as a vehicle (cited with approval in *Nichol* v. *Leach and Another* [1973] R.T.R. 476); nor does a passenger who is ignorant of the lack of insurance cover and does not procure the making of a journey (*D.* v. *Parsons* [1960] 2 All E.R. 493), nor a person sitting in the driving-seat, drunk, when the car is stationary and the ignition-key and insurance are held by the owner also present in the car (*Fisher* v. *Kearton* (1964), 108 S.J. 258). And see *Hamilton* v. *Blair and Meechan; Windle* v. *Dunning & Son, Ltd.; Carmichael & Sons* v. *Cottle; Crawford* v. *Haughton* and *Cobb* v. *Williams, infra.*

Turning to the cases, a driver of a vehicle may be convicted of using it with his load improperly secured, contrary to the Construction and Use Regulations, although the loading was done under the supervision of the hirer's servant and the driver took no part in it (*Gifford* v. *Whittaker* [1942] 1 All E.R. 604). A driver who ought to have known his brakes were defective was also convicted of using his vehicle with defective brakes (*Adair* v. *Donaldson* [1935] S.C.(J.) 23). A trade licence issued to a company forbade the carrying of an excessive number of passengers in a vehicle; the company drew its drivers' attention to the licence and ordered them to observe that term. A car driven by an employee carried an excessive number of passengers; the company was convicted of using it and it was said that it would make no difference if the employer had been an individual (*Griffiths* v. *Studebakers* (1924), 87 J.P. 199). However, where a vehicle was used without licence as an express carriage and the illegality arose through the action of some people who were not the vehicle owner's servants or agents, which action was unknown to him, he should not be convicted of using; a person is not guilty if he does an act lawful in itself but which has become unlawful, unbeknown to him, through the actions of such people (*Reynolds* v. *Austin* [1951] 1 All E.R. 606).

A leading case on " using " is *Green* v. *Burnett* [1954] 3 All E.R. 273. In this case, an employee used a vehicle with defective brakes; there was some evidence of negligence by the defendant-owner's servant in maintaining the brakes but the owner had given him general instructions to take the vehicle to motor engineers whenever he felt it needed maintenance or some defect manifested itself. The vehicle was used on the owner's business and it was held that he (the owner) was guilty of " using ", as the Construction and Use Regulations (with a few exceptions) impose an absolute prohibition on use in breach of them, although the owner was quite unaware of the defect. Liability for contravention of an absolute prohibition depends on the fact of contravention and not upon the intention to contravene. Neither *mens rea* in its true sense of importing a blameworthy mind nor negligence in the form of a failure to take reasonable steps to prevent the offence is relevant save on the question of punishment.

A vehicle owner who hired it out was held not to be a user of it whilst the hirer had it, and the hirer also, when not in the vehicle, was held not to be using it (*Hamilton* v. *Blair and Meechan* [1962] S.L.T. 69). It was agreed that passengers, including possibly the hirer, were not users in breach of Pt. III of the 1960 Act, relating to public service vehicles (see p. 566). In *Windle* v. *Dunning & Son, Ltd.* [1968] 2 All E.R. 46, the defendants hired vehicles from a firm of haulage contractors; the drivers, although they spent a lot of time on the defendants' work, were paid by the contractors, and the defendants' servants loaded the vehicles and directed the drivers where to go. The defendants' servants sent them out with overloaded vehicles and it was held that only the drivers and not the defendants were using them as opposed to causing them to be used. " Using " might also cover, it was said, an employer where the driver was about that employer's business. *Hamilton's* case (under the name of *Macleod* v. *Penman*) was followed.

Where an owner lends his car to a friend on condition that he renews the licence when it expires, the owner does not use the car after expiry of the licence (*Abercromby* v. *Morris* (1932), 96 J.P. 392). It is doubtful, indeed, if a person who lends his car to a friend for social purposes, abandoning all control, uses it at all but, if he knows of defects, he might be liable for aiding and abetting

the friend. An unreported case (*Stone* v. *Horton* (1935)) is mentioned at 113 J.P.Jo. 674, however, in which an owner was held
to be " using " where he had hired or lent his car to a customer.
Apparently, this case was under (what is now) the Vehicles (Excise)
Act and the courts often take a stricter view in Revenue prosecutions than they do in criminal cases (*cf. Strutt* v. *Clift* (1911), 74 J.P.
471, and see *Hamilton* v. *Blair and Meechan, supra*). A further
distinction between " using " a vehicle without a licence contrary
to the Vehicles (Excise) Act and " using " a vehicle without insurance (s. 143) or in contravention of a Construction and Use
Regulation (s. 40 (5)) is that there is no offence of " causing " or
" permitting " the use of an untaxed vehicle contrary to s. 8 of the
Vehicles (Excise) Act (see *Carmichael & Sons* v. *Cottle* and *Crawford*
v. *Haughton, infra*). A garage company which lent a car to a customer, while his car was being repaired, was not guilty of using the
lent car when he later drove it with defective tyres, *semble*, even
though they may have been defective when the company handed
it over (*L. F. Dove, Ltd.* v. *Tarvin* (1964), 108 S.J. 404). Where
the conditions of A, B or C licences applied, it was held that they
must be observed at all times (save where use without a licence was
lawful) and the licence-holder was criminally responsible for their
non-observance, even though he was not using the vehicle nor being
paid for its use (*Lloyd* v. *Lee* [1951] 1 All E.R. 589). See also
Strutt v. *Clift* and *Phelon* v. *Keel* on p. 49, as to use without authority.
    A vehicle is in use when it is stationary on a road for loading or
unloading (*Andrews* v. *Kershaw* [1951] 2 All E.R. 764) and is in use
and requires to be insured even where it has been left immobile
with an engine which does not work and without petrol or battery,
so long as it can be moved, e.g., by pushing or releasing the brake
(*Elliott* v. *Grey* [1959] 3 All E.R. 733). Where a vehicle had been
left in a gateway of a rural road (but, *semble*, on the road) for so
long that the green grass grew all around, it was held that it was
still used on the road for insurance and test certificate purposes
(*Another* v. *Howard*, J.P.Jo. Supp., 11th June, 1968). A person who
had abandoned a car in a lay-by " uses " it and requires a policy
of insurance under s. 201 of the 1960 Act (*Williams* v. *Jones*, W.L.R.,
7th March, 1969, Recent Points). It might be that user in breach
of other provisions would not necessarily be established in like
circumstances. Also, the court said in *Another* v. *Howard* that their
finding might be otherwise if the car was totally immobilised by
removal of its wheels, i.e., that the vehicle might have ceased to be
a " motor vehicle," and, indeed, in *Hewer* v. *Cutler* [1973] R.T.R.
155, for these reasons *Elliott* v. *Grey* was not applied in a case of
" using " a motor vehicle without a current test certificate contrary

to s. 44 of the Act of 1972: it was held that a totally immobilised vehicle left on a road could not be said to be " used " for the purposes of s. 44. It was doubted, *obiter*, whether the test as to whether a vehicle is " used " is the same in s. 44 as in s. 143: in *Elliott* v. *Grey* it was said that " use " for the purpose of s. 143 was equivalent to " have the use of the vehicle on the road ". For excise duty purposes, a motor vehicle kept on a public road is chargeable with duty while not used thereon, as well as when used (Vehicles (Excise) Act, 1971, s. 1 (1)); see p. 487 as to " keeping ". The driver of a towing vehicle causes the towed vehicle to be used and presumably therefore the towed vehicle is also " used " (*Milstead* v. *Sexton* [1964] Crim.L.R. 474). In *Cobb* v. *Whorton* [1971] R.T.R. 392 it was held that a van which was on tow on a road was " used " and if it was untaxed the user, who was in charge of and responsible for the van, was guilty of an offence under s. 7 of the Vehicles (Excise) Act, 1962 (now s. 8 of the 1971 Act). It was pointed out that it was inconsistent for the justices, having come to the conclusion that the van was " used " while stationary, then to hold that it ceased to be used the moment it began to be towed (at p. 395). *Cobb* v. *Whorton* was applied in *Nichol* v. *Leach* [1973] R.T.R. 476. It was held that both the driver of a vehicle being towed by another vehicle and the driver of the towing vehicle could be convicted of " using " whilst uninsured (contrary to s. 201 of the Act of 1960, now s. 143 of the Act of 1972) and without an excise licence contrary to s. 8 of the Vehicles (Excise) Act, 1971. A vehicle does not have to be driven under its own power to be " used " on a road (*ibid.*).

In *Brown* v. *Grange Tours, Ltd.* (1968), 112 S.J. 1010, a limited company was charged with using but the magistrates, without hearing any evidence, dismissed the case on the ground that a limited company could not use; the case was sent back to the magistrates with a direction to hear the evidence. It does not seem to be a helpful authority on " using ".

Employers can be convicted of " using " contrary to (what is now) s. 40 of the Act of 1972, a vehicle which contravenes a Construction and Use Regulation when the vehicle is being driven as directed by police or a vehicle examiner (*Drysdale and Others* v. *Harrison* [1973] R.T.R. 45). Use of a vehicle by the employer does not cease through an incident of driving such as a police direction to the driver to stop or to take a certain course, or an examiner directing the vehicle to proceed to a weighbridge to be weighed (*ibid.*).

In *Carmichael & Sons, Ltd.* v. *Cottle* [1971] R.T.R. 11 a company hired out one of their cars to a hirer who was found driving it with a badly worn tyre contrary to what is now reg. 99 of the Construction and Use Regulations (and what is now s. 40 of the 1972 Act). The company was convicted of " using " the vehicle in contravention of the regulation but the conviction was set aside on the ground that the only person who could be said to be " using " the vehicle was the driver. It was argued before the Divisional Court that the company could be convicted as an accessory because the tyre must have been in a poor condition when the car was first hired out. This argument was dismissed on the ground that it had not been raised before the justices, but in the course of his judgment Lord Parker, C.J., suggested (supported by Ashworth, J.) that the argument could also be dismissed on the ground that where the words in a statute creating the offence are " using or causing or permitting " the latter words provide for the offences of being an aider and abettor or an accessory and that if the defendant is an accessory or aider and abettor he should be specifically charged with " causing " or " permitting " the user and not with " using ". This latter approach was specifically adopted by the present Lord Chief Justice, Lord Widgery, in *Crawford* v. *Haughton* [1972] 1 All E.R. 535, where the owner of a stock car had been convicted by the magistrates' court of using the vehicle in contravention of seven separate Construction and Use Regulations, using it whilst uninsured, using it without a vehicle excise licence and using it displaying trade plates without being the holder of the trade licence. The convictions were set aside on the ground that he should have been charged with " permitting ". Where the statute provides alternative offences of " causing or permitting " the only persons who can be convicted of " using " are the driver or an employer if the vehicle was being driven on the employer's business by his employee. The Divisional Court refused to extend the meaning of " using " to include the owner where the person driving the vehicle was not his servant even though that person was driving at his specific request on a specific journey. Note that the convictions under the Vehicles (Excise) Act for using the vehicle without an excise licence and displaying trade plates were also set aside, because no distinction had been made in the magistrates' court between these offences and the remainder. Lord Widgery suggested that different considerations might apply if these two offences had been considered in isolation, as the sections creating the offence do not contain the alternatives of " causing or permitting " the use. It is submitted that, at any rate so far as an offence under s. 8 of the Vehicles (Excise) Act is concerned, where a vehicle is driven on behalf of the owner by another on a journey at his request and on his business, the owner may be found guilty of " using ". Not only is the Vehicles (Excise)

Act a taxation statute where a stricter view is often adopted by the courts, but more importantly there is no offence of " causing " or " permitting " the use of an unlicensed vehicle. Moreover an " aider and abettor " or accessory may be convicted as a principal (Magistrates' Courts Act, 1952, s. 35; *Du Cros* v. *Lambourne* (1907), 70 J.P. 525). The purpose of the Vehicles (Excise) Act is to tax the person who uses or keeps a vehicle on a road; the Act is silent and uncaring as to who is the driver. In *Stone* v. *Horton*, unreported except for a mention at 113 J.P.Jo. 674, an owner was held to be " using " where he had lent or hired his vehicle to a customer.

The court applied *Crawford* v. *Haughton, supra*, and again refused to extend the category of person who can be said to be " using " a vehicle in *Garrett* v. *Hooper* [1973] R.T.R. 1. A partner who is not the driver of a vehicle owned by the partnership does not " use " the vehicle if he is not the driver of the vehicle (*ibid.*). But in *Cobb* v. *Williams* [1973] R.T.R. 113 it was explained that *Crawford* v. *Haughton* and the other cases supporting it were cases of vicarious liability; a restricted meaning of " use " had been adopted in those cases where the defendant was not himself driving the car. Where a defendant is himself a passenger in his own car driven by a friend directly for the defendant's own purposes, then the defendant is " using " and may be convicted of using the vehicle whilst not insured contrary to s. 143 of the Act of 1972 (*Cobb* v. *Williams, supra*).

Where works contractors hired a vehicle plus driver from another company, it was held that the contractors could not be said to be " using " the vehicle which was in contravention of various Construction and Use Regulations, Lighting Regulations and s. 22 of the Vehicles (Excise) Act, 1971 (*Balfour Beatty & Co., Ltd.* v. *Grindey* [1975] R.T.R. 156). The defendant company could have been convicted of causing or permitting the use of the vehicle in contravention of the Construction and Use Regulations (*ibid.*). Similarly it was held in *Howard* v. *G.T. Jones & Co. Ltd.* [1975] R.T.R. 150, a company could not be held to be "using " a motor vehicle contravening a Construction and Use Regulation if the driver was not employed by the company charged with " using ".

Employers are often prosecuted for offences under the Construction and Use Regulations because of the defective condition of the vehicle (note the special defence as to speedometers) and the defence that there is a proper system of maintenance is advanced. Can it prevail? One can only refer to the various cases cited; some of them certainly have a strong leaning towards absolute liability, e.g., in *Gifford* v. *Whittaker, supra*, the vehicle had been loaded by experienced men and yet the driver, who had had no hand in it, was convicted. Again, cases on other (but not all)

parts of the Road Traffic Act establish absolute liability on the
employer, and in *Griffiths* v. *Studebakers, supra,* the convicted employers seem to have done all that could reasonably be expected
of them to ensure compliance with the law. These Regulations
can certainly be said to be for the protection of the public and, if
there is evidence that a vehicle was sent out on the road by the
company's employees in an unlawful condition, the company is
liable (*Provincial Motor Cab Co.* v. *Dunning,* (1909), 73 J.P. 387).
In *Churchill* v. *Norris* and *Prosser* v. *Richings,* p. 40, *supra* (both
cases on these Regulations), the facts showed that the convicted
employers took some risk of the driver's accepting an excessive load,
i.e., both could be called slight cases of *mens rea.* Whatever the
position may be in law, it is submitted that the justices should
inquire carefully into the facts. Rust, loose bolts and other defects
are not usually things that come about in a moment, in the twinkling
of an eye; they point to defective maintenance. If so, surely the
employer is liable, however good he may have imagined his system
of maintenance to be (*Provincial Motor Cab Co.* v. *Dunning, supra*).
Even if a vehicle goes out in perfect condition and a defect occurs
suddenly, e.g., a rod snaps through a fault in the metal, *Griffiths*
v. *Studebakers* suggests that the employer is still using the vehicle
while it continues to be driven on the road although he may have
told his drivers to take vehicles off the road immediately such a
defect occurs. Indeed, it is hinted at 113 J.P.Jo. 472, that it is
difficult to defend a charge of " using " under the Regulations and
Green v. *Burnett* [1954] 3 All E.R. 273 reinforces that view. Whether
there should in fact be a prosecution, however, is another matter;
see *Hart* v. *Bex* [1957] Crim.L.R. 622, noted on p. 42, *supra.*

Is an employer who duly authorises his driver to drive the firm's
vehicle on the firm's business liable for using if the driver, without
permission, lets some other person drive it on the firm's business?
It is submitted, with some hesitation, that the owner is not liable
when an act is done by a trespasser and in those circumstances
would not be liable under s. 143 if the insurance policy did not cover
the unauthorised driver.

A special defence for employees charged with using a vehicle
without insurance is given by the Road Traffic Act, 1972, s. 143 (2)
(see p. 377).

It should be noted that there is no offence of " using " a vehicle
contravening the Lighting Regulations contrary to s. 81 of the
Act of 1972, nor is there an offence of " using " a vehicle without
a number plate contrary to s. 22 of the Vehicles (Excise) Act, 1971.
Convictions in such cases were quashed (*Balfour Beatty & Co., Ltd.*
v. *Grindey* [1975] R.T.R. 156). Section 22 of the Act of 1971

makes it an offence only to " drive or keep " and s. 81 of the 1972 Act to " cause or permit ". When, however, s. 9 (4) of the Act of 1974 is brought into operation, s. 81 will be repealed and any existing regulations will have effect as if made under s. 40 of the Act of 1972. It would seem, therefore, that when s. 9 (4) is brought into operation, persons may be prosecuted for " using " a vehicle which is in contravention of the Lighting Regulations under s. 40 of the Act of 1972 and the law applicable to " causing ", " permitting " or " using " contrary to s. 40 will apply in the same way as a contravention of the Lighting Regulations as at present in respect of a contravention of the Construction and Use Regultaions.

The following propositions are submitted:—

(1) Absolute liability for use is imposed by certain statutes and regulations, e.g., use without third-party insurance or without most licences or contrary to most of the Construction and Use Regulations, and the fact that the person using is quite unaware of the breach of the law and has not been negligent is immaterial. It is a question of construction in each case whether absolute liability is imposed. (Note the paragraph above as to uninsured employees; there is also a special defence as to speedometers—see p. 415.)

(2) A master may be liable for use by his servant on the master's business and, if the statute or regulation imposes an absolute prohibition, lack of knowledge or of negligence on the master's part is no defence, though it may be mitigation. Again, it is a question of construction whether absolute liability for his servant's acts is imposed on the master. In *Strutt* v. *Clift* (1911), 74 J.P. 471, a master entrusted a van to his servant to use legally on his (the master's) business, but the servant illegally used it for his own pleasure; the master was held liable in a Revenue prosecution. On the other hand, in *Phelon* v. *Keel* (1914), 78 J.P. 247, " use " in the then Regulations relating to trade plates was held to mean use by or on behalf of the holder and not unauthorised use by a trespasser. It is suggested that the very strict liability laid down in *Strutt* v. *Clift* does not necessarily apply in road traffic cases and that it will often be a question of fact whether a servant's deviation from his duty and instructions is sufficiently gross to show that the use of a vehicle was no longer on the master's behalf.

(3) Where the statute creates the offence of " causing " or " permitting " as well as " using ", only the driver, a person in the vehicle controlling the driver and the driver's

employer, while it is being used on the employer's business, " use " it. Hirers may cause or permit it to be used if the driver is not in their employ. An aider and abettor, and an accessory before the fact, should be charged with " permitting " or " causing ". Where the only offence is " using " and there is no offence of " causing " or " permitting " as in the Vehicles (Excise) Act, 1971, then it may be possible for the owner of a vehicle to be charged with using if he caused it to be used by another on his behalf.

See generally Edwards, *Mens Rea* and Statutory Offences (1955) and Glanville Williams, Criminal Law: The General Part, 2nd ed., p. 277 et seq.

The owner is deemed to have been using the vehicle in the absence of contrary evidence (*Watson* v. *Paterson*, noted at 121 J.P.Jo. 336; *Ende* v. *Cassidy* (1964), 108 S.J. 522; but see the qualifications given on p. 121). On the other hand ownership or proof of ownership is not essential either for proof of " using " a vehicle without being insured under s. 143 of the Act of 1972 or " using " it without an excise licence contrary to s. 8 of the Act of 1971 (*Napthen* v. *Place* [1970] R.T.R. 248). For the purposes of Pt. V of the Transport Act, 1968 (carriage of goods by road, operators' licences, etc.), the driver of a vehicle if he owns it or possesses under a loan or hire-purchase agreement is deemed to use the vehicle, and in any other case the person whose servant or agent the driver is is the user of the vehicle (Transport Act, 1968, s. 92 (2)). This is, it is submitted, essentially a question of fact. Thus where justices found as a fact that a driver who had been provided for a haulage company by the defendant employment agency was employed by the haulage company and not by the employment agency, the justices' decision of fact could not be impugned (*Alderton* v. *Richard Burgon Associates, Ltd.* [1974] R.T.R. 422). Nor was the justices' finding reversed when they came to an opposite conclusion, viz.: that an employment agency employed the driver and not the company to whom the driver was supplied (*Howard* v. *G. T. Jones & Co. Ltd.* [1975] R.T.R. 150).

Quarter sessions have held that it is not " using " a licence with intent to deceive to send it to the council for renewal; such use must be in connection with the driving or attempted driving of a motor vehicle (*R.* v. *McCardle* [1958] Crim.L.R. 50) but the language of s. 233 of the 1960 Act (now re-enacted in s. 169 of the 1972 Act) does not seem to contain any restriction on the meaning of " use " in that section.

See *Pawley* v. *Wharldall* on p. 283 as to persons " using the road "

under s. 3 of the 1972 Act (driving without reasonable consideration).

" Agriculture "

Some statutes and regulations refer to vehicles used in the business
of agriculture or some such phrase.   The Road Traffic Act, 1972,
and the Road Traffic Regulation Act, 1967, contain no general
definition;   the Vehicles (Excise) Act, 1971, defines " agricultural machine " in Sched. 3, para. 2 (see p. 492 and *Bullen* v.
Picking, p. 493).   There is a definition in s. 75 of the Road Traffic
Act, 1972, which is applicable to that section only, and there is a
definition in s. 103 (1) of the Transport Act, 1968.   " Agricultural
trailer " and " land " implements, locomotives and tractors are
defined by reg. 3 of the Construction and Use Regulations (see
p. 766).   The relevant definition should be consulted in every
case, but there have been these decisions.   Unprocessed hides
imported from abroad are " agricultural produce " (*Scarr* v. *Wurzal*
[1951] 1 All E.R. 1014).   Taking a pony to a show is not use for
hauling agricultural produce (*Henderson* v. *Robson* (1949), 113 J.P.
313).   A wholesale greengrocer who buys crops growing in a field
does not use a vehicle sent to take them away in the business of
agriculture (*Leach* v. *Cooper* (1950), 48 L.G.R. 526).   A vehicle
licensed as a farm goods vehicle and used to carry furniture from a
sale room to a farm worker's cottage is not used solely for the conveyance of articles required for the purpose of agricultural land
(*M'Boyle* v. *Hatton Estate Co.* [1951] S.L.T.(Sh.) 101; certain relevant cases cited are mentioned at Jo.Crim.L. (1952) 170).   A tractor hauling a trailer loaded with bricks and a fireplace for installation at a farm worker's cottage, part of the farm, is not hauling
" articles required for the farm " under (now) the Vehicles (Excise)
Act, 1971, Sched. 3, para. 2 (*Brook* v. *Friend* [1954] Crim.L.R. 942).
A market gardener taking vegetables in his car to retail customers
uses it in the business of agriculture (*Manley* v. *Dabson* [1949] 2 All
E.R. 578); *Fillingham* v. *Hall* (1935), unreported, deciding that
agriculture does not include selling and distributing milk by retail,
may be compared so far as farmers so doing are concerned.   Moving
agricultural implements and furniture from one farm to another is
use in the business of agriculture (*Flatman* v. *Poole* [1937] 1 All E.R.
495).   See also 117 J.P.Jo. 18.   A policy covering use "solely for
agricultural or forestry purposes including the hauling of . . . articles
required for agriculture " did not cover use of a tractor to convey
household furniture of a newly engaged farm servant to the farm
(*Agnew* v. *Robertson* [1956] S.L.T.(Sh.) 90).   See also *Bruce* v. *Odell*

(1939), 27 Traff.Cas. 135, and Jo.Crim.L. (1960) 57. "Agriculture" seems to include chicken and livestock farming as well as cultivating the soil (*J. M. Knowles, Ltd.* v. *Rand* [1962] 2 All E.R. 926) and hatching eggs can be articles required for agricultural land (*ibid.*). And see *London County Council* v. *Lee* on p. 498. Turf can be an agricultural product (*A.-G.* (*McCloskey*) v. *East*, Jo. Crim.L. (1964) 123).

" Aiding and Abetting "

Little can be added to that which already is in the text-books on this subject except that reference to some recent cases may be helpful. It was suggested by Lord Parker, C.J., *obiter* with Ashworth, J., expressing his agreement that where the statute creating the offence employs the words " using or causing or permitting " the latter two verbal nouns provide for the offences of being an accessory or aiding and abetting and in such cases the aider and abettor or accessory should be more properly charged with " permitting " or " causing " (*Carmichael & Sons, Ltd.* v. *Cottle* [1971] R.T.R. 11, at pp. 14, 15). Although Lord Parker remarked that he did not wish to come to a conclusion to this effect, this reasoning of Lord Parker and Ashworth, J., was specifically approved in *Crawford* v. *Haughton*, p. 46, *supra*.

If a person knows all the circumstances and those circumstances constitute an offence and he helps in the actions which constitute the offence, that may be enough to convict him of aiding and abetting, although he does not realise that those circumstances constitute an offence (*Ackroyds* v. *D.P.P.* [1950] 1 All E.R. 933). A person who carries on the business of a transport clearing house, hiring lorries to carry goods for other firms, must inquire whether the A or B licence held by the lorry owner so engaged entitles him to carry the goods in question; if he fails in his duty to see whether the lorry owner can lawfully carry those goods, he aids and abets the lorry owner in failing to comply with a condition of his licence should it be infringed by so carrying the goods (*Carter* v. *Mace* [1949] 2 All E.R. 714; see below). A man who does not know of the essential matters constituting an offence does not aid and abet its commission (*Johnson* v. *Youden* [1950] 1 All E.R. 300). In *Ferguson* v. *Weaving* [1951] 1 All E.R. 412 it was held on the facts that knowledge to constitute aiding and abetting could not be imputed to an employer because his servants knew. *Carter* v. *Mace*, *supra*, was distinguished in *Davies, Turner & Co.* v. *Brodie* [1954] 3 All E.R. 283; there the defendant had made proper inquiries as to whether goods could be carried in another firm's lorry without contravening the terms of an A licence, but had been given false information. It was held that the defendant was not guilty of aiding and abetting the other firm in the illegal use of the vehicle. In *Smith* v. *Jenner* (1968), 112 S.J. 52, a driving instructor was shown his pupil's then valid driving licence and he told him to renew when necessary; the instructor gave lessons without further inquiry and was charged with aiding and abetting the pupil to drive when unlicensed, the licence having expired. It was held that the instructor should not be convicted. See also *Stanton & Sons, Ltd.* v. *Webber* (1972), 116 S.J. 667 (firm acquitted where there was no actual knowledge that the employee was a learner driver). In *Bateman* v. *Evans* (1964), 108 S.J. 522, where the defendant allowed a disqualified person to drive his car in the belief that he was not disqualified, it was held that he was not guilty but that he would be if he shut his eyes to the obvious or perhaps refrained from making the inquiries which a reasonably sensible man would make. Deliberate abstention from obtaining knowledge can be aiding and abetting (*Poultry World* v. *Conder* [1957] Crim.L.R. 803). A person may be guilty of aiding and abetting where he is under a legal duty to act to prevent an offence and he remains passive (*Rubie* v. *Faulkner* [1940] 1 All E.R. 285). A supervisor can be convicted of aiding and abetting the learner driver to drive with excess blood alcohol. He cannot escape conviction by arguing that he cannot know that the learner driver is above the limit unless and until the blood alcohol level has been scientifically determined (*Crampton* v. *Fish* (1969), 113 S.J. 1003). The learner driver and supervisor had been out drinking together that evening; the vehicle had hit the bank on three occasions and had been swerving from side to side. In *Carter* v. *Richardson* [1974] R.T.R. 314, a supervisor of a learner driver was similarly convicted of aiding and abetting the learner driver to drive with alcohol in excess of the prescribed limit. It was held that it suffices if the aider and abetter was aware that the principal had had an excessive amount of alcohol or was reckless whether he had done so. The aider and abetter does not have to know the precise amount (*ibid.*). The supervisor attempted to deceive the police that he had been driving and not his pupil. The justices were entitled to infer from that deception that he knew or believed his pupil had too much alcohol in his blood (*per* Mackenna, J., on p. 318, *ibid.*).

As to the liability of a master for his employees' acts, contrast *John Henshall (Quarries), Ltd.* v. *Harvey* [1965] 1 All E.R. 725 with *National Coal Board* v. *Gamble* [1958] 3 All E.R. 203, where a private firm's lorry went to a Coal Board depôt and was loaded with coal there. The Board's servant weighed the loaded lorry at a weighbridge of which he was in charge and found that the laden weight exceeded that allowed by the Construction and Use Regulations. Nevertheless he gave the weight ticket to the driver, who knew of the overweight. It was held, on a charge against the Board of aiding and abetting the use by the firm of an overweight lorry, that the crime of aiding and abetting was committed on proof of a positive act of assistance voluntarily done and a knowledge of the circumstances constituting the offence and that the question of motive was irrelevant. The handing of the weight ticket by the attendant at the weighbridge to the driver with knowledge that an offence was going to be committed made the Board aiders and abettors. A special feature of this case is that the Board called no evidence. In the *Henshall* case it was held that the knowledge of a subordinate employee, who was under the general supervision of a manager, was not enough to make his employer guilty of aiding and abetting an illegal act contributed to by the employee and unknown to the manager; to make the master, whether a company or an individual, liable the employee should be a responsible officer, part of the " brains " of the company. It might be otherwise if the master had handed over the effective management to an employee.

In *Pope* v. *Minton* [1954] Crim.L.R. 711, the defendant knew that his friend had been disqualified from driving, but told him that he could use his (defendant's) car if he wanted. Defendant was not present when the friend used the car, nor (*semble*) did he do any more to assist him to take and use it. It was held that the defendant was guilty of aiding and abetting the friend to drive while disqualified, but it would be otherwise if the car owner was genuinely unaware of the disqualification (*Bateman* v. *Evans*, on p. 653). A bus owner who put an inexperienced conductor in charge of the bus without proper supervision was held guilty of aiding and abetting the conductor in allowing overcrowding (*Gough* v. *Rees* (1929), 94 J.P. 53). A lorry driver employed by a Scottish company set off on a long journey into England with a dangerously worn front offside tyre the condition of which he knew. The state of the tyre was also known to the managing director of the Scottish company. The tyre burst and the lorry crashed into a motor car, killing its occupants. It was held that the company and the managing director were guilty of counselling and procuring the offence of causing death by dangerous driving because the managing director knew of the dangerous state of the tyre (*R.* v. *Robert Millar (Contractors), Ltd., and Robert Millar* [1970] 1 All E.R. 577). Moreover, as the crime of the lorry driver was committed in England, and as counselling and procuring was not a crime on its own account but rather participating in a crime, they could be tried in England; an alternative reason for trial in England was that the counselling and procuring was a continuous act and continued as long as the driver drove the lorry with the dangerous tyre. A person cannot be guilty of aiding and abetting a crime if it be shown that no crime was committed (*Thornton* v. *Mitchell* [1940] 1 All E.R. 339), but this case is distinguishable where *A* is charged with aiding and abetting the commission of an offence by *B* and it is shown that the offence was committed though not by *B*; *cf. R.* v. *Anthony* [1965] 1 All E.R. 440 and *R.* v. *Humphreys* [1965] 3 All E.R. 689. Evidence that a person charged as an aider and abettor has previously been warned about the same matters is admissible to show that he knew what might be going on (*Duxley* v. *Gilmore* (1959), 123 J.P.Jo. 331). Merely riding in a vehicle, without more, does not show that the rider is aiding and abetting its illegal use; there should be some evidence of a joint enterprise (*D.* v. *Parsons* [1960] 2 All E.R. 493); and in *Smith* v. *Baker* [1972] Crim.L.R. 25 a passenger in a stolen car was held not to be guilty of aiding and abetting its uninsured use when he had not assisted in its use in any way even though he had " a fair idea it was stolen " and ran away when the police arrived.

Surreptitiously lacing a motorist's drink knowing that he would drive with excess alcohol as a result is " procuring " (*Attorney General's Reference No. 1 of 1975, The Times*, 25th April, 1975). It seems that a person charged as a principal can be convicted although the evidence shows that he only aided and abetted (*Du Cros* v. *Lambourne* (1907), 70 J.P. 525; *Cooper* v. *Leeke* (1968), 112 S.J. 46).

See pp. 613 and 623 as to endorsing the licences of, and disqualifying, aiders and abettors.

" Owner "

The term " owner," in relation to a vehicle which is the subject of a hiring agreement or hire-purchase agreement, means the person in possession under that agreement (Road Traffic Act, 1972, s. 196 (1); Road Traffic Regulation Act, 1967, s. 104 (1)). For the purposes of giving information as to insurance under ss. 162 (1) and 166 the term in relation to a vehicle which is the subject of a hiring agreement includes each party to the agreement (Road Traffic Act, 1972, ss. 162(4), 167(2); see pp. 381 and 461).

" Owner " is not defined in the Vehicles (Excise) Act, 1971, but it is defined in relation to regulations thereunder (see p. 517).

CHAPTER II

PROCEDURE AND EVIDENCE

1. COMMENCING PROCEEDINGS

THE majority of road traffic prosecutions are begun by summons and most courts require that the informant should attend before a magistrate or justices' clerk to apply for it. The information may, however, be laid on behalf of the informant by an agent or solicitor or counsel (Magistrates' Courts Rules, 1968, r. 1 (1)). Magistrates may refuse to issue a summons if they think fit on reasonable grounds; if a summons is unreasonably refused, mandamus may be granted to compel its issue (Stone (1975), p. 538). Complaints and informations not on oath may be to a justices' clerk, who may issue the summons (Justices' Clerks Rules, 1970 (S.I. 1970 No. 231)). An oral or written information is vital to the validity of any proceedings, but the reading in court of an otherwise invalid summons can constitute a valid oral information if within time when read (*R.* v. *Brentford Justices* [1975] 2 All E.R. 201). A fascimile rubber stamp signature may comply with r. 81 of the Magistrates' Courts Rules, 1968 (*ibid.*). See p. 647, *infra*, as to removals of disqualification. By the Criminal Justice Act, 1967, s. 24 (1) and (2), a warrant to arrest a defendant in the first instance may not be issued for any offence unless it is indictable, or punishable with imprisonment, or his address is not sufficiently established to enable a summons to be served on him; nor may a warrant be issued on his non-appearance unless the offence is punishable with imprisonment or the court, having convicted him, proposes to disqualify him.

Unless a statute otherwise requires, a prosecution may be commenced by any person. Exceptions are under Pt. III of the Road Traffic Act, 1960 (see s. 161), and for not paying the proper duties under the Vehicles (Excise) Act, 1971, and (possibly) for driving to the common danger under the Public Health Act, 1925, s. 74, and obstruction and other offences under the Town Police Clauses Act, 1847, s. 28. The view that a constable who witnessed the offence may prosecute under s. 28 is advanced in Stone (1975), p. 4287.

The power to prosecute generally is discussed at [1955] Crim.L.R. 668. Where the authority of some person or body to prosecute is required, the magistrates' clerk should satisfy himself that such authority has been duly given before issuing the summons; at the hearing the summons is presumed to have been duly authorised and the prosecutor need take no further steps unless the defence raise objection. Then, he must satisfy the court of the authorisation. Such an objection should be taken before the prosecutor's case is closed (*Price* v. *Humphries* [1958] 2 All E.R. 725).

Juveniles

Subject to the exceptions below, only a juvenile court may deal with an offence by a juvenile under seventeen. Unless the offence is one of " homicide " (and it is submitted that causing death by dangerous driving comes within this term: see p. 258) or is punishable if committed by an adult with fourteen years' imprisonment or more, the court cannot commit the juvenile for trial at the Crown Court even if the prosecution or the defence wish to have the charge tried before a jury (Children and Young Persons Act, 1969, s. 6). A juvenile may however be tried by a magistrates' court if he is charged jointly with an adult; either the juvenile or the adult is a principal offender and the other is an aider or abettor of the offence; the juvenile is charged with an offence arising out of the circumstances or connected with the circumstances giving rise to an offence for which an adult is charged (Children and Young Persons Act, 1933, s. 46; Children and Young Persons Act, 1963, s. 18). Provided the juvenile is charged jointly with an adult, the magistrates' court may commit them both for trial if the court considers it necessary in the interests of justice to do so and if there is sufficient evidence to commit them for trial. The court may also now commit them under s. 1 of the Criminal Justice Act, 1967, without consideration of the evidence (Children and Young Persons Act, 1969, s. 6, as amended by the Criminal Justice Act, 1972) provided, also, the court considers it to be in the interests of justice.

Section 7 (8) of the Children and Young Persons Act, 1969, provides that where a magistrates' court tries a person who at the time the proceedings in question were begun has not attained the age of seventeen, the magistrates' court is required to remit the offender to a juvenile court, unless the court deals with the case by exercising one or more of the following powers: absolute or conditional discharge, a fine or order for costs or damages, an order for his parent to enter into a recognizance, an order of disqualification or endorsement of a driving licence under s. 5 or s. 7 of the Road Traffic Act, 1962 (now ss. 93 and 101 of the 1972 Act). It should be noted that the determining date of the age of the offender is for the purposes of s. 7 (8) of the 1969 Act the date when the proceedings

were begun. If, for example, the magistrates' court wishes to send
to a detention centre an offender who has since become seventeen
he must be remitted to the juvenile court to be sentenced. On the
other hand, if a fresh charge is preferred after the juvenile attains
seventeen, *R.* v. *Chelsea JJ., ex parte D.P.P.* [1963] 3 All E.R. 657
still seems to be authority for the proposition that a juvenile court
cannot deal with the fresh charge if at the time of preferment it
was known he was then seventeen. Section 7 of the 1969 Act
does not define the moment at which it may be said " proceedings
are begun ". This presumably means when an information is laid
or the juvenile is charged.

In England a person attains an age on the day which is the
anniversary of his birth and not, as formerly, on the preceding day
(Family Law Reform Act, 1969, s. 9). See [1962] S.L.T.N. 16 as
to Scotland. For presuming and determining age see s. 99 of the
Children and Young Persons Act, 1933, and s. 126 (5) of the Magistrates' Courts Act, 1952. The procedure under s. 1 of the Magistrates' Courts Act, 1957, whereby an offender may plead guilty
by post does not apply to juvenile courts, but s. 46 (1A of the
Children and Young Persons Act, 1933 (as amended by the like-
named Act of 1969) has the effect of preserving a conviction under
that Act of a juvenile if the magistrates' court had no reason to
believe he was a juvenile.

See p. 95 as to disregarding findings of guilt while under fourteen
against a person who has attained the age of twenty-one and *R.* v.
Blandford JJ. [1966] 1 All E.R. 1021 as to accepting pleas of guilty
from juveniles.

Empire and Foreign Servicemen

Where the defendant is a serviceman of a British Dominion or
allied country, such as U.S.A., the Visiting Forces Act, 1952, as
extended by the International Headquarters and Defence Organisations Act, 1964, will enable magistrates' courts to try him for a
road traffic offence, generally speaking, unless it arose out of, and
in the course of, his duty (see s. 3). Thus, an American Army
officer driving on manoeuvres would be acting in the course of his
duty and would normally not be triable in an English court, but,
if he were on a domestic shopping trip with his family, he would
not be acting in the course of his duty and would be triable for a
road traffic offence by an English court. The Act is discussed in
the *Modern Law Review*, January, 1953, at 103 L.J.News. 149,
and at 119 J.P.Jo. 99. It applies to American servicemen and those
of the countries listed in Stone (1975), p. 1093. The Motor

Vehicles (Construction and Use) Regulations, 1973, reg. 4 (9) (see p. 775), the Motor Vehicles (Construction and Use) (Track Laying Vehicles) Regulations, 1955, reg. 4, the Motor Vehicles (Variation of Speed Limit) (Amendment) Regulations, 1954, and the Road Vehicles Lighting Regulations, 1971, regs. 57 to 60, give certain exemptions for the vehicles of visiting forces. As to insurance, see p. 369, and excise licences, p. 500.

The Visiting Forces and International Headquarters (Application of Law) Order, 1965 (S.I. 1965 No. 1536), applies many provisions of the Road Traffic Act, 1960, to vehicles of visiting forces and their drivers when on duty, but offences committed on duty would be tried by the service courts. The general position is that drivers and vehicles of visiting forces are subject to the same provisions of the Road Traffic Acts as persons and vehicles in the service of the Crown (see *infra*). The Interpretation Act, 1889, s. 38 (1), applies the provisions of the Road Traffic Regulation Act, 1967, and the Road Traffic Act, 1972, replacing those of the 1960 Act, to the relevant parts of the 1965 Order.

A civil court may not try for the same crime a person already tried by the service court of a visiting force and, where the civil court tries him for a different crime but he has already been tried by the service court wholly or partly for the acts or omissions in respect of which the civil court convicts him, the latter court must have regard to the sentence already passed (Visiting Forces Act, 1952, s. 4).

Diplomatic Privilege

By the Diplomatic Privileges Act, 1964, Sched. 1, arts. 31 and 37, members of the diplomatic, administrative and technical staff of a mission and members of the family of such staff forming part of their household are exempt from criminal proceedings, and members of the domestic service staff enjoy like immunity in respect of acts performed in the course of their duties. All such immunities may be waived. Private servants of members of the mission, as opposed to those of the mission itself, are not exempt; nor are members of the family of the diplomatic staff and members of the administrative and technical staff and their families who are British nationals or permanently resident here. See 7 Halsbury, 3rd ed., pp. 274–9, as to representatives of Commonwealth countries and of international organisations. Where a person is a member of a diplomatic mission of a Commonwealth country or Eire or a private servant of such a person, and is a citizen both of that country and of the United Kingdom, he has the same privileges and immunities as he would have if he were not a citizen of the United Kingdom (Diplomatic Privileges (Citizens of the United Kingdom and Colonies) Order, 1964 (S.I. 1964 No. 2043)). Similar privilege may also exist under the International Organisations Act, 1968. Consular officers and consular employees, as defined in art. 1 of the Schedule to the Consular Relations Act, 1968, are not subject to the jurisdiction of British courts in respect of acts performed in the course of consular functions but such immunity may be waived (arts. 43, 45).

The waiver of diplomatic privilege must be made by or on behalf of the representative of the country concerned and cannot be made by the defendant himself; until there is due waiver, proceedings are without jurisdiction and null and void (*R.* v. *Madan* [1961] Crim.L.R. 253).

The Crown

Parts I, II, III and IV of the Road Traffic Act, 1972, apply, to the extent stated in s. 188 thereof, to persons and vehicles in the public service of the Crown and, for the purpose of proceedings for an offence in connection with any such vehicle against any person other than the driver, the person nominated in that behalf by the Government department in whose service the vehicle is used shall be deemed to be the person actually responsible unless it is shown that the driver only was responsible (Road Traffic Act, 1972, s. 187 (8)). Section 97 of the Road Traffic Regulation Act, 1967, is in like terms. Other Parts of the Act do not apply to the Crown (*Adair* v. *Feist* [1936] S.L.T.(Sh.) 22). Drivers of Crown vehicles (including British servicemen on duty) are thus fully responsible for offences of bad or drunken driving, disobeying traffic signs, not reporting accidents, breaches of the Construction and Use and Pedestrian Crossings Regulations, speeding (with certain exceptions) and so on; the position as to insurance is mentioned on p. 369. The nationalised industries are not Crown emanations (*Tamlin* v. *Hannaford* [1949] 2 All E.R. 327) and the B.B.C. is not a Crown Department (*British Broadcasting Corporation* v. *Johns* [1964] 1 All E.R. 923) nor is the British Airports Authority (Airports Authority Act, 1965, s. 1 (7)). On the other hand, a hospital management committee acts on behalf of the Crown (*Nottingham No. 1 Area Hospital Management Committee* v. *Owen* [1957] 3 All E.R. 358). The Post Office Corporation is not a Crown Department (Post Office Act, 1969, s. 6 (5)).

A British serviceman may be convicted by court-martial of committing a civil offence of a road traffic type abroad contrary to s. 70 of the Army Act (*Cox* v. *Army Council* [1962] 1 All E.R. 880). The offence in question was careless driving on a road in Germany and it was said that there may be offences under the Road Traffic and Highway Acts which cannot be committed abroad. The provisions of the Road Traffic Act, 1972, ss. 5 and 6, as to driving, etc., when unfit through drink or with alcohol above the prescribed limit in the blood are applied to servicemen in Great Britain and abroad (1972 Act, s. 188). Where a person subject to the Naval Discipline Act, 1957, is acquitted or convicted of an offence by a Naval tribunal, a civil court shall by s. 129 (1) be debarred from trying him subsequently for the same offence and by s. 129 (2) acquittal or conviction by a civil court bars subsequent trial by a Naval tribunal. By the Armed Forces Act, 1966, s. 25, substituting a new s. 133 in the Army and the Air Force Acts, 1955, where a person subject to military or Air Force law has been tried for an offence by a court-martial or by his commanding officer or had it taken into consideration at a court-martial, a civil court is debarred from trying him subsequently for an offence substantially the same as that offence. See p. 653 as to disqualification.

Enactments Not Specifically Naming the Crown

As stated, many of the provisions of the Road Traffic Acts apply to the Crown and its servants but the provisions of s. 25 of the Road Traffic Regulation Act, 1967 (stopping for school crossing patrols) are not mentioned in s. 97 nor do the Highway Act, 1835, the Town Police Clauses Act, 1847, and the Highways Act, 1959, s. 121 (obstruction), contain provisions binding the Crown.

A statute which does not name the Crown does not bind it unless it is an enactment of paramount importance to public safety which requires that Crown servants should be responsible if, in performance of their duties and acting under orders, they contravene its terms (*Cooper* v. *Hawkins* (1904), 68 J.P. 25). It is submitted that the provisions of s. 25 of the Road Traffic Regulation Act, 1967, and of s. 78 of the Highway Act, 1835 (relating to school crossing patrols and negligent opening of car doors respectively) are enactments of sufficient importance to public safety to override the rule that Crown servants acting on duty are not liable under them. Even if they do not override that rule, where there is a personal element in a charge against a man under a statute which does not bind the Crown or an individual act by a driver apart from the performance of his duty as a servant of the Crown (*per* Lord Alverstone, C.J., in *Cooper* v. *Hawkins*, *supra*), or an act by a driver which is his own personal act, e.g., being drunk or in a condition or under circumstances in which he was not performing a public duty or acting in accordance with superior orders (*per* Wills and Channell, JJ., *ibid.*), it is submitted that the driver in such a case cannot claim the benefit of any Crown exemption. Although in *Cooper* v. *Hawkins, supra,* a conviction of an Army driver for exceeding a local speed limit was quashed because he was acting under orders and it was necessary both in the particular circumstances and in the interests of the Army generally that a low speed limit should not be observed, the cited dicta of the judges in the case are, it is argued, sufficient authority for saying that Crown drivers are in the same position as civilian drivers in regard to obeying school crossing patrols and taking precautions before opening car doors, for these are personal matters in the drivers and save, perhaps, in exceptional circumstances, in no way hinder the performance of the functions of any Crown department. Examples of exceptional circumstances in which a Crown servant might not be liable would be a policeman opening the door of his car as quickly as possible to save life or the driver of an R.A.F. ambulance, under orders to get to a crashed aircraft without delay, ignoring a school crossing patrolman's signal. It is submitted that it is only if the driver's personal act is in direct performance of his public duty that the exemption applies. Accordingly, Crown drivers cannot, if this argument is right, claim any exemption for the acts and omissions mentioned above or others arising under the same statutes. See also *Salt* v. *Macknight* on p. 369. Prosecutions for " opening car doors " will generally now be brought under the Construction and Use Regulations, which apply to the Crown. See p. 400.

As regards obstruction, there is no exemption for the Crown under the Motor Vehicles (Construction and Use) Regulations, which relate to motor vehicles and trailers, but it might sometimes be necessary to prosecute Crown drivers and their superior officers under the Highways Act, 1959, s. 121. Here a defence that it was necessary to leave vehicles near a particular Government building for the department's work to be done more efficiently might be successful.

As regards school crossing patrols, it is submitted that the omission of s. 25 from s. 97 of the Road Traffic Regulation Act, 1967, which specifies the provisions of that Act which bind the Crown, is not conclusive in showing that s. 25 does not anyhow itself bind the Crown. Section 97 is a re-enactment of a provision in the Road Traffic Act, 1930, and s. 25 is a re-enactment of the original School Crossing Patrols Act, 1953; the 1953 Act contained no reference to the Crown so that the omission of s. 25 of the 1967 Act from s. 97, it is argued, does not expressly mean that it does not bind the Crown but merely that the position under the 1953 Act, which may or may not have bound the Crown, is preserved.

Crown roads are subject to the general statutory provisions which apply to roads generally, it is submitted. Those particular statutory provisions which apply to roads only if particular steps are taken as by the making of an order, may be applied to Crown roads by order under s. 149 of the Transport Act, 1968 (see p. 31), e.g., restricted waiting orders, pedestrian crossings, etc.

Drivers from Abroad

Where a solicitor is instructed in a case relating to the duty payable on, the insurance cover for, or the application of the Construction and Use Regulations to a car brought from abroad or as to the driving licences of overseas visitors, he should refer, *inter alia*, to the Motor Vehicles (International Circulation) Act, 1952; the Motor Vehicles (International Circulation) Orders, 1957 (S.I. 1957 No. 1074); 1962 (S.I. 1962 No. 1344); 1969 (S.I. 1969 No. 1086); and 1971 (S.I. 1971 No. 869); the Motor Vehicles (International Circulation) Regulations, 1971 (S.I. 1971 No. 937); the Motor Vehicles (International Motor Insurance Card) Regulations, 1971 (S.I. 1971 No. 792); the Motor Vehicles (Driving Licences) Regulations, 1971 (S.I. 1971 No. 451), reg. 21; the Road Vehicles Lighting Regulations, 1971 (S.I. 1971 No. 694), reg. 63; the Motor Vehicles (Construction and Use) Regulations, 1973, reg. 4 (6) (*infra*, p. 774); and the Goods Vehicles (Plating and Testing) Regulations, 1971 (S.I. 1971 No. 352), Sched. 2, para. 24. As to drivers' hours and records where the E.E.C. international rules apply, see Drivers' Hours (Passenger and Goods Vehicles) (International Rules) Regulations, 1973 (S.I. 1973 No. 379) and similarly named regulations relating to drivers' records (S.I. 1973 No. 380). International passenger services are governed by the Road Transport (International Passenger Services) Regulations, 1973 (S.I. 1973 No. 806). These regulations are made in implementation of E.E.C. regulations (see further p. 554).

In *British Road Services* v. *Wurzal* [1971] 3 All E.R. 480 it was held in relation to the Goods Vehicles (Plating and Testing) Regulations, 1968, that a vehicle is not " temporarily in Great Britain " if its presence in England although intermittent is regular and repeated. This decision has wider implications than at first appears and was based on the dictum of Lord M'Laren when he said in *Inland Revenue* v. *Cadwalader* (1904), 42 Sc.L.Rep. 117, at p. 120: " Taking the ordinary meaning of the word I should say that temporary purposes means casual purposes as distinguished from the case of a person who is here in pursuance of his regular habits of life." If this decision is applied to the Regulations as to driving licences for foreign and Commonwealth visitors (see art. 2 of the Motor Vehicles (International Circulation) Order of 1957 as added by the 1962 Order, *supra*), many citizens of Eire in particular may no longer be able to drive on their Eireann driving licences. Many Irishmen have worked regularly in England for a number of years, returning only for Christmas or other holidays. Although they often retain their Eire residence, they cannot be said to be " temporarily in Great Britain " if the decision of *B.R.S.* v. *Wurzal* applies. It is submitted that it does, and if there is doubt in the matter the headnote to art. 2 refers to " Visitors' Driving Permits ". It is difficult to describe a national of another country who has worked in the United Kingdom regularly for a number of years as a " visitor ".

Waiving Summons

The court may deal with a defendant actually before it, though not in answer to a summons, unless he seeks time to prepare his defence (Stone (1975), p. 507). Sometimes, when a defendant has come in answer to a summons, the prosecution desire to prefer a further or alternative charge. The defendant may waive having a summons for the new charge and declare himself ready to meet it then and there, and, if he does, the new charge can be proceeded with immediately (*Eggington* v. *Pearl* (1875), 40 J.P. 56). But the defendant is entitled to insist on a summons and should be told of his right to an adjournment to consider the new charge. *Semble*, a defendant who contends that he has been wrongfully arrested or that his summons is defective may properly object to being tried until proper process summoning him has been issued (*Dixon* v. *Wells* (1890), 54 J.P. 308, 725), but it was remarked in that case that it had been held by some of the judges in *R.* v. *Hughes* (1879), 4 Q.B.D. 614, and *R.* v. *Shaw* (1865), 34 L.J.(M.C.) 169, that, if the accused were present and the court had jurisdiction, his protest against any defect in process or wrongful arrest might be of no avail. *Semble*, a summons returnable forthwith, if the time-limit had not expired, could be sought and issued by the magistrates but the defendant should be allowed time to prepare his defence if he wants it. Where the prosecution agree with the defence to " accept a plea " to careless driving on a summons for dangerous driving, the defendant may waive having the summons for the lesser charge, but the procedure to be followed in these particular cases is mentioned on p. 266. Generally, a court cannot deal with a defendant who appears under protest, unless the protest be properly overruled (Paley on Summary Convictions, 10th ed., p. 64). The court must, of course, in every case have jurisdiction to deal with the offence— see " Venue ", *infra*.

Form of Summons

An irregularity or illegality in the mode of bringing a defendant before the court, if not objected to at the hearing, does not invalidate the conviction (*Grays* v. *Customs Commissioners* (1884), 48 J.P. 343).

By r. 81 (3) of the Magistrates' Courts Rules, 1968, a single summons can be issued on more than one information, and r. 12 of the Magistrates' Courts Rules, 1968, expressly provides that two or more informations may be set out in one document. The cases where more than one charge has been included in the information should be read with these provisions in mind. The summons should specify the statute or regulation infringed. As to the particulars in the summons generally see the Magistrates' Courts Rules, 1968, r. 83, and Brian Harris, Criminal Jurisdiction of Magistrates, 4th ed., p. 396, and elsewhere. Examples of insufficient detail in summonses are found in *Stephenson* v. *Johnson* [1954] 1 All E.R. 369 and *Cording* v. *Halse* [1954] 3 All E.R. 287. The summons does not have to show the date of the laying of the information (see *R.* v. *Godstone Justices* on p. 69) and it is perfectly proper for the signature to be affixed by a rubber stamp (*R.* v. *Brentford Justices, ex parte, Catlin* [1975] 2 All E.R. 201).

See p. 91 as to duplicity and charging alternative offences and p. 88 as to amending a summons.

2. VENUE

The venue for indictable offences is regulated, so far as magistrates' courts are concerned, by the Magistrates' Courts Act, 1952, s. 2. By s. 2 (3) and (4) magistrates may try summarily under s. 19 an offence mentioned in Sched. 1 to that Act, e.g., taking a conveyance, which has been committed by a person who appears or is brought before the court, although it has been committed outside their jurisdiction. In the case of a hybrid offence, i.e., one expressed to be triable either summarily or on indictment such as driving dangerously or while disqualified, the offender may, it is submitted, be tried summarily from the start although it was committed outside the magistrates' jurisdiction, provided that he is already before the court for another offence committed within its jurisdiction (Criminal Justice Act, 1967, ss. 28 and 36 (2)); otherwise, a hybrid offence committed outside the magistrates' area must be started with depositions and then switched to summary trial. A magistrates' court for any area by which a person is tried for an offence shall have jurisdiction to try him for any summary offence for which he could be tried by a magistrates' court for any other area (Criminal Justice Act, 1967, s. 28); it is submitted that he must lawfully have first come before the court for an offence in that court's area or be otherwise lawfully triable by it by issue of a summons for an offence within the court's jurisdiction before he can be dealt with for a summary offence committed outside it.

Otherwise, unless the statute which creates the offence provides differently, the venue for offences which can only be tried summarily is where the offence was committed. Thus, where a driving offence is committed by an unknown person in Brighton and the owner of the vehicle concerned refuses to give information, contrary to the Road Traffic Act, 1972, s. 168, when interviewed in Dover, the owner's offence is committed in Dover (but see the Magistrates' Courts Act, 1952, s. 1 (2), *infra*). Again, where a driver exceeds the speed limit on a Kent road, but is not stopped by his pursuers till he is one mile inside Sussex, and he then fails to produce his licence, the speeding is committed in Kent and the non-production offence in Sussex (see *infra* as to offences within 500 yards of a boundary), but under s. 28 of the Criminal Justice Act, 1967, he can be tried for both offences together in Sussex or in Kent.

The Magistrates' Courts Act, 1952, s. 1 (2) (*b*), enables a person to be tried for his offences in the same court as some other person charged with some other offence, where a magistrate considers it expedient so to do, although the former's offence may have been outside the jurisdiction of the court which is trying the latter's, e.g., a person who gave in London general permission to use a vehicle could be tried for permitting an illegal use in Brighton along with the user. Further, a person charged with aiding, abetting, counselling and procuring may be tried either in the same court as the principal offender or where the aiding, etc., took place (Magistrates' Courts Act, 1952, s. 35). Proceedings against a second defendant under s. 1 (2) (*b*) may be brought where there is some *nexus* between his offence and the first defendant's, but a magistrate should consider the interests of a defendant living at a distance before issuing process under s. 1 (2) (*b*) (*R.* v. *Blandford* [1955] 1 All E.R. 681). It is submitted that there must be a special application to a magistrate under s. 1 (2) (*b*) before issuing a summons pursuant to it and that it cannot be relied on to give jurisdiction where there has not been such an application.

The jurisdiction of county justices extends throughout their county (*R.* v. *Beacontree JJ.* (1915), 79 J.P. 461), and so they can try offences committed in another petty sessional division of the same county. The former commissions of the peace for counties and boroughs were replaced on 1st April, 1974, by new commissions for " commission areas " by virtue of s. 1 of the Administration of Justice Act, 1973. " Commission areas " are the London commission areas (as specified by s. 2 of the Administration of Justice Act, 1964, as amended), the City of London and a commission area for each of the metropolitan and non-metropolitan counties in England and Wales (see Scheds. 1 and 4 to the Local Government Act, 1972). Borough commissions (other than the City of London) no longer exist. Section 2 (1) of the Magistrates' Courts Act, 1952, states that magistrates' courts for a county shall have jurisdiction to try all summary offences committed within the county. (It is submitted that " county " for this purpose now means a metropolitan or non-metropolitan county in accordance with the Local Government Act, 1972). Stone (1974), on p. 42, footnote (*p*), stated that the power of a justice of the peace to sit is not restricted to the magistrates' court in the county in which he ordinarily sits. A metropolitan stipendiary magistrate is a justice of the peace for Greater London and for Essex, Hertfordshire, Kent and Surrey (Administration of Justice Act, 1964, s. 10). As to offences under the Metropolitan Police Act, 1839, see 108 J.P. Jo. 203.

By the Magistrates' Courts Act, 1952, s. 3, where an offence is committed on the boundary of two or more local jurisdictions or within 500 yards of such boundary, or is begun in one jurisdiction and finished in another, the offence may be treated as having been committed in any of these jurisdictions. The measurement, under s. 3 of the 1952 Act, will be in a straight line on a horizontal plane (Interpretation Act, 1889, s. 34). An offence of demanding an excessive taxi fare at *A* for a journey begun at *B* cannot be tried at *B*, as the offence was not in any sense commenced at *B* (*Ely* v. *Godfrey* (1922), 86 J.P. 82).

By s. 3 (3), where an offence has been committed on any person, or on or in respect of any property in or on a vehicle on a journey through two or more jurisdictions or along any road forming the boundary between two or more jurisdictions, the offence may be treated as having been committed in any of them. To give jurisdiction in respect of offences committed on a journey the offence must relate to a person or property carried in the vehicle, e.g., theft or wilful damage; an illegal user of the vehicle for carrying goods, where nothing is done to the goods, did not give jurisdiction under this section in any place save where the goods were carried, although the vehicle was on a continuous journey

and carried them during part of it (*Wardhaugh* v. *Mace* [1952]
2 All E.R. 28).

A firm charged with failing to comply with the terms of a carrier's
licence may properly be dealt with in the court in whose area its
offices or headquarters are situate and at or from which it controls
its drivers and to which the drivers have to hand in their reports
although the contravention was elsewhere (*Entwhistle* v. *Woodford*
(1937), King's Bench Division, unreported). A stipendiary
magistrate has held that a failure to comply with the terms of a
carrier's licence by carrying goods illegally cannot be tried where
the goods were carried, but should be tried where the defendant
firm's operating centre is. He has further held that, where a
servant is charged with committing an offence and the master
with permitting it, the offences occur simultaneously in the place
where the servant was at the time of the offence and *Entwhistle* v.
Woodford does not apply to give jurisdiction at the place where the
master's office is and where he first gave permission.

For a case where a Scottish managing director and Scottish
limited company were found guilty of counselling and procuring
an offence in England, see *R.* v. *Robert Millar* (*Contractors*), *Ltd. and
Robert Millar* [1970] 1 All E.R. 577.

Special cases on venue are dealt with under " Records " and the
Vehicles (Excise) Act, 1971 (pp. 544 and 489, *infra*). As to refusal
of breath, blood and urine samples, see p. 229.

3. LIMITATION OF TIME

If the offences are indictable, there is no time-limit applicable
to road traffic offences but, if they are offences expressed by statute
to be triable either summarily or on indictment (such as driving
dangerously), they should be committed for trial if more than six
months have elapsed between the offence and the laying of the
information or the arrest and charge. The prosecutor in such
offences must apply for trial on indictment before his case is closed,
so far as limitation is concerned.

For all summary offences the information (in the absence of a
special provision) must be laid within six calendar months of the
offence (Magistrates' Courts Act, 1952, s. 104). Time runs (in
the absence of a special provision) from the commission of the
offence, not from its discovery (*Teall* v. *Teall* [1938] 3 All E.R.
349). Provided the information is laid within six months the
hearing, the issue and service of the summons and the conviction
may all be outside that period (*Abraham* v. *Jutson* (1962), 106
S.J. 880; *R.* v. *Fairford J.J.*, *ex parte Brewster* (1975), *The Times*,

22nd April). The date of the information need not be stated in the summons unless there was some question of its being out of time (*R.* v. *Godstone JJ.*, *ex parte Secretary of State for the Environment* [1974] Crim.L.R. 110). The day of the offence is excluded in computing the time (*Radcliffe* v. *Bartholomew* (1892), 56 J.P. 262; *Stewart* v. *Chapman* [1951] 2 All E.R. 613) unless the relevant statute expressly provides otherwise, as in *Hare* v. *Gocher* [1962] 2 All E.R. 763. Thus, if an offence is committed at any hour on 1st January, the information may be laid at any hour up to 11.59 p.m. on 1st July. A month ends on the day on the next month corresponding in number to that from which the computation begins or, if there is no corresponding one, to the one next before it. Where there is doubt as to whether an information was laid in time, it is for the prosecutor to satisfy the court that it was and the court is entitled to dismiss the case if he fails to do so (*Lloyd* v. *Young* [1963] Crim.L.R. 703). A summons or warrant shall not cease to have effect by reason of the death of the justice or his ceasing to be a justice (Magistrates' Courts Act, 1952, s. 101). This provision would presumably apply to a summons issued by a justices' clerk by virtue of the Justices' Clerks Rules, 1970 (S.I. 1970 No. 231), because the wording of s. 5 (1) of the Justices of the Peace Act, 1968, shows the clerk's power is equated with that of a single justice for such purposes.

In view of ss. 104 and 125 (*b*) of the Magistrates' Courts Act, 1952, it is submitted that an offence triable on indictment only at the election of the accused (i.e., an offence to which s. 25 of the Magistrates' Courts Act, 1952, applies because, though expressed to be triable summarily, the punishment exceeds three months' imprisonment) is a summary offence so far as limitation of time is concerned and the information for it must have been laid within six months whether or not the defendant elects to be tried by jury.

Section 180 of the Act of 1972 lays down a special time-limit for certain offences under that Act. It reads:—

" Summary proceedings for an offence under this Act to which this section is applied by column 7 of Part I of Schedule 4 to this Act may be brought within a period of six months from the date on which evidence sufficient in the opinion of the prosecutor to warrant the proceedings came to his knowledge; but no such proceedings shall be brought by virtue of this section more than three years after the commission of the offence.

For the purposes of this section a certificate signed by or on behalf of the prosecutor and stating the date on which such evidence as aforesaid came to his knowledge shall be conclusive evidence of that fact; and a certificate stating that matter and purporting to be so signed shall be deemed to be so signed unless the contrary is proved."

The main offences to which s. 180 applies are s. 89 (3) (driving licence holder failing to surrender his licence and give particulars when particulars become incorrect), s. 99 (obtaining a driving licence, or driving, while disqualified), s. 143 (uninsured use of a motor vehicle), ss. 169, 170, 171 (forgery, issuing and making false statements in relation to driving licences, test certificates, insurance certificates). With minor alterations s. 28 of the Vehicles (Excise) Act, 1971, is identical in wording to s. 180 of the Act of 1972 and applies a similar time limit to specified offences under that Act, viz., s. 8 (using and keeping a vehicle without an excise licence), s. 16 (7) (misuse of trade licences), s. 18 (4) (using a vehicle for a purpose attracting a higher rate of duty), s. 26 (1) or (2) (forgery of and false statements relating to licences and registration marks) and " regulations made in pursuance (of the Vehicles (Excise) Act ". Section 29 imposes a similar limitation for vehicle excise offences in Scotland. If an offence has a special time-limit, the time-limit applies to an aider and abettor of the offence whether the period be longer (*Homolka* v. *Osmond* [1939] 1 All E.R. 154) or shorter (*Gould* v. *Houghton* (1921), 85 J.P. 93).

The subject of continuing offences is discussed at 107 J.P.Jo. 183 and 93 S.J. 671; later cases are *R.* v. *Wimbledon JJ.*, *ex parte Derwent* [1953] 1 All E.R. 390 and *R.* v. *Chertsey JJ.*, *ex parte Franks* [1961] 1 All E.R. 825.

The question may arise where a person neglects to give information as to the identity of a driver, and relevant considerations may be whether a penalty is provided for default after conviction and the absence of a provision declaring it to be a continuing offence (*cf.* the Mines and Quarries Act, 1954, s. 163 (5), and the Restrictive Trade Practices Act, 1956, s. 16 (3)). While " maintaining " may be a continuing offence (*Edwards* v. *Bull* (1956), 54 L.G.R. 338), an offence of " depositing and leaving " is not complete unless both the deposit and the leaving were within the limitation period (*Vaughan* v. *Biggs* [1960] 2 All E.R. 473). See p. 396 as to abandoning under the Civic Amenities Act, 1967, s. 19. Where a regulation requires an action to be done " forthwith," e.g., signing a driving licence, generally this is not a continuing offence and the six months run from the date of the issue of the licence (*A. & C. McLennan (Blairgowrie), Ltd.* v. *MacMillan* [1964] S.L.T. 2). For the same reason offences of failing to notify forthwith a change of ownership, etc., under reg. 12 (1), (2) (*a*) and (*b*), of the Road Vehicles (Registration and Licensing) Regulations, 1971 (S.I. 1971 No. 450), appear not to be continuing offences. It should be noted, however, that the time-limit for these offences is governed not by s. 104 of the Magistrates' Courts Act, 1952, but by s. 28 of the Vehicles (Excise) Act, 1971 (see above) as s. 28 applies not only to various offences under the Vehicles (Excise) Act (see above), but also to offences under regulations made in pursuance of that Act.

Where persons have conspired together to evade a statute creating summary offences, they may be tried on indictment for conspiracy even though some of the acts of evasion were more than six months ago (*R. v. Blamires Transport Services, Ltd.* [1963] 3 All E.R. 170), unless the statute itself makes the conspiracy to evade it a summary offence (*R. v. Barnett* [1951] 1 All E.R. 917).

Mere delay in taking proceedings does not seem to be a ground for refusing to hear them, but a case where magistrates did so refuse is discussed at 128 J.P.Jo. 634.

4. THE HEARING

The Court

The hearing must be in public, and examining justices taking depositions should sit in open court except where it appears to them as respects the whole or any part of the proceedings that the ends of justice would not be served by so sitting (Criminal Justice Act, 1967, s. 6); juvenile courts admit only the press. A single magistrate may sit as an examining justice to take depositions but, unless expressly provided otherwise by statute, at least two justices must sit to try a case summarily (Magistrates' Courts Act, 1952, s. 98 (1)). Not more than seven justices may sit in an adult court and not more than three in the juvenile court. However, Metropolitan and stipendiary magistrates may sit alone. If the justices are equally divided in their findings, the case may be reheard by other justices. A single magistrate may adjourn a case and, subject to the consent of both parties, a clerk to the justices may further adjourn a case (Justices' Clerks Rules, 1970 (S.I. 1970 No. 231)).

If any evidence is taken, the whole case must be heard by the same justices or two of them, and, if another magistrate joins them, the witnesses must be recalled and testify again (*R. v. Manchester JJ., ex parte Burke* (1961), 125 J.P. 387; Magistrates' Courts Act, 1952, s. 98 (6)). It does not suffice to read their evidence over again to the witnesses who have already given evidence, unless it be a deposition (see Stone (1975), p. 523). Thus, if a hearing begins on Monday before three justices, the hearing of the same case on Tuesday must be before them or two of them (only one, though, if depositions are being taken); if another magistrate sits with the two or one who come again on Tuesday, witnesses called on Monday must be recalled and give their evidence again. A differently constituted court, however, may sentence a person after he has been convicted by another court, provided there is full inquiry into the facts and circumstances of the case (Magistrates' Courts Act, 1952, s. 98 (7)).

Proof of Service; Attendance of Defendant

A summons may be served personally, by leaving it with some person at the defendant's usual or last known place of abode or by registered or recorded delivery letter addressed to such place of abode (Magistrates' Courts Rules, 1968, r. 82). The court may proceed in the defendant's absence only if he was served personally a reasonable time before the hearing, unless satisfied, e.g., by a letter from him, that the summons has come to his knowledge though served in one of the other ways specified, save that, where the summons is for an offence which is not triable on indictment (save on the election of the accused), the fact that the summons came to his knowledge need not be proved. By s. 24 (3) of the Criminal Justice Act, 1967, the defendant may have an adjudication set aside if he makes a statutory declaration that the summons had not come to his notice until a date specified in the declaration, and within fourteen days of that date, the declaration is served on the clerk to the justices. See p. 630 as to the effect on a disqualification. A warrant may not be issued for the arrest of a defendant charged with an offence which is not an indictable one or punishable with imprisonment unless his address is not sufficiently established for a summons to be served on him; on his non-appearance, a warrant may not be issued unless the offence is punishable with imprisonment or the court, having convicted him, proposes to disqualify him (Criminal Justice Act, 1967, s. 24).

A summons may be served on a corporation by leaving it at, or sending it by ordinary post to, the registered office, if such office is in England or Wales; if there is no such office in England or Wales, it may be so served at any place in England or Wales where the corporation trades or conducts its business. Summonses may be served for offences in England by persons who are in Scotland or the Isle of Man under the Summary Jurisdiction (Process) Act, 1881; if such person is in any part of Ireland or in the Channel Islands, a summons may not, but a warrant may, be issued (Magistrates' Courts Act, 1952, s. 103).

If a person is outside the British Isles just named, he cannot be summoned or arrested by warrant save in so far as the procedure relating to fugitive offenders and extradition applies (16 Halsbury, 3rd ed., p. 582 and Supplement).

Where a person is convicted in his absence due to his belief that the case is to be adjourned to a later day, the High Court will not generally grant certiorari to quash his conviction but will intervene only if it is clear that he had done everything in his power to make sure he was not required to attend on the first day and that any mistake about a possible adjournment was due solely to the court or the prosecution (*R.* v. *Pembroke JJ., ex parte Perrins* (1961), *The Guardian*, 26th October); the defendant should appeal to quarter sessions (i.e., now the Crown Court) (*ibid.*). Where a defendant has been notified that a case is to be adjourned to a certain date, the case should not be heard in his absence on an earlier date without his being given notice of the change, even though he has told the court that he will not be attending (*R.* v. *Haverfordwest JJ., ex parte George* (1964), 108 S.J. 199). Where a court has convicted or sentenced a defendant in his absence through mistake or inadvertence either on the part of the court or on the part of the defendant, the defendant may instead of appealing, ask the magistrates' court to exercise its power under s. 41 of the Criminal Justice Act, 1972, to re-open the case to rectify the mistake rather than lodging an appeal. The power of a magistrates' court to re-open the case has to be exercised within fourteen days (see s. 41 (4) of the Criminal Justice Act, 1972).

Plea of Guilty

A corporation or limited company may enter a plea by a representative appointed pursuant to s. 33 (6) of the Criminal Justice Act, 1925 (Criminal Justice Act, 1967, s. 29). He need not be a solicitor or barrister but the section is silent on whether the representative may examine and cross-examine witnesses or, indeed, address the court. The extent to which he may do so is, it is submitted, at the discretion of the court (*O'Toole* v. *Scott* [1965] 2 All E.R. 240). Where the defendant appears, s. 13 of the Magistrates' Courts Act, 1952, requires the court to *ask* him his plea. A plea of guilty by a solicitor on behalf of his client without the question having been put was, for this reason, quashed in *R.* v. *Wakefield JJ., ex parte Butterworth* [1970] 1 All E.R. 1181 and, similarly, where there was doubt as to whether the charge was properly put, the case was remitted back to the justices for rehearing (*R.* v. *Gowerton JJ., ex parte Davies* [1974] Crim.L.R. 253), but it was said that if the charge had been properly put, there would be no objection to the plea being given by the solicitor and further that such pleas would be valid even if not justified by the solicitor's instructions if the client did not show dissatisfaction with the pleas at the time. A magistrates' court may allow a defendant to change his plea at any stage up to the moment sentence is pronounced (*S.* v. *Manchester City Recorder* [1969] 3 All E.R. 1230). Where a defendant has been committed to the Crown Court for sentence, the case may be remitted back to the justices for them to determine whether his plea of guilty was unequivocal or whether there was material throwing doubt on the plea (*R.* v. *Tottenham JJ., ex parte Rubens* [1970] 1 All E.R. 879), but where the plea was unequivocal, and the stipendiary magistrate sought to ensure that the defendant understood the plea, the Crown Courts have no power to remit the case back to the magistrates' court (*R.* v. *Marylebone JJ., ex parte Westminster City Council* [1971] 1 All E.R. 1025). See p. 98 as to pleas in writing.

Hearing Charges Together

The law as to whether a number of charges against a single defendant or similar charges against two or more defendants can be heard together is now clear. A defendant may consent impliedly or expressly to a number of informations against him being heard together by the magistrates' court, but if he does not so consent he is entitled to a separate trial on each information (*Brangwynne* v. *Evans* [1962] 1 All E.R. 446) and the magistrates should announce their convictions or acquittals on each before starting on the next (see p. 77). Where a number of defendants are charged on separate but similar informations arising from one set of facts, in the absence of their consent to be tried together each is entitled to a separate trial (*Aldus and Another* v. *Watson* [1973] R.T.R. 466). If, however, a number of defendants are charged jointly on one information, then it is a matter for the discretion of the justices as to whether the defendants are tried together (*ibid.*). On exercising their powers under para. 4 of Sched. 4 to the Act of 1972 (see p. 266), the justices, seemingly could have ordered one joint information against all four defendants (*ibid.*).

Where two defendants are charged with separate offences, e.g., one with using and the other with permitting the use of the same vehicle on the same occasion, and are not tried together, the whole of the relevant evidence must be given in each case, even though most of it is repetition from the first hearing (*Taylor's Central Garages* v. *Roper* (1951), 115 J.P. 445).

Cases against different defendants or several charges against the same defendant, if the facts are substantially the same, may be heard together, provided all parties consent (*R.* v. *Ashbourne JJ.* (1950), 48 L.G.R. 268; *Taylor's Central Garages* v. *Roper, supra*). Where two defendants are being tried together on different charges, e.g., for careless driving in a cross-roads collision, should the court allow the solicitor defending the one to cross-examine the other or the witnesses called for that other's defence? The defending solicitor may undoubtedly do so where there is a joint charge and the other accused's evidence is unfavourable to his client (*R.* v. *Hadwen* (1902), 66 J.P. 456; *Rigby* v. *Woodward* [1957] 1 All E.R. 391), and even if it is not unfavourable (*R.* v. *Hilton, infra*). The procedure where separate charges are being tried together is considered at 120 J.P.Jo. 38. In *R.* v. *Hadwen* (*supra*) it was said that evidence for one defendant might incriminate the other and become tacked, as it were, to the case for the prosecution. That case, as stated, related to a joint trial, where neither defendant can insist on separate trials, as they can in separate careless driving cases. On the other hand, the High Court encourages the hearing of such charges together. It is submitted, with some hesitation, that, where two defendants are tried together on separate charges, each should be allowed to cross-examine the other and his witnesses, on the ground that the evidence for one defendant may become tacked to the case for the prosecution against the other. The main justification for this opinion is that, if one defendant is not allowed to cross-examine the other, notwithstanding that the latter's evidence helps the prosecutor, a serious injustice may result; support for it may be found in *Lord* v. *Colvin* (1855), 24 L.J.Ch. 517, and *Dryden* v. *Surrey C.C.* [1936] 2 All E.R. 535 (both civil cases). If defendants are allowed to cross-examine each other, it is unlikely that any injustice will result. In *R.* v. *Hadwen* (*supra*) reference was made to the difficulty the jury would have in distinguishing between the evidence given for the one and the other. However, in *Hedley* v. *Sparrow* [1964] N.I. 72; Jo.Crim.L. (1965) 210, a conviction of one defendant was quashed where he and the other driver had been tried together; the appellant had not given evidence but the other defendant had and had not been cross-examined. The judgments are difficult to understand in so far as they say that the other's evidence would be inadmissible and could not be the subject of cross-examination. Lord McDermott, C.J., said trials together, while allowable, should not allow admission of evidence not otherwise permitted. If magistrates who had not allowed such cross-examination, however, satisfied the High Court that they had regarded only the evidence for the prosecution in convicting a defendant incriminated by another defendant, it might well be that the High Court would not interfere. To overcome these difficulties it is suggested that, as consent is necessary before two defendants separately charged can be heard together, the defendants should also be asked at the outset if they consent to be cross-examined by the other. The general question of hearing charges of dangerous or careless driving against two defendants together, e.g., in a crossroads collision, is discussed at 120 J.P.Jo. 38, where the view is advanced that they should be heard separately, but there is cited a dictum of Lord Hewart, C.J., that it is the proper course that they should be heard together, so long as the parties consent. See also Cross on Evidence, 3rd ed., p. 212, as to mutual cross-examination. One co-defendant may cross-examine another even if the other co-defendant had given no evidence adverse to him (*R.* v. *Hilton* [1971] 3 All E.R. 541).

The further question of trying charges against one person of dangerous and careless driving together is discussed at 112 J.P.Jo. 226 and 305, and 113 J.P.Jo. 201. If the magistrates convict on both charges and impose penalties on both, their decision might be open to challenge as being equivalent in effect to punishing a person for both murder and manslaughter; if they convict on both and impose a penalty for dangerous driving only, the defendant, on appeal to the Crown Court against the conviction for dangerous driving, escapes all penalties if his appeal succeeds. Magistrates might think it best to convict for dangerous driving only and mark the other charges " no adjudication " or " adjourned ". Obviously, a safe course for the prosecution is to prefer a charge of dangerous driving only and let the court reduce it, if thought fit, under Sched. 4, Pt. IV, para. 4, or, with consent, charges of both " dangerous " and " careless " can be heard together. And see *R.* v. *Hawarden JJ.* on p. 267. Where there is a charge of dangerous driving and the prosecution agree with the defence to " accept a plea " of guilty to careless driving only and not to proceed with the graver charge, it is submitted that the proper course is for the facts to be related by the prosecuting solicitor to the magistrates and their approval obtained to this course before applying to withdraw the charge of dangerous driving and before any plea is taken. In *R.* v. *Bedwellty JJ., ex parte Munday* [1970] Crim.L.R. 601 the prosecution agreed with the defence not to offer evidence on a dangerous driving charge if the defendant pleaded guilty to the lesser charge of careless driving. The transcript of the judgments of the Divisional Court shows that the consent of the prosecution to this course was given subject to the court's consent. The magistrates' court insisted on hearing an outline of the facts and after hearing the facts refused to accept the dismissal of the " dangerous " driving charge. Their insistence was upheld by the Divisional Court, but the magistrates were directed to allow the defendant to elect trial by jury on the dangerous driving charge as he had only consented to summary trial on the basis that he would have the charge dismissed. If there is a charge of dangerous driving only, the court cannot reduce the charge under the Road Traffic Act, 1972, Sched. 4, Pt. IV, para. 4, until the " hearing " has begun, though there would be no objection to a summons for careless driving, returnable forthwith, being preferred. Where charges for dangerous and careless driving are preferred together, it is argued at 112 J.P.Jo. 226 that a plea of " guilty " to careless driving may bar proceedings for dangerous driving, but a defendant who agrees to two charges being heard together cannot say that the court cannot convict and punish him on both (*Williams* v. *Hallam* (1943), 59 T.L.R. 287).

A charge of driving while disqualified should not be heard along with other charges under the Road Traffic Act because of the possible prejudice to the defendant (*R.* v. *Pomeroy* (1935), 25 Cr. App.R. 147). But a contrary view is argued at [1961] Crim.L.R. 275 in respect of magistrates' courts. Some magistrates' clerks get over the difficulty by omitting the charge of driving whilst disqualified from the court list put before the magistrates until the defendant has pleaded guilty or been found guilty on the other charges. However, an indictment may properly be drawn containing a count for this offence and one for another offence and, if the defence is that the accused was not driving at all, he would not (according to the Court of Appeal) be prejudiced by the jury's knowing of his conviction for the offence for which he was disqualified. On indictment, he may always apply for separate trials and he is entitled to insist on them before magistrates (*R.* v. *Andrews* [1967] 1 All E.R. 170). Where the issue was, whether the defendant was the driver, counts of dangerous driving and driving while disqualified were heard together at a Crown Court (unreported) notwithstanding *R.* v. *Pomeroy, supra.*

Where charges against the same defendant are heard separately, the justices should convict or acquit on the first charge before starting on the second, but may postpone sentence (*Hamilton* v. *Walker* (1892), 56 J.P. 583; *R.* v. *Fry* (1898), 62 J.P. 457). Where two defendants are being tried separately on charges arising out of the same facts, e.g., careless driving causing an accident, the magistrates should announce their finding in the first case before starting to hear the second (*R.* v. *Chambers* (1939), 83 S.J. 439). *Quaere*, whether they should do the same where defendants on separate charges are tried together. Where the charge is a joint one, they hear both defendants before coming to a decision (*cf. R.* v. *Hadwen, supra*), and if, in their discretion, they feel that the allegations made by the first-testifying defendant against the other require answering and generally the facts and evidence are so intermingled as to make it desirable to hear both defendants in order to arrive at a proper decision, it may be that they can defer deciding separate charges tried together until both defendants have concluded their cases.

A person charged under the Road Traffic Act, 1972, s. 33, with selling a defective protective helmet may himself summon the person actually responsible for the offence in the same proceedings pursuant to Sched. 1. The procedure to follow in such " third-party proceedings " is indicated in the notes in Stone to s. 113 of the Food and Drugs Act, 1955.

Committal for Trial or Sentence

Where a defendant has a right to elect to be tried by a jury, he must be informed of it personally and by clear words telling him of his rights (*R.* v. *Kettering JJ.*, *ex parte Patmore* [1968] 3 All E.R. 167); his solicitor may elect on his behalf (*R.* v. *Salisbury, etc., JJ.* [1954] 2 All E.R. 326). Omission to tell the defendant of his right is fatal even though it is known that he intended to plead guilty before the magistrates (*R.* v. *Berkeley (Gloucestershire) JJ.*, *ex parte Higgins* (1965), 109 S.J. 77). But if the defendant is absent the magistrates' court may try the case in his absence, as the right of election for trial by jury can only be exercised by a defendant in person (*R.* v. *Bishop's Stortford JJ.*, *ex parte Shields* [1969] Crim.L.R. 201; and see s. 25 (2) of the Magistrates' Courts Act, 1952). It is submitted that, where a defendant has elected for trial by jury or consented to summary trial, and the case is adjourned without any evidence being taken, he should be given a fresh election or opportunity to consent at the adjournment if another magistrate not present on the first occasion is then sitting. On the other hand, it can be argued that his election or consent is binding on him, once he has exercised his right, being of a general nature and not concerned with the composition of a particular court. He can anyhow withdraw his consent to a summary trial, on a plea of not guilty, until evidence has been called (*R.* v. *Craske* [1957] 2 All E.R. 772; *R.* v. *Southampton City JJ.*, *ex parte Briggs* [1972] 1 All E.R. 573). A defendant who had consented to summary trial on a charge of dangerous driving on the basis that the court would be asked to dismiss it and proceed on the lesser charge of careless driving was allowed to elect for trial by jury after the magistrates' insistence on the charge of dangerous driving being heard had been upheld by the Divisional Court (*R.* v. *Bedwellty JJ.*, *ex parte Munday* [1970] Crim.L.R. 601).

The procedure in offences punishable summarily or on indictment (e.g., dangerous driving and drunken driving) is regulated by the Magistrates' Courts Act, 1952, s. 18, and the prosecutor, if desiring summary trial, may apply for it at the outset; the application may be made expressly or be implied from his conduct (*James* v. *Bowkett* [1952] 2 All E.R. 320; see also p. 80). The procedure of s. 19 of the Magistrates' Courts Act, 1952, applies only to the offences listed in Stone (1974), pp. 121–3; the main offences so far as this book is concerned are taking or attempting to take conveyances and criminal damage under the Criminal Damage Act, 1971 (see p. 364). Any person convicted of a " s. 19 " offence may be committed for sentence, if appropriate, on pleading or being found guilty, whether or not depositions were taken. Where the charge is a " s. 18 " offence, and the defendant has a bad record and it is considered that he should be sent to the Crown Court for sentence, he can only be committed for sentence if the proceedings are commenced by the taking of depositions and then subsequently switched to summary proceedings in accordance with s. 18 (3) of the Magistrates' Courts Act, 1952 (*R.* v. *Moore* (1968), *The Times*, 20th August, as explained in *R.* v. *Jones* (*Gwyn*) [1969] 1 All E.R. 325). If the case is a serious one, it should be committed for trial. There is power to commit for sentence under the Criminal Justice Act, 1967, s. 56, any road traffic summary offences (including " s. 18 " cases tried summarily) so long as they carry either disqualification or endorsement or imprisonment, if the offender is at the same time being committed for sentence for another offence under s. 28 or 29 of the Magistrates' Courts Act, 1952, the Vagrancy Act, 1824, or the Criminal Justice Act, 1967, s. 41 (2) or s. 62 (6), which relate respectively to suspended sentences, revocation of parole, or for an offence committed during probation or conditional discharge. On committal under s. 56 to the Crown Court, the court has only the same power to punish as the committing justices (*R.* v. *Ronald Ward* (1968), 53 Cr.App.R. 23). Once the justices have decided to commit the defendant for sentence under s. 29 there is no power to make any ancillary order such as an order of compensation (*R.* v. *Blackpool JJ.* [1972] 3 All E.R. 854) other than an interim order of disqualification (see p. 636). It was held in *R.* v. *Phillips* [1953] 1 All E.R. 968 that where the defendant elects for trial by jury, fresh charges arising from the same facts should not be preferred, but this case was not followed in *R.* v. *Nisbet* [1971] 3 All E.R. 307, where the defendant had elected trial on a charge under s. 235 of the 1960 Act (now s. 170 of the 1972 Act). Other charges were added at quarter sessions. His convictions were upheld by the Court of Appeal.

Additional counts may be added to the indictment, even if the original charge is one which would not have been tried by a jury except at the defendant's election. But such additional counts to an indictment may not be made if it is unfair or oppressive to the defendant. Moreover such additional counts may only be added if disclosed in the depositions of the examining justices (*R.* v. *Nisbet, supra*). Hitherto many " hybrid " offences were triable on indictment either on election by the prosecution under s. 18 (1) of the Magistrates' Courts Act, 1952, or by the defence under s. 25 of the Act because the offence is punishable summarily with more than three months' imprisonment. The only road traffic offences under the Act of 1972 which now come within this category are s. 2 (1) (dangerous, etc., driving), s. 5 (1) (driving or attempting to drive while unfit) and s. 6 (1) (driving or attempting to drive with excess blood/alcohol level). All other " hybrid " offences, notably driving while disqualified (s. 99 (*b*)), refusing to supply a specimen for laboratory testing (s. 9 (3)), in charge of a motor vehicle while drunk or with excess blood/alcohol (s. 5 (2) and s. 6 (2)) are offences for which the defendant has no longer any right to elect trial by jury under s. 25 because all these offences can no longer be punished by imprisonment on summary conviction at all or for a term exceeding three months. The fact, however, that the prosecutor asks the magistrates' court to deal with such an offence summarily does not, it is submitted, necessarily mean that the defendant has no possibility of securing trial by jury. It would appear from the wording of s. 18 (1) that the magistrates' court has a discretion as to whether to accede to an application by the prosecutor for the matter to be dealt with summarily. Additionally s. 18 (5) enables a magistrates' court to revert to committal proceedings at any time before the conclusion of the evidence for the prosecution. It is, therefore, clear that a defendant's advocate has two opportunities to seek to persuade the magistrates' court not to deal with an offence summarily. The first is at the outset of the proceedings when the prosecutor applies for summary trial under s. 18 (1) and the second is at any time before the conclusion of the evidence for the prosecution. Section 18 is silent as to how the magistrates' court should exercise its discretion (but see *Collins* v. *Spring,* below). It is submitted that the primary criteria are the interests of justice. An obvious example is where a defendant is additionally charged with an offence for which the magistrates' court has no alternative but to commit for trial (e.g., a defendant charged with refusing a specimen for laboratory testing and who is additionally charged with dangerous driving for which he elects trial by jury). In *Collins* v. *Spring* [1975] Crim.L.R. 100, it was held that there was no onus on the prosecution to satisfy magistrates that the case should be dealt with summarily; once the prosecution has made application for summary trial, the justices should consider whether they have adequate powers of punishment and in other respects it is a proper case for summary trial (*ibid.*).

A defendant who is not personally present cannot claim trial by jury under s. 25 of the Magistrates' Courts Act (*R.* v. *Bishop's Stortford JJ.* (1969), 113 S.J. 124) but a defendant must be present to consent to summary trial under s. 19; such cases cannot be dealt with in his absence.

Advantages of being tried by a jury are the disclosure of the Crown case in advance and the recognised tendency of some juries to acquit in road traffic cases. Disadvantages are the greater expense, the very real danger of a heavier sentence and the liability, on an acquittal for dangerous driving by a jury, still to be tried summarily for careless driving (*R.* v. *Cardiff JJ.* (1959), on p. 264). Also, the chances of a successful appeal from a magistrates' conviction to the Crown Court are greater, for the Crown Court will re-hear the whole case and other witnesses can be called; on an appeal from a conviction on indictment, the Court of Appeal will interfere only if there has been a serious irregularity in the trial or a defective summing-up or the jury's verdict is clearly insupportable. See generally as to the respective advantages of trial by jury or summarily: 99 S.J. 667.

Where a prosecution for a " s. 18 " or " s. 19 " (of the Magistrates' Courts Act) offence is being carried on by the Director of Public Prosecutions, it cannot be tried summarily without his consent. Nor can a " s. 19 " offence affecting the property or affairs of the Crown or of a public body be tried summarily without the prosecutor's consent.

Where a magistrates' court has begun to try an indictable offence summarily under s. 18 or s. 19, the defendant may still be committed for trial, depositions being duly taken and witnesses recalled for this purpose so far as necessary, in accordance with the Magistrates' Courts Act, 1952, s. 18 (5), and the Criminal Justice Administration Act, 1962, s. 13, provided this is done before the conclusion of the prosecution's evidence.

See p. 636 as to disqualification on committal for sentence.

Depositions

Save where the Criminal Justice Act, 1967, s. 1 (*infra*), applies, evidence on a committal for trial may be wholly oral or a mixture or oral and written or wholly written; the latter would seldom

occur but might where the defence wished to submit that even the
unchallenged evidence for the prosecution disclosed no case.
Written evidence, by s. 2 of the Act, must contain the declarations,
etc., indicated in s. 2 (2) and (3) and should be read aloud at the
hearing, unless the court directs that an account shall be given
orally of it; the court of its own motion or on the application of
any party may require the maker of the statement to attend and
give oral evidence. Admissions made in court pursuant to s. 10
of the 1967 Act should be written down and signed by the person
making them (Magistrates' Courts Rules, 1968, r. 59). By s. 2 (2)
(d) also a party may object to a particular written statement given
in evidence, in which case the witness must attend. It suffices
if a written statement is given in advance to the defending solicitor
but there must be a copy for each defendant whom he represents
(*R.* v. *Bott* [1968] 1 All E.R. 1119). The Magistrates' Courts
Rules, 1968, r. 58, further deals with written evidence. Though
no minimum time for the defendant to see the written statements
is laid down, obviously it must be long enough to enable proper
consideration to be given to them.

Under s. 1 of the Criminal Justice Act, 1967, where the defendant
or all the defendants, if more than one, are legally represented
and all the evidence for the prosecution has been tendered to the
defence before the hearing, the defence may consent to a committal
for trial without the court considering the evidence; this course
may not be taken when any one of the defendants is not legally
represented or does not consent. The Criminal Justice Act, 1972,
s. 44, now allows a juvenile to be committed for trial under s. 1
of the Criminal Justice Act, 1967.

Unless one of the defendants applies for the restrictions on
publicity at the preliminary hearing to be lifted, the evidence will
not be reported in the press prior to the trial on indictment, save
where no defendant is committed for trial (Criminal Justice Act,
1967, s. 3).

If the defendant gives evidence at the preliminary hearing before
the magistrates, his deposition may be read to the jury at the trial
before the close of the prosecution's case, even if he does not give
evidence at the trial (*R.* v. *Boyle* (1904), 20 T.L.R. 192), but he
should be told of the prosecution's right (*R.* v. *Warren* (1909), 73
J.P. 359). See 114 J.P.Jo. 62 as to recording relevant remarks
made by the defendant at the preliminary hearing.

Speeches and No Case to Answer

The informant may conduct the case for the prosecution and
cross-examine witnesses for the defence, and r. 13 of the Magistrates'

Courts Rules, 1968, gives both the informant and the defendant in a trial the right to address the court. Where a defendant was denied her right to address a stipendiary matistrate, her conviction was set aside (*R.* v. *Great Marlborough St. Magistrate, ex parte Fraser* [1974] Crim.L.R. 47). In many courts a senior police officer in fact conducts the case though he may not always be the informant; police advocacy was disapproved of in *May* v. *Beeley* (1910), 74 J.P. 111, but in *O'Toole* v. *Scott* [1965] 2 All E.R. 240 the Privy Council held that the New South Wales legislation (which is similar to s. 99 of the Magistrates' Courts Act, 1952) gave a discretion to a court of summary jurisdiction to allow the prosecutor or defendant to be represented by someone other than a barrister or solicitor. On the other hand the court are required to allow any party to proceedings in a magistrates' court to be represented by a solicitor or barrister (Magistrates' Courts Act, 1952, s. 99). See generally as to the police prosecutor, Brian Harris, Criminal Jurisdiction of Magistrates, 4th ed., p. 372. Where a solicitor appears to prosecute, he may make an opening speech, reply to points of law and intervene to correct misstatements of fact made by the defending solicitor. The defendant or the defending solicitor may address the court either at the end of the prosecution's case or at the end of his case; he may address the court a second time, if the court permits, but then the prosecution are entitled to a second speech, to be delivered prior to the second speech for the defence (Magistrates' Courts Rules, 1968, r. 13). Rule 13 in fact gives these rights of address to the " prosecutor " and the " accused " and so apparently applies to those appearing in person and to prosecutors not legally qualified who are allowed to appear, e.g., under the Local Government Act, 1972, s. 223.

The rules make no mention of submitting " No case to answer ", but this seems to be a well-recognised procedure now and in a criminal case the court should not put a defendant to his election whether to give evidence or rest on a submission of " no case " (*Jones* v. *Metcalfe* [1967] 3 All E.R. 205); evidence may be called if it is overruled. It is submitted that the prosecutor may reply to a submission that there is in law no case to answer but should not reply to a like submission on facts alone, e.g., that the witnesses have been so discredited that their evidence cannot be safely relied on. And see *Saunders* v. *Johns* on p. 87.

Where the defence submit that there is no case to answer, the court should, before ruling, ask: " Are you calling evidence? " so that there is no misunderstanding as to whether it is the final speech or a mere submission (*R.* v. *Birkenhead JJ., ex parte Fisher* [1962] 3 All E.R. 837; *R.* v. *Gravesend JJ., ex parte Sheldon* [1968] Crim.L.R.

506).   Where in reply to a submission of " no case " the magistrates use words intended to amount to a conviction, their decision will be quashed (*ibid.*, but see now *S.* v. *Manchester City Recorder, infra*). But such words must be intended to amount to a conviction and if, through infelicity of expression, the chairman has announced a conviction in reply to a submission but his colleagues intended merely that he should announce that they overrule the submission, this verbal error can be corrected since it is a " slip of the tongue " as in *R.* v. *Newcastle-upon-Tyne JJ., ex parte Swales* [1972] Crim.L.R. 111.   It is suggested that in such a case the prosecutor should immediately ask all the magistrates if it is the decision of the whole Bench that there should be a conviction.

In a Practice Direction at [1962] 1 All E.R. 448 [" All justices' clerks should keep on their table a copy (of this Practice Direction) and make a practice of putting it before the presiding justice for guidance on every submission of no case ": *per* Lord Widgery, C.J. in *Stoneley* v. *Coleman* [1974] Crim.L.R. 254], the Divisional Court stated that a submission that there is no case to answer may properly be made and upheld: (*a*) when there has been no evidence to prove an essential element in the alleged offence; or (*b*) when the evidence adduced by the prosecution has been so discredited as a result of cross-examination or is so manifestly unreliable that no reasonable tribunal could safely convict on it.

Apart from these two situations, the Practice Direction continues, a tribunal should not in general be called on to reach a decision as to conviction or acquittal until the whole of the evidence which either side wishes to tender has been placed before it. If, however, a submission is made that there is no case to answer, the decision should depend not so much on whether the adjudicating tribunal (if compelled to do so) would at that stage convict or acquit but on whether the evidence is such that a reasonable tribunal might convict. If a reasonable tribunal might convict on the evidence so far laid before it, there is a case to answer. Convictions were quashed where submissions of no case were mistaken for final speeches in *R.* v. *Birkenhead JJ.* and *R.* v. *Gravesend JJ., supra,* but it is now submitted that if the court has not pronounced sentence, it may, as soon as it realises its mistake, adjourn the case to be reheard by a different bench. The House of Lords in *S.* v. *Manchester City Recorder* [1969] 3 All E.R. 1230 held that a magistrates' court is not *functus officio* until sentence is pronounced. The latter case allowed a defendant to change his plea after it had been accepted and the case adjourned. There is no difference in principle between a defendant being allowed to change his mind and a court being allowed to do so when the court has made a finding of guilt on a mistaken premise. The House of Lords in *S*'s case, *supra*, held that magistrates have only one duty, that of carrying a case to its conclusion. This involves a conviction or finding of guilt followed by a further decision as to sentence. Therefore where a magistrates' court mistook a submission of no case for a final speech, announced conviction and did not pronounce sentence, it was held that the case could be reheard *de novo* by a differently constituted bench (*R.* v. *Midhurst JJ.*, *ex parte Thompson and Another* (1973), *The Times*, 3rd October). If it is argued that a fresh bench cannot hear the case because the defendant has already been convicted, the answer to such a plea of *autrefois convict* is that the conviction is a nullity because the defendant was given no opportunity of defending the case. Section 41 of the Criminal Justice Act, 1972, enables a court to reopen the case where the defendant has pleaded not guilty or has been convicted in his absence. The section also enables a court to vary or rescind any sentence or order made by the court, whether the defendant pleaded guilty or otherwise. The powers under the section are only exercisable within fourteen days. It should be noted that the section does not enable a court to reopen the case for the purposes of a re-trial where the defendant has pleaded guilty and has been sentenced.

In *Lonnkuist* v. *Lonnkuist* (1952), 96 S.J. 135, a civil case, it was held that, when a defendant has begun to give evidence after an unsuccessful submission of " no case ", the court should not stop the case until his cross-examination is concluded. *Quaere*, whether this rule applies in criminal cases; it may be that it would be limited to cross-examination on the vital issue, e.g., if the magistrates are satisfied that the defendant was not the driver in a s. 2 case after he has been cross-examined on that issue, it seems pointless to continue cross-examining on any other issues.

The defendant or his advocate may further address the court on rejection of his submission of " No case to answer " (*Disher* v. *Disher* [1963] 3 All E.R. 933, a civil case). The magistrates may still dismiss a case after rejecting a submission of " No case to answer " even though no evidence is given for the defence (*De Filippo* v. *De Filippo* (1964), 108 S.J. 56, a civil case; see also *Rabjohns* v. *Burgar* [1972] Crim.L.R. p. 46 where the justices' decision was overruled on other grounds). In *Walker* v. *Walker* (1966), 110 S.J. 270, magistrates were enjoined to allow advocates to address them on questions of custody of children after the main issue had been determined and no doubt they should allow advocates and defendants to address them on such questions as disqualification also.

Reopening

The prosecution may properly be allowed to reopen their case where some formal proof has not been given of, say, a statutory instrument or (subject to what is said below) to hear evidence which owing to mistake or accident or want of foresight has not been given; if the statutory instrument is not immediately available, the court should adjourn (*Duffin* v. *Markham* (1918), 82 J.P. 281; *Palastanga* v. *Salman* [1962] Crim.L.R. 334). Justices have a discretion whether to allow a prosecutor to call evidence, after he has closed his case, to fill a gap and their discretion will not be interfered with by the High Court if they exercise it judicially (*Middleton* v. *Rowlett* [1954] 2 All E.R. 277). In *Middleton's* case the magistrates refused to allow the prosecution to reopen the case to prove the identity of the driver on a charge of dangerous driving. As they had exercised their discretion judicially, their decision was upheld. *Middleton's* case was applied and approved in *Piggott* v. *Sims* [1973] R.T.R. 15, where on the other hand the justices had allowed the prosecution to reopen the case to adduce in evidence the certificate of the police surgeon as to the voluntary taking of blood from the defendant and the certificate of the analyst as to the blood/alcohol level. Melford Stephenson, J., emphasised that the justices have a discretion to allow the prosecution to reopen their case even if the evidence, as was the case, was a vital part of the prosecution's case and was no mere error of procedure on the prosecution's part. *Piggott's* case makes it clear that provided the justices exercise their discretion judicially, essential prosecution evidence can be admitted even if the evidence is more than of a formal or procedural nature. The justices' decision was " abundantly justified " (*per* Melford Stephenson, J., on p. 18). The justices were aware that copies of the certificates had already been tendered to the defence under (what is now) s. 10 (3) of the Act of 1972 and had not been objected to by the defendant. It was said in *Royal* v. *Prescott-Clarke* [1966] 2 All E.R. 366, that magistrates should normally grant an adjournment to the prosecution after the close of their case to allow them to satisfy a formal requirement as to proof (though evidence should not be allowed merely to strengthen the case against the defendant) unless there is misconduct by the prosecutor or he elects to call no further evidence or there is potential prejudice to the defendant; in *Royal's* case formal evidence was allowed to prove that a restriction applied to a motorway even though the defence had given notice to the prosecution well in advance of the hearing that they would require proof of such formal requirements.

It is not essential to produce all exhibits (though some, such as statements, must be produced) but the absence of exhibits may be a matter for comment (*Hockin* v. *Ahlquist* [1943] 2 All E.R. 722). And see further as to reopening under " Irregularity ", *infra*, and *Price* v. *Humphries* [1958] 2 All E.R. 725, where the prosecutor was allowed to reopen to prove the consent to the prosecution. It was said there that cases can properly be reopened where there is an objection which goes only to procedure, but magistrates must be very careful about allowing the prosecution to call more evidence, after closing their case, to prove something which goes to the merits and upon which the guilt or innocence of the defendant depends. Thus, if there has been no proof that the defendant was the driver of the vehicle, the prosecutor should generally, it seems, not be allowed to reopen to prove this, for it is a matter on which he obviously should have had evidence available. But, if the necessary witness has been called and, through a slip of memory, the prosecutor has omitted to ask him the formal question " Who was the driver? ", it is submitted following the views of the judges both in *Middlleton*'s case and *Piggott*'s case that it would be unfair and a wrong exercise of discretion not to allow him to reopen in such circumstances. If a prosecutor finds during the hearing that a vital matter is likely to be unproved through the non-appearance or hostility of witnesses, he should seek an adjournment. See also *Jones* v. *Carter* on p. 122. However, in *Saunders* v. *Johns* [1965] Crim.L.R. 49, as explained in *Brake* v. *Taylor* (1967), 1st June, unreported, Lord Parker, C.J., said that, on a submission of " no case " because of failure to identify the defendant, the prosecutor or the court could have recalled the relevant witness as soon as the submission had been made and obtained evidence which would have completed the identification. In the *Saunders* case there had been a failure to state certain facts which would have identified the defendant. Although it was said in *Brake* v. *Taylor, supra,* that there had been several unreported cases which showed that it was only in the event of a technical omission in a prosecution case that the magistrates were under any obligation to permit the calling of further evidence, *Piggott*'s case makes it clear that where there is no merit in the defence objection, essential evidence should be admitted where the defence are aware of the nature of that evidence and are not challenging it. Further evidence should not be admitted after both sides have completed their case and the magistrates have retired to consider their decision (*Webb* v. *Leadbetter* [1966] 2 All E.R. 114), and a conviction was quashed where the justices, after retiring, returned and heard a prosecution witness whose evidence had already been given by the reading of her statement made by that witness under s. 9 of the Criminal Justice Act, 1967 (*French's Dairies* (*Sevenoaks*), *Ltd.* v. *Davis* [1973] Crim.L.R. 630). Where a vital witness turns up at that stage, one course would be for the whole case to be adjourned for hearing by a different bench but this cannot be done if the magistrates have announced the sentence.

Amending Summonses

Section 100 of the Magistrates' Courts Act, 1952, reads:—

(1) No objection shall be allowed to any information or complaint, or to any summons or warrant to procure the presence of the defendant, for any defect in it in substance or in form, or for any variance between it and the evidence adduced on behalf of the prosecutor or complainant at the hearing of the information or complaint.

(2) If it appears to a magistrates' court that any variance between a summons or warrant and the evidence adduced on behalf of the prosecutor or complainant is such that the defendant has been misled by the variance, the court shall, on the application of the defendant, adjourn the hearing.

This means in effect that the summons can be amended (*per* Byrne, J., in *Meek* v. *Powell* [1952] 1 All E.R. 347); it was also said the concept of amendment at an appellate stage was foreign to our criminal law and in *Garfield* v. *Maddocks* [1973] Crim.L.R. 231 it was held that s. 100 had no application to a Crown Court hearing on appeal from a magistrates' court. Section 100 was held to obviate the necessity for a summons to repeat the date upon which the information was laid (*R.* v. *Godstone JJ.*, *ex parte Secretary of State for the Environment* [1974] Crim.L.R. 110); *aliter* if there was any question as to the information being out of time. In *Atterton* v. *Browne* (1945), 109 J.P. 25, magistrates were held entitled to dismiss the summons altogether for a serious defect, but apparently there were other grounds also for dismissing it. And see *Westminster City Council* v. *Peart* [1968] Crim.L.R. 504 for a case where a magistrate was justified in dismissing an insufficiently detailed summons. In *Wright* v. *Nicholson* [1970] 1 All E.R. 12, it was held that the words of s. 100 (1) of the Magistrates' Courts Act should not be read literally as meaning that there can be no attack on an information however fundamental the defect. Each case depends on its own merits and circumstances are infinitely variable. It depends in every case whether the variance is of such a character as to require amendment. If the defendant has been misled or the variance is fundamental so that there might be injustice to an accused, an amendment is required. Once an amendment is required s. 100 (2) operates and requires the court to adjourn if the defence applies. If the defendant does not require an adjournment, the amendment may be made forthwith and the case proceeded with on the amended summons.

The variance may be so trivial that no amendment at all is required. In *Darnell* v. *Holliday* [1973] R.T.R. 276 the defendant was charged on five informations with using a car in " South Parade ". The justices dismissed the case on the grounds that the offences occurred not in South Parade but in an unnamed cul-de-sac opposite. The justices were directed to convict by the Divisional Court as no sort of injustice was suffered by the defendant because of the misnaming of the road. Similarly in *Taylor* v. *Grey* [1973] R.T.R. 281 a stipendiary magistrate was directed to hear and determine a case where the road was described as " Princes' Street, London, W.1 " instead of " Princess Street, London, W.1 ", the Divisional Court again holding that no amendment was required; " it was a simple typing error which could confuse nobody " (*per* Lord Widgery at p. 280). In *Moulder* v. *Judd* [1974] Crim.L.R. 111 a defendant was charged with speeding on the M1 on an information that it was " at Bushey . . . on the south bound carriageway of the M1 "; on it being shown that no part of the speed check took place in the parish of Bushey, on a submission by the defendant the case was dismissed. The justices were ordered to continue the hearing—" it was inconceivable that the defendant was misled."

At the other extreme, one can have a defect that is so fundamental that, far from it being required to be cured by amendment, it is in fact incapable of being cured. Thus the summons cannot be amended to a different offence altogether (*Loadman* v. *Cragg* (1862), 26 J.P. 743—from " drunk and disorderly " to " drunk "; *Lawrence* v. *Fisher*, Jo.Crim.L. (1947) 356; *Atterton* v. *Browne* (1945), 109 J.P. 25). But it is proper to amend a summons, subject to the defendant's right to an adjournment if he has been deceived or misled, where the ownership of property maliciously damaged has been wrongly described (*Ralph* v. *Hurrell* (1875), 40 J.P. 119); where the date of the offence has been wrongly stated so long as it is within the six-month period (*Exeter Corporation* v. *Heaman* (1877), 42 J.P. 503); where the defendant appearing in court has been wrongly named in the summons (*Dring* v. *Mann* (1948), 112 J.P. 270); by deleting superfluous words (*Rogerson* v. *Stephens* [1950] 2 All E.R. 144) or where the defendant is charged under the wrong section and the charge is inadequately stated (*Hunter* v. *Coombs* [1962] 1 All E.R. 904). Section 100 can be used after conviction and before sentence (*Allan* v. *Wiseman* [1975] Crim.L.R. 37) (defendant convicted in the name of "Jeffrey Thomas Loach "—real name "Jeffrey Thomas Allan "

—arrested—name amended to Allan on appearance for sentence). Where a defendant is charged with an offence under a repealed statute he cannot be convicted unless the summons has first been amended, even if the statutes are word for word the same. Paragraph 3 of Sched. 10 to the Act of 1972 does not entitle a court to convict on the repealed statute (*Stowers* v. *Darnell* [1973] R.T.R. 459). Where the defence ask for further particulars, the prosecution would often be wise to supply them (*Robertson* v. *Rosenberg* (1951), 115 J.P. 128). Where offences are charged in the alternative, the prosecutor must elect at the outset on which he will proceed and it is too late after that to amend the information (*Hargreaves* v. *Alderson* [1962] 3 All E.R. 1019), but where justices convicted an employer of failing to cause a current record of driving to be kept between dates in August and dates in September, it was held that while an information bad for duplicity could not be cured on appeal, the circumstances of the justices' finding of guilt showed that they had found the offence to have been committed on the first date mentioned in the information and that the words " between " and " September 25th " could be treated as mere surplusage (*Blakey Transport, Ltd.* v. *Baggott* [1973] Crim.L.R. 776). See *R.* v. *Aylesbury JJ., ex parte Wisbey* [1965] 1 All E.R. 602 as to the amount of information to which a defendant is entitled prior to the hearing, and see below. In *Cross* v. *Oliver* (1964), 108 S.J. 583 a defendant was charged with speeding in a road controlled as to part by 1957 Regulations and as to part by 1958 ones. The speeding had occurred in both parts and the information alleged one offence of speeding contrary to both Regulations. The prosecutor declined to elect to proceed for one offence against one of the Regulations only and the conviction was quashed on the ground that the information was bad for duplicity as charging two offences.

A defendant who disputes the case on merits is generally deemed to waive objection to irregularities in the summons, etc. Justices are not deprived of jurisdiction because a summons is insufficiently detailed (*Neal* v. *Devenish* (1894), 58 J.P. 246); contrast *Stephenson* v. *Johnson* [1954] 1 All E.R. 369, where the particulars of the offence were so lacking that the justices " should not have entertained it ". *Semble*, they could at their discretion have adjourned for further and better particulars to be given.

Where the prosecutor does not avail himself of his chance to seek amendment of a defective information, a conviction on that information will be bad (*Hunter* v. *Coombs, supra*).

A defective summons can be withdrawn and a regular one issued in its place, if within the time-limit and if there has been no adjudication on the first one. See pp. 64–65.

Duplicity

An information should charge one offence only and, if more than one offence is charged in one information in the alternative, e.g., driving without due care and attention or without reasonable consideration, it is out of order; the court should call on the prosecutor to elect on which charge to proceed (*R.* v. *Surrey JJ., ex parte Witherick* (1932), 95 J.P. 219; *Fox* v. *Dingley, Ware* v. *Fox* [1967] 1 All E.R. 100). See *R.* v. *Clow*, p. 265, for cases where a charge of driving in a dangerous manner and (not " or ") at a dangerous speed have been held to be good. If a statute forbids the doing of act *A* or act *B*, it creates two offences and a conviction of both offences on one information is bad for uncertainty (*Field* v. *Hopkinson* (1944), 108 J.P. 21, but contrast *Davis* v. *Loach* (1886), 51 J.P. 118, where a byelaw forbade the emission of " smoke or steam " and a conviction for emitting " smoke and steam " (they being mingled together) was upheld). But if there is one single incident *R.* v. *Clow* (see p. 265) is authority for allowing alternatives to be charged conjunctively. Thus in *Vernon* v. *Paddon* (1972), *The Times*, 11th February, a charge under s. 5 of the Public Order Act of insulting words *and* insulting behaviour was upheld where it arose out of a single incident. If a statute creates a duty to do either act *A* or act *B*, in order to constitute the offence there must be a failure to do both acts (*Field* v. *Hopkinson, supra*), and an information charging failure to do *A* or *B* is good. A charge of being unfit to drive through " drink or drug " is not bad for duplicity (*Thomson* v. *Knights* [1947] 1 All E.R. 112), nor is one for " wilfully or negligently " failing to comply with a condition under s. 134 of the Act of 1960 (*G. Newton, Ltd.* v. *Smith* [1962] 2 All E.R. 19), nor one for drunken driving in " a road or other public place " (*Montgomery* v. *Loney* [1959] N.I. 171). An information bad for duplicity cannot be cured on appeal (see *Blakey Transport, Ltd.* v. *Baggott* on p. 90).

See generally Stone (1975), pp. 502–503.

Irregularity

Where an irregularity occurs during a trial, the court may start the hearing all over again on the same day (*R.* v. *Marsham* (1912), 76 J.P. 284) or permit the summons to be withdrawn and a fresh one issued, if in time (*Davis* v. *Morton* (1913), 77 J.P. 223). If the irregularity prejudices the accused, e.g., disclosure of previous convictions, the case should be adjourned to a fresh bench (see p. 92, *infra*). Magistrates should not interview a witness privately, either before or after conviction (*R.* v. *Bodmin JJ.* [1947] 1 All E.R. 109) nor allow an informant into their retiring room after retirement

(*R.* v. *Stratford-upon-Avon JJ.*, *ex parte Edmonds* [1973] Crim.L.R. 241);
nor a social worker in their retiring room (*R.* v. *Averdare JJ.*, *ex
parte Jones* (1973), J.P.News. 57).

R. v. *Guest, ex parte Anthony* [1964] 3 All E.R. 385, *R.* v. *Blandford
JJ.* [1966] 1 All E.R. 1021 and *R.* v. *Gore JJ.* [1966] 3 All E.R.
991 were disapproved by the House of Lords in the case of *S.* v.
Manchester City Recorder [1969] 3 All E.R. 1230 in so far as these
decisions held that a magistrates' court was *functus officio* as soon as a
conviction or finding of guilt was announced.   The House of Lords
held that magistrates only have one *officium*, that of carrying a case
to a conclusion.   Where therefore a defendant pleads guilty and
his plea is accepted and the case is adjourned, the defendant may
change his plea to one of not guilty.   The House of Lords decision
has, it is submitted, a much wider and more fundamental effect on
the practice and procedure in magistrates' courts than may at first
have been thought by commentators and other legal writers.   It
is submitted that, provided the court has not pronounced sentence, a
magistrates' court may quite properly allow a defendant to change
his plea of guilty at any stage of the proceedings.   If prejudice is
likely to be caused to the defendant by trial by the same justices
(e.g., if evidence of previous convictions has been given) the case
should be heard by a differently constituted bench.   On the other
hand, once the justices have pronounced sentence they are *functus
officio* even if their sentence has not been entered in the court
register.   The entry in the court register is an administrative
act recording the decision of the court.   If the court has by a slip
of the tongue announced the sentence wrongly, then, provided
it is a slip of the tongue and not a change of mind, the sentence may
be changed (*R.* v. *Newcastle-upon-Tyne JJ.*, *ex parte Swales* [1972]
Crim.L.R. 111).   If the defendant is allowed to change his plea,
the fact that he originally pleaded guilty may have some probative
value and evidence of his original plea may be admitted on the trial
of his not guilty plea, but before allowing such evidence, it should
be decided by the judge whether it has any probative value, and
if it has, whether its probative value would exceed the prejudice
caused by its admission.   If the charge is heard before a jury, the
admissibility of the previous plea of guilty should be decided by the
judge holding a " trial within a trial " (*R.* v. *Rimmer* [1972] 1 All
E.R. 604) (but see *R.* v. *Hetherington* [1972] Crim.L.R. 703).

Autrefois Acquit or Convict

A withdrawal of a summons does not bar subsequent proceedings
(*Owens* v. *Minoprio* [1942] 1 All E.R. 30), and in *R.* v. *Bedford and*

Sharnbrook JJ., ex parte Ward (1973), J.P.News. 40, justices were
held to be entitled to hear a charge of driving with excess blood/
alcohol against a Mr. B. C. Ward who because he had been mistaken for a Colin Ward had been previously told that he would
be required no further by the court.   A conviction for dangerous
driving, where the justices have taken into consideration the
defendant's speed, bars proceedings for speeding (*Welton* v. *Taneborne* (1908), 72 J.P. 419); *aliter,* it seems, an acquittal on the
graver charge.   A conviction or acquittal in Ireland on merits for
driving in a dangerous manner bars subsequent proceedings for
driving recklessly or at a dangerous speed (*R.* v. *Beattie* [1946]
Ir.Jur.R. 62).   An acquittal on indictment for dangerous driving
does not bar proceedings for careless driving (see p. 264), but
different considerations might arise where a magistrates' court has
acquitted of dangerous driving, in view of the Road Traffic Act,
1972, Sched. 4, Pt. IV, para. 4.   As to the plea of *autrefois acquit*
where there has been a dismissal without a hearing on merits, see
114 J.P.Jo. 49 and 116 J.P.Jo. 785.   The text-books contain many
other cases on these pleas; see Paley on Summary Convictions,
10th ed., p. 77, and Rouse Jones on Magistrates' Courts, p. 215
et seq., and the law generally was reviewed in *Connelly* v. *Director
of Public Prosecutions* [1964] 2 All E.R. 401.   See also 120 J.P.Jo. 533
and 110 L.J.News. 441.   In *R.* v. *Burnham JJ., ex parte Ansorge*
[1959] 3 All E.R. 505, it was said that where two informations,
though alleging offences under different enactments, relate to the
same facts and a plea of guilty to one information is accepted, the
magistrates have jurisdiction to inquire into the matter but, if they
find that the facts are the very facts which gave rise to the first
conviction, they should proceed no further; if they did convict,
appeal would lie.   In that case the defendant had been charged
with obstruction and breach of a "no-waiting" order and both
informations related to the same facts.

No person may be convicted of an offence if he has paid a fixed
penalty for it without prosecution under the Road Traffic Regulation Act, 1967, s. 80, before proceedings are begun.

As to servicemen and members of visiting forces already dealt
with by their own courts, see pp. 59 and 61.

Where magistrates have adjudicated on a case on which they
had no power to adjudicate, the case may properly be later heard
before a court which can adjudicate upon it (*R.* v. *West* [1962]
2 All E.R. 624).

Where the right to recovery of a charge for towing away depends
on the fact of an offence having been committed and the summons
for that offence is dismissed without evidence having been offered,

the charge cannot be recovered (*Commissioner of Police of the Metropolis* v. *Meller* [1963] Crim.L.R. 856).

Evidence of Character and Record

Defendant's Previous Convictions

Where there was a reference to a previous conviction for dangerous driving during a hearing before magistrates but they announced that they would disregard such reference, and did disregard it, the conviction was upheld (*Cholerton* v. *Copping* (1906), 70 J.P. 484; see also *Barker* v. *Arnold* (1911), 75 J.P. 364). *Aliter* where the High Court are not satisfied that the previous conviction has been disregarded (*R.* v. *Grimsby Borough Quarter Sessions* [1955] 3 All E.R. 300). Where the defendant had been wrongly cross-examined as to a previous conviction, his conviction was quashed although the magistrates stated that their minds had not been in any way affected by the revelation of his previous court appearance; the cases of *Cholerton* v. *Copping* and *Barker* v. *Arnold*, above, were not apparently cited (*R.* v. *South Holderness JJ.*, *ex parte Bonner* [1964] Crim.L.R. 537). A certificate of conviction to prove a disqualification should mention only the offence (or, *semble*, one of the offences) for which the defendant was disqualified (*Stone* v. *Bastick* [1965] 3 All E.R. 713). If an endorsed licence is used for this purpose, it is submitted that any other endorsements on it should be covered up before the magistrates see it. Generally, if an irregularity of this kind occurs during a trial and the justices feel that they cannot disregard it, they should adjourn the trial to a different bench (*Elkington* v. *Kesley* [1948] 1 All E.R. 786). It seems to be the better opinion that, where the defendant is absent, previous convictions should not be mentioned on his being convicted unless, perhaps, he has clearly admitted them to a witness. If he is present, he should be asked if he admits them; if he denies them, they must either be strictly proved or ignored. The prosecution now, however, may (save in juvenile courts) use s. 3 of the Magistrates' Courts Act, 1957: under it, where a person is convicted by magistrates of a summary offence, then, if it is proved that he has been served personally or by registered post with a list of previous convictions for summary offences (as defined by the Magistrates' Courts Act, 1952, s. 125) not less than seven days previously, the court may in his absence take account of such convictions. This list, by virtue of the definition in s. 125, can show, in effect, previous traffic offences but not generally crimes of dishonesty. This procedure may be used whether the case has been proven by a written plea of guilty under s. 1 of the 1957 Act or by evidence in the defendant's absence. His attendance cannot be enforced by warrant, after he has been convicted in his absence, for the mere purpose of proving his record (*R.* v. *Montgomery* (1910), 74 J.P. 110). It should be noted that proof of previous convictions under the procedure set out in s. 3 suffers from two defects from the point of view of the prosecutor for a road traffic endorsable offence. The notice under s. 3 has to be served seven days previous to the conviction. If, therefore, a prosecutor becomes aware of previous convictions after the conviction, it is useless then to serve a notice under s. 3. The other defect is that the notice cannot cite any previous convictions other than a summary offence. A summary offence for this purpose is defined in s. 125 of the Magistrates' Courts Act, 1952, as excluding indictable cases tried summarily under s. 19. Thus a notice under s. 3 cannot cite many endorsable traffic offences, including causing death by dangerous driving (s. 1 of the Act of 1972), stealing a motor vehicle under the Theft Act, taking a motor vehicle (s. 12 of the Theft Act), and any " hybrid offence " which has been dealt with by the Crown Court (e.g., dangerous driving, drunken driving, etc.). To get over these difficulties the Act of 1974 inserted a new subsection (2A) in s. 182 of the Act of 1972 in order that details of previous convictions for endorsable offences might be proved to a court in the absence of the defendant and after conviction (for s. 182 as amended see p. 108).

Particulars of an endorsement on the defendant's licence noted by the police prior to the hearing may be so given in evidence in his absence without a notice to produce it (*Martin* v. *White* (1910), 74 J.P. 106). Where a conviction has to be proved by other means, it can be done by producing a record or extract of such conviction with proof of identity or by finger prints. It was suggested by the late author that s. 16 (2) of the Children and Young Persons Act, 1963, requires previous findings of guilt whilst under fourteen to be disregarded where the defendant has attained the age of twenty-one. It is submitted that s. 16 (2) applies only where the defendant is examined as a witness as to his previous offences (as on p. 97). If relevant, such previous findings of guilt can and should be contained in the defendant's antecedent history and previous offences prepared by the police; *cf.* the Practice Direction at [1966] 2 All E.R. 929. Any doubts that existed as to whether a court is entitled to look at a driving licence have been resolved by s. 101 (4A) of the Act of 1972 (inserted by para. 10 (1) of Sched. 3 to the Road Traffic Act, 1974), which provides that where a person is convicted of an obligatorily endorsable offence, the court may take into consideration particulars

of any previous conviction or disqualification endorsed on the
licence when deciding what order to make in pursuance of the
conviction. (See also p. 607.)

The payment of a fixed penalty without prosecution under the
Road Traffic Regulation Act, 1967, s. 80, or a mitigated penalty
to a council under the Vehicles (Excise) Act, 1971, does not count
as a previous conviction for the purpose of inflicting a higher
penalty where this is permitted on second or subsequent convictions.
Nor may such cases be included in a record of convictions submitted
under the Magistrates' Courts Act, 1957, s. 3 (*supra*). In the
debate on the Road Traffic and Roads Improvement Bill of 1960
(on which s. 80 was based) the Government spokesmen stated
emphatically that cases of payment of fines without prosecution
should not be mentioned as part of a defendant's record. Section
80 (10) of the Road Traffic Regulation Act, 1967, provides that
in any proceedings for an offence for which a fine without prosecution may be demanded under s. 80 no reference shall be made
after the conviction of the accused to any such demand for a penalty
or to its payment or non-payment unless in the course of the
proceedings or in some document before the court in the proceedings
reference has been made to it by or on behalf of the accused. But
s. 80 (10) ceased to have effect on the bringing into force of vehicle
owner liability (see pp. 584–593) (s. 4 (5), Road Traffic Act, 1974).

Magistrates should announce their decision to convict before
inquiring into the defendant's record, but their failure to do so
is not necessarily fatal, if they have actually so decided (*Davies*
v. *Griffiths* [1937] 2 All E.R. 671).

To prove guilty knowledge, previous convictions and even
acquittals may in certain circumstances be mentioned and so may
cautions (*Duxley* v. *Gilmore* (1959), 123 J.P.Jo. 331); this power
should be used sparingly, however, and only where it is essential
to prove a guilty state of mind and knowledge.

In giving the defendant's record after conviction, the police
may, in addition to previous convictions, inform the court of matters,
whether or not the subject of charges which are to be taken into
consideration, which are not disputed by the defendant and ought to
be known by the court (*R.* v. *Van Pelz* [1943] 1 All E.R. 36). *Semble*,
this seems wide enough to allow them to mention undisputed
cautions for motoring offences but not fixed penalty offences.

Cross-examination as to Character

Evidence of the defendant's bad character and his cross-examination thereon is not permitted prior to conviction unless its admissibility falls within one of the recognised exceptions. A defendant

who merely says that he does not like driving at an excessive speed is not setting up his good character (*R.* v. *Beecham* (1921), 85 J.P. 276) and it is doubtful if he is setting it up if he says that he has driven for many years (see 125 J.P.Jo. 774). If he merely makes imputations on the witnesses for the prosecution, evidence-in-chief of his bad character or previous convictions may not be given and the prosecution's rights are limited to cross-examining him if he chooses to give evidence (*R.* v. *Butterwasser* [1947] 2 All E.R. 415). Merely to deny in strong terms a witness's statement does not alone permit the prosecution to cross-examine the defendant as to his character (*R.* v. *Rouse* (1904), 68 J.P. 14) but they may do so, at the discretion of the court, if there are allegations of manu- facturing evidence additional to those that the witness is not speaking the truth (*R.* v. *Clark* [1955] 3 All E.R. 29). The cases were reviewed in *Selvey* v. *Director of Public Prosecutions* [1968] 2 All E.R. 497, where the House of Lords laid down that, where the defence attack the character of a prosecution witness, the court has an unfettered discretion to permit or exclude cross-examination of the defendant as to his record and that there is no general rule that it should not be allowed if the defence necessarily involves imputations against the character of a prosecution witness. Cross- examination of the defendant should not be so conducted as to induce him to attack the prosecution witnesses' characters (*R.* v. *Baldwin* (1925), 89 J.P. 116). Where an unrepresented defendant in a magistrates' court begins to attack the character of a prosecu- tion witness, the prosecutor should warn him of the risk of being himself cross-examined as to character; such warning should not be given in open court but an adjournment should be requested and the help of the magistrates' clerk enlisted to explain it all to the defendant in the magistrates' absence during the adjournment (*R.* v. *Weston-super-Mare JJ., ex parte Townsend* [1968] 3 All E.R. 225).

A defendant who has attained the age of twenty-one may not be cross-examined as to offences of which he was found guilty prior to his becoming fourteen (Children and Young Persons Act, 1963, s. 16 (2)).

Second or Subsequent Offence

Section 21 of and Sched. 5 to the Road Traffic Act, 1974, re- moved from virtually every provision under the Road Traffic Acts of 1960 and 1972, the Road Traffic Regulation Act, 1967, and the Transport Act, 1968, a heavier penalty on a " second or sub- sequent conviction ", and the reader is referred to pages 85 and

86 of the 7th edition of this work should a question arise as to whether a heavier penalty may be attracted by reason of a " second or subsequent conviction ".

Presence of Defendant

Minor cases are often dealt with in the absence of the defendant (Magistrates' Courts Act, 1952, s. 15). However, the defendant must be present if he is to be committed for trial. The defendant should always be given an adjournment, if he asks for it, when he has had the summons in insufficient time before the hearing. Any defendant may sufficiently answer a summons by solicitor, save where his presence is required to take depositions or consent to summary trial. (Note there is a distinction between " consenting to summary trial " and " electing for trial by jury ", the former coming under s. 19 of the Magistrates' Courts Act, 1952, and the latter under s. 25.) Save in the cases of taking depositions or consenting, the attendance of the defendant for trial cannot be enforced if a solicitor appears for him. A corporation or limited company can plead by a representative or solicitor (see p. 73; the Magistrates' Courts Act, 1952, Sched. 2 makes provision as to election for summary trial by a corporation and its committal. A defendant cannot be sentenced to imprisonment or detention in his absence and he may not be disqualified if absent at the first hearing unless and until he has been given the chance to attend at an adjourned hearing; the notice to him of the adjournment should show the intention of the court to consider disqualification (Criminal Justice Act, 1967, s. 26 (3)).

Save where the defendant is represented by a solicitor who pleads guilty on his behalf, the case must be proved by evidence, if he is absent, and letters to the court or police admitting the offence, if used at all to prove guilt, should only be used to supplement such evidence on proof that such letters are in the defendant's handwriting. No evidence need be given on a plea of guilty, although, where the defendant disputes the facts, magistrates may call for evidence (Magistrates' Courts Act, 1952, s. 13). A defendant cannot be arrested on non-appearance, personally or by solicitor (where this suffices), unless the offence is punishable with imprisonment or, having convicted him, the magistrates propose to disqualify (Criminal Justice Act, 1967, s. 24 (2)).

Pleading Guilty in Writing

As is well known, however, the Magistrates' Courts Act, 1957, s. 1, now enables pleas of guilty for summary offences (meaning here offences not triable on indictment and also those for which

the defendant cannot be given more than three months' imprisonment) to be received in writing in magistrates' courts, other than
juvenile courts, in the absence of the defendant.   The defendant is
served in the usual way with the summons, an explanatory form
and a statement of the facts of the offence. If he wishes to dispute
the case, he or his solicitor must attend the court on the day for
which the summons is returnable and the hearing will proceed in
the usual way with sworn oral evidence or s. 9 statements.   If he
does nothing, the prosecutor, on proof of service of the summons,
proves his case by oral evidence or s. 9 statements.   If the defendant
or his solicitor writes to the court pleading guilty, then the statement
of facts is read aloud to the court and his letter is also read aloud;
no oral evidence is allowed to supplement the written statement of
facts and the prosecutor may not add anything to the statement
(*R.* v. *Malden JJ.* [1966] Crim.L.R. 387; *R.* v. *Liskerret JJ., ex parte
Child* [1972] R.T.R. 141).

A corporation or limited company may plead guilty in writing
signed by a director or secretary under the 1957 Act (Criminal
Justice Act, 1967, s. 29 (3)).   The plea must clearly refer to all
the offences charged (*R.* v. *Burnham JJ.* [1959] 3 All E.R. 505).
If the letter does not amount to a plea of guilty, oral evidence of
the offence must be given at an adjourned court.   Both the statement
and the reply of the defendant must be read aloud (*R.* v. *Oldham
JJ.* [1958] 3 All E.R. 559); the onus of proving the contrary is
on the defendant (*R.* v. *Davis, ex parte Brough* [1959] 1 W.L.R.
59*n*).   His licence may be ordered to be endorsed under the 1957
Act procedure but he may not be disqualified from driving in his
absence, where he has pleaded guilty in writing pursuant to that
procedure, unless and until the court has given him the opportunity
of attending on an adjourned hearing (1957 Act, s. 1 (2) (iii);
R. v. *Totton JJ.* [1958] Crim.L.R. 543; *R.* v. *Llandrindod Wells
JJ., ex parte Gibson* [1968] 2 All E.R. 20).   The 1957 Act is discussed at 101 S.J. 685.   If a case under the 1957 Act procedure
has been adjourned without a hearing and the accused has not
been required to attend at the adjourned hearing, only the statement of facts served on him may be read out and no witness may be
called by the prosecution at the adjourned hearing, unless the
accused is present or represented (*R.* v. *Norham JJ.* [1961] 1 All
E.R. 455).   A notice of adjournment should give the reason for
it, e.g., where it is intended that the court will disqualify (1957
Act, s. 1 (3); Criminal Justice Act, 1967, s. 26 (3)) and if the reason
for adjournment was to consider disqualification and this was not
stated, the disqualification will be quashed (*R.* v. *Mason* [1965]
2 All E.R. 308).

Legal Aid

Legal aid is now granted under Pt. II of the Legal Aid Act, 1974, and the defendant may be called upon for a contribution. It is available for proceedings concerned with the sentence only as well as for a trial and for binding-over proceedings. It should generally be given to a person committed for trial or sentence even though a plea of guilty is expected and any doubt as to whether it should be granted or not is to be resolved in the defendant's favour (Legal Aid Act, 1974, s. 29 (6)). Application for legal aid is made to the relevant court under s. 73 and not to The Law Society. The Departmental Committee on Legal Aid under the chairmanship of Lord Widgery (1966) recommended that, so far as the offences in this book are concerned, legal aid should be considered for grant where the accused is in real danger of losing his liberty or livelihood or there is a substantial question of law, or the accused has insufficient knowledge of English or is mentally disabled, or the nature of the defence involves the tracing of witnesses or expert cross-examination. Of these criteria, the one most frequently applicable to users of this book is the likelihood of a defendant losing his livelihood if he is disqualified from holding or obtaining a driving licence.

Mitigation

Where justices have retired to consider whether to convict or acquit and have decided on the defendant's guilt, they should not on their return immediately announce their penalty. After they have announced a conviction, the prosecution should have an opportunity of citing any previous convictions and making any application for costs, and the court, if it is an endorsable offence, should see the defendant's driving licence and, most importantly, the defendant or his solicitor or counsel should have an opportunity of putting forward any matter in mitigation. Justices decided on a person's guilt and immediately announced a penalty of £100 without giving the defence an opportunity of a speech in mitigation. After remonstrations from defence counsel they then heard a speech in mitigation, retired and announced a reduced penalty of £80 plus £21 costs. The justices' sentence was quashed and the case was sent back for sentence to be reconsidered by a different bench (*R.* v. *Southampton JJ., ex parte Atherton* [1974] Crim.L.R. 108).

It may be wise to support a plea in mitigation by evidence, particularly where the mitigation adduced is of an unusual nature or extraordinary character; in some cases, sworn evidence is essential: e.g., " special reasons " for not endorsing or disqualifying (see p. 664). Where, however, such sworn evidence is required, a statement under s. 9 of the Criminal Justice Act, 1967, is admissible as evidence to the like extent as oral evidence (s. 9 (1)). Section 9 statements can be tendered by either party including the defendant. Admissions by the prosecutor may also be obtained (see p. 120).

5. EVIDENCE

Enforcing Attendance

The attendance of witnesses and the production of documents may be secured by witness summons. Under the Magistrates' Courts Act, 1952, s. 77, application for a witness summons may be made without oath, but oath is necessary for a warrant; a reasonable sum must be tendered to the witness for costs and expenses when he is served with the summons. Applications for a witness summons may be made to a justices' clerk, who may issue it (Justices' Clerks Rules, 1970 (S.I. 1970 No. 231)). Any witness may be committed for seven days (not fined any sum) if he refuses to be sworn, give evidence or produce a document, whether he attends on summons or not. Witness process granted when a witness is in England or Wales may be enforced by warrant in any other part of the British Isles under the Magistrates' Courts Act, 1952, s. 103, if he goes there. See Archbold, 37th ed., para. 1364, as to enforcing attendance of witnesses outside England and Wales, at the Crown Court. The attendance of a witness in prison may be obtained by Home Office order (Prison Act, 1952, s. 22).

The Criminal Procedure (Attendance of Witnesses) Act, 1965 (as amended by the Courts Act, 1971) regulates the procedure for the attendance of witnesses at the Crown Court.

Where documents are in the defendant's possession, he cannot be ordered to produce them, but should be given notice to produce them. If he has been given such notice and fails to produce them in court, secondary evidence may be given of their contents (see Stone (1975), pp. 570–571). Notice is unnecessary where the summons by its very character puts the accused on notice that a document will be required, e.g., the certificate of insurance on a charge of uninsured driving (*Williams* v. *Russell* (1933), 97 J.P. 128).

Sworn Evidence

The witnesses must attend and be sworn in court save that the evidence of a child of tender age who is not intelligent enough to understand the oath may be received unsworn in a criminal case (Children and Young Persons Act, 1933, s. 38) and by the Criminal Justice Act, 1967, ss. 2 and 9, written evidence is permitted on the conditions there specified. In *Chapman* v. *Ingleton* (1973), J.P.News. 204, it was held that while it was vital for a statement under s. 9 to contain the required declaration as to its truth, etc., it did not matter whether the declaration appeared at the head or foot of the statement. It would seem that a child under ten years of age cannot make a statement under s. 2 or s. 9 of the Criminal Justice Act, 1967, since a child under ten is not liable to prosecution. Where unsworn evidence of a child is admitted for the prosecution, the defendant must not be convicted unless that evidence is corroborated by some other material evidence in support implicating him (Children and Young Persons Act, 1933, s. 38). This section and the previous authorities were reviewed and considered by the House of Lords in *D.P.P.* v. *Hester* [1973] 3 All E.R. 1056. The unsworn evidence of a child can be supported by the sworn evidence of another child and this evidence can be corroborative of each other, but this evidence must be weighed with special care. The sworn evidence of a child need not be corroborated in law, but although there is a risk in convicting on the child's evidence alone a court may do so if convinced that the child is telling the truth (*ibid.*). The unsworn evidence of a child cannot be corroborated merely by the unsworn evidence of another child (*ibid.*). Unsworn evidence of a child can be treated as corroboration of other evidence provided the court is satisfied that the child is a truthful witness (*ibid.*). Otherwise, all evidence (save where permitted in documentary form) must be given on oath (or affirmation, if oaths are contrary to the witness's religious belief or he has none or the Oaths Act, 1961, is applied: see *infra*), although a witness producing documents only need not be sworn (other rare exceptions are given in Phipson's Manual of Evidence, 10th ed.). If a witness refuses to be sworn or is of insufficient mental capacity to understand the oath, his evidence is not receivable. Magistrates, while entitled to convict on the sworn evidence of young children corroborating one another, should warn themselves of the risk of acting on such evidence (*R.* v. *Campbell* [1956] 2 All E.R. 272).

Under the Oaths Act, 1961, affirmation in lieu of oath is permitted where it is not reasonably practicable without delay or inconvenience to administer an oath to a person in the manner appropriate to his religious belief. The Children and Young Persons Act, 1963, s. 28, prescribes the form of oath to be taken by lla witnesses in juvenile courts and by juveniles in any court and enacts that the proper oath shall be deemed to have been taken although one of the forms prescribed by s. 28 has been used instead of the other.

Sick Witnesses

In the trial of a summary offence, the evidence of a witness who is too ill to come to court cannot be received in writing, on oath or not, even under s. 9 of the Criminal Justice Act, 1967, if the other side claims that the witness should attend; it may be received under s. 9 if his attendance is not required. It is suggested at 95 S.J. 178 that in such cases the place where a witness (on either side) lies ill should be designated an occasional court house and the magistrates and all the parties should attend at his bedside to hear his evidence; the rest of the case can be heard in the ordinary court house. If the case is indictable, the witness's deposition may be taken by the magistrate who takes the other depositions at his bedside in the defendant's presence, provided the witness is either in the county or borough for which that magistrate acts or in an adjoining county or borough (*R.* v. *Bros, ex parte Hardy* (1911), 74 J.P. 483; Magistrates' Courts Act, 1952, s. 116). Where an important witness is ill and unlikely to be well enough to attend a court within a reasonable time, in practice it is suggested that, if the case be indictable, it should be committed for trial, as his deposition is receivable (see *infra*). Occasionally, in summary and indictable cases, the defendant's reply in the presence of the witness to the latter's statement might be usable in evidence as showing his acceptance of the truth of the statement. If it is desired to designate a place as an occasional court house, the procedure indicated in the Magistrates' Courts Act, 1952, s.123, must be followed; licensed premises cannot be so designated.

In trials on indictment, the deposition of a witness for either side before the examining justices may be read if he is insane or too ill to attend (Criminal Justice Act, 1925, s. 13 (3)). See Archbold, 38th ed., paras. 466–8a, as to this provision.

By the Criminal Law Amendment Act, 1867, s. 6, and the Magistrates' Courts Act, 1952, s. 41, the evidence of a witness relating to an indictable offence may be taken at his bedside if he is dangerously ill and unlikely to recover. Reasonable notice must have been given to the defendant or prosecutor—for the procedure is available to both sides—so that he can be present and cross-examine, if he wishes. No one need actually have been charged but, if a charge is likely, the proposed defendant (if the

witness is for the prosecution) or the chief constable (if he is a
defence one) should be notified and given the chance to attend.
The deposition so taken will then be available at the trial, if the
witness is still ill or is dead, and at the preliminary hearing (Magistrates' Courts Act, 1952, s. 41; Magistrates' Courts Rules, 1968,
r. 29). The 1867 Act is discussed at 109 J.P.Jo. 195 and 95 S.J.
178, and it is emphasised that it can be used by both sides and
relates not only to persons injured as a result of the offence, e.g., a
victim of dangerous driving, but also to those seriously ill from other
causes. The magistrate who takes the deposition need not be the
one who commits the defendant for trial and the witness may be
in his (the magistrate's) or an adjoining county or borough. The
procedure is commended to defending solicitors who have reserved their client's defence and then find a material witness
in danger of dying. See 118 J.P.Jo. 276 as to witnesses ill outside a magistrates' area, and 120 J.P.Jo. 439 and 453 generally
as to the depositions of sick witnesses. Written evidence may
now be allowed under s. 2 or s. 9 of the Criminal Justice Act,
1967, but the 1867 Act does not require the consent of the other
side.

Where the charge is one involving bodily injury to a juvenile
under seventeen, his evidence may be taken out of court (on
notice to the defendant) if his attendance would endanger his
health (Children and Young Persons Act, 1933, s. 42). This
provision obviously applies to the offence of causing bodily harm
to a juvenile by furious driving (Offences against the Person Act,
1861, s. 35) but it is doubtful if dangerous and careless driving
alone contrary to the Road Traffic Act, 1972, ss. 2 and 3, are
offences involving bodily injury, though a juvenile may have been
injured in the accident. It was held in *R.* v. *Moore* [1954] 2 All
E.R. 189 that arson of a house in which were some children (who
were not injured by the fire) was not an offence " involving bodily
injury " to them and that those words referred to offences *ejusdem
generis* with those set out in Sched. 1 to the 1933 Act, which relates
to assaults and other crimes of sex and violence.

It would seem that even in magistrates' courts the evidence of
a witness who has already given evidence in proceedings on the
same issue may be read at the second trial if he is too ill to attend,
e.g., where careless driving is tried again because the magistrates
could not agree (Cross on Evidence, 3rd ed., p. 453). But see
Bishop v. *Hosier* on p. 698. On a re-trial ordered under the Criminal
Appeal Act, 1968, evidence may, in the circumstances given in
Sched. 2, be read from the transcript.

Dead Witnesses

The deposition of a witness for either side taken under the Criminal Law Amendment Act, 1867, *supra,* may be read at the trial or preliminary hearing, though he has since died (Magistrates' Courts Act, 1952, s. 41). It would seem that, if he died before his evidence was complete, the deposition would be inadmissible (*cf. Waugh* v. *R.* [1950] A.C. 203). The deposition of a witness for either side at the preliminary hearing before the justices may be read at the trial on indictment if he has died (Criminal Justice Act, 1925, s. 13 (3)). As to dying declarations in homicide cases, see p. 253. See Archbold, 38th ed., paras. 466–8a, as to s. 13 (3).

The evidence of a witness who has died cannot otherwise be brought before the court unless it comes within certain exceptions (given in Phipson's Manual of Evidence, 8th ed., ch. 19), viz., declarations against interest, declarations in the course of duty and declarations as to public rights (see 115 J.P.Jo. 599). Also, where he has already given evidence in the same proceedings and they are begun again, his evidence to the court can be read (Cross on Evidence, 3rd ed., p. 453). But see *Bishop* v. *Hosier* on p. 698.

Witnesses Abroad

The attendance of witnesses from Scotland, Ireland, the Isle of Man and the Channel Islands can be secured by process (see p. 101). The evidence of a witness outside the United Kingdom may be given before a judge or magistrate in the British Empire or before a British consul elsewhere and such depositions are admissible here (Merchant Shipping Act, 1894, s. 691). The defendant in a criminal case must be present at the examination of the witness and have the opportunity to cross-examine him; the statute seemingly requires the defendant's presence (but not the prosecutor's) even where the evidence is for the defence, but possibly this requirement would be construed to give a more sensible result. Section 691 applies to all criminal and civil proceedings and refers to a deposition " previously " made; *quaere* whether this means previously to the commencement of the proceedings or to the hearing itself. On the question whether written evidence under s. 2 or s. 9 of the Criminal Justice Act, 1967, can be received from witnesses outside England and Wales the matter has now been resolved by s. 46 (2) of the Criminal Justice Act, 1972. The section enables statements made by witnesses outside the United Kingdom to be receivable in evidence in committal proceedings but not in respect of summary proceedings under s. 9. Statements made by witnesses in Scotland and Northern Ireland are however admissible in the same way as if they had been made in England or Wales (s. 46 (1) of the Criminal Justice Act, 1972).

Documentary Evidence

By the Road Traffic Act, 1972, s. 181, in any proceedings for an offence under that Act specified in column 7 of Pt. I of Sched. 4 to the Act, or under any other enactment relating to the use of vehicles on roads, a certificate in the form prescribed by the Evidence by Certificate Rules, 1961 (S.I. 1961 No. 248, as amended by S.I. 1962 No. 2319), signed by a constable and certifying that a person specified in the certificate stated to him—

(a) that a particular motor vehicle was being driven or used by, or belonged to, that person on a particular occasion; or

(b) that a particular motor vehicle was used by, or belonged on a particular occasion to, a firm in which that person also stated that he was at the time of the statement a partner; or

(c) that a particular motor vehicle was used by, or belonged on a particular occasion to, a corporation of which that person also stated that he was at the time of the statement a director or officer or employee,

shall be admissible as evidence for the purpose of determining by whom the vehicle was being driven or used, or to whom it belonged, as the case may be, on that occasion. Nothing in s. 181 shall be deemed to make such certificate admissible as evidence in proceedings for an offence except in a case where and to the extent to which oral evidence to the like effect would have been admissible in those proceedings. A copy of the certificate must have been served on the defendant in the manner indicated in r. 3 of the Evidence by Certificate Rules, 1961, not less than seven days before the hearing and the defendant may require, not later than three days before the hearing, the attendance of the constable who gives the certificate (see s. 181 (3)). It would seem that, as leaving a vehicle on the road can be " using " it (see p. 44), s. 181 applies to all charges of obstruction and parking. It applies to proceedings on indictment as well as before magistrates. The view is advanced at 122 J.P.Jo. 131 that the certificate of a Scottish constable is admissible under (what is now) s. 181 in England. Section 181 applies only to motor vehicles and not to pedal cycles.

Offences under regulations made under any Act mentioned in s. 181 are offences under that Act and s. 181 applies to such offences (cf. *Bingham* v. *Bruce* [1962] 1 All E.R. 136; *Rathbone* v. *Bundock* [1962] 2 All E.R. 257).

Note the limitations on the matters statable in such certificates, e.g., a constable can certify only that the person interviewed said he was driving a motor vehicle on a named occasion and not that that person said that some other person was driving. Although a certificate can be used to show that a particular person was driving, it cannot be used to prove that the vehicle was used or driven on the particular road or place alleged. Sections 181 and 183 are useful to prove ownership of a particular vehicle or to prove that a defendant admitted he was driving it, where the defendant or the owners are interviewed in a town a long way from the court, e.g., when a Durham lorry driver is summoned for an offence in Sussex and his firm, also in Durham, is summoned for permitting the offence. The evidence of the Durham constable who interviewed the defendant and the firm is thus receivable, without his (the constable's) attendance in Sussex, on the matters set out in s. 181. It is submitted that the only persons who can answer for a firm or company are those with sufficient authority to make admissions on its behalf.

Further powers of proving by writing that the defendant was the driver are given by the Road Traffic Act, 1972, s. 183, and the Road Traffic Regulation Act, 1967, s. 90. On the summary trial of an information for an offence under the Road Traffic Act, 1972, or any regulations made or continued thereunder to which s. 183 is applied by virtue of column 7 of Pt. I of Sched. 4 to the Act, or under any enactment relating to the use of vehicles on roads, if it is proved that a requirement under s. 168 (2) of the Road Traffic Act, 1972 (see 461), to give information as to the identity of the driver of the particular vehicle on the particular occasion to which the information relates has been served on the defendant by post and a statement in writing, purporting to be signed by the defendant, that he was the driver of the vehicle on that occasion is produced to the court, that statement may be treated as evidence that he was the driver. Section 183 does not apply to committal proceedings or to trials on indictment. It can be used only to prove that the defendant himself was the driver; it cannot be used to prove that he was the owner or that someone else was driving. Section 183 applies to all types of vehicles and, it seems, to riders of cycles (cf. s. 168 (2)). All the above powers are additional to the power to use written statements in evidence under ss. 2 and 9 of the Criminal Justice Act, 1967.

Registration Particulars and Driving Licence Records

Section 31 of the Vehicles (Excise) Act, 1971, and s. 182 of the

Road Traffic Act, 1972, enable evidence as to registration particulars and driving licence records to be given by certificate.

The sections in each Act are a re-enactment of s. 27 of the Vehicle and Driving Licences Act, 1969, and read identically (save that s. 31 of the Vehicles (Excise) Act does not contain subsection (2A)) as follows:—

" (1) A statement contained in a document purporting to be—

(a) a part of the records maintained by the Secretary of State in connection with any functions exercisable by the Secretary of State by virtue [of the Vehicles (Excise) Act, 1971, or of Pt. III of the Road Traffic Act, 1972, or a part of any other records maintained by the Secretary of State with respect to vehicles]; or

(b) a copy of a document forming part of those records; or

(c) a note of any information contained in those records,

and to be authenticated by a person authorised in that behalf by the Secretary of State shall be admissible in any proceedings as evidence of any fact stated therein to the same extent as oral evidence of that fact is admissible in those proceedings.

(2) In subsection (1) above 'document' and 'statement' have the same meanings as in subsection (1) of section 10 of the Civil Evidence Act, 1968, and the reference to a copy of a document shall be construed in accordance with subsection (2) of that section; but nothing in this subsection shall be construed as limiting to civil proceedings the references to proceedings in subsection (1) above.

[(2A) In any case where—

(a) any such statement as is referred to in subsection (1) above is produced to a magistrates' court in any proceedings for an offence involving obligatory or discretionary disqualification, within the meaning of Part III of this Act, and

(b) the statement specifies an alleged previous conviction of an accused person of any such offence, and

(c) it is proved to the satisfaction of the court, on oath or in such manner as may be prescribed by rules under section 15 of the Justices of the Peace Act 1949, that not less than 7 days before the statement is so produced a notice was served on the accused, in such form and manner as may be so prescribed, specifying the previous conviction and stating that it is proposed to bring it to the notice of the court in the event of, or, as the case may be, in view of his conviction, and

(d) the accused is not present in person before the court when the statement is so produced,

the court may take account of the previous conviction as if the accused had appeared and admitted it.]

(3) Nothing in the foregoing provisions of this section shall enable evidence to be given with respect to any matter other than a matter of the prescribed description.

(4) In its application to Scotland this section shall have effect as if—

(a) in subsection (1), for the words from ' as evidence ' onwards there were substituted the words ' as sufficient evidence of any fact stated therein, so however that nothing in this subsection shall be deemed to make such a statement evidence in any proceedings except where oral evidence to the like effect would have been admissible in those proceedings '; and

(b) in subsection (2), for the references to subsections (1) and (2) of section 10 of the Civil Evidence Act, 1968, there were substituted references to subsections (3) and (4) respectively of section 17 of the Law Reform (Miscellaneous Provisions) (Scotland) Act, 1968."

Other than in the circumstances specified in s. 182 (2A) above, it will be noted that there seems to be no procedural provision requiring the other party to be served with a copy of the certificate before the proceedings. As soon as the certificate is produced it proves itself. Moreover there is no limitation on the nature or type of proceedings for which a certificate may be used. It appears that the sections may be used for any civil or criminal proceedings and are not limited to proceedings under the Vehicles (Excise) Act, 1971, and the Road Traffic Act, 1972. The only apparent limitation is that the matters for which evidence may be given are only those of a prescribed description (subs. (3), *supra*) and that the evidence of any fact is admissible only to the same extent as oral evidence. If, therefore, the certificate contains inadmissible evidence, e.g., hearsay, neither s. 31 nor s. 182 renders it admissible.

The Vehicle and Driving Licences Records (Evidence) Regulations, 1970 (S.I. 1970 No. 1997), prescribe the matters for which certificates may be given as follows:—

" (1) in connection with the licensing of drivers under Part II of the Road Traffic Act, 1960—

(a) a document being, forming part of, or submitted in connection with, an application for a driving licence;

(b) a driving licence;

(c) a certificate of competence to drive;

(d) the conviction of an offence specified in Part I or Part II of Schedule 1 to the Road Traffic Act, 1962, or of an offence treated as so specified by virtue of section 5 of the Road Safety Act, 1967, of any person or any order made by the court as a result of any such conviction;

(2) in connection with the licensing and registration of mechanically propelled vehicles under the 1962 Act—

(a) a document being, forming part of, or submitted in connection with, an application for—

(i) a vehicle licence;

(ii) a trade licence;

(iii) a repayment of duty under section 9 of the 1962 Act or the recovery of underpayments or overpayments of duty under section 11 of that Act;

(b) a vehicle licence, trade licence, registration book or registration mark;

(c) a document containing a declaration and particulars such as are prescribed under the 1962 Act in relation to vehicles exempted from duty under that Act;

(*d*) the conviction of an offence under the 1962 Act of any person;

(3) in connection with the examination of a goods vehicle under regulations under section 9 of the Road Safety Act, 1967—

(*a*) an application for an examination of a vehicle under the said regulations;

(*b*) a notifiable alteration made to a vehicle and required by the said regulations to be notified to the Secretary of State;

(*c*) a plating certificate, goods vehicle test certificate, notification of the refusal of a goods vehicle test certificate, Ministry plate, Ministry test date disc or certificate of temporary exemption."

The above regulations are preserved by para. 1 of Pt. II of Sched. 7 to the Vehicles (Excise) Act, 1971, and para. 1 of Sched. 10 to the Road Traffic Act, 1972; references to the 1962 Act should be construed as referring to the Vehicles (Excise) Act, 1971, and the reference to Pt. II of the Road Traffic Act, 1960, as referring to Pt. III of the 1972 Act. The other references in the regulations should be similarly construed as referring to the corresponding provisions in the Vehicles (Excise) Act, 1971, or the Road Traffic Act, 1972.

Subsection (2A) of s. 182 was inserted by s. 13 (3) of the Road Traffic Act, 1974. Its purpose is to enable the prosecution to cite previous convictions for endorsable offences in the absence of the defendant. Although a defendant is required to produce his licence to a court on conviction of an endorsable offence and risk prosecution if he fails to do so (see p. 607), a magistrates' court frequently finds that a licence is not forthcoming even when the court has specifically adjourned sentence in order to obtain it. In the absence of a driving licence and in the absence of a notice under s. 3 of the Magistrates' Courts Act, 1957 (see p. 94), there was no way for a prosecutor to inform the court of a defendant's previous convictions in the absence of the defendant (see also p. 94). The new subsection enables a statement to be produced to the court specifying the previous endorsable convictions of the defendant in order that a court may take into account any previous convictions when sentencing the defendant in his absence. If the notice discloses two or more endorsable convictions so that s. 93 (3) of the Act of 1972 applies, it will be necessary for the court to further adjourn the case and serve notice on the defendant giving the reason for adjournment (see p. 98). It should be noted that if a court convicts and adjourns sentence in order that the prosecution may have an opportunity of serving a notice under subs. (2A), sufficient time must be given to enable the notice to be served " not less than seven days before " the notice is produced, i.e., the notice must arrive in the ordinary course of post so that there are seven clear days between the date of service of the notice and the date of hearing at which the statement is produced. Justices may not adjourn after conviction for a period exceeding four weeks at a time (*R.* v. *Talgarth JJ.* [1973] 2 All E.R. 717).

Weight Tickets and Timetables

A weight ticket given under the Road Traffic Act, 1960, s. 224 (3) (now s. 160 (3) of the 1972 Act) was admitted by magistrates as showing weight, but their decision as to this was not mentioned by the High Court on appeal in *Churchill* v. *Norris* (1938), 158 L.T. 255. Obviously, it could be used to refresh the memory of some-one who saw the weights shown on the dials.

Timetables, etc., are admissible against employers charged with procuring or inciting their drivers to exceed the speed limit (Road Traffic Regulation Act, 1967, s. 78A (4)). Records of hours of driving kept by a firm's drivers are admissible against the firm on a charge of permitting them to drive for excessive periods contrary to the Road Traffic Act, 1960, s. 73 (*Beer* v. *Clench* [1936] 1 All E.R. 449; *Adair* v. *Craighouse* [1937] S.C.(J.) 89). The fact that the numbers on log sheets tally with the numbers of vehicles may suffice to relate the sheets to those vehicles (*Hogg* v. *Burnet* [1938] S.C.(J.) 160). Where letters are sent by a witness to a particular person on a particular matter and an answer is received in due course, there is a presumption that the answer has been written by the person in whose writing (or, *semble*, on whose headed letter-paper) it purports to be (see cases in the English and Empire Digest, Repl. vol. 22, p. 190).

Manufacturers' Records

The Criminal Evidence Act, 1965, provides that, where direct oral evidence of a fact would be admissible, any statement contained in a document and tending to establish that fact shall on production of the document be admissible as evidence of that fact if the document is, or forms part of, a record relating to any trade or business compiled, in the course of that trade or business, from information supplied by persons who have or may reasonably be supposed to have personal knowledge of the matters dealt with in the information they supply, and the person who supplied that information is dead, abroad or ill, or has disappeared or, having regard to the lapse of time, cannot be reasonably expected to have any recollection of the matters dealt with in the information which he supplied. This Act reverses the decision in *Myers* v. *Director of Public Prosecutions* [1964] 2 All E.R. 881 as to motor manufacturers' records. The admissibility of documents in evidence and the hear-say rule generally are discussed in that case. The Act indicates

the considerations to be applied in assessing the weight of such
evidence. The work of a Government department is not a trade
or business (*R.* v. *Gwilliam* [1968] 3 All E.R. 821).

Refreshing Memory

A witness may refresh his memory from any writing made or
verified by himself contemporaneously with, and concerning, the
facts to which he testifies; " contemporaneously " includes so
shortly afterwards that the facts were fresh in the memory, e.g.,
a fortnight but not several weeks or more (Cross on Evidence,
3rd ed., p. 189 et seq.). Thus, a witness may refresh his memory
from police notes taken from his lips and signed by him (*R.* v.
Mullins (1848), 12 J.P. 776). In *Gleed* v. *Stroud*, Jo.Crim.L.
(1962) 161, a witness had written a lorry's number on an envelope
at the time of an offence by the lorry-driver. Two hours later,
the witness made a statement to the police and included the lorry's
number in it. When he gave evidence, the envelope had been
lost. The High Court held that it was proper to allow him to refresh his memory of the number from his signed statement to the
police. But where a witness wrote a car's number down at the
request of someone who saw the car but the latter did not see what
the witness wrote, it was held that the witness should not give
evidence of the number which he wrote, for it was hearsay (*R.*
v. *McLean* (1967), 111 S.J. 925). And see *Jones* v. *Metcalfe* on
p. 122. A witness may also speak from records kept by him as
part of his duty and say, " I am satisfied I kept this record and that
this or that happened as it is duly recorded," even though he may
not actually remember the occurrence (*R.* v. *Bryant* (1946), 110
J.P. 267). Notes made with a view to subsequent litigation may
be used to refresh memory and it is not necessary that the witness
should have any independent recollection of the incident (*Buckeridge*
v. *Buckeridge* (1962), 106 S.J. 471). A copy checked months later
by the witness from an original record contemporaneously made
by him may be used if the original be lost or even if its absence is
not explained (*Talbot* v. *Cusack* (1864), 12 L.T. 678). The record
need not actually have been made by the witness provided he
checked it contemporaneously (*Burrough* v. *Martin* (1809), 2 Camp.
12, N.P.). The document, even if a confidential one, used to
refresh memory must be made available to the other side (*Betts*
v. *Betts* (1917), 33 T.L.R. 200), but, if no reference is made to any
document to refresh memory, the other side cannot insist on seeing
confidential documents, such as police notebooks (*Hinshelwood* v.
Auld [1926] S.C.(J.) 4, but *cf. R.* v. *Bass* [1953] 1 All E.R. 1064,

where police notebooks should have been called for). In *R.* v. *Richardson* [1971] 2 All E.R. 773 the Court of Appeal held that there could be no general rule that prosecution witnesses should not see their statements before going into court to give evidence. Such a rule could militate against the interests of justice if there has been lengthy delay in bringing the case to trial (*ibid.*). Summary trials by their very nature are normally not subject to the same delay as trials on indictment (in *Richardson's* case the delay was eighteen months) and whether it is proper for prosecution witnesses to be shown their statements will depend on the length of the delay and the complexity and nature of their evidence. A pro-forma witness statement made and signed contemporaneously by a doctor when asked by a constable for his consent to the patient supplying breath or blood samples can be used by him to refresh his memory (*Taylor* v. *Armand* [1975] R.T.R. 225) (see also *Groves* v. *Redbart* on p. 319). By a Home Office Circular, No. 82/1969, issued with the approval of the Lord Chief Justice and the judges of the Queen's Bench Division, witnesses for the prosecution are normally (though not in all circumstances) entitled, if they so request, to be supplied with copies of any statements taken from them by the police. A tape-recording may also be used to refresh memory (*R.* v. *Mills* [1962] 3 All E.R. 298). See further as to tape-recordings, pp. 115, 126.

Plans and Photographs

Plans and sketches are frequently used in careless driving cases—some cases would be incomprehensible without them. A map or plan prepared for the purpose of a trial ought not to contain any reference to transactions and occurrences which are the subject-matter of the investigation before the court and were not existing when the survey was made; if it does and *objection is taken*, the court should not look at it (*R.* v. *Mitchell* (1852), 6 Cox C.C. 82). In *Tarbox* v. *St. Pancras Borough Council* [1952] 1 All E.R. 1306 (a civil case), however, particulars of the place where the plaintiff said he was walking, the position of the defendant's servant and the position where the plaintiff fell were ordered to be put on a plan rather than in a statement of claim. If no objection is taken by the other side, a plan or sketch showing both things existing at the time it was made (e.g., traffic lights, white lines, skid marks, piles of mud) and also things surmised by the artist (e.g., the course of a car prior to stopping) can, it seems, be put in evidence, but the other side should first be given a sight of the drawing. Provided that it is made clear to the court that some of it is surmise, that it is for guidance only and that it must be carefully checked with the evidence, a plan or sketch not objected to, put in before the court for guidance only, seems to be no more inadmissible than a sketch made by a magistrate as the case unfolds. If a sketch not to a scale and showing only things existing and no surmised tracks, etc., is objected to, it would seem that the person who prepared it can still put it in when called as a witness for what it is worth but, if it is such a bad sketch as to be completely out of proportion—as some are—it is submitted that the other side could successfully object to its being put in at all because it is so misleading. If it is a plan to scale, however, and shows only things existing when it is made, it must be admitted when the person who prepared it swears to it in the witness box. Further, by the Criminal Justice Act, 1948, s. 41, in any criminal proceedings a plan prepared by a constable, architect, chartered surveyor, civil engineer, municipal engineer or land agent and certified by him to be correctly drawn to a specified scale shall be evidence of the relative position of the things shown thereon; the person who prepared the plan need not be called as a witness, but a copy of the plan and certificate must have been served on the defendant at least seven days before the hearing and, not less than three days before the hearing, the defendant can require that person to be called as a witness (see s. 41 (5)). Sketches are discussed in an article at 121 J.P.Jo. 754.

It was held in *Hogg* v. *Clark* [1959] S.C. 7 that a plan could be put by the defence to a prosecution witness although the plan had not at that time been proved.

Maps, such as the Ordnance Survey, are admissible as to matters deducible from them, such as whether a road is in existence, and distances (see cases in E. and E. Dig., Repl. vol. 22, pp. 374–6). A rotameter may be used on a map to show distances travelled. In statutes passed after 1st January, 1890, distance is measured in a straight line on a horizontal plane unless the contrary intention appears (Interpretation Act, 1889, s. 34). Distance in general is measured as the crow flies (39 Halsbury, 3rd ed., p. 792). Ordnance maps are not in themselves evidence that a forecourt is part of the highway (*Baxter* v. *Middlesex County Council* [1956] Crim.L.R. 561), nor of the boundaries of the highway (*Webb* v. *Eastleigh Borough Council* (1957), 56 L.G.R. 124). The Highways Act, 1959, s. 35, however, allows maps, plans and local histories to be put in evidence as to the dedication of a highway. Moreover some Ordnance Survey maps show the footpaths, bridleways and roads used as public paths as on a "definitive map" prepared under the National Parks and Access to the Countryside Act, 1949 (see

p. 32 as to the effect if a right of way is so shown on a definitive map).

Photographs are proved by the oath of the person who took them, he producing the negatives at the same time. Their value is discussed at [1958] Crim.L.R. 6. A film of a reconstruction of an accident or piece of driving would generally not be admissible, for it would not be the best evidence (*R.* v. *Quinn* [1961] 3 All E.R. 88). A tape-recording which may not be the original recording is similarly inadmissible unless it can be proved to be the original tape or it can be compared with the original. The prosecution must prove that a tape-recording is the original if it is to be admitted in evidence (*R.* v. *Robson*, p. 126).

The police will normally supply a copy of any photograph taken by them on payment of the cost.

Inspection of Vehicles

Where vehicles are near the court, the justices may inspect them provided they have sworn evidence as to whether they are in a different condition from that at the time of the offence (*Keeble* v. *Miller* [1950] 1 All E.R. 261). Witnesses taking part in a view should be recalled for cross-examination, if desired (*Karamat* v. *R.* [1956] 1 All E.R. 415, where views generally are discussed). In *R.* v. *Knight* (1961), *The Times*, 14th June, the jury, in a case of taking and driving away a lorry, asked if they could inspect a similar lorry and were allowed to do so. The Court of Criminal Appeal said that applications for inspection should be regarded with great caution, especially when the conditions of the inspection differed. See also Cross on Evidence, 3rd ed., p. 8.

A conviction was quashed in *R.* v. *Lawrence* [1968] 1 All E.R. 579, where the jury inspected a vehicle after they had retired, but not quashed in *R.* v. *Nixon* [1968] 2 All E.R. 33, where the same had happened but defending counsel had said that he desired the jury to do so.

See p. 173 as to magistrates using their own knowledge.

Spouses

The spouses of defendants may not be called for the prosecution in any road traffic cases save those of causing the death of, or bodily injury to, a juvenile under seventeen. The spouse is competent but not compellable in such cases (Children and Young Persons Act, 1933, s. 15). (See p. 104 as to whether this includes dangerous and careless driving under ss. 2 and 3 of the Road Traffic Act, 1972, merely because a child has been injured.) The spouses of any defendants being tried jointly cannot be called for the prosecution even though their evidence does not relate to the particular defendant who is the husband or wife in question (*R.* v. *Mount* (1934), 24 Cr.App.R. 135). This point should be watched where two defendants are being tried together on separate charges and the prosecution wish to call one defendant's spouse to prove facts against the other defendant. See Roscoe's Criminal Evidence, 16th ed., p. 133. In *Parson* v. *Tomlin* (1956), 120 J.P. 129, the evidence of a spouse was held inadmissible for the Crown in a dangerous driving charge involving a child's death. As her evidence was of no weight, the conviction was not quashed, but it would have been had her evidence been material (*R.* v. *Boucher* (1952), 36 Cr.App.R. 152). Section 15 of the Children and Young Persons Act, 1933, mentioned at the start of this paragraph, was not cited in *Parson* v. *Tomlin* (*supra*).

May one spouse give evidence for the prosecution where the other has committed a road traffic offence deliberately directed against her? The point actually arose before a Metropolitan magistrate when a husband was charged with failing to accord precedence to his wife on a pedestrian crossing, it being suggested that he was trying to frighten her. The magistrate did not allow her to give evidence. It is submitted that a spouse may testify for the prosecution in such circumstances only where a charge under the Offences against the Person Act or for an attempt to commit an offence under that Act has been brought in respect of harm or threatened harm to her or binding-over is sought.

Spouses are competent witnesses for the defence but can only be called on the defendant's application—here again watch the point where two defendants are being tried together and it is desired to call the spouse of one to testify for the other defendant. Failure of a spouse to give evidence for the defence must not be made the subject of any comment by the prosecution; comment would seem to include such questions in cross-examination as, " And yet your wife, who was sitting by you in the car, is not being called? " The Criminal Evidence Act, 1898, s. 1, which deals with the evidence of spouses, also provides that spouses are not compellable to disclose communications made to the witness-spouse by the other during marriage. This privilege (of non-disclosure of communications) does not extend to communications made by the witness-spouse to the other nor to evidence given by widows, widowers and divorced persons lawfully called (*Shenton* v. *Tyler* [1939] 1 All E.R. 827). A communication privileged between spouses may be given in evidence by someone who overheard it or read it (*Rumping* v. *Director of Public Prosecutions* [1962]

3 All E.R. 256). A divorced spouse cannot be called (save in the excepted cases) to testify against the other spouse in respect of any matters arising or conversations which passed during the marriage; the same rule applies where the marriage was voidable and has been annulled but not, *semble*, where it was void from the start (*R.* v. *Algar* [1953] 2 All E.R. 1381). Nor is the evidence of one spouse admissible in a road traffic prosecution against the other where they are judicially separated (*Moss* v. *Moss* [1963] 2 All E.R. 829). If the prosecutor does comment on the failure of the defendant or his wife to give evidence the defence should be offered an adjournment to a different bench (*R.* v. *Allerton* (1953), 117 J.P.Jo. 421) but in *R.* v. *Hunter* (1969), 113 S.J. 161, a conviction was upheld where a trial proceeded after prosecution commented on the spouse not being called. The prosecutor may ask the defendant in cross-examination if his wife is at the trial so long as he does not comment on it (*R.* v. *Scales*, W.L.R., 7th March, 1969, Recent Points).

See generally, as to evidence of spouses in criminal cases, 99 S.J. 551.

Statements

The defendant's admission that he was driving will suffice to show that he was the driver. Statements by the defendant to the police are admissible in evidence without a caution having been administered and a constable may properly ask a person if he was driving on a particular occasion (*Hennell* v. *Cuthbert* [1962] Crim.L.R. 104). The person's answers will still be admissible provided that they were obtained without unfairness and that the constable had not reasonable grounds for thinking that he had committed an offence (*Berry* v. *Robson* (1964), 108 S.J. 259). But if he has been charged with or informed that he may be prosecuted for an offence or the constable has reasonable grounds for suspecting that he may have committed an offence, then he should first be cautioned. A statement by a defendant, which he had acknowledged but not signed, was held admissible in *The People* v. *Wickham* [1949] Ir.R. 180, discussed at Jo.Crim.L. (1950), 183. Indeed it is customary for all relevant remarks made by the defendant after an accident to be given in evidence anyhow. See generally the Judges' Rules, 1964. For r. III (*a*) to apply, the defendant must actually have been charged or, though not arrested, be likely to be summoned; even where r. III does not apply as above, no questioning after caution should take place if the constable concerned has enough evidence to prefer a charge

(*R.* v. *Collier* [1965] 3 All E.R. 136). Arrest on suspicion does not necessarily mean that there is enough evidence to charge (*ibid.*).

Where a statement is made without caution in circumstances where compliance with the Judges' Rules would necessitate a caution, it is for the judge or magistrates in exercise of their discretion to decide whether the statement should be admitted or not (*R.* v. *Ovenell* [1968] 1 All E.R. 933). The dictum in that case that the Rules are directed to the police alone overlooks r. VI, which says that persons other than police officers charged with the duty of investigating offences shall, so far as practicable, comply with them, so the Rules may apply to Ministry of Transport examiners and government officers investigating excise licence offences. In Scotland it has been held that an admission by the defendant to a constable that he was the driver at the relevant time is not admissible if the constable had not been authorised by a chief officer of police to demand the information under s. 232 of the 1960 Act (now s. 168 of the 1972 Act on p. 461) (*Foster* v. *Farrell* [1963] S.L.T. 182). The English decisions just cited suggest that this case would not be followed in England, and *Foster* v. *Farrell* was distinguished in *Miln* v. *Cullen* [1967] S.L.T. 35, where it was held that the admission of the defendant at the scene of an accident in reply to a question by a constable whether he was the driver may be allowed in evidence if there is no unfairness to him. It was said obiter in *Berry* v. *Robson, supra,* that the question " Are you the driver? " must be answered because of s. 167 or s. 168 but those sections apply only when the constable has been authorised to demand the information by or on behalf of a chief officer of police. It may be that statements made in breach of the Judges' Rules are anyhow admissible at the court's discretion (*Hennell* v. *Cuthbert, supra*).

The police should supply a copy of the defendant's statement to them to the defence on request (110 J.P.Jo. 435) and the Home Secretary has said that it is the practice of the police to supply to the solicitor of an accused person on request copies of statements made by him, unless the police think that to do so would impede the course of justice (105 S.J. 133). Abstracts of the police report of an accident will generally be supplied at a charge of £2·50 unless a prosecution is pending. The charge for interviewing a police officer is £4 and for a copy of a witness's statement £1·75. A police report containing limited particulars costs £1·75. The police will also supply a copy of a photograph at 50p a copy. The *Law Society's Gazette*, August, 1967, p. 418, indicates the recommended police procedure for interviewing police officers and supplying statements, etc., for civil proceedings.

It is not customary for the police to supply copies of statements, made by witnesses who are to be called by them, to the defence in advance (*R.* v. *Bryant* (1946), 110 J.P. 267). If the prosecution know of a credible witness who can speak of material facts which tend to show the defendant's innocence, his statement, if he is not to be called for the prosecution, should be made available to the defence (*Dallison* v. *Caffery* [1964] 2 All E.R. 610). A practice seems to have been growing up, however, at any rate at trials on indictment, of letting the defence see (*semble*, at the trial) the statements of witnesses called for the Crown, and how far this will extend to magistrates' courts is not clear (see *R.* v. *Hall* (1958), 43 Cr.App.R. 29; *R.* v. *Fenn*, Jo.Crim.L. (1959) 253). In the latter case Pilcher, J., said that, where a witness's evidence differs materially from that given in his statement to the police, that statement ought to be shown to the defence, so that there may be cross-examination on that issue, it being the prosecutor's duty to place all the facts before the court. See generally Archbold, 38th ed., paras. 443 and 443a. The police should supply to the defending solicitor, on his request, a list of the defendant's previous convictions, without waiting for the latter's permission. Witnesses or prospective witnesses may be interviewed before trial by either side, whether or not they have been seen already by the other side; once the defendant has been committed for trial, the defence may still interview the prosecution witnesses but the occasions when such a course is necessary must be rare and, if there is to be an interview after committal, the prosecutor should be invited to attend (*Law Society's Gazette*, February, 1963). See also 118 N.L.J. 913. By Home Office Circular No. 82/1969 (issued with the approval of the Lord Chief Justice and the judges of the Queen's Bench Division) witnesses for the prosecution are normally, though not in all circumstances, entitled, if they so request, to be supplied with copies of any statement taken from them by the police.

The practice of the police in interviewing and obtaining a further statement from a defendant, when he has already made or declined to make one at the time of occurrence, was criticised by a Metropolitan magistrate (Jo.Crim.L. (1955) 291).

Statements in the defendant's presence are evidence against him of the truth of the matters stated so far as by words or conduct he has acquiesced in their contents. But where no admission can be reasonably inferred, it is in criminal cases a rule of practice that such statements should, in order to avoid prejudice to the prisoner, not be given in evidence at all (Phipson's Manual of Evidence, 8th ed., p. 130). The working of this rule can be shown thus: Tate is charged with using a vehicle with defective brakes.

In the presence of Tate and the police constable, a mechanic (not called as a witness) examines the brakes and mentions certain defects. If Tate then admitted the truth of the mechanic's remarks by words or conduct, the mechanic's statement and Tate's reply may be given in evidence; if Tate by words or conduct then denied their truth, the mechanic's remarks should not generally be given in evidence. Evidence of what has been said to the defendant by persons not called as witnesses may be given if relevant to show the defendant's state of mind (*Subramaniam* v. *Public Prosecutor* [1956] 1 W.L.R. 965; *R.* v. *Willis* [1960] 1 All E.R. 331), e.g., that what he had been told by a person not called as a witness induced in him a belief that the owner of a motor vehicle would have consented to his taking it.

Admissions

Admissions by either side before or at the hearing are allowed in the circumstances given in s. 10 of the Criminal Justice Act, 1967. A defendant may thus be asked to admit in court that he was the driver or what his reply to a constable was; his admission in a magistrates' court must be put in writing and signed by him (Magistrates' Courts Rules, 1968, r. 59) but no doubt the magistrates will control a prosecutor who tries to get the defendant to admit his case for him. Save so far as admissions are made in advance, each side should be ready to prove its case by ordinary evidence; an admission may only be withdrawn by leave of the court and the side relying on it would no doubt be granted an adjournment to call the necessary evidence. In *R.* v. *Lewis* [1971] Crim.L.R. 414, defending counsel admitted the facts as stated in the prosecutor's opening speech. The Court of Appeal said it was a practice which should be adopted rarely and with extreme caution.

Proof Generally

Where it is a matter of notorious local knowledge that a journey of $1\frac{1}{2}$ miles from point A to point B necessarily involved using several different public roads, the justices were held to be entitled to use this knowledge in rejecting a submission of no case and convicting the defendant where the prosecution had been unable to prove the precise route taken by the offending vehicle (*Borthwick* v. *Vickers* [1973] R.T.R. 390).

The owner of a motor vehicle is presumed in law to be the user, in the absence of contrary evidence (*Watson* v. *Paterson*, noted at 121 J.P.Jo. 336). In *Barnard* v. *Sully* (1931), 47 T.L.R. 557, it was held that proof of a defendant being owner of a car was *prima facie* evidence that it was being driven at the material time by him or his servant or agent. This was a civil case and, in a reference to it in *Ende* v. *Cassidy* (1964), 108 S.J. 522, it was said that there would be a higher standard of proof in criminal cases, but it was held in *Ende's* case that ownership was some evidence that the defendant was responsible for an obstruction with his car, especially as it had been left outside a block of flats where he lived. It is submitted that these cases, while sufficient to convict a defendant owner (in the absence of his denial) of offences of using, including obstruction, where there is no evidence as to the identity of the driver, are not necessarily sufficient to convict him of " driving ". One has only to consider, as an example, whether a High Court judge would allow the conviction of a car-owner for manslaughter where the sole evidence implicating him personally was that he owned the vehicle involved. In seeking proof as to the identity of a driver, the police should remember their powers of requiring the owner or any other person to give information as to this (see p. 461). If the name and address of an offending motorist have been obtained from a driving licence produced by the offender at the time of the offence, the appearance at court of a defendant of that name in answer to the summons is *prima facie* evidence that he is the driver. See *Cooke* v. *McCann* [1974] R.T.R. 131 where a traffic warden was unable to identify in court the defendant as the driver he had seen driving the wrong way down a one-way street and the resulting summons was issued in the name and address shown on the driving licence produced at the time. In *Edwards* v. *Brookes (Milk), Ltd.* [1963] 3 All E.R. 62 it was held that admissions by employees may be used in evidence against their master when there is *prima facie* evidence that they are the master's agents and they have an ostensible status qualifying them to make statements on behalf of the master; in that case the employee concerned was a depôt manager and there was evidence to imply that he had authority. Admissions made by a subordinate employee, however, would not generally be allowed in evidence (*Roberts* v. *Morris* [1965] Crim.L.R. 46; here it was a lorry-driver). And *cf. John Henshall (Quarries), Ltd.* v. *Harvey* on p. 53. See p. 106 as to certificates of admission; it is submitted that the above rules apply to written admissions also. See generally Cross on Evidence, 3rd ed., p. 443. *Watson* v. *Paterson, supra*, shows that, anyhow, a vehicle-owner is presumed to be its user and evidence of ownership, if not obtained from the firm's directors, is obtainable from the Department of the Environment and from the name and address painted on the vehicle itself (*cf. Martin* v. *White*

(1910), 74 J.P. 106). A partner's admissions are evidence against the firm (Partnership Act, 1890, s. 15). Note also s. 10 of the Criminal Justice Act, 1967, on p. 120, which allows admissions before and at the hearing by a defendant or by the prosecution; where the defendant is an individual, only his lawyer may make them for him, prior to the hearing, under s. 10. A corporation may make written admissions by its directors, manager, secretary or clerk under s. 10.

In a case where the defendant was found to be driving a car seven miles from a town, it was presumed, in the absence of contrary evidence, that he was driving on the same journey and road when three miles from the town shortly before (*Beresford* v. *St. Albans JJ.* (1905), 22 T.L.R. 1). Where a witness observed a lorry and caused his wife to write down its number, she should be called to say what number she wrote down or the husband should produce and identify the piece of paper used as the one on which the number was written (*Grew* v. *Cubitt* (1951), 49 L.G.R. 650). This case was distinguished in *Jones* v. *Metcalfe* [1967] 3 All E.R. 205, where it was held that, although an eye-witness had told the police the registration number of the defendant's vehicle and that it was the vehicle involved in an accident, there was no written evidence of the number or anything to identify the defendant. And see *R.* v. *McLean* on p. 112. In *Jones* v. *Carter* [1956] Crim.L.R. 275, an acquittal was directed in a careless driving case where the prosecutor had not proved that the defendant was driving, although there had been no cross-examination by the defence as to identity and the case had been conducted on the basis that the defendant (who did not testify) was driving. The court may properly infer that traffic lights work correctly (*Wells* v. *Woodward* (1956), 54 L.G.R. 142). In *Farrell* v. *Feighan* (1961), 76 Sh.Ct. Rep. 141, the owner of a car was found in the road beside it, unconscious; it was held to be sufficient proof that he had been driving but not that he had been driving carelessly. See *Platt* v. *Green* [1965] Crim.L.R. 311 and *Dickens* v. *Smith* [1965] Crim.L.R. 312 for cases where the High Court refused to interfere with convictions in road traffic cases notwithstanding discrepancies in the evidence of identification. The defendant's appearance in court in answer to the summons is not an admission that he was the driver or user at the time of the offence (*Saunders* v. *Johns* [1965] Crim.L.R. 49).

Where several men are found together in a vehicle, which has been taken without the owner's consent, in suspicious circumstances, that may be *prima facie* evidence that they were acting in concert and they can all be properly charged with taking it and with using it without insurance (*Ross* v. *Rivenall* [1959] 2 All E.R. 376). The presumption of guilt would be less strong, however, against a passenger where the circumstances were not suspicious. See p. 356.   See also *R.* v. *Baldessare*, cited on p. 357.

The prosecution must prove their case. In some road traffic cases it suffices to show that the defendant did the forbidden act without any evidence of a guilty mind: see, for example, *Hawkins* v. *Holmes* on p. 416 (failing to maintain brakes); in others, *mens rea* must be shown. In dangerous and careless driving cases it is not sufficient to show an accident which may well have occurred through negligence; the defendant's guilt must be established by positive evidence (*Alexander* v. *Adair* [1938] S.C.(J.) 28); see further p. 271. But any exception, exemption, proviso, excuse or qualification for a defendant should be proved by him and need not be negatived by police evidence in opening (Magistrates' Courts Act, 1952, s. 81; see *Baker* v. *Sweet* on p. 319). The defendant must prove facts peculiarly within his own knowledge, e.g., that he has a licence (*R.* v. *Oliver* [1943] 2 All E.R. 800) or policy of insurance (*Leathley* v. *Drummond, infra*). Where it is an offence to do an act without lawful authority, the defendant must prove that he had such authority and the prosecution need not prove its absence (*Williams* v. *Russell* (1933), 97 J.P. 128). On a charge of driving without a licence or insurance, it suffices if the prosecutor proves that the defendant drove a motor vehicle on a road on the day in question and, in law, no further evidence, e.g., that he was asked for, and failed to produce his licence or insurance certificate, as the case may be, is required; the onus then shifts to the defendant to show that he had the licence (*John* v. *Humphreys* [1955] 1 All E.R. 793) or insurance policy (*Leathley* v. *Drummond* [1972] Crim.L.R. 227). More proof, however, appears to be required in Eire (*A.-G.* (*McGowan*) v. *Carville* (1961), 95 I.L.T.R. 41). It would in fact be improper, however, to institute a prosecution on the sole ground that the defendant was seen to drive; the prosecutor should have some reason for thinking that no licence or insurance was in force. In *Howey* v. *Bradley* [1970] Crim.L.R. 223 the court left open the question whether the onus is on the prosecution to prove that an otherwise valid insurance policy produced by the defendant does not cover the particular use of the vehicle. See *Baker* v. *Sweet* on p. 319 as to proof that a speed limit applies to a particular road. It should, however, be remembered that where the onus of proof lies upon the defendant, the onus is that of a balance of probabilities—a defendant does not have to prove the matter in question beyond a doubt based on reason.

Where two defendants each are separately charged with careless driving in a cross-roads collision or with certain other offences involving both, it seems that the prosecution can call one defendant to testify against the other, provided they are tried separately; the witness need not answer any questions tending to incriminate him (*A.-G.* v. *Egan* [1948] Ir.R. 433; Jo.Crim.L. (1949) 207). But a defendant jointly charged with another should not be called for the prosecution and, even where two defendants are charged with separate offences, it is suggested at 109 J.P.Jo. 39 that one should not be called against the other if there is something linking the two offences, e.g., using and permitting. But see *R.* v. *Norfolk Quarter Sessions, ex parte Brunson* [1953] 1 All E.R. 346. Any defendant may be called after he has been sentenced, acquitted or pardoned.

Evidence Generally

While the court can call and recall witnesses itself, it was held in *R.* v. *Owen* [1952] 1 All E.R. 1040 (discussed at Jo.Crim.L. (1952) 249) that this should not be done in jury cases after the summing-up, though this rule may be relaxed for the defence (*R.* v. *Sanderson* [1953] 1 All E.R. 485). But a witness may be recalled at a trial before justices or on appeal from such a trial where no shorthand note is taken, provided that the witness was recalled solely for the purpose of refreshing the court's memory (*Phelan* v. *Back* [1972] Crim.L.R. 104). It is submitted that justices should exercise such a power with extreme caution and should first endeavour to avoid having to do so by seeking agreement from the parties as to what the evidence was. And see the cases on inspecting vehicles on p. 115. Magistrates have a discretion to admit further evidence at least until the close of the case for the defence, but should not do so after they have retired save in very special circumstances (*Webb* v. *Leadbetter* [1966] 2 All E.R. 114). In *Phelan* v. *Back* [1972] 1 All E.R. 901 following *Webb* v. *Leadbetter* a recorder hearing an appeal was upheld when he recalled a witness for the prosecution to refresh his memory as he had taken no note of his evidence. Justices should be careful not to call for any evidence which might fill a gap in the police case, but see *Saunders* v. *Johns* and *Piggott* v. *Simms* on p. 86 as to calling evidence after a submission of "no case". On indictment the presiding judge has a discretion whether to recall a witness after a submission of "no case" (*R.* v. *McKenna* (1956), 40 Cr.App.R. 65).

In cases of dangerous and careless driving a view of the *locus* by the advocate is obviously helpful. Skid marks and other marks, damage, the visibility and obstructions at corners, the light, the state of the road at the time and mud or other indications where the point of impact was, are all things which may prove very significant at the hearing and it should be remembered that the view of a driver from a low, long-bonneted car may differ from that of a tall policeman on foot. The observance or non-observance of the Highway Code may be relied on in any civil or criminal proceedings as tending to establish or negative liability (Road Traffic Act, 1972, s. 37; see further, however, on p. 286 where this provision is discussed in the light of recent cases). A table of braking distances taken, by permission, from the Highway Code appears inside the front cover of this book, along with mileage per hour converted to feet per second. The Highway Code makes no reference to the question whether disc brakes are more efficient than other types. As to views generally, see p. 115.

Leading questions may not normally be asked in examination-in-chief save to prove introductory matters and contradiction but it is a common practice to allow a witness in a criminal case to be led as to matters not actually in controversy (Cross on Evidence, 3rd ed., p. 187 *et seq.*). A question may nevertheless be leading even if the witness is presented with a question in an alternative form. The primary test as to whether a question is leading is whether it suggests to the witness what the answer should be. The court also may relax the rule against asking leading questions if the court thinks it necessary in the interests of justice, although it is difficult to think of circumstances when the question could not to be asked just as well in the alternative form. If the court exercises its discretion to allow leading questions, a higher court will not normally interfere (*Ex parte Bottomley* (1909), 73 J.P. 246). Cases where leading questions have been allowed are *Acerro* v. *Petroni* (1815), 1 Stark. 100 (witness said he could not remember the names of members of a firm but thought he would if they were read to him; reading them to him was allowed), *Rivers* v. *Hague* (1837), cited in Phipson, *op. cit.*, 7th ed., p. 202 (witness called to testify as to entries in the Bankruptcy List and the Gazette but mentioned only the List; the court allowed the question: " Was anything said about the Gazette? ") and *Courteen* v. *Touse* (1807), 1 Camp. 43 (witness called to contradict another about the contents of a letter, which had been destroyed, allowed to have the particular passage suggested to him after he had exhausted his memory). See generally as to evidence-in-chief 98 S.J. 547. Failure to cross-examine a witness generally amounts to acceptance of his version (Cross on Evidence, 3rd ed., p. 212), but justices were held entitled to convict because they disbelieved the defence witnesses even though the evidence of the defendant and his witnesses had

not been challenged (*O'Connell* v. *Adams* [1973] R.T.R. 150).
Unlike professional judges, justices are under no obligation to test
witnesses in respect of evidence they disbelieve (*ibid.*). Leading
questions may not be asked in re-examination.

It is the normal practice of a criminal court for all witnesses to be
out of court until called to give evidence. If, however, through
inadvertence or any other reason the witness was in court, his evidence is admissible, with the court making such deductions as to
its weight as may be appropriate in the circumstances.

As to corroboration in speeding cases, see p. 318. As to corroboration by defendant's own statements in court prior to the
close of the Crown case, see 114 J.P.Jo. 62. As to corroborating
the evidence of children, see p. 102.

See pp. 274–275 as to giving evidence in dangerous and careless
driving cases when the defendant had been drinking.

Evidence of acts of driving some distance away may be given
in certain circumstances (see p. 276).

Evidence obtained by illegal means (other than confessions) is
admissible for the prosecution, unless admitting it would be unfair
to the defendant (*Kuruma* v. *R.* [1955] 1 All E.R. 236), or it was
obtained by a trick or misrepresentation (*Callis* v. *Gunn* [1963]
3 All E.R. 677; *R.* v. *Murphy* [1965] N.I. 138, where evidence of
spies was admitted). The court has a discretion to refuse to admit
it if there was unfairness. See [1963] Crim.L.R. 15 and Cross on
Evidence, 3rd ed., p. 266, and as to Scotland, *The Juridical Review*,
August, 1966.

As to exhibits, see p. 86 and *R.* v. *Orrell* at p. 179.

The High Court of Justiciary have admitted a tape-recording
in evidence (*Hopes* v. *Lord Advocate* [1960] S.L.T. 264) and a tape-
recording of an overheard conversation can be used to refresh the
hearer's memory (*R.* v. *Mills* [1962] 3 All E.R. 298). In *R.* v.
Maqsud Ali [1965] 2 All E.R. 464 it was held that a tape-recording
of remarks made by a defendant is admissible if the recording
can be properly proved and his voice identified; a properly proved
transcript of the recording may be used to assist the court. The
prosecution must prove on the balance of probabilities that the
recordings are original and authentic before they can be admitted
as evidence (*R.* v. *Robson* [1972] 2 All E.R. 699, considering *R.*
v. *Stevenson, Hulse and Whitney* [1971] 1 All E.R. 678 and *R.* v.
Maqsud Ali, supra).

CHAPTER III

NOTICES OF INTENDED PROSECUTION

THE Road Traffic Act, 1972, s. 179 (replacing s. 241 of the Road Traffic Act, 1960, as amended), requires that for certain offences the defendant must have been warned at the time of the possibility of a prosecution for those offences or have been served with the summons within fourteen days of the offence. Alternatively the prosecutor is required to have sent notice of the possibility of the prosecution within fourteen days of the offence, either to the driver or to the registered owner of a motor vehicle, or in cases under s. 17 or 18 of the Act (dangerous or careless cycling) to the rider of the cycle.

Section 179 reads:—

" (1) This section applies to—

- (a) any offence under this Act to which it is applied by column 7 of Part I of Schedule 4 to this Act; and
- (b) any offence under section 77 (7) of the Road Traffic Regulation Act, 1967, or punishable by virtue of section 78A of that Act.

(2) Subject to the following provisions of this section and to the provisions of paragraphs 5, 6 and 7 of Part IV of the said Schedule 4 where a person is prosecuted for an offence to which this section applies he shall not be convicted unless either—

- (a) he was warned at the time the offence was committed that the question of prosecuting him for some one or other of the offences to which this section applies would be taken into consideration; or
- (b) within fourteen days of the commission of the offence a summons (or, in Scotland, a complaint) for the offence was served on him; or
- (c) within the said fourteen days a notice of the intended prosecution specifying the nature of the alleged offence and the time and place where it is alleged to have been committed, was—
  - (i) in the case of an offence against section 17 or 18 of this Act, served on him;
  - (ii) in the case of any other offence served on him or on the person, if any, registered as the keeper of the vehicle at the time of the commission of the offence;

and the notice shall be deemed for the purposes of paragraph (c) above to have been served on any person if it was sent by registered post or recorded delivery service addressed to him at his last known address, notwithstanding that the notice was returned as undelivered or was for any other reason not received by him.

127

(3) The requirement of subsection (2) above shall in every case be deemed to have been complied with unless and until the contrary is proved.

[(3A) The requirement of subsection (2) above shall not apply in relation to an offence if, at the time of the offence or immediately thereafter, an accident occurs owing to the presence on a road of the vehicle in respect of which the offence was committed.]

(4) Failure to comply with the requirement of subsection (2) above shall not be a bar to the conviction of the accused in a case where the court is satisfied—

(a) that neither the name and address of the accused nor the name and address of the registered owner, if any, could with reasonable diligence have been ascertained in time for a summons or, as the case may be, a complaint to be served or for a notice to be served or sent in compliance with the said requirement; or

(b) that the accused by his own conduct contributed to the failure."

Paragraphs 5, 6 and 7 of Pt. IV of Sched. 4 to the Act read as follows:—

" 5. Where a person is prosecuted on indictment in England or Wales for an offence to which section 179 does not apply, section 179 (2) shall not be taken to prejudice any power of the jury on the charge for that offence, if they find him not guilty of it, to find him guilty of an offence against section 2.

6. In Scotland a person may be convicted of an offence against section 2 by virtue of paragraph 1 or 2 above notwithstanding that the requirement of section 179 (2) has not been satisfied as respects that offence.

7. A person may be convicted of an offence against section 3 or 18 notwithstanding that the requirement of section 179 (2) has not been satisfied as respects that offence where—

(a) the charge for the offence has been preferred against him by virtue of paragraph 4* above, and

(b) the said requirement has been satisfied, or does not apply as respects the alleged offence against section 2 or, as the case may be, section 17."

Subsection (3A), above, was inserted by the Road Traffic Act, 1974.

Application of Section 179

Section 179 applies to the following offences:—

(i) Driving a motor vehicle recklessly, in a dangerous manner, at a dangerous speed (s. 2), without due care and attention or without reasonable consideration (s. 3), at a speed exceeding a statutory speed limit or at a speed exceeding that lawful for

---

*Paragraph 4 (formerly s. 3 (2) of the 1960 Act) contains the procedure whereby a magistrates' court may direct a charge of careless driving (or cycling) to be preferred where the court are of the opinion that a charge of dangerous driving (or cycling) has not been proved (see p. 266).

vehicles of the particular type (s. 78A of the Road Traffic Regulation Act, 1967) (as to exceeding 70 m.p.h. on a motorway see below) or at a speed less than the minimum prescribed under s. 77 (7) of the Road Traffic Regulation Act, 1967;

(ii) Dangerous, reckless or careless riding by cyclists (ss. 17 and 18) (in which case the notice is required to be sent to the alleged offender);

(iii) Offences under s. 22 (disobeying certain traffic signs and police signals) and s. 24 (leaving a vehicle in a dangerous position) of the 1972 Act; in *Sulston* v. *Hammond* [1970] 2 All E.R. 830 it was held that s. 179 has no application to an offence under s. 23 of the Road Traffic Regulation Act, 1967, of failing to comply with the requirement of a pedestrian crossing Regulation;

(iv) Aiding and abetting the commission of any of the above-named offences (*The People* (*A.-G.*) v. *Carroll* [1950] Ir.Jur.R. 20).

It does not apply to any of the offences (i), (iii) and (iv) above when committed by the driver of a tram or trolley vehicle operated under statutory powers (s. 198 (6)). It applies to horse-drawn vehicles under (iii).

It does not apply to other road traffic offences by the driver of any vehicle (*cf. Staunton* v. *Coates* (1924), 88 J.P. 193). Nor does it apply to other road traffic offences even if they are similar in character to those enumerated in Sched. 4, e.g., pedestrian crossing offences (see *Sulston* v. *Hammond, supra*). See also " Offences Causing Death and Courts-Martial " (*infra*). Failure to comply with s. 179 means that there cannot be a conviction for the offences to which it applies.

It suffices if any one of the requirements of s. 179 is fulfilled, e.g., if the defendant was adequately warned at the time, there is no need for a notice (see also *Shield* v. *Crighton* on p. 134). Many police forces, from abundant caution, do in fact send the notice in all cases although there may have been warning at the time. It will also be noted that, in the case of motor vehicles, the notice can be given either to the driver or to the registered owner.

Speeding

Section 179 applies to all speeding offences " punishable by virtue of s. 78A of the Road Traffic Regulation Act, 1967 " (see s. 179 (1) (*b*) above). This definition is sufficiently wide to cover all offences of speeding with one possible exception. A magistrates' court has held that s. 179 does not apply to an offence of exceeding 70 m.p.h. on a motorway on the ground that as the offence was contrary to the Motorways Traffic (Speed Limit) (England) Regulations, 1967 (S.I. 1967 No. 1041) the offence was punishable not by virtue of s. 78A but by virtue of s. 13(4) of the 1967 Act. The 1967 Regulations have now been replaced by the Motorways Traffic (Speed Limit) Regulations, 1974 (S.I. 1974 No. 502) and these regulations are similarly made by virtue of s. 13 (2) of the Road Traffic Regulation Act, 1967, and offences under the regulations so made are similarly punishable under s. 13 (4). Although the magistrates' court were required to state a case for the opinion of the High Court, the appeal was not persisted in. It should be noted that the decision only has application to offences of exceeding the overall limit of 70 m.p.h. on motorways or 60 or 50 m.p.h. on certain lengths of particular motorways specified by the same regulations. It does not apply to offences of exceeding 60, 50, or 40 m.p.h. in respect of certain goods vehicles and vehicles drawing trailers under the Motor Vehicles (Speed Limits on Motorways) Regulations, 1973 (S.I. 1973 No. 748) as these offences are clearly punishable by virtue of s. 78A and not s. 13 (4).

Waiver

May a defendant waive a failure to comply with s. 179 and submit to judgment? It is submitted that he may (Maxwell on the Interpretation of Statutes, 11th ed., p. 377, citing *R.* v. *Hughes* (1879), 4 Q.B.D. 614; see also cases on p. 90 and Craies on Statute Law, 6th ed., p. 269).

Subsection (3A)—Accidents

Subsection (3A) was inserted into s. 179 by para. 22 of Sched. 6 to the Road Traffic Act, 1974, and came into effect on 1st January, 1975. The subsection exempts the prosecution from complying with the requirements of s. 179 (2) if, owing to the presence on a road of the vehicle in respect of which the offence was committed, an accident occurred at the time of the offence or immediately thereafter.

The primary purpose of the enactment of the subsection was to relieve the police of having to serve numerous notices of intended prosecution whenever a series of multiple accidents occurred on a motorway. The subsection clearly will apply, however, to any accident, no matter how trivial, and even if one vehicle only is involved. An " accident " was defined for the purposes of ss. 5–12 of the Act of 1972 as " an unintended occurrence which has an adverse physical result " in *R.* v. *Morris* [1972] R.T.R. 201, at

p. 204 (where two vehicles became locked together when the front bumper of one car which was pushing another slipped under the rear bumper of the vehicle it was pushing). It is understood that notwithstanding the wide terms of the subsection many police forces may continue to comply with s. 179 in simple accident cases. It would seem that the fact that a prosecutor endeavoured to comply with the requirements of s. 179 but failed to do so will not debar him subsequently from claiming exemption from the requirements of s. 179 if the subsection applies. The subsection will also allow a defendant who has been summoned under s. 2 or s. 3 following an accident to apply for a cross-summons against the other party to the accident. In many cases in the past a defendant was unable to do so because he was outside the time-limits imposed by s. 179.

The subsection will chiefly apply to dangerous, etc., driving under s. 2 and careless or inconsiderate driving under s. 3 where accidents have occurred. It should be observed, however, that the subsection applies to all offences to which s. 179 is otherwise applicable; accidents may occur, for example, as a result of an offence of failing to comply with a traffic signal (s. 22) or causing or permitting a vehicle to remain at rest in a dangerous position, etc. (s. 24). The accident must occur " owing to the presence on a road of the vehicle ". These words were considered in *Quelch* v. *Phipps* [1955] 2 All E.R. 302 in respect of an offence of failing to report an accident (see p. 346). It was held that there must be some direct causal connection between the vehicle on the road and the occurrence of the accident. Difficulties of causation may arise in respect of an offending vehicle which is not itself involved in the resulting accident, e.g., a vehicle left in a dangerous position on a road as a result of which another vehicle has to pull out to overtake and collides with a vehicle coming in the opposite direction. It is submitted that as long as the accident occurs as a direct result of the offending vehicle's presence subs. (3A) applies but not if the accident occurs only incidentally or indirectly. Section 24 itself requires the offending vehicle " to cause danger " and it may therefore be difficult to envisage a conviction under s. 24 if the vehicle only indirectly causes danger. The accident must occur " at the time of the offence or immediately thereafter", and particularly in the case of a s. 24 offence difficulties of interpretation may arise. The offence under s. 24 is committed if a person " causes or permits " a vehicle " to remain at rest " in a dangerous position, etc. If a vehicle is allowed to remain at rest in a dangerous position and the accident does not occur immediately after the vehicle was left on the road, the subsection may apply if a s. 24 offence is regarded as a continuing offence. It would seem, however, that an offence under s. 24 is complete as soon as the offender has caused or permitted the vehicle to remain at rest.

Presumption of Conformity with Section 179

As appears from subs. (3) of s. 179, it is unnecessary for the prosecution to give any evidence that its requirements have been fulfilled. It is for the defence to allege that they have not, and to call evidence to that effect; while it is a convenient practice to decide this issue as a preliminary point, the issue can be raised at any relevant stage of the proceedings (*R.* v. *Edmonton JJ., ex parte Brooks* [1960] 2 All E.R. 475). The defence must show that the driver and the registered " keeper " of a motor vehicle have not had the notice under under s. 179 (2) (*c*) and both the driver and the keeper should give evidence to that effect; it is not enough for the defendant alone, when he is not also the keeper, to give evidence that he has not had it (*Sanders* v. *Scott* [1961] 2 All E.R. 403). If the defendant proves that neither he nor the registered " keeper " has had the notice, it is for the prosecutor to prove its posting by registered or recorded delivery post, if he can, to the last-known address (*Archer* v. *Blacker* (1965), 109 S.J. 113). *Semble*, it would be unnecessary to call the " keeper " if the police were to admit in evidence that no notice had been given to him. See *infra* under " Notice " as to non-receipt of a notice sent by post and under " Reasonable Diligence " as to excusing non-compliance with s. 179. Where a case is to be sent for trial on indictment, the magistrates should normally not deal with the issue whether s. 179 has been complied with; that is a matter for the court of trial (*Card* v. *Salmon* [1953] 1 All E.R. 324).

In *Rogerson* v. *Edwards* (1951), 49 L.G.R. 358, the owners of the vehicle concerned were Greenwoods (Contractors), Ltd., Bury Road, Ramsey, and there was another company named Greenwoods (Transport), Ltd., in the same street. The police sent a notice addressed to " Messrs. Greenwoods, Bury Road, Ramsey ". It was held that the defendant must show that the right company had not had the notice and, in the absence of evidence that Greenwoods (Contractors), Ltd., had not received it, the case should proceed. It is submitted that, if it can be proved by evidence given for the prosecution or by the defendant's admission in cross-examination or prior to the hearing that he did receive a notice of intended prosecution within fourteen days of the offence, the proceedings should not be dismissed although there may have been mistakes in the addressing and stamping of the envelope or it came by ordinary post or it was left at the wrong house or with the wrong person; the defendant, however, should also have known, in the case of an incorrectly named or addressed notice, that he was in fact the person for whom it was intended (*cf. Re Poyser and Mills' Arbitration* [1963] 1 All E.R. 612, at p. 617, a case on another statute).

A similar provision to s. 179 in Irish legislation has been interpreted more strictly than s. 179 has in England. The Irish cases, which are reviewed at 88 I.L.T.N. 123 and 129, are therefore of little authority here, though some are cited in this chapter on points where there is no English or Scottish authority.

Offences Causing Death and Courts-Martial

The presumed effect of para. 5 of Pt. IV of Sched. 4 to the Act is that a person charged on indictment with manslaughter or causing death by dangerous driving need not have received a warning or notice if the jury convict him, pursuant to s. 6 (3) of the Criminal Law Act, 1967, of dangerous or reckless driving. Where a charge of reckless or dangerous driving under the Road Traffic Act, 1972, s. 2, is reduced to careless driving or driving without reasonable consideration under s. 3 pursuant to para. 4 of Pt. IV of Sched. 4 to the Act, notice or warning of the substituted charge need not have been given (para. 7, *ibid.*). Like provision applies to cyclists (para. 7, *ibid.*). Section 179 does not apply in favour of a soldier charged at a court-martial with committing a civil offence, viz., careless driving contrary to the Army Act, 1955, s. 70, so that warning or notice need not have been given (*R. v. Jennings* [1956] 3 All E.R. 429).

Warning at the Time

This may be oral or written. Where an accident occurred at 11.45 a.m., the police arrived at 12.15 p.m., and the defendant was given an oral warning at the scene of the accident at 12.20 p.m., this was held to be " warning at the time ", it having been given at the earliest time reasonably possible after the arrival of the police and while the parties were still at the scene of the accident (*Jeffs* v. *Wells* (1936), 100 J.P.Jo. 406; see also *Shield* v. *Crighton, infra*). A warning at 4 p.m. in respect of an offence at 8.30 a.m. the same day is not a warning at the time (*Cuthbert* v. *Hollis* [1958] S.L.T.(Sh.) 51; [1958] Crim.L.R. 814). In *Jollye* v. *Dale* [1960] 2 All E.R. 369, a driver was pursued by the police for 30 minutes after an act of dangerous driving and then arrested. An hour later he was medically examined and, very soon after, the first oral warning was given. It was held that the words " at the time of the offence " were not limited to the point of time when the offence was committed and it was a question of fact whether there had been a warning at the time: the High Court refused to interfere with the magistrates' finding that there had been a proper warning under s. 179. It was added, however, that where the earliest possible time for warning the driver was several hours later, this would not generally be a warning at the time. After an accident in the country, a car driver took the victim to two hospitals and did not report to the police until four hours after the accident; a warning then sufficed (*Sinclair* v. *Clark* [1962] S.L.T. 307). In *Shield* v. *Crighton* [1974] Crim.L.R. 605 it was held that the phrase " at the time " had to be construed " sensibly " and it was held that an oral warning was " at the time the offence occurred " where the constable arrived at the scene of the accident giving rise to the offence ten minutes after it occurred and gave the oral warning only after having first taken a written statement from the defendant under caution.

The form of words necessary to constitute a warning has been the subject of many decisions, which are discussed at 213 L.T. News. 204; most of them were under an earlier Act which required that the defendant be "warned of the intended prosecution". The words, " I think you are exceeding the limit but if (on checking) I find I am wrong, you will hear no more about it," were held sufficient (*Jessopp* v. *Clarke* (1908), 72 J.P. 358; and see *Taylor* v. *Horn* [1929] S.L.T. 600). Is it necessary to state for what offence or offences prosecution may be considered? In *Watt* v. *Smith* [1942] S.C.(J.) 109; Jo.Crim.L. (1942) 293, it was held that the words, " The circumstances of the accident will be reported to the fiscal for the purpose of considering a prosecution," were insufficient though they were spoken at the scene of the accident; they might have been thought to refer to a common-law offence or some other contravention of the Road Traffic Acts. It was also said that the constable need not select the particular offence for which there might be a prosecution, but he must so word his warning as to direct attention to ss. 2 and 3. In *Alston* v. *Nurse* (1933), unreported), the King's Bench Division upheld as a good warning the words, " I will have to report the matter to my superior officer with a view to prosecution "; they gave, it was said, the information which s. 179 intends the motorist to have. In *A.-G.* v. *Foley* (1952), 86 I.L.T.R. 30, it was held to be unnecessary to specify for what offences the prosecution would be (see also Jo.Crim.L. (1953)

170). In view of the infinite variety of warning formulae usable, every case must be decided on its facts. In *Parkes* v. *Cole* (1922), 86 J.P. 122, however, it was held that warning of a charge of dangerous driving did not amount to a warning of a charge of exceeding the speed limit.

If a defendant has been orally warned at the time, can he say that the warning was ineffective because he did not or could not take it in? Defendants have successfully so pleaded in Ireland (see Jo.Crim.L. (1954) 275) but here, it is submitted, it would be a question of fact, a heavy onus being on the defendant to show that the warning was ineffective. Obviously, bawling formulae into the ear of an unconscious or seriously injured man is insufficient; on the other hand, if the defendant was apparently in full possession of his faculties, can he plead that he was so worried by the accident that he failed to understand what the policeman said to him? In *Day* v. *Harris* (1953), 117 J.P. 313, a civil case on a different statute, it was held that a provision requiring a notice to be read and explained was satisfied if this was done, although the listener was mentally incapable of understanding it. It might also be argued that a defendant at the scene of an accident, who never took in an oral warning, contributed to the failure to comply with s. 179 by his own conduct in not listening properly. See also 126 J.P.Jo. 262 and *Wheatley* v. *Lodge* [1971] 1 All E.R. 173 as to stating the reason for arrest to a deaf person. In *A.-G.* v. *Wallace* [1964] I.L.T. 117, a notice written in a language which the defendant did not understand was held to be valid.

Service of the Summons

A drunken driver, on awaking from his stupor, will sometimes find himself charged with reckless driving without a summons being served on him. Does this suffice, for the purposes of s. 179, as being equivalent to a summons being served on him? It is submitted that, while he can insist on a summons, he can also waive having one and, as the charges are as fully apparent to him as if he had had a summons, s. 179 is sufficiently complied with. But the police would be wise to serve a summons or notice all the same. Where the defendant was committed for trial on a charge of driving under the influence of drink, and a charge of reckless driving was added for the first time at sessions more than fourteen days after his arrest, the omission to comply with s. 179 was fatal to the prosecution (Jo.Crim.L. (1953) 22). The effect of s. 37 of the Magistrates' Courts Act, 1952, and r. 82 (1) and (2) of the Magistrates' Courts Rules, 1968, would appear to be that the prosecutor, once he has sent a summons by post which in the ordinary course of post should have arrived within fourteen days, may, if the defendant fails to appear or otherwise has not acknowledged he has had the summons, serve another summons within fourteen days of the return date of the original summons if the offence is under s. 2 of the Road Traffic Act, 1972 (dangerous, etc., driving) and provided the second summons is so served it will be sufficient compliance with s. 179 (2). If the offence is in respect of any of the other offences to which s. 179 applies (all of which are purely summary offences) it would appear that notwithstanding there was no acknowledgement or proof of receipt, if it is shown that it was posted at such time as to enable it to be delivered in the ordinary course of post within fourteen days of the offence, this will be sufficient service to satisfy s. 179 (2).

Notice

The notice must be in writing. If the notice was sent by registered post or recorded delivery service addressed to the defendant or the registered owner of a motor vehicle at his last-known address, para. (c) of s. 179 (2) declares that that is in effect due service under, and compliance with, s. 179, notwithstanding that the notice was returned as undelivered or was for any other reason not received by him. *Beer* v. *Davies* [1958] 2 All E.R. 255 is overruled on this issue. The motorist cannot object if the notice arrives late if it has been sent timeously. In *Groome* v. *Driscoll* [1969] 3 All E.R. 1638n. the offence occurred on 4th September and the notice of intended prosecution was posted by recorded delivery the following day but was not actually delivered until 21st September. The justices dismissed the case, apparently overlooking the proviso to s. 179 (2) (c), and the Divisional Court directed a conviction. Section 179 is, however, not complied with if a notice arrives outside the fourteen-day period because it was posted so late—e.g., the fourteenth day—that the notice could not be expected to arrive within the fourteen days in the normal course of post (*Nicholson* v. *Tapp* (1972), 116 S.J. 527). In *Groome* v. *Driscoll* the Divisional Court interpreted the proviso as if the words " in time " were added to the end of the proviso and it was held in *Nicholson* v. *Tapp* that the proviso only applies if the notice was sent at such a time that it could be reasonably expected to arrive in time in the normal course of post. *Stewart* v. *Chapman, infra,* p. 138, although decided before the proviso to s. 179 (2) (c) was inserted by the Road Traffic Act, 1962, would therefore still appear to be good law. It was held in *Layton* v. *Shires* [1959] 3 All E.R. 587 that it was

good service of a notice if it was sent by registered post to the defendant's address so that it arrived within fourteen days after the
offence and was taken in there by some person authorised to receive
letters on his behalf, e.g., a member of his family or a domestic servant, even though the defendant did not see the notice till more
than a fortnight after the offence.

A notice may also be served personally, provided it is served
within fourteen days of the offence. If the defendant and the
registered owner have no fixed abode, e.g., they are gipsies, and
dodge personal service, it seems that s. 179 (4) would apply to
excuse the police from serving the notice, provided some effort
had been made to reach them. Where the notice was handed by
a constable to the defendant's wife, who was authorised to accept
letters for him, this was held to be valid service (*Burt* v. *Kircaldy*
[1965] 1 All E.R. 741). Indeed, it is an irresistible inference that
a wife living with her husband is fully authorised to take in and
deal with mail addressed to her husband (*Hosier* v. *Goodall* [1962]
1 All E.R. 30; in this case the defendant was in hospital at the
time). In *Burt's* case, it was doubted whether delivery to a hall-
porter would be sufficient. The case of *Martin* v. *Brooman* (1909),
73 J.P. 484, was not cited in *Burt's* case; it was held there that it
sufficed to leave a notice with a hall-porter under a statute which
required the notice to be " sent ", not " served ". *Martin's* case,
however, is out of harmony with modern cases which suggest the
test to be receipt by a person authorised to deal with a notice,
although in *Layton* v. *Shires* [1959] 3 All E.R. 587 receipt by a
servant of the defendant's household was held valid. If a notice
is validly served within fourteen days of the offence, it will not matter
if the defendant does not see it until later.

If service of a notice has been by leaving with an adult, the new
para. (*c*) of s. 179 (2) will not of itself apply to overcome its non-
receipt, as para. (*c*) in regard to non-receipt applies only to postal
service. The police would be wise to serve always personally or
by registered post or recorded delivery, as, if the defendant proves
that he did not himself get a notice left by a constable with an adult
within fourteen days and it was not given to a person authorised
to take in letters and other documents for him, such service does
not comply with s. 179: *Hosier* v. *Goodall, supra*, where the defendant
was in hospital and the notice was sent to his home address and
there taken in and received on his behalf by his wife. This was
held to be good service. In *Phipps* v. *McCormick* [1971] Crim.L.R.
541 it was argued (and accepted by the justices) that as the police
knew the defendant had been taken to hospital following the accident, the hospital was the correct address for the purposes of s. 179

(2) (c) as this was his last address that the police knew and that notice should therefore have been sent to the hospital rather than to his home. The Divisional Court overruled the justices and held that " his last known address " for the purposes of s. 179 meant the place where the person concerned would normally expect to receive correspondence, an address which had some degree of permanence.

A notice may be served on a Sunday as, unlike a summons, it is not " process " (*Maher* v. *Prendergast* [1948] Ir.R. 339) but this decision is now otiose in England as a summons may now be served on a Sunday as a result of the repeal of the Sunday Observance Act, 1677, by s. 1 of the Statute Law (Repeals) Act, 1969. Earlier cases on non-receipt of a notice because the defendant, being in hospital, did not receive a notice addressed to him at home were overruled in *Hosier* v. *Goodall, supra.* The significance of the latter case is abrogated by the new provision of s. 179 declaring that it suffices to post the notice to the driver or keeper by registered or recorded delivery post (see *supra*); *Hosier's* case had held that the reasonableness of the police action in sending the notice to a particular address was no longer the test. It might still be held, however, that s. 179 is not complied with if the prosecutor posts the notice to an address which he well knows is no longer the defendant's permanent address unless he had left no address and it is the only address to which the prosecutor can send. The address must be the " last known " address, notwithstanding that this may differ from the one in the register or given to the police but " last known " address should not be interpreted too literally and means, in effect, the last known permanent address at which he may be expected to receive correspondence (*Phipps* v. *McCormick, supra*). In *Price* v. *West London Investment Building Society, Ltd.* [1964] 2 All E.R. 318, a case on another statute, it was said that " last known " place of abode means that last known to the person sending the notice and might include a place which the defendant had left if the change was unknown to the sender of the notice.

The notice, if sent by registered or recorded delivery post, should be posted within such a time that, in the ordinary course of post, it would reach the person to whom it is addressed within the fourteen days (*Stewart* v. *Chapman* [1951] 2 All E.R. 613; *Nicholson* v. *Tapp, supra*). The day of the offence is not counted in computing the fourteen days. Thus, if an offence occurs on 1st January, the notice should be posted so that it reaches the defendant's address not later than last post on 15th January. The state of the postal service near Christmas and the difference in the time of delivery between first-class and second-class mail should be remembered. A properly addressed letter sent by post will be deemed to have been received, unless the contrary is proved, when it would be delivered in the ordinary course of post (Interpretation Act, 1889, s. 26); *aliter,* where it is wrongly addressed (*Getreide, etc., Co.* v. *Contimar, etc., Co.* [1953] 2 All E.R. 223). In a case before a Metropolitan magistrate, the envelope was postmarked so as to be outside the fourteen days but there was sworn evidence that it was posted on the ninth day. The magistrate accepted the sworn evidence but, as the envelope had been addressed to the defendant's son, and the defendant, who saw it six-teen days after the offence, had claimed that he did not realise it was meant for him (his son was aged $3\frac{1}{2}$ years,) the magistrate held that the notice had not been served on the defendant (Jo.Crim.L. (1965) 153).

The prosecutor, in cases where non-receipt of a notice is put forward, should always make sure that a warning at the time of the offence was not given as, if it was, it will not matter when the notice was received. He should remember, too, to ask the defendant expressly, if he has the chance, when the notice was received as it may transpire that, notwithstanding wrong addressing or receipt by another, the defendant did have it within the fortnight. See p. 132 as to the need for the defendant to prove non-receipt by him and the keeper.

See under " Reasonable Diligence ", below, as to the defendant's conduct contributing to the failure to comply with s. 179.

Notice may be either to the defendant or to the person registered as keeper of the vehicle at the time of the offence, save that in cases of dangerous or careless cycling it should be given to the defendant. One doubts if there is any " register " of owners of horse-drawn vehicles. If given to the owner, the notice need not specify the name of the person to be summoned (*R.* v. *Bolkis* (1932), 97 J.P. 10). The police should, it seems, and generally will, send it to the driver, where he is known; if they serve the owner, they probably need not show that they did not know who the driver was (*Rogerson* v. *Edwards* (1951), 49 L.G.R. 358, at p. 360). A notice sent to the owner stating that " you " will be prosecuted for dangerous driving of a lorry is good, although the actual intention is to prosecute the driver and not the owner (*Taylor* v. *Campbell* [1956] Crim.L.R. 342). See *infra* as to mistakes in the notice. Delivery at the registered office of a company is good and valid service of a notice to the owner, if the company is the owner, but all that is necessary is that the notice should be in the hands of a responsible officer of the company within the fourteen days (*R.* v. *Bilton* (1964), 108 S.J. 880). There, the notice had been brought to the manager at a local office, which was not the registered office; he accepted it after he had consulted the company's solicitors and the notice was in the hands of the assistant secretary and the solicitors within a fortnight of the offence. This was held to be good service.

Notice of intended prosecution was duly served on the defendant. The police then wrote to him saying that he would not be prosecuted. Later the police decided to prosecute him. It was held that cancellation of the notice did not affect the matter and that he was rightly convicted (*Lund* v. *Thompson* [1958] 3 All E.R. 356).

The cases are reviewed at 104 S.J. 397.

Reasonable Diligence

Section 179 provides that the police need not have complied with it if neither the driver's nor the registered owner's identity could with reasonable diligence be ascertained in time for a summons or notice to be served or sent. A defendant drove on after an accident but his number was taken; it was held that, as the police actually ascertained the owner's identity in time for a notice to be sent to him, the fact that the driver's identity was unknown did not excuse them from so doing and, as no notices had been sent at all, the defendant was acquitted (*R.* v. *Bolkis, supra*). The question of reasonable diligence is for the judge, not the jury (*ibid.*). The position seems to be that, if the police have time to find out the identity of, and serve, either the driver or (if he is unknown) the keeper within fourteen days, the driver's conduct at the time of the offence does not contribute to their failure to do so. But, if the defendant drives away before his number can be taken, the provisions of subs. (4) excuse the police from complying with the section unless they could have discovered his or the owner's identity with reasonable diligence, or, *a fortiori*, do discover it within fourteen days. It will not suffice if the defendant is interviewed and given an oral warning within that time; a summons must be served or written notice given when he was not warned at the time of the offence. Giving a false address or information or deliberately evading service is conduct contributing to the failure of the police to comply with s. 179 and excuses them. Giving an address at which the defendant knows he will not be at the likely time is also such conduct (Jo.Crim.L. (1959) 2) but not merely going away on holiday with no intent to evade service (*Beer* v. *Davies* [1958] 2 All E.R. 255). A person who goes away without arranging for mail to be forwarded is not normally evading service (*Macleod* v. *Anderson* [1961] S.C.(J.) 32). See, however, now the new provision of s. 179 that posting a notice suffices. If the police hear of an accident more than two weeks after its occurrence and the driver concerned has been under no duty to report it to them, it is sub-

mitted that he had not been guilty of conduct contributing to their
failure to give him notice, though it would be otherwise if he had
not reported to the police an accident which he should have reported under s. 25 or had given a false name and address to a person
involved in the accident. Nor, it is submitted, could the police
be said to have been unable to ascertain his or the owner's name
and address with reasonable diligence in the fortnight, for s. 179 (4)
(a) presupposes that the police have some information to work on
about an accident or act of bad driving; the idea of s. 179 is to allow
the defendant the chance to collect witnesses and ascertain facts
while his recollection is fresh (see p. 143).

Where the police made inquiry of the Motor Licences Department
in good time but were given wrong information, it was held that they
had shown reasonable diligence and their failure to send the notice
to the correct person was in those circumstances no bar to conviction
(*Clarke* v. *Mould* [1945] 2 All E.R. 551; see also *Rogerson* v. *Edwards*,
on p. 139, and *Carr* v. *Harrison* (1966), *The Times*, 18th November,
the only report on this point, where it was held that the police in
approaching the licensing authority in good time had shown
reasonable diligence, though the authority had been slow in
supplying the information).

Notice addressed to a firm cannot be regarded as notice to every
individual in a firm, and the fact that the owner had caused the
vehicle to be registered in the firm's name was not conduct on his
part contributing to the police failing to comply with s. 179 (*Clarke* v.
Mould, supra). There the owner had actually received the notice
and, though *Clarke's* case was mentioned in *Rogerson* v. *Edwards*,
supra, it was not distinguished. Notice addressed to a limited
company omitting the word " Limited " is good (*Springate* v.
Questier [1952] 2 All E.R. 21). A notice addressed to " O'Loughlin "
was served on the defendant McLoughlin. He signed it and the
policeman then put the correct name on it. It was held to be a good
notice (*The State* (*McLoughlin*) v. *The President of the Circuit Court*
[1948] Ir.R.439). If a notice is otherwise good and the defendant
obviously knows to what incident it relates, a mistake in the number of his car is immaterial (*A.-G.* (*O'Gara*) v. *Callanan* (1958), 92
I.L.T.R. 74). See also *Taylor* v. *Campbell, supra*, on p. 139. A
notice in the name " Hornet " sent to a defendant Horne was
held not to have misled him and the error was not sufficient to
invalidate the notice (*Camp* v. *Horne*, noted at Jo.Crim.L. (1965) 153).

Nature of the Offence

Where a charge of dangerous or reckless driving is reduced to one under s. 3 of the 1972 Act, pursuant to para. 4 of Pt. IV of Sched. 4 to the Act, the defendant may be convicted although s. 179 has not been complied with as respects the new charge (para. 7, *ibid.*).   A notice stating that the defendant would be reported for dangerous driving and specifying his conduct, e.g., overtaking and cutting-in, is good although he is subsequently charged with careless driving only (*Milner* v. *Allen* (1933), 97 J.P. 111).   The view is advanced at 123 J.P.Jo. 35 that a notice specifying a charge of careless driving suffices for a prosecution for dangerous driving.   A notice alleging driving without due care and attention but not specifying the acts of bad driving is good (*Percival* v. *Ball* [1937] W.N. 106).   So is a notice stating that it was intended to prosecute the defendant " for an offence against s. 12 of the Road Traffic Act, 1930, in that you did drive a motor car " at a specified time and place, despite the omission of the words " without due care and attention " or of any alleged acts of bad driving (*Venn* v. *Morgan* [1949] 2 All E.R. 562).   In *Venn's* case the car's number was not given.   Section 12 of the 1930 Act is now s. 3 of the 1972 Act.

Date, Time and Place

A notice referred in error to dangerous driving at " 1.15 p.m."; in fact, the accident from which the charge arose was at 11.15 a.m. It was held that the mere fact that the time was wrongly stated made no difference and the notice was valid, for the notice mentioned the place where the accident occurred and the defendant could have been under no doubt that the notice related to it; different considerations might apply where he had had two accidents on the same day or, *semble*, when the charge was speeding and he had been on the same road more than once that day without being accosted by the police (*Pope* v. *Clarke* [1953] 2 All E.R. 704; *Carr* v. *Harrison* [1967] Crim.L.R. 54, where, although the notice referred to 8.40 p.m. instead of a.m., the defendant, having been interviewed about the incident and knowing all about it, was not prejudiced by the mistake).   In *Walton* v. *Hawkins* [1973] R.T.R. 366 and 369 the Divisional Court approved the abandonment by an appellant that a notice was bad in that the occurrence took place south of a junction when in fact the road ran east and west, citing *Pope* v. *Clarke, supra.*   In *Goody* v. *Fletcher* [1962] Crim.L.R. 324, a mistake of one day in stating the date was held not to invalidate the notice; the time and place were correctly given in the notice and the defendant was in no doubt as to the incident referred to.   A notice cannot be " amended "; if time permits, a fresh notice should be served or sent in lieu of the defective one.   It was said *obiter* in *R.* v.

Budd [1962] Crim.L.R. 49, that there can be a conviction for dangerous driving only if it occurred in the road named in the warning of intended prosecution. In *Shield* v. *Crighton* [1974] Crim.L.R. 605 a notice erroneously stated the name of a road some eighty yards distant from the road where the offence was committed; it was said *obiter* that a written document mis-stating the place could be misleading, but as an oral warning had been given at the scene at the time (see p. 138), s. 179 had been complied with; *semble aliter* if the defendant had received no oral warning. The time, apparently, need not be mentioned in a summons. A notice alleging excessive speed " between " two places more than ten miles apart was held good in *Beresford* v. *St. Albans JJ.* (1905), 22 T.L.R. 1, but the then statute did not require, as s. 179 does, that the " place " of offence be specified. In Ireland a notice alleging dangerous driving in a road a mile-and-a-quarter long was held to be too vague; there had been no accident (*Duffy* v. *Lovegrove*, Jo.Crim.L. (1955) 172). Likewise, in *Young* v. *Day* (1959), 123 J.P. 317, a notice alleging dangerous driving by nearly colliding with a stationary car on the offside in " the Hothfield to Bethersden road " was held insufficient; there had been no accident and the defendant had not been stopped. The High Court said that it was a question of fact for the magistrates, using their local knowledge, to decide if a " place " was sufficiently specified. The road named is about four miles long.

It was said in *Beresford's* case, *supra*, that the notice is intended to give an idea of the offence of which the defendant will be accused and to guard against the possibility of his being taken unawares (see also *Pope* v. *Clarke* [1953] 2 All E.R. 704), and in *Milner* v. *Allen* (1933), 97 J.P. 111, that the test of the validity of the notice is whether the defendant is in any way prejudiced in his defence by the defect. In *R.* v. *Bilton* (1964), 108 S.J. 880, it was said that the object of the notice is to ensure that the driver is not taken by surprise long after the offence, when his recollection is dulled and witnesses may be difficult to trace.

CHAPTER IV

DRINK/DRIVING OFFENCES

THIS chapter is solely concerned with the various drink/driving offences, viz., driving or being in charge of a motor vehicle whilst unfit to drive through drink or drugs (Road Traffic Act, 1972, s. 5); driving or being in charge of a motor vehicle with a blood/alcohol level in excess of the prescribed limit (s. 6); failing without reasonable excuse to supply a specimen of breath (s. 8 (3)); failing without reasonable excuse to supply a specimen of blood or urine for laboratory testing (s. 9 (3)); cycling when under the influence of drink or drugs (s. 19) and offences under s. 12 of the Licensing Act, 1872.

The drink/driving offences under the Act of 1972 have assumed an importance and have attracted a body of case law sufficient to justify treatment of these offences separately from the other road traffic offences which are dealt with in Chapter V.

It was in *Scott* v. *Baker* [1969] 1 Q.B. 659 that the High Court first enunciated the principle that before a person can be convicted of an offence under s. 6 (1) or s. 6 (2) or s. 9(3) (driving or being in charge of a motor vehicle with excess blood/alcohol, and failing to supply a specimen for laboratory testing), the prosecution must show that the procedural requirements of the relevant statutory provisions have been strictly followed. In order to assist the user of this book both to follow the correct path through the statutory maze and to be able to inspect the thick hedge of case law at any particular point along that path, a summary of the procedural provisions of the Act is set out on pp. 145–146 together with the page reference where each particular statutory requirement is more fully discussed. The text of the statutory provisions is set out on pp. 150–158.

The Road Traffic Act, 1972, consolidated both the offence of driving or being in charge of a motor vehicle while unfit to drive through drink or drugs contained in s. 6 of the Road Traffic Act, 1960, as amended by the Road Traffic Act, 1962, and also the provisions relating to the offence of driving or attempting to drive with excess alcohol in the blood created by Pt. I of the Road Safety Act, 1967. The consolidated provisions are almost wholly contained in ss. 5 to 13 of, and Sched. 4 to, the Act, and (with minor drafting corrections) re-enact the former legislation in a consolidated and different sequence but are otherwise almost *verbatim*. The Act does not alter substantially the former law. The major alteration was to include the provisions as to the punishment and procedure relating to the offences in a schedule (Sched. 4) set out in tabular form. This involved the creation, as a separate offence, of the offence of refusal to supply a specimen of blood or urine.

The Road Traffic Act, 1974, did not amend in any way the provisions of the 1972 Act relating to drink/driving offences other than to amend the penalties which may be imposed on conviction by a magistrates' court. Whether a defendant has a right to elect trial by jury depends, by virtue of s. 25 of the Magistrates' Courts Act, 1952, on whether the offence is punishable on summary conviction with more than three months' imprisonment. The Road Traffic Act, 1974, by amending Sched. 4 to the 1972 Act removed from magistrates the power to impose imprisonment in respect of the offences of s. 5 (2) (being in charge of a motor vehicle while unfit through drink or drugs), s. 6 (2) (being in charge of a motor vehicle with excess blood/alcohol) and s. 9 (3) (refusing without reasonable excuse to supply a specimen for laboratory testing). Defendants have thus been deprived of this right to elect trial by jury under s. 25 in respect of these offences and can only attempt to claim trial by jury by virtue of s. 18 of the Magistrates' Courts Act, 1952 (see further, Trial Court and Procedure, on pp. 159–163).

Summary

(The following pages contain a summary of the law and all the matters raised are discussed more fully and with authorities cited at p. 163 et seq., infra.)

The Road Safety Act, 1967, Pt. I (now largely embodied in ss. 6 to 13 of the Road Traffic Act, 1972: see pp. 150–158) created the offences of:—

    I. Driving or attempting to drive a motor vehicle with more than the prescribed limit of alcohol in the blood or urine (now s. 6 (1) of the Act of 1972); and

   II. Being in charge of a motor vehicle with more than the prescribed limit in blood or urine (s. 6 (2)); and

  III. Failing or refusing to provide, without reasonable excuse, a specimen of breath for a breath test (now s. 8 (3)); and

  IV. Failing or refusing to provide, without reasonable excuse, a specimen of blood or urine for laboratory analysis (now s. 9 (3)).

The text of the whole of the statutory provisions relating to all the drink/driving offences is set out on pp. 150–158 immediately following this summary.

The Road Safety Act, 1967, left unrepealed the former offence of driving, attempting to drive or being in charge of a motor vehicle whilst unfit to drive through drink or drugs contrary to s. 6 of the Act of 1960. Although the intention was said to be to allow the prosecution of motorists whose ability to drive was impaired through drink but whose blood/alcohol level did not exceed the prescribed limit, the offence (now under s. 5 of the 1972 Act) has been frequently used to obtain a conviction of a person whose blood/alcohol level is above the limit but who, because of procedural defects, could not be convicted under s. 6. The statutory provisions of the two sets of offences are so inter-related that it is possible under some circumstances for a person who has been arrested under one section to be subsequently charged and convicted under the other section (see " Interaction of ss. 5 and 6 ", *post*, p. 235). Section 5 also remains of importance to deal with motorists whose driving ability is impaired by drugs. The medical examination of drunken motorists under s. 7 of the Act is now almost confined to drugs cases and for alcohol has been superseded by the taking of specimens of blood or urine for laboratory analysis under s. 9. Those practitioners who wish to examine the matter in greater detail are referred to the sixth edition. For the same reason the Report of a Special Committee of the British Medical Association on " The Medico-Legal Investigation of the Drinking Driver " (set out in Appendix II to the sixth edition) has been largely omitted. The law relating to offences of driving or being in charge of a vehicle while unfit to drive under s. 5 is procedurally simpler than the provisions for the offences under s. 6, s. 8, and s. 9, and is discussed on p. 235 onwards. As a result of the adoption by the courts of the principle first stated in *Scott* v. *Baker* [1969] 1 Q.B. 659 (viz., that before a person can be convicted it is necessary for the prosecution to prove that the certificate of analysis has been lawfully obtained and that a certificate cannot be lawfully obtained unless all the procedural provisions of the statute have been strictly followed) an intelligible exposition of the statutory provisions and the accompanying case law is best illustrated by summarising the procedural provisions followed by a detailed discussion of each particular statutory requirement in the light of the relevant case law.

I. *Driving or Attempting to Drive with Excess Blood or Urine/Alcohol* (*s.* 6 (1))

The prosecution must prove that the defendant drove or attempted to drive—

" a motor vehicle " (see pp. 2–9);
" on a road or other public place " (see pp. 173–175);
with excess blood or urine/alcohol content " as ascertained from
a laboratory test " (for the ascertainment of the laboratory test
and method of obtaining the analysis and proof of analysis by
certificate, see pp. 175–183).

For the certificate of analysis to be admissible in evidence, the
prosecution must show that the sample of blood or urine for the
laboratory test was lawfully obtained. For the test to be lawfully
obtained the defendant must first have been " required " (see
p. 197) to take a lawful breath test. A constable is only entitled
lawfully to require a breath test if one of two basic situations occurs.
The first (contained in s. 8 (1) of the Act) is if a constable in
uniform (for definition of " constable in uniform ", see p. 199) has
reasonable cause to suspect a person " driving or attempting to
drive " either of having alcohol in his body or of having committed
a traffic offence while the vehicle was in motion. The constable's
suspicion must arise while the person was " driving or attempting
to drive ". " Driving or attempting to drive " does not mean
that the vehicle necessarily has to be in motion on the road or
other public place. The phrase has perhaps given rise to more
High Court cases than any other and for the meaning given " driving or attempting to drive " in this context, see pp. 184–192.
Whether a person is " driving or attempting to drive " is a
question of fact, not law (see R. v. Guttridge and other cases cited
on pp. 186–187). Whichever is the ground of suspicion under
s. 8 (1) (see " Suspicion of alcohol or moving traffic offence " on
p. 192) the breath test must be administered " there or nearby ", and
if the ground of suspicion is that of a traffic offence the breath test
must also be " as soon as is reasonably practicable " (for " there or
nearby " and " as soon as reasonably practicable ", see pp. 197–198).
The power of a constable to stop a vehicle exists independently
of the statutory provisions relating to drink/driving offences;
a motorist can be stopped at random without any grounds of
suspicion whatsoever that he has been drinking; provided that the
constable's suspicion of alcohol arose while the motorist was still
" driving or attempting to drive ", a breath test may lawfully be
required (see further " Driving or attempting to drive " on
pp. 184–192).
The constable's suspicions must arise while the vehicle is " on a
road or public place ", but provided there is an unbroken chain of
events between the time the constable's suspicions occurred and the
time the breath test was required, the actual requirement to take

the test does not have to be on a road or other public place (see *Sakhuja* v. *Allen* on p. 185).

The other basic situation entitling a constable to require a breath test is under s. 8 (2) where " owing to the presence of a motor vehicle on a road " (see *Quelch* v. *Phipps* on p. 196) an accident occurs. As in s. 8 (1) the constable has to be in uniform (see p. 199). There has to be an accident which has been defined as an " unintended occurrence having an adverse physical result " (see *R.* v. *Morris* and other cases on the meaning of " accident " on pp. 196–197).

The breath test following an accident must be made either at or near where the breath test requirement was made or at a police station specified by the constable or, where the person has been taken to hospital as a patient, at the hospital (see " Hospital patients ", p. 222). The breath test under s. 8 (1) or s. 8 (2) must be lawfully administered. For the breath test to be lawfully *administered*, it must be by a device approved by the Secretary of State (see p. 200) and evidence should be given that it was taken by such a device (see p. 200). The constable when administering the breath test must comply with the manufacturer's instructions as to its assembly but, provided he acts *bona fide* and not negligently, non-compliance with any of the manufacturer's other instructions does not invalidate the test (see pp. 201–203).

If the breath specimen provided proves positive (see p. 204), the motorist is then liable to arrest under s. 8 (4) except while he is at a hospital as a patient. If, on the other hand, a person fails (and a failure includes a refusal for this purpose by virtue of the statutory definition in s. 12 (1)) to supply a specimen he is liable, unless a hospital patient, to arrest under s. 8 (5) provided that the constable has reasonable cause to suspect him of consumption of alcohol (see pp. 204–208). Although the power of arrest under s. 8 (4) and s. 8 (5) appears discretionary, the police constable must actually arrest the motorist in order to obtain a specimen of blood or urine for laboratory testing at a police station. The motorist must be arrested under the correct subsection (see *R.* v. *Holah* on p. 207). He must, as in any other type of arrest, be told of the reason for his arrest as soon as is reasonably practicable.

After a lawful arrest under s. 8 (4) or s. 8 (5), *supra*, or after an arrest for driving or attempting to drive or being in charge of a motor vehicle while unfit to drive through drink or drugs under s. 5 (5) (see " Interaction of ss. 5 and 6 " on p. 235), the motorist may be required to supply a specimen of blood or urine for laboratory analysis. He must first be offered another breath test at the police station to which he has been brought for the purpose of obtaining a specimen. It is only if the breath test gives a positive result, or he declines to give a specimen of breath (see " Second breath test at police station ", pp. 212–214), that the police can then require a specimen of blood or urine. The defendant should be warned of the consequences of his failure to supply a specimen of blood or urine, but failure to give such a warning will not necessarily be a ground for acquittal (see pp. 214–215).

The motorist should first be required to provide blood, then if he fails or refuses, urine, then, if he fails to supply specimens of urine, blood (see pp. 216–217). The prosecution must prove that the defendant was offered " an adequate sample in a suitable container " (see pp. 217–222) of the specimen of blood or urine supplied by him. Evidence of the analysis may be given by certificate (see pp. 215–217). Any specimen of blood must be taken by a qualified medical practitioner and that it was taken by a medical practitioner may be proved by certificate (see pp. 215–217). The certificate of analysis must relate to the amount of alcohol in the blood at the time of the commission of the offence (see pp. 181–183).

There are special provisions which must be complied with safeguarding the treatment of the motorist while at a hospital as a patient. The doctor in charge of the motorist while a patient at the hospital must be asked by the constable for his consent to the constable's requiring the patient to take a breath test and for the patient actually providing it. The doctor must also give prior consent to the requirement to supply the specimen of blood or urine, the actual provision by the patient of the specimen of blood or urine and the warning by the constable under s. 9 (7) of the consequences of the failure to supply a specimen. Doctors (unlike laymen) are not presumed to know the law and for this reason the constable must first explain to the doctor that a patient may be required to provide either a specimen of urine or of blood, together with the terms of warning to be given to the patient under s. 9 (7) (for a detailed discussion of all these provisions see " Hospital patients " on pp. 222–227).

It is possible for the motorist, if he has been arrested under s. 5 (5) (drinking or in charge of a car while unfit through drink), to be convicted of the offence of excess blood/alcohol (and *vice versa*). In such a case the requirements relating to breath tests prior to arrest (*supra*) do not have to be complied with. On the other hand, the procedure after arrest (set out above) does have to be strictly followed (see " Interaction of ss. 5 and 6 ", pp. 235–237).

II. *In Charge of a Motor Vehicle with Excess Blood/Alcohol (s. 6 (2))*

A person cannot be required to take a breath test under s. 8 (1) if he is only " in charge " of a motor vehicle. (For the meaning of " in charge ", see pp. 163–173.) To secure a conviction of this offence, the person must first have been arrested under s. 5 (5) through being unfit through drink or drugs, or have been arrested under s. 8 (2) following an accident (see *R.* v. *Lawrence* on p. 168). On his being arrested under s. 5 (5) he may then be taken to a police station for the purpose of supplying a specimen for laboratory testing. The procedure after arrest set out in section I, above, for supplying a specimen of blood or urine must then be strictly followed. If the specimen when analysed is above the limit, the person in charge may then be summoned for an offence under s. 6 (2) as well as an offence under s. 5 (2) (see "In charge " on pp. 163–173 and " Interaction of ss. 5 and 6 " on pp. 235–237). The defendant has a defence under s. 6 (3) if he proves that there was no likelihood of his driving with blood/alcohol above the limit.

III. *Failing to Provide a Specimen of Breath for a Breath Test*

This offence is committed whenever a constable in uniform (see p. 199) has by virtue of s. 8 (1) or s. 8 (2) (see section I, above) been lawfully entitled to require the defendant to supply a specimen of breath and the defendant without reasonable excuse (see " Reasonable excuse " on pp. 231–234) failed (or refused) to supply a specimen of breath (see pp. 227–229).

IV. *Failing or Refusing to Provide a Specimen of Blood or Urine for Laboratory Analysis (s. 9 (3))*

This offence is committed when the defendant fails or refuses to provide a specimen of blood or urine for laboratory analysis " without reasonable excuse " (see pp. 231–234). The only difference in law between this offence and the offence under s. 6 (1) (driving a motor vehicle with excess blood/alcohol) or s. 6 (2) (in charge of a motor vehicle with excess blood/alcohol) is that the defendant will necessarily have supplied a specimen of blood or urine in the latter instance, but for this offence he necessarily must have failed or refused to supply such a specimen. The procedural requirements as to the offences are otherwise identical, and must similarly be proved by the police to have been followed before there can be a conviction. Punishment for the offence varies according to whether the defendant was " driving or attempting to drive" or merely " in charge " at the relevant time (see pp. 234–235).

Sections 5 to 13 of the 1972 Act read as follows:—

Driving, or being in charge, when under influence of drink or drugs

5.—(1) A person who, when driving or attempting to drive a motor vehicle on a road or other public place, is unfit to drive through drink or drugs shall be guilty of an offence.

(2) Without prejudice to subsection (1) above, a person who, when in charge of a motor vehicle which is on a road or other public place, is unfit to drive through drink or drugs shall be guilty of an offence.

(3) For the purposes of this section a person shall be deemed not to have been in charge of a motor vehicle if he proves that at the material time the circumstances were such that there was no likelihood of his driving it so long as he remained unfit to drive through drink or drugs.

(4) For the purposes of this section a person shall be taken to be unfit to drive if his ability to drive properly is for the time being impaired.

(5) A constable may arrest without warrant a person committing an offence under this section.

Driving, or being in charge, with blood-alcohol concentration above the prescribed limit

6.—(1) If a person drives or attempts to drive a motor vehicle on a road or other public place, having consumed alcohol in such a quantity that the proportion thereof in his blood, as ascertained from a laboratory test for which he subsequently provides a specimen under section 9 of this Act, exceeds the prescribed limit at the time he provides the specimen, he shall be guilty of an offence.

(2) Without prejudice to subsection (1) above, if a person is in charge of a motor vehicle on a road or other public place having consumed alcohol as aforesaid, he shall be guilty of an offence.

(3) A person shall not be convicted under this section of being in charge of a motor vehicle if he proves that at the material time the circumstances were such that there was no likelihood of his driving it so long as there was any probability of his having alcohol in his blood in a proportion exceeding the prescribed limit.

(4) In determining for the purposes of subsection (3) above the likelihood of a person's driving a motor vehicle when he is injured or the vehicle is damaged, the jury, in the case of proceedings on indictment, may be directed to disregard, and the court in any other case may disregard, the fact that he had been injured or that the vehicle had been damaged.

Evidence on charge of unfitness to drive

7.—(1) In any proceedings for an offence under section 5 of this Act, the court shall, subject to section 10 (5) thereof, have regard to any evidence which may be given of the proportion or quantity of alcohol or of any drug which was contained in the blood or present in the body of the accused, as ascertained by analysis of a specimen of blood taken from him with his consent by a medical practitioner, or of urine provided by him, at any material time; and if it is proved that the accused, when so requested by a constable at any such time, refused to consent to the taking of or to provide a specimen for analysis, his refusal may, unless reasonable cause therefor is shown, be treated as supporting any evidence given on behalf of the prosecution, or as rebutting any evidence given on behalf of the defence, with respect to his condition at that time.

(2) A person shall not be treated for the purposes of subsection (1) above as refusing to provide a specimen unless—

(*a*) he is first requested to provide a specimen of blood, but refuses to do so;

(*b*) he is then requested to provide two specimens of urine within one hour of the request, but fails to provide them within the hour or refuses at any time within the hour to provide them; and

(c) he is again requested to provide a specimen of blood, but refuses to do so.

(3) The first specimen of urine provided in pursuance of a request under subsection (2) (b) above shall be disregarded for the purposes of subsection (1) above.

Breath tests

8.—(1) A constable in uniform may require any person driving or attempting to drive a motor vehicle on a road or other public place to provide a specimen of breath for a breath test there or nearby, if the constable has reasonable cause—

    (a) to suspect him of having alcohol in his body, or
    (b) to suspect him of having committed a traffic offence while the vehicle was in motion;

but no requirement may be made by virtue of paragraph (b) above unless it is made as soon as reasonably practicable after the commission of the traffic offence.

(2) If an accident occurs owing to the presence of a motor vehicle on a road or other public place, a constable in uniform may require any person who he has reasonable cause to believe was driving or attempting to drive the vehicle at the time of the accident to provide a specimen of breath for a breath test—

    (a) except while that person is at a hospital as a patient, either at or near the place where the requirement is made or, if the constable thinks fit, at a police station specified by the constable;
    (b) in the said excepted case, at the hospital:

but a person shall not be required to provide such a specimen while at a hospital as a patient if the medical practitioner in immediate charge of his case is not first notified of the proposal to make the requirement or objects to the provision of a specimen on the ground that its provision or the requirement to provide it would be prejudicial to the proper care or treatment of the patient.

(3) A person who, without reasonable excuse, fails to provide a specimen of breath for a breath test under subsection (1) or (2) above shall be guilty of an offence.

(4) If it appears to a constable in consequence of a breath test carried out by him on any person under subsection (1) or (2) above that the device by means of which the test is carried out indicates that the proportion of alcohol in that person's blood exceeds the prescribed limit, the constable may arrest that person without warrant except while that person is at a hospital as a patient.

(5) If a person required by a constable under subsection (1) or (2) above to provide a specimen of breath for a breath test fails to do so and the constable has reasonable cause to suspect him of having alcohol in his body, the constable may arrest him without warrant except while he is at a hospital as a patient.

(6) Subsections (4) and (5) above shall not be construed as prejudicing the provisions of section 5 (5) of this Act.

(7) A person arrested under this section, or under the said section 5 (5), shall, while at a police station, be given an opportunity to provide a specimen of breath for a breath test there.

(8) In this section " traffic offence " means an offence under any provision of this Act except Part V thereof or under any provision of Part III of the Road Traffic Act, 1960, or the Road Traffic Regulation Act, 1967.

Laboratory tests

9.—(1) A person who has been arrested under section 5 (5) or 8 of this Act may, while at a police station, be required by a constable to provide a specimen for a laboratory test (which may be a specimen of blood or of urine), if he has previously been given an opportunity to provide a specimen of breath for a breath test at that station under subsection (7) of the said section 8, and either—

(a) it appears to a constable in consequence of the breath test that the device by means of which the test is carried out indicates that the proportion of alcohol in his blood exceeds the prescribed limit, or

(b) when given the opportunity to provide that specimen, he fails to do so.

(2) A person while at a hospital as a patient may be required by a constable to provide at the hospital a specimen for a laboratory test—

(a) if it appears to a constable in consequence of a breath test carried out on that person under section 8 (2) of this Act that the device by means of which the test is carried out indicates that the proportion of alcohol in his blood exceeds the prescribed limit, or

(b) if that person has been required, whether at the hospital or elsewhere, to provide a specimen of breath for a breath test, but fails to do so and a constable has reasonable cause to suspect him of having alcohol in his body;

but a person shall not be required to provide a specimen for a laboratory test under this subsection if the medical practitioner in immediate charge of his case is not first notified of the proposal to make the requirement or objects to the provision of a specimen on the ground that its provision, the requirement to provide it or a warning under subsection (7) below would be prejudicial to the proper care or treatment of the patient.

(3) A person who, without reasonable excuse, fails to provide a specimen for a laboratory test in pursuance of a requirement imposed under this section shall be guilty of an offence.

(4) Nothing in the foregoing provisions of this section shall affect the provisions of section 7 (1) of this Act.

(5) A person shall not be treated for the purposes of subsection (3) above as failing to provide a specimen unless—

(a) he is first requested to provide a specimen of blood, but refuses to do so;

(b) he is then requested to provide two specimens of urine within one hour of the request, but fails to provide them within the hour or refuses at any time within the hour to provide them; and

(c) he is again requested to provide a specimen of blood, but refuses to do so.

(6) The first specimen of urine provided in pursuance of a request under subsection (5) (b) above shall be disregarded for the purposes of section 6 of this Act.

(7) A constable shall on requiring any person under this section to provide a specimen for a laboratory test warn him that failure to provide

a specimen of blood or urine may make him liable to imprisonment, a fine and disqualification, and, if the constable fails to do so, the court before which that person is charged with an offence under section 6 of this Act or this section may direct an acquittal or dismiss the charge, as the case may require.

In this subsection "disqualification" means disqualification for holding or obtaining a licence to drive a motor vehicle granted under Part III of this Act.

Ancillary provisions as to evidence in proceedings for an offence under s. 5 or 6

10.—(1) For the purposes of any proceedings for an offence under section 5 or 6 of this Act, a certificate purporting to be signed by an authorised analyst, and certifying—

(a) the proportion of alcohol or any drug found in a specimen identified by the certificate, and

(b) for the purposes only of proceedings for an offence under the said section 5, in the case of a specimen of urine, the proportion of alcohol or of that drug in the blood which corresponds to the proportion found in the specimen,

shall, subject to subsection (3) below, be evidence of the matters so certified and of the qualification of the analyst.

(2) For the purposes of any proceedings for an offence under the said section 5 or 6, a certificate purporting to be signed by a medical practitioner that he took a specimen of blood from a person with his consent shall, subject to subsection (3) below, be evidence of the matters so certified and of the qualification of the medical practitioner.

(3) Subjections (1) and (2) above shall not apply to a certificate tendered on behalf of the prosecution unless a copy has been served on the accused not less than seven days before the hearing or trial, nor if the accused, not less than three days before the hearing or trial, or within such further time as the court may in special circumstances allow, has served notice on the prosecutor requiring the attendance at the hearing or trial of the person by whom the certificate was signed.

A copy of a certificate required by this subsection to be served on the accused or of a notice required by this subsection to be served on the prosecutor may either be personally served on the accused or the prosecutor (as the case may be) or sent to him by registered post or the recorded delivery service.

(4) In any proceedings in Scotland for an offence under the said section 5 or 6, a certificate complying with subsection (1) or (2) above and, where the person by whom such a certificate was signed is called as a witness, the evidence of that person, shall be sufficient evidence of the facts stated in the certificate.

(5) Where, in proceedings for an offence under the said section 5 or 6 the accused, at the time a specimen of blood or urine was taken from or provided by him, asked to be supplied with such a specimen, evidence of the proportion of alcohol or any drug found in the specimen shall not be admissible on behalf of the prosecution unless—

(a) the specimen is either one of two taken or provided on the same occasion or is part of a single specimen which was divided into two parts at the time it was taken or provided, and

(b) the other specimen or part was supplied to the accused.

(6) A constable requesting any person to consent to the taking of or to provide a specimen of blood or urine for analysis shall offer to supply to him, in a suitable container, part of the specimen or, in the case of a specimen of blood which it is not practicable to divide, another specimen which he may consent to have taken.

(7) In this section " authorised analyst " means any person possessing the qualifications prescribed by regulations made under section 89 of the Food and Drugs Act, 1955, or section 27 of the Food and Drugs (Scotland) Act, 1956, as qualifying persons for appointment as public analysts under those Acts, and any other person authorised by the Secretary of State to make analyses for the purposes of this section.

Detention of persons while affected by alcohol

11. Any person required to provide a specimen for a laboratory test under section 9 (1) of this Act may thereafter be detained at the police station until he provides a specimen of breath for a breath test and it appears to a constable that the device by means of which the test is carried out indicates that the proportion of alcohol in that person's blood does not exceed the prescribed limit.

Interpretation of ss. 6 to 11

12.—(1) In sections 6 to 11 of this Act, except so far as the context otherwise requires—

" breath test " means a test for the purpose of obtaining an indication of the proportion of alcohol in a person's blood carried out by means of a device of a type approved for the purpose of such a test by the Secretary of State, on a specimen of breath provided by that person;

" fail," in relation to providing a specimen, includes refuse and " failure " shall be construed accordingly;

" hospital " means an institution which provides medical or surgical treatment for in-patients or out-patients;

" laboratory test " means the analysis of a specimen provided for the purpose;

" the prescribed limit " means 80 milligrammes of alcohol in 100 millilitres of blood or such other proportion as may be prescribed by regulations made by the Secretary of State.

(2) A person shall be treated for the purposes of sections 6 and 9 of this Act as providing a specimen of blood if, but only if, he consents to the specimen being taken by a medical practitioner and it is so taken and shall be treated for those purposes as providing it at the time it is so taken.

(3) References in sections 8, 9 and 11 of this Act to providing a specimen of breath for a breath test are references to providing a specimen thereof in sufficient quantity to enable that test to be carried out.

(4) For the purposes of the said section 6 and this section 107 milligrammes of alcohol in 100 millilitres of urine shall be treated as equivalent to 80 milligrammes of alcohol in 100 millilitres of blood, and the power conferred by subsection (1) above to prescribe some other proportion of alcohol in the blood shall include power to prescribe a proportion of alcohol in urine which is to be treated as equivalent to the prescribed proportion of alcohol in the blood.   [Section 13: see p. 158]

SCHEDULE IV

PART I

1 Provision Creating Offence	2 General Nature Offence	3 Mode of Prosecution	4 Punishment	5 Disqualification	6 Endorsement	7 Additional Provisions
5 (1)	Driving or attempting to drive when unfit to drive through drink or drugs.	(a) Summarily.	£400 or 4 months' imprisonment.	Obligatory.	Obligatory.	Sections 181 and 183 and paragraph 3 of Part IV of this Schedule apply.
		(b) On indictment.	2 years or a fine or both.			
5 (2)	Being in charge of a motor vehicle when unfit to drive through drink or drugs.	(a) Summarily.	£200.	Discretionary.	Obligatory.	Sections 181 and 183 and paragraph 3 of Part IV of this Schedule apply.
		(b) On indictment.	12 months or a fine or both.			
6 (1)	Driving or attempting to drive with blood/alcohol concentration above the prescribed limit.	(a) Summarily.	£400 or 4 months' imprisonment.	Obligatory.	Obligatory.	Sections 181 and 183 and paragraph 3 of Part IV of this Schedule apply.
		(b) On indictment.	2 years or a fine or both.			
6 (2)	Being in charge of a motor vehicle with blood/alcohol concentration above the prescribed limit.	(a) Summarily.	£200.	Discretionary.	Obligatory.	Sections 181 and 183 and paragraph 3 of Part IV of this Schedule apply.
		(b) On indictment.	12 months or a fine or both.			

For an offence charged with an offence under ss. 5, 6 and 8 the following offences ——

		Obligatory.	Sections 181 and 183 apply.
		—	Sections 181 and 183 and paragraph 3 of Part IV of this Schedule apply.
8 (3) Failing to provide a specimen of breath for a breath test.	Summarily. £50.	—	Sections 181 and 183 apply.
9 Failing to provide a specimen of blood or urine for a laboratory test.	(a) Summarily. (i) Where it is shown that at the relevant time (as defined in Part V of this Schedule)* the offender was driving or attempting to drive a motor vehicle on a road or other public place, £400. (ii) Where in any other case it is shown that at that time the offender was in charge of a motor vehicle on a road or other public place, £200. (b) On indictment. (iii) 2 years or a fine or both in the case of a conviction where it is shown in paragraph (i) above. (iv) 12 months or a fine or both in the case of a conviction where it is shown as mentioned in paragraph (ii) above.	(a) Obligatory if it is shown as mentioned in paragraph (i) of column 4. (b) Discretionary if it is not so shown.	
19 Cycling when unfit through drink or drugs	£50.	—	Sections 181 and 183 apply.

* For Part V see overleaf.

Person liable to be charged with offence under s. 5, 6 or 9 not liable to be charged with certain other offences

13. A person liable to be charged with an offence under section 5, 6 or 9 of this Act shall not be liable to be charged—

(*a*) under section 12 of the Licensing Act 1872, with the offence of being drunk while in charge, on a highway or other public place, of a carriage, or

(*b*) under section 70 of the Licensing (Scotland) Act 1903, with the offence of being drunk while in charge, in a street or other place, of a carriage.

SCHEDULE IV

PART V

Interpretation

1. For the purposes of the entries in Part I of this Schedule relating to an offence under section 5 (1), 6 (1) or 9 (3) " the relevant time " means—

(*a*) in relation to a person required under section 8 (1) to provide a specimen of breath for a breath test, the time when he was so required;

(*b*) in relation to a person required under section 8 (2) to provide such a specimen, the time of the accident;

(*c*) in relation to a person arrested under section 5 (5), the time of his arrest.

Cycles

By the Road Traffic Act, 1972, s. 19, a person riding a bicycle, tricycle or cycle having four or more wheels, not being a motor vehicle (s. 195), on a road (including a bridleway) or other public place, and unfit through drink or drugs to ride it, is guilty of an offence. Section 19 (2) exempts such a person from being charged under the Licensing Act, 1872, s. 12 (p. 252) or the like Scottish enactment and s. 19 (3) gives constables a power of arrest. Section 19 (4) defines " unfit to ride " as being under the influence of drink or a drug to such an extent as to be incapable of having proper control of the vehicle. As to cyclists attempting to ride, or in charge of, their machines see p. 252. See p. 247 for penalties.

Section 19 was not amended by references to the rider's ability to ride properly being impaired as was done in respect of offences in respect of a motor vehicle under s. 5. Section 7 (1) and (2) of the 1972 Act plainly refer to offences under s. 5 only. While a blood or urine test may still be properly taken in respect of a cyclist, with his consent, as could have been done for motorists or cyclists before the Act, the support arising under s. 7 (1) for the prosecution's case from his refusal of the test does not apply (but see p. 240) and the analyst's certificate will not be admissible in evidence; the analyst himself must testify either orally or by written evidence under the Criminal Justice Act, 1967, s. 9. Although the requirement in s. 10 (5) to supply to a defendant requesting it a sample of the blood or urine taken for analysis does not apply, it is submitted that the police would be wise to comply with this requirement and also the requirement as to a suitable container in s. 10 (6).

The offences contained in ss. 6, 8 and 9 as to driving, etc., on the road with more than 80 mg. of alcohol per 100 ml. of blood, offences of refusing breath, blood and urine specimens, etc., do not apply to pedal cycles and cyclists. It is submitted that a constable can properly ask a cyclist to consent to take a breath test; the cyclist commits no offence by refusing and the fact that the test is positive should not be given in evidence save in rebuttal of the cyclist's allegation that he had not drunk any alcohol at all or as part justification for arresting him. A breath test does not have to be offered or taken before an arrest under s. 5 and it was held in *Wimperis* v. *Griffin* [1973] Crim.L.R. 533 that the fact that a breath test was required did not invalidate the arrest under s. 5.

Whether the person behind the wheel of a towed vehicle is " driving " is a question of fact that must be left to the jury (*R.* v. *Shaw (Kenneth)* [1975] R.T.R. 160) (see further as to " driving " on p. 23).

A person pedalling a moped because the engine has failed temporarily can be convicted of driving a motor vehicle whilst unfit through drink and also of driving with excess blood/alcohol. A moped does not lose its character of a " mechanically propelled vehicle " merely because at the relevant time it is being propelled by means other than the engine (*R.* v. *Tahsin* [1970] R.T.R. 88, applying and approving *Floyd* v. *Bush* [1953] 1 All E.R. 265). The test of whether a pedal cycle with a means of mechanical propulsion attached to it can be said to have lost its character of mechanically propelled motor vehicle is whether the mechanically propelled part of the vehicle had in any sense ceased to be in existence (see also pp. 6–7).

Trial Court and Procedure

A charge of riding a cycle or tricycle when unfit through drink or drug under s. 19 and a charge under s. 8 (3) of failing to provide breath for a breath test under s. 8 (1) or (2) may be tried by magistrates only and there is no right to claim trial by jury. Sometimes a case under s. 6 of the Act (driving or in charge with more than 80 mg.) or under s. 9 (3) (refusing to provide a blood or urine specimen) will be charged along with one of refusing a breath test under s. 8 (3); the latter charge cannot be committed

for trial or sentence but should be adjourned until the verdict
on the other charge at the Crown Court is known: *R.* v. *Haslam*,
infra. The Crown Court might indeed rule during the latter
proceedings that the breath test was not properly done and, if it
does, it is suggested that, in fairness to the accused, the breath
test charge should not then normally be proceeded with. In
R. v. *Haslam* [1972] R.T.R. 297 the defendant was charged on two
counts of an indictment, refusing a breath test and refusing to
supply a specimen for laboratory testing. The jury failed to
agree on the first count but convicted on the second. An appeal
against conviction on the second count was heard by the Court
of Appeal, who subsequently authorised the Registrar to state that
the fact that no comment was made by the Court of Appeal should
not be taken as approval of the inclusion of the purely summary
offence of refusing a breath test—or indeed any other purely
summary offence—in an indictment: (1972), 136 J.P.Jo. 391.

Charges under s. 5 (1) and s. 6 (1) (driving or attempting to
drive while unfit through drink or drugs or with a blood/alcohol
level above the prescribed limit) are punishable on summary conviction with more than three months' imprisonment and thus by
virtue of s. 25 of the Magistrates' Courts Act, 1952, defendants
have a complete and unfettered right of election for trial by jury
at the Crown Court. If a defendant is not given the right of
election, a subsequent conviction may be set aside; moreover
there can be no waiver of that right (see Stone (1975), p. 76,
note (*m*), and Brian Harris, Criminal Jurisdiction of Magistrates,
4th ed., p. 38). On the other hand if the charge is under s. 5 (2),
s. 6 (2) (" in charge " only of a motor vehicle whilst unfit or
with excess blood/alcohol) or s. 9 (3) (refusing without reasonable
excuse to supply a specimen for laboratory testing even if at the
relevant time the motorist was driving or attempting to drive)
the defendant no longer has any right of election under s. 25 of the
Magistrates' Courts Act, 1952, because the magistrates' power to
impose imprisonment has been removed by the Road Traffic
Act, 1974. All the offences whether " in charge " only or " driving
or attempting to drive " are, however, " hybrid " offences and the
procedure is thus governed by s. 18 of the Magistrates' Courts
Act, 1952. Under s. 18 the prosecution are entitled to ask the
magistrates to commit the defendant for trial and the magistrates
cannot try the case summarily without the prosecutor's consent if
the case affects the property or affairs of Her Majesty or a public
body as defined by the Public Bodies Corrupt Practices Act, 1899,
or the prosecution is carried on by the Director of Public Prosecutions. Cases may occur, however, where the prosecution ask for

summary trial but the defence wish to elect trial by jury but because the charge is under s. 5 (2), s. 6 (2) or s. 9 (3) can no longer elect trial by jury under s. 25. Under s. 18 (1) it is clear that the justices have a discretion whether to accede to the prosecution's request for summary trial. As the court has a discretion whether to commit for trial, clearly the defence have the right to address the court as to the manner in which they should exercise their discretion. Section 18 is silent as to the criteria which the court should apply when deciding to exercise its discretion. It is submitted that the primary criterion is whether it is in the interests of justice for there to be a trial by jury. If, for example, the defendant is additionally or alternatively charged with other offences for which the defendant has the right to elect trial by jury and is exercising that right, then it is clearly in the interests of justice for the magistrates' court to commit him to the same Crown Court which will try the alternative or additional charges for which he is electing trial by jury. It is in the interests of justice for the same court to deal with charges which are either in the alternative or arise out of one set of circumstances. It would also obviously appear in the interests of justice if the case was of such a grave character that on a conviction the court should have the opportunity of considering imposing an immediate or suspended sentence of imprisonment and as the magistrates' courts have no power of imprisonment, it should therefore be tried on indictment. In *Collins* v. *Spring* [1975] Crim.L.R. 100 it was held that there was no onus on the prosecution when making an application for a case to be tried summarily under s. 18 (1) to satisfy the justices that it should be dealt with summarily. The justices should consider whether it was a proper case to be dealt with summarily, whether they had adequate powers of punishment and whether in other respects it was a proper case for summary trial (*ibid.*) The defendant or his advocate has two opportunities to make representations that the case should be dealt with on indictment. First at the commencement of the proceedings under s. 18 (1), before any evidence is called and secondly at some further stage before the close of the prosecution's case by virtue of s. 18 (5), which allows the magistrates' court where it has begun to try the case summarily to discontinue the summary trial at any time before the close of the prosecution's evidence. The magistrates' court may not be able to adequately judge the seriousness or otherwise of the case without hearing the actual evidence. If the magistrates exercise their power under s. 18 (5), the witnesses will have to be recalled in order that the evidence can be taken in the form of depositions unless it is possible for this evidence to be given in the form of

statements under s. 2 of the Criminal Justice Act, 1967. A charge
of driving whilst disqualified should not, in some circumstances, be
tried in any court along with one under s. 5 (*cf. R.* v. *Pomeroy* (1935),
25 Cr.App.R. 147), but see p. 77.

A conviction for driving " under the influence of drink or drug ",
the former phrase, is not bad for duplicity (*Thomson* v. *Knights*
[1947] 1 All E.R. 112), but a conviction based on a verdict of a jury
that the defendant was " guilty of being under the influence of
drink " with no reference to proper control was quashed (*R.* v.
Hawkes (1931), 22 Cr.App.R. 172).

It would seem that offences under s. 5 (1) and (2) can properly
be charged and (with consent) tried together, so long as there is a
conviction for only one. An analysis of a specimen obtained after a
warning given under s. 9 (7) of the Act is admissible in a subsequent
charge under s. 5 (*R.* v. *Palfrey, infra*).

Under s. 9 (7) the warning that is to be administered is that
" failure to provide a specimen of blood or urine may make you
liable to imprisonment, a fine and disqualification " (*R.* v. *Palfrey*;
R. v. *Sadler* [1970] 2 All E.R. 12). In each of these cases the
defendant had been acquitted by the jury after a successful submission of " no case " in respect of a count on the indictment under
s. 1 of the 1967 Act. Each defendant had been originally arrested
under the Road Safety Act and had supplied a laboratory specimen
after being warned as required by the Act. Alternative counts
had been inserted in the indictment under s. 6 of the 1960 Act.
Each quarter sessions had then proceeded on the count of driving
whilst unfit to drive through drink or drugs and allowed the
analyst's certificate of blood/alcohol to be used in evidence in
support of the charge. The Court of Appeal said that an analyst's
certificate is not analogous to a confession. It is material, real
evidence and the strict rules excluding admissions or confessions
made on inducement or promise by a person in authority were
limited. Although the Court of Appeal certified the point as one of
public importance and granted legal aid to one of the defendants to
appeal to the House of Lords, the House of Lords refused leave to
appeal.

A charge under s. 5 may be included in an indictment for motor
manslaughter, causing death by dangerous driving or dangerous
driving provided that the amount of drink was such that the driver
would be or was adversely affected (*R.* v. *McBride* [1961] 3 All E.R.
6). Similarly a charge under s. 6 may also be included (*R.* v. *Thorpe*
[1972] R.T.R. 118).

A court cannot call the analyst at the end of the defendant's
case unless it is to give evidence in rebuttal (*R.* v. *Godstone JJ.*,

ex parte Dickson (1971), 115 S.J. 246), although if the analyst's certificate is defective (in this case it referred to "Joan Grierson Dickson" instead of "John Grierson Dickson") the court might call the analyst at the conclusion of the prosecution case. (For a case where justices should have allowed the analyst to be called in rebuttal, see *Hudson* v. *Hornsby* on p. 219.)

The police cannot bail a defendant who has been arrested under s. 8 of the Act under s. 38 of the Magistrates' Courts Act, 1952, to come back to the police station after the analyst's result is known. The purpose of the arrest under s. 8 is to obtain the provision of a specimen of blood or urine for laboratory testing, and he may only be detained thereafter under s. 11 of the Act (*R.* v. *McKenzie* [1971] 1 All E.R. 729).

Attempting to Drive

This is an offence under s. 5 and s. 6 of the Act and can be relevant under s. 9 (3) of the Act. A drunken person went to the front of a car and turned the starting handle; he then opened the offside door, leaned inside and appeared to touch the dashboard instruments. He returned to the starting handle and then sat in the driver's seat; the engine was heard to turn over but failed to start. The court found that he had the immediate intention of driving and it was held that this was an attempt to drive (*The State (Prendergast)* v. *Porter* [1961] Ir.Jur.Rep. 15; Jo.Crim.L. (1962) 217). And see *R.* v. *Cook* and *Jones* v. *Brooks* on p. 358; also *Shaw* v. *Knill* on p. 655. In *Harman* v. *Wardrop* [1971] R.T.R. 127 a motorist gave up his ignition keys to a person who he mistakenly thought was a police constable. When he realised his mistake he asked for his keys back with the intention of driving the car. He was refused. Lord Parker doubted whether the motorist would ever be said to be attempting to drive if he merely asked for his keys. There should, it is submitted, be a sufficiently proximate act in order to constitute the attempt to commit the offence. On the other hand an intending motorist may attempt to drive without having the keys: for example, he may be able to short circuit the ignition and start the engine.

The meaning of "drive" is discussed on pp. 21 and 184.

In Charge

The decided cases are given below. Most (but see *Woodage* v. *Jones* (*No. 2*) (see p. 166)) were decided prior to the enactment of s. 6 (2) of the Act, but it is felt that they will be of help to the court in deciding whether or not a defendant was in charge. It will be necessary in every case for the prosecutor to prove this and, if he fails to prove that the defendant was in charge, the charge should be dismissed without calling on the defendant to raise any defence under the last part of s. 5 (3) or s. 6 (3) of the Act. Similarly, if, in the case of a person accused under s. 9 (3) of the Act of refusing a blood or urine specimen, it is not shown that he was in charge when arrested, he should be acquitted.

A policeman has no power under s. 8 (1) to require a person " in charge " of a motor vehicle to take a breath test; a breath test may only be required, under s. 8 (1), of a person " driving or attempting to drive " (see pp. 184–192), although seemingly a breath test can be required of a motorist in charge of a motor vehicle following an accident under s. 8 (2) (*R.* v. *Lawrence* [1973] R.T.R. 64). If, however, a policeman does require a motorist who is only " in charge " to take a breath test, the requirement does not invalidate an arrest under (what is now) s. 5 (5) for being in charge while unfit to drive through drink or drugs. Where a motorist was so arrested following a positive breath test, the High Court directed the magistrates to convict him of a charge under s. 6 (2) (*Wimperis* v. *Griffin* [1973] Crim.L.R. 533).

Is it a question of fact or law as to whether a person is " in charge " ? It is submitted that it is primarily a fact for a jury or the magistrates to decide. In a case, *R.* v. *Short,* reported only in *The Times* (10th December, 1955) Lord Goddard, C.J., said: " Curiously enough, for a long time there seems to have been abroad the idea that the question of whether or not a man is in charge of a car is a matter of law. It seems to me it is entirely a question of fact. And questions of fact have to be resolved by a jury." Lord Goddard in this case was following himself when two months earlier in *R.* v. *Harnett* [1955] Crim.L.R. 793 he said that the question of " in charge " was a question of fact for the jury to try.

In *Crichton* v. *Burrell* [1951] S.L.T. 365, Lord Keith said: " The words ' in charge ' mean being responsible for the control or driving and do not necessarily mean that the person was actually driving or attempting to drive." In *MacDonald* v. *Bain* [1954] S.L.T.(Sh.) 30, it was said that the words " in charge " had to be read in the light of the later words " incapable of having proper control of the vehicle " and " proper control " meant " proper driving control ", the word " proper " referring to some specific relationship between the person and the vehicle.

A man who was supervising a learner-driver and was himself under the influence of drink was held to be in charge of the vehicle (*Clark* v. *Clark* [1950] S.L.T.(Sh.) 68) but it is a question of fact

which must be proved in each individual case whether the supervisor
had or had not " care and control " when the learner was driving
(*R.* v. *Lumiala* (1957), 25 C.R. 361, a case on a Canadian statute
making it an offence to have " care and control "). In respect of
a charge under (what is now) s. 6 (2) of the Act the Divisional
Court in *Sheldon* v. *Jones* (1969), 113 S.J. 942, found it unnecessary
to decide whether a supervisor was " in charge " of a motor vehicle
driven by his wife who was a learner-driver (but a supervisor
can be found guilty of aiding and abetting a learner-driver to
commit an offence contrary to s. 6 of the Act: see *Crampton* v. *Fish*
(1969), 113 S.J. 1003). In *Adair* v. *M'Kenna* [1951] S.L.T.(Sh.) 40
a mechanic repairing a car at the roadside was summoned under
s. 5 (2) of the Act as being in charge of the car but was acquitted on
the ground that he had no authority to drive and no ignition key.
In *Leach* v. *Evans* [1952] 2 All E.R. 264 a van driver under the influence of drink came out of an inn and said that he was looking for
his van, when he was about three yards from it. He then pointed
to it and said he was going home, an ignition key being in his
possession. He was arrested before he got into the van. It was
held that there was evidence that he was in charge of the van. In
Dean v. *Wishart* [1952] S.L.T. 86 the defendant, who owned the car,
got so drunk that his friends put him in the back seat of his car
while it was in the car park, immobilised the car and left him there
in a stupor from which the police woke him ninety minutes later.
He did not know that he was in the car when he was awakened. It
was held that, as he was not a free agent in any sense and had been
put in the back of the car insensible, he could not be fairly and
properly described as being in charge; it was also said to be a
difficult case. In *Macdonald* v. *Crawford* [1952] S.L.T.(Sh.) 92
the defendant was held to be in charge where his car had broken
down and been parked by the roadway to await a tow and he
was found sitting in the driving seat under the influence of drink.
In *Crichton* v. *Burrell* (*supra*) the owner of a car, who had an ignition
key on him, was standing by the car but not trying to enter it;
it had been arranged that another man with a duplicate key
should drive it, but this man did not arrive until after the owner's
arrest. The High Court of Justiciary quashed the conviction,
it being stated that " in charge " meant " in *de facto* control ".
Any attempt to include the owner merely because he was present
or because he had the key of a car which he had arranged for a
chauffeur to drive, it was said, would lead to extravagant results,
e.g., where a drunk owner and a drunk driver were both in the
car at the same time. In *Fisher* v. *Kearton* [1964] Crim.L.R. 470,
the defendant, who had no driving licence or insurance, was found

drunk in the driving seat of a car; a person who held an insurance and driving licence and the car's ignition keys was in the passenger seat. It was held that the defendant was not in charge.

But contrast *Haines* v. *Roberts* [1953] 1 All E.R. 344, where the defendant had left his motor cycle in a public place and then got drunk. His friends, realising his condition, intended to prevent his riding the machine and took him to the parking place to douse his head in water. At the same time they tried to arrange for someone else to ride the motor cycle. Nearly two hours later the defendant was found by the police, still under the influence of drink, about five feet from his cycle. He told them to leave it alone and added that, if he wanted to ride it, no one would stop him. When accused by the police of an offence under s. 5 (2) he succinctly paraphrased his counsel's arguments by replying: " I was not in charge of any bloody bike." It was held that he was in charge of it, it being said that, until he had given it into somebody else's charge, he remained in charge. In *Woodage* v. *Jones* (*No. 2*) [1975] R.T.R. 119, *Haines* v. *Roberts* was applied and it was held that a motorist stopped by other motorists who requested him to pull in and who had then put his car on a garage forecourt and on learning that the police were summoned, then walked half-a-mile away before being arrested, was held still to be " in charge " as he had not put his vehicle in charge of somebody else. In *R.* v. *Paul* [1952] N.I. 61, a man borrowed his son's car; he was later found sitting in the driving seat but he did not intend to drive, and the car was mechanically incapable of being started. He was held to be in charge of it. A bus driver who leaves a bus on the road and goes off duty remains in charge of it until he hands over the charge to another person (*Ellis* v. *Smith* [1962] 3 All E.R. 954).

A decision of the High Court of Justiciary is noted at Jo.Crim.L. (1954) 63 in which a defendant was held guilty of being in charge. He had parked and left his car and he then became under the influence of drink. He later went back to the car to get some papers; noticing that a sidelight was out, he pressed the self-starter so that the vibration might restore the connection. He did not take the ignition key out of his pocket. The High Court specifically said that a motorist could be in charge although he was not intending to drive, but s. 5 (3) of the 1972 Act now allows a defence. In *Winter* v. *Morrison* [1954] S.C.(J.) 7, a conviction was quashed where the defendant had been found in the front passenger seat and his wife was in the driver's seat. It was said that it was a question of fact who was in charge and there was no justification for the view that anyone save his wife was in charge at the relevant time; it was quite immaterial that she held only an expired provisional driving licence. In *R.* v. *Harnett* [1955] Crim.L.R. 793, it was said that whether or not a person was in charge was a question of fact in each case and possession of the ignition key was not the only factor, and in *Walker* v. *Rountree* [1963] N.I. 23 that proof of possession of the ignition key by the defendant is not essential.

A Metropolitan magistrate acquitted a man who had handled a car, not his own, solely because he (the defendant) was so bemused by drink that he did not know what he was doing (*The Solicitor*, October, 1952; and see Jo.Crim.L. (1956) 6, where the defendant had no intention of driving). Another magistrate acquitted a man who was so drunk that he was incapable of forming any intention in regard to the car in which he was a passenger (Jo.Crim.L. (1955) 111).

At 98 S.J. 275 it is said that in Scotland persons have been held not guilty of being in charge although they have not put their vehicles in charge of anyone else, but in England it has been said that a person remains in charge until he has given the vehicle into another's charge (*Haines* v. *Roberts, supra*). Lord Goddard, C.J., in *R.* v. *Short* (1955), *The Times*, 10th December, repeated this view, saying: " Somebody must be in charge of a car when it is on a road unless it has been abandoned altogether." It is submitted that a vehicle can be taken out of the owner's charge against his will, e.g., by a thief or even by friends who, realising his drunken condition, forcibly prevent him from entering. Again, what of a person who leaves his car for the night and goes to bed? Cannot he cease to be in charge of a vehicle if he has temporarily abandoned it for a period of (say) eight hours or more? It seems that in the circumstances of the man in bed, he is clearly not in charge for there was no likelihood of his driving whilst unfit (see s. 5 (3)). Even in cases where s. 5 (3) does not directly apply, it is submitted that, as both *Haines* v. *Roberts* and *Leach* v. *Evans* (both *supra*) were concerned with cases where the defendant was actually close to the vehicle, the point is still open to argument in England where the circumstances are different and show an abandonment for a substantial period. In many cases now, of course, the defendant will be able to plead under s. 5 (3) or s. 6 (3) of the Act that he did not intend to drive, and defending solicitors may sometimes think it better to rely on that defence rather than on a submission that their client was not in charge; should the court accept the submission at the close of the prosecutor's case, the defendant may find that an appeal by case stated is lodged against him. If the court, on the other hand, hear the defence and acquit on the facts, the prosecutor generally has no appeal; if the court hear the

defence and convict, the point as to being in charge is still open to
the defendant on appeal.

To give up being in charge, the driver should place his car in
charge of a suitable person, giving him authority to drive or garage
it; merely to hand the ignition key to a drinking companion may
not suffice (*Thaw* v. *Segar* [1962] S.L.T.(Sh.) 63).

Normally a motorist involved in an accident and required to take
a breath test by virtue of s. 8 (2) of the Act (see pp. 195–197) will
be convicted under s. 6 (1) of *driving* with excess blood/alcohol.
If, however, the motorist consumes alcohol after the accident but
before he supplies a specimen of blood or urine he cannot be
convicted under s. 6 (1) as the analysis must relate to the amount of
alcohol he had while driving or attempting to drive (see *Rowlands* v.
Hamilton on pp. 181–183). Where, however, a motorist had an
accident, then went to a nearby public house and consumed
alcohol to fortify himself, he was convicted under s. 6 (2) of being
in charge of the motor vehicle (*R.* v. *Lawrence* [1973] R.T.R. 64).

Defences in Cases of Being in Charge

Section 5 (3) and s. 6 (3) of the Act indicate a defence which is
not available in charges under s. 5 (1) or s. 6 (1), and it may be
that some prosecutors will now accuse persons of attempting to
drive where formerly the accusation would have been that they
were in charge. It is submitted that, if the defendant proves that
he had no intention of driving, he is not guilty of attempting to
drive, for the mind must go with the attempt.

The former requirement of s. 6 (2) (ii) of the 1960 Act that, to
establish a defence under that subsection, the defendant had to
prove that he had not driven a motor vehicle since he became
impaired was repealed by the Road Safety Act, 1967; all he need
now show is that there was no likelihood of his driving whilst
unfit.

A similar defence applies where the defendant is accused of
being in charge of a motor vehicle when he had a blood/alcohol
concentration exceeding 80 mg. He should be acquitted on proof
that at the material time the circumstances were such that there
was no likelihood of his driving it so long as there was any probability of his having alcohol in his blood above the limit. See
Northfield v. *Pinder* on p. 172.

By s. 6 (4) of the Act, in cases under s. 6 (2) of the Act (in charge
with more than 80 mg.), the fact that the defendant had been
injured or his vehicle damaged may be disregarded in determining
the likelihood of his driving, i.e., his plea that he was too badly
hurt to drive or his car was too damaged can be disregarded and

the court can find that he would have driven if he had not had an accident. No such statutory provision relates to the defence of no likelihood under s. 5 (2) of the Act and in *R.* v. *Jephcott* [1967] Crim.L.R. 52 it was held that damage to the defendant's car could be raised as a defence under s. 5 (3) that its damage precluded him from driving it so that there was no likelihood of its being driven whilst he was still unfit. Although *Jephcott's* case was not cited in argument or referred to in the judgment, it was similarly held in *R.* v. *Lawrence* [1973] R.T.R. 64 that in respect of an offence under s. 5 (2) the jury are not entitled to disregard the fact that the defendant might not have been able to drive as a result of personal injury or damage to the vehicle following an accident.

The defence of no likelihood of driving must generally be established by evidence given by the defence, although, rarely, precise admissions obtained in cross-examination of the witnesses for the prosecution might suffice (*cf. McCrone* v. *Rigby* (1952), 50 L.G.R. 115, at p. 119, noted on pp. 514–515, *infra*). To establish a defence under s. 5 (3) the defendant must show on a balance of probabilities that the circumstances were such that there was no likelihood of his driving while unfit (*Morton* v. *Confer* [1963] 2 All E.R. 765; *R.* v. *Lawrence, supra*; see also *R.* v. *Rivers, infra*). Proof beyond reasonable doubt by the defendant is not required in England (*Morton* v. *Confer, supra*) or Scotland (*Neish* v. *Stevenson* [1970] Crim.L.R. 161, where balance of probabilities was accepted). It was further said in *Morton* v. *Confer* (*supra*) that the court should not accept merely what the defendant says was his intention but must consider whether, having regard to all relevant evidence, including his testimony, the court is satisfied that there was no likelihood of his driving while he remained unfit. In that case the driver had said that he stopped his car when the " drinks hit him " and then he went to sleep. When awakened, he immediately switched on the ignition. The magistrates accepted his sworn evidence that he would not have driven until he felt fit but the High Court said that this was insufficient; they should have considered all the circumstances, including his switching on of the ignition, but a court would be entitled in some cases to say that his intent not to drive would be fulfilled notwithstanding contrary actions or, it is submitted, the lack of any evidence other than his own where there was no other evidence.

It must be made clear to a jury that the standard of proof which a defendant has to satisfy when raising the special defence under s. 5 (3) is no more than a balance of probabilities. Where, therefore, a judge merely read to a jury the words of s. 5 (3) without directing them that the defendant had only to satisfy them as to his defence under s. 5 (3) on a balance of probabilities, the conviction of the defendant under s. 5 (2) was set aside (*R.* v. *Rivers* [1974] R.T.R. 31). Seemingly if the charge were under s. 6 (2) a conviction would be similarly set aside if the judge merely read s. 6 (3) without directing the jury on the standard of the burden of proof which lies on a defendant following *R.* v. *Rivers.* It has been long established that where in a criminal trial the burden of proof of any matter lies upon the defendant he has only to prove that matter on the balance of probabilities.

The defendant is limited to showing that there was no likelihood of his driving the particular vehicle of which he was in charge whilst unfit or over 80 mg.; ss. 5 (3) and 6 (3) expressly say this. If he shows this, he should be acquitted even though there is evidence that he was going to drive another car.

In *Farrell* v. *Campbell* (1958), 75 Sh.Ct.Rep. 24, the defendant, who was drinking in a public house, was told that the police were outside. He left his car where it was outside the public house and took a bus to a friend's house and gave him the ignition key. The friend agreed to drive the car home. It was held that the defendant had shown that he had no intention of driving and had brought himself within the defence. A Resident Magistrate has held that the term " no likelihood " of driving whilst under the influence means that the court can, on the evidence, come to the conclusion that the preponderance of probability is that the defendant would have in fact refrained from driving. A state of mind alone is not enough and there should be some evidence of the pursuit of a line of conduct by him; in the particular case he had walked by his car and not tried to enter it, which was sufficient evidence to establish " no likelihood " (Jo.Crim.L. (1959) 296). Nevertheless, there may be some cases where there is no evidence available of pursuit of a line of conduct and it is submitted that, if magistrates have no evidence before them pointing either way, other than the defendant's own testimony, they must be left in doubt as to whether the prosecution's case has been proved and are entitled to acquit, assuming that they accept his evidence.

The defendant under s. 5 (2) or s. 6 (2) is not limited to proving that he had no intention of driving. He can call evidence, for example, that his friends would have forcibly prevented him from getting into the driving seat; mere inability to start the engine, due to the removal of the rotor arm or hiding of the ignition key, may not suffice because a man can " drive " without the engine being started (*Saycell* v. *Bool* [1948] 2 All E.R. 83, and cases cited on pp. 21–26). Defences that the defendant would not have contemplated driving the vehicle in question because he was unlicensed or disqualified, so that driving would have meant breaking the law, would have evidential value.

Note that under s. 6 (4) damage to the vehicle or injury to the driver may be disregarded in assessing the likelihood of his driving whilst with more than 80 mg. but it is otherwise under s. 5 (2); see p. 169 and *R.* v. *Lawrence* in particular.

Normally, the defendant's intention at the time will be material and it may be that if he was so drunk as to be incapable of forming any intention it will be difficult to tell whether or not there was any likelihood of his driving. Each case must be decided on its own facts and the court obtains such help as it can from the defendant's action and declarations and even from the possibility that he might become unconscious before he began to drive and would be rescued by friends. Possibly a man might plead s. 6 (2) even after the intervention of the police, as where a man is called by a constable from a bar to switch on his car lights and is then discovered to be intoxicated; can he plead to the court that his intoxication would have become apparent to himself as soon as he went into the open air and he would not have driven his car? The defence does not specifically refer to his intention but to " the circumstances "; it is submitted that his state of mind and his absence from the car can be " circumstances ". One may compare the *locus poenitentiae* allowed to those contemplating other crimes— crimes which admittedly require more overt acts than being in charge does. The defence has been raised that the intervention of the police, who stopped a drunken man getting into his car, can establish that there would be no likelihood of his driving it (Jo.Crim. L. (1957) 291). In the old larceny and receiving cases, certainly, the intervention of the police could sometimes result in persons with guilty minds being acquitted—see Archbold, 36th ed., paras. 1510 and 2101. In *John* v. *Bentley* (1961), *The Times*, 20th April, the defendant was found dead drunk in charge of a car; his condition was such that he slept all through the medical examination and for several hours after. Quarter sessions held that, as he was so drunk that it was most unlikely that he could have driven at all and there was some evidence of a previous decision not to drive if too drunk, he had shown on the balance of probabilities that there was no likelihood of his driving whilst unfit. The High Court refused to interfere with the decision of sessions, though Lord Parker, C.J., said that he was far from saying that he would have come to the same conclusion as sessions had. This seems to have been an extreme case and often it would not suffice for a person in charge of a car to show that he was unconscious through drink for a short time, since he might recover the ability to drive whilst still under the influence of drink. In *Northfield* v. *Pinder* [1968] 3 All E.R. 854, where *John* v. *Bentley* was not cited, the defendant was accused of being in charge under s. 6 (2) of the Act with more than 80 mg. of alcohol in his blood; he had 240 mg. He was found by his car at 9.14 p.m. and the magistrates considered that he was at that time so hopelessly drunk as to be incapable of driving his car or even of finding it or walking to it, so they dismissed the charge. The High Court quashed their decision and directed a conviction, saying that he must show that there was no likelihood of his driving whilst his level exceeded 80 mg. and that there had been no evidence that he would not have driven when the worst effects of the drink had worn off. The term " material time " in s. 6 (3) clearly included the time when he was found near his car. Medical evidence would probably be needed to show when his level would decrease to 80 mg. but other evidence such as arranging for someone else to drive it or taking a bedroom at a hotel nearby would prove the unlikelihood better. A very material factor in almost every case will be the level of alcohol in the blood as found by the analyst. If the level is only just over the limit, the defendant's blood/alcohol level will comparatively quickly recede below 80 mg. If, on the other hand, the blood/alcohol level is grossly above the limit, medical evidence may be required even if the defendant can show that he had arranged overnight accommodation. It is perfectly possible for a person to be still over the prescribed limit the morning after the night before, particularly if the night before had involved a very large amount of alcohol. In *Pugsley* v. *Hunter* (see p. 676) it was held that it was only if it were obvious to a layman that the " lacing " of the defendant's drink accounted for the defendant being above the limit that medical evidence is not required to be called by the defence. It is thought likely that a similar approach to this problem may be adopted.

In *Sheldon* v. *Jones* (1969), 113 S.J. 942, the prosecution sought to argue that it was impossible for a supervisor to establish that there was no likelihood of his driving since at any moment he might have to take over the driving. The justices found as a fact that there was no such likelihood and the Divisional Court, although stating that they themselves might have come to a different conclusion, felt unable to disturb the justices' finding to that effect. It is, however, submitted that a supervisor will usually have a difficult task in proving that there was no likelihood of his driving. It is submitted that momentarily taking over control of the steering or the engine may well amount to " driving " and this is one of the main duties of a supervisor of a learner-driver (see p. 21 as to " driving ").

In *R.* v. *Curran* (1975), *The Times*, 8th May, the Court of Appeal have certified the point for consideration by the House of Lords as to whether a person who is deemed not to be in charge of a motor vehicle by reason of s. 5 (3) (see p. 168) can nevertheless be convicted of refusing laboratory specimens under s. 9 (3) where the constable had reasonable cause to believe he was " in charge " and was subsequently lawfully entitled to require the provision of laboratory specimens.   There are two previous decisions of the Court of Appeal directly in conflict on the point (*Williams* v. *Osborne* [1975] R.T.R. 181 and *R.* v. *Richardson* (*John*) [1975] R.T.R. 173).   The House of Lords will thus have to consider whether on a charge under s. 9 (3) of refusing, the prosecution have to prove whether the defendant was " driving or attempting to drive " or " in charge " at the relevant time on the one hand or whether it suffices for the prosecution on the other hand merely to prove that the constable was lawfully entitled to require the defendant to provide laboratory specimens on the ground he had reasonable cause to believe the driver was " in charge " or " driving or attempting to drive " as the case may be.

" Road or Other Public Place "

Offences under s. 5 or s. 6 may be committed " on a road or other public place ".   " Road " is defined by s. 196 of the Act of 1972 and bears a wider meaning than a public highway: see *Harrison* v. *Hill* and other cases on the meaning of " road " on p. 26–32.

The term " or other public place " is not defined; it is discussed at Jo.Crim.L. (1955) 12, in Stroud's Judicial Dictionary and Saunders' Words and Phrases Legally Defined, and at 127 J.P.Jo. 563. It is a question of degree and fact whether a place is public or private; if only a restricted class of persons is permitted or invited to have access, the case would fall on the side of the place being private but if only a restricted class is excluded, the place would be public (*R.* v. *Waters* (1963), 47 Cr.App.R. 149).   It is for the prosecution to prove that a place is public (*Pugh* v. *Knipe, infra*).

Magistrates may make use of their general local knowledge in deciding whether a car-park is a public place under s. 5 or s. 6 (*Clift* v. *Long* [1961] Crim.L.R. 121).   See also *Thomas* v. *Thomas* [1961] 1 All E.R. 19 as to magistrates using their own knowledge.   But knowledge of one magistrate only need not be accepted by the other magistrates; the prosecution must prove that the place was a public place at the time of the offence, and evidence that it is normally public may not suffice where it is not clear that at the time it was (*Williams* v. *Boyle* (1962), 106 S.J. 939).

Examples

A private field to which the public were temporarily invited to watch racing was held to be a public place under s. 5, although it could be closed at any time and particular persons could be refused admission (*R.* v. *Collinson* (1931), 23 Cr.App.R. 49). *Paterson* v. *Ogilvy* [1957] S.C.(J.) 42 is a case to the like effect. Conversely a car-park attached to a public house may be regarded as a public place during general licensing hours but it may well be no longer a public place outside those hours. In *Sandy* v. *Martins* [1974] Crim.L.R. 258 justices were held entitled to acquit after the prosecution had failed to prove that the invitation to the public to use the car-park extended one hour after closing time. In *Montgomery* v. *Loney* [1959] N.I. 171, where a Northern Irish statutory definition of " road " was considered, it was held that the forecourt of a petrol-filling station, with carriageways with unobstructed entrances to, and exits from the highway, was a " road or public place ", it being said that, though the forecourt was open only to those members of the public who wished to do business with the station-owner, they were enough to show that the public had access. It was also said that an offence charged as being " in a road or other public place " was not bad for duplicity. In *Elkins* v. *Cartlidge* [1947] 1 All E.R. 829 there was at the side of an inn a well-defined parking ground from which an open gateway gave access to an enclosure. Cars went into this enclosure and parked there. The enclosure was held to be a public place, as being a place to which the public had access in fact, but a car-park attached to a club can only be regarded as public if there is evidence of public use of the car-park (*Pugh* v. *Knipe* [1972] R.T.R. 286). A public house offers its services to the public but a private club does not (*ibid.*, distinguishing *Elkins* v. *Cartlidge*). A vacant piece of land used as an overflow parking ground was held to be a public place in *McDonald* v. *M'Ewen* [1953] S.L.T.(Sh.) 26. In *White* v. *Cubitt* (1930), 94 J.P. 60, a case under another statute, a piece of private ground adjoining an inn and separated from the highway only by a level row of stone setts was held to be a public place. The public did not have access to this ground save to enter the inn and it was not a car-park. A Metropolitan magistrate has held that a bombed site, on which buildings once stood and which was private property, was " a public place " under s. 5 when there was evidence that the public used it as a short cut and as a children's playground and that vehicles often parked there, all apparently without objection by the owner (Jo.Crim.L. (1955) 10).

Quarter sessions have held that Hyde Park is not a public place during the time it is closed to the public in the small hours (*R.* v.

Arthur, Jo.Crim.L. (1961) 97). A part of the grounds of a hospital into which part visitors and their friends were permitted to enter was held to be a public place under the Prevention of Crime Act, 1953, where " public place " is defined as including any highway or place to which at the material time the public have or are permitted to have access whether on payment or otherwise (*R.* v. *Powell* [1963] Crim.L.R. 511). In *R.* v. *Kane* [1965] 1 All E.R. 705, an affray case, it was said that a public place was one to which the public could and did have access, whether at the invitation of the occupier or only with his permission and whether or not some payment or other formality was required; it would not be public if restricted to members of a club and their guests, other people who entered being trespassers.

Driving with Blood/Alcohol Concentration above the Prescribed Limit of 80 mg.

The offence of driving or attempted driving of a motor vehicle with more than 80 mg. of alcohol per 100 ml. of blood (or 107 mg. of alcohol per 100 ml. of urine—see s. 12 (4) of the Act) comes under s. 6 (1). The Secretary of State may by Regulation prescribe some other proportion of blood or urine/alcohol level (s. 12). Up to the time to which this edition states the law, the Secretary of State has not done so. The offence is triable either summarily or on indictment and the defendant may claim trial by jury; the driving or attempted driving offence carries an obligatory disqualification of at least twelve months, unless there are special reasons. The Magistrates' Association recommends a longer disqualification where the blood alcohol is 120 mg. per 100 ml. or more (see p. 594). For the penalties generally, see pp. 243–252.

The prosecutor must show, under s. 6 (1), that the defendant was driving or attempting to drive a motor vehicle on a road or public place; see Chapter I and also pp. 175–177 as to these terms. The section does not apply to pedal cycles but does apply to auto-assisted cycles or mopeds. For the meaning of " motor vehicle " see pp. 2–9 and in particular *R.* v. *Tahsin* on p. 6.

Results of Laboratory Tests

The prosecutor must show that the analysis of the specimen taken for the purpose of the laboratory test not only exceeds 80 mg. of alcohol per 100 ml. of blood or 107 mg. of alcohol per 100 ml. of urine (or such other proportions as may be prescribed by Regulation by the Secretary of State) but also that the actual analysis is correct.

The analysis may be proved by the production of the certificate or calling the analyst. Section 6 (1) requires the defendant to be above the limit " *as ascertained* " from the laboratory test. It was held in *R.* v. *Bowell* [1974] R.T.R. 273 that this means that the prosecution had to prove that the particular ascertainment of the blood/alcohol level by the analyst was correct; it did not suffice merely to prove that the defendant's blood/alcohol level exceeded 80 mg. The analyst's certificate in *Bowell*'s case showed the defendant to have 192 mg. in 100 ml. of blood. The defendant adduced evidence in an attempt to disprove the figure of 192 as being correct. The judge directed the jury to convict if they were satisfied the defendant had over 80 mg. even if they were not satisfied the blood/alcohol level was as high as 192. The direction was held to be incorrect and the conviction was quashed.

Proof of the blood/alcohol or urine/alcohol concentration can be given only by analysis of a blood or urine specimen and not by any other means; if there has been no proper analysis, even the defendant's admission that he has drunk so much alcohol that he must obviously have had more than 80 mg. will not suffice for a conviction under s. 6, though it will be valuable evidence under s. 5. Reactions of the breathalyser are of no evidential value under s. 6. In *R.* v. *Bowell, supra,* the defence sought to challenge the accuracy of the official analysis of the defendant's blood which showed 192 mg. when the sample was taken at midnight. The defendant, in order to be released from the police station under s. 11 gave a specimen of breath on the Alcotest device at 1.35 a.m. which proved negative. The defendant's expert witness said in evidence that the analysis of 192 mg. could not be accurate for the defendant to have given a negative breath test only one and a half hours later. The Court of Appeal in directing the defendant's conviction to be quashed were careful not to express any view on whether it is possible to challenge a certificate of analysis in this way. It is clearly a matter to be judged in the light of technical expert evidence, but the approved breath test is primarily a screening device; if the approved breath test device were as accurate as a laboratory analysis of blood or urine, there would be no need for the law to require a separate laboratory analysis of blood or urine.

Whether evidence of analysis be given orally or by certificate in writing, it must be shown by evidence of taking or posting to, and receipt at the laboratory that the specimen taken is the same as the one analysed; this applies to the defence, too, and specimens sent to a laboratory should be marked for identification on their containers.

The specimen analysed must be the specimen supplied by

the defendant in accordance with the procedure under s. 9. Where a defendant agreed to supply specimens of urine and the second specimen was thrown away by the station sergeant because he wrongly thought it was of insufficient quantity, the analysis of a specimen of blood which the defendant afterwards supplied could not be used for a subsequent prosecution under (what is now) s. 6; the Act did not contemplate that once a requirement had been made and complied with, there might be further requirements (*R.* v. *Hyams* [1972] 3 All E.R. 651); but if the requirement has *not* been complied with, the police are entitled to make a further requirement. In *R.* v. *Paduch* [1973] R.T.R. 493, the defendant agreed to provide blood, but because a police surgeon was unavailable, was subsequently asked by the police to supply urine which on analysis showed his urine/alcohol to be above the limit. His conviction on the urine analysis was upheld by the Court of Appeal.

Oral evidence of analysis of a specimen of blood or urine may be given by any person qualified to do so. By s. 10 (1) a certificate given by an authorised analyst may be admitted in evidence to show the proportion of alcohol or drug in the blood, whether it is a specimen of blood or urine. An " authorised analyst " by s. 10 (7) means any person possessing the qualifications prescribed under s. 89 of the Food and Drugs Act, 1955 (or s. 27 of the Food and Drugs (Scotland) Act, 1956), as qualifying persons for appointment as public analysts under these Acts. The Secretary of State may also authorise other persons to make analyses for the purposes of this section. Such authority has been given to named persons at various Home Office Forensic Science Laboratories and at the Metropolitan Police Laboratory. The certificate, provided it has been served in accordance with s. 10 (3), is evidence of the matters certified and of the qualifications of the analyst.

The evidence given in the certificate of the authorised analyst should be accepted by the court, so far as it falls within s. 10 and is uncontradicted by other evidence (*cf. McCulloch* v. *Hannam* [1951] 1 All E.R. 402, a case on the Food and Drugs Act, 1955, s. 110 (1), declaring a certificate to be " sufficient evidence "; see also the other cases cited in Stone on that provision). If evidence is brought contradicting the certificate, the court or jury must decide which to accept (*cf. Preston* v. *Fennell* [1950] 1 All E.R. 1099) and the benefit of any doubt be given to the defendant. If the certificate goes beyond the matters in s. 10, the magistrates should be asked to ignore the additional matter and if they do so, it seems that a conviction by them would not be quashed; see the cases on mentioning previous convictions at p. 94. The certificate is admissible in s. 5 cases both for the defence and, subject to the proviso in s. 10 (3), for the prosecution, but either side can, if preferred, call the analyst to give oral evidence. A certificate of urine analysis under s. 5 must show the corresponding alcohol content in the blood (*MacLeod* v. *Nicol*, Jo.Crim.L. (1964) 119) but for the purposes of an offence under s. 6, 107 mg. of alcohol per 100 ml. of urine is treated by s. 12 (4) as equivalent to 80 mg. of alcohol per 100 ml. of blood. A mistake in a certificate as to the place where the specimen was taken was held in *Douglas* v. *Wilkinson* [1964] S.L.T.(Sh.) 68 to render it inadmissible, as it therefore did not correctly identify the specimen, but this decision was disapproved in *Lawrie* v. *Stevenson* [1968] S.L.T. (Notes) 79, where it was said that the analyst's certificate is not evidence that the specimen was taken from a particular person at a particular time and place. The origin of the specimen must be proved by other evidence. Where the certificate sufficiently indicated the defendant and the prosecutor, a mistake of one day on it was held immaterial (*Alexander* v. *Clatworthy* (1969), 113 S.J. 387). In *R.* v. *Godstone JJ., ex parte Dickson* (1971), 115 S.J. 246, it was apparently accepted that a certificate referring to " Joan Grierson Dickson " did not sufficiently indicate the defendant, whose name was " John Grierson Dickson". The justices were prohibited from themselves calling the analyst to repair the deficiency of the prosecution's case after the close of the defence. The court did, however, say that the justices could have done so immediately after the close of the prosecution's case. But a better approach to the problem of identification is contained, it is submitted, in *Dickson* v. *Atkins* [1972] R.T.R. 209, where it was held that an analyst's certificate cannot be evidence that a sample was taken from a particular person at a particular place. What it is necessary for the prosecution to prove is:—

(a) that the specimen taken from the defendant was sent to the analyst; and

(b) that the analyst's certificate refers to the specimen sent to the analyst by the police.

It was therefore held that the fact that the certificate showed typographical errors (defendant named " Joan " instead of " John " and the police officer " Faul " instead of " Gaul ") was irrelevant and the court was satisfied by other evidence that the specimen analysed was that of the defendant (*ibid.*). It was also held (*per* Lord Widgery, C.J.) that a certificate which in no way identifies the sample does not satisfy the statutory requirements. It was pointed out in *R.* v. *Shaw* (*Derek*) [1974] R.T.R. 458 that s. 10 (1) (a) permits identification of the sample by the certificate. A certificate repeating the name of the defendant, the time it was taken from the label of the container of the sample, together with a recorded delivery certificate giving the name of addressee and date and place of posting of the sample, was held to be evidence from which a jury could infer that the sample given by the defendant at the police station was that analysed by the official analyst. An issue as to whether the sample given by the defendant has been identified as the sample which was analysed at the laboratory should be left to the jury (*ibid.*).

The Court of Appeal held in relation to a sample of urine that it was sufficient for the prosecution to prove by written markings on the bottle that the sample of urine that had been taken from the defendant was that received by the laboratory and analysed by them (*R.* v. *Orrell* [1972] R.T.R. 14). It is not necessary to produce the bottle or label (*ibid.*) because, the bottle being a chattel, the best evidence rule does not apply. By s. 10 (2) of the Act a doctor's certificate that he took a blood specimen is evidence of the matters so certified and of the doctor's qualifications; the proviso contained in s. 10 (3) also applies to it.

The requirements in the proviso as to service of the certificate, in so far as its admissibility for the prosecution is concerned, will be noted. The service must not be less than seven days before " the hearing or trial " and not the first return day of the summons; " not less than seven days " seems to mean seven clear days, i.e., excluding the day of service and the day of the hearing (*R.* v. *Long* [1959] 3 All E.R. 559). It will be seen that the court may allow an extension of time to the defence for requiring the calling of the analyst. A copy of the certificate required by the proviso in s. 10 (3) of the Act to be served on the accused or of a notice so required to be served on the prosecutor may either be personally served on the accused or prosecutor, as the case may be, or sent by registered or recorded delivery post (s. 10 (3)).

If the certificate of the analysis is not served within the time limited, it seems that this omission can be waived by the defence, and, if objection is to be taken to the omission, it should be taken immediately at the opening of the hearing; if it is taken successfully, it seems plain that the certificate cannot be admitted in those proceedings (*cf. Grimble & Co.* v. *Preston* (1914), 78 J.P. 72; this case was applied in *R.* v. *Banks* [1972] R.T.R. 179, where it was held that if the defence do not object to the admissibility of the certificate before the close of the prosecution, the defence will be deemed to have waived proof of the requirements as to service).

May the prosecution call the analyst in person where they have omitted to comply with the proviso in s. 10 (3)? It seems that he can properly be called, for the proviso is limited to evidence by certificate under s. 10 (1) and (2). Cases under the Food and Drugs Act, 1955, s. 108 (3), relating to service of a certificate of analysis with the summons were concerned with a provision which made it essential to the validity of the whole proceedings that there should be such service. Section 10 of the Act is in a quite different form and, it is submitted, plainly refers to evidence by certificate only. *Semble*, if objection is taken to an analyst's certificate on the ground of non-compliance with the proviso in s. 10 (3), and the prosecution do not call him, a fresh summons can be issued on a new or the same information and on the second summons the analyst's certificate, if duly served, will then be admissible, provided the first summons is withdrawn or adjourned (*Williams* v. *Letheren* (1919), 83 J.P. 159) but not if the first summons has been dismissed (*Haynes* v. *Davis* (1915), 79 J.P. 187). It is doubtful how far these principles apply to a trial on indictment. *Quaere*, if the analyst had died, whether his certificate would be admissible as that of a statement made by a person in the course of his duty.

It is of course possible for the defence to seek to establish that the analysis is incorrect because the sample of blood or urine has been placed in a contaminated or dirty container or a container which is not empty of other material, or that a proper specimen was not taken. This is a matter of fact to be determined by the court of trial. In *Rowlands* v. *Harper* [1972] R.T.R. 469 a police sergeant, contrary to instructions, assembled the syringe, needle and capsules for the taking of the blood specimen. The justices had doubts whether a true specimen had been taken, and the High Court dismissed an appeal by way of case stated. Lord Widgery was careful to state that the justices' doubt as to the taking of a true specimen was not to be justified simply on the footing that the sergeant had failed to carry out the instructions. The true *ratio decidendi* of the case is simply that the prosecution have to prove beyond reasonable doubt that the sample has been properly taken, and if the evidence is such that a reasonable tribunal might have a doubt, the Divisional Court will not disturb such a finding, which is one of fact, by the magistrates. Although the onus is on the prosecution, if the defence have not required the presence of the analyst or medical practitioner, the burden of proof that the sample was properly taken is sufficiently discharged by the prosecution by the production of the certificates. Even where the doctor taking the specimen of blood actually gives evidence, a court may infer that it has been properly taken even if the evidence is very scanty. Thus in *Braddock* v. *Whittaker* [1970] Crim.L.R. 112, the defendant was held to be rightly convicted under s. 1 of the Road

Safety Act on an analyst's certificate although the sample of blood produced at court was not identified by the doctor and the cups into which the blood had been placed contained crystals which the doctor had merely assumed to be anti-coagulant crystals without any evidence being adduced as to what the crystals actually were.

The certificate of analysis is, of course, conclusive. The defendant cannot seek an acquittal on the ground that his driving ability was unimpaired. Nor can he seek to argue that his blood/alcohol level was rising, so that although by the time he reached the police station and gave a specimen of blood for analysis his blood was above the limit, it was not above the limit at the time he ceased driving (*Ferriby* v. *Sharman* [1971] R.T.R. 163). The words of the section specifically say " as ascertained from a laboratory test for which he subsequently provides a specimen ". It was pointed out in this case by Widgery, L.C.J., that the only time which is relevant is the time at which the defendant provided the specimen and that this normally works to the advantage of a defendant in that the level of blood/alcohol usually declines. It was also held in this case that the fact that the blood/alcohol level may have risen between the time when the defendant was arrested and the time when he gave the blood specimen for laboratory analysis was not a special reason for refraining from disqualifying.

The certificate of analysis must, however, *relate* to the amount of alcohol in the defendant's blood when he was driving. It was held by the House of Lords in *Rowlands* v. *Hamilton* [1971] 1 All E.R. 1089, that if a defendant consumes alcohol after he ceases driving but before the specimen for laboratory testing is given, this invalidates the analysis even if the prosecution are able to show that, even if he had not consumed the additional alcohol, his blood would still have been above the limit. The defendant had been involved in an accident and went to a public house and consumed three single measures of whisky. Expert evidence was called to the effect that, even if he had not consumed the whisky after he had ceased driving, the result of the test would have shown that his blood was in excess of the limit. Nevertheless the House of Lords, by a majority, held that the conviction should be quashed; the analysis could not be adjusted by subsequent evidence. The " ascertainment " of the blood/alcohol level must be established by the result of the test alone; it cannot be established in any other way. In Scotland, however, the High Court of Justiciary allowed a conviction where the accused consumed alcohol after an accident, on the ground that the evidence of alcohol after the accident was insufficient to rebut the analyst's certificate (*Ritchie* v. *Pirie* [1972] Crim.L.R. 251).

It should, however, be noted that *Rowlands* v. *Hamilton* is a case where the consumption of alcohol occurred after the defendant was involved in an accident (see " Accident", pp. 196–197). If the motorist is stopped while " driving or attempting to drive " (see pp. 184–192) and consumes alcohol on seeing the constable and before the constable has time to require him to take a breath test by virtue of s. 8 (1), this is unlikely to invalidate the analysis as he will normally be " driving or attempting to drive ". Lord Diplock pointed out *obiter* in *D.P.P.* v. *Carey* [1969] 3 All E.R. 1662 that as in accordance with *Pinner* v. *Everett* [1969] 3 All E.R. 257, the motorist must still be " driving or attempting to drive " up to the time of the administration of the breath test, if he takes a hasty drink before the breath test, as he is still in law " driving or attempting to drive ", any alcohol that he manages to consume becomes part of the relevant alcohol for the purposes of s. 6 of the Act. The Scottish High Court of Justiciary decided (before *D.P.P.* v. *Carey* and *Pinner* v. *Everett*) in *Wood* v. *Brown* [1969] S.L.T. 297 that evidence that, after finishing his journey and before providing a blood specimen, the defendant had consumed further alcohol was relevant, and the court quashed a conviction following a ruling by the Sheriff-Substitute that such evidence was not relevant.

It is submitted that the *obiter dicta* of Lord Diplock in *D.P.P.* v. *Carey* must be correct if the facts show that the motorist is still " driving or attempting to drive " when he consumed the additional alcohol. However, the facts might show that the defendant was only " in charge " and was no longer " driving or attempting to drive " (see pp. 184–192); any alcohol he consumes will no longer be relevant to a charge under s. 6 (1) but may well be relevant to an offence under s. 6 (2) of being " in charge " of a motor vehicle with excess blood/alcohol. If the alcohol is consumed while he is still " in charge ", even if he is no longer driving or attempting to drive, the plain words of s. 6 (2) require him to be convicted. Indeed, in *R.* v. *Lawrence* [1973] R.T.R. 64 because of such post-accident consumption of alcohol, the prosecution charged the defendant under s. 6 (2) for being in charge. The case was considered on appeal by the Court of Appeal on other grounds, and Lord Widgery, C.J., recited the reason for the prosecution doing so without comment (at p. 66, letters C and D). It may also be noted that where the defendant is charged with driving while unfit to drive through drink or drugs under s. 5 (1) and consumes alcohol after the accident but before supplying a specimen for analysis, the analyst's certificate is admissible evidence as to the impairment of the defendant's driving ability together with medical evidence as to the extent to which the analysis should be adjusted by reason of the consumption of the post-accident alcohol (*R.* v. *Richards (Stanley)* [1974] R.T.R. 520).

Because it might be very easy for the defence of post-accident consumption of alcohol to be advanced, Lord Parker remarked in *R.* v. *Durrant* [1969] 3 All E.R. 1357, at p. 1359: " No doubt justices or juries at quarter sessions will in these circumstances look with very great care at the evidence produced." In *Rowlands* v. *Hamilton* it was the prosecution who produced the evidence of the consumption of alcohol after the accident. It is submitted that, following Lord Parker's *dicta*, provided it is made clear to the jury that the burden of proof that the motorist has not consumed alcohol after the accident is still on the prosecution, a jury may be reminded by the presiding judge that evidence from the defendant alone that he has consumed alcohol should be examined with care and caution.

The principle of Scott v. Baker

The principle in *Scott* v. *Baker* [1969] 1 Q.B. 659 is that before a motorist can be convicted of an offence under s. 6 (1), s. 6 (2) or s. 9 (3) the prosecution must show that the sample of blood or urine for analysis was lawfully obtained. A sample may only be lawfully obtained if the police can prove that the specimen was lawfully taken at the hospital or police station. If the specimen is taken at a police station, it can only be lawfully taken if the police can show that the defendant was lawfully arrested under s. 8 (4) or s. 8 (5) or s. 5 (5). A lawful arrest under s. 8 (4) (following a positive breath test) or s. 8 (5) (following a failure to supply a specimen of breath) in turn depends on the police having first lawfully required a breath test from a defendant under s. 8 (1) or s. 8 (2). Similarly where the motorist is a patient at a hospital after an accident, the lawfulness of any sample of blood or urine supplied depends on whether the police can prove that the procedural requirements as to the breath test and the supply and the requirement to supply a sample of blood or urine for analysis have been strictly followed together with the special statutory safeguards applicable while the motorist is at a hospital as a patient (see " Hospital Patients " on pp. 222–227). Omission of any one of the statutory requirements contained in ss. 6 to 12 of the Act is usually fatal to a prosecution. The statutory requirements which the police must adhere to will now follow, starting with the two basic situations which alone entitle the police to require a breath test. A constable is enpowered to stop a motor vehicle under s. 159 of the Act of 1972. His power to do so is not dependent on his suspecting the driver of an offence under s. 5 or s. 6. A driver stopped at random, however, cannot randomly be required to take a breath test (see further as to " random tests " on p. 189). A motorist can only be required to take a breath test where there are grounds for doing so under s. 8 (1) or s. 8 (2). The right to stop a vehicle and the right to administer a breath test are two separate things and should not be confused (*Adams* v. *Valentine* [1975] Crim.L.R. 238).

Requirement of Breath Test under s. 8 (1)

A police constable in uniform may require a motorist to take a breath test while:—

(*a*) " driving or attempting to drive ";
(*b*) either the constable has reasonable cause to suspect him " of having alcohol in his body "; or
(*c*) the constable has reasonable cause to suspect him of having committed a traffic offence whilst the vehicle was in motion.

(*a*) " *Driving or Attempting to Drive* "

A constable can only require a breath test under s. 8 (1) of a person who is " driving or attempting to drive ". If a constable purports to make a requirement under s. 8 (1) and the constable's suspicion arose while the motorist was not " driving or attempting to drive " he should be acquitted notwithstanding that the constable had reasonable cause to suspect the consumption of alcohol and notwithstanding the fact that the constable's suspicions were shown to be amply justified by the results of the subsequent laboratory analysis. Whether a person is " driving or attempting to drive " is a question of fact not of law, and the issue must be left to the jury if disputed in any way (see *R.* v. *Guttridge* on p. 186).

The first of two decisions of the House of Lords on what is " driving or attempting to drive " is *Pinner* v. *Everett* [1969] 3 All E.R. 257. The facts of the case are that the motorist was stopped by the police at 1 a.m. because his rear number plate was not illuminated. (This is an offence under Regulations made under the Vehicles (Excise) Act, 1971, and was not therefore a " traffic offence " while the vehicle was in motion.) The constables spoke to the defendant for some time and then noticed his breath smelt of alcohol. By a majority, with one dissentient, the House of Lords allowed an appeal against a conviction under what is now s. 9 (3) of the 1972 Act. The speeches of the House of Lords are not consistent in holding whether the *requirement* for the breath test or whether the *suspicion* of alcohol by the police constable must be contemporaneous with the " driving or attempting to drive " but it was held that certainly either the requirement and/or the suspicion must arise while the motorist was " driving or attempting to drive " (see *Sakhuja* v. *Allen, infra*, p. 185). The House of Lords held the words " driving or at-

tempting to drive " must not be equated with " driver " or the person
" actually driving " nor should the test be whether the defendant has
finished his journey. These latter tests as expressed in *R.* v. *Price*
[1968] 3 All E.R. 814, *Campbell* v. *Tormey* [1969] 1 All E.R. 961 and
R. v. *Wall* [1969] 1 All E.R. 968n. were inappropriate. It is an
offence to be " in charge " and this can be contrasted with the offence
of " driving or attempting to drive ". For a person to be " driving "
the vehicle need not be in motion. The motorist may be in the
driving seat of a vehicle stationary at a traffic jam or he may have
got out to clean his windscreen, nor might it make a difference if he
got out to buy a newspaper from a pavement vendor (but it would if
he stopped and got out to go shopping or if his passenger did—he
would then not be driving but waiting for his passenger) (Lord Reid).
He may be stationary at traffic lights, in traffic congestion, or at a
railway crossing (Lord Guest). He may still be said to be driving
when he leaves the vehicle for a purpose connected with the driving
of the vehicle such as filling up with petrol or changing a wheel.
But different considerations arise if he dismounts for a purpose
unconnected with the driving (Lord Guest): see below. A person
is obviously driving although held up in an almost interminable
traffic block, or at a level crossing or at traffic lights or if he merely
fills up with petrol, nor would it make any difference if in a traffic
block he switched off the engine (Lord Upjohn).

These judgments were analysed by the Divisional Court in
Stevens v. *Thornborrow* [1969] 3 All E.R. 1487 (motorist, although
still in driving seat, held not to be " driving or attempting to drive "
after he had stopped and switched off the engine and continued a
discussion for twenty minutes with his passengers). The following
propositions were extracted from *Pinner* v. *Everett* by the Divisional
Court:—

(1) Whether a person is " driving or attempting to drive " is a
question of fact.

(2) It is far easier to find as a fact that a motorist is driving if he is
still at the wheel, more difficult if he has dismounted.

(3) The overriding principle, whether or not he is at the wheel,
is whether he is doing something connected with driving.

The second of the two cases to go to the House of Lords is
Sakhuja v. *Allen* [1972] 2 All E.R. 311. The defendant in the case
was observed exceeding the speed limit; he evaded the attempts of
the police to stop him on the road, was chased by the police and
by the time he could be required to take a breath test had reached
home. The question certified by the Court of Appeal was:
" Whether, on the true construction of section 2 (1) of the Road
Safety Act, 1967 [now s. 8 (1) of the Act of 1972] in cases where a

suspicion arises with respect to a person driving while his vehicle is in motion, that person, if immediately pursued by a constable in uniform, may be required to provide a specimen of breath for a breath test, notwithstanding that at the conclusion of the pursuit he is no longer a person driving or attempting to drive a motor vehicle on a road or other public place." All five members of the Appellate Committee of the House of Lords were unanimous in holding that while the *suspicion* of the commission of a traffic offence or consumption of alcohol must arise while the motorist was " driving or attempting to drive ", the actual *requirement* does not have to be given while the defendant was " driving or attempting to drive " so long as it formed part of a relevant single transaction or chain of events flowing from the driving. The members of the Appellate Committee differed, however, in the grounds upon which they arrived at their decision. Lord Hailsham, L.C., and Viscount Dilhorne disapproved of the grounds of the majority in the decision of *Pinner* v. *Everett*. The majority however in *Sakhuja* considered themselves bound by *Pinner* v. *Everett*, and it must be regarded as settled, unless and until *Pinner* v. *Everett* is reconsidered by the House of Lords, that the suspicion of the constable in uniform must arise while the motorist is still " driving or attempting to drive ".

Whether a person is " driving or attempting to drive " is a question of fact. As it is a question of fact, it must normally be left to be decided by the jury. It is only if there is an admission under s. 10 of the Criminal Justice Act, 1967, or where the issue of whether the motorist was driving has not been contested that it is permissible for the judge to direct the jury that the motorist was driving; if the accused disputes the question as to whether he was driving, the issue must be left to the jury (*R.* v. *Guttridge* [1973] R.T.R. 135). The judge is entitled to comment on the issue in strong language, if the facts justify him so doing, provided he makes it clear that he is merely commenting and not directing the jury (*ibid.*). But in *R.* v. *Kelly* [1970] R.T.R. 301 a differently constituted Court of Appeal held that where the primary facts as to whether a person is " driving or attempting to drive " are not in dispute the presiding judge was entitled to direct the jury as to their verdict. The Court of Appeal in *Guttridge, supra,* said that in such circumstances the only safe course was nevertheless to leave the matter to the jury. In *R.* v. *Herd* [1973] R.T.R. 165 the Court of Appeal, Lord Widgery, C. J., James, L. J., and Nield, J., declined to follow *R.* v. *Guttridge* and preferred *R.* v. *Kelly*. In *R.* v. *Herd* the facts were agreed, and at the conclusion of the prosecution case on a submission that these facts did not constitute a case for the defendant to answer inasmuch as on these facts the defendant was not " driving or attempting to drive ", the judge overruled the submission and directed the jury to convict. In upholding the conviction, Lord Widgery, C.J. (at p. 169, letter G) followed *R.* v. *Kelly* and stated that the difference in judicial opinion will be resolved in the fullness of time. A yet further differently constituted Court of Appeal in *R.* v. *Martin* [1973] R.T.R. 171, heard some six months before *Herd,* held that where a jury had to draw an inference from undisputed primary facts, the jury should not be directed as to their verdict, and the conviction was quashed. It was said in this case that it was only in some cases that a jury should be directed to convict. Finally the difference in judicial opinion referred to by Lord Widgery in *R.* v. *Herd* now seems to be resolved by the decision of *R.* v. *Bates* [1973] R.T.R. 264 where a Court of Appeal presided over by Lord Widgery decided that the principle stated in *R.* v. *Kelly* should be regarded as erroneous and the principle of *R.* v. *Jones (E.J.M.)* [1970] R.T.R. 56 should be followed, that the paramount consideration is the constitutional requirement that issues of fact should always ultimately be decided by a jury and not be the subject of a direction. The final paragraph of the judgment of Lord Widgery deserves quotation as providing a summary of the position. At p. 267 he stated:

" We think, therefore, that when a trial involves the question whether the motorist was or was not driving at the appropriate time, the issue should, in the end, be left to the jury. There will, of course, be cases in which the judge, with his knowledge of the authorities, may have to indicate to the jury that the argument is really all one way. In *Edkins* v. *Knowles* [1973] R.T.R. 257 the court summarized the main principles upon which this issue depends, and if the judge finds that applying those principles a conclusion one way or the other seems to him virtually inevitable, he is entitled in his discretion to make his views clear. We think, however, that in the end, the matter should be left to the jury, and that for the future at any rate, the principle of *R.* v. *Jones (E.J.M.)* should be preferred ".

The principle of *R.* v. *Jones* is simply that unless there are admissions the issue is one of fact that must be left to the jury.

The phrase " driving or attempting to drive " despite the explanation of its meaning in the various speeches of the Appellate Committee members in *Pinner* v. *Everett* and *Sakhuja* v. *Allen* continued to give rise to a large number of appeals to the Divisional Court and the Court of Appeal. All the cases were reviewed by a five-member Divisional Court in *Edkins* v. *Knowles* [1973] R.T.R. 257. In order to ensure that the matter was adequately considered not only were the court assisted by leading counsel for both parties to the appeal but also leading counsel was instructed by the Treasury Solicitor as *amicus curiae.*

Possibly to avoid any confusion as to the grounds of the decision, only one judgment was given, that of Griffiths, J. Having regard to the composition of the court and the manner in which the case was considered, his judgment was clearly intended to be and, it is submitted, is, a definitive judgment as to when a person is, or is not, " driving or attempting to drive ". There are some earlier cases which may appear to conflict with *Edkins* v. *Knowles*; it is submitted that, even if this is so, and even if the decision is one of the Court of Appeal, it is difficult to rely on them in preference to *Edkins* v. *Knowles* as many of such cases may have been decided without other cases of equal standing being cited. As was said in *R.* v. *Herd* [1973] R.T.R. at pp. 167 and 169 " [The decisions] present a morass to judges and counsel, rationalisation of all the earlier cases ' on driving or attempting to drive ' is impossible." After stating that all the cases had been considered and that it was not necessary for there to be an elaborate citation of authority (p. 262, letter J) and that it was not possible to reconcile all the decisions one with another, the court summarised the collective effect of the two House of Lords decisions of *Pinner* v. *Everett* and *Sakhuja* v. *Allen* and all the various Court of Appeal and Divisional Court cases in five propositions as follows:—

1. The vehicle does not have to be in motion; there will always be a brief interval of time after the vehicle has been brought to rest and before the motorist has completed those operations necessarily connected with driving, such as applying the handbrake, switching off the ignition and securing the vehicle, during which he must still be considered to be driving.

2. When a motorist stops before he has completed his journey he may still be driving; an obvious example is when he is halted at traffic lights. Each case will depend upon its own facts, but generally the following questions will be relevant: (*a*) What was the purpose of the stop? If it is connected with the driving, and not for some purpose unconnected with the driving, the facts may justify a finding that the drving is continuing although the vehicle is stationary. (*b*) How long was he stopped? The longer he is stopped the more difficult it becomes to regard him as still driving. (*c*) Did he get out of the vehicle? If he remains in the vehicle it is some though not a conclusive indication that he is still driving.

3. If a motorist is stopped by a constable in uniform who immediately forms the suspicion that the motorist has alcohol in his body, the motorist should be regarded as still driving at the moment when the suspicion is formed: but if an appreciable time elapses before the constable's suspicion is aroused it will be a question of fact and degree whether the motorist is still to be considered as driving at that time.

4. When a motorist has arrived at the end of his journey then subject to the brief interval referred to in 1 above he can no longer be regarded as driving.
5. When a motorist has been effectively prevented or persuaded from driving he can no longer be considered to be driving.

A close examination of these five principles, particularly 1 and 3 above, demonstrates that the police are not prohibited from " random testing " in any way. The power of stopping a motor vehicle under s. 159 of the Act of 1972 is not related in any way to the operation of the drink/driving provisions in the Act. Once, however, a vehicle is stopped, it is possible then for the first time for a constable to suspect the motorist of consuming alcohol. Provided at the time the constable's suspicions arose the motorist is still " driving or attempting to drive ", the constable is lawfully entitled to require the motorist to take a breath test even though the motorist was stopped " at random ". In *R.* v. *Needham* [1974] R.T.R. 201, the Court of Appeal, three weeks after the decision of *Edkins* v. *Knowles*, arrived at the same conclusion on this point and specifically held there was nothing in the statutory provisions to prevent random stopping; they declined to introduce any further provision as to the circumstances of the stopping of the vehicle which could lead to a lawful demand for a breath test. The matter may, it is submitted, be summarised by stating that the police are not prohibited from random stopping of motor vehicles but are prohibited from requiring breath tests " at random " because a breath test can only be required if the constable's suspicion arose while the motorist was " driving or attempting to drive " (for further authority supporting the decision in *R.* v. *Needham*, see *Harris* v. *Croson* [1973] R.T.R. 57 and *R.* v. *Gaughan* [1974] R.T.R. 195 and *Adams* v. *Valentine* [1975] Crim.L.R. 239 where it was emphasised that the power to stop a vehicle and the power to administer a breath test are not to be confused, once a vehicle is stopped and the constable's suspicion of alcohol immediately arises, the driver is still " driving or attempting to drive ").

In *Newsome* v. *Hayton* [1974] R.T.R. 9, the Divisional Court refused to disturb a finding of fact by a Crown Court hearing an appeal from a magistrates' court that because an appreciable interval of time " had elapsed between the stopping of the vehicle and when the constable's suspicion of alcohol first arose ", the motorist was therefore not " driving or attempting to drive ". The court nevertheless observed that if principles 2 and 3 of *Edkins* had been brought to the attention of the Crown Court a different conclusion of fact might have been reached. In *R.* v. *Gready* [1974] R.T.R. 16 leave to appeal was refused by the Court of Appeal where a constable smelt alcohol on a defendant's breath " almost immediately " after the vehicle had been stopped by him.   In *R.* v. *Reid (Philip)* [1973] R.T.R. 536, the Court of Appeal confirmed that a motorist did not cease to be " driving or attempting to drive " when he got out of his car to answer the questions of a constable who believed some kind of offence might have been committed and was making routine enquiries as to the motorist's name and address, when he then smelt drink on the appellant's breath.   The fifth principle in *Edkins* v. *Knowles* was applied in *R.* v. *Bates* [1973] R.T.R. 264, where the defendant had been effectively prevented from driving by another motorist who detained him until a police patrol came on the scene.   But the fact that a constable asks the motorist to wait until the breath test equipment is brought does not break the chain of events nor does it amount to an arrest, even though a constable has power to arrest under s. 8 (5) for failing to supply a breath test if the motorist had attempted to run away before the equipment arrived (*R.* v. *Coleman* [1974] R.T.R. 359).   A combination of unspoken thoughts and physical inaction place no man under restraint (*ibid.*).   In *Hay* v. *Shepherd* [1974] R.T.R. 64 also it was held that a motorist cannot argue that he was effectively prevented or stopped from driving (see proposition 5 in *Edkins* v. *Knowles*) once a motorist has been stopped by a constable if the circumstances fit proposition 3 in *Edkins* v. *Knowles*.

It will be seen that the time when the suspicion of alcohol arose is vital.   The suspicion of alcohol must not arise after the motorist has ceased to drive or attempt to drive, but there appears nothing to prevent a constable's suspicion of alcohol arising before the motorist began driving.   In *R.* v. *Furness* [1973] Crim.L.R. 759 a defendant who was unsteady on his feet outside a public house told the constable he was going home by taxi.   Half an hour later the constable saw him driving out of the car-park, stopped him and required him to take a breath test.   The Court of Appeal upheld his conviction, holding that the constable could rely on the suspicion he formed earlier.   Where one police officer suspects alcohol and communicates his suspicions to another officer who as a result requires the motorist to take a breath test, the relevant time at which the suspicion arose was not when the suspicion was communicated to the other officer but when the first constable's suspicion arose (*R.* v. *Evans (Terence)* [1974] R.T.R. 232).   If the motorist was driving when he was seen by the first constable, the sole question is whether there was a continuous chain of events from that time up to the time the second constable required the breath test (*ibid.*).

In *Trigg* v. *Griffin* (1969), 113 S.J. 962, the conviction of the defendant was quashed by the Divisional Court on the ground that, although the defendant was a person " driving or attempting to drive ", he was not " on a road or public place " because he had driven from the road onto a private forecourt of lock-up garages, one of which was used by him. In *R. v. Jones E.J.M.* [1970] 1 All E.R. 209, the Court of Appeal disapproved of *Trigg* v. *Griffin.* A motorist cannot, said the Court of Appeal, stultify police action by turning a few feet off the highway. As long as the police have reasonable suspicion of the driver having consumed alcohol or having committed a moving traffic offence, the police may pursue the driver in order to make a breath test requirement. Following the line of decisions relating to arrest and " fresh pursuit " the Court of Appeal in *R. v. Jones* ruled that a driver cannot escape the requirement by driving onto private property. The breath test may thus be " off the road ", provided it is made " in the course of actions following sufficiently closely on an observed driving on the road ".

The same point arose for consideration by the Divisional Court in *Sasson* v. *Taverner* [1970] 1 All E.R. 215. A constable, having reasonable cause to suspect the motorist of having committed a moving traffic offence, chased the car into the car-park of the motorist's residence and made the breath test requirement after he had switched off the engine and lights and got out of the driver's door. The Divisional Court followed *R.* v. *Jones,* holding that the whole sequence of events was so closely related as to form a single transaction.

Sasson v. *Taverner* and *R.* v. *Jones* were unanimously upheld by the House of Lords in *Sakhuja* v. *Allen,* where it was held that as long as the suspicion of alcohol or moving traffic offence arose while the motorist was " driving or attempting to drive " the actual requirement could be made after he had ceased to be regarded as " driving or attempting to drive " as long as there was a continuous chain of events from the time when the suspicion first arose up to the time of the requirement. It would appear that whether there is a continuous chain of events is essentially a matter of fact to be determined by the jury. In *R.* v. *Coleman* [1974] R.T.R. 359 the jury were directed that it was for them to be satisfied by the prosecution that there was no break in the chain of events. Indeed, as was said by Lord Hailsham, L.C., in *Sakhuja* v. *Allen* (at p. 330, letter C), whether the chain is broken is a question of fact and degree.

In *Edkins* v. *Knowles* itself the motorist was followed by two plain clothes officers, and it would appear that their suspicions of alcohol were not communicated to a police officer in uniform until some five minutes after the motorist had ceased " driving and attempting to drive ". For this reason the conviction of the motorist was set aside. If ignition keys are removed by another person, this will usually effectively prevent the motorist from further driving and in accordance with principle (5) enunciated in *Edkins* v. *Knowles* on p. 189 he can no longer be said to be "driving or attempting to drive".

In Scotland a motorist was acquitted of an offence under s. 6 (1) in such circumstances (*Cruickshank* v. *Devlin* [1973] S.L.T. (Sh.Ct.) 81). Similarly in England a motorist was held no longer to be " driving or attempting to drive " when he had been effectively prevented from going any further by handing over the ignition keys to a security guard before the arrival of the police (*Harman* v. *Wardrop* [1971] R.T.R. 127), but the fact that the keys are handed over is not necessarily in all cases sufficient to amount to a cesser of " driving or attempting to drive "; each case depends on why the keys were handed over and in what circumstances (*R.* v. *Cooper* [1974] R.T.R. 489).

Reasonable Cause to Suspect Alcohol or Moving Traffic Offence

Before a constable can require a breath test under s. 8 (1) he must have reasonable cause to suspect the motorist either of having alcohol in his body or of having committed a traffic offence whilst the vehicle was in motion.

It is clear that the test is not whether the motorist has actually consumed alcohol or actually committed a traffic offence. What matters is whether the constable has reason to suspect consumption of alcohol or a moving traffic offence. It is for the prosecution to prove that the constable had reasonable cause to suspect but it may be no defence (nor is it a reasonable excuse for failing to supply a specimen for laboratory testing) that in fact alcohol may not have been consumed (see *McNicol* v. *Peters* [1969] S.L.T. 261). If a moving traffic offence is suspected then it is not a reasonable excuse for failing to supply a specimen for laboratory testing for the defendant to believe that he had not committed a moving traffic offence. All that the prosecution must prove is that the constable had reasonable cause to suspect he had committed a traffic offence while the vehicle was in motion (*R.* v. *Downey* [1970] Crim.L.R. 287).

Nor is it necessary for the constable's grounds of suspicion to be first-hand. A constable has been held by the English High Court to have reasonable ground for suspecting a motorist of having consumed alcohol when his only source of knowledge is what he has been told by another constable (*Erskine* v. *Hollin* [1971] R.T.R. 199). The Scottish High Court came to a similar conclusion when it was held that a uniformed officer could have reasonable cause for suspicion when he has been called in for this purpose by

plain-clothes police officers (*Copeland* v. *McPherson* [1970] S.L.T.
87). In *R.* v. *Moore* [1970] Crim.L.R. 650 it was held that when
a police constable received a wireless message to the effect that the
driver was believed to be drunk it was not possible for it to be
argued that the constable had no reasonable cause to suspect
alcohol and, although the judge should have left the matter to the
jury, the Court of Appeal applied the proviso and dismissed the
appeal. *Erskine* v. *Hollin, supra,* was applied in *R.* v. *Evans* (*Terence*)
[1974] R.T.R. 232 where it was held that a police patrolman who
had been informed by radio of a foot constable's suspicion of alcohol
of a motorist seen driving erratically could thereby himself have
reasonable cause to suspect the motorist.

Can a constable have reasonable cause to suspect if his informant
is not a police officer? It is submitted that this is primarily a
question of fact, not law, and the answer in practice will depend
entirely on who was the informant, the precise nature of the information given and all the surrounding circumstances. However, it
would be customary for a constable to state the grounds of his suspicion to the motorist before making the requirement and if there
is any truth in the allegation either the answer of the motorist
or the manner in which the answer is given might well provide
sufficient justification for the constable to confirm his suspicions.

A " U " turn in a road, wrong indicator and excess speed do
not of themselves indicate a reasonable suspicion of alcohol and if
these are the only facts the court will quash a conviction based on
these facts alone being held as sufficient to constitute a suspicion
of alcohol (*Williams* v. *Jones* [1972] R.T.R. 4). If it is a matter of
fact primarily for the jury, a conviction will only be quashed where
the evidence as a matter of law could not support reasonable
grounds for suspicion (*R.* v. *Fardy* [1973] R.T.R 268). In considering whether a constable had reasonable grounds for forming a
suspicion regard was to be had to all the circumstances, and the
fact that the incident occurred at 3.30 a.m. was not to be overlooked
(*ibid.*). Even where a constable may not have reasonable cause to
suspect alcohol from the defendant's driving (circling a roundabout
very slowly early in the morning and turning very hesitantly into
a road already passed) the constable's initial suspicions may be
confirmed by his smelling alcohol after stopping the motorist
provided the motorist was still " driving or attempting to drive "
(in accordance with *Edkins* v. *Knowles*: see p. 188) when the constable
smelt the alcohol (*Hay* v. *Shepherd* [1974] R.T.R. 64). In *R.* v.
McGall [1974] R.T.R. 216 it was again held that all the circumstances had to be considered as to whether a constable had reasonable cause to suspect a motorist of alcohol; abnormally slow driving

for no apparent reason late at night with a trafficator unjustifiably repeated after correction could give rise to reasonable suspicion; *R.* v. *Fardy, supra,* and *Williams* v. *Jones, supra,* should be regarded as illustrations of the principle that if there is insufficient evidence to go before a jury, it should not go before a jury but on the other hand if there is sufficient evidence to go to a jury, an appellate court should be slow to interfere (*ibid.*). Twice driving over a central white line could not possibly give rise by itself to suspicion of alcohol, but where a motorist was stopped as a result by constables who then smelt alcohol, his conviction was upheld as the defendant when stopped was still " driving or attempting to drive " in accordance with *Edkins* v. *Knowles* (*R.* v. *McGall, supra*).

The constable only has to have reasonable cause to suspect consumption of alcohol *or* the commission of a traffic offence while the vehicle is in motion. He does not have to suspect both. In practice a constable rarely requires a motorist to take a breath test merely because he sees the motorist committing a traffic offence, but he almost certainly will only require a motorist to take a breath test if he has some sort of reason to suppose the motorist has been consuming alcohol. Nevertheless the commission of a moving traffic offence by itself provides a legal justification for a requirement to take a breath test. The suspicion of alcohol may arise after the motorist has ceased to be " driving or attempting to drive " while suspicion of a traffic offence will necessarily have arisen while the vehicle is being driven. In such an instance the policeman is entitled to rely on the suspicion of a traffic offence in order legally to require a breath test. In *Timmins* v. *Perry* [1970] R.T.R. 477 a constable saw the defendant, who was alone in the vehicle, driving a motor van with " L " plates. The van stopped, and the constable went up to it and questioned the defendant whether or not he had a full licence. The suspicion of alcohol arose after the defendant had got out of the van. The Divisional Court held that, although the suspicion of alcohol may have arisen when the driver was no longer driving or attempting to drive, it was an " irresistible inference " that the constable had suspected a traffic offence while the van was in motion because the defendant was the only person in the van when it was driven bearing " L " plates.

A conviction was set aside on the ground that the facts were such that a constable could have no reasonable cause to suspect the consumption of alcohol (*Williams* v. *Jones* (see p. 193). In that case the defendant had undoubtedly committed a moving traffic offence but because the case throughout had been presented on the basis that suspicion of alcohol was the sole consideration the Court of Appeal nevertheless quashed the conviction.

Traffic Offence

A traffic offence is defined as any offence under any provision of the Act except Pt. V (which relates to the registration, etc., of driving instructors), any offence under any provision of Pt. III of the Road Traffic Act, 1960 (which relates to public service vehicles), and any offence under any provision of the Road Traffic Regulation Act, 1967. Offences under the regulations made under those Acts are probably included (*Bingham* v. *Bruce* [1962] 1 All E.R. 136; *Rathbone* v. *Bundock* [1962] 2 All E.R. 257), but offences under any other Acts or regulations made thereunder are not.

The traffic offence must have been committed while the vehicle was in motion. Thus driving without lights justifies a test (see, e.g., *R.* v. *Price* [1968] 3 All E.R. 814 and *Witts* v. *Williams* on p. 198) but not driving with an unilluminated rear number plate, as for example in *Pinner* v. *Everett* [1969] 3 All E.R. 257, because this offence is contrary to Regulations made under the Vehicles (Excise) Act, 1971. Is taking a conveyance (s. 12 of the Theft Act, 1968, which replaced the offence of taking and driving away under the Road Traffic Act, 1960 in England and Wales) still included in the definition? It is thought that s. 38 (1) of the Interpretation Act, 1889, may have the effect of including s. 12 of the Theft Act in the definition (for a case on s. 38 (1) which might be helpful in this context, see *Lovell* v. *Duckett*; *Lovell* v. *Archer* [1971] R.T.R. 237).

In *Anthony* v. *Jenkins* [1971] R.T.R. 19 the defendant was actually arrested under s. 12 of the Theft Act. The case was dealt with on the basis that the constable suspected the consumption of alcohol after the defendant had been arrested and the point whether the constable had reasonable cause to suspect the defendant of having committed a moving traffic offence, namely, taking a conveyance, was not mooted.

Requirement of Breath Test Following Accident (s. 8 (2))

The other situation entitling a constable lawfully to require a breath test is where there has been an accident.

A constable may require a breath test of a person who he has reasonable cause to believe *was* driving or attempting to drive a vehicle owing to the presence of which on a road or other public place an accident occurred. Unlike a requirement under s. 8 (1), the motorist is not required to *be* driving or attempting to drive; the past tense is used in s. 8 (2). The motorist may still be " driving or attempting to drive ", he may merely be " in charge " or he may even be neither. There is no requirement that the breath test should be made as soon as reasonably practicable. It is irrelevant whether, at the time when the breath test was required, the person was " driving or attempting to drive " (R. v. Warr (1969), 113 S.J. 287). The constable may require the " post-accident " test solely on his belief that the motorist was driving a vehicle involved in an accident perhaps even hours before: it is immaterial that the constable has no evidence that the driver had consumed alcohol or had driven carelessly or dangerously or had committed any traffic offence. The sole criterion as to the lawfulness of the requirement is whether the constable had a reasonable belief that the motorist had been driving the vehicle, and that as a result of the vehicle being present on a road or other public place an accident had occurred. (Nevertheless, of course, a person cannot be convicted under s. 6 (1) or s. 9 (3) unless the prosecution prove that he was driving or attempting to drive at the relevant time.)

Accident

There has to be an " accident ". This is a question of fact which should be left to the jury and should not be decided as a preliminary point by the presiding judge (R. v. Seward [1970] 1 W.L.R. 323). Although it was held in R. v. Pico [1971] Crim.L.R. 599, that if the facts are not really in dispute (applying R. v. Kelly, supra), a conviction will not be set aside if the defendant was merely deprived of the chance of the jury returning a thoroughly perverse verdict and in R. v. Morris [1972] 1 All E.R. 384, Lord Widgery, C.J., stated that, where matters of law only were important, the judge could give a ruling, these cases were decided before R. v. Bates (see p. 187). It is suggested that because R. v. Kelly was disapproved, the principle of R. v. Jones (E.J.M.) [1970] R.T.R. 56 should also be applied, so that wherever there is a question of whether there was an accident (i.e., unless an admission is made) the question must be left to the jury. The meaning of the word " accident " was considered in R. v. Morris. " Accident " in the section should bear its ordinary meaning and the court unanimously agreed that it might be defined for the purposes of the section as " an unintended occurrence which had an adverse physical result ". No other vehicle need be involved, as in R. v. Pico, supra, where the defendant's car hit the kerb and a gatepost, injuring the defendant and damaging the gate. Similarly in R. v. Harling [1970] R.T.R. 441 no other vehicle was apparently involved. Where an accident occurs it is not necessary for the defendant's vehicle to be physically involved in the accident; it is only necessary for there to be a direct causal connection between the presence of the defendant's vehicle on the road and the accident occurring (see Quelch v. Phipps [1955] 2 All E.R. 302 and the discussion of the words " owing to the presence of a motor vehicle on a road " on p. 346).

The subsequent analysis of the blood or urine obtained as a result of a requirement under s. 8 (2) following an accident must relate to the blood/alcohol level at the time of the accident. If, therefore, a motorist consumes alcohol after the accident but before supplying a specimen of blood or urine for analysis, this invalidates the analysis and he must be acquitted even if the prosecution can show that his blood/alcohol level would have been in excess despite allowance being made for his post-accident consumption of alcohol (*Rowlands* v. *Hamilton, supra,* p. 181; although this case, despite its being a House of Lords case, has not been strictly followed in Scotland (see *Ritchie* v. *Pirie,* p. 181)). If, however, a defendant returns to the scene of the accident after fortifying himself at a public house, he will normally be "in charge" and may be convicted under s. 6 (2) (see *R.* v. *Lawrence* on p. 182).

"Requirement" of the Breath Test

Both under s. 8 (1) and under s. 8 (2) the statute states that a police constable may "require" the motorist to take a breath test. The constable does not have to use a particular formula when he requires the motorist to take a breath test. The words "I intend to give you a breath test" were held sufficient in *R.* v. *O'Boyle* [1973] R.T.R. 445, and "I wish to give you a breath test" were held sufficient in *R.* v. *Clarke (Christopher)* (1969), 113 S.J. 428. As long as the language used can fairly be said to be capable of amounting to a requirement, it is a question of fact for the jury as to whether a constable required the motorist to take a breath test (*R.* v. *O'Boyle, supra*). It is not necessary for the words used by the constable to have been heard or understood by the motorist if they were spoken to him in the honest and reasonable belief that they were heard and understood, provided that the constable did not act in bad faith (*R.* v. *Nicholls* [1974] R.T.R. 308) (see also p. 205).

There or Nearby

The breath test under s. 8 (1) must be made "there or nearby". This is a matter of fact and degree in all the circumstances of the particular case and, as it is a question of fact, the High Court will regard itself as bound by a finding of fact by the magistrates (*Arnold* v. *Hull Chief Constable* [1969] 3 All E.R. 646, where a charge was dismissed on the ground that a police station one and a half miles away was not "there or nearby"). In *Donegani* v. *Ward* [1969] 3 All E.R. 636 the Divisional Court again refused to disturb a finding by the justices, this time that 160 yards away was not "there or nearby". Although the Divisional Court held themselves to be bound by a finding of fact by the magistrates it is submitted that the

Divisional Court would review a perverse finding of fact by magistrates as a point of law.

As Soon as Reasonably Practicable

Where a defendant has been stopped by reason of a traffic offence the breath test must be made as soon as reasonably practicable. This question is again one of fact and degree for the magistrates or jury. " As soon as reasonably practicable " does not have to be explained to the jury, it is a matter of pure commonsense; cases on " reasonably practicable " under the Factory Acts have no relevance to the Road Traffic Act (*R.* v. *Pearson (Donald)* [1974] R.T.R. 92). In *Arnold* v. *Hull Chief Constable, supra,* the charge was also dismissed because the requirement was more than twenty-five minutes after the offence. Failing to carry proper lights is a continuing offence. Where, therefore, a constable followed a vehicle with defective lights for 2½ miles and did not attempt to stop him until the defendant drove off the road into his own property, it was held that the requirement had been made as soon as reasonably practicable (*Witts* v. *Williams* [1974] Crim.L.R. 259). Many constables on foot or cycle patrol will not carry breathalysers and will have to telephone or radio for one to be brought by police car or motorcycle; it is suggested that this is the most immediately practicable way of getting a breathalyser to the scene and that any resultant delay is excusable. The breath test may be made off the public road provided that the suspicion of alcohol or committing a traffic offence arose while the defendant was driving on a public road and that the requirement was made following an unbroken chain of events (see *Sakhuja* v. *Allen* and other cases on p. 185, and *R.* v. *Coleman* on p. 191).

There is no requirement that the breath test should be made as soon as reasonably practicable where the ground for the requirement is the suspicion of alcohol under s. 8 (1) (*a*).

If the breath test is made under s. 8 (2) following an accident the breath test may be made at a hospital if the motorist is at the hospital as a patient, or if not at the hospital it may be either at or near the place where the requirement is made or, if the constable thinks fit, at a police station specified by him. A motorist may be required by a constable to take a breath test in the ambulance which is taking him to hospital; an ambulance is not " a hospital " for this purpose and no consent of a doctor is required (*Hollingsworth* v. *Howard* [1974] R.T.R. 58). A breath test made following an accident does not have to be made as soon as reasonably practicable.

The constable requiring the breath test following an accident must have reasonable cause to believe the defendant was driving the motor vehicle at the time of the accident. Where a defendant voluntarily accompanied the police officer to a police station and the station sergeant then required the breath test, it was held that the defendant was entitled to be acquitted of a charge under s. 6 (1) as the prosecution had not proved that the station sergeant had such a reasonable belief (*Moss* v. *Jenkins* [1975] R.T.R. 25). *Aliter* if the station sergeant had said in evidence what he had been told by the constable, because one police officer can form a reasonable belief on what he had been told by another police officer.

" Constable in Uniform "

The only person who may require a breath test is a " constable in uniform ". Whether a constable is " in uniform " is a question of fact to be proved by the prosecution and determined by the magistrates or jury. In *Wallwork* v. *Giles* (1969), 114 S.J. 36, it was held that a police constable who was not wearing a helmet but who otherwise was in his normal uniform was nevertheless " in uniform ". It was said that the object of the provision was to ensure that the constable might be easily identified as a police constable. It was further suggested that the fact that the constable was driving a police car with a police sign was relevant. It is submitted, with respect, that the nature of the police vehicle is irrelevant. Surely a constable in uniform may require a breath test even if the constable has been driving his own private car? Likewise a detective constable in civilian dress may not make a requirement even though he is driving a standard police patrol car.

The Scottish High Court of Justiciary have held that a constable in uniform may make the requirement in consequence of information received from a constable not in uniform (*Copeland* v. *McPherson* [1970] S.L.T. 87). The Divisional Court in *Erskine* v. *Hollin* [1971] R.T.R. 199 held that a constable in uniform could validly require a breath test on information supplied to him by another police constable, and it was held in *R.* v. *Evans* [1974] R.T.R. 232 that the material time for considering when the suspicion arose was when it arose in the mind of the officer who observed the driving (see p. 190). A " constable " in the section, it is suggested, must refer not to the rank of constable but to any constable of whatever rank and that " constable " refers to any member of any police force within the jurisdiction, including special constables (see s. 19 of the Police Act, 1964). If the constable omits to state that he was in uniform a court are entitled to assume that he was in uniform when he has stated that he was on duty as a motor patrol officer (*Cooper* v. *Rowlands* [1971] R.T.R. 291).

Lawful Administration of the Breath Test Device

For a defendant to have been properly arrested because the breath test was positive under s. 8 (4), the breath test is required to have been properly administered by the police constable.

The breath test device is required to be approved by the Secretary of State (s. 12 of the Act) and the Secretary of State signified his formal approval (as a result of *Scott* v. *Baker* [1968] 2 All E.R. 993) of the Alcotest Device by making the Breath Test Device (Approval) (No. 1) Order, 1968 (a like No. 2 Order was made by the Minister of Defence in respect of servicemen).   The constable giving evidence of the administration of a breath test or a refusal or failure to take a test should always say that the device used was the one so approved. Proof to that effect is essential to prove the preliminary steps necessary to secure a conviction under s. 6 (*Scott* v. *Baker*, *supra*), but so many cases have come before the courts that judicial notice can be taken of the fact that the Alcotest is the device approved by the Home Secretary and proof of the order is unnecessary (*R.* v. *Jones (Reginald)* [1969] 3 All E.R. 1559).   Indeed it has now been held that if a constable simply states that he produced a breathalyser and required the defendant to take a test, the court is entitled to assume, in the absence of the point being challenged by the defence, that the device referred to was the approved Alcotest (R) 80 device (*Cooper* v. *Rowlands* [1971] R.T.R. 291).

The law on the administration of the Alcotest was reviewed by the House of Lords in *D.P.P.* v. *Carey* [1969] 3 All E.R. 1662.

In each box of the device (which contains ten ampoules) there is an instruction leaflet.   In addition to the leaflet the manufacturers print short instructions on the lid of the box.

The short instructions are as follows (the words underlined are as underlined in the instructions):—

" At least 20 minutes should elapse between the consumption of alcoholic drinks and using the ALCOTEST 80.   Smoking during or immediately prior to the test should not be permitted.
1. Scratch both ends of the tube on the built in ampoule saw and break off tips in the snap hole.
2. Insert the green end of the tube into the collar of the empty measuring bag and the white end into the mouthpiece.   Confirm correct assembly by observing that the arrow points towards the bag.
3. The measuring bag must be fully inflated by <u>one single breath in not less than 10 and not more than 20 seconds.</u>
4. The test is positive if a green stain shows past the yellow ring."

The booklet states (*inter alia*):—

(1) General
The <u>ALCOTEST 80</u> objectively determines whether or not the blood

alcohol concentration of a tested person appears to exceed a prescribed limit. Provided the test is correctly carried out the ALCOTEST 80 indicates the order of the alcohol concentration in the blood at the time of the test. If the ALCOTEST 80 gives a positive result, the taking of a subsequent blood sample for legal purposes is justified. . . .

(3) How to use the ALCOTEST 80

. . . The subject being tested must blow through the mouthpiece and tube into the bag until the latter is fully inflated.   This should be done with one single breath in not less than 10 and not more than 20 seconds.

(4) Evaluation of the results

. . . The result is therefore limited to the one observation, i.e. does the green reaction stain pass the yellow ring or not?

*   *   *   *   *

Special points to be observed when testing:

It is essential that at least 20 minutes should elapse between the drinking of alcohol and using the ALCOTEST 80.   This delay should also be observed if mouth sprays have been used or aromatic drinks consumed.

Immediately after the consumption of an alcoholic drink the alcohol remaining in the mouth and in the saliva will cause a falsely high indication which bears no relation to the true blood alcohol level.   After 20 minutes the distorting influence of the mouth alcohol disappears, and the blood alcohol content is thus accurately indicated by the expired air.

A high concentration of tobacco smoke tends to colour the reagent brown. Smoking during or immediately prior to the test should not therefore be permitted.

(5) General Remarks

Packets of ALCOTEST 80 should always be kept closed and protected from strong light, excessive heat, damp or cold.   In these conditions their shelf life is at least three years.

Before use the colour of the indicator reagent should be checked.   This should be a clear yellow colour; any green discolouration indicates a possible leak in the tube, and such a tube should not be used for testing purposes. . . . ''

On the box cover is written:—

" To be stored below
30° C (86° F)
Please protect from
light ''

In *D.P.P.* v. *Carey, supra,* the justices found that the defendant had consumed alcohol within twenty minutes of the test, that he had smoked shortly before and neither police officer had instructed him to fill the bag in not less than 10 nor more than 20 seconds and the question that arose in the case was " *how far does non-compliance with the manufacturers' instructions invalidate a breath test?* '' The House of Lords held:—

(1) That the manufacturers' instructions supplied with the Alcotest formed no part of the device as approved by the Home Secretary.

(2) That the only manufacturers' instructions which necessarily had to be complied with were those as to the assembly of the device.

(3) That provided there was a *bona fide* use of the device by the constable subsequent proof of failure to comply with the other instructions would not invalidate the breath test, and in particular—

(a) *As to the instructions relating to recent consumption of alcohol, i.e., 20 minutes should elapse between consumption of alcohol and the test—*

If the constable had no knowledge of or reasonable cause to suspect the consumption of alcohol within 20 minutes preceding the test (if he had he should wait) or recent smoking it was a valid test even if the motorist had consumed alcohol within 20 minutes of the test. Moreover a police officer had no duty to inquire when a motorist last consumed alcohol.

(b) *As to the instructions relating to inflating the bag in not less than* 10 *seconds or more than* 20 *seconds—*

A direction to the motorist to take a deep breath and blow in the bag was adequate; the officers could see for themselves whether or not the bag had been inflated in 10 or 20 seconds.

(4) (*Per* Lord Diplock) The only relevance of non-compliance with any of the instructions for the use of the Alcotest (other than those relating to its assembly) was that it might be evidence from which the *mala fides* of the constable could be inferred.

Although in *D.P.P.* v. *Carey* the defendant apparently smoked immediately prior to the test, the speeches of the members of the House of Lords Appellate Committee only dealt with this breach of the manufacturers' instructions generally and not specifically. The point, however, arose directly in *Darnell* v. *Portal* [1972] R.T.R. 483, where it was observed that smoking prior to the test should be regarded as irrelevant unless it was so immediate as to raise the possibility of contamination of the specimen of breath. In *Watkinson* v. *Barley* [1975] R.T.R. 136 it was held that a breath test was not to be invalidated by non-compliance with the manufacturers' instructions as to the smoking (see above) unless it was first established that the failure to comply with these instructions could adversely affect the test. The test could only be adversely affected if the amount of smoke in his lungs when he took the test was of sufficiently high concentration (*ibid.*). In *Attorney-General's Reference* (*No. 2* of 1974) [1975] R.T.R. 142 it was pointed out following *Watkinson* v. *Barley* that a high concentration of smoke sufficient to affect the test is not likely to be achieved unless the motorist inhales through the cigarette and exhales into the bag, and that two or three normal inhalations of breath would usually be sufficient for the Alcotest device not to be affected. But where the Alcotest is so affected (and the jury or magistrates must first find this as a fact) then a breath test is invalidated if the constable fails to delay giving the test to a driver whom he knows was smoking very shortly before the test even if the constable was acting in good faith and in ignorance of the manufacturers' instructions (*Attorney-General's Reference* (*No. 2* of 1974)) and, it is submitted, *a fortiori* if the constable knew the driver was still smoking at the time of the test. The mischief which the manufacturers' instruction is aimed to prevent is that smoke stains the Alcotest crystals brown thus obscuring whether the alcohol in the driver's breath has also stained the crystals green. For this reason where there is a question as to whether smoking may have affected the ascertainment of a positive result of a test, it was said (*per* Lord Widgery, L.C.J., in *Butcher* v. *Catteral* (1975), *The Times*, 11th June) that the test could only be challenged by the defence if it was first put to the officer in cross-examination that the crystals either turned brown or were difficult to read and might have turned brown.

The manufacturers advise that the Alcotest must not be stored above a certain temperature. In *Sayer* v. *Johnson* [1970] R.T.R. 286 it was held that unless the defence raised the question whether the device had been properly stored in accordance with the manufacturers' instructions it was unnecessary for the prosecution to prove that the storage requirements had been complied with. In *Gill* v. *Forster* [1970] R.T.R. 372 a constable agreed that it was possible that there might have been occasions when the Alcotest in his car might have been subject to a temperature in excess of that advised by the manufacturers. On this evidence the recorder allowed an appeal. The Divisional Court corrected the recorder and directed him to continue the appeal and apply the test in *D.P.P.* v. *Carey*, *supra*, viz., whether there was any dishonesty or lack of *bona fides* on the part of the constable.

Cases have arisen where the device has been incorrectly assembled. It is clear that a test on an incorrectly assembled or defective device is not a breath test (see *D.P.P.* v. *Carey*, finding (2), p. 202). If as a result the defendant is arrested under s. 8 (4) because the device indicated excess alcohol, then any conviction is invalid. The constable must show that the device was correctly assembled, for example that the tube was inserted the correct way round. Thus in *R.* v. *Coates* [1971] Crim.L.R. 370 the constable made a slip when asked in cross-examination how he assembled the device, but said that he followed the instructions carefully. The conviction was quashed on the ground that the issue of whether it had been correctly assembled had not been left to the jury. If the device indicates excess alcohol when the bag has a hole in it, then if the defendant is then arrested under s. 8 (4) his conviction will be quashed (*Rayner* v. *Hampshire Chief Constable* [1971] R.T.R. 15). While a bag with a hole in it is defective and thus not an approved device (*ibid.*), a device which is slightly corroded, which the constable acting *bona fide* did not notice, is an approved device and a conviction will be affirmed (*R.* v. *Parsons* [1972] R.T.R. 425). The Alcotest has an inbuilt potential to corrode; the relevance of the manufacturers' instructions (see 5 on p. 201) is merely (applying *D.P.P.* v. *Carey*) as to the constable's *bona fides* (*ibid.*).

Conversely, as a breath test on an incorrectly assembled or defective device is not in law a breath test, it is submitted that if the constable realises that the equipment is defective or he has assembled it incorrectly, he may require the motorist to take another breath test on another device. If the motorist then fails or refuses to take the breath test or if the fresh device then indicates excessive alcohol he may then be validly arrested. In *Wright* v. *Brobyn* [1971] R.T.R. 204 a constable administered a breath test within twenty minutes of the motorist consuming alcohol. The breath test proved positive. The constable waited for a sergeant, who arrived in a matter of minutes and, hearing that the defendant had consumed alcohol only ten minutes before, waited until twenty minutes had elapsed, when the defendant was requested to take another breath test. This second test again proved positive. It was held that the first abortive test did not invalidate the conviction following an arrest as a result of the second test.

Positive Breath Test; Failing to Take Breath Test

After being required under either s. 8 (1) or s. 8 (2) to take a breath test, unless the motorist is a patient at a hospital he may be arrested either if the Alcotest gives an indication of excess alcohol or if he fails to supply a specimen of breath.

The Alcotest consists of a glass tube of yellow crystals. Alcoholic breath stains the crystals green and a positive result is shown if the green stain passes the yellow ring marked on the tube. The Alcotest is of no evidential value in showing whether the motorist is guilty of an offence under s. 6. This can be decided only as a result of a laboratory analysis subsequently obtained under the provisions of s. 9. The Alcotest is merely a screening device in order to prevent motorists being unnecessarily arrested and having to undergo the indignity of supplying specimens of blood or urine. It is nevertheless necessary for the constable who has arrested a motorist under s. 8 (4) as a result of a positive breath test to state in evidence that the test was positive. He need not produce the device which was used; evidence can be given of a chattel without it actually being produced (*Miller* v. *Howe* [1969] 3 All E.R. 451). It is normal police practice to destroy the used Alcotest ampoules as they contain corrosive substances. Moreover it is believed that once a tube of crystals has been used, the green may in the course of time creep along the tube. In any event as the tube has been broken at each end, the crystals will be exposed to the atmosphere and may corrode and deteriorate.

By virtue of s. 12 " fail " in relation to providing a specimen (whether of breath or blood or urine) includes " refuse ", and " failure " shall be construed accordingly. So long as clear words are used to show to the defendant that he is being required to give a sample of breath, that suffices, and no particular form of words is needed to show that he is refusing (*R.* v. *Clarke* [1969] 2 All E.R. 1008). So long as the constable when making the requirement honestly and reasonably believes that he is heard and understood, the person concerned may be said to have been " required " to take the test even if that person may not in fact have heard or understood because he was in a dazed or confused state (*R.* v. *Nicholls* [1972] 2 All E.R. 186). *R.* v. *Clarke* and *R.* v. *Nicholls* were applied in *R.* v. *O'Boyle* [1973] R.T.R. 445 where it was held that so long as the words used by the constable could fairly be said to be capable of amounting to a requirement, no set formula had to be used and it was a question of fact for the jury to be satisfied that the defendant was required by the police constable to take a test (see " requirement " on p. 197). It was held in *R.* v. *Ferguson* (1971), 54 Cr.App.R. 415, that once a person had been given the opportunity to do something and did not do it, there was a " failure " to do it. Thus where a motorist refused to wait until the Alcotest arrived and suddenly pushed the constable in the chest and knocked him against the side of the car and said, " I am not waiting," it was held by the Divisional Court in *R.* v. *Wagner* [1970] Crim.L.R. 535 that he had refused the test and the constable was thus justified in arresting him under s. 8 (5). It was also said in the case that a time-lag will often occur between the requirement to take the breath test and its administration. The Alcotest (as in *R.* v. *Wagner*) may not be immediately to hand or it may be necessary to wait because of the fact that the constable had reason to believe that the defendant had consumed alcohol less than twenty minutes before. If a defendant shows by his actions, either by running away or otherwise, that he is refusing the test, he may be arrested under s. 8 (5). He may be convicted of wilfully obstructing the police if he deliberately snatches a drink to render a breath test abortive (*Ingleton* v. *Dibble* [1972] 1 All E.R. 275), and also of the rather more serious offence of attempting to pervert the course of justice. After being lawfully required to take a breath test, a defendant went into his house and took a drink asking his mother to keep the constable out. In upholding the conviction, the Court of Appeal held that once the statutory course of action had been started by a constable having required a breath test, any action thereafter deliberately taken by a motorist to frustrate the statutory procedure could amount to an attempt to pervert the course of justice (*R.* v. *Britton* [1973] R.T.R. 502). Consumption of alcohol is not the only manner in which a person may frustrate the statutory procedure. In *R.* v. *Welsh* [1974] R.T.R. 478 a defendant was also convicted of attempting to pervert the course of justice, because he emptied down the sink the sample of urine he had supplied to the constable for laboratory analysis.

The constable must be careful to arrest the defendant under the right subsection, namely under s. 8 (5) if he " fails " the test or under s. 8 (4) if the test is valid and positive. The House of Lords in *D.P.P.* v. *Carey* [1969] 3 All E.R. 1662 left open the conflict between *R.* v. *Chapman* [1969] 2 Q.B. 436, where it was held that a motorist who failed to inflate the bag in one breath " failed " the breath test under s. 8 (5), and *Brennan* v. *Farrell* [1969] Crim.L.R. 494, where the High Court of Justiciary in Scotland held that a motorist had discharged his obligations under the Act by inflating the bag " albeit in two exhalations ". The position was reviewed in *Rendell* v. *Hooper* [1970] 2 All E.R. 72. In this case the defendant only partly inflated the bag; the constable then handed it back to him and asked him to blow again. He did so and filled it. The breath test then proved positive. It was held that arrest of the defendant was justified under s. 8 (4) of the Act in that it was a valid breath test as the device gave an indication of an excess over the limit. On the other hand it was held that to inflate the bag in two breaths did not amount to a failure under s. 8 (5). It was held in *R.* v. *Thorpe* (*Thomas*) [1974] R.T.R. 465 that the test as laid down by the House of Lords in *D.P.P.* v. *Carey*, viz., whether a constable administered a test in good faith, only applies to a case where there is a positive reading and the defendant is arrested under s. 8 (4) for giving a positive test. Section 8 (4) states: " If it appears to a constable. . . . " but in contrast in s. 8 (5) the test is simply whether or not the person " fails ". It is therefore an objective test and a matter of fact as to whether a person fails a breath test. Although the manufacturers' instructions for the administration of the breath test device state that the bag should be inflated in one single blow of between ten and twenty seconds (see p. 201), s. 12 (3) of the Act states (see p. 155) that references to providing a specimen of breath are references to providing a specimen of breath in sufficient quantity to enable the test to be carried out. In practice, a motorist may not inflate the bag or he may take two or more blows to inflate the bag. A policeman who is of the opinion that the motorist did not inflate the bag or took more than one blow to inflate it, should always inspect the tube to see whether it gives a positive reading before deciding to arrest the defendant under s. 8 (5) for failing the breath test. If the bag although only partly inflated gives a positive reading, the breath may, nevertheless (in accordance with s. 12 (3)), have been of sufficient quantity to provide a positive reading (*R.* v. *Holah* [1973] R.T.R. 74) and the defendant will therefore not have failed to provide a specimen of breath under s. 8 (5). Similarly in *R.* v. *Thorpe* (*Thomas*), *supra*, a conviction was set aside where the defendant made two attempts to inflate the bag and either partly or wholly inflated it, and was arrested for failing to provide a specimen of breath by the constable who did not look to see whether the crystals in the tube had nevertheless given a positive result. *R.* v. *Holah* and *R.* v. *Thorpe* were applied in *Walker* v. *Lovell* [1975] R.T.R. 61. The motorist blew twice for four seconds each time into the bag which did not inflate. As the constable arrested the defendant under s. 8 (5) for failing to provide a specimen instead of s. 8 (4) for giving a positive test, the Divisional Court quashed the conviction because the device had in fact indicated a positive result. Leave to appeal to the House of Lords was granted.

A breath test on an incorrectly assembled device is a nullity. In *Rayner* v. *Hampshire Chief Constable* [1970] Crim.L.R. 703, a motorist was given a breath test on the Alcotest. It was noticed that the bag was not being inflated, because of a hole. The ampoule used with the defective bag gave a positive reading. The defendant subsequently refused another test on a perfect piece of equipment. The constable did not then arrest the defendant for his failing to supply a specimen of breath, but instead used the positive result obtained by the defective first test as the ground for arrest. The conviction was quashed: he could not be validly arrested for failing a test on a defective device. The court made it clear that if he had been arrested for refusing the second test his conviction would have stood. A second breath test can be administered if the first is honestly but mistakenly administered. In *Wright* v. *Brobyn* [1971] R.T.R. 204 a breath test was innocently administered by a constable within twenty minutes of the consumption of alcohol by the driver, but a sergeant arrived who realised (see *D.P.P.* v. *Carey*, p. 201) that the breath test might thus be inaccurate. After the requisite time had elapsed a further test was administered which was again positive and a subsequent arrest under s. 8 (4) and conviction were upheld by the Divisional Court.

Section 8 (5) creates no offence of failing to supply a specimen of breath. It is merely the justification for arrest of the defendant in order to obtain laboratory specimens of blood or urine for analysis. If, therefore, a motorist fails to supply a specimen of breath because of a bronchitic condition he " fails " and may validly be arrested under s. 8 (5), even though his bronchitic condition provides a reasonable excuse for his failure and thus he would not be guilty of an offence under s. 8 (3) (see p. 227). The two subsections (3) and (5) of s. 8 are distinct and separate. The latter is a justification for arrest in order to obtain laboratory specimens; the former creates a summary offence for which a defendant may only be convicted if he has no reasonable excuse for his failure to supply a specimen of breath (*Hirst* v. *Wilson* [1969] 3 All E.R. 1566). In *R.* v. *Kelly* [1972] R.T.R. 447 the defendant was unable to provide a breath test as he had a permanent tracheotomy; in *Hirst* the defendant suffered from bronchitis. Each, no doubt, had a reasonable excuse for failing to provide a specimen of breath, but each nevertheless failed to provide a breath specimen and was validly arrested under s. 8 (5) and convicted. Similarly if there is doubt whether he has a " reasonable excuse " but there is no doubt that he failed to supply a specimen of his breath, his arrest is valid and he may be subsequently convicted of failing to supply a specimen of blood or urine (*R.* v. *Haslam* [1972] R.T.R. 297).

Section 12 (3) states that references to the provision of a specimen of breath are references to the provision of " a specimen thereof in sufficient quantity to enable that test to be carried out " (see *R.* v. *Holah*, *R.* v. *Thorpe*, and *Walker* v. *Lovell*, *supra*).

Arrest

For a defendant to be convicted under s. 6 (1) (" driving or attempting to drive " a motor vehicle with excess blood/alcohol) he must have been arrested, unless he was a patient at a hospital. A conviction under either subsection requires an analysis of a specimen of blood or urine to be taken under s. 9 of the Act. Section 9 only allows a constable to require a specimen for a laboratory test where the defendant has been arrested " under section 5 (5) or 8 ". In

Alderson v. *Booth* [1969] 2 Q.B. 216 it was therefore decided that
there must be an actual arrest. This case was followed in *Campbell*
v. *Tormey* [1969] 1 All E.R. 961, where a conviction was quashed
because the motorist went voluntarily to the police station and was
thus not under arrest. In *Christie* v. *Leachinsky* [1947] A.C. 573 the
House of Lords made plain that where a person is arrested the arresting constable must in ordinary circumstances inform the person
arrested of the true ground of arrest. There are, however, exceptions to this proposition. The first occurs where the defendant by
his own conduct produces the situation which makes it practically
impossible to inform him of the ground of arrest. Thus in *R.* v.
Gordon [1970] R.T.R. 125 the defendant was arrested simultaneously
for insulting behaviour, assault and driving whilst unfit to drive
through drink. One constable managed to say to him: " I am
arresting you for insulting behaviour," but because of his violent,
abusive and excitable behaviour it was not possible to inform
him of the other two grounds of arrest until he arrived at the police
station. The Court of Appeal upheld a conviction under s. 9 (3)
of refusing without reasonable excuse to supply a specimen of blood
or urine for laboratory testing. It was said in *Alderson* v. *Booth*,
supra, at pp. 220–221, that the ground of arrest should be brought
to the defendant's notice, but in *Wheatley* v. *Lodge* [1971] R.T.R. 22
it was held that there was a further exception to the rule that the
ground of arrest must be brought to the defendant's notice. The
defendant in this case was deaf and for that reason did not realise he
had been arrested nor the reason for his arrest, while the constable
for his part rightly thought the defendant was drunk but did not
realise that he was also deaf. Following the dicta in *Alderson* v.
Booth the justices had dismissed the charge, but the Divisional Court
directed a conviction and held that a constable arresting a deaf
person is only required to do that which a reasonable person would
have done in the circumstances.

The question will sooner or later arise as to how the police,
after having arrested the defendant on another charge, for example,
taking a motor vehicle (Theft Act, 1968, s. 12) or driving whilst
disqualified (s. 100 of the 1972 Act), are able to proceed for an offence
of driving with excess blood/alcohol. The late G. S. Wilkinson in his
last edition of this book rightly stated: " Arrest for any other offence,
e.g., stealing a car, does not suffice." Is it possible for the police to
arrest a man for an offence under s. 5 or s. 6 when he has already
been arrested on another charge? There has been no direct
authority on the point. It has been stated that the probable
position is that the police cannot re-arrest a man on a fresh charge
until he is released from custody on the former charge (*per* Lord

Parker in *R.* v. *Gordon, supra,* at p. 126). The question was reserved for a future occasion in *Rooney* v. *Haughton* [1970] 1 All E.R. 1001 and also in *Anthony* v. *Jenkins* [1971] R.T.R. 19. It is quite clear that a person may be validly arrested for a number of offences simultaneously and if one of the offences is under s. 5 or s. 6 of the Act a subsequent conviction will be upheld (*R.* v. *Gordon, supra*). It is therefore difficult to understand why if a simultaneous arrest is valid a subsequent arrest is not. In *R.* v. *Weir* [1972] 3 All E.R. 906 it was pointed out by Judge Bingham that an arrest consists of two elements, (*a*) physical restraint and (*b*) the stated reason for arrest. It was therefore suggested *obiter,* that for a person already arrested for another offence to be arrested under s. 5 or s. 6 the person need only be told of the new reason for his arrest; he does not have to be released in respect of the original offence to be re-arrested under s. 5 or s. 6. It is not uncommon for a criminal to be arrested originally for a minor offence and subsequently to be charged with a graver offence; he is under arrest for the graver offence as soon as he is told of the graver offence.

The prosecution are required to prove that there was an arrest. This is essentially a matter of fact, and where the judge withdraws the question of arrest from the jury a conviction will be quashed (*R.* v. *Veevers* [1971] R.T.R. 47). Likewise where the question of the legality of the arrest arises, e.g., because the defendant asserts that he was not told the reason for his arrest, this again is a matter of fact for the jury to determine and a conviction will be quashed where the legality of the arrest was withdrawn from the jury by the presiding judge (*R.* v. *Coates* [1971] R.T.R. 74). A conviction will also be quashed where the question of arrest is determined as a preliminary point by a " trial within a trial " and the defendant is thereby deprived of raising the issue of whether he was arrested (*R.* v. *Ayres* [1970] R.T.R. 398). The defendant must also be told of the reason for his arrest (*Christie* v. *Leachinsky, supra*). If he is arrested for the wrong reason, he has not been validly arrested for the purpose of securing laboratory specimens. Thus in *R.* v. *Holah* [1973] R.T.R. 74 the defendant was arrested under s. 8 (5) for failing to supply a specimen of breath when he should have been arrested under s. 8 (4) as the Alcotest gave a positive reading. In *R.* v. *Mayne* [1973] R.T.R. 448 a conviction was quashed as the indictment alleged that the defendant had been arrested under s. 6 (4) of the Act of 1960 (now s. 5 (5) of the Act of 1972) when in fact the evidence at his trial was that he had been arrested under the Road Safety Act, 1967 (now s. 8 of the Act of 1972).

Read literally, s. 8 (4) and s. 8 (5) enable only the actual constable who made the breath test requirement to arrest the defendant. No other constable on a literal reading of the two subsections would seem able to do so. In *R.* v. *Tulsiani* [1973] Crim.L.R. 186, a submission of no case to answer was upheld by Judge Graham Hall, where the defendant after being required to take a breath test by one officer fled and was subsequently arrested for failing to supply a specimen of breath by other officers who had been informed by radio of what had happened by the officer who had made the original requirement. It was further observed that the other officers should have again required the defendant to take a breath test and if he then failed they might then arrest him. There is no doubt that on a literal reading of the subsections *R.* v. *Tulsiani* is correct, but *quaere* whether a constable cannot arrest a defendant on another's behalf if he has been authorised or requested to do so by the constable who made the original requirement.

The defendant does not have to be arrested for a specimen for laboratory testing to be validly requested and supplied if the defendant is a patient at a hospital. A person who is no longer a patient at the hospital, may nevertheless be arrested on his being discharged as a patient and supply the sample at the hospital (*Bourlet* v. *Porter* [1973] R.T.R. 293). The fact that a motorist gave a positive breath test and was not arrested because the constable, immediately after the test, was told that the motorist was going to hospital for observation did not invalidate the subsequent procedure at the hospital, where the motorist gave another breath test and subsequently a sample of blood for laboratory analysis (*Goodley* v. *Kelly* [1973] R.T.R. 125). (For the special procedure applicable to hospital patients, see p. 222.)

An arrest under s. 2 (4) of the Road Safety Act, 1967 (now s. 8 (4) of the Act of 1972) is an arrest only for the limited purpose of obtaining a specimen for laboratory testing and the arrested person is entitled to be released as soon as he has supplied a specimen unless detained under s. 4 of the Act (now s. 11 of the Act of 1972). After having supplied a specimen, a motorist entered into a recognizance under s. 38 (2) of the Magistrates' Courts Act, 1952, in a false name. No offence under s. 34 of the Forgery Act, 1861 (acknowledging recognizance in the name of another) was committed as the constable, who had not detained the defendant under s. 4, could not require the defendant to enter into a recognizance. *Quaere* whether, if the constable had detained the defendant under s. 4 (now s. 11), he would have any right to require a recognizance. It is submitted that there is no such right; the only right the constable has is to detain the motorist under s. 11 until he provides a negative breath test.

It does not matter whether the arrest was under s. 5 or s. 8. A valid arrest under one section will often result in a valid conviction under the other section (see " Interaction of ss. 5 and 6 ", pp. 235–237). In *R.* v. *Wall* [1969] 1 All E.R. 968 it was suggested that it was proper for a motorist to be arrested simultaneously both under s. 5 and under s. 8.

Second Breath Test at Police Station

After lawful arrest under s. 8 or arrest under s. 5 (driving whilst unfit through drink) the motorist may be required to supply a specimen of blood or urine for laboratory analysis provided he has been offered a second breath test at the police station.

The second breath test must be offered at the police station to which he is brought for the purpose of acquiring the specimen of blood or urine. Thus he cannot be brought to one police station and there offered another breath test and then taken to another police station where there is a police surgeon available to take a specimen of blood (*Butler* v. *Easton* (1969), 113 S.J. 906). The second breath test, the requirement to provide a specimen for a laboratory test and the actual provision of the specimen are all required to take place at the same station according to *Butler* v. *Easton*, but the Scottish High Court have pointed out in *Milne* v. *McDonald* [1971] S.L.T. 291 that there is " nothing in the statutory provisions to necessitate the actual specimen being taken in the same police station as that in which the requirement [to provide one] was made." With respect, it is submitted that the Scottish decision is correct. Therefore while the offer of the second breath test and the requirement to provide a specimen must be made at the same police station (*Butler* v. *Easton*) the defendant may be taken to another police station to provide it.

The second breath test must be " offered ". It does not have to be accepted, nor is it an offence if it is refused. It is a question of fact whether an opportunity to take a breath test was offered to the motorist, and the burden of proof is upon the prosecution. It is also a question of fact whether the motorist refused or failed to take up the offer. However, if there is no dispute on the facts, the question of whether those facts amount to a refusal then becomes a matter of law (*R.* v. *Ferguson* (1971), 54 Cr.App.R. 415), but *quaere* whether this issue of fact should not be left to the jury unless there are admissions: see *R.* v. *Bates* on p. 187. In this case it was also held that there is a " failure " on the part of a person when that person is given the opportunity to do something and does not do it. Accordingly where the defendant, on being offered the test, simply said he would give a test " when the doctor arrived " it was held that he failed to supply a specimen of breath.

If the defendant takes the breath test and the result is positive the police may then require him to supply a specimen of blood or urine for laboratory testing. Failure to offer a second breath test at the police station is fatal to a prosecution under s. 6 (1) or s. 9 (3). It has not been settled whether the omission of an offer of a breath test is also fatal to a prosecution under s. 5. It is submitted that it is fatal only to the extent that it renders a subsequent laboratory analysis obtained by virtue of s. 9 inadmissible. The police are not required to follow the procedure contained in s. 9 after an arrest for driving whilst unfit to drive through drink or drugs and may rely instead on the procedure for obtaining laboratory specimens contained in s. 7 (1). Where the police suspect that the motorist's ability to drive is impaired because of drugs rather than alcohol the procedure for obtaining laboratory specimens under s. 9 is wholly inappropriate as this section is designed for cases of excessive consumption of alcohol.

It should be noted that it is only if the defendant has been brought to a police station after arrest that he must be offered a second breath test. Where a patient at a hospital gave a positive breath test, consented to supply a specimen for laboratory testing and discharged himself as a patient before providing the laboratory specimen and had thereupon been arrested, it was held by the House of Lords that the Act did not require him to be taken to a police station after arrest, only that if he was taken to a police station the Act required him to be offered a breath test there (*Bourlet* v. *Porter* [1973] R.T.R. 293, reversing *R.* v. *Porter* [1973] R.T.R. 117) (see further " hospital patients ", pp. 222–227).

It should also be noted that after an accident the constable may require the breath test to be provided at a police station specified by him. If this is the situation and the breath test proves positive or the defendant fails or refuses to supply a specimen as a result of which the constable arrests the defendant under s. 8 (4) or s. 8 (5) at the police station, does the law require the defendant to be offered yet another breath test? It was held in *Rooney* v. *Haughton* [1970] R.T.R. 119 that on the true construction of s. 8 (7) he does not have to be offered a second breath test at the same station to which he was brought and subsequently arrested. In *Rooney* the constable, after arresting him at the first police station, took him to another where he gave a second positive test and subsequently provided a specimen of blood for laboratory testing, and the case does not deal with the situation where the police wish to make the requirement at the police station to which the motorist is first brought. It is submitted that on a literal construction of s. 8 (7) and s. 9 (1) the police are under no obligation to provide a second breath test in such a situation where a breath test has been given at a police station specified by the constable under s. 8 (2) following an accident.

Provision of Laboratory Specimens

After the offer of the second breath test and its either being positive or having been refused, a constable may then require the motorist to supply a specimen of blood or urine for laboratory testing.   The requirement has to be made by a constable.   The section does not specify that he need be in uniform, but the requirement cannot, presumably, be made by anyone other than a constable, for example the police doctor.   It is also submitted that the word " constable " refers to anyone holding the office of constable irrespective of rank.

Warning under s. 9 (7)

The constable who makes the requirement is required by s. 9 (7) to warn the motorist that failure to supply a specimen of blood or urine " may make him liable to imprisonment, a fine and disqualification ".   If the constable fails to give the warning the court *may* direct an acquittal or dismiss the charge (s. 9 (7)).

If the warning is not given and the motorist provides a specimen of blood or urine, this is not fatal to a conviction under s. 6 (*R*. v. *Brush* [1968] 3 All E.R. 467).   The court is given a discretion under s. 9 (7) as to whether to direct an acquittal or dismiss the charge, and it should be exercised in favour of the defendant if he has been prejudiced by not being warned of the consequences of his refusal. The court observed that it is difficult to see how a motorist can normally be said to be prejudiced if he gives a specimen despite the fact that he was never warned of the consequences of failure.   On the other hand failure to give the warning is very relevant where the defendant refuses a specimen because it may well provide a " reasonable excuse " for refusing (see *R*. v. *Dolan*, p. 234).   The warning should be given by the constable who requires the motorist to provide the specimen.   According to the wording of the section, the warning may not be given by anyone else, for example, the station sergeant.   However, since failure to give the warning at all is not necessarily fatal to a conviction under s. 6, it is difficult to see how it could ever be fatal for the station sergeant to give the warning instead of the constable who required the specimen.

The constable should warn the defendant that failure to supply a specimen of blood *or* urine renders him liable to the penalties. It is misleading for a constable to demand blood only and then warn the accused that failure to supply blood may lead to the penalties being exacted. Where a defendant provided a specimen of blood in such circumstances, it was held that he was not prejudiced and a conviction under s. 6 was upheld (*R. v. Moore* [1970] Crim.L.R. 650). A similar case with a similar finding that the defendant was not prejudiced is *R. v. Forbes* [1971] Crim.L.R. 174. According to *R. v. Brush, supra*, if a question arises as to whether the warning was given this should be determined by a trial within a trial.

The request for a specimen for laboratory testing may be either for blood or urine (*R. v. Moore, supra*).

The warning under s. 9 (7) refers to the initial " requirement " under s. 9 (1) to provide a specimen of blood or urine for laboratory testing. It does not refer to s. 9 (5) where it is provided that a person shall not be treated as failing to provide a specimen unless he is first " requested " to provide a specimen of blood and if he refuses he is then " requested " to provide specimens of urine but fails to provide them and he is again " requested " to supply a blood specimen. It was thus held in *R. v. Chippendale* [1973] R.T.R. 236 that the warning under s. 9 (7) only had to be given as the initial requirement under s. 9 (1) and did not have to be repeated each time a "request" was made for a specimen in the sequence provided under s. 9 (5)).

Taking of Specimens

Any specimen of blood must be taken by a medical practitioner. Section 12 (2) states that a person may be treated as providing a specimen of blood only if he consents to its being taken by a medical practitioner and it is in fact taken by a medical practitioner. It is clear that if the consent is obtained improperly, the defendant does not consent and a conviction can be quashed. In *R. v. Palfrey*; *R. v. Sadler* [1970] 2 All E.R. 12 the Court of Appeal made it clear that if there was some real substance in an assertion that the specimen of blood or urine was improperly taken either against the will of the defendant or without his true consent, it was for the defendant to raise the issue and show that, at least, there was some substance in it. If some substance was shown the court had a discretion to exclude the evidence improperly obtained. The court referred to *R. v. Payne* [1963] 1 All E.R. 848 (a case on a s. 5 offence), where the defendant before consenting to examination by the police surgeon was told by him that the results of the examination would not be given in evidence, with the result that the court held that the evidence of the examination should be excluded. It is for the doctor to say how the blood specimen should be taken. The defendant cannot insist on the blood being taken from a particular portion of his anatomy selected by him (*Solesbury* v. *Pugh* [1969] 2 All E.R. 1171). If the doctor asks for an intravenous specimen from the arm and the defendant only consents to a capillary specimen from his finger, this is a refusal: *Rushton* v. *Higgins* [1972] Crim.L.R. 440. It was said, *per* Lord Widgery, C.J., that the true *ratio* in *Solesbury* v. *Pugh* was that if a doctor asked to take a specimen in accordance with ordinary medical practice and was met by an offer to provide in a different way, that was a refusal. A motorist refused the initial request for blood, refused to supply specimens of urine but then consented to the final request for blood. The constable thereupon asked the defendant to sign a form consenting to a doctor taking a sample of blood. The motorist on asking and being told by the constable that it would have to be taken from the forearm, indicated he would only allow it to be taken from his thumb. The constable treated this as a refusal. It was held that the constable was justified in asking the motorist to sign a form signifying his consent to save calling the police doctor unnecessarily (*R.* v. *McAllister* [1974] Crim.L.R. 716). Under s. 10 (2) a certificate purporting to be signed by a medical practitioner that he took a specimen of blood from the defendant with his consent is evidence of the qualifications of the medical practitioner and that the defendant consented, etc. A copy must have been served on the defendant not less than seven days before the hearing or trial by personal service or by recorded delivery service or registered post. Rule 55 of the Magistrates' Courts Rules, 1968, prescribes how such service may be proved. " Not less than seven days " seems to mean seven clear days, i.e., excluding the day of service and the day of hearing (*R.* v. *Long* [1959] 3 All E.R. 559). The accused is entitled to require the attendance of the doctor and can do so by similarly serving notice on the prosecutor to that effect " not less than three days " before the hearing or trial or within such further time as the court may in special circumstances allow. Where the doctor's certificate and analyst's certificate had been properly served on the defence in accordance with s. 10 (3) but the prosecution forgot to tender the certificates in evidence before closing the prosecution case at the trial, the justices were held to be "abundantly justified " in exercising their discretion to allow the prosecution to re-open their case to put the certificates in evidence even though it was no mere procedural error but went to the root of the prosecution case (*Piggott* v. *Sims* [1973] R.T.R. 15).

The procedure under s. 9 (5) is for the defendant to be asked for a specimen of blood, and if he fails, then two specimens of urine within one hour of the request, and if he fails or refuses to supply urine specimens he will again be asked for a specimen of blood.

The constable may require the specimen under s. 9 (1) in any order, and if he obtains a specimen, the conviction under s. 6 will be upheld (see *R.* v. *Moore* [1970] Crim.L.R. 650), but the order of specimen-taking set out in s. 9 (5) must be followed for there to be a successful conviction under s. 9 (3) should the defendant refuse to supply a specimen at all. Once a defendant has consented *and supplied* a specimen for laboratory testing, he cannot be requested to supply another specimen (*R.* v. *Hyams* [1972] 3 All E.R. 651, where a constable threw away the sample of urine, wrongly thinking it was of insufficient quantity, and went on to request a sample of blood). But where a defendant has consented *and not supplied* a specimen for laboratory testing, he may then be requested to supply specimens of urine and if he does so he may be convicted (*R.* v. *Paduch* [1973] R.T.R. 493, where the defendant agreed to supply blood but because no police surgeon could be obtained to take the specimen, was then asked by the constable for specimens of urine, which he provided). Section 9 (6) provides that the first specimen of urine provided shall be disregarded, and it was accordingly held in *R.* v. *Walsby* [1972] R.T.R. 301 that there is no requirement for the police to retain the first specimen of urine. Where a defendant sufficiently filled a jar for the second specimen but which fell from the defendant's hand as the police officer reached out for it, he has not " provided " the second specimen (*Ross* v. *Hodges* [1975] R.T.R. 55). The certificate of analysis, if it relates to a urine specimen, must be of the second specimen. The urine specimen does not have to be taken by a medical practitioner. Evidence should be given that the correct specimen of urine was sent for analysis. If the wrong specimen was sent, s. 9 (6) will automatically result in an acquittal of a charge made under s. 6. If there is any substantial doubt raised as to whether the right specimen of urine was sent, it is submitted that it is for the prosecution to prove that it was (see *Dickson* v. *Atkins* and *R.* v. *Shaw* on p. 178, as to evidence of identification that the defendant's sample was subsequently analysed by the analyst). Section 9 (5) requires the second urine specimen to be given within one hour of a request therefor, but the Court of Appeal has allowed two police appeals from the dismissal by two different magistrates' courts where a prosecution under s. 6 (1) was based on a second urine specimen provided more than one hour after the request and in *Standen* v. *Robertson* (1975), *The Times*, 23rd May, certified the point for consideration by the House of Lords.

Supply of Sample of Specimen to Defendant

Section 10 (5) of the Act provides that evidence of the amount of alcohol or drug in a specimen of blood or urine shall not be admissible for the prosecution if the defendant, at the time of the taking of the specimen, asked to be supplied with such a specimen and was not given one in accordance with the subsection. This provision applies whether the case is under s. 5 of the Act (unfit to drive) or s. 6 (more than 80 mg.). The exclusion of such evidence occurs whether the proposed evidence is oral or by certificate and it seems from the use of the words " shall not be admissible " that, once the court is satisfied that the police or doctor failed to comply with s. 10 (5), the court must exclude such evidence and has no discretion as to whether or not to admit it save that presumably the defendant may, if properly advised, waive the benefit of the subsection where it has not been complied with and agree to evidence of the analysis being given. Where the only charge is under s. 6, the defence are hardly likely to waive the matter, as a conviction under s. 6 depends upon there being an analysis. Section 10 (5) does not apply to cases under s. 19 of the Act (drunken cyclists). It does not exclude evidence of analysis of a specimen obtained in breach of s. 10 (5) if this evidence is to be given for the defence in a charge under s. 5.

Section 10 (5) applies where the defendant asked for the specimen of blood or urine at the time of its taking but not where he asked for it afterwards. While it is a wise and proper practice to supply the part of the specimen to the accused before he leaves the police station, it need not necessarily be supplied to him before he does, so long as it is supplied within a reasonable time; the trial judge or magistrates should review all the circumstances, including the reasons why the police did not give it to him before he left, e.g., because he was too drunk to accept it, and the question whether he was prejudiced by the failure to get it when he left and whether the time when he did get it was within a reasonable period (*R.* v. *Sharp* [1968] 3 All E.R. 182). Whether a defendant has been supplied with a part specimen under s. 10 (5) is essentially a question of fact to be determined by the jury (*R.* v. *Jones* (*Colin*) [1974] R.T.R. 117). Although the matter was not left to the jury, who were directed to convict, the facts were such that the conviction was not set aside because the jury could only have come to one conclusion. It was held that the principle in *R.* v. *Bates* (see p. 187) applied, viz., that an issue of fact such as this must be left to the jury unless admissions have been made. Although *R.* v. *Sharp, supra,* was not considered, it is submitted that *R.* v. *Sharp* should be reconsidered in so far as it implies that the question of whether a sample was supplied is a matter for the judge rather than the jury. Where justices refused to allow the prosecution to call rebutting evidence after a defence analyst had given evidence that the defendant's part specimen was incapable of analysis and the prosecution's evidence as to analysis had not been challenged, the case was sent back to be re-tried by a differently constituted bench (*Hudson* v. *Hornsby* [1973] R.T.R. 4). The defence should have made it clear before the prosecution's evidence as to analysis was given, that its admissibility would be challenged on the ground that the defendant's part specimen was incapable of analysis (*ibid.*).

It is however submitted that, like other points which are essential for a successful prosecution under s. 6, although the judge may be entitled to withdraw the question of whether the defendant asked for a specimen if the facts are not in dispute, where the facts are in any material way in dispute the question, which is one of fact, must be left to the jury (see *R.* v. *Jones (Colin)*, *supra*).

The words " a single specimen " in s. 10 (5) (*a*) of the Act may appropriately refer to any aliquot part of the total quantity of blood which was in the syringe used to take a blood specimen and it is not essential that the totality of blood in the syringe be divided into two parts (*Kidd* v. *Kidd*; *Ley* v. *Donegani* [1968] 3 All E.R. 226, where the contents of the syringe had been divided into three and one of the three given to the defendant; this was in order). The specimen given to him should be sufficient to enable him to have a proper analysis made of it (*ibid.*). The normal method of analysis is now by gas chromatography. This permits microscopic portions of the specimen to be analysed. Several such portions are usually analysed and, in preparing the report, the average of the analyses will be calculated. In order to safeguard the motorist, a standard deviation of 2 per cent. is assumed and 6 mg. per 100 ml. is subtracted from all averages less than 100 mg. and 6 per cent. from all averages over 100 mg. Thus an analytical average of 97 will be reported as " not less than 91 " and a figure of 250 as " not less than 235 ". Usually, therefore, a motorist who sends his sample privately for analysis will receive an analysis 6 per cent. higher than the police forensic laboratory's analysis. If the defence analysis gives a much lower figure, the defence should be questioned as to how long, and as to the places where, the specimen was kept before being sent for analysis because blood specimens should be kept in a cool place and their alcohol content will decrease according to the temperature in which they are kept.

There have been a large number of cases on whether, in accordance with s. 10 (5), the sample of blood supplied to the defendant is adequate. The purpose of the section is to allow the defendant to have an independent analysis. It is submitted that the following propositions adequately summarise the law:—

(1) Each part of the specimen, including the sample given to the

defendant, must be of a quantity and quality " capable of analysis by the use of ordinary equipment and ordinary skill by a reasonably competent analyst " (*Smith* v. *Cole* [1971] 1 All E.R. 200*n*.). Whether equipment is " ordinary " is a matter of fact and degree (*Nugent* v. *Hobday* [1972] Crim.L.R. 569).

(2) The sample handed to the defendant must also be capable of analysis within a reasonable time (*Thompson* v. *Charlwood* (1969), 113 S.J. 1004; *Ward* v. *Keene* [1970] R.T.R. 177).

(3) The adequacy of a sample is a question of fact, not of law, and must be decided by the court of trial on the evidence presented to it in each case. The burden of proof of the adequacy of the samples is on the prosecution (*Cronkshaw* v. *Rydeheard* (1969), 113 S.J. 673; *Ward* v. *Keene, supra*; *Smith* v. *Cole, supra*), but it was decided in *Kierman* v. *Willcock* [1972] R.T.R. 270 that the fact that the prosecution's samples, which were chosen at random, were capable of analysis was evidence (but not conclusive evidence) that the defendant's sample was also capable of analysis.

(4) The time at which the part specimen should have the quality of remaining suitable for analysis for a reasonable time (see (2) above) to enable the defendant to send it away for an independant analysis, is the time at which the police supply it to the defendant (*R.* v. *Wright* (*John*) [1975] R.T.R. 193).

Defendants who are anxious to obtain an analysis of the part specimen can obtain advice as to how to keep the sample, where and to whom it should be sent for analysis, from the Royal Institute of Chemistry, 30 Russell Square, London WC1B 5DT, who also publish a leaflet designed to help enquirers on the matter.

Offer of Container

Section 10 (6) requires a constable who requests a person to consent to give a specimen of blood or urine to offer to supply to him part of the specimen in a suitable container; this seems to apply to offences under s. 19 (cyclists) as well as under ss. 5 and 6 (motorists). If a constable has omitted to make this offer, it is suggested that this failure to comply with s. 10 (6) will not matter where a properly advised defendant has waived it or the defendant was in fact supplied with a suitable container for his part of the specimen, so that he was in no way prejudiced. The offer of a container under s. 10 (6) can be made in a written form handed to the defendant (*Farrell* v. *Nivett* [1967] S.L.T. 33). When a request is made under s. 10 (6) by a constable to supply a specimen, the offer to supply a container should be made simultaneously, or, if not simultaneously, at an earlier time so proximate that it will still be clearly in the mind of the person to whom it was addressed (*R.* v. *Price* [1963] 3 All E.R. 938).

It will be noted that, although the police are required under s. 10 (6) to offer the accused a container, they are not obliged to supply a part of the specimen to him if he does not ask for it after such an offer, because s. 10 (5) requires him to ask for it (*Farrell* v. *Nivett* [1967] S.L.T. 33).

The section requires the sample to be given in a " suitable " container.

Where the sample given to a defendant was in a clean, airtight container but contrary to usual police practice the container was not in a sealed and signed envelope, two laboratories to which the defendant sent his sample refused to analyse it because it was " open to interference ". It was held in *Moore* v. *Wilkinson* [1969] Crim.L.R. 493 that the defendant had been given a sample in a " suitable container " (s. 10 (6)) and it was impossible to say that a " suitable container " meant a proper container inside a sealed envelope. A " suitable container " was held to mean a container which is suitable to act as a container for transit of the blood sample from the police station to the analyst (*Langridge* v. *Taylor* [1972] R.T.R. 157) and in *Clark* v. *Stenlake* [1972] R.T.R. 276 it was held that the fact that the police specimen was sent in an identical container and that the police sample arrived so that it could be properly analysed was evidence from which it could be inferred that the container given to the defendant was also suitable.

In *R.* v. *Sodo* (1975), *The Times*, 6th May, the sample analysed by the police was certified as not less than 86 mg. per 100 ml. but the sample supplied to the defendant was analysed at 48 mg. It was held that the jury should have acquitted if the cause of the discrepancy between the two analyses was due to the fact that the defendant's container leaked. A leaky container is not a " suitable container " (*ibid.*). It is submitted that the question of whether s. 10 (6) has been complied with is a question of fact which must be left to the jury in a manner similar to other questions of fact that arise in prosecutions under s. 6 (see *R.* v. *Jones* and other cases on p. 187).

After the accused has supplied a specimen of blood or urine, s. 11 of the Act allows the police to continue to detain him at the police station until he provides a breath test which is no longer positive. In *R.* v. *McKenzie* [1971] 1 All E.R. 729 it was held that the Act only allowed the arrest and detention of a motorist for the purpose of supplying a specimen of blood or urine for laboratory testing and that the police may thereafter detain him only under s. 11. The police had no power to require the defendant to enter into a recognizance under s. 38 of the Magistrates' Courts Act, 1952, as he had not been detained under s. 11.   It is submitted that the police have no power to bail a defendant under s. 38 of the Magistrates' Courts Act, 1952, even if he was detained under s. 11.

Hospital Patients

There are special provisions in the Act for obtaining breath tests and specimens of blood or urine for laboratory testing from a person "while at a hospital as a patient".   The provisions for breath tests for hospital patients are contained in s. 8 (2) and for blood or urine specimens in s. 9 (2).   Hospital means an institution which provides medical or surgical treatment for in-patients or out-patients (s. 12) (see p. 155).   It does not include an ambulance conveying a person to hospital (*Hollingsworth* v. *Howard, infra*).

It is a question of fact whether a person is at a hospital as a patient.   Fortunately the question is usually simple in that most hospitals have a strict routine as to the keeping of records.   Casualty departments normally keep registers of the details of the admission and discharge of patients.   Once a person is admitted as a patient, he will be regarded by the hospital as a patient until he is discharged either by a doctor or by himself.   If he discharges himself, normally the hospital routine will require the person to sign his discharge.

A motorist being taken to hospital in an ambulance is not "at a hospital as a patient", and a constable has a discretion to require a breath test in an ambulance if in his judgment the motorist was capable of providing it (*Hollingsworth* v. *Howard* [1974] R.T.R. 58), and such a breath test is valid (*ibid.*).   Where a constable administered a positive breath test and did not arrest the defendant because he was being removed to hospital, it was held that this did not vitiate another breath test and subsequent supply of a laboratory specimen at the hospital (*Goodley* v. *Kelly* [1973] R.T.R. 125).

Both s. 8 (2) (breath tests) and s. 9 (2) (blood or urine specimens) require "the medical practitioner in immediate charge of his case" to be first notified of the proposal to take the tests.   The police do not have to produce medical lists to prove that the person whom they notified is a medical practitioner.   Both in *R.* v. *Chapman* [1969] 2 All E.R. 321, where the point was not pressed, and in *Jones* v. *Brazil* [1970] R.T.R. 449 it was held or agreed that, while each case depends on its own particular facts, if the constable simply gives evidence that *M* appeared to be the casualty officer on duty in the casualty department with nurses and orderlies being on duty there with him, this is sufficient to raise a *prima facie* case that *M* was the "medical practitioner in immediate charge" of the case.   Nor do

the police have to call the doctor to prove that he did not object
to breath or blood tests.   The constable may give evidence that the
doctor did not object.   It is not hearsay (*Burn* v. *Kernohan* [1973]
R.T.R. 82).

Breath Test

Section 8 (2) provides that where the person who was driving or
attempting to drive a vehicle owing to the presence of which an
accident had occurred (see " Accident ", p. 196) is at a hospital
as a patient, the constable (who must be in uniform: see p. 199)
may require the patient to provide a specimen of breath at " the
hospital ".   It must be at the hospital where the person is for the
time being a patient; he cannot be required to take the test at
any other place, e.g., a police station or, seemingly, another
hospital.

The constable, before making the requirement for a breath test,
is first required to notify the doctor that he proposes to make the
requirement.

The doctor on being notified may object to the breath test on the
ground that the breath test or the requirement to provide it would be
prejudicial to the proper care or treatment of the patient.   If he
objects the constable may not require the breath test.   The doctor
may object not only to the breath test but also to the " requirement
to provide it ".   The condition of a patient may be such that a
doctor may consider it prejudicial to his proper care or treatment
merely to be *asked* for a breath test.   The Act does not require the
constable to warn the patient that if he fails or refuses to take the
breath test he may be fined.   Many police forces, however, incorporate in the requirement to take the test a warning that failure or
refusal to take the breath test may render the patient liable to a fine
and in *Bryant* v. *Morris* [1972] R.T.R. 214 the Lord Chief Justice
stated that the court did not wish to discourage the practice of giving
such a warning.   Where the constable proposes to give such a
warning (following *R.* v. *Knightley, infra*) it is submitted that the
constable should explain beforehand to the doctor that he will be
giving the warning.

Blood or Urine Tests

As in breath tests, there are similar safeguards where a constable
wishes to require a patient at a hospital to supply a specimen of
blood or urine for laboratory testing.   Before a constable can make
such a requirement, the patient must either have failed to supply a
specimen of breath and the constable has reasonable cause to

suspect him of having consumed alcohol (see s. 9 (2) (*b*)) or he has supplied a specimen of breath which has given a positive result (see s. 9 (2) (*a*)). It should be noted that the failure to supply a specimen of breath, or the provision of a positive breath test, need not have occurred while the motorist was a patient at the hospital (see s. 9 (2)). There are two stages: what might be termed the breath test stage, and the stage at which a specimen of blood or urine for laboratory testing is required. Sometimes, both stages may take place while the motorist is at the hospital as a patient, sometimes the motorist does not become a patient at a hospital until after he has provided or failed to provide a breath test. A positive breath test while not a hospital patient was held by the High Court in *Hollingsworth* v. *Howard* [1974] R.T.R. 58 to constitute a valid justification for a subsequent requirement of a laboratory specimen at the hospital, without the necessity for another breath test when he arrived at the hospital. If, however, the motorist is a patient at the hospital and has not been asked for a breath test, there is no reason why the doctor in immediate charge of the patient should not be asked simultaneously if he objects to the requirement of the breath test, the provision of the breath specimen and of the requirement for the supply of a specimen of blood or urine, the actual provision of a specimen of blood or urine and the warning under s. 9 (7) of the consequences of a failure to supply such a specimen (*Ratledge* v. *Oliver* [1974] R.T.R. 394). It was said that the safeguard to the motorist is that the doctor can decide that his permission should be obtained in two stages (*per* Lord Widgery, C.J., p. 398, letter H). The doctor may object not only to the requirement to provide a specimen but also to the warning under s. 9 (7). In *R.* v. *Knightley* [1971] 2 All E.R. 1041 the doctor was not notified beforehand that the warning under s. 9 (7) would be given. The conviction was quashed on the ground that " the proposal to make the requirement " means the proposal to make the requirement as required by the Act, i.e., the requirement to provide the specimen together with the statutory warning. It was not sufficient for the police to give the warning in the presence of the doctor; he had to be told beforehand that the warning would be given. If the patient suffered from a heart condition, once the warning was given it would be too late to avoid the heart attack. The doctor is required to know that the warning is to be given, and the wide variety in the patients admitted to hospital after road accidents and in the experience of the casualty officers renders the presumption that everyone knows the law an inadequate protection for patients suspected of driving with excess alcohol. *R.* v. *Knightley* followed and approved a case at Hampshire Assizes, *R.* v. *Green*

[1970] 1 All E.R. 408, where it was held that the doctor must also be told that the requirement to obtain a laboratory specimen could involve the taking of a specimen of urine as well as blood. Although *Knightley* was followed with reluctance and doubted in *Burke* v. *Jobson* [1972] R.T.R. 59 the principle in *Knightley*, that the doctor must give his consent not only to the taking of a specimen but also to the terms of the warning, was applied by Bridge, J., in *R.* v. *Walters* [1972] Crim.L.R. 381, where an acquittal was directed because the defendant had or could have heard the terms of the proposed warning before the doctor had an opportunity of deciding whether the warning could be prejudicial to the health of the patient. *Knightley* was followed and applied in *Foulkes* v. *Baker* [1975] R.T.R. 50 where a conviction was quashed on the ground that the prosecution had not adduced evidence that the doctor had been told of the warning to be given under s. 9 (7). But in *Taylor* v. *Armand* [1975] Crim.L.R. 227 justices were held to be wrong in refusing to admit in evidence a proforma witness statement setting out the relevant information and questions for complying with the requirements of s. 8 (2) and s. 9 (2) which the constable and doctor had read together. The constable should also have been allowed to refresh his memory from it (*ibid.*).

The doctor need not be called by the police to say that he did not object to the requirement to supply a specimen of blood or urine. The constable may give evidence that the doctor consented both as to the breath test requirement and as to the requirement and warning, etc., as to the supply of a specimen of blood or urine (*Burn* v. *Kernohan* [1973] R.T.R. 82).

The provisions as to the offer and supply to the motorist of a sample of the specimen of blood or urine supplied by him apply to a hospital patient in exactly the same manner as to the motorist who supplies a specimen at the police station (see pp. 214–222).

A conviction may be quashed if the special provisions relating to hospital patients are not complied with, even if it can be subsequently shown that the patient either did not suffer or would not have suffered any ill effects as a result of the non-compliance. In *R.* v. *Knightley, supra,* there was no suggestion that the defendant had a weak heart and that, therefore, the doctor might have objected to the warning under s. 9 (7) being given.

It will be noted that the police have no power of arrest of a hospital patient, and therefore the provisions as to arrest (see p. 208) do not apply while the motorist is a hospital patient. The hospital has, of course, no power to detain a patient. Where a patient absconded after agreeing initially to supply blood, it was held that he could not be convicted of failing to supply a specimen for laboratory testing, because a person cannot be treated as failing until he has not complied with all three requests in accordance with s. 9 (5) (*Cunliffe* v. *Bleasdale* [1972] Crim.L.R. 567).

Difficulties have arisen where a motorist ceases to be a patient at the hospital. In *Bosley* v. *Long* [1970] R.T.R. 432, the defendant, who had been at hospital as a patient, discharged himself after having consented, but not having actually provided, specimens of urine; he subsequently provided a specimen of blood at a police station, and it was held that his conviction should be set aside on the ground that the Act provides two sets of procedures, one following arrest at a police station and the other while a patient at a hospital and if either of the two procedures is not carried to a conclusion, the other must be followed. The actual decision of *Bosley* v. *Long* was approved by the House of Lords in *Bourlet* v. *Porter* [1973] R.T.R. 293 but the ground upon which the Divisional Court reached their decision was disapproved. The true ground for decision in *Bosley* v. *Long* was that the defendant when at the police station had not been offered a second breath test as required under s. 9 (1). In *Bourlet* the facts were that the motorist following a road accident was taken to a hospital. While at the hospital as a patient, he provided a positive breath test, and subsequently, after having been required to provide a specimen of blood or urine for laboratory testing, agreed to provide a specimen of blood, but before he actually provided it discharged himself from hospital. On his discharge he was then arrested on the ground that he had provided a positive breath test and was no longer a hospital patient. After being arrested he provided a blood sample to the police surgeon at the hospital and was then re-admitted to the ward at the hospital as a patient. The House of Lords with one dissentient (Lord Morris) reversed the Court of Appeal decision and held that the defendant was rightly convicted of driving with excess blood/alcohol contrary to s. 6 (1) of the Act. Section 9 (2) specifies that a specimen of blood or urine can be provided at a hospital only if the person providing it is a patient at a hospital. On the other hand s. 9 (1), concerning a person who following arrest has been brought to a police station, states that the arrested person, following the offer of a breath test (see " Second Breath Test " at p. 212), may at the police station be required to provide a specimen of blood or urine but does not specify the actual place at which the specimen of blood or urine is to be given. If, indeed, s. 9 (1) stated that he had actually to provide it at a police station, then a motorist taken ill at a police station could not be taken to hospital to provide it. *Bourlet* v. *Porter* can be summarised as stating that a specimen for laboratory testing may, after arrest, be provided either at a hospital or at a police station; if at the police station then he must first have been offered a breath test.

Failing to Supply Specimen of Breath

It is an offence under s. 8 (3) for a person to fail " without reasonable excuse " to provide a specimen of breath under s. 8 (1) (suspicion of moving traffic offence or consumption of alcohol: see p. 192); while driving or attempting to drive (see " driving or attempting to drive ", p. 184); or s. 8 (2) (following an " accident ": see p. 196).

The breath test must be lawfully required (see pp. 184–199).

The offence is only committed if the defendant has no reasonable excuse, and many of the cases on what is, or is not, a reasonable excuse for failing to supply a specimen of blood or urine for a laboratory test may be applied to this offence of failing to supply a specimen of breath (see p. 231). Thus a person's belief that he has not consumed any alcohol is not a reasonable excuse for failing to take a breath test. All that is necessary is for the constable to prove that he had reasonable cause to suspect the consumption of alcohol (*McNicol* v. *Peters*, p. 192). Nor is it a reasonable excuse that the defendant thought he had not committed a moving traffic offence; all that is necessary is for the constable to prove he had reasonable cause to suspect that the defendant had committed a moving traffic offence (*R.* v. *Downey*, p. 192). The question raised in that case ([1970] R.T.R. 257, at p. 260) was whether it would be a defence if the police had misled the defendant into thinking that he was under no obligation to supply a specimen of breath. It is submitted that it would be a reasonable excuse if the policeman misled the defendant into thinking that if he refused he would not incur a penalty (following *R.* v. *Dolan*, p. 234). Nevertheless it is not a reasonable excuse if the constable mistakenly gives the warning which is appropriate only to a requirement to provide a specimen of blood or urine for laboratory testing. If, therefore, the constable warns the accused that failure to supply a specimen of breath " will render you liable to fine, imprisonment and disqualification ", a conviction under s. 8 (3) will be affirmed even though the offence is neither disqualifiable nor punishable with imprisonment (*Bryant* v. *Morris* [1972] R.T.R. 214). It may be a reasonable excuse that the defendant was concussed and did not appreciate what was being said to him (*R.* v. *Knightley*, p. 233). A medical condition, such as a bronchitic condition of the chest, is a " reasonable excuse " (*Hirst* v. *Wilson* [1969] 3 All E.R. 1566) and also, no doubt, a permanent tracheotomy (*R.* v. *Kelly* [1972] R.T.R. 447).

"Fail" includes "refuses", and "failure" has to be construed accordingly (s. 12 (1)). For cases on "failing" see p. 229. Although a person can only "fail" (in the ordinary sense of the word) if he does not do that which he has an opportunity of doing, as "fail" includes "refuses" a person fails both in accordance with s. 8 (3) and s. 8 (5) if his conduct is such as to show that he is refusing a breath test, even though because the constable has not the Alcotest with him he has not yet been given the opportunity of providing a breath test. In *R.* v. *Wagner* [1970] R.T.R. 422 a motorist having agreed to a breath test and having been asked to wait until the Alcotest arrived, after three minutes suddenly pushed the constable in the chest and said "I am not waiting . . ." It was held that this amounted to a refusal and was thus a failure in accordance with s. 8 (5). It is submitted that the only difference between failing to provide a specimen of breath under s. 8 (5) and s. 8 (3) is that a person may only be convicted under s. 8 (3) if he has no reasonable excuse. So long as clear words are used to show to the defendant that he is being required to take a breath test, that suffices, and no particular form of words is needed to show he is refusing (see *R.* v. *Clarke* and other cases on p. 197). "Providing a specimen of breath" means providing a specimen of breath in sufficient quantity to enable the test to be carried out (s. 12 (3)). Following *R.* v. *Holah,* and *Walker* v. *Lovell* (see p. 207) if a person takes two breaths or only partly inflates the bag, yet nevertheless the breath is of sufficient quantity to provide a positive result, he has not "failed" and cannot therefore be convicted under s. 8 (3).

If the motorist is a patient at a hospital, he may only be required to take a breath test if the doctor in charge does not object to the requirement to provide a specimen of breath and its actual provision by the patient (see p. 223).

The offence is punishable only with a fine, the maximum being £50. It is only triable summarily and there can be no endorsement or disqualification. After failing to supply a specimen of breath the accused will be arrested and taken to a police station, or if ill or injured to a hospital. He may then refuse or fail to supply a specimen of blood or urine at the police station or hospital and thus commit an offence under s. 9 (3). If the hospital or police station are in a different petty sessional division, it is submitted that either court has jurisdiction to try both offences by virtue of s. 28 of the Criminal Justice Act, 1967.

Failing without Reasonable Excuse to Provide Specimen for Laboratory Testing

It is an offence to fail to provide a specimen of blood or urine for laboratory testing. Although it was held in *R.* v. *Moore* [1970] Crim.L.R. 650 that a constable may initially request under s. 9 (1) either blood or urine at his discretion, the offence of failing to supply a specimen for laboratory testing can only be committed if the constable initially asks for blood *by following the procedure set out in s. 9 (5)*. This requires the constable first to ask for blood. If the defendant refuses, then the constable must ask him to supply two specimens of urine within one hour of the request, and if the defendant fails or refuses at any time within the hour to provide them, then the constable must again ask for a specimen of blood. Once all three requests have been refused—blood, urine, blood again—the offence is complete. In *Procaj* v. *Johnstone* [1970] Crim.L.R. 110 the defendant refused all three requests made to him by the station sergeant. Before being charged, the defendant changed his mind. The Divisional Court held that it was then too late. On the other hand a person cannot be convicted of refusing unless all three requests have been made (*Cunliffe* v. *Bleasdale* [1972] Crim.L.R. 567—hospital patient absconded after agreeing to initial blood request).

It was said *obiter* in *R.* v. *Reid (Philip)* [1973] R.T.R. 536 that s. 9 (5) of the Act does not equate refusal with failure. The Act merely lays down that there shall be no failure unless there is first a refusal (see s. 9 (5) (*a*)). In *R.* v. *Paduch* [1973] R.T.R. 493, the motorist consented to supply a sample of blood, but because no police surgeon could be found, the constable requested the defendant to supply specimens of urine. The defendant did so and it was held that provided the request was made before the motorist had complied with the initial request such a request was lawful. Following *R.* v. *Reid* and *R.* v. *Paduch* it is submitted that if a motorist agrees to the initial request for blood he cannot be convicted under s. 9 (3) of failing if he fails or refuses to supply urine. In *R.* v. *Hyams* [1973] R.T.R. 68 the defendant consented to and did supply blood, after having supplied specimens of urine the second of which was thrown away by the station sergeant who mistakenly thought it was of insufficient quantity. His conviction under s. 6 (1) was set aside. It is clear, it is submitted, that his conviction would be also set aside if he had refused the subsequent request for blood. It seems illogical that Parliament should lay down that a motorist who co-operates with the police to provide specimens of urine because a police surgeon cannot be found to take a blood sample (*R.* v.

Hyams) can be convicted under s. 6 (1) if the urine sample is above the prescribed limit, but cannot be convicted of failing under s. 9 (3) if he refuses to co-operate any further. Such, however, seems to be the position.

In *R.* v. *Pursehouse* [1970] 3 All E.R. 218 it was held that there was no need for the constable to spell out the exact requirements as to two urine specimens after there had been a clear unequivocal refusal to give any specimen followed by a refusal to give a specimen of urine. Evasion of a constable's request for two specimens of urine by repeatedly saying " I have done nothing wrong " was held by justices to be tantamount to a refusal, and the justices were held by the High Court to be entitled to take that view (*Jones* v. *Roberts* [1973] R.T.R. 26). It should also be noted from the wording of s. 9 (5) (*b*) that the police only have to wait an hour where the defendant consents to supply specimens of urine. If he refuses to supply specimens of urine, the police do not have to wait for an hour to elapse (*Jones* v. *Roberts, supra*). It is a question of fact whether there has been a refusal which should be left to the jury. Although in *R.* v. *Godden* [1971] Crim.L.R. 656 it was held that the matter could be withdrawn from the jury if the evidence was such that only one conclusion could be drawn, in *R.* v. *Reid* (*Philip*) [1973] R.T.R. 536 it was stated that it was a question of fact for the jury and it is now clear that as in similar questions of fact in drinking/driving cases the matter must be left to the jury unless there are admissions (following *R.* v. *Bates* and other cases on p. 187) (*R.* v. *McAllister* [1974] Crim.L.R. 716).

It would appear that a conditional acceptance is no acceptance and amounts to a refusal. When a defendant answered on the first request by saying " I am not interested until I have spoken to my solicitor," when asked for urine said " No, I want legal advice," and when asked again for blood refused, saying " Not without my solicitor here," the magistrates' finding that this amounted to a refusal was upheld by the Divisional Court in *Law* v. *Stephens, infra.* [For a criticism of *Law* v. *Stephens* based on the right to be advised by a solicitor, see " Solicitors at the police station ", Crim.L.R. 1975, p. 189.] Where a request for a breath test was answered: " I will give one in front of the doctor " when no doctor was present, there was held to be a " failure " (*R.* v. *Ferguson* (1971), 54 Cr.App.R. 415). Also the magistrates' apparent acceptance that the defendant had refused specimens of urine when he said " I want to see a solicitor. I am not giving anything until he gets here " was not commented upon in *Hockin* v. *Weston* [1972] R.T.R. 136, the Divisional Court apparently holding that this must amount to a refusal. *Law* v. *Stephens, infra*, was followed in *R.* v. *Seaman* [1971]

R.T.R. 456, where it was again held that if a defendant lays down
conditions as to giving a specimen that amounts to a refusal by him.

For the offence under s. 9 (3) to be committed otherwise than at a
hospital it is necessary for the arrest under s. 8 to be lawful.   If the
arrest is unlawful, a conviction under s. 9 (3) will be quashed (*R. v.
Bove* [1970] 2 All E.R. 20).   All the necessary preliminaries to a
conviction under s. 6 are equally necessary to a conviction under
s. 9 (3).   Thus if the arrest is under s. 8 all the requirements as to
" constable in uniform " (p. 199), " there or nearby " (p. 197),
" accident " (p. 196), etc., apply to the offence under s. 9 (3) just
as they do to that under s. 6.   There must also be an " arrest " (see
p. 204).   Whether the arrest was under s. 8 or s. 5, the defendant
must have been offered a breath test at the police station (see *R. v.
Withecombe* [1969] 1 All E.R. 157: see p. 212).   If the motorist
was required to take a breath test under s. 8 (1) as a result of the
constable suspecting alcohol or commission of a traffic offence, the
suspicion must arise while the motorist was " driving or attempting
to drive " (see p. 184).   The provisions safeguarding hospital
patients apply (see " Hospital Patients ", p. 222).

The offence is committed only if the defendant failed or refused to
supply the specimen of blood or urine " without reasonable excuse ".
Once the defence of " reasonable excuse " is advanced, it is for the
prosecution to negative the defence (*Rowland* v. *Thorpe* [1970] 3 All
E.R. 195, at p. 197).   It is a question of fact as to whether there was
a " reasonable excuse " and the jury must be satisfied beyond
reasonable doubt that the defendant had no " reasonable excuse "
(*R. v. Harling* [1970] R.T.R. 441; also *R. v. Knightley* [1971] 3 All
E.R. 1041), but whether facts are capable of amounting to a
reasonable excuse is a matter of law.   If the excuse is capable of
amounting to a reasonable excuse, then it becomes a matter of fact
and degree whether or not it does so, and the burden is on the
prosecution to negative it (*Law* v. *Stephens, infra*).   But a judge
cannot rule an excuse put forward by the defence as incapable of
amounting to a reasonable excuse in law and so directing a jury,
before the defence has had an opportunity of giving evidence as to
the matter.   A conviction was set aside, where the judge directed
there could be no reasonable excuse at the close of the prosecution
case and before the defence had been opened (*R. v. Brown (John)*
[1974] R.T.R. 377).   Where there are facts which are such that
they might possibly amount to a reasonable excuse, the judge must
leave the question to be decided by the jury.   A conviction was set
aside where a jury might have found that the defendant was so
afraid of a hypodermic needle as to be incapacitated from submitting to it (*R. v. Harding* [1974] R.T.R. 325).   It was said in this

case that fear of providing blood to amount to a reasonable excuse must, in most, if not all cases, be supported by medical evidence.

For an excuse to be held in law as capable of amounting to a reasonable excuse, the excuse must relate to a person's physical or mental condition being such that it affects his ability to supply a specimen for laboratory testing. The drink/driving provisions contained in ss. 6 to 12 of the Act involve a statutory interference with the liberty of the subject and a true and conscientious refusal based on religious or other grounds will usually be held to be incapable of amounting to a reasonable excuse for refusing. Thus it is not a reasonable excuse that a person will only do so after seeing a solicitor (*Law* v. *Stephens*, *infra*) or that he is a follower of Mesmer and sincerely opposed to the shedding of blood (*R.* v. *John*, p. 234).

The reasonable excuse must be a reasonable excuse for refusing *both* blood and urine. Thus in *Rowland* v. *Thorpe*, *supra*, the woman accused was or might have been embarrassed to supply a specimen of urine because no policewoman was present, but it was held that she should be convicted as she had no reasonable excuse for refusing to supply a specimen of blood. Similarly in *R.* v. *Harling* [1970] R.T.R. 441 the defendant lost confidence in the doctor after three unsuccessful attempts by the doctor to obtain a specimen of blood, and it was held that, although he might have a reasonable excuse for refusing to supply blood, his conviction should be upheld because the jury had found that he had no reasonable excuse not to supply urine.

In the case of a defendant arrested under s. 8 (1) (*b*), all that is necessary is for the prosecution to prove that the constable had reasonable cause to suspect that the defendant had committed a moving traffic offence. Once the prosecution have proved this, it is not a reasonable excuse for the defendant to refuse to supply specimens on the ground that he thought he had not committed a moving traffic offence (*R.* v. *Downey* [1970] Crim.L.R. 287). It is not a reasonable excuse for refusing for a defendant to believe he was not " in charge " of the motor vehicle (*Williams* v. *Osborne* [1975] R.T.R. 181). Similarly the Scottish High Court have held it not a reasonable excuse for the defendant to refuse to supply specimens on the ground that he believed he had not consumed any alcohol (*McNicol* v. *Peters* [1969] S.L.T. 231). It is not a reasonable excuse for refusal is the accused will only consent to the blood sample being taken from a particular portion of his anatomy (his big toe) rather than from where the doctor requires (*Solesbury* v. *Pugh* [1969] 2 All E.R. 1171) or capillary instead of intravenous blood (*Rushton* v. *Higgins* [1972] Crim.L.R. 441). It was said in that case that the true *ratio* of *Solesbury* v. *Pugh* was that if a doctor asked to take a specimen in accordance with ordinary medical practice and was met by an offer to provide in a different way, that was a refusal. In *R.* v. *McAllister* [1974] Crim.L.R. 716 it was held that a police officer was entitled to regard a motorist as refusing to supply blood, who had refused to sign a form signifying his consent to give a blood sample and had made it clear he would only allow it to be taken from his thumb, not his forearm.

It can be a reasonable excuse for a defendant to refuse or fail to supply specimens if he is concussed (*R.* v. *Knightley* [1971] 2 All E.R. 1041). Mental condition or physical injuries can also amount to a reasonable excuse (*Rowland* v. *Thorpe* [1970] 3 All E.R. 195, at p. 196), but in that case it was said that the mental condition or physical injuries must be of an extreme character to constitute a reasonable excuse and in *R.* v. *Knightley, supra*, at p. 1045, the court said that they did not wish in any way to qualify that statement. In *R.* v. *Wallace* [1972] R.T.R. 9, a " not very serious assault " was held incapable of amounting to a reasonable excuse. The court was, however, careful not to say that under no circumstances could an assault by a police officer amount to a reasonable excuse (*ibid.*).

A request for a solicitor to be present for legal advice was held in *Law* v. *Stephens* [1971] Crim.L.R. 36 not to be capable of amounting to a reasonable excuse for refusing to supply laboratory specimens, following and approving *dicta* to that effect in *R.* v. *Clarke (Christopher)* [1969] 2 All E.R. 1008. *Law* v. *Stephens* was followed in *R.* v. *Seaman* [1971] R.T.R. 456, where an Australian wished first to contact his High Commissioner. This was held not to amount to a reasonable excuse for refusal.

In *Glendinning* v. *Bell* [1973] R.T.R. 52, following an accident a motorist on his way to hospital in an ambulance was given alcohol. At the hospital he refused a breath test and subsequently a specimen of blood or urine for laboratory testing because he had had alcohol after he had ceased driving. The High Court set aside the conviction on the ground that the consumption of alcohol subsequent to the accident would have rendered any specimen supplied by him unreliable (following *Rowland* v. *Thorpe* on p. 181) and therefore subsequent consumption of alcohol could amount to a reasonable excuse for refusing to supply a specimen for laboratory analysis. Subsequently, however, the Court of Appeal in *R.* v. *Lennard* [1973] R.T.R. 252 declined to follow *Glendinning* v. *Bell* and held the excuse put forward by the defendant, that he had consumed alcohol after ceasing to drive, was incapable of amounting to a reasonable excuse, as a reasonable excuse must arise out of a physical inability to provide one or a substantial risk to health in its provision. In *R.* v. *Najran* [1973] R.T.R. 451 the reasonable excuse put

forward was that because of his religious views the defendant had a
reasonable excuse to refuse to supply blood. *R.* v. *Lennard* and
R. v. *Najran* were considered by the Court of Appeal in *R.* v. *John*
[1974] R.T.R. 332, where it was held following *R.* v. *Lennard* that a
sincerely held belief precluding a motorist from supplying a specimen
cannot amount to a reasonable excuse. It was said ([1974] R.T.R.,
at p. 337) that some of the language used in the judgment of *R.* v.
Lennard if construed too strictly might involve " an over-rigid
approach ". A distinction must be drawn between a person who
cannot supply a specimen because of some physical or mental
condition, and one who is physically and mentally able to do so,
but whose beliefs albeit sincere preclude him from doing so.

The constable is required under s. 9 (7) to warn the defendant
that failure to supply a specimen of blood or urine renders him liable
to fine, imprisonment and disqualification. It is misleading for the
constable to request a sample of blood and then to say that failure
to supply a specimen of blood renders the defendant liable to the
penalties. The warning should relate to blood *or* urine (*R.* v.
Moore [1970] Crim.L.R. 650) but as the procedure will require
the constable subsequently to require urine it is difficult to see how
prejudice might result to the defendant after refusing all three
requests or how he would have a reasonable excuse. If, however,
the warning under s. 9 (7) is not given at all this would constitute
a reasonable excuse for the defendant to refuse laboratory specimens.
A dispute as to whether the warning was given should be decided by
the jury. If the jury come to the conclusion that the defendant
had not been warned (and the onus of proving the warning lies
on the prosecution) the defendant would have a reasonable excuse
and thus should be acquitted (*R.* v. *Dolan* (1969), 113 S.J. 818).

Punishment for the offence of refusing laboratory specimens
depends on whether " at the relevant time " the defendant was
" driving or attempting to drive " or whether he was " in charge "
of a motor vehicle. If the former the punishment is the same as if
convicted under s. 6 (1), if the latter the punishment is the same as
if convicted under s. 6 (2). The " relevant time " is defined by
Pt. V of Sched. 4 (see p. 158). In the case of a person who has been
required to provide a breath test by a constable under s. 8 (1)
(suspicion of alcohol or moving traffic offence: see p. 192) the
relevant time is " the time when he was so required ". This was
held in *Brooks* v. *Ellis* [1972] R.T.R. 361 to mean (following a
remark of Lord Dilhorne in *Sakhuja* v. *Allen*) the occasion which
gave rise to the requirement rather than the exact moment of time
at which the requirement was made. If any other interpretation
were adopted there would be a premium on non-compliance (*ibid.*).

It will not infrequently happen that a motorist has been observed driving in such a manner or committing a traffic offence which will justify a constable requiring a breath test under s. 8 (1), but because the motorist attempts to evade the police, the police cannot actually make the requirement to the motorist until after he has ceased to be " driving or attempting to drive ".   Provided there is an unbroken chain of events (see p. 191) such a requirement is lawful even if made off a public road and when the motorist has ceased driving. *Brooks* v. *Ellis, supra*, is authority for saying that if the motorist subsequently refuses to supply a specimen for laboratory testing, the relevant time is not when the requirement was made, but when the occasion for the requirement first arose.

It is not clear whether the prosecution have to prove not only that the constable was lawfully entitled to require specimens of breath and subsequently lawfully entitled to require specimens for laboratory testing, but also that the defendant was actually " driving or attempting to drive " or " in charge " of the motor vehicle as the case may be at the relevant time (see *R.* v. *Curran* on p. 173).

In *R.* v. *Jackson*; *R.* v. *Hart* [1969] 2 All E.R. 453, at p. 460, it was said to be difficult to envisage what could be a special reason for not disqualifying in relation to an unreasonable refusal.   This *dictum* was followed in *Scobie* v. *Graham* [1970] Crim.L.R. 589, when it was decided that, once the magistrates had, by accepting the defendant's plea of guilty, impliedly held that the defendant's pain and injuries could not amount to a reasonable excuse, it was impossible for those injuries to amount to a special reason for not disqualifying.   Similarly in *Hockin* v. *Weston* [1972] R.T.R. 136, the magistrates were directed to disqualify, the Divisional Court holding that if the defendant's mental anguish and physical injuries did not amount to a reasonable excuse for refusing to supply laboratory specimens, they could not amount to special reasons for not disqualifying (see further on special reasons, pp. 678–679).

Driving Whilst Unfit to Drive through Drink or Drugs

Interaction of ss. 5 *and* 6

When Parliament enacted Pt. I of the Road Safety Act, 1967, not only was the old offence of driving whilst unfit to drive through drink or drugs (now s. 5 of the 1972 Act) left unrepealed, but the new procedure of obtaining an analysis of the motorist's blood/alcohol level contained in s. 3 of the Road Safety Act (now s. 9 of the 1972 Act) was applied to cases where the accused was arrested under the old offence of being unfit to drive through drink or drugs.

Where a person has been arrested under s. 5 (5), without a

roadside or post-accident breath test being taken prior to his arrest, he may still be proceeded against under s. 6 so long as he was offered a breath test at the police station under s. 8 (7) and lawfully gave a blood or urine specimen in accordance with s. 9 (*Roberts* v. *Jones* (1968), 112 S.J. 884). *Coneys* v. *Nicholson* (1968), 112 S.J. 787, is to the same effect but it was questioned whether the police could proceed under s. 6 if they had abandoned their intention to proceed under s. 5. The same question was canvassed in *Humphreys* v. *Thompson* [1970] R.T.R. 228, where it was held that since there was no suggestion of the constable concluding that the driver's ability to drive was unimpaired and the constable for this reason deciding to abandon his intention to proceed against him under s. 5, there was no defence to a charge under s. 6. It was also suggested in *Campbell* v. *Tormey* [1969] 1 All E.R. 961 that it was possible for a person arrested under s. 6 (4) of the Road Traffic Act (now s. 5 of the 1972 Act) to be convicted under s. 1 of the Road Safety Act, 1967 (now s. 6 of the 1972 Act); see also *per* Lord Dilhorne *obiter* in *D.P.P.* v. *Carey* [1969] 3 All E.R. 1662. In *R.* v. *Wall* [1969] 1 All E.R. 968 Lord Parker, correcting slightly what he said in *Campbell* v. *Tormey*, said that where impairment is reasonably suspected the arresting officer should make it clear that he is arresting under both (what is now) s. 8 of the 1972 Act and (what is now) s. 5 of the 1972 Act. *Campbell* v. *Tormey* was followed in this respect in *Norman* v. *Magill* [1972] R.T.R. 81 where the motorist was arrested under what is now s. 5 of the 1972 Act for being " in charge " of a motor vehicle while unfit to drive. The defendant sought to argue that at the time the police officer approached he was not driving. It was held that as he was arrested under s. 5 it was irrelevant whether he was driving or attempting to drive at the time the police officer approached and a conviction (under what is now s. 6 (1)) of driving with an excess blood/alcohol level was affirmed. It was also again held that no roadside breath test was necessary where the arrest was under s. 5. Similarly it was held in *Woodage* v. *Jones* (*No. 2*) [1975] R.T.R. 119 that where a motorist was validly arrested under s. 5 for being " in charge " of a motor vehicle, he might then be requested to supply a laboratory specimen under s. 9 (1) and he could then be proceeded against under s. 6 (1) as there was evidence that he had driven the car. While a roadside breath test is not a necessary pre-condition of an arrest under s. 5, if the police do in fact make a request for a breath test prior to an arrest, this does not invalidate either the arrest or the subsequent proceedings (*Wimperis* v. *Griffin* [1973] Crim.L.R. 533). The Court of Appeal in *R.* v. *Jones* (*R. W.*) [1969] 2 All E.R. 1559 had no hesitation in upholding a conviction under s. 1 (1) of the

Road Safety Act for attempting to drive with excess blood/alcohol (now s. 6 (1)) when the defendant had been arrested for being in charge of a motor vehicle whilst unfit to drive under s. 6 (4) of the 1960 Act (now s. 5 (5) of the 1972 Act).

Indeed it may be observed that except where there has been an accident the police have no power to arrest a person who is " in charge " of a motor vehicle with excess blood/alcohol contrary to s. 6 (2).   Under s. 8 (1) he may only be arrested for driving or attempting to drive.   Since the police cannot require a motorist to supply a specimen for laboratory testing unless there is an arrest, the only method by which a conviction under s. 6 (2) may be obtained is for the defendant to be arrested under s. 5 (5) for being in charge while unfit to drive or following an accident, failing to give a breath test or giving a positive test following a requirement under s. 8 (2).

The converse is also correct.   A person arrested under s. 2 of the Road Safety Act, 1967 (now s. 8 of the 1972 Act), may be convicted under s. 6 of the 1960 Act (now s. 5 of the 1972 Act) for being unfit to drive through drink or drugs and the certificate of analysis obtained is admissible in the proceedings.   The fact that the defendant has been warned of the consequences of his refusal to supply a sample for laboratory testing (under s. 9 (7)) does not render the certificate inadmissible in a charge under s. 5 (*R.* v. *Palfrey*; *R.* v. *Sadler* [1970] 2 All E.R. 12).   The certificate of analysis is admissible evidence of a defendant's impaired ability to drive.   Although a certificate of analysis cannot be adjusted to discount any subsequent consumption of alcohol in a charge under s. 6 (1) since the certificate of analysis must relate to the amount of alcohol when driving or attempting to drive (see *Rowlands* v. *Hamilton* on p. 181) it can be adjusted where the defendant is charged under s. 5 (*R.* v. *Richards* (*Stanley*) [1974] R.T.R. 520.)   The power of arrest under s. 5 (5) is to be construed as meaning that a constable may arrest without warrant a person apparently committing an offence under s. 5 (*Woodage* v. *Jones* (*No. 2*), *supra*).

Impairment of Ability to Drive Properly

Under s. 5 (4) of the 1972 Act, a person shall be taken to be unfit to drive if his ability to drive properly is for the time being impaired. The law before 1962 required that he should be under the influence of drink or drugs to such an extent as to be incapable of having proper control of a motor vehicle and this is still the requirement under s. 19 in respect of cyclists who are under such influence.   The fact that the defendant had driven for 200 yards in a proper way did not create a presumption of sobriety which medical evidence could not displace in a charge under the old law (*Murray* v. *Muir*

[1949] S.C.(J.) 127). In *R.* v. *Carlson* (1956), 19 W.W.R. 574, a Canadian case, it was said that "impaired by alcohol" meant impaired in the sense that it was impaired in the field of judgment, i.e., in the ability to make and act upon accurately and quickly those decisions which are required of a driver; and see *Louden* v. *British Merchants Insurance Co.* on p. 241.

Impairment of ability to drive properly can be proved by evidence that a car was being driven erratically or had an accident at a spot where there was no hazard for a normal driver, provided, of course, that there is also evidence of drink or drugs. It can be assumed from evidence of the defendant's condition, e.g., frequently falling asleep or inability to stand or mental confusion, provided, again, that there is some evidence that his condition was due to drink or drugs and not to illness. It will be noted that the test is ability to "drive properly" and that the prosecutor need not prove that the defendant could not drive. Impairment can also be shown by evidence of the amount of alcohol taken by the defendant as revealed by a test of his blood or urine, if the analysis shows a high blood/ alcohol content; even a high content may still be disregarded by the jury or court in a charge under s. 5 at its discretion (see *MacNeill* v. *Fletcher* on p. 242). Evidence of analysis, whether above or below 80 mg., will usually be relevant, though the lower the content, the more it favours the defence in a charge under s. 5.

The 1965 Report of a Special Committee of the British Medical Association (which preceded the enactment of the Road Safety Act, 1967) did not retain conversion tables to enable courts to estimate the minimum amount of alcohol which must have been taken by the suspect, because, as is stated in the summary of the Report, "the relationship between the amount of alcohol taken and the blood alcohol concentration varies greatly, both as between different individuals, and in the same individual at different times. It is not possible to give the courts more than a very rough figure and this must often be a gross underestimate. Impairment of driving ability depends primarily upon the concentration of alcohol in the body and not on the amount of alcohol taken, and we recommend that attempts to translate the blood alcohol concentration into the quantity of alcohol consumed should be limited to the purpose of confirming or rejecting a plea that the suspect has taken little or no alcohol before he was detained. For this purpose detailed conversion tables are not necessary. All that need be said is that a male weighing 11 st. with a blood alcohol concentration of 50 mg./100 ml. cannot possibly have taken less than $1\frac{1}{2}$ pints of ordinary beer or 3 single whiskies, and that he has almost certainly had very much more."

Refusal of Consent under s. 7

The police, after arresting the motorist under s. 5 of the 1972 Act, will normally adopt the procedure under s. 9 to obtain a specimen for laboratory analysis. The procedure has the advantage (from the police point of view) that if the accused fails or refuses without reasonable excuse he commits an offence which is punished similarly to an offence under s. 5 or s. 6 of the Act. The procedure requires the police to offer the accused a breath test at the police station (see p. 212) and either the defendant to fail to provide a specimen or the Alcotest to prove positive.

Where the police suspect that the motorist is unfit to drive because of drugs rather than alcohol, the procedure under s. 9 is inappropriate, because the Alcotest measures alcohol only and does not determine whether a motorist is under the influence of a drug. In such a case the police may use the provisions formerly set out in s. 2 (1) of the Road Traffic Act, 1962 (now s. 7 (1) of the 1972 Act), to obtain an analysis. It would appear that the police may also use the same section if the accused has been offered a breath test under s. 9 (1) and the breath test does not prove positive and the police are of the opinion that the evidence that they have already as to the impairment of the accused's ability to drive is such as to justify further enquiries into the possibility of an offence under s. 5.

Section 7 provides (see p. 151) that a court shall have regard to any evidence of the proportion or quantity of alcohol or of any drug which was contained in the blood or present in the body of the accused as ascertained by analysis of a specimen of blood taken with his consent by a doctor or of urine provided by him. The accused commits no offence under s. 7 if he refuses to supply a specimen of blood or urine but, unless he has reasonable cause to refuse, his refusal may be treated as supporting the prosecution's evidence as to his condition or rebutting the defence evidence as to his condition at the time. The request for a specimen must be made by a constable and, as in s. 9, he must follow the " triple requirement ", i.e., blood, then two specimens of urine, then blood. Similarly, as in s. 9, the first specimen of urine is to be disregarded. The provisions as to the supply to the accused of a sample of the specimen in a suitable container (see p. 217) apply to s. 7 in the same manner as to s. 9. The identical provisions in s. 10 as to the admissibility of an analyst's certificate (see p. 218) and the taking of a specimen of blood with the consent of the accused by a medical practitioner (see p. 215) apply to the provision of a specimen under s. 7 in the same way as under s. 9.

Section 7 states that the accused's refusal to supply a specimen for analysis may be treated as supporting the prosecution's evidence as to his condition " unless reasonable cause [for his refusal] is shown ". This may be compared with the offence under s. 9 (3) which is committed if the accused "without reasonable excuse " fails to supply a specimen for laboratory testing. How far do the numerous cases on " reasonable excuse " in s. 9 apply to a refusal under s. 7? It is submitted that there is little material difference between the two phrases. In particular it is submitted that the wording of s. 7, like s. 9, requires there to be reasonable cause for refusing both blood and urine. A reasonable cause for refusing only blood, or only urine, does not suffice. It is also submitted that in s. 7, as in s. 9, once something capable of amounting to a reasonable excuse or cause for refusal is raised, it is for the prosecution to negative it.

In *R.* v. *Dick-Cleland* (1965), 109 S.J. 377, the defendant had refused to give a sample and had said in evidence that he did so because he had an unfortunate medical history, had not wished to explain the matter to a strange doctor and had thought that the sample was required for an examination of that medical condition; it was held to have been a misdirection to tell the jury that they were to hold this against him and not merely that they could hold the refusal against him.

The provisions of s. 7 (1) of the Act as to refusal of a test being in support of the prosecution's case in charges under s. 5 do not apply where the request for a specimen was made by a person who was not a constable, e.g., a doctor. Nor do they apply to charges against cyclists under s. 19 of the 1972 Act. It is submitted that in all cases, whether under s. 5 or s. 19 of the Act, the accused's refusal to provide a specimen or submit to a test or full medical examination can be taken into account by the court, if thought fit, just as any other suspicious action of a defendant can and always could at common law be taken into account by the court, e.g., in a theft case unreasonably refusing to answer questions when first seen by the policeman who was making the preliminary enquiries, or hiding the stolen property or destroying evidence or running away. Whether the court should, apart from s. 7 (1), take his refusal to provide a specimen or submit to examination as a matter, if unexplained, to be held against him would be a question for the court in each case in the light of all the circumstances. Often its value to the prosecution would be negligible but it might be a circumstance of considerable suspicion if a lawyer, doctor or analyst, who would obviously know the value of analysis to him if he had taken only a little alcohol, refused to provide a specimen of his blood or urine. The effect of s. 7 (1) of the Act is to require the court in all cases under

s. 5, where a constable has requested a specimen and the provisions of s. 10 are satisfied, to take into account the defendant's unexplained refusal to give it; what weight the court will attach to it is a matter for the court in the light of the circumstances.

Meaning of Drink or Drug

" Drink " means alcoholic drink and " drug " means a medicament or medicine, something given to cure, alleviate or assist an ailing body (*Armstrong* v. *Clark* [1957] 1 All E.R. 433). In that case it was held that a diabetic who took a wrong dose of insulin and thereby became incapable of proper control of a car could be charged with driving under the influence of a drug. On special facts, it was held in *Watmore* v. *Jenkins* [1962] 2 All E.R. 868 that, where the taking of a proper dose of insulin was a mere predisposing cause and a change in the body's working was the effective cause of the defendant's coma, it was justifiable to acquit him. In *Louden* v. *British Merchants Insurance Co.* [1961] 1 All E.R. 705, Lawton, J., held that the words " under the influence of intoxicating liquor " in a policy meant such influence of liquor as to disturb the quiet, calm and intelligent exercise of faculties. See also p. 237, as to impairment.

Magistrates have held that " drink " includes fumes from a brewery vat. See also *Brewer* v. *Metropolitan Police Commissioner* [1969] 1 All E.R. 513 (fumes of alcohol coming from a heated chemical which accumulated in the defendant's body with the three whiskies later taken).

A certificate of analysis obtained under s. 9 may be used in evidence in a charge under s. 5 (see *R.* v. *Palfrey*; *R.* v. *Sadler*, p. 237).

Evidence Generally

A witness who is not an expert can give his general impression as to whether a person has taken drink and must describe the facts on which he founds that impression (*R.* v. *Davies* [1962] 3 All E.R. 97; *Sherrard* v. *Jacob* [1965] N.I. 151). He may not, merely because he is an experienced driver, give his impression as to whether such a person was fit to drive (*ibid.*). Where the court have disregarded opinions as to unfitness to drive given by laymen, a conviction may be upheld (*R.* v. *Neal* [1962] Crim.L.R. 698). Where a driver, before consenting to examination by the police surgeon, has been told that the results of the examination will not be given in evidence, evidence of those results should not be admitted (*R.* v. *Payne* [1963] 1 All E.R. 848). A doctor may sometimes be called to examine a person arrested under s. 5. The police normally tell a defendant that he can have his own doctor as well and a Metropolitan magistrate commented unfavourably on the calling by the prosecution of the defendant's own doctor against him (Jo.Crim.L. (1955) 115). Where a defendant was found by the doctor to be very much under the influence of drink half an hour after his arrest, it was held that the charge should not have been dismissed merely because the doctor's evidence did not relate to the time of the arrest (*Dryden* v. *Johnson* [1961] Crim.L.R. 551). The fact that the defendant drove for 200 yards in a proper way did not create a presumption of sobriety which medical evidence could not displace (*Murray* v. *Muir* [1949] S.C.(J.) 127). The evidence of a doctor who, in a proper manner, persuaded the accused, after protests, to be examined is admissible; the evidence of a doctor, police surgeon or not, should be treated as that of a professional man giving independent expert evidence with no other desire than to assist the court unless the doctor himself shows that it ought not to be (*R.* v. *Nowell* [1948] 1 All E.R. 794; *R.* v. *Lanfear* [1968] 1 All E.R. 683). In Scotland and Ireland, however, the rule is that the accused's voluntary submission to test and questioning must be proved (*Reid* v. *Nixon* [1948] S.C.(J.) 68; *Gallacher* v. *H.M. Advocate* [1963] S.L.T. 217; *The State (Sullivan)* v. *Robinson* (1954), 88 I.L.T.R. 169). But evidence of a doctor's observations can be given even where consent to a medical examination has been refused (*Wishart* v. *Fenwick* [1968] S.L.T. 263).

In *MacNeill* v. *Fletcher* [1966] S.C.(J.) 18, an acquittal was upheld on a s. 5 charge where, though analysis of the one sample of urine taken showed a high alcohol content, the doctor on the medical examination called it a borderline case and did not certify the defendant as unfit and there was doubt of the reliability of analysis of one urine sample.

For a case in which a proforma witness statement could be put in evidence and referred to by a constable to refresh his memory, see *Taylor* v. *Armand* on p. 225.

Evidence of the manner of driving three miles away was admitted under s. 5 in *R.* v. *Burdon* (1927), 20 Cr.App.R. 80. See also *R.* v. *Taylor* and *Hallett* v. *Warren* on p. 276.

Quarter sessions have held that a person cannot be convicted of aiding and abetting an offence under s. 5 when he was himself so drunk as not to possess the necessary knowledge to aid and abet ([1955] Crim.L.R. 183). But in *Crampton* v. *Fish* [1970] Crim.L.R. 235 it was held that a supervisor of a learner-driver charged under s. 6 (1) (excess blood/alcohol level) can be convicted of aiding and abetting the offence. An aider and abettor cannot escape conviction on the ground that no one can know that a person's blood is above the statutory limit until his blood is analysed. In

R. v. *Tinsley* [1963] Crim.L.R. 520, a conviction for aiding and abetting a driver to drive when unfit through drink was quashed for lack of direction to the jury as to the ingredients of the offence of aiding and abetting.

As the man at the steering wheel of a towed vehicle is not " driving " it (see p. 21), it seems that he may not be guilty of an offence under s. 5 (1) or s. 6 (1) if he is drunk. The issue of whether the person behind the wheel of a towed vehicle is " driving " must be left to the jury (*R.* v. *Shaw (Kenneth)* [1975] R.T.R. 160). If he is charged under s. 5 (2) or s. 6 (2) it seems that he can show that there would be no likelihood of his driving it either (121 J.P. Jo. 238). *Semble,* if he was drunk, he still could not be charged under the Licensing Act, 1872, s. 12, because by s. 13 he would be " liable to be charged " under s. 5 (2).

Fine and Imprisonment

Motor Vehicle

An offence of refusing or failing a breath test under s. 8 (3) of the Act without reasonable excuse carries a fine of £50 but no disqualification or endorsement. The penalties for the offences suggested by the Magistrates' Association are set out on p. 878 et seq.

On conviction under s. 5 (1) of the Act, for driving or attempting to drive a motor vehicle under the influence of drink or drug, the penalty (apart from disqualification, etc., *infra*) is:—

   (*a*) on indictment, a fine of unlimited amount or two years' imprisonment or both;

   (*b*) on summary conviction, a fine of £400 *or* four months' imprisonment.

On conviction under s. 5 (2) for being in charge of a motor vehicle, the penalty (apart from disqualification, etc., *infra*) is:—

   (*a*) on indictment, a fine of unlimited amount or twelve months' imprisonment or both;

   (*b*) on summary conviction, a fine of £200.

On conviction under s. 6 (1) of the Act (driving or attempted driving with a blood/alcohol content exceeding 80 mg.), the fine and imprisonment are the same as for an offence of driving under s. 5 (1) of the Act; see two paragraphs above.

On conviction under s. 6 (2) of the Act (in charge with blood/alcohol concentration exceeding 80 mg.), the fine and imprisonment are the same as for an offence of " in charge " under s. 5 (2) of the Act; see (*a*) and (*b*), above. The Magistrates' Association recommend a longer disqualification where the blood/alcohol is 120 mg. per 100 ml. or more (see p. 879).

On conviction under s. 9 (3) of the 1972 Act (refusing without reasonable excuse to provide a specimen of blood or urine), if at the " relevant time " (see p. 234) the defendant was driving or attempting to drive:—

    (*a*) on indictment, two years' imprisonment and/or a fine of unlimited amount;

    (*b*) summarily, a fine of £400.

If at the " relevant time " (see p. 234) the defendant was in charge:—

    (*a*) on indictment, twelve months' imprisonment and/or an unlimited fine;

    (*b*) summarily, a fine of £200.

It will be noted that offences under s. 9 (3), s. 5 (2) and s. 6 (2) are no longer punishable with imprisonment if tried summarily, nor will the magistrates' court have power to commit offenders to the Crown Court for sentence if the proceedings were commenced at the outset as a summary offence (*R.* v. *South Greenhoe JJ., ex parte Director of Public Prosecutions* [1950] 2 K.B. 558). As a consequence of the removal of the power of imprisonment, defendants may not elect for trial by jury under s. 25 of the Magistrates' Courts Act, 1952 (see p. 160).

It was formerly considered that *R.* v. *Bignell* (see p. 635) was sufficient authority for holding that a court is under no obligation to impose any further sentence of a fine or imprisonment if the defendant is disqualified; the question is further discussed in Chapter VI on p. 635).

In *R.* v. *Lavin* (1967), 51 Cr.App.R. 378, it was said that it is normal practice to fine and not imprison for drink/driving offences. The facts in that case were not very serious (four whiskies, 20 m.p.h., 1 a.m. in Manchester), but it is now clear that the policy as exemplified by recent Court of Appeal cases is that where there is evidence of a really excessive amount of alcohol a custodial sentence of immediate imprisonment is justified. In *R.* v. *Tupa* [1974] R.T.R. 153, Roskill, L.J., said *obiter*, at p. 154, H—J:—

" It has been suggested to us in argument that it would in any event have been wrong in this case, where the blood-alcohol content exceeded by some three times the permitted limit, [298 mg. in 100 ml. of blood] to have passed a custodial sentence. If that view is in any way prevalent at the present time, this court wishes to make it as clear as it can that, in many cases of this kind where the amount of alcohol imbibed and found in a person's blood after he has been breathalysed is anything like the quantity in the present case, whatever the conviction is at a Crown Court or in a magistrates' court, a custodial sentence is entirely proper and ought not to be interfered with on appeal."

These remarks albeit *obiter* have been applied and adopted by the Court of Appeal in *R.* v. *Pashley* [1974] R.T.R. 149 and in *R.* v. *Horton* [1974] R.T.R. 399. Where, however, imprisonment is imposed it would seem that unless the circumstances are otherwise extraordinary, the length of imprisonment is normally not long. Thus in *R.* v. *Horton, supra,* where the defendant had refused to supply a sample of blood or urine and thus had been charged and convicted under s. 9 (3), the defendant who was in a "fairly advanced state of intoxication" had a period of twelve months' imprisonment reduced on appeal to six months. In *R.* v. *Gormley* [1973] R.T.R. 483, the defendant assaulted a constable when required to undergo a breath test, and while the Court of Appeal upheld the sentence of nine months' imprisonment for the offence of assault on the constable in execution of his duty, directed the sentence of six months for refusing to supply a sample of blood or urine to run concurrently with the nine months for the other offence instead of consecutively. In so doing it should be noted that the Court of Appeal observed that to argue from the fact that the two offences arose out of one incident and that therefore the assault was "part and parcel" of the offence of refusing was untenable.

The penalties for these offences when dealt with on indictment were unaltered by the Road Traffic Act, 1974, but the penalties on summary conviction were altered by that Act in that the higher maximum of six months' imprisonment for a second or subsequent offence was removed in respect of s. 5 (1) and s. 6 (1) offences (driving or attempting to drive while unfit or with excess blood/alcohol), but for the offence of refusing to supply a specimen for laboratory testing even when driving or attempting to drive at the relevant time, the Road Traffic Act, 1974, completely removed the power of imprisonment on summary conviction. The 1974 Act also removed the power of imprisonment on summary conviction in the "in charge" offences contrary to s. 5 (2) and s. 6 (2). How far are the cases of the Court of Appeal relevant in summary convictions? It is submitted that where excessive levels of alcohol are shown in driving cases, a custodial sentence is still justifiable. Only in cases of refusing will magistrates no longer be able to consider imprisonment. Magistrates cannot commit an offender to the Crown Court for sentence under s. 29 of the Magistrates' Courts Act, 1952, in respect of any of these offences if an offence was dealt with at the outset as a summary offence in accordance with s. 18 (1) of the Magistrates' Courts Act, 1952. Prosecutors may have regard to the power of magistrates adequately to punish an offence in deciding whether to apply for summary trial, and as the magistrates' court has a discretion (see p. 160) whether to accede to such a request the magistrates may have regard to this consideration, among others, in deciding whether to accede to the prosecution's request.

The level of fines imposed on indictment should not necessarily be equated with summary cases, as on indictment the fine can be of unlimited amount while maxima are laid down on summary convictions. The Road Traffic Act, 1974, increased the maxima from £100 to £400 in respect of driving or attempting to drive while unfit or with excess alcohol (s. 5 (1), s. 6 (1)) and similarly for refusing to supply a sample of blood or urine when driving or attempting to drive at the relevant time (s. 9 (3)). The Act of 1974 increased the maxima of the " in charge " offences on summary conviction (s. 5 (2), s. 6 (2)) from £100 to £200 only.

In *R.* v. *Tupa, supra,* the offender deserved a custodial sentence but the sentencing court instead decided to impose a fine of £1,000. The Court of Appeal, although confirming that a custodial sentence might well have been appropriate, reduced the fine to £250. In *R.* v. *Najran* [1973] R.T.R. 451, the defendant's fine of £250 for refusing to supply a sample of blood or urine was reduced to £75 by the Court of Appeal, who observed that fines " are normally very much less " than £250 for such an offence. In *R.* v. *Welsh* [1974] R.T.R. 478 a conviction for attempting to pervert the course of justice was treated as "a bad case " of refusing to supply a specimen for laboratory testing and a fine of £90 was substituted for twelve months' imprisonment. The level of fine will generally depend on three factors, the seriousness of the offence particularly the blood or urine/alcohol level, the previous convictions, if any, of the defendant and the circumstances and means of the offender. It may also be relevant to consider the length of the disqualification imposed, as this may considerably affect the defendant's earning capacity or may increase substantially his commitments in that he himself can no longer drive. A defendant is perfectly entitled to contest an extremely strong prosecution case and the penalties should not be increased if he does so, but in such a case he can properly be ordered to pay or contribute to the prosecution costs (*R.* v. *Yoxall* [1973] Crim.L.R. 63). Fines for cases of driving with excess blood/alcohol tried on indictment and considered by the Court of Appeal have ranged between £50 and £250 (see *R.* v. *Yoxall* [1973] Crim.L.R. 63; in the 1973 Road Traffic Reports *R.* v. *Thomas,* p. 325 and *R.* v. *Najran,* p. 451; and in the 1974 Road

Traffic Reports, *R.* v. *Tupa*, p. 153, *R.* v. *Slade*, p. 20, *R.* v. *Sharman*, p. 213 and *R.* v. *Newton*, p. 451).

Magistrates' courts in fixing the amount of fine " shall take into consideration among other things the means of the person on whom the fine is imposed so far as they appear or are known to the court" (Magistrates' Courts Act, 1952, s. 31). On summary conviction of a defendant convicted under s. 5 (1) or s. 6 (1) (driving or attempting to drive while unfit or with excess blood/alcohol) a magistrates' court cannot now both imprison and impose a fine as the penalty is " £400 *or* four months' imprisonment ". Imprisonment in this context refers to a suspended sentence of imprisonment as well as to an immediate prison sentence.

Cycles

A person convicted under s. 19 of riding a bicycle, tricycle or cycle with four or more wheels is liable to a fine of £50. The maximum of £50 applies even if it is the defendant's second or subsequent offence. The power of imprisonment for a second or subsequent offence was removed by the Road Traffic Act, 1974.

Endorsement, Disqualification and Driving Test

The following provisions relate only to persons convicted in respect of motor vehicles and do not relate to cyclists or to drivers of motor vehicles convicted of failing to provide a specimen of breath under s. 8 (3).

Endorsement must be ordered on conviction under s. 5 (unfit to drive), s. 6 (more than 80 mg.) and s. 9 (3) (refusing to give a blood or urine specimen), unless there are special reasons (see Chapter VII), whether the accused was driving, attempting to drive or only in charge at the material time (Road Traffic Act, 1972, s. 101 and Sched. 4).

The endorsement will be in code form on the new type of driving licences and also on many of the licences issued by local councils, and the endorsement code is as follows:—

DR 10 Driving or attempting to drive with blood/alcohol level above limit.

DR 20 Driving or attempting to drive when unfit through drink or drugs.

DR 30 Failing to provide a specimen of blood or urine for laboratory testing when driving or attempting to drive at the relevant time.

DR 40 In charge of a motor vehicle with blood/alcohol above
       limit.

DR 50 In charge of a motor vehicle when unfit through drink or
       drugs.

DR 60 Failing to provide a specimen of blood or urine for labora-
       tory testing when in charge of a motor vehicle at the relevant
       time.

Disqualification Obligatory for Driving or Attempted Driving

On conviction under s. 5 (1) (driving or attempted driving when
unfit), s. 6 (1) (driving or attempted driving with more than 80 mg.)
or s. 9 (3) (refusing a blood or urine specimen when driving or
attempting to drive at the relevant time), the defendant must be
disqualified for *at least* twelve months unless the court for special
reasons orders him not to be disqualified or to be disqualified for a
shorter period (Road Traffic Act, 1972, s. 93 and Sched. 4, column
5). [The Magistrates' Association recommend a longer disqualification where the blood/alcohol is 120 mg. per 100 ml. or more
(see p. 879).] Where there is a previous *conviction* within a period
of ten years prior to the *commission* of such an offence, the minimum
period for which the court is required to disqualify the offender is
increased to three years by virtue of s. 93 (4), which reads as
follows:—

(4) Where a person convicted of an offence under any of the following
provisions of this Act, namely section 5 (1), 6 (1) or 9 (3) (where the latter
is an offence involving obligatory disqualification), has within the ten years
immediately preceding the commission of the offence been convicted of any
such offence, subsection (1) above shall apply in relation to him with the
substitution of three years for twelve months.

Paragraph 5 of Sched. 10 to the 1972 Act has the effect of including previous convictions under s. 6 (1) of the Road Traffic
Act, 1960, or s. 1 (1) or s. 3 (3) (when driving or attempting to
drive) as previous convictions for the purposes of s. 93 (4) provided,
of course, such previous convictions are within the ten-year period.

Previous convictions under the Act of 1960, the Road Safety
Act, 1967, or the Act of 1972 or in respect of being *in charge* or as a
cyclist do not count as previous convictions for the purposes of
s. 93 (4). Thus, a person previously convicted in 1968 of driving
when unfit will get a disqualification of at least three years if
he is convicted in 1972 of driving with more than 80 mg. under s. 6 (1)
of the 1972 Act or of refusing a blood or urine sample under s. 9 (3)
thereof while driving. Similarly, a person convicted in 1972 under
s. 6 (1) or s. 9 (3) (if a driver) will get a three-year disqualification
if he is convicted in 1978 of driving when unfit under s. 5 (1) of the

Act. " Driving ", it is submitted, includes attempted driving, both being offences under ss. 5 (1) and 6 (1), and *vice versa*. See p. 621 as to " within ". It should be particularly noted that the wording of s. 93 (4) makes it clear that the ten-year period has to be calculated from the date of the *commission* of the subsequent offence back to the date of the *conviction* of the earlier offence. This has a number of consequences; a person appearing before a court charged with two offences committed on different dates is only liable to a minimum of twelve months on each as he will necessarily not have been *convicted* for the earlier offence when he *committed* the second offence. (It should also be noted in such an instance that the court cannot make the two orders of disqualification consecutive: see *R.* v. *Bain* and other cases on p. 623). The method of calculating the ten-year period in accordance with s. 93 (4) can however also work to the disadvantage of the defendant. Thus if the later offence occurred on 1st January, 1973, and the earlier offence was committed in December, 1962, for which the defendant was convicted on 1st February, 1963, he is liable to the three-year compulsory disqualification. On the other hand if the earlier offence was committed in December, 1972, and he was convicted on 1st February, 1973, the compulsory three-year period does not apply to an offence committed in January, 1973, because he had not previous to the second offence been *convicted*. In such a case there is nothing, however, to prevent a court disqualifying the person for three years if the court thinks it just to do so.

The compulsory disqualification of twelve months or three years, like all other orders of disqualification whether compulsory or not, commences from the date when it is imposed and cannot be made to run consecutively to any other period of disqualification (see *R.* v. *Bain* and other cases on p. 623.) The only exception to this rule is a period of disqualification under " totting-up ". In *R.* v. *Middlesex Area Quarter Sessions, ex parte Bull* [1972] R.T.R. 205 it was said *obiter* that where a defendant was liable to obligatory disqualification for the offence and also liable to obligatory disqualification for " totting-up " under s. 93 (3) it was logical and proper for a court to impose one entire order of disqualification (see further p. 629). A " totting-up " disqualification cannot be ordered to run concurrently with any other order of disqualification. It must run consecutively to any other order of disqualification whether imposed on the occasion of the conviction for the particular offence or any other occasion (s. 93 (5) of the Road Traffic Act, 1972). An order of disqualification may be suspended pending the hearing of an appeal.

Section 26 (2) of the Criminal Justice Act, 1967, prohibits a court from disqualifying a person in his absence unless the court has previously adjourned under s. 14 (3) of the Magistrates' Courts Act, 1952. The notice of adjournment must include notice of the reason for the adjournment (Criminal Justice Act, 1967, s. 26 (3)). Where a magistrates' court, without first adjourning under s. 14 (3) of the Magistrates' Courts Act, 1952, convicted and disqualified a defendant in his absence for driving with excess blood/alcohol, the disqualification (but not the conviction) was quashed (*R*. v. *Bishops Stortford JJ*. [1969] Crim.L.R.201).

It should perhaps be emphasised that the period of twelve months' or three years' disqualification is a minimum period. It was held in *Delaroy-Hall* v. *Tadman* [1969] 2 Q.B. 208 that, even if a defendant is only 2 mg. above the prescribed limit, he must still be disqualified for the minimum period of twelve months. The policy of the Court of Appeal has been to uphold periods of disqualification in excess of the minimum period where the defendant's blood/alcohol level is substantially in excess of the minimum or where there has been bad driving or bad behaviour. The courts have increasingly recognised that an order of disqualification is the chief penalty for most offenders and have wished to show a distinction in the period of disqualification between an offender only slightly above the limit whose driving ability is only slightly impaired, if at all, and an offender whose blood/alcohol level is greatly in excess of the prescribed limit and whose driving has clearly been affected by his consumption of alcohol. In *R*. v. *Sakhuja* [1972] R.T.R. 315, Lord Hailsham, L.C., in his speech in that case remarked ". . . it may well be that circuit judges and recorders will do well to bear in mind that they have a discretion to impose longer periods of disqualification when bad driving and bad behaviour follow the drink. In this way they can differentiate between drivers whose excessive drinking is substantial . . . and those where the drinking is only slightly above the limit and has not been accompanied by bad driving or bad behaviour." These remarks were approved and applied in *R*. v. *Slade* [1974] R.T.R. 20 where a disqualification of thirty months was upheld. Despite the hardship caused by disqualification (living in remote area, wife unwell and not able to drive, daughter having to be driven to school, defendant driving 25,000 to 30,000 miles a year) the period of disqualification was " wholly right " as the defendant's blood/alcohol level was 165 mg. of alcohol in 100 ml. of blood.

In *R*. v. *Yoxall* [1973] Crim.L.R. 63 a period of three years' disqualification was upheld (236 mg. of alcohol in 100 ml. of blood); in *R*. v. *Thomas* [1973] R.T.R. 325 a two-year period was upheld (292 mg. of alcohol in 100 ml. of urine); in *R*. v. *Tupa* [1974]

R.T.R. 153 a period of five years was upheld (289 mg. of alcohol in 100 ml. of blood); in *R.* v. *Sharman* [1974] R.T.R. 213 a period of two years was upheld (143 mg. of alcohol in 100 ml. of blood); in *R.* v. *Mills* [1974] R.T.R. 215 a period of two years was upheld (118 mg. of alcohol in 100 ml. of blood: *per* Lord Widgery, C.J., on p. 216: " it is quite wrong to talk about the tariff disqualification being twelve months. . . . It cannot be less than twelve months and it is a matter within the discretion of the court and a fairly wide discretion how long a disqualification is imposed "); in *R.* v. *Newton* [1974] R.T.R. 451 an eighteen-month period was upheld even though the defendant's drink had been laced.

On the other hand it is the policy of the Court of Appeal not to approve excessively long periods of disqualification particularly where there is a risk of the offender being thereby tempted to drive while disqualified and there are no considerations of public safety involved. In *R.* v. *Calhoun* [1974] Crim. L.R. 436 a period of fifteen years' disqualification was reduced to the minimum of three years for this reason. In *R.* v. *Pashley* [1974] R.T.R. 149 a sentence of twelve months' imprisonment was upheld but a disqualification of three years was reduced to twelve months because of the risk of the defendant being tempted to drive while disqualified on coming out of prison. On the other hand if there has been persistent disregard of motoring laws and it was in the public interest for the offender not to be allowed to drive again, a long period of disqualification will be upheld (*R.* v. *Davitt* [1974] Crim. L.R. 719).

Disqualification Optional for Being in Charge

On conviction under s. 5 (2), s. 6 (2) or s. 9 (3) of the Act, viz., when the defendant was in charge but not driving or attempting to drive at the material time, he may be disqualified for any period, at the court's option; the court may also refrain from disqualifying him, if so minded, however bad his record and even if he had previous " drunken-driving " or " in charge " convictions, unless totting-up (see next paragraph) applies.

Totting-up

Section 93 (3) of the Act applies to offences under s. 5, s. 6 and s. 9 (3), so that, if a defendant convicted under any of these provisions has, within the three years immediately preceding the commission of the offence, been convicted on not less than two occasions of an endorsed disqualifiable offence, he shall be disqualified for not less than six months unless, having regard to all the circumstances, the court considers that there are grounds for mitigating the normal consequences of the conviction (see pp. 624–629). The disqualification imposed under s. 93 (3) is additional and consecutive to any disqualification imposed for the offence itself or for another offence on the same occasion or for any previous offence (s. 93 (5)).

See Chapter VII and pp. 670–679 particularly as to special reasons for not disqualifying.

Aiders and Abettors

A person convicted of aiding and abetting an offence under s. 5 (1), s. 6 (1) or s. 9 (3) is not liable to compulsory disqualification save in so far as s. 93 (3) of the Act applies (see above and s. 93 (6)).

Driving Test

A driving test may be ordered on first or subsequent conviction under s. 5, s. 6 or s. 9 (3) (s. 93 (7)). It may be particularly appropriate to make such an order where the defendant has not had much experience of driving and the defendant is otherwise disqualified for a period but such an order must not be imposed as a punishment (see *R.* v. *Guilfoyle* and other cases on p. 661).

There is, as stated, no power to disqualify or endorse for refusing a breath test.

Other Vehicles

By the Licensing Act, 1872, s. 12, as amended by the Penalties for Drunkenness Act, 1962, a person who is drunk while in charge on any highway or other public place of any carriage, horse or cattle is liable to a fine of £10 or one month's imprisonment; this section does not apply to motor vehicles (Road Traffic Act, 1972, s. 13). Section 12 applies to cyclists (*Corkery* v. *Carpenter* [1950] 2 All E.R. 745) and, *semble*, to barrows (Jo.Crim.L. (1939) 338; and see p. 343). The prosecutor must prove that the defendant was drunk, not merely under the influence of drink. The legal dictionaries suggest that the term " cattle " generally includes horned domestic animals, horses, asses, pigs and sheep. A pedal cyclist or tricyclist riding (not attempting to ride) his machine when under the influence of drink or drugs should be charged under s. 19 of the 1972 Act; an attempt to ride should be charged under s. 12 of the 1872 Act. Section 12 does not apply to persons under the influence of a drug.

CHAPTER V

OTHER ROAD TRAFFIC OFFENCES

1. CAUSING DEATH AND INJURY BY DRIVING

MANSLAUGHTER, whether committed by an adult or a juvenile, is a Class 2 offence* triable at the Crown Court. It need not have been committed on a road. For a general statement of the law relating to the offence, see Archbold, 38th ed., para. 2558. A higher standard of negligence than that to prove dangerous driving is required. For a case where the Court of Appeal observed a defendant could have been charged with manslaughter instead of causing death by dangerous driving, see *R.* v. *Milburn* [1974] R.T.R. 431 (defendant raced another through main streets of Middlesbrough at 7 p.m. on a Saturday in July, killing a pedestrian on the pavement). By the Road Traffic Act, 1972, s. 37, observance or non-observance of the Highway Code may tend to negative or establish liability for the offence. (For text of s. 37 (5) and discussion as to its effect on careless and dangerous driving offences, see p. 258.) By the Road Traffic Act, 1972, Sched. 4, Pt. IV, para. 1, the jury, on a charge of culpable homicide in Scotland, may convict of dangerous driving. Where the charge is motor manslaughter on a road in England, it seems that s. 6 (3) of the Criminal Law Act, 1967, allows the jury to convict either of causing death by dangerous or reckless driving or of dangerous or reckless driving; that Act repealed s. 2 (3) of the Road Traffic Act, 1960, in relation to manslaughter in England. A constable, on reasonable suspicion that manslaughter has been committed, may arrest without warrant any person suspected with reasonable cause by him of committing the offence (Criminal Law Act, 1967, s. 2). The death must occur within a year and a day of the offence.

Spouses are competent but not compellable witnesses for the prosecution against each other where the deceased was under seventeen (Children and Young Persons Act, 1933, s. 15), but not otherwise. Dying declarations by the deceased are admissible to prove the circumstances of the crime, provided they are complete (*Waugh* v. *R.* [1950] A.C. 203) and provided the charge is homicide.

* See Directions of the Lord Chief Justice (Stone (1975) pp. 5326–30).

The prosecution should be careful to see that there is evidence of the death of the actual victim, i.e., it may not suffice for a police witness to say that John Smith was knocked down by a car on Sunday and removed to hospital and then for a doctor to say that John Smith died there on Monday.   There must be evidence to show that the two John Smiths are the same person.   See p. 258 as to notifying the coroner of committal.   See p. 260 as to penalty, disqualification, etc.

Hit-and-run Drivers

It is submitted that there may be one other instance where manslaughter might possibly be committed by a motorist.   One of the purposes of Parliament when enacting the duty to stop after an accident and to report that accident now contained in s. 25 of the Road Traffic Act, 1972, was, it is submitted, the saving of life.   If therefore a motorist knowing of the possibility of serious injury fails to stop or fails to report that accident and as a result of that failure the person whom he has hit with his motor vehicle dies, it could be argued that his deliberate or reckless failure to comply with the duty might be sufficient to warrant a charge of manslaughter even if there is no evidence of dangerous driving.   It should be noted that the duty to stop means to stop sufficiently long to exchange particulars with anyone requiring the same (*Lee* v. *Knapp*: see p. 347).   The duty of reporting an accident is required to be exercised " as soon as reasonably practicable ".   As was held in *Bulman* v. *Bennett* [1974] R.T.R.1, this means exactly this, it does not mean that the motorist has twenty-four hours within which to report the accident.

Causing Death by Dangerous Driving

The Road Traffic Act, 1972, s. 1, creates the offence of causing the death of another person by driving a motor vehicle on a road recklessly or at a dangerous speed or in a dangerous manner; the offence is a Class 4 offence* triable only at the Crown Court. Although s. 2 (2) of the Road Traffic Act, 1960, was repealed by the Criminal Law Act, 1967, it seems that under s. 6 (3) of that 1967 Act, a jury on a charge under s. 1 may convict the defendant of dangerous or reckless driving under s. 2 (1) of the 1972 Act and possibly of causing bodily harm by furious driving under s. 35 of the Offences against the Person Act, 1861 (see p. 258), but the latter offence does not carry disqualification.   Reference should be made to s. 198 as to whether tramcars or trolley vehicles come within the

* See Directions of the Lord Chief Justice (Stone (1975) pp. 5326–30).

ambit of s. 1.   As s. 2 is specifically not applied to tramcars operated under statutory powers it is doubtful if s. 1 applies to them either (see s. 198 (1)).   Warning of intended prosecution under s. 179 (see Chapter III) is not required for offences under s. 1 and by Sched. 4, Pt. IV, para. 5, a conviction under s. 2 is good on indictment under s. 1 although no warning or notice of intended prosecution under s. 2 was given.

An indictment containing a charge of " motor manslaughter " or of causing death by dangerous driving should not include a charge of driving under the influence of drink (*R.* v. *McBride* [1961] 3 All E.R. 6), but in *R.* v. *Thorpe* [1972] R.T.R. 118 an indictment containing a count of causing death by dangerous driving and also a count of driving with excess blood/alcohol was not questioned.   These two cases, discussed on p. 274, deal with the admissibility of evidence that the accused had been drinking. *Quaere*, whether a dying declaration by the deceased would be admissible; such declarations so far have been admitted only in murder and manslaughter cases.

In *R.* v. *Courtley*, Jo.Crim.L. (1958) 200, Stable, J., ruled that an indictment containing counts for causing death by driving in a dangerous manner and for causing death by driving at a dangerous speed was not in a proper form and directed the substitution of an indictment for causing death by driving at a speed and in a manner dangerous to the public.   A charge of causing death by driving at a speed and in a manner which was dangerous to the public is good if the matter relates to one single incident (*R.* v. *Clow* [1963] 2 All E.R. 216) and it would seem that a charge of driving recklessly and at a dangerous speed is also good (*cf. R.* v. *Jones, ex parte Thomas* (1921), 85 J.P. 112).   See p. 265 as to charges in the alternative.

In *R.* v. *Curphey* [1957] Crim.L.R. 191 it was held that a jury might properly be directed to convict if they considered the defendant's driving was *the substantial* cause of death but not the sole one. In *R.* v. *Gould* [1963] 2 All E.R. 847 a jury were directed that they might convict if the defendant's driving was *a* substantial cause and not *the* substantial cause.   These cases were reviewed by the Court of Appeal in *R.* v. *Hennigan* [1971] 3 All E.R. 133.   The defendant's car was driven in a restricted area at estimated speeds of up to 80 m.p.h.   It crashed into another car which was astride the centre of the road having emerged from a minor road.   The defendant was going dangerously fast but it might be held that the other driver was substantially to blame as she was clearly at fault in emerging from the minor road.   The jury were directed that they could convict even if the appellant was only a little more than one-fifth to blame. The Court of Appeal ruled that this was an incorrect approach.

The proper way for a jury to be directed is for them to be told to consider whether the defendant's driving is *a* cause, and it no longer has to be a *substantial* cause. Lord Parker, C.J., stated (p. 135): "The court would like to emphasise that there is nothing in the statute which requires the manner of the driving to be a substantial cause or a major cause or any other description of cause, of the accident. So long as the dangerous driving is a cause and something more than *de minimis*, the statute operates."

Death, if the rule as to other forms of homicide applies, must occur within a year and a day. Spouses are competent witnesses for the Crown Court against the other where the victim was under seventeen years of age (Children and Young Persons Act, 1933, s. 15 and Sched. 1, as " bodily injury " must include a fatal injury). In *McKie* v. *Lord Advocate* [1958] S.L.T. 152 evidence of an examination of the defendant by a doctor with a view to preferring a charge of drunken driving was admitted in a charge under s. 1, the death not having been discovered until after the examination. Evidence that the defendant had pleaded guilty to a charge of excess blood/alcohol (now s. 6 of the 1972 Act) was held admissible in a trial on a charge of causing death by dangerous driving (see *R.* v. *Thorpe*, p. 274). See p. 269 as to driving in a state of automatism.

The question how far the injury itself and how far external factors can cause the death is discussed in the *Modern Law Review*, October, 1959, at p. 517, citing *R.* v. *Jordan* (1956), 40 Cr.App.R. 152, and *R.* v. *Smith* [1959] 2 All E.R. 193. See also articles at [1957] Crim.L.R. 429, 510 and 576.

In *R.* v. *Stern* [1967] Crim.L.R. 421, it was emphasised that the jury must be satisfied that there was dangerous driving. On a charge of causing death by dangerous driving, the court should not allow questions and argument on the subject whether the defendant's conduct amounted to careless driving only; while all careless driving is not necessarily dangerous driving, careless driving may well be dangerous and it is not correct to say that, if the offence were one of careless driving, that in fact would exclude it from being one of dangerous driving (*R.* v. *Scammell* [1967] 3 All E.R. 97) and in *R.* v. *Stevens* [1970] Crim.L.R. 158 a jury were directed as to an offence of causing death by dangerous driving in accordance with *R.* v. *Evans*, below. The jury sent a note to the judge: " The members of the jury feel that the defendant is not guilty of dangerous driving but guilty of driving without due care and attention." The judge then further directed the jury that if the jury concluded the car was driven dangerously it did not matter that the defendant had only been careless. " If you decide that there had not been due care and attention and the manner of driving was dangerous then you would convict." The further direction was upheld by the Court of Appeal.

While it may be necessary to prove that the defendant's state of mind was reckless where the charge is reckless driving, on a charge of dangerous driving he is guilty if he adopted a manner of driving which was dangerous to other road users and it matters not whether he was deliberately reckless, careless, momentarily inattentive or even doing his incompetent best, though such considerations are highly relevant when it comes to sentence or to considering whether a prosecution is justified (*R.* v. *Evans* [1962] 3 All E.R. 1086, where the defendant's manner of driving would be deemed to have amounted to dangerous driving anyhow). See further p. 280. In *R.* v. *Parker* (1957), 41 Cr.App.R. 134, a jury had been directed that a momentary disregard of safety precautions or a momentary act of negligence on the part of a driver (here going over a dangerous crossing against the red light) could amount to dangerous driving; the Court of Criminal Appeal approved the direction. In *R.* v. *Ball and Loughlin* (1966), 50 Cr.App.R. 266, it was said that driving in a dangerous manner means the manner of the actual driving; the offence is absolute and a driver is liable if the result of his driving is a dangerous situation or manœuvre, but this case was disapproved in *R.* v. *Gosney* [1971] 3 All E.R. 220 (see p. 280 for the facts of this case and *R.* v. *Ball and Loughlin*). The driver to be convicted of dangerous driving must be at " fault ", which, following *R.* v. *Evans*, means " falling below the standard of care of a competent and experienced driver ": see further p. 281. In *R.* v. *Spurge* (see p. 277) it was held to be dangerous driving, if the dangerous manœuvre was caused by a mechanical defect of which the defendant was aware. This principle, i.e., that a driver who, knowing of the defect, drives a defective vehicle, is guilty, where danger results, of dangerous driving, has been applied to the offence of causing death by dangerous driving: *R.* v. *Robert Millar (Contractors), and Robert Millar* [1970] 1 All E.R. 577. The defendant drove a lorry with a dangerously worn tyre which burst. The lorry as a result hit a motor car, killing the occupants. The defendant company and the managing director were also convicted of aiding and abetting the offence even though resident in Scotland. Aiding, abetting, counselling and procuring is a continuing offence and the company sent the vehicle into England knowing of the defective tyre.

The offence can be committed only on a " road " (see p. 26) and relates only to motor vehicles. Carters (drivers of a " four in hand " and pony traps) and cyclists may be charged with manslaughter.

The cases on dangerous driving at pp. 280-282 are relevant to charges under s. 1. Note particularly those on p. 276 as to driving in the period prior to the main incident.

For the purposes of s. 1, "driver" does not include a separate person acting as steersman (s. 195 (1)) but such a person might, if the facts warrant, be prosecuted for aiding and abetting an offence under s. 1.

A constable, on reasonable suspicion that an offence under s. 1 has been committed, may arrest without warrant a person suspected by him with reasonable cause of having committed it (Criminal Law Act, 1967, s. 2).

A juvenile court may not try homicide (Children and Young Persons Act, 1969, s. 6). The legal dictionaries define it as " killing a person " and do not limit it to murder and manslaughter; homicide thus includes any offence an essential element of which is that the accused caused the death of another person. Causing death by dangerous driving contrary to s. 1 of the 1972 Act satisfies this test as well as the more usual forms of homicide such as murder, manslaughter or infanticide. It is therefore submitted that a juvenile charged with causing death by dangerous driving can only be tried at the Crown Court.

Inquests

Where a coroner has begun an inquest touching a death, the police should not prefer a lesser charge, e.g., dangerous driving, before the inquest is concluded and, if such a charge has been preferred, it should not be heard and determined until such conclusion (*R.* v. *Beresford* (1952), 36 Cr.App.R. 1). Likewise, the coroner will adjourn the inquest when a charge of manslaughter or causing death by dangerous driving has been brought by the police (Coroners (Amendment) Act, 1926, s. 20; Road Traffic Act, 1972, s. 1 (2)). As to inquests generally, see also the Coroners Rules, 1953 (97 S.J. 159). The magistrates' clerk must inform the coroner of a committal by his magistrates for manslaughter or causing death by dangerous driving (Coroners (Amendment) Act, 1926, s. 20 (5); s. 1 (2) of the Act of 1972).

Causing Bodily Harm by Furious Driving, etc.

One may notice here also that s. 35 of the Offences against the Person Act, 1861, is still occasionally used. Section 35 reads as follows:—

" Whosoever having the charge of any carriage or vehicle, shall, by wanton or furious driving or racing, or other wilful misconduct, or by wilful neglect, do or cause to be done any bodily harm to any person whatsoever, shall be guilty of an offence. . . ."

This offence, when committed by an adult, is triable only on indictment and is punishable with a maximum of two years' imprisonment. It need not have been committed on a road: see *R. v. Philip Cooke, infra*, where the offence was committed on a track or footpath of a public recreation ground. Section 35 applies to pedal cycles as well as to other vehicles (*R. v. Parker* (1895), 59 J.P. 793). Where the victim is a juvenile, spouses are competent witnesses for the prosecution against each other (Children and Young Persons Act, 1933, s. 15). Quarter sessions have held that, on a charge under s. 35, the Crown must prove a degree of lack of care which would amount to dangerous driving; " wanton driving " indicates a positive lack of care and " wilful neglect " implies something of a negative nature ([1954] Crim.L.R. 137). In *R. v. Philip Cooke* [1971] Crim.L.R. 44 the charge under s. 35 was that the defendant having charge of a motor vehicle caused bodily harm by " wilful misconduct ". The jury at quarter sessions were directed that there was no need for the prosecution to prove an intention to cause injury or bodily harm. If the defendant's driving was intended it was " wilful " and if it fell below the normal standard so that it could be called " misconduct " it sufficed if the " wilful misconduct " amounted to a substantial cause of the injury. Failure to have a light at night on a horse-drawn vehicle can be " wilful neglect " under s. 35 (*A.-G. v. Joyce* (1956), 90 I.L.T.R. 47). A conviction under s. 35 was upheld where the jury had found that the defendant was driving in a wanton way by reason of the amount of liquor he had taken; there was also evidence of reckless driving (*R. v. Burdon* (1927), 20 Cr.App.R. 80). Disqualification and endorsement may not be ordered for this offence (*quaere* whether s. 24 of the Criminal Justice Act, 1972, may be used: see p. 640) and its only useful purposes now seem to be for dealing with horse-drawn vehicles and cyclists and as a reserve charge for motorists who cannot be prosecuted for dangerous driving either because notice of intended prosecution was not given or the offence was not committed on a road within the meaning of the Act of 1972. There is no power of arrest without warrant save of a person found committing the offence at night or at any time in the Metropolitan Police District.

Evidence

Two persons pursuing a common purpose in a motor car may be guilty of criminal negligence by driving, though only one of them drives (*R.* v. *Baldessare* (1930), 22 Cr.App.R. 70). Evidence of the manner of driving prior to the accident and some miles away can, presumably, be given on the analogy of similar cases quoted on p. 276. The qualifications to *Baldessare's* case given on p. 277 should be noted. Persons in different vehicles racing each other or inciting each other to drive fast may both be guilty of causing death although it was caused by only one of the vehicles (*R.* v. *Swindall* (1846), 2 Car. & Kir. 230). But it may be noted that in the more modern case of *R.* v. *Milburn* [1974] R.T.R. 431 where two motorists raced each other and one of them killed a pedestrian on the pavement, the other defendant was only charged with aiding and abetting offences under s. 1 of the Road Traffic Act, 1972, and s. 35 of the Offences against the Person Act, 1861.

Disqualification, Endorsement and Penalty

Disqualification and endorsement must be ordered for offences by motor-drivers of manslaughter, culpable homicide and causing death by dangerous driving (Road Traffic Act, 1972, ss. 93 (1), 177 (2), Sched. 4, Pts. I and II) unless there are special reasons (see Chapter VII). The disqualification must be for not less than twelve months and, if the accused has been convicted within the three years preceding the offences for which endorsement was ordered on at least two occasions (see pp. 624–629), a further six months' disqualification consecutive to the period imposed (and to any disqualification previously ordered) must be ordered, unless having regard to all the circumstances there are grounds for mitigating the normal consequences of the conviction (see pp. 688–695) (Road Traffic Act, 1972, s. 93 (3)). As stated, disqualification and endorsement cannot be ordered for offences under the Offences against the Person Act, 1861, s. 35 (above), as the 1972 Act does not include them in Sched. 4.

The maximum penalty for manslaughter is life imprisonment and for causing death by dangerous driving five years' imprisonment (two years' imprisonment if tried by a sheriff court). There would seem to be a power to fine also (Archbold, 38th ed., para. 667; Criminal Law Act, 1967, s. 7 (3)). The sentence under the Offences against the Person Act is two years' imprisonment or a fine.

The court may also order the defendant to be disqualified till he takes a driving test (Road Traffic Act, 1972, s. 93 (7)), save for offences under the 1861 Act (see *R.* v. *Guilfoyle* and other cases below).

The endorsement code for manslaughter is DD60, and for causing death by dangerous driving DD50.

Principles of Punishment

In *R.* v. *Mabley* (1965), 109 S.J. 296, the defendant was a youth with an excellent character and there was no question of drink or of his skylarking about and being in need of discipline; the Court of Criminal Appeal substituted a fine for detention. In *R.* v. *Rous* [1965] Crim.L.R. 378, a disqualification of a chauffeur with an excellent record was reduced from five to three years. In *R.* v. *McCarthy* [1964] Crim.L.R. 330 the Court of Criminal Appeal substituted a fine for detention and upheld a seven-year disqualification on a previously unconvicted young man who had driven at 70 m.p.h. on a road limited to 40 m.p.h. In *R.* v. *Challoner* (1964), 108 S.J. 1049, and in *R.* v. *Worrell* [1965] Crim.L.R. 561, sentences of nine months' imprisonment and ten-year disqualifications were approved on drivers (Challoner had a record but Worrell did not) who had in one case driven on side-lights on the crown of a country road without stopping after the accident and in the other repeatedly overtaken where it was prohibited and had been drinking. In *R.* v. *Boe* [1968] Crim.L.R. 171 sentences of two years' imprisonment and disqualification for five years were upheld on young men who had been racing each other at 60 m.p.h. in ten-year-old cars in a restricted area: both had records; and in *R.* v. *Milburn* [1974] R.T.R. 431 a two-year prison sentence would have been upheld (or indeed three years if charged with manslaughter) for racing through the main streets of Middlesbrough with another motor car and killing a pedestrian on the pavement if his co-defendant had received a comparable sentence. In *R.* v. *Hazell* [1965] Crim.L.R. 120, a racing case on a motorway, a sentence of three months' imprisonment was upheld and a disqualification reduced to five years on a young man with no record. Where the defendant is under the influence of drink a custodial sentence is generally held necessary (*R.* v. *Worrell, supra*) even where the defendant is of previous good character and would lose his job as an airline pilot but had a blood/alcohol level of 292 mg. per 100 ml. (*R.* v. *Kashyap* [1972] Crim.L.R. 257; see also *R.* v. *Sullivan* [1974] Crim.L.R. 56 where a sentence of eighteen months was upheld even though his expectation of life was uncertain following an operation for cancer). In *R.* v. *Tyrer* [1972] Crim.L.R. 55 it was again stated that the gravity of the offence was less where it arose from inadvertence rather than a deliberate and calculated judgment. In *R.* v. *Guilfoyle* [1973] R.T.R. 272 the Court of Appeal suggested guide-lines for sentencing offenders convicted of s. 1 offences (*per* James, L.J., in *R.* v. *Lobley*

[1974] R.T.R., at p. 553: "But let this be said, *R.* v. *Guilfoyle* was not laying down any rule of law but only guide-lines, and in the end each case has to be visited with a period of disqualification which is appropriate to the facts of that particular case "). Where there has been recklessness or selfish disregard for the safety of others, a custodial sentence may be appropriate. Where the accident was caused by momentary inattention a fine will suffice. If the offender's driving record is good he should be disqualified for the minimum period, if indifferent two to four years and if bad for a long time. A period of disqualification should be fixed without regard to the right of a defendant to apply for its removal under s. 95 of the Road Traffic Act, 1972 (*R.* v. *Lobley* [1974] R.T.R. 550).

Where the offender is young, the principle that young offenders should normally not be disqualified for very long periods applies to s. 1 offences (see generally p. 638). On the other hand a young offender has less experience of driving and it is therefore more appropriate to order the offender to take a driving test at the end of a period of disqualification (*R.* v. *Guilfoyle,* where a period of disqualification for three years was reduced to one but the order under s. 93 (7) was upheld). It was further suggested in R. v. *Guilfoyle* that the longer a person is disqualified the more important it is that he be ordered to undergo a driving test, before he again obtains a full licence. In *R.* v. *Lobley* [1974] R.T.R. 550, an order under s. 93 (7) was imposed on appeal by the Court of Appeal when reducing a period of disqualification from four to two years, because the facts of the case raised serious doubts as to his driving ability and qualifications. In *R.* v. *Rowe* [1975] Crim.L.R. 245 an order to pass a test was upheld on a man who would be 67 when his term of disqualification expired and where there were indications that his powers of concentration were declining. A fine of £250 was upheld, but although he was a man of means an order to pay prosecution costs of £1,500 as well was quashed.

2. DANGEROUS AND CARELESS DRIVING AND CYCLING

These offences are dealt with together, as many of the cases apply to both.

Dangerous driving includes driving in a dangerous manner, driving at a dangerous speed and driving recklessly, and arises under the Road Traffic Act, 1972, s. 2 (formerly s. 2 of the 1960 Act); it reads:—

" (1) If a person drives a motor vehicle on a road recklessly, or at a speed or in a manner which is dangerous to the public, having regard to all the circumstances of the case, including the nature, condition and use of the road, and the amount of traffic which is actually at the time, or which might reasonably be expected to be, on the road, he shall be guilty of an offence." (For penalty see p. 292.)

The Criminal Law Act, 1967, repealed s. 2 (2) and (3) of the 1960 Act save for the reference in s. 2 (3) to culpable homicide in Scotland. In Scotland the Road Traffic Act, 1972, Sched. 4, Pt. IV, para. 2, allows conviction for dangerous driving on a s. 1 charge.

Careless driving includes driving without due care and attention and driving without reasonable consideration for other persons using the road, and arises under the Road Traffic Act, 1972, s. 3 (formerly s. 3 of the 1960 Act); it reads:—

" (1) If a person drives a motor vehicle on a road without due care and attention, or without reasonable consideration for other persons using the road, he shall be guilty of an offence." (For penalty see p. 293.)

The difference between dangerous driving and careless driving is discussed on p. 278.

As to pedal cyclists see p. 291.

Offences under ss. 2 and 3 can be committed only on a road as defined in the 1972 Act (see p. 26).

Sections 2 and 3 apply to trolley vehicles but not to tramcars operated under statutory powers (Road Traffic Act, 1972, s. 198 (1)).

Warning of intended prosecution (see Chapter III) is required for offences under ss. 2 and 3 unless an accident occurred (see Chapter III).

As to venue see p. 65.

A constable may arrest without a warrant a driver who within his view commits an offence under s. 2 or s. 3 unless he has given his name and address or produced his licence (Road Traffic Act, 1972, s. 164 (2)). As offences of dangerous or reckless driving are indictable offences, any constable or other person may arrest any person " found committing " an offence under s. 2 at night (Prevention of Offences Act, 1851, s. 11), and a Metropolitan police constable may arrest any person found committing such an offence at any hour in the District (Metropolitan Police Act, 1839, s. 66).

All offences of dangerous and careless driving and cycling apply to servants of the Crown (s. 188).

To produce false evidence with a view to misleading a court and perverting the course of justice constitutes the common-law offence of perverting the course of justice. It is also an offence to incite a person to do so (*R.* v. *Andrews* [1973] 1 All E.R. 857, where the defendant offered *R* in return for a reward from him to make a false statement to the police regarding an accident in which *R* was involved).

Procedure for Trial

Dangerous driving is triable on indictment or by magistrates and the procedure is that indicated by the Magistrates' Courts Act, 1952, s. 18 (see p. 79). Where the prosecution is being carried on by the Director of Public Prosecutions, his consent to summary trial is necessary. It is a Class 4 offence* for trial at the Crown Court. Dangerous cycling is triable summarily only.

The defendant may under s. 2 elect to be tried by jury under s. 25 of the Magistrates' Courts Act, 1952 (see p. 78), and the prosecutor should ask for summary trial at the outset, if he wants it. If a non-indictable offence, such as careless driving, speeding or disobeying a traffic sign, is charged along with dangerous driving, only the latter may be tried on indictment and the other offences will usually be adjourned until the Crown Court has dealt with the charge under s. 2. If there is an acquittal on indictment for dangerous driving, it seems that the police can still proceed (provided the information was laid in time and the warning of intended prosecution, where necessary, was given) with a lesser charge like speeding or disobeying a traffic sign and even with a charge of careless driving arising from the same facts. In *R.* v. *Cardiff JJ.* (1959), Queen's Bench Division, 20th January, a magistrate was directed by mandamus to hear a charge of careless driving after an acquittal on indictment on a charge of dangerous driving arising from the same facts. It may or may not be significant that, after the acquittal by the jury, the defendant would, unknown to the magistrate, have pleaded guilty to the lesser charge. Where there has been a conviction under s. 2 on indictment and the jury have taken into consideration the facts of the lesser offence in convicting under s. 2 this generally would bar further proceedings on the lesser charge (*Welton* v. *Tanebourne* (1908), 72 J.P. 419). See p. 93.

A charge of dangerous or careless driving may be tried along with one of driving under the influence of drink (*R.* v. *McBride* on p. 274), provided that in a magistrates' court the parties consent.

If a defendant charged with dangerous driving elects to be tried by jury and the magistrates find no case to answer against him, the court (if consisting of two or more magistrates) may proceed to hear a charge for careless driving or some other lesser offence on the same facts if the defendant has been duly summoned, or waives having a summons on such a charge. The evidence would all have to be given again, however, unless there was a plea of guilty. It may be, however, that para. 4 of Pt. IV of Sched. 4 (allowing pre-

* See Directions of the Lord Chief Justice (Stone (1975) pp. 5326–30).

ferment of a s. 3 charge on failure of a s. 2 one) would apply (see *infra*, p. 266), so that a charge of careless driving (but not of any other offence) could be heard without recalling the witnesses, unless requested.

Careless driving can only be tried by magistrates. The consent of both sides should be obtained where more than one charge is being tried together even if both charges arise from the same incident, though such consent is often impliable (*R*. v. *Ashbourne JJ.* (1950), 48 L.G.R. 268; *Brangwynne* v. *Evans* [1962] 1 All E.R. 446).

It is for the prosecutor, not the magistrates, to decide at the first instance whether the charge shall be dangerous or careless driving and the magistrates should not refuse to issue a summons for careless driving if he applies for that only (*R*. v. *Nuneaton JJ.* [1954] 3 All E.R. 251) but where the prosecution have preferred both dangerous and careless driving charges, the magistrates may refuse to consent to the withdrawal of the more serious charge (see *R*. v. *Bedwellty JJ.*, p. 76).

See p. 74 *et seq.* as to trying charges against separate defendants together with p. 77 as to trial of charges of driving whilst disqualified along with s. 2 or s. 3 charges.

A serviceman may properly be tried by court-martial for dangerous or careless driving on a road abroad on a charge of committing a civil offence contrary to the Army Act, 1955, s. 70 (*Cox* v. *Army Council* [1962] 1 All E.R. 880).

Alternative Charges

Section 2 creates three distinct offences and the defendant should not be charged with driving at a dangerous speed or in a dangerous manner in one information, as this creates duplicity (*R*. v. *Wilmot* (1933), 97 J.P. 149). A conviction, however, for driving recklessly *and* at a dangerous speed was upheld on the ground that the defendant's act was one and indivisible (*R*. v. *Jones, ex parte Thomas* (1921), 85 J.P. 112, not followed in *R*. v. *Belfast JJ.* [1952] N.I. 91). In *R*. v. *Clow* [1963] 2 All E.R. 216, an indictment for causing death by driving at a speed *and* in a manner dangerous to the public was upheld. In *Vernon* v. *Paddon* (1972), *The Times*, 11th February, *R*. v. *Clow* was followed. It is permissible to charge conjunctively provided that the matter relates to a single incident (*ibid.*). Where more than one offence under s. 2 or s. 3 is charged before magistrates, otherwise than in the alternative, in one information, it is submitted that the defendant can properly ask that the prosecutor elect on which limb he wishes to proceed; where the charges are in the alternative, the prosecutor should elect on which limb he wishes to proceed (*Edwards* v. *Jones* [1947] 1 All E.R. 830).   He must elect at the outset (*Hargreaves* v. *Alderson* [1962] 3 All E.R. 1019).

Section 3 creates two separate offences, and a conviction for driving without due care or without reasonable consideration is bad (*R.* v. *Surrey JJ.* (1932), 95 J.P. 219).   In *Hutton* v. *Casey* (1952), 116 J.P.Jo. 223, however, convictions under both limbs of s. 3, not in the alternative, were upheld in respect of an act of driving lasting only a few seconds.   In Scotland it seems that a charge under both limbs of s. 3 in the alternative is good (*Archibald* v. *Keiller* [1931] S.C.(J.) 34).

Co-defendants

Where a number of defendants are charged on separate informations with identical offences all arising out of one set of circumstances, the consent of each defendant is required for them to be tried together by a magistrates' court (*Aldus* v. *Watson* [1973] R.T.R. 466).   If on the other hand there is one information charging the defendants jointly, the defendants' consent is not required (*ibid.*).

Reduction of Dangerous Driving Charge to Careless Driving

Paragraph 4 of Pt. IV of Sched. 4 to the Road Traffic Act, 1972, makes provision as to this in magistrates' courts in England and Wales and reads:—

" Where a person is charged in England or Wales before a magistrates' court with an offence under section 2 or with an offence under section 17, and the court is of opinion that the offence is not proved, then, at any time during the hearing or immediately thereafter the court may, without prejudice to any other powers possessed by the court, direct or allow a charge for an offence under section 3 or, as the case may be, section 18 to be preferred forthwith against the defendant and may thereupon proceed with that charge, so however that he or his solicitor or counsel shall be informed of the new charge and be given an opportunity, whether by way of cross-examining any witness whose evidence has already been given against the defendant or otherwise, of answering the new charge, and the court shall, if it considers that the defendant is prejudiced in his defence by reason of the new charge's being so preferred, adjourn the hearing."

It is not clear if the paragraph applies when the defendant is neither present nor represented.   By para. 7 warning of intended prosecution need not have been given in such a case so far as the charge under s. 3 is concerned.   No charge save one under s. 3 can be preferred pursuant to this procedure—not, e.g., disobeying a traffic sign.   Paragraph 4 does not apply to trials on indictment and it is, of course, unnecessary to apply it in a magistrates' court where a charge of careless driving has been tried simultaneously with the one under s. 2. It is also not clear whether a magistrates' court, consisting of two or more magistrates, which has refused to commit a defendant for trial for dangerous driving, may then apply the subsection and direct the preferment of a charge of careless driving, without recalling any of the prosecution witnesses, unless requested.

The wording of para. 4 does not seem to be limited to trials as opposed to committals, however. If there is already a charge under s. 3 before the magistrates to which a plea has not been taken, the prosecutor, if he chooses to proceed on that charge and not make use of para. 4, must call his witnesses again, unless the defendant pleads guilty to careless driving. Where a dangerous driving charge alone has been tried summarily and the magistrates decide to reduce it under para. 4, it is submitted that the magistrates, besides giving the defence the chance of recalling prosecution witnesses for cross-examination and of adjourning, should allow, if desired, a further address by the defendant or his advocate and the recall of defence witnesses, in view of the words " or otherwise " in para. 4. *Semble*, on reducing a charge under para. 4, the defendant should also be asked if he pleads guilty to the new charge. There is no power, on a charge under s. 2, to convict under s. 3 unless the procedure of para. 4 has been followed or a charge under s. 3 has been specifically tried before the court; *cf. Ex parte Newsham* [1964] Crim.L.R. 57. A person was charged with dangerous driving and, alternatively, with careless driving. The s. 2 charge was then heard alone; after evidence had been heard on that dangerous driving charge, it was dismissed. The defendant had pleaded not guilty to careless driving but the magistrates purported to convict him of it without hearing any more evidence. The conviction was quashed (*R. v. Hawarden JJ., ex parte Leo* (1966), *The Guardian*, 4th February). If a charge of careless driving has been heard simultaneously with one of dangerous, the magistrates would be justified in dismissing the s. 2 charge and convicting on the s. 3 one at the end of the hearing; if the dangerous driving charge had been heard alone, they should either use the procedure of para. 4 on dismissing the " dangerous " charge or re-hear all the evidence when the " careless " charge is put, if there is a plea of not guilty to it.

The view has been advanced that quarter sessions (now the Crown Court), when hearing an appeal from a magistrates' court against a conviction for dangerous driving, cannot operate para. 4, as there can be no appeal on facts from a finding of guilt under s. 3 from the Crown Court. It is arguable that the Crown Court could use para. 4 if there was a plea of guilty to the new charge, for there is no appeal from a plea of guilty (though there is against sentence). It is accordingly submitted that the absence of a right of appeal is not necessarily a fatal objection to a conviction by the Crown Court even on a plea of not guilty. A way out of the difficulty might be for the Crown Court to remit the matter with their opinion thereon to the magistrates.

It is common for some police forces to prefer separate information for charges under ss. 2 and 3 together. Where this is done, the consent of the defendant and of the court to the charges being heard together should be obtained (*R.* v. *Ashbourne JJ.* (1950), 48 L.G.R. 268). *Edwards* v. *Jones*, *supra*, is distinguishable, as in that case there were two offences in one summons.

Section 104 of the Magistrates' Courts Act, 1952, provides that a magistrates' court shall not try an information unless it was laid within six months of the offence. If the dangerous driving charge occurred more than six months before the court hearing, does s. 104 prevent the magistrates exercising their power under para. 4 to direct or to allow a charge under s. 3 to be preferred? It may well do so: " charge " in the paragraph is, it is submitted, synonymous with " information ". In *Aldus* v. *Watson* [1973] R.T.R. 466 where the use of para. 4 was involved, Lord Widgery throughout referred to " informations " rather than " charges ". Support for this view can also be obtained from the judgment of Humphreys, J., in *Arnell* v. *Harris* [1945] K.B. 60, at p. 63. It may also be observed that para. 7 of Pt. IV of Sched. 4 contains an express exclusion of s. 179 (necessity of warning of intended prosecution, etc.) where the charge under s. 3 has been preferred against a defendant by virtue of para. 4. If it was thought necessary to expressly exclude s. 179 (2), Parliament could have similarly thought it necessary to exclude s. 104 if it wished.

Evidence

Public Emergencies

There is no exemption for police, fire-engine or ambulance drivers from prosecution for dangerous or careless driving and prosecutions are reported at 113 J.P.Jo. 374; 114 J.P.Jo. 54 and Jo.Crim.L. (1961) 1; and see also *R.* v. *Lundt-Smith* and *R.* v. *O'Toole* on p. 669 (two cases of ambulance drivers driving dangerously in an emergency). In *Gaynor* v. *Allen* [1959] 2 All E.R. 644, a civil case, it was held that a police officer driving in the course of his duty owes the same duty as a civilian driver to the public to drive with due care, and in *Wardell-Yerburgh* v. *Surrey County Council* [1973] R.T.R. 462 it was held that the driver of a fire tender responding to an emergency call owed to the public the same duty of care as any other driver. See *infra* as to any sudden emergency confronting a driver.

Objective Standard of Danger and Care

Section 2 contains an absolute prohibition against driving dangerously in that the prosecution does not have to prove an intention on the part of the driver to drive dangerously (see Megaw, L.J.'s comment on *Hill* v. *Baxter* in *R.* v. *Gosney*, p. 280; if his defence is that he was in a state of automatism through a fit or had lost control because of an attack by bees, he must bring evidence to show this: *Hill* v. *Baxter* [1958] 1 All E.R. 193). Magistrates cannot theorise that a dangerous course of driving arose because the defendant had a " black-out " in the absence of any evidence to that effect (*Richards* v. *Gardner* [1974] Crim.L.R. 119). It may be, however, that recklessness in his mind must be shown where the charge is one of reckless driving, though his manner of driving would be good evidence of his state of mind. If an explanation of automatism is suggested and supported by evidence of sufficient substance to merit consideration, the onus on the prosecution (of proof of guilt) is not discharged unless the court or jury, having considered this explanation, are still left in no reasonable doubt of the driver's guilt (*R.* v. *Budd* [1962] Crim.L.R. 49). If a man who knows that he is subject to dizzy spells or black-outs drives, it is no defence that his dangerous driving was caused by his having an attack (*R.* v. *Sibbles* [1959] Crim.L.R. 660); similarly, a man cannot plead the effect of high blood pressure bringing on a black-out and causing his car to be driven dangerously if he has aggravated his condition by drinking beforehand (*ibid.*). Where a diabetic in a state of confusion through his illness had driven for five miles but there was no evidence to show that the movements of his body and legs in driving were involuntary and wholly uncontrolled and uninitiated by any function of conscious will, the High Court directed a conviction (*Watmore* v. *Jenkins* [1962] 2 All E.R. 868). Where a diabetic's state of mind was caused by his taking too much insulin rather than by the disease itself, he is entitled to put forward a defence of automatism (*R.* v. *Quick* [1973] 3 All E.R. 347, where the Court of Appeal approved the following direction to a jury in the Scottish case of *H.M. Advocate* v. *Ritchie* [1926] J.C. 45: " Automatism is a defence to a charge of dangerous driving provided that a person takes reasonable steps to prevent himself from acting involuntarily in a manner dangerous to the public. It must be caused by some factor which he could not reasonably foresee and not by a self induced incapacity. . . ."). (It should, however, be noted that this may not be the law in Scotland as *Ritchie* was over-ruled in *H.M. Advocate* v. *Cunningham* [1963] J.C. 80. It should also be noted that *R.* v. *Quick* was apparently decided without *Cunningham* being cited to the Court of Appeal. It is, with respect, suggested that the distinction between impairment caused by the disease itself and impairment caused by too much insulin is unreal.) There was a conviction where the defendant failed to prove that he had been in a state of automatism (*Stevenson* v. *Beatson* [1965] S.L.T.(Sh.) 11), and in *Cook* v. *Atchison* (1968), 112 S.J. 235, magistrates were directed to convict where a defendant gave evidence that he thought he must have had a mild black-out because of his inability to brake on seeing that the traffic lights were red but no medical evidence was called. The mere fact that the magistrates thought that his evidence was apparently credible was not a sufficient foundation for the defence of automatism. Overtaking in dangerous circumstances under the mistaken belief that one is in the proper lane in a dual carriageway has been held to be dangerous driving (*R.* v. *Johnson* [1960] Crim.L.R. 430) but for it to be dangerous driving to do so, the defendant must nevertheless be " at fault " (see *R.* v. *Gosney* on p. 280). But a conviction for dangerous driving was quashed where there had been, in the words of the jury, " a mere error of judgment " (*R.* v. *Howell* (1938), 103 J.P. 9, a case later said to lay down no principle of law).

The driving need not actually cause danger; it is sufficient if the manner or speed of the driving is potentially dangerous. In *Trentham* v. *Rowlands* [1974] R.T.R. 164 the defendant, after flashing his headlights, followed a car at 70 m.p.h. keeping to the outer lane of a motorway, and after about a mile overtook on the inside. The driver of the other vehicle knew of the defendant's vehicle behind and was not jeopardised or endangered by the defendant overtaking. The defendant's conviction was affirmed by the High Court as overtaking at that speed and in that manner was potentially danger-ous as the driver in front could at the moment of overtaking have decided to resume his proper lane.

It is submitted that the standard of care demanded by the criminal law cannot be higher than that demanded by the civil law of negligence. In *Scott* v. *Warren* [1974] R.T.R. 104 the obligation of a following car to avoid hitting a car in front was examined and the civil case of *Brown & Lynn* v. *Western S.M.T. Co., Ltd.* [1945] S.C. 31 was applied (see p. 287).

With careless driving also, the test is an objective one. If the defendant fails to exercise due care, he is guilty whether or not his failure is due to his inexperience (*McCrone* v. *Riding* [1938] 1 All E.R. 157; learner-driver guilty) and whether or not it was a deliberate act or an error of judgment (*Taylor* v. *Rogers* (1960),

124 J.P. 217). Nor is knowledge of his carelessness an essential element of careless driving. A lorry driver who was not aware that he had hit a stationary vehicle was held to be rightly convicted of careless driving, although his conviction for failing to report the accident was quashed because he did not know of the accident (*Hampson* v. *Powell* [1970] 1 All E.R. 929). If a driver does not exercise that degree of care and attention which a reasonably prudent man would exercise in the circumstances, he is guilty whether or not he is committing an error of judgment (*Simpson* v. *Peat* [1952] 1 All E.R. 447, discussed at 102 L.J.News. 146; 213 L.T.News. 176 and 121 J.P.Jo. 591). Where magistrates had dismissed a charge of careless driving because they thought that the driver must have had a dizzy spell or been hit by a stone or a bird, there being no evidence before them to that effect, they were directed to convict, it being said that theirs was a fanciful doubt, not a reasonable one (*Oakes* v. *Foster* [1961] Crim.L.R. 628). See also *Johnson* v. *Fowler* and *Rabjohns* v. *Burgar*, *infra*, under " *Res Ipsa Loquitur* ". If the charge is one of driving without reasonable consideration for other road users, it is submitted that the test here would also be objective.

A wrong action in the agony of the collision will not suffice alone to prove an offence under s. 2 or s. 3 (*Simpson* v. *Peat*, *supra*), if the defendant had been driving properly beforehand and his actions prior to the time when the collision became imminent had been those of a prudent driver.

Res Ipsa Loquitur

Frequently the only evidence which the police are able to bring is evidence of the defendant's vehicle leaving the road and a collision occurring with a wall or a pole or the vehicle ending up in a ditch or upside down in a field. In the absence of any explanation by the defendant, if the only conclusion which it is possible to draw is that the defendant was negligent or had departed from what a reasonably prudent and competent driver would have done in the circumstances, a court should convict. The doctrine of *res ipsa loquitur* is a rule of evidence applicable to the tort of negligence and as such has no application to the criminal law. But the fact that *res ipsa loquitur* has no application to criminal law does not mean that the prosecution have to negative every possible explanation of a defendant before he can be convicted of careless driving where the facts at the scene of an accident are such that, in the absence of any explanation by the defendant, a court can have no alternative but to convict. Thus in *Rabjohns* v. *Burgar* [1972] Crim.L.R. 46 the defendant's car on a dry road collided with the concrete wall of a bridge on a fine clear day with no other vehicle apparently involved. There were two skid marks behind the car. There were no witnesses to the accident and the defendant gave no explanation as to how the accident occurred. The justices found that there was sufficient evidence for the defendant to be required to answer the prosecution's case but, on the defendant declining to give or call any evidence, ruled that there was insufficient evidence to convict. The Divisional Court held that the facts were so strong that the defendant should be convicted and pointed out that the prosecution did not have to show there was nothing wrong with the steering as the defendant had not raised the matter. A magistrates' court was directed to find that there was a case for the defendant to answer in *Watts* v. *Carter* [1971] R.T.R. 232, where the defendant's car was found to have hit a Post Office support pole two feet nine inches from the edge of the road and his suggestion that there was something wrong with his steering was shown to be wrong. This case was applied in *Wright* v. *Wenlock* [1972] Crim.L.R. 49, where the defendant's vehicle hit a telegraph pole near to the road's edge. In the absence of any explanation of the accident, the justices were directed by the Divisional Court to find that there was a case for the defendant to answer. Similarly in *Bensley* v. *Smith* [1972] Crim.L.R. 239 justices were directed to convict a defendant who had crossed a central white line and collided with a car coming in the opposite direction. Crossing a white line was itself evidence of careless driving and in the absence of explanation the justices must convict (*ibid.*). In *Richards* v. *Gardner* [1974] Crim.L.R. 119 the driver of a motor tractor unit pulled out to overtake, but braked on seeing a motor coach coming in the opposite direction, and the rear wheels then hopped and juddered for fifty feet causing the unit to turn to the right, go over the central white line and collide with the oncoming motor coach. The justices dismissed a charge of dangerous driving on the ground that the cause of the tractor unit going into the path of the motor coach was due to some factor beyond the control of the driver. He might have had a black-out. The justices were directed to convict; braking of such a kind as to cause hopping and juddering inferred that the driver had got into such a situation as to require violent braking. In the absence of evidence of a black-out or mechanical cause, this was clear evidence of dangerous driving.

But if an explanation, other than a fanciful explanation, is given by the defendant it is for the prosecution to disprove it and unless it is disproved the defendant is entitled to the benefit of the doubt (see *R.* v. *Spurge*, on p. 277). Thus in *Butty* v. *Davey* [1972] Crim.L.R. 48 the defendant's car after negotiating one sharp bend failed to negotiate a slight left-hand bend and slid on to the wrong side of the road and collided with an oncoming lorry. The defendant contended that he could only have done so because of some unexpected slipperiness of the road due to rain. The justices were upheld in dismissing the case as the defendant's explanation was not fanciful. It was also said that it was not incumbent on a defendant in a criminal case to show that he had skidded without fault (although it should be noted that in this particular case the defendant had given an explanation which was upheld by the justices). Where a vehicle takes a dangerous course and there is an accident, magistrates should refrain from theorising about its causes in the absence of any evidence and should not assume that the steering-column must have broken just before the accident, when there is evidence that the vehicle was in good condition prior to the accident (*Johnson* v. *Fowler* [1959] Crim.L.R. 463). In *Griffin* v. *Williams* [1964] Crim.L.R. 60 a conviction was directed where a car went out of control and there was no evidence of any defect. In *Hougham* v. *Martin* (1964), 108 S.J. 138, a car inexplicably veered off its course and collided with another vehicle: it was said that magistrates were not entitled to assume, without evidence, that, because it was a modern, mass-produced car, it was prone to mechanical defects. See *Oakes* v. *Foster*, under " Objective Standard ", p. 269, and " Mechanical Defects ", p. 277.

On the other hand, it should perhaps be emphasised that the facts must be so strong that in the absence of any evidence of mechanical defect, illness or other explanation that is given, the facts must give rise to an inference that the defendant was guilty of careless or dangerous driving. The facts have to be such as to show that the defendant's standard of driving was less than that required of a prudent and competent driver in all the circumstances of the case (see p. 286 and in particular *Scott* v. *Warren*—following car hitting car in front which had made an emergency stop; and *Jarvis* v. *Fuller*—colliding at night with cyclist without lights).

Falling Asleep

A driver who allows himself to be overcome by sleep, so that the car mounts the pavement or goes to the wrong side, is guilty of dangerous or careless driving, for he should have stopped when he felt sleep overtaking him (*Kay* v. *Butterworth* (1946), 110 J.P. 75; *Henderson* v. *Jones* (1955), 119 J.P. 305). In the latter case *Edwards* v. *Clarke* (1951), 115 J.P.Jo. 426, was explained as showing only that a driver's statement that he was asleep without other evidence of careless driving is insufficient for a conviction under s. 3, for he had not said nor was it shown that he went to sleep while driving. There are articles at 114 J.P.Jo. 16 and 119 J.P.Jo. 113 as to drivers overcome by *petit mal* and diabetes respectively and a case of heart trouble causing unconsciousness is at Jo.Crim.L. (1958) 181. In *Kay* v. *Butterworth*, *supra*, it was said that a driver should not be found guilty because he loses control through sudden illness or being hit by a stone. See also *Hill* v. *Baxter* and *R.* v. *Sibbles*, *supra*, under " Objective Standard ".

Drink

Where there is no charge of driving under the influence of drink and the accused is being tried for dangerous or careless driving only, evidence that he was at the time adversely affected by drink is of probative value and admissible, and its admissibility is not limited to rebuttal of such a defence as that he was not in control through no fault of his own. Such evidence must tend to show that the amount of drink taken was such as adversely to affect a driver or that he was in fact adversely affected, but the court has an overriding discretion to exclude such evidence where its prejudicial effect outweighs its probative value (*R.* v. *McBride* [1962] 2 Q.B. 167). Ashworth, J., said that no general rule could be laid down as to the way in which the discretion could be exercised, as each case must be considered on its own particular facts, but, if such evidence is introduced, it should at least appear of substantial weight (*ibid.*, at p. 172). Cases where such evidence has been allowed are *R.* v. *McBride*, *supra* (enough drink taken to justify a charge of driving under the influence of drink), *R.* v. *Richardson* [1960] Crim.L.R. 135 (visits to public houses before driving) and *R.* v. *Fisher* (*ibid.*; practically the whole day spent in public houses prior to driving). In *R.* v. *Thorpe* [1972] R.T.R. 118, following *R.* v. *McBride*, *supra*, evidence that the defendant was guilty of an offence of having more than the prescribed blood/alcohol level contrary to s. 6 of the 1972 Act was held to be admissible on a charge of causing death by dangerous driving because a blood/alcohol level of over 80 mg. per 100 ml. was such that it could tend to prove that it could affect a driver even if, for a particular driver, it might or might not affect his ability to drive. The test of whether evidence of drink is admissible was said in *R.* v. *Thorpe* to be (quoting Ashworth, J., in *R.* v. *McBride*, *supra*, at p. 172, with approval) that " such evidence must tend to show that the amount of drink taken was such as would adversely affect a driver or alternatively that the driver was in fact adversely affected." Thus evidence merely that the driver's breath smelled of drink or that he had been in one bar for a short while would not, it is submitted, generally be of sufficient probative value to justify its admission. As stated, the court has a discretion to exclude any such evidence, and the test to be applied is that already quoted.

It would seem that like principles might apply where it is alleged that the defendant's driving was affected by his having taken a drug or even by severe pain or emotional upset, if such evidence is of substantial weight.

A like rule as to admissibility of evidence of drinking applies in Scotland (*Burrell* v. *Hunter* [1956] S.L.T.(Sh.) 75). In Eire there is a conflict of decisions; see Jo.Crim.L. (1965) 53.

A charge of driving under the influence of drink or drugs may be tried along with one of dangerous or careless driving (*R.* v. *McBride*, *supra*), provided that in a magistrates' court the parties consent. Charges of causing death by dangerous driving should be tried separately from one under s. 5 (*ibid.*).

The fact that the driver is under the influence of drink so as to be incapable of having proper control of his vehicle is not of itself evidence of dangerous driving; dangerous driving has to be considered objectively having regard to what he is doing with his vehicle (*R.* v. *Ward* [1954] Crim.L.R. 940).

State of Traffic

The reference in s. 2 (1) to the traffic which is actually at the time, or might reasonably be expected to be on the road, should be noted in dangerous driving cases. Evidence as to traffic which might normally be expected to be on the road is receivable (*Durnell* v. *Scott* [1939] 1 All E.R. 183), and in *Parson* v. *Tomlin* (1956), 120 J.P. 129, evidence by a policeman of his estimate of the amount of traffic on a road at the time of the offence (*semble*, he was not there) and of the amount of traffic observed by him to pass the spot on a summer day was held admissible. See p. 173 as to magistrates using their own knowledge of the area. It is submitted that magistrates may properly be expected to know things of common knowledge, e.g., that the main roads to Brighton and Blackpool will be crowded at Bank Holiday week-ends and that traffic on motorways goes fast.

Dangerous Manner and Speed

A charge of driving in a dangerous manner seems to cover most sins of driving, since evidence of the vehicle's speed can be taken into consideration on such a charge, speed being an element of danger (*Hargreaves* v. *Baldwin* (1905), 69 J.P. 397; *Beresford* v. *Richardson* (1921), 85 J.P. 60). In *Bracegirdle* v. *Oxley* [1947] 1 All E.R. 126 and in *Baker* v. *Williams* (1956), 54 L.G.R. 197, evidence of cutting-in and overtaking was admitted on charges of driving at a dangerous speed, although in Scotland it has been held that on the latter charge evidence of speed only should be given and not of " jumping " traffic lights and cutting-in (*Galloway* v. *Adair* [1947] S.C.(J.) 7).

Evidence of Previous Driving

Evidence of dangerous driving a few minutes before but two miles from the scene of the accident was held to be admissible in *Hallett* v. *Warren* (1929), 93 J.P. 225; and in *R.* v. *Taylor* (1927), 20 Cr.App.R. 71, evidence of reckless driving five miles away was given. It is submitted, however, that the evidence of the earlier acts of driving must have some relevance to those charged, e.g., fast driving in the Strand is not necessarily relevant on a charge of careless driving in Piccadilly if the only allegation in Piccadilly is that the defendant, while driving slowly and on his correct side, was frequently glancing at shop windows as he drove. Assize judges, on trials for causing death by dangerous driving, have sometimes rejected evidence of the defendant's fast driving a mile from the accident; in one case there was a roundabout between the two spots. Indeed, evidence that the defendant was driving fast at a place where it was not unsafe to drive fast seems irrelevant and might be unfairly prejudicial and it is submitted that only acts of dangerous or careless driving within a reasonable distance and time should be allowed in evidence. It seems to be in order to charge the offence as having been committed in all the roads where the defendant drove dangerously or carelessly. If the charge relates to driving in the last road only and evidence is tendered of driving in other roads so that the defendant is misled or taken by surprise, he should be granted an adjournment, if he asks for it (*Hallett* v. *Warren, supra*). That case suggests that, if dangerous driving within the jurisdiction is proved, the court should convict even if there is no proof of an offence on the road actually charged as the scene of the offence, e.g., a charge of dangerous driving in Piccadilly should not be dismissed even if there is no evidence of dangerous driving there, so long as there is proof of dangerous driving in Trafalgar Square and Lower Regent Street. The prosecutor, however, would be wise to name all the roads in his information, as *Hallett* v. *Warren, supra*, may yet be distinguished and it was said *obiter* in *R.* v. *Budd* (1961), *The Times*, 8th November, that there can be a conviction for dangerous driving only if it occurred in the road named in the warning of intended prosecution under s. 241 (now s. 179 of the 1972 Act) (but see further Chapter III on p. 143).

Aiders and Abettors and Supervisors

In *Du Cros* v. *Lambourne* (1907), 70 J.P. 525, it was held that a person charged with dangerous driving could be convicted although the evidence might show only that he was aiding, abetting, counselling and procuring, and the actual driver had not been summoned (see also Jo.Crim.L. (1953) 173). In that case the lower court had found it unnecessary to decide whether the defendant had been driving; he had been sitting in the front of the car, and, being its owner, could control the manner of its driving. Two persons pursuing a common purpose may be guilty of criminal negligence in driving, although only one of them drives (*R.* v. *Baldessare* (1930), 22 Cr.App.R. 70). In that case the jury found that the passenger joined in responsibility with the driver for the way in which the vehicle was driven, but the doctrine of joint responsibility should not be applied indiscriminately where it is not clear who drove or that the passenger joined in responsibility for the way it was driven (*Webster* v. *Wishart* [1955] S.L.T. 243). See also *R.* v. *Swindall* on p. 260, *supra.* A managing director of a haulage company, together with the haulage company in Scotland, were held to be rightly convicted of aiding and abetting causing death by dangerous driving in England where the defendant lorry driver had been sent on a journey from Scotland into England when the managing director knew that the lorry had a dangerously worn tyre (*R.* v. *Robert Millar, infra*).

The supervisor of a learner-driver may be found guilty of aiding and abetting careless driving by the learner if he has failed to supervise him properly (*Rubie* v. *Faulkner* [1940] 1 All E.R. 285). He must not be passive where his supervisory duties require him to be active and he must advise the learner what to do to avoid accidents and risks (*ibid.*). If he does so advise and takes other available steps to avoid danger, it is submitted that the supervisor should not be found guilty merely because there has nevertheless been an accident because of the learner's failure to heed his advice, or because of a sudden and unexpected action. See p. 21 as to a supervisor being regarded as a driver. Driving-test examiners are there to observe the driver's mistakes and are not in the position of a driving instructor or supervisor (*B.S.M., Ltd.* v. *Simms* [1971] R.T.R. 190).

Mechanical Defects

It is a defence to charges of dangerous or careless driving that the driver, without fault of his own, was deprived of control of his vehicle by a mechanical defect therein of which he did not know and which was not such as he should have discovered if he had exercised reasonable prudence and, once there is some evidence of such a defect, the accused should be acquitted if his explanation leaves a real doubt in the minds of the jury or magistrates (*R.* v. *Spurge* [1961] 2 All E.R. 688). In that case the conviction was

+ PTO

upheld because, although a defect causing the car to pull to its offside was proved, the driver knew of this defect and yet continued to drive in a manner which was dangerous in those circumstances. Where a lorry driver knew that a tyre was dangerously worn and drove, his conviction for causing death by dangerous driving was upheld after the tyre had burst, causing the lorry to swerve and kill the occupants of an oncoming car (*R.* v. *Robert Millar (Contractors), Ltd., and Robert Millar* [1970] 1 All E.R. 577, following and approving the principle of *R.* v. *Spurge, supra*). The principle in *R.* v. *Spurge* is that if the danger was created by a sudden loss of control in no way due to any fault on the part of the driver (see *R.* v. *Gosney*, p. 280) the defendant should be acquitted. Once there is evidence of a mechanical defect which the driver neither knew of nor ought to have known, " the onus of disproving [it] undoubtedly rests on the prosecution " (*per* Salmon, J., [1961] 2 All E.R., at p. 692, expressly cited with approval by the Court of Appeal in *R.* v. *Gosney*, p. 280). Once it has been found as a fact that the motorist knows or ought to have known of the mechanical defect, he cannot avail himself of the defence even if the car has been subsequently serviced by a garage (*Haynes* v. *Swain* [1975] R.T.R. 40). Where a car has been serviced by a garage all that can be assumed is that the car has been serviced, nothing else (*ibid.*).

The corollary to the principle that an unexpected mechanical defect is a defence is that if the motorist drives a car having a mechanical defect of which he knows or ought to know, and danger results, he should be convicted of careless or dangerous driving. No reasonable, prudent and competent driver will knowingly drive a motor vehicle with a worn tyre, defective steering or defective brakes, and if a driver does so he is *ipso facto* departing from the standard of a prudent, reasonable and competent driver, it is submitted. *R.* v. *Spurge* was expressly upheld not only in *R.* v. *Gosney* (see p. 280) but also in *R.* v. *Atkinson* [1970] Crim.L.R. 405, where a motorist's conviction was quashed when he had not been allowed to call evidence to rebut the prosecution's evidence that he should have known his brakes were defective.

The court should not assume, without evidence, that a vehicle must have developed defects: see *Rabjohns* v. *Burgar, Richards* v. *Gardner, Johnson* v. *Fowler* and *Bensley* v. *Smith* on p. 271 under " *Res Ipsa Loquitur* ". See also *Burns* v. *Bidder* on p. 449.

The Difference between Dangerous and Careless Driving

Prior to the Road Traffic Act, 1930, persons were charged with reckless or negligent driving or driving in a manner or at a speed which was dangerous; these offences were under one section and carried the same penalty. The 1930 Act created offences of dangerous or reckless driving and driving carelessly or without reasonable consideration, the latter carrying then much lower penalties. It was obviously intended that the more serious charge should be brought where the defendant was plainly reckless or gravely irresponsible or had driven in a way which an onlooker could call " wicked ". The lesser charge would be brought, for example, where the defendant had been foolish or had committed an error of judgment. Where both offences are charged (i.e., 1972 Act, s. 2 and s. 3), it is submitted that it is for the magistrates, as a tribunal of fact, to say which offence has been committed and that no High Court decision can help on this question, which is essentially one of fact. Winn, J. (as he then was) has said, at *nisi prius*, that dangerous driving was a deliberate choice of a course of conduct whereby danger arose. Although *R.* v. *Evans*, on p. 257, *R.* v. *Parker*, on p. 257, *R.* v. *Gosney*, on p. 280 and *R.* v. *Stevens* on p. 256, clearly suggest that acts normally regarded as careless can be dangerous driving, those cases were not dealing with the distinction between the two offences and were not intended to lay down that mere foolish acts or errors of judgment alone are dangerous driving, otherwise the offence of careless driving might just as well not exist if practically everything is automatically dangerous driving. Parliament clearly intended there to be a distinction between the two offences otherwise magistrates would not have been given the power of directing a charge of careless driving to be brought where the magistrates' court find a charge of dangerous driving not proven. It is submitted that justice can be served if a conviction for dangerous driving is affirmed by magistrates only if the driving has been reckless or the defendant has intentionally taken risks, or, in the words of Winn, J., the defendant's driving was a deliberate choice of a course of conduct whereby danger arose. This appears sometimes to be the view of the Director of Public Prosecutions and many police officers who decide on prosecutions. Where a defendant has been merely careless, doing his incompetent best or momentarily inattentive both the Director and police forces have been known to charge the defendant with careless driving only, despite the fact that the defendant's carelessness has resulted in the death of an innocent party and despite the fact that in accordance with *R.* v. *Stevens* (see p. 256) and *R.* v. *Evans* (see p. 257) a conviction for causing death by dangerous driving would appear inevitable. See generally 117 J.P.Jo. 776 and [1955] Crim.L.R. 238.

Dangerous and Careless Driving and Civil Negligence Cases

The dangerous driver must be " at fault " (R. *v.* Gosney).—The leading case on dangerous driving may now be said to be *R.* v. *Gosney*
[1971] 3 All E.R. 220—at least so far as charges tried before a jury
at the Crown Court are concerned (see the second paragraph on
p. 281, *infra*). In *R.* v. *Gosney* the defendant turned right out of
a minor road and drove her car in the wrong direction along
the carriageway of a dual carriageway road. She sought to show
that she was not at fault because she was a stranger to the area
coming to the road at night and there was nothing to indicate
to a reasonable and competent driver in the prevailing circumstances that the main road was a dual carriageway rather than
a single carriageway. Her evidence was ruled irrelevant and
inadmissible following *R.* v. *Ball and Loughlin* (1966), 50 Cr.App.R.
266. Ball was the driver of an army scout car so designed that
he had no side vision and he relied on Loughlin for advice and
directions as to whether it was safe to proceed. He drove from
a minor road into a major road after being told by Loughlin it
was safe to proceed, Ball being unable to see that he was driving
into the path of an approaching vehicle on the major road. He
was convicted but given an absolute discharge. After this case
it became customary to add to the direction to the jury in *R.* v.
Evans, infra, " or whether (when the dangerous driving arose) he
was a good driver doing his best in very difficult circumstances "
and the offence of dangerous driving was said to be an " absolute
offence "; the only defences to the charge being " automatism "
or " mechanical defect " (see *R.* v. *Spurge*, on p. 277). Because
Mrs. Gosney's evidence was ruled inadmissible the jury convicted,
as it is unquestionably dangerous to drive the wrong way down the
fast lane of a dual carriageway at night. The Court of Appeal
set aside Mrs. Gosney's conviction on the ground that she should
have been allowed to give or call evidence that she was not at fault.
The Court of Appeal held that for the offence of dangerous driving
to be committed the defendant must be shown to be " at fault ".
" Fault " does not necessarily involve deliberate misconduct, recklessness or intention to drive in a manner inconsistent with proper
standards of driving. In *Hill* v. *Baxter* [1958] 1 Q.B. 277, at p. 282,
Lord Goddard, C.J., said that " no question of *mens rea* enters into
the offence." He meant by this (according to Megaw, L.J., in *R.* v.
Gosney, at p. 223) no more than that the prosecution did not have
to prove an intention to drive badly. Fault involved failure,
i.e., falling below the standard of care or skill of a competent and
experienced driver. The test is that the defendant's driving must

be measured against that of a competent and experienced driver in the circumstances of the case (*R.* v. *Gosney*). *R.* v. *Evans* [1962] 3 All E.R. 1086 was approved and followed, where the judge's direction to a jury was to the effect that if the jury were satisfied that the defendant's vehicle was driven dangerously, the defendant was guilty even if the dangerous driving arose from his " mere carelessness, momentary inattention or lack of skill or even though he was doing his incompetent best."

It follows from *R.* v. *Gosney* and *R.* v. *Evans* that as far as trial by jury is concerned there is no distinction between dangerous driving caused by recklessness or intentional bad driving, and dangerous driving caused by the driver driving without due care and attention (see for example *R.* v. *Stevens*, on p. 256).

The Court of Appeal expressly approved *R.* v. *Spurge* together with the statement in *R.* v. *Spurge* as to the onus of proof (see p. 278). If therefore a defendant raises a defence of mechanical defect or lack of fault it is for the prosecution to disprove it. In *R.* v. *Atkinson* [1970] Crim.L.R. 405 the prosecution called evidence that the motorist's car had defective brakes and, in reliance on *R.* v. *Spurge* (see p. 277), he should have known of the defect. Mechanical defect was ruled irrelevant and the defendant was not allowed to call expert evidence to rebut the prosecution evidence. The Court of Appeal held the judge to be wrong. *R.* v. *Evans, supra*, had in no way overruled *R.* v. *Spurge*.

Cases on Dangerous or Careless Driving

The following cases do not necessarily lay down principles of law applicable in all circumstances; a slight variation in facts, e.g., the time of day or the traffic, may make a difference.

Dangerous driving.—In *Troughton* v. *Manning* (1905), 69 J.P. 207, it was held that the intention of the statute is to prevent misconduct in the management of the vehicle towards the people outside it on the highway, and not towards persons in the vehicle. It was said in *Pawley* v. *Wharldall* [1965] 2 All E.R. 757 that the judgment of Kennedy, J., in *Troughton's* case went too far. Potential danger, having regard to the traffic which might reasonably be expected to be on the road (see p. 275), may suffice for a conviction, even though no other traffic was in fact endangered (*Bracegirdle* v. *Oxley* [1947] 1 All E.R. 126—lorry going at more than twice the speed permitted for it along a road normally carrying heavy traffic, overtaking without a signal on a bend and " charging at narrow bridges "). In *Marson* v. *Thompson* (1955), *The Times*, 8th March, magistrates were directed by the High Court to convict a motorist under s. 2 where he had " cut in " in a dangerous way, ignoring a signal not to do so.   Driving a motor cycle along an unrestricted road in a built-up area at 64 m.p.h. in heavy traffic and making a third line of traffic when overtaking a vehicle itself overtaking was held to be dangerous driving (*Baker* v. *Williams* (1956), 54 L.G.R. 197).   Overtaking two lines of traffic at speed, when traffic is approaching from the other direction, can be dangerous driving (*Squire* v. *Metropolitan Police Commissioner* [1957] Crim.L.R. 817). Overtaking in dangerous circumstances under the mistaken belief that the driver is in one lane of a dual carriageway was held by a judge to be dangerous driving (*R.* v. *Johnson* [1960] Crim.L.R. 430). In *Johnstone* v. *Hawkins* [1959] Crim.L.R. 854, the High Court refused to quash an acquittal for dangerous driving at 85 m.p.h. along a main road past a road junction controlled by a " slow " sign, where the driver had a long view down the minor road when twenty yards from it, but it was said (*ibid.*, at p. 459) that passing a junction at that speed was *prima facie* dangerous driving.   In *Tribe* v. *Jones* (1961), 59 L.G.R. 582, the High Court refused to interfere with an acquittal for driving at a dangerous speed where a car had been driven along a restricted road at speeds between 45 and 65 m.p.h.; it was a wide road, well surfaced and bounded by common land, the road was not busy at the time (7.20 a.m.) and the visibility and weather were good.   Momentary inattention, resulting in a failure to see traffic lights, can amount to dangerous driving (*R.* v. *Parker* (1957), 41 Cr. App.R. 134, discussed on p. 257). In a case noted on p. 4 of the *Guardian* of 28th January, 1966, magistrates were directed to convict a motor cyclist who had driven at a speed of 60 m.p.h. with his hands off the handlebars for four seconds, on a road with fairly heavy traffic.   In *Anderson* v. *Transport Board* [1964] N.Z.L.R. 881, the driver of a towing vehicle drove it in such a manner that the trailer snaked dangerously about the road; he was convicted of dangerous driving.

Careless driving.—Mounting the verge and hitting a pole nearly three feet from the edge of the road is *prima facie* evidence of careless driving, unless explained, e.g., a skid (*Watts* v. *Carter* (1959), *The Times*, 22nd October).   A driver who signals that he will turn right and then turns left without taking any precautions to see if anything is coming behind is guilty of careless driving (*Pratt* v. *Bloom* [1958] Crim.L.R. 817).   Failing to stop and look at a " T " junction was held to be careless driving in *Baker* v. *Spence* (1960), *The Times*, 27th May.   The driver's duty is not confined to making signals; he must see, so far as he can, that they have been understood and he may be guilty of careless driving if he drives on after making one without so seeing (*Sorrie* v. *Robertson* [1944] S.C.(J.) 95). The High Court reluctantly upheld a conviction of a motorist who edged from a park on to a road when his view of it was obstructed by parked vehicles (*O'Connel* v. *Fraser* (1963), 107 S.J. 95). A defendant who gave misleading signals that he was going to turn but did not in fact turn was held guilty of careless driving (*Another* v. *Probert* [1968] Crim.L.R. 564). It is submitted that this case is not necessarily an authority for the view that a driver who is, without negligence, un-aware that his indicators are flashing is therefore guilty of careless or inconsiderate driving. A conviction was directed when a car was driven at 25 m.p.h. past an obscured halt sign, and though the driver must have seen the white lines to mark the junction, he failed to see a car on the main road (*Spencer* v. *Silvester* (1963), 107 S.J. 1024). Crossing a central white line is itself evidence of careless driving in the absence of an explanation (*Bensley* v. *Smith* [1972] Crim.L.R. 239). A Metropolitan magistrate convicted a driver who was reading a newspaper and the case was likened to a driver who kept kissing his passenger (Jo.Crim.L. (1954) 204). A driver of a bus who is reversing and relying on his conductor's signals must satisfy himself that the conductor is so positioned that he can see what he ought to see; if that person is not so positioned, the driver may be guilty of careless driving (*Liddon* v. *Stringer* [1967] Crim.L.R. 371).

Driving without reasonable consideration.—Drivers have been prose-cuted for driving without reasonable consideration for other road users where they have had brilliant headlights which they have not dipped for oncoming traffic, or they have driven through puddles at speed, drenching pedestrians (129 J.P.Jo. 338). In *Saville* v. *Bache* (1969), *The Times*, 28th February, a civil case, it was said by the Court of Appeal that, if a motorist drove with undipped headlights in circumstances where he should know that they might dazzle an oncoming driver, it was for the former motorist to disprove his *prima facie* negligence in doing so by giving evidence of a good reason for not dipping. See p. 290 as to driving with uncorrected defective eyesight. A conviction was directed where the only road users affected were passengers in the defendant's vehicle; " other road users " include persons in or outside the vehicle (*Pawley* v. *Wharldall* [1965] 2 All E.R. 757). *Semble*, it must be proved that there actually were other road users; there is no reference, as there is in s. 2 (1), to persons who might reasonably be expected to be on the road. The defendant in *Pawley's* case had driven a bus in a way which scared the passengers. It may be necessary on this charge to show that the defendant was knowingly acting without consideration for others;

his acts or omissions will often establish a *prima facie* case to this effect. A motorist who kicked out at a pedal cyclist was held not guilty of this offence as there was no evidence that his machine came near enough to the pedal cycle to constitute the offence (*Downes* v. *Fell* (1969), 113 S.J. 387).

Civil cases.—The obligation of a following driver to exercise due care and attention when charged with a criminal offence under s. 3 of the 1972 Act cannot be higher than that imposed by the tort of negligence (*per* Lord Widgery, C.J., *Scott* v. *Warren* [1974] R.T.R. 104). A skid is not necessarily evidence of negligence (*Laurie* v. *Raglan, etc., Co.* [1941] 3 All E.R. 332), and in *Custins* v. *Nottingham Corporation* [1970] R.T.R. 365 a bus driver was found not to be negligent in allowing his bus to get out of control on an icy road, but in *Richley* v. *Faull* [1965] 3 All E.R. 109 an unexplained and violent skid was said to be in itself evidence of negligent driving. There is an article at 130 J.P.Jo. 283. Stopping suddenly is not necessarily evidence of negligent driving (*Parkinson* v. *Liverpool Corporation* [1950] 1 All E.R. 367). Automatic stop lights may not be in themselves sufficient warning to following traffic (*Croston* v. *Vaughan* [1937] 4 All E.R. 249). Hitting an unlit obstruction in the road does not necessarily show that the driver is negligent (*Tidy* v. *Battman* [1934] 1 K.B. 319) and in *Hill* v. *Phillips* (1963), 107 S.J. 890, it was said that persons driving along country roads with dipped headlights should keep an especially careful look-out, as the presence of unlit obstructions should be anticipated there. In *Grange Motors (Cwmbran), Ltd.* v. *Spencer* [1969] 1 All E.R. 340 it was held that a driver is not necessarily negligent in acting on the signals of another person, here a postman-driver as opposed to a casual onlooker; para. 70 of the 1969 Highway Code says that one should rely only on signals by policemen or traffic wardens. In *Clarke* v. *Winchurch* [1969] 1 All E.R. 275 the Court of Appeal said that flashing headlights could mean " come on ", notwithstanding para. 96 of the 1969 Highway Code, which says it means merely advising other road users of one's presence. If a driver is proceeding slowly and carefully where his view is obstructed, it is a counsel of perfection to require him to stop and look again when his bonnet is one foot out (*ibid.*) but Russell, L.J., dissented where the situation was potentially dangerous. A driver on a major road must still take precautions as to traffic emerging from minor roads and take due care to avoid colliding with it or endangering it (*Lang* v. *London Transport Executive* [1959] 3 All E.R. 609) and it is a question of fact whether he has been negligent in regard to it. While entitled to assume that drivers on the minor road will behave properly, he must take precautions if it is apparent they will not (*Browne* v. *Central S.M.T. Co.* [1949] S.C. 9). It was said in *Butters* v. *J. H. Fenner & Co.* (1967), *The Times*, 6th February, that a driver on a major road must still watch minor roads. It may be negligent to enter another road without ensuring that there is no traffic hidden by other vehicles in that road (*Harding* v. *Hinchcliffe* (1964), *The Times*, 8th April. It was a dark and stormy night and a lorry was being backed into a car park; it was at right angles to the carriageway and totally obstructed it and it showed no lights to the side. The plaintiff, driving along the road, collided with it and it was held that there was negligence by the lorry driver (*Barber* v. *British Road Services* (1964), *The Times*, 18th November). Similarly in *Jordan* v. *North Hampshire Plant Hire* [1970] R.T.R. 212 the driver of an articulated lorry was held to be negligent to drive in the dark his 35-feet-long lorry out of a drive and across a fast stretch of road where there were double white lines and a gradual bend. It was said to be a most dangerous manœuvre despite the fact that the sides of the lorry were not required by law to be lit. It is submitted that both in *Barber* v. *B.R.S.* and in *Jordan, supra,* either defendant could be charged with driving without reasonable consideration. If a driver is in doubt whether he has room to pass a stationary vehicle or obstruction, he should stop and check up (*Randall* v. *Tarrant* [1955] 1 All E.R. 600). To drive a motor vehicle along a country road when the driver knows that the vehicle has no front light is negligent (*Dawrant* v. *Nutt* [1960] 3 All E.R. 681). A motorist who disregards a white line at an uncontrolled road junction is not negligent (*Homewood* v. *Spiller* (1962), 106 S.J. 900) but (*per* Pearson, L.J.) it might indicate a junction where extra care is needed. Now, under reg. 22 (2) of the Traffic Signs Regulations and General Directions, 1964, double broken lines at a road-mouth mean that the driver must take precautions; see p. 311. It may therefore be that *Homewood* v. *Spiller* (*supra*) is now of less authority. It is not necessarily negligent to drive at a very high speed on a motorway but the driver should not assume that all overtaken vehicles will invariably observe lane discipline (*Hurlock* v. *Inglis* (1963), 107 S.J. 1023; see also *Trentham* v. *Rowlands* on p. 287 where it was held to be dangerous driving to overtake on the inside lane of a motorway at 70 m.p.h.). In *Quinn* v. *Scott* [1965] 2 All E.R. 588 a speed of 75 m.p.h. on a three-lane country road, when traffic was not heavy, was held not to be negligent in the circumstances. A speed of 25 to 30 m.p.h. in a quiet residential road on a Sunday and not sounding a horn or slowing down when passing a large coach parked on the nearside is not negligent (*Moore* v. *Poyner* [1975]

R.T.R. 127). Deceleration without warning to following traffic is not an act of negligence, even on a motorway, but a driver should signal his intention to make a sudden heavy stop (*Jungnickel* v. *Laing* (1967), 111 S.J. 19) and in *Goke* v. *Willett and Another* [1973] R.T.R. 422 a driver was held to be negligent in relying solely on his indicator and stop lights when slowing down in the centre lane of a three-lane busy trunk road to turn right into a service station.

Roundabouts and precedence for traffic on the right.—The 1969 Highway Code, para. 81, says that on a roundabout one should give way to vehicles coming from the right. The Highway Code does not say that one should give way to vehicles already on a roundabout, as the Ministry of Transport once advised; presumably para. 81 now applies, assuming that there is no " Give Way " sign. If a motorist fails to give way on a roundabout to traffic on his right, a charge of driving without reasonable consideration for other road users might be the appropriate one. As to giving way to traffic on the right generally, the Court of Appeal has said that it is a very salutary guiding rule that, where vehicles are approaching in risk of collision or where there is doubt as to priority, the vehicle which has the other on its right-hand side is the one to give way (*McIntyre* v. *Coles* [1966] 1 All E.R. 723, an accident at a " Y " junction). The 1969 Highway Code has no ruling on this point but the prosecution might argue that motorists should know the law as laid down by the Court of Appeal and ignorance of it, on this argument, is no defence to a charge of dangerous or careless driving.

Dangerous and Careless Driving Generally
Highway Code

It is emphasised again that dangerous and careless driving are questions of fact, and decisions of the High Court will generally be of little value because it is the facts in the particular case before the magistrates which must be considered and, even if a High Court decision can be found to fit them, there will almost certainly be some material variation in weather, state of traffic or other matter. The test as to whether a driver charged with dangerous or careless driving is " at fault " may be said to be *whether the prosecution have proved that the defendant departed from the standard of care and skill that in the particular circumstances of the case would have been exercised by a reasonable, prudent, competent and experienced driver.*

The best *guide* for those engaged in dangerous and careless driving cases is the Highway Code itself; its observance or non-observance can be relied on as tending to negative or establish liability in such cases. Section 37 (5) of the Road Traffic Act, 1972, reads as follows:—

" A failure on the part of a person to observe a provision of the Highway Code shall not of itself render that person liable to criminal proceedings of any kind, but any such failure may in any proceedings (whether civil or criminal and including proceedings for an offence under this Act, the Road Traffic Act, 1960 or the Road Traffic Act, 1967) be relied upon by any party to the proceedings as tending to establish or to negative any liabilities which is in question in those proceedings."

The Highway Code is only a guide. While the table of braking distances may be used in cross-examination to prove a breach of the code, it is otherwise inadmissible by itself to prove speed as it is hearsay (*R.* v. *Chadwick* [1975] Crim.L.R. 105). Prosecutions occasionally are brought on the basis that because a defendant is in breach of a provision of the Highway Code, he should automatically be convicted of careless driving in the absence of any other explanation. The facts of the case may, of course, be so overwhelming that in the absence of any explanation the defendant should be convicted (see " *Res Ipsa Loquitur* " on p. 273), but the mere breach of a provision of the Code by itself is not sufficient (see s. 37 (5), above). In *Scott* v. *Warren* [1974] R.T.R. 104 the defendant driving in a line of moving traffic was unable to avoid hitting the van in front which had made an emergency stop to avoid hitting a piece of metal which had fallen off a lorry in front of the van. The magistrates dismissed the case and it was suggested on the hearing of the case stated before the High Court that if a driver did not leave sufficient space between himself and the vehicle in front to avoid a collision then the defendant was *prima facie* guilty of careless driving as he would be in breach of rules 34 and 35 of the Highway Code. The Divisional Court disagreed, holding that whether a person has driven carelessly is primarily a matter of fact; the duty of a driver following another vehicle was, as far as reasonably possible, to take up such a position and to drive in such a fashion as to be able to deal with all traffic exigencies reasonably to be expected (applying *Brown & Lynn* v. *Western S.M.T. Co., Ltd.* [1945] S.C. 31). Another case where the justices' dismissal of a careless driving charge was upheld by the High Court where the defendant was in breach of the Highway Code is *Jarvis* v. *Fuller* [1974] R.T.R. 160. The defendant drove at 50 m.p.h. in drizzle at night with dipped headlights and failed to avoid hitting a pedal cyclist wearing dark clothing and whose rear light was probably not working. The Divisional Court again emphasised that whether a defendant was driving carelessly is primarily a question of fact. A breach of the Highway Code is, in accordance with s. 37 (5), *supra*, only evidential in its effect. On the other hand, the evidential effect of a failure to observe the Code may be strongly relied on to prove carelessness, dangerous or potentially dangerous driving. In *Trentham* v. *Rowlands* [1974]

R.T.R. 164, the Divisional Court relied, *inter alia*, on rule 116
(" overtake only on the right . . . never move to a lane on your left
to overtake . . .") in holding that it was potentially dangerous and
thus dangerous driving for a motorist to overtake another on the
outside lane at 70 m.p.h. by moving over to the inner lanes to do so,
particularly having regard to the obligation imposed by rule 114
on the driver being overtaken to return to the inside lane. It
should also be noted that under s. 37 (5) only a *failure* to observe
the Code is of evidential value. The fact that a defendant or
prosecution witness has complied with the Code does not mean that
that person cannot have been careless or negligent. In *Goke* v.
Willett [1973] R.T.R. 422, a driver who gave no hand signal but
relied only on his indicator and stop lights to show he was slowing
in the middle lane of a three-lane trunk road to turn right, was
held to be negligent even though the Highway Code can be read
as indicating that if trafficators and stop lights are both fitted
and are in good working order, hand signals need never be used.
In so far as the Code indicates that hand signals need never be used,
this is unwise advice (*ibid.*, *per* Edmund Davies, L.J., at p. 425).

Visibility

Where a driver finds himself unexpectedly blinded by headlights
or the sun or for any other reason he cannot see properly or control
the car, e.g., his dog suddenly jumps on his lap, then, unless the loss
of vision or control immediately ceases, he should stop at once.
If during the literal second or two while he has not proper vision
or control, an accident occurs which is due entirely to that loss of
vision or control, it is submitted that he is not guilty of careless
driving. But if the accident occurs ten seconds or more after the
loss of vision or control began and the driver has not done anything
about reducing speed or stopping, he should, it is submitted,
generally be found guilty of careless driving at least, not so much
for running into something because he could not see it but rather
for continuing to drive when he could not see or control the car
properly. In *S.* v. *Lombard* [1964] (4) South African L.R. 346,
it was held that a reasonable driver, if a horse-fly or any insect
which could perhaps cause trouble flies in at the window, will
immediately apply his brakes and stop. Again, the driver should
keep his eyes on the road, but must occasionally look aside to watch
his dashboard or pedestrians or police signals from the pavement
or to observe direction signs. It is submitted that no criminal
liability should attach to a driver for not keeping a proper look-out
during the second or two while he necessarily glances away from the
road ahead, provided he is driving at a reasonable speed. If he is

travelling at a speed of 30 m.p.h., a glance away for even four seconds may be dangerous; certainly gazing up at signposts while approaching a busy road junction could be, and a driver's failure to stop or slow down might amount to careless driving. The late author recalled a very experienced solicitor advising a driver to plead guilty to a charge of careless driving where the latter had reversed a few yards from a stationary position and collided with something because she had not made sure that the road behind was clear. Somewhat similar cases are reported at Jo.Crim.L. (1954) 120 and 121 J.P.Jo. 421. A driver who intends to reverse and cannot see from the driving seat whether he safely can, should, it is submitted, alight and satisfy himself that the road will be clear; if there are children about, even that might not suffice and he should wait until some reliable person can be found to signal him. It was held in *S. v. Lalla* [1964] (4) South African L.R. 320 that the reasonable driver who intends to reverse out of his garage or backyard where small children are or may be playing in close proximity to his line of travel knows that he must not begin to reverse before satisfying himself that no child has walked or crawled behind the car, for he is alive to that possibility and to the fact that he may not observe such a child by merely looking behind him from the driver's seat.

In *R. v. Parker* (1957), 41 Cr.App.R. 134, it was held that it was not a misdirection to tell a jury that a momentary inattention resulting in a failure to see traffic lights can amount to dangerous driving; the defendant was driving in a busy main street and went over a dangerous crossing, colliding with a bus. It is submitted that the case is not an authority for charging everyone who fails to see traffic lights with dangerous driving.

Use of Headlights

It is obviously dangerous to drive at night with sidelights only, on an unlit road, and by reg. 21 of the Road Vehicles Lighting Regulations (p. 745) it is now an offence if the street is not illuminated by street lamps. The Court of Appeal in *Hill* v. *Phillips* (1963), 107 S.J. 890 (a civil case), held that, when driving with dipped headlights in country roads, motorists should drive so that they could see unlighted obstructions the presence of which might be anticipated, e.g., cycles without lights or people in dark clothes. See *Clarke* v. *Winchurch* on p. 284 as to signalling by headlights.

The Road Vehicles Lighting Regulations, 1971 (S.I. 1971 No. 694) require that all moving vehicles having four or more wheels which are required to carry headlamps shall use a matched pair of headlamps except when on a road furnished with street lamps not more than 200 yards apart, such street lamps being lit; certain exceptions arise for public service, road clearance and towed vehicles, and foglamps and spotlamps may be used in fog and snow. Regulation 21 is set out on p. 745. Breach of the Regulations is an offence under s. 81 of the Road Traffic Act, 1972, and carries a fine of £50 but not endorsement or disqualification. Non-use of headlamps alone does not show dangerous or careless driving; there should be other evidence to sustain a s. 2 or s. 3 charge, e.g., fast driving or a collision suggesting that the driver was not driving within the limits of his vision. See also p. 283 as to driving without reasonable consideration with undipped headlamps.

It is also now an offence not to display headlamps, or fog lights or spotlights in conditions of poor visibility (see p. 403, and for the text of the Regulations, p. 764).

Two Offences from One Incident

The police sometimes charge a driver with both careless driving and disobedience to traffic lights or a stop sign in respect of the same incident. It is submitted that it is proper to convict on both charges where there has been some carelessness over and above the disobedience to the sign, e.g., approaching the junction too fast or not keeping a proper look-out for approaching traffic, but the penalty should be generally on the s. 3 charge and the other charge can be marked " no adjudication " or " adjourned " *sine die* if there is a conviction on the graver offence, so as to preserve, if desired, the position on appeal. Like principles would apply where there are charges of failing to accord precedence on a crossing and of careless driving from one incident or of crossing double white lines and careless driving from one incident. If there is nothing more to the case than disobedience to the red light (or other minor charge) and the driver has otherwise been careful, it is submitted that a conviction on the lights charge suffices and the careless driving one can properly be dismissed. Similarly it is also submitted that if the only carelessness is to fail to observe the lights or traffic sign, conviction on the graver charge only is sufficient. *R.* v. *Parker*, on p. 257, is not overlooked but it is submitted that to convict on both is oppressive, especially as it can lead to two endorsements and two penalties for one incident which might properly have been charged as a traffic light offence at the start. *Cf. R.* v. *Burnham JJ.*, on p. 93.

Driving with Uncorrected Defective Eyesight

The Road Traffic Act, 1972, s. 91, reads:—

" (1) If a person drives a motor vehicle on a road while his eyesight is such (whether through a defect which cannot be or one which is not for the time being sufficiently corrected) that he cannot comply with any requirement as to eyesight prescribed under this Part of this Act for the purposes of tests of competence to drive, he shall be guilty of an offence.

(2) A constable having reason to suspect that a person driving a motor vehicle may be guilty of an offence under subsection (1) above may require him to submit to a test for the purpose of ascertaining whether, using no other means of correction than he used at the time of driving, he can comply with the said requirement as to eyesight; and if that person refuses to submit to the test he shall be guilty of an offence."

The requirement as to eyesight mentioned in s. 91 is that the driver, whether wearing glasses or not, can read a car's number plate at a distance of 75 feet in good daylight, and 45 feet for pedestrian controlled vehicles; or, where the letters or figures are $3\frac{1}{8}$ inches in height instead of $3\frac{1}{2}$ inches, the minimum reading distance is reduced from 75 to 67 feet, and for pedestrian-controlled vehicles from 45 to 40 feet (Motor Vehicles (Driving Licences) Regulations, 1971 (S.I. 1971 No. 451), reg. 20 (1) (h)). The section makes it clear that, if he needs glasses to read the plate at 25 yards and he was not wearing them when he was driving, he is guilty and that he is to be tested in the same state as to wearing or not wearing them as when he was driving. It is submitted that the police may require the motorist under s. 91 (2) to take an eyesight test subsequent to the occasion which gave rise to the constable's suspicions. A person may be seen driving at night or in conditions of poor visibility and the prescribed test as to eyesight has to be taken in good daylight.

Penalties under s. 91 (1) and s. 91 (2) are now identical; both are punishable with a fine of £100 and are non-imprisonable. Offences under s. 91 carry obligatory endorsement unless there are " special reasons " (see Chapter VII) and optional disqualification. Section 93 (3) applies to them (see p. 624).

The endorsement code for the two offences under s. 91 is MS 40.

If the defendant's eyesight has not been corrected by spectacles or is incapable of being corrected by spectacles, a court should consider notifying the Secretary of State with a view to the licence being revoked under s. 92 of the 1972 Act. Alternatively the court may consider disqualifying the defendant under s. 93 (7) until he passes a test.

Cyclists

The Road Traffic Act, 1972, ss. 17 and 18, contain similar provisions to ss. 2 and 3 in respect of dangerous or careless riding of bicycles, tricycles and (s. 196) cycles having four or more wheels. An auto-assisted cycle may be a cycle for the purposes of ss. 17 and 18, if its engine is disconnected and essential parts have been removed (*Lawrence* v. *Howlett* [1952] 2 All E.R. 74; see the discussion of that case on p. 6). Otherwise, it is a motor vehicle whether the engine is running or not, and the definition of " cycle " contained in s. 196 specifically excludes cycles which are motor vehicles. The Concise Oxford Dictionary defines " ride " as " sit on and be carried by ", including " sit or go or be on something as on a horse, especially astride ". It is not clear whether a cyclist who is propelling himself by standing with one foot on the pedal and by touching the ground occasionally with the other " rides "; it can certainly be said that he is being " carried by " his machine. By contrast, s. 22 of the 1972 Act (failing to conform to traffic directions or signs) refers to persons " driving or propelling vehicles ". Offences under ss. 17 and 18 are triable by magistrates only; warning of intended prosecution is required (see Chapter III). Paragraph 4 of Pt. IV of Sched. 4 allows reduction of a charge of dangerous cycling to one of careless cycling as well as the reduction of dangerous driving to careless driving: see p. 266.

Driving to Common Danger, etc.

Offences akin to dangerous and careless driving arise also under the Highway Act, 1835, s. 78, the Metropolitan Police Act, 1839, s. 54, the Town Police Clauses Act, 1847, s. 28, and the Public Health Act, 1925, s. 74. These Acts would apply to motor vehicles, cycles and horse-drawn vehicles and (except for s. 28) to equestrians, mahouts, cameleers and outward-bound ladies from Riga (*Williams* v. *Evans* (1876), 41 J.P. 151) but see 119 J.P.Jo. 746, and p. 56, *supra*, as to who may prosecute under s. 28 and s. 74. As to Crown drivers, see p. 61.

The only value of these Acts so far as cases against motorists and cyclists are concerned is that warning of intended prosecution need not have been given (see Chapter III). Disqualification and endorsement cannot be ordered as these offences are not mentioned in Sched. 4 to the Road Traffic Act, 1972.

Penalties, Endorsement and Disqualification

Dangerous Driving of Motor Vehicles—Fines, &c.

On indictment the defendant, under s. 2, may be imprisoned for two years or fined an unlimited amount or both. The Court of Criminal Appeal reduced a sentence of imprisonment passed for dangerous driving where the defendant, in addition to driving dangerously, had been offensive to the police and carried out various manœuvres to irritate them; disrespect to authority is not a ground for passing a longer sentence than would otherwise have been awarded (*R.* v. *Thomas* [1961] Crim.L.R. 839). In *R.* v. *Storey* [1973] Crim.L.R. 189 a sentence of imprisonment of nine months was upheld in a bad case of deliberate dangerous driving where the defendant had been drinking. A sentence of imprisonment for a first offence of dangerous driving was severe (*ibid.*). See *R.* v. *Mabley* on p. 261 for a case where a fine was substituted for detention on a person of good character and generally as to sentencing at p. 594.

On conviction by magistrates he may be imprisoned for four months or fined £400. Magistrates no longer have the alternative of fining *and* imposing a sentence of imprisonment even if the latter is suspended.

The suggested penalty of the Magistrates' Association is " £100 and six months' disqualification " (see p. 879 and also generally, p. 594).

Dangerous Cycling

The penalty under s. 17 is a fine of £50. A second or subsequent offence is no longer imprisonable.

Careless or Inconsiderate Driving of Motor Vehicles—Fines, &c.

The fine on conviction under s. 3 is £200. Similarly a second or subsequent offence can no longer be punished by imprisonment.

The suggested penalty of the Magistrates' Association is " £50 and consider disqualification "; see p. 879 and, generally, p. 594.

Careless or Inconsiderate Cycling

The fine on conviction under s. 18 is £50 whether or not it is a first, second or subsequent conviction.

Dangerous Driving—Disqualification and Endorsement

On first conviction under s. 2 the defendant may, at the court's discretion, be disqualified for such period as the court directs. Whether or not disqualification is ordered on first conviction, the licence must be endorsed unless there are special reasons (Road Traffic Act, 1972, s. 101). See Chapter VII as to special reasons. If the defendant is subsequently convicted of an offence which was *committed* within three years after the date on which he was previously *convicted*, he must be disqualified (unless there are special reasons) for at least twelve months. Thus if the second offence occurred after the first offence, but at the time of commission of the second offence he had not yet been convicted of the first offence, the court is not obliged to disqualify him (although, of course, in such a case it is thought that ordinarily a court would consider exercising its discretionary power to disqualify). The previous conviction may be either under s. 1 (causing death by dangerous driving) or s. 2 (dangerous driving), but not for motor manslaughter or culpable homicide. If it is a first offence or the previous conviction was more than three years ago, the court has a discretion whether or not to disqualify. Offences under s. 2 are offences to which s. 93 (3) of the Road Traffic Act, 1972, applies, viz., on conviction under s. 2, there must be a disqualification for six months at least if the defendant has within three years immediately before the offence been convicted on not less than two occasions of an endorsed disqualifiable offence in respect of a motor vehicle (see p. 624) unless, having regard to all the circumstances, there are grounds for mitigating the normal consequences of the conviction (see p. 688). The six months' disqualification under s. 93 (3) must be additional and consecutive to any period of disqualification ordered on the same occasion or for an earlier offence (s. 93 (5)). The endorsement code for dangerous driving is as follows:—

Driving in a dangerous manner DD10
Driving at a dangerous speed DD20
Reckless driving DD30

Careless Driving—Disqualification and Endorsement

On first or subsequent conviction under s. 3, the defendant may at the court's discretion be disqualified for such period as it directs. His licence must be endorsed unless there are special reasons (s. 101). The endorsement code for driving without due care and attention is CD10 and for driving without reasonable consideration is CD20.

Offences under s. 3 are offences to which s. 93 (3) of the Act applies, and carry compulsory disqualification, if there are two previous convictions for offences within the last three years for which the licence was ordered to be endorsed; see above.

Driving Tests

A person convicted under s. 2 or s. 3 may be ordered to be disqualified until he passes a driving test (1972 Act, s. 93 (7); see p. 262 and Chapter VI, p. 660).

3. TRAFFIC SIGNS AND POLICE SIGNALS

The Road Traffic Regulation Act, 1967, s. 55, authorises the highway authority to place traffic signs on or near any road and s. 57 of the same Act authorises constables, or any person acting under the instructions (general or specific) of a chief officer of police, to place on any highway or on any structure on a highway authorised signs relating to special traffic regulations. By s. 58 of the Act of 1967 constables, or any person acting under the instructions (general or specific) of a chief officer of police, may place on a highway or on a structure on a highway authorised signs to prevent or mitigate congestion or obstruction of, or danger to or from traffic in consequence of extraordinary circumstances, but such signs by s. 58 (1) may not be maintained for longer than seven days.

The Road Traffic Act, 1972, s. 22, reads:—

" (1) Where a constable is for the time being engaged in the regulation of traffic in a road, or where a traffic sign, being a sign of the prescribed size, colour and type, or of another character authorised by the Secretary of State under the provisions in that behalf of the Road Traffic Regulation Act, 1967, has been lawfully placed on or near a road, a person driving or propelling a vehicle who—

(a) neglects or refuses to stop the vehicle or to make it proceed in, or keep to, a particular line of traffic when directed so to do by the constable in the execution of his duty, or

(b) fails to comply with the indication given by the sign,

shall be guilty of an offence [for penalty see p. 314].

(2) A traffic sign shall not be treated for the purposes of this section as having been lawfully placed unless either—

(a) the indication given by the sign is an indication of a statutory prohibition, restriction or requirement, or

(b) it is expressly provided by or under any provision of this Act or of the Road Traffic Regulation Act, 1967, that this section shall apply to the sign or to signs of a type of which the sign is one;

and where the indication mentioned in paragraph (a) of this subsection is of the general nature only of the prohibition, restriction or requirement to which the sign relates a person shall not be convicted of failure to comply with the indication unless he has failed to comply with the said prohibition, restriction or requirement.

(3) For the purposes of this section a traffic sign placed on or near a road shall be deemed to be of the prescribed size, colour and type, or of another character authorised as mentioned in subsection (1) above, and (subject to subsection (2) above) to have been lawfully so placed, unless the contrary is proved.

(4) It shall be lawful in Scotland to convict a person of a contravention of this section on the evidence of one witness."

[The reference to a constable also includes a traffic warden (see p. 305, *infra*).]

Section 22A (inserted by s. 6 of the Road Traffic Act, 1974) reads:—

" (1) If a traffic survey of any description is carried out on or in the vicinity of a road, then—

(a) for the purposes of section 22 of this Act, a traffic direction given by a constable to a person driving or propelling a vehicle, being a direction given for the purposes of the survey, shall be treated as a direction given by him in the execution of his duty and at a time when he is engaged in the regulation of traffic; and

(*b*) section 22 of this Act shall apply to a traffic sign by which a traffic direction is given for the purpose of the survey.

(2) In this section ' traffic direction ' means a direction to stop a vehicle, to make it proceed in, or keep to, a particular line of traffic or to proceed to a particular point on or near the road on which the vehicle is being driven or propelled, but does not include a direction requiring any person to furnish any information for the purposes of a traffic survey.

(3) In relation to a traffic direction given by a constable by virtue of this section and requiring a vehicle to proceed to a particular point, paragraph (*a*) of subsection (1) of section 22 of this Act shall have effect as if, after the words ' line of traffic ' there were inserted the words ' or to proceed to a particular point '.

(4) The power to give a traffic direction for the purposes of a traffic survey shall be so exercised as not to cause any unreasonable delay to a person who indicates that he is unwilling to furnish any information for the purposes of the survey."

Section 54 of the Road Traffic Regulation Act, 1967, defines " traffic sign " and reads:—

" (1) In this Act ' traffic sign ' means any object or device (whether fixed or portable) for conveying, to traffic on roads or any specified class of traffic, warnings, information, requirements restrictions, or prohibitions of any description specified by regulations made by the Minister and the Secretary of State acting jointly or authorised by the appropriate Minister, and any line or mark on a road for so conveying such warnings, information, requirements, restrictions or prohibitions.

(2) Traffic signs shall be of the size, colour and type prescribed by regulations made as aforesaid except where the appropriate Minister authorises the erection or retention of a sign of another character; and for the purposes of this subsection illumination, whether by lighting or by the use of reflectors or reflecting material, or the absence of such illumination, shall be part of the type or character of a sign.

(3) Regulations under this section may be made so as to apply either generally or in such circumstances only as may be specified in the regulations.

(4) Except as provided by this Act, no traffic sign shall be placed on or near a road except—

(*a*) a notice in respect of the use of a bridge;

(*b*) a traffic sign placed, in pursuance of powers conferred by a special Act of Parliament or order having the force of an Act, by the owners or workers of a tramway, light railway, or trolley vehicle undertaking, a dock undertaking or a harbour undertaking;

(*c*) a traffic sign placed on any land by a person authorised under the following provisions of this Part of this Act to place the sign on a highway, being a sign placed on that land for a purpose for which that person is authorised to place it on a highway.

(5) Regulations under this section, or any authorisation under subsection (2) above, may provide that section 14 of the Road Traffic Act, 1960 (drivers to comply with traffic directions) [*Now* s. 22 *of the Act of* 1972: *Ed.*] shall apply to signs of a type specified in that behalf by the regulations, or as the case may be to the sign to which the authorisation relates.

(6) References in any enactment (including any enactment contained in this Act) to the erection or placing of traffic signs shall include references to the display thereof in any manner, whether or not involving fixing or placing."

The present Regulations and Directions are the Traffic Signs Regulations and General Directions, 1964 (S.I. 1964 No. 1857), as amended by S.I. 1964 No. 2069, S.I. 1966 Nos. 489 and 490, S.I. 1969 No. 1269, S.I. 1970 Nos. 468 and 1972, and S.I. 1971 No. 2095, together with the Traffic Signs (Disqualification for Offences) Regulations, 1969 (S.I. 1969 No. 1270). Relevant extracts from the Regulations are set out in Appendix I to this book; see p. 709.

Section 22 applies to Crown vehicles (s. 188).

Offences under Section 22

It is an offence under s. 22 (1) and (2) of the 1972 Act to fail to comply with the indication given by a sign if it indicates a statutory prohibition, restriction or requirement or if it is expressly provided by or under any provision of the Act that s. 22 applies to that sign or type of sign. Section 22 (2) is curiously worded in that it says that a sign shall not be deemed to have been " lawfully placed " unless it indicates the statutory prohibition, etc., or it is expressly provided that s. 22 applies to the sign; it does not expressly say that it is not an offence to disobey any other sign. The term " statutory prohibition, restriction or requirement " means, it is submitted, one having effect pursuant to a public or local Act of Parliament and does not extend to signs, such as " No Waiting ", having effect under an order or regulation: cf. the meaning of "enactment " in s. 168; see p. 461. Regulation 7 of the 1964 Regulations, as amended, provides that s. 22 applies to the signs listed in that regulation, so that it is an offence under s. 22 to fail to comply with such a sign. They are " Stop " (at junction of major road), " Give Way " (at junction of major road), " Stop " (at road works), the straight arrow to indicate that traffic is to proceed in a particular direction, the diagonal arrow for " keep left " or " right ", red traffic lights (not including the motorway flashing red signals, but including the flashing red lights used at automatic level crossings), the double white lines (either both unbroken or a continuous line and broken line), the round red sign with the white band meaning " No Entry " and the " Drivers of Large or 5 ton Vehicles Must Phone " sign at automatic level crossings. Temporary signs erected by the police (see p. 310) in the exercise of the powers conferred by s. 58 of the Act of 1967 are expressly included in the category of signs to which s. 22 applies by virtue of s. 58 (2). The red flashing traffic signs erected on motorways are individually authorised by the Secretary of State under ss. 54 and 55 of the Act of 1967. It is understood that all the authorisations of such motorway red flashing lights expressly applied s. 22 to the signs but in any case where a contravention occurs a defending solicitor may wish to insist on production of the authorisation before advising his client to plead guilty to a prosecution under s. 22. (For an article setting out rather more fully the legal position of these motorway signs, see *Justice of the Peace*, 1974, pp. 634–635.) Although contravention of them is punishable under s. 22, an offence in respect of these signs carries no risk of disqualification or endorsement because these signals are not included amongst those attracting possible disqualification and obligatory endorsement (see Traffic Signs (Disqualification for Offences) Regulations, 1969 (S.I. 1969 No. 1270) on p. 728).

" One Way ", " No Right Turn ", etc., Orders

Is it an offence under s. 22 to fail to comply with any other sign prescribed by the Regulations, such as " One Way Traffic ", " No Waiting ", or " No Right Turn "? It is submitted that disobedience to any such sign should be prosecuted under s. 1 (8) of the Act of 1967 in respect of the particular traffic regulation order whereby waiting in, entry to the street, etc., is forbidden and not under s. 22. If any sign indicates a "statutory prohibition, restriction or requirement " (see s. 22 (2) (*a*)), then reg. 7 which sets out certain signs to which s. 22 does apply, is completely unnecessary. The signs in reg. 7 have effect under the Traffic Signs Regulations and General Directions, 1964 just as other signs have effect under the 1964 Regulations and (usually) some other order as well. Indeed, if a person stopped to unload goods in a " no waiting " area where unloading was allowed, to charge him with contravention of the " no waiting " sign might be to deprive him of the benefit of the unloading exemption unless it can be said that the latter part of s. 22 (2) preserves his rights.

Where defendants are prosecuted under s. 1 (8) of using a vehicle, or causing or permitting a vehicle to be used (for " using, causing or permitting ", see Chapter I) in contravention of a traffic regulation order, the defence may properly insist on production of the relevant order. If the order has not been published in accordance with regulations made under s. 84C of the Act of 1967 no offence will have been committed (*James* v. *Cavey* [1967]

1 All E.R. 1048). If the prosecution, even after notice from the defence, omit to prove proper publication, the court should normally grant the prosecution an adjournment to do so, it is submitted, as such evidence is of a formal nature (see *Royal* v. *Prescott-Clarke* [1966] 2 All E.R. 366 where the High Court similarly interpreted comparable regulations made under s. 72 (5) of the Act of 1967 in respect of motorways).

In *Wright* v. *Howard* [1973] R.T.R. 12 the High Court considered the effect of a " no right turn " order. The relevant order prohibited motorists emerging from Turl Street, Oxford, to " make a right hand turn into " High Street. The right hand kerb of Turl Street was in line with the left hand kerb of Alfred Street. The defendant therefore had to veer slightly to the right across High Street to enter Alfred Street. The High Court held that no offence was committed; giving importance to the word " into " it was held that making a right turn " into " meant proceeding right " into " High Street, not virtually going straight across High Street but veering slightly right to enter Alfred Street.

Pushing Cycles and Hand Carts

Section 22 applies to cyclists, trams, trolley vehicles, horse-drawn vehicles and hand carts as well as to motor vehicles, but not to equestrians. As to persons pushing cycles, see 114 J.P.Jo. 160; a person who pushed a lorry to try to make it start was held to be guilty of taking and driving it away (*Shimmell* v. *Fisher* [1951] 2 All E.R. 672) and so it can be argued that persons pushing bicycles and hand carts are guilty of an offence if they disobey a traffic sign. On the other hand, there is the argument that " Stop " signs and traffic lights do not apply to persons pushing pedal cycles and hand carts because, presumably, such signs are not meant to affect pedestrians, who can walk into main roads and against traffic signs at their pleasure. If a pedestrian can do that, cannot a pedestrian pushing a pram, or a child with a scooter, do the same? And if a pram-pusher can, why should not a cycle-pusher? A counter-argument is that the mischief aimed at by s. 22 is to prevent any type of vehicle being in a major road in disobedience of the sign or going against the red light and that it is immaterial whether such a vehicle arrives there by mechanical or muscular power, the offence being " driving or propelling " a vehicle. Compare *McKerrell* v. *Robertson* on p. 449—woman and go-cart which she was pushing held to be one entity under the Pedestrian Crossings Regulations.

Warning of Intended Prosecution

Warning of intended prosecution (see Chapter III) is required for all offences under s. 22 (Road Traffic Act, 1972, s. 179 and Sched. 4) whether committed by the driver of a motor vehicle or by the rider or propeller of any other type of vehicle, including pedal cyclists and tricyclists, or by the driver of a horse-drawn vehicle unless s. 179 (3A) applies in the particular case (see pp. 128 and 130). In *Walton* v. *Hawkins* [1973] R.T.R. 366, at p. 369, a contention that the notice of intended prosecution did not comply with the statutory requirements in that the failure to observe double white lines according to the notice occurred south of a junction when in fact the road ran east and west, was abandoned by the appellant with the approval of the court as the appellant had not been prejudiced by the error (following *Pope* v. *Clarke* [1953] 2 All E.R. 704).

Presumption of Conformity

A traffic sign placed on or near a road shall be deemed to be of the prescribed size, colour and type, or of another character authorised by the Secretary of State for the Environment, and to have been lawfully so placed, unless the contrary is proved (Road Traffic Act, 1972, s. 22 (3)). See *infra* as to defective signs. See also *Woodriffe* v. *Plowman* under " Traffic Lights ", *infra*.

Traffic lights are presumed to be working properly (see *Wells* v. *Woodward* on p. 303).

For the purposes of a traffic regulation order made under the Road Traffic Regulation Act, 1967, s. 1, a traffic sign is deemed to be lawfully in place unless the contrary is proved and certain other evidential presumptions may be made (Transport Act, 1968, Sched. 14).

Liability of Driver

It is no defence that the defendant did not see the sign; *mens rea* is not essential (*Rees* v. *Taylor* (1939), unreported, cited in Stone (1974), p. 3317; *Hill* v. *Baxter* [1958] 1 All E.R. 193). As to proving that a sign does not conform, see the *Justices' Clerk*, June, 1953. Illumination of signs is dealt with *infra* in respect of particular signs and by regs. 15 to 19 of the Traffic Signs Regulations and General Directions, 1964.

An information under s. 22 is not bad because it uses the word " fail " instead of " neglect " (*Pontin* v. *Price* (1933), 97 J.P. 315).

In *R.* v. *Spurge* [1961] 2 All E.R. 688 it was held that it is a defence to a charge of dangerous driving if it occurred owing to a defect in the vehicle of which the driver did not know and which he could not previously have discovered by the exercise of reasonable prudence, and in *Burns* v. *Bidder* [1966] 3 All E.R. 29 it was said that being pushed by another vehicle on to a crossing or a latent defect might afford a defence to a charge of not according precedence on a pedestrian crossing. The same principles presumably apply as defences to charges of disobeying police signals and traffic signs.

Traffic Lights

Regulations 31 to 35 of the Traffic Signs Regulations and General Directions, 1964, deal with light signals for traffic and pedestrians. Regulation 34 (3) requires drivers passing signals to proceed with due regard for the safety of other road users and subject to the directions of any uniformed constable or other duly authorised person who may be engaged in the regulation of traffic. Traffic wardens may regulate traffic and so be duly authorised persons (see p. 305).

In *Eva* v. *Reeves* [1938] 2 All E.R. 115 (a civil case) it was held that a driver who has the green light in his favour owes no duty to traffic entering a crossing in disobedience to the lights save that, if he actually sees such traffic, he must take all reasonable steps to avoid a collision.

Fire engines (and, *semble*, police cars and ambulances) may not disregard traffic lights when answering emergency calls (*Ward* v. *L.C.C.* [1938] 2 All E.R. 341, a civil case). In *Buckoke and Others* v. *Greater London Council* [1971] 2 All E.R. 254, it was held that, although the law was clear that it was an offence for the driver of a fire appliance to pass a traffic light at red, a fire authority could lawfully issue a fire brigade order giving the driver responding to an emergency call a discretion to pass lights at red. If the driver uses all care and there is no danger to others and he is prosecuted he should be given an absolute discharge under s. 7 of the Powers of Criminal Courts Act, 1973 (*per* Lord Denning, M.R., at p. 258), and (presumably) not have his licence endorsed on the ground of the emergency. By reg. 34 (1) (*b*) of the 1964 Regulations the amber-with-red signal shall not alter the prohibitions conveyed by the red signal; by reg. 34 (1) (*d*) the amber alone signal shall convey the prohibition that traffic shall not proceed beyond the stop line or, if there is no stop line visible, beyond the signals except in the case of any vehicle which, when the signal first appears, is so close to the line or signals that it cannot safely be stopped before passing the line or signals. As reg. 7 does not say

that disobedience to the amber-alone signal is an offence against
s. 22, it may be that disobeying an amber signal is not an offence,
notwithstanding the terms of reg. 34, just cited, if it can be shown
that the driver was never subject to a red light. He might still be
liable for careless driving, however. A Metropolitan magistrate
has dismissed a case under s. 22 of crossing on amber alone
(Jo.Crim.L. (1959) 87). Where lights have apparently stuck at red,
a District Justice has held that a driver who has waited a reasonable
time for them to change in his favour may then proceed with caution
against them (Jo.Crim.L. (1959) 222); a prosecution against a
careful driver in such circumstances would rightly be criticised but
he might have no defence in a civil case. The liability of a driver
where the traffic light nearest to him is not working, but the further
one is, is discussed at 122 J.P.Jo. 82. A civil case in which a driver
who had the lights in his favour was held guilty of negligence in
entering a crossing too fast just after the lights had changed and in
which a lorry-driver who was crossing the car's path on the amber
was also held negligent in not paying enough regard to crossing
traffic, although he could not have safely stopped at the amber, is
Godsmark v. *Knight Bros.* (1960), 124 J.P.Jo. 422.

Portable lights are authorised by reg. 33 (1) in the following cases:
(*a*) where because of roadworks or some other reason the width of
the carriageway is so restricted that it will only carry one line of
traffic, (*b*) temporary schemes of traffic control where the signals
are in the control of the police. A temporary light signal for road
works is, it seems, presumed to have been lawfully placed and it is not
necessary to prove that it was lawfully maintained; s. 58 of the Road
Traffic Regulation Act, 1967, relating to emergency signs, does not
apply (*Woodriffe* v. *Plowman* (1962), 60 L.G.R. 183). Portable
signals have to comply with the specifications applicable to permanent lights contained in reg. 31 (2) (*a*), (*b*), (*c*), (*e*), (*f*) and (*g*)
and reg. 33 (3) (*d*). The main effect is that portable lights have
to be of the same dimensions, include an amber light and show the
lights in the same sequence as permanent lights.

The prohibition on passing over the stop-line applies to any part
of the vehicle when the red light is showing; if the front of a
vehicle has already crossed that line when the light goes red, it is an
offence under s. 22 for it to proceed further (*Ryan* v. *Smith* [1967]
1 All E.R. 611).

On the question whether it is an offence to cross the light at
red if the line has been passed at green, see Jo.Crim.L. (1955)
113; the wording of the Regulations of 1964 differs by referring to
the stop line being " not for the time being visible "; *quaere*, if
this includes not being visible to the driver because he has passed it

or only means not visible generally, i.e., faded or tarred-over. If the lights are showing green for east-west traffic, magistrates are entitled to infer, unless the contrary be shown, that they are red for north-south traffic (*Wells* v. *Woodward* (1956), 54 L.G.R. 142; *Pacitti* v. *Copeland* [1963] S.L.T. (Notes) 52); for a similar finding in a South African case, see *S.* v. *Grandin* [1970] 2 S.A.L.R. 621; [1971] 4 C.L. 319. Intermittent red signals under reg. 31 (3A) (which are for use at automatic level crossings) convey the prohibition that a vehicle shall not proceed beyond the stop line or if there is no stop line, or if it is not visible, the signals (reg. 34 (4A (*b*), see p. 724) (see also Automatic Level Crossings, on p. 308).

Police Signals

By s. 22 it is an offence if any person driving or propelling a vehicle of any kind (including a pedal cycle) neglects or refuses to stop the vehicle or make it proceed in or keep to a particular line of traffic when directed so to do by a constable or traffic warden engaged in regulating traffic on a road; the vehicle itself need not be on a road. See p. 314 as to the penalty. By the Road Traffic Act, 1972, s. 159, a person driving a motor vehicle and a person riding on a road a bicycle or tricycle shall stop on being so required by a constable in uniform; see p. 314 for the penalty. It will be noted that offences under s. 22 arise only where the constable (or traffic warden) is engaged in regulating traffic, and there is no such limitation under s. 159. In both sections, however, before an offence can be said to have been committed, the constable must have been acting in execution of his duty. Section 22 (1) (*a*) (see p. 295) explicitly so states and it was held in *R.* v. *Waterfield* [1963] 3 All E.R. 659 that s. 159 does not confer statutory power on a police constable to stop a vehicle where a constable would not have power under the common law to do so. *R.* v. *Waterfield* was applied to s. 22 in *Hoffman* v. *Thomas* [1974] R.T.R. 182 where it was held that the power of a constable to regulate traffic in execution of his duty stems from the constable's duty and right at common law to act in protection of life and property and that a constable has no right to regulate traffic for personal motives or other extraneous reason; his right and duty solely arise because of the danger to life and limb which unregulated traffic can present. The conviction under s. 22 of a motorist who refused to proceed to a census point in accordance with the direction of a constable who was engaged in selecting vehicles at random on a motorway and directing the selected vehicles to a census point was accordingly set aside. Conducting a traffic census is not part of a constable's duty to regulate traffic in execution of his right to protect life and property (*ibid.*) (but see now s. 22A on p. 295 and Census Points on p. 309).

Notwithstanding *R.* v. *Oliver* on p. 394 and the reference in s. 25 (2) of the Road Traffic Regulation Act, 1967, to starting up again after being required to halt by a school crossing patrol, it is submitted that a driver who has stopped at a constable's signal may not start again until he has been signalled or otherwise permitted to proceed. If the constable is still holding up his hand, the driver offends in the second after he has started again by not stopping; in other cases, the constable will often in fact have made a second signal to him. It is suggested that " stop " in these sections means both " bring to a halt " and "remain at rest ". The requirement to stop may be a verbal one as well as by hand signal. See also p. 347. The reference to a police constable in both ss. 22 and 23 of the 1972 Act includes a traffic warden (see p. 305, *infra*).

Pedestrians

The Road Traffic Act, 1972, s. 23, reads:—

" Where a constable [this includes a traffic warden: see p. 305, *infra*] in uniform is for the time being engaged in the regulation of vehicular traffic in a road, a person on foot who proceeds across or along the carriageway in contravention of a direction to stop given by the constable, in the execution of his duty, either to persons on foot or to persons on foot and other traffic, shall be guilty of an offence."

Section 165 gives to constables (and traffic wardens) the right to require names and addresses from offenders against s. 23.

Failure to See Signals of Constable

Is it a defence that the defendant in any of the above cases never saw the constable's signal? In *R.* v. *Ellis* [1947] 1 W.W.R. 717, a Canadian case, it was held that a driver could not be guilty of failing to stop at a junction when " signalled " to do so by a policeman unless the signal was consciously received by him, although his failure to see it was due to the fact that he was not keeping a proper look-out in the direction in which he was going. In *R.* v. *Barber* [1963] 3 S. African L.R. 700, a defendant who had not in fact seen the constable's signal was held to have been properly acquitted, after reference to English cases including *Harding* v. *Price, infra*. On the other hand, it may be thought that a signal can be made without necessarily being seen and it is no defence here that a driver failed to see a traffic sign (*Rees* v. *Taylor*, p. 300, *supra*). It can be argued, however, that traffic signs are placed in positions where they can easily be seen and at places, such as road junctions, where a driver would expect to find them, and it is a different matter where a driver without negligence and in conditions of bad visibility fails to see a policeman's signal from a crowded footpath or in an ill-lit street. There was once no offence in like circumstances under the Pedestrian Crossings Regulations (*Leicester* v. *Pearson* [1952] 2 All E.R. 71; see p. 450) and the law does not call on persons to perform a duty on an event happening unless they know that the event has happened (*Harding* v. *Price* [1948] 1 All E.R. 283 and cases there cited; see p. 344, *infra*). Magistrates in a case reported at 119 J.P.Jo. 659 dismissed a charge of failing to stop in response to a lamp signal given by a policeman at night where the motorist had not understood the meaning of the signal. The view is advanced at Jo.Crim.L. (1956) 192 that a defendant may be excused if he does not see a constable's signal through no fault of his own, but the onus of proving his lack of negligence lies on him.

See p. 347 for cases on the meaning of " stop ".

See p. 452 as to defects in the vehicle making compliance with a signal impossible.

The Police Act, 1964, s. 19, allows a constable to act as such anywhere in England and a special constable to act as a constable in his own and adjoining areas. Under the Road Traffic Act, 1972, ss. 23 and 159, offences arise only if the constable is in uniform; under s. 22 he need not be in uniform but, if he is not, it must be proved that the defendant knew him to be a constable. On the other hand, it can be argued that the liability under s. 22 is absolute, so that it is unnecessary to prove that the defendant knew a person in plain clothes to be a constable and his ignorance is no defence: *cf. Kenlin* v. *Gardiner* [1966] 3 All E.R. 931, at p. 934, where it was said that, on a charge of assaulting a police officer, knowledge that he was one is not necessary. The Highway Code, however, says that a driver should not rely on signals given by unauthorised persons to go ahead; see also p. 284.

Traffic wardens appointed under the Road Traffic Regulation Act, 1967, s. 18, are not constables but by virtue of the Functions of Traffic Wardens Order, 1970 (S.I. 1970 No. 1958) and s. 81 (4A) of the 1967 Act references to a constable in ss. 22 and 23 include traffic wardens. If a motorist ignores a traffic warden's direction under s. 22, he can thus be prosecuted and convicted exactly as if a constable had been on duty. Moreover the traffic warden is empowered (also by virtue of the Functions of Traffic Wardens Order and s. 81 (4A)) to demand the offending motorist's name and address under s. 161. The traffic warden (unlike a constable) cannot, however, demand to see the offending motorist's driving documents, as reg. 3 (3) only applies s. 161 so far as it relates to " the furnishing of names and addresses ". The functions prescribed for Scottish traffic wardens are set out in S.I. 1962 No. 1271 and S.I. 1966 No. 222.

Horse Riders

The Road Traffic Act, 1972, contains no provision requiring equestrians, mahouts and other riders of animals to obey police signals. If an accident occurs or might occur because of a horseman's disregard of a constable's signal, it might be that this would be obstructing the police in that an accident could be a breach of the peace (*cf. Duncan* v. *Jones* (1936), 99 J.P. 399). Also, he might be charged, if the facts warrant, with interrupting by negligence or by misbehaviour the free passage of another person or of a vehicle (Highway Act, 1835, s. 78; see *Baldwin* v. *Pearson* on p. 400).

" Stop " Signs at Major Roads

The " Stop " sign presumably requires that a vehicle subject to it be brought to a standstill; it was so held in relation to the former " Halt " sign (*Tolhurst* v. *Webster* [1936] 3 All E.R. 1020), where it was also said that the vehicle should stop (see reg. 11 (2) on p. 711) at the major road or line provided and not at the sign itself. Justices were directed to convict where a driver had stopped at the sign and not at the major road (*Brooks* v. *Jefferies* [1936] 3 All E.R. 232).

The " Stop " sign placed near the junction of a major and a minor road is No. 601 in Sched. 1 to the 1964 Regulations. By Direction 10 of the 1964 Directions it may be used on a road only in conjunction with the road marking of solid transverse lines to indicate the position beyond which vehicles must not proceed (diagram 1002) and with the painted letters " Stop " on the carriageway (diagram 1022), save where road works temporarily require their removal or the " Stop " sign itself was erected temporarily because of road works. The sign is a white circle with a red border and an inverted red triangle within the border broken by the word " Stop " in black letters of proportionate dimensions (see reg. 14); the internal diameter of the circle may be 30 inches, 45 inches or 60 inches (see digaram 601) but variation in dimensions, by reg. 8 (1), is permitted if it does not exceed $2\frac{1}{2}$ per cent. of that dimension. By reg. 15 (9) the sign, when erected within 50 yards of a street lamp lit by electricity, shall be illuminated throughout the hours of darkness by internal or external lighting unless the sign is temporary. If the sign is not within 50 yards of such a lamp, it must, by reg. 18, be illuminated by the use of reflecting material save that no reflecting material shall be applied to the black part (the word " Stop "). The post should be coloured grey, unless it is

concrete (Direction 36). The back of the sign shall be grey
(Direction 37) but as the back of the sign is not the side designed
to give the indication and guidance for which it was erected,
presumably the High Court would hold that the sign would not be
invalidated if it were painted a different colour (see *Sharples* v.
Blackmore [1973] R.T.R. 249, where it was held that a speed
limit sign was not invalidated by its back not being painted grey).

The requirement of this " Stop " sign is that every vehicle shall
before entering the major road stop at the transverse lines or, if
they are not visible, at the major road, and shall not go past those
lines or, if they are invisible, enter the major road in such a manner
or at such a time as to endanger a vehicle on the major road or to
necessitate the latter vehicle changing speed or course to avoid
an accident with the minor road vehicle (1964 Regulations, reg. 11
(2); see p. 711). By reg. 7 failure to comply with the " Stop "
sign is an offence against s. 22.

" Give Way " Signs

The " Give Way " sign is No. 602 in the 1964 Regulations and
it is an offence under reg. 7 to disobey it. It is an inverted white
triangle and can be 27 or 48 or 72 inches in height; its borders
are red and the lettering black and, by reg. 14, the size of the
letters is proportionate. The provisions as to illumination and
colour of post are the same as for " Stop " signs at major roads.
By Direction 10 of the 1964 Directions the " Give Way " sign
may be used only in conjunction with the road-marking of broken
transverse lines (diagram 1003) and the triangle painted on the
road (diagram 1023), save where road works temporarily require
the removal of the lines and triangle. By reg. 11 (2) of the 1964
Regulations (see p. 711) the requirement conveyed by the " Give
Way " sign is that no vehicle shall pass the transverse lines or,
if they are invisible, enter the major road in such a manner or at
such a time as is likely to cause danger to the driver of any other
vehicle on the major road or as to necessitate the driver of any such
other vehicle to change its speed or course in order to avoid an
accident with the minor road vehicle.

" Keep Left " Signs and Arrows

A roundabout bore a " Keep Left " sign but a motorist approaching made a " U " turn in the road 62 feet short of it. It was
held that in those circumstances he had not committed an offence
of disobeying the sign (*Brazier* v. *Alabaster* [1962] Crim.L.R. 173).
Semble, if he had been very close to the sign, he would have had to
obey it and go round the roundabout in order to turn back.

It is an offence under reg. 7 of the 1964 Regulations to disobey the white arrow on a blue circle, with white border (diagram 606—proceed in direction indicated by arrow) and the diagonal white arrow on a blue circle, with white border (diagram 610—keep left or right). The internal diameter of the circle for 606 is $10\frac{1}{2}$ or 12 or 24 or 48 or 72 inches and that for 610 is $10\frac{1}{2}$ or 24 or 48 or 72 inches; there is a permitted variation of $2\frac{1}{2}$ per cent. under reg. 8 (1). Sign 606 may be used only on the central island of roundabouts, with the dual carriageway sign (diagram 608) or to indicate the effect of an order, regulation, byelaw or notice. By reg. 15 sign 606, when mounted in a bollard or fixed to light signals, shall be illuminated during darkness, and in other cases shall be illuminated during darkness if within 50 yards of an electric street lamp, unless placed only temporarily; by reg. 19 the dual carriageway plate should also be illuminated. By reg. 15, sign 610, when mounted in a bollard, shall also be illuminated during darkness and similarly if within 50 yards of an electric street lamp, unless placed temporarily. By reg. 18 (2) both signs must otherwise be illuminated by reflecting material.

It is not an offence contrary to s. 22 to contravene a requirement of diagram 609 (Vehicular Traffic must turn left (or right)) because reg. 7 does not list this sign as one to which s. 22 applies even though diagram 609 is somewhat similar to diagrams 606 and 610.

Automatic Level Crossings

The sign requiring drivers of abnormally large or slow vehicles to telephone the railway signalman to obtain permission to cross at automatic railway level crossings is diagram 649 and is governed by reg. 11A of the regulations (added and amended by S.I. 1969 No. 1269, S.I. 1970 No. 468 and S.I. 1971 No. 2095) and is incorporated in the regulations set out at p. 712. Note that the person who must telephone is the actual driver of the vehicle; if there is more than one driver, the driver of the foremost motor vehicle forming part of the vehicle must telephone. The railway signalman can impose any terms on the driver before allowing the vehicle to cross and if these terms are not complied with the regulation is contravened (reg. 11A (2) (b)). Note also the proviso at the end of the regulation which requires the driver on receiving no answer to try for not less than two minutes to telephone the signalman and to cross the crossing during the times which may be shown near the telephone during which trains do not normally travel. If no such times are exhibited, the driver has no alternative but to wait until the signalman answers the telephone and gives him permission to cross. The 1971 amendment regulations require the driver to receive an indication that the phone is being rung in the signalman's box. If therefore the phone is " dead," he is not allowed to cross. The approaches to many railway level crossings (whether or not they are automatic) are marked by double white lines. These double white lines are not part of the signs of an automatic level crossing. Regulation 23 governs all double white lines whether at railway level crossings or elsewhere (see p. 716), and prosecutions for failing to conform to double white lines at level crossings will be by virtue of that regulation and not reg. 11A. Similarly a driver who disobeys the red lights at the automatic level crossing will contravene reg. 31 (3A) and not reg. 11A. The red lights consist of two horizontal red lights with an amber light below the centre point between the two red lights. The sequence of lights (amber followed by red) the flashing of the red lights (one must be on while the other is off), the rate of flashing and dimensions are set out in reg. 31 (3A) (see p. 721).

Census Points

Section 22A (see p. 295) was passed as a result of the decision in *Hoffman* v. *Thomas* [1974] R.T.R. 182 (see p. 303) where it was held that a constable was not acting in execution of his duty of regulating traffic in selecting vehicles at random from a motorway to go to a census point. A motorist who refused to comply with the constable's signal directing him to stop and proceed to the census point was not guilty of an offence under s. 22. It was also held that the sign " Stop at Census Point " was informatory only in its effect, and non-compliance with it could also not give rise to an offence contrary to s. 22.

Section 22A reverses the decision of *Hoffman* v. *Thomas*. The existing " informatory " traffic sign " Stop at Census Point " becomes mandatory by virtue of s. 22 A (1) (*b*). It is also made an offence by s. 22A (1) (*a*) to fail to comply with traffic directions given by a constable for the purpose of a traffic census. Subsection (2) gives a wide definition of a " traffic direction " for this purpose and subs. (3) amends s. 22 (1) (*a*) for this purpose so that a motorist commits an offence not only if he neglects or refuses to stop, make the vehicle proceed in, or keep to, a particular line of traffic as directed but also if he fails " to proceed to a particular point". Parliament was anxious that motorists should not be compelled to give census information and that any information should only be given voluntarily. Not only is it not an offence to refuse to supply information for the purposes of a survey (see definition of " traffic direction " in subs. (3)), but also the power to give a traffic direction must, in accordance with subs. (4), be exercised so as not to cause unreasonable delay to a person who indicates he is unwilling to participate in the census.   Nevertheless it would seem that a motorist who is unwilling to participate in the census must comply with traffic directions unless and until he indicates he is unwilling to furnish information.   On the other hand it would seem that a constable will not be acting in execution of his duty and a conviction under s. 22 will be set aside if the power to give a traffic direction is exercised in contravention of subs. (4) of s. 22A.   Although a traffic direction for the purpose of a traffic census is treated by virtue of s. 22A (1) (*a*) as a direction by a police constable in the execution of his duty, a constable cannot be said to be acting in execution of his duty if he acts in contravention of the wishes of Parliament as enacted in subs. (4).

Contravention of a traffic direction for the purpose of a traffic census or of the sign is by virtue of s. 22A an offence contrary to s. 22 and is punishable accordingly (see p. 314).

Other Signs

A portable sign of an authorised nature requiring a vehicle to stop must be obeyed although the person using it is not a policeman in uniform (*Langley Cartage Co.* v. *Jenks* [1937] 2 All E.R. 525). Such signs are now only the round red " Stop " sign used at road works (diagram 603 in the 1964 Regulations).   Sign 603 may be used only where one-way working is necessary owing to temporary closure of a width of the carriageway of the road.   Sign 605 (Stop-Weight Check) is obsolescent although continuing to be included amongst the signs listed in reg. 7.   Emergency traffic signs placed by the police pursuant to s. 58 of the Road Traffic Regulation Act, 1967, seem to be those referred to in regs. 27 to 29 of the 1964 Regulations for diversions, alternative routes and traffic congestion; disobedience to such a mandatory sign is an offence against s. 22—see s. 58 (2).   It should be noted that s. 22 is also specifically applied to signs used for the purpose of a traffic census by s. 22A (1) (*b*) and therefore persons not complying with such a sign can be prosecuted under s. 22 notwithstanding that the signs are not listed in reg. 7 (see further " Census Points," *supra*).

White Lines and Double White Lines

By the Road Traffic Regulation Act, 1967, s. 54, lines or marks on roads may be traffic signs if they indicate a warning, prohibition,

restriction or requirement prescribed or authorised under s. 54; it
had been held previously in *Evans* v. *Cross* [1938] 1 All E.R. 751 that
a white line on a bend or down the centre of a road was not a traffic
sign. Single white lines, if disobeyed, create no offence under
s. 22, although a charge of careless driving is justified for a central
white line (see *Bensley* v. *Smith* on p. 272), but reg. 22 (2) specifically
provides that the transverse lines at the mouth of a minor road
(diagram 1003), where it enters a major road, whether or not used
with the " Give Way " sign (602), create the requirement that no
vehicle shall pass them into the major road in such a manner or
at such a time as is likely to cause danger to a vehicle on the major
road or to cause it to change speed or course to avoid it. A driver
who disobeyed this requirement, however, would not seem to offend
against s. 22 where there was no " Give Way " sign, as reg. 7 does
not apply s. 22 to diagram 1003, only to the " Give Way " sign,
but he could properly be charged, if the facts warranted, with
careless or dangerous driving and it may be that he could be charged
with disobeying reg. 22 (2) contrary to s. 87 of the Road Traffic
Regulation Act, 1967.

Double Lines

Regulation 23 of the 1964 Regulations (see p. 716) deals with the
double white lines (diagram 1013). Double white lines consist
either of two continuous white lines or one continuous white line
together with a broken white line. Two continuous white lines
require vehicles in either direction at all times to keep to the nearside of the nearest continuous line, and a broken line with a con-
tinous white line requires a vehicle to keep to the nearside of
the continuous white line when the continuous white line is the
nearer of the two lines to his vehicle. The lines must comply with
the Regulations and if they do not a person contravening them
commits no offence even if the lines are readily recognisable as
double white lines (*Davies* v. *Heatley* [1971] R.T.R. 145, where
the lines were not in accordance with diagram 1013 in so far as an
intermittent white line had been placed between two continuous
white lines and the continuous lines were too far apart). In *Walton*
v. *Hawkins* [1973] R.T.R. 366 it was held that diagram 1013 of the
1964 Regulations was not one unit but consists of three separate
markings each having a different purpose and the sequence in which
they are imposed is matter for the highway authority to suit the requirements of the road in question. It was therefore held that the
defendant was properly convicted under s. 22 when he drove on the
offside of double white lines, although the sequence in which the
three types of double lines appeared was the exact reverse of that

shown in the diagram and which is normally applied.   Regulation 7 applies so that contravention of the requirements of reg. 23 becomes an offence contrary to s. 22.   It is an offence to stop anywhere on either side of a road within a double white line system, whether the lines are both continuous or only one of the two lines is continuous.   It is also a requirement that the driver must keep his moving vehicle in a position on a road governed by a double white line system so that at all times the offside of the vehicle is on the nearside of the white lines while both white lines are continuous or where the nearside white line is continuous and the offside line is broken.   On the other hand if the broken line of a double white line is nearest to the vehicle viewed in the direction of travel, the double line may be crossed if it is seen to be safe to do so (reg. 23 (5)); if it was crossed when unsafe, the charge should not be under s. 22, for reg. 7 does not apply to breach of reg. 23 (5), but careless or dangerous driving or, possibly, breach of reg. 23 (5) contrary to s. 87 of the Road Traffic Regulation Act, 1967, could be charged. Stopping is permitted by reg. 23 (3) to enable a person to board or alight from the vehicle or to load or unload goods (see p. 717), for building operations, road and public utility works, for fire, ambulance and police vehicles, for pedal cycles without sidecars, whether or not auto-assisted, for exigencies of traffic, to avoid an accident or with police permission.   It is an offence to drive on the wrong side of double white lines when both lines are continuous or only the nearside is continuous even if it is perfectly safe to do so.   Defences are set out in reg. 23 (4).   These allow a vehicle to cross or straddle the continuous line in order to obtain access to side roads or land or premises adjoining the road; to pass a stationary vehicle; to avoid an accident or in circumstances beyond the driver's control or under police direction.   In *R.* v. *Blything (Suffolk) Justices, ex parte Knight* [1970] R.T.R. 218 the justices were advised by their clerk that reg. 23 (4) only gave a defence where the vehicle actually crossed or straddled the white lines and that therefore the defendant, who was on the offside of the road before the double white lines began, could not avail himself of the defence contained in the Regulations.   It was held that this was wrong and that " crossing or straddling " did not have this restricted meaning.   On the facts the Divisional Court held that the defendant, who had commenced overtaking two vehicles before the double white lines, could not have a defence under reg. 23 (4), but it was said by Lord Parker (at pp. 220, 221) that he could not avail himself of the defence because he had " put himself in the wrong " by endeavouring to overtake vehicles.   With respect, it is submitted that this case cannot be relied on as authority for the legal proposition that a motorist who commences to overtake vehicles before double white lines begin can in no circumstances rely on the defence of " circumstances beyond his control " or " in order to avoid an accident ", if he finds himself contravening the double white lines because (for example) the vehicle being overtaken unexpectedly accelerates. It is submitted that it is essentially a question of fact, but the mere fact that the vehicle being overtaken unexpectedly accelerates will normally be insufficient to show that the circumstances were beyond the defendant's control, because the contravention of the Regulation may well have been caused as much by his decision to overtake as the fact that the other vehicle accelerated.

The lines must, by reg. 24 (1), be white and, by reg. 25 (1), illuminated by reflecting material and studs incorporating reflections between the two lines. The variations in dimensions allowed by reg. 8 (3) apply.

Under the 1964 Regulations and Directions the warning arrows (diagram 1014) do not appear to be mandatory. It would not, therefore, appear to be a defence to a charge of failing to conform to a double white line, that there were no such warning arrows or that they did not comply with the regulations.

Non-Conforming and Damaged Signs

The colour, dimensions, etc., of signs are dealt with by regs. 9, 10, 12, 13 and 14 of the 1964 Regulations, and reg. 8 (see p. 710) allows certain variations in dimensions. Where a no-waiting order or other traffic regulation order, e.g., a clearway, has been made, normally it must be indicated by traffic signs which conform with the 1964 Regulations, even though the local authority have a discretion whether to erect such signs; if it is not so indicated or the signs do not conform, *MacLeod* v. *Hamilton* [1965] S.L.T. 305 seemed to be authority for the proposition that there might be no offence against the order. It is now clear from *Davies* v. *Heatley* [1971] R.T.R. 145, that, because by s. 54 (2) of the Road Traffic Regulation Act, 1967, traffic signs shall be of the size, colour and type prescribed by regulation, if the sign is not as prescribed by the Regulation, no offence is committed if the sign is contravened even if the sign is clearly recognisable to a reasonable man as a sign of that kind (but see *Sharples* v. *Blackmore*, *infra*). The facts of *Davies* v. *Heatley* were that a single intermittent line had originally been placed in the centre of the road. Double white lines were subsequently placed on the road but the intermittent line was insufficiently defaced. Although the court might possibly have been able to hold that the old line could be subtracted from the existing double lines and thus form no part of them, in any event the existing double lines were more widely spread than was permitted by the regulation. In *Sharples* v. *Blackmore* [1973] R.T.R. 249 the Divisional Court held that the colour of the back of a speed limit sign was immaterial as it was the front of the sign which of course conveyed the warning to the motorist.   Where, therefore, a speed limit sign's back was painted black instead of grey, the sign was nevertheless held to be a sign prescribed under the Traffic Signs (Speed Limits) Regulations and General Directions, 1969.   It would seem that a sign not complying with direction 37 of the 1964 Directions which requires the back of signs to be grey (or black in the case of signs mounted on traffic lights) would, following *Sharples* v. *Blackmore*, be held to comply with the 1964 Regulations and Directions, where the back of the sign is immaterial for its purpose of regulating traffic.   *R.* v. *Priest* (1961), 35 C.R. 31, a decision of the Ontario Court of Appeal that a non-conforming stop sign was binding on the driver providing he could have seen it if he was keeping a proper look-out, was distinguished in *Davies* v. *Heatley* on the ground that the Canadian legislation did not make it an offence to comply with " a prescribed stop sign " but only with a stop sign.

Previous Conviction for Dangerous, etc., Driving

Where a court has taken into consideration disobedience to traffic signs on convicting for dangerous or careless driving, the conviction would seem to be a bar to further proceedings under s. 22 (*cf. Welton* v. *Taneborne* (1908), 72 J.P. 419) but it would be otherwise if there had been an acquittal under s. 2 or s. 3   See p. 290 as to convicting for both offences.

Penalty, Disqualification and Endorsement

The penalty for an offence against s. 22 is a fine of £100 on first or subsequent conviction (Road Traffic Act, 1972, Sched. 4 as amended by the 1974 Act).

The penalty for failing to stop at a constable's signal contrary to s. 159 is a fine of £100 on first or subsequent conviction (1972 Act, Sched. 4 as amended by the 1974 Act).   Disqualification and endorsement may not be ordered.

Pedestrians disobeying police signals are liable to a fine of £50 on first or subsequent conviction.

Disqualification may be ordered and endorsement is obliged to be ordered (in the absence of " special reasons ": see Chapter VII) on conviction for an offence under s. 22 of failing to comply with a constable's traffic direction or with a specified sign: see below.   It would seem however that a motorist convicted of failing to conform to a traffic warden's directions is not liable to be disqualified nor is his licence liable to endorsement as column 5 of Sched. 4 to the 1972 Act refers only to a " police constable " and s. 81 (4A) of the Road Traffic Regulation Act, 1967, does not include Sched. 4 in the list of statutory provisions where references to a police constable are deemed to include references to a traffic warden.

Offences of disobedience of " one-way street ", " no right turn ", etc., orders carry a fine of £100 (Road Traffic Regulation Act, 1967, s. 1 (8) as amended by the Act of 1974). Neither disqualification nor endorsement can be ordered for such offences.

The signs, disobedience to which under s. 22 carries optional disqualification and obligatory endorsement, are the " Stop " at major road sign, red traffic lights (not including motorway flashing red lights but including the flashing red lights at automatic level crossings and the portable red lights at road works), any contravention of double white lines (whether by stopping within the system or driving a vehicle on the wrong side of double lines or the wrong side of a continuous line if it is on the nearside of the road) and failing to obtain permission for a large or slow vehicle to cross an automatic level crossing (Traffic Signs (Disqualification for Offences) Regulations, 1969). Neither disqualification nor endorsement may be ordered for any other offence under s. 22 such as disobedience to a " No Entry," " Give Way " or " Keep Left " sign or arrow, temporary traffic signs erected under s. 58 of the Act of 1967, or red flashing lights on motorways, or any of the Traffic Census signs. Nor may disqualification or endorsement be ordered for contravention of a " one way street " or " no right turn " order. The endorsement codes for traffic sign offences are as follows:—

Traffic lights signals	TS10
Double white lines	TS20
" Stop " sign	TS30
Police constable's traffic directions	TS40
Any other sign	TS50

The Magistrates' Association's suggested penalties (see p. 594 and p. 880) are for contravention of traffic lights or double white lines " £25 and consider disqualification " and a fine of £20 for failure to comply with police or traffic signs other than traffic lights or double white lines.

Section 93 (3) of the 1972 Act applies to offences under s. 22, so that, if a person convicted of a disqualifiable offence under s. 22 in respect of a motor vehicle has been previously convicted on not less than two occasions of an endorsed disqualifiable offence in respect of a motor vehicle within the three years immediately before the offence, he must be disqualified for at least six months (see p. 624) unless, having regard to all the circumstances, there are grounds for mitigating the normal consequences of a conviction (see p. 688). The six-month disqualification is additional and consecutive to any period of disqualification imposed on the same occasion, or for any previous offence.

The court may also order the defendant to be disqualified until he passes the test (Road Traffic Act, 1972, s. 93 (7)); this power is limited to the offences for which disqualification may be ordered.

4. SPEED LIMITS

Offences of exceeding the speed limit fall into four classes, (a) exceeding the limit on a restricted road; (b) exceeding on any road the limit applicable to the class of vehicle; (c) exceeding the temporary limits of 50 and 60 m.p.h. on roads other than motorways and (d) exceeding the limits of speed applicable to motorways only. Heavy lorries, for example, are subject to speed limits under all four; ordinary motor cars and motor cycles with pneumatic tyres, not being goods vehicles or drawing trailers are subject to a limit only on a restricted road and to the overall 50, 60 and 70 m.p.h. maxima on single carriageway roads, dual carriageway roads and motorways respectively. There may also be some speed limits of local application, e.g., in Royal Parks. Section 199 (4) of the Port of London Act, 1968, has the effect of imposing a speed limit of 30 m.p.h. on all vehicles in the Port of London Authority area. Offences of contravening any such limits are offences against s. 78A of the Road Traffic Regulation Act, 1967 (as added by s. 203 of the Road Traffic Act, 1972).

The Road Traffic Regulation Act, 1967, s. 77, authorises certain temporary or experimental speed limits and minimum speed limits on specified roads. Offences against orders under s. 77 (1) (b) imposing a minimum speed limit are offences against s. 77 (7). Temporary speed limit orders made under s. 77 can be made in respect of all types of road other than motorways (s. 77 (9)).

The overall temporary limits of 50 m.p.h. and 60 m.p.h. in respect of non-dual carriageway and dual carriageway roads were imposed by virtue of the 60 m.p.h. and 50 m.p.h. (Temporary Speed Limit) Order, 1974, made by virtue of s. 77, *supra*, and the Fuel Control (Modification of Enactments) (Speed Limits) Order, 1973 (S.I. 1973 No. 2051). The order revoked the 70 m.p.h. and 60 mp.h. (Temporary Speed Limit) Order, 1974. The order came

into effect on Sunday, 15th December, 1974, and unless extended
ends at midnight on Sunday, 30th November, 1975 (the text of the
order is set out on p. 729). The order does not (and could not because of s. 77 (9) of the Road Traffic Regulation Act, 1967) apply to
motorways. An order made under s. 77, applying to all roads does
not need to be indicated by signs (Road Traffic Regulation Act,
1967, s. 77 (5) (a)). The order (see p. 729) imposes a limit of 60
m.p.h. on " any dual carriageway road " and 50 m.p.h. on any road
not a dual carriageway road. No definition is contained in the order
or in the Road Traffic Regulation Act, 1967, of " dual carriageway
road ".

The relevant orders relating to motorways are dealt with and
discussed on p. 336 under the heading " Motorway Speed Limits ".
The provisions of Sched. 5 to the Road Traffic Regulation Act,
1967, which lays down various limits of speed for certain classes
of vehicle, are substantially varied and altered to impose different
limits of speed for vehicles travelling on the motorway. The
temporary speed limits of 50 and 60 m.p.h. do not of course apply
to motorways where an overall limit of 70 m.p.h. is applicable
(see p. 336).

The Road Traffic Regulation Act, 1967, s. 77, as amended by the
Transport Act, 1968, s. 126, allows the making of orders valid for
eighteen months at a time imposing speed limits on roads of a
specified class or on all roads other than roads of a specified class.

The limit of 30 m.p.h. on restricted roads is imposed by the Road
Traffic Regulation Act, 1967, s. 71; s. 74 of that Act allows the
proper authorities to fix other speed limits for designated roads in
all areas. The offences in relation to the class of vehicle on all
roads fall under the Road Traffic Regulation Act, 1967, s. 78, and
the limits for the various classes are indicated in Sched. 5 to the
1967 Act. That Schedule is set out on pp. 325–332 and as varied
for motorways on p. 337. Speed limits under those sections do not
apply to tramcars or trolley vehicles operated under statutory
powers (s. 106). The sections apply only on roads and to motor
vehicles (as defined in Chapter I). Save as mentioned on pp.
338–339, the limits apply to vehicles of the Crown and visiting
forces.

Warning of intended prosecution is required for offences of exceeding speed limits punishable by virtue of s. 78A of the Road Traffic Regulation Act, 1967, and offences of failing to observe a minimum speed
limit (see Chapter III). Offences may be tried by magistrates only.

The term " restricted road " is defined on p. 321.

The British Transport Commission Act, 1956, s. 27 (4), relates
to speed limits in the Commission's docks.

Evidence

By the Road Traffic Regulation Act, 1967, s. 78A (2), a person prosecuted for driving a motor vehicle at a speed exceeding the limit imposed by or under any enactment shall not be convicted solely on the evidence of one witness to the effect that, in the opinion of the witness, the defendant was driving at a speed exceeding that limit. A like provision applies to offences of not attaining minimum speed limits (1967 Act, s. 77 (7)). The corroborative witness must speak as to speeding at the same moment of time as the first witness, so one police officer who saw the defendant on one part of the road did not corroborate another who saw him some moments later at a place further along the same road (*Brighty* v. *Pearson* [1938] 4 All E.R. 127). Corroboration is usually provided nowadays by the speedometer of a police car, a radar set, or *vascar*. In *Nicholas* v. *Penny* [1950] 2 All E.R. 89, it was held that a person could be convicted on the evidence of one policeman supported by evidence by him of the reading of a speedometer or other mechanical means, even though there was no evidence that the speedometer had been tested. In that case the defendant was said to be going 10 m.p.h. in excess of the limit and the court commented on the amount of the excess; had the speed been only, say, 2 m.p.h. in excess of the limit, they might have called for evidence of the accuracy of the speedo- meter. In any case, it is in the discretion of the magistrates to accept or reject evidence tendered in speeding as in all other cases (see 114 J.P.Jo. 309). Applying *Nicholas* v. *Penny* it was held in *Swain* v. *Gillett* [1974] R.T.R. 446 that for the purposes of s. 78A (2), *supra*, a speedometer reading was capable of amounting to corro- boration of a police officer's opinion evidence about the speed of a vehicle without proof of testing of the accuracy of the speedometer. Two police officers independently forming an opinion about the speed of an offending vehicle is sufficient as a matter of law to satisfy s. 78A (2) (*ibid.*), but it is for the magistrates as a tribunal of fact to consider how much weight should be attached to the evidence adduced. The magistrates, who had dismissed a case of speeding on accepting a submission of no case to answer on the ground that the officer's evidence as to speeding was not corroborated by a speedometer for which no evidence as to its accuracy had been produced, were directed to continue the hearing of the case. *Melhuish* v. *Morris* [1938] 4 All E.R. 98, which implies that a speedo- meter has to be tested before its reading can be used in evidence, was not followed. In *Houston* v. *Leslie* [1958] S.L.T. 109; [1958] Crim.L.R. 477, a variation between the evidence of two constables as to the vehicle's position behind another vehicle was held enough to justify a doubt as to the proving of the case, on its particular facts. In *Gillespie* v. *Macmillan* [1957] S.L.T. 283; Jo.Crim.L. (1957) 341, a conviction was upheld where a constable, on a measured length of road, had started a stop-watch when a car passed; another constable further along the same length had started his watch when the car passed him and, on the watches being stopped when the car was stopped, a comparison of the two watches showed a speed of 52 m.p.h.

A person may refresh his memory from a contemporaneous record compiled by another provided it was checked at the time by him and adopted as his own. The constable who had observed the speed recorded by the radar meter of an offending vehicle, checked and countersigned a record compiled by the constable responsible for later stopping the offending vehicle, was held to be entitled to refresh his memory from the other constable's record of the offence (*Groves* v. *Redbart* [1975] Crim.L.R. 158.)

In *Baker* v. *Sweet* [1966] Crim.L.R. 51 a temporary speed limit order restricted speeds on all roads save motorways and dual-carriageways; on the hearing of a charge of exceeding the limit, the order was not produced and no evidence was given that it applied to the road in question and it was held that it was for the defendant to show, pursuant to s. 81 of the Magistrates' Courts Act, 1952, that the order did not apply to the road. As the order was not even published as a statutory instrument, this is an unsatisfactory decision in that magistrates seem to be expected to take their law from what they have read about speed limits in the newspapers or from the " *ipse dixit* " of the prosecutor.

Radar speed meters.—These are discussed at 101 S.J. 761, 765 and 820, in *The Times* of 21st April, 1965, and at 129 J.P.Jo. 341 and 388, and there is an article by an electrical engineer at [1958] Crim.L.R. 349. In *Farrell* v. *Simpson* [1959] S.L.T.(Sh.) 23; Jo.Crim.L. (1959) 278, a sheriff convicted on the evidence of a reading of such a meter by two constables, who also gave their opinion that the car was exceeding 30 m.p.h. The evidence showed that the road was straight and level for a long distance, that the car was the only vehicle about, that the meter had been tested that day and the speed recorded on the meter of 42 m.p.h. had been shown thereon for over two-and-a-half seconds. The notes at 101 S.J. 761 and 820 give instances where evidence by meter has been rejected by a superior court in Canada and accepted by superior courts in U.S.A. respectively. Evidence of mechanical devices such as speedometers and stop-watches is always acceptable in English courts (*Nicholas* v. *Penny* [1950] 2 All E.R. 89) and, where radar is used, it is a question of fact for the magistrates whether or not its evidence on the particular facts before them should be accepted. Such cases and opinions as have been reported or given seem to show that meters are very accurate if working under good conditions and operated by experienced constables. Such cases as are dismissed by magistrates are almost invariably dismissed not because the magistrates are not satisfied as to the accuracy of the radar meter but because they are not satisfied as to the accuracy of the evidence of the police officers operating the radar trap. Instances have occurred where the police officer has been unable to satisfy the magistrates that either he has read the radar meter correctly or the meter reading he has given in evidence referred to the defendant's motor vehicle. Radar traps are usually operated so that one constable is stationed by the radar set observing the speed of the vehicle as it passes through the radar beam, and another constable is stationed considerably further down the road to stop an offending vehicle. The constable stopping an offending vehicle will usually be told by radio of that vehicle's registration number and the type of vehicle; occasionally magistrates have dismissed a case where they have not been satisfied that the correct vehicle was stopped, either because of a possible error on the part of the constable at the radar set in identifying the vehicle, or an error on the part of the constable responsible for stopping the vehicle.

Vascar

Some police forces have equipped traffic police vehicles with *vascar* (Visual Average Speed Computer and Recorder). Like radar meters, *vascar* is technically extremely accurate. Unlike radar meters which record the vehicle's speed in the fraction of a second it takes a vehicle to pass through the radar beam, the *vascar* device records the speed as averaged by the vehicle over the distance recorded; but like radar meters, it will usually be extremely difficult to obtain an acquittal of a charge of speeding on technical grounds where *vascar* is used. The degree of training required of a police constable for the proper operation of *vascar* is, if anything, rather more than that required for radar, and it is believed most forces require a constable to pass a stringent test programme before allowing the constable to operate the device for the purposes of prosecution. The proper operation of *vascar* depends on the police constable accurately operating the switches and being able to satisfy the court that there has been no mistake in relation to the identification of the offending vehicle and no misjudgment of the exact moment the vehicle passed the relevant landmark used in its operation sufficient to render unreliable the speed as recorded by the device.

Generally

Time-tables, schedules and directions issued by an employer may be produced as evidence in a prosecution of the employer for procuring or inciting his drivers to exceed a speed limit imposed under any enactment, where they show that the driver is bound to exceed the limit if he is to comply with the document issued to him (Road Traffic Regulation Act, 1967, s. 78A (4); and see *Newman* v. *Overington* (1928), 93 J.P. 46).

Measurement of a distance on a map by a rotameter, to show that the distances given in the driver's records could not be covered without exceeding the limit, was held admissible in *Morrison* v. *M'Cowan* [1939] S.C.(J.) 45.

The opinion of any witness as to speed is receivable (Cross on Evidence, 3rd ed., p. 360). Magistrates have convicted on the evidence of policemen on foot alone, without stop-watches or speedometers, in a case of exceeding the limit on a restricted road, for, while it is unwise to accept such evidence as to what a vehicle's speed was, it is relatively easy to accept that a vehicle which is going very fast is going in excess of 30 m.p.h. (118 J.P.Jo. 105 and 104 S.J. 20) but it is in their discretion whether or not to accept such evidence.

Restricted Roads

The term " built-up ", which appeared in former Acts, is not used in the Road Traffic Regulation Act, 1967; s. 71 of that Act makes it an offence to drive a motor vehicle on " a restricted road " at a speed exceeding 30 m.p.h. Where a limit had been imposed under s. 74 of the 1967 Act (generally a limit other than 30 m.p.h.), such road is not deemed to be a restricted road for the purposes of s. 71 (s. 74 (1)). By s. 72 of the Road Traffic Regulation Act, 1967, a restricted road is a road where there is provided a system of street lighting furnished by means of lamps placed not more than 200 yards apart (see as to distance on p. 114) or a road in respect of which the relevant authority has made a direction that it shall be a restricted road notwithstanding the absence of such street lighting. In the following paragraphs the term means roads subject to speed limits whether of 30 m.p.h. or otherwise.

Where a lamp is temporarily missing, e.g., it has been knocked down, so that at one place two lamps are more than 200 yards apart, it is suggested that a " system of street lighting " is still provided as above (see 114 J.P.Jo. 627). Where there is a direction in force imposing a limit under s. 72 on a road without the requisite lamp-posts, the presence of the speed limit signs is *prima facie* evidence that the speed limit applies to that road, and the police need not call evidence to prove the direction unless the defence call evidence that the road is not restricted (*Boyd-Gibbins* v. *Skinner* [1951] 1 All E.R. 1049). A conviction was upheld where a defendant had exceeded the limit on a road on which there were four lamps, two of which were 201½ yards apart and the others 200 yards apart (*Briere* v. *Hailstone* (1968), 112 S.J. 767); the " *de minimis* " principle was applied. It might be otherwise if all or nearly all the lamps were more than 201 yards apart. Indeed, it is respectfully submitted that *Briere's* case was not really a correct application of the " *de minimis* " rule; part of the road in question there had got the relevant system of street lighting and it was thus irrelevant that the limit was also exceeded on a part where the lamps were more than the prescribed distance apart. It may also be pointed out that s. 72 refers to a " system " of street lighting furnished by lamps placed not more than 200 yards apart. If some of the gaps between lights are slightly more than 200 yards it is possible to argue that there is still a " system " of street lighting if the number of lights is such that the gaps average less than 200 yards.

In *Roberts* v. *Croxford* (1969), 113 S.J. 269, magistrates, on inspecting a road, found that the system of street lighting was for lighting a promenade nearby and not for lighting the road; their action in inspecting and their finding that the road had not the necessary system in contradiction of a certificate of an officer of the highway authority under s. 72 (4) was upheld.

By the Road Traffic Regulation Act, 1967, s. 75 (4), if a road has the relevant system of street lighting, evidence of the absence of derestriction signs shall be evidence that it is deemed to be a road which is restricted. If the road has not the relevant system of street lighting but is restricted, a person shall not be convicted unless there are the necessary restriction signs (s. 75 (3)). By s. 72 (2) a length of trunk road or classified road (generally a major road as opposed to a side-street) is not deemed to be a road which is restricted by reason only of the system of street lighting thereon if no system, with lamps not more than 200 yards apart, was provided thereon before 1st July, 1957. By s. 72 (4) a certificate by an officer of the highway authority stating whether the relevant system was provided before that date and a certificate of an officer of the appropriate Secretary of State, stating that a road is or is not a trunk road or classified road shall be evidence of the facts certified. It is not conclusive evidence (*Roberts* v. *Croxford, supra*).

Where different lengths of one road are governed by different regulations applying to one length only, even though imposing the same limit, an information alleging an offence against both regulations is bad for duplicity; there should either be separate, fresh informations for each length or the prosecutor should have elected on the original information to proceed in respect of one length only (*Cross* v. *Oliver* (1964), 62 L.G.R. 501).

The signs to indicate that a road is restricted are set out in the Traffic Signs (Speed Limits) Regulations and General Directions, 1969 (S.I. 1969 No. 1487). The Regulations allow for variations in the dimensions of the overall diameter of the signs, which is the only measurement prescribed. Speed limit signs should be illuminated by lighting or " reflecting material " (see *Bursey* v. *Barron, infra*), unless the Secretary of State has agreed otherwise. The table at the end of the Directions indicates the maximum distances there must be between signs. There is a saving for signs which conform to previous Regulations and Directions, but note s. 75 (4) (on p. 322) as to roads which have not the necessary lamps. Where some lamps were more than 200 yards apart and there were no intermediate signs as required by the relevant Traffic Signs (Speed Limits) Regulations and General Directions, a conviction for exceeding the limit was quashed (*Mackereth* v. *Madge* (1968), 66 L.G.R. 69). The erection of repeater signs in a 30 m.p.h. area governed by a system of street lighting is specifically prohibited by the 1969 Regulations. It is submitted that where there are such illegal repeater signs, a conviction for exceeding 30 m.p.h. will not be invalidated. Only the converse applies (see s. 75 (3) and (4) of the 1967 Act).

See s. 77 (5) of the Road Traffic Regulation Act, 1967, and 106 S.J. 864 as to indicating special temporary speed limits, particularly in relation to signs indicating that a limit is to be observed in any " area."

As special limit signs must, in accordance with s. 75 (1) (*a*) and s. 54 (1) and (2), be the " prescribed " traffic signs it would appear that, if the sign is not in accordance with the Regulations, the defendant is entitled to be acquitted unless the offence took place in an area restricted to 30 m.p.h. by reason of a system of street lamps not more than 200 yards apart. Under reg. 4 (4) of Pt. II of the regulations, signs not illuminated by external lighting must be illuminated by " reflecting material " but by reg. 6 (4) no reflecting material is to be applied to any part of the sign coloured black. In *Bursey* v. *Barron* (1971), 115 S.J. 469, it was held that reflecting material in this context meant reflecting material designed to illuminate the sign, and a coat of varnish which had been applied to the black " 50 " of the sign and which reflected direct light was held not to invalidate the sign.

The only signs which are required to be illuminated are those " terminal " signs erected on a trunk or principal road where there is an electrical street lamp within 50 metres. Such " terminal " signs are required either to be continuously illuminated throughout the hours of darkness, or illuminated while the street lamp is lit providing the sign is also illuminated by reflecting material (i.e., reflecting material designed to illuminate: see *Bursey* v. *Barron, supra*). A " terminal " sign is defined by reg. 4 as those required at the beginning of the speed limit in accordance with directions 2 (1), 2 (2) and 4 but does not include speed limit signs at junctions or signs under directions 2 (3) or 2 (4). Where a terminal sign required to be illuminated under reg. 4 was in such a condition that it could not be illuminated, justices dismissed a case of speeding during daylight hours on the ground that as the sign could not comply with reg. 4 it did not comply with s. 54 (2) of the Road Traffic Regulation Act, 1967. The justices were directed to convict where the speeding took place in daylight: the requirement that the sign should be illuminated was not contravened, as there was no requirement that during daylight hours the sign should be in a state fit for illumination during the hours of darkness (*Stubbs* v. *Morgan* [1972] R.T.R. 459).

Direction 9 requires the back of any speed limit sign to be grey. The justices dismissed a case of speeding where the back of a speed limit sign was painted black instead of grey because s. 54 (2) of the Road Traffic Regulation Act, 1967, requires speed limit signs to be not only of the prescribed size and type but also of the prescribed colour. The High Court, in directing the justices to convict, held that the requirements of s. 75 of the Road Traffic Regulation Act only apply to the front of the prescribed sign and the colour of the back of the sign is immaterial (*Sharples* v. *Blackmore* [1973] R.T.R. 249). The colour of the back of a sign (which no driver sees until he passes it and only then if he turns round) does not make an otherwise restricted road into an unrestricted road (*ibid.*).

Minimum Speed Limits

These may be imposed for specified roads by orders under the Road Traffic Regulation Act, 1967, s. 77 (1) (*b*). The penalty for not observing a minimum limit is a fine of £50; endorsement and disqualification may not be ordered. No person may be convicted solely on the evidence of one witness; see p. 318. By s. 77 (5) signs must be displayed. The relevant order, when made, should be consulted to see if it contains any exception allowing lower speeds for safety reasons.

Class of Vehicle

Certain vehicles are restricted as to speed, whether on restricted roads or not, by the Road Traffic Regulation Act, 1967, Sched. 5. See p. 337 as to vehicles on motorways. There are special limits for trailers constructed as grass cutters and hedge-trimmers, straddle carriers, land tractors used for threshing and reaping, hay and straw balers, vehicles for moving excavated material or for carrying abnormal indivisible loads and engineering plant and loads exceeding 14 feet in width (Motor Vehicles (Authorisation of Special Types) General Order, 1973 (S.I. 1973 No. 1101), arts. 10, 13, 14, 15, 16 and 23). *Semble,* if a vehicle to which the Special Types Order applies exceeds its special limit under that order but keeps within the limit laid down by Sched. 5 to the 1967 Act, no speeding offence is committed, but the driver may be prosecuted under the Construction and Use Regulations in respect of matters, such as width, length, etc., to which they apply, for the protection of the Special Types Order is lost when it is breached; see p. 430.

The limits for classes of vehicle, which, save as stated on p. 337, do not apply on motorways, are indicated in Sched. 5 to the Road Traffic Regulation Act, 1967. Schedule 5 (as varied by the Motor Vehicles (Variation of Speed Limits) Regulations, 1973 (S.I. 1973 No. 747)) reads as follows:—

SCHEDULE 5

LIMITS OF SPEED FOR VEHICLES OF CERTAIN CLASSES

Class of vehicle (*See also paragraph* 13)	*Maximum speed, miles per hour*

VEHICLES OTHER THAN TRACK-LAYING VEHICLES

1. Passenger vehicles, that is to say, vehicles constructed solely for the carriage of passengers and their effects, and dual purpose vehicles:—

(1) a passenger vehicle having an unladen weight exceeding 3 tons, or adapted to carry more than 7 passengers exclusive of the driver, in respect of which a public service vehicle licence granted under section 127 of the Road Traffic Act 1960 is in force.. .. **50**

(2) a passenger vehicle having an unladen weight not exceeding 30 hundredweight, adapted to carry more than 7 passengers exclusive of the driver and in respect of which a public service vehicle licence granted under section 127 of the Road Traffic Act 1960 is not in force **50**

(3) a vehicle having an unladen weight exceeding 3 tons, or adapted to carry more than 7 passengers exclusive of the driver, not being a vehicle which falls within sub-paragraph (1) or (2) above .. **40**

(4) a vehicle drawing one trailer when the drawing vehicle is either a motor car adapted to carry not more than 7 passengers exclusive of the driver or a passenger vehicle which has an unladen weight not exceeding 30 hundredweight and is adapted to carry more than 7 passengers exclusive of the driver—

Class of vehicle	*Maximum speed, miles per hour*
(*a*) in a case where the relevant conditions specified in paragraph 25 below are satisfied, or the drawing vehicle is a foreign vehicle	50
(*b*) in any other case	40
(5) a vehicle drawing one trailer in circumstances not falling within sub-paragraph (4) above—	
(*a*) in the case of a passenger vehicle having an unladen weight exceeding 3 tons, or adapted to carry more than 7 passengers exclusive of the driver, in respect of which a public service vehicle licence granted under section 127 of the Road Traffic Act 1960 is in force	40
(*b*) in the case of a vehicle not falling within sub-paragraph (*a*) above	30
(6) a vehicle drawing more than one trailer	20
(7) a vehicle not fitted with pneumatic tyres and a vehicle drawing a trailer not so fitted	20
(8) an invalid carriage	20

2. Goods vehicles, that is to say, vehicles constructed or adapted for use for the conveyance of goods or burden of any description, but not including dual-purpose vehicles—

(1) generally, except for vehicles falling within sub-paragraph (2) or (3) (*a*) below	40
(2) vehicles having an unladen weight not exceeding 30 hundredweight, when not drawing a trailer ..	50
(3) vehicles drawing a trailer, not being articulated vehicles—	
(*a*) in the case of a trailer drawn by a motor car having an unladen weight not exceeding 30 hundredweight when the relevant conditions specified in paragraph 25 below are satisfied or the drawing vehicle is a foreign vehicle	50
(*b*) in the case of a trailer drawn by a heavy motor car or by a motor cycle	30
(*c*) in the case of a trailer drawn by a motor car having an unladen weight exceeding 30 hundredweight if the trailer—	
(i) being a load-carrying trailer, has an unladen weight exceeding 5 hundredweight, or	
(ii) being neither a living van nor a load-carrying trailer, has an unladen weight exceeding 15 hundredweight	30
(4) vehicles drawing more than one trailer	20
(5) vehicles not fitted with pneumatic tyres, if drawing trailers or having an unladen weight exceeding 1 ton, and vehicles drawing trailers not fitted with pneumatic tyres	20
(6) vehicles not fitted with resilient tyres and vehicles drawing trailers not so fitted..	5

| *Class of vehicle* | *Maximum speed, miles per hour* |

3. Motor tractors:—

(1) generally, except for vehicles falling within the following sub-paragraph **20**

(2) vehicles fitted with pneumatic tyres, equipped with springs and wings and which satisfy the conditions as to brakes specified in paragraph 20 (*a*) below or such vehicles drawing a trailer so fitted and equipped and which satisfies the conditions as to brakes specified in paragraph 20 (*b*) below **30**

(3) if drawing two or more trailers **12**

(4) if not fitted with resilient tyres or drawing trailers not so fitted **5**

4. Heavy locomotives and light locomotives:—

(1) generally, except for vehicles falling within the following sub-paragraph **12**

(2) vehicles fitted with pneumatic tyres, equipped with springs and wings and which satisfy the conditions as to brakes and weight specified in paragraph 20 (*a*), (*c*) and (*d*) below or such vehicles drawing a trailer so fitted and equipped and which satisfies the conditions as to brakes specified in paragraph 20 (*b*) below if the further conditions as to the weight of a vehicle and trailer specified in paragraph 20 (*e*) below are complied with **20**

(3) if drawing two or more trailers **12**

(4) if not fitted with resilient tyres or drawing trailers not so fitted **5**

Track-Laying Vehicles

5. Motor cars and heavy motor cars **20**

6. Motor tractors:—

(1) generally **20**

(2) if drawing two or more trailers **5**

7. Light locomotives:—

(1) generally **12**

(2) if drawing more than two trailers **5**

8. Heavy locomotives **5**

9. Track-laying vehicles which do not satisfy both of the following conditions—

(*a*) that the vehicle is fitted with springs between its frame and the weight-carrying rollers, and

(*b*) that the vehicle is fitted with resilient material between the rims of the weight-carrying rollers and the road surface,

and vehicles drawing track-laying trailers which do not satisfy both of those conditions **12**

	Maximum speed, miles per hour

Class of vehicle

10. Track-laying vehicles satisfying neither of the said conditions, and vehicles drawing track-laying trailers satisfying neither of those conditions   5

11. Combined track-and-wheel vehicles not fitted with resilient tyres, and vehicles drawing trailers which are combined track-and-wheel vehicles not fitted with resilient tyres   5

12. Vehicles drawing trailers, where the drawing or any of the drawn vehicles, not being a track-laying vehicle, is not fitted with resilient tyres   5

INTERPRETATION AND APPLICATION

13. A vehicle falling within two or more classes specified in this Schedule shall be treated as falling within that class for which the lowest limit of speed is specified.

14.—(1) In this Schedule " dual-purpose vehicle " means a vehicle constructed or adapted for the carriage both of passengers and of goods or burden of any description being a vehicle of which the unladen weight does not exceed 2 tons and which either—

    (*a*) satisfies the conditions as to construction specified in the following sub-paragraph; or

    (*b*) is so constructed or adapted that the driving power of the engine is, or by the appropriate use of the controls of the vehicle can be, transmitted to all the wheels of the vehicle.

(2) The conditions as to construction referred to in sub-paragraph (1) above are the following:—

    (*a*) the vehicle must be permanently fitted with a rigid roof, with or without a sliding panel;

    (*b*) the area of the vehicle to the rear of the driver's seat must—

        (i) be permanently fitted with at least one row of transverse seats (fixed or folding) for two or more passengers and those seats must be properly sprung or cushioned and provided with upholstered backrests, attached either to the seats or to a side or the floor of the vehicle, and

        (ii) be lit on each side and at the rear by a window or windows of glass or other transparent material having an area or aggregate area of not less than 2 square feet on each side and not less than 120 square inches at the rear;

    (*c*) the distance between the rearmost part of the steering wheel and the backrests of the row of transverse seats satisfying the requirements specified in head (*b*) (i) of this sub-paragraph (or, if there is more than one such row of seats, the distance between the rearmost part of the steering wheel and the backrests of the rearmost such row) must, when the seats are ready for use, be not less than one-third of the distance between the rearmost part of the steering wheel and the rearmost part of the floor of the vehicle.

15. In this Schedule "load-carrying trailer" means a trailer, not being a living van which is constructed or adapted for use for the conveyance of goods or burden of any description.

16. [Revoked.]

17. In this Schedule " articulated vehicle " means a vehicle which consists of a motor vehicle drawing a trailer where the trailer is so attached to the drawing vehicle that part of the trailer is superimposed upon the drawing vehicle, and when the trailer is uniformly loaded not less than 20 per cent. of the weight of its load is borne by the drawing vehicle.

18. In this Schedule, in relation to a vehicle (including a trailer)—

(a) " fitted with pneumatic tyres " means that every wheel of the vehicle is fitted with pneumatic tyres;

(b) " fitted with resilient tyres " means that every wheel of the vehicle is fitted either with pneumatic tyres or with other soft or elastic tyres; and

(c) " equipped with springs and wings " means that the vehicle —

(i) is equipped with suitable and sufficient springs between each wheel and the frame of the vehicle, and

(ii) unless adequate protection is afforded by the body of the vehicle, is provided with wings or other similar fittings to catch, so far as practicable, mud or water thrown up by the rotation of the wheels.

19. In this Schedule " track-laying " means so designed and constructed that the weight is transmitted to the road surface either by means of continuous tracks or by a combination of wheels and continuous tracks, and " combined track-and-wheel vehicle " means a vehicle so designed and constructed that its weight is transmitted to the road surface by a combination of wheels and continuous tracks.

20. The conditions referred to in paragraphs 3 (2) and 4 (2) above are as follows:—

(a) the motor tractor, or, as the case may be, the locomotive, shall be equipped with an efficient braking system having two means of operation or with two efficient braking systems each having a separate means of operation, the system or systems being so designed and constructed that, notwithstanding the failure of any part (other than a fixed member or a brake shoe anchor pin) through or by means of which the force necessary to apply the brakes is transmitted, there is still available for application by the driver to not less than half the number of the wheels of the vehicle brakes sufficient under the most adverse conditions to bring it to rest within a reasonable distance;

(b) the trailer shall be equipped with an efficient braking system so constructed—

(i) that when the trailer is being drawn the brakes are capable of being applied by the driver of the drawing vehicle to at least two of the wheels of a trailer having not more than four wheels and to at least four, but not less than half, of the wheels of a trailer having more than four wheels, and

(ii) that it is not rendered ineffective by the non-rotation of the engine of the drawing vehicle;

(c) the weight transmitted to the road surface by any one wheel of the locomotive, where no other wheel is in the same line transversely, shall not exceed 4½ tons, the total weight so transmitted by any two wheels in line transversely shall not exceed 9 tons and the sum of the weights so transmitted by all the wheels shall not exceed—

    (i) in the case of a vehicle having not more than four wheels, 14 tons,

    (ii) in the case of a vehicle having more than four but not more than six wheels, 20 tons, and

    (iii) in the case of a vehicle having more than six wheels, 24 tons;

(d) the weight transmitted by the locomotive (whether laden or unladen) to any strip of the surface of a road on which it rests contained between any two parallel lines drawn 2 feet apart on that surface at right angles to the longitudinal axis of the vehicle shall not exceed 11 tons; and

(e) the maximum laden weight of the locomotive and trailer shall not exceed 22 tons or, if the trailer is fitted with power-assisted brakes which can be operated by the driver of the drawing vehicle and are not rendered ineffective by the non-rotation of its engine, and if that vehicle is equipped with a warning device so placed as to be readily visible to the driver when in the driving seat of the vehicle in order to indicate an impending failure or deficiency in the vacuum or pressure system, 32 tons.

21. For the purposes of this Schedule measuring or testing apparatus, and any ballast necessary in connection therewith, drawn upon one wheel by a vehicle, when used solely for or in connection with testing or measurement purposes, shall not, if the wheel is fitted with a pneumatic tyre and does not transmit to the road surface a weight exceeding 2 hundredweight, be treated as a trailer.

22. For the purposes of paragraphs 20 and 21 above, two wheels of a vehicle shall be regarded as one wheel if the distance between the centres of their respective areas of contact with the road is less than 18 inches.

23. A heavy motor car or motor car drawing a trailer and being used as a public service vehicle or as a goods vehicle shall be treated as not drawing a trailer if the trailer is used solely for the carriage of a container or containers for holding, or plant and materials for producing, for the purpose of the propulsion of the drawing vehicle, any fuel that is wholly gaseous at 60 degrees Fahrenheit under pressure of 30 inches of mercury.

24.—(1) Paragraphs 1 to 4 above do not apply to, and paragraphs 5 to 12 above apply only to, track-laying vehicles and vehicles drawing track-laying trailers or trailers some of which are track-laying.

(2) Paragraphs 1 to 12 above do not apply to vehicles for the time being used in the conduct of experiments or trials under section 6 of the Roads Improvement Act 1925 or section 249 of the Highways Act 1959.

25. The relevant conditions referred to in paragraphs 1 (4) and 2 (3) above in relation to a vehicle drawing a trailer and the trailer so drawn are as follows:—

(a) appropriate weights shall be displayed as follows:—

    (i) in the case of the drawing vehicle, its kerbside weight shall be legibly marked in a conspicuous and readily accessible position—

        (A) inside the vehicle, or

        (B) outside the vehicle and on its left or near side, and

    (ii) in the case of the trailer being a living van, or being neither a living van nor a load-carrying trailer, its maximum gross weight shall be legibly marked in a conspicuous and readily

accessible position on the left or near side of, and on the
outside of, the trailer;

(b) the appropriate weights referred to in (a) above may be stated in
imperial units or in metric units but the same units shall be employed for both the drawing vehicle and the trailer, and if metric
units are employed the weights shall be stated in kilograms.

(c) there shall be exhibited in a conspicuous position at the rear of
the trailer a plate which complies in all respects with the following
requirements—

  (i) the plate shall be circular or elliptical, shall be fixed in a
  vertical position facing squarely to the rear of the trailer,
  shall, if elliptical, be placed so that the major axis is in the
  horizontal position, and shall be kept clean and unobscured
  so as to be plainly visible from behind the trailer,

  (ii) the surface facing to the rear shall be black and shall display
  thereon the number " 50 " in white or silver or light grey
  figures,

  (iii) the plate, if circular, shall be not less than 4 inches in diameter,
  and, if elliptical, shall be not less than 3 inches in height and
  $4\frac{1}{4}$ inches in width,

  (iv) each figure of the said number shall be not less than $1\frac{3}{4}$ inches
  in height and $1\frac{1}{4}$ inches in total width, the width of every part
  of each figure shall be not less than $\frac{5}{16}$ inch, and the space
  between the nearest parts of the two figures shall be not less
  than $\frac{1}{4}$ inch, and

  (v) no part of any such figure shall project from the surface of
  the said plate by more than $\frac{3}{16}$ inch;

(d) the following weight ratios shall be observed—

  (i) where the trailer drawn is a living van, its maximum gross
  weight shall not exceed the kerbside weight of the drawing
  vehicle,

  (ii) where the trailer drawn is a braked load-carrying trailer, its
  laden weight shall not exceed the kerbside weight of the
  drawing vehicle,

  (iii) where the trailer drawn is an unbraked load-carrying trailer, its
  laden weight shall not exceed 60 per cent. of the kerbside
  weight of the drawing vehicle,

  (iv) where the trailer drawn is a braked trailer, being neither a
  living van nor a load-carrying trailer, its maximum gross
  weight shall not exceed the kerbside weight of the drawing
  vehicle, and

  (v) where the trailer drawn is an unbraked trailer, being neither
  a living van nor a load-carrying trailer, its maximum gross
  weight shall not exceed 60 per cent. of the kerbside weight of
  the drawing vehicle.

26. In this Schedule—

" braked trailer " means a trailer which is equipped with a braking
system in accordance with Regulation 70 of the Motor Vehicles (Construction and Use) Regulations 1973 whether or not the Regulation applies to
it;

" unbraked trailer " means a trailer which is not so equipped;

" foreign vehicle " means—

(a) a motor vehicle brought into Great Britain and displaying a registration mark mentioned in Regulation 5 of the Motor Vehicles (International Circulation) Regulations 1971, a period of twelve months not having elapsed since the vehicle in question was last brought into Great Britain; or

(b) a vehicle in the service of a visiting force or of a headquarters.

" kerbside weight " means, in relation to a motor vehicle, the weight of the vehicle (inclusive of any towing bracket with which it is normally equipped) when it carries—

(i) no person thereon, and

(ii) a full supply of fuel in its tank, an adequate supply of other liquids incidental to its propulsion and no load other than the loose tools and equipment with which the vehicle is normally equipped;

" maximum gross weight " means, in relation to a trailer, the weight which it is designed or adapted not to exceed when in normal use and travelling on a road laden;

" vehicle in the service of a visiting force or of a headquarters " has the same meaning as in Article 8 (6) of the Visiting Forces and International Headquarters (Application of Law) Order 1965.

The terms " motor car ", " heavy motor car ", " light (and) heavy locomotive ", " motor tractor " and " invalid carriage " are defined in s. 190 of the 1972 Act (see p. 2), the definitions in s. 99 of the Road Traffic Regulation Act being the same. The definition of an " articulated vehicle " is identical with that in the Construction and Use Regulations (see p. 11 and in particular *Hunter* v. *Towers*).

In para. 2 of the Schedule (relating to goods vehicles) set out above, " constructed " means " as originally constructed " (*Hubbard* v. *Messenger* [1937] 4 All E.R. 48), but a vehicle can be reconstructed so that it joins another class (*Keeble* v. *Miller* [1950] 1 All E.R. 261). Adaptation, seemingly, is insufficient to change a goods vehicle to a passenger one, however; there must be a major reconstruction (*Fry* v. *Bevan* (1937), 81 S.J. 60). Fitting a different body could be a major reconstruction (*Burrows* v. *Berry* (1949), 113 J.P.Jo. 492). Fitting a container to a tractor or locomotive would not convert it to a goods vehicle and, in view of para. 13, it seems doubtful if such an adaptation would allow such vehicles to go at the same speed as goods vehicles. See below and pp. 495–497 as to adaptation.

Weight is calculated pursuant to the Road Traffic Act, 1972, s. 194 (see p. 15), even though this may result in a vehicle being of a different unladen weight under the Vehicles (Excise) Act.

Passenger Vehicles

Ordinary, i.e., passenger-carrying motor cars of an unladen weight not exceeding three tons and motor cycles and motor cycle combinations, provided they are adapted to carry not more than seven passengers exclusive of the driver, are not subject to any special speed limit when not on restricted roads, unless drawing trailers.   The speed limits for other passenger-carrying vehicles are indicated in Sched. 5   Under para. 1 the vehicle must be " constructed solely for the carriage of passengers and their effects " and a goods vehicle adapted to carry passengers is not so " constructed ".   Further, a vehicle must be constructed " solely " to carry passengers and a utility vehicle made to carry passengers or goods is not constructed " solely " to carry passengers even if goods are never in fact carried (*Hubbard* v. *Messenger* [1937] 4 All E.R. 48). Unless, as will often be the case now, it is a dual-purpose vehicle, as defined in para. 14, a utility vehicle will generally be classed as a goods vehicle under para. 2; *cf. Taylor* v. *Thompson* [1956] 1 All E.R. 352.

The 1973 Regulations have inserted a new sub-para. (2) in para. 1 the effect of which is to allow minibuses, i.e., passenger vehicles not exceeding 30 cwt adapted to carry more than seven passengers exclusive of the driver to drive at up to 50 m.p.h. if the minibus does not have a public service vehicle licence; passenger vehicles which do have a public service vehicle licence and which *either* exceed three tons unladen *or* carry more than seven passengers exclusive of the driver are also subject to 50 m.p.h. limit only (see sub-para. (1)) but passenger vehicles and dual-purpose vehicles exceeding 3 tons or adapted to carry more than seven passengers not coming within either of the two categories (see sub-paras. (1) and (2)) are subject to a 40 m.p.h. limit (e.g., a minibus of more than 30 cwt not having a public service vehicle licence).

" Adapted " in para. 1 (1) means suitable for the carriage of eight or more passengers whether by original construction or subsequent alteration (*Maddox* v. *Storer* [1962] 1 All E.R. 831). " Adapted " in para. 1 (1) and (3) of Sched. 5 to the 1967 Act was held to mean " fit and apt for the purpose ", not merely " altered so as to be apt ", although, *semble*, it can include both vehicles originally constructed to be fit and apt and those subsequently altered so that they then are fit and apt.   It would seem that a similar construction should be placed on the word " adapted " in the new sub-para. (2).

It should be noted that the position varies if a trailer is being drawn.

Goods Vehicles

These are defined in para. 2 as vehicles constructed or adapted for use for the conveyance of goods or burden of any description, and the limits laid down apply whether the vehicle is carrying goods or not and whether it has a goods vehicle licence or not and whatever its unladen weight, save that dual-purpose vehicles, as defined below, are exempt. Note that goods vehicles not drawing a trailer and having an unladen weight not exceeding 30 cwt are subject to a maximum speed limit of 50 m.p.h. The speed limit for tower-wagons, sound-recording vans, breakdown lorries and vehicles fitted with a special appliance or apparatus is discussed at 121 J.P.Jo. 479; as such apparatus is, by s. 99 (10), not now a " burden ", the case of *Burningham* v. *Lindsell* [1936] 2 All E.R. 159 is no longer of authority. Generally, such vehicles will carry goods also and can be found to be goods vehicles. A chassis, while remaining a motor vehicle, is not subject to any limit under Sched. 5, as it does not come within any of the types there specified (*Millard* v. *Turvey* [1968] 2 All E.R. 7). A vehicle constructed solely to carry passengers and their effects and not adapted to carry goods will remain a passenger vehicle and subject to the limits (if any) prescribed by para. 1 of Sched. 1, however, even though it carries goods which are not the " effects " of the passengers. Dual-purpose vehicles (*infra*) are also exempt.

In *Bryson* v. *Rogers* [1956] 2 All E.R. 826, a farmer's Austin pick-up van, which did not conform to the definition of dual-purpose vehicle, as defined below, was held to be subject to a speed limit of (now) 40 m.p.h. under para. 2, although it was not carrying goods. A van adapted to carry passengers and with no shelves for goods was held not to be a goods vehicle (see *Tait* v. *Odhams Press*, p. 543, *infra*, a case on goods vehicle licensing). In *Levinson* v. *Powell* [1967] 3 All E.R. 796, a taxi was held not to be a goods vehicle, though it may be a dual-purpose one.

" Adapted " was said in *Taylor* v. *Mead* [1961] 1 All E.R. 626 to mean some amount of alteration of the original construction; the term is discussed above and at p. 496. Addition of a luggage rack to a passenger vehicle, if not so big as to be out of keeping with the number of passengers, and so long as it does not involve interference with the structure, does not convert it to a goods vehicle (*Flower Freight Co., Ltd.* v. *Hammond* [1962] 3 All E.R. 950). The term " adapted " has a different meaning in para. 2 from that in para. 1. Whilst in para. 1 it means merely " suitable for " with or without alteration (*Maddox* v. *Storer* [1962] 1 All E.R. 831), it is in para. 2 contrasted with the term " constructed " and means " altered by some form of reconstruction " as in *Taylor* v. *Mead*, *supra* (*Maddox* v. *Storer*, *supra*).

Goods vehicles must comply with speed limits at all times, whether or not they are carrying goods, because the test is not whether goods are actually carried but whether the vehicle is constructed or adapted for the carriage of goods or burden of any description, not including dual-purpose vehicles (see para. 2 of Sched. 5 to the Road Traffic Regulation Act, 1967, *supra*, p. 326, and *Bryson* v. *Rogers*, *supra*). " Goods " is not confined to goods for sale or delivery: it includes a window-cleaner's ladders, rags and buckets (*Clarke* v. *Cherry* [1953] 1 All E.R. 267) and effluent (*Sweetway Sanitary Cleansers* v. *Bradley* [1961] 2 All E.R. 821); in *Bourne* v. *Norwich Crematorium, Ltd.* [1967] 1 W.L.R., at p. 695 (a tax case), it was held that corpses are not " goods," though it was argued that coffins and shrouds might be and reference was made to a case where dogs were held to be goods.

Motor cycles with side-cars made to carry goods fall under para. 2 and when drawing a trailer were formerly subject to a limit of 40 m.p.h. Motorcycles when drawing a trailer are now subject to a 30 m.p.h. limit whether falling under para. 1 (see para. 1 (5) (*b*)) or para. 2 (see para. 2 (3) (*b*)).

Dual-Purpose Vehicles

These are defined in para. 14 of Sched. 5 to the Road Traffic Regulation Act, 1967 (see p. 328), and vehicles falling within the definition given are exempt from speed limits when not on restricted roads, whether or not they are carrying goods. They are mainly shooting-brakes and utility vehicles, but vehicles so constructed or adapted that the driving power of the engine is, or by the appropriate use of the controls can be, transmitted to all the wheels are also included under para. 14 (1) (*b*). Such vehicles are Land Rovers, Jeeps and those designed to go over rough ground as well as on roads, not being track-laying vehicles, and they are exempt from speed limits when not on restricted roads, whether or not they comply with the conditions as to construction specified in para. 14 (2), e.g., rigid roofs, transverse seats, etc. (*Kidson* v. *Swatridge* [1957] Crim.L.R. 193). Shooting-brakes and utility vehicles without four-wheel drive must comply with those conditions to obtain exemption from speed limits when not on restricted roads. A van had been adapted to be a " dual-purpose vehicle " by adding windows, but its windows were covered by panels of wood screwed into the windows so as to obscure them entirely. It was held that the van had been adapted to become a dual-purpose vehicle and that it was not subject to any limit as a goods vehicle (*Popperwell* v. *Cockerton* [1968] 1 All E.R. 1038). In *Levinson* v. *Powell* [1967] 3 All E.R. 796, a taxi was held to be a dual-purpose vehicle, but each vehicle would have to be inspected to see if it did fall within the definition in para. 14.

If a vehicle, though constructed to carry goods and passengers, does not come within the definitions given, e.g., because its unladen weight exceeds 2 tons or it has a non-rigid roof or its seats run lengthways and not transversely, it will fall under para. 2 of Sched. 1 to the Road Traffic Act, 1960 (now Sched. 5 to the Road Traffic Regulation Act, 1967) as a goods vehicle, whether or not it is carrying goods (*Bryson* v. *Rogers* [1956] 2 All E.R. 826).

Articulated Vehicles and Trailers

The lower limits laid down when a vehicle draws a trailer will be noted. An articulated vehicle as defined in para. 17 of Sched. 5 to the Act of 1967 is not now treated, for speed-limit purposes, as a vehicle drawing a trailer and, unless within para. 2 (4) or any later paragraph, will generally be subject to the same limits as goods vehicles under para. 2 (1), unless the whole articulated vehicle is itself drawing a trailer behind it. The definition in para. 17 differs slightly from that in s. 190 (9) of the Act of 1972 (see p. 3) but is identical with the definition in the Construction and Use Regulations. A four-wheeled vehicle being towed with two wheels in the air is not a " two-wheeled trailer " (*Cary* v. *Heath* [1951] 2 All E.R. 774). A vehicle and trailer closely coupled together, not being an articulated vehicle, do not thereby become one vehicle (*Dixon* v. *B.R.S.* (*Pickford*), *Ltd.* [1959] 1 All E.R. 449).

A car towing a two-wheeled caravan with the aid of a " van-dolly ", i.e., a small chassis with two wheels, is towing a four-wheeled trailer and subject to the limit laid down pursuant to Sched. 5 (*Brown* v. *Dando* (1954), 118 J.P.Jo. 319). A trailer and car amalgamated into one four-wheeled rigid unit is one trailer not two (*Baker* v. *Esau* [1972] Crim.L.R. 559).

Note the increase in the limit to 50 m.p.h. conferred on passenger and dual purpose vehicles drawing a trailer by para. 1 (4) (*a*) and on goods vehicles drawing a trailer conferred by para. 2 (3) (*a*). The 50 m.p.h. limit in such cases only applies either when the relevant conditions in para. 25 are satisfied or the drawing vehicle is a foreign vehicle (note the definition of " foreign vehicle " in para. 26). The wording of paras. 1 (4) (*a*) and 2 (3) (*a*) appears quite categoric and if any of the conditions of para. 25 are not satisfied, e.g., no 50 plate, the weight ratio exceeded, the kerbside weight of the drawing vehicle not marked as required, the appropriate lower speed limits of 40 or 30 m.p.h. will be applicable.

Motorway Speed Limits

The Motor Vehicles (Speed Limits on Motorways) Regulations, 1973 (S.I. 1973 No. 748) as amended by like named Amendment

Regulations (S.I. 1973 No. 2058) substitute the following Schedule for vehicles while being driven on motorways in place of the ordinary Sched. 5:—

SCHEDULE
LIMITS OF SPEED

Class of Vehicle

Maximum speed, miles per hour

1. A goods vehicle having an unladen weight exceeding 3 tons   50

2. Any motor vehicle drawing a trailer (not being an articulated vehicle) if the trailer has less than 4 wheels or is a close-coupled four-wheeled trailer, except when falling within paragraph 3 below   50

3. Any motor vehicle having an unladen weight not exceeding 30 hundredweight, when drawing such a trailer as is referred to in paragraph 2 above in circumstances where the speed limit under Schedule 5 to the Act (as varied) for such a vehicle when drawing such a trailer and being driven on a road which is not a special road is 40 miles per hour or less   ..   40

INTERPRETATION

4. In this Schedule " close-coupled ", in relation to a trailer, means that the wheels on the same side of the trailer are so fitted that at all times while it is in motion they remain parallel to the longitudinal axis of the trailer and that the distance between the centres of the respective areas of contact with the road surface does not exceed 33 inches.

5. Any expression which is used in this Schedule and to which a meaning is given in Schedule 5 to the Act has the same meaning in this Schedule as it has in the said Schedule 5.

For the vehicles which may lawfully travel on a motorway see p. 580. It will be noted that by virtue of para. 5, terms such as " articulated vehicle ", " goods vehicle " or other terms which have particular meanings, bear the same meaning as in Sched. 5 to the Act (see pp. 325–332). It will also be noted that vehicles not exceeding 30 cwt. drawing a trailer which are subject to a 50 m.p.h. limit on ordinary roads so long as the provisions of para. 25 of the Schedule are complied with will be subject to a 40 m.p.h. limit on a motorway if the provisions of para. 25 are not complied with on the motorway (see the exception to para. 2 above and para. 3).

The temporary speed limits of 50 and 60 m.p.h. do not and could not apply to motorways as the enabling section of the Act under which the order was made does not apply to motorways (s. 77 of the Road Traffic Regulation Act, 1967). Vehicles not already subject to a lower speed limit by virtue of the Schedule referred to above are subject to an overall limit of 70 m.p.h. on motorways by virtue of the Motorways Traffic (Speed Limit) Regulations, 1974 (S.I.

1974 No. 502). These regulations provide for an overall limit of 70 m.p.h. and special overall limits of 50 and 60 m.p.h. on particular stretches of various motorways as set out in Schedules to the order. The 1974 Regulations are not temporary or limited in time and are made by virtue of s. 13 of the Road Traffic Regulation Act, 1967. (For necessity of notice of intended prosecution, see pp. 129 and 130.)

Exemptions from Speed Limits

Vehicles being used for fire brigade, ambulance or police purposes are not subject to any speed limit either on a restricted road or by virtue of their class if observance of the limit would be likely to hinder their use for the purpose for which they are being used on that occasion (Road Traffic Regulation Act, 1967, s. 79), but are otherwise. A private person who is trailing a police car with a view to obtaining evidence to prosecute its driver for speeding cannot plead s. 79 as a defence (*Strathern* v. *Gladstone* [1937] S.C.(J.) 11). If, in a particular case and a particular set of special circumstances, it is established that, solely in order to enable a police purpose to be performed, or solely to ensure that a police purpose requiring to be performed is not frustrated, use must be made of a vehicle and the use being made of it would be hindered by observance of the provisions restricting the speed at which vehicles can travel, then in such circumstances s. 79 excuses the offence of travelling too fast (*Aitken* v. *Yarwood* [1964] 2 All E.R. 537). In that case, the car taking a policeman to court to give evidence broke down and it was held that in those circumstances he was entitled to exceed the limit in order to get to court in time. Normally, however, a constable should start for court in time to get there without exceeding the limit and it would only be in unforeseen circumstances, e.g., a breakdown or stopping to give first aid at an accident, that he would be entitled to exceed the limit. Like considerations apply to fire and ambulance vehicles; they may exceed the limit only if it would hinder the relevant use on the particular occasion, e.g., the chief fire officer in his car must obviously get to the fire as quickly as possible but there is no need to hurry home on going off duty. *Semble*, a car taking a casualty to hospital in an urgent case is being used for ambulance purposes but it is doubtful if a doctor hurrying to an urgent case is using his car for ambulance purposes; an ambulance, according to the Oxford Dictionary, is a vehicle for conveying wounded.

The Motor Vehicles (Variation of Speed Limit) Regulations, 1947 (S.R. & O. 1947 No. 2192) and the like Amendment Regulations, 1954 (S.I. 1954 No. 943), provide that Sched. 5 to the 1967 Act (*supra*) shall have effect as though it imposed no speed limits in relation to certain types of vehicles owned by the Secretary of State for Defence and used for naval, military or air force purposes or which are so used whilst being driven by persons subject to the orders of a member of the armed forces of the Crown. There is a similar exemption (by the 1954 Regulations) for like vehicles in the service of a visiting force (see p. 58). The types of vehicles so exempted are ones constructed or adapted for combative purposes or training in connection therewith, for conveyance of personnel, for use with or to carry or draw guns and machine guns, certain track-laying vehicles, fire tenders and ambulances. Vehicles used for salvage purposes pursuant to Pt. IX of the Merchant Shipping Act, 1894, are also exempt from Sched. 5 under the 1947 Regulations and so are vehicles used in the conduct of experiments or trials for road improvements (see para. 24 (2) of Sched. 5).

The 1947 Regulations, *supra*, only exempt the vehicles referred to therein from the provisions of Sched. 5. The Regulations do not confer exemption on these vehicles in respect of roads subject to restricted speeds. Section 79 would seem to confer exemption from such restrictions in respect of service ambulances and fire brigade vehicles, and (possibly) service police vehicles if it can be argued that military, naval or air force police purposes come within " police purposes " in s. 79.

Autrefois Convict

In *Welton* v. *Taneborne* (1908), 72 J.P. 419, a conviction for driving in a dangerous manner, where the court had taken into consideration the defendant's speed, was held to bar a subsequent prosecution for exceeding the speed limit. In that case both summonses had been preferred together, but the dangerous driving charge was heard first and, upon the conviction being announced, the police desired to proceed on the speeding charge also. It would seem, however, that, if there had been an acquittal on the graver charge, this would not necessarily bar the speeding one.

Endorsement, Disqualification and Penalty

On first or subsequent conviction for an offence of exceeding a speed limit imposed by or under the Road Traffic Regulation Act, 1967, the Parks Regulation (Amendment) Act, 1926, s. 2, or any Act passed after 1st September, 1960, the offender's driving licence must be endorsed unless there are special reasons (see Chapter VII).

There is no power to order endorsement (or disqualification) for an offence of failure to observe a minimum speed limit under the 1967 Act.

A person convicted of exceeding a speed limit mentioned in the last paragraph but one may be disqualified for any period at the court's discretion. The court may also order the defendant to be disqualified till he passes the test (Road Traffic Act, 1972, s. 93 (7)).

Section 93 (3) of the 1972 Act applies to offences of exceeding a speed limit, so that if a person convicted of that offence has been previously convicted on not less than two occasions of an endorsed disqualifiable offence within the three years immediately before the offence he must be disqualified for at least six months (see p. 624) unless, having regard to all the circumstances, there are grounds for mitigating the normal consequences of the conviction (see p. 688). The mere fact that a previous or present offence is for speeding is not a mitigating circumstance justifying a court not disqualifying under s. 93 (3) (see *Lambie* v. *Woodage* and *Baker* v. *Cole*, pp. 689, 691). The six-month disqualification is additional and consecutive to any period of disqualification imposed on the same occasion or for any previous offence.

The fine is £100 on first or subsequent conviction. The same penalty applies to aiders, abettors and inciters of speeding offences. The maximum fine for offences of failing to observe a minimum speed limit is £50 (Road Traffic Regulation Act, 1967, s. 77 (7)).

Warning of intended prosecution is required for speeding offences " punishable " by virtue of s. 78A of the Road Traffic Regulation Act, 1967, and offences of failing to observe a minimum speed limit under s. 77 (7) (see Chapter III). Exceeding the overall motorway limit of 70 m.p.h. (or 60 or 50 m.p.h. on certain specified stretches of various motorways) contrary to the Motorways Traffic (Speed Limit) Regulations, 1974, may, possibly, not be subject to the requirements of s. 179 of the Act of 1972 as such offences can be said to be punishable by virtue of s. 13 of the Road Traffic Regulation Act, 1967, and not by virtue of s. 78A (see p. 129).

The endorsement codes for speeding offences are as follows:—

Exceeding speed limit for type of vehicle   SP20
Exceeding statutory limit on a road   SP30
Exceeding passenger vehicle speed limit   SP40
Exceeding speed limit on a motorway.   SP50

The Magistrates' Association's suggested penalties (see p. 594 and p. 879) for speeding offences read as follows:—" £1.50 per m.p.h. over any limit. More for heavy vehicles. Consider disqualification particularly if 30 m.p.h. over limit."

5. REPORTING ACCIDENTS

Accidents Involving Injury—Production of Certificates

Under the Road Traffic Act, 1972, s. 166 (1) and (2), where, owing to the presence of a motor vehicle (other than an invalid carriage) on a road, an accident occurs involving personal injury to another person and the driver does not at the time produce his certificate of insurance to the police or to some person who has on reasonable grounds required its production, the driver shall, as soon as possible and in any case within twenty-four hours of the accident, report it to the police and thereupon produce his certificate, provided that he may within five days after the accident produce it at such police station as he specifies at the time of reporting. Note that the driver no longer has to produce the certificate in person. This section has been amended by the Act of 1974 (para. 20, Sched. 6) to bring it into line with the requirement to produce a certificate under s. 162 (2) (see p. 380), which need not be in person. In *Tremelling* v. *Martin* [1971] R.T.R. 196 the defendant produced his driving licence and certificate of insurance at a police station. The clerk was called to the telephone before the documents could be examined. The defendant did not wait and walked out of the station. Directing a conviction under both sections, the Divisional Court held that the purpose of producing driving licences was to enable the police to ascertain the name and address of the holder of the licence, the date of issue and the authority that issued it, and the purpose of s. 162 was to enable a constable to inspect the certificate of insurance and see that it was a proper certificate. The case would appear to apply to s. 166 also, because the object of the section would appear to be basically similar to that of s. 162.

The requirements under s. 166, which only arise on an accident involving personal injury to another person, must be obeyed although the driver has given his name and address to some person reasonably requiring it under s. 25, *infra*. The section would not apply where the driver was quite unaware of the accident or the injury and had not wilfully or negligently shut his eyes to it (*Harding* v. *Price* [1948] 1 All E.R. 283). In *Hampson* v. *Powell* [1970] 1 All E.R. 929 a lorry driver was held not to be guilty under s. 25 of failing to stop and failing to report an accident of which he was not aware, although he was convicted of careless driving as the evidence, although insufficient to show that he knew of the accident, was sufficient to show that he drove the vehicle without due care and attention. Nor does it apply to Crown vehicles. It would seem to apply where a passenger was injured and it could be particularly important now that passenger liability is compulsorily insurable. It is an offence under s. 162 to fail to produce the certificate to a policeman at the time (subject to the same five days of grace as above), but no offence to fail to produce it to any other person. Section 166 does not apply to drivers of trams and trolley vehicles operated under statutory powers (s. 197 (4)). *Semble*, if the driver has no certificate of insurance, he does not " produce " one and so must report to the police.

The penalty under s. 166 is a fine of £100 on first or subsequent conviction and there is no power to order disqualification or endorsement.

Note that the " driver " has the obligation, not the owner or anyone else, save so far as he may aid and abet the driver's failure.

Accidents to Persons, Animals, Vehicles or Property

The Road Traffic Act, 1972, s. 25, replacing s. 77 of the 1960 Act, reads:—

" (1) If in any case, owing to the presence of a motor vehicle on a road, an accident occurs whereby personal injury is caused to a person other than the driver of that motor vehicle or damage is caused to a vehicle other than that motor vehicle or a trailer drawn thereby or to an animal other than an animal in or on that motor vehicle or a trailer drawn thereby [or to any other property constructed on, fixed to, growing in or otherwise forming part of the land on which the road in question is situated or land adjacent thereto] the driver of the motor vehicle shall stop and, if required so to do by any person having reasonable grounds for so requiring, give his name and address, and also the name and address of the owner and the identification marks of the vehicle.

(2) If in the case of any such accident as aforesaid the driver of the motor vehicle for any reason does not give his name and address to any such person as aforesaid, he shall report the accident at a police station or to a constable as soon as reasonably practicable, and in any case within twenty-four hours of the occurrence thereof.

(3) In this section ' animal ' means any horse, cattle, ass, mule, sheep, pig, goat or dog.

(4) A person who fails to comply with this section shall be guilty of an offence."

(The words in square brackets in subs. (1) were added by para. 12 of Sched. 6 to the Act of 1974.)

For penalties see p. 348.

Section 25 applies to the drivers of trams and trolley vehicles operated under statutory powers. The section casts no duties on the drivers or riders of vehicles which are not " motor vehicles ", as defined on p. 2.

The words of the section make it clear that it does not apply where the only damage is to the motor vehicle concerned or its trailer or an animal therein or the only person injured is the driver himself. It applies where a passenger is injured and to Crown drivers. Note that the term " animal " does not include cats or any other beast not mentioned above or bird. See p. 252 as to the meaning of " cattle ". The obligations of s. 25 arise only where there has been injury to a person or an animal as defined above or damage to another vehicle, motor vehicle or not, or to the road or roadside property particularised in the amendment to subs. (1). A bicycle is a vehicle (*Ellis* v. *Nott-Bower* (1896), 60 J.P. 760). Trams and trolley vehicles are also vehicles within the meaning of s. 25 where damage is caused *to* them by a motor vehicle. Horse-drawn carts are, too. It may be that " vehicle " in s. 25 means one normally used on the carriageway as opposed to the footway. A Metropolitan magistrate has held a barrow to be a " carriage " (Jo.Crim.L. (1939) 338). See also 210 L.T. News 201. A motorised invalid carriage is clearly a vehicle. Whether a pram or a child's fairy-cycle is a vehicle has not been decided; the case of *R.* v. *Mathias* (1861), 2 F. & F. 570, cited in some earlier editions of this book as to a pram not being a " carriage ", is not now put forward as an authority either way. Any wheeled vehicle, pram, doll's pram, or fairy-cycle, which is not within the " *de minimis* " rule, however, appears to be within the dictionary definition of " vehicle ".

The section formerly applied only where there had been injury or damage to another vehicle or person or " animal ", and if any other form of property, e.g., a wall or lamp-post was damaged, s. 25 did not apply (*Pagett* v. *Mayo* [1939] 2 All E.R. 362).

The effect of *Pagett* v. *Mayo* has been reversed by the inclusion of the words in square brackets in subs. (1) by the Road Traffic Act, 1974. Damage to property growing in, constructed on, fixed to or forming part of the land of the road or land adjacent thereto, now gives rise to the obligations contained in s. 25. The words " growing in " quite clearly bring damage to trees, crops and plants within the ambit of the section. The amendment does not include property not fixed, etc., on the road or roadside, and it would therefore appear that if the damage was, for example, only to the load of another vehicle, or to the clothing only of a pedestrian he being unhurt, s. 25 as amended would not apply. If a traffic sign or other roadside property is damaged, there will usually be no one to whom the motorist can reasonably be required to give his name and address, and in such a case he will therefore be under an obligation to report the accident to the police (see *Peek* v. *Towle* on p. 345).

REPORTING ACCIDENTS

Section 25 applies only where the accident has been due to the presence of the defendant's motor vehicle " on a road ". It does not apply to accidents on a car park or private property. *Semble*, if only part of the defendant's vehicle is on a road, the section applies, e.g., where he is emerging from his private drive.

The driver is under the obligations imposed by s. 25 even though the accident may have been caused entirely by the fault of someone else.

Knowledge of Driver

It is the " driver " who has the duties under s. 25, not the owner or anyone else save so far as the latter may aid, abet, counsel or procure the driver's failure.

The requirement imposed by the provisions of s. 25 only applies if the defendant knows or suspects that an accident has occurred (*Harding* v. *Price* [1948] 1 All E.R. 283), but usually the prosecution can show either that he actually knew of it or that he ought reasonably to have known of it, e.g., by there being a severe jolt or a loud crash at the time. It is submitted that, once the damage or injury has been proved, the onus shifts to the defence to produce some evidence of the defendant's genuine unawareness of them. If, after hearing all the evidence, the court is in doubt whether or not he knew or suspected that he was involved, he should be acquitted. The principle of *Harding* v. *Price* was applied in *Hampson* v. *Powell* [1970] 1 All E.R. 929, where convictions of a lorry driver were quashed for failing to stop and failing to report an accident. In this case it was held that the knowledge of the driver was a " necessary ingredient " of the offence. No damage could be seen on the lorry; when the driver was seen by the police he admitted he was in the relevant area at the time but denied all knowledge of an accident.

Quarter sessions have held that a driver who was aware of the accident but was unaware of any injury to the victim, such belief being based on reasonable grounds, commits no offence if he fails to comply with s. 25, e.g., where an apparently unhurt victim assures him that he is unhurt ([1955] Crim.L.R. 317). A contrary view appears at 121 J.P.Jo. 554.

On a similarly-worded Rhodesian statute, it was held that, where the driver is aware that he has been involved in an accident, ignorance that it had one of the consequences of injury or damage mentioned in the section will only be a defence if he establishes on a balance of probabilities that he believed honestly and on reasonable grounds that the accident was not one falling within the section (*R.* v. *Breingan* [1966] (3) S.A. 410).

Duty to Exchange Names or Report

If the motorist for any reason has not given his name and address to any person who has reasonable grounds for requiring it, s. 25 (2) requires him to report the accident at a police station or to a police constable " as soon as reasonably practicable and in any case within twenty-four hours. . . .". " As soon as reasonably practicable " was held to mean precisely what it says: a motorist who did not report the accident as soon as it was reasonably practicable for him to do so was held to have committed the offence even though he made admissions about the accident within twenty-four hours to a constable who came to interview him (*Bulman* v. *Bennett* [1974] R.T.R. 1). The additional words " and in any case within twenty-four hours " do not qualify the obligation to report as soon as reasonably practicable and thus give a motorist the right to wait twenty-four hours before reporting; the words " in any case " were held to be equivalent to " without prejudice to the foregoing " (*ibid.*). It is thus clear that (*a*) the motorist must report as soon as reasonably practicable (and this, it is submitted, is a matter of fact for the court to determine depending on the particular circumstances of each case) and (*b*) the motorist must in any event report it within twenty-four hours, seemingly, even if not reasonably practicable to do so within that time.

It has also been held that if the driver refuses his name and address to a person reasonably requiring it, he commits an offence although he reports to the police within twenty-four hours (*Dawson* v. *Winter* (1932), 49 T.L.R. 128). If he does give his name and address, etc., to such a person, he need not report to the police (*Adair* v. *Fleming* [1932] S.C.(J.) 51; *Green* v. *Dunn* [1953] 1 All E.R. 550), unless there has been personal injury and the insurance certificate has not been produced, so that s. 166, *supra*, applies. If an accident occurs and the driver does not give his name and address, etc., because no one asks for it, or because there is no one at the scene, or for any other reason, he must report to the police (*Peek* v. *Towle* [1945] 2 All E.R. 611).

In *R.* v. *Togo* [1966] (3) S.A. 695, a case on a like-worded Rhodesian statute, it was held that, if within twenty-four hours of its occurrence a driver becomes aware that he has been involved in an accident of the type specified in the section, it is still his duty to report to the police, even though he was unaware of the accident when it occurred; it might be, however, that it would be a defence if he had reasonable grounds for believing that the information given to him was not accurate.

The words " owing to the presence of a motor vehicle on a road " were considered in *Quelch* v. *Phipps* [1955] 2 All E.R. 302. It was held that there must be some direct causal connection between the vehicle and the occurrence of the accident and the section applied where a passenger jumped off a moving bus and hurt himself. The presence of the vehicle must be more than a mere *sine qua non* and an indirect connection is insufficient, e.g., a pedestrian stepping back to avoid a car and injuring another pedestrian. The section is not limited to collisions. Questions can arise as to how far the presence of a stationary car can be said to cause an accident; its presence probably does where a cyclist runs into it but it might be otherwise if he swerved to avoid it and fell off his machine. See generally 108 S.J. 249; often the driver will not have been in the car so that in that case there might be no duty on him.

It can be argued that the defendant driver's vehicle need not even have been involved in the accident if his driving has been the primary cause of collision between two other vehicles, if such accident would never have happened but for the defendant's own bad driving. In such a case the prosecutor would have to prove that the defendant knew both that there had been a collision and that injury or damage had been caused. On the other hand, it could be said that, if the collision of the pedestrians need not be reported (see above), nor need the collision of two other vehicles by a third driver whose conduct caused the collision.

There is a *dictum* by Avory, J., in *Dawson* v. *Winter* (1932), 49 T.L.R. 128, that it would not be reporting to the police if the defendant had told them of the incident only as a result of their coming to interview him during their investigations after he had left the scene, but in *Bulman* v. *Bennett, supra,* the Divisional Court did not on this ground criticise magistrates who had held that admissions about an accident by the defendant to a constable who had come to interview him constituted a report to a constable for the purpose of s. 25 (2).

The onus of proof that a driver failed to report to the police does not seem to lie on the police; it is a matter peculiarly within the driver's own knowledge whether he did so (see p. 123). Otherwise every constable from miles around would have to be called to say that the driver did not report to him.

The obligation under s. 25 (2) is to report " at " a police station or " to " a constable; this appears to imply that the motorist must report in person at a police station or personally make the report to a constable—telephoning a police station or police constable seems insufficient compliance with s. 25 (2); moreover ss. 161 and 162 specifically empower a constable to require a motorist whom he has reasonable cause to believe was involved in an accident to produce his driving licence, insurance certificate, etc., and one of the purposes of these sections is seemingly to enable a policeman to require a motorist reporting an accident to produce these documents.

If either element of s. 25 (1) is missing, i.e., if a person fails to stop but later gives his particulars or if he stops but refuses those particulars, an offence is committed (*North* v. *Gerrish* (1959), 123 J.P. 313).

The question whether the former s. 22 of the 1930 Act created only one offence or two, i.e., failing to stop and failing to report to the police, is argued at 123 J.P.Jo. 633 and 635 and 124 J.P.Jo. 120. Section 77 (4) of the 1960 Act did not use the words " guilty of an offence ", however, which were in s. 22 (4) and are now in s. 25 of the 1972 Act. Compare *Butterworth* v. *Shorthouse* on p. 421. It is submitted that a person may be charged either with failing to stop and with failing to report or with failing to give his particulars and with failing to report.

Meaning of " Stop ", " Driver " and " Injury "

In *Lee* v. *Knapp* [1966] 3 All E.R. 961, it was held that " stop " in s. 25 (1) means stop and remain at the scene of the accident for such a time as in the prevailing circumstances, having regard in particular to the character of the road or place in which the accident happened, would provide a sufficient period to enable persons who had a right so to do, and reasonable ground for so doing, to require of the driver direct and personally the information which might be required under the section. It does not suffice if an employee or agent of the driver waits at the scene (*ibid.*). The driver does not have to wait indefinitely (*Norling* v. *Woolacott* [1964] S.A.S.R. 377; accident involving an unattended vehicle, no other people or houses near). In *Jarman* v. *Walsh* [1936] S.A.S.R. 25, a case on an Australian statute requiring a driver to stop and, if required, give his name and address, it was held that a driver who had gone on for 300 yards and then returned to the scene of the accident had not complied with the statute.

Where the motor vehicle is stationary when the accident occurs, it is submitted that the driver must remain at the scene until he has ascertained or done the things required to be done when he stops (see the last paragraph and Jo.Crim.L. (1937) 499), i.e., that " stop " in s. 25 (1) means both " bring to a stop " and " remain stopped ".

" Driver " in s. 25 means the person who takes the vehicle out on the road; he remains the driver until he finishes the journey, although he may have stopped and switched off the engine some

minutes before (*Jones* v. *Prothero* [1952] 1 All E.R. 434—driver
convicted for not reporting accident to cyclist knocked over by a
car door opening suddenly; he was still in the car). However,
a person ceases to be a " driver " when he has finished his journey
and there would seem to be no obligations under s. 25 on him if
he has left the car at the conclusion of the journey; *cf.* s. 5 of the
1972 Act, which contrasts those driving with those in charge when
unfit through drink. It is presumably a question of fact, when he
is not in the car, whether he has finished his journey. If he drives
to the cinema, that is the end of that journey even though he
intends to drive home later, but the journey to the cinema would
not be over if he got out on the way to buy cigarettes at a shop.
However, it could be said that here there were two journeys—from
home to shop and from shop to cinema; also, the usual meaning of
" driver " in the Road Traffic Acts is a person at the steering wheel
and not someone out of the car altogether; see p. 21.

" Injury " has been held by a stipendiary magistrate to include
shock, citing *Hay (or Bourhill)* v. *Young* [1943] A.C. 92 (115 J.P.Jo.
250). A hysterical and nervous condition can be " actual bodily
harm " (*R.* v. *Miller* [1954] 2 All E.R. 529). In *Clements* v. *Gill*
[1953] S.A.S.R. 25, an Australian case, a pedestrian was struck
and thrown to the ground by a motor vehicle. Evidence was given
that he was shaken and dazed, but there was no evidence of any
actual physical injury. It was held that the evidence was insufficient
to prove that injury had been caused to him.

The term " accident " can include a deliberate collision (*Trim
Joint District School* v. *Kelly* [1914] A.C. 667). It has been held that
an accident for the purpose of s. 8 of the Act is " an unintended
occurrence which has an adverse physical result " (see *R.* v. *Morris*
and other cases on p. 196).

Penalty, Endorsement and Disqualification

A person convicted under s. 25 may be fined £100 (Road
Traffic Act, 1972, Sched. 4, as amended by the Road Traffic Act,
1974). There is now no longer any power of imprisonment.
The offence can only be tried summarily.

The defendant's licence must be endorsed on first or subsequent
conviction unless there are special reasons (see Chapter VII).

He may be disqualified at the court's option for any period on
first or subsequent conviction.

Section 93 (3) of the 1972 Act applies to convictions under s. 25
so that, if a person convicted of that offence has been previously
convicted on not less than two occasions of an endorsed disqualifiable

offence within the three years immediately before the offence, he must be disqualified for at least six months (see p. 624) unless having regard to all the circumstances there are grounds for mitigating the normal consequences of the conviction (see p. 688). The court may also order the defendant to be disqualified until he passes a test (s. 93 (7)).

The endorsement offence codes for offences under s. 25 are as follows:—

Failing to stop/and or give particulars after an accident AC 10
Failing to report the accident to the police   AC 20

The Magistrates' Association's suggested penalties (see p. 594 and p. 880) for these offences read as follows:—" failing to stop: £25 if later reported; otherwise £45 and consider disqualification.   Failing to report accident, £25."

6. PROTECTIVE MOTOR CYCLE HELMETS

Section 32 of the Act of 1972 empowers the Secretary of State to make regulations requiring persons driving or riding on motor cycles of any class specified in the regulations to wear protective headgear, and by s. 32 (3) any person who drives or rides on a motor cycle in contravention of the regulations is guilty of an offence.   A " motor cycle " is defined as a mechanically propelled vehicle, not being an invalid carriage, with less than four wheels and an unladen weight not exceeding 8 cwt. (s. 190 (4): see p. 3) but it will be seen *infra* that the regulations limit the necessity of wearing protective headgear to persons riding or driving a " motor bicycle " as defined in the Regulations.

The Regulations are the Motor Cycles (Wearing of Helmets) Regulations, 1973 (S.I. 1973 No. 180), and are set out on p. 728. It will be seen that protective headgear does not have to be worn while the driver is propelling the motor bicycle while on foot (reg. 3) nor do the Regulations apply to certain motor mowers which may otherwise come within the definition of " motor bicycle " in the Regulations.

Regulation 3 requires every person driving " or riding on " a motor bicycle to wear protective headgear. Thus both the driver and a pillion passenger are required to wear helmets. The definition of motor bicycle in reg. 2 includes all two-wheeled motor cycles whether having a sidecar or not, but persons riding " in " a sidecar are exempt (for a case on the meaning of sidecar, see *Cox* v. *Harrison* on p. 476).

The definition of protective headgear in reg. 2 (1) (*b*) makes it clear that if the helmet is worn unfastened or improperly fastened,

an offence is committed. The helmet must either comply with the
British Standards set out in reg. 2 (1) (*a*) (i) or be reasonably to be
expected to afford a similar or greater degree of protection than
the Standards specified. A new British Standard has since been
issued (B.S. 2001: 1972) and presumably comes within this latter
category (see Regulations made under s. 33, *infra*).

Section 33 empowers the Secretary of State to make Regulations
prescribing types of helmets recommended as affording protection to
persons on or in motor cycles. The regulations are the Motor
Cycles (Protective Helmets) Regulations, 1974 (S.I. 1974 No. 2000)
which revoked like-named regulations of 1968 (S.I. 1968 No. 844).
The helmets are specified in the Schedule to the Regulations and
are British Standards (B.S. 2001: 1956, B.S. 1869: 1960, B.S. 2495:
1960, and B.S. 2001: 1972). The helmets are required to conform
to one of these British Standards subject to any amendments to
that standard at the date of manufacture. They must also be
marked with the number of the British Standard and the certification mark of the British Standards Institution. Helmets conforming
to B.S. 2001 of 1962 are no longer recommended headgear and thus
cannot be sold as such if manufactured on or after 1st March, 1975.

It is an offence under s. 33 (2) for a person to sell, offer for sale,
let on hire or offer to let on hire, a helmet for affording protection
from injury in the event of accident for persons driving or riding
on motor cycles if the helmet is either not of a type prescribed by the
Regulations or if of a type authorised by the Regulations, it is sold
or offered for sale, etc., subject to any conditions prohibited in
the authorisation. By s. 33 (6) " helmet " includes any head-dress.
Puggarees together with hats worn at Ascot are thus included in
the definition. A person may not be convicted if he proves (*semble*
on the balance of probabilities) that the helmet was sold or offered
for sale for export from Great Britain.

A person charged with selling or offering for sale, etc., under
s. 33, a helmet which does not conform with a type set out in the
Regulations may himself summon the person actually responsible
for the offence in the same proceedings by following the procedure
set out for the purpose in Sched. 1. Schedule 1 is almost identical
to ss. 113 to 116 of the Food and Drugs Act, 1955, and reference
may usefully be made to the extensive case law upon these sections
as set out in Stone, 1975, pp. 1982–1988. Paragraph 2 (3) of
Sched. 1 gives the prosecutor the right to proceed directly
against a person whose act or default gave rise to the offence
and thus proceed in an appropriate case directly against the whole-
saler or manufacturer instead of the retailer (see also s. 113 (3)
of the Food and Drugs Act, 1955, in Stone, 1975, pp. 1983–1984).

The penalty for a first or subsequent offence under s. 32 is £50 and for a first or subsequent offence under s. 33 is £100. Both offences are triable summarily only and endorsement, disqualification or imprisonment may not be ordered for either offence. The Magistrates' Association's suggested penalty for an offence under s. 32 is £10 (see p. 594 and p. 881).

Both ss. 32 and 33 apply to vehicles and persons in the public service of the Crown (s. 188).

7. TAKING CONVEYANCES

The Theft Act, 1968, s. 12 (replacing s. 217 of the Road Traffic Act, 1960, in England and Wales) reads:—

Taking motor vehicle or other conveyance without authority

(1) Subject to subsections (5) and (6) below, a person shall be guilty of an offence if, without having the consent of the owner or other lawful authority, he takes any conveyance for his own or another's use or, knowing that any conveyance has been taken without such authority, drives it or allows himself to be carried in or on it.

(2) A person guilty of an offence under subsection (1) above shall on conviction on indictment be liable to imprisonment for a term not exceeding three years.

(3) Offences under subsection (1) above and attempts to commit them shall be deemed for all purposes to be arrestable offences within the meaning of section 2 of the Criminal Law Act, 1967.

(4) If on the trial of an indictment for theft the jury are not satisfied that the accused committed theft, but it is proved that the accused committed an offence under subsection (1) above, the jury may find him guilty of the offence under subsection (1).

(5) Subsection (1) above shall not apply in relation to pedal cycles; but, subject to subsection (6) below, a person who, without having the consent of the owner or other lawful authority, takes a pedal cycle for his own or another's use, or rides a pedal cycle knowing it to have been taken without such authority, shall on summary conviction be liable to a fine not exceeding fifty pounds.

(6) A person does not commit an offence under this section by anything done in the belief that he has lawful authority to do it or that he would have the owner's consent if the owner knew of his doing it and the circumstances of it.

(7) For the purposes of this section—

(a) " conveyance " means any conveyance constructed or adapted for the carriage of a person or persons whether by land, water or air, except that it does not include a conveyance constructed or adapted for use only under the control of a person not carried in or on it, and " drive " shall be construed accordingly; and

(b) " owner ", in relation to a conveyance which is the subject of a hiring agreement or hire-purchase agreement, means the person in possession of the conveyance under that agreement.

Section 217 of the Road Traffic Act, 1960 (now s. 175 of the 1972 Act), continues to apply to Scotland and s. 12 does not.

Changes from the previous law are that the belief of the accused that he had authority need not be reasonable and the onus is not on him to prove it; the offence is now complete if the defendant " takes " not " takes and drives away " the conveyance (see *R.* v. *Bogacki and Others* and *R.* v. *Pearce*, below, and also, in relation to employee-drivers, *McKnight* v. *Davies* on p. 359). The section extends to ships, rubber dinghies, aircraft, vehicles whether mechanically propelled or not, e.g., carts and trams and trolley vehicles, railway rolling-stock, and, as indicated in s. 12 (5), cycles; the Concise Oxford Dictionary defines " cycle " as including a bicycle, tricycle or similar machine. In *R.* v. *Bogacki and Others* [1973] R.T.R. 384 it was held that to " take " as expressed in s. 12 of the Theft Act was not equivalent to " use ", nor could it consist of a mere assumption of possession adverse to the rights of the true owner; to constitute the offence of taking there must be an unauthorised taking possession or control of the conveyance adverse to the rights of the true owner or person otherwise entitled to such possession or control coupled with some movement of the conveyance no matter how small. Accidentally putting a foot on the accelerator of an automatic drive vehicle which had the engine running with the result that the vehicle drove all over the road, is not " taking " for the purpose of s. 12 (*Blayney* v. *Knight* [1975] Crim.L.R. 237). The construction placed on " drive " in s. 12 (7) does not mean that the movement of the conveyance has to be in the element for which the conveyance is designed to travel; thus, in *R.* v. *Pearce* [1973] Crim.L.R. 321 a defendant's conviction was upheld for taking an inflatable rubber dinghy from a life-boat depôt, and putting it on a trailer which he then drove away.

The definition of " conveyance " in s. 12 (7) suggests that there is no offence if a person takes a remotely-controlled aircraft or vehicle (see *R.* v. *Roberts* on p. 21). The conveyance must be constructed or adapted for the carriage of a person or persons, so that a goods-trailer, milkfloat or porter's trolley or hand-barrow is not covered. Presumably, the presence of a seat for the driver shows that a conveyance is constructed for the carriage of " a person "; otherwise it would not be an offence to take a lorry. It is submitted that an excavator or bulldozer which has a seat for the driver is constructed or adapted for the carriage of a person and so is a conveyance under s. 12, but the point is arguable.

The offence is properly charged where there is no evidence of an intention permanently to deprive the owner of his conveyance; sometimes a person who takes a car or motor-vessel is accused of stealing the petrol also but it is submitted that he should not be punished for both offences (see [1968] Crim.L.R. 282; *R.* v. *Burnham JJ.* on p. 93). On summary trial the punishment is the same anyhow. A person charged under s. 12 may still, it is submitted, be convicted even if the facts show that he is guilty of theft because he took the conveyance with the intention of permanently depriving the owner of it. It is no defence to the alternative offence of driving or allowing oneself to be carried, when not a party to the original taking, that the defendant knew that the vehicle had been *stolen* and not just taken (*Tolley* v. *Giddings* [1964] 1 All E.R. 201).

Procedure for Trial

The offence under s. 12 (1) and any attempt to commit it are indictable offences triable at the Crown Court and may be tried by magistrates pursuant to s. 19 of the Magistrates' Courts Act, 1952 (Theft Act, 1968, s. 29). The defendant must consent to summary trial and, if the conveyance belongs to the Crown or a public body, the prosecutor's consent is also required to summary trial. In *R.* v. *Wakefield JJ., ex parte Butterworth* [1970] Crim.L.R. 102 a solicitor consented on behalf of his client to summary trial on a charge under s. 12 and added " and he pleads guilty " before the court could ask for the plea. As the court did not *ask* the plea (Magistrates' Courts Act, 1952, s. 13) the case was sent back to the justices for the court to ask the plea. Taking a pedal cycle is a summary offence only (s. 12 (5)) but an attempt to take a pedal cycle seems to be an indictable offence only, not triable by magistrates because an attempt to commit a purely summary offence is only triable on indictment.

If the accused, being of the age of seventeen or over, has a firearm or imitation firearm in his possession when committing an offence under s. 12 (1) of the Theft Act or attempting such an offence, or uses one with intent to resist arrest, he must be sent for trial at the Crown Court (Firearms Act, 1968, Sched. 6, Pt. II, para. 3; Theft Act, 1968, Sched. 2). This provision does not apply where a pedal cycle is taken.

It is submitted that a conveyance taken in breach of s. 12 is not stolen goods so that a person who dishonestly receives one which he knows to have been so taken is not guilty of handling under s. 22 of the Theft Act.

Where an offence under s. 12 is committed, attempted, abetted or procured by a member of a visiting force (see p. 58) in respect of a conveyance which belongs to that force or to a member, or dependant of a member of that force, he may not be tried by a British civil court, save where the visiting force consents (Visiting Forces Act, 1952, s. 3). "Dependant" does not include a person who is a British citizen or ordinarily resident here.

Offences and attempts to commit offences under s. 12 (1) are by s. 12 (3) "arrestable offences" so that the "suspected person loitering" limb of s. 4 of the Vagrancy Act, 1824, is applicable save where taking a pedal cycle is in contemplation. They would also be an "unlawful purpose" within the other limb of s. 4 of the 1824 Act relating to persons found in certain buildings or enclosed places and this limb applies in respect of taking pedal cycles also.

Arrest

The offence under s. 12 being by s. 12 (3) an "arrestable offence", by the Criminal Law Act, 1967, s. 2 (2), any person may arrest without warrant anyone whom he with reasonable cause suspects to be in the act of committing such an offence; by s. 2 (4) a constable who with reasonable cause suspects that this offence has been committed may arrest without warrant anyone reasonably suspected by him of an offence under s. 12 (1) or of an attempt to commit it, and by s. 2 (5) a constable may arrest without warrant anyone reasonably suspected by him of being about to commit such an offence. These powers of arrest do not apply to persons taking pedal cycles.

Defences

Unlike the former offence in England and Wales, and present offence in Scotland, under s. 175 of the Act of 1972, the onus of proving that the accused did not believe under s. 12 (6) that he had lawful authority to take the conveyance or that he would have had the owner's consent if the latter knew of his doing it and the circumstances of it is on the prosecution; the latter can usually show this by calling the owner to deny his consent or the likelihood of its being given. It was held in *R.* v. *McPherson* [1973] R.T.R. 157 that if an issue arises as to whether a defendant under s. 12 (6) had a belief of lawful authority, etc., the onus is on the prosecution to prove that the defendant had no such authority or consent. On the other hand the prosecution do not have to prove a specific intent on the part of the defendant to take the vehicle (*ibid.*). Thus where the defendant was drunk (but not so drunk as to raise the defence of insanity) a judge was entitled to direct the jury that self-induced drunkenness was no defence, and that, unless an issue under s. 12 (6) was raised, the only matters that the jury had to be satisfied about were (*a*) that the vehicle was taken by the defendant and (*b*) that it was without the owner's consent.

The statute does not apparently require the defendant's belief under s. 12 (6) that he had lawful authority or consent to be reasonable. The very absurdity of some factors for the belief can show that he did not really hold it, but it need not be reasonable; a person under drugs might have some literally fantastic belief but, if the prosecution do not disprove that he had such a belief, it seems to be a defence. Magistrates acquitted a defendant who took a car in the belief that the owner, a friend, would have consented; the owner testified that, while normally he would have consented, he would not have done so on that occasion as the fan belt was broken (Jo.Crim.L. (1968) 3). Moving a motor vehicle simply for one's own convenience, e.g., because it is blocking a doorway, is not normally an offence under s. 12 (*Shimmell* v. *Fisher* [1951] 2 All E.R. 672).

The section was primarily designed to deal with people who took cars for " joy rides " and then abandoned them, thus escaping a charge of larceny of the car on the ground that there was no intention permanently to deprive the owner of it. Where a person is charged on indictment with theft of a conveyance (other than a pedal cycle) the jury may, by s. 12 (4), convict him of an offence under s. 12 (1), but this power does not extend to magistrates' courts. In the latter courts it would no doubt be wise to bring charges both of theft and under s. 12 (1) where the circumstances warrant it.

A person who enters a building as a trespasser with intent to take a conveyance does not commit burglary under s. 9 of the Theft Act because offences under s. 12 are not comprised in s. 9 (1) or (2). By s. 25 (5) of the Theft Act, 1968, the offence of having an article for use in connection with any theft applies to offences under s. 12 (1); a person who had with him (otherwise than at his place of abode) a set of car-keys or a car-park attendant's uniform with a view to facilitating an offence under s. 12 would be guilty—see s. 25 (3) as to burden of proof. This does not apply to persons equipped to take pedal cycles.

If the owner's consent were obtained by intimidation seemingly this would not be " consent " under s. 12 (*R.* v. *Hogdon* [1962] Crim.L.R. 563) but in *R.* v. *Peart* [1970] 2 All E.R. 823 it was held that consent of the owner as to the use of the car by another was not vitiated by the fact that the defendant obtained the owner's consent by falsely pretending that he needed the car to go to Alnwick when in fact he went to Burnley instead. The court held that when s. 12 was enacted there was no intention by Parliament to create a new offence of taking conveyances by false pretences. If therefore the owner's consent is obtained by means of a false pretence either as to the destination or purpose of the journey, no offence under s. 12 appears to be committed. The court, however, reserved for a future occasion the legal position where the consent of the owner was obtained by a fundamental mis-representation, as for example where *B* pretended to the owner that he was *C*. In such a case, it is submitted that the owner's consent is no consent for *B* to take the conveyance and if he does so he is guilty of an offence under s. 12 because the owner has given no consent to *B*, only to *C*. It should be noted, also, that *Peart* is inconsistent with *R.* v. *Phipps, R.* v. *McGill* [1970] R.T.R. 209, a case under the 1960 Act where *M* obtained permission to borrow the car to go to the railway station. He did not return and used it next day to go to Hastings. It was held that, he having once failed to return the car, his use was unlawful unless he reasonably believed that the owner in the circumstances would have given his consent if asked. It seems that if the defendant in *Peart* had in fact gone to Alnwick and then on to Burnley he would be guilty in accordance with *Phipps*. For further criticism of *Peart* see [1970] Crim.L.R., p. 480. It should also be noted that *Phipps* was followed and applied in *McKnight* v. *Davies* (see p. 359). The distinction between a person obtaining permission to use a vehicle for a limited purpose and not using it for that purpose and there-fore being held guilty of an offence under s. 217 or s. 12 (*Phipps*) and a person obtaining permission for a different purpose than the one he actually used it for (*Peart*) is a fine one. *Peart* was cited in argument to the court in *McKnight* v. *Davies* but there is no mention of it in the judgment. (*Phipps*, contrary to the state-ment in the judgment of *McKnight* v. *Davies* [1974] R.T.R. 4, at p. 7G, was a case under s. 217 of the Act of 1960, not s. 12 of the Theft Act.)

Knowledge of Passengers

In *Shimmell* v. *Fisher* [1951] 2 All E.R. 627 three men approached a parked lorry and the hand-brake was released; two of the men pushed it and the third held the steering wheel and they tried unsuccessfully to start the engine. On a charge under s. 217 of the Road Traffic Act, 1960, of taking and driving away the lorry, it was held that " driving away " meant causing the vehicle to move from the place where it was standing and that a vehicle could be said to be driven if one man pushed and another steered. It is submitted that under s. 12 all three would be joint offenders en-gaged in a common purpose and should be convicted. But merely releasing the brake of a lorry, so that it ran downhill driverless, is not taking and driving away (*R*. v. *Roberts* [1964] 2 All E.R. 541). It can be argued that letting a vehicle run downhill unattended or a vessel drift away unmanned is likewise not " taking " it under s. 12 and that there should be some measure of control by the accused over it. The case of *R*. v. *Roberts*, however, turned partly on the question whether what the defendant did was " driving away " and it was suggested in the judgment of Lord Parker, C.J., that this might be taking. The taking, by s. 12 (1), must anyhow be for " the use of " the defendant or another; letting a vehicle run away is hardly for anyone's use, and it would now seem from *R*. v. *Bogacki and Others* (see p. 352) that the unauthorised possession or control of the conveyance is the essential element in such cases. Letting a vehicle run downhill or a boat downstream unattended would not constitute possession or control, but otherwise if the offender was in the driving seat or on the boat. In *R*. v. *Baldessare* (1930), 22 Cr.App.R. 70, two persons engaged in a common purpose were both held guilty of criminal negligence in driving though only one drove. Passengers are, it seems, counsellors and procurers of the offence by the driver if they all act together in taking the car, and they can all properly be convicted along with him. The matter is now put beyond doubt by s. 12 (1), which extends to a person who, " knowing that any conveyance has been taken without [the owner's consent or other lawful] authority, drives it or allows himself to be carried in or on it ". It is submitted that the prosecution must still prove that where any such driver or passenger was not a party to the original taking the driver or passenger knew that the vehicle had been taken without consent. There is a clear case to answer against passengers as well as against the driver where a car is found at 2 a.m. without petrol and the passengers give an unsatisfactory explanation to the police of the reason for their presence in the car (*Ross* v. *Rivenall* [1959] 2 All E.R. 376) but Donovan, J. (as he then was), doubted if mere presence in a car as a passenger, without any suspicious circumstances, was enough (*ibid.*). It does not matter whether the driver or a passenger took the car, so long as they were acting in concert, or even if they had it from another person (*R*. v. *Richardson* [1958] Crim.L.R. 480), but to convict a passenger of taking there must be some evidence to show that each accused was a party to the taking or knew of the unlawful taking; entering a car after it has been taken, without evidence that the passenger was a party to, or knew of the taking, is not enough (*R*. v. *Stally* [1959] 3 All E.R. 814). If evidence to show that a passenger was a party to the taking is produced, it need not be shown that he was present

at the taking (*ibid.*).   It was said in *R.* v. *Pearce* [1961] Crim.L.R.
122 that it was not correct to say that there was a new taking
and driving away every time the car was moved.   Convictions
were quashed where there was no evidence to show that a passenger
was concerned in the original taking (*D.* v. *Parsons* [1960] 2 All
E.R. 493;   *A.* v. *Bundy* (1960), 125 J.P. 89), but see now the express
reference in s. 12 (1) to knowledge that a conveyance has been
taken without authority.   A person not a party to the taking who,
knowing that a motor vehicle has been *stolen*, drives or travels in
it commits an offence (*Tolley* v. *Giddings* [1964] 1 All E.R. 201).

Where a person takes an auto-assisted pedal cycle, he should be
charged with taking a conveyance under s. 12 (1) and not with
taking a pedal cycle under s. 12 (5);   such a machine is a motor
vehicle unless vital parts are disconnected (see *Floyd* v. *Bush*,
Lawrence v. *Howlett*, *R.* v. *Tahsin* and other cases on pp. 6, 7).

Attempts

See the cases on p. 163 as to attempting to drive.   In *R.* v.
Cook [1964] Crim.L.R. 56 it was held that a man who was found
in the front seat of a car fiddling with the ignition, the dashboard being lit, and who later said that, if not caught, in another
minute he would have got away with the car, could properly be
convicted of an attempt to take it.   In *R.* v. *Bogacki and Others*
(see p. 352) the defendants acting in concert entered a bus with
the intention of driving it away; one of them turned the engine
over with the starter, but the engine never started and the bus
did not move; their conviction of attempting to take the bus was
quashed because the jury were wrongly directed as to the meaning
of the word " take ", but it is clear from the judgment of the
Court of Appeal that if the jury had been properly directed there
was ample evidence to constitute an attempt.   The act of endeavouring to open a car door is capable of amounting to an attempt
to take and drive it away without authority; in deciding if such
an equivocal act does amount to an attempt, the court should
take into consideration any evidence of the defendant's actual
intention, including any statement made by him (*Jones* v. *Brooks*
(1968), *The Times*, 26th June).

Employees and Hirers

It was held that a van driver, in lawful possession of his employer's
van, who drives it on a frolic of his own, committed no offence in
Mowe v. *Perraton* [1952] 1 All E.R. 423.   It would be otherwise,
if he had put the vehicle back into his employer's possession,

e.g., by leaving it in the employer's garage, and then took it out of such possession without leave. The reason for the decision was that an employee, being in lawful possession of his employer's vehicle whilst on duty, cannot " take " what he already has, but this reasoning was inconsistent with *R.* v. *Phipps, R.* v. *McGill* [1970] R.T.R. 209, and the latter case was followed in preference to *Mowe* v. *Perraton* in *McKnight* v. *Davies, infra.*

In *R.* v. *Wibberley* [1965] 3 All E.R. 718, the defendant, a truck-driver, was supposed to return the truck to his employer's premises at the end of the day's work but, instead, he took it home and parked it outside his house for two hours. He then drove it away on a purpose of his own. The employers would not have objected to him parking outside his house for the night and taking the truck to work next morning. His conviction for taking it for his own purposes, after he had parked it, was upheld, as he had no authority to use it, after parking it outside his home, until the next day's work began. There was a distinction between deviation from employment during working hours, when he still intended to carry out his instructions to drive the vehicle to his employer's premises, and taking it after working hours with no such intention and after an interruption in time.

In *McKnight* v. *Davies* [1974] R.T.R. 4 a lorry driver returning to his employer's depôt struck a low bridge with the roof of his lorry. He was not permitted to use the lorry for his own purposes, but, being scared on seeing the damage to the lorry's roof, he drove to a public house and had a drink, then drove three men to their homes and returned to the centre of the city, had a drink at another public house and drove home leaving his lorry nearby, in all driving 30 miles in excess of his proper delivery route. *R.* v. *Wibberley, supra,* and *R.* v. *Phipps* [1970] R.T.R. 209 were followed in preference to *Mowe* v. *Perraton,* which was held to be inconsistent in particular with *Phipps.* (In *Phipps* it was held that where a defendant had been given permission to take and use a vehicle for a limited purpose, and thereafter used it for another purpose, he was guilty of the offence; see also p. 356.) The court went on in *McKnight* v. *Davies* to consider to what extent the unauthorised use by an employee of his employer's vehicle could in law amount to a " taking " for the purposes of s. 12. Not every brief un-authorised diversion from his proper route would necessarily involve a " taking " for use (*ibid.,* p. 8); if, however, he returned the vehicle and parked it for the night and drove off on an unauthorised errand (as in *R.* v. *Wibberley*) that would be a sufficient " taking " (*ibid.*). It was suggested that to constitute a " taking " of the vehicle during his working day or while he has authority to use the vehicle, he must have appropriated it in a manner which repudiated his employer's true rights or as also cited with approval (Smith's Law of Theft, 2nd ed., p. 113) he has " altered the character of his control over the vehicle, so that he was no longer held as servant but assumed possession of it in the legal sense ". In the opinion of the court, the defendant " took " the vehicle not when he first went to a public house after the accident, but when he left it to drive the three men home.

A person who takes away a conveyance on hire-purchase with the hirer's consent but without the consent of the dealer or finance company which owns it does not offend against s. 12 because, by s. 12 (7) (b), " owner ", in relation to a vehicle which is the subject of a hiring agreement or hire-purchase agreement, means the person in possession of the vehicle under that agreement (R. v. Tolhurst [1962] Crim.L.R. 489).

Penalty, Endorsement and Disqualification

The penalty on summary conviction under s. 12 (1) or for an attempt is a fine of £400 or six months' imprisonment, or both (Magistrates' Courts Act, 1952, s. 19). A person convicted of taking a pedal cycle may be fined £50 but not sent to prison or detention or committed for sentence.

On indictment the penalty is a fine of unlimited amount or three years' imprisonment (Theft Act, 1968, s. 12 (2)).

A person found guilty under s. 12 by magistrates may be committed to the Crown Court for sentence under s. 29 of the Magistrates' Courts Act, 1952. He may, if of the relevant age, be so committed for borstal training under s. 28 of that Act. Magistrates should not order disqualification and endorsement before committing for sentence (see the Criminal Justice Act, 1967, s. 56, and p. 636) but leave that to the Crown Court; they may order an interim disqualification (see p. 636).

It is improper for one incident to sentence both for stealing and for an offence under s. 12 (R. v. Gibbs [1960] Crim.L.R. 197).

If under the age of seventeen, an offender under s. 12 (1) may be sent to a detention centre for three months (neither more nor less) by a juvenile court (if convicted by a magistrates' court he must be remitted to the juvenile court for sentence if detention is thought appropriate; this applies if he was under seventeen at the time proceedings were commenced even if he has subsequently attained that age); if he has attained the age of seventeen, magistrates may sentence him to detention for a period up to six months.

If convicted on indictment he may be sent for six months (Criminal Justice Act, 1961, s. 4). Semble, if committed for sentence under s. 28, he may be sent by the Crown Court for three months only but, if under s. 29, for six months.

The penalty for going equipped for stealing or for taking conveyances under s. 25 of the Theft Act is £400 or six months' imprisonment or both on summary conviction and an unlimited fine or three years' imprisonment on indictment; this offence is triable summarily pursuant to s. 19 of the Magistrates' Courts Act, 1952 (Theft Act, 1968, s. 29). The offender may also be committed for sentence.

Compensation may be ordered, on conviction of any offence in respect of personal injury, loss or damage resulting from that offence, of up to £400 if convicted by magistrates or of an unlimited amount if convicted on indictment (s. 35 of the Powers of Criminal Courts Act, 1973). The court are required to have regard to an offender's means, so far as they are known, in fixing the amount of compensation (s. 35 (4)). No application by or on behalf of the loser is necessary. Although ordinarily no compensation is payable in respect of injury, loss or damage which results from a road accident (s. 35 (3)), if the offence is under the Theft Act and the property is recovered any damage occurring to the property while out of the owner's possession shall be treated as resulting from the Theft Act offence no matter who caused the damage or how it occurred (s. 35 (2)). Thus if a person is convicted of stealing or taking a motor vehicle, or allowing himself to be carried on or in it under the Theft Act and it is damaged, whether in a road accident or any other way, that person can be ordered to pay compensation for that damage. Compensation may be awarded not only in respect of an offence for which the defendant is convicted but also an offence taken into consideration (in such a case a magistrates' court is still limited to a maximum sum of £400 for each offence for which the offender is *convicted*. See (s. 35 (5)).

Endorsement and Disqualification

The provisions as to endorsement and disqualification apply to passengers convicted under s. 12 as well as to drivers, provided in all cases the offence was in respect of a motor vehicle. It is appropriate to disqualify the passenger as well as the driver in a joint venture (*R.* v. *Reed* [1975] R.T.R. 313; *R.* v. *Saunders* [1975] R.T.R. 315).

On conviction under s. 12 in respect of a motor vehicle and also for an offence under s. 25 committed with reference to the theft or taking of motor vehicles, the defendant's driving licence must be endorsed unless there are special reasons. On first or subsequent conviction he may be disqualified at the court's option for any period and a driving test may be ordered (1972 Act, s. 93 (2) and (7)). And see below as to attempts.

Section 93 (3) of the 1972 Act applies to offences under s. 12 and s. 25 so that if a person convicted of the full offence under it in respect of a motor vehicle has been previously convicted on not less than two occasions of an endorsed disqualifiable offence in respect of a motor vehicle within the three years immediately before the offence, he must be disqualified for at least six months (see p. 624) unless having regard to all the circumstances there are grounds for mitigating the normal consequences of the conviction (see p. 688). The six-month disqualification is additional and consecutive to any period of disqualification imposed on the same occasion or for any previous offence. See p. 638 as to the undesirability of very long disqualifications on young men.

Disqualification may, and endorsement must, also be ordered for attempting to steal or for stealing a motor vehicle, and s. 93 (3) likewise applies to that offence (1972 Act, Sched. 4, Pt. III, para. 1). It would seem that a person convicted of burglary involving the theft of a motor vehicle is liable to obligatory endorsement and optional disqualification. Paragraph 1 of Sched. 4, Pt. III, to the 1972 Act does not specify a section of the Theft Act and refers simply to " stealing or attempting to steal ". Contrast paras. 2 and 3 of the same Part of the Schedule.

Attempts to commit offences under s. 12 in respect of a motor vehicle are expressly made subject to obligatory endorsement and optional disqualification (or obligatory under s. 93 (3) of the 1972 Act for third offence in three years after two endorsements) (see paras. 1 and 2 of Pt. III of Sched. 4 to the 1972 Act). For a case in which a person had been wrongly disqualified for an attempt to commit an offence under s. 217 of the 1960 Act and subsequently convicted of driving whilst disqualified for that offence, see *R*. v. *Cockermouth JJ., ex parte Patterson* [1971] Crim.L.R. 287.

The endorsement code for offences under the Theft Act or s. 175 (see below) are as follows:—

Taking and driving away without consent or attempting
    to do so (s. 175: Scotland only)   UT 10
Stealing or attempting to steal a motor vehicle   UT 20
Going equipped for stealing or taking a motor vehicle UT 30
Taking or attempting to take a motor vehicle or allowing
    oneself to be carried knowing it to be unlawfully taken,
  etc.   UT 40

The Magistrates' Association's suggested penalties for offences under s. 12 in respect of motor vehicles read:— " Taking vehicle without consent: £60 and 12 months' disqualification or consider detention centre or prison. Carried in taken vehicle: £50 and 6 months' disqualification " (see further p. 594 and p. 880).

Scotland

The provisions of the Theft Act, 1968, s. 12, do not apply to Scotland, where s. 175 of the 1972 Act applies. This section is a re-enactment, almost *ipsissimis verbis*, of s. 217 of the Road Traffic Act, 1960, as amended by s. 44 of the Road Traffic Act, 1962. The section relates to motor vehicles only. Most of the cases cited above were on s. 217 of the 1960 Act. The punishment under s. 175 is three months' imprisonment or a fine of £50 on summary conviction and twelve months' imprisonment on indictment and a fine. See generally Gordon on the Criminal Law, pp. 482–483, and pp. 481–482 of that work as to taking and using cycles. The offence or attempted offence under s. 175 carries compulsory endorsement and optional disqualification and driving test and the liability to compulsory disqualification under s. 93 (3) (see p. 624).

Getting on Vehicles or Tampering with Mechanism

Where a potential offender is caught before he has done anything amounting to the complete offence or an attempt under s. 12 of the Theft Act, he may, if the facts warrant, be charged under the Road Traffic Act, 1972, s. 29, with getting on a motor vehicle or tampering with the brake or other part of its mechanism without lawful authority or reasonable cause. It is submitted, as the brake alone is mentioned and no other category of equipment, the *ejusdem generis* rule is excluded and " other part of its mechanism " includes parts nothing to do with the brakes. This offence arises only if the vehicle is on a road or on a parking place *provided by a local authority*; the penalty under s. 29 for a first or subsequent offence is a fine of £100 (1972 Act, Sched. 4 as amended by the 1974 Act). Disqualification and endorsement may not be ordered. It is submitted that the term " local authority " includes parish councils as well as county, district councils and London boroughs (*cf.* Local Government Act, 1972, s. 270, albeit that district and county councils and London boroughs only are authorised under ss. 26 to 31 of the Road Traffic Regulation Act, 1967, to provide parking places). It seems that it need not be a parking place open to the public; if a local authority provides a parking place for its employees' cars, that is within s. 29. Car parks provided by Government departments and public utility boards are not within s. 29.

It is also an offence under the 1972 Act (s. 30 (1)) for a person otherwise than with lawful authority or with reasonable cause to take or retain control of or get on to a motor vehicle while in motion on a road, for the purpose of being carried. It would seem that once an issue has been raised in a charge under s. 29 or s. 30 as to whether a defendant has lawful authority or reasonable cause, it is for the prosecution to disprove it. An offence can only be committed under s. 30 (1) if the person got on or took or retained control of the vehicle while it was in motion on a road. If it was stationary, he should be charged under s. 29. The penalty under s. 30 (1) for a first or subsequent offence is £20 (1972 Act, Sched. 4, as amended by the 1974 Act). Disqualification and endorsement may not be ordered.

Committing Damage Whilst Driving

A driver who drives recklessly may sometimes cause damage to other property in consequence. Or the taker of a car without authority may damage it whilst it is in his possession. Apart from the liability to be sued civilly for the damage, what is the criminal liability of such people?

This is now dealt with by the Criminal Damage Act, 1971. The Act was passed as a result of recommendations of the Law Commission and repealed the over-detailed and out-of-date statutory provisions relating to damage (including arson) contained in a large number of Acts of Parliament and replaced them with one offence of intentionally or recklessly destroying or damaging property (s. 1 (1)) together with an aggravated offence of destroying or damaging property with the intention of endangering life or being reckless as to whether someone else's life would be endangered (s. 1 (2)).

The offence is committed if the defendant either had an intention to destroy or damage property or was reckless as to whether the property would be destroyed or damaged. It should be noted that the intention relates to the destruction or damage not of the particular property intended to be damaged but of any property belonging to another, and therefore the fact that the defendant may not have intended to damage or destroy the particular property that was in fact destroyed is not a defence. The prosecution only has to prove either an intention to destroy or damage property of another or that the defendant was reckless in that regard. It would therefore appear that a person who drives recklessly and damages or destroys another vehicle could theoretically be charged with and convicted of an offence under s. 1 (1), but Parliament presumably did not intend reckless drivers to be charged under the Criminal Damage Act, 1971, rather than s. 2 of the Road Traffic Act. However there are obvious examples where the police may well wish to use the Criminal Damage Act; where, for example, the thief or joyrider damages the car to break into it in order to drive it away, or if through recklessness the car is damaged. It might also be used, it would seem, in cases where s. 2 of the Road Traffic Act cannot apply because the vehicle has not been driven on a road as defined in the Road Traffic Act, or the vehicle is not a motor vehicle.

It would seem from *R.* v. *Smith (D.R.)* [1974] 1 All E.R. 632 that a person who honestly believes, whether it is a justifiable belief or not, that the property he damages is his own, cannot be convicted under the Criminal Damage Act, 1971.

Offences under s. 1 (1) are indictable offences triable summarily with the consent of the accused and are punishable summarily with a fine of £400 and/or six months' imprisonment. Arson is now triable summarily (s. 47 of the Criminal Justice Act, 1972). There is no power of disqualification or endorsement.

The offence under s. 1 (2) (destroying or damaging property either intending another's life to be endangered or reckless in that regard) can only be tried on indictment, the maximum punishment being life.

Under s. 35 of the Powers of Criminal Courts Act, 1973, compensation up to £400 may be ordered to be paid by the defendant to the person whose property was damaged. The court has power to award compensation of its own motion under s. 35 and its power to do so does not depend on an application by the loser. No compensation is payable under the Act in respect of loss or damage due to an accident arising out of the presence of a motor vehicle on a road (s. 35 (3)) unless the damage is as a result of an offence under the Theft Act, 1968 (see p. 361).

" Property " includes any property of a tangible nature whether real or personal (s. 10) but does not include the flowers, fruit or foliage of a plant growing wild on any land.

8. INSURANCE

The Road Traffic Act, 1972, s. 143 (1) (replacing s. 201 (1) of the 1960 Act), reads:—

" Subject to the provisions of this Part of this Act, it shall not be lawful for a person to use, or to cause or permit any other person to use, a motor vehicle on a road unless there is in force in relation to the use of the vehicle by that person or that other person, as the case may be, such a policy of insurance or such a security in respect of third-party risks as complies with the requirements of this Part of this Act; and if a person acts in contravention of this section he shall be guilty of an offence."

Section 145 provides as follows:—

" (1) In order to comply with the requirements of this Part of this Act, a policy of insurance must satisfy the following conditions.

(2) The policy must be issued by an authorised insurer, that is to say, a person or body of persons carrying on motor vehicle insurance business in Great Britain.

(3) Subject to subsection (4) below, the policy—

> (a) must insure such person, persons or classes of persons as may be specified in the policy in respect of any liability which may be incurred by him or them in respect of the death of or bodily injury to any person caused by, or arising out of, the use of the vehicle on a road; and
>
> (b) must also insure him or them in respect of any liability which may be incurred by him or them under the provisions of this Part of this Act relating to payment for emergency treatment.

(4) The policy shall not, by virtue of subsection (3) (a) above, be required to cover—

> (a) liability in respect of the death, arising out of and in the course of his employment, of a person in the employment of a person insured by the policy or of bodily injury sustained by such a person arising out of and in the course of his employment; or
>
> (b) any contractual liability."

By s. 20 of the Act of 1974 all authorised insurers (see s. 145 (2), *supra*) in Great Britain were from 1st March, 1975, required to be members of the Motor Insurers' Bureau.

Social and Business Purposes

Policies often refer to use for social, domestic and pleasure purposes; this does not cover a trip by the proprietor of a business to negotiate a contract (*Wood* v. *General, etc., Assurance Co.* (1949), 65 T.L.R. 53). A car lent to a friend for a pleasure trip, the friend paying the owner for the petrol in it, is being used for social and domestic purposes and is not " hired " (*McCarthy* v. *British Oak Insurance Co.* [1938] 3 All E.R. 1). A policy limited to use " in the assured's business " does not cover him when he and another member of his firm are using the car on their respective businesses (*Passmore* v. *Vulcan, etc., Insurance Co.* (1935), 52 T.L.R. 193). But giving a lift out of courtesy to a person on business rounds is use for social purposes (*ibid.*), and in *D. H. R. Moody (Chemists)* v. *Iron Trades Mutual Insurance Co.* [1971] R.T.R. 120 it was held that a council in trying to encourage contacts with a foreign town were using a car for a social purpose even if the driver, who was the clerk of the council, was fulfilling a duty to his employers by driving the car for that purpose. Use by a farmer to move an employee's furniture to another house is not use under a policy " for agricultural purposes " (117 J.P.Jo. 18, Q.S.; and see p. 51). Carrying furniture, without payment, for a friend is use for " social, domestic and pleasure purposes " (*Lee* v. *Poole*

[1954] Crim.L.R. 942). Use of a tractor to convey household furniture of a newly-engaged farm servant to the farm was not within a policy covering use " solely for agricultural or forestry purposes including the haulage of articles required for agriculture " (*Agnew* v. *Robertson* [1956] S.L.T.(Sh.) 90). Carrying cattle food for cows is not use for domestic purposes though it might be otherwise if it was food for a pet dog or canary (*Whitehead* v. *Unwins* (*York*), *Ltd.* [1962] Crim.L.R. 323). The court reserved its opinion whether lending a lorry to a person out of friendship would be for " social " purposes even where the borrower's employee was driving. In *A.-G.* (*McCloskey*) v. *East* (1964), 98 I.L.T.N. 33, a farmer loaded his vehicle with turf and was taking it to a neighbour to use as fuel; his policy permitted carriage of agricultural produce and it was held that he was insured. If a car is insured in respect of use on the owner's business and that business is specified in the policy, use for another business which he also carries on would not be covered (*Jones* v. *Welsh Insurance Co.* [1937] 4 All E.R. 149). Where a car owner was insured for use in his business, specified as a builder's labourer, and used his car to carry swill in connection with his other business of pig-farming, he was held covered on the facts as he was returning from his building work at the time (*Kelleher* v. *Christopherson* (1957), 91 I.L.T.R. 191). Pig-farming was said to be a business, not a hobby or amusement (*ibid.*). When a car-owner allowed the foreman of a garage, where his car had been left for certain work, to use the car on a condition and the foreman used it in breach of that condition, the insurers, on the terms of the policy, were held not liable (*Browning* v. *Phoenix Assurance Co.* [1960] 2 Lloyd's Rep. 360). And see the *Justices' Clerk*, September, 1965, p. 104.

Servants and Agents

Where a policy covered the assured " or his paid driver " this was held to cover a driver who was driving for the assured and was paid as a driver, though not necessarily being paid by, or being in the general employment of the assured (*Bryan* v. *Forrow* [1950] 1 All E.R. 294). An agent employed by the assured under a contract of service and using the car to try to sell it for him was held to be in his employment (*Burton* v. *Road Transport, etc., Insurance Co.* (1939), 63 Lloyd's Rep. 253). Where an employee had the option of using his employer's vehicle to return from a job and was injured while so riding in it, this injury did not arise out of and in the course of his employment under a policy but he was nevertheless being carried on the vehicle by reason or in pursuance of his

contract of employment (*McSteen* v. *McCarthy* [1952] N.I. 33;
cf. the English workmen's compensation cases). A garage proprietor driving a lorry to the assured's premises after effecting
repairs is not a person " in the assured's employment " (*Lyons* v.
May [1948] 2 All E.R. 1062). If a policy covers employees,
driving by one in an unauthorised manner, if within the scope of
his employment, will normally be covered (*Marsh* v. *Moores* [1949]
2 All E.R. 27). A garage proprietor with whom an owner has
left his car is not in the owner's employment (*Lyons* v. *May, supra*).

A vehicle owner had frequent business deals with the defendant
and one day asked him to drive the vehicle home and collect the
owner next day to go on a business journey; the defendant deviated
from the quickest way home to give a girl a lift. It was held that
the defendant was in the owner's employment and was not on a
frolic of his own in going 2½ miles more with the girl (*Ballance* v.
Brown [1955] Crim.L.R. 384).

See *infra* under " Absolute Liability " (p. 377) for the special
defence for employees using a vehicle in ignorance of the lack of cover.

A common form of policy allows driving, with the permission of
the insured person, by any person " who holds or has held a driving
licence " and is not disqualified. Thus, if the driver has once held
a driving licence, he will be covered even though it may have expired
and even though it was only provisional. A driving licence would
normally include a provisional driving licence (Road Traffic
Act, 1972, s. 110) and in *Rendlesham* v. *Dunne* [1964] 1 Lloyd's Rep.
192 it was held in a county court that the policy still covered
use by a learner-driver although he was driving in breach of the
terms of his provisional licence. It will depend on the terms of the
policy whether he is covered if his licence extends to certain classes of
motor vehicle and the insured vehicle is not in one of those classes.
If a person who does not hold a licence commits an offence and the
court lawfully orders his licence to be endorsed, a licence subsequently obtained by him is of no effect if he did not disclose
particulars of the endorsement (Road Traffic Act, 1972, s. 101 (6)).
Consequently he might not be covered by a policy of the kind
mentioned above. In regard to policies which allow driving by a
person " who holds a driving licence ", it is submitted that this
includes a foreign driving licence, unless the terms of the policy
make it clear that it does not. Persons are permitted to drive in
Great Britain on foreign and international licences, and insurance
companies must know that such people may well drive the insured
vehicle with the policy-holder's permission, particularly if he is
himself a foreigner. Moreover, a policy will normally be construed
against the insurer. In *Kinsey* v. *Herts County Council* [1972] Crim.

L.R. 564, a sixteen-year-old was held not to " hold " a driving licence which had been issued to him a month before his sixteenth birthday to come into effect on his birthday.

Where a policy allows driving by a person who " is not disqualified from holding or obtaining a driving licence ", this means " disqualified by order of a court ", and a person who has been refused renewal of a driving licence because he is mentally defective is not " disqualified " within the meaning of the policy (*Edwards* v. *Griffiths* [1953] 2 All E.R. 874). But a person is " disqualified from holding a licence " if he is, under s. 96 of the Road Traffic Act, 1972, prohibited from driving by reason of his age (*Mumford* v. *Hardy* [1956] 1 All E.R. 337; *R.* v. *Saddleworth JJ.* [1968] 1 All E.R. 1189).

A case of special facts as to associated companies and liquidation is *Biddle* v. *Johnston* (1965), 109 S.J. 395.

Public Authorities and Other Special Cases

It seems that s. 143 does not apply to Crown vehicles, because s. 188 of the 1972 Act does not mention s. 143, and Crown vehicles, it is gathered, are in fact not insured. But a Government servant who uses a Government vehicle for purposes other than the public service of the Crown without being insured offends against s. 143 (*Salt* v. *MacKnight* [1947] S.C.(J.) 99). A Metropolitan magistrate has held that a postman not employed to drive who drives a mail van on post office business without authority offends against s. 143 (Jo.Crim.L. (1946) 168). Reference to s. 144 shows that that section contains special exemptions for the vehicles of local and police authorities, for those of persons who have deposited £15,000 in the Supreme Court and for merchant navy salvage vehicles. Nor is insurance required for invalid carriages, or for trams and trolley vehicles the use of which is authorised by special Act (ss. 143 (3) and 198), or for vehicles requisitioned by the Army or R.A.F. (s. 144 (2) (*d*)). Section 143 does not apply to vehicles which are not mechanically propelled vehicles intended or adapted for use on roads, such as dumpers, or have ceased to be such vehicles. See further p. 7.

The use of motor vehicles of visiting forces (see p. 58) on duty need not be covered by insurance, but members of such forces, when off duty, must comply with s. 143 (Visiting Forces and International Headquarters (Application of Law) Order, 1965). The Motor Vehicles (International Motor Insurance Card) Regulations, 1971 (S.I. 1971 No. 792), relate to the insurance of vehicles brought here temporarily by visitors.

Void Conditions

By the Road Traffic Act, 1972, s. 148 (2), a condition in a policy that liability shall not arise or shall cease because of something done or omitted after the event giving rise to a claim is void, but a condition in a policy that pillion passengers should not be carried is valid and is not made void by s. 148 (2) if such a passenger is carried (*Bright* v. *Ashfold* (1932), 96 J.P. 182). But see the next paragraph. Further, by s. 148 (1) of that Act, so much of a third-party policy as purports to restrict the insurance by reference to—

(a) the age or physical or mental condition of persons driving the vehicle; or

(b) the condition of the vehicle; or

(c) the number of persons that the vehicle carries; or

(d) the weight or physical characteristics of the goods that the vehicle carries; or

(e) the times at which or the areas within which the vehicle is used; or

(f) the horse power or cylinder capacity or value of the vehicle; or

(g) the carrying on the vehicle of any particular apparatus; or

(h) the carrying on the vehicle of any particular means of identification other than any means of identification required to be carried by or under the Vehicles (Excise) Act,

is of no effect as respects the liabilities to be covered by s. 143 of the 1972 Act. A person holding a policy which contains a condition rendered void by s. 148 and using the insured vehicle in breach of that condition only may therefore have a good defence to a prosecution under s. 143 (but see a contrary opinion at 110 J.P.Jo. 498) and, even if he has not, s. 148 provides good grounds for arguing lenient treatment in cases to which it applies. The various pre-1934 decisions on terms of the nature mentioned in s. 148 should now be read, so far as third-party insurance is concerned, in the light of that section. Section 148 (1) (d), relating to the physical characteristics of the goods carried, does not prevent the insurers limiting the policy to cover goods carried for the assured's business only (*Jones* v. *Welsh Insurance Corpn.* [1937] 4 All E.R. 149). A term in a policy that only steady and sober drivers should be employed is not one restricting it by reference to the physical or mental condition of persons driving the vehicle within s. 148 (1) (a) (*National Farmers' Insurance Society* v. *Dawson* [1941] 2 K.B. 424).

Quaere, if a condition that a pillion passenger shall not be carried on a motor cycle or combination is rendered void by s. 148 (1) in that it is a condition " as to the number of persons that the vehicle carries ".   It was submitted in the sixth edition that it is a condition as to the manner in which a passenger is carried and therefore it is not void.   The importance of this condition has been increased in that passenger liability was made compulsorily insurable from December, 1972.   It is submitted that if a policy purports to exclude liability when a passenger is carried this may be held to be a void condition in that it restricts the number of persons carried if the vehicle is constructed or adapted to carry one or more passengers. On the other hand if a motor cycle does not, for example, have a pillion seat a condition in a policy that the motor cycle should not be adapted for the carriage of a passenger would appear to be lawful.

A policy which prohibits the carrying of a load in excess of that for which the vehicle was constructed refers to the weight-load specified for lorries and vans and is not infringed by carrying excess passengers (*Houghton* v. *Trafalgar Insurance Co.* [1953] 2 All E.R. 1409).   An overloaded vehicle can be in an " unsafe and unroad-worthy condition " within the meaning of an exception clause and this condition can be permanent or temporary (*Clarke* v. *National Insurance and Guarantee Corporation* [1963] 3 All E.R. 375, C.A.). " Maintaining a car in an efficient condition " generally means that it should be capable of doing what is normally and reasonably required of it (*McInnes* v. *National Motor &c. Union* [1963] 2 Lloyd's Rep. 415).   A policy required the insured to take all reasonable steps to maintain the vehicle in an efficient condition; this means in roadworthy condition.   The tyres had no tread and this was obvious to anyone looking at them; it was held that the vehicle was not maintained in an efficient condition (*Conn* v. *Westminster Motor Insurance Association, Ltd.* [1966] 1 Lloyd's Rep. 407).

Under a somewhat similar Irish statute, a side-car was held not to be " equipment " of a motor cycle but part of the motor cycle itself (*Higgins* v. *Feeney* (1954), 88 I.L.T.R. 152).

Trailers

A policy which excepts from cover any use while drawing more trailers than is permitted by law is avoided where the vehicle is so used, and the driver offends against s. 143 (*Kerridge* v. *Rush* [1952] 2 Lloyd's Rep. 305).   Use when drawing a trailer is an offence if the policy expressly does not cover use with a trailer (*Robb* v. *M'Kechnie* [1936] S.C.(J.) 25).   But a policy which insures against the consequences of negligent driving is valid under s. 143 although it may permit the vehicle to be used illegally by drawing laden trailers (*Leggate* v. *Brown* [1950] 2 All E.R. 564).   See also *Jenkins* v. *Deane* on p. 10.   A charge of using " a motor vehicle and trailer " in breach of s. 143 is bad; the reference to the trailer should be deleted (*Rogerson* v. *Stephens* [1950] 2 All E.R. 144).

A motor vehicle which is being towed remains a motor vehicle and its use on the road must be covered by insurance (*Milstead* v. *Sexton* [1964] Crim.L.R. 474). See generally p. 10.

General Conditions of Liability of Insurers

The policy is the document which the court must consider and, where a policy clearly does not cover the risk, an offence is committed although the insurers may be willing, as an act of grace, to accept liability (*Egan* v. *Bowler* (1939), 63 Lloyd's Rep. 266, where it was also held that a letter from the insurers should be disregarded). But, where there was a question before magistrates whether a vehicle in its particular state was covered by the policy and evidence was given on behalf of the insurers that they regarded themselves as still liable on the policy, such being a reasonable interpretation thereof, the magistrates' dismissal of a charge under s. 143 was not upset by the High Court (*Carnill* v. *Rowland* [1953] 1 All E.R. 486). On the other hand, an offence will be committed where a policy does not cover a risk notwithstanding that the insurers accept liability on a mistaken view of the law (*Mumford* v. *Hardy* [1956] 1 All E.R. 337). It is the policy of insurance that matters; if there is no insurance policy covering the use of the vehicle by the defendant, rights at law under contract, whether between the defendant and another or with the insurance company, cannot make good the deficiency of a policy (*Roberts* v. *Warne* [1973] R.T.R. 217). While it is desirable that the policy should be seen in most cases, it need not be seen if the court is satisfied that all the required information can be obtained from the certificate (*Borders* v. *Swift* [1957] Crim.L.R. 194). In *Leathley* v. *Drummond* [1972] R.T.R. 293 a case was remitted back to the justices who had dismissed it on a submission of no case after only a certificate of insurance but no policy had been produced; it was for the defendants to prove that the use of the vehicle in question was covered by insurance (*ibid.*). The policy overrides the certificate where there is inconsistency between the two (*Biddle* v. *Johnston* (1965), 109 S.J. 395); not only cannot the certificate override the policy but the certificate itself is not a policy (*Roberts* v. *Warne, supra*). In *Howey* v. *Bradley* [1970] Crim.L.R. 223 the Divisional Court left open the question whether, once a policy of insurance is produced which purports to cover the use of the vehicle, the burden is on the prosecution to show that the use of the vehicle is not within the uses covered by the policy. Section 81 of the Magistrates' Courts

Act, 1952, it is submitted, has the effect of requiring the defendant to produce a certificate of insurance or policy to show that he was insured (see also *Williams* v. *Russell* (1933), 97 J.P. 128; *Leathley* v. *Drummond* and *Davey* v. *Towle*, *supra*). Once he has done this, it is for the prosecution to prove that that particular policy does not cover the defendant because of an exception clause in the policy (see the test in an Irish case, *Shehan* v. *Cork JJ.*, quoted in Brian Harris, Criminal Jurisdiction of Magistrates, 2nd ed., p. 5).

Where a policy covers a named vehicle and " any other vehicle not belonging to or hired by " the assured, the policy lapses on the sale of the named vehicle, unless rights of user of it are retained (*Boss* v. *Kingston* [1963] 1 All E.R. 177; and see *Smith* v. *Ralph*, *infra*). But a policy for third party risks only may not lapse on the sale of the vehicle, unless the terms of the policy show that it does (*ibid.*). See also *Tattersall* v. *Drysdale* [1935] 2 K.B. 174 and *Rogerson* v. *Scottish Automobile, etc., Insurance Co.* (1931), 48 T.L.R. 17, as to vehicles being used " instead of " the insured car.

A car-hire firm held a policy which excluded publicans from driving hired cars. The defendant, who was a publican, completed the firm's form for hirer-driving insurance by giving his occupation as a printer. It was held that he was guilty of uninsured use in driving a car hired from the firm (*Evans* v. *Lewis* [1964] Crim.L.R. 472); there was no question of false representation being made to the insurance company by the publican, the policy was effected between the insurance company and the garage and therefore there was no question of s. 149 applying.

Where the defendant has a policy covering the driving of any car by him, stipendiary magistrates have held that this covers driving of a car which he has illegally taken without the owner's consent (*The Times*, 25th May, 1954, and 28th March, 1961; at 124 J.P.Jo. 109 quarter sessions apparently reached a like conclusion). But some policies cover only driving with the leave of the other car-owner. See 125 J.P.Jo. 108.

Where cover has run out and the insurers give an extended cover-note, the defendant must accept that cover-note before he is validly insured under it and, if he is shown not to have relied on it, e.g., by later insuring with another company and never paying the first company, that cover-note will not insure him (*Taylor* v. *Allon* [1965] 1 All E.R. 557).

A cover-note was issued at 6.30 p.m. on 25th March expressed to cover from 6.45 p.m. and later the policy was issued stating that the insurance commenced on 25th March. It was held that the insured was not covered at 6.5 p.m. on that day (*Smith* v. *Alexander* [1965] 1 Lloyd's Rep. 283).

The cover required by s. 143 includes cover against intentional criminal acts (*Hardy* v. *Motor Insurers' Bureau* [1964] 2 All E.R. 742).

In *Police* v. *Bishop* [1956] Crim.L.R. 569 a policy covering motor vehicles not belonging to the defendant was held to cover a vehicle which the defendant had taken without the owner's consent.

A policy which covers persons driving a vehicle by the order, or with the permission, of the assured does not extend to a purchaser from him even though the purchase price has not been paid in full (*Peters* v. *General, etc., Assurance Co.* [1938] 2 All E.R. 267). Where the assured's business was taken over by a company in which she was the chief shareholder, a policy in her name did not insure the company's vehicles (*Levinger* v. *Licences, etc., Insurance Co.* (1936), 54 Lloyd's Rep. 68). Permission to drive granted by the policy-holder is not necessarily revoked by his death (*Kelly* v. *Cornhill Insurance Co.* [1964] 1 All E.R. 321) but permission to drive given by a policy-holder cannot extend beyond the time when he ceases to have an insurable interest because he has sold the car (*Smith* v. *Ralph* [1963] 2 Lloyd's Rep. 439).

If a policy of insurance is in force covering the use of the vehicle, a policy covering the personal liability of the driver is not required (*Marsh* v. *Moores* [1949] 2 All E.R. 27, a case which also deals with questions of driving within the scope of employment). An exceptions clause in a policy relating to persons who "to the knowledge of the assured" were unlicensed means that the assured must have actually known of that or not wilfully shut his eyes to the obvious; the fact that the assured was reckless in not making inquiries does not mean that he actually had knowledge, and it was held that he was covered by the policy (*Ellis* v. *Hinds* [1947] 1 All E.R. 337). A policy which did not cover driving by an unlicensed person was held to cover driving of a car by such a person where a licensed person sat by her and retained effective control (*Langman* v. *Valentine* [1952] 2 All E.R. 803); it would be otherwise if the licensed person gave merely passive supervision (*Evans* v. *Walkden* [1956] 3 All E.R. 64). The facts of these two cases are given on p. 21.

Passengers in a car who know that it is being used without insurance may be guilty under s. 143 (*Ross* v. *Rivenall* [1959] 2 All E.R. 376, where there was evidence of all the car's occupants having been concerned together in unlawfully taking it) but not, it seems, if they are ignorant of the lack of cover and do not procure the use of the vehicle (*D.* v. *Parsons* [1960] 2 All E.R. 493, and other cases cited on p. 358). See also as to passengers in the next paragraph.

Meaning of " Use "

" Use " under s. 143 means that there must be an element of controlling, managing and operating the vehicle as a vehicle and the term " use " does not include the relationship of a passenger to a vehicle or part of it (*Brown* v. *Roberts* [1963] 2 All E.R. 263). An owner sitting by the driver would normally retain control of his vehicle, as would an employer not in it when the vehicle was being used on his business and with his permission, so both would be users along with the driver under s. 143. But passengers who had no power of control over the driver would not be users under s. 143 and, it is submitted, would not aid and abet his uninsured use merely by letting themselves be driven even if they knew of the lack of insurance unless they had procured the making of the journey. For example, a passenger who said, " I accede to your unsolicited invitation to drive me to London in your uninsured car " would not offend against s. 143 or, in the absence of any form of procurement or assistance, aid and abet but he would aid and abet if he said to the driver, " Please take me to London in your uninsured car." It is appreciated that the number of persons who would use such language is probably small. In *Carmichael & Sons* v. *Cottle* [1971] R.T.R. 11, it was suggested that the only person who could be said to " use " a vehicle was either the driver or an employee when driven on the employer's business. This suggestion was followed in *Crawford* v. *Haughton* [1972] R.T.R. 125, where the court declined to extend the " user " to include the owner of a car when it was driven by another at his request. In such cases he should be charged with " causing " or " permitting ", which was said in *Carmichael's* case to provide for the offences of aiding and abetting or being an accessory (see p. 46). But where the owner was actually in his motor vehicle as a passenger, and the vehicle was driven for him by a friend, it was held that the owner was " using " the vehicle; *Crawford* v. *Haughton* was explained as dealing with the situation of vicarious responsibility, where the owner was not present personally in the vehicle (*Cobb* v. *Williams* [1973] R.T.R. 113). The fact that a passenger in a motor vehicle runs away on seeing the police does not justify on its own the inference that he was knowingly helping the driver to commit the offence of no insurance, and a conviction of aiding and abetting the driver's uninsured use was set aside (*Smith* v. *Baker* [1971] R.T.R. 350). In *Fisher* v. *Kearton* (1964), 108 S.J. 258, it was held that a passenger, found drunk in the driving seat, was not a user under s. 143 when a policy and the ignition keys were held by another person in the car.

A vehicle is in use on the road even when it is stationary and unattended and it must be insured (*Elliott* v. *Grey* [1959] 3 All E.R.

733, followed in *Adams* v. *Evans* [1971] 12 C.L. 339, a case at quarter sessions where the vehicle had no rear axle or rear wheels and was parked in a cul-de-sac. As to the meaning of " to use " generally, see the discussion of the cases on pp. 41–51.

Policy Obtained by Misrepresentation

A policy obtained by a false and material representation remains valid so far as the criminal liability under s. 143 is concerned, unless the insurers have taken steps to avoid it; it makes no difference whether it is void or voidable (*Durrant* v. *MacLaren* [1956] Crim.L.R. 632; [1956] 2 Lloyd's Rep. 70). It had already been held that a voidable policy satisfied s. 143 unless and until it was avoided (*Goodbarne* v. *Buck* [1940] 1 All E.R. 613). In neither case, however, was reference made to *Guardian Assurance Co.* v. *Sutherland* [1939] 2 All E.R. 246, where it had been held that a policy obtained by a false and material representation insured no one and was not a policy within s. 145 (3). This conflict is discussed at Jo.Crim.L. (1965) 81.

Insurance Certificates and Policies

By s. 147 (1) of the 1972 Act, a policy is of no effect unless and until the insurer delivers to the assured a certificate in the prescribed form. For a conviction for using a vehicle contrary to s. 143 because the certificate had not been delivered, see *Starkey* v. *Hall* [1936] 2 All E.R. 18, a case on special facts. The Motor Vehicles (Third Party Risks) Regulations, 1972 (S.I. 1972 No. 1217) prescribe the forms of certificate. Form B in the Schedule to the Regulations is in such a form that the registered number of the vehicle does not have to be shown. By reg. 10 every company issuing a policy or security is required to keep a record as to specified details of the policies and of any certificate issued therewith and all such companies are required without charge to furnish to the Secretary of State or any chief officer of police any particulars of such records. Regulation 13 requires an insurance company to issue on demand a fresh certificate to the loser if they are satisfied it has been lost or destroyed.

By s. 158 (1) " policy of insurance " includes a covering note. Every such policy " in the form of a cover note has to bear a certificate (Form C in the Schedule) that it satisfies the requirements of the relevant law in Great Britain (reg. 5 (3) of the Regulations above). A policy covering use of " any farm implement or machine not constructed or adapted for the conveyance of goods " means " any farm implement or farm machine " and does not cover a cement-mixer, as that is not a farm machine (*J. R. M. (Plant), Ltd.* v. *Hodgson* [1960] 1 Lloyd's Rep. 538).

Absolute Liability

The offence under s. 143 arises if a person " uses " a motor vehicle on a road or " causes " or " permits " any other person to use it on a road while uninsured. Subject to the special defence for employees, it was expressly held in *Tapsell* v. *Maslen* [1967] Crim.L.R. 53, following *Morris* v. *Williams* (1952), 50 L.G.R. 308, and *Lyons* v. *May* [1948] 2 All E.R. 1062, that s. 143 imposes an absolute prohibition on using an uninsured vehicle or causing or permitting it to be used on a road. A conviction must follow if it be shown that a defendant used it or caused or permitted its use, irrespective of whether he knew or not that the vehicle was uninsured (unless the special defence under s. 143 (2) of the 1972 Act (*infra*) applies). But a person does not " permit " a vehicle to be used uninsured if he allows another to use it only on the express condition that that person would first insure it. When the borrower used the vehicle without having insured it it was held that as he was using it without having insured the vehicle as required by the owner, he was using it without the owner's permission and thus the owner could not be convicted of " permitting " (*Newbury* v. *Davis* [1974] R.T.R. 367). *Lyons* v. *May* and *Tapsell* v. *Maslen, supra,* were distinguished for the reason that in both those cases there was no question that the defendants had given permission for the respective vehicles to be used. The question in both those cases was as to whether it was also necessary to prove the defendants knew there was no insurance covering the permitted use. *Sheldon Deliveries* v. *Willis* [1972] R.T.R. 217 was explained in support of the view that no one can be convicted of permitting a vehicle to be used unless that person has allowed the vehicle to be used. In *Sheldon*, a car delivery firm were held not to have permitted the uninsured use of a vehicle being delivered by them, when their delivery car driver had, contrary to instructions and unknown to the delivery company, driven the car on a Sunday for his own purposes and without the trade plates. It was held in *Sheldon* that the car delivery firm could not be convicted of permitting as they had no knowledge, actual or constructive, of the unauthorised use of the car. In *Newbury* v. *Davis, supra*, it was pointed out that a distinction must be drawn between lack of knowledge of the fact that a vehicle was being used as in *Sheldon* and lack of knowledge of the fact that when a vehicle was being used it was in contravention of s. 143 because it was uninsured (*Lyons* v. *May*; *Tapsell* v. *Maslen*). In *British School of Motoring, Ltd.* v. *Simms* [1971] 1 All E.R. 317 it was held to be an implied term of a contract between a driving school and a pupil that the vehicle provided by the school for the pupil to take the test should be insured. It is submitted that criminal liability under s. 143 for " permitting " would also attach. Any person using a vehicle in breach of s. 143 offends against it, whether he be its owner or not (*Williamson* v. *O'Keefe* [1947] 1 All E.R. 307), and in *Napthen* v. *Place* [1970] R.T.R. 248 it was held that ownership or proof of ownership of a vehicle was not essential to proof of an offence under s. 143. The test is whether the prosecution can prove that the defendant " used or permitted the use of it " (see p. 375). But it will be a defence if the employer is covered by his policy of insurance in respect of his employee's driving, even if the employee-driver himself is not covered because of his age (*Ellis, Ltd.* v. *Hinds* [1947] 1 All E.R. 337). There is an article at 97 S.J. 396. A person may " permit " though he is not the owner (*Lloyd* v. *Singleton* [1953] 1 All E.R. 291). On a charge of permitting the use of a car without insurance the defendant's counsel submitted that since the defendant was not the registered owner he could not be convicted of the offence. The prosecuting inspector referred to p. 202 of the fifth edition of this textbook, where it was stated (*supra*): " A person may permit though he is not the owner," citing *Lloyd* v. *Singleton*. Counsel persuaded the justices that unless the inspector could produce *Lloyd* v. *Singleton* they could not refer to this book. In remitting the case back to the justices for the hearing to be continued, Lord Parker stated: " In my judgment that is wholly wrong. They are entitled to and should look at the textbook; and if they then feel in doubt they should, of their own motion, send for the authority and, if necessary, adjourn for it to be obtained " (*Boys* v. *Blenkinsop* [1968] Crim.L.R. 513).

A passenger who is ignorant of the lack of cover and does not procure the making of the journey should not be prosecuted (*D.* v. *Parsons* [1960] 2 All E.R. 493). See p. 375 as to " use " by passengers, and *Smith* v. *Baker*, p. 375.

Special Defence for Employees

The Road Traffic Act, 1972, s. 143 (2), provides a special defence for employees using in ignorance of the lack of cover. It reads:—

" A person charged with using a motor vehicle in contravention of this section shall not be convicted if he proves that the vehicle did not belong to him and was not in his possession under a contract of hiring or of loan, that he was using the vehicle in the course of his employment and that he neither knew nor had reason to believe that there was not in force in relation to the vehicle such a policy of insurance or security as is mentioned in subsection (1) above."

The acquittal of a servant pursuant to s. 143 (2) does not prevent the conviction of his master for causing or permitting under s. 143

(1) (*A.-G.* v. *Downes* (1959), 93 I.L.T.R. 121), or, presumably, using the vehicle.

Procedure, Penalty, Endorsements and Disqualification

Evidence

Notice to produce the policy is not required and evidence may be given by a policeman who saw the insurance certificate of its terms, if the defendant does not produce it in court (*Williams* v. *Russell* (1933), 97 J.P. 128; *Machin* v. *Ash* (1950), 94 S.J. 705). The onus of proving possession of a policy is on the defendant once it is shown that he has used a motor vehicle on a road (*Philcox* v. *Carberry* [1960] Crim.L.R. 563, following *John* v. *Humphreys* [1955] 1 All E.R. 793). In *Leathley* v. *Drummond, Leathley* v. *Irving* [1972] R.T.R. 293 it was again affirmed that the onus is on the defendant, once it has been shown that a vehicle has been used on a road, to show that the use of the vehicle was covered by insurance. The onus is on the defendant to show that the vehicle's use in question was covered by an insurance policy, even though he is not the owner. A driver charged with using a vehicle without insurance must still show that the vehicle's use was insured even though, because he is not the owner, he might find it difficult to obtain the owner's certificate of insurance or insurance policy (*Davey* v. *Towle* [1974] R.T.R. 329). In *Howey* v. *Bradley* [1970] Crim.L.R. 223 the court left open the question of whether the onus is on the prosecution to prove that the use of a vehicle is not covered by an insurance policy which the defendant has produced. It is submitted that, once a defendant has produced a policy that *prima facie* shows the use of the vehicle by him to be insured, it is for the prosecution to prove that the particular use of that particular vehicle on the occasion of the charge was not covered by the terms of the policy.

Limitation of Time

By s. 180 proceedings may be brought for an offence under s. 143 within six months from the date on which the offence came to the prosecutor's knowledge subject to an overall time limit of three years from the commission of the offence. A certificate signed by or on behalf of the prosecutor as to when evidence of the offence came to his knowledge is conclusive evidence of that fact. A certificate purporting to be so signed shall be deemed to be so signed unless the contrary is proved. The offence can only be tried summarily.

Penalty, etc.

The penalty for a first or subsequent offence contrary to s. 143 is a fine of £200 (1972 Act, Sched. 4, as amended by the 1974 Act). The 1974 Act removed the power of magistrates to impose imprisonment for this offence.

Endorsement of the offender's driving licence must be ordered on his conviction under s. 143 unless there are special reasons (see Chapter VII).

Disqualification for any period may at the court's option be ordered on a first or subsequent conviction under s. 143. The court may also disqualify an offender until he passes a test (s. 93 (7)).

Section 93 (3) of the 1972 Act applies to offences under s. 143 so that, if a person convicted under it has been previously convicted on not less than two occasions of an endorsed disqualifiable offence in respect of a motor vehicle within the three years immediately before the commission of the s. 143 offence, he must be disqualified for at least six months (see p. 624) unless, having regard to all the circumstances, there are grounds for mitigating the normal consequences of the conviction (see p. 688). The six-month disqualification is additional and consecutive to any period of disqualification on the same occasion or for a previous offence.

Where there is deliberate uninsured use, an absolute or conditional discharge should be given only in exceptional circumstances (*Taylor* v. *Saycell* [1950] 2 All E.R. 887). Where a defendant is placed on probation, or conditionally or absolutely discharged, his licence, in the absence of " special reasons ", is obliged to be endorsed and he may also be disqualified (Powers of Criminal Courts Act, 1973, s. 13).

The endorsement code for an offence under s. 143 is IN 10.

The Magistrates' Association's suggested penalty for the offence (see p. 594 and p. 879) reads: "£50 and consider disqualification".

Production of Certificate

Section 162 of the Road Traffic Act, 1972, makes provision for the production to the police of insurance certificates by drivers and suspected drivers and offenders. No offence is committed if the certificate is produced within five days at a named police station by the person concerned or on his behalf. In *Tremelling* v. *Martin* [1971] R.T.R. 196 it was held that production for this purpose must be long enough to enable the police to inspect it and see that it is a proper certificate of insurance. The Motor Vehicles (International Motor Insurance Card) Regulations, 1971 (S.I. 1971

No. 792), apply this provision to such cards (reg. 6 (1)). Section 162 also requires the giving of names and addresses of persons interrogated and vehicle-owners. The term " owner ", in relation to a vehicle which is the subject of a hiring agreement, includes both parties to the agreement (s. 162 (4)).

The penalty on a first or subsequent conviction of an offence under s. 162 is £50. It is only triable summarily.

Forgery and Fraudulent Applications

The Road Traffic Act, 1972, ss. 169, 170 and 171, respectively penalise a person (1) who, with intent to deceive, forges within the meaning of the Forgery Act, 1913, s. 1, or alters or uses or allows the use of a certificate of insurance or security issued pursuant to s. 145 or makes or has in his possession a document so closely resembling a certificate as to be calculated to deceive, or (2) who makes a false statement or withholds any material information for the purpose of obtaining such a certificate, or (3) who issues one knowing it to be false in a material particular.   Offences under (1) may be tried either summarily or on indictment pursuant to the Magistrates' Courts Act, 1952, s. 18, and for all the offences the defendant now no longer has the right to elect trial by jury under s. 25 of the Magistrates' Courts Act, 1952, as the power of magistrates to impose imprisonment on summary conviction has been removed by the Act of 1974.   An extended time-limit for summary proceedings, i.e., within six months from the time when the offence came to the prosecutor's knowledge but not more than three years from its commission, is provided by the Road Traffic Act, 1972, s. 180.   There is no time-limit for proceedings on indictment under s. 169 ([1958] Crim.L.R. 50) but the limit given in s. 180 applies to cases under ss. 170 (1) and (6) and 171.   See *R.* v. *McCardle* on p. 50 as to " use. "

The case of *R.* v. *Cleghorn* [1938] 3 All E.R. 398 is sometimes cited as showing that a certificate of insurance which was once valid but has ceased to be so because of the cancellation of a policy is a document so closely resembling a certificate as to be calculated to deceive.   " Calculated to deceive " seems to mean " likely to deceive " as well as " intended to deceive " (82 J.P.Jo. 447, and see Stroud's Judicial Dictionary).   In *R.* v. *Davison* [1972] 1 W.L.R. 1540 " calculated to deceive " in the House to House Collections Act, 1939, was held to mean " likely to deceive ".   An expired certificate would still seem to be a certificate under s. 169 (*cf. Taylor* v. *Emerson* (1962), 106 S.J. 552).   Under a similarly-worded provision in another context, it was held that, on a charge of possessing documents resembling clothing coupons with intent to deceive, it sufficed if the prosecutor established the intent to deceive and he was not also put to proof that the defendant knew of the falsity of the documents (*R.* v. *Greenberg* [1942] 2 All E.R. 344), but the defendant may set up the defence that he acted in good faith (*Brend* v. *Wood* (1946), 110 J.P. 317). It is immaterial, in a charge under s. 170 of making a false statement, that no gain accrued to the defendant from it (*Jones* v. *Meatyard* [1939] 1 All E.R. 140). The offence under s. 170 (6) of making a false statement for the purpose of obtaining the issue of a certificate of insurance is an absolute offence and consciousness by the defendant of the statement's falsity need not be shown, so long as it was false; the offence of withholding material information for the same purpose may, however, predicate a conscious withholding on his part (*R.* v. *Cummerson* [1968] 2 All E.R. 863). It is doubtful how far, if at all, the Criminal Justice Act, 1967, s. 8 (proof of criminal intent), applies a subjective test as to what a defendant intended or foresaw in these cases. On a charge under s. 171 of issuing a certificate which is to the knowledge of the defendant false, the prosecutor must show not only that it was false but also that the defendant knew it to be so (*Ocean Accident &c. Co.* v. *Cole* (1932), 96 J.P. 191). A person who commonly uses another name than his proper name may be guilty of an offence if in completing a proposal form for insurance he uses the adopted name and does not reveal his real one (*Clark* v. *Chalmers* [1961] S.L.T. 325). It might be otherwise if he had lawfully changed his name (*ibid.*). On a charge against a car-owner of making a false declaration that a car had not been used within a particular period, it will not suffice for the prosecutor to show that some unidentified person was seen to use it within the period and rely on the presumption that a car is being used by its owner (*A.-G. (Connor)* v. *Shorten* (1959), 93 I.L.T.R. 168).

By s. 173 power of seizure of documents contravening ss. 169 to 171 is given to the police.

The penalty under s. 169 is a fine only of £200 on summary conviction, but on indictment two years' imprisonment may be imposed. The penalty under s. 170 (6) (false statement to obtain insurance certificate) is a fine only of £200. The penalty under s. 171 (issuing false insurance certificates) is also a fine only of £200. The accused may no longer elect trial by jury for any of these offences under s. 25 of the Magistrates' Courts Act, 1952, as none are any longer punishable with imprisonment by magistrates. Disqualification and endorsement may not be ordered for any of these offences.

9. OBSTRUCTION

Proceedings for obstructing the highway can be brought under the Highways Act, 1959, s. 121 (wilfully obstructing the free passage of a highway), the Town Police Clauses Act, 1847, s. 28 (wilfully causing an obstruction in any public footpath or public thorough-fare), and reg. 114 (p. 839, *infra*) of the Motor Vehicles (Construction and Use) Regulations, 1973 (causing or permitting a motor vehicle or trailer to stand on a road so as to cause any un-necessary obstruction thereof). The Regulations extend to the whole of Great Britain and the Highways Act to England and Wales, including London (London Government Act, 1963, s. 16 (2)). See *infra* as to the 1847 Act. The law is discussed at 94 S.J. 811 and, with particular reference to Irish cases, at Jo.Crim.L. (1953) 78 and 168 and at 99 I.L.T.N. 181, 187, 197, 207, 217 and 227. The Acts apply to all vehicles but the Regulations only to motor vehicles (not being trolley vehicles) and trailers.

The Regulations apply to a " road " as defined on p. 26. The Highways Act applies to ways over which all members of the public are entitled to pass and repass. A decision of quarter sessions under s. 31 (1) of the National Parks and Access to the Countryside Act, 1949, is a judgment *in rem* and binding on a magistrates' court. An owner cannot therefore dispute the status of a public path declared to be such by quarter sessions when prosecuted under the Highways Act for wilful obstruction (*Armstrong* v. *Whitfield* [1973] 2 All E.R. 546). The Town Police Clauses Act, 1847, s. 28, did not usually apply outside boroughs and urban districts and an obstruction under it must be shown to have been to the obstruction, annoyance or danger of the residents or passengers in the street.

The question as to who may prosecute under the Town Police Clauses Act is discussed at 119 J.P.Jo. 746 and Stone (1975), pp. 4286–4287, where it is suggested that the constable who saw the offence should be the informant. That Act, other than the pro-visions relating to hackney carriages, seems now to apply to all dis-tricts, whether they were formerly boroughs, urban districts or rural districts (see s. 171 of the Public Health Act, 1875, and para. 23 of Sched. 14 to the Local Government Act, 1972). A prosecution under the Highways Act or the Regulations may be brought by any person.

Regulation 114 does not apply to trams and trolley vehicles (see s. 198, excluding s. 40, of the 1972 Act), but the other two Acts do.

The position as to the application of the Highways and Town Police Clauses Acts to Crown vehicles is discussed on pp. 60–63. The Regulations apply to Crown vehicles.

Parking Meters

The Road Traffic Regulation Act, 1967, ss. 35 to 44, deal with parking on the highway and parking meters and have been amended by the Transport Act, 1968, s. 127. Apart from those sections and the Parking Meters (Description and Testing) (England and Wales) Orders, 1957 and 1961 (see art. 2 of the 1961 Order as to the application of the 1957 Order, and see S.I. 1959 No. 1348 as to Scotland), the orders designating parking areas are local ones and information about them should be obtained from the local authority or police. " Parking places " are provided on the highway, marked with lines, and some may accommodate several vehicles. Each driver, on putting the appropriate coin in the meter, may park there for a specified time but no longer; if the vehicle stays for longer than that time, an excess charge must be paid to the local authority. If it is there for more than four hours, an offence is committed. A motorist may not put more money in the meter to extend his period, unless the order permits. He may go to another " parking place " but may not return to his original one or sometimes one within the same zone until he has been gone from it for a prescribed period. The cited provisions are taken from one particular order and other orders differ. The police or council may prosecute for offences. Section 42 specifies a number of offences and makes the driver who first left the vehicle generally responsible (s. 42 (2)). By s. 42 (6) a meter is presumed to be of the approved type and design. The Westminster Order contains exemptions for loading and unloading. A case under the Order of two vehicles parking in one space is reported at Jo.Crim.L. (1959) 98. By s. 42 (3) acceptance of the excess charge bars proceedings for failing to pay an initial charge. An order regulating the use of a parking place may make provision for treating the indications given by a meter or ticket as evidence of such facts as may be provided by the order (s. 36 (2)). By s. 41 a designation order, setting aside parking places on the highway, may not be challenged in any legal proceedings, save that it allows a challenge in the High Court only for a period after the order has been made. The definition of " driver " for the purposes of s. 42 is limited by s. 104. A defendant accused of failing to pay an excess charge may in the circumstances given in s. 42 (7) be convicted of failing to pay an initial charge.

The provisions of s. 41 (as to challenging orders in the High Court) are extended to certain other orders under the 1967 Act (Transport Act, 1968, Sched. 14).

If a motor vehicle is left in a parking bay, no time is allowed for delaying the insertion of the coin in the meter unless it be merely to alight from the car and walk to the meter. Payment must be made as soon as the car is left in the bay, whether the driver stays in it or not, and he must not go off looking for change if he has not the right coin on him (*Strong* v. *Dawtry* [1961] 1 All E.R. 926). The relevant order should always be scrutinised, however, to see if it contains exemptions not in the order considered in *Strong's* case, where the High Court expressed surprise that a motorist who had left his car for only a minute or so to get change for the meter had been fined at all.

In *Roberts* v. *Powell* (1966), 64 L.G.R. 173, it was held, on the terms of a particular order, that where a meter had been temporarily suspended or removed by the local authority a prosecution under the order failed.

Where tickets were issued by a machine for use in an unattended car-park and had to be fixed to the vehicle parked, the fact that the machine *might* be out of order was not a defence to a charge of not fixing a ticket (*Rawlinson* v. *Broadley* (1969), 113 S.J. 310).

There is an article on parking meters at [1962] Crim.L.R. 947. On and after 1st January, 1963, parking meters first installed at a parking place in England or Wales must be of a design and type approved by the Minister of Transport (Parking Meters (Type and Design Approval) (Appointed Day) Order, 1962 (S.I. 1962 No. 947).)

" Bank holiday " in a parking order means an official public holiday, not a day when the banks have shut pursuant to a royal proclamation (*O'Neill* v. *George* (1969), 113 S.J. 128).

When operative, ss. 1 and 2 of the Road Traffic Act, 1974, together with the related Sched. 1 to that Act, will fix the liability for the payment of excess meter charges and offences for which fixed penalty notices have been issued in the first instance on the owner of the vehicle (see Vehicle Owner Liability, pp. 584–593).

What Amounts to Obstruction

Obstruction can be caused by actual physical obstruction of an essential line of traffic, e.g., taking up half of a narrow, busy road, so that single-line working has to be employed. Or it may be unreasonable use of the right of stopping even though there is plenty of room for other traffic to pass. An example of the former is *Wall* v. *Williams* [1966] Crim.L.R. 50, where a vehicle making a forbidden " U " turn in a very crowded street held up the traffic for fifty seconds; the conviction under (what is now) reg. 114 was upheld.

While there is obviously an offence if there is a serious obstruction in fact, unreasonable use of the highway calculated to obstruct and whereby persons might be obstructed may suffice for a conviction without evidence that anyone has actually been obstructed (*Gill* v. *Carson* (1917), 81 J.P. 250, a case under the 1847 Act, s. 28). In *Nagy* v. *Weston* [1965] 1 All E.R. 78 parking a van for five minutes in a wide, busy street near a bus stop and refusing to move was held to be an obstruction under s. 121.

Lord Parker, C.J., said that, *while there must be proof of unreasonable use, whether or not user amounting to an obstruction was or was not unreasonable use was a question of fact, depending on all the circumstances, including the length of time the obstruction continued, the place where it occurred, the purpose for which it was done and whether it caused an actual as opposed to a potential obstruction.* These words of Lord Parker, C.J., as quoted were expressly approved by Ashworth, J., in *Evans* v. *Barker* [1971] R.T.R. 453, on p. 456, where it was held, following *Solomon* v. *Durbridge, infra,* that leaving a car for a reasonable time, although amounting to an obstruction, did not amount to an unnecessary obstruction within the meaning of reg. 114 of the Construction and Use Regulations. The facts were that the defendant had left his car on a Wednesday, which was the market day, between 2.45 p.m. and 4 p.m. in Welsh Walls, Oswestry, leaving 20 feet of the width of the road clear. The justices' finding that this was not an " unnecessary " obstruction was upheld by the Divisional Court. It is primarily a question of fact, applying a test such as is adduced by Lord Parker as quoted, whether the circumstances in which a car is left are " unreasonable ". If the obstruction is " unreasonable " it would appear to be " unnecessary " within the meaning of reg. 114. In *Absalom* v. *Martin* [1974] R.T.R. 145, a bill poster parked his van with two wheels on a footpath and the other two on the roadway while posting a bill. The justices found as a fact that the obstruction was not an unreasonable use of the highway and their dismissal of a charge under s. 121 (1) of the Highways Act, 1959, was upheld by the High Court who again cited with approval the words of Lord Parker, C.J., in *Nagy* v. *Weston* set out above. The court reserved for a future occasion whether it is more difficult to justify reasonable use when parking on a footpath rather than on the carriageway. In *Pitcher* v. *Lockett* (1966), 64 L.G.R. 477, it was held that it was not a reasonable use of the highway to park a van on a busy road to sell hot dogs from it. It was said also that, normally, if what is done is nothing to do with the passage to and fro, that is not making a use of the highway which is reasonable, but that a milkman on his rounds was making a reasonable use of the road even though he might occasionally sell a bottle of milk. Whether particular facts amount to an unreasonable use would depend very much on the magistrates' local knowledge of the importance of the particular road; a long stay may not be out of order in a quiet residential side road, but it would be otherwise in a busy shopping street. An obstruction only comes into existence if there is an unreasonable use of the right of stopping (*Nagy* v. *Weston, supra*), and it is a matter of degree (*Dunn* v. *Holt* (1904), 68 J.P. 271). In *Gill's* case a vehicle had been left unattended for five minutes in such a position as to block one out of four lines of traffic in a street carrying a tram route, and the High Court held that those facts showed no evidence of unreasonable use of the highway; it was added, however, that, had the vehicle been left for a long period, there would have been an obstruction. In *Dunn's* case, where there was an acquittal, no one was obstructed and the vehicle, though stationary for several hours, took up less than 3 feet in a carriageway 30 feet wide. It is doubtful how far *Dunn's* case is still of authority in relation to obstructions lasting several hours. In *Absalom* v. *Martin* the nearest public car park was several hundred yards away, the defendant parked partly on the carriageway and partly on the footpath and was endeavouring to carry on his business of bill posting in such a way as to cause the least inconvenience to pedestrians and other road users. A defendant who sold fruit from a barrow for fifteen minutes, the barrow taking up 5 feet in a 24 foot road and customers causing further obstruction, was held to have been rightly convicted, as continuous selling does not mean that the barrow was not standing longer than was necessary (*Whiteside* v. *Watson* [1952] S.L.T. 367). In *Bego* v. *Gardner* [1933] S.L.T. 110 the conviction was upheld of a man who sold ices from his van parked in a cul-de-sac frequented by the public. Leaving a car unattended for three hours, which was found to cause danger to the public and annoyance to the residents but which was not specifically found to cause an obstruction, was held to constitute the offence of leaving a car unattended for longer than was necessary to load or unload it (*Henderson* v. *Gray* [1927] S.C.(J.) 43). A motorist parked his car in a line of cars in a street and left it there for five hours. He argued that, as he parked in a line of cars, he was not causing an unnecessary obstruction. The High Court held that he clearly caused one (*Solomon* v. *Durbridge* (1956), 120 J.P. 231). In *Gelberg* v. *Miller* [1961] 1 All E.R. 291, at pp. 295–296, it was said that to leave a car for the luncheon period in Jermyn Street, London, was plainly an obstruction. Parking for five hours on a grass verge between the footpath and the wall was held to cause an unnecessary obstruction in *Worth* v. *Brooks* (1959), *The Times*, 13th October, but in *Police* v. *O'Connor* [1957] Crim.L.R. 478, quarter sessions held that it was not an unreasonable use of the highway to park a large vehicle outside the driver's own house in a cul-de-sac. In *Worth's* case it was said that, if a car was immobile through a breakdown, the obstruction might be "necessary". In *London Borough of Redbridge* v. *Jaques* [1971] 1 All E.R. 260 it was held that the fact that a street trader had for many years sold from a fruit stall erected on the back of his stationary vehicle without objection from the local authority and without inconveniencing the public use of the highway was not a reason for dismissing a charge of wilful obstruction under s. 121 of the Highways Act. This case was applied in *Cambridgeshire County Council* v. *Rust* [1972] 3 All E.R. 232, where it was held not to be a "lawful excuse" for a person, prosecuted under s. 127 of the Highways Act, 1959, for setting up a stall on the highway, to believe he could lawfully do so because he made reasonable enquiries and had paid rates on the stall to the district council. Once a highway always a highway, and a council cannot grant a licence to perform an unlawful act.

Scotland.—The judgment of the Sheriff-Substitute in *Macmillan* v. *Gibson* [1966] S.L.T.(Sh.) 84 suggests that, when there is no actual physical obstruction, a conviction should follow only if it has been brought to the motorist's attention, e.g., by a police warning or by a notice or sign, that there is a regulation against the stopping of vehicles in the particular street, i.e., that the obligation imposed on the driver is not absolute but the prosecutor should show *mens rea*. That case (see p. 393) concerned parking in breach of byelaws, not of reg. 114, and *Watson* v. *Ross* (1920), 1 S.L.T. 65, on which reliance was placed, concerned a charge of standing longer than necessary.

It was held in *Arrowsmith* v. *Jenkins* [1963] 2 All E.R. 210, a case of causing a crowd to collect, that, if a person intentionally by exercise of his will does something which causes an obstruction of a highway, this constitutes wilful obstruction under s. 121 and it is no defence that the person believes that he has genuine authority to do what he is doing if he has not lawful authority or reasonable excuse.

In *Seekings* v. *Clarke* (1961), 59 L.G.R. 268, a case under s. 121 of the Highways Act, 1959, not involving a motor vehicle, it was said that anything which substantially prevented the public from passing over the whole of the highway (including the footway) and which was not purely temporary was an unlawful obstruction, subject to an exception on the *de minimis* principle. This case is discussed in *Wolverton U.D.C.* v. *Willis* [1962] 1 All E.R. 243.

The driver of a slow vehicle does not "negligently interrupt the free passage" of overtaking vehicles merely because they have to go to the offside of the road to pass him (*Sleith* v. *Godfrey* (1920), 85 J.P. 46). In a case noted at 85 J.P.Jo. 500, the High Court upheld the conviction for obstruction where a lorry driver refused to draw into his nearside but drove along the centre of the road so that traffic could not overtake him.   Obstruction of the footway can be an offence under the Regulations (*Bryant* v. *Marx* (1932), 96 J.P. 383).   Other earlier cases on obstruction, mainly civil, are collected at E. & E. Dig., Repl. vol. 26, p. 466 *et seq.*   On a charge of having deposited without lawful authority or excuse anything on a highway in consequence whereof a user of the highway was injured or endangered, it is no defence that it was commercially convenient to do so (*Gatland* v. *Metropolitan Police Commissioner* [1968] 2 All E.R. 100—hopper, 6 feet wide, left at night on 43-foot-road, only place where it could conveniently be placed). Builders' skips became, however, subject to control by ss. 31 and 32 of the Highways Act, 1971, on 17th January, 1972 (see p. 399).

The right of an occupier of premises abutting on a highway to make use of it for the purpose of obtaining access to his premises and of loading and unloading goods there is subject to the right of the public to use the highway (*Vanderpant* v. *Mayfair Hotel Co.* (1930), 94 J.P. 23, a civil case).   In *Trevett* v. *Lee* [1955] 1 All E.R. 406, a civil case, a landowner laid a small hosepipe across the road to other land; it was held that whether or not he was obstructing the highway was to be judged by reasonableness both from his point of view and from that of other members of the public.   In *Marr* v. *Turpie*, Jo.Crim.L. (1949) 416, the High Court of Justiciary upheld the conviction of a motorist who had left his car for thirty minutes outside his own premises in a narrow street.   The question whether a moving vehicle can be said to " stand " on a road within the meaning of reg. 114 of the Construction and Use Regulations was raised but not decided in *Carpenter* v. *Fox* (1929), 93 J.P. 239; Lord Hewart, C.J., thought, however, that it was not a very strong argument to say that a moving vehicle was not " standing ".   The fact that someone is left in charge of a vehicle does not prevent there being an offence of obstruction if there is in fact an obstruction (*Hinde* v. *Evans* (1906), 70 J.P. 548).

An act which in fact causes an obstruction cannot be justified by the motive or purpose which inspires or induces its commission (*W. R. Anderson (Motors), Ltd.* v. *Hargreaves* [1962] 1 All E.R. 129). It is submitted, however, that to constitute an offence the obstruction must be unlawful and the motive might make it not unlawful because it is a necessary or reasonable obstruction, e.g., a fire engine where there is no other place from which it can operate; *aliter*, if there is some such place and it is not moved to it within a reasonable time.

When lorries were parked on a grass verge and the drivers went

to a café to get meals, it was held that they did not obstruct the
highway merely by a temporary call for a legitimate purpose
provided that they did not stop in a place where the mere presence
of a stationary vehicle would create an obstruction (*Rodgers* v.
Ministry of Transport [1952] 1 All E.R. 634).   But to leave a large
roller on the highway, even when it belongs to the owner of the land
on each side, is not a reasonable use of the highway (*Wilkins* v.
Day (1883), 48 J.P. 6).   (As to the parking of vehicles on verges
now see s. 36A and s. 36B of the Road Traffic Act, 1972, on p. 395).
In *Baxter* v. *Middlesex County Council* [1956] Crim.L.R. 561, a forecourt was held on the facts not to be part of the highway; it was
used as a display park for cars.   A claim by an innkeeper for standing his guests' vehicles on the highway cannot be supported, even
though it has been so used for more than twenty years (*Gerring* v.
Barfield (1864), 28 J.P. 615).   If a local authority have designated
part of a street as a parking place under the Public Health Act,
1925, s. 68, or other legislation, no offence of unnecessary obstruction
is committed by leaving vehicles in that part during the period
allowed by the order and the motive in leaving them there, e.g.,
to relieve congestion in the owner's premises, is irrelevant (*W. R.
Anderson (Motors), Ltd.* v. *Hargreaves* [1962] 1 All E.R. 129) but it is
submitted that if the vehicle is parked in such a way as to cause a
physical obstruction in a busy street where proper parking would
not cause it, then the offender could properly be charged notwithstanding the street's designation for parking.   If a vehicle
breaks down and causes an obstruction, there is no wilful obstruction, it seems, if the driver does his best to get it moved out of the
way within a reasonable time (*Original Hartlepool Collieries* v. *Gibb*
(1877), 41 J.P. 660).   A van driver who stops it to sell ices has not
" pitched a stall on the highway " contrary to the Highways Act,
1959, s. 127 (*Divito* v. *Stickings* [1948] 1 All E.R. 207).   A bus
driver who left a bus in the road and went off duty without giving
its charge to any other person caused an obstruction under reg. 114
(*Ellis* v. *Smith* [1962] 3 All E.R. 954).   In *Reed* v. *Wastie and Another*
[1972] Crim.L.R. 221, an arrest of a lorry driver whose vehicle was
standing on the motorway was held justified under s. 121 of the
Highways Act, 1959, as it was an obstruction of a highway.

" No waiting " Streets

Local Acts and orders sometimes permit vehicles to stop in
" no-waiting " streets while loading or unloading goods.   The
question was raised but not decided in *Kirkland* v. *Cairns* [1951]
S.C.(J.) 61, whether the goods must be limited to those not sold

from the vehicle; in that case fish and chips were sold from the vehicle. In *Whiteside* v. *Watson* [1952] S.L.T. 367 it was doubted if selling to customers is " unloading ". " Unloading " was held by a Metropolitan magistrate to include taking a large sum of money from a car into a bank (Jo.Crim.L. (1952) 193). Money in bulk can be " goods " (112 J.P.Jo. 49, Q.S.). It is not " loading goods " to put a small parcel in a private car, but it might be if an object not easily portable was put in a car, e.g., a laundry basket or several chairs (*Sprake* v. *Tester* (1955), 53 L.G.R. 194). A Metropolitan magistrate has held that, where a van is left in a restricted street for eighteen minutes and during most of that time the driver is not engaged in loading or unloading, he is not within an exemption for delivering or loading, etc. The van must be engaged, as distinct from the driver, in loading or delivering during the whole time. Further, the regulations in question required the driver to be with the van all the time (102 S.J. 358). In *McLeod* v. *Wajkowska* [1963] S.L.T. (Notes) 51, it was held that an exemption in an order for loading and unloading goods extended to taking goods from the vehicle into premises and depositing them there. Where an order permits waiting " while loading ", the defendant must show that his actions were covered by the latter words; if he had merely been asking customers if they had goods for loading but no goods had been loaded, he was not within the permission (*Holder* v. *Walker* [1964] Crim.L.R. 61). A Metropolitan magistrate has held that waiting in expectation of a load is not within the exemption ([1963] Crim.L.R. 706). In *Chafen* v. *Another*, Supplement to the *Justice of the Peace and Local Government Review*, 21st March, 1970, it was held that an exemption for the loading or unloading of goods did not extend to leaving a vehicle for so long as might be necessary for the goods to be located. No criticism could be made of a finding that thirty-five minutes' parking was unreasonable. It was held in *Hunter* v. *Hammond* [1964] Crim.L.R. 145 to be no defence to a charge of waiting for longer than the permitted period that the defendant was delayed by having to dry his coat, when coffee had been spilt upon it. Nor is it a defence to a charge of breach of a no-waiting order that a taxi-driver would otherwise find it very difficult to carry on his legitimate business (*Levinson* v. *Powell* [1967] 3 All E.R. 796). Orders forbade waiting in roads *A* and *B* but exempted unloading; a driver unloaded goods outside premises in *A* and then moved to *B* to park there, as *B* was a wider road. He was held guilty, as the unloading was finished even though the business connected with it was not; on the facts the High Court recommended leniency (*Pratt* v. *Hayward* [1969] 3 All E.R. 1094).

Where an order in respect of a no-waiting street forbade a vehicle to wait but contained an exemption for waiting " for so long as may be necessary to enable any person to board or alight from the vehicle ", it was held that this allowed a car to stop for only so long as necessary to allow someone to get in or out; taking parcels into a nearby house and returning, all within five minutes, was not within the exemption (*Clifford-Turner* v. *Waterman* [1961] 3 All E.R. 974). In *Kaye* v. *Hougham* (1964), 62 L.G.R. 457, it was likewise held not to be within that exemption where a taximan went to get change for a £5 note from his fare at the end of the fare's journey, but it was said that prosecutions should not be brought in such circumstances. The relevant order should always be scrutinised to see the precise form of exemption. A case of a constable purporting to give herself permission to park in a " no-waiting " area is discussed at 131 J.P.Jo. 627.

The prosecution need not show that the defendant's conduct in parking did not fall within any of the exemptions, such as unloading; it is for the defendant to establish that the waiting was for a per-mitted purpose (*Funnell* v. *Johnson* [1962] Crim.L.R. 488).

These and other traffic regulation orders are made under ss. 1 to 8 of the Road Traffic Regulation Act, 1967 (replacing ss. 26 and 34 of the Road Traffic Act, 1960, and other provisions); these provisions are amended by the Transport Act, 1968, s. 126. The Heavy Commercial Vehicles (Controls and Regulations) Act, 1973, added two new subsections (3AA) and (3AB) to s. 1. These subsections enable county councils to make orders specifying through routes for heavy commercial vehicles and prohibiting or restricting their use in specified zones or on particular roads. The same Act also added s. 1A which requires the local authority to formulate proposals for such control of heavy commercial vehicles. The penalty for breach of a traffic regulation order, where the breach is proceeding or not proceeding in a specified direction or along a specified part of the carriageway, or otherwise is now £100 (ss. 1 (8) and 6 (9), as amended by the Act of 1974). There is now no difference in the penalty between breach of a one-way street and any other type of order made under the statutory provisions referred to. By s. 1 (5), relating to places outside Greater London, an order may not restrict access to premises adjoining the road at any time for persons on foot and for no more than eight hours out of every twenty-four in respect of vehicles; if it does, presumably it is *ultra vires* to that extent. Further, by s. 1 (3), outside Greater London a traffic regulation order imposing restrictions on waiting shall not apply to a stage carriage or express carriage, viz., a bus or coach carrying passengers at separate fares (not one used to carry an employer's workmen free or, it seems, a bus company's bus not actually carrying passengers, e.g., returning empty to the depôt). A no-waiting order presumably does not affect a bus or coach in service to carry passengers for fares but does otherwise. By s. 15 of the Road Traffic Regulation Act, 1967, orders may be made determining the highways which may be or may not be used by public service vehicles, viz., ones carrying passengers for hire or reward; the section prescribes no penalty and it is argued at 132 J.P.Jo. 664 that breach of it would be disobedience to traffic sign 621 and an offence against s. 14 of the Road Traffic Act, 1960 (now s. 22 of the Road Traffic Act, 1972). However, it can also be argued that, as s. 15 lays down no penalty, breach of order can be dealt with only by proceedings on indictment (Archbold (38 ed., §10, p. 4.) 6) or by injunction or complaint to the Traffic Commissioners; see p. 298 as to disobedience to signs not being an offence. The Transport Act, 1968, s. 128, amends s. 15.

The former restrictions on prosecutions by the police or private persons in respect of orders and byelaws made under the Public Health Act, 1925, s. 68, or the Road Traffic Act, 1960, s. 81, were removed by the Road Traffic and Roads Improvement Act, 1960, s. 11. Any person or constable may now bring such a prosecution.

Signs.—If signs to indicate the effect of a " No-waiting " order have not been erected or signs have been erected not conforming to s. 54 of the Road Traffic Regulation Act and the Traffic Signs Regulations and General Directions, 1964, no offence against the " No-waiting " order is committed (*MacLeod* v. *Hamilton* [1965] S.L.T. 305). See also *Davies* v. *Heatley*, on p. 311. Even though the Highway Code may give a different impression, a single yellow line supplemented by the authorised indication of the duration of the prohibition is sufficient indication that parking is prohibited on a Sunday as well as working days, and a conviction will be directed if the local order so prohibits parking on a Sunday (*Derrick* v. *Ryder* [1972] R.T.R. 480). In *James* v. *Cavey* [1967] 1 All E.R. 1048 a motorist parked at 6 a.m., when the sign indicated that parking was permitted under an " alternative day waiting " order. At 9 a.m. the sign was changed to forbid parking. It was held that, as the sign did not forbid parking when he left his car, he committed no offence under the order by waiting after 9 a.m. The placing of signs to mark the effect of orders is discretionary in Greater London and mandatory elsewhere, though this position can be changed by Regulation (*Cooper* v. *Hall* (1967), 111 S.J. 928). In *Macmillan* v. *Gibson* [1966] S.L.T.(Sh.) 84 a person parked his vehicle in breach of byelaws made under the

Roads and Bridges Act, 1878; as there were no notices to warn him of the byelaws and no evidence that he knew of them, he was acquitted. It is possible that the application of *Cooper* v. *Hall*, *supra*, in London may have been affected by s. 126 (7) of the Transport Act, 1968.

For the purposes of a traffic regulation order made under the Road Traffic Regulation Act, 1967, s. 1, traffic signs shall be deemed to be lawfully in place unless the contrary is proved, and certain other evidential presumptions may be made (Transport Act, 1968, Sched. 14).

In *Kierman* v. *Howard* [1971] Crim.L.R. 286 it was held that a local authority had erected signs near the road ". . . where parking was allowed" in accordance with reg. 17 (1) (*f*) of the Local Authorities' Traffic Orders (Procedure) (England and Wales) Regulations, 1969 (S.I. 1969 No. 463), when the only signs they had erected informing motorists of a disc parking scheme were at the entrances to and exits from the zone. "Near" should be interpreted in the light of all the circumstances and in the case of a zone or area could be aptly treated as meaning at the entrance to the zone or area (*ibid.*).

A byelaw prohibited "stopping" in a street between 4 p.m. and 6 p.m. A driver left his car there before 4 p.m. and it remained after that hour. It was held that he was not guilty as the byelaw made no reference to remaining at rest (*R.* v. *Oliver* (1958), 119 C.C.C. 394, a Canadian case).

The Metropolitan police have special powers to arrest persons obstructing the highway who refuse their names and addresses; refusal is not otherwise obstructing the police (*Gelberg* v. *Miller* [1961] 1 All E.R. 291).

Clearways

The Various Trunk Roads (Prohibition of Waiting) (Clearways) Order, 1963 (S.I. 1963 No. 1172) (see p. 730), and the like London Order (S.I. 1963 No. 1347) forbid vehicles to stop on the main carriageways of certain named roads unless with police permission, for building, road or public utility works, fire, ambulance or police purposes, postal collections and deliveries or local authority cesspool and refuse vehicles, to close gates and barriers, to avoid accidents or in circumstances beyond the driver's control. "Main carriageway" means any carriageway of that road primarily used by through traffic and excludes lay-bys. The acceleration lanes at the junction of minor roads with the clearway would appear to be excluded from the operation of the order by this definition.

A vehicle may not wait on a lay-by or verge of any such named road for the purpose of selling goods from that vehicle unless they are at once delivered to premises adjacent to that vehicle. Other clearways orders have been made.

Breach of a clearways order is punishable under s. 1 (8) (or in the case of the London Order s. 6 (9)) of the Road Traffic Regulation Act, 1967, with a fine of £100 for a first or subsequent offence. No endorsement or disqualification may be ordered.

Parking on Verges, Footpaths and Central Reservations

The Heavy Commercial Vehicles (Controls and Regulations) Act, 1973, inserted a new section (s. 36A) in the Act of 1972 prohibiting the parking of heavy commercial vehicles on verges, footpaths or central reservations of roads, and the Act of 1974 inserted a similar section (s. 36B) prohibiting the parking of vehicles other than heavy motor vehicles on the verges, footpaths or central reservations of " urban roads ".

A heavy commercial vehicle is defined by s. 36A (5) as any vehicle whether mechanically propelled or not which is constructed or adapted for the carriage of goods (see p. 333) and has an unladen weight exceeding three tons. Under s. 36A (6) to (8) the Secretary of State may by Regulation amend this definition. Under s. 36A (3A) the Secretary of State may exempt certain classes of vehicle from the provisions of s. 36A or apply the section subject to specified conditions.

Section 36B applies to all vehicles other than heavy commercial vehicles and makes it an offence for a person to park a vehicle on the verge, central reservation or footpath of an " urban road ". " Urban road " is defined as a road subject to a speed-limit not exceeding 40 m.p.h. imposed by s. 71 or s. 74 of the Road Traffic Regulation Act, 1967, or any local Act.

The prohibition under s. 36A or 36B applies to " the verge " of the road, " any land which is situated between two carriageways . . ." of the road and any " footway ", i.e., a way over which the public have a right on foot only and which is comprised in a highway consisting of a carriageway (see s. 295 of the Highways Act, 1959).

Provided it is not left unattended, it is a defence to a charge under either section if the vehicle was parked for loading or unloading on the footway or verge and the loading or unloading could only be satisfactorily performed by being so parked. It is also a defence to either section if the vehicle was parked with police permission or for life saving, fire fighting or in a like emergency.

Local authorities may prosecute offenders under s. 36A and
s. 36B. A first or subsequent offence under either section is punishable with a fine of £100. There is no power of imprisonment,
nor are the offences endorsable or disqualifiable. Evidence may
be given by way of certificate under s. 181 of the Act of 1972 (see
p. 69) and proof of identity of the driver may be given by s. 183
(see p. 107). Local authorities can make orders either wholly
exempting, or partially exempting during specified hours, roads
in their area from the operation of s. 36A.

Removal of Vehicles

By s. 19 (1) of the Civic Amenities Act, 1967, any person who,
without lawful authority, abandons on any land in the open air,
or on any other land forming part of a highway, a motor vehicle
or anything which formed part of a motor vehicle and was removed
from it in the course of dismantling the vehicle on the land, is
liable to a fine of £100 and on second or subsequent conviction
to a fine of £200 or three months' imprisonment or both. By s. 19
(2), a person who leaves anything on any land in such circumstances
or for such a period that he may reasonably be assumed to have
abandoned it or to have brought it to the land for the purpose of
abandoning it there shall be deemed to have abandoned it there
or, as the case may be, to have brought it to the land for that
purpose unless the contrary is shown. Proof of the contrary seems
to be on the defendant. The offence does not carry disqualification or endorsement but may be prosecuted by any person, e.g.,
an aggrieved landowner. In view of the wording of s. 19 (2), it
may be that the time-limit for proceedings runs from the date of
the leaving of the vehicle and that the offence is not a continuing
one; cf. *R* v. *Boulden* (1957), 41 Cr.App.R. 105; *Vaughan* v. *Biggs*
[1960] 2 All E.R. 473. " Motor vehicle " is widely defined in
s. 27 (1) as including trailers and contraptions which have ceased
to be motor vehicles under the Road Traffic Act.

By ss. 20 to 22 as amended by Sched. 19 to the Local Government Act, 1972, power is given to local authorities to remove
vehicles appearing to have been abandoned on any land in the open
air or on any other land forming part of a highway, to dispose of
abandoned vehicles and to recover their expenses.

" Abandon ", according to the Concise Oxford Dictionary,
means to give up or forsake; it is not " abandoning children in a
manner likely to cause them unnecessary suffering " to leave them
in Chatham Juvenile Court whilst in session (*R.* v. *Whibley* [1938]
3 All E.R. 777).

Further powers of removing and disposing of vehicles are given by the Road Traffic Regulation Act, 1967, ss. 20, 52 and 53, as amended by the Removal and Disposal of Vehicles (Alteration of Enactments) Order, 1967 (S.I. 1967 No. 1900), and by the Removal and Disposal of Vehicles Regulations, 1968 (S.I. 1968 No. 43) and Sched. 19 to the Local Government Act, 1972.

Driving on the Footway and on Common or Private Land

Under the Highway Act, 1835, s. 72, it is an offence to drive on the footway, even though the driving may last for only a few seconds (*M'Arthur* v. *Jack* [1950] S.C.(J.) 29). Driving across the footway to get to a private car park was held to be an offence in the absence of proof of long user or of its being a way of necessity (*Curtis* v. *Geeves* (1930), 94 J.P. 71) but in *Vestry of St. Mary, Newington* v. *Jacobs* (1871), L.R. 7 Q.B. 47, the owner of land adjoining the highway was held to be entitled to convey machinery on trolleys over the pavement into his premises.

The Road Traffic Act, 1972, s. 36, relates to driving motor vehicles on footpaths, bridleways, common land, moorland or other land not part of a road, with an exception for parking within fifteen yards of a road or for emergencies. The penalty is a fine of £20; disqualification and endorsement cannot be ordered. It reads:—

" (1) Subject to the provisions of this section, if without lawful authority a person drives a motor vehicle on to or upon any common land, moorland or other land of whatsoever description, not being land forming part of a road, or on any road being a footpath or bridleway, he shall be guilty of an offence.

(2) It shall not be an offence under this section to drive a motor vehicle on any land within fifteen yards of a road, being a road on which a motor vehicle may lawfully be driven, for the purpose only of parking the vehicle on that land.

(3) (*No offence in emergencies such as fire and rescue.*)

(4) (*Saving for s. 193 of the Law of Property Act, 1925, and byelaws and for law of trespass.*)"

The effect of s. 36, it is submitted, is that a motorist may drive on common or moorland off a public road for 15 yards, so long as he intends to park; if he goes more than 15 yards, he commits an offence whether he parks or not. If he goes on private land, he commits no offence so long as he parks there and does not go more than 15 yards, although the landowner does not consent to the vehicle going on the land; the landowner should sue for trespass. If the motorist parks, say, 20 yards from the road on private land, he commits an offence under s. 36 and he also commits an offence if he drives less than 15 yards on private land for the purpose of turning his car round. *Quaere*, if a defence of *de minimis* could be raised for a move lasting four or five seconds only 3 feet up a private drive. It seems to be an offence to drive on private land under s. 36, unless within the exceptions; consequently, motoring trespassers can be prosecuted if, say, they drive up the approach to a country house or a farm purely from motives of curiosity and with no intention of visiting the occupant. The motorists' passengers could be charged if aiding, abetting, counselling and procuring can be proved. Persons coming to a house on lawful business, however, have an implied licence to go through an unlocked gate (if motorists, perhaps not to open a closed gate) and up to the door (*Robson* v. *Hallett* [1967] 2 All E.R. 407) but not, it is suggested, to deviate from a driveway or roadway on to grassland. The opinion is advanced that s. 36 extends to any private land and that such land need not be *ejusdem generis* with a common or moorland—it could be a factory yard or private car-park as well as a field—the words " other land of whatsoever description " being wide enough to exclude the *ejusdem generis* rule (Maxwell on the Interpretation of Statutes, 11th ed., pp. 332–333).

The question is discussed at 125 J.P.Jo. 251 whether s. 36 applies to all footpaths, both those at the side of carriageways and those ways for pedestrians and cyclists only. It is submitted there, following earlier opinions cited, that s. 36 is aimed at persons who drive motor vehicles on footpaths and bridleways which are not at the side of a carriageway and that the section applies to such ways for foot passengers and cyclists in towns as well as in the country. See p. 32 as to offences by cyclists on bridleways and as to the meaning of that term.

The Highway Act, 1835, s. 72, *supra*, applies to footpaths at the side of a road.

Certain local authority vehicles are exempt (Public Health Act, 1961, s. 49; Vehicles (Conditions of Use on Footpaths) Regulations, 1963 (S.I. 1963 No. 2126) and 1966 (S.I. 1966 No. 864)).

The Law of Property Act, 1925, s. 193 (4), penalises with a fine of £20 (Criminal Justice Act, 1967, Sched. 3) any person who without lawful authority draws or drives upon any metropolitan common, manorial waste, common wholly or partly within a borough or urban district, or any land subject to rights of common to which the section may be applied under s. 193 (2), any carriage, cart, caravan, truck or other vehicle or who camps or lights a fire thereon.

Builders' Skips

The Highways Act, 1971, s. 31 (1) and (3), makes it an offence, punishable with a fine of £100 to be the " owner " (see definition below) of a builder's skip which has been deposited on the highway without permission of the highway authority. It is also an offence punishable by a fine of £100 for the owner to fail to comply with a condition imposed by the permission or to fail to secure that the skip is properly lighted at night, to fail to remove the skip as soon as practicable after it has been filled and to fail to secure that the skip is clearly and indelibly marked with his name and address or telephone number.

Under s. 31 (5) proceedings may be taken against any other person whose act or default resulted in the offence being committed whether or not proceedings are also taken against the owner.

It is a defence to a charge under s. 31 that the commission of the offence was due to the act or default of another and that the defendant took all reasonable precautions and exercised all due diligence to avoid the commission of the offence (s. 31 (6)). To avail oneself of the defence notice has to be given to the prosecutor seven clear days before the hearing identifying that other person (s. 31 (7)). A defendant giving notice under s. 31 (7) identifying that other person has to give as full information as he was able honestly to provide in accordance with the facts in his possession at the time he gave the notice (*Barnet London B.C.* v. *S. & W. Transport Ltd.* [1975] Crim.L.R. 171). It was held in *Lambeth London B.C.* v. *Saunders Transport, Ltd.* [1974] R.T.R. 319 that the owner of a skip who had hired it out could avail himself of the defence as he had taken all reasonable precautions and had used due diligence to see that the hirers were aware of their duties as to lighting it. The purpose of s. 31 (6) was to provide a defence for owners of skips who were accustomed to hire out skips and took the necessary steps to see that the hirers complied with their duties such as lighting (*ibid.*). Section 31 (11) defines a builder's skip as a container designed to be carried on a road vehicle and to be placed on a highway or other land for the storage of builder's materials, or for the removal and disposal of builder's rubble, waste, household and other rubbish or earth. " Owner " is defined as the hirer where the skip is hired for not less than one month or is hired under a hire purchase agreement.

Negligent Opening of Car Doors

It is convenient to mention here prosecutions of motorists and their passengers who suddenly open a car door and strike a passing cyclist or pedestrian. The position is now covered, so far as motor vehicles and trailers are concerned, by reg. 117 of the Motor Vehicles (Construction and Use) Regulations, 1973, discussed *infra*. Prosecutions may still be brought under the Highway Act, 1835, s. 78, however, and persons on cycles and in horse-drawn vehicles who cause hurt can only be charged under that Act. They should not be charged under the limb of s. 78 of the Highway Act, 1835, which deals with drivers on the highway causing hurt by negligence; that limb is concerned with negligence in driving and not with things done after the vehicle has stopped (*Shears* v. *Matthews* [1948] 2 All E.R. 1064). But the driver or any passenger who opens a car door in a negligent way may be convicted of interrupting by negligence the free passage of a person or vehicle on the highway under another limb of s. 78 (*Watson* v. *Lowe* [1950] 1 All E.R. 100). Where a defendant had taken precautions to see if traffic was coming and nevertheless an accident occurred when he opened the door, it was held on those facts that he should not be convicted of " wilful obstruction " (*Eaton* v. *Cobb* [1950] 1 All E.R. 1016). It may be that the "interrupting by negligence " limb of s. 78 covers cases where cigarette ash is carelessly flicked into a cyclist's face causing him to have an accident. " Car door " accidents, if a person or animal is injured or another vehicle damaged, should be reported to the police by the driver where s. 25 or s. 166 of the Road Traffic Act, 1972, applies (*Jones* v. *Prothero* [1952] 1 All E.R. 434). See p. 348. A passenger may properly be convicted of hindering the free passage of a person on the highway by negligently opening a car door (*Baldwin* v. *Pearson* (1958), 122 J.P. 321).

Regulation 117 of the Motor Vehicles (Construction and Use) Regulations, 1973, reads:—

" No person shall open or cause or permit to be opened any door of a motor vehicle or trailer on a road so as to cause injury or danger to any person."

The Regulation applies to any person, e.g., a commissionaire, as well as to people in the vehicle. It applies only on a road (see p. 26) and it is submitted, as " trailer " is defined in s. 190 (1) of the 1972 Act as a vehicle drawn by a motor vehicle, that it applies to caravans and other trailers only whilst they are attached to a motor vehicle. In *R.* v. *Cowley* [1971] 6 C.L. 257, a case at Middlesex Quarter Sessions, the words " cause injury or danger " were held to be merely descriptive and the summons was thus not held to be bad for duplicity. *Quaere*, if the defendant is liable to conviction if he has not been negligent. While there is a presumption that *mens rea* is required for all offences, this can be displaced by the subject-matter with which the regulation deals. Normally, unless *mens rea* is clearly or by necessary implication ruled out, proof of it is required (*Brend* v. *Wood* (1946), 110 J.P. 317). On the other hand, it can be argued that it is the duty of every door-opener to satisfy himself that no cyclist or other person can possibly be endangered and to make allowance for blind spots in his view behind, e.g., by using another door, so that an almost undischarge-able burden is on the defendant; support for this strict view may come from the need to suppress the mischief at which reg. 117 is obviously aimed, as decisions establishing absolute liability often arise from statutes which strike at an evil affecting the public welfare.

See p. 62 as to drivers in Crown service committing these offences.

The penalty under s. 78 is a fine of £20 (Criminal Justice Act, 1967, Sched. 3), and that under reg. 117 a fine of £100. Dis-qualification, driving test and endorsement may not be ordered.

Leaving Vehicle in Dangerous Position

The Road Traffic Act, 1972, s. 24, replacing s. 16 of the 1960 Act, reads:—

" If a person in charge of a vehicle causes or permits the vehicle or a trailer drawn thereby to remain at rest on a road in such a position or in such condition or in such circumstances as to be likely to cause danger to other persons using the road, he shall be guilty of an offence."

Warning of intended prosecution (see Chapter III) is required (Road Traffic Act, 1972, s. 179) for all vehicles; s. 24 applies to Crown vehicles, trams and trolley vehicles operated under statutory powers, cycles and carts as well as to motor vehicles on roads but not off them.

This includes not only leaving a vehicle just around a blind corner, but also leaving one in a position which is safe while it is at rest but dangerous if it moves (*Maguire* v. *Crouch* (1940), 104 J.P. 445: driver leaving a vehicle without setting the brake so that it ran away). The penalty is a fine of £100 on first or subsequent conviction (Road Traffic Act, 1972, Sched. 4, as amended by the Act of 1974). Disqualification and a driving test may be ordered (1972 Act, s. 93 and Sched. 4), and endorsement must be ordered unless there are special reasons. Section 93 (3) of the Act of 1972 applies (see p. 624: six months' compulsory disqualification if two endorsed disqualifiable offences within three years preceding offence under s. 24, unless, having regard to all the circumstances, there are grounds for mitigating the normal consequences of the

conviction (see p. 688); such disqualification is consecutive to
any other period imposed or previously imposed). The endorsement code for an offence contrary to s. 24 is MS 10.

By reg. 115 of the Construction and Use Regulations, 1973
(p. 839, *infra*), no person shall cause or permit a motor vehicle to
stand on any road during the hours of darkness otherwise than
with its left or near side as close as may be to the edge of the carriageway. Exceptions are (*a*) leave of a policeman in uniform, (*b*) fire,
police, defence and ambulance vehicles, (*c*) car parks, taxi stands
and bus stops, (*d*) one-way streets, and (*e*) vehicles on building
work, repair work or road work (see 118 J.P.Jo. 101). The fine
is £100; disqualification, endorsement and driving test cannot be
ordered. A case is discussed at 131 J.P.Jo. 627 of a policewoman
in uniform purporting to give herself leave to park in a " no-
waiting " area; vehicles used for police purposes are exempt
anyhow under reg. 115.

Mud on Highways

Byelaws are in force in some areas prohibiting the dropping of
mud from a vehicle upon the highway (see [1954] Crim.L.R. 213).
See Local Government Act, 1972, s. 238, for proof of byelaws.

Penalties for Obstruction

The power to disqualify from driving and the power to endorse
a driving licence under ss. 93 and 101 of the 1972 Act do not
extend to obstruction and parking cases and offences under traffic
regulation orders (though they do extend to parking within the limits
of a pedestrian crossing (p. 455) and to leaving in a dangerous
position, *supra*). The penalty under the Highways Act, 1959,
is a fine of £50, under the Town Police Clauses Act, 1847, a fine
of £20 or fourteen days' imprisonment and under the Construction
and Use Regulations a fine of £100. The penalty for stopping on a
clearway or breach of an order made under s. 1 is a fine of £100
(Road Traffic Regulation Act, 1967, s. 1 (8)). All such offences
can only be tried by magistrates. (The fines under the 1847 and
1959 Acts were increased by the Criminal Justice Act, 1967,
Sched. 3; the others were increased by the Act of 1974.)

The Magistrates' Association suggested penalties (see p. 594 and
p. 879) for certain obstruction offences read:

" (a) Dangerous Position: £25
  (b) On zigzags by Pedestrian Crossing: £20
  (c) Obstruction: £8 minimum ".

10. LIGHTS ON VEHICLES

The statute law on this subject is at present wholly contained in ss. 68–82 of the Road Traffic Act, 1972, which repealed and replaced the Road Transport Lighting Act, 1957, the Road Transport Lighting (Amendment) Act, 1958, and the Road Transport Lighting Act, 1967. Most of the subordinate legislation is now contained in the Road Vehicles Lighting Regulations, 1971 (S.I. 1971 No. 694) (for extracts from the Regulations see pp. 731–764) which revoked all the previous numerous lighting Regulations, including the Headlamps Regulations and also those Construction and Use Regulations relating to stop lights and direction indicators.

Section 9 (1) and (2) of the Road Traffic Act, 1974, now in force enables the Secretary of State to include amongst the Construction and Use Regulations made under s. 40 of the Act of 1972 Regulations relating to lights on vehicles and trailers. Section 9 (2) enables any such Regulations to require lights to be displayed under certain conditions or at certain times. This enables Regulations to be made requiring vehicles to display lights during daylight hours and the Road Vehicles (Use of Lights during Daytime) Regulations, 1975, have been made. The text of the Regulations is set out on p. 764. It will be noted that vehicles have to display "obligatory lights" during " poor visibility conditions " (these terms are defined in reg. 1 (2)). " Obligatory lights " include " obligatory headlamps " (see regs. 16 and 17 of the Lighting Regulations on pp. 742, 744), but instead of displaying headlamps motorists by reg. 2 (3) are permitted to display instead of headlamps either two matching fog-lamps or a matching fog-lamp and spot-lamp as may be allowed under reg. 21 or 22. As the Regulations are made under s. 40 of the Act of 1972 (as amended), breach of the Regulations is punishable under s. 40 (5) of the Act of 1972 and not under s. 81 of the Act (as are offences contrary to the Lighting Regulations). Although the maximum fine under both sections is the same (£100), there is no offence of " using " under s. 81 (see *Balfour Beatty & Co., Ltd.* v. *Grindey* on p. 405) but under s. 40 (5) the offence is either " using " or " causing " or " permitting " the vehicle to be used in contravention of the Regulations (see Chapter I for the meaning of those terms).

Sections 68 to 82 of the 1972 Act are prospectively repealed by the 1974 Act but the provision doing so is not yet in force. Even when ss. 68–82 are repealed, s. 9 (4) of the Act of 1974 will enable any Regulations under the repealed provisions to continue in force as if made under s. 40 of the Act of 1972.

" Sunset " means sunset according to local, not Greenwich, time (*Gordon* v. *Cann* (1899), 63 J.P. 324, and see 95 J.P.Jo. 772

as to evidence to determine sunset and sunrise). Some cases on
the reasonableness of local byelaws as to lights are given in the
E. and E. Dig., Repl. vol. 45, pp. 27–28. The words " visible
from a reasonable distance " in s. 1 of the 1957 Act (now s. 68
of the 1972 Act) were held to require no more than that another
road user could see at a distance that there were lights ahead and
not that he should be able to identify the type of vehicle (*Silke*
v. *Whelan* (1939), 73 I.L.T.R. 248). In *Howman* v. *Russell* [1923]
S.L.T. 336 it was held to be no defence that the lamp had blown
out unknown to the driver of a moving vehicle.

The Motor Vehicles (Construction and Use) Regulations, 1973,
reg. 38 (see p. 794) require motor vehicles to be equipped with
such lighting equipment and reflectors as to render the vehicle
capable of being driven on a road at night without contravening
the provisions of the 1972 Act and its Regulations as to the obligatory lamps and reflectors to be carried, but a motor vehicle
" not provided with any front or rear lamp " is exempt; it is
argued at 124 J.P.Jo. 478 that this means that reg. 38 does not
apply where the vehicle is not provided with lamps, e.g., a racing
car, though it would still have to show lights to the front and rear
under the 1972 Act at night. " Motor vehicle " in reg. 38 refers
only to the motive unit of a composite vehicle. It was held in
Johnston v. *Cruickshank* [1962] S.L.T. 409 that provided the drawing unit of an articulated vehicle carries the obligatory front and
rear lamps and reflectors at all times, the rear or superimposed
part of it need not carry lights and reflectors during daylight.
Regulation 97 of the Construction and Use Regulations requires
the lamps and reflectors required under reg. 38 to be maintained
in proper condition at all times, day and night, so that the vehicle
can be driven at night without contravening the 1972 Act and
Regulations under it. The Motor Vehicles (Construction and
Use) (Track Laying Vehicles) Regulations, 1955, as amended, contain a similar provision (reg. 54A) in relation to track laying vehicles.
It is a defence to a charge under reg. 97 or 54A that contravention in respect of use on a road by day arose from a defect in the
lights or reflector which occurred in the course of the journey
during which the contravention occurred or that that contravention arose from a defect in the lights or reflector and, before
it occurred, steps had already been taken to remedy the defect
with all reasonable expedition.

The obligations of the Road Traffic Act, 1972, relating to lights on
vehicles and of the above reg. 97 apply only on a " road " (see p. 26.)

The term " hours of darkness " means the time between half-
an-hour after sunset and half-an-hour before sunrise (1972 Act, s. 82).

Defences

There is no offence of "using" a vehicle contrary to s. 81 (*Balfour Beatty & Co., Ltd.* v. *Grindey* [1974] Crim.L.R. 120). Section 81 of the 1972 Act makes it an offence for any person to "cause or permit" any vehicle to be on any road in contravention of the Act and Regulations or "otherwise to fail to comply" therewith, provided that it is a defence for a driver or person in charge to prove that the offence arose through the negligence or default of some other person whose duty it was to provide the vehicle with a lamp or lamps or reflector. While some of the cases to which this proviso applies are obvious, it does not *per se* exempt a motorist who leaves his car outside his house with the lights burning and then finds that they have been switched off without his knowledge by some naughty boy. Compare *Howman* v. *Russell* [1923] S.L.T. 336, where the cause of the rear lamp going out was that a stone had broken the glass while the car was moving and the driver drove it for only 300 yards further, it being quite impossible for him to have known of the mishap. Yet he was convicted. It is difficult to distinguish between a stone breaking a lamp and a boy switching it off, and it seems that the strictest liability is established by the Road Transport Lighting Act as now re-enacted in the Road Traffic Act, 1972. The whole question of criminal liability under that Act is discussed in the *Journal of Criminal Law*, October, 1955. For a contrary view, see the *Modern Law Review*, 1962, p. 741. *Howman* v. *Russell*, *supra*, was, however, decided on different statutory provisions and it may be distinguishable.

The proviso refers to persons whose duty it is to "provide lamps or reflectors", and s. 81 casts that duty on the person who causes or permits the vehicle to be on any road during the hours of darkness. The proviso is not confined, it is submitted, to cases where lamps have been fitted, as they are to all cars, whether the lamps work or not; the duty is to provide lamps which show light visible from a reasonable distance. Thus, to take one example, a borrower of a car, who unexpectedly found that the lights would not work owing to the car owner's neglect to get the battery recharged or dud bulbs replaced, might have a defence under the proviso where he had the car with the owner's permission and with no foreknowledge of the defects. Also, for the special defence where there is a charge of not illuminating the rear number plate, see *infra*, p. 408, and for not having lighting equipment and reflectors by day, see p. 404.

There have been successful prosecutions for driving without reasonable consideration for other road users where drivers have wilfully refused to reduce strong headlights which have tended to dazzle oncoming traffic. And see *Saville* v. *Bache* on p. 283.

The Act's lighting provisions and the Regulations apply to vehicles of the Crown (s. 188 of the 1972 Act) but regs. 57 to 60 make special provision as to vehicles of the home forces and of visiting forces. By s. 188 the person named by the Government department concerned shall be deemed to be the person who causes or permits the vehicle to be on a road.

The lighting provisions of the Act apply to trolley vehicles but not to trams (s. 197).

See reg. 63 (p. 757) of the 1971 Regulations as to vehicles brought temporarily into Great Britain, reg. 64 (p. 757) as to blue and amber flashing lamps, reg. 65 (p. 759) as to breakdown vehicles and reg. 67 (p. 759) as to vehicles with movable platforms.

General Requirements

The number and position of lamps showing to the front and the requirements relating thereto are prescribed by the 1972 Act, ss. 68 to 77, and Pt. II of the Road Vehicles Lighting Regulations, 1971. As to solo motor cycles and solo cycles and tricycles, see s. 74, as to horse-drawn vehicles, see s. 75, as to overhanging loads, see s. 76 and Pt. VII of the Regulations, as to towed and towing vehicles, see s. 77. Regulation 13 requires front lights exceeding seven watts in power to be extinguished while a vehicle is stationary, with exceptions for enforced stoppages, public service vehicles, interior lights, breakdown vehicles, searchlights on fire engines, military and other public utility vehicles and direction indicators. Spotlights and movable lamps are dealt with by regs. 9 and 10; otherwise, lamps should not be movable by swivelling or deflection (s. 71). Spotlights under the former Regulations are discussed at 116 J.P.Jo. 690, 118 J.P.Jo. 523, 119 J.P.Jo 355 and 120 J.P.Jo. 749.

By s. 74 (*d*) of the 1972 Act, bicycles and tricycles not propelled by mechanical power need not show lights while stationary owing to the exigencies of traffic or to comply with traffic signals or directions, provided they keep as near as possible to the near or left-hand edge of the carriageway. By s. 74 (*c*), in the case of bicycles not having a side-car attached (whether motor cycles or not) and pedal tricycles, no lamp need be carried while the vehicle is being wheeled by a person on foot as near as possible to the near or left-hand edge of the carriageway.

Reflectors are made compulsory by s. 68 (2) of the 1972 Act for all vehicles and are dealt with by Pt. VI of and Sched. 2 to the Regulations save that, by reg. 63, vehicles brought temporarily into Great Britain by persons resident outside the United Kingdom are exempt. Pedal cycles and tricycles, whether with or without side-cars, and solo motor cycles must carry one reflector in addition to the rear lamp (save where that lamp itself serves as a reflector); all other vehicles must carry two reflectors. Reflectors must be kept clean and otherwise comply with the requirements of Pt. VI. Section 77 (1) (c) of the 1972 Act makes provision as to the reflectors where vehicles are being towed and by s. 72 (3) it is enacted that, where a vehicle's tail light is so constructed that, when not showing a light, it is an efficient reflector complying with the Regulations, it shall be treated as being such a reflector when it is, as well as when it is not, showing a light. Section 81 (2) of the 1972 Act makes it an offence to sell, offer for sale or expose for sale any appliance adapted for use as a reflector or tail lamp which offends the Act or Regulations. The penalty is £50. By virtue of reg. 32 reflectors must carry certain markings to show that they comply with the standard laid down by the Regulations.

Reversing white lights are dealt with by Pt. V of the Regulations.

Multi-purpose lamps are allowed by s. 72 of the 1972 Act. By reg. 3, " dual-purpose lamp " means one showing to the front and rear and reg. 7 deals with these.

Rear lights come under ss. 68, 70, 74, 75, 76 and 78 of the 1972 Act, and Pt. IV of and Sched. 1 to the Regulations. Two rear lamps must normally be carried but there are exemptions for passenger vehicles adapted to carry eight or more passengers, exclusive of the driver, and registered before 1st October, 1954, or if not requiring registration, supplied before that date, for pedal cycles, and for motor cycles without side-cars, while vehicles brought temporarily from abroad are dealt with by reg. 63. Part VII of the Regulations relates to overhanging and projecting loads; see also s. 76. Provided the drawing unit of an articulated vehicle carries the obligatory front and rear lamps and reflectors at all times, the rear or superimposed part of it need not carry them during daylight under reg. 38 of the Construction and Use Regulations but appropriate rear lights and reflectors must be on it during darkness (*Johnston* v. *Cruickshank* [1962] S.L.T. 409).

Hand-propelled vehicles come under reg. 61 and by s. 193 (1) of the 1972 Act pedestrian-controlled motor mowers are to be treated as not being motor vehicles.

Miscellaneous

By s. 60 of the Road Traffic Act, 1972, it is an offence to sell or supply a motor vehicle which does not comply with the law's requirements as to lighting equipment and reflectors; see p. 424.

By s. 68 of the 1972 Act lamps must be kept in a clean and efficient condition and properly trimmed.

Illuminating Number Plates

The Road Vehicles (Registration and Licensing) Regulations, 1971, reg. 19 (2) and (for vehicles registered before 1st October, 1938) para. 4 of Sched. 3, make it an offence not to illuminate the rear number plates of vehicles on " public roads ", i.e., roads repairable at the public expense (Vehicles (Excise) Act, 1971, s. 22), the penalty for a first offence being a fine of £20 or in any other case £50. By s. 22 of the latter Act it is a defence for a person charged with such an offence or any other offence of allowing a number plate to be obscured or become not easily distinguishable to prove that he took all reasonable steps to prevent it being obscured or rendered not easily distinguishable (*Printz* v. *Sewell* (1912), 76 J.P. 295, a case on lighting the rear number plate). But this special defence does not apply to charges under the Road Traffic Act, 1972. Rear number plates do not have to be illuminated when a parked vehicle is exempt from displaying lights (Road Vehicles (Registration and Licensing) Regulations, 1971, reg.19 (3)).

Parked Vehicles

Whether or not a parked vehicle is required to display lights no longer varies from locality to locality and there is now one code for displaying lights on parked vehicles applicable throughout the whole of England and Wales. The Regulations (the Road Vehicles Lighting (Standing Vehicles) (Exemption) (General) No. 2 Regulations, 1972 (S.I. 1972 No. 557)) replaced and revoked all the existing Regulations. Parked vehicles are no longer required to display lights provided that the road in question is subject to a speed limit of 30 m.p.h. or lower. The exemption only applies if the vehicle is parked facing the correct way and as near as may be to the left-hand side of the road (or in the case of a one-way street either side of the road) and also no part of the vehicle is within fifteen yards of a highway junction whether that junction is on the same side of the road as the parked vehicle or not. The exemption from lights only applies to passenger vehicles adapted to carry not more than seven passengers exclusive of the driver, goods vehicles having an unladen weight not exceeding 30 cwt. (Home Office Circular 81/1972 is inaccurate in that it states invalid carriages, motor cycles or stationary goods vehicles weighing 30 cwt. or more unladen are not exempted; the regulations exempt goods vehicles which *do not exceed* 30 cwt.), tricycles and pedal cycles (or tricycles). Front and rear lights must be displayed if the vehicle has an overhanging or projecting load to which s. 76 of the Road Traffic Act, 1972, applies. Lights also must be displayed on vehicles to which a trailer is attached. The previous Regulations which allowed parking lights to be displayed on one side of the vehicle have been revoked. The effect of this is that where lights are required by the present Regulations to be displayed on a parked vehicle, that vehicle is required to display all four lights, front and rear.

Headlamps

Part III of the Road Vehicles (Lighting) Regulations, 1971 (see p. 740) governs the use of headlamps. Regulations 14 to 16 prescribe what headlamps shall be carried by what vehicles, reg. 17 allows combined side lamp and headlamp units and reg. 18 requires every headlamp to be securely fixed, adjustable so that when stationary the beam may be adjusted and kept in a clean and efficient condition. Regulation 19 requires matched headlamps to be of the same area and shape, to emit the same colour light and to " dip " or be on main beam simultaneously. Regulation 20 requires all headlamps to emit only white or yellow light.

Regulation 21 governs the use of headlamps by vehicles having four or more wheels. Matched headlamps are required to be lit while a vehicle is in motion on a road during the hours of darkness unless that road has street lamps actually illuminated not more than 200 yards apart. In conditions of fog or snow the driver may use instead of his headlamps either two fog lights or a fog light and a spot light which are level with each other and equally spaced not more than 350 mm. from the outermost part of the vehicle or 400 mm. if the vehicle was first used on or after 1st January, 1971. The effect of reg. 21 (see pp. 745–746) is that a single fog lamp or spot lamp may be used if the matched headlamps are also kept lit. Regulation 22 deals with the use of headlamps for vehicles having two or three wheels and is in similar terms to reg. 21. It similarly requires the illumination of headlamps, or a headlamp, for vehicles moving during the hours of darkness on unlit roads and where a three-wheeled vehicle has matched headlamps it is unlawful for a single fog lamp to be displayed even in conditions of fog or snow unless the matched headlamps are on at the same time.

Stop Lights, Direction Indicators and Hazard Warnings

The maintenance of stop lights and direction indicators is now governed by the Lighting Regulations and no longer by the

Construction and Use Regulations. Perhaps the most important regulation is 76, which reads as follows:—

" Every direction indicator and every stop lamp fitted to a motor vehicle or trailer shall at all times while the vehicle is used on a road be maintained in a clean condition and in good and efficient working order."

The word " fitted " in reg. 76 presumably includes stop lamps and direction indicators actually fitted to a motor vehicle whether or not the other regulations require stop lamps or direction indicators to be fitted to the particular motor vehicle or trailer concerned. Regulations 70 and 71 detail the classes of vehicle and trailers which are required to be fitted with direction indicators, and Sched. 5 specifies the types and dimensions of the direction indicators. Regulation 69 and Sched. 5 specify the requirements as to direction indicators when fitted. Stop lights are dealt with by regs. 72 to 75.

Regulation 77 (p. 764) allows a hazard warning to be fitted enabling direction indicators to flash simultaneously on both sides of the vehicle. The device must incorporate a warning light warning the driver it is in operation. The device may only be used " when the motor vehicle is stationary on a road due to a breakdown of the vehicle or any other vehicle, a road accident or any other emergency, for the purpose of warning other road users by the simultaneous illumination of the indicators of a temporary obstruction on the carriageway of a road." For the text of the Lighting Regulations see pp. 731–764.

Penalties

The penalty for breach of the Act or Regulations under s. 81 is a fine of £100 on first or subsequent conviction (Road Traffic Act, 1972, Sched. 4, as amended by the Act of 1974). Disqualification and endorsement may not be ordered.

Breach of Construction and Use Regulations, e.g. regs. 38 and 97 (see p. 404), and of the Use of Lights during Daytime Regulations (see p. 403) is also punishable with a fine of £100 under s. 40 (5). The Magistrates' Association's suggested penalties for lighting offences are set out on p. 881 (see also p. 594).

11. THE MOTOR VEHICLES (CONSTRUCTION AND USE) REGULATIONS, 1973

These Regulations (S.I. 1973 No. 24) as amended are printed at p. 766 *et seq*. Certain of the regulations to which reference rarely requires to be made are omitted or summarised.

Regulation 3 contains the definitions, and definitions in the 1972 Act also apply where the Regulations do not have a specific one.

Regulation 4 contains exemptions for road rollers and vehicles going to a port for export; it also provides that certain regulations shall apply only to vehicles used on " highways ", a narrower term than " road ".   It was held in *Borthwick* v. *Vickers* [1973] R.T.R. 390 that justices were entitled to use their own knowledge in deciding that a vehicle which contravened reg. 142 when travelling from one local works to another local works in their area necessarily had to make the journey by travelling on public roads.   By reg. 4 (5) certain vehicles registered before the expiration of one year from the making of the Regulations have certain exemptions for five years if complying with the previous regulations.   Other exemptions in reg. 4 are for vehicles in the service of a visiting force and for vehicles on test.   Motor vehicles and trailers brought temporarily into Great Britain are also exempted.   " Temporarily " means " casually " and does not include a trailer brought intermittently but regularly into this country (see *B.R.S.* v. *Wurzal*, on p. 63).   " Works trucks " are exempted from some of the regulations, e.g., reg. 27 (horns) and reg. 61 (wings).   A works truck is defined in reg. 3 as one which is used in " the immediate neighbourhood " of the premises.   It was held that in " the immediate neighbourhood " had to be construed with reference to the amount of user on the road involved.   Land adjacent or nearly adjacent to the main premises may not be in the " immediate neighbourhood " if it nevertheless involves having to travel a considerable distance on a public road (*Hayes* v. *Kingsworthy Foundry Co., Ltd.* [1971] Crim.L.R. 239).   Regulation 4 (10) and (11) qualifies the case of *Wilkinson* v. *Barrett* (1958), 122 J.P. 349 (see p. 9).   The Regulations apply only to wheeled vehicles, not being trolley vehicles, and additional obligations are imposed by the Public Service Vehicles (Equipment and Use) Regulations, 1958 (S.I. 1958 No. 926), as amended in 1966 (S.I. 1966 No. 676) and 1968 (S.I. 1968 No. 826).   Track-laying vehicles are subject to the Motor Vehicles (Construction and Use) (Track Laying Vehicles) Regulations, 1955 (S.I. 1955 No. 990, as amended by like (Amendment) Regulations, S.I. 1957 Nos. 439 and 972 and S.I. 1959 Nos. 2053 and 2231).   Generally, the 1973 Regulations would seem to apply, with certain exceptions as to roads being highways in certain cases (see reg. 4 (4)), only to motor vehicles and trailers while used on a road as defined on p. 26;   strange results would flow if they applied to them off the road.   See s. 40 (5) of the 1972 Act.   The reason why the Regulations do not apply to trams and trolley vehicles is that they were made under s. 64 of the Road Traffic Act, 1960, which, by s. 259, did not apply to such vehicles (see now ss. 40 and 198 of the 1972 Act).

The power to make these Regulations is now contained in s. 40 of the 1972 Act.

As to " roads ", a judge in *Davidson* v. *Adair* [1934] S.C.(J.) 37 did say *obiter* that the offence of quitting a vehicle without setting the brake under reg. 116 could be committed on a common or public seashore; another judge, however, disagreed. Regulation 116 does not now mention " quitting ". The Regulations and definitions are detailed and should always be carefully consulted. Offences under the Regulations are generally for " using " or " causing " or " permitting " use: see pp. 32–51 as to these expressions. Of the cases there cited *Rushton* v. *Martin* [1952] W.N. 258, *F. Austin (Leyton), Ltd.* v. *East* [1961] Crim.L.R. 119 and *Magna Plant, Ltd.* v. *Mitchell* (1966), 110 S.J. 349 (all dangerous condition); *Prosser* v. *Richings* (1936), 100 J.P. 390, *Churchill* v. *Norris* (1938), 158 L.T. 255, *Morrison* v. *Sinclair* [1937] S.L.T.(Sh.) 15, *Gifford* v. *Whittaker* [1942] 1 All E.R. 604, *Windle* v. *Dunning* [1968] 2 All E.R. 46, *Wurzal* v. *Reader Bros., Ltd.* [1974] R.T.R. 383, *Thurrock District Council* v. *L. A. and A. Pinch* [1974] R.T.R. 269, and *Ross Hillman, Ltd.* v. *Bond* [1974] R.T.R. 279 (all overloading); *Adair* v. *Donaldson* [1935] S.L.T. 76, *Muir* v. *Lawrence* [1951] S.L.T.(Sh.) 88, *James* v. *Smee* [1954] 3 All E.R. 273, *Green* v. *Burnett* [1954] 3 All E.R. 273, *Hutchings* v. *Giles* [1955] Crim.L.R. 784, *Clark* v. *Hunter* [1956] S.L.T. 188, *Hart* v. *Bex* [1957] Crim.L.R. 622, *Fransman* v. *Sexton* [1965] *The Guardian,* 9th July, and *Hill & Sons (Botley and Denmead), Ltd.* v. *Hampshire Chief Constable* [1971] Crim.L.R. 538 (all brakes); and *Carmichael & Sons, Ltd.* v. *Cottle* [1971] Crim.L.R. 45 (tyres); *Garrett* v. *Hooper* [1973] R.T.R. 1 (silencer and tyres); *Balfour Beatty & Co., Ltd.* v. *Grindey* [1974] Crim.L.R. 120 (reflectors, lights, windscreen wiper, audible warning instrument) were on these Regulations.

Failure to comply with the Regulations is an offence (*Mogg* v. *Skirton* (1952), 116 J.P.Jo. 351).

The summons should indicate that it is contrary to s. 40 (5) of the 1972 Act and the particular regulation (*Simmons* v. *Fowler* (1950), 48 L.G.R. 623, discussed at 115 J.P.Jo. 322). See generally Oke's Magisterial Formulist, 18th ed., p. 950, and the forms there for the appropriate charge. The prohibition on " use " (as opposed to permitting use) in s. 40 (5) is absolute in the sense that no *mens rea*, apart from user, need be shown unless a regulation is so worded as to show that the exercise of proper care and absence of knowledge are defences, as in the regulations on speedometers and excessive noise (*Green* v. *Burnett, supra*). Where, however, the charge is causing or permitting, this necessarily requires prior knowledge of the unlawful user on the part of the person causing or permitting (see *Ross Hillman, Ltd.* v. *Bond* [1974] R.T.R. 279 and other cases cited on p. 33 *et seq.*). But where a regulation casts a duty only upon the vehicle-owner, it may be that user by another is not an offence (126 J.P.Jo. 93), save so far as it is aiding and abetting. As to the various provisions relating to weighbridges, ascertainment and transmission of weight, plated weights and defences to weight prosecutions, see pp. 16–21.

As to unnecessary obstruction (reg. 114) see p. 383; as to opening car doors (reg. 117) see p. 399; as to maintenance of lights and reflectors (regs. 38 and 97) see p. 404; as to the use of lights in conditions of poor visibility see p. 403.

Crown Vehicles

The Regulations apply to Crown vehicles and drivers and (with the exceptions detailed in reg. 4, p. 774, *infra*) to vehicles and drivers of visiting forces. There are certain exemptions for Crown vehicles of special types (see p. 430).

Land Implements

Opinions as to land implements and crop sprayers appear at 125 J.P.Jo. 314 and 341; " land implement " is defined in reg. 3 (p. 768). An elevator capable by adaptation of being worked by belt and pulley from a tractor but designed to be run and driven by its own engine and having rubber wheels is not a land implement (*Hockin* v. *Reed & Co.* (*Torquay*), *Ltd.* (1962), 60 L.G.R. 203). A trailer, in this instance a " Webb Masterspread ", can fall within the definition of " land implement " in reg. 3 irrespective of the manner in which it is drawn and it can be within the exemptions given by the Regulations whether or not it is for the time being used with a land locomotive or land tractor (*Amalgamated Roadstone Corporation* v. *Bond* [1963] 1 All E.R. 682). Land tractors are specially dealt with by reg. 5 and are exempted by it from certain of the Regulations. A land implement under reg. 3 does not include a machine used for scraping earth and carrying it from one place to another; it must be connected with agriculture and use with a land tractor is confined to farming and forestry land and does not cover engineering work on building sites (*Markham* v. *Stacey* [1968] 3 All E.R. 758).

Overhang, Length and Rear Markings

A vehicle complies with the Regulations as to overhang although the load projects beyond the permitted distance (*Marston Services* v. *Police* (1934), 98 J.P.Jo. 848), but there might be a prosecution for a dangerous load under reg. 90 (see p. 418). If a vehicle conforms with the Regulations as to overhang when the tailboard is up, letting it down does not contravene them in this respect (*Andrews* v. *Kershaw* [1951] 2 All E.R. 764). See also the definition of " overall length " in reg. 3 (p. 769). Here again an offence might arise under reg. 90. Note the reference to hoods and luggage racks in the definition of " overhang " in reg. 3 (p. 770, *infra*). The term " overhang " is explained at 115 J.P.Jo. 254. The definition of " overall length " in reg. 3 now requires that account shall be taken of any device or any receptacle on or attached to the vehicle which increases its carrying capacity, and *Bason* v. *Vipond* [1962] 1 All E.R. 520 should be read in the light of this change.

Andrews v. *Kershaw* and *Bason* v. *Vipond* were distinguished in *Guest Scottish Carriers, Ltd.* v. *Trend* [1967] 3 All E.R. 52, where it was held that, where the tailboard of a van had been constructed in order to be used for increasing the van's carrying capacity, the overall length and the overhang should be measured with the tailboard let down. A conviction for using the van with overhang exceeding that permitted was upheld where it had been driven with the tailboard down and loaded with goods.

In the proviso to reg. 9 (1) (see p. 780) the word " normally " has its ordinary meaning and is used in contradistinction to abnormal or exceptional; where a vehicle carried exceptionally long loads on forty-six journeys out of one hundred and seventy-seven, it was held that these forty-six journeys could not be said to be exceptional or abnormal (*Peak Trailer & Chassis, Ltd.* v. *Jackson* [1967] 1 All E.R. 172). An " indivisible " load is not of " exceptional " length if it would go in a vehicle of standard length (15 metres) (*Cook and Anor.* v. *Briddon* (1975), 119 S.J. 462; see also p. 432).

By reg. 3, account should not be taken, in computing overall length, of a receptacle constructed or adapted for the purpose of being lifted on or off vehicles with goods or burden contained therein and from time to time actually used for that purpose in the ordinary course of business; *Claude Hughes & Co. (Carlisle), Ltd.* v. *Hyde* [1963] 1 All E.R. 598 and *John Stamper (Farms), Ltd.* v. *Hyde* (1963), 107 S.J. 982, should likewise be read in the light of this change. By the Special Types Order of 1973 and regs. 130 and 131, where a vehicle carries long or wide loads or a combination of vehicles exceeds certain lengths or there are certain projections, an attendant must be carried, two clear days' notice to the police must be given and projections must be marked. A movable cattle-container on an articulated vehicle does not make it a vehicle constructed to carry indivisible loads under reg. 9 (1) (*Fellside Transport* v. *Hyde* (1962), unreported).

A case on the width of a vehicle (*Gwennap* v. *Amphlett*) is discussed on p. 431.

Rear Markings

Motor vehicles exceeding 3 tons unladen and trailers exceeding 1 ton are required to display special rear markings by virtue of the Motor Vehicles (Rear Markings) Regulations, 1970 (S.I. 1970 No. 1700) as amended by like named amendment regulations (S.I. 1972 No. 842 and S.I. 1975 No. 29). Regulation 2 exempts certain vehicles. Regulation 4 prescribes which rear markings are fitted to which type of vehicle, while Pts. I and II of the Schedule prescribe their size and colour. Part III of the Schedule details their position and requires them to be maintained in a clean and efficient condition while on a road. Regulation 5 modifies Pt. III and reg. 4 enables rear markings to be fitted to the load of a vehicle when the load projects beyond the rear of the vehicle so as to obscure the vehicle's rear markings.

Speedometers

Regulation 18 (p. 785, *infra*) requires a speedometer, as defined, to be fitted to every public service vehicle used as an express carriage and to every motor vehicle registered on or after 1st October, 1937, except land tractors, invalid carriages, works trucks, motor cycles with engines not exceeding 100 c.c. cylindrical capacity, and certain other vehicles of low speed. If a car has no speedometer but a revolution counter, it is doubtful if it would comply (*Sellwood* v. *Butt* [1962] Crim.L.R. 841), especially as, under the present regulation, the instrument must " readily indicate the speed ". Regulation 91 (p. 828, *infra*) requires the speedometer to be at all material times maintained in good working order and free from obstruction, but it is a defence that (*a*) the defect occurred in the course of a journey during which the contravention was detected or (*b*) at the time of detection steps had already been taken to have the defect remedied with all reasonable expedition. The term " registered on or after 1st October, 1937 ", means registered for the first time on or after that day (*Mackinnon* v. *Peate* [1936] 2 All E.R. 240).

Brakes

See regs. 13, 14, 46, 47, 50, 54, 59, 62, 66, 70 and Sched. 4 as to the brakes to be fitted. In most cases each brake must be able to stop the vehicle in a reasonable distance under the most adverse conditions. For the Highway Code braking distance table, see inside cover: although this table has been unaltered for several years it is still considered valid despite modern tyres and modern brakes and is likely to be repeated in a new Highway Code.   In *R.* v. *Chadwick* [1975] Crim.L.R. 105 it was held that the table of stopping distances in the Highway Code was inadmissible as being hearsay unless there was a failure to observe a relevant provision of the Highway Code.   By reg. 94 (p. 829, *infra*) every part of the braking system and of the means of operation thereof must be maintained in good and efficient working order and properly adjusted; this means exactly what it says; in *Kennett* v. *British Airports Authority* [1975] Crim.L.R. 106 justices who had dismissed a charge because the overall braking system of a car was efficient, were directed to convict the defendant because the disc brake on one wheel was badly worn; justices on a charge of this nature should examine every part of the braking system as it applied to each wheel (*ibid.*). The regulation contains a number of other requirements.   It seems that the fact that the brakes failed to work on one occasion does not prove that the braking system is improperly constructed contrary to Pt. II and in such a case a prosecution should be brought under reg. 94 for bad maintenance (*Cole* v. *Young* [1938] 4 All E.R. 39). Similarly, where the brakes do not comply with Pt. II but they are properly maintained, it is wrong to charge under reg. 94 (*Unwin* v. *Gayton* (1949), 93 S.J. 72).   A missing handbrake ratchet can be a defect of construction, as well as of maintenance (*Smith* v. *Nugent* [1955] S.L.T.(Sh.) 60).   The method of calculating the number of wheels on which a braking system is deemed to operate under reg. 54 was considered in *Langton* v. *Johnson* [1956] 3 All E.R. 474; see the relevant Regulations now as to the inclusion of front wheels in calculating the wheels on which a braking system operates.   The prosecution should prove that a trailer exceeds 2 cwt. in unladen weight where its brakes are defective (*Muir* v. *Lawrence* [1951] S.L.T.(Sh.) 88).   A brake drum for the purposes of the Regulations is part of the wheel and not of the braking system (reg. 3 (4)).

The obligation to maintain the brakes in good and efficient working order is an absolute one (*Green* v. *Burnett* [1954] 3 All E.R. 273); it is not a defence that the defendant ensured that the brakes were regularly maintained or that he had done all he could to see his brakes were in order (*Hawkins* v. *Holmes* [1974] R.T.R. 436), otherwise the exemption for endorsement conferred in column 5 of Sched. 4 would not be necessary (*ibid.*) (see p. 434).   All that a driver can assume after a car has been serviced by a garage is that it has been serviced.   He cannot assume it is in good mechanical order; *per* Park, J., in *Haynes* v. *Swain* [1975] R.T.R. 40, at p. 44.

Cases on motor-scooter brakes are at [1957] Crim.L.R. 709 and Jo. Crim.L. (1965) 155. It is suggested at the latter place that in the case of vehicles to which Sched. 5 of the Construction and Use Regulations applies (viz., motor cycles, motor cars, heavy motor cars and goods vehicles not exceeding 30 cwt. in unladen weight but not public service vehicles carrying eight or more passengers, articulated vehicles, works trucks, pedestrian-controlled vehicles, locomotives or motor tractors) the prosecutor must show both that the brakes are not in good and efficient working order and properly adjusted and also that they do not have the efficiency required by the relevant Regulations. But it may be that breach of either requirement suffices (*cf. Butterworth* v. *Shorthouse* on p. 421). Tests on stationary vehicles are also discussed.

The fact that brakes are inefficient does not have to be proved as a result of a test by an authorised examiner. In *Stoneley* v. *Richardson* [1973] R.T.R. 229 a constable, with the permission of the defendant, was able to push the defendant's car along the road with the handbrake fully applied; the justices were directed to convict even though the constable was not an authorised examiner. It is submitted that whether or not brakes are maintained in good and efficient working order is a simple question of fact, albeit in some cases technical evidence may be necessary. Normally, evidence improperly obtained is nevertheless admissible. In *Stoneley* there was no suggestion that the evidence was improperly obtained, as the test was made with the defendant's consent.

Some of the older cases on brakes are collected at p. 131 of the second edition of this book; they may be of some value in relation to " vintage cars " as there are certain exemptions for vehicles registered many years ago (see reg. 4 (9)).

The Road Traffic and Roads Improvement Act, 1960, s. 21 (now s. 41 (2) of the 1972 Act) provided that no provision in the Regulations imposing or varying requirements in respect of the brakes with which a motor vehicle must be equipped shall be taken to relate to the construction of vehicles. The reason is explained in *Hansard*, 27th July, 1960, cols. 1734–1738.

Pedal Cycles

The Brakes on Pedal Cycles Regulations, 1954 (S.I. 1954 No. 966) indicate the brakes with which pedal cycles and pedal tricycles must be equipped and give the police powers of testing. A person who rides a cycle or tricycle, or causes or permits one to be ridden, on the road in contravention of these Regulations, may be fined £50 by magistrates under s. 178 of the Road Traffic Act, 1972. Magistrates have held parents liable under these Regulations in respect of their children's cycles (99 S.J. 602). The power to make Regulations as to cycles arises under s. 66 of the 1972 Act. Under s. 66 (5) it is an offence punishable with a fine of £100 to sell, supply or offer to sell or supply a cycle in contravention of the Regulations unless it is sold for export or in the belief that it would not be used until it had been put in a condition complying with the Regulations.

There are articles on the braking requirements in the *Police Review* of 11th March, 1966, and 24th March, 1967.

Vehicle or Load in Dangerous Condition

This offence arises under reg. 90 (see p. 828, *infra*). As in any other Construction and Use Regulation the defendant may either be charged with " using " a vehicle in contravention of the Regulation or " causing or permitting " the vehicle to be used. In the former case it is an absolute offence and the driver and the employer of a vehicle being driven on the employer's business may both be convicted of " using " even though the latter is unaware of the contravention (see " using " at p. 41 *et seq.*). In *Cornish* v. *Ferry Masters Ltd. and Another* [1975] R.T.R. 292 a drum fell off a lorry onto the road because the pallet upon which it was loaded collapsed due to some extraordinary, unexplained, inherent defect. The lorry's owners and driver were both charged with " using " and the justices dismissed the charges against both defendants as both were neither at fault nor negligent. The High Court directed both to be convicted: the offence of "using " is an absolute offence, the defendants' knowledge or lack of knowledge of the defect is irrelevant. The likelihood or otherwise of danger being caused was to be adjudged according to the factual circumstances as they were, regardless of the knowledge of the person using the vehicle (see also *Keyse* v. *Sainsbury, infra*). On the other hand where an employer is charged with " permitting " a vehicle with an insecure load contrary to reg. 90 (2) the prosecution must prove that a director or " brain " of the company knew of the contravention (*P. Lowery & Sons, Ltd.* v. *Wark* [1975] R.T.R. 45, applying *Ross Hillman, Ltd.* v. *Bond* (see p. 40)).

Where crates fall off a lorry when going round a sharp bend, an offence arises and the driver may be convicted though the crates were loaded by another person (*Gifford* v. *Whittaker* [1942] 1 All E.R. 604). Where trees protruded 32 feet beyond the back of a trailer, an offence against reg. 90 arose, and the proviso to reg. 68 (as to trailers carrying indivisible loads) was no defence (*Cripps* v. *Cooper* [1936] 2 All E.R. 48). There was a conviction under this Regulation where the blades of a bulldozer being carried on a vehicle projected 3½ feet beyond the offside of the vehicle; the blades being detachable, the bulldozer was not an " indivisible " load (*Newstead* v. *Hearn* (1950), 114 J.P.Jo. 690). It was stated in *Andrews* v. *Kershaw* [1951] 2 All E.R. 764, at p. 768, that, if a large van was driven with the tailboard down, this might be an offence under reg. 90. But evidence merely that many milk cans rattled on a lorry and made a great noise does not suffice to show that their loading or adjustment was faulty (*Re Scottish Farmers' Dairy Co.* (1934), 98 J.P.Jo. 848).

Regulation 90 is absolute in terms and the vehicle must at all times on the road be in such condition that no danger is caused to road users; if it is not in such condition, an offence arises even though the dangerous condition is due to a latent defect (*F. Austin (Leyton), Ltd.* v. *East* [1961] Crim.L.R. 119), and in *Keyse* v. *Sainsbury* [1971] Crim.L.R. 291 it was held that reg. 90 (1) was absolute. The fact that a defect was a latent defect and there was no negligence is a mitigating circumstance, however (*F. Austin (Leyton), Ltd.* v. *East, supra*). The dangerous condition in reg. 90 (1) does not necessarily have to arise through lack of maintenance; where a motorcyclist added extension pieces to his exhaust to a height of 2 ft. 8 in. causing danger in that passers by could be burnt if they touched the exhaust or find the exhaust fumes directed at their faces, it was held that the motorcyclist should be convicted of an offence under reg. 90 (1) (*Reeve* v. *Webb* [1973] R.T.R. 130).

Regulation 90 (1) creates three separate offences in respect of condition, of passengers and of load, and all three should not be charged in one information (*Dickson* v. *Brown* [1959] S.L.T. 207). The Regulation now applies to the manner in which passengers are carried and *Dickson* v. *Brown* and *Houghton* v. *Trafalgar Insurance Co.* [1953] 2 All E.R. 1409 are no longer of authority in relation to that point. Where an examiner found excessive play in the steering-joint and pivot of the steering arm due to wear, causing one-third free play in the steering wheel, it was held that the charge was not improperly brought under reg. 90 (dangerous condition) rather than under reg. 95 (defective steering) (*Bason* v. *Eayrs* [1958] Crim.L.R. 397). In *Jenkins* v. *Deane* (1933), 103 L.J.K.B. 250, an insurance case, a tow-chain was held not to be part of the vehicle and a condition of the policy in respect of driving " in an unsafe condition " was not breached by using a defective chain to tow another vehicle, and in *Keyse* v. *Sainsbury, supra*, a heavy weight of concrete and steel attached by two hooks to a steel bar at the back of a tractor were held not to be part of the tractor as such and the charge, which was so framed that it related solely to the condition of the tractor, was held to be rightly dismissed.

Even if parts and accessories are in good repair, they must also be in proper working order; where, for example, a tow bar was of good construction and in good repair but became uncoupled because someone failed to ensure it was properly engaged, the user of the vehicle was guilty under reg. 90 (*O'Neill* v. *Brown* [1961] 1 All E.R. 571).

Regulation 90 (1) makes it an offence if the " weight, distribution, packing and adjustment of the load " are dangerous; reg. 90 (2) provides that " the load carried . . . shall at all times be so secured or be carried in such a position " that no danger is caused. Offences under reg. 90 (1) carry compulsory endorsement and optional disqualification; those under reg. 90 (2) and under reg. 90 (3), now, also carry compulsory endorsement and optional disqualification (s. 21 (4) of the Act of 1974, reversing *Beighton* v. *Brown* [1965] 1 All E.R. 793 and *R.* v. *Bromley JJ.* [1970] Crim.L.R. 103); possibly offences under reg. 90 (1) as to " manner " do not (see p. 433). It may be thought that " securing " and " carrying " a load are often akin to " packing " and " adjustment " and that it will be difficult to judge whether the offence is under reg. 90 (1) or 90 (2). It is submitted that, where a load is not adequately tied by ropes or kept from falling overboard by other means, it is not " secured " and that if it is placed on the edge of the vehicle or on top of it and is likely to bounce off, it is not " carried in a [safe] position ". If it is packed in such a way that parts of it burst out of the packing and fall on the road or if it is distributed in such a way that heavier parts push other parts off the vehicle or if it is adjusted in such a way as to import a dangerous bias to one side, then reg. 90 (1) applies. The Oxford Dictionary defines " adjustment " as including " settling, harmonising or properly disposing " and " putting in proper order ". " Packing " is defined as including " the putting of things together compactly as for transport . . . the filling (of a receptacle) with things so put in."

Regulation 90 (3) (see p. 828) forbids a motor vehicle to be used for any purpose for which it is unsuitable so as to cause or be likely to cause danger. In *Hollis Brothers, Ltd.* v. *Bailey, Buttwell* v. *Bailey* [1968] 1 W.L.R. 663 a lorry's load was badly stacked, causing it to topple over; the conviction was set aside; the fact that the load was unsuitably stacked did not necessarily cause the vehicle to be unsuitable to carry that load. This case may be contrasted with *British Road Services* v. *Owen* [1971] 2 All E.R. 999, in which a lorry was loaded with two forklifts which were too high to go under a footbridge, causing a collision. The load was properly secured and stable, and the lorry mechanically sound. The lorry was held to be unsuitable for the purpose, as when assessing the purpose for which a vehicle is to be used regard must be had to the nature and features of the route to be taken by that vehicle.

The summons should specify the defects in the parts and accessories (*Simmons* v. *Fowler* (1950), 48 L.G.R. 623). A stipendiary magistrate has held that reg. 90 is aimed at the maintenance of a vehicle, not its construction, so that a manufacturer's fitting on top of the bonnet is not within reg. 90 as being dangerous ([1957] Crim.L.R. 562).

Attendants on Trailers

Regulation 135 (p. 849, *infra*) relates to attendants on trailers and gives a special exemption for certain meat-carrying trailers. According to the headnote in *Union Cartage Co.* v. *Heamon* [1937] 1 All E.R. 538 the exemption applies only when the trailer is actually carrying meat or, *semble*, returning empty from a journey to carry meat and not when it is carrying something else, such as tiles. This was the view of the magistrates, but the judgment in the High Court does not in fact refer to the point beyond saying that their decision was upheld, the judgment being on another point.

Quitting Vehicles

By reg. 116 (p. 840, *infra*) it is an offence for a person to cause or permit a motor vehicle to be on a road unattended by a person duly licensed to drive it unless the engine has been stopped and the brake set or it is a fire engine at work or a gas-driven vehicle or being used for police or ambulance purposes. A motorist who leaves a vehicle without setting the brake may also be convicted under s. 24 of the Act (see p. 401) if the vehicle is on a slope so that it runs away and causes danger (*Maguire* v. *Crouch* (1940), 104 J.P. 445). A motorist was charged with not stopping his engine and not setting the brake but the magistrates found that he had stopped the engine. He argued that the information was bad for duplicity and that reg. 116 required both failures to be proved. The High Court upheld his conviction (*Butterworth* v. *Shorthouse* (1956), 120 J.P.Jo. 97). It is submitted at 119 J.P.Jo. 262 that a person offends against this Regulation if the vehicle has run on to the road from private land. See also *Davidson* v. *Adair* on p. 412 and 122 J.P.Jo. 48. For a car to be " attended ", there must be a person able to keep it under observation, see any attempt to interfere with it and have a reasonable prospect of preventing interference (*Starfire Diamond Rings, Ltd.* v. *Angel* (1962), 106 S.J. 854, followed in *Ingleton of Ilford, Ltd.* v. *General Accident &c. Co.* [1967] 2 Lloyd's

Rep. 179, where a van was deemed unattended when the driver
was in a place where he could not see it and had no reasonable
prospect of being able to reach it in time). In *Attridge* v. *Attwood*
[1964] Crim.L.R. 45 the defendant had left a taxi in the street and
taken the ignition key with him; the taxi was in his view from the
building nearby, where he was. His conviction, for leaving the taxi
without someone proper to take care of it under the Town Police
Clauses Act, 1847, s. 62, was upheld. On the terms of a policy,
a vehicle was deemed to be " not unattended " when the driver was
in it, asleep (*Plaistow Transport, Ltd.* v. *Graham* [1966] 1 Lloyd's
Rep. 639). Regulation 116 is not a Construction and Use Regulation relating to brakes and an offender against it cannot be disqualified or have his licence endorsed (*Kenyon* v. *Thorley* [1973]
R.T.R. 60).

Regulation 109 requires the engine to be stopped when the
vehicle is stationary, so far as may be necessary for the prevention
of noise; there are exceptions for examination, working for another purpose and gas-propelled vehicles.

Mirrors, Mascots, Tyres, Seat Belts and Petrol Tanks, etc.

By reg. 23 every passenger vehicle adapted to carry more than
seven passengers, exclusive of the driver, and every goods and dual-
purpose vehicle, shall be equipped with at least two mirrors fitted
as therein indicated to assist the driver, if he so desires, to become
aware of traffic to the rear and on both sides rearwards, and every
other motor vehicle (except a motor cycle with or without a sidecar, a land locomotive, a pedestrian-controlled vehicle and a motor
vehicle drawing a trailer in which is an attendant who can clearly
signal to the driver) shall be equipped either internally or externally
with one mirror to assist the driver, if he so desires, to become aware
of traffic to the rear. The two mirrors on large passenger vehicles
and goods and dual-purpose vehicles must show not merely traffic
to the rear but on both sides rearwards; if the two mirrors are so
adjusted that there is not a view on both sides rearwards, there may
be an offence. Regulation 23 (1) (*b*) makes special provision as to
land tractors. Although the exceptional size of the load may for
the time being obscure the driver's view in his mirror, there is no
offence if the vehicle is in fact equipped with the mirror or mirrors
required by reg. 23 and he can see in them to the rear when the
vehicle is carrying a normal load or is unloaded (*Mawdsley* v.
Walter Cox (*Transport*), *Ltd.* [1965] 3 All E.R. 728).

Mascot.—A manufacturer's fitting on a car has been held by a
stipendiary magistrate not to be a " mascot " within reg. 132;

the term means something supposed to bring luck ([1957] Crim.L.R. 563).

Seat belts.—Motor cars registered on or after 1st January, 1965, and three-wheeled vehicles exceeding 5 cwt. first used on or after 1st September, 1970, must be provided with anchorage points and seat belts, as described in reg. 17; the excepted vehicles are named in reg. 17 (2). The Regulation does not require any person to use a seat belt.

Tyres.—Regulation 99 (1) specifies six different types of defect in tyres (see sub-paragraphs (*a*) to (*f*) on p. 832). In *Saines* v. *Woodhouse* [1970] 2 All E.R. 388 it was held that there must be a separate information in respect of each tyre which is alleged to contravene any of the six sub-paragraphs. The justices had dismissed an information in respect of the rear offside tyre under reg. 99 (1) (*a*) after they had convicted the defendant in respect of the rear nearside tyre under reg. 99 (1) (*f*). Their reason was that reg. 99 (4) (which reproduces the wording of former Regulations) required one information in respect of all the tyres of the vehicle. It is submitted that one information relating to a number of tyres under reg. 99 (4) is still valid. It is believed some police forces continue to charge under reg. 99 (4). It is submitted they may do so provided there is no charge in respect of any of the same tyres under reg. 99 (1). In *Goosey* v. *Adams* [1972] Crim.L.R. 49 it was held that, although close-coupled wheels are required by reg. 3 (5) (see p. 774) to be treated as one wheel, this has no application to tyres, and that each tyre on a close-coupled wheel should be looked at in isolation to see whether it complies with reg. 99 (1) (*f*). In *Renouf* v. *Franklin* [1971] R.T.R. 489 a tyre had a V-shaped tear producing a triangular flap of rubber which could be lifted by the finger, exposing the tyre cord. A conviction under reg. 99 (1) (*e*) was set aside, because for a tyre to have the " ply or cord structure exposed " meant exposed to view. The court indicated that in such a case if the dimensions of the cut were sufficient sub-paragraph (*c*) would have been the appropriate sub-paragraph; on the other hand, if the tyre had a worn patch exposing the cords, sub-paragraph (*e*) would be appropriate.

Regulation 99 (1) (*a*) deals with mixed tyres generally but reg. 100 prohibits the mixing of certain types of tyre (see p. 833). For a case where a lorry dirver was held guilty of causing death by dangerous driving, and his employers guilty of aiding and abetting, when he knowingly drove a lorry with an unsafe tyre, see *R.* v. *Robert Millar (Contractors), Ltd.,* on p. 257.

Whether a tyre complies with the regulations is a question of fact; it does not matter that the constable who examined the tyre and gave evidence as to its condition is not an authorised examiner (*Phillips* v. *Thomas* [1974] R.T.R. 28, following *Stoneley* v. *Richardson* (see p. 417)).

Emission of oil.—The reference in reg. 101 to the emission of oily substances, etc., covers not only the actual discharge but dripping which follows it (*Tidswell* v. *Llewellyn* [1965] Crim.L.R. 732).

Noise.—Regulations 106 to 108 and Sched. 9 relate to noise and noise measurement; they are discussed in the *Police Review*, 14th June and 12th July, 1968. Regulations 28 and 98 relate to silencers and regs. 27 and 110 to use of audible warning instruments. Three-toned horns, provided they do not sound similar to two-toned horns (see definition in reg. 3 on p. 772), which are limited to fire brigade, ambulance and police vehicles, etc., would appear not to offend against the Regulations (but see reg. 27 (2) on p. 788 which requires any instrument on a vehicle first used on or after 1st August, 1973, to be continuous and uniform and not strident).

Petrol tanks.—By reg. 96 (see p. 831) every motor vehicle shall at all times be so maintained that (*a*) the petrol tank is reasonably secure against it being damaged, and (*b*) petrol leakage from the tank is adequately prevented. The wording of the new Regulation appears to be absolute.

Sale of Unroadworthy Vehicles

The Road Traffic Act, 1972, s. 60, makes it an offence (punishable on summary conviction with a fine of £200 on first or subsequent conviction) to sell or supply or offer to sell or supply [or expose for sale] a motor vehicle or trailer for delivery in such a condition that its use on a road would be unlawful under s. 40 of the Act, or under Regulations as to brakes, steering or tyres or as to construction, weight or equipment and lighting of vehicles [or maintenance of vehicles, their parts and accessories in such a condition that no danger is likely to be caused]. (The words in square brackets above were inserted in s. 60 by s. 11 of the Act of 1974.) It is also an offence to alter one so as to render its condition such that its use on a road would be unlawful under s. 40 or the cited Regulations. An auctioneer does not offer to sell the goods auctioned, he invites those present to make offers to buy. Accordingly auctioneers of an unroadworthy vehicle which was driven away by the successful bidder cannot be convicted of an " offer to sell " contrary to s. 60 (*British Car Auctions, Ltd.* v. *Wright* [1972] Crim.L.R. 562 (for criticism of the case see *ibid.*, p. 563)). If the vehicle or trailer had been constructed and equipped in accordance with Pt. II of the Construction and Use Regulations, it was no offence to sell or supply it with defects which only indicated a failure to maintain it properly in breach of Pt. III of those Regulations, unless it contravened a Regulation as to the maintenance of brakes (see reg. 94), tyres (reg. 99) or steering gear (reg. 95). Section 11 of the Act of 1974 has now added to the Regulations contravention of which gives rise to an offence under s. 60, the Regulation which requires vehicles, their parts and accessories to be maintained in such a condition that no danger is, or is likely to be caused (see reg. 90 (1)). This amendment reverses the effect of *Keyte* v. *Dew* [1970] R.T.R. 481 where it was held that reg. 90 (1) was a regulation as to the maintenance of a vehicle and not as to construction, and the sale of a vehicle which was dangerous as a result of lack of maintenance was held not to contravene s. 60. There are, however, other Regulations as to maintenance, and no offence can arise under s. 60 unless it can be shown that the vehicle contravenes the Regulations specified in the section, i.e., brakes, tyres, steering gear and dangerous condition of vehicle, parts or accessories. Danger may be caused or likely to be caused as a result of the breach of other maintenance Regulations (e.g., 91 (speedometer), 93 (windscreen), 98 (silencer), 101 (smoke)), but it is submitted that unless it can be shown that there is also a contravention of reg. 90 (1) or a contravention of the Regulations as to the maintenance of brakes, steering or tyres, no offence is committed under s. 60 as the amendment made by the 1974 Act follows almost word for word the relevant wording of reg. 90 (1).

The liability of a seller under s. 60 is absolute and he is guilty if he sells or supplies a vehicle in breach of it, whether or not he had guilty knowledge (*Sandford Motor Sales* v. *Habgood* [1962] Crim.L.R. 487). Section 60 extends to lighting equipment and reflectors on motor vehicles, but it is a defence if the seller or supplier reasonably believed that there would be no use on roads here during darkness.

See s. 61 of the 1972 Act as to entering sale-rooms to test vehicles.

By s. 62 of the 1972 Act, selling, supplying or offering to sell or supply or exposing for sale a goods vehicle or goods vehicle part without the manufacturer's or Minister's approval certificate required is an offence carrying a fine of £200. It is a defence that the defendant sold, etc., it for export from Great Britain or reasonably believed that it would not be used on a road in Great Britain till the certificate was given or only in an area where use without a certificate is lawful (s. 60 (4)).

Section 12 of the Act of 1974 inserted a new s. 60A in the Act of 1972. It is an offence under s. 60A (1) for a person to fit or cause or permit a vehicle part to be fitted, if by reason of that part being fitted, the use of the vehicle on a road would thereby constitute a contravention of or a failure to comply with *any* of the Construction and Use Regulations. It is similarly an offence under s. 60A (3) for a person to sell, supply, offer to sell or supply a vehicle part, or to cause or permit a vehicle part to be sold, supplied or offered for sale or supply when he has reasonable cause to believe it will be fitted to a motor vehicle so as to give rise to a contravention of or non-compliance with a Construction and Use Regulation. Offences under s. 60A (1) and (3) are punishable with a fine of £200 for a first or subsequent offence.

Testing Vehicles

Regulation 137 (p. 851, *infra*) provides for the testing of brakes, silencers, tyres, lights, reflectors and steering gear of motor vehicles and trailers by constables and authorised examiners on the premises where the vehicle is, with the consent of the owner of the premises. Section 43 of the Road Traffic Act, 1972, authorises the testing of such equipment on roads. Sections 43 and 44, as extended by the Motor Vehicles (Tests) (Extension) Order, 1966 (S.I. 1966 No. 973), require every motor vehicle first registered more than three years before the time at which it is being used on the road to pass a test under s. 43. Section 44 (2) and (3) ensures that vehicles manufactured more than three years earlier also require test certificates once they are brought into the United Kingdom and registered here. The Motor Vehicles (Tests) Regulations, 1968 (S.I. 1968 No. 1714), as amended by amendment regulations of 1969 (S.I. 1969 No. 1171), of 1971 (S.I. 1971 No. 165) and of 1972 (S.I. 1972 No. 898), and the Motor Vehicles (Tests) (Exemption) Regulations, 1969 (S.I. 1969 No. 419) apply and regulate the procedure, etc., and exempt loco-motives, motor tractors, track-laying vehicles, public service vehicles, goods vehicles of an unladen weight exceeding 30 cwt. (other than dual-purpose vehicles), articulated vehicles, works trucks, pedestrian-controlled vehicles, invalids' vehicles of 6 cwt. or less, hackney carriages in London and certain other towns, vehicles for export or belonging to a visiting force, land tractors, certain police vehicles, vehicles temporarily in Great Britain and vehicles exempt from duty because of minimal use of the road from the operation of s. 44. Also exempted are vehicles going to and from tests and to be repaired as a result of faults found on a test, vehicles officially seized in certain circumstances and vehicles on certain small islands reachable by ship or plane only. Sections 43 and 44 bind the Crown.

Sections 45 and 46 contain the provisions relating to the testing of goods vehicles formerly contained in Pt. II of the Road Safety Act. The Construction and Use Regulations which are prescribed for the purpose of the annual test of goods vehicles are regs. 13, 14, 18, 22, 23, 25–27, 39, 54, 59, 60, 64, 70, 72, 90, 93–95, 99, 101, 103, 140 and 146 (see p. 781 *et seq.*). Unlike the testing of vehicles under ss. 43 and 44, the testing of goods vehicles is carried out by the Department of the Environment at Government testing stations. The relevant Regulations are now the Goods Vehicles (Plating and Testing) Regulations, 1971 (S.I. 1971 No. 352), as amended by like-named amendment regulations (S.I. 1971 No. 2074, S.I. 1972 Nos. 195 and 806, S.I. 1974 No. 99 and S.I. 1975 No. 36). Schedule 2 to the Regulations lists the vehicles which are exempt from the necessity of plating and test certificates. The exemption includes dual-purpose vehicles not forming part of an articulated vehicle, mobile cranes, breakdown vehicles, engineering plant, road construction vehicles, road rollers, asphalt or tar trailers, fire fighting vehicles, works trucks and trailers, snow ploughs, etc., living vans, hearses, land implements, land locomotives and land tractors, goods vehicles in the service of a visiting force, goods vehicles proceeding to a port for export, track laying vehicles and police vehicles. Also included are tower wagons as defined in Sched. 3 to the Vehicles (Excise) Act, 1971. In *Anderson and Heeley Ltd.* v. *Paterson* [1975] R.T.R. 248 a van fitted with an extensible high loader was held not to be a tower wagon as it could and did carry a load contrary to one of the requirements of the definition in Sched. 3 to the 1971 Act.

Using a goods vehicle on a road, or causing or permitting it to be so used, without the necessary test certificate (s. 46 (2)) is an offence subject to a penalty of £200 for a first or subsequent offence and similarly using, etc., a goods vehicle without a plating certificate (s. 46 (1)) is an offence punishable by a fine of £100 for a first or subsequent offence. It is also an offence to use a goods vehicle on a road, or cause or permit it to be so used, with an alteration to the vehicle or equipment without the Secretary of State having been notified of the alteration as required by the Regulations (s. 46 (3)). It is a defence to s. 46 (3) that the alteration was not specified in the relevant plating certificate (s. 46 (4)). An offence under s. 46 (3) is punishable with a fine of £100 for a first or subsequent offence.

Section 53 enables an authorised examiner to make a roadside test of a motor vehicle as to its brakes, silencer, steering gear, tyres, emission of smoke or fumes and lighting equipment and reflectors and noise. " Authorised examiner " for the purposes of this section may include both a constable appointed as such by his chief constable and a person appointed by the police authority for the purposes of this section acting under the directions of the chief constable. The driver may elect for the test to be deferred unless the constable thinks that the vehicle is so defective that the test should be carried out forthwith or that the vehicle has caused an accident (s. 53 (3)). Failing to comply with the requirements of the section or obstructing an examiner is punishable with a fine of £50. Prosecution for contravention of a Construction and Use Regulation as to tyres or brakes does not depend on whether the evidence as to the contravention has been obtained as a result of a test by an authorised examiner (*Stoneley* v. *Richardson* [1973] R.T.R. 229; *Phillips* v. *Thomas* [1974] R.T.R. 28). Similarly, production of a traffic examiner's authority is not a pre-requisite of a conviction of being overweight contrary to reg. 142 of the Construction and Use Regulations (*Wurzal* v. *Reader Bros., Ltd.* [1974] R.T.R. 383).

Section 54 contains the procedure for remedying defects discovered by the road-side test. It enables the examiner to give the owner (the person driving the vehicle can be required to state the name and address of the owner) a notice specifying the defect and requiring the owner to have the defect remedied. The owner is then required to give a certificate within twenty-eight days countersigned by an authorised tester that the defect no longer exists. Alternatively the owner can make a declaration that he has sold or disposed of the vehicle to a person named in the declaration or that he no longer intends to use the vehicle on a road (s. 54 (3), (4)). Failure to give the certificate or declaration within the specified time attracts a fine of £50 as does failure by the driver to give the owner's name and address. Neither under s. 53 nor under s. 54 is there power to disqualify an offender or endorse his driving licence.

Sections 56 and 57 contain parallel provisions relating to goods vehicles. Section 56 enables a goods vehicle examiner to inspect goods vehicles and to enter premises on which he has reason to believe that goods vehicles are kept. Section 57 enables the examiner to prohibit the driving of a goods vehicle which either is unfit for service or " is likely to become unfit for service ". Such prohibition notices may either be immediate or delayed in their effect. Section 58 governs the procedure for removal of a goods vehicle prohibition order. Obstructing a goods vehicle examiner under s. 56 (3) is punishable with a fine of £50 on a first conviction or subsequent conviction. Driving a goods vehicle in contravention of a prohibition order or refusing to proceed to a place of inspection is punishable with a fine of £400. Offences under s. 56 or s. 57 are not punishable with endorsement or disqualification.

Regulation 15 (1) of the Motor Vehicles (Tests) Regulations, 1968, provides that examiners shall issue a test certificate or notification of its refusal on the same date as that on which the examination is completed. If it cannot be issued on that day, it must be issued on the next day (not being a Sunday or public holiday) and the vehicle must not have been moved from the testing station or its condition changed.

The certificates under s. 44 must be issued annually.

The option to defer the test given to a driver under s. 53 of the 1972 Act extends to him only and not to the owner, nor need the examiner tell the driver of his option (*Brown* v. *McIndoe* [1963] S.L.T. 233). The material date for deciding if a test certificate is false in a material particular contrary to s. 171 of the Act of 1972 is the date of issue, even though the examination may have taken place earlier (*R.* v. *Evans* [1964] 3 All E.R. 666); see also reg. 15 (1) above. A test certificate which has been backdated is false in a material particular (*Murphy* v. *Griffiths* [1967] 1 All E.R. 424).

By s. 162 (which extends to Crown drivers) test certificates must be produced to constables. It is no defence to a charge under s. 162 that the driver would find it difficult if not impossible to obtain the test certificate from the owner (*Davey* v. *Towle* [1973] R.T.R. 326). An offence under s. 162 is punishable with a fine of £50 on a first or subsequent conviction. By s. 44 it is an offence to use, or cause or permit to be used, on a road a vehicle as respects which no requisite test certificate has been issued within a period of twelve months. The fine for a first or subsequent offence is £100 (Road Traffic Act, 1972, Sched. 4); disqualification and endorsement may not be ordered. No offence arises from mere failure to submit the vehicle to test. It is use on the road that gives rise to the offence of causing or permitting use without a test certificate being in force; see as to these terms pp. 32–51. In a case at quarter sessions *Elliott* v. *Grey* (see p. 10) was applied to a vehicle which was left in a cul-de-sac without rear wheels and a rear axle and the defendant's conviction of " using " the vehicle without a test certificate was upheld, but in *Hewer* v. *Cutler* [1974] R.T.R. 155 it was held that a car parked on a road with disconnected gearbox linkage so that the car could be neither driven nor moved did not require a test certificate. *Elliott* v. *Grey* was distinguished and it was doubted whether the test as to whether a car requires a test certificate is the same as the test to be applied in determining whether an insurance certificate is required. It is submitted that the purpose of a test certificate is to ensure that a car is periodically tested to see whether it may safely move on roads; on the other hand third party liability may arise when a car is stationary and completely immobile.   In construing the word " use " it is proper to have regard to the mischief against which the statutory provision creating the offence is aimed.

Foreign Goods Vehicles

The Road Traffic (Foreign Vehicles) Act, 1972, gives additional powers to authorised examiners to issue prohibition orders in respect of foreign goods vehicles and foreign public service vehicles.   Where the examiner exercises any function under s. 128 (3) of the Road Traffic Act, 1960 (entry and inspection of public service vehicle), s. 99 of the Transport Act, 1968 (inspection of drivers' records, etc.), ss. 53 and 56 of the 1972 Act (powers of testing, etc., *supra*) and s. 160 of the Act of 1972 (weighing of motor vehicles), he may issue a prohibition order should there be *any* contravention of any of the regulations or enactments in Sched. 2 to the Act.   Schedule 2 includes the whole of the Construction and Use Regulations, and all the requirements relating to lights on vehicles.   The Schedule also includes s. 60 (operators' licences) and ss. 96 to 98 of the Transport Act, 1968 (drivers' hours) and Regulations under s. 91 (1) (*c*) of the same Act (requiring plates and marks, etc.).   A prohibition order may also be made if the driver obstructs the examiner.

Any person who drives a vehicle or causes or permits one to be driven in contravention of such a prohibition or does not comply with the direction made as a result of a prohibition order is liable on summary conviction to a fine of £200 (s. 3 (1), *ibid.*), and can be arrested by a constable without warrant (s. 3 (2)).   The constable is also given powers of impounding a vehicle where he suspects an offence under s. 3 (1).   He may authorise an appropriate person to remove the vehicle for that purpose (s. 3 (3)–(6)).

A foreign goods vehicle or foreign public service vehicle is one brought into the United Kingdom and not registered in the United Kingdom (s. 7), and any vehicle not displaying a licence or trade plates issued under the Vehicles (Excise) Act, 1971, shall be presumed unless the contrary be proved not to be registered in the United Kingdom (s. 7 (4)).

Special Types of Vehicles

The 1973 Construction and Use Regulations and the Construction and Use (Track Laying Vehicles) Regulations, 1955, are qualified as to particular types of vehicles by the Motor Vehicles (Authorisation of Special Types) General Order, 1973 (S.I. 1973 No. 1101). Part II of the Order relates to track-laying vehicles, naval, military, air force and aviation vehicles, vehicles used for saving life at sea, grass-cutting machines and hedge trimmers, pedestrian-controlled road maintenance vehicles, vehicles used for experiments or trials under the Roads Improvement Act, 1925, straddle carriers, land tractors for reaping and threshing, hay and straw binding and baling vehicles, vehicles for moving excavated materials, vehicles fitted with movable platforms and vehicles constructed for use abroad and new improved types of vehicle constructed for tests. Part III of the Order relates to abnormal and indivisible loads, engineering plant, and vehicles carrying wide loads. Notice to the police and highway and bridge authorities and to the Department of the Environment must be given before a vehicle carrying an abnormal indivisible load or engineering plant exceeding certain widths and weights is used on roads and there are restrictions on speed and on such vehicles using or waiting on bridges. Attendants are required pursuant to art. 24. Forms of notice to the police and to highway and bridge authorities are given in Sched. 2 to the Order and notice is also required for certain other vehicles.

The Special Types Orders may give exemption for certain vehicles as to width, length, weight, etc., provided certain conditions—e.g., notice to the police and highway authority—are fulfilled. A highway authority is empowered under art. 28 (2) of the Order to dispense with the requirements relating to the length of notice and as to the form of notice and as to the particulars given but has no power to dispense altogether with the giving of a notice (*George Cohen 600 Group, Ltd.* v. *Hird* [1970] 2 All E.R. 650). Convictions under the Construction and Use Regulations were upheld even though the highway authority concerned (the G.L.C.) apparently had never before required notices to be given or prosecuted where notices had not been given. If the conditions are not fulfilled—notices, attendants, etc.—an offence may arise under the general law as to those matters, e.g., reg. 48 (as to width of tractors) of the Construction and Use Regulations, but no offence would arise under the Special Types Order (*Gwennap* v. *Amphlett* [1957] 2 All E.R. 605) and it is submitted that it may be inappropriate to charge a breach of that Order at all, even if the speed limit laid down by any of the articles of the Special Types Order is exceeded. Certainly, s. 40 (5) of the 1972 Act does not apply in respect of the Order, for the Order is made under s. 42 and s. 40 (5) creates offences under Regulations " under this section ". Nor does s. 177 apply, it seems, as that relates to a contravention of " Regulations ". Convictions under the Construction and Use Regulations were upheld in respect of use of vehicles of special types in *Sunter Bros., Ltd.* v. *Arlidge, Siddle C. Cook, Ltd.* v. *Arlidge* and *Smith* v. *North West Traffic Area Licensing Authority*, all *infra*, and *George Cohen 600*

Group, Ltd. v. *Hird, supra.* In art. 24 " vehicles " does not mean a combination of vehicles and covers a trailer (*Dixon* v. *B.R.S.* [1959] 1 All E.R. 449); this case related to attendants. And see *Siddle C. Cook, Ltd.* v. *Holden* on p. 18. A motor tractor and combine harvester coupled together constitute two vehicles (*Gwenapp* v. *Amphlett, supra*).

In deciding whether a load cannot without undue expense or risk of damage be divided into two or more loads and so is an abnormal indivisible load under the Special Types Order and exempt from weight and width restrictions, etc., the only undue expense or risk of damage to which the court may have regard is that likely to be incurred in dividing the load; any additional expense or risk involved in carrying the load in two vehicles is irrelevant (*Sunter Bros., Ltd.* v. *Arlidge* [1962] 1 W.L.R. 199; [1962] 1 All E.R. 510). The load there was two steel plates loaded on one vehicle for convenience. A like decision is *Siddle C. Cook, Ltd.* v. *Arlidge* [1962] 1 W.L.R. 203, where the magistrates had found that a load of ten steel boxes could have been divided without undue expense or risk of damage. A vehicle carried a hopper, which was an abnormal indivisible load in the main, but valves, etc., had been detached from the hopper and left in the vehicle; the total weight exceeded that allowed by reg. 81. It was held that the exemption for an abnormal load did not apply, as the hopper was divisible in respect of the valves, so that the carriage of the valves was not allowed; it was suggested that tarpaulins and plant battens might be allowed as being " in connection with the carriage " of the load (*Crabtree* v. *McKelvie & Co.* (1964), 62 L.G.R. 192). In *Smith* v. *North-West Area Licensing Authority* [1974] R.T.R. 236 it was similarly held that twelve separate pre-stressed concrete beams could not constitute an abnormal indivisible load; as the load was capable of being reduced into twelve separate beams, the company were accordingly rightly convicted of exceeding the plated train weight of the vehicle contrary to reg. 142 (see also p. 414).

Penalties, Endorsement and Disqualification

An offence of breach of the Regulations of 1973 carries a fine of £100 but is £400 in the case of an offence of using, or causing or permitting the use of, a goods vehicle

(*a*) so as to cause, or to be likely to cause, danger by the condition of the vehicle or its parts or accessories, the number of passengers carried by it, or the weight, distribution, packing or adjustment of its load; or

(b) in breach of a construction and use requirement as to brakes, steering-gear, tyres or any description of weight; or

(c) for any purpose for which it is so unsuitable as to cause or to be likely to cause danger.

The fine is also £400 in the case of an offence of carrying on a goods vehicle a load which, by reason of its insecurity or position, is likely to cause danger.

Endorsement

Limited powers of endorsement and disqualification are given by Sched. 4 to the 1972 Act. Endorsement must be ordered, unless there are special reasons or the defendant had no reason to suspect that an offence was being committed (see under " Exceptions from Endorsement "), for an offence under the Regulations in using a vehicle or trailer or causing or permitting its use in the following circumstances:—

(a) so as to cause or be likely to cause danger by the condition of the vehicle or its parts or accessories, the number of passengers carried by it, or the weight, distribution, packing or adjustment of its load;

(b) in breach of a requirement as to brakes, steering gear or tyres;

(c) for any purpose for which it is so unsuitable as to cause or be likely to cause danger; or

(d) an offence of carrying on a goods vehicle a load which, by reason of its insecurity or position, is likely to cause danger (1972 Act, Sched. 4, column 5 of the entry relating to s. 40 (5), as amended by s. 21 (4) of the Act of 1974).

Regulation 90 (1) relates to (a) above and regs. 94, 95 and 99 to (b), and also it seems that regulations as to brakes and tyres in Pt. II come under (b). Offences under reg. 90 (1) as to " weight, distribution, packing and adjustment of the load ", as well as the other matters mentioned in reg. 90 (1), carry compulsory endorsement. Offences under reg. 90 (2) as to " security and position " of the load relate to (d) above, and also now carry compulsory endorsement and discretionary disqualification. Offences contrary to reg. 90 (3) relate to (c) above and also now carry compulsory endorsement and discretionary disqualification. In other words only offences under regs. 90 (1) (other than as to " manner " of carriage of passengers), 90 (2), 90 (3), 94, 95 and 99 and under the regulations in Pt. II as to brakes and tyres carry endorsement and it may not be ordered for any other offence under the Regulations. Like considerations would apply in respect of offences under the Track Laying Vehicles Regulations. An offence under reg. 116 of leaving a vehicle unattended without setting the brake does not carry endorsement because it is not an offence as to use of the vehicle but as to the duties of the driver and also because it would be anomalous if this did carry endorsement while the offence under the same regulation of not stopping the engine did not (*Kenyon* v. *Thorley* [1973] R.T.R. 60) (see p. 422).

Paragraphs (*c*) (reg. 90 (3)) and (*d*) (reg. 90 (2)) above were added by s. 21 (4) of the Act of 1974, thus reversing *Beighton* v. *Brown* [1965] 1 All E.R. 793 where it had been held that an offence under reg. 90 (2) was not endorsable and *R.* v. *Bromley JJ.* [1970] Crim.L.R. 655 where it had been held that an offence under reg. 90 (3) was not endorsable.

Column 4 of Sched. 4 to the Road Traffic Act, 1972, for offences contrary to s. 40 (5), which indicates the offences of " dangerous condition " for which endorsement may be ordered, does not mention the " manner " in which passengers are carried and it is submitted that there is thus no power to endorse for an offence under reg. 90 (1) as to the manner of such carriage. Nor is there any power to endorse for offences of overloading a motor vehicle unless the charge is under reg. 90 (1), viz., that the weight of the load was such as to cause danger.

Exceptions from Endorsement

By the Road Traffic (Amendment) Act, 1967, s. 7 (now column 5 of the entry relating to s. 40 (5) contained in Pt. I of Sched. 4 to the 1972 Act) where a person is convicted of the offences which carry compulsory endorsement under the Construction and Use Regulations, i.e., those relating to brakes, tyres and steering, dangerous condition, insecure load (see (*a*), (*b*), (*c*) and (*d*), *supra*), his licence shall not be endorsed if he proves (*semble*, on a balance of probabilities) that he did not know, and had no reasonable cause to suspect that the facts of the case were such that that offence would be committed. The effect of this is to exempt from endorsement, driving test and disqualification, including totting-up (but not from conviction and fine), a driver who shows that he had taken out his vehicle in reliance on his foreman's or its owner's assurance that the brakes, steering, etc., were in order or in reliance on the load being properly packed by his firm's loaders; likewise it will exempt an employer who sends out his driver with properly maintained vehicles and proper instructions to take them off the road if defects appear but whose drivers disobey those instructions, so that the employer, though physically absent, is charged with using with defective brakes, etc. It may well exempt sons and daughters who drive their parents' cars on the assumption that they are in good running order; it will be a question of fact in each case whether they had any reasonable cause to suspect that there was anything wrong with the brakes, steering or tyres. It will certainly exempt those who drive defective vehicles relying on the owner's assurance that they are in good condition and those who drive vehicles which have just come back from a check at a garage, provided that in these and the earlier cited cases they do not go on driving after the defect has become obvious. The defendant's evidence will always be required and he must show not only that he did not know of the defect but also that he had no reasonable cause to suspect it. The test of reasonableness is, it is submitted, subjective; the standard of knowledge expected of the driver of the Clapham omnibus will be higher than that of the man on it, when driving his own car, unless he is in the motor trade, but there must come a time when it is obvious to anyone that something is wrong. A motorist who genuinely believes his steering to be in order, having just had it repaired, but finds it fails in Piccadilly Circus, may claim the benefit of the exception if he stops at once but he cannot dodge the column if, knowing of the defect, he continues to drive into Trafalgar Square. It will also exempt a lorry driver convicted of using the lorry with an insecure load which has been caused by a latent defect of which he neither knew nor could have known (e.g. *Cornish* v. *Ferry Masters* and *Keyse* v. *Sainsbury* on pp. 418, 419).

Endorsement need not be ordered in any event if there are special reasons (see Chapter VII). Since s. 7 of the Road Traffic (Amendment) Act, 1967, said that, if a person proves that he did not know or have reasonable cause to suspect that an offence arose, " he shall not be liable to be disqualified . . . nor shall particulars of his conviction be endorsed," it seemed that the court was forbidden to endorse or disqualify on such proof, even if it wished to do so.   The Road Traffic Act, 1972, now sets out the matter less clearly in columnar form but no doubt the law is unchanged in this respect because it will presumably be held that the 1972 Act, being primarily a consolidation Act, intended no change.

Disqualification

Disqualification for any period and a driving test may be ordered for any offence for which endorsement is obligatory but not for any other offence under the Regulations. Section 93 (3) of the 1972 Act applies to offences for which disqualification may be ordered but not to any other offences under the Regulations. If a person is convicted of a disqualifiable offence under them and he has been previously convicted of an endorsed disqualifiable offence

436 CONSTRUCTION AND USE REGULATIONS

within the three years immediately before the commission of this third offence he must be disqualified for at least six months, unless having regard to all the circumstances there are grounds for mitigating the normal consequences of the conviction (see p. 688). Such grounds would obviously include the fact that he had no reason to suspect that an offence was being committed; see " Exceptions from Endorsement ", *supra*. If such is proved, the court, it is submitted, is forbidden to disqualify or endorse (see last paragraph) even if it wants to do so. The six-month disqualification is additional and consecutive to any period of disqualification imposed on the same occasion or for a previous offence.

Like provisions as to fines, endorsement, driving tests and disqualification, etc., apply to offences under the Motor Vehicles (Construction and Use) (Track Laying Vehicles) Regulations.

" Trailer " is defined by s. 190 (1) of the Act of 1972 as a " vehicle ", so it is submitted that offences of use, etc., of trailers in a dangerous condition, with defective brakes, etc., attract compulsory endorsement and optional disqualification. The draftsman of the consolidating 1972 Act apparently takes the same view. Column 5 of Sched. 4 where it relates to offences contrary to s. 40 (5) refers to " any motor vehicle or trailer ".

The penalties suggested by the Magistrates' Association for breach of Construction and Use Regulations are set out on p. 880 (see also generally p. 594).

Endorsement Code

The endorsement codes for offences contrary to the Construction and Use Regulations are as follows:—

Using a vehicle with defective brakes	CU 10
Causing or likely to cause danger by reason of use of unsuitable vehicle or using a vehicle with parts or accessories (excluding brakes, steering or tyres) in a dangerous condition.	CU 20
Using a vehicle with defective tyres	CU 30
Using a vehicle with defective steering	CU 40
Causing or likely to cause danger by reason of load or passengers	CU 50

12. THE PEDESTRIAN CROSSINGS REGULATIONS

The Pedestrian Crossings Regulations of 1954, as amended by numerous subsequent amending regulations, were revoked and replaced by the " Zebra " Pedestrian Crossings Regulations, 1971 (S.I. 1971 No. 1524). " Pelican " crossings (see the " Pelican "

Pedestrian Crossings Regulations and General Directions, 1969 (S.I. 1969 No. 888)) are operated by push buttons and replaced the push-button controlled crossings under the 1967 Regulations: see p. 445. The text of the 1971 Regulations reads:—

"**1.** (*Commencement and citation.*)

2. (*Saving for crossings under the* 1954 *Regulations—now spent.*)

Interpretation

" **3.**—(1) In these Regulations, unless the context otherwise requires, the following expressions have the meanings hereby respectively assigned to them:—

'the appropriate Secretary of State' means, in relation to a crossing established on a road in England excluding Monmouthshire, the Secretary of State for the Environment, in relation to a crossing established on a road in Scotland, the Secretary of State for Scotland, and, in relation to a crossing established on a road in Wales or Monmouthshire, the Secretary of State for Wales;

'appropriate authority' means, in relation to a crossing on a trunk road, the appropriate Secretary of State, and in relation to any other crossing the local authority in whose scheme submitted and approved under section 21 of the Act of 1967 the crossing is for the time being included;

'carriageway' does not include that part of any road which consists of a street refuge or central reservation, whether within the limits of a crossing or not;

'central reservation' means any provision, not consisting of a street refuge, made in a road for separating one part of the carriageway of that road from another part of that carriageway for the safety or guidance of vehicular traffic using that road;

'crossing' means a crossing for foot passengers established either—

(*a*) by a local authority in accordance with the provisions for the time being in force of a scheme submitted and approved under section 21 of the Act of 1967, or

(*b*) in the case of a trunk road, by the appropriate Secretary of State in the discharge of the duty imposed on him by section 22 of the Act of 1967;

but does not include a 'Pelican' crossing within the meaning of the 'Pelican' Pedestrian Crossings Regulations, 1969;

'dual-carriageway road' means a length of road on which a part of the carriageway thereof is separated from another part thereof by a central reservation;

'give-way line' has the meaning assigned to it by paragraph 2 of Schedule 3;

'one-way street' means any road in which the driving of all vehicles otherwise than in one direction is prohibited at all times;

'stud' means a mark or device on the carriageway, whether or not projecting above the surface thereof;

'zebra controlled area' means, in relation to a zebra crossing, the area of the carriageway in the vicinity of the crossing and lying on both sides of the crossing or only one side of the crossing, being an area the presence and limits of which are indicated in accordance with Schedule 3;

'zebra crossing' means a crossing the presence and limits of which are indicated in accordance with the provisions of Schedule 2;

'uncontrolled zebra crossing' means a zebra crossing at which traffic is not for the time being controlled by a police constable in uniform or by a traffic warden.

(2) Any reference in these Regulations to a numbered Regulation or Schedule is a reference to the Regulation or Schedule bearing that number in these Regulations except where otherwise expressly provided.

(3) Any reference in these Regulations to any enactment shall be construed as a reference to that enactment as amended by any subsequent enactment.

(4) The Interpretation Act, 1889, shall apply for the interpretation of these Regulations as it applies for the interpretation of an Act of Parliament, and as if for the purposes of section 38 of that Act these Regulations were an Act of Parliament and the Regulations revoked by Regulation 2 were Acts of Parliament thereby repealed.

Part II

Marks, Signs and other Particulars as Respects Zebra Crossings

Zebra crossings

4.—(1) The provisions of Part I of Schedule 2 shall have effect for regulating the manner in which the presence and limits of a crossing are to be indicated by marks or studs on the carriageway for the purpose of constituting it a zebra crossing.

(2) The provisions of Part II of Schedule 2 shall have effect as respects the size, colour and type of the traffic signs which are to be placed at or near a crossing for the purpose of constituting it a zebra crossing.

Zebra controlled areas and give-way lines

5.—(1) Subject to paragraph (3) of this Regulation, the provisions of Schedule 3 shall have effect as respects the size, colour and type of the traffic signs which shall be placed in the vicinity of a zebra crossing for the purpose of constituting a zebra controlled area in relation to that crossing and of indicating the presence and limits of that area.

(2) A give-way line (included among the said signs) shall, where provided, also convey to vehicular traffic proceeding towards a zebra crossing the position at or before which a driver of a vehicle should stop it for the purpose of complying with Regulation 8.

(3) Where the appropriate authority is satisfied in relation to a particular area of carriageway in the vicinity of a zebra crossing that, by reason of the layout of, or character of, the roads in the vicinity of the crossing, the application of such a prohibition as is mentioned in Regulation 10 or 12 to that particular area or the constitution of that particular area as a zebra controlled area by the placing of traffic signs in accordance with Schedule 3 would be impracticable, it shall not be necessary for that area to be constituted a zebra controlled area but, if by virtue of this paragraph it is proposed that no area, on either side of the limits of a zebra crossing (not on a trunk road), is to be constituted a zebra controlled area by the 30th November, 1973, a notice in writing shall be sent by the appropriate authority before that date to the appropriate Secretary of State stating the reasons why it is proposed that no such area should be so constituted.

Variations in dimensions shown in Schedule 3

6. Any variations in a dimension specified in the diagram in Schedule 3 or otherwise specified in that Schedule shall be treated as permitted by these Regulations if the variation—

    (*a*) in the case of a dimension of 300 millimetres or more, does not exceed 20% of that dimension; or

    (*b*) in the case of a dimension of less than 300 millimetres, where the actual dimension exceeds the dimension so specified, does not exceed 30% of the dimension so specified, and where the actual dimension is less than the dimension so specified, does not exceed 10% of the dimension so specified."

[*Regulation 7 empowers the appropriate authority to illuminate pedestrian crossings during the hours of darkness.*]

Precedence of passengers over vehicles

" **8.** Every foot passenger on the carriageway within the limits of an uncontrolled zebra crossing shall have precedence within those limits over any vehicle and the driver of the vehicle shall accord such precedence to the foot passenger, if the foot passenger is on the carriageway within those limits before the vehicle or any part thereof has come on to the carriageway within those limits.

For the purpose of this Regulation, in the case of such a crossing on which there is a street refuge or central reservation the parts of the crossing which are situated on each side of the street refuge or central reservation as the case may be shall each be treated as a separate crossing.

Prohibition against the waiting of vehicles and pedestrians on zebra crossings

9.—(1) The driver of a vehicle shall not cause the vehicle or any part thereof to stop within the limits of a zebra crossing unless either he is prevented from proceeding by circumstances beyond his control or it is necessary for him to stop in order to avoid an accident.

(2) No foot passenger shall remain on the carriageway within the limits of a zebra crossing longer than is necessary for the purpose of passing over the crossing with reasonable despatch.

Prohibition against overtaking at zebra crossings

10. The driver of a vehicle while it or any part of it is in a zebra controlled area and it is proceeding towards the limits of an uncontrolled zebra crossing in relation to which that area is indicated (which vehicle is in this and the next succeeding Regulation referred to as ' the approaching vehicle ') shall not cause the vehicle, or any part of it—

    (*a*) to pass ahead of the foremost part of another moving motor vehicle, being a vehicle proceeding in the same direction wholly or partly within that area, or

    (*b*) subject to the next succeeding Regulation, to pass ahead of the foremost part of a stationary vehicle on the same side of the crossing as the approaching vehicle, which stationary vehicle is stopped for the purpose of complying with Regulation 8.

For the purposes of this Regulation—

    (i) the reference to another moving motor vehicle is, in a case where only one other motor vehicle is proceeding in the same direction in a zebra controlled area, a reference to that vehicle, and, in a case where more than one other motor vehicle is so proceeding, a reference to such one of those vehicles as is nearest to the limits of the crossing;

(ii) the reference to a stationary vehicle is, in a case where only one other vehicle is stopped for the purpose of complying with Regulation 8, a reference to that vehicle and, in a case where more than one other vehicle is stopped for the purpose of complying with that Regulation, a reference to such one of those vehicles as is nearest to the limits of the crossing.

11.—(1) For the purposes of this Regulation, in the case of an uncontrolled zebra crossing, which is on a road, being a one-way street, and on which there is a street refuge or central reservation, the parts of the crossing which are situated on each side of the street refuge or central reservation as the case may be shall each be treated as a separate crossing.

(2) Nothing in paragraph (*b*) of the last preceding Regulation shall apply so as to prevent the approaching vehicle from passing ahead of the foremost part of a stationary vehicle within the meaning of that paragraph, if the stationary vehicle is stopped for the purpose of complying with Regulation 8 in relation to an uncontrolled zebra crossing which by virtue of this Regulation is treated as a separate crossing from the uncontrolled zebra crossing towards the limits of which the approaching vehicle is proceeding.

Prohibition on stopping in areas adjacent to zebra crossings

12.—(1) For the purposes of this Regulation and the next two following Regulations, the expression ' vehicle ' shall not include a pedal bicycle not having a sidecar attached thereto, whether additional means of propulsion by mechanical power are attached to the bicycle or not.

(2) Save as provided in Regulations 14 and 15, the driver of a vehicle shall not cause the vehicle or any part thereof to stop in a zebra controlled area ".

13. (*This Regulation has ceased to have effect.*)

" **14.** A vehicle shall not by Regulation 12 or 13 be prevented from stopping in any length of road on any side thereof—

(*a*) if the driver has stopped for the purpose of complying with Regulation 8 or Regulation 10 (*b*);

(*b*) if the driver is prevented from proceeding by circumstances beyond his control or it is necessary for him to stop in order to avoid an accident; or

(*c*) for so long as may be necessary to enable the vehicle, if it cannot be used for such purpose without stopping in that length of road, to be used for fire brigade, ambulance or police purposes or in connection with any building operation, demolition or excavation, the removal of any obstruction to traffic, the maintenance, improvement or reconstruction of that length of road, or the laying, erection, alteration, repair or cleaning in or near to that length of road of any traffic sign or sewer or of any main, pipe or apparatus for the supply of gas, water or electricity, or of any telegraph or telephone wires, cables, posts or supports.

15. A vehicle shall not by Regulation 12 be prevented from stopping in a zebra controlled area—

(a) if the vehicle is stopped for the purpose of making a left or right turn;

(b) if the vehicle is a public service vehicle, being a stage carriage or an express carriage being used otherwise than on an excursion or tour within the meaning of section 159 (1) of the Transport Act 1968, and the vehicle is waiting, after having proceeded past the zebra crossing in relation to which the zebra controlled area is indicated, for the purpose of enabling persons to board or alight from the vehicle."

[*Schedule* 1 *lists the Regulations repealed.*]

SCHEDULE 2   Regulation 4

MANNER OF INDICATING PRESENCE AND LIMITS OF ZEBRA CROSSINGS

PART I

Studs and Marks

" 1.—(1) Every crossing and its limits shall be indicated by two lines of studs placed across the carriageway in accordance with the following provisions of this paragraph.

(2) Each line formed by the outside edges of the studs shall be so separated from the other line so formed that no point on one line shall be less than 2.4 metres nor more than 5 metres or such greater distance (not being more than 10.1 metres) as the appropriate Secretary of State may authorise in writing in the case of any particular crossing from the nearest point on the other line:

Provided that the preceding provisions of this sub-paragraph shall be regarded as having been complied with in the case of any crossing which for the most part complies with those provisions notwithstanding that those provisions may not be so complied with as respects the distance from one or more points on one line to the nearest point on the other line, so long as the general indication of the lines is not thereby materially impaired.

(3) The studs of which each line is constituted shall be so placed that the distance from the centre of any one stud to the centre of the next stud in the line is not less than 250 millimetres nor more than 715 millimetres, and a distance of not more than 1.3 metres is left between the edge of the carriageway at either end of the line and the centre of the stud nearest thereto:

Provided that the preceding provisions of this sub-paragraph shall be regarded as having been complied with in the case of any line where most of the studs constituting it comply with those provisions notwithstanding that those provisions may not be complied with as respects one or more such studs, so long as the general indication of the line is not thereby materially impaired.

(4) Studs shall not be fitted with reflecting lenses and shall be—

(a) white, silver or light grey in colour;

(b) square or circular in plan, the sides of a square stud not being less than 95 millimetres nor more than 110 millimetres in length and the diameter of a circular stud not being less than 95 millimetres nor more than 110 millimetres, and

(c) so fixed that they do not project more than 16 millimetres above the carriageway at their highest points nor more than 7 millimetres at their edges.

2. A crossing or its limits shall not be deemed to have ceased to be indicated in accordance with the preceding provisions of this Part of this Schedule by reason only of the discoloration or temporary removal or displacement of one or more studs in any line so long as the general indication of the line is not thereby materially impaired.

3. Without derogation from the provisions of the preceding paragraphs of this Part of this Schedule, every crossing shall be further indicated in accordance with the following provisions of this Part and of Part II of this Schedule.

4.—(1) The carriageway shall be marked within the limits of every such crossing with a pattern of alternate black and white stripes:

Provided that where the colour of the surface of the carriageway provides a reasonable contrast with the colour of white that surface may itself be utilised for providing stripes which would otherwise be required to be black.

(2) Every stripe shall—

(a) extend along the carriageway from one line formed by the inside edges of the studs or from a part of the crossing which is not more than 155 millimetres from that line to the other line so formed or to a part of the crossing which is not more than 155 millimetres from that line; and

(b) be of a width of not less than 500 millimetres or of such smaller width not being less than 380 millimetres as in the case of any particular crossing the appropriate authority may consider necessary having regard to the layout of the carriageway and, in the case of the first stripe at each end of the crossing, not more than 1.3 metres, or in the case of any other stripe, not more than 715 millimetres or of such greater width not being more than 840 millimetres as in the case of any particular crossing the appropriate authority may consider necessary having regard to the layout of the carriageway.

(3) The preceding provisions of this paragraph shall be regarded as having been complied with in the case of any crossing which for the most part complies with those provisions notwithstanding that those provisions may not be complied with as respects one or more stripes and a crossing shall not be deemed to have ceased to be indicated in accordance with those provisions by reason only of the imperfection, discoloration or partial displacement of one or more of the stripes, so long as the general appearance of the pattern of stripes is not materially impaired.

PART II

Traffic Signs

1. The traffic signs which are to be placed at or near a crossing for the purpose of constituting it and indicating it as a zebra crossing shall consist of globes in relation to which the following provisions in this Part of this Schedule are complied with.

2.—(1) At or near each end of every crossing there shall be placed, and in the case of a crossing on which there is a street refuge or central reservation there may be placed on the refuge or reservation, in accordance with the following provisions of this paragraph globes mounted on posts or brackets.

(2) Globes shall be—

- (a) yellow in colour;
- (b) not less than 275 millimetres nor more than 335 millimetres in diameter; and
- (c) so mounted that the height of the lowest part of the globe is not less than 2.1 metres nor more than 3.1 metres above the surface of the ground in the immediate vicinity.

(3) Globes shall be illuminated by a flashing light or, where the appropriate Secretary of State so authorises in writing in the case of any particular crossing, by a constant light.

(4) Where globes are mounted on or attached to posts specially provided for the purpose, every such post shall, in so far as it extends above ground level, be coloured black and white in alternate horizontal bands, the lowest band visible to approaching traffic being coloured black and not less than 275 millimetres nor more than 1 metre in width and each other band being not less than 275 millimetres nor more than 335 millimetres in width:

Provided that nothing in this sub-paragraph shall apply to any container fixed on any such post which encloses the apparatus for providing the illumination of a globe.

3. A crossing shall not be deemed to have ceased to be indicated in accordance with the preceding provisions of this Part of this Schedule by reason only of—

- (a) the imperfection, discoloration or disfigurement of any of the globes, posts or brackets; or
- (b) the failure of the illumination of any of the globes:
  Provided that this sub-paragraph shall not apply unless at least one globe is illuminated in accordance with the provisions of sub-paragraph (3) of the last preceding paragraph ".

SCHEDULE 3 — Regulation 5

MANNER OF INDICATING ZEBRA CONTROLLED AREA AND PROVISION AS TO PLACING OF GIVE-WAY LINE

PART I

Traffic Signs

" 1. Subject to the provisions of Regulation 5 (3), the traffic signs which are to be placed on a road in the vicinity of a zebra crossing for the purpose of constituting a zebra controlled area lying on both sides of the limits of the crossing or on only one side of such limits and indicating the presence and limits of such an area shall consist of a pattern of lines of the size and type shown in the diagram in Part II of this Schedule and so placed as hereinafter provided.

2. A pattern of lines shall, subject as hereinafter provided, consist of:—

(*a*) a transverse white broken line (hereinafter referred to as a " give-way line ") placed on the carriageway 1 metre from and parallel to the nearer line of studs indicating the limits of the crossing and shall extend across the carriageway in the manner indicated in the said diagram; and

(*b*) two or more longitudinal white broken lines (hereinafter referred to as " zig-zag lines ") placed on the carriageway or, where the road is a dual-carriageway road, on each part of the carriageway, each zig-zag line containing not less than 8 nor more than 18 marks and extending away from the crossing at a point 150 millimetres from the nearest part of the give-way line on the same side of the crossing to a point 150 millimetres from the nearest part of a terminal line of the size and type shown in the said diagram (hereinafter referred to as a " terminal line ").

3. Where the appropriate authority is satisfied in relation to a particular area of carriageway in the vicinity of a zebra crossing that by reason of the layout of, or character of, the roads in the vicinity of the crossing it would be impracticable to lay the pattern of lines as shown in the diagram in Part II of this Schedule and in accordance with the preceding paragraph any of the following variations as respects the pattern shall be permitted—

(*a*) the number of marks contained in each zig-zag line may be reduced from 8 to not less than 2;

(*b*) a mark contained in a zig-zag line may be varied in length so as to extend for a distance not less than 1 metre and less than 2 metres, but where such a variation is made as respects a mark each other mark in each zig-zag line shall be of the same or substantially the same length as that mark, so however that the number of marks in each zig-zag line shall not be more than 8 nor less than 2.

4. The angle of the give-way line (if any) in relation to and its distance from the nearer line of studs indicating the limits of a crossing may be varied, if the appropriate authority is satisfied that such variation is necessary having regard to the angle of the crossing in relation to the edge of the carriageway at the place where the crossing is situated.

5. Where by reason of Regulation 5 (3) an area of carriageway in the vicinity of a zebra crossing is not constituted a zebra controlled area by the placing of a pattern of lines as provided in the foregoing provisions of this Schedule, a give-way line shall nevertheless be placed on the carriageway as previously provided in this Schedule unless the appropriate authority is satisfied that by reason of the position of that crossing it is impracticable so to place the line.

6. Each mark contained in a give-way line or in a zig-zag line and each terminal line may be illuminated by the use of reflecting material.

7. A zebra controlled area or its limits shall not be deemed to have ceased to be indicated in accordance with the provisions of this Schedule by reason only of the imperfection, discoloration or partial displacement of either a terminal line or one or more of the marks comprised in a give-way line or a zig-zag line, so long as the general indication of any such line is not thereby materially impaired."

The regulations apply to the drivers of motor vehicles, trams, trolley vehicles and horse-drawn vehicles and to the riders of motor cycles and cycles (save as indicated in reg. 12) but not to equestrians. Save as provided in reg. 14, there is no exemption for fire engines, ambulances or police cars. The regulations are made under the Road Traffic Regulation Act, 1967, ss. 21 to 23.

The regulations apply to Crown vehicles (s. 97 of the 1967 Act).

Pelican Crossings

These are regulated by the " Pelican " Pedestrian Crossings Regulations and General Directions, 1969 (S.I. 1969 No. 888). By reg. 6 when a steady amber light is showing vehicles must stop at the stop line unless the vehicle is so close to the stop line that it cannot safely stop; when the red light is showing a vehicle is prohibited from proceeding over the stop line. When a flashing amber light shows, the driver shall accord precedence to a pedestrian if the latter is on the carriageway within the limits of the crossing before any part of the vehicle has entered those limits (reg. 11 is in almost identical terms to reg. 8 of the " Zebra " Crossings Regulations, *supra*). Regulation 9 prohibits the stopping of vehicles on the approach to a pelican crossing (this is in rather similar terms to reg. 14 of the " Zebra " Crossings Regulations). Regulation 12 forbids either vehicles or pedestrians to wait on the crossing.

Section 179 of the Road Traffic Act, 1972, does not apply to offences under the " Pelican " Crossings Regulations and the police do not have to serve a notice of intended prosecution (*Sulston* v. *Hammond* [1970] 2 All E.R. 830).

Controlled Areas

The Controlled Areas (Pedestrians) Regulations, 1965 (S.I. 1965 No. 545), made special provisions as to pedestrians going on parts of the carriageway of certain streets in London.

Proof of Conformity of Crossings

By the Road Traffic Regulation Act, 1967, s. 23 (6), for the purposes of a prosecution under the Regulations a crossing shall be deemed to be duly established and indicated unless the contrary is proved.

By reg. 4 every crossing and its limits shall be indicated in accordance with the provisions of Sched. 2. This means that every crossing shall be indicated by two lines of studs placed across the roadway in accordance with Pt. I of Sched. 2. There the distances apart, the colour, size, shape and permitted projection of the studs are prescribed and by para. 2 a crossing or its limits shall not be deemed to have ceased to be indicated by reason only of the discoloration or temporary removal or displacing of one or more studs in any line so long as the general indication of the line is not thereby materially impaired. Paragraph 1 (2) and (3) saves crossings which comply for the most part as respects the studs and distances apart.

The crossing must also be indicated by yellow globes and black and white stripes on the crossing.

Paragraph 4 (1) allows the omission of black painted stripes where the surface of the road provides a reasonable contrast to the white stripes.

By para. 4 (3) the provisions as to the width and extent of the stripes shall be regarded as having been complied with though they may not have been so complied with as respects one or more of the stripes, and disregarding any imperfection, discoloration or partial displacement of one or more of the stripes, so long as the general appearance of the stripes is not materially impaired.

Paragraph 1 and para. 2 (1) of Pt. II of Sched. 2 require the crossing also to be indicated by yellow globes mounted on posts or brackets. Although there must be a yellow globe at or near each end of the crossing, there need not be globes on any central reservation or street refuge but such globes *may* be placed there. If globes are not placed on a central reservation, the crossing would appear to be sufficiently indicated. The globes are required to be illuminated by flashing lights or, where so authorised by the Secretary of State, by a constant light. But by para. 3 a crossing shall not cease to be properly indicated by reason only of the imperfection, discoloration or disfigurement of any of the posts, globes or brackets or the failure of the illumination of the globes. If, however, the illumination of *all* the globes fails, then the proviso to para. 3 (*b*) has the effect of removing the protection of para. 3. Where therefore there is not at least one globe illuminated, the crossing is not indicated as required by the Regulations and a motorist may not be convicted of failing to accord precedence. Paragraph 2 (2) and (4) prescribe the limits of dimensions of the globes, their height above ground, and the alternate black and white horizontal stripes on the posts. Where a globe is mounted on a bracket, the bracket does not have to be striped. It is only posts specially provided for the purpose of bearing globes which are required to be painted black and white.

Schedule 3 contains provisions prescribing the manner in which the zebra controlled area and " give-way " lines are to be indicated. Regulation 5 (3) enabled the appropriate authority to dispense with the necessity of a controlled area by the giving of a notice before 30th November, 1973, to the Secretary of State. A broken white line (the " give-way " line) must be placed one metre each side of the crossing and two or more longitudinal white lines (" zig-zag " lines) must be placed on each side of the crossing indicating the controlled area. The Schedule prescribes the dimensions of the signs and reg. 6 prescribes the permitted variations in the dimensions. By para. 7 of Sched. 3 the controlled area and its limits are sufficiently indicated despite the imperfection, discoloration or displacement of any of the lines so long as the general indication of such line is not materially impaired.

The failure of the illumination of a lamp provided under reg. 7 would not appear to invalidate the crossing because the Regulation does not make it mandatory to provide such a lamp.

The Road Traffic Regulation Act, 1967, s. 23 (4), allows special provisions to be made in regard to particular crossings.

Proceedings for Other Offences

The Regulations do not bar any proceedings for disobeying police signals or traffic lights or for dangerous or careless driving or cycling; if, however, in proceedings for dangerous or careless driving the justices convict and take into account the defendant's conduct in so far as it was a breach of the Regulations, even though no such breach was charged, it is arguable that the conviction might be a bar to further proceedings under the Regulations (see p. 92). Certainly, a conviction and the imposition of a penalty for dangerous or careless driving might be held to be a good ground for not inflicting a penalty under the Regulations pursuant to the Interpretation Act, 1889, s. 33 (provision as to offences under two or more laws). An acquittal for dangerous or careless driving would generally be no bar to proceedings under the Regulations (see generally p. 92). See p. 290 as to failure to accord precedence being charged along with careless driving.

According Precedence

This is dealt with by reg. 8 of the 1971 Regulations. The definition of " uncontrolled crossing " is in reg. 3 (1). If the crossing is for the time being controlled by a policeman in uniform or by a traffic warden the crossing ceases to be " uncontrolled " and the provisions relating to pedestrians being afforded precedence and motorists being forbidden to overtake cease, but vehicles and pedestrians must obey the policeman's or traffic warden's signals and failure to do so may result in prosecution under the Road Traffic Act, 1972, s. 22, s. 23 or s. 159.

Liability under reg. 8 arises only if the pedestrian is on the carriageway within the limits of the crossing before the vehicle or any part of it has come on the carriageway within those limits, i.e., the black and white striped area inside the innermost lines of studs. See p. 453 under " Limits of Crossing " as to that term. A pedestrian waiting on the kerb or walking along the roadway towards the crossing is thus not within reg. 8. It is essential not to be confused between the " Limits of Crossing " and the zebra controlled area, i.e., the area of carriageway, bordered by zig-zag lines both sides of the actual crossing (see p. 453 under " Zebra Controlled Area " for meaning of that term). Justices who dismissed a case of failing to accord precedence under reg. 8 because they were not certain whether the motorist reached the beginnings of the zebra controlled area before the pedestrian stepped on the actual crossing were directed to convict the motorist (*Moulder* v. *Neville* [1974] R.T.R. 53); a case can only be dismissed under reg. 8 if the prosecution fail to prove that the foot passenger stepped onto the actual crossing before the car reached the actual limits of the crossing, i.e., the black and white striped area.

Regulation 5 (2) requires the motorist to stop at or before the " give-way " line which is one metre from the limits of the crossing in order to afford the pedestrian precedence, and he will offend against reg. 8 if he does not do so.

Where there is a central reservation or street refuge in a crossing, the parts on each side of the reservation or refuge are treated as separate crossings (reg. 8). A motorist approaching a crossing on the left-hand side of a road thus owes no duty under reg. 8 to a pedestrian who is walking from the right-hand kerb towards a central reservation.

If a zebra crossing is for the time being controlled by a police officer or traffic warden, again reg. 8 will not apply, and the driver or rider of a vehicle must obey the police officer's signals. The reason for this provision seems to be that pedestrians who themselves disobey the warning gestures of a police officer thereby put themselves in peril, and to cast a double duty on a motorist of both obeying a police officer and according precedence to a pedestrian would be unfair. A High Court decision noted at 130 J.P.Jo. 759 (1966) is that a crossing is not controlled by a police officer when the latter is standing on the pavement at the crossing but has not begun controlling the traffic, even if he is about to do so.

In *Kayser* v. *L.P.T.B.* [1950] 1 All E.R. 231, a case on the pre-1951 Regulations, it was held that, where a driver is satisfied that persons on the crossing are out of danger from him, he may proceed at a reasonable speed. Compare *Wishart* v. *McDonald* on p. 451.

In *McKerrell* v. *Robertson* [1956] S.L.T. 290 it was held that precedence must be accorded to a woman pushing a go-chair when the go-chair is on the crossing, although she is still on the pavement; she and the go-chair are one entity. The case is discussed at 125 J.P.Jo. 341 of a pedestrian on a crossing who does not wish to cross.

A magistrates' court has held that a child on roller-skates is not a " foot passenger ". It is submitted that this decision is correct. In the absence of a definition a " foot passenger " must mean someone on foot. Cyclists have been known to push their cycles across uncontrolled pedestrian crossings. It can be argued that a cyclist, although dismounted, is still a cyclist and may not become a " foot passenger " merely because he dismounts. On the other hand *McKerrell* v. *Robertson, supra,* could be applied; if a pram pusher is one entity why not a cycle pusher? The distinction may lie in the fact that a cycle is a vehicle for the carriage of the cyclist, a pram may only carry a child and is required at all times to be propelled by someone on foot.

Absolute Liability of Driver

Subject to the limited exceptions given in *Burns* v. *Bidder, infra,* the duty of the motorist, cyclist or other driver to accord precedence is absolute.

In *Neal* v. *Reynolds* (1966), 110 S.J. 353, it was said that magistrates should not approach these prosecutions on the basis whether the defendant driver was negligent or not. In *Burns* v. *Bidder* [1966] 3 All E.R. 29, the cases were all reviewed again and James, J., said:—

" Regulation 4 must be read ' subject to the principle of impossibility ' . . . In my judgment the regulation does not impose an absolute duty come what may, and there is no breach [of it] in circumstances where the driver fails to accord precedence to a pedestrian solely because his control of the vehicle is taken from him by the occurrence of an event which is outside his possible or reasonable control and in respect of which he is in no way at fault." [He instanced the driver being stung by bees or having an epileptic fit or his vehicle being propelled forward by being hit from behind as illustrations of the vehicle's being taken out of the driver's control, so that his failure then to accord precedence would be no offence, and continued] ". . . a sudden removal of control over the vehicle occasioned by a latent defect of which the driver did not know and could not reasonably be expected to know would render the resulting failure to accord precedence no offence, provided he is in no way at fault himself. But beyond that limited sphere, the obligation of the driver under the regulations can properly be described . . . as an absolute one."

This case settled the law fairly conclusively as to reg. 4 of the 1954 Regulations. Regulation 8 of the 1971 Regulations does not differ materially from reg. 4 and it is submitted that *Burns* v. *Bidder* still expresses the law.

In *Gibbons* v. *Kahl* [1955] 3 All E.R. 345 it was said that it is the duty of a driver to be able to stop before he gets to a crossing unless he can see that there is no one on it. If he cannot see if there is anybody on it, he must drive in such a way that he can stop if there is a person on it masked from him by other traffic. In *Gibbons'* case, the defendant overtook a bus, which had stopped at a crossing to allow pedestrians to proceed; the pedestrians were hidden from the defendant by the bus and he did not see them until they had passed in front of the bus. He was then too near the crossing to stop and he was held guilty of not according precedence. This case was followed in *Lockie* v. *Lawton* (1960), 124 J.P. 24, where it was said that a driver approaching a crossing must drive in such a way that he can stop if there is a pedestrian on the crossing, although his view of the crossing may be blocked by other vehicles until he is right on it. In *Hughes* v. *Hall* [1960] 2 All E.R. 504 it was said that there was an absolute duty under the Regulations, and it is immaterial whether there is any evidence of negligence or failure to take care by the driver. In *Scott* v. *Clint* (1960), *The Times*, 28th October, a driver was approaching a crossing at 15 to 20 m.p.h. and, when he was 10 yards from it, two children stepped on it without looking. He swerved but could not avoid hitting one of them. It was held that he was guilty but that it was a proper case for an absolute discharge. The case of *Leicester* v. *Pearson* [1952] 2 All E.R. 71, holding that a driver could be excused if he was driving reasonably and with care in bad visibility, no longer seems to be of authority. In *Hughes* v. *Hall*, *supra*, the driver was approaching the crossing at a proper speed and had passed or partly passed over the approach studs when a pedestrian stepped on the crossing without looking and walked 9 or 10 feet before being hit by the car, which was rapidly pulling up. As stated, the driver was held guilty and, unless the High Court is prepared to draw a distinction between the cases cited above and cases where a pedestrian steps practically in front of a slow-moving car when it is a foot or so from the crossing, it seems that the driver must always be found guilty if he had not in fact accorded precedence, although an absolute discharge is often justifiable, where the driver is not negligent, and " special reasons " could be found.

The meaning of the term " accord precedence " was considered by two Metropolitan magistrates, whose views are reported at Jo.Crim.L. (1952) 105 and 110, but should now be read in the light of the cases cited in the last paragraph. In one case the defendant drove between two pedestrians on a zebra crossing; he was driving cautiously and neither pedestrian was endangered. Sir Wilfred Bennett dismissed the charge, holding that " according precedence " meant much the same as " not interrupting the free passage of a pedestrian ", the term in the pre-1951 Regulations. He said that the new Regulation required that a driver must not cause a pedestrian to stop once he has started to cross. In the other case, the facts accepted were that the pedestrians were on the crossing but so far away from the defendant's car that he could not have interrupted their crossing. Mr. T. F. Davis apparently did not agree that the law had not been altered and, save for " suicide cases " (*semble*, people who stepped practically in front of a fast-moving car), held that a motorist who could reasonably stop must stop if there are pedestrians on the crossing. In *Rhind* v. *Irvine* [1940] 2 W.W.R. 333, a Canadian case, it was held that the motorist's duty to " yield the right of way " to a pedestrian on a crossing did not give a pedestrian a right to walk into or against an obstructing car or to walk over the crossing with his eyes shut. In *Wishart* v. *McDonald* (1962), 78 Sh.Ct.Rep. 3, a driver passed over a crossing while a blind pedestrian was walking over it, the pedestrian being neither impeded by the car nor even aware of it; the sheriff acquitted the driver of not according precedence. The sheriff rejected the view that the Regulation means that the pedestrian shall go first over the crossing before the vehicle goes over it. Precedence, he said, means " go before " or " in front of " and the Regulation means that the vehicle shall not prevent a foot-passenger from crossing; the issue of precedence would arise only where there was a likely encounter between vehicle and pedestrian. A New Zealand Regulation required the motorist when approaching a pedestrian crossing to " yield the right of way " to a pedestrian on it. It was held that a motorist approaching a crossing on which there was a pedestrian must surrender to the latter any priority in passage ahead which he might otherwise have had whether or not a collision might seem likely or however far the pedestrian might be on the crossing to his left and that a pedestrian who had begun to cross and then paused and stopped was still within the protection of the Regulation (*Torok* v. *Lake* [1964] N.Z.L.R. 824). In *Kozimor* v. *Adey* [1962] Crim.L.R. 564, a civil case, Megaw, J., said that the only way a motorist can be certain of avoiding a breach of the Regulations is to approach the crossing at such a slow speed that he can stop in the event of any conceivable use of the crossing by any conceivable pedestrian except a suicidal one who deliberately walked in front of a car. If, therefore, a motorist driving in the centre of a wide street sees a pedestrian step off the kerb, the motorist, it is submitted, must stop if there is any reasonable possibility that the pedestrian might get in the car's path; the fact that the pedestrian is walking so slowly that it is unlikely that he will get in the car's path would not necessarily be an excuse, for he might panic and break into a run. If a pedestrian signals a car to come on and himself stops, it still seems that the driver should accord him precedence as a matter of strict law (*Neal* v. *Bedford* [1965] 3 All E.R. 250), though no doubt it would be strong mitigation if the driver accepted the pedestrian's signal to him to proceed and then the pedestrian dashed forward. In that case pedestrians had stopped to allow a car ahead of the defendant's car to pass in front of them; they moved on when the first car had passed and the defendant's car also came on and struck one of them. The High Court said that reg. 4 of the 1954 Regulations imposed an absolute duty to accord precedence and whether the defendant genuinely thought that the pedestrians would let him pass was irrelevant; they had not waived their precedence by signalling to him to pass but had started walking. A conviction was directed. However, in most cases it will turn out to be a question of fact and a motorist, even if he is held to have broken the law, may still have many matters to urge in mitigation of penalty. The question of liability under the 1954 Regulations is discussed in the *Criminal Law Review*, March, 1967.

Defence of Mechanical Failure

See *Burns* v. *Bidder*, on p. 449, where it was said that it would be a defence if a vehicle went on to a crossing because of the driver's excusable loss of control, through being stung or being pushed forward by a vehicle behind or through a latent defect in the brakes of which the driver could not reasonably be expected to know, so long as he was in no way at fault himself.

The Regulations are in a quite different form from the pre-1951 Regulations and the decisions on the latter are not necessarily of any help in deciding points arising on the present law; the old cases were reviewed in *L.P.T.B.* v. *Upson* [1949] 1 All E.R. 60. The latter case also deals with the question of a pedestrian's contributory negligence in a civil action.

Limits of Crossing

The limits of the crossing in reg. 4 of the 1971 Regulations means the striped parts and the lines of studs bordering them only and a vehicle has not come " within the limits of a crossing " under reg. 4 if it has come within the zig-zag lines marking the approach to the crossing but has not reached the studs bordering the black and white stripes (*Moulder* v. *Neville* [1974] R.T.R. 53, a case on the 1971 Regulations and following *Hughes* v. *Hall* [1960] 2 All E.R. 504 which was a similar decision on the 1954 Regulations). Under the 1971 Regulations the limits of the crossing are defined by the studs across the road on each side of the black and white stripes (Sched. 2, Pt. I, para. 1 (1)). A pedestrian is seemingly outside the limits of the crossing if he is outside the studs but within the " give-way " line which is one metre away. It seems that the effect of the " give-way " line is not to extend the limits of the crossing but to indicate to the motorist where he should stop to afford precedence to a pedestrian who is on the black and white stripes of the crossing.

Note the provision in reg. 8 as to the parts of a zebra crossing on each side of a street refuge or central reservation being treated as separate crossings for the purposes of that Regulation.

Stopping in the Zebra Controlled Area

Regulation 9 relates to stopping on crossings; circumstances beyond the driver's control and stopping to avoid an accident are defences. The Regulation also forbids pedestrians to loiter on the crossing. Regulation 12 forbids the driver of a vehicle to stop in the zebra controlled area. Note the definition of " zebra controlled area " in reg. 3 (1). It is the area bordered by zig-zag lines as required by Pts. I and II of Sched. 3. Note Pt. I of Sched. 3 and reg. 6 as to variations and in particular para. 7 of Pt. I of Sched. 3 as to imperfections. Bicycles are exempted from the regulation even if additional means of propulsion are attached. The bicycle must not, however, have a sidecar. It should be noted that the controlled area normally extends to both sides of the crossing, and unlike the former Regulations, it is an offence to stop on the further side of the crossing, as well as on its approach. Regulations 14 and 15 contain various exemptions from reg. 12: fire, ambulance, police and defence purposes, building works, road works, emergencies, etc. Stopping for the purpose of turning right or left is exempted. Public service vehicles are also exempted for the purpose of picking up or dropping passengers on the far side of the crossing but not on the approach to the crossing. Stopping for reasons beyond a driver's control or to avoid an accident is also exempted. The Regulations forbidding stopping in the area controlled by a zebra crossing apply even if the zebra crossing is for the time being controlled by a policeman or traffic warden.

Overtaking in the Controlled Area

It is an offence when approaching a zebra crossing to overtake a moving motor vehicle (reg. 10 (a)) or a stationary vehicle (reg. 10 (b)) in the area controlled by the crossing. It is not an offence to overtake a vehicle in the controlled area on the further side of the crossing. Regulation 10 is phrased in such a way that a vehicle " overtakes " another once any part of the vehicle passes ahead of the foremost part of the other vehicle. It would appear, therefore, that an offence is committed even if the overtaking vehicle subsequently drops back. However, it is only an offence if the vehicle overtaken is either the only other vehicle on the approach to the crossing or, if there is more than one, it is the nearest vehicle to the crossing. The vehicle being overtaken may be either moving or stationary but if it is stationary the overtaking is only an offence if the vehicle overtaken " has stopped for the purpose of complying with reg. 8 " (see reg. 10 (b)). It was held in *Gullen* v. *Ford*; *Prowse* v. *Clark* [1975] R.T.R. 303 that " stopped for the purpose of complying with reg. 8 " did not mean that the stationary vehicle must have stopped because a pedestrian had a foot on the crossing and the driver would thus have committed an offence under reg. 8 if the car had not stopped. Stopping for the purpose of reg. 8 includes a car which had stopped out of courtesy only to a pedestrian who was waiting to cross but who had not actually placed his foot on the carriageway. It was said *obiter* by Lord Widgery, C.J., that he was concerned in the case of very long crossings when no danger was caused by reason of a technical breach of reg. 10 (b). He suggested that the prosecution in such a case should refrain from prosecuting on a purely technical charge when no danger of any kind was created.

A further distinction between the offence under reg. 10 (a) of overtaking a moving motor vehicle and under reg. 10 (b) of overtaking a stationary vehicle is that an offence is only committed in overtaking a moving vehicle if the vehicle which is overtaken is a motor vehicle. An offence under reg. 10 (*b*) on the other hand is committed if the vehicle overtaken is any type of vehicle including a bicycle (see " vehicle " on p. 4).

If the crossing is controlled for the time being by a policeman or traffic warden, the provisions forbidding overtaking do not apply. Regulation 11 treats a crossing in a one-way street which has a central reservation as two separate crossings and allows a vehicle on one side of the crossing to overtake a vehicle which has stopped on the other side of the reservation to allow a passenger to cross.

Penalties, Endorsement and Disqualification

The penalty for a breach of the 1969 or 1971 Regulations on first or subsequent conviction is a fine of £100 (Road Traffic Regulation Act, 1967, s. 23 (5) as amended by the 1974 Act).

The Magistrates' Association suggested penalties for pedestrian crossing offences are (see pp. 879–880) £20 for parking within the limits of a pedestrian crossing and "£25 and consider disqualification " for the other offences under the Regulations (see generally p. 594).

The following provisions as to disqualification, tests and endorsement only apply where the defendant is convicted in respect of a motor vehicle.

Endorsement

The defendant's driving licence must be endorsed unless there are special reasons (1972 Act, s. 101 (2) and Sched. 4). See Chapter VII as to special reasons.

The endorsement codes in respect of pedestrian crossing offences are as follows:—

Undefined contravention of pedestrian crossing regulation (Scottish Courts only)	PC 10
Contravention of regulations with moving vehicle	PC 20
Contravention of regulations with stationary vehicle	PC 30

Disqualification

The defendant may be disqualified for any period on first or subsequent conviction (1972 Act, s. 93 (2)). Section 93 (3) applies so that a person convicted of an offence under the regulations who has been previously convicted on two occasions of an endorsed disqualifiable offence within the three years immediately preceding the commission of the pedestrian crossing offence must be disqualified for at least six months, unless having regard to all the circumstances there are grounds for mitigating the normal consequences of the conviction (see p. 688). The six-month disqualification is additional and consecutive to any period of disqualification imposed then or for a previous offence.

" Special reasons " in respect of pedestrian crossing offences are discussed in Chapter VII, at p. 680.

A driving test may be ordered on conviction (s. 93 (7)).

13. SCHOOL CROSSING PATROLS

These come under the Road Traffic Regulation Act, 1967, ss. 24 and 25. Section 25 reads:—

" *Stopping of vehicles at school crossings*

25.—(1) When between the hours of eight in the morning and half-past five in the afternoon a vehicle is approaching a place in a road where children on their way to or from school [or on their way from one part of a school to another] are crossing or seeking to cross the road, a school crossing patrol wearing a uniform approved by the Secretary of State shall have power, by exhibiting a prescribed sign, to require the person driving or propelling the vehicle to stop it.

(2) When a person has been required under subsection (1) above to stop a vehicle—

    (*a*) he shall cause the vehicle to stop before reaching the place where the children are crossing or seeking to cross and so as not to stop or impede their crossing; and

    (*b*) the vehicle shall not be put in motion again so as to reach the place in question so long as the sign continues to be exhibited;

and a person who fails to comply with paragraph (*a*) above, or who causes a vehicle to be put in motion in contravention of paragraph (*b*) above, shall be liable on summary conviction to a fine not exceeding [£100.]

(3) In this section—

    (*a*) ' prescribed sign ' means a sign of a size, colour and type prescribed by regulations made by the appropriate Minister, or, if authorisation is given by the appropriate Minister for the use of signs of a description not so prescribed, a sign of that description; and regulations under this subsection may provide for the attachment of reflectors to signs, or for the illumination of signs; and

    (*b*) ' school crossing patrol ' means a person appointed to patrol in accordance with arrangements made under section 24 of this Act.

(4) For the purposes of this section—

    (*a*) where it is proved that a sign was exhibited by a school crossing patrol, it shall be presumed to be of a size, colour and type prescribed, or of a description authorised, under the foregoing provisions of this section, and if it was exhibited in circumstances in which it was required by the regulations to be illuminated, to have been illuminated in the prescribed manner, unless the contrary is proved;

(b) where it is proved that a school crossing patrol was wearing uniform, the uniform shall be presumed, unless the contrary is proved, to be a uniform approved by the Secretary of State; and

(c) where it is proved that a prescribed sign was exhibited by a school crossing patrol at a place in a road where children were crossing or seeking to cross the road, it shall be presumed, unless the contrary is proved, that those children were on their way to or from school."

The words in square brackets in subss. (1) and (2) were inserted by the Road Traffic Act, 1974.

A person required to stop by the sign must " cause the vehicle to stop before reaching the place where the children are crossing or seeking to cross and so as not to stop or impede their crossing." It should be noted that before a person may be convicted under s. 25 (2) (a) of failing to stop or under s. 25 (2) (b) of putting the vehicle in motion again while the sign continues to be exhibited, the person must first have been required to stop in accordance with s. 25 (1).

In *Franklin* v. *Langdown* [1971] 3 All E.R. 662 a party of children with two or three adults were crossing a road under the protection of a school crossing patrol sign. When the last of the children had passed over the crown of the road, the defendant drove out of a side turning and passed behind the last of the adults, causing her to hasten her steps. At the time of so doing, the sign continued to be exhibited. The magistrates' court dismissed the case because they were of the opinion that a conviction under s. 25 (2) (a) could only be obtained if the motorist acted so as to stop or impede the children crossing. The justices were directed to convict and it was held that the words in s. 25 (2) (a), " and so as not to stop or impede their crossing ", were merely descriptive of the manner in which a motorist is required to stop (see further, below). In *R.* v. *Greenwood* [1962] Crim.L.R. 639 a motorist was acquitted where there were no children on the crossing and none, apparently, seeking to cross. This decision, which was criticised in *Franklin* v. *Langdown, supra,* may possibly be explained on the ground that the motorist in that case had not been lawfully required to stop under s. 25 (1) because, when he was required to do so, there were no children crossing or seeking to cross and the patrolman could not therefore display his sign in accordance with s. 25 (1). Nevertheless, the case was again criticised in *Wall* v. *Walwyn* [1974] R.T.R. 24, where following *Franklin* v. *Langdown* justices were again directed to convict a motorist whom they had acquitted because the children had not been impeded. Lord Widgery in *Wall* v. *Walwyn*, at p. 27, repeated his view as to the duty of a driver as he expressed it in *Franklin* in the following terms:—

"In my judgment the reference to 'and so as not to stop or impede their crossing' in s. 25 (1) (*a*) is merely descriptive of the manner in which the driver should stop. My reading of the section, therefore, is that once the sign has been properly exhibited in accordance with s. 25 (1) the driver must stop, unless indeed by the time he reaches the crossing the prescribed sign had already been removed. Of course, if he approaches slowly and the patrol had taken the sign down before the driver gets there, naturally he can proceed. But if the sign is still exhibited there is in my judgment an obligation to stop, which obligation cannot be released until s. 25 (2) (*b*) has been satisfied, namely, that the sign no longer continues to be exhibited."

It is submitted that the liability under s. 25 is absolute and that a driver must stop even if it is very difficult for him to do so because of the lateness of the signal; compare the cases on according precedence at p. 449. Where it is desired to exempt drivers from an absolute duty to stop, the Regulations say so, e.g., as to amber lights on p. 301. The sign must be exhibited by the patrol in such a way that the approaching driver can see the words on the sign but it need not be full face to oncoming traffic (*Hoy* v. *Smith* [1964] 3 All E.R. 670). The sign has been altered from " Stop Children Crossing " to " STOP = Children ", but *Hoy* v. *Smith* seems as applicable to the new signs as to the old.

Section 25 (2) (*b*) creates a separate offence of again putting the vehicle in motion so as to reach the place while the sign continues to be exhibited. It should be noted that this is a separate offence from s. 25 (2) (*a*) and that an information charging both offences would be bad for duplicity. It would appear that an offence can only be committed under s. 25 (2) (*b*) after the motorist has stopped. If he does not stop at all he should be charged with not stopping contrary to s. 25 (2) (*a*). It may also be noted that the vehicle must move sufficiently " so as to reach the place in question ", i.e., the place where children are crossing or seeking to cross.

By s. 25 (4) signs are presumed to be of the prescribed size, colour and type and to have been illuminated as prescribed.

The signs are prescribed by the Traffic Signs (School Crossing Patrols) Regulations, 1968 (S.I. 1968 No. 1826), applicable throughout Great Britain.

By s. 25 (1) the patrolman must wear the approved uniform. The uniform worn is deemed to be approved by the Secretary of State unless otherwise proved (s. 25 (4)). No statutory instrument approving any uniform has been found but by Home Office Circular No. 119 of 1954 it was stated that the approved uniform was a cap for men (or a beret for a woman) with a white dust coat or macintosh. By Home Office Circular No. 108 of 1966 fluorescent jerkins or sleeves were allowed to be worn over the approved uniform. Having regard to the presumption contained in s. 25 (4) (*b*) it is not necessary for the prosecution to prove that the Secretary of State's approval has been given to the uniform. The prosecution only has to prove that the school crossing patrol is wearing *a* uniform. *Semble* the defence would succeed if the school crossing patrol did not wear a white dust coat or macintosh, but it is submitted that the wearing of the cap or beret is not essential (see (*Wallwork* v. *Giles* as to a police constable in " uniform "). (As to traffic wardens acting at school crossings see below.)

The question of proceedings against Crown drivers is discussed on p. 61.

" School " is not defined and the term seems to include private and nursery schools and Sunday schools as well as those of education authorities. Section 25 (1) applies, however, only when children are crossing or seeking to cross and are on their way to or from school. It does not apply where adults alone are crossing or children shown not to be on the way to or from school. Note that, by s. 25 (4) (*c*), unless the contrary is shown, there is a presumption that children at a crossing are on their way to or from school, if it is proved that a prescribed sign was exhibited by a patrol. It will be noted that s. 25 applies only between 8 a.m. and 5.30 p.m.

On the analogy of *Burns* v. *Bidder*, cited on p. 449, inability of a motorist or cyclist to stop because of a latent defect in his brakes, undiscoverable on a reasonable examination, or because he was pushed forward by a vehicle colliding with his vehicle's rear, or because he lost control under attack by a swarm of bees, would probably be a defence.

" Road " has the same meaning as elsewhere in the Road Traffic Act (see p. 26). Section 25 applies to all vehicles, including trams, trolley vehicles and cycles, but not to equestrians, mahouts and cameleers.

The term " children " is not defined for the purposes of s. 25. While a child under the Children and Young Persons Act, 1933, means one under the age of fourteen, it is submitted that for the purposes of s. 25 the definition should not exclude children of fourteen or above but should at least extend to all children of compulsory school age, and that it would be within the spirit and object of s. 25 if it extended to all pupils at secondary schools, whether above or below compulsory school age. " Child ", in the

context of s. 25, it is submitted, means any child of any age who
goes to school.

Sometimes the school crossing patrol displays his sign for the
benefit of children cycling to school. There appears to be nothing
in s. 25 (1) to limit the protection given by the school crossing
patrol to children on foot only and it is submitted that a motorist
can be lawfully required to stop whether the children are crossing
the road on foot or on bicycles.

Traffic wardens appointed under the Road Traffic Regulation
Act, 1967, s. 81, may act as school crossing patrols (see S.I. 1970
No. 1958) and when so doing it is not essential for them to wear the
white coat prescribed in the Home Office Circular No. 119 of 1954,
but they must when so doing exhibit the prescribed sign and be
wearing the approved traffic wardens' uniform (see Home Office
Circular 110/1965 which was addressed to Police Authorities and
Chief Constables only; presumably the Home Office will be prepared to supply a copy if applied to).

Nothing in s. 25 prevents proceedings being taken against
motorists and all cyclists for dangerous or careless driving or riding
or against drivers or riders of any vehicles and equestrians for
driving or riding to the common danger under the Public Health
Act, 1925, s. 74, or under the Highway Act, 1835 (see p. 292).

Penalty, Endorsement and Disqualification

The penalty is a fine of £100 (Road Traffic Regulation Act, 1967,
s. 25 (2) as amended by the Act of 1974). The Magistrates'
Association suggested penalty is " £25 and consider disqualification " (see p. 880 and, generally, p. 594). The following
provisions as to endorsement, disqualification and driving test
apply only to drivers of motor vehicles.

Endorsement must be ordered unless there are special reasons, as
defined in Chapter VII (1972 Act, s. 101 (2), Sched. 4).

The endorsement code for an offence contrary to s. 25 (2) is
TS 60.

Disqualification may be ordered for any period on first or subsequent conviction (s. 93 (2)). Section 93 (3) applies so that a
person convicted under s. 25 who has been previously convicted
on two occasions of endorsed disqualifiable offences within the
three years immediately preceding the commission of the s. 25
offence must be disqualified for at least six months, unless having
regard to all the circumstances there are grounds for mitigating the
normal consequences of the conviction (see p. 688). The six-month
disqualification is additional and consecutive to any period of

disqualification imposed on the same occasion or for any previous offence. A driving test may be ordered (s. 93 (7)).

14. REFUSAL TO GIVE INFORMATION AS TO DRIVER

As to the duty to state the ownership of a vehicle for fixed penalty offences and excess meter charges see Vehicle Owner Liability on pp. 584 to 593.

It is the duty of the owner of a motor vehicle under penalty to give such information as he may be required by or on behalf of a chief officer of police to give for the purposes of determining whether the vehicle was or was not being driven in contravention of s. 143 of the Road Traffic Act, 1972 (no insurance), on any occasion when the driver was required to produce his certificate of insurance (Road Traffic Act, 1972, s. 167). The penalty is a fine of £200 on first or subsequent conviction, but endorsement, test and disqualification cannot be ordered. " Owner ", in relation to a vehicle which is the subject of a hiring agreement, includes each party to the agreement (s. 167 (2)). And see p. 55.

By s. 168 (2) of the Road Traffic Act, 1972, where the driver of a vehicle (whether it be a motor vehicle or not) is alleged to be guilty of an offence to which the section applies, (a) the person keeping the vehicle shall give such information as to the identity of the driver as he may be required to give by or on behalf of a chief officer of police and (b) any other person shall if required as aforesaid give any information which it is in his power to give and which may lead to the identification of the driver. The reference in the statute to " in his power to give " is in para. (b) only, but by s. 168 (3) the person keeping the vehicle required under (a) is not guilty if he shows that he did not know and could not with reasonable diligence have ascertained who the driver was. The section extends to any offence under the Road Traffic Act, 1972, other than offences under Pt. V (registration of driving instructors), ss. 169 to 174 (these relate mainly to offences of dishonesty or forgery of driving documents, etc.) and ss. 15, 32, 45 (7), 50 (5), 53 (4), 55 (5), 56 (3), 91, 119. It also extends to offences against any other enactment relating to the use of vehicles on roads and, by virtue of the Act of 1974, also extends to ss. 36A and 36B of the Act (parking of vehicles on footpaths, verges and central reservations: see p. 395), in which case the local authority are empowered to make the requirement. See *infra* as to s. 168 extending to Regulations.

In Scotland, s. 168 extends to offences under s. 175 (taking and

driving away) also; it is submitted that, by virtue of the Interpretation Act, 1889, s. 38 (1), it extends also to offences under s. 12
of the Theft Act, 1968 (taking conveyances) in England and Wales.
Quaere, if s. 168 extends to offences under s. 12 in respect of conveyances which are vehicles but not motor vehicles; as s. 12
extended the scope of s. 175 to them, it is argued that it does
(*Stevens* v. *General Steam Navigation Co.* [1903] 1 K.B. 890), so long
as they are " vehicles".

The Road Traffic Regulation Act, 1967, s. 85, is in like terms to
s. 168 and extends to offences under ss. 1 to 84 of that Act, save
those under ss. 17 (5), 31 (5) (in England and Wales), 77 (7) and
80 (8). Neither s. 85 of the Road Traffic Regulation Act, 1967, nor
ss. 167 and 168 of the Road Traffic Act apply to persons and
vehicles in the public service of the Crown.

The Vehicles (Excise) Act, 1971, s. 27, is in like terms to s. 168
and extends to offences under ss. 8, 16 (7) or 18 (4). In relation
to offences of using a vehicle in contravention of these sections,
both the driver and the person using the vehicle shall be treated
as the persons concerned whose identities are required to be given,
and, where the offence alleged is keeping a vehicle, the person
whose identity has to be given is the person keeping it. The
persons who can demand information under s. 27 are the chief
officer of police or the Secretary of State for the Environment.

The cases cited below with reference to s. 168 presumably apply
to s. 167 and in principle also to s. 85 of the Road Traffic Regulation
Act and s. 27 of the Vehicles (Excise) Act.

There are two types of case which can arise under s. 168 (or
indeed under s. 27 of the 1971 Act or s. 85 of the 1967 Act, *supra*).
The first and more usual situation is that once a good notice under
the section has been served or sufficient requirement made, the
person to whom the demand is made is then under the statutory
obligation to give the information; once he is told of the fact that
the vehicle in question was seen at a particular place at a particular
time, the police do not have to prove the offence alleged or, indeed,
any further information about the allegation (*Pulton* v. *Leader* [1949]
2 All E.R. 747; *Jacob* v. *Garland* [1974] R.T.R. 40). If the person
fails to give the information required he may only escape conviction
if he can avail himself of the defence in s. 168 (3) if he is owner or
if the other person in (*b*), *supra*, that it is not in his power to give
the information. (The owner can properly be summoned under
s. 168 (2) (*b*) as well as (*a*) (*Hodgson* v. *Burn* (1966), 110 S.J. 151).)
The other type of case which can arise under s. 168 is where the
person from whom the information is demanded denies that the
vehicle in question was at the place at the time alleged, and accord-

ingly refuses to give the information required on the ground that it is impossible for him to do so as the vehicle was elsewhere at the time.   In this case, the police are required to prove that the vehicle was at the place at the time specified in the notice (*Neal* v. *Fior* [1968] 3 All E.R. 865; *Jacob* v. *Garland, supra*).

The question has been raised (see *Justice of the Peace*, 1974, pp. 66, 137) as to the legality of a requirement under s. 168 of the 1972 Act or s. 85 of the Road Traffic Regulation Act or s. 27 of the Vehicles (Excise) Act, 1971, being made by post, and in particular if the requirement has been so made, whether the prosecution have to prove that the defendant has received the requirement which has been posted to him.   The answer would seem to depend on whether s. 26 of the Interpretation Act, 1889 applies.   If s. 26 applies, the prosecution have only to show that the requirement was sent by post to the defendant's address because, by virtue of s. 26, the defendant is deemed to have received it when it would have arrived in the normal course of post (provided that the letter is not subsequently returned to the sender as undelivered: *R.* v. *London County Quarter Sessions, ex parte Rossi* [1956] 1 All E.R. 670). Section 26 applies " Where an Act . . . authorises or requires any document to be served by post, whether the expression ' serve ' or the expression ' give ' or ' send ' or other expression is used." Although not one of the three sections referred to itself authorises or requires the demand for the requirement for information to be made by post, s. 183 in the case of a requirement under s. 168, s. 90 of the 1967 Act in the case of a requirement under s. 85 of the Road Traffic Regulation Act, 1967, and s. 32 of the 1971 Act in the case of a requirement made under s. 27 of the Vehicles (Excise) Act, 1971, all envisage requirements under the respective sections being made by post and further provide that a statement purporting to come from the accused admitting that he was the person driving, using or keeping the vehicle on the day in question is admissible in evidence of that fact.   Proof of the posting has to be given in each case by rules made under s. 15 of the Justices of the Peace Act, 1949 (r. 55 of the Magistrates' Courts Rules, 1968, is the relevant rule).   It is also clear that a requirement under the sections cited can be in the form of a " document "; it would be difficult to make a requirement sent by post in any other form. In *Pulton* v. *Leader, supra*, the request for information was in the form of a document.

In *Record Tower Cranes, Ltd.* v. *Gisbey* [1969] 1 W.L.R. 148, enquiring of only 12 out of 25 drivers was said not to show due diligence under s. 168 (3).   It is not a condition precedent to the owner being required to give information that the driver should previously have refused his own name and address (*R.* v. *Hankey* (1905), 69 J.P. 219). The person who was the offending driver must give the required information if it is demanded under s. 168 (2) (*b*) and cannot claim the privilege of not incriminating himself (*Bingham* v. *Bruce* [1962] 1 All E.R. 136).

The obligation under s. 168 (2) (*b*) to give any information " which it is in his power to give " applies to a doctor who has the information as a result of a professional consultation. He cannot say that by reason of the ethics of the medical profession it is not within his power to give the required information (*Hunter* v. *Mann* [1974] R.T.R. 338). The court (*per* Lord Widgery, C.J., at p. 345) cited with approval the B.M.A. Handbook which states, " A doctor should refrain from disclosing to a third party information which he has learnt professionally or indirectly in his professional relationship with a patient . . . subject to (the following exceptions) . . . where the information is required by law." The court in *Hunter* accordingly upheld a conviction under s. 168 of a doctor who had refused to disclose the identity of a man and a girl who had been treated by him following an accident in which a motor car which had been taken without the owner's consent had been involved. In *Hawkes* v. *Hinckley* (noted at 120 J.P.Jo. 642) the High Court held that the obligation to give information continues even after the person from whom it is required has himself been summoned for dangerous driving. The police may thus use s. 168 to obtain information as to the identity of a driver at any time. The obligation imposed by s. 168 on the person keeping the vehicle is a personal one and cannot be discharged by some other person, such as a solicitor, giving the information on his behalf (*Hodgson* v. *Burn* (1966), 110 S.J. 151). A person becomes owner of a vehicle on hire-purchase when he takes possession on the signing of the agreement; he must then answer questions under s. 168 in respect of matters before that date, when he had in fact had possession of it (*Hateley* v. *Greenough* [1962] Crim.L.R. 329).

See *Ex parte Jefferson* on p. 470 as to a person deliberately taking an inordinately long time to give information.

Extension

In the case of offences under the Road Traffic Regulation Act, 1967, s. 42, in relation to parking places, and s. 31 (5) (plying for hire on parking places), the power to require information shall be exercised in writing by the local authority. Section 168 (2) would generally extend to offences under Regulations made under any provisions of the 1972 Act mentioned in s. 168 (1), e.g., the

Pedestrian Crossings Regulations, the Motor Vehicles (Construction and Use) Regulations, etc. (*Bingham* v. *Bruce* [1962] 1 All E.R. 136; *Rathbone* v. *Bundock* [1962] 2 All E.R. 257), but not to Regulations made under any other enactment (*Rathbone* v. *Bundock, supra*). Section 85 of the Road Traffic Regulation Act, 1967, would likewise extend to offences under orders and Regulations made under that Act. " Use " includes leaving a vehicle stationary (*Elliott* v. *Grey* [1959] 3 All E.R. 733) (but see " using " for the purposes of a requirement under s. 27 of the 1971 Act, *supra*).

It seems that the police can make more than one duly authorised demand, e.g., where a person says on Monday that he can ascertain by Friday who the driver was and fails to give the information when demanded again on Friday, he can be summoned for the Friday offence.

If a person duly required to give information under s. 168 or s. 85 knowingly gives false information, he seems to be guilty of an offence against the section because he has failed to give " information which he is required to give " and which it is " in his power to give ". He is likewise guilty if he pretends not to know the answer to the questions put.

Sections 168 and 85 apply where the " driver " of a vehicle is alleged to be guilty of an offence. *Semble,* it does not extend to enquiries as to offences by persons who were not " drivers " (see p. 21 as to this term) or riders, e.g., to the supervisor of a learner.

It seems that a constable may not use s. 168 on his own initiative; he must be authorised by or on behalf of his chief constable and the prosecution should prove this (*Osgerby* v. *Walden* [1967] Crim.L.R. 307, where the silence of the defendant was held on the particular facts to amount to an admission as to this). Where information was demanded in writing on a form signed by a police sergeant and there were added after his signature the words " on behalf of the Commissioner " this was held not to be proof that the sergeant had the necessary authority (*Record Tower Cranes, Ltd.* v. *Gisbey* [1969] 1 W.L.R. 148), but this case was distinguished in *Nelms* v. *Roe* [1969] 3 All E.R. 1379, where evidence was given that the inspector who made the request was authorised to do so by his sub-divisional police superintendent. Although it was held that the Commissioner of Police was not in the position of a Minister of the Crown who can act through an officer of the department of the Crown, the Commissioner of Police in entrusting the superintendence of the sub-division to the police superintendent impliedly authorised the superintendent to act on his behalf through a responsible officer in the sub-division. It was therefore held that the superintendent's delegation to the inspector of the power to make the request was done with the implied authority of the Commissioner of the Metropolitan Police. This principle would seem to apply also to the delegation by chief constables of provincial police forces to their divisional officers. It has been held in Scotland that statements obtained by constables not authorised under s. 168 may be inadmissible (*Foster* v. *Farrell* [1963] S.L.T. 182), but this decision was distinguished in *Miln* v. *Cullen* [1967] S.L.T. 35, on the question of admissibility in other proceedings of statements made. One should distinguish between the admissibility in other proceedings of statements made pursuant to requests purporting to be made under s. 168 or s. 85, whether *intra vires* or *ultra vires* the requesting constable, and the commission of an offence under those sections by refusing to answer. " Chief officer of police " is now defined in Sched. 8 to the Police Act, 1964, as the Commissioner of the City or Metropolitan Police or the chief constable of a county, borough or combined force but does not, it seems, include the chief constable of a special force such as a Ministry of Defence Police Force or the British Transport Police. Compare *Westminster Coaching Services* v. *Piddlesden* on p. 572 as to delegation by the chief officer of police on a differently worded section.

All these offences may be tried by magistrates only. They do not extend to Crown drivers (see s. 187 of the 1972 Act and s. 97 of the 1967 Act).

See p. 463 as to enabling information obtained under s. 168 to be given in writing pursuant to s. 183 of the Act.

It is submitted that refusal to give information is not a continuing offence and that the six months' limitation period starts with each demand. See generally p. 68.

A person who refuses information or his name and address to the police is not guilty of obstructing the police (*Gelberg* v. *Miller* [1961] 1 All E.R. 291), but it may be obstructing the police to give false information as to the identity of an offender (*R.* v. *Field* [1964] 3 All E.R. 269, at p. 280).

Section 161 of the 1972 Act enables the police when requiring the driver to produce his driving licence to require him also in certain circumstances to state his date of birth: see p. 470. Likewise where a person is convicted of an endorsable offence, the court, unless his date of birth is known, are required to order the defendant to state his date of birth (s. 104). Where a person has stated his date of birth either to a constable or to a court, the Secretary of State may serve a notice on the person requiring him to verify the date of birth (ss. 104 (5), 161 (5)).

Section 162 of the 1972 Act also confers powers on constables, whether authorised by a superior officer or not, to require information as to drivers, owners and insurance in the case of accidents and suspected offences.

Penalty

Offences under s. 168 of the Road Traffic Act, 1972, s. 85 of the Road Traffic Regulation Act, 1967, and s. 27 of the Vehicles (Excise) Act, 1971, carry a fine of £50 on first or subsequent conviction. There is no power to endorse or disqualify.

15. DRIVING LICENCES

Ordinary driving licences are dealt with by Pt. III of the Road Traffic Act, 1972, and driving licences for drivers of heavy goods vehicles (HGV licences) by Pt. IV of the Act. The Motor Vehicles (Driving Licences) Regulations, 1971 (S.I. 1971 No. 451) as amended by like named Amendment Regulations (S.I. 1973 No. 2051 and S.I. 1975 No. 521) deal with ordinary driving licences and HGV licences are regulated by the Heavy Goods Vehicles (Drivers' Licences) Regulations, 1975 (S.I. 1975 No. 739). Other Regulations have also been made, relating to persons from abroad (see *infra*) and to other matters not within the scope of this book.

Section 144 of the Road Traffic Act, 1960, relates to driving licences for public service vehicles. Proceedings for breach of s. 144 (drivers' licences for public service vehicles) or of Pt. IV of the Road Traffic Act, 1972 (licensing of drivers of heavy goods vehicles), may, by s. 161 of the Road Traffic Act, 1960, and s. 123 of the 1972 Act, be instituted only by the Director of Public Prosecutions or by a person authorised in that behalf by the traffic commissioners, a chief officer of police or a local authority (see *Westminister Coaching Services, Ltd.* v. *Piddlesden* (1933), 97 J.P. 185, at p. 572, *infra*). Part IV of the 1972 Act does apply to drivers in the service of the Crown (see s. 188), but the licensing authority for the issue of HGV licences and their revocation or suspension is to be exercised in the case of army, navy or air force vehicles by the South East Traffic Area Commissioners (reg. 25). By s. 188 (3), s. 4 (restricting the driving of heavy vehicles by persons under twenty-one) shall not apply in respect of such vehicles to drivers in H.M. Forces or subject to the orders of H.M. Forces.

It should be noted that the law has been changed as to the physical fitness of drivers (p. 477, *infra*) and that the passing of a test on automatic transmission cars only confers exemption for other classes of vehicles which also have automatic transmission (see Sched. 3 to the Regulations). It should also be noted (see

" Learner-drivers ", *infra*) that the holder of a " full " licence does not need to take out a provisional licence in respect of vehicles for which he has not passed a test. Subject to minor exceptions relating to handicapped or disabled drivers, a full licence confers provisional licence entitlement for the vehicle classes not otherwise covered by the full licence. A provisional licence holder may not drive a motor bicycle with an engine capacity exceeding 250 c.c. " not being a vehicle having three wheels " (see " Learner-drivers ", *infra*).

Driving permits issued by H.M. Forces are not driving licences (121 J.P.Jo. 732). Permits issued by visiting forces may be valid as licences in respect of the holder but do not qualify him to be the " qualified driver " to accompany a learner (*Urey* v. *Lummis* [1962] 2 All E.R. 463). See, however, under " Drivers from Abroad ", *infra*, p. 480, as to non-resident holders of British Forces' Driving Permits.

The opinion is given in Stone (1975), p. 3886, that an employer who employs a person to drive on a road offends against s. 84 (2) of the 1972 Act unless he proves he is licensed, the cases of *Griffiths* v. *Studebakers* and *Provincial Cab Co.* v. *Dunning* being cited. But aiding and abetting imports *mens rea* and an employer cannot be convicted of aiding and abetting his employee not to display L-plates and to drive unsupervised when the employer had no knowledge that the employee was a learner-driver only and had not shut his eyes to the fact (*Stanton & Sons, Ltd.* v. *Webber* (1972), 116 S.J. 667).

Expiry and Production of Licences

The power to require production of a driving licence under s. 161 (1) (or insurance or test certificates under s. 162 which is in like terms) applies s. 161 (1) to (*a*) a person driving a motor vehicle on a road; (*b*) a person whom a constable has reasonable cause to believe was the driver of a motor vehicle involved in an accident; (*c*) a person whom the constable has reasonable cause to believe has committed an offence in relation to the use of the motor vehicle on a road; and (*d*) a person who is supervising a learner driver or whom the constable reasonably believed was supervising when an accident occurred or an offence was suspected. It will be noted that s. 161 (1) (*a*) and (*b*) are in similar terms to s. 8 (1) and (2) of the Act of 1972 (" driving or attempting to drive ": see p. 184), and in *Boyce* v. *Absalom* [1974] R.T.R. 248 the question arose for consideration as to whether a person who had ceased driving at the time of the constable's request could be validly required to produce his driving licence under s. 161 or test or insurance certificate under s. 162. Following *Edkins* v. *Knowles* (see p. 188) it was held that the test of the word " driving " in s. 161 (1) (*a*) and s. 162 (1) (*a*) should be the same as in that case and as it was agreed that the defendant had ceased driving when the request was made, the dismissal of the charge was upheld. On the other hand where there was a suspicion of a traffic offence under s. 161 (1) (*c*), the test is whether there has been a continuous chain of events from the suspicion to the requirement, and the fact that the driving has then ceased is irrelevant. It would seem that where the requirement is based on suspicion of the vehicle having been involved in an accident under s. 161 (1) (*b*) the requirement (as in a requirement for a breath test following an accident (see p. 196)) may be made at any time.

At present a full licence is renewable every three years but on para. 5 (1) of Sched. 3 to the 1974 Act being brought into force driving licences may be issued until the holder attains the age of 70 and will thereafter be renewable every three years.

Where a driver fails to produce his licence to a constable and names a police station at which he wishes to produce it within five days under s. 161 (4), it is, it is submitted, unnecessary for the police to call any witnesses from that police station to show that he did not, for that is a fact peculiarly within his own knowledge; further, the Magistrates' Courts Act, 1952, s. 81, applies. In *Tremelling* v. *Martin* [1971] R.T.R. 196 it was held that in order to avail himself of the defence of producing his licence at the police station, a person must produce it at a police station for a sufficient time for the constable to ascertain the matters set out in s. 161 (1), viz., that person's name and address, the date of issue of the licence and the authority that issued it. The court also held that the similar proviso to s. 162 as to the production of a certificate of insurance requires the defendant to produce the certificate of insurance for a sufficient time to enable the police to examine it.

Section 164 (2) enables a constable to arrest without warrant a driver seen by him to commit an offence of careless or dangerous driving (ss. 2 and 3) unless the driver either gives his name and address or produces for examination his driving licence. It was said *obiter* in *Squires* v. *Botwright* [1972] R.T.R. 462 that the driver must have been asked for his name and address and for his driving licence and have failed to supply either for the constable to be able to arrest him under the section.

A police constable, when he makes a requirement for production of a driving licence, may additionally under s. 161 require the motorist to state his date of birth under any of the following circumstances: when he does not produce his licence, where the licence produced is issued by a local authority, or where the constable has reason to suspect that the licence was not issued to the motorist, was issued in error or has been altered with intent to deceive (reg. 22 of the Motor Vehicles (Driving Licences) Regulations, 1971 (S.I. 1971 No. 451)). Section 161 (4) has been amended by the Act of 1974 to make it clear that the fact that a person produces a driving licence at the police station in five days is only a defence to a charge of not producing the licence, it is not a defence to a charge under the section of not stating his date of birth.

It may be that the time limit for an offence under s. 161 or s. 162 does not begin to run until the five days have expired. See 115 J.P.Jo. 254.

On a charge of driving without a driving licence, the prosecutor need in law prove only the act of driving a motor vehicle on a road and the defendant must prove he had the licence; in fact, the prosecutor should have some grounds for thinking that the defendant was unlicensed (*John* v. *Humphreys* [1955] 1 All E.R. 793). In Eire there must be more evidence than the mere fact of driving (*A.-G. (McGowan)* v. *Carville* (1961), 95 I.L.T.R. 41). By s. 161 (1) the police may demand production of driving licences; this power extends to foreign and international driving permits and British Forces' driving licences (Motor Vehicles (International Circulation) Order, 1957 (S.I. 1957 No. 1074), Sched. 3). Powers to seize revoked licences and to require the production of licences obtained by false statements are also given by s. 161 (2) and (3).

In *Ex parte Jefferson* (1966), *The Times*, 5th November, the High Court declined to interfere with the conviction of a man who had spelt out the letters of his name one at a time and had taken an inordinate time in giving his name under s. 161.

The driver must produce his licence " in person " at the police station. He cannot, seemingly, avail himself of the defence if it is produced by someone else on his behalf. A constable may not be able to ascertain the name and address of the holder under s. 161 (1) if it is not produced in person and, following *Tremelling* v. *Martin, supra*, this is the purpose of its production. Moreover s. 161 (4) may be contrasted with the parallel provisions as to production of a certificate of insurance contained in s. 162 (2) and s. 166 (2) as amended by the Act of 1974 where, clearly, the sections allow the certificate of insurance to be produced by someone on behalf of the driver.

It is the duty of the licence-holder to renew the licence on expiry and it is no excuse that no reminder has been sent to him (*Caldwell* v. *Hague* (1914), 79 J.P. 152). A person is unlicensed if he has no licence at 11 a.m. even though he takes one out later the same day (*Campbell* v. *Strangeways* (1877), 42 J.P. 39; and *cf. Wharton* v. *Taylor* (1965), 109 S.J. 475). There are no " days of grace " for renewing driving licences. It was held in *Nattrass* v. *Gibson* (1968), 112 S.J. 866, that a person is not licensed even if his cheque and application for a licence or renewal have been sent to the licensing authority so long as the licence has not been issued, but the position now is altered by virtue of s. 84 (4). The position may be summarised by saying that a person may now drive notwithstanding he has not received his licence provided that a valid application for the grant or renewal of the licence has been received by the licensing authority except in the following circumstances:—

(*a*) where the application is for a first provisional licence (in which case the person concerned cannot drive until the licence is issued);

(*b*) where the application is to drive further classes of motor vehicle for which the existing licence carried no full or provisional licence entitlement (again, he cannot drive until the licence is issued);

(*c*) when the application for a full or provisional licence follows a lapse of ten years from the date of expiry of the previous licence or, if disqualified, the date of disqualification (see s. 85 (1)) (again, he cannot drive until the licence is issued);

(*d*) the applicant has not in effect disqualified himself from obtaining a licence by stating on his application form that he is suffering from a relevant disability (s. 87);

(*e*) the applicant has been disqualified until he passes a test of competence to drive under s. 93 (7), in which case again he cannot drive until a provisional licence has been issued (see s. 98 (3)).

Section 84 requires not merely that a driver shall be licensed but that his licence extend to the type of vehicle he is driving; these types are grouped in Sched. 3 of the Motor Vehicles (Driving Licences) Regulations, 1971 (S.I. 1971 No. 451), and also appear on the licence itself. Section 84 (3) exempts the second driver or steersman of vehicles with a speed limit of 5 m.p.h. Where a licence at the time of issue allowed a person under twenty-one years to drive a motor vehicle not exceeding $2\frac{1}{2}$ tons in weight and, on a re-issue, the law had been changed to allow persons under twenty-one years to drive 3-ton vehicles, it was held on the special facts that his licence was not extended to driving the heavier types (*White* v. *Trainor* [1959] N.I. 147).

The table contained in s. 4 allows persons under twenty-one years of age to drive motor tractors used primarily for work on land in connection with agriculture, although such persons may normally not drive tractors, locomotives or heavy motor cars; an agricultural tractor may not, however, be driven by a person under sixteen years of age (*Watts* v. *Berryman* [1958] Crim.L.R. 56, decided when the age was seventeen). The Motor Vehicles (Minimum Age for Driving) Regulations, 1963, indicate the types of tractors which may be so driven. The table of age limits for driving motor vehicles set out in what is now s. 4 (1) was also changed on 16th December, 1971, by the Motor Vehicles (Minimum Age for Driving) (Motor Cycles) Regulations, 1971: S.I. 1971 No. 1979. The minimum age for driving motor cycles was raised from sixteen to seventeen other than motor cycles of less than 50 cc. equipped with pedals or those motor cycles which are motor mowers or are vehicles controlled by a pedestrian. Section 4 restricts driving by persons under certain ages and s. 96 declares that a person so restricted is disqualified from holding or obtaining a licence save to drive vehicles which he is permitted to drive. The table in s. 4 has been further amended with effect from 1st January, 1975, by s. 15 of the Act of 1974 to allow drivers of eighteen but under twenty-one years of age to drive heavy goods vehicles other than road rollers provided they comply with certain prescribed conditions. A person who is disqualified from holding a licence to drive motor vehicles by reason of his age offends against s. 99 of the Road Traffic Act, 1972, if he applies for or obtains a driving licence and offends against s. 4 (driving under age) as well as under s. 99 if he drives a motor vehicle on a road; he should not be punished under both sections if he does drive (*R*. v. *Saddleworth JJ.*, *ex parte Staples* [1968] 1 All E.R. 1189).

Licences not produced pursuant to s. 101 (4) of the Road Traffic Act, 1972, as amended by the Act of 1974, are suspended and a person who fails to produce or send it to the court after being so required commits an offence punishable by a fine of £100 in respect of a first or subsequent conviction unless he satisfies the court that he has applied for a new licence and not received it (s. 101 (4)). If after being required to produce the licence he then drives without having produced the licence to the court, he commits the offence of driving without a licence.

Section 89 (3) requires a licence holder to surrender his driving licence forthwith to the Secretary of State on a change of name or address at the same time giving particulars of the change; if he fails to do so he is guilty of an offence. Under s. 89 (2) the Secretary of State may revoke a licence and require the holder by service of a notice to deliver it up where it was granted in error or there is an error or omission either in the licence particulars or in respect of any endorsement. On surrender of a licence under s. 89 (3) following a change of name and address or under s. 89 (2) because of an error or omission, the Secretary of State will then deliver a new and correct licence free of charge unless the error or omission under s. 89 (2) was attributable to the licence holder.

An offence under s. 89 (3) is punishable with a fine of £50 for a first or subsequent offence. The extended time limit provided by s. 180 applies to this offence. No offence is seemingly committed if a person fails to surrender a licence after service of a notice under s. 89 (2). As however the licence is revoked by service of the notice under s. 89 (2), the offender commits an offence under s. 84 of driving without a licence should he drive after failing to comply with the notice.

By virtue of s. 101 (6) an applicant for a driving licence who applies for or obtains a driving licence without giving particulars of an order of endorsement (unless he is entitled to have a licence issued free of the endorsement under s. 101 (7) because 3, 4, 10 or 11 years as the case may be have elapsed since the date of the endorsement (see p. 615)) commits an offence and any licence so obtained is of no effect. If such a person then drives, he can be convicted under s. 84 (1) of driving without holding a driving licence.

Learner-drivers

The Road Traffic (Driving Instruction) Act, 1967, provided for the registration of persons engaged in giving instruction in the driving of motor vehicles and for instruction for payment being given only by registered instructors. The Act has been repealed and has been re-enacted as Pt. V (ss. 126 to 142) of the Road Traffic Act, 1972. The sections require driving instructors to be registered and provide for the examination of persons applying to be registered. It is only the driving instruction given for money or money's worth that is controlled by Pt. V. Provided neither money nor money's worth is given, any unregistered person may give driving instruction, but free driving instruction given by someone engaged in the business of buying and selling motor cars shall be deemed to be for the payment of money if given in connection with the supply of a motor vehicle (s. 126 (2)). Exemption is given to police driving instructors giving instruction under the authority of a chief officer of police under arrangements made by him or a local authority.

The duties of provisional licence holders (including full licence holders who are driving a vehicle for which they only have a provisional licence entitlement) are set out in reg. 6 of the Motor Vehicles (Driving Licences) Regulations, 1971 (S.I. 1971 No. 451, as amended by S.I. 1973 No. 2015, which substituted a new subpara. (1) (*b*) in square brackets below), which reads:—

" (1) Subject to the provisions of paragraphs (2), (3) and (4) of this Regulation the holder of a provisional licence shall comply with the following conditions in relation to motor vehicles of a class or description which he is authorised to drive by virtue of the provisional licence, that is to say he shall not drive or ride such a motor vehicle—

    (*a*) otherwise than under the supervision of a qualified driver who is present with him in or on the vehicle;

    (*b*) [unless a distinguishing mark in the form set out in Schedule 2 to these Regulations is displayed on the vehicle in such a manner as to be clearly visible to other persons using the road from within a reasonable distance from the front and from the back of the vehicle];

    (*c*) while it is being used to draw a trailer; and

    (*d*) in the case of a motor bicycle not having attached thereto a side-car, while carrying on it a person who is not a qualified driver:

Provided that where the holder of a provisional licence has passed a test which authorises him to be granted a full licence to drive or ride a particular class or description of vehicles the above-mentioned conditions shall cease to apply in relation to the driving or riding (as the case may be) by him of motor vehicles of that class or description.

(2) The condition specified in paragraph (1) (*a*) of this Regulation shall not apply when the holder of the provisional licence—

    (*a*) is undergoing a test or a test of competence to drive heavy goods vehicles under Part V of the Act of 1960; or

    (*b*) is driving a vehicle (not being a motor car) constructed to carry only one person and not adapted to carry more than one person; or

    (*c*) is driving a vehicle the unladen weight of which does not exceed 16 hundredweight, being a vehicle propelled by electrical power, constructed or adapted to carry only one person and constructed or adapted for the carriage of goods or burden of any description; or

    (*d*) is driving a road roller the unladen weight of which does not exceed 3 tons, being a vehicle constructed or adapted for the carriage of goods or burden of any description; or

    (*e*) is riding a motor bicycle, whether or not having attached thereto a side-car.

(3) The condition specified in paragraph (1) (*c*) of this Regulation shall not apply when the holder of the provisional licence is driving an agricultural tractor, nor shall it prevent the holder of a provisional licence from driving an articulated vehicle.

(4) The condition specified in paragraph (1) (*d*) of this Regulation shall not apply when the holder of the provisional licence is riding a pedal cycle of the tandem type to which additional means of propulsion by mechanical power are attached.

(5) In this Regulation ' qualified driver ' means a person who holds a full licence authorising him to drive as a full licence holder a motor vehicle of the same class or description as the vehicle being driven by the holder of the provisional licence."

The supervisor's duties were considered in *Rubie* v. *Faulkner* [1940] 1 All E.R. 285; it is his duty, when necessary, to do whatever can reasonably be expected to be done by a person supervising the acts of another to prevent that other from acting unskilfully or carelessly or in a manner likely to cause danger to others, and to this extent to participate in the driving. It would be a question of fact in each case whether the position and actions of the qualified driver were such that the learner was under his supervision. If the learner was not, he could be charged with driving when not under supervision and the supervisor with aiding and abetting him. A supervisor may also be convicted of aiding and abetting the learner-driver to drive with excess blood/alcohol, contrary to s. 6 of the 1972 Act. It is not a defence that he did not know that the defendant had consumed too much, because no one can know until his blood has been analysed. The justices were directed to convict the supervisor when the evidence was that the vehicle had been swerving from side to side, that it had hit the bank on three occasions, and that the supervisor had told the police that he and the learner-driver had been out drinking together that evening (*Crampton* v. *Fish* (1969), 113 S.J. 1003). It was similarly held in *Carter* v. *Richardson* [1974] R.T.R. 314 that to convict a supervisor of aiding and abetting the learner driver to drive with an excess blood/ alcohol level, it is sufficient for the justices to be satisfied that he knew the learner driver had an excessive amount of alcohol, even though he could not know the precise alcohol content of his blood.

The holder of a U.S. Forces' driving permit is not a qualified driver under reg. 6 (5) for the purposes of supervising a learner (*Urey* v. *Lummis* [1962] 2 All E.R. 463). A provisional licence holder cannot carry any passenger on a solo motor bicycle other than a qualified driver. If he is driving a motor car, as defined on p. 2, whether a goods vehicle or a passenger vehicle, of an unladen weight between 8 cwt. and 3 tons, he must be accompanied by a qualified driver, and if the car is so constructed that there is no room for the supervisor, it must not be used by a learner-driver. If he is driving a heavy motor car, a locomotive or a tractor, as defined respectively on pp. 2–3, he should be under supervision unless the vehicle is made so as to accommodate the driver only. If he is driving a motor tricycle (i.e., not exceeding 8 cwt. in unladen weight) he should be accompanied by a qualified driver unless the vehicle is so constructed that there is no room for one; such a vehicle is not a " motor bicycle " under reg. 6 (2) (e), as that means a two-wheeled machine, though it is a " motor cycle " under s. 189 (4) (*Brown* v. *Anderson* [1965] 2 All E.R. 1). The driver of a motor bicycle with a sidecar attached may carry an unqualified passenger. A flat tubular framework attached to a motor bicycle, with a wheel on an axle welded to that framework, is not a sidecar under reg. 6 (1) (d); to be a sidecar the structure must be capable of carrying (*Cox* v. *Harrison* [1968] 3 All E.R. 811), but such a structure attached to a motor bicycle may, it is submitted, enable a learner-driver to drive a motor cycle with an engine exceeding 250 cc., since s. 88 (2) (c) only applies to motor cycles " not being a vehicle having three wheels ". Note the special provisions as to small electric vehicles, road rollers and tandems.

In *Vincent* v. *Whitehead* [1966] 1 All E.R. 917, a learner-driver was in a mini-car fitted with only one seat but the vehicle was designed with space for another seat, which could easily be added. It was held that the vehicle was constructed to carry more than one person and that the driver should have been accompanied by a qualified driver under reg. 6 (2) (b) of the Motor Vehicles (Driving Licences) Regulations (see p. 474). The vehicle was not a " motor car " but a " motor tricycle " under s. 198 (4), being under 8 cwt. and having three wheels.

A supervisor who has ascertained that his pupil has a valid provisional licence and has warned him to renew it is not under a duty to see that the licence is still valid every time they go out together (*Smith* v. *Jenner* (1968), 112 S.J. 52). It is submitted that the mere presence of an unqualified person in a car or on the pillion of a motor bicycle driven by a provisional licence holder does not show that the former is guilty of aiding and abetting the latter's offence. As indicated on p. 52 there must be some knowledge of the illegality shown by the prosecutor or a failure to make enquiries which a reasonable person would make (see also *Stanton & Sons, Ltd.* v. *Webber* on p. 53).

It has been argued that a Ministry of Transport examiner has not the duties of a supervisor, and in *B.S.M., Ltd.* v. *Simms and Another* [1971] R.T.R. 190, a case of civil negligence, it was held that an examiner was not a driving instructor or a passenger supervising a learner-driver. His duty is to examine the applicant and see if he passes the test. This sometimes means that he must not interfere in the driving in order to see if the applicant makes a mistake.

The duration of a provisional licence is now twelve months (s. 89). This section, which is a re-enactment of the new sections substituted by the Vehicle and Driving Licences Act, 1969, no longer allows the licensing authority to refuse to renew provisional licences on the ground, in effect, that it appears that the applicant does not intend to submit himself for a test within a reasonable time.

A person who has never held a provisional licence or whose provisional licence has expired and who drives without supervision or L plates commits only one offence, viz., driving without a driving licence, contrary to s. 84, but it is more serious because of his non-compliance with the conditions which would otherwise apply to him. Endorsement in such a case must be ordered (*infra*). Only persons actually holding a current driving licence at the time of the offence can be charged under reg. 6. A learner-driver who drives a solo motor bicycle, without a sidecar, the engine capacity of which exceeds 250 cc. does not offend any of the Motor Vehicles (Driving Licences) Regulations; the effect of s. 88 (2) (*c*) is that he is only guilty of an offence contrary to s. 84 of driving without a licence. Endorsement in such a case must also be ordered (*infra*). By the Motor Vehicles (Minimum Age for Driving) (Motor Cycles) Regulations, 1971 (S.I. 1971 No. 1979), the age for taking out a licence to drive motor cycles is raised from sixteen to seventeen except for mopeds of up to 50 cc. which are fitted with pedals capable of propelling the machine.

Revocation or Refusal of Licence

Section 90 of the 1972 Act gives a right of appeal against the refusal or revocation of a licence or the refusal to grant a full licence for the full three years or a provisional licence for a period less than the prescribed period. There is an article at 111 S.J. 610.

Regulation 20 of the Motor Vehicles (Driving Licences) Regulations, 1971, sets out the diseases and disabilities justifying refusal of a licence (mental disorder or subnormality, epilepsy, sudden attacks of disabling giddiness or fainting (including liability to such attacks by reason of a heart condition or that a person has a heart pace-maker implanted in his body), and inability to read a number plate within the prescribed distance). By s. 87 of the Road Traffic Act, 1972, a licence may be refused because of other diseases or physical disabilities which would make the applicant a source of danger to the public, e.g., deafness (*Woodward* v. *Dykes* (1968), 112 S.J. 787). Section 87 (6) defines " disability " as including a " disease ".

As to revoking a licence because of physical unfitness, see s. 87 (5) of the 1972 Act. A person who drives after his licence has been revoked by the licensing authority under s. 87 (5) appears to commit only the offence of driving without a licence contrary to s. 84. It does not appear that he commits the offence of driving whilst disqualified, since he is not disqualified either by order of a court or by age. A person who is refused a licence because of defective eyesight which he had himself disclosed on his application form cannot appeal to a magistrates' court under s. 90 (*R.* v. *Cumberland JJ.* (1931), 95 J.P. 206). But, if a licence is refused because of information disclosed otherwise than on the form which the applicant has completed, e.g., from enquiries made by the authority, the applicant may appeal to the magistrates against refusal (*R.* v. *Cardiff JJ., ex parte Cardiff City Council* [1962] 1 All E.R. 751). He may likewise appeal against revocation under s. 87 (5) (*ibid.*) or, save for certain disabilities, demand a test on revocation. Licensing of drivers is now by the Department of the Environment and not by county or county borough councils. The Regulations allow a licence to be revoked if a holder suffers from "sudden attacks of disabling giddiness or fainting". A person had attacks which allowed sufficient warning for her to stop and park the car; it was held that these, being attacks which came on unexpectedly, were "sudden attacks" (*Swift* v. *Norfolk C.C.* [1955] Crim.L.R. 785). Regulation 20 has been amended by the 1973 Regulations to provide that liability to sudden attacks of disabling giddiness or fainting by reason of a heart condition or that a person has a heart pace-maker implanted in his body are prescribed conditions justifying revocation or refusal of a licence. By reg. 20 (2A), however, a person having such a heart condition or having a heart pace-maker implanted, is entitled to a licence under s. 87 (3) (*b*) if he can show that the driving by him of a motor vehicle is unlikely to be a source of danger to the public and that he has made adequate arrangements to receive supervision from a hospital cardiologist throughout the period he holds the licence.

A person had suffered from periodic epileptic fits, the last being about two years ago. He claimed that, so long as he continued to take the necessary drugs, the chance of another attack was practically eliminated. It was held that he should be refused a licence, for, so long as drugs were necessary to prevent the manifestation of the disease, the disease remained (*Devon County Council* v. *Hawkins* [1967] 1 All E.R. 235), but by virtue of s. 87 (3) (*b*) an epileptic may obtain a driving licence if he satisfies the following conditions which are prescribed by reg. 20 (2):—

"(*a*) he shall have been free from any epileptic attack while awake for at least three years from the date when the licence is to have effect;

(*b*) in the case of an applicant who has had such attacks whilst asleep during that period he shall have been subject to such attacks whilst asleep but not whilst awake since before the beginning of that period;

(*c*) the driving of a vehicle by him in pursuance of the licence is not likely to be a source of danger to the public."

Before a person may appeal under s. 90 to the magistrates' court acting for the petty sessions area in which he resides against the refusal or revocation of his licence he is required to be a " person aggrieved ". It was held in *R.* v. *Cumberland JJ., supra*, that the applicant could not be said to be a " person aggrieved " where the disability which he himself disclosed on his application form was such that the authority had no choice but to refuse his application. The appellate court has no greater authority to grant a licence than has the licensing authority. *R.* v. *Cumberland JJ.*, was followed in *R.* v. *Ipswich Justices, ex parte Robson*, p. 485, *infra*. On appeal the magistrates' court is not entitled to entertain any question of the applicant's competence to drive if the examiner has declared that he failed the test (s. 90 (2)).

Section 92 of the 1972 Act requires a court before which proceedings for an offence in respect of a motor vehicle are being taken to notify the licensing authority if it appears that the defendant may have a disease or disability which would be likely to cause his driving to be a source of public danger. It is submitted that the duty of a court under s. 92 arises whether the accused is convicted or not. The section states " If, in any proceedings for an offence committed in respect of a motor vehicle, it appears . . . " An offence may be committed, it is submitted, even though the accused may not be convicted because for example he had a blackout or was driving in a state of automatism (see p. 269). The words " committed in respect of a motor vehicle " are merely descriptive of the type of offence giving rise to the proceedings and do not imply that a conviction has to take place. In any event it would seem to be in order for a court to report to the licensing authority any driver, defendant or witness who appears to be a menace on the road because of disease or disability, with a view to revocation of his licence.

See p. 290 as to driving with defective eyesight.

Schedule 3 to the Act of 1974 inserts a new section, s. 87A, in the Act of 1972, placing drivers under a duty to notify the Secretary of State, and empowering the Secretary of State to revoke licences or impose conditions, where the driver becomes aware that he is suffering from a previously undisclosed relevant disability unless he has reasonable grounds for believing that its duration will not be more than three months from when he became aware of it. The driver must also notify the Secretary of State (who can also on this motion revoke the licence) if a previously disclosed disability becomes more acute since the licence was granted. When operative, the Road Traffic Act, 1974, by amending s. 87 and s. 88A requires a driver to notify the Secretary of State (and the Secretary of State to revoke or issue conditional licences) where the driver although not suffering from a disability suffers from a condition that by virtue of its intermittent or progressive nature may become a prescribed disability.

Miscellaneous Matters

As to appeal against a driving test, see p. 477. The Road Traffic Act, 1972, ss. 169 and 170, provide heavy penalties for forgery and fraudulent use of and fraudulent applications for driving licences; see p. 381 as to these sections. The extended time-limit for proceedings contained in s. 180 applies to these proceedings: six months after the offence came to the knowledge of the prosecutor, subject to an overriding limit of three years. A false answer on the application form for a driving licence is an offence whether or not the question asked is *intra vires* (*Woodward* v. *Dykes* (1968), 112 S.J. 787). These sections extend to badges of, and applications to become, approved driving instructors and the penalty under s. 169 on summary conviction is a fine of £200. There is no time-limit for proceedings on indictment under s. 169 ([1958] Crim.L.R. 50). Proceedings under s. 170 carry similar maximum penalties to s. 169 but, except on the application of the defendant, cannot be tried on indictment. Use of a licence with intent to deceive means use in connection with driving or attempted driving and not merely sending it for renewal (*ibid.*) but this decision of quarter sessions is respectfully doubted as putting too narrow a meaning on " use ". For a case of conspiracy by impersonation at a driving test see *R.* v. *Potter* [1958] 2 All E.R. 51. The term " licence " would include an expired licence (*Taylor* v. *Emerson* (1962), 106 S.J. 552).

Section 173 of the 1972 Act gives to the police power to seize licences and other documents; this section and s. 169 extend to visitors', etc., driving permits (Motor Vehicles (International Circulation) Order, 1957, Sched. 3).

Drivers from Abroad

By reg. 21 (1) a person from abroad must within three months of becoming resident here take out a provisional driving licence, if he wishes to drive, unless he has previously passed an official driving test here or has held a full licence here in the last ten years (s. 85 (1)). Persons from Northern Ireland, the Isle of Man and the Channel Islands who have within the last ten years held the equivalent of full driving licences under their own countries' legislation are exempt from tests. A person who is resident outside the U.K. and is here temporarily is allowed by the Motor Vehicles (International Circulation) Order, 1957, art. 2 (S.I. 1957 No. 1074, as substituted by S.I. 1962 No. 1344), to drive without a driving licence for twelve months from his last arrival here while his international driving licence or his foreign licence remains valid, and provided he is within the appropriate U.K. age limits.   If he is disqualified from holding or obtaining a driving licence by an English court, his right to drive ceases.   Article 3 of the 1957 Order cited above deals with visiting forces.

Penalties, Endorsement and Disqualification

Driving without a licence or employing an unlicensed person to drive under s. 84 (1) and (2) carries a fine of £100 on first or subsequent conviction (1972 Act, Sched. 4, as amended by the Act of 1974).

The suggested penalty for no driving licence by the Magistrates' Association (see p. 880 and, generally, p. 594) is £5 except where it is endorsable (see below) when a penalty of £30 is suggested.

Failure to produce a driving licence or state date of birth under s. 161 carries a fine of £50 (1972 Act, Sched. 4), but failure to produce a licence to a court under s. 101 (4) (or in the case of a Northern Ireland licence, s. 111 (2)) carries a fine of £100 (1972 Act, Sched. 4, as amended).

Failure to sign a driving licence carries a fine of £50.   It is not a continuing offence: see p. 70.

An offence by a learner-driver of disobeying the terms of his provisional licence carries a fine of £100.   The suggested penalties by the Magistrates' Association are £25 driving without supervision, £15 motor cyclist carrying unauthorised passenger and £15 no L plates (see p. 879 and, generally, p. 594).

Failure to surrender a licence on change of address or name under s. 89 (3) is punishable with a fine of £50 on first or subsequent conviction.

The offence of applying for or obtaining a licence without giving particulars of a current endorsement under s. 101 (6) is punishable with a fine of £100 on a first or subsequent conviction.

Endorsement and disqualification may not be ordered for any of the above offences except (1) an offence under s. 84 (1) committed by driving a motor vehicle in a case where either no licence authorising the driving of that vehicle could have been granted to the offender (e.g., a learner-driver riding a solo motor cycle with an engine exceeding 250 cc.) or, if a provisional (but no other) licence to drive it could have been granted to him, the driving would not have complied with the conditions thereof; or (2) the offence of a learner-driver who fails to comply with a condition of his provisional licence or of a full licence holder who likewise fails to comply with a provisional licence condition when the vehicle he drives is not covered by his full licence but, instead, confers a provisional licence entitlement. Apart from disqualified drivers (who commit an offence anyhow by driving), a licence cannot be granted to persons under the minimum ages specified in s. 4 (as amended by the Motor Vehicles (Minimum Age for Driving) (Motor Cycles) Regulations, 1971 (S.I. 1971 No. 1979), which raised the age-limit for motor cycles (except mopeds not exceeding 50 cc. fitted with pedals capable of propelling the machine) from sixteen to seventeen), so that a lad of seventeen may be disqualified if he drives a heavy motor car; nor may it be granted to a physically unfit person. An employer who employs a person who cannot obtain (e.g., because he is under age) a driving licence offends against s. 84 but, although the employee's licence must be endorsed and he may be disqualified, the employer is not so liable. A person of any age who has not passed a test to drive the particular type of vehicle in use, or is not otherwise qualified to drive, is liable to disqualification if he drives unaccompanied by a competent driver or without L plates. The holder of a provisional licence who drives unaccompanied or without L plates may also be disqualified. *Semble*, endorsement must, and disqualification may be ordered if a provisional licence holder or a person who holds no licence and has not passed a test drives a solo motor bicycle with an engine of a cylinder capacity exceeding 250 cc.

The Endorsement Code for driving licence offences is as follows:—

Driving without a licence	LC10
Driving under age	LC20
No L plates	PL10
L-driver not accompanied by qualified driver	PL20
L-motor-cyclist carrying a person not qualified	PL30
L-driver drawing a trailer	PL40

Endorsement under s. 101 must be ordered for offenders who can be disqualified, as above, unless there are special reasons (see Chapter VII). Disqualification for any period may be ordered at the court's discretion (s. 93). Section 93 (3) applies (see p. 624), so that if there are two endorsed convictions in the three years preceding the offence, there must be a six-month disqualification additional to any disqualification then or previously imposed, unless, having regard to all the circumstances, there are grounds for mitigating the normal consequences of the conviction (see p. 688).

Endorsement and disqualification may thus not be ordered for an offence of driving without a licence, full or provisional, if the offender has omitted to renew it, so long as that licence would have covered driving the class of motor vehicle which he was driving. Nor may it be ordered for a person who formerly held a full licence unless he has not taken out a licence for ten years from the expiry of his previous licence. (The effect of s. 85 (1) is that he would then only be entitled to take out a provisional licence, and he will then be liable to endorsement if he failed to comply with a provisional licence condition when driving.) Nor may it be ordered for employing unlicensed drivers. In the case of an expired provisional licence, as stated, the driver must be accompanied by the competent driver and show L plates to avoid liability to disqualification and endorsement. References above to learner-drivers being accompanied should be applied with the necessary modifications to those riding motor bicycles. A driving test may be ordered for any of the above offences for which disqualification may be ordered. It would seem that a full licence holder, when relying on his provisional licence entitlement to drive a vehicle not covered by his full licence, will not only have his licence endorsed if he fails to comply with a provisional licence condition, but may also be ordered to be disqualified until he passes another test. The effect of such an order will be that his full licence is revoked, and that he has to take out a provisional licence for all groups.

Heavy Goods Vehicle Licences

Heavy goods vehicle licences (HGV licences) are required for the driving of heavy goods vehicles (Pt. IV of the 1972 Act; Heavy Goods Vehicles (Drivers' Licences) Regulations, 1975 (S.I. 1975 No. 739).

A heavy goods vehicle is defined for this purpose as:—

" a vehicle of any of the following classes which is constructed or adapted for hauling or carrying goods or burden of any description, that is to say, a heavy locomotive, a light locomotive, a motor tractor, a heavy motor car and a motor car so constructed that a trailer may by partial superimposition be attached thereto in such a manner as to cause a substantial part of the weight of the trailer to be borne thereby " (s. 124).

It is an offence under s. 112 of the Act of 1972 to drive a heavy goods vehicle or to employ another person to drive a heavy goods vehicle unless the driver has a heavy goods vehicle driver's licence authorising him to drive goods vehicles of that class. The penalty is £100 for a first or subsequent conviction (Road Traffic Act,

1972, Sched. 4, as amended). The licences are issued by the chairman of the Traffic Commissioners. Provisional licences may be issued for drivers who have not passed an HGV licence test. Provisional licence holders can only drive if thIy comply with the conditions prescribed by reg. 9, i.e., displaying HGV L plates, driving only when under the supervision of the holder of a full HGV licence and not drawing a trailer (other than the trailer of an articulated vehicle). Failure to comply with a provisional licence condition is an offence under s. 114 (3) and punishable with a fine of £100 on a first or subsequent conviction. Proceedings for offences under s. 112 or s. 114 may only be instituted by or on behalf of the Director of Public Prosecutions, the Traffic Commissioners, the chief officer of police or the council of a county or county district. The Regulations (Sched. 1) specify eight different classes of heavy goods vehicle drivers' licences.

Section 15 of the Act of 1975 (see p. 472) allows a person aged eighteen but under twenty-one to drive heavy goods vehicles provided certain prescribed conditions are complied with. Section 15 also makes consequential amendments to ss. 114–116 of the Act of 1972 to enable both provisional and, after passing the test, full HGV licences to be obtained by persons under twenty-one. It is an offence punishable with a fine of £100 under s. 114 (4) to employ a driver under twenty-one to drive a heavy goods vehicle in contravention of the prescribed conditions.

HGV licences are additional to the ordinary driving licence. An HGV driver must have an ordinary licence as well as his HGV licence. Regulation 12 provides that where the holder is disqualified from holding or obtaining an ordinary driving licence he must notify, and deliver up his heavy goods vehicle driving licence to, the Traffic Commissioners, who will retain it until he is no longer under an order of disqualification.

If the HGV driver is convicted of an offence which is ordinarily endorsable under s. 101 of the Act of 1972 it is his ordinary driving licence which is required to be produced to the court for endorsement. Although the HGV licence has pages for " endorsements " these pages are to record particulars of suspension or revocation of the HGV licence by the licensing authority. Under s. 115 (1) the licensing authority may revoke or suspend a licence holder if by reason of his conduct as a driver of a motor vehicle or by reason of physical disability the driver is not a fit person to hold a licence.

An applicant may appeal to the licensing authority to reconsider the refusal or failure to grant a licence or its suspension, revocation, etc. (s. 118). If still dissatisfied the applicant may appeal to the magistrates' court acting for the petty sessions area in which he resides (or in Scotland the sheriff's court). The magistrates' court has no greater power than the licensing authority and cannot grant on appeal an HGV licence which the licensing authority could not grant, nor may the applicant be a " person aggrieved " if he has been deprived of something the licensing authority could not grant (*R.* v. *Ipswich JJ.*, *ex parte Robson* [1971] 2 All E.R. 1395). A magistrates' court may determine whether a test for an HGV licence has been properly conducted in accordance with the Regulations and, if it is found not to have been so conducted, the court may order the applicant to be allowed another test immediately without his having to wait the prescribed period of one month which he would otherwise have to wait before he took another test (s. 117).

Failure to comply with certain of the Regulations is an offence punishable with a fine of £50 (Road Traffic Act, 1972, s. 119 (2), Sched. 4, as amended by the Act of 1974), e.g., reg. 3 (3)—applying for an HGV licence when disqualified or suspended; reg. 7—failing forthwith to sign the licence; reg. 10 (1)—failing to deliver up licence and notice of suspension or revocation; reg. 12 (1)—failing to notify and deliver HGV licence on disqualification of his Pt. III licence (see above); reg. 13 (2)—failing to surrender HGV licence on its being found after a duplicate licence has been issued on its being lost; and reg. 14—failure to produce an HGV licence to a police constable (this Regulation is similar to s. 161 of the Act of 1972 in relation to Pt. III licences; see p. 468).

16. VEHICLE EXCISE LICENCES

The statute law is now to be found in the Vehicles (Excise) Act, 1971. This Act consolidates the existing statutes and incorporates all the changes effected by the Vehicle and Driving Licences Act, 1969. It came into force on 1st April, 1971, when the power to issue licences was transferred from county and county borough councils to the Department of the Environment. Many of the provisions of the Vehicle and Driving Licences Act, 1969, had not been brought into force on the date when the Vehicles (Excise) Act, 1971, came into force. The interpretation of the Vehicles (Excise) Act, 1971, is complicated in that the practitioner will need to refer first to the main text of the Act and then to Sched. 7 to the Act to see what transitional modifications are made. (Indeed, many of the transitional modifications may continue until 1977, when it is envisaged that the centralised computer for the issue of driving and vehicle excise licences will be fully operational.) Sections 2 (commencement and duration of licences and rate of duty), 8–20, 23–26 and 37 (liability to pay duty and issue, exhibition, exchange and registration, etc., of licences) all have to be read in conjunction with Pt. I of Sched. 7.

Among the changes made by the Vehicle and Driving Licences Act, 1969, incorporated in the main text of the Vehicles (Excise) Act, 1971, and still not yet brought into force are the licensing of vehicles from day to day instead of month to month (s. 2), continuous liability for duty unless the Secretary of State is first notified (s. 10), the statutory enactments of " days of grace " (ss. 8 (2), 12 (5)), the marking of vehicle engines and bodies (s. 24) and temporary fourteen-day licences (s. 13).

The Road Vehicles (Registration and Licensing) Regulations, 1971 (S.I. 1971 No. 450) came into force simultaneously with the Vehicles (Excise) Act, 1971. These Regulations replaced the similarly named Regulations of 1964 and the eight sets of Amending Regulations made since 1964. The main alteration in the 1971 Regulations was to reflect the transfer of the licensing functions to the Secretary of State for the Department of the Environment. The 1971 Regulations have been amended by like named Amendment Regulations (S.I. 1971 No. 1285 and S.I. 1972 No. 1865). The Road Vehicles (Index Marks) Regulations, 1964, and four sets of Amending Regulations were revoked because, as the Department of the Environment is the licensing authority, index marks no longer needed to be allocated to the various local authorities. The only change not a direct consequence of the transfer of functions was to require the rear number plates of agricultural vehicles to be illuminated with effect from 1st April, 1972.

Prosecutions, Venue and Limitation

Practically all the offences under the Act and Regulations are limited to matters arising on " public roads ", i.e., roads which are repairable at the public expense (s. 38 (1)), a definition narrower than that of " road " in the Road Traffic Act (see p. 26). By the Finance Act, 1953, s. 33 (nullifying *Brown* v. *Allweather Mechanical Grouting Co.* [1953] 1 All E.R. 474), any acts or omissions in respect of which a pecuniary penalty is imposed under the Customs or Excise Acts (which term here includes ss. 8, 18 (4) and 16 (7) of the Vehicles (Excise) Act) are offences under those Acts within the meaning of Pt. XI of the Customs and Excise Act, 1952, and proceedings may be brought in a magistrates' court and against aiders and abettors accordingly.

It suffices in law for the prosecutor to show that the defendant used the vehicle on a road; the defendant must show that it was licensed (*John* v. *Humphreys* [1955] 1 All E.R. 793). It is submitted that where the defendant is charged with " keeping " it is similarly sufficient for the prosecutor to prove that the defendant kept the vehicle on a road and that it is then for the defendant to show that it was licensed.

Duty is chargeable on mechanically propelled vehicles kept or used on public roads, even though they are never driven (Vehicles (Excise) Act, 1971, s. 1 (1)). A motor vehicle separated from the road surface by roller skates is nevertheless " on " a road (*Holliday* v. *Henry* [1974] R.T.R. 101). A person " keeps " a vehicle on a road if he causes it to be on a road when not in use, no matter how short the period may be (s. 38 (2), nullifying the effect of *Dudley* v. *Holland* [1963] 3 All E.R. 732). It is submitted, therefore, that the mere sight of a vehicle stationary and unattended on a public road is now sufficient evidence of its being kept there. Ownership or proof of ownership is not essential to proof of the offence of " keeping " or " using " (*Napthen* v. *Place* [1970] Crim. L.R. 474). It is a question of fact in each case whether the vehicle remains a " mechanically propelled vehicle " (see p. 6); removal of most of its essential parts might cause it to cease to be, but a vehicle which resembles a car is presumed to be a mechanically propelled vehicle still, even though essential parts have been removed, if there is a possibility of their replacement in a reasonable time (see *Newberry* v. *Simmonds* on p. 6; *aliter*, if there is no conceivable prospect of it being made mobile: see *Smart* v. *Allan* on p. 6. In *Binks* v. *Department of the Environment* [1975] Crim.L.R. 244, a vehicle without an engine was held to be mechanically propelled because it was the intention of the owner to make it mobile again. If it is shown that a motor vehicle has been used without an excise licence, the case must not be dismissed even though the breach of the law is highly technical and trivial and there are mitigating circumstances as well. The defendant must be found guilty but the penalty may properly be light in such a case (*Patterson* v. *Helling* [1960] Crim.L.R. 562). And see *Nattrass* v. *Gibson* on p. 506 (no excuse that cheque in post).

See pp. 41–51 as to " using ", and in particular p. 45.

Where an employed driver is found using a vehicle on his employer's business and the proper duty has not been paid, generally the employer and not the driver should be summoned (*Carpenter* v. *Campbell* [1953] 1 All E.R. 280). If a vehicle is used on the road, there is a presumption that the use is by or on behalf of the registered owner and he may properly be summoned if the driver's identity is unknown (*Watson* v. *Paterson* (1957), 121 J.P.Jo. 336), though the person summoned may still show that he knew nothing of the use and so be not guilty.

Who may Prosecute and Authorisation to do so

Section 28 reads:—

" (1) Subject to the provisions of this section, summary proceedings for an offence under section 8, 11 (2), 16 (7), 18 (4) or 26 (1) or (2) of this Act or under regulations made in pursuance of this Act may be instituted in England and Wales by the Secretary of State or a constable (in this section severally referred to as ' the authorised prosecutor ') at any time within six months from the date on which evidence sufficient in the opinion of the authorised prosecutor to warrant the proceedings came to his knowledge; but no proceedings for any offence shall be instituted by virtue of this subsection more than three years after the commission of the offence.

(2) No proceedings for an offence under section 8, 16 (7) or 18 (4) of this Act shall be instituted in England and Wales except by the authorised prosecutor; and no proceedings for such an offence shall be so instituted by a constable except with the approval of the Secretary of State.

(3) A certificate stating—

 (*a*) the date on which such evidence as is mentioned in subsection (1) above came to the knowledge of the authorised prosecutor; or

 (*b*) that the Secretary of State's approval is given for the institution by a constable of any proceedings specified in the certificate,

and signed by or on behalf of the authorised prosecutor or, as the case may be, the Secretary of State shall for the purposes of this section be conclusive evidence of the date or approval in question; and a certificate purporting to be given in pursuance of this subsection and to be signed as aforesaid shall be deemed to be so signed unless the contrary is proved.

(4) In a magistrates' court or before the registrar of a county court any proceedings by or against the Secretary of State under this Act may be conducted on behalf of the Secretary of State by a person authorised by him for the purposes of this subsection.

(5) Section 281 of the Customs and Excise Act, 1952 (which restricts the bringing of proceedings under that Act) and section 283 (1) of that Act (which extends the time for bringing such proceedings) shall not apply to proceedings in England or Wales for offences under this Act."

If the information is laid by an official and not by a constable and it alleges that the proceedings are instituted by that official on behalf of the Secretary of State, it seems that this is sufficient proof that they are so instituted unless the contrary is proved (*Dyer* v. *Tulley* (1894), 58 J.P. 656; Customs and Excise Act, 1952, s. 290 (1)). The magistrates' clerk or justice issuing a summons to a constable should satisfy himself by the production of the certificate under s. 28 (2) that the proceedings are brought by the constable with the approval of the Secretary of State. There is no need for the prosecutor to take any further step to prove authorisation in open court unless the defence object that it has not been proved. Such objection by the defence should be taken before the close of the prosecution's case, and if objection is made the prosecution should be given the opportunity to prove the consent (*Price* v. *Humphries* [1958] 2 All E.R. 725); if necessary, an adjournment can properly be granted. It is submitted that as the matter is of a technical or formal nature, the adjournment should be granted almost as a matter of course (see *Royal* v. *Prescott Clarke* [1966] 2 All E.R. 366). Where an information is laid by an officer who has not been generally or specially authorised to take those proceedings, an authorisation given after the laying of the information would not, it seems, validate the proceedings (*Bowyer, Philpot and Payne* v. *Mather* (1919), 83 J.P. 50), and from the wording of s. 28 (3) (*b*) it would seem that the Secretary of State cannot give subsequent approval to a constable who has already instituted proceedings.

The Vehicles (Excise) Act, 1971, s. 3 (2), confers on the Secretary of State the powers of the Commissioners of Customs and Excise, and the relevant Acts, e.g., the Customs and Excise Act, 1952, in relation to the duties of excise and to punishments and penalties in connection therewith, apply. This may refer only to penalties for not paying duty and not to penalties for other offences, e.g., not exhibiting a licence (*M'Millan* v. *Grant* [1924] S.C.(J.) 13); in *Pilgram* v. *Dean* (see p. 503), the court laid stress on the fact that an offence under s. 8 attracted an excise penalty and an offence under s. 12 (4) was punishable by fine.

Venue

The Customs and Excise Act, 1952, s. 284, appears to apply to offences under the Vehicles (Excise) Act and Regulations made thereunder; consequently, proceedings may also be taken where the offender resides or is found or in any part of England in cases where the offence was committed in England (similarly in Scotland)—see Jo.Crim.L. (1958) 269—as well as where the offence was committed. The view is, however, held in some authoritative circles that s. 284 applies only to offences which are " excise offences ", i.e., where payment of duty is in issue, and not, e.g., to failing to illuminate a number plate. This view is based on s. 3 (2) of the Vehicles (Excise) Act, which applies the Customs and Excise Act in relation to " duties of excise " and punishments and penalties in connection therewith. See *M'Millan* v. *Grant*, *supra*.

Where a false statement was knowingly made in one jurisdiction in an application for a licence and it was sent by post to the licensing authority in another jurisdiction, it was held in Scotland that the *locus* for the offence could only be where it was received (*Gibb* v. *Hill*, Jo.Crim.L. (1948) 185). In England, however, it would seem that there could be a prosecution in either place, provided the form was received by the council (*R.* v. *Burdett* (1820), 4 B. & Ald. 95; *Grimble* v. *Preston* (1914), 78 J.P. 72; Magistrates' Courts Act, 1952, s. 3 (2)). Under the Regulations various offences arise of failing to notify change of ownership; it is submitted that such defaulters can be prosecuted either where they are when they make default or where the offices which should be notified are, but it is understood that the former Ministry of Transport have recommended that proceedings should be taken in the place where the offender resides.

The general rules as to venue set out on p. 65 supplement the above provisions.

Limitation

Offences of failure to notify change of ownership are not continuing offences; see p. 518.

It should be noted that the special time-limit only applies to the particular offences specified in s. 28 together with any offence under Regulations made in pursuance of the Act. The period of six months runs from the date of the discovery of the offence although the overriding limit of three years runs from the date of the commission of the offence. It may also be noted that a certificate of the authorised prosecutor shall be conclusive evidence of the date of discovery of the offence by him and the approval of the institution of proceedings by the Secretary of State. This may be contrasted with the signature of the certificate, which is deemed to be signed on behalf of the Secretary of State " unless the contrary is proved ".

A right of appeal by the prosecutor to the Crown Court is given by the Customs and Excise Act, 1952, s. 283 (4); *quaere* whether this applies only to " excise duties " (see *supra* under " Venue ").

In *R.* v. *Godstone JJ., ex parte Secretary of State for the Environment* [1974] Crim.L.R. 110 it was held that a summons which did not bear the date upon which the information was laid was not ineffectual. It is only where there is some question as to whether the information was laid in time that it is material. It is submitted that if there is any question whether the information was laid in time, it is the duty of the prosecution to give proof of the date of laying of the information because an information for a purely summary offence laid out of time renders the proceedings a nullity.

The Vehicles (Excise) Act, 1971

The provisions of this Act will now be briefly reviewed, but the reader is reminded that its provisions are often long and complicated and reference should always be made to the text itself, not forgetting a reference to Sched. 7, which may modify the particular section. The Act applies to Scotland but not to Northern Ireland. By s. 1 it is declared that the duties set out in Scheds. 1 to 5 to the Act shall be charged in respect of mechanically propelled vehicles used or kept on public roads in Great Britain and paid upon a licence to be taken out by the person keeping the vehicle. The mechanically propelled vehicles mentioned in the Act include electrical, steam and gas driven vehicles as well as vehicles which run on petrol. The Finance (No. 2) Act, 1975, s. 5, exempts from duty tramcars used for the conveyance of passengers. See generally pp. 2–14 as to the meaning of " motor vehicles ", but, if a mechanically propelled vehicle is in fact used on a public road, duty will be chargeable, unless the Act itself exempts it, whether or not the vehicle is intended or adapted for use on the roads.

In so far as duty is chargeable in respect of the keeping of a vehicle on a road, the vehicle is chargeable with the like duty as on the occasion of the licence last issued or, if no licence has been issued, with the duty applicable under Sched. 5.

By the Customs and Excise Act, 1952, s. 234, a licence is void from the time it is granted if it is paid for by a cheque which is dishonoured.

Motor Bicycles and Three Wheeled Vehicles

The duties in respect of motor cycles, motor scooters, electrically propelled bicycles, motor tricycles and vehicles, other than mowing machines, with more than three wheels neither constructed or adapted for use nor used for the carriage of a driver or passenger, are specified in Sched. 1; definitions are also in Sched. 1. Auto-assisted cycles are included. The duty varies according to the cylinder capacity of the engine. Vehicles so chargeable with duty are not chargeable with duty under Sched. 2 as hackney carriages or Sched. 4 as goods vehicles. The Finance (No. 2) Act, 1974, s. 5, raised the permissible unladen weight of such vehicles from 8 cwt. to $8\frac{1}{4}$ cwt.

Hackney Carriages

Schedule 2 relates to the duties on hackney carriages exceeding 8 cwt. in unladen weight. Passenger-carrying trams are subject to duty under Sched. 2, but other vehicles used on tram lines are exempt from duty under s. 4 (1) (e). Other vehicles caught by Sched. 2 include not only ordinary taxi-cabs but also omnibuses and motor coaches. Duty is calculated by seating capacity (except for trams) in accordance with reg. 42 of the Road Vehicles (Registration and Licensing) Regulations, 1971. "Hackney carriage" by s. 38 (1) means a mechanically propelled vehicle standing or plying for hire and includes any mechanically propelled vehicle let for hire by a person whose trade it is to sell mechanically propelled vehicles or to let mechanically propelled vehicles for hire, but a letting under a hire-purchase agreement is not treated as a letting for hire. To use a vehicle, licensed for private use only, as a hackney carriage renders the user liable to prosecution under s. 18 if the hackney carriage rate is higher, and, conversely, use of a vehicle, licensed as a hackney carriage, for private purposes renders the user liable to prosecution also if the "private rate" is higher. See 99 S.J. 312 for a report of a successful prosecution of a taxi-driver who was giving a free lift to his family.

Cars hired out with or without a driver may be taxed under Sched. 2 but, if so taxed, they must carry the hackney carriage plate under s. 21 of the Act and reg. 41 of and Sched. 4 to the Regulations. In fact, many firms lawfully tax their private hire cars at the higher "private" rate under Sched. 5 so that the plate need not be carried.

By para. 3 of Pt. I of Sched. 2, the "private" rate may be chargeable under Sched. 5 where a hackney carriage is partly used for private purposes; "used for private purposes" means used otherwise than to carry passengers for hire or reward or on hire.

Tractors, Agricultural Vehicles, etc.

Schedule 3 specifies the rates of duty for vehicles dealt with in this paragraph. Paragraph 5 of Pt. I of the Schedule defines "works truck" in similar terms to those contained in reg. 3 (1) of the Construction and Use Regulations, save that the vehicle must be a "goods vehicle" as defined in Sched. 4 and that the definition refers to "the immediate vicinity" instead of "the immediate neighbourhood". It was held in *Hayes* v. *Kingsworthy Foundry Co., Ltd.* [1971] Crim.L.R. 239 that a vehicle was not a "works truck" within the meaning of the Construction and Use Regulations where the vehicle had to travel six-tenths of a mile along a road even though the two sites were very close together. "Immediate neighbourhood" had to be measured by reference to the amount of user of the road involved, not in relation to the distance which two sites are apart "as the crow flies". Similarly, a journey between two premises two miles apart by road was held not be be "in the immediate neighbourhood" (*G. Greaves & Son, Ltd.* v. *Dean* [1972] R.T.R. 146, applying *Hayes'* case, *supra*). Schedule 3 applies to:—

(*a*) locomotive ploughing engines, tractors, agricultural tractors and other agricultural engines which are not used on public roads for hauling any objects (with exceptions too numerous to detail here but mainly to do with farming); the Finance Act, 1971, s. 6, states, however, that a motor vehicle shall not be treated as a tractor within Sched. 3 unless it was designed and constructed primarily for use otherwise than on roads and is incapable by reason of its construction of exceeding 25 m.p.h. on the level under its own power. The exemption under para. 2 (1) (*d*) for " agricultural machines " for hauling articles required for a farm only applies if the vehicle is registered in the name of the owner or occupier of the farm or in the name of a contractor engaged by the owner or occupier. In *Bullen* v. *Picking* [1974] R.T.R. 46, a tractor hauling bricks for doing piping on and for the purposes of the farm was held to be within the exemption. Although the tractor was not registered in the contractor's name, because the tractor used was one which had been lent by the farmer to the contractor, it came within the first part of the exemption in that it was registered in the farmer's name and used for the purpose of hauling articles required for the farm;

(*b*) vehicles designed, constructed and used for trench digging, shovelling and excavating and vehicles designed and constructed as mobile cranes, provided they are used on public roads only for work of excavating, etc. (or, if cranes, for work on a site in the immediate vicinity), or for proceeding to and from the place of work, and carry or haul no load;

(*c*) mowing machines; and

(*d*) vehicles, not being ones already referred to, constructed and used on public roads for haulage solely, e.g., tractors, and not constructed and used to carry loads other than necessary for their own propulsion and equipment.

In deciding whether a vehicle is an agricultural machine, no account shall be taken of certain uses of that vehicle on public roads in snow clearance. By Sched. 4, para. 3 (*b*), an agricultural machine falling under (*a*) above is not chargeable as a goods vehicle by reason of the fact that it is constructed or adapted for use and used for the conveyance of farming or forestry implements fitted thereto for operation while so fitted. In *R. v. Berkshire County Council, ex parte Berkshire Lime Co. (Childrey), Ltd.* [1953] 2 All E.R. 779 it was said that the lower rate for class (*a*) above applies only so long as the vehicles mentioned in it are used for hauling and a vehicle consisting of a driver's cab mounted on a chassis on which was also imposed a large receptacle for holding lime was a goods vehicle chargeable under Sched. 4 and not under Sched. 3, because it carried goods, viz., lime, although the vehicle was used in the business of spreading lime on agricultural land and was thus an agricultural engine. This case was decided prior to the operation of the exemption given by Sched. 4, para. 3 (*b*), but it is doubtful if it is affected thereby. It is provided by Sched. 3, para. 2 (2) (*a*), that references in Sched. 3 to a farm include a market garden and there are further definitions relating to woodland and articles required for farm and forestry estates.

A tractor fitted with a winch, jib and anchor used for loading tree trunks on a trailer drawn by it, the tractor being incapable of carrying any goods, is constructed and used for haulage solely under Sched. 3 and is not a goods vehicle under Sched. 4 (*Worgan v. Gloucestershire County Council* [1961] 2 All E.R. 301). See further the definition of a tractor contained in s. 6 of the Finance Act, 1971, *supra*.

A vehicle carrying a built-in air compressor used only to supply power to pneumatic drills falls under Sched. 3 as a trench digger and, *semble*, is not a road construction vehicle under s. 4, which exempts the latter type from duty (*N.W. Construction Co. v. Lancashire County Council*, a county court decision of 1939). See under s. 4, *infra*, as to dumpers and excavators.

As to "farmers' goods vehicles", see p. 498.

In *London County Council v. Hay's Wharf Cartage Co.* [1953] 2 All E.R. 34, a Scammell heavy duty tractor, used for towing, was held, on the facts, to be a haulage vehicle and it did not become a goods vehicle merely because such things as tools, blocks and ballast were carried by it to render it more fit for haulage work. In *Brook v. Friend* [1954] Crim.L.R. 942, it was held that use of a farmer's tractor to haul a trailer loaded with bricks and a fireplace to one of his farmworkers' cottages was not within the exemption given by Sched. 3, para. 2 (1) (*b*), for hauling "articles required for the farm". Nor is taking a pony to a show for exhibition (*Henderson v. Robson* (1949), 113 J.P. 313). In *Thornton v. Proudlock* (Queen's Bench Division, 1952, unreported) it was held that a tractor fitted with a transport box is a vehicle adapted for use for conveyance of goods or burden and in *A.-G. (Croke) v. O'Sullivan*

(1958), 92 I.L.T.R. 21, it was held that a tractor adapted to carry sacks by fitting a detachable wooden platform was "hauling" goods, so as to attract the rate of duty for a goods vehicle. The effect of these cases is now qualified in Great Britain by Sched. 4, para. 7 (2), which relates to removable appliances fitted at the front or back of agricultural tractors. Where a farmer was contractually bound to supply firewood to his employees, it was held that use of his tractor to haul it was use for agricultural purposes (*East Lothian County Council* v. *Lambert* [1950] S.L.T.(Sh.) 41; this case cites two earlier English decisions which are to much the same effect as *Brook* v. *Friend, supra*; see also Jo.Crim.L. (1952) 170, and *Agnew* v. *Robertson* on p. 51 and *Armitage* v. *Mountain* on p. 498.

Schedule 4, para. 7 (6), relates to vehicles of this type with a double front wheel.

"Agriculture" in the Vehicles (Excise) Act seems to include chicken and livestock farming as well as cultivating the soil (*J. M. Knowles, Ltd.* v. *Rand* [1962] 2 All E.R. 926).

Goods Vehicles

Schedule 4 relates to the duties on goods vehicles. It also refers to goods vehicles used for drawing trailers and to vehicles conveying a machine or contrivance only and no other load (not being chargeable under Sched. 3). Schedule 4 refers, *inter alia*, to works trucks (which has the same meaning as in Sched. 3), farmers' goods vehicles and showmen's goods vehicles and trailers. "Goods vehicle", by para. 9, means a mechanically propelled vehicle (including a tricycle weighing more than 8 cwt. unladen) constructed or adapted for use and used for the conveyance of goods or burden of any description, whether in the course of trade or otherwise. Thus, a private car, not constructed or adapted for the conveyance of goods, is still taxable at the private rate although it may carry goods in the course of trade—see *Taylor* v. *Mead, infra*. Further, by Sched. 4, para. 3 (*d*), a vehicle constructed or adapted for use for the conveyance of goods or burden but not used for the conveyance thereof for hire or reward or for or in connection with a trade or business is not treated as a goods vehicle. This provision is especially useful for owners of utility vehicles, shooting-brakes and Land Rovers, who do not use them for their trade or business. But where the director of a firm of photographers carried photographic equipment in a shooting-brake on the firm's business, it was held that the vehicle was a goods vehicle and taxable accordingly; para. 3 (*d*) of Sched. 4 did not apply as it was used for a trade or business (*Taylor* v. *Thompson* [1956] 1 All E.R. 352). A shooting-brake is constructed or adapted for use to convey goods (*ibid.*). Carriage of personal luggage or farm produce for the owner's own use would not attract the " goods rate " duty; the court left open whether carriage of a doctor's bag or a lawyer's robes and books in such a vehicle would attract it. In *Armitage* v. *Mountain* [1957] Crim.L.R. 257, use of a farmer's goods vehicle to carry the furniture of a newly engaged farm-labourer as an act of kindness and not for payment was held not to be use for the farmer's trade or business. See also *R.* v. *Berkshire County Council, Worgan* v. *Gloucestershire County Council* and *London County Council* v. *Hay's Wharf Cartage Co.*, on p. 494. The term " goods vehicle " in the Road Traffic Act is discussed on p. 333. The term " hire or reward " is discussed on pp. 542–544.

By para. 2 of Pt. I of Sched. 4, a goods vehicle taxed at a lower rate than the " private " rate must pay the private rate, if it is higher, when it is partly used for private purposes. This catches particularly dual-purpose vehicles of or under 12 cwt. unladen weight taxed under Sched. 4 when used for a family outing or other purpose not involving the carriage of goods for hire or reward or in the course of trade or business. " Used for private purposes " means used otherwise than for the conveyance of goods or burden for hire or reward or for or in connection with a trade or business including the performance by a local or public authority of its functions.

In *James* v. *Davies* [1952] 2 All E.R. 758 it was held that haulage by a Land Rover, itself empty, of a trailer laden with goods on the owner's business was a conveyance of the goods and that it mattered not that the towing vehicle carried no goods; duty was payable under both para. 1 (1) and 1 (2) of Sched. 4. The Land Rover was a vehicle constructed for the conveyance of both goods and passengers and was therefore itself within the definition of " goods vehicle ". In *Pearson* v. *Boyes* [1953] 1 All E.R. 492, however, an empty van towing an empty caravan was held not to be carrying goods or burden; the court pointed out that the Act seemed to differentiate between hauling and towing on the one hand and carriage on the other, and stressed that clear words imposing a higher rate of taxation must be used to authorise it. By s. 18 (6), if duty has been paid under Sched. 4, higher duty is not payable on goods vehicles substantially used to carry loads if also used to carry employees of the owner of the loads.

In *Taylor* v. *Mead* [1961] 1 All E.R. 626, the defendant's saloon car was fitted in the rear part of the interior with rails from which dresses were hung, he himself having put in those rails and the screws for their support. When dresses were not hung inside, passengers could sit in the back seats in the normal way. On the question whether the car was adapted for use for conveying goods, the High Court refused to interfere with a finding of magistrates that the car had not been so adapted but did not say whether they (the judges) would have come to the same conclusion. Lord Parker, C.J., said that " constructed or adapted " in para. 9 (1) meant " originally constructed or where the structure is subsequently altered " and approved two earlier cases on the Customs and Inland Revenue Act, 1888, s. 4, holding that adapting meant some amount of alteration of the original construction. Making a small fitting or attachment involving the boring of holes for screws in the structure would not be altering the structure but fitting stronger springs and widening the wheels would be (*ibid.*). See also *Thornton* v. *Proudlock* on p. 494. The question whether an adaptation is such as to make a passenger vehicle into a goods vehicle is resolved by assuming that it had originally been constructed in its altered condition and then deciding whether as such it would be a passenger or goods vehicle; actual use is irrelevant (*Flower Freight Co.* v. *Hammond* [1962] 3 All E.R. 950). In some contexts, however, " adapted " means " suitable for " without any work of reconstruction (*Maddox* v. *Storer* on p. 334).

" Tower Wagons " attract a lower rate of duty (see para. 3 in Table A of Pt. II of Sched. 4). A " tower wagon " is defined in para. 9 of Pt. I of Sched. 4 as a goods vehicle into which there is built any expanding or extensible contrivance for the erection, inspection, repair or maintenance of overhead structures or equipment provided that it is neither constructed nor adapted for use nor used for the conveyance of any load other than the extensible contrivance or articles used in connection therewith. A vehicle with such an extensible contrivance was held not to be a " tower wagon " as it was being used for the conveyance of a load, namely, a pillar for a lamp standard (*Anderson & Heeley, Ltd.* v. *Paterson* [1975] 1 All E.R. 523).

Trailers

By Sched. 4, para. 9 (2), the term " trailer " does not include grit-throwers not exceeding 5 cwt. in weight, snow ploughs, certain road construction vehicles, trailers used solely to carry or produce gas for the propulsion of the towing vehicle, or farming implements not constructed or adapted for the conveyance of goods or burden of any description when drawn by a farmer's goods vehicle (as defined in Sched. 4). The term " trailer " has been held to include an empty poultry shed being drawn by a tractor (*Garner* v. *Burr* [1950] 2 All E.R. 683) and a hut used as an office towed along the highway (*Horn* v. *Dobson* [1933] S.C.(J.) 1);

for the purposes of Sched. 4, para. 1 (2), to the Vehicles (Excise) Act (additional duty where trailer drawn), this duty is chargeable only when the drawing vehicle is a " goods vehicle " as defined, *supra*. An articulated vehicle, by para. 6 (1), is deemed to be one vehicle. No increased duty is charged for drawing a trailer when the drawing vehicle is exempt from duty as a tower wagon or council watering vehicle (para. 6 (2)).

A mechanically propelled vehicle can be both a " mechanically propelled " vehicle and a trailer. There is nothing in the Vehicles (Excise) Act, 1971, to exempt a mechanically propelled vehicle from taxation when it is being towed on a publicly repairable road. Where, therefore, a van was towed without its having been licensed, the justices were directed to convict the defendant even though the towing vehicle was itself licensed (*Cobb* v. *Whorton* [1971] Crim.L.R. 372). It is only if the vehicle is in such a condition that it can no longer be said to be mechanically propelled that no licence is needed (see meaning of " mechanically propelled " on pp. 6–7).

Farmers' Goods Vehicles

It is not use as a " farmer's goods vehicle " as defined *infra* to take furniture from a saleroom to the cottage of one of the farmer's employees (*M'Boyle* v. *Hatton Estate Co.* [1951] S.L.T.(Sh.) 101); see also *Agnew* v. *Robertson* on p. 51. The term " articles required for the purposes of the agricultural land " includes livestock and eggs as well as seeds, fertilisers and tools where a vehicle is being used by a chicken-farmer (*J. M. Knowles, Ltd.* v. *Rand* [1962] 2 All E.R. 926). A different view prevails in Northern Ireland (*Porter* v. *Bloomer* [1957] N.I. 123, discussed at Jo.Crim.L. (1960) 57). In *Armitage* v. *Mountain* [1957] Crim.L.R. 257, it was held that carrying furniture for a newly-engaged farm servant did not come within the uses for which a farmer's goods vehicle may lawfully be used as such, but on the facts higher duty was not payable. The term " articles required for the purposes of the agricultural land which [the farmer] occupies " does not include the carriage of agricultural implements which have been sold by the farmer and are being taken to the purchaser (*Mac-Millan* v. *Butter* [1963] S.L.T.(Sh.) 44). On an earlier statute it was held that a locomotive drawing to market some trolleys laden with farm produce was employed by the farmer " for the purposes of his farm " (*London County Council* v. *Lee* (1914), 78 J.P. 396). So where a locomotive was being used to take manure to a farm (*Cole Bros.* v. *Harrop* (1915), 79 J.P. 519).

The term " farmer's goods vehicle " means a goods vehicle

registered in the name of a person engaged in agriculture and used on public roads solely by him for the purpose of the conveyance of the produce of, or of articles required for the purposes of, the agricultural land which he occupies, and for no other purpose (Vehicles (Excise) Act, 1971, Sched. 4, para. 9 (1)). Thus, a vehicle licensed as a farmer's goods vehicle may not be used either simultaneously or separately for any purpose not caught by the definition just cited; if it is so used, and the unauthorised purpose is one which attracts a higher rate of duty, an offence arises under s. 18 (4). An example of an unauthorised use not attracting higher duty is *Armitage* v. *Mountain, supra*. In *Howard* v. *Grass Products, Ltd.* [1972] R.T.R. 552 a company agreed to cut a farmer's grass and remove it for dehydration. The work took three and a half days. The company's lorry which was used was registered as a farmer's goods vehicle. It was held that the vehicle was improperly registered and attracted a higher rate of duty as the " occupier " for the purpose of para. 9 (1), *supra*, meant a person in possession of agricultural land with some prospect of remaining in possession. The vehicle carried the produce of agricultural land but not of land of which the company was the " occupier ". Certain exemptions also arise under s. 18 (7) for occasional carriage of another farmer's goods of small amount and without payment. There may also be special exemptions pursuant to s. 18 (8), which appears to relate to use of vehicles at harvest time.

Paragraph 4 of Sched. 4 reads:—

" Without prejudice to paragraph 2 above a vehicle shall be treated for the purposes of this Schedule as a farmer's goods vehicle notwithstanding that it is partly used for private purposes as defined in the said paragraph 2 if, apart from that use, it would be a farmer's goods vehicle as defined in this Schedule."

This seems to mean that, where a vehicle taxed as a farmer's goods vehicle is partly used for a private purpose, e.g., a family outing, and it is of or under $2\frac{1}{2}$ tons unladen weight, the " private " rate of £40 will be payable under Sched. 5 but not the much higher " goods " rate under Sched. 4, Pt. II, para. 4.

By Sched. 4, para. 5 (1), a vehicle constructed or adapted to carry a machine or contrivance and no other load, though it be built in, is chargeable as a goods vehicle, but the machine or contrivance is not included in the unladen weight.

Private Cars

The duties on mechanically propelled vehicles not caught by the other Schedules are set out in Sched. 5. It is under this provision that private cars fall to be taxed. See p. 496 as to utility vehicles, shooting-brakes and Land Rovers. Cars not exceeding seven horse-power and first registered before 1947 pay less duty than the sum of £40 which all others pay per year.

Exemptions from Duty

Vehicles exempted from duty under s. 4 of the Vehicles (Excise) Act include fire engines (whether kept by a public authority or any other person), vehicles kept by a local authority for the purposes of their fire brigade service, ambulances for humans and animals (but not, *semble*, cars for sitting cases), road rollers, vehicles used on tram lines (not being passenger-carrying trams), lifeboat haulage vehicles, vehicles not exceeding 8 cwt. unladen specially adapted for invalids, road construction vehicles used solely for the conveyance of road construction machinery which is built in or permanently attached to the vehicle and is used for no purpose other than the construction or repair of roads at the public expense, gritthrowing vehicles, tower wagons used by a street lighting authority or by a contractor with the authority (see definition in Sched. 4 and *Anderson & Heeley, Ltd.* v. *Paterson* on p. 497) and local authority's watering vehicles. By s. 7 (3) there is an exemption for snowclearance vehicles. By s. 7 (1) the Secretary of State with the consent of the Treasury may exempt from duty a vehicle intended to be used on public roads only in passing from land of the owner to other land of his and for distances not exceeding six miles in the aggregate in any week. The Motor Vehicles (International Circulation) (Amendment) Order, 1971 (S.I. 1971 No. 869), relates to vehicles brought into the country by persons making only a temporary stay and to vehicles carrying foreign tourists. Vehicles used only at elections, without payment by the passengers, are also exempt (Representation of the People Act, 1949, s. 89), as are vehicles used by a public or local authority for civil defence purposes (Vehicles (Excise) Act, 1971, s. 7 (4); Civil Defence Vehicles (Relief from Duty) Regulations, 1953), and vehicles in the service of visiting forces (see p. 59) (Visiting Forces and International Headquarters (Application of Law) Order, 1965). By s. 6 exemption is also given for vehicles exempted from purchase tax with a view to being taken abroad by an overseas resident, but duty is payable if they are not taken abroad.

By s. 5 of the 1971 Act a vehicle is exempt from duty when proceeding to and from a previously arranged vehicle test either under s. 43 (ordinary vehicles) or s. 45 (goods vehicles subject to plated weights) of the Road Traffic Act, 1972, or to or from a place where a defect revealed by that test is by previous arrangement remedied. Section 5 only grants exemption where the vehicle is being used solely for the purpose of proceeding to and from the test or place of repair. This appears to prevent an impecunious holiday maker in London from arranging for his car carrying him and his family on holiday to Cornwall to be tested in Penzance and thus exempting the vehicle from being taxed.

Questions arise from time to time whether certain machinery used in connection with road works is exempt from duty under s. 4 as a road construction vehicle or is chargeable under Sched. 3 as a vehicle used for trench digging or excavating. In *Orr* v. *Carmichael* [1941] S.C.(J.) 27, a dumper used solely in connection with road construction was held to be exempt from duty as a road construction vehicle, as the law then stood. In *Cowan* v. *Hale* [1966] N.I. 31 it was held, on a statute of Northern Ireland, in relation to a dumper fitted with a metal tipping skip, that the skip was road construction machinery, that, though capable of carrying loads nothing to do with road construction, the skip carried articles used for the purposes of road construction machinery and that the dumper was a road construction vehicle; it was said that the question of exemption from duty depends on the actual use of the vehicle and not on its obvious characteristics of function and design. The decision is criticised at Jo.Crim.L. (1966), 210. In *McCrone* v. *J. & L. Rigby (Wigan), Ltd.* (1952), 50 L.G.R. 115, however, a dumper and an excavator were both held to be chargeable under Sched. 3, but the decision proceeded partly on the view that the vehicle owners had not discharged the burden of proof cast on them by s. 33 of the Act to show that the dumper was used " for no purpose other than the construction of roads ". It was also held that the excavator was specifically taxable under Sched. 3, which refers to vehicles used for trench digging or any kind of excavating or shovelling work. The legal position as to dumpers still remains unsettled and the two cases should be carefully studied when any point arises. They are discussed at 119 J.P.Jo. 458. See also p. 7.

Mitigated Penalties

By s. 3 of the Vehicles (Excise) Act it is provided that the duties imposed by the Act shall be levied by the Secretary of State. Section 3 (3) empowers the Secretary of State to mitigate or remit penalties, and this power is frequently exercised by asking offenders in less serious cases to pay a penalty and avoid court proceedings. It is submitted that it is proper for the prosecutor to tell the court, after conviction, what mitigated penalty was imposed when there is a prosecution on failure to pay that penalty and the magistrates themselves have a discretion whether to make their fine more or less than it.

False Declarations

By s. 26 (2) it is declared to be an offence, punishable with a fine not exceeding £200, if a person in connection with an application for an excise licence makes a declaration which is to his knowledge false or in any material respect misleading. The offence is triable summarily but may be tried on indictment pursuant to the Magistrates' Courts Act, 1952, s. 18. If tried summarily it is punishable on a first or subsequent conviction by a fine only, of up to £200 and on indictment by two years' imprisonment or fine of an unlimited amount. The onus of proving his declaration true is cast on the defendant by s. 33 to the extent set out therein (see p. 514). As s. 26 requires that the declaration be false or misleading " to the knowledge " of the declarant, such knowledge must be shown, subject to s. 33, and it does not suffice to convict merely on proof of the falsity; *R.* v. *Cummerson,* on p. 382, is not applicable. A defendant who signed an application form completed by his daughter and failed to read it and thus notice that it contained a false declaration was not guilty of making a declaration which to his knowledge was false (*Bloomfield* v. *Williams* [1970] Crim.L.R. 292). It was said *obiter* by Donaldson, J., that if someone signs an application he impliedly says that he knows what is in the particulars and he must be guilty of making a declaration which to his knowledge is misleading (another offence under the subsection) if he has not bothered to check. With respect, it is submitted that " knowledge " is the same for the offence of making a false declaration as it is for making a declaration " in any material respect misleading ". " Knowledge " in this context means either actual knowledge or second degree knowledge " where a man deliberately shuts his eyes to information which he fears will give him knowledge he does not wish to acquire " (*per* Devlin, J., in *Roper* v. *Taylor's Central Garages (Exeter), Ltd.* [1951] 2 T.L.R. 284, at p. 288, referred to in *Bloomfield* v. *Williams* (1970), *The Times,* 24th February). Section 26 (2) extends to applications for trade licences.

Persons applying for licences must do so on the appropriate form as prescribed by the Road Vehicles (Excise) (Prescribed Particulars) Regulations, 1972 (S.I. 1972 No. 850).

Failing to Display Licence

By s. 12 (4) of the 1971 Act, the excise licence shall be fixed to and exhibited on the vehicle in the manner prescribed by the Regulations.

It is an offence under s. 12 (4) to fail to exhibit a licence whether a licence is in force for the vehicle or not. If there is no licence for the vehicle, the user may be prosecuted and incur the excise penalty under s. 8 of using the vehicle without a licence and may also be fined for the offence of not exhibiting a licence under s. 12 (4) (*Pilgram* v. *Dean* [1974] R.T.R. 299). When subs. (5) comes into force it will be a defence to a charge under s. 12 (4) if (*a*) application has been made for renewal of an existing licence and (*b*) the old licence is displayed, and (*c*) no more than fourteen days have elapsed since the previous licence has expired. The only existing defence is the limited defence set out in the proviso to reg. 16 (1) of the 1971 Regulations (see p. 517).

A New Zealand regulation read: " No person shall permit a motor vehicle to be on a road . . . unless there is carried on the vehicle a current warrant of fitness." A car exhibited the necessary warrant on the windscreen and the owner left the car for a short time; when he returned, he found that a trespasser had removed the warrant and that a traffic-offence notice had been stuck to the windscreen. It was held, after reference to Halsbury, 3rd ed., vol. 10, p. 272, and to Russell on Crime, 11th ed., p. 25, that the owner was not guilty as the omission to carry the warrant was not within his conduct, knowledge or control (*Kilbride* v. *Lake* [1962] N.Z.L.R. 590).

This New Zealand case was considered in *Strowger* v. *John* [1974] R.T.R. 124. It was held that the offence under s. 12 (4) was absolute and no *mens rea* was required. A motorist left his car locked and while away the plastic holder containing the licence fell from the windscreen out of sight on to the floor of the car; the justices were directed to convict the motorist in that the car and its accessories were at all times under his control (*ibid.*). *Kilbride* was distinguished because in *Kilbride* the removal of the licence was totally unexplained—it had disappeared from the car. Lord Widgery, C.J., in *Strowger*, at p. 130, specifically reserved for future consideration whether a driver would have a defence to a charge under s. 12 (4) if the car is broken into and the licence stolen.

An offence under s. 12 (4) is punishable by a fine of £20 for a first or subsequent conviction. Where the failure to exhibit is without fault or blame on the part of the defendant an absolute discharge may be the appropriate penalty. In *Strowger* v. *John*, *supra*, the Divisional Court remitted the case back to the recorder of the Crown Court to enable him to give " (with a clear lack of discouragement) the opportunity of imposing an absolute discharge as the only possible penalty ".

Trade licences for motor traders are dealt with under s. 16 of the 1971 Act and Pt. V of the Road Vehicles (Registration and Licensing) Regulations, 1971 (see p. 519).

Under-Payment of Duty

By s. 18 (1) it is provided that, where a licence has been taken out in respect of a vehicle at a certain rate and the vehicle is at any time used on a public road in an altered condition or in a manner or for a purpose which brings it within or which, if it was used solely in that condition or in that manner or for that purpose, would bring it within a class or description of vehicle to which a higher rate of duty is applicable, duty at that higher rate shall become chargeable. By s. 18 (4), where by virtue of such user a higher rate of duty becomes chargeable and duty at the higher rate was not paid before the vehicle was used on a public road, the person so using the vehicle shall be liable to whichever is the greater of the following penalties, viz:—

(a) an excise penalty of £50; or

(b) an excise penalty of an amount equal to five times the difference between the duty actually paid and the amount of duty at that higher rate (calculated, *semble*, at the annual rate; see p. 506).

A magistrates' court may, however, mitigate the penalty to such extent as it thinks fit (Magistrates' Courts Act, 1952, s. 27). The burden of proof as to user is not laid on the defendant in proceedings under s. 18, since s. 33 of the Act (p. 514) does not apply to them. But see s. 290 (2) of the Customs and Excise Act, 1952, on p. 515.

Section 18 (2) makes provision as to the payment of extra duty when, because of a change of use, a licence has to be exchanged.

By s. 18 (5), duty at a higher rate applicable to vehicles of some other class or description shall not become chargeable by reason of such user of a vehicle as is mentioned in s. 18 (1), unless the vehicle as so used while the licence at the lower rate is in force complies with all the conditions which must be satisfied in order to bring it into the other class. In *Payne* v. *Allcock* (1932), 96 J.P. 283, it was held that use of a private car of the ordinary passenger type to convey goods in the course of trade attracted the " goods " duty, but this decision no longer applies since s. 18 (5) requires the vehicle to satisfy all the conditions which would bring it into the other class before it becomes taxable at the higher rate for that other class; a private car does not satisfy the condition in Sched. 4, para. 9 (1), that it is a goods vehicle constructed or adapted for use for conveying goods (*cf. Flower Freight Co.* v. *Hammond* [1962] 3

All E.R., at p. 952, letter G). The decision, however, would probably still apply in respect of shooting-brakes and like vehicles which can carry either goods or passengers. See also p. 495.

Where boards were fitted to the side of a lorry to enable it to carry more coal, this was held to be use in an altered condition, attracting more duty (*Lowe* v. *Stone* [1948] 2 All E.R. 1076). See also *Blaikie* v. *Morrison* on p. 16.

The liability to prosecution under s. 18 for a use not covered by the licence and to pay higher duty for it arises where the duty payable in respect of that other use is higher than the proper duty actually paid in respect of that vehicle. Thus, use for a private purpose of a twenty-seater bus, licensed under Sched. 2 as a hackney carriage (duty £20), will be an offence, as the duty under Sched. 5 would be £40. There would be no offence if it was a sixty-seater bus, as the duty under Sched. 2 would be £40, for the " private rate " is also £40. Again, if an Oxford eccentric uses a 3-ton lorry as his private conveyance, the duty is at the private rate (£40) and he will become liable to pay the goods rate only if he uses it to convey goods for hire or reward or in the course of trade or business.

By s. 18 (6) and (7) there are special exemptions for goods vehicles used to carry employees, provided such vehicles are mainly used to convey goods, and for farmers' goods vehicles used occasionally to carry small amounts of agricultural goods, without payment, for other agriculturists at the same time as they carry agricultural goods for the owner. Section 18 (8) also gives exemptions for farmers' goods vehicles in circumstances specified by statutory instruments; these instruments, if issued, generally relate to harvesting. See pp. 498–499 as to such vehicles.

The time-limit for proceedings under s. 18 is six months from the date when the offence comes to the knowledge of the authorised prosecutor, subject to an over-riding time-limit of three years from the commission of the offence (see s. 28 on p. 488). A prosecution may be instituted only by the Secretary of State or by a constable with his approval (*ibid.*).

By s. 30, under-payments of duty may be recovered by the Secretary of State (*semble*, in the county court), provided that the action is begun before the expiration of the twelve months beginning with the end of the period in respect of which the licence was taken out. A similar time-limit applies to proceedings by a vehicle owner who has overpaid duty.

The power of a criminal court under s. 1 of the Criminal Justice Act, 1972, to award compensation could in law possibly be used to order compensation for any duty lost as a result of the offence, but the section was drafted following publication of the Report by the Advisory Council on the Penal System on Reparation by the Offender who made it clear that it was expected that compensation should only be awarded in respect of truly criminal offences and not regulatory offences (see *The Magistrate*, vol. 30, p. 58).

Non-Payment of Duty and Payment of Back-Duty

It is provided that a person who uses or keeps on a public road a vehicle for which a licence is not in force, shall be liable by s. 8—

  (1) to whichever is the greater of the following penalties, viz.:—

    (*a*) an excise penalty of £50; or

    (*b*) an excise penalty equal to five times the amount of duty chargeable;

and also by s. 9—

(2) to back-duty (see p. 509 as to this); unless the vehicle is exempt from duty under the Act or any other enactment. Proceedings under s. 8 may be brought within six months of the offence coming to the knowledge of the prosecutor, subject to an over-riding time-limit of three years from the date of the offence. Proceedings may only be brought by the Secretary of State or a constable with his approval (see s. 28, *supra*).

The Magistrates' Association's penalty for an offence under s. 8 is " Actual duty lost plus fine of approximately twice that amount (minimum £25) " (see p. 881 and, generally, p. 594).

If use without payment of duty is established, the defendant must be found guilty, however trivial the case—see *Patterson* v. *Helling* on p. 487. Ownership or proof of ownership of the vehicle is not essential to proof of the offence of " keeping " or " using " (*Napthen* v. *Place* [1970] Crim.L.R. 474). It is no defence that a cheque has been posted to the licensing authority prior to the use of the vehicle on the road (*Nattrass* v. *Gibson* (1968), 112 S.J. 866), but s. 8 (2), when no longer modified by Sched. 7, will alter this.

Section 16 (7) imposes like penalties on a holder of a trade licence or licences who uses on a public road at any one time a greater number of vehicles than he is authorised to use by virtue of that or those licences. The same time-limit applies under s. 28.

A licence is void from the time it is granted if it is paid for by a cheque which is dishonoured (Customs and Excise Act, 1952, s. 234).

Calculation of Penalty

The penalty under s. 8 (1) (*b*) is calculated as five times the annual rate of duty applicable to the vehicle at the date of the offence and, in the case of a continuing offence, the offence shall be deemed to have been committed on the date or latest date to which the conviction relates (ss. 8 (3) (*b*), 16 (7)). Where in the case of a vehicle kept on a road, the rate of duty at the date of the offence differs from the annual rate by which the vehicle was chargeable, viz., that applicable at the date of issue of its last licence, the duty shall be calculated at the latter rate (*ibid.*). It would seem that s. 8 (3) (*b*) nullifies the decision in *Holland* v. *Perry* [1952] 2 All E.R. 720 in that the maximum penalty is five times the annual rate of duty or £50, whichever is the greater. Any duty actually paid by the defendant would seem not to alter the maximum penalty; only the amount of any back duty payable under s. 9 would be affected (see p. 509). Where a licence has not been taken out at all, the defendant cannot plead that he would have licensed the car for, say, four months only and that the quintuple duty should be calculated for that period only (*Holland* v. *Perry*, *supra*). The court may mitigate the penalty to whatever extent it wishes and is no longer limited to an amount not less than a quarter of the duty (Customs and Excise Act, 1952, s. 286 (2)). The burden of proof as to user, etc., is thrown on the defendant by s. 33 (p. 514) in proceedings under s. 8. Days of grace are in fact allowed for the renewal of licences (not trade licences) but, if a licence is not taken out after they have passed, it is proper to charge unlicensed use during them (*Sly* v. *Randall* (1916), 80 J.P. 199). (Section 8 (2) gives statutory effect to fourteen days of grace, but it is not yet in force.) It is the duty of the licence-holder to renew it when it expires and it is no defence that he has not been given a reminder by the authorities (*Caldwell* v. *Hague* (1914), 79 J.P. 152). A person who is detected using an unlicensed vehicle on a public road at any time commits an offence and cannot plead as a defence that he took out a licence five minutes later (*Campbell* v. *Strangeways* (1877), 42 J.P. 39; *Wharton* v. *Taylor* (1965), 109 S.J. 475), nor that a cheque had been posted to the licensing authority before the vehicle was used on the road (*Nattrass* v. *Gibson* (1968), 112 S.J. 866).

In *Flack* v. *Church* (1918), 82 J.P. 59, it was held that the fact that in a particular year a person had been convicted of keeping a dog without a licence did not prevent a further conviction for keeping the same dog without a licence on another day later in the same year. Liability under taxing statutes can sometimes be strict. In *Strutt* v. *Clift* (1911), 74 J.P. 471, a master sent his servant out in a carriage on lawful business; the servant used it for a frolic of his own in an unlawful way which attracted higher duty. The master was held liable. In *Stone* v. *Horton* (1949), 113 J.P.Jo. 674, an owner was likewise held liable under what is now the Vehicles (Excise) Act where he had hired or lent the car to a customer. On the other hand, it was held in *Abercromby* v. *Morris* (1932), 96 J.P. 392, that an owner who lends his car to a friend for a period, on the understanding that the friend will renew the licence, is not liable for unauthorised use by the friend on expiry of the licence. And see *Dove* v. *Tarvin* and *Carmichael & Sons, Ltd.* v. *Cottle*, cases on the Construction and Use Regulations, on pp. 44, 45.

By s. 27 owners and other persons are required, under penalty of £50, to furnish information to the police or licensing authority as to the identity of users of a vehicle, where it is alleged that a vehicle has been used in contravention of s. 8, s. 16 (7) or s. 18 (4). This and the similar provision in the Road Traffic Act, 1972, s. 168, are discussed on p. 462. Any person may prosecute under s. 27 (1) and the time-limit is six months. Information may be demanded under s. 18 in writing (s. 32).

The Vehicles (Excise) Act, 1971, s. 26 (1), declares it to be an offence (punishable summarily with a fine of £200 or two years' imprisonment on indictment) for a person to forge or " fraudulently " alter, use, lend or allow to be used a number plate, trade plate, licence or registration document. It was held in *R.* v. *Manners-Astley* [1967] 3 All E.R. 899 that " fraudulently " means an attempt to avoid paying the proper duty and the court must consider whether the defendant's intention was to defraud the Excise. In *Cook* v. *Lanyon* [1972] R.T.R. 496, it was said that " fraudulently " in relation to a licence meant using one licence with intention to avoid paying for another. The vehicle had been left on a piece of land not a public road, displaying an excise licence belonging to another vehicle. As there was no evidence as to how the car came to be left on the land or what its future movement might be, and the only way a licence could be used was by exhibiting on a vehicle while on a public road, the justices' dismissal was upheld although it was said to be a " borderline " case. Section 26 (2) declares it to be an offence (punishable similarly as under s. 26 (1)) if a person in connection with a change of registration furnishes any particulars which are to his knowledge false or in any material respect misleading. The onus is cast on him by s. 33, to the extent set out therein (see p. 514). The defendant's knowledge that what he has done was false must, on the words of s. 26 (2) itself, be shown; there may not be a conviction on proof of the falsity, etc., without proof of his knowledge of it (see also *Bloomfield* v. *Williams* on p. 502).

Effect of Failure to Transfer Licence

Section 8 (3) (*a*) reads:—

"Where a vehicle for which a vehicle licence is in force is transferred by the holder of the licence to another person, the licence shall be treated as no longer in force unless it is delivered to that other person with the vehicle."

If, therefore, a licensed vehicle is transferred by the holder of the licence to another person without the licence being handed over at the same time, any use of that vehicle on a public road is deemed to be an unlicensed use. *Quaere*, if the vehicle becomes re-licensed, as it were, once the licence has been delivered; it is arguable on the wording of s. 8 (3) (*a*) that it still remains unlicensed, especially from the omission of "and until" after "unless". On the other hand, this subsection imposes a taxing burden in making duty payable possibly twice and it can be said that only clear words can justify such an interpretation against the transferee.

Payment of Back-Duty

By s. 9 of the Vehicles (Excise) Act, 1971, where a person convicted of an offence of using or keeping an unlicensed vehicle is the person by whom that vehicle was kept at the time of the offence, the court shall order him to pay, in addition to any penalty, back-duty calculated in accordance with s. 9 (2) to (4); this provision applies also where the defendant is put on probation or discharged absolutely or conditionally (see s. 9 (5)). The amount of back-duty is, subject to s. 9 (3), an amount equal to one-twelfth of the annual rate of duty for each calendar month or part of a calendar month in the relevant period. "The relevant period", by s. 9 (2), is one ending with the date of the offence and beginning:—

    (*a*) if the defendant has before that date notified the licensing authority of his acquisition of the vehicle, with the date of receipt of that notification or, if later, with the expiry of the licence last in force for the vehicle, or

    (*b*) in any other case, with the expiry of the licence last in force for the vehicle before the date of the offence or, if there has not at any time before that date been a licence in force for the vehicle, with the date on which the vehicle was first kept by that person.

By a proviso to s. 9 (2), if a person has been previously ordered to pay back-duty for the same vehicle, the relevant period begins with the month following that in which the first offence was committed.

By s. 9 (3), where the defendant proves (*semble*, on balance of probabilities and not beyond reasonable doubt) that (*a*) throughout

any month or part of a month in the relevant period the vehicle wa
not kept by him, or was neither used nor kept by him on a publi
road, or was not chargeable with duty, or (b) that he has paid dut
in respect of the vehicle for any such month or part, whether o
not on a licence, the amount payable under s. 9 (2) shall be cal
culated as if that month or part were not comprised in the relevan
period.

Note that s. 9 applies only to the person convicted under s. 8
and only if he was the person by whom the vehicle was kept at th
time of the offence. Thus, if A's son uses A's unlicensed car, th
son cannot, on conviction under s. 8, be made to pay back-duty
under s. 9 of the Act of 1971. If A has been convicted of aidin
and abetting his son's unlicensed use, A has, it is submitted, bee
himself " convicted of an offence " under s. 8; s. 35 of the Magi
strates' Courts Act, 1952, says that an aider and abettor is " guilt
of the like offence ". Then A must be ordered to pay back-duty.

Home Office Circular 158/1967, of 29th August, 1967, and th
Justices' Clerk, April, 1968, p. 74, give guidance as to s. 9.

By far the great majority of cases under s. 8 are brought under th
procedure set out in the Magistrates' Courts Act, 1957, by which
defendant may plead guilty by post. Section 34 of the Vehicle
(Excise) Act adapts the procedure to allow the prosecutor to serv
with the summons a notice stating that, in the event of the defendan
being convicted, he will be required to pay the amount of back-duty
specified in the notice unless he states that it is inappropriate. I
he pleads guilty and does not state that the amount is inappropriat
s. 30 requires the court to order payment of the back-duty. Fre
quently, defendants delete on the form the wrong alternative
leaving the other alternative: " I do not wish to challenge th
accuracy of the amount alleged to be due . . .", and then procee
to write as mitigating circumstances a statement that the vehicl
has only just been purchased, that the vehicle has been kept in th
garage or some other statement showing that the amount of back
duty is inappropriate. It is submitted that the court can an
should adjourn such cases to give the defendant an opportunity o
disputing the back-duty. Section 34, it is submitted, only require
the court to order payment of back-duty where the defendan
unequivocally accepts the amount of back-duty.

Summary and Examples

The provisions of s. 9 as to back-duty apply only where ther
is a conviction under s. 8 of the Vehicles (Excise) Act for using o
keeping an unlicensed vehicle on a public road; if the conviction i
under s. 18 (alteration of use of vehicle) or s. 16 (trade licences), th

Act does not apply in respect of back-duty; in these circumstances back-duty is recoverable as a civil debt.

If, however, there is a conviction (including an order of absolute or conditional discharge or probation but not a finding under the Mental Health Act, 1959, s. 60 (2)) under s. 8, the court has a discretion as to the amount of the fine or penalty (up to £50 or five times the annual duty) but must order the full back-duty, however great the financial hardship to the defendant and however impecunious he is, unless the defendant can show that for some or all of the relevant period he was not the keeper of the vehicle or that it was not used or kept on a public road or chargeable with duty or that the relevant back-duty has in fact been paid.

The Courts Act, 1971, amended s. 44 of the Criminal Justice Act, 1967. The effect of the amendment is, that although a court after non-payment of a fine or enquiring into the offender's means may ordinarily remit the whole or part of a fine because of a change in his circumstances, this power of remission cannot be exercised either in respect of orders for the payment of back-duty under s. 9 or in respect of any penalties imposed under s. 8 or s. 18 (4) as these do not come within the definition of " fine " in s. 44 (11) of the Criminal Justice Act, 1967, as amended (see also p. 516).

The statement of facts normally indicates the amount of back-duty claimed and the licensing authority will, of course, know when any was last paid. A defendant who seeks to prove that he was not the keeper during any part of the relevant period should adduce evidence to that effect; the then owner of the vehicle may give evidence as to this but is in danger of incriminating himself both for not notifying the change and for not paying duty. Or the defendant may give and call evidence that the vehicle was not used or kept on a public road during the period before the offence or some of that period; members of his household or neighbours can often help on this point.

The defendant may also show that he has paid duty for the relevant period or some of it and in that case the period is calculated as if the month or part of a month for which he has paid were not comprised in the relevant period (s. 9 (3)). Or it may be shown that he has already been ordered to pay back-duty for the same vehicle on a previous conviction, in which case the back-duty now payable by him begins to run with the month following the previous conviction. The defendant may, possibly, appeal to the Crown Court against the amount ordered (see further on this point on p. 697 in Chapter VIII). Some examples may assist:—

    (1) *A* commits the offence of using a motor vehicle on a public
        road on 18th February, 1976. The licence ran out on

31st December, 1974 and *A* calls no evidence to suggest that the vehicle was not on a public road during 1975–76. In addition to the fine, the amount of which is at the magistrates' discretion, he must be ordered to pay full back-duty for the twelve months of 1975 and two months of 1976. The duty to be claimed, by s. 9 (4), is the annual rate applicable to it at the beginning of each month, or part; the Finance (No. 2) Act, 1975, s. 5, increased duties on licences taken out after 15th April, 1975— see s. 5 (6). The duty charged will be thus at the pre-15th April rate for the first four months of 1975 and at the increased rate under the 1975 Act for May, 1975, and subsequent months.

(2) The same facts but *A* notified the licensing authority that he had become the owner on 22nd June, 1975. Then he is liable to pay back-duty only for the months commencing 1st June, 1975. It seems on the wording of s. 9 (2) (*a*) that it is only notification by the person convicted that counts; a notification by the previous owner does not. Notification must be before the offence, not the conviction.

(3) The same facts but *A* proves in court that on 31st December, 1974, he put the car in his garage and the car was first put on the road a week before 18th February, 1976, the day of the offence. He pays back-duty for February, 1976, only. *Quaere*, if he first got the car out on 18th February; by s. 9 (2) the relevant period is one " ending with the date of the offence ". Does that period " end " at 0001 hours on 18th February or at 23.59 hours on that day? It is suggested that the construction against the Revenue should be adopted both because a taxing statute is so construed and because there is ambiguity, so that no back-duty for February is payable. The licensing authority can always obtain the February duty by other means.

(4) The same facts but *A* shows that he has in fact paid the back-duty before he came to court, e.g., he called at the appropriate office and paid it on the way to the hearing. Then no back-duty is orderable by the court; if he paid only part of the back-duty, the court should order payment of the part unpaid. *A* can also prove that the vehicle was exempt from duty in the relevant period or part of it.

(5) *B's* last licence expired on 30th June, 1975; he commits the offence of using his car on a public road on 21st March, 1976, and is later convicted of it at Oxford. He proves

to the Oxford court that he was convicted of a like offence committed at Cambridge in January, 1976, and that the Cambridge court ordered him to pay back-duty for July to December, 1975, and for January, 1976. The Oxford court should order him to pay back-duty for February and March, 1976, under the proviso to s. 9 (2).

In all the above cases the court should order a fine or absolute or conditional discharge in addition to the back-duty. By s. 9 (4) a vehicle is deemed to have belonged to the same duty-class throughout, unless otherwise proved; the prosecution may elect to treat it as being in the class in which it was when a licence was last taken out.

A defence under s. 9 (3) (b) arises only if the defendant paid the back-duty prior to the hearing. If someone else paid it, it is arguable that there is no back-duty " appropriate to the vehicle " under s. 9 (2).

See s. 6 as to back-duty on vehicles exempted from purchase tax because they are to be taken abroad, and then becoming chargeable with duty because not taken abroad.

Registration Marks

By s. 21 hackney carriages are required to exhibit distinctive signs showing that they are hackney carriages and their seating capacity, in the form indicated in Pt. VI of the Regulations. These signs must be exhibited in addition to any signs of a *different* kind required by a local Act or byelaw (*Eccles* v. *Kirke* [1949] 1 All E.R. 428).

By s. 22 (1) it is provided that, if a mark or sign required by s. 19 or s. 21 is not fixed to the vehicle as required, the *driver* of the vehicle or, if it is not being driven, the person keeping the vehicle, shall be liable to a fine of £20 or, for a second or subsequent offence, £50; it shall be a defence that the defendant had no reasonable opportunity of registering the vehicle and that it was being driven for the purpose of being registered.

By s. 22 (2), if any mark or sign fixed on a vehicle pursuant to s. 19 or s. 21 is in any way obscured or allowed to become not easily distinguishable, the *driver* or, if it is not being driven, the person keeping the vehicle, shall be liable to the penalties just mentioned but it shall be a defence that he took all steps reasonably practicable to prevent it being obscured or rendered not easily distinguishable. On a somewhat similarly worded provision in earlier legislation it was held in *Printz* v. *Sewell* (1912), 76 J.P. 295, that this defence could be invoked where the charge was failing to illuminate the rear number-plate, so that its numbers and letters were not easily distinguishable. Of course, this defence would not apply in charges under the Road Traffic Act for not having a rear light, even though the same light might serve both as a rear light and to illuminate the number plate, so the defendant could properly be convicted on the one charge and acquitted on the other.

By s. 26 (1) it is an offence if any person forges, or fraudulently alters or uses, or fraudulently lends or allows to be used by any other person any registration mark or sign or any licence or any registration book; the penalty is a fine of £200 on summary conviction and on indictment two years' imprisonment. " Forge " is not defined in the Act but there is a comprehensive definition in the Forgery Act, 1913, s. 1. The term " licence " includes an expired licence under s. 26 (*Taylor* v. *Emerson* (1962), 106 S.J. 552). " Fraudulently " in s. 26 means with intent to defraud the Revenue of duty, so that it may be that a fraudulent use of a licence to avoid police enquiries about stolen cars would not come under s. 26 (*R.* v. *Manners-Astley* [1967] 3 All E.R. 899), or to use the words of Lord Widgery, C.J., in *Cook* v. *Lanyon* [1972] R.T.R. 496, at pp. 497–498: " unquestionably means intent to use one licence in order to avoid having to pay for another . . .". Section 26 (1) extends to trade plates.

Burden of Proof

By s. 33 it is provided that if, in proceedings under s. 26 (2) (false declarations on applications for licences and false information on change of registration), under s. 8 (using and keeping vehicles without a licence) or under s. 16 (7) (using excess vehicles under trade licence), any question arises—

    (*a*) as to the number of vehicles used, or
    (*b*) as to the character, weight, horse-power or cylinder capacity of any vehicle, or
    (*c*) as to the number of persons for which a vehicle has seating capacity, or
    (*d*) as to the purpose for which any vehicle has been used,

the burden of proof in respect of the matter in question shall lie on the defendant. The section was discussed in *McCrone* v. *J. & L. Rigby (Wigan), Ltd.* (1952), 50 L.G.R. 115, and it should be noted that it applies only to proceedings under s. 8, s. 16 (7) or s. 26 (2); in summary proceedings under other sections, e.g., s. 18, the normal rule as to the burden of proof applies. Generally, a defendant must prove facts peculiarly within his own knowledge, e.g., that he has a licence (*John* v. *Humphreys* [1955] 1 All E.R. 793), and by the Magistrates' Courts Act, 1952, s. 81, any exception, exemption, proviso, excuse or qualification for a defendant should be proved by him and need not be negatived by the prosecution in opening. The defendant's burden under s. 33 may be discharged by evidence for the defence or by precise admissions made by the witnesses for the prosecution (*McCrone* v. *Rigby*, *supra*) and would seem to be less than that on a prosecutor generally to prove a criminal charge; he may satisfy the court of the probability of what he alleges, it seems (*R.* v. *Carr-Briant* [1943] 2 All E.R. 156).

By the Customs and Excise Act, 1952, s. 290 (2), where in any proceedings relating to excise any question arises as to whether duty has been paid on any goods or as to whether any goods or other things whatsoever are of the description or nature alleged in the information, the burden of proof lies on the defendant.

Section 31 of the Act enables evidence of prescribed matters to be given by the production of a document authenticated by a person authorised in that behalf by the Secretary of State (see p. 108).

Weight of Vehicles

Schedule 6 indicates the manner in which the weight of the vehicle is to be ascertained; it provides a code which may differ in some respects from that provided by the Road Traffic Act, 1972, s. 194, for ascertaining weight for the purposes of that Act (*Mackie* v. *Waugh* [1940] S.C.(J.) 49). The Schedule should be carefully studied. Unladen weight for the purposes of the Act shall be taken to be the weight of the vehicle inclusive of the body and all parts (the heavier being taken where alternative bodies or parts are used) which are necessary to or ordinarily used with the vehicle when working on a road, but exclusive of the weight of water, fuel or accumulators used for the purpose of the supply of power for the propulsion of the vehicle, and of loose tools and loose equipment. The meaning of " loose equipment " is discussed on p. 15. A vehicle with a detachable body is treated as being of the heavier weight unless it is re-weighed and re-registered, save so far as Sched. 6, para. 3, applies (*Scott* v. *Dickson* (1939), 83 S.J. 317, a case on the Road Traffic Act).

By para. 3, in computing the unladen weight of a goods vehicle, there shall be included the weight of any receptacle, being an additional body, placed on the vehicle to carry goods or burden, if the latter are loaded into, carried in and unloaded from the receptacle without the receptacle being removed from the vehicle, provided that the weight of the receptacle shall not be included—

(a) unless it is placed on the vehicle by or on behalf of the person in whose name the vehicle is registered; or

(b) if it is constructed or adapted for the purpose of being lifted on or off the vehicle with goods or burden contained therein and is from time to time actually used for that purpose in the ordinary course of business; it shall be deemed, by para. 3 (2), not to be so used until the contrary is shown; or

(c) if it is specially constructed or specially adapted for carrying livestock and is used solely for that purpose; by para. 3 (3), on journeys the main purpose of which is transport of livestock or on the way to the start of, or from the finish of, such journeys, however, agricultural produce or requisites may also be carried.

Paragraph 2 of Sched. 6 provides, in relation to a vehicle having a body constructed or adapted for the purpose of being lifted on or off the vehicle with goods or burden contained therein which is for the time being actually used for that purpose in the ordinary course of business, that the unladen weight of the vehicle shall, for the purposes of the Vehicles (Excise) Act, be taken exclusive of the weight of any such body and, where alternative bodies are used, any such body shall be disregarded for the purposes of Sched. 6. If any question arises as to whether the body is so used in the ordinary course of business, it shall be deemed not to be so used until the contrary is shown.

By para. 4 of Sched. 6 for the purposes of Scheds. 3 and 4 the weight of towing contrivances, to an amount of 1 cwt., if there is one such contrivance, or 2 cwt., if there is one at each end, is excluded in computing unladen weight, save in respect of tractors and goods vehicles used for drawing trailers. By para. 5 provision is made for excluding the weight of gas propulsion gear. See generally as to " weight " on p. 14, where the cases are reviewed.

By Sched. 4, para. 5, if a vehicle is constructed to carry a machine or contrivance, the weight of the latter is not included in the unladen weight, even though it is built in.

Definitions are found in s. 38 and the Schedules.

Endorsement and Disqualification

There is no power to endorse or disqualify for offences under the Vehicles (Excise) Act.

Remission of Fine or Penalty

By reason of the definition of " fine " contained in s. 44 (11) of the Criminal Justice Act, 1967, as amended, on an enquiry into a defendant's means after non-payment of a fine where there has been a change in the defendant's circumstances magistrates may remit the whole or part of a fine imposed under s. 12 (4) (failure to exhibit a licence), s. 26 (1) and s. 26 (2) (false declarations, forgery and fraudulent use of licences), s. 22 (failure to display number plates), s. 27 (failure to give information) and s. 37 (breach of Regulations), but magistrates may not do so in respect of any penalties imposed under s. 8 (no excise licence), s. 18 (4) (using a vehicle without paying a higher rate of duty), any order for payment of back-duty under s. 9 and any penalty under s. 16 (7) (Trade Licence Offences) (see p. 519).

The Road Vehicles (Registration and Licensing) Regulations

The relevant Regulations are now those of 1971 (S.I. 1971 No. 450), as amended by like-named Amendment Regulations of 1971 and 1972 (S.I. 1971 No. 1285 and S.I. 1972 No. 1865).

The 1971 Regulations define " works truck " as in reg. 3 of the Construction and Use Regulations (see p. 772); Sched. 3 to the Act is similar but uses the word " vicinity " instead of " neighbourhood ". (See p. 411.)

By reg. 3 (1) of the 1971 Regulations " owner " means in relation to a vehicle the person by whom it is kept or used. By reg. 16 the licence in force shall be fixed to and exhibited on the vehicle at all times while it is kept or used on a public road (see *Pilgram* v. *Dean* and *Strowger* v. *John* on p. 503, *Elliott* v. *Grey* on p. 44 as to " use " when stationary, and as to " keeping " see s. 38 (2) on p. 487). The only defence at present to a charge of failing to exhibit a licence, contrary to s. 12 (until s. 12 (5) is brought into force), is contained in the proviso to reg. 16 (1), which allows an applicant at a post office to detach the licence in order to apply for a new licence, and allows the new licence to be displayed in place of the old licence even though the new licence may not be in force. The manner and place of exhibition are also prescribed. Regulation 7 forbids alteration of a licence or exhibition of a faded or altered licence or document which could be mistaken for a licence. Other Regulations relate to the production of registration books (reg. 8 (2)) and to the duty of vendors and purchasers of motor vehicles to notify the registration authority of the sale and of changes of address and of alterations to the vehicle (regs. 10 to 15). Many of these duties are cast on " the owner " and a summons alleging an offence by the owner under these Regulations, committed after he had ceased to be owner, is bad, although he has omitted to notify the change of ownership and the vehicle is still registered in his name (*Spain* v. *Johns* (1950), 48 L.G.R. 532). Of course, by reg. 12 (1) he committed an offence as " the previous owner " by failing to report the change. Failure to notify the registration authority is not a continuing offence and time runs from a day or two after the change of ownership (*A. & C. McLennan (Blairgowrie), Ltd.* v. *MacMillan* [1964] S.L.T. 2) but the special time limit of s. 28 applies (see p. 490). See s. 8 (3) (*a*) on p. 509 as to the effect of non-delivery of the licence on transfer.

Regulations 17 to 22 and Scheds. 2 and 3 relate to the exhibition and position of registration marks; the figures and letters must be white, silver or light grey, indelible and on a black surface, save where translucent; or where the plate is constructed of reflex reflecting material the letters and figures must be black, and the front number must have a white reflex reflecting background and the rear a yellow reflex reflecting background. It is submitted that these paragraphs (paras. 6, 7 and 8 of Pt. II of Sched. 2) do not prohibit a vehicle from displaying a white plate in front and a black one at the rear or a black plate in front and a yellow one at the rear; otherwise there would be the absurd result that, while a vehicle with black plates front and rear would be legal, one with a white plate in front and a black at the rear (or a black in front and a yellow at the rear) would not, notwithstanding that the white and yellow plates are better, visibility-wise, than the black and consequently the vehicle would be safer than one with two black plates. By reg. 19 rear number plates must be illuminated at night. Schedule 3 makes special provision as to the position, visibility and illumination of registration marks on vehicles registered before 1st October, 1938. Vehicles need not have their rear number plates illuminated when they are exempt wholly or partially by the Road Transport Lighting Regulations (see p. 408) from showing lights to the front and rear (reg. 19 (3)). The Vehicles (Excise) Act, 1971, s. 22, applies to all vehicles; it provides certain defences in respect of obscured, unfixed or unlit marks. The case of *Printz* v. *Sewell* (p. 408, *supra*) relates to the latter.

Part VI and Sched. 4 prescribe the additional marks to be displayed by hackney carriages and the method of computing their seating capacity; Pt. IV relates to vehicles exempt from duty, and requires certain declarations to be made in respect of them, and Pt. VII indicates the method of calculating horse-power, cylinder capacity and unladen weight.

Regulation 45 empowers the Secretary of State to require a certificate of weight of a vehicle or to have the vehicle made available for weighing.

Breach of the present Regulations is punishable with a fine of £20. There is no power to endorse or disqualify.

Finally, it is emphasised that, like the Act, the Regulations require to be carefully studied in respect of any matters arising under them.

17. TRADE LICENCES

The law relating to trade licences is contained in s. 16 of the Vehicles (Excise) Act, 1971, and Pt. V of the Road Vehicles (Registration and Licensing) Regulations, 1971. A trade licence is issued to motor traders, vehicle testers and vehicle manufacturers. Section 16 is modified in respect of subss. (4) and (5) by Sched. 7 to the Act.

Section 16 as modified reads:—

" (1) If a motor trader or a vehicle tester applies in the prescribed manner to the Secretary of State to take out a licence under this section (in this Act referred to as a " trade licence ")—

    (i) in the case of a motor trader, for all mechanically propelled vehicles which are from time to time temporarily in his possession in the course of his business as a motor trader and all recovery vehicles kept by him for the purpose of dealing with disabled vehicles in the course of that business; or

    (ii) in the case of a vehicle tester, for all mechanically propelled vehicles which are from time to time submitted to him for testing in the course of his business as a vehicle tester; or

    (iii) in the case of a motor trader who is a manufacturer of mechanically propelled vehicles, for all vehicles kept and used by him solely for purposes of conducting research and development in the course of his business as such a manufacturer,

the Secretary of State may, subject to the prescribed conditions, issue to him a trade licence on payment of duty at the rate applicable to the licence in accordance with the following provisions of this section:

Provided that the holder of a trade licence shall not be entitled by virtue of that licence—

    (a) to use more than one mechanically propelled vehicle at any one time, except in the case of a recovery vehicle drawing a disabled vehicle; or

    (b) to use any vehicle for any purpose other than such purposes as may be prescribed; or

    (c) to keep any vehicle on a road if it is not being used thereon.

(2) Regulations shall be made under this section prescribing the conditions subject to which trade licences are to be issued and the purposes for which the holder of a trade licence may use a vehicle under the licence.

(3) The purposes which may be prescribed as those for which the holder of a trade licence may use a vehicle under the licence shall not include the conveyance of goods or burden of any description other than—

    (a) a load which is carried solely for the purpose of testing or demonstrating the vehicle or any of its accessories or equipment and which is returned to the place of loading without having been removed from the vehicle except for such purpose or in the case of accident; or

(b) in the case of a recovery vehicle, any such load as is referred to in the definition of such a vehicle contained in subsection (8) below or a load consisting of a disabled vehicle; or

(c) any load built in as part of the vehicle or permanently attached thereto; or

(d) a load consisting of parts, accessories or equipment designed to be fitted to the vehicle and of tools for so fitting them; or

(e) a load consisting of a trailer;

and, for the purposes of this subsection, where a vehicle is so constructed that a trailer may by partial superimposition be attached to the vehicle in such a manner as to cause a substantial part of the weight of the trailer to be borne by the vehicle, the vehicle and the trailer shall be deemed to constitute a single vehicle.

[(4) A trade licence may be taken out either for one calendar year or, except in the case of a licence which is to be used only for vehicles to which Schedule 1 to this Act relates, for a period of three months beginning with the first day of January, of April, of July or of October.]

[(5) The rate of duty applicable to a trade licence taken out for a calendar year shall be [£20] or, if the licence is to be used only for vehicles to which Schedule 1 to this Act relates, [£2·50;] and the rate of duty applicable to a licence taken out for a period of three months shall be eleven fortieths of the rate applicable to the corresponding trade licence taken out for a calendar year, any fraction of 5p being treated as 5p if it exceeds 2·5p but otherwise being disregarded.]

(6) Nothing in this section shall operate to prevent a person entitled to take out a trade licence from holding two or more trade licences.

(7) If any person holding a trade licence or trade licences issued under this section uses on a public road by virtue of that licence or those licences—

(i) a greater number of vehicles at any one time than he is authorised to use by virtue of that licence or those licences; or

(ii) any vehicle for any purpose other than such purposes as may have been prescribed under subsection (2) above;

or if that person uses that licence or any of those licences for the purpose of keeping on a road a vehicle which is not being used on that road, he shall be liable to the greater of the following penalties, namely—

(a) an excise penalty of £50; or

(b) an excise penalty equal to five times the amount of the duty chargeable in respect of the vehicle or vehicles.

The amount of the duty chargeable in respect of a vehicle shall be calculated for the purposes of this subsection in the same manner as it is calculated for the purposes of section 8 of this Act by virtue of subsection (3) thereof.

(8) In this section—

'motor trader' means a manufacturer or repairer of, or dealer in, mechanically propelled vehicles; and a person shall be treated for the purposes of this section as a dealer in such vehicles if he carries on a business consisting wholly or mainly of collecting and delivering mechanically propelled vehicles, and not including any other activities except activities as a manufacturer or repairer of, or dealer in, such vehicles;

'vehicle tester' means a person, other than a motor trader, who regularly in the course of his business engages in the testing on

roads of mechanically propelled vehicles belonging to other persons; and
'recovery vehicle' means a vehicle on which there is mounted, or which is drawing, or which is carrying as part of its equipment, apparatus designed for raising a disabled vehicle wholly or partly from the ground or for drawing a disabled vehicle when so raised, and which is not used for the conveyance of goods other than a disabled vehicle wholly raised by that apparatus, and which carries no other load than articles required for the operation of, or in connection with, that apparatus or otherwise for dealing with disabled vehicles."

The Regulations which have been issued are now contained in Pt. V of the Road Vehicles (Registration and Licensing) Regulations, 1971. Regulation 28 relates to applications for trade licences, reg. 29 prescribes twenty-eight days as the period for requesting review of a decision refusing a trade licence, reg. 30 requires the holder to notify the Secretary of State of any change in the name or address of his business, reg. 31 prescribes the issue and replacement of trade plates, reg. 32 forbids the alteration or mutilation of trade plates or the exhibition of anything which might be mistaken for a trade plate and reg. 33 governs the manner in which trade plates should be fixed and displayed on vehicles.

The remaining Regulations read as follows:—

"*Restriction on use of trade plates and licences*

34. No person, not being the holder of a trade licence, shall use on a public road a vehicle on which there is displayed a trade plate or a trade licence, so, however, that nothing in this Regulation shall apply so as to prevent a person with the consent of the holder of the trade licence from driving a vehicle when the vehicle is being used on a public road by virtue of a trade licence and by the holder thereof.

Purposes for which a vehicle may be used

35.—(1) In this Regulation, ' business purpose ', in relation to a motor trader, means—

(a) a purpose connected with his business as a manufacturer or repairer of or dealer in mechanically propelled vehicles, or

(b) a purpose connected with his business as a manufacturer or repairer of or dealer in trailers carried on in conjunction with his business as a motor trader.

(2) For the purposes of sub-paragraphs (a) to (k) of paragraph (4) of this Regulation, where a mechanically propelled vehicle is used on a public road by virtue of a trade licence and that vehicle is drawing a trailer, the vehicle and trailer shall be deemed to constitute a single vehicle.

(3) Save as provided in Regulation 36 of these Regulations, no person, being a motor trader and the holder of a trade licence, shall use any mechanically propelled vehicle on a public road by virtue of that licence unless it is a vehicle which is temporarily in his possession in the course of his business as a motor trader or a recovery vehicle kept by him for the purpose of dealing with disabled vehicles in the course of that business.

(4) Save as provided in the said Regulation 36 and without derogation from the provisions of the last preceding paragraph of this Regulation, no person, being a motor trader and the holder of a trade licence, shall use any mechanically propelled vehicle on a public road by virtue of that licence for a purpose other than a business purpose and other than one of the following purposes:—

(a) for its test or trial or the test or trial of its accessories or equipment in the ordinary course of construction or repair or after completion in either such case;

(b) for proceeding to or from a public weighbridge for ascertaining its unladen weight or to or from any place for its registration or inspection by a person acting on behalf of the Secretary of State;

(c) for its test or trial for the benefit of a prospective purchaser, for proceeding at the instance of a prospective purchaser to any place for the purpose of such test or trial, or for returning after such test or trial;

(d) for its test or trial for the benefit of a person interested in promoting publicity in regard to it, for proceeding at the instance of such a person to any place for the purpose of such test or trial, or for returning after such test or trial;

(e) for delivering it to the place where the purchaser intends to keep it;

(f) for demonstrating its operation or the operation of its accessories or equipment when being handed over to the purchaser;

(g) for delivering it from one part of his premises to another part of his premises, or for delivering it from his premises to the premises of, or between parts of premises of, another manufacturer or repairer of or dealer in mechanically propelled vehicles or removing it from the premises of another manufacturer or repairer of or dealer in mechanically propelled vehicles direct to his own premises;

(h) for proceeding to or returning from a workshop in which a body or a special type of equipment or accessory is to be or has been fitted to it or in which it is to be or has been painted or repaired;

(i) for proceeding from the premises of a manufacturer or repairer of or dealer in mechanically propelled vehicles to a place from which it is to be transported by train, ship or aircraft or for proceeding to the premises of such a manuacturer, repairer or dealer from a place to which it has been so transported;

(j) for proceeding to or returning from any garage, auction room or other place at which vehicles are usually stored or usually or periodically offered for sale and at which the vehicle is to be or has been stored or is to be or has been offered for sale as the case may be;

(k) for proceeding to or returning from a place where it is to be or has been tested, or for proceeding to a place where it is to be broken up or otherwise dismantled; or

(l) in the case of a recovery vehicle—

(i) for proceeding to or returning from a place where assistance is to be, or has been, rendered to a disabled vehicle,

(ii) for proceeding to or returning from a place where it is to be, or has been, held available for rendering assistance to a disabled vehicle, or

(iii) for carrying a disabled vehicle, or for towing such a vehicle (whether with the assistance of a trailer or not), from the place where it has broken down or from such other place where it is subsequently for the time being situated to a place for repair or storage or breaking up.

36. No person, being a motor trader and who is a manufacturer of mechanically propelled vehicles and the holder of a trade licence, shall use any mechanically propelled vehicle, kept by him solely for the purposes of conducting research and development in the course of his business as such a manufacturer, on a public road by virtue of that licence except for such a purpose.

37. No person, being a vehicle tester and the holder of a trade licence, shall use any mechanically propelled vehicle on a public road by virtue of that licence for any purpose other than testing it or any trailer drawn thereby or any of the accessories or equipment on such vehicle or trailer in the course of his business as a vehicle tester.

Conveyance of goods or burden

38.—(1) No person, being a motor trader and the holder of a trade licence, shall use a mechanically propelled vehicle on a public road by virtue of that licence for the conveyance of goods or burden of any description other than—

(*a*) a load which is carried by a vehicle being used for a relevant purpose and is carried solely for the purpose of testing or demonstrating the vehicle or any of its accessories or equipment and which is returned to the place of loading without having been removed from the vehicle except for such last mentioned purpose or in the case of accident:
In this sub-paragraph ' relevant purpose ' means a purpose mentioned in Regulation 35 (4) (*a*), (*c*), (*d*) and (*f*) of these Regulations; or

(*b*) in the case of a recovery vehicle, being used for a relevant purpose, any such load as is referred to in the definition of such a vehicle contained in section 16 (8) of the Act or a load consisting of a disabled vehicle:
In this sub-paragraph ' relevant purpose ' means a purpose mentioned in Regulation 35 (4) (*l*) of these Regulations; or

(*c*) any load built in as part of the vehicle or permanently attached thereto: or

(*d*) a load consisting of parts, accessories or equipment designed to be fitted to the vehicle and of tools for so fitting them, the vehicle being used for a relevant purpose:
In this sub-paragraph ' relevant purpose ' means a purpose mentioned in Regulation 35 (4) (*g*), (*h*) or (*i*) of these Regulations; or

(*e*) a load consisting of a trailer, the vehicle carrying the trailer being used for a relevant purpose:
In this sub-paragraph ' relevant purpose ' means a purpose mentioned in Regulation 35 (4) (*e*), (*h*) or (*i*) of these Regulations.

(2) No person, being a motor trader and who is a manufacturer of mechanically propelled vehicles and the holder of a trade licence, shall

use any mechanically propelled vehicle, kept by him solely for the purposes of conducting research and development in the course of his business as such a manufacturer, on a public road by virtue of that licence for the conveyance of goods or burden of any description other than—

    (*a*) a load which is carried solely for the purpose of testing the vehicle or any of its accessories or equipment and which is returned to the place of loading without having been removed from the vehicle except for such purpose or in the case of accident; or

    (*b*) any load built in as part of the vehicle or permanently attached thereto,

and nothing in the last preceding paragraph of this Regulation shall be taken as applying to a mechanically propelled vehicle the use of which is restricted by this paragraph.

(3) For the purposes of this Regulation and the next succeeding Regulation, where a vehicle is so constructed that a trailer may by partial superimposition be attached to the vehicle in such a manner as to cause a substantial part of the weight of the trailer to be borne by the vehicle, the vehicle and the trailer shall be deemed to constitute a single vehicle.

39. No person, being a vehicle tester and the holder of a trade licence, shall use a mechanically propelled vehicle on a public road by virtue of that licence for the conveyance of goods or burden of any description other than—

    (*a*) a load which is carried solely for the purpose of testing or demonstrating the vehicle or any of its accessories or equipment and which is returned to the place of loading without having been removed from the vehicle except for such purpose or in the case of accident; or

    (*b*) any load built in as part of the vehicle or permanently attached thereto.

Carriage of passengers

40.—(1) No person, being the holder of a trade licence, shall use a mechanically propelled vehicle on a public road by virtue of that licence for carrying any person on the vehicle or on any trailer drawn thereby other than—

    (*a*) the driver of the vehicle, being the holder of the licence, an employee of the holder, or any other person driving with the consent of the holder while (except in the case of a vehicle which is constructed to carry only one person) accompanied by the holder or an employee of his;

    (*b*) any person required to be on the vehicle or trailer by, or by virtue of, the Road Traffic Act, 1960;

    (*c*) any person carried for the purpose of fulfilling his statutory duties in connection with an inspection of the vehicle or trailer;

    (*d*) any person in a disabled vehicle being towed;

    (*e*) the holder of the trade licence or an employee of his, if in either case his presence is necessary for the purpose for which the vehicle is being used;

    (*f*) an employee of the holder of the trade licence proceeding to a place for the purpose of driving vehicles on behalf of the holder of the trade licence in the course of his business as a motor trader;

(*g*) a prospective purchaser or his servant or agent or any person requested to accompany the said prospective purchaser, or in the case of a vehicle being used for the purpose mentioned in Regulation 35 (4) (*f*) of these Regulations, the purchaser or his servant or agent or any person requested to accompany the said purchaser; or

(*h*) a person mentioned in Regulation 35 (4) (*d*) of these Regulations.

(2) Where a person coming within sub-paragraph (*g*) or (*h*) of the preceding paragraph of this Regulation is carried he shall be accompanied (except in the case of a vehicle which is constructed to carry only one person) by the holder of the trade licence or an employee of his."

Under the former Regulations not only was a holder allowed to use trade plates for a " business purpose ", which was defined in identical terms to those now set out in reg. 35 (1) (*a*) and (*b*), but also he could use the trade licence for any additional purpose as long as it was used at the same time for a " business purpose ". This was found difficult to control, and the present Regulations, instead of allowing the additional purposes to be unspecified, specify the purposes in detail in reg. 35 (4) (*a*) to (*l*). It should also be noted that, except for recovery vehicles and vehicles used by motor manufacturers under reg. 36 solely for the purposes of research and development, a vehicle may not be used under trade plates unless it is temporarily in the possession of the motor trader (reg. 35 (3)). A motor trader who carries on the business of collecting and delivering vehicles may legitimately use trade plates for this purpose (see reg. 35 (4) (*g*) to (*k*)) but where part of the business of the motor trader was to collect and deliver trailers from one factory where they were partly assembled to another factory where the trailers were completed, a magistrates' court has held that the motor trader could not use trade plates on the vehicles which towed the trailers unless the towing vehicles as well as the trailers were temporarily in the possession of the motor trader. Excise duty does not have to be paid on trailers, only on mechanically propelled vehicles; reg. 35 (2), which requires the towing vehicle and trailer to be treated as one vehicle, could not therefore be construed so that the towing vehicle could thus be said to be temporarily in the possession of the motor trader merely because the trailer was.

Recovery Vehicles

" Recovery vehicle " is defined in s. 16 (8), *supra*. A Land Rover with a towing buoy secured to its rear supporting a crane that was able to produce a suspended tow for a disabled car was held to be a " recovery vehicle " as formerly defined in s. 12 of the Vehicles

(Excise) Act, 1962, when the buoy had been detached from the Land Rover only once during the preceding eight months (*Seeney* v. *Dean* [1971] Crim.L.R. 545). Section 16 (8) repeats the definition in the 1962 Act as modified by s. 9 (3) of the Finance Act, 1970. The modification makes it clear that the apparatus for raising the vehicle no longer has to be mounted on the recovery vehicle. Indeed it would now appear that the definition is so wide as to enable practically any vehicle which carries a jack to be used as a recovery vehicle, and in *E. Pearson & Son (Teesside), Ltd.* v. *Richardson* [1972] R.T.R. 552 a vehicle equipped with heavy duty lifting jacks but not capable of suspended towing was held to be a "recovery vehicle". On the true construction of s. 16 (8) there are two sub-categories of vehicle, those equipped for drawing and those so equipped that they were only able to raise a disabled vehicle wholly or partly from the ground (*ibid.*).

In *Hunter the Bakers, Ltd.* v. *Hills* [1973] R.T.R. 361, *Pearson* was followed and applied. It was held that a platform lorry with a detachable rigid tow bar with a bracket for it, four 4 cwt. concrete ballast slabs, ropes and 5 ton hydraulic jack was a recovery vehicle. The justices who had held that it was not a recovery vehicle because, *inter alia*, it could only be a recovery vehicle if it was used in conjunction with a vehicle capable of suspended towing, were directed to convict.

The definition in s. 16 (8) requires the recovery vehicle not to be used "for the conveyance of goods other than a disabled vehicle wholly raised by that apparatus". A 15-ton tracked shovel climbed on to a low loader under its own power and was then secured by a winch. It was held that as the tracked shovel had climbed on to the low loader under its own power, the tracked shovel was "not wholly raised by that apparatus" and the low loader could therefore not be classed as a "recovery vehicle" (*Scott* v. *Gutteridge Plant Hire, Ltd.* [1974] R.T.R. 292).

The cases on the pre-1970 Regulations are generally of little use on the present Regulations. Although most of them turned on the question of "business purpose", they are now of little help because the present Regulations only allow trade plates to be used for one of the purposes set out in reg. 35 (4) (*a*) to (*l*) in addition to a "business purpose".

In the pre-1970 Regulations the term "prospective purchaser" includes a possible purchaser (*Helson* v. *Barnard* [1922] S.L.T. 40), and this decision would appear to apply to reg. 35 (4) (*c*) of the 1971 Regulations.

Employers have been held criminally liable for illegal use of trade plates by their servants, though against their instructions

(*Griffiths* v. *Studebakers* (1923), 87 J.P. 199). Days of grace are not allowed to renew trade licences.

Persons who use trade licences in contravention of the Regulations offend against them; liability is not confined to the licence-holder (*Waugh* v. *Paterson* [1924] S.C.(J.) 52) save, *semble*, so far as particular Regulations apply to the holder alone. In such cases, only he and those who aid and abet him should be charged.

Penalty and Procedure

The penalty is £50 or five times the actual duty (for calculation of the penalty see pp. 506–508). The penalty for a breach of the Regulations is a fine of £20 (Vehicles (Excise) Act, 1971, s. 37 (3) (*b*) as modified by Sched. 7).

Offences may be tried by magistrates only. Any person may prosecute for an offence under the Regulations. For offences under s. 16 (7) the time-limit is six months from the discovery of the offence by the prosecutor, subject to an overriding time-limit of three years from the date of the offence and only the Secretary of State or a constable with his approval may prosecute (see s. 28 on p. 488). Magistrates cannot remit payment wholly or partly of a penalty under s. 16 (7) on a means enquiry under s. 44 of the Criminal Justice Act, 1967, as the penalty is not a " fine ": *aliter* a fine for breach of the Regulations (see p. 516). The special time-limit under s. 28 applies to breach of the Regulations.

There is no power to endorse or disqualify.

18.   OPERATOR'S LICENCE FOR CARRIAGE OF GOODS

The licensing of a goods vehicle for the carriage of goods for hire or reward or for or in connection with a trade or business now comes under Pt. V of the Transport Act, 1968.

An operator's licence is required under s. 60 from the Area Chairman of the Traffic Commissioners (see s. 59) for the use on a road of a goods vehicle (see s. 92 (1) and (5) on p. 540, whereby goods-carrying trailers are included and trams and trolley-vehicles operated under statutory powers excluded) for the carriage of goods (*a*) for hire or reward, or (*b*) for or in connection with any trade or business carried on by the applicant. The Regulations under which operators' licences are obtained are the Goods Vehicles (Operators' Licences) Regulations, 1969 (S.I. 1969 No. 1656), and the fees for licences are prescribed by the Goods Vehicles (Operators' Licences) (Fees) Regulations, 1971 (S.I. 1971 No.

149). By s. 60 (2) an operator's licence is not required in cases specified in the Regulations or for the use of a " small goods vehicle ". " Small goods vehicle " is defined in s. 60 (4) as being, in the case of a lone vehicle without a trailer, one with a plated (i.e., laden) weight of $3\frac{1}{2}$ tons or less or, if it has no plated weight, with an unladen weight of 30 cwt. or less; see s. 60 (4) as to the term " relevant plated weight " and also as to the definition of " small goods vehicle " in relation to an articulated vehicle or a goods vehicle linked with a trailer or trailers.

Regulation 3 of the Regulations, together with Sched. 1, exempts twenty-three classes of vehicle from the necessity of obtaining operators' licences. These include dual-purpose vehicles (as defined in reg. 3 (1) of the Construction and Use Regulations), public service vehicles, hackney carriages, road-cleansing vehicles, vehicles used for police, fire brigade or ambulance purposes, and vehicles used for the purposes of funerals.

The Goods Vehicles (Operators' Licences) (Temporary Use in Great Britain) Regulations, 1972 (S.I. 1972 No. 716) as amended by like named Amendment Regulations (S.I. 1972 No. 1535) modify the relevant sections of the Transport Act in respect of foreign and Northern Ireland goods vehicles. Regulation 3 defines a " foreign goods vehicle " as a vehicle—

" (a) which has been brought temporarily into Great Britain and does not remain in Great Britain for more than three months; and
(b) which is engaged in carrying goods by road on a journey, some part of which has taken place, or will take place, outside the United Kingdom; and
(c) which is not used at any time during the said journey for the carriage of goods loaded at one place in the United Kingdom and delivered at another place in the United Kingdom."

" Temporarily " in reg. 27 of the Construction and Use Regulations was construed as " casually ". If the vehicle is brought regularly, although intermittently, into Great Britain it is not " temporarily " in Great Britain (B.R.S. v. Wurzal [1971] 3 All E.R. 480). The Regulations make special provision for Austrian, Belgian, Bulgarian, Czechoslovakian, Danish, Dutch, French, German, Hungarian, Italian, Norwegian, Rumanian, Spanish, Swedish and Yugoslavian goods vehicles by dispensing with the need for such vehicles to have operators' licences and substituting a requirement in certain circumstances for the carrying of other permits or documents.

Section 60 of the Transport Act, 1968, reads:—

" (1) Subject to subsection (2) of this section and to the other provisions of this Part of this Act, no person shall, after the appointed day for the purposes of this section, use a goods vehicle on a road for the carriage of goods—

   (*a*) for hire or reward; or

   (*b*) for or in connection with any trade or business carried on by him,

except under a licence granted under this Part of this Act (hereafter in this Part of this Act referred to as an ' operator's licence ').

   (2) Subsection (1) of this section shall not apply—

   (*a*) to the use of a small goods vehicle as defined in subsection (4) of this section; or

   (*b*) to the use of a vehicle of any class specified in regulations.

   (3) It is hereby declared that, for the purposes of this Part of this Act, the performance by a local or public authority of their functions constitutes the carrying on of a business.

   (4) For the purposes of subsection (2) (*a*) of this section a small goods vehicle is a goods vehicle which—

   (*a*) does not form part of a vehicle combination and has a relevant plated weight not exceeding $3\frac{1}{2}$ tons or (not having a relevant plated weight) has an unladen weight not exceeding 30 hundredweight; or

   (*b*) forms part of a vehicle combination (not being an articulated combination) which is such that—

     (i) if all the vehicles comprised in the combination (or all of them except any small trailer) have relevant plated weights, the aggregate of the relevant plated weights of the vehicles comprised in the combination (exclusive of any such trailer) does not exceed $3\frac{1}{2}$ tons;

     (ii) in any other case, the aggregate of the unladen weights of those vehicles (exclusive of any such trailer) does not exceed 30 hundredweight; or

   (*c*) forms part of an articulated combination which is such that—

     (i) if the trailer comprised in the combination has a relevant plated weight, the aggregate of the unladen weight of the motor vehicle comprised in the combination and the relevant plated weight of that trailer does not exceed $3\frac{1}{2}$ tons;

     (ii) in any other case, the aggregate of the unladen weights of the motor vehicle and the trailer comprised in the combination does not exceed 30 hundredweight.

In any provision of this subsection ' relevant plated weight ' means a plated weight of the description specified in relation to that provision by regulations; and in paragraph (*b*) of this subsection ' small trailer ' means a trailer having an unladen weight not exceeding 1 ton.

   (5) A person who uses a vehicle in contravention of this section shall be liable on summary conviction to a fine not exceeding £200."

Note that an offence under s. 60 can be committed by a person who " uses " in contravention of s. 60; any person who is not a " user " can be charged only with aiding and abetting use. By s. 92 (2) the driver, if he is the owner or is in possession under a hire-purchase agreement, etc., and in any other case the person whose servant or agent the driver is, is deemed to be the user; normally therefore an employed driver should not be charged under s. 60 and the High Court said in *Carpenter* v. *Campbell* [1953] 1 All E.R. 280 that, where it is the employer's duty to get the licence, the driver should not be prosecuted anyhow. For a case in which an employment agency who introduced drivers to haulage companies were held not to be the employers of the drivers and thus could not be prosecuted by virtue of s. 92 (2) when a client haulage company had no operator's licence, see *Alderton* v. *Richard Burgon Associates, Ltd.* [1974] R.T.R. 422. And see p. 50. Section 61 of the 1968 Act reads:—

" (1) Subject to subsection (2) of this section, the vehicles authorised to be used under an operator's licence shall be—

(a) such motor vehicles, being vehicles belonging to the holder of the licence or in his possession under an agreement for hire-purchase, hire or loan, as are specified in the licence;

(b) trailers from time to time belonging to the holder of the licence or in his possession under an agreement for hire-purchase, hire or loan, not exceeding at any time such maximum number as is specified in the licence;

(c) unless the licence does not permit the addition of authorised vehicles under this paragraph and subject to subsection (3) of this section, motor vehicles not exceeding such maximum number as is specified in the licence, being vehicles belonging to the holder of the licence or in his possession under an agreement for hire-purchase, hire or loan, but acquired by him, or coming into his possession under such an agreement, only after the grant of the licence.

For the purposes of paragraphs (b) and (c) of this subsection different types of trailers or different types of motor vehicles, as the case may be, may be distinguished in a licence and a maximum number may be specified in the licence for trailers or vehicles of each type.

(2) An operator's licence shall not authorise the use of any vehicle unless the place which is for the time being its operating centre—

(a) is in the area of the licensing authority by whom the licence was granted; or

(b) is outside that area and has not been the operating centre of that vehicle for a period of more than three months.

For the purposes of paragraph (b) of this subsection, two or more successive periods which are not separated from each other by an interval of at least three months shall be treated as a single period having a duration equal to the total duration of those periods.

(3) A motor vehicle which, after the grant of an operator's licence, is acquired by the holder of the licence, or comes into his possession under an agreement for hire-purchase, hire or loan, and thereupon becomes an authorised vehicle by virtue of subsection (1) (c) of this section, shall cease to be an authorised vehicle on the expiration of one month from the date on which it was acquired by him or came into his possession unless before the expiration of that period he delivers to the licensing authority a notice in such form as the authority may require to the effect that the vehicle

has been acquired by him, or has come into his possession, as the case may be.

(4) (*Licensing authority to vary licence on receipt of such notice.*)

(5) A motor vehicle specified in an operator's licence shall not, while it remains so specified, be capable of being effectively specified in any other operator's licence.

(6) (*Power to vary licence by removing vehicle therefrom.*)"

Note that by s. 61 (5) a motor vehicle can be specified in only one licence. *Semble*, if two licences are issued for one vehicle, the second one may be void and any conditions attached to the second one issued in point of time may be void also, so that it may not be an offence to fail to comply with a condition of the second one.

Later sections of Pt. V of the Transport Act indicate the procedure for applying to the Area Chairman of the Traffic Commissioners for an operator's licence and by s. 66 conditions as to notifying certain matters may be attached to such a licence; s. 66 (2) reads:—

" Any person who contravenes any condition attached under this section to a licence of which he is the holder shall be liable on summary conviction to a fine not exceeding £200."

An offence under s. 66 can be committed only by the holder of an operator's licence or by a person who aids and abets him, as indicated on p. 52. Some knowledge of the fact that the condition is being breached or wilful shutting of eyes to it is generally needed to prove aiding and abetting. As the licence-holder will almost always know of the matters to be notified, when they arise, it seems unnecessary to discuss whether his liability is absolute or not; see p. 68 as to whether this would be a continuing offence.

Save under ss. 65 (conditions as to transport managers, *infra*) and 66 (see above), no express power to attach conditions to an operator's licence is conferred.

Part V of the Transport Act, 1968, is not applied to vehicles of the Crown or of visiting forces; the like provisions under Pt. VI of the Road Traffic Act, 1960, did not apply either.

Provision is made by s. 85 of the Transport Act, 1968, and reg. 20 of and Sched. 3 to the Goods Vehicles (Operators' Licences) Regulations, 1969, as to operators' licences in respect of holding companies and subsidiaries.

Transport Managers

The law as to transport managers is governed by s. 65 of the 1968 Act. This section is not yet in force. Section 65 reads:—

" (1) In every operator's licence granted by a licensing authority on an application made after the appointed day for the purposes of this section there shall be specified, in relation to each place in the area of the authority which, when the licence is granted, will be an operating centre of the holder of the licence, a person (being the holder of the licence, if an individual, or a person employed by him) who is to be responsible for the operation and maintenance of the authorised vehicles normally used from that centre, and it shall be a condition of the licence—

(a) that the person so specified shall be the holder of a transport manager's licence of the prescribed class; and

(b) if the person so specified is an employee of the holder of the operator's licence, that that person is employed by him in a position of responsibility specified in the licence.

(2) Where, at any time after an operator's licence has been granted as mentioned in subsection (1) of this section by the licensing authority for any area, a place in that area becomes an operating centre of the holder of the licence, that subsection shall, at the expiration of the period of three months beginning at that time, apply to the new operating centre as it applies to any operating centre which the holder of the licence has when the licence is granted.

(3) Unless in any case the licensing authority in his discretion otherwise determines, the person specified in any licence for the purposes of subsection (1) of this section in relation to any operating centre of any person shall not be the same as the person specified for those purposes in relation to any other operating centre of that person, whether in that licence or in any other operator's licence which is then held by him.

(4) The licensing authority may, if he thinks fit, permit the responsibility for the operation and maintenance of the authorised vehicles normally used from any particular operating centre to be shared between two or more persons; and, in any such case, subsection (1) of this section shall have effect—

(a) as if it required both or all of these persons to be specified in the licence, together with the manner in which the responsibility is to be shared between them; and

(b) as if references in paragraphs (a) and (b) to the person specified in the licence were references to each of the persons so specified by virtue of this subsection.

(5) In specifying for the purposes of subsection (1) of this section a position of responsibility to be held by any person, the licensing authority shall secure that that person thereby carries direct responsibility for the operation and maintenance of the authorised vehicles normally used from the operating centre in question or such share of that responsibility as may have been allocated to him under the last foregoing subsection.

(6) For the purposes of subsection (1) of this section a director of a company shall be deemed to be employed by it; and where the authorised vehicles are to be operated by the holder of an operator's licence in partnership with other persons, any of those other persons may be specified in the licence for the purposes of that subsection, but, if any of them is so specified, it shall be an additional condition of the licence that the authorised vehicles are operated by the holder of the licence in partnership with the person so specified.

(7) Where at any time a person specified in an operator's licence for the purposes of any condition imposed by or under this section dies, or ceases to be employed by the holder of the licence in a position of responsibility specified therein, or ceases to hold a transport manager's licence of the prescribed class, or any other event occurs whereby such a condition

is contravened, that condition shall nevertheless be deemed not to have been contravened—

    (a) during the period of three months beginning at that time or such longer period as the licensing authority who issued the operator's licence may in any particular case allow; and

    (b) if before the expiration of that period the holder of the operator's licence duly applies for the licence to be varied for the purpose of bringing the contravention to an end, during the period until the application, and any appeal arising out of it, have been disposed of.

(8) (*Power to make regulations.*)

(9) Subject to subsection (7) of this section, any person who uses an authorised vehicle from an operating centre of his for a purpose for which it cannot lawfully be used without the authority of an operator's licence—

    (a) at a time when a condition under this section of an operator's licence held by him is contravened in relation to that operating centre; or

    (b) at a time when the matters required by virtue of subsection (1) or (2) of this section to be specified in relation to that operating centre in an operator's licence held by him are not so specified,

shall be liable on summary conviction to a fine not exceeding £200.

(10) Schedule 9 to this Act shall have effect in relation to transport managers' licences.

(11) In this section references to responsibility for the operation of any vehicles include (without prejudice to the generality of that expression) references to responsibility for securing that the drivers of the vehicles are properly licensed and comply with Part VI of this Act or, so long as those sections remain in force, sections 73 and 186 of the Act of 1960."

The clause was debated in the House of Commons on 28th May, 1968.

What is the criminal liability of a transport manager if a vehicle goes on the road in a defective condition or the driver works excessive hours or some other road traffic offence is committed? The section does not specifically mention or impose any criminal liability greater than that ordinarily imposed on an owner or foreman who has a general responsibility for the actions of his staff and the safety of his vehicles, though it can be argued that a somewhat higher duty than the ordinary is imposed on a transport manager in respect of licences and drivers' hours by s. 65 (11). However, s. 65 (1) does declare that the transport manager " is to be responsible for the operation and maintenance " of the authorised vehicles and s. 65 (5) refers to carrying " direct responsibility ". It is submitted that every case must be decided on its facts; if the transport manager can show that an offence occurred without his knowledge or negligence, e.g., when he was away ill or in defiance of his instructions, it may be that he is not criminally liable. In a prosecution of a transport manager, his appointment as such must be established but an admission under the Criminal Justice Act, 1967, s. 10, will often do this. Another question is whether s. 65, in putting liability on the transport manager, exempts people like the owner and his head mechanic who would otherwise be liable; it is submitted that it does not, though, on particular facts, the obligations of the section coupled with an actual allocation of responsibilities might exempt a head mechanic as well as going to mitigate the penalty on the owner.

Section 65 relates to authorised vehicles, as defined in s. 92, but, once the transport manager has been given responsibility in fact for his firm's fleet of vehicles, it seems that in practice he is equally responsible for both authorised and unauthorised vehicles; however, there may be cases where there is one statutory transport manager for authorised vehicles and another non-statutory one for the smaller ones and the non-application of s. 65 to the latter manager might lessen his criminal liability. *Semble*, a transport manager would not normally " use " vehicles; the firm and the driver are the users. He would usually " cause " or " permit " or aid and abet use.

In the Parliamentary debates it was said that a local garage proprietor might be appointed transport manager under s. 65 where the operator had only two or three vehicles. Assuming that such proprietor can be a person " employed " by an individual operator (see s. 65 (1)), it seems difficult to pin criminal liability on him for acts or omissions of drivers and staff not employed or controlled by him unless directly attributable to his own fault, e.g., failure to service vehicles or to inspect them.

The words " from an operating centre of his " in s. 65 (9) ensure that, when an operator has more than one operating centre specified in his operator's licence, it is an offence to use a vehicle only from any of those centres which does not have the necessary licensed transport manager in post (*Hansard*, House of Lords, 3rd July, 1968, col. 381).

Special Authorisation for Long Journeys by Large Goods Vehicles and Carriage of Heavy Loads

When s. 71 of the Transport Act, 1968, is operative, special authorisation from the Area Chairman of the Traffic Commissioners will be required for operators of large goods vehicles undertaking journeys in Great Britain (England, Scotland and Wales) exceeding 100 miles for carrying goods and it will also be required for carrying a load of prescribed goods on a shorter journey if the load exceeds 11 tons in weight; " large goods vehicle " is defined in s. 71 (6). By s. 71 (9) the section does not apply to the use of a vehicle for the carriage of goods otherwise than for hire or reward or for or in connection with any trade or business carried on by the user. " Prescribed goods " will be those prescribed by Regulations. Section 71 reads:—

" (1) Subject to the provisions of this section and to the other provisions of this Part of this Act, no person shall, after the appointed day for the purposes of this section, use a large goods vehicle on a road—

> (a) to carry any goods on, or on any part of, a controlled journey; or
>
> (b) to carry an amount exceeding 11 tons in weight of any prescribed goods otherwise than on a controlled journey

except under a special authorisation granted under this Part of this Act.

(2) For the purposes of the foregoing subsection, a controlled journey is a journey between places in Great Britain separated by a distance exceeding one hundred miles, being—

> (a) in relation to goods to which paragraph (b) of this subsection does not apply, a journey for the whole of which the goods are carried on the same large goods vehicle without being taken off it;
>
> (b) in relation to goods in a container having a volume (ascertained by external measurement) of not less than 600 cubic feet or on a pallet having a surface area of not less than 50 square feet, a journey for every part of which they are carried by a large goods vehicle (whether the same vehicle or successive vehicles) without being taken out of the container or off the pallet;

and, where the vehicle on which the goods are carried is a trailer, it is immaterial whether it is drawn on the journey by the same vehicle or different vehicles.

(3) For the purposes of this section goods shall be treated as carried on a vehicle notwithstanding the fact that the vehicle is itself being carried on a vessel, aircraft or other means of transport, but, in relation to a journey in the course of which a vehicle is so carried, the distance to be taken into account for the purposes of subsection (2) of this section shall be the aggregate of the distances separating the points between which the vehicle is not so carried on the journey.

(4) Where in the case of any controlled journey—

> (a) no one person uses a vehicle or vehicles to carry the goods in question between places separated by a distance exceeding 100 miles; and
>
> (b) a special authorisation applicable to that journey is held by any one of the persons who use a vehicle or vehicles to carry those goods in the course of that journey

then, if under that authorisation the journey is one which may be undertaken in part by persons other than the holder of the licence, it shall not be necessary for the purposes of subsection (1) (a) of this section for any of those other persons to hold a special authorisation.

(5) The Minister may by regulations direct—

> (a) that subsection (1) of this section shall not apply—
>
>> (i) to carriage on journeys in the case of which the distances specified in the regulations are not exceeded;

(ii) to carriage by vehicles of any class specified in the regulations;

(b) that paragraph (a) of that subsection shall not apply to the carriage of any prescribed goods;

and regulations under paragraph (b) of this subsection or prescribing goods for the purposes of subsection (1) (b) of this section may describe the goods in question by reference to their nature, to the amount in which, or the places between which, they are carried, or by reference to any other circumstances.

(6) For the purposes of this section and the subsequent provisions o this Part of this Act, a large goods vehicle is a goods vehicle (other than a hauling vehicle) which—

(a) has a relevant plated weight exceeding 16 tons or (not having a relevant plated weight) has an unladen weight exceeding 5 tons; or

(b) forms part of a vehicle combination (not being an articulated combination) which is such that—

(i) if all the vehicles comprised in the combination (or all of them except any small trailer) have relevant plated weights, the aggregate of the relevant plated weights of the vehicles comprised in the combination (exclusive of any such trailer) exceeds 16 tons;

(ii) in any other case, the aggregate of the unladen weights of those vehicles (exclusive of any such trailer) exceeds 5 tons; or

(c) forms part of an articulated combination which is such that—

(i) if the trailer comprised in the combination has a relevant plated weight, the aggregate of the unladen weight of the motor vehicle comprised in the combination and the relevant plated weight of that trailer exceeds 16 tons;

(ii) in any other case, the aggregate of the unladen weights of the motor vehicle and the trailer comprised in the combination exceeds 5 tons.

In any provision of this subsection 'relevant plated weight' means a plated weight of the description specified in relation to that provision by regulations; and in paragraph (b) of this subsection 'small trailer' means a trailer having an unladen weight not exceeding 1 ton.

(7) Subsection (1) (b) of this section shall apply to the carriage of an amount exceeding 11 tons in weight of any prescribed goods in two or more vehicles forming part of a vehicle combination such as is mentioned in subsection (6) (b) or (c) of this section as it applies to the carriage of such an amount in a single vehicle, whether forming part of such a combination or not.

(8) In this section—

'hauling vehicle' means a motor tractor, a light locomotive, a heavy locomotive or the motor vehicle comprised in an articulated combination;

'pallet' means a movable deck on which a quantity of goods can be assembled for the purpose of being handled, loaded or transported as a single unit, and 'surface area' in relation to a pallet means the area on which the goods can be assembled as aforesaid.

(9) Nothing in this section shall apply to the use of a vehicle by any person for the carriage of goods otherwise than for hire or reward or for or in connection with any trade or business carried on by him.

(10) Any person who uses a vehicle in contravention of this section shall be liable on summary conviction to a fine not exceeding £200."

Note s. 71 (3), where the vehicle is taken part of the way by sea or air or rail, and s. 71 (4), where not all the operators hold special authorisations.   Regulations under s. 71 (5) have yet to be made. Any person who uses or aids and abets use of a vehicle in contravention of s. 71 is liable to a fine of £200 under s. 71 (10); causing and permitting cannot be charged and endorsement and disqualification under ss. 93 and 101 of the Road Traffic Act, 1972, cannot be ordered.

By s. 92 (2) the driver can be charged as a user only if he owns the vehicle or possesses it under hire-purchase; see the subsection on p. 541.   Provision as to subsidiaries and holding companies may be made by Regulations under s. 85.   Sections 72 to 80 deal with the grant, duration, variation and revocation of special authorisations under s. 71; by s. 76 conditions as to certain matters may be attached to special authorisations.   Breach of such conditions by the holder of the special authorisation or by anyone aiding and abetting him and by the other persons named in s. 76 (3) is an offence carrying a fine of £200 but not disqualification or endorsement under ss. 93 and 101 of the Road Traffic Act, 1972.

Cases on the old law on breach of conditions may be of some relevance but should be read in the light of the different wording of the new Act.   In *Lloyd* v. *Lee* [1951] 1 All E.R. 589, it was held that, if a condition of a licence is not complied with, the licence-holder commits an offence although he is not himself then using the vehicle and receives no reward for its use; this may be distinguishable as to conditions of a special authorisation, which applies only to carriage for hire or reward or on the licence-holder's business. A person who hires a vehicle to carry goods, whether for himself or another, must see that the licence, etc., covers its proposed use and, if a vehicle is used under this arrangement in breach of the licence (or, *semble*, of a condition under s. 71), the hirer aids and abets the lorry owner in his offence; *quaere*, though, if the owner " uses " (*Carter* v. *Mace* [1949] 2 All E.R. 714).   But no offence would be committed by a defendant hirer if proper enquiries had been made and he had been given wrong information (*Davies, Turner & Co., Ltd.* v. *Brodie* [1954] 3 All E.R. 283).   See *Arthur Sanderson, etc.* v. *Vickers* on p. 544 as to specifying the type of vehicle and number of trailers.

Consignment Notes

Section 81, which is not yet in force, provides that a signed consignment note in the form to be prescribed by Regulations must be carried by the driver of a large goods vehicle (defined in s. 71 (6), *supra*) while it is in use to carry goods but this provision does not apply in cases exempted by Regulations yet to be made or to a carriage of goods which is lawful without the authority of an operator's licence, e.g., free. By s. 81 (3) consignment notes must be preserved for a period to be specified and by s. 81 (4) a person who uses or drives a vehicle when a proper consignment note is not carried or who does not preserve it is liable to a fine of £200. Here liability is cast upon the driver who is employed as well as upon the owner; an aider and abettor can also be charged but " causing " and " permitting " cannot be alleged. Section 81 reads:—

" (1) Subject to subsection (2) of this section, no goods shall be carried on a large goods vehicle unless a document (in this section referred to as a ' consignment note ') in the prescribed form and containing the prescribed particulars has been completed and signed in the prescribed manner and is carried by the driver of the vehicle.

(2) Subsection (1) of this section shall not apply—

(*a*) to the carriage of goods on any journey or in a vehicle of any class exempted from that subsection by regulations; or

(*b*) to any carriage of goods which is lawful without the authority of an operator's licence;

and, subject to the provisions of regulations, a licensing authority may dispense with the observance, as respects the carriage of goods under an operator's licence granted by him, of any requirement of that subsection, and may grant such a dispensation either generally, or as respects a particular vehicle, or as respects the use of vehicles for a particular purpose, but he shall not grant such a dispensation unless satisfied that it is not reasonably practicable for the requirement dispensed with to be observed.

(3) The consignment note relating to the goods carried by a vehicle on any journey shall, at the conclusion of that journey, be preserved for the prescribed period by the person who used the vehicle (or if the journey was a controlled journey within the meaning of section 71 of this Act, the last vehicle) for carrying the goods on that journey.

(4) Any person who uses or drives a vehicle in contravention of subsection (1) of this section or who fails to comply with subsection (3) thereof shall be liable on summary conviction to a fine not exceeding £200."

Evidence

Examiners appointed under the Road Traffic Act, 1972, other persons authorised by the Chairman of the Area Traffic Commissioners and constables are given powers of entry and inspection by s. 82 of the Transport Act, 1968, and may seize documents

Falsification of consignment notes and records is made an offence triable summarily or on indictment by s. 83; the defendant has no right to demand trial by jury as the offence is punishable by fine only on summary conviction. Evidence by certificate as to certain matters is allowed by s. 84, which reads:—

" In any proceedings for an offence under this Part of this Act or Schedule 9 thereto a certificate signed by or on behalf of a licensing authority and stating—

(a) that, on any date, a person was or was not the holder of an operator's licence, a special authorisation or a transport manager's licence granted by the authority;

(b) the dates of the coming into force and expiration of any such licence or authorisation granted by the authority;

(c) the terms and conditions of any operator's licence or special authorisation granted by the authority;

(d) that a person is by virtue of an order of the authority disqualified from holding or obtaining an operator's licence, a special authorisation or a transport manager's licence indefinitely or for a specified period;

(e) that a direction, having effect indefinitely or for a specified period, has been given by the licensing authority under section 69 (6) of this Act in relation to any person;

(f) that, on any date or during any specified period, any such licence or authorisation granted by the authority was of no effect by reason of a direction that it be suspended,

shall be evidence, and in Scotland sufficient evidence, of the facts stated; and a certificate stating any of the matters aforesaid and purporting to be signed by or on behalf of a licensing authority shall be deemed to be so signed unless the contrary is proved."

See *McCulloch* v. *Hannam* and *Preston* v. *Fennell* on p. 177 as to the evidential value of a certificate.

Schedule 9 relates to transport managers' licences. " The licensing authority " is defined by s. 59 as the Chairman of the Area Traffic Commissioners (but see s. 92 (6), *infra*) and the certificate under s. 84 may be signed by him or " on his behalf " and shall be deemed to be so signed unless the contrary is proved. Consequently, a certificate signed in the name of the chairman by his blonde typist or signed by her in her name " on behalf of " him is admissible unless and until the defence establish that she had no authority to sign. *Semble*, if this was established, in some circumstances the prosecution might be permitted to call oral evidence as to the matters stated in the certificate or to produce a proper certificate but normally the prosecution should have their tackle in order at the start and permission to re-open, once their case was closed, could properly be refused. Normally, the proof that a person holds a licence is on him once he has been shown to have done something for which that licence is required.

It seems that any person may prosecute for offences under Pt. V of the Transport Act.

Transitional provisions are in s. 94.

Definitions

The definition section for the purposes of Pt. V of the Transport Act, 1968, is s. 92; the latter part of s. 92 (1) applies definitions in the Road Traffic Act, 1960, e.g., "road", "light locomotive" and so on.   It reads:—

" (1) In this Part of this Act and Schedule 9 thereto, unless the context otherwise requires—

'articulated combination' means a combination made up of—

> (a) a motor vehicle which is so constructed that a trailer may by partial superimposition be attached to the vehicle in such a manner as to cause a substantial part of the weight of the trailer to be borne by the vehicle, and
> (b) a trailer attached to it as aforesaid;

'authorised vehicle' means, in relation to an operator's licence, a vehicle authorised to be used thereunder, whether or not it is for the time being in use for a purpose for which an operator's licence is required and whether it is specified therein as so authorised or, being of a type so authorised subject to a maximum number, belongs to the holder of the licence or is in his possession under an agreement for hire-purchase, hire or loan;

'carriage of goods' includes haulage of goods;

'carrier's licence' means a licence granted under Part IV of the Act of 1960;

'contravention', in relation to any condition or provision, includes a failure to comply with the condition or provision, and 'contravenes' shall be construed accordingly;

'driver' means, in relation to a trailer, the driver of the vehicle by which the trailer is drawn and 'drive' shall be construed accordingly;

'goods' includes goods or burden of any description;

'goods vehicle' means, subject to subsection (5) of this section, a motor vehicle constructed or adapted for use for the carriage of goods, or a trailer so constructed or adapted;

'large goods vehicle' shall be construed in accordance with section 71 of this Act;

'operating centre' means, in relation to any vehicles, the base or centre from which the vehicles are, or are intended to be, normally used;

'prescribed' means prescribed by regulations;

'regulations' means regulations made by the Minister under this Part of this Act;

'subsidiary' means a subsidiary as defined by section 154 of the Companies Act 1948;

'vehicle combination' means a combination of goods vehicles made up of one or more motor vehicles and one or more trailers all of which are linked together when travelling;

and any expression not defined above which is also used in the Act of 1960 has the same meaning as in that Act.

(2) For the purposes of this Part of this Act, the driver of a vehicle, if it belongs to him or is in his possession under an agreement for hire, hire-purchase or loan, and in any other case the person whose servant or agent the driver is, shall be deemed to be the person using the vehicle; and references to using a vehicle shall be construed accordingly.

(3) In this Part of this Act references to directing that an operator's licence be curtailed are references to directing (with effect for the remainder of the duration of the licence or for any shorter period) all or any of the following, that is to say—

(a) that any one or more of the vehicles specified in the licence be removed therefrom;

(b) that the maximum number of trailers or of motor vehicles specified in the licence in pursuance of section 61 (1) (b) or (c) of this Act be reduced;

(c) that the addition of authorised vehicles under the said section 61 (1) (c) be no longer permitted.

(4) (*Bankruptcy includes sequestration in Scotland.*)

(5) In this Part of this Act and Schedule 9 thereto, references to goods vehicles do not include references to tramcars or trolley vehicles operated under statutory powers within the meaning of section 259 of the Act of 1960.

(6) Anything required or authorised by this Part of this Act to be done to or by a licensing authority by whom a licence or authorisation was granted may be done to or by any person for the time being acting as licensing authority for the area for which the first-mentioned authority was acting at the time of the granting of the licence or authorisation."

A B licensee hired out his vehicle and driver to a C licensee and the latter used it, with the driver, for a purpose lawful under the C licence but unlawful under the B licence. As the driver remained the servant of the B licensee the latter was held to be guilty of contravening his B licence (*Sykes* v. *Millington* [1953] 1 All E.R. 1098). In Northern Ireland there is a special statutory provision as to transferred drivers (see *Ulster Transport Authority* v. *Ardill* [1955] N.I. 34). Where a B licence authorised the carriage of fish from *B* to *A*, this did not permit the licensee to pick up goods at an intermediate point and take them to *A* (*Brown* v. *Dougal* [1960] S.L.T. 19) (see also pp. 529 and 50 as to who " uses ").

It is very doubtful whether a lorry returning from a place where it has carried goods for hire or reward or going to a place where it will carry goods for hire or reward can be said at such times to be used on the road for carriage of goods for hire or reward (*per* Lord Parker, C.J., in *Roberts* v. *Morris* [1965] Crim.L.R. 46). By the definition in s. 92 of the Transport Act on p. 540, *supra*, " authorised vehicle " means one authorised to be used under an operator's licence whether or not it is for the time being in use for a purpose for which an operator's licence is required and whether it is specified therein as so authorised.

Hire or Reward

The leading case on the meaning of " hire or reward " is *Albert* v. *Motor Insurers' Bureau* [1971] 2 All E.R. 1345. This was not a case on an operator's licence but on s. 203 (4) of the Road Traffic Act, 1960, which exempted a driver of a motor vehicle from being required to insure against passenger liability provided the passengers were not carried for " hire or reward ". The House of Lords disapproved *Coward* v. *Motor Insurers' Bureau* [1962] 1 All E.R. 531, where it was held that " hire or reward " meant a monetary reward legally recoverable under a contract express or implied, and held that the test as to whether a vehicle was being used for " hire or reward " was whether there had been a systematic carrying of passengers for reward which went beyond the bounds of mere social kindness. It was immaterial that no contractual relationship was intended. The words " hire or reward " must be read disjunctively.

A defendant trained horses for reward and it was his duty to see that they reached the racecourses; he carried a horse to a race meeting in an unlicensed vehicle. It was at the owner's discretion whether he paid the defendant for the transport and in fact he was not paid. The defendant was held not guilty under a corresponding Irish statute (*A.-G.* v. *Brogan* (1953), 87 I.L.T.R. 181). A company owning a vehicle with a C licence agreed for an expected reward to arrange for the transport of goods from London to Northumberland; a vehicle belonging to another firm, with an A licence, was to take them from East London to Northumberland but the company's vehicle took them from North London to the starting point. A Metropolitan magistrate held this journey to be part of the whole journey for arranging which the company was being paid and convicted the company of carrying goods without an A or B licence (Jo.Crim.L. (1954) 219). Where a vehicle was used at a standard charge to empty a septic tank and dumped the effluent emptied from the tank on farmland some distance away, it was held that the effluent was " goods " and that it was a carriage for reward (*Sweetway Sanitary Cleansers, Ltd.* v. *Bradley* [1961] 2 All E.R. 821).

A C licence allowed the holder to use the vehicles for or in connection with any trade or business carried on by him but not for carrying goods for hire or reward. The vehicles were used to remove surplus excavated earth at an agreed price from a building site for the builders (third parties). The vehicle owner paid someone else to tip it. It was held that, as a large part of the payment was for the carriage of the rubbish, the vehicles were used to carry goods for reward, it being immaterial that the property in the earth passed to the vehicle owners when it was loaded (*Spittle* v. *Thames Grit and Aggregates, Ltd*. [1937] 4 All E.R. 101). This case was distinguished by a Metropolitan magistrate in *Metropolitan Traffic Commissioner* v. *Alexander Thomson & Co*., Jo.Crim.L. (1952) 194, where the vehicle owners were themselves also the contractors who did the work of laying cables as well as removing the surplus earth. He held that this was not carrying goods for hire or reward requiring a B licence but was used in connection with the company's trade or business and was covered by their C licence. The prosecution did not appeal by case stated. A firm of sand and gravel merchants excavating those materials from a pit were required by a planning condition to fill up the parts excavated. To do this, they took rubbish from a building site, the builder paying them 8s. 6d. per cubic yard of rubbish. The House of Lords held that, by virtue of s. 164 (5) (*a*) of the Road Traffic Act, 1960, the rubbish was being used in the course of the sand merchant's business and was not being carried for reward (*Hammond* v. *Hall and Ham River, Ltd*. [1965] 2 All E.R. 811, overruling *Corbett* v. *Barham* [1965] 1 W.L.R. 187). A lorry owner went from *C* to *B* in Ireland to borrow some planks. The plank owner agreed to lend them but said they were at *F* and asked the lorry owner, when bringing them to *C*, to take some scaffolding for him at the same time. The lorry owner, when charged with carrying the scaffolding "for reward", pleaded that he did so merely to oblige and he was found not guilty (*A.-G. (Holland)* v. *Hurley*, Jo.Crim.L. (1960) 59, where conflicting views are discussed). In *Stewart* v. *McFadyen* [1958] S.L.T.(Sh.) 7 it was held that a licence to carry building materials included granite chips for road making, as being road-building materials. A stipendiary magistrate acquitted a coal-merchant who had loaded his vehicle with scrap iron to see if it was likely in the future to be fit for use for carrying coal ([1958] Crim.L.R. 693).

Other cases on use in the course of the licence-holder's business, carrying goods for process or treatment, use in agriculture and farmers' goods vehicles appear in the fifth edition of this book.

Only goods vehicles, i.e., vehicles and trailers constructed or adapted to carry goods, need licences under the Transport Act, and a van adapted for the carriage of passengers and used only to carry samples to the owner's place of business was held not to be a goods vehicle in *Tait* v. *Odhams Press* (1937), 26 Traff.Cas. 80, where certain exempting Regulations were also in point. Remember, however, that trailers constructed or adapted to carry goods need licences. Where a passenger vehicle has been altered to carry goods, the test whether the vehicle is a goods or passenger one is whether it would, if it had been constructed in its altered condition, still be regarded as a vehicle used to carry passengers and their effects (*Flower Freight Co.* v. *Hammond* [1962] 3 All E.R. 950, further discussed on p. 334). Passengers' effects are not goods (*ibid.*). A shooting-brake or other utility vehicle would be within the Act if used to carry goods for reward or in connection with a trade or business (*cf. Taylor* v. *Thompson* [1956] 1 All E.R. 352), but many will be exempt as being under 30 cwt. (s. 60 (4) (*a*)). The term " goods vehicle " includes a van used only for carrying a window-cleaner's ladders, rags and buckets, as these are goods (*Clarke* v. *Cherry* [1953] 1 All E.R. 267). A decision of magistrates that a car adapted to carry dresses hung on rails at the back was not adapted to carry goods was upheld in *Taylor* v. *Mead* [1961] 1 All E.R. 626. It is submitted that, as in s. 92 the term " adapted " is contrasted with " constructed ", the former means " altered physically so as to make fit for the purpose " (*Maddox* v. *Storer* [1962] 1 All E.R. 831) (see p. 334).

See also p. 334, as to " goods ".

An incorporated society, consisting of miners at one colliery, delivering coal to one of its members at a charge to be deducted from his wages, uses the vehicle for hire or reward; *aliter*, where it is an unincorporated society delivering to a member (*Wurzal* v. *Houghton Main Home Delivery Service, Ltd.* [1936] 3 All E.R. 311).

The licensing authority under the 1960 Act could lawfully specify the type as well as the number of trailers to be used under an A licence and specify a particular trailer by the maker's number (*Arthur Sanderson (Great Broughton), Ltd.* v. *Vickers* (1964), 108 S.J. 425).

Schedule 10 to the Transport Act, 1968, applies provisions of the Road Traffic Act, 1960, as to powers of vehicle examiners, duty to give information as to driver's identity, forgery, false statements and calculation of weight for the purposes of Pt. V of the 1968 Act.

19. RECORDS

The provisions in the Transport Act, 1968, as to the keeping of records by drivers have been brought into force only in respect of the drivers of goods vehicles. The provisions do not apply to drivers of passenger-carrying vehicles except that a driver who drives both a goods vehicle and a passenger-carrying vehicle must record his passenger-vehicle driving in his goods vehicle record book (reg. 3 (4)). The Regulations are the Drivers' Hours (Goods

Vehicles) (Keeping of Records) Regulations, 1970 (S.I. 1970 No. 123) as amended in a minor particular by like-named Amendment Regulations of 1971 (S.I. 1971 No. 847). Drivers must keep in their current driver's record book a record of their driving, duty and rest in the course of their employment as drivers of such vehicles, and must carry their record books with them at all times when driving such vehicles on duty (regs. 3 (1) and 7). By reg. 12 (1) drivers of vehicles exempted from operators' licences, i.e., small goods vehicles not exceeding 3½ tons plated weight or 30 cwt. unladen weight if unplated, dual purpose vehicles and certain specialised vehicles, do not have to record their hours of driving. If, however, the driver also drives during any period of twenty-four hours commencing at midnight a vehicle not exempted, he is required to enter the hours of driving both of that vehicle and the exempted vehicle. Regulation 12 (2) exempts drivers from keeping records if the driver does not drive for more than four hours and not outside a radius of twenty-five miles from the vehicle's operating centre. By s. 98 (1) a duty to keep records is cast on drivers and employers of employee-drivers and to keep registers on owner-drivers and employers of employee-drivers; see ss. 95 (3) and 103 (1) and (3) for definitions in relation to drivers and employers. Section 95 reads:—

" (1) This Part of this Act shall have effect with a view to securing the observance of proper hours of work by persons engaged in the carriage of passengers or goods by road and thereby protecting the public against the risks which arise in cases where the drivers of motor vehicles are suffering from fatigue [but the Secretary of State may by regulations make such provision supplemental or incidental to, or by way of adaptation of, this Part of this Act as is in his opinion called for to take account, in relation to journeys and work to which the international rules apply, of the operation of those rules and to ensure compatibility of operation between section 96 (1) to (9) as they apply to other journeys and work and the international rules; and regulations made under this subsection—

(a) may in particular make exceptions from the operation of section 96 (1) to (6), and include provision as to the circumstances in which a period of driving or duty to which the international rules apply is to be included or excluded in reckoning any period for purposes of section 96 (1) to (6); and

(b) may contain such transitional and supplementary provisions as the Secretary of State thinks necessary or expedient;

and a reference to the international rules shall be deemed to be included in any reference to this Part of this Act in sections 35 (2) (b), 62 (4) (b) and 64 (2) (c) of this Act and in paragraph 2 (5) of Schedule 9 thereto.]

(2) This Part of this Act applies to—

(a) passenger vehicles, that is to say—

(i) public service vehicles; and

        (ii) motor vehicles (other than public service vehicles) constructed or adapted to carry more than twelve passengers;

   (b) goods vehicles, that is to say—

        (i) heavy locomotives, light locomotives, motor tractors and any motor vehicle so constructed that a trailer may by partial superimposition be attached to the vehicle in such a manner as to cause a substantial part of the weight of the trailer to be borne by the vehicle; and
        (ii) motor vehicles (except those mentioned in paragraph (a) of this subsection) constructed or adapted to carry goods other than the effects of passengers.

(3) This Part of this Act applies to any such person as follows (in this Part of this Act referred to as ' a driver '), that is to say—

   (a) a person who drives a vehicle to which this Part of this Act applies in the course of his employment (in this Part of this Act referred to as ' an employee-driver '); and
   (b) a person who drives such a vehicle for the purposes of a trade or business carried on by him (in this Part of this Act referred to as ' an owner-driver ');

and in this Part of this Act references to driving by any person are references to his driving as aforesaid."

The words in square brackets in subs. (1) above were inserted by Sched. 4 to the European Communities Act, 1972 (see "E.E.C. and Foreign Vehicles", on p. 554).

By s. 98 (4) contravention of the Regulations carries a fine of £200 (not endorsement or disqualification) but the employer of an employee-driver can escape conviction for a contravention of the Regulations whereby he is required to cause any records to be kept on proof that he has given proper instructions to his employees with respect to the keeping of the records and has from time to time taken reasonable steps to secure that those instructions are being carried out. The licensing authorities are empowered to revoke, suspend or curtail an operator's licence if the licence-holder or his driver has been convicted under Pt. VI of the Act or convicted of conspiracy to contravene Pt. VI of the Act (s. 69 (4) (c)). In R. v. *Blamires Transport Services* [1964] 1 Q.B. 278 a haulage company's conviction on indictment of conspiring with the company's drivers to make false records under s. 186 of the Road Traffic Act, 1960, was upheld on appeal. By s. 102 (1) the requirements as to records will apply to Crown vehicles and drivers, other than vehicles owned or used by the Army, Royal Navy or R.A.F., and vehicles being used for police or fire brigade purposes. Drivers of foreign goods vehicles are required to keep records of hours (see "E.E.C. and Foreign Vehicles", on p. 554).

Section 98 of the Transport Act, 1968, reads:—

" (1) The Minister may make regulations—

    (a) for requiring drivers to keep, and employers of employee-drivers to cause to be kept, in such books as may be specified in the regulations records with respect to such matters relevant to the enforcement of this Part of this Act as may be so specified; and

    (b) for requiring owner-drivers and the employers of employee-drivers to maintain such registers as may be so specified with respect to any such books as aforesaid which are in their possession or in that of any employee-drivers in their employment.

(2) Regulations under this section may contain such supplementary and incidental provisions [including provisions supplementary and incidental to the requirements of the international rules as to books and records] as the Minister thinks necessary or expedient, including in particular provisions—

    (a) specifying the person or persons from whom books and registers required for the purposes of the regulations [or of the international rules] are to be obtained and, if provision is made for them to be obtained from the Minister, charging a fee for their issue by him (which shall be payable into the Consolidated Fund);

    (b) as to the form and manner of making of entries in such books and registers;

    (c) as to the issue by and return to the employers of employee-drivers of books required to be kept by the latter for the purposes of the regulations;

    (d) requiring any book in current use for the purposes of the regulations to be carried on, or by the driver of, any vehicle, as to the preservation of any books and registers used for those purposes, and otherwise as to the maner in which those books and registers are to be dealt with;

    (e) for exemptions from all or any of the requirements of the regulations in respect of drivers of small goods vehicles as defined in section 103 (6) of this Act and for other exemptions from all or any of those requirements.

(3) Subject to the provisions of any regulations made by the Minister, the traffic commissioners or licensing authority for any area may dispense with the observance by any employee-driver or his employer, or by any owner-driver, of any requirement imposed under this section, either generally or in such circumstances or to such extent as the commissioners or authority think fit, but the traffic commissioners or licensing authority shall not grant such a dispensation unless satisfied that it is not reasonably practicable for the requirement dispensed with to be observed.

(4) Any person who contravenes any regulations made under this section [or any requirement as to books and records of the international rules] shall be liable on summary conviction to a fine not exceeding £200; but the employer of any employee-driver shall not be liable to be convicted under this subsection by reason of contravening any such regulation whereby he is required to cause any records to be kept if he proves to the court that he has given proper instructions to his employees with respect to the keeping of the records and has from time to time taken reasonable steps to secure that those instructions are being carried out.

(5) Any entry made by an employee-driver for the purposes of regulations under this section [or of the international rules] shall, in any proceedings under this Part of this Act, be admissible in evidence against his employer."

For the defence available to an employer by s. 98 (4) see p. 553.

Regulation 5 (8) requires the driver to return the book sheets to his employer within seven days of completion. An employer should not be convicted of aiding and abetting a breach of reg. 5 (8) by his driver unless the employer knowingly encouraged such a breach in some way (*Cassady* v. *Reg. Morris* (*Transport*), *Ltd.* [1975] Crim.L.R. 398).

Regulation 8 (1) requires employers to "preserve . . . intact" a driver's record book for six months. An employer issued a book to one employee who duly completed the required records on the first five pages and then returned it to his employer, who then re-issued it to another driver, who used it and produced it to a police officer when stopped. It was held in *Blakey Transport* v. *Casebourne* [1975] R.T.R. 221 that the employer did not preserve the book intact in accordance with reg. 8 (1) by re-issuing the book to another employee for use by him; nor in such a case is it a " new " book as is required by reg. 3 (2) (*Cassady* v. *Ward & Smith, Ltd.* [1975] Crim.L.R. 399).

Section 99 reads:—

" (1) An officer may, on production if so required of his authority, require any person to produce, and permit him to inspect and copy—

> (*a*) any book or register which that person is required by regulations under section 98 of this Act to carry or have in his possession for the purpose of making in it any entry required by those regulations or which is required under those regulations to be carried on any vehicle of which that person is the driver;
>
> (*b*) any record, book or register which that person is required by regulations under section 97 or 98 of this Act to preserve;
>
> (*c*) if that person is the owner of a vehicle to which this Part of this Act applies, any other document of that person which the officer may reasonably require to inspect for the purpose of ascertaining whether the provisions of this Part of this Act or of regulations made thereunder have been complied with;
>
> [(*d*)any corresponding book, register or document required by the international rules or which the officer may reasonably require to inspect for the purpose of ascertaining whether the requirements of the international rules have been complied with;]

and that record, book, register or document shall, if the officer so requires by notice in writing served on that person, be produced at the office of the traffic commissioners or licensing authority specified in the notice within such time (not being less than ten days) from the service of the notice as may be so specified.

(2) An officer may, on production if so required of his authority—

> (*a*) at any time, enter any vehicle to which this Part of this Act applies and inspect that vehicle and any equipment installed in it for the purposes of section 97 of this Act and inspect and copy any record on the vehicle which has been produced by means of that equipment;

(b) at any time which is reasonable having regard to the circumstances of the case, enter any premises on which he has reason to believe that such a vehicle is kept or that any such records, books, registers or other documents as are mentioned in subsection (1) of this section are to be found, and inspect any such vehicle, and inspect and copy any such record, book, register or document which he finds there.

(3) For the purpose of exercising his powers under subsection (2) (a) and, in respect of a document carried on, or by the driver of, a vehicle, under subsection (1) (a) [or (d)] of this section, an officer may detain the vehicle in question during such time as is required for the exercise of that power.

(4) Any person who—

(a) fails to comply with any requirement under subsection (1) of this section; or

(b) obstructs an officer in the exercise of his powers under subsection (2) or (3) of this section,

shall be liable on summary conviction to a fine not exceeding £100.

(5) Any person who makes, or causes to be made, any such record as is mentioned in section 97 of this Act or any entry in a book or register kept for the purposes of regulations under section 98 thereof [or the international rules] which he knows to be false or, with intent to deceive, alters or causes to be altered any such record or entry shall be liable—

(a) on summary conviction, to a fine not exceeding £200;

(b) on conviction on indictment, to imprisonment for a term not exceeding two years.

(6) If an officer has reason to believe that an offence under subsection (5) of this section has been committed in respect of any record or document inspected by him under this section, he may seize that record or document; and where a record or document is seized as aforesaid and within six months of the date on which it was seized no person has been charged since that date with an offence in relation to that record or document under that subsection and the record or document has not been returned to the person from whom it was taken, a magistrates' court shall, on an application made for the purpose by that person or by an officer, make such order respecting the disposal of the record or document and award such costs as the justice of the case may require.

(7) Any proceedings in Scotland under subsection (6) of this section shall be taken by way of summary application in the sheriff court; and in the application of that subsection to Scotland references to costs shall be construed as references to expenses.

(8) In this section 'officer' means a certifying officer appointed under section 56 of the Road Traffic Act 1972, a public service vehicle examiner, an examiner appointed under Part IV of that Act and any person authorised for the purposes of this section by the traffic commissioners or licensing authority for any area.

(9) The powers conferred by this section on an officer as defined in subsection (8) of this section shall be exercisable also by a police constable, who shall not, if wearing uniform, be required to produce any authority.

(10) In this section references to the inspection and copying of any record produced by means of equipment installed for the purposes of section 97 of this Act in a vehicle include references to the application to the record

of any process for eliciting the information recorded thereby and to taking down the information elicited from it."

The words in square brackets in subss. (1) (*d*), (3) and (5) above were inserted by the European Communities Act, 1972, Sched. 4 (see "E.E.C. and Foreign Vehicles", on p. 554).

The falsification offences under s. 99 (5) are hybrid offences (see p. 80) and the defendant cannot insist on trial by jury. An extended time-limit for offences against s. 99 (5) is provided by s. 244 of the Road Traffic Act, 1960, as amended by Sched. 11 to the Transport Act, 1968, and Sched. 9 to the Road Traffic Act, 1972 (s. 244 is in identical terms to s. 180 of the Act of 1972: see p. 69).

The application to Crown, military, police and fire brigade vehicles comes under s. 102, which reads:—

" (1) Subject to subsection (2) of this section, this Part of this Act shall apply to vehicles and persons in the public service of the Crown.

(2) This Part of this Act shall not apply in the case of motor vehicles owned by the Secretary of State for Defence and used for naval, military or air force purposes or in the case of vehicles so used while being driven by persons for the time being subject to the orders of a member of the armed forces of the Crown.

(3) For the purpose of proceedings for an offence under this Part of this Act in connection with a vehicle in the public service of the Crown, being proceedings against a person other than the driver of the vehicle, the person nominated in that behalf by the department in whose service the vehicle is used shall be deemed to be the person actually responsible unless it is shown to the satisfaction of the court that the driver only was responsible.

(4) This Part of this Act shall not apply in the case of motor vehicles while being used for police or fire brigade purposes."

Note that s. 102 (2) refers to vehicles "used" and s. 102 (4) to vehicles "while being used".

Definitions for the purposes of Pt. VI come under s. 103, which reads:—

" (1) In this Part of this Act—
    ' agriculture ' has the meaning assigned by section 109 (3) of the Agriculture Act, 1947, or, in relation to Scotland, section 86 (3) of the Agriculture (Scotland) Act, 1948;
    ' driver ', ' employee-driver ' and ' owner-driver ' have the meaning assigned by section 95 (3) of this Act;
    ' employer ', in relation to an employee-driver, means the employer of that driver in the employment by virtue of which that driver is an employee-driver;
    [' the international rules ' means any directly applicable Community provision relating to the driving of road vehicles on international journeys;]
    ' licensing authority ' has the same meaning as in Part V of this Act;

' prescribed ' means prescribed by regulations made by the Minister;
' working day ', in relation to any driver, means—

    (*a*) any period during which he is on duty and which does not fall to be aggregated with any other such period by virtue of paragraph (*b*) of this definition; and

    (*b*) where a period during which he is on duty is not followed by an interval for rest of not less than eleven hours or (where permitted by virtue of section 96 (4) (*b*) of this Act) of not less than nine and a half hours, the aggregate of that period and each successive such period until there is such an interval as aforesaid, together with any interval or intervals between periods so aggregated;

' working week ' means, subject to subsection (5) of this section, a week beginning at midnight between Saturday and Sunday;

and any expression not defined above which is also used in the Act of 1960 has the same meaning as in that Act.

(2) For the purposes of this Part of this Act a director of a company shall be deemed to be employed by it.

(3) In this Part of this Act references to a person driving a vehicle are references to his being at the driving controls of the vehicle for the purpose of controlling its movement, whether it is in motion or is stationary with the engine running.

(4) In this Part of this Act references to a driver being on duty are references—

    (*a*) in the case of an employee-driver, to his being on duty (whether for the purpose of driving a vehicle to which this Part of this Act applies or for other purposes) in the employment by virtue of which he is an employee-driver, or in any other employment under the person who is his employer in the first-mentioned employment; and

    (*b*) in the case of an owner-driver, to his driving a vehicle to which this Part of this Act applies for the purposes of a trade or business carried on by him or being otherwise engaged in work for the purposes of that trade or business, being work in connection with such a vehicle or the load carried thereby.

(5) The traffic commissioners or licensing authority for any area may, on the application of an owner-driver or of the employer of an employee-driver, from time to time direct that a week beginning at midnight between two days other than Saturday and Sunday shall be, or be deemed to have been, a working week in relation to that owner-driver or employee-driver; but where by virtue of any such direction a new working week begins before the expiration of a previous working week then, without prejudice to the application of the provisions of this Part of this Act in relation to the new working week, those provisions shall continue to apply in relation to the previous working week until its expiration.

(6) In sections 97 (2) (*a*) and 98 (2) (*e*) of this Act ' a small goods vehicle ' means a goods vehicle which has a plated weight of the prescribed description not exceeding $3\frac{1}{2}$ tons or (not having a plated weight) has an unladen weight not exceeding 30 hundredweight; but the Minister may by regulations direct that the foregoing provisions of this subsection shall have effect, in relation to either or both of those sections—

(a) with the substitution for either of the weights there specified of such other weight as may be specified in the regulations;

(b) with the substitution for either of those weights or for any other weight for the time being specified as aforesaid of a weight expressed in terms of the metric system, being a weight which is equivalent to that for which it is substituted or does not differ from it by more than 5 per cent. thereof.

(7) Without prejudice to any jurisdiction of any court under any other enactment, proceedings for an offence under this Part of this Act may be commenced in any court having jurisdiction in the place where the person charged with the offence is for the time being.

(8) The enactments specified in Schedule 11 to this Act shall have effect subject to the amendments there specified.

(9) Any order made under section 166 (2) of this Act appointing a day for the purposes of any of the provisions of this Part of this Act may contain such transitional provisions as the Minister thinks necessary or expedient as respects the application of any particular provision of this Part of this Act to a working week or working day falling partly before and partly after the date on which that provision comes into operation."

The definition of " the international rules " was inserted by Sched. 4 to the European Communities Act, 1972 (see "E.E.C. and Foreign Vehicles ", on p. 554).

Cases under the Old Law

The cases which follow were decided on the 1960 Act and Regulations thereunder and may still be of relevance. A fitter was employed to do running repairs to vehicles broken down in the highway; it was held that, when he drove to that work, he was a part-time driver and should keep records (*Mackie* v. *MacLeod* [1956] S.L.T. 116). In *Gross Cash Registers, Ltd.* v. *Vogt* [1965] 3 All E.R. 832 a salesman was free to do his travelling in any way he chose—on foot, by bus or in the firm's van; if he used the van, he was allowed to drive it and did so; it was held that, when he drove it in the course of his employment, he was a part-time driver and should keep records.

Under the old Regulations, no licence-holder need keep records in respect of driving by him of a licensed vehicle on journeys which were in no way connected with any trade or business carried on by him, and there was no duty to keep records outside the scope of an employed driver's work. The court should ask itself whether the driver was working in an irregular and unauthorised manner or was acting wholly outside the scope of his employment. In the latter case the employer was not liable for not keeping records (*Jack Motors, Ltd.* v. *Fazackerley* [1962] Crim.L.R. 486). See *Flatman* v. *Poole* [1937] 1 All E.R. 495, *Manley* v. *Dabson* [1949] 2 All E.R. 578, *Leach* v. *Cooper* (1950), 48 L.G.R. 526, and *Fillingham* v. *Hall* (1935), unreported, on p. 305 of the fifth edition of this book, as to exemptions in respect of agricultural use of vehicles.   It is proper to charge a defendant, where appropriate, with " failing to keep or to cause to be kept " the necessary records in one information (*Field* v. *Hopkinson* (1944), 108 J.P. 21).

Liability of Employer for Staff Defaults

Under the old Regulations it had been held that a guilty intent was not a necessary ingredient in the offence of not causing a true record to be kept and employers were convicted where a driver had made an incorrect entry, although the employer had had no chance to check it (*Cox* v. *Sidery* (1935), 24 Traff. Cas. 69; *Mitchell* v. *Morrison* [1938] S.C.(J.) 64).   In *Nelson* v. *Coventry Swaging Co.* (1936), 25 Traff. Cas. 68, employers were convicted where a driver had made an entry, which proved to be correct, in advance. However, the employer now has the defence provided by s. 98 (4), *supra*, that he had given proper instructions to his employees and checked from time to time; the onus is on the employer and the prosecution do not have to disprove this in advance.   It is for the court to say, after hearing the employer, whether he has given " proper " instructions and taken " reasonable steps " from time to time.   Under the previous law it was a defence if an employer had been able to show " due diligence " in seeing that the law had been complied with.   In *Series* v. *Poole* [1967] 3 All E.R. 849 it was held that where the employer had delegated his duties to ensure compliance with the law to a competent employee, that employee then became his *alter ego*, and if that employee was negligent the employer could not therefore avail himself of the defence. *Series* v. *Poole* was overruled in *Tesco Supermarkets* v. *Nattrass* [1971] 2 All E.R. 127; in the case of a large-scale organisation the owner, whether it be a limited company or an individual, cannot personally supervise the activities of all his servants, and it would be consistent with the taking of reasonable precautions and the exercise of all due diligence to institute an effective system to prevent the commission of offences under which superior servants were instructed to supervise inferior servants whose acts might otherwise lead to the commission of an offence.   It is submitted that the approach to the problem posed under the Trade Descriptions Act shown by the House of Lords in *Tesco* is of relevance in considering whether a defence under s. 98 (4) is made out.   It is submitted that whether the employer has given "proper" instructions and taken "reasonable steps" is essentially a question of fact and degree.

The records are admissible in evidence against the employers, whether on charges under s. 98 or otherwise (*Beer* v. *Clench* [1936] 1 All E.R. 449; *Adair* v. *Craighouse & Co.* [1937] S.L.T. 499).

When the number of a vehicle appears in the record, that may suffice to identify that vehicle (*Hogg* v. *Burnet* [1938] S.C.(J). 160). Such records were not made admissible previously by any statute but are now made specifically so by s. 98 (5), when entered by an employee-driver, in proceedings under Pt. V against his employer. It is submitted that this does not cut down their admissibility generally under the cases just cited.

It seems that the venue for the offence by a driver of " making " a false entry is where it is made (*Waugh* v. *Mentiplay* [1938] S.C. (J.) 117). Section 103 (7) (*supra*) allows proceedings for an offence as to records of drivers' hours to be brought where the person charged with the offence " is for the time being " or in any other court having jurisdiction. This would appear to allow proceedings to be brought where a company has its registered office or principal place of business. " Is for the time being " refers to the moment of time when the proceedings are commenced, i.e. by laying an information. It does not apply to the place where the driver was for the time being stopped by the police. Accordingly, where it appeared that an offence, *inter alia*, of failing to keep records was not committed within the area of a magistrates' court in which the driver was stopped by the police, it was held that the justices were correct in declining to hear the case on the ground of lack of jurisdiction (*R.* v. *Hitchin JJ., ex parte Hilton* [1974] R.T.R. 380). See generally as to venue, p. 65.

An indictable charge at common law of conspiracy to contravene these provisions may properly be brought (*R.* v. *Blamires Transport Services, Ltd.* [1963] 3 All E.R. 170).

Penalty, etc.

Contravention of the Regulations, including contravention of the rules relating to international journeys, is punishable under s. 98 (4) on a first or subsequent conviction with a fine of £200. The venue for proceedings includes any court having jurisdiction in the place where the defendant is for the time being (see s. 103 (7), on p. 552, and *R.* v. *Hitchin JJ., supra*). Disqualification and endorsement cannot be ordered.

E.E.C. and Foreign Vehicles

As a result of the United Kingdom's accession to the Treaty of Rome and the consequent enactment of the European Communities Act, 1972, the law relating to road traffic on international journeys, in respect of both British and foreign vehicles, is amended. Perhaps the most important alteration so far as this book is concerned is the provisions relating to drivers' records and hours while on international journeys. Article 74 of the Treaty of Rome requires member countries to work towards a common transport policy and art. 75 is directed towards the establishment of common rules for international transport. Substantial progress had been made towards harmonisation at the time of the United Kingdom's accession, and the European Communities Act, 1972, accordingly amended the relevant provisions of the Transport Act, 1968 (and where the text of that Act is set out in this book, the amendments made by the European Communities Act are set out in square brackets). In implementation of E.E.C. Regulation 543/69 the Drivers' Hours (Passenger and Goods Vehicles) (Keeping of Records) (International Rules) Regulations, 1973 (S.I. 1973 No. 380) were made. Where a driver or employer contravenes the international rules (see the definition on p. 550) the offender may be dealt with in this country by prosecution under s. 98 (4). The E.E.C. Regulation is, as already mentioned, reg. 543/69/E.E.C. of the Council of 25th March, 1969, as amended by regs. 514/72/E.E.C. and 515/E.E.C.

Similarly, where contravention of the international rules relating to hours occurs, an offence in this country may be prosecuted under s. 96 (11A) (see p. 558). The E.E.C. Regulation directly applicable is the E.E.C. Regulation 543, as amended, referred to above. The corresponding United Kingdom Regulation in implementation is the Drivers' Hours (Passenger and Goods Vehicles) (International Rules) Regulations, 1973 (S.I. 1973 No. 379). The international rules, both in respect of hours and records, will normally apply not only to E.E.C. and British vehicles but also to vehicles of a third foreign country. However, when the European Agreement concerning the Work of Crews of Vehicles Engaged in International Transport is in force, any international transport from and to a third country which is party to that agreement will be governed by the provisions of that agreement.

20. DRIVERS' HOURS

Section 73 of the Road Traffic Act, 1960, and the orders deemed to be made thereunder, were replaced by Pt. VI of the Transport Act, 1968, and Regulations made thereunder.

The main new provision as to drivers' hours and rest periods is s. 96 of the Transport Act, 1968. It applies to public service vehicles, passenger vehicles constructed or adapted to carry more than twelve passengers, and goods vehicles, as all defined in s. 95, which relates to drivers' hours as well as to records. Section 95 is set out on p. 545, and s. 98 on p. 547. Definitions appear in s. 103, set out on p. 550, and the application of s. 98 to Crown, military, police and fire brigade vehicles is indicated in s. 102 on p. 550. The main operative section is s. 96. This section has been extensively modified in respect of passenger-vehicle hours, and the modifications for this purpose are set out on p. 563. Section 96 reads:—

" (1) Subject to the provisions of this section, a driver shall not on any working day drive a vehicle or vehicles to which this Part of this Act applies for periods amounting in the aggregate to more than ten hours.

(2) Subject to the provisions of this section, if on any working day a driver has been on duty for a period of, or for periods amounting in the aggregate to, five and a half hours and—

    (*a*) there has not been during that period, or during or between any of those periods, an interval of not less than half an hour in which he was able to obtain rest and refreshment; and

    (*b*) the end of that period, or of the last of those periods, does not mark the end of that working day,

there shall at the end of that period, or of the last of those periods, be such an interval as aforesaid.

(3) Subject to the provisions of this section, the working day of a driver—

    (*a*) except where paragraph (*b*) or (*c*) of this subsection applies, shall not exceed eleven hours;

    (*b*) if during that day he is off duty for a period which is, or periods which taken together are, not less than the time by which his working day exceeds eleven hours, shall not exceed twelve and a half hours;

    (*c*) if during that day—

        (i) all the time when he is driving vehicles to which this Part of this Act applies is spent in driving one or more express carriages or contract carriages; and

        (ii) he is able for a period of not less than four hours to obtain rest and refreshment,

    shall not exceed fourteen hours.

(4) Subject to the provisions of this section, there shall be, between any two successive working days of a driver, an interval for rest which—

    (*a*) subject to paragraph (*b*) of this subsection, shall not be of less than eleven hours;

    (*b*) if during both those days all or the greater part of the time when he is driving vehicles to which this Part of this Act applies is spent in driving one or more passenger vehicles, may, on one occasion in each working week, be of less than eleven hours but not of less than nine and a half hours;

and for the purposes of this Part of this Act a period of time shall not be treated, in the case of an employee-driver, as not being an interval for rest by reason only that he may be called upon to report for duty if required.

(5) Subject to the provisions of this section a driver shall not be on duty in any working week for periods amounting in the aggregate to more than sixty hours.

(6) Subject to the provisions of this section, there shall be, in the case of each working week of a driver, a period of not less than twenty-four hours for which he is off duty, being a period either falling wholly in that week or beginning in that week and ending in the next week; but—

(a) where the requirements of the foregoing provisions of this subsection have been satisfied in the case of any week by reference to a period ending in the next week, no part of that period (except any part after the expiration of the first twenty-four hours of it) shall be taken into account for the purpose of satisfying those requirements in the case of the next week; and

(b) those requirements need not be satisfied in the case of any working week of a driver who on each working day falling wholly or partly in that week drives one or more stage carriages if that week is immediately preceded by a week in the case of which those requirements have been satisfied as respects that driver or during which he has not at any time been on duty.

(7) If in the case of the working week of any driver the following requirement is satisfied, that is to say, that, in each of the periods of twenty-four hours beginning at midnight which make up that week, the driver does not drive a vehicle to which this Part of this Act applies for a period of, or periods amounting in the aggregate to, more than four hours, the foregoing provisions of this section shall not apply to him in that week, except that the provisions of subsections (1), (2) and (3) shall nevertheless have effect in relation to the whole of any working day falling partly in that week and partly in a working week in the case of which that requirement is not satisfied.

(8) If on any working day a driver does not drive any vehicle to which this Part of this Act applies—

(a) subsections (2) and (3) of this section shall not apply to that day, and

(b) the period or periods of duty attributable to that day for the purposes of subsection (5) of this section shall, if amounting to more than eleven hours, be treated as amounting to eleven hours only.

(9) For the purposes of subsections (1) and (7) of this section no account shall be taken of any time spent driving a vehicle elsewhere than on a road if the vehicle is being so driven in the course of operations of agriculture or forestry, of quarrying or of carrying out any work in the construction, reconstruction, alteration, extension or maintenance of, or of a part of, a building, or of any other fixed works of construction or civil engineering (including works for the construction, improvement or maintenance of a road) and, for the purposes of this exemption, where the vehicle is being driven on, or on a part of, a road in the course of carrying out any work for the improvement or maintenance of, or of that part of, that road, it shall be treated as if it were being driven elsewhere than on a road.

(10) For the purpose of enabling drivers to deal with cases of emergency or otherwise to meet a special need, the Minister may by regulations—

(a) create exemptions from all or any of the requirements of subsections (1) to (6) of this section in such cases and subject to such conditions as may be specified in the regulations;

(b) empower the traffic commissioners or licensing authority for any area, subject to the provisions of the regulations—

(i) to dispense with the observance of all or any of those requirements (either generally or in such circumstances or to such extent as the commissioners or authority think fit) in any particular case for which provision is not made under paragraph (a) of this subsection;

(ii) to grant a certificate (which, for the purposes of any proceedings under this Part of this Act, shall be conclusive evidence of the facts therein stated) that any particular case falls or fell within any exemption created under the said paragraph (a);

and regulations under this subsection may enable any dispensation under paragraph (b) (i) of this subsection to be granted retrospectively and provide for a document purporting to be a certificate granted by virtue of paragraph (b) (ii) of this subsection to be accepted in evidence without further proof.

(11) If any of the requirements of subsections (1) to (6) of this section, or any condition having effect by virtue of regulations made under subsection (10) thereof, is contravened in the case of any driver—

(a) that driver; and

(b) any other person (being that driver's employer or a person to whose orders that driver was subject) who caused or permitted the contravention,

shall be liable on summary conviction to a fine not exceeding £200; but a person shall not be liable to be convicted under this subsection if he proves to the court—

(i) that the contravention was due to unavoidable delay in the completion of a journey arising out of circumstances which he could not reasonably have foreseen; or

(ii) in the case of a person charged under paragraph (b) of this subsection, that the contravention was due to the fact that the driver had for any particular period or periods driven or been on duty otherwise than in the employment of that person or, as the case may be, otherwise than in the employment in which he is subject to the orders of that person and that the person charged was not, and could not reasonably have become, aware of that fact.

[(11A) Where, in the case of a driver or member of the crew of a motor vehicle, there is in Great Britain a contravention of any requirement of the international rules as to periods of driving or distance driven, or periods on or off duty, then the offender and any other person (being the offender's employer or a person to whose orders the offender was subject) who caused or permitted the contravention shall be liable on summary conviction to a fine not exceeding £200.]

(12) (*Power of Minister by order to vary hours and modify requirements.*) "

Subsection 11A above was inserted by the European Communities Act, 1972 (see "E.E.C. and Foreign Vehicles", on p. 554).

Goods Vehicles

Orders have been made under subs. (12) modifying s. 96 in respect of both goods vehicles and passenger vehicles. The order relating to goods vehicles is the Drivers' Hours (Goods Vehicles) (Modifications) Order, 1970 (S.I. 1970 No. 257), as amended by S.I. 1971 No. 818.   The effect of the modification is that drivers of light vans (not exceeding $3\frac{1}{2}$ tons plated weight or 30 cwt. unplated) used for professional purposes (doctors, dentists, midwives, nurses or vets) or for services of maintenance, repair, installation, cleaning or fitting, or by commercial travellers, or by employees of the A.A. or R.A.C., are exempted from all the provisions of s. 96 other than the requirement in s. 96 (1) not to drive for more than ten hours. The order also modifies the text of s. 96 (9), and the text on p. 557 is as modified by the order.

Exemptions for drivers of goods vehicles for various purposes are set out in the Drivers' Hours (Goods Vehicles) (Exemptions) Regulations, 1972 (S.I. 1972 No. 574).   The purposes include an "emergency" (Pt. I of the Schedule), and "emergencies" are defined as events which cause or are likely to cause danger to the life or health of a human being or an animal, serious interruption to public water, gas, electricity, drainage, telecommunication or postal services, serious interruption in the use of roads or airports, or serious damage to property so as to necessitate the taking of immediate action.   The other exemptions relate to cases of special need which are set out in Pt. II of the Schedule.   They include the handling of Christmas mail, the carriage of perishable food in holiday periods, the carriage of animals, fish and agricultural produce and requirements, newspapers, building and engineering materials, furniture removal and shopfittings, explosives, radioactive substances, ships' stores and exceptional loads accompanied by the police.   Reference in each case must be made to the Schedule as to the extent of the exemption and the circumstances which confer the exemption.

The definitions of "working day" and "working week" are in s. 103 (1), on p. 550, and s. 103 (4) explains references to a driver being on duty, so that he is deemed to be on duty for purposes other than driving when engaged in the course of his employment by his employer; there is special provision as to owner-drivers.   Note s. 96 (9) as to drivers engaged in agricultural, forestry, quarrying or road construction operations.   The section applies to empty vehicles of the types specified in s. 95 as well as to loaded ones, seemingly, even when on joy-rides.

Criminal liability under s. 96 or for breach of conditions under Regulations is cast by s. 96 (11) on the driver and on any other person, being that driver's employer or a person to whose orders that driver was subject, who caused or permitted the contravention; consequently a transport manager might be liable for causing or permitting.   Aiding and abetting can also be charged.   Cases on causing and permitting are set out on pp. 33–41 and *Sidcup Building Estates* v. *Sidery, Forsyth* v. *Phillips, Grays Haulage Co., Ltd.* v. *Arnold* and *Dixon Bool Transport, Ltd.* v. *Forsyth* on pp. 37–38 were on this subject. The most recent case is *Knowles Transport, Ltd.* v. *Russell* [1975] R.T.R. 87.

Knowledge of the irregularities is an essential requisite before an employer can be said to have " caused " or " permitted " contravention of the Regulations. Where the defendant is a corporation, such guilty knowledge must be imputed to a "reasonable officer " of the corporation, i.e., " one whose duty included some measure of control of the company's business " (*per* Melford Stevenson, J., at p. 93). Two checking clerks could have detected the excessive hours worked by the company's drivers when they checked the drivers' time sheets and calculated their wages, but as there was no evidence that the matter was brought to the attention of a responsible officer of the company or that any matter came to his notice which should have put him on enquiry, the company's conviction was set aside.

The defence under s. 96 (11) (i) as to unavoidable delay applies to any person, driver or not.

In *Whitby* v. *Stead* [1975] R.T.R. 169, a driver was delayed for an hour while attempting to deliver some goods and again delayed while helping in an accident to other vehicles. He was charged with exceeding the working day of fourteen hours and driving for a period exceeding ten hours, because by s. 103 (1) (*b*) (see p. 551) his two periods of driving became aggregated, since they were not separated by an interval of rest of at least eleven hours. The justices acquitted because of unavoidable delay under s. 96 (11) (i). The Divisional Court directed a conviction because the problems caused to the defendant by the delays could have been avoided by the defendant starting his second period of driving later. The defence of unavoidable delay is not available to excuse a failure to have an interval of eleven hours rest (*ibid.*). The defence under s. 96 (11) (ii) applies to employers, transport managers and other directing staff. In a case under s. 96 (11) (ii) the defendant must show not only that he was unaware that a driver had been driving otherwise than in his employment with the defendant's firm but also that the defendant could not reasonably have become aware of that fact. This suggests that employers and transport managers may have some duty to instruct their drivers to report to them if the drivers have been driving outside their employment. It seems to be no defence under s. 96 (11) (assuming a defence is not available under s. 96 (11) (ii)) if the driver had been on duty in his employer's business for an excessive period even though directly against his master's orders: the master

should supervise properly, but it may be a defence if he did supervise properly and his orders were still disobeyed unknown to him
him (*Grays Haulage Co., Ltd.* v. *Arnold* [1966] 1 All E.R. 896); see
p. 36.

Where a driver is engaged in canvassing and delivering during
his journey, this was held under the old law to be time spent in
driving (*M'Callum* v. *Adair* [1937] S.C.(J.) 114) and clearly still is
time on duty under s. 96 of the Transport Act—see s. 103 (4) (*a*).
As, by s. 103 (4), time spent on other " employment under the
person who is his employer " is time spent on duty, as is time spent
in the employment as a driver, cases such as *Jesner* v. *Waugh* [1936]
S.C.(J.) 47 (time spent by driver at the depôt awaiting orders),
Wells v. *Sidery* [1939] 3 All E.R. 54 (watching his lorry being
unloaded) and *Parkinson* v. *Axon* [1951] 2 All E.R. 647 (working
on a different job, sorting parcels) are probably no longer of
authority, where the driver is working or acting for the employer
who employs him as a driver. Subject to the next paragraph, it
may be that time spent on work for another employer does not count
and, since questions may arise as to who is the employer, e.g.,
where there are several sub-contractors on a site, the common-law
cases as to who is the employer may be of relevance.

It was held in *Beer* v. *Fairclough* (1937), 101 J.P. 157, on the old
law, that, provided employers allowed their driver proper time for
resting, they did not have to see that he actually spent it in resting
and they committed no offence if he did not, but it might be otherwise if he had, to their knowledge, to spend part of his rest-period in
travelling to the place at which he had orders to resume work. This
rule is not expressly reversed by s. 96, but s. 96 (11) (*b*) suggests
that an employer or transport manager might be liable if a driver
had been working for someone else to the defendant's knowledge
and would therefore be driving for the defendant for an excessive
period or would not have enough rest. However, to impose a new
criminal liability by spelling it out from a subsection enacted to
provide a defence is an odd procedure, and the case of *Beer* may still
bring aid and comfort to defendants in these circumstances.

A driver, after driving a goods vehicle for the maximum permitted
period, used his employers' car to get home; sometimes he drove
it and sometimes he was a passenger in it, but his employers gave
him a genuine option to stay overnight at the place where he left
his goods vehicle. It was held that, in view of this option, he
had been given his rest period and no offence was committed if
he chose to use the car (*Witchell* v. *Abbott* [1966] 2 All E.R. 657, at
p. 659), but this case was distinguished in *Potter* v. *Gorbould* [1969]
3 All E.R. 828. The defendant was allowed by his employer,

when he had finished his normal day's work, to earn overtime by cutting up scrap in his employer's scrapyard if he wished. As a result the defendant had less than the period for rest required. It was held that, as what was being done was not purely for the benefit of the driver but equally for the benefit of the employer and he was bound by the terms of his employment to obey the employer's directions and it was within the general terms of his employment, it could not be held that he had been given his period of rest.

Where a driver worked for a number of periods which in the aggregate exceeded eleven hours, an offence was held to have been committed, though each separate period was separated from the next by an interval of at least thirty minutes (*Cook* v. *Plumpton* (1935), 99 J.P. 308).

Where the driver's records show that he was working for a particular period and that period exceeds the permitted period of work, there is a *prima facie* case against him and against his employers for permitting him to work excessive hours; he or his employers must show that he was in fact resting or off duty (*Smith* v. *All-Wheel Drive Co., Ltd.* (1962), *The Guardian*, 12th February). The magistrates should not infer that it was unlikely that he was working without such evidence (*ibid.*).

The records of the driver's hours are admissible against his employer in a charge under s. 96 (Transport Act, 1968, s. 98 (5), on p. 547). They appear to be admissible anyhow at common law against the driver himself and possibly against the transport manager, if the court holds that the latter has the duty of seeing that his firm's drivers obey the requirements of s. 96. If the manager is charged with aiding and abetting the employer, it could be argued that by s. 35 of the Magistrates' Courts Act, 1952, the manager is " guilty of the like offence ", so that evidence admissible against the employer is likewise admissible against the manager; on the other hand, there are cases every day where evidence against one defendant is not admissible against another. Certainly, if the manager is charged as the principal offender, it can be said that, as against him, the driver's records are hearsay and not admissible. The prosecutor might be wise to call the driver to give oral evidence or submit his written evidence under s. 9 of the Criminal Justice Act, 1967, the driver refreshing his memory from his records (*R.* v. *Bryant* on p. 112). Relevant cases are *Beer* v. *Clench* and *Adair* v. *Craighouse & Co.* on p. 553; also *Hogg* v. *Burnet* on p. 554 as to a vehicle number on a record identifying it. An indictable charge of conspiracy to contravene s. 98 may properly be brought (*R.* v. *Blamires Transport Services, Ltd.* [1963] 3 All E.R. 170).

Passenger Vehicles

Section 96 is extensively modified by the Drivers' Hours (Passenger and Goods Vehicles) (Modifications) Order, 1971 (S.I. 1971 No. 818). Where passenger vehicles' hours are alleged to be contravened and the driver spends all or the greater part of the time in driving passenger vehicles during a working day, s. 96 (1) is unmodified (see p. 556) but s. 96 (2) must be read as follows:—

" (2) Subject to the provisions of this section if on any working day a driver has been driving a vehicle or vehicles to which this Part of this Act applies—

    (*a*) for a period of five and a half hours and the end of that period does not mark the end of the working day; or

    (*b*) for periods amounting in the aggregate to five and a half hours and there has not been between any of those periods an interval of not less than half an hour in which the driver was able to obtain rest and refreshment and the end of the last of those periods does not mark the end of the working day,

there shall, as respects the period mentioned in paragraph (*a*) above, at the end of that period or, in the case of the periods mentioned in paragraph (*b*) above, at the end of the last of those periods, be such an interval as aforesaid; but the requirements of the foregoing provisions of this subsection need not be satisfied in relation to a driver who, within any continuous period of eight and a half hours in the working day, drives for periods amounting in the aggregate to not more than seven and three-quarter hours, being periods of driving between which there is a period of, or there are periods amounting in the aggregate to, not less than forty-five minutes during which the driver has not been driving, if—

    (i) the end of the last of those periods of driving marks the end of the working day, or

    (ii) at the end of the last of those periods there is such an interval as is mentioned in paragraph (*b*) above."

Section 96 (3) is modified by the substitution of a new para. (*c*):—

" (*c*) if during that day all or the greater part of the time when he is driving vehicles to which this Part of this Act applies is spent in driving one or more passenger vehicles, shall not exceed sixteen hours."

In s. 96 (4), in place of paras. (*a*) and (*b*), the following words are substituted:—

" shall not be of less than ten hours except that on not more than three occasions in any working week the said interval may be of less than ten hours but not of less than eight and a half hours."

Section 96 (5) does not apply.

Section 96 (6) reads as follows:—

" (6) Subject to the provisions of this section, there shall be, in the case of every two successive working weeks of a driver, a period of not less than twenty-four hours, for which he is off duty, being a period either falling wholly in those weeks or beginning in the second of those weeks and ending in the first of the next two successive weeks; but where the requirements of the foregoing provisions of this subsection have been satisfied in the case of any two successive working weeks by reference to a period ending in the first of the next two successive weeks, no part of that period (except any part after the expiration of the first twenty-four hours of it) shall be taken into account for the purpose of satisfying those requirements in the case of the said next two successive weeks."

Section 96 (7) is replaced by the following subsections:—

" (7) If in the case of the working week of any driver the following requirements are satisfied, that is to say, that—

(a) the driver does not drive any vehicle to which this Part of this Act applies for a period of, or for periods amounting in the aggregate to, more than four hours in more than two of the periods of twenty-four hours beginning at midnight which make up that working week (any such period of twenty-four hours in which the driver does drive for a period of, or for periods amounting in the aggregate to, more than four hours being in this subsection, and in subsection (7B) below, referred to as ' " a full time day " '); and

(b) the provisions of subsection (7B) of this section are complied with in relation to him as respects each full time day in that week,

then, subject to subsection (7A) of this section, the provisions of subsections (1) to (4) of this section shall not apply to that driver in that week, and where the said requirements are satisfied in the case of two successive working weeks of that driver the provisions of subsection (6) of this section shall not apply to him as respects those working weeks.

(7A) Where in the case of the working week of a driver the requirements mentioned in subsection (7) above are satisfied but there is a working day of the driver which falls partly in that working week and partly in a working week in the case of which the said requirements are not satisfied, then the provisions of subsections (1), (2) and (3) of this section shall nevertheless have effect in relation to the whole of that working day.

(7B) The following provisions shall apply as respects each full time day in a working week of a driver in the case of which the requirement mentioned in subsection (7) (a) above is satisfied, that is to say—

(a) each period of duty of that driver shall fall wholly within the full time day;

(b) there shall be an interval for rest of not less than ten hours immediately before his first period of duty and immediately after his last period of duty in the full time day or, if there is only one such period of duty therein, immediately before and after that period of duty;

(c) the driver shall not in the full time day drive a vehicle or vehicles to which this Part of this Act applies for periods amounting in the aggregate to more than ten hours;

(d) if in the full time day the driver has been driving a vehicle or vehicles to which this Part of this Act applies—

(i) for a period of five and a half hours and the end of that period of driving does not mark the end of his period of duty, or of the last of his periods of duty, in that day, or

(ii) for periods amounting in the aggregate to five and a half hours and there has not been between any of those periods of driving an interval of not less than half an hour in which the driver was able to obtain rest and refreshment and the end of the last of those periods of driving does not mark the end of his period of duty, or of the last of his periods of duty, in that day,

there shall be such an interval as aforesaid at the end of the period of driving mentioned in sub-paragraph (i) above or of the last of the periods of driving mentioned in sub-paragraph (ii) above: provided however that the foregoing requirements of this paragraph need not be satisfied in relation to a driver who, within any continuous period of eight and a half hours falling wholly within the full time day, drives for periods amounting in the aggregate to not more than seven and three-quarter hours, being periods of driving between which there is a period of, or there are periods amounting in the aggregate to, not less than forty-five minutes during which the driver has not been driving, if the end of the last of those periods of driving marks the end of his period, or of the last of his periods, of duty in that day, or at the end of the last of those periods of driving there is such an interval as is mentioned in sub-paragraph (ii) above; and

(e) the period during which the driver is on duty in the full time day or, if there is more than one such period, the period between the beginning of his first period of duty in that day and the end of his last period of duty therein, shall not exceed sixteen hours."

Section 96 (8) (b) does not apply.

The definition of " working day " in s. 103 (see p. 551) is also modified by the substitution of " ten hours " for " eleven hours " and " eight and a half hours " for " nine and a half hours ".

Installation and Operation of Recording Equipment

Provision is made by s. 97 (when operative) for installing and operating equipment for recording information, which must be kept in working order, in vehicles mentioned in s. 95 (on p. 545), other than small goods vehicles, as defined in s. 103 (6) (on p. 551), and other vehicles exempted by Regulations. By s. 97 (5) a record made by such equipment is, in proceedings under Pt. VI (hours and records), evidence of the matters appearing from the record. Offences arise under s. 97 (4) but a defence to a charge that the equipment was not in working order while the vehicle was being driven is provided by that subsection where the breakdown occurred during a journey and was not due to the defendant or the driver and the journey was not continued after it had become reasonably practicable to mend it. Section 97 has not yet been brought into force. Regulations have been made by the Council of the E.E.C. (Regulation 1463/70/E.E.C. of the Council) concerning such recording equipment within the European Economic Community but there has been no specific implementation of these Regulations in the United Kingdom.

Penalty

The penalty is a fine of £200 under s. 96 (11) or s. 96 (11A) for contravening the hours. Offences can be tried by magistrates only. There is no power to endorse or disqualify.

An indictable charge at common law of conspiracy to contravene s. 96 may properly be brought (*R. v. Blamires Transport Services, Ltd.* [1963] 3 All E.R. 170).

By s. 103 (7) (see p. 552) proceedings may be brought not only in the court normally having jurisdiction but also in any other court where the person charged with the offence " for the time being is " (see also *R. v. Hitchin JJ.*, on p. 554).

21. PUBLIC SERVICE VEHICLES

The law as to the licensing of public service vehicles is found in Pt. III of and Sched. 12 to the Road Traffic Act, 1960. This Part of the 1960 Act remains in force and has not been consolidated with the other provisions into the 1972 Act. The relevant provisions now follow and an attempt to explain the law appears on p. 570.

The Road Traffic Act, 1960, s. 117, reads:—

" (1) For the purposes of this Act a public service vehicle is a motor vehicle used for carrying passengers for hire or reward which either—

 (*a*) is carrying passengers at separate fares, or
 (*b*) is not carrying passengers at separate fares but is adapted to carry eight or more passengers.

In this subsection ' motor vehicle ' does not include a tramcar or a trolley vehicle.

(2) For the purposes of this Act a stage carriage is a public service vehicle carrying passengers at separate fares, not being an express carriage.

(3) For the purposes of this Act an express carriage is a public service vehicle carrying passengers at separate fares none of which is less than one shilling or such greater sum as may be prescribed; and for the purposes of this subsection—

 (*a*) a composite fare for more than one journey shall not be regarded as representing the aggregate of fares of any less amount, and
 (*b*) no account shall be taken of any fare which is charged in the case of passengers of particular descriptions if a fare of not less than one shilling, or such greater sum as may for the time being be prescribed by virtue of the foregoing provisions of this subsection, is charged for the like service in the case of all passengers not falling within any of those descriptions.

(4) For the purposes of this Act a contract carriage is a public service vehicle not carrying passengers at separate fares.

(5) This section has effect subject to the next following section."

The difference between stage and express carriages is in the minimum fare. Stage and express carriages are those in which passengers each pay separate fares, though not necessarily to the vehicle-owner; a contract carriage is one hired by one person or body, the cost falling entirely on the hirer, e.g., father hiring a taxi for his family, when he obviously pays the whole cost of the hire himself, or a philanthropist hiring a motor-coach to give a free outing to the blind.

The term " adapted " in s. 117 (1) means " suitable " with or without alteration (*Maddox* v. *Storer* [1962] 1 All E.R. 831; *Wurzal* v. *Addison* [1965] 1 All E.R. 20). See p. 542 as to " hire or reward ".

By the Road Traffic Act, 1960, s. 127, a " public service vehicle licence " is required for all motor vehicles which are used on a road (see p. 26) as stage, express or contract carriages, save that a vehicle with seats for less than eight passengers does not require one when used as a contract carriage. By s. 134 a " road service licence " in addition is required for use as a stage or express carriage, i.e., at separate fares, but not as a contract carriage; the Transport Act, 1968, s. 30, provides that no road service licence is required for the provision of any bus service operated wholly within an area to which s. 30 applies and restricts the conditions imposable as to passengers taken up and set down in that area. Part III of the Act of 1960 deals with public service vehicles generally.

Section 118 of the Road Traffic Act, 1960, reads:—

" (1) A vehicle carrying passengers at separate fares in circumstances in which the conditions set out in Part I, II, III or IV of the Twelfth Schedule to this Act are fulfilled shall be treated as not being a public service vehicle unless it is adapted to carry eight or more passengers.

(2) A public service vehicle carrying passengers at separate fares shall be treated as a contract carriage, and not as a stage carriage or an express carriage, when used in circumstances in which the conditions set out in either Part III or Part IV of the Twelfth Schedule to this Act are fulfilled.

(3) For the purposes of this and the last foregoing section and of the Twelfth Schedule to this Act—

    (*a*) a vehicle is to be treated as carrying passengers for hire or reward if payment is made for, or for matters which include, the carrying of passengers, irrespective of the person to whom the payment is made and, in the case of a transaction effected by or on behalf of a member of any association of persons (whether incorporated or not) on the one hand and the association or another member thereof on the other hand, notwithstanding any rule of law as to such transactions;

    (*b*) a payment made for the carrying of a passenger shall be treated as a fare notwithstanding that it is made in consideration of other matters in addition to the journey and irrespective of the person by or to whom it is made;

(c) a payment shall be treated as made for the carrying of a passenger if made in consideration of a person's being given a right to be carried, whether for one or more journeys and whether or not the right is exercised;

(d) in a case where one or more passengers are being carried for hire or reward otherwise than in the course of a business of carrying passengers, the vehicle shall be treated as carrying passengers at separate fares."

The remainder of s. 118 contains exemptions for vehicles belonging to, or hired by education authorities, e.g., " school buses ", vehicles used to carry agricultural workers during the six months starting on 1st June and vehicles used for certain Health Service purposes.

Schedule 12 to the 1960 Act reads:—

" CONDITIONS AFFECTING CLASSIFICATION OF PUBLIC SERVICE VEHICLES

PART I

Race meetings, public gatherings, etc.

1. The journey on which the passengers are being carried must be made on the occasion of a race meeting, public gathering or other like special occasion.

PART II

Conditions relating to certain journeys for vehicles carrying four passengers or less

2. The number of passengers carried must not exceed four.

3. The making of the agreement for the payment of separate fares must not have been initiated by the driver or by the owner of the vehicle, by the person who has let the vehicle for hire by any hiring agreement or hire-purchase agreement, or by any person who receives any remuneration in respect of the arrangements for the journey:

Provided that the agreement may have been initiated by the driver or owner if the passengers are not being carried in the course of a business of carrying passengers.

4. The journey must be made without previous advertisement to the public of facilities for its being made by passengers to be carried at separate fares.

5. The journey must not be one on which passengers are carried at separate fares frequently, or as a matter of routine, in the same vehicle or in vehicles (other than vehicles used under a road service licence) belonging to the same owner or belonging partly to one person and partly to another who is a party to a hiring agreement or hire-purchase agreement of which any of the vehicles is the subject.

6. The journey must not be made in conjunction with, or in extension of, a service provided under a road service licence if the vehicle is owned by, or made available under any arrangement (including a hiring agreement or hire-purchase agreement) with, the holder of the licence or any person

who receives any remuneration in respect of the service provided thereunder or in respect of arrangements for that service.

PART III

Parties of overseas visitors

7. Each of the passengers making the journey must have been outside Great Britain at the time of concluding his arrangements to make the journey.

PART IV

Alternative conditions affecting classification

8. Arrangements for the bringing together of all the passengers for the purpose of making the journey must have been made otherwise than by, or by a person acting on behalf of,—

 (a) the holder of the public service vehicle licence in respect of the vehicle, if such a licence is in force,

 (b) the driver or the owner of the vehicle or the person who has let the vehicle for hire by any hiring agreement or hire-purchase agreement, if no such licence is in force,

and otherwise than by any person who receives any remuneration in respect of the arrangements.

9. The journey must be made without previous advertisement to the public of the arrangements therefor.

10. All the passengers must, in the case of a journey to a particular destination, be carried to, or to the vicinity of, that destination, or, in the case of a tour, be carried for the greater part of the journey.

11. No differentiation of fares for the journey on the basis of distance or of time must be made.

12. In the case of a journey to a particular destination the passengers must not include any person who frequently, or as a matter of routine, travels, at or about the time of day at which the journey is made, to or to the vicinity of that destination from a place from or through which the journey is made.

PART V

Supplementary

13. For the purposes of paragraphs 4 and 9 of this Schedule no account shall be taken of any such advertisement as follows, that is to say—

 (a) a notice displayed or announcement made at or in any place of worship in the manner in which notices or announcements for the information of persons attending that place of worship are normally displayed or made, or

 (b) a notice displayed in any periodical published for the information of persons who attend a particular place of worship or a place of worship in a particular place, and circulating wholly or mainly among persons who attend or might reasonably be expected to attend there.

14.—(1) A vehicle adapted to carry eight or more passengers shall not be treated as having been used in circumstances in which the conditions set out in Part III or Part IV of this Schedule were fulfilled unless, within such time as may be prescribed, the holder of the public service vehicle licence in respect of the vehicle makes, or causes to be made, a record in such form as may be prescribed containing such particulars, other than particulars of fares or prices, relating to the journey and the circumstances in which it was arranged as may be prescribed.

(2) A vehicle adapted to carry eight or more passengers shall not be treated as being used as aforesaid unless the driver of the vehicle carries a work ticket in such form and containing such particulars as may be prescribed,* being particulars appearing to the Minister requisite for enabling records made under the last foregoing sub-paragraph to be traced and identified.

(3) (*Driver to produce work ticket on demand by constable or person authorised by Traffic Commissioners.*)

(4) (*Records to be preserved for six months and produced to person authorised by Traffic Commissioners.*)

15. In this Schedule ' owner ', in relation to a vehicle which is the subject of a hiring agreement or hire-purchase agreement, means the person in possession of the vehicle under that agreement."

Foreign public service vehicles and British vehicles on international journeys are now controlled by the Road Transport (International Passenger Services) Regulations, 1973 (S.I. 1973 No. 806). These Regulations were made under s. 160 of the 1960 Act, as amended by the European Communities Act, 1972. The Regulations extensively modify Pt. III of the Act of 1960 in relation to public service vehicles on international journeys. It is an offence to provide a regular or shuttle service otherwise than in accordance with the appropriate E.E.C. authorisation (reg. 5 (*a*), (*b*)). It is also an offence to provide a service for the carriage of the undertaking's own workers without the appropriate E.E.C. certificate (reg. 5 (*c*)). It is also an offence to obstruct an examiner in the exercise of his powers, or to fail to carry or produce the relevant documents required to be carried with the vehicle under the Regulations (reg. 16).

Offences under regulations made under s. 160 are triable by magistrates only and are perishable by a fine of £50.

Examples

Perhaps it would be well to try to explain the law by examples. It will be noted that the criterion in ss. 117 and 118 is whether a vehicle is adapted to carry eight or more passengers, not the number in fact carried. Whether the driver should be counted among the passengers is not clear; in Pt. II of Sched. 12 " driver " is contrasted with " passenger ". In Sched. 5 to the Road Traffic

* See Public Service Vehicles (Contract Carriage Records) Regulations, 1960 (S.I. 1960 No. 1503).

Regulation Act, 1967 (see p. 325, *supra*) the term " passengers exclusive of the driver " is used, which suggests that he is a passenger. In *Wurzal* v. *Addison* [1965] 1 All E.R. 20, a finding of magistrates that a Volkswagen minibus, seating six passengers behind and with a bench seat seating the driver and two passengers in front, was not adapted to carry eight passengers was upheld because the gear lever was in the central position, but Lord Parker, C.J., said that, in other cases involving similar vehicles, magistrates would, on proper evidence, be almost bound to find that they were adapted to carry eight passengers. For the purpose of Pt. II of Sched. 12 it is submitted that four persons plus the driver may be carried. The law is also discussed at 121 J.P.Jo. 21.

Smith owns a seven-seater car. The question of hackney carriage licences is not dealt with in this book but guidance on that subject will be found in Stone (1975), pp. 4280–4286. Smith will not require either a public service vehicle licence or a road service licence (*a*) for any use as a contract carriage, or (*b*) for any use which falls within Pt. I, II, III or IV of Sched. 12 to the Road Traffic Act, 1960, although separate fares are paid by his passengers. If, on a special occasion such as the Derby (see *infra*), he takes passengers, however many, at separate fares, he is exempt from both licences by Pt. I. If, again, he takes not more than four passengers on any journey at separate fares and does not previously advertise the journey and otherwise complies with Pt. II, he is exempt from both licences. But if he takes five or more passengers (it not being a special occasion or within Pt. III or IV) at separate fares or (when taking only four) otherwise fails to comply with Pt. II, he will require both licences. Again, if he carries overseas visitors, however many, on any journey at separate fares he will not require either licence provided that each passenger must have been outside Great Britain (i.e., England, Wales and Scotland but not the Channel Islands or the Isle of Man) at the time of concluding the arrangements for the journey (Pt. III of Sched. 12). Lastly, if Smith carries passengers, however many, at separate fares but complies in respect of this journey with Pt. IV of Sched. 12, he will not require a public service vehicle licence or a road service licence. It is assumed in these examples that Smith carries on business as a taxi-proprietor or car-hirer. If he does not, s. 118 (3) (*d*) provides that the vehicle shall be treated as carrying passengers at separate fares: see p. 568.

Jones owns a 24-seater motor coach. For use as a stage carriage, as an express carriage or as a contract carriage he will require a public service vehicle licence under the Road Traffic Act, 1960, s. 127. He will require a road service licence under s. 134 in

addition whenever passengers are carried at separate fares, unless
Pt. III or IV of Sched. 12 is applicable.   See *supra* as to Pt. III.   As
to Pt. IV, the exemption from having a road service licence will
apply although the journey is not on a " special occasion "; the
party carried is not expressly required by the Act to be a " private
party " but the restrictions on advertising practically make it so.
Parts I and II of Sched. 12 have no application to motor coaches.

If the conditions of any Part of Sched. 12 applicable to the
journeys of the vehicles of Smith or Jones are not complied with, a
licence under s. 127 and/or s. 134 of the 1960 Act may become
necessary and an offence may arise (see *infra*).   An offence might
be committed in respect of a Pt. IV trip if the driver did not carry
a work ticket (*Evans* v. *Hassan* [1936] 2 All E.R. 107) or if that trip
were publicly advertised; several announcements taken together
can constitute an advertisement (*Poole* v. *Ibbotson* (1949), 113 J.P.
466).

Proceedings

By the Road Traffic Act, 1960, s. 161, proceedings for an offence
under s. 127 or s. 134 (below) or any other provisions in Pt. III of the
cited 1960 Act or any Regulations made thereunder (other than
as to the conduct of passengers) shall not in England be instituted
except by or on behalf of the Director of Public Prosecutions or by
a person authorised in that behalf by commissioners of a traffic
area, a chief officer of police or the council of a county or county
district.   Where a police sergeant laid an information which was
signed by an Assistant Commissioner of the Metropolitan Police
and by a superintendent, and the Commissioner had given a general
authorisation in writing to prosecute, it was held in *Westminster
Coaching Services* v. *Piddlesden* (1933), 97 J.P. 185, that the sergeant
had authority to take proceedings under s. 161.   Contrast *Record
Tower Cranes* v. *Gisbey* and *Nelms* v. *Roe* on p. 465.   See *Price* v.
Humphries on p. 57 as to proving the authority to prosecute.   Section
161 also does not apply to proceedings under Regulations for control
of the number of passengers.

If any person causes or permits a motor vehicle to be used on a
road as a stage, express or contract carriage without a public service
vehicle licence he offends against the Road Traffic Act, 1960,
s. 127, but by s. 127 (2) and (3) the licence to use as one type of
such carriage in certain cases allows use as another type.   " Using "
in itself does not seem to be an offence under s. 127.   Further, by
s. 134, a person who uses or causes or permits a vehicle to be used as a
stage or express carriage without a road service licence or contrary to

a condition of such licence commits an offence. Where it is the employer's duty to get any licence under Pt. III of the 1960 Act, and he has failed to do so, the driver should not be prosecuted (*Carpenter* v. *Campbell* [1953] 1 All E.R. 280). Where the owner of a bus drives it without a licence, he is causing it to be used in breach of s. 127 (*Baker* v. *Chapman* (1963), 61 L.G.R. 527). Actual knowledge in the owner of payments being made by passengers to the company which employed them and which hired the bus from the owner is not essential on a charge of " causing use " against the owner if he never made any inquiry as to whether they were paying anything to the company (*Wurzal* v. *Wilson* [1965] 1 All E.R. 26).

By the Transport Act, 1947, s. 65, a road service licence was not required for a service provided under a scheme by the British Transport Commission or its agent; where the Commission itself hired a bus and gave all the directions as to its movements, it was held to provide the transport itself (*Railway Executive* v. *Henson* (1949), 113 J.P. 333). Section 65 is now repealed.

See p. 568 as to exemptions for school buses, transport for agricultural workers and certain Health Service vehicles.

As to " causing " and " permitting " and " using ", see pp. 32–51.

Generally, a vehicle owner offends if he lets out his vehicle to a person who, he knows, may use it in contravention of s. 127 or s. 134 or if he (the owner) does not take adequate steps to prevent the contravention (*Goldsmith* v. *Deakin* (1933), 98 J.P. 4; *Webb* v. *Maidstone, etc., Services* (1934), 78 S.J. 336; *Clydebank Co-operative Society* v. *Binnie* [1937] S.C.(J.) 17). But he is not guilty if he does not know of the illegal use and does not deliberately refrain from making inquiries or shut his eyes to the obvious (*Evans* v. *Dell* [1937] 1 All E.R. 349). Nor is he liable when the trip has been made illegal by the action, unknown to him, of a person not subject to his control (*Reynolds* v. *Austin* [1951] 1 All E.R. 606). On the other hand, inadequate supervision as to the persons who travel on a journey may show that the vehicle owner has not taken adequate steps to prevent unauthorised persons going on it (*Browning* v. *J. W. H. Watson (Rochester), Ltd.* [1953] 2 All E.R. 775) or he may be guilty if he has not made proper inquiry as to whether separate fares will be paid (*Wurzal* v. *Wilson* [1965] 1 All E.R. 26). An owner who has let his vehicle out on hire may not be liable for unauthorised use nor may the hirer, when not present on the illegal journey (*Hamilton* v. *Blair and Meecham* [1962] S.L.T. 69; English decisions were not cited). See Jo.Crim.L. (1962) 292, and p. 43 of this book.

If a condition imposed by the Commissioners is *ultra vires*, its breach is no offence (*Ellis* v. *Dubowski* (1921), 85 J.P. 230). If an employee wilfully or negligently disobeys a term of his master's road service licence, e.g., by diverting from the authorised route, the master may be liable for a breach of s. 134 (*G. Newton, Ltd.* v. *Smith* [1962] 2 All E.R. 19). In that case, the charge was failure to comply with a condition of the licence and it was held that s. 134 (3) imposes on a master liability for a failure by him or his servant to comply with the conditions of the licence, provided the driver acted wilfully or negligently.

A charge under s. 134 (3) is not bad for duplicity if it is for " wilful or negligent " failure (*ibid.*).

The Road Traffic Act, 1960, s. 118 (3), makes special provision as to arrangements between a society and its members or between members for transport being deemed a carriage for hire or reward; otherwise, a member of an unincorporated society could be said to be using his own vehicle if the society owned it. The principle laid down in *Wurzal* v. *Houghton Main Home Delivery Service, Ltd.*, p. 544, *supra*, therefore seems inapplicable.

Stage and Express Carriages

A road service licence is necessary for either type, but not for a contract carriage; the only difference between stage and express carriages is in the minimum fare. The original definition in the 1930 Act (now repealed) showed the stage carriage to be the ordinary bus picking up and setting down passengers frequently along its route, e.g., the bus along the Strand, and the express carriage to be one such as the London to Brighton regular bus service.

The cases which follow were decided on the old law and s. 40 of the 1956 Act (now s. 118) made more stringent provision as to the payment of separate fares. The cases should be read in the light of it.

A bus proprietor hired a bus out to a football club and it stood in a street awaiting any passengers who might come along; there was no question of a private party. Each passenger paid a separate fare, which went to the club secretary. It was held to be used as a stage carriage, as s. 118 makes it immaterial to whom the fares are paid (*Osborne* v. *Richards* (1932), 96 J.P. 377). A railway company ran excursions to a certain station, where the defendants' buses met the passengers and conveyed them to a chocolate factory, the railway company receiving an inclusive fare from each excursionist; the railway company afterwards paid to the defendants a sum exceeding one shilling for each passenger carried in the buses. It was held that the buses were express carriages, it being immaterial, in view of s. 118, that the excursionists paid nothing to the defendants (*Birmingham, etc., Omnibus Co.* v. *Nelson* (1932), 96 J.P. 385). Where a company hired a bus to take employees to work and the employees made payments to the company, this was held to be carriage at separate fares requiring a road service licence for an express carriage although the passengers paid nothing themselves to the owner of the bus (*Wurzal* v. *Wilson* [1965] 1 All E.R. 26). " Separate fares " simply means payments for carriage by individual passengers and it is immaterial whether there is a firm arrangement as to the amount of the payment or a tariff of payments (*Aitken* v. *Hamilton* [1964] S.L.T. 125). Tips unsolicited by the driver were held on the facts not to be separate fares (*McLean* v. *Fearn* [1954] S.L.T.(Sh.) 37). Coaches hired from the defendants by a stadium proprietor picked up casual passengers at several points and took them to the stadium; the passengers paid nothing for their rides and were free not to go into the stadium, if they wished, the charge for admission being the same for them as for anyone else. It was held that the coaches were stage, not contract carriages, as the passengers were carried in consideration of separate payments made by them to the stadium proprietor and were thus caught by s. 118 (3) (*Westminster Coaching Services* v. *Piddlesden* (1933), 97 J.P. 185). A lorry owner who used his lorry to carry other people's goods to market and also carried as passengers the people whose goods were in the lorry was held to offend against s. 127 and s. 134 (as an express carriage) although he contended that the payments were for carriage of the goods only (*Drew* v. *Dingle* (1934), 98 J.P. 1). Public advertisement of a trip can convert what would otherwise be a trip for which a licence is unnecessary, under Sched. 12 to the Act of 1960, into one requiring a licence under s. 134 (*Evans* v. *Dell* [1937] 1 All E.R. 349; and see *Goldsmith* v. *Deakin* (1933), 98 J.P. 4). A car owner regularly drove three fellow-employees to work at a factory and back; the expenses of oil and petrol were shared by each paying 5s. per week. It was held that the friends were carried in consideration of separate payments and the vehicle was an express carriage (*East Midlands, etc., Commissioners* v. *Tyler* [1938] 3 All E.R. 39; paras. 3 and 5 of Sched. 12 to the Act of 1960 obviously were not complied with so as to bring the journey within that saving). A club hired a taxi to take members to work regularly and each member made separate payments, covering both transport charges and other purposes; it was held that, under s. 118 (3) *(d)*, these were separate fares (*Hawthorn* v. *Knight* [1962] S.L.T. 69). Where a hirer of a mini-bus agreed to pay to its owner seven shillings per day to take her and her fellow-workers to work, however many were carried, and she herself collected separate fares from the other passengers, it was held that, under s. 118 (3) (*b*), there was a payment of separate fares and the owner was guilty of use as an express carriage without a public service vehicle licence (*Wurzal* v. *Addison* [1965] 1 All E.R. 20). *Lyons* v. *Denscombe* [1949] 1 All E.R. 977 was declared to be no longer of authority. The leading case on the meaning of " hire or reward " is *Albert* v. *Motor Insurers' Bureau* [1971] 2 All E.R. 1345. This was not a case on a public service vehicle licence but on s. 203 (4) of the Road Traffic Act, 1960, which exempted a driver of a motor vehicle from being required to insure against passenger liability provided the passengers were not carried for " hire or reward ". The House of Lords (Lord Cross dissenting) disapproved *Coward* v. *Motor Insurers' Bureau* [1962] 1 All E.R. 531, where it was held that " hire or reward " meant a monetary reward legally recoverable under a contract express or implied, and held that the test as to whether a vehicle was being used for " hire or reward " was whether there had been a systematic carrying of passengers for reward which went beyond the bounds of mere social kindness. It is immaterial that no contractual relationship was intended. The words " hire or reward " must be read disjunctively.

The reference in para. 12 of Sched. 12, on p. 569, to frequent and routine travelling refers to those who regularly use the relevant vehicle as well as to those who generally use other methods of transport (*MacLeod* v. *Penman* [1962] S.L.T. 69).

A bus hired to take people back after a dance went to their various homes; it was held that this was not a " journey to a particular destination " under para. 10 of Sched. 12 (*Clark* v. *Dundee Council* [1957] S.L.T. 306).

Special Occasion

The term " special occasion " now occurs only in Pt. I of Sched. 12 to the Road Traffic Act, 1960, and applies only to trips by vehicles seating less than eight passengers. The journey must be to an event which is a special occasion in the locality to which the journey is made, e.g., an annual angling match, the Derby, or the unveiling of a statue (*Wurzal* v. *Dowker* [1953] 2 All E.R. 88). Twice-monthly league football matches can be special occasions, the test being the amount of extra public transport required for such events, but matches played more frequently than fortnightly might cease to be by reason of their frequency (*Browning* v. *J. W. H. Watson (Rochester), Ltd.* [1953] 2 All E.R. 775). A regular Saturday bus service from a railway station to a holiday camp is not a special occasion (*Victoria Motors* v. *Wurzal* [1951] 1 All E.R. 1016). Nor is a regular weekly or fortnightly market a special occasion (*Miller* v.

Pill (1933), 97 J.P. 197). Nor is a journey to a football ground every time the team played at home (*Sidery* v. *Evans* [1938] 4 All E.R. 137). Nor are Blackpool illuminations, which last for forty-nine days, as they are not analogous to a race meeting or a public gathering (*Nelson* v. *Blackford* [1936] 2 All E.R. 109). *Sidery* v. *Evans*, *supra*, appears distinguishable from *Browning* v. *Watson*, *supra*, in that in the former case club members travelled frequently to football matches, but on the issue of " special occasion " the two seem to conflict. The cases mentioned in this paragraph were on the old law and in the main are not now of authority save on the meaning of the term " special occasion ".

It would seem that all the prosecution need do is to prove that a trip was made by passengers paying separate fares, and the defendant must show that he had no need of a licence.

Paterson's Licensing Acts contains decisions on the meaning of " special occasions " under another Act.

Part III of the 1960 Act does not apply to the Crown.

Penalty

The penalty for an offence, whether a first or subsequent conviction, under s. 127 or s. 134 is a fine of £100.

These offences are triable by magistrates only.

There is no power in the court to endorse a driving licence or disqualify from driving motor vehicles.

Under s. 127 (7) of the Act of 1960 the Traffic Commissioner may suspend a public service vehicle licence. A public service vehicle licence may not be suspended as a penalty for past conduct; the power of suspension under s. 127 (7) may only be exercised for the reason that the licence holder is not a fit and proper person (*Robinson* v. *Secretary of State for the Environment* [1973] R.T.R. 511). There is also power under s. 133 (as amended by the 1974 Act) to suspend a public service vehicle licence in respect of a particular vehicle because of defects in that vehicle.

22. CONDUCT ON PUBLIC SERVICE VEHICLES

The Public Service Vehicles (Conduct of Drivers, Conductors and Passengers) Regulations, 1936 (S.R. & O. 1936 No. 619) are deemed to have been made pursuant to the Road Traffic Act, 1960, ss. 146 and 147, and regulate behaviour on public service vehicles, not being trams or trolley vehicles or contract carriages carrying less than eight passengers. The Stage Carriages Act, 1832, applies to trams and trolley vehicles (*Chapman* v. *Kirke* [1948] 2 All E.R. 556). Proceedings for an offence by a passenger may be instituted by any person, but those for an offence by a driver or conductor only by a person mentioned in the Road Traffic Act, 1960, s. 161 (see p. 572), so far as the Regulations are concerned. Offences by drivers and conductors under s. 48 of the 1832 Act may be prosecuted within six months, as may all offences under the Regulations (*Orr* v. *Strathern* [1929] S.C.(J.) 30). Only s. 48 of the 1832 Act and part of s. 103 remain unrepealed. The Regulations are in Stone, Part VI, p. 6401.

" Disorderly conduct " includes something less aggressive than a breach of the peace (*Campbell* v. *Adair* [1945] S.L.T. 135).

The provisions of reg. 11 (as amended by S.R. & O. 1946 No. 357) as to non-payment of fares appear to be valid and have been drafted to avoid the difficulty raised by the decision in *L.P.T.B.* v. *Sumner* (1935), 99 J.P. 387. The railway ticket fraud cases are cited in Stone (1975), p. 3519. For cases on the term " passengers " including " intending passengers ", see Jo.Crim.L. (1952) 102, and 116 J.P.Jo. 280, and as to "entering" and "alighting", see Jo.Crim.L. (1952) 116. In *Reid* v. *MacNicol* [1958] S.L.T. 42, the driver of a bus was charged with failing to take precautions for the safety of passengers entering it in that he did not halt at a bus stop and a person stumbled on boarding the bus. It was held that the Regulations only imposed a duty towards persons entitled to enter the bus and no person was entitled to enter a moving bus.

The legal position as to boarding buses between stops is discussed at 119 J.P.Jo. 98. A Metropolitan magistrate has held that it is not obstructing a conductor under the Regulations to board a bus ahead of one's place in the queue and to refuse to alight when the conductor tells one to get back in the queue (Jo.Crim.L. (1961) 9). It might be that the passenger would be guilty of conducting himself in a disorderly manner or of unreasonably impeding other passengers seeking to enter the bus under reg. 9 or under local byelaws directed against disorderly conduct or in an extreme case breach of the peace.

" Driver " and " conductor " in the 1936 Regulations mean persons licensed to act as such, and magistrates dismissed a case where it was not proved that a conductor was licensed (120 J.P.Jo. 110 and reg. 2).

In *Askew* v. *Bowtell* [1947] 1 All E.R. 883, a tram conductor was charged with endangering the safety of a passenger by negligence contrary to the Stage Carriages Act, 1832, s. 48. The conductor was on top of the tram as it approached a compulsory stop and the driver slowed to a speed of one m.p.h. A lady began to get off when the driver accelerated and she was thrown. The conductor was unaware that she wished to alight. It was held that the conductor was entitled to assume that the driver would stop at the compulsory stop and that passengers would not alight before the tram halted; the conductor was therefore not guilty of negligence. It was also said that, if the tram had stopped, it would be his duty to see that passengers were safely off and on before it started again. Civil cases on the duties of conductors are *Mottram* v. *S. Lancs. Transport Co.* [1942] 2 All E.R. 452, *Davies* v. *Liverpool Corporation* [1949] 2 All E.R. 175, *Prescott* v. *Lancashire United Transport Co.* [1953] 1 All E.R. 288 and *Wingroves C.B.* v. *Scottish Omnibuses, Ltd.* [1965] S.L.T.N. 55. Other cases are in Bingham's Motor Claims Cases. A conductor should not open the door for passengers to alight until the vehicle has stopped (*Nicholson* v. *Goddard* [1954] Crim.L.R. 474, a prosecution). Where a Mrs. Entwistle fell off a bus and the conductress was charged with failing to take reasonable precautions for the safety of the passengers, it was held that whether " reasonable precautions " had been taken was a question of fact for the court and it was immaterial that the Regulations do not define them (*Marshall* v. *Clark* [1958] S.L.T. 19).

The 1936 Regulations are not intended to deal with traffic offences by a driver, e.g., where he has driven without reasonable consideration for his passengers (*Pawley* v. *Wharldall* [1965] 2 All E.R. 757).

The number of passengers to be carried in a public service vehicle is regulated by the Public Service Vehicles and Trolley Vehicles (Carrying Capacity) Regulations, 1954 (S.I. 1954 No. 1612), 1958 (S.I. 1958 No. 472) and 1966 (S.I. 1966 No. 674). Special provision is made as to special hardship, peak traffic hours and children. A bus owner, who had appointed a young and in-experienced conductor and had not provided for adequate inspection, was convicted of aiding and abetting the conductor to allow overcrowding, although the owner was not present on the bus at the material time (*Gough* v. *Rees* (1930), 94 J.P. 53). The offence of " carrying " excess passengers is committed by the operator, not by the driver or conductor; the latter might be liable for aiding and abetting the operator; but it is wrong to charge the conductor with " permitting " overcrowding (*Spires* v. *Smith* [1956] 2 All E.R. 277). The Regulations are in Stone, Part VI, p. 6398. Any person may prosecute under them.

The penalty under the 1936 Regulations has been increased by the Road Traffic Act, 1974, to £20 in respect of offending drivers or conductors, and the conviction may be endorsed on the public service vehicle licence of the offending driver or conductor (Road Traffic Act, 1960, ss. 146 and 147). The penalty for offending passengers has been increased by the Road Traffic Act, 1974, to

£100. The penalty under the Carrying Capacity Regulations of 1954 has been increased to £50 (s. 148 (2)), and the penalty under the Stage Carriages Act is £5. All such offences are triable by magistrates.

There is no power to disqualify from driving or to endorse a driving licence.

The Public Service Vehicles (Arrest of Offenders) Act, 1975, was enacted as a result of increasingly violent and disorderly behaviour on public service vehicles particularly at night.

By s. 1 of the Act a constable who with reasonable cause suspects a person of contravening or failing to comply with a provision of the Regulations having effect by virtue of s. 147 of the 1960 Act (i.e., the 1936 Regulations in so far as they relate to passengers: see p. 577), or of byelaws made under the Tramways Act, 1870, may require that person to give his name and address. The constable may then arrest him if that person—

(a) refuses to give his name and address to the constable; or
(b) gives a name and address to the constable but does not answer to the satisfaction of the constable questions put to him by the constable for the purpose of ascertaining whether the name and address are correct.

On receiving the Royal Assent the whole of the Act came into force at once except in respect of persons suspected of offending the Tramway byelaws. (This latter provision will be brought into force on such date as the Secretary of State appoints: s. 2 (3)).

The Act does not apply to Scotland and Northern Ireland.

23. MOTORWAYS

The only vehicles which may lawfully use the motorways at all times are those in Classes I and II in Sched. 4 to the Highways Act, 1959, or Sched. 2 to the Special Roads Act, 1949, as varied by the Special Roads (Classes of Traffic) Order, 1971 (S.I. 1971 No. 1156). These two Schedules as varied by the 1971 order are in identical terms and read, in part, as follows:—

" CLASSES OF TRAFFIC FOR PURPOSES OF SPECIAL ROADS

Class I:

Heavy and light locomotives, motor tractors, heavy motor cars, motor cars and motor cycles whereof the cylinder capacity of the engine is not less than 50 cubic centimetres, and trailers drawn thereby, which comply with general regulations as to construction and use made under section 64 of the Road Traffic Act, 1960 and in the case of which the following conditions are satisfied, that is to say:—

    (i) that the whole weight of the vehicle is transmitted to the road surface by means of wheels;

   (ii) that all wheels of the vehicle are equipped with pneumatic tyres;

   (iii) that the vehicle is not controlled by a pedestrian;

   (iv) that the vehicle is not a vehicle chargeable with duty under paragraph 2 of Part I of Schedule 3 to the Vehicles (Excise) Act, 1971; and

   (v) in the case of a motor vehicle it is so constructed as to be capable of attaining a speed of twenty-five miles per hour on the level under its own power, when unladen and not drawing a trailer.

Class II:

Motor vehicles and trailers the use of which for or in connection with the conveyance of abnormal indivisible loads is authorised by order made by the Secretary of State for the Environment under section 64 (4) of the Road Traffic Act, 1960.

Motor vehicles and trailers constructed for naval, military, air force or other defence purposes, the use of which is authorised by order made by the said Secretary of State under section 64 (4) of the Road Traffic Act, 1960.

Motor vehicles and trailers, to which any of the following Articles of the Motor Vehicles (Authorisation of Special Types) General Order, 1969, as amended, namely, Article 16 (which relates to vehicles for moving excavated material), Article 17 (which relates *inter alia* to vehicles constructed for use outside the United Kingdom) and Article 21 (which relates to engineering plant) relate and which are authorised to be used by any of those articles of the said Order or by any other Order under section 64 (4) of the Road Traffic Act, 1960, the said motor vehicles being vehicles in respect of which the following condition is satisfied, that is to say, that the vehicle is so constructed as to be capable of attaining a speed of twenty-five miles per hour on the level under its own power, when unladen and not drawing a trailer."

The remaining Classes may only use a motorway in accordance with reg. 14 of the Motorways Traffic Regulations, 1959 (see p. 708). Class III consists of motor vehicles controlled by pedestrians and Class IV of all motor vehicles (other than invalid carriages and motor cycles less than 50 c.c.) not comprised in Classes I to III. " Abnormal indivisible load " in Class II has the same meaning as in the Motor Vehicles (Authorisation of Special Types) General Order, 1969 (S.I. 1969 No. 344) (see p. 432).

Special speed limits for vehicles on motorways are prescribed by the Motor Vehicles (Speed Limits on Motorways) Regulations, 1973 (S.I. 1973 No. 748), but the law relating to speed limits generally is otherwise applicable. For this reason motorway speed limits are discussed in the section of this book relating to speed limits (see p. 316 and pp. 336–338).

The Motorways Traffic Regulations, 1959, as amended, are set out on pp. 704–709.

Contravention of the red flashing motorway signs is dealt with in the section relating to Traffic Signs and Police Signals on p. 298.

Certain of the cases in the section on Dangerous and Careless Driving relate to motorways: see notably *Trentham* v. *Rowlands* p. 287).

Where the prosecution omitted before closing their case to prove that a motorway was a " special road " in accordance with the Special Roads (Notice of Opening) Regulations, 1962, made under what is now s. 72 (5) of the Road Traffic Regulation Act, 1967, and also to prove the Regulations, the justices were directed that they had a discretion to allow the prosecution to re-open their case and should exercise their discretion in favour of the prosecution as the evidence was purely of a formal nature (*Royal* v. *Prescott-Clarke* [1966] 2 All E.R. 366), despite the fact that the defence had given the prosecution notice prior to the hearing that formal proof of these matters would have to be given.

Standing on any part of a motorway is an offence contrary to reg. 12 of the Motorways Traffic Regulations, 1959, but in *Reed* v. *Wastie and Another* [1972] Crim.L.R. 221 it was held that it was also wilful obstruction of a highway contrary to s. 121 of the Highways Act, 1959, and that a constable could therefore lawfully arrest a person who was standing on the carriageway causing danger to himself and others and who had refused to move when requested to do so.

The Motorways Traffic Regulations, 1959, contain many prohibitions and the Regulations should in each particular case be referred to (see pp. 704–709). Regulation 7 contains restrictions on stopping on carriageways, and where a vehicle has to stop on a motorway by reason of an emergency or other circumstances set out in reg. 7 (2), it is required to be driven or moved on to a verge. Regulation 9 makes it an offence for a vehicle to be driven or to stop on a verge unless the circumstances set out in reg. 7 (2) exist.

Where the defendant stopped on the hard shoulder of a slip road leading to the motorway to eat his sandwiches, he was prosecuted under reg. 7 (1) for stopping on a carriageway. His conviction under reg. 7 was set aside on the ground that he should have been prosecuted under reg. 9 for stopping on the verge, the Divisional Court holding that the hard shoulder adjoining a carriageway is not part of the " carriageway " as defined by reg. 3 (1) (*a*), nor is it the " marginal strip " (it was held that this refers to the line running along the nearside of the carriageway); it is in fact part of the " verge " as defined by reg. 3 (*Wallwork* v. *Rowland* [1972] 1 All E.R. 53).

One of the grounds set out in reg. 7 (2) justifying a motorist stopping on the verge is " by reason of any accident, illness or other emergency " (reg. 7 (2) (b)). A motorist when a mile from a motorway began to feel drowsy but reached the slip road to the motorway before he saw a place to park his car. Knowing that the next motorway intersection was ten miles further on he parked his car at the side of the slip road. It was held that the element of suddenness was not to be emphasised in the meaning of " emergency " in reg. 7 (2) (b) but the emergency must arise after the defendant had entered the motorway system (*Higgins* v. *Bernard* [1972] R.T.R. 304) and he should therefore be convicted as he felt drowsy before he reached the motorway slip road.

Other offences contained in the Regulations are reversing (reg. 8), using the central reservation (reg. 10), driving by learner drivers (reg. 11), goods vehicles of more than three tons laden weight and vehicles drawing trailers using the outside lane of a three-lane carriageway (reg. 11 A). Regulation 14 allows vehicles otherwise excluded from the motorway to use it in the circumstances set out in the Regulation and reg. 15 contains exceptions and relaxations of the Regulations for certain purposes or in certain circumstances.

All offences under the Motorways Regulations and under s. 13 of the Road Traffic Regulation Act, 1967 (this includes the driving of excluded vehicles on motorways) are purely summary offences punishable under s. 13 (4) of the Road Traffic Regulation Act, 1967. All offences under s. 13 (4) are now punishable with a fine of £100 whether on a first or subsequent conviction. Offences committed in respect of motor vehicles carry obligatory endorsement (in the absence of " special reasons ": see p. 664) and optional disqualification unless the offence is one under reg. 9 of unlawfully stopping on the hard shoulder where vehicles are in certain circumstances allowed to stop. Offences committed not in respect of a motor vehicle (e.g., reg. 12) are not endorsable or disqualifiable but now attract the same penalty (£100) as offences committed in respect of motor vehicles. Where a court is required to endorse the offender's licence the court may also disqualify, and, under s. 93 (7), order the offender to take a test. Section 93 (3) of the 1972 Act also applies to a conviction for an endorsable motorway offence so that if a person convicted has been previously convicted on not less than two occasions and his licence has been ordered to be endorsed within three years prior to the commission of the motorway offence he must be disqualified for at least six months unless having regard to all circumstances there are grounds for mitigation (see p. 624).

The endorsement code for all motorway offences other than speed limits is MW 10. Exceeding a speed limit on a motorway is SP 50.

Motorway offences are included in the list of recommended penalties published by the Magistrates' Association (see p. 594 and Items 26 to 34 on p. 882). It should also be noted that the list recommends heavier penalties for contravention of the Construction and Use Regulations committed on motorways (see Item 17 on p. 880).

24. VEHICLE OWNER LIABILITY

Sections 1 to 5 of the Road Traffic Act, 1974, were enacted to deal with the situation caused by the increasing proportion of excess meter charges and fixed penalties found to be uncollectable in London and the other large urban centres. The solution adopted by the Act is to fix the liability for the payment of the excess meter charge or fixed penalty in the first instance on the owner of the vehicle. The following is a brief summary and an attempted explanation of the provisions.

Where an excess meter charge or fixed penalty is unpaid, the police or local authority will serve on the registered owner of the vehicle a notice in respect of a fixed penalty under s. 1 (6) or a notice under s. 2 (6) if it is in respect of excess meter charge. (It will be noted from the text of the relevant part of the Act (set out on pp. 587–593), that ss. 1 and 2 are identical except that s. 1 refers to fixed penalties and s. 2 to excess meter charges.) The notice must be in a prescribed form (these and all other notices are prescribed by the Road Traffic (Owner Liability) Regulations, 1975 (S.I. 1975 No. 324)) and contain particulars of the offence and fixed penalty or excess meter charge. The notice requires the person served, unless he pays the fixed penalty or excess meter charge, to send to the police or local authority who served the notice a statement as to the ownership of the vehicle at the relevant time, i.e., at the time the offence giving rise to the fixed penalty was committed or the vehicle was left at the parking meter (see definitions of " relevant time " in s. 5 (1)). The requirements as to " the statement of ownership " are set out in Pt. I of Sched. 1 to the Act. The " owner " is the person by whom the vehicle was kept at the relevant time and for the purposes of ss. 1 to 4 of the Act of 1974 is presumed to be the registered owner (s. 5 (3)) but by virtue of s. 5 (4) it is open to the defence and prosecution notwithstanding this presumption to prove that the vehicle was in fact kept by some person other than the registered owner at the particular time. The statement of ownership is required to be signed by the person furnishing it and if he admits he was the owner the statement can be used by the prosecutor to prove his ownership (s. 4 (4)). If, on the other hand, he was not the owner at the relevant time, he is required, in so far as the information is in his possession, to give the name and address of the person from whom he bought or to whom he sold the vehicle as the case may be, together with the date of sale or purchase. If he states that he was not the owner then the presumption that he was the driver under s. 1 (2) or s. 2 (2) no longer applies (ss. 1 (4) and 2 (4)).

The person served with a notice under s. 1 (6) or s. 2 (6) can also serve with the statement as to ownership " a statement of facts " as set out in Pt. II of Sched. 1 giving the name and address of the driver at the relevant time. The advantage from the owner's point of view of serving such a notice is that, provided the statement of facts is counter-signed by the driver, the police or local authority can then proceed to prosecute the driver. If he is convicted, the original person served with the notice under s. 1 (6) or s. 2 (6) then escapes any further liability for an offence under s. 1 (7) or s. 2 (7) (see s. 1 (9) (b) or s. 2 (9) (b)). It should be noted that it is only if the driver is convicted that the person served with the original notice escapes liability; if the driver goes abroad or cannot be found or for any other reason escapes conviction, the person served with the notice remains liable. " Driver " is defined by s. 5 (1).

If the person served with a notice under s. 1 (6) or s. 2 (6) fails without reasonable excuse to furnish a statement of ownership he commits an offence under s. 1 (7) or s. 2 (7) punishable summarily with a fine of £100 unless the fixed penalty or excess meter charge is paid within the appropriate period, i.e., fourteen days from service of the notice or such longer period as is specified in the notice. This is so even if the person served was not the owner of the vehicle at the relevant time. However, notwithstanding the fact that the fixed penalty or excess meter charge is not paid within this time limit, a person served with a notice can still escape liability under s. 1 (7) or s. 2 (7) if the amount due is paid before proceedings under s. 1 (7) or s. 2 (7) are " commenced " against him (ss. 1 (9) (a) and 2 (9) (a)). The Act is silent as to the exact moment of time when it can be said proceedings are commenced. It is submitted that proceedings are commenced when the information is laid before a magistrate or justices' clerk in order to obtain a summons. Where a person is convicted under s. 1 (7) or s. 2 (7) this discharges any liability for the excess meter charge or for the offence for which the fixed penalty was incurred (ss. 1 (9) (c) and 2 (9) (c)).

The presumption under s. 1 (2) or s. 2 (2) that the owner was the driver does not apply if it is proved that the vehicle was in the possession of some other person without the accused's consent or that the accused was not the owner of the vehicle at the relevant time and had a reasonable excuse for not complying with the notice served on him under s. 1 (6) or s. 2 (6) (see ss. 1 (5) and 2 (5)).

Where in response to a notice under s. 1 (6) or s. 2 (6) a person furnishes a statement which is false in a material particular and does so recklessly or knowing it to be false he is liable to proceedings under s. 1 (8) or s. 2 (8) and, on conviction, to a fine of £400. It would appear that "a statement" in s. 1 (8) or s. 2 (8) includes a statutory statement as to ownership, a statement of facts as to the driver of the vehicle under Sched. 1 and a statement as to the hiring of the vehicle under s. 3. Proceedings under s. 1 (8) or s. 2 (8) for an offence in England and Wales may be commenced within six months of the date upon which evidence sufficient to warrant the bringing of proceedings comes to the notice of the prosecutor (s. 4 (1) and (3)). Subsections (1) and (3) of s. 4 are in almost identical terms to s. 180 of the Act of 1972 (see p. 69). Section 4 (2) provides a similar time-limit in respect of offences in Scotland.

Car-Hire Firms

Section 3 of the Act deals with vehicles hired out under a " hiring agreement " by " a vehicle-hire " firm. A " hiring agreement " does not include hire-purchase agreements. It is an agreement containing the particulars as are prescribed by the Road Traffic (Owner Liability) Regulations, 1975, and a " vehicle-hire firm" is defined as " any person engaged in hiring vehicles in the course of a business " (s. 3 (7)). The effect of s. 3 is that where a vehicle is hired out by a car-hire firm the car-hire firm escapes all liability under the vehicle owner provisions as soon as the firm produces to the police or local authority a signed statement as prescribed by the Regulations that the vehicle concerned was hired under a hiring agreement, together with copies of the hiring agreement and of a " statement of liability " signed by the hirer. (The " statement of liability" is a statement signed by the hirer acknowledging that he will be liable in respect of any excess meter charges and fixed penalties during the currency of his hiring agreement.) By virtue of s. 3 (5) a person authorised by the local authority or police may, at any reasonable time within six months after the service on the vehicle-hire firm of a notice under s. 1 (6) or s. 2 (6), inspect the originals of the hiring agreement and statement of liability signed by the hirer, and if the documents are not produced, the firm becomes liable as not having complied with the notice under s. 1 (6) or s. 2 (6).

Where a statement under s. 3 together with copies of the hiring agreement and the hirer's statement of liability have been furnished by the vehicle-hire firm, the vehicle owner provisions of s. 1 or s. 2 then operate as if references to the owner of the vehicle referred to the hirer. The hirer, when in turn served with a notice under s. 1 (6) or s. 2 (6), is then under a duty to serve a statutory statement of hiring under para. 2 of Pt. I of Sched. 1. This statutory statement (which should not be confused with a statement under s. 3 by the vehicle-hire firm) requires him to state whether at the relevant time the vehicle was let to him under the hiring agreement and, if not, the date when he returned the vehicle to the vehicle-hire firm. The Regulations require the statement under s. 3 of the hiring of the vehicle to give the full name and address.

Regulation 4 and Sched. 2 to the Owner Liability Regulations (S.I. 1975 No. 324) require the statement of hiring given by a vehicle-hire firm under s. 3 to contain the registration number and make of the vehicle and of any other vehicle substituted during the currency of a hiring agreement together with the times and dates of any change of vehicle, the commencement and expiry of the hiring and the commencement and expiry of any extension of the hiring. The statement of liability signed by the hirer is required to contain the full name, date of birth and permanent address of the hirer, his address at the time of hiring if different, together with the driving licence number, its issuing authority and its date of expiry.

Service of Notices

Service of notices is dealt with by s. 5 (5) and (6). It should be noted that s. 26 of the Interpretation Act, 1889, applies. The effect of s. 26 is that the service of any notice is deemed to have been effected when it would have arrived in the ordinary course of post. It would seem that by virtue of these provisions the prosecution can prove an offence under s. 1 (7) or s. 2 (7) by giving evidence that a notice under s. 1 (6) or s. 2 (6) has been posted and has not been returned, that no statutory statement of ownership has been furnished and that the excess meter charge or fixed penalty has not been paid. (For a brief discussion of s. 26 see p. 139.)

The text of ss. 1 to 5 of the Road Traffic Act, 1974, together with Sched. 1, is as follows:—

" LIABILITY OF VEHICLE OWNERS

Liability of vehicle owner in respect of certain fixed penalty offences

1.—(1) This section applies where—

    (*a*) a fixed penalty notice has been given under subsection (2), or affixed to a vehicle under subsection (7), of section 80 of the 1967 Act; and

(b) the fixed penalty notice relates to an offence committed in respect of a stationary vehicle and falling within any of paragraphs (a) to (c) and (f) of subsection (1) of that section, other than the offence mentioned in paragraph (b) of that subsection of obstructing a road; and

(c) the fixed penalty has not been paid within the period of 21 days mentioned in subsection (3) of that section or, if it is longer, the period fixed for payment by the fixed penalty notice.

(2) Subject to the following provisions of this section,—

(a) for the purposes of the institution of proceedings in respect of the alleged offence against any person as being the owner of the vehicle at the relevant time, and

(b) in any proceedings in respect of the alleged offence brought against any person as being the owner of the vehicle at the relevant time,

it shall be conclusively presumed (notwithstanding that that person may not be an individual) that he was the driver of the vehicle at that time and, accordingly, that acts or omissions of the driver of the vehicle at that time were his acts or omissions.

(3) Subsection (2) above shall not apply in relation to any person unless, within the period of 6 months beginning on the day on which the fixed penalty notice was given or affixed as mentioned in subsection (1) (a) above, a notice under subsection (6) below has been served on him by or on behalf of the chief officer of police.

(4) If the person on whom a notice under subsection (6) below is served in accordance with subsection (3) above was not the owner of the vehicle at the relevant time, subsection (2) above shall not apply in relation to him if he furnishes a statutory statement of ownership to that effect in compliance with the notice.

(5) The presumption in subsection (2) above shall not apply in any proceedings brought against any person as being the owner of the vehicle at the relevant time if, in those proceedings, it is proved—

(a) that at the relevant time the vehicle was in the possession of some other person without the consent of the accused; or

(b) that the accused was not the owner of the vehicle at the relevant time and that he has a reasonable excuse for failing to comply with the notice under subsection (6) below served on him in accordance with subsection (3) above.

(6) A notice under this subsection shall be in the prescribed form, shall give particulars of the alleged offence and of the fixed penalty concerned and shall provide that, unless the fixed penalty is paid before the expiry of the appropriate period, the person on whom the notice is served—

(a) is required, before the expiry of that period, to furnish to the chief officer of police by or on behalf of whom the notice was served a statutory statement of ownership (as defined in Part I of Schedule 1 to this Act); and

(b) is invited, before the expiry of that period, to furnish to that chief officer of police a statutory statement of facts (as defined in Part II of Schedule 1 to this Act).

(7) If, in any case where—

(a) a notice under subsection (6) above has been served on any person, and

(b) the fixed penalty specified in the notice is not paid within the appropriate period, the person so served fails without reasonable excuse to comply with the notice by furnishing a statutory statement of ownership, he shall be liable on summary conviction to a fine not exceeding £100.

(8) If, in compliance with or in response to a notice under subsection (6) above, any person furnishes a statement which is false in a material particular and does so recklessly or knowing it to be so false, he shall be liable on summary conviction to a fine not exceeding £400.

(9) Without prejudice to section 80 (2) of the 1967 Act (payment of fixed penalty before proceedings are begun a bar to conviction) where a notice under subsection (6) above has been served on any person,—

(a) payment of the fixed penalty by any person before the date on which proceedings are begun against the person so served for an offence under subsection (7) above in respect of a failure to comply with the notice shall discharge any liability of his for that offence; and

(b) conviction of any person of the offence specified in the notice shall discharge the liability of any other person (under this or any other enactment) for that offence and the liability of any person for an offence under subsection (7) above in respect of a failure to comply with the notice; and

(c) conviction of the person so served of an offence under subsection (7) above in respect of a failure to comply with the notice shall discharge the liability of any person for the offence specified in the notice;

but, except as provided by this subsection, nothing in this section shall affect the liability of any person for an offence specified in a notice under subsection (6) above.

Liability of vehicle owner in respect of excess parking charges

2.—(1) This section applies where—

(a) an excess charge has been incurred in pursuance of an order under sections 35 and 36 of the 1967 Act (provision on highways of parking places where charges are made); and

(b) notice of the incurring of the excess charge has been given or affixed as provided in the order; and

(c) the excess charge has not been duly paid in accordance with the order;

and in the following provisions of this section ' the excess charge offence ' means the offence under section 42 of the 1967 Act of failing duly to pay the excess charge.

(2) Subject to the following provisions of this section,—

(a) for the purposes of the institution of proceedings in respect of the excess charge offence against any person as being the owner of the vehicle at the relevant time, and

(b) in any proceedings in respect of the excess charge offence brought against any person as being the owner of the vehicle at the relevant time,

it shall be conclusively presumed (notwithstanding that that person may not be an individual) that he was the driver of the vehicle at that time and, accordingly, that acts or omissions of the driver of the vehicle at that time were his acts or omissions.

(3) Subsection (2) above shall not apply in relation to any person unless, within the period of 6 months beginning on the day on which the notice of the incurring of the excess charge was given or affixed as mentioned in subsection (1) (b) above, a notice under subsection (6) below has been served on him by or on behalf of the authority which is the local authority for the purposes of sections 35 and 36 of the 1967 Act in relation to the parking place concerned or, as the case may be, by or on behalf of the chief officer of police.

(4) If the person on whom a notice under subsection (6) below is served in accordance with subsection (3) above was not the owner of the vehicle at the relevant time, subsection (2) above shall not apply in relation to him if he furnishes a statutory statement of ownership to that effect in compliance with the notice.

(5) The presumption in subsection (2) above shall not apply in any proceedings brought against any person as being the owner of the vehicle at the relevant time if, in those proceedings, it is proved—

(a) that at the relevant time the vehicle was in the possession of some other person without the consent of the accused; or

(b) that the accused was not the owner of the vehicle at the relevant time and that he has a reasonable excuse for failing to comply with the notice under subsection (6) below served on him in accordance with subsection (3) above.

(6) A notice under this subsection shall be in the prescribed form, shall give particulars of the excess charge and shall provide that, unless the excess charge is paid before the expiry of the appropriate period, the person on whom the notice is served—

(a) is required, before the expiry of that period, to furnish to the authority or chief officer of police by or on behalf of whom the notice was served a statutory statement of ownership (as defined in Part I of Schedule 1 to this Act); and

(b) is invited, before the expiry of that period, to furnish to that authority or chief officer of police a statutory statement of facts (as defined in Part II of Schedule 1 to this Act).

(7) If, in any case where—

(a) a notice under subsection (6) above has been served on any person, and

(b) the excess charge specified in the notice is not paid within the appropriate period,

the person so served fails without reasonable excuse to comply with the notice by furnishing a statutory statement of ownership, he shall be liable on summary conviction to a fine not exceeding £100.

(8) If, in compliance with or in response to a notice under subsection (6) above, any person furnishes a statement which is false in a material particular and does so recklessly or knowing it to be so false, he shall be liable on summary conviction to a fine not exceeding £400.

(9) Where a notice under this section has been served on any person in respect of any excess charge,—

(a) payment of the charge by any person before the date on which proceedings are begun for the excess charge offence or, as the case may be, for an offence under subsection (7) above in respect of a failure to comply with the notice shall discharge the liability of that or any other person (under this or any other enactment) for the excess charge offence or, as the case may be, for the offence under subsection (7) above;

(b) conviction of any person of the excess charge offence shall discharge the liability of any other person (under this or any other enactment) for that offence and the liability of any person for an offence under subsection (7) above in respect of a failure to comply with the notice; and

(c) conviction of the person so served of an offence under subsection (7) above in respect of a failure to comply with the notice shall discharge the liability of any person for the excess charge offence;

but, except as provided by this subsection, nothing in this section shall affect the liability of any person for the excess charge offence.

3.—*This section relates to vehicles hired out by a vehicle-hire firm.*

4.—(1) to (3). *These subsections set out the time limit for bringing proceedings under s.* 1 (8) *or s.* 2 (8) *in England and Wales and in Scotland.*

(4) Where any person is charged with any such offence as is specified in section 1 (1) (b) above or with the offence of failing duly to pay an excess charge and the prosecutor produces to the court any of the statutory statements in Schedule 1 to this Act or a copy of a statement of liability, within the meaning of section 3 above, purporting—

(a) to have been furnished in compliance with or in response to a notice under section 1 (6) or section 2 (6) above, and

(b) to have been signed by the accused,

the statement shall be presumed, unless the contrary is proved, to have been signed by the accused and shall be evidence (and in Scotland sufficient evidence) in the proceedings of any facts stated in it tending to show that the accused was the owner, the hirer or the driver of the vehicle concerned at a particular time.

Provisions supplementary to sections 1 *to* 4 *and Schedule* 1

5.—(1) In sections 1 to 4 above and Schedule 1 to this Act,—

' appropriate period ', in relation to a notice under section 1 (6) or section 2 (6) above, means the period of 14 days from the date on which the notice is served, or such longer period as may be specified in the notice or as may be allowed by the chief officer of police or authority by or on behalf of whom the notice was served;

' driver ',—

(a) in relation to the alleged offence referred to in section 1 (1) above, means the person by whom, assuming the alleged offence to have been committed, it was committed; and

(b) in relation to an excess charge, as defined below, and in relation to an offence of failing duly to pay such a charge, means the person driving the vehicle at the time it was left in the parking place concerned;

' excess charge ' has the same meaning as in section 36 of the 1967 Act;

' fixed penalty ' means a fixed penalty under section 80 of the 1967 Act and ' fixed penalty notice ' means a notice under that section offering a person the opportunity of the discharge of any liability to conviction of an offence by payment of such a fixed penalty;

' prescribed ' means prescribed by regulations made by the Secretary of State contained in a statutory instrument subject to annulment by a resolution of either House of Parliament;

' relevant time ',—

(a) in relation to the alleged offence referred to in section 1 (1) above, means the time at which the offence is alleged to have been committed; and

(b) in relation to an excess charge, as defined above, means the time when the vehicle was left in the parking place concerned, notwithstanding that the period in respect of which the excess charge was incurred did not begin at that time.

(2) Any reference in sections 1 to 4 above to a statutory statement of any description shall be construed in accordance with Schedule 1 to this Act.

(3) For the purposes of the provisions of this Act referred to in subsection (1) above, the owner of a vehicle shall be taken to be the person by whom the vehicle is kept; and for the purpose of determining, in the course of any proceedings brought by virtue of those provisions, who was the owner of a vehicle at any time, it shall be presumed that the owner was the person in whose name the vehicle was at that time registered under the Vehicles (Excise) Act, 1971.

(4) Notwithstanding the presumption in subsection (3) above, it shall be open to the defence in any proceedings to prove that the person in whose name a vehicle was so registered at a particular time was not the person by whom the vehicle was kept at that time and to the prosecution to prove that the vehicle was kept by some other person at that time.

(5) A notice under section 1 (6) or section 2 (6) above may be served on any person—

(a) by delivering it to him or by leaving it at his proper address, or

(b) by sending it to him by post,

and where the person on whom such a notice is to be served is a body corporate it shall be duly served if it is served on the secretary or clerk of that body.

(6) For the purposes of subsection (5) above and of section 26 of the Interpretation Act 1889 (service of documents by post) in its application to that subsection, the proper address of any person on whom such a notice is to be served shall, in the case of the secretary or clerk of a body corporate, be that of the registered or principal office of that body, and in any other case shall be the last known address of the person to be served.

*　　*　　*　　*　　*

SCHEDULE 1

Statutory Statements

Part I

Statutory Statement of Ownership or Hiring

1. For the purposes of sections 1 to 4 of this Act, a statutory statement of ownership is a statement in the prescribed form, signed by the person furnishing it and stating—

(a) whether he was the owner of the vehicle at the relevant time; and

(b) if he was not the owner of the vehicle at the relevant time, whether he ceased to be the owner before, or became the owner after, the relevant time and, if the information is in his possession, the name and address of the person to whom, and the date on which, he disposed of the vehicle or, as the case may be, the name and address of the person from whom, and the date on which he acquired it.

2.—(1) For the purposes of sections 1 to 4 of this Act, a statutory statement of hiring is a statement in the prescribed form, signed by the person furnishing it, being the person by whom a statement of liability was signed, and stating—

    (a) whether at the relevant time the vehicle was let to him under the hiring agreement to which the statement of liability refers; and

    (b) if it was not, the date on which he returned the vehicle to the possession of the vehicle-hire firm concerned.

(2) In sub-paragraph (1) above 'statement of liability', 'hiring agreement' and 'vehicle-hire firm' have the same meanings as in section 3 of this Act.

PART II
STATUTORY STATEMENT OF FACTS

3. For the purposes of sections 1 to 4 of this Act, a statutory statement of facts is a statement which is in the prescribed form and which either—

    (a) states that the person furnishing it was the driver of the vehicle at the relevant time and is signed by him; or

    (b) states that that person was not the driver of the vehicle at the relevant time, states the name and address at the time the statement is furnished of the person who was the driver of the vehicle at the relevant time and is signed both by the person furnishing it and by the person stated to be the driver of the vehicle at the relevant time."

Penalty

As already stated, offences under ss. 1 (7) and 2 (7) are punishable by magistrates only and with a fine of £100 for a first or subsequent conviction. Offences under ss. 1 (8) and 2 (8) are punishable by magistrates only and with a fine of £400 for a first or subsequent offence. There is no power to endorse or disqualify until the offender passes a test.

None of the offences under ss. 1 and 2 are included in the list of recommended penalties published by the Magistrates' Association.

CHAPTER VI

PENALTIES, ENDORSEMENT AND DISQUALIFICATION

Fines and Imprisonment, etc.

FINES may be imposed by magistrates' courts up to the maximum amount set out in the statute or regulation for the particular offence. In fixing the amount of the fine a magistrates' court is required to take into consideration among other things the means of the offender so far as they are known to the court (Magistrates' Courts Act, 1952, s. 31). Notwithstanding the maximum for adults, there is an over-riding maximum of £10 for children (i.e., under fourteen) or £50 for young persons (i.e., under seventeen).

The Magistrates' Association for a number of years has circulated amongst its members suggestions for assessing penalties for the more common road traffic offences. Hitherto the list has been confidential but the latest issue, which was revised to take account of the increase in penalties made by the Road Traffic Act, 1974, has been made public and is reproduced in Appendix III on pp. 878–882. The list is not designed to ensure uniformity of penalty but consistency in the level of sentencing between one magistrates' court and another. The suggestions should not therefore be regarded as a tariff, and any figure suggested is required to be assessed in accordance with the explanation which is printed at the beginning on p. 878. This makes it clear beyond doubt that the court is required to sentence each case on its merits and adjust the penalty appropriately. It should also be noted that many, if not most, magistrates' courts will themselves revise the suggested starting points in accordance with local considerations. The suggestions have been approved in principle by both the Lord Chancellor and the Lord Chief Justice.

Enforcement of payment of fines imposed by magistrates is dealt with by the Magistrates' Courts Act, 1952, Pt. III, and the Criminal Justice Act, 1967, ss. 44 to 50. An offender cannot be committed to prison by a magistrates' court for non-payment of a fine unless a means enquiry has subsequently been held in his presence, but exceptions to this rule are where he is at the time of his conviction serving imprisonment or detention or is at that time sentenced to imprisonment or detention for an offence, or appears to have enough money to pay the fine immediately or appears to be unlikely to stay long enough at a place of abode in Great Britain or Northern Ireland to enable payment to be enforced by other methods. If on the means enquiry the only evidence is that the defendant has never had the money to pay, he cannot be imprisoned for non-payment (*R.* v. *Woking JJ., ex parte Johnstone* [1942] 2 All E.R. 179), but it is otherwise if the magistrates are the same at both hearings and there was evidence of means at the first hearing (*R.* v. *Dunne, ex parte Sinnatt* [1943] 2 All E.R. 222). A defendant may be searched in court and money found used for his fine. Schedule 3 to the Magistrates' Courts Act as amended by the Criminal Justice Act, 1967, indicates the calculation of reduction in imprisonment for part-payment of fines and the periods of imprisonment in default of payment; note the special provisions as to excise penalties; note also that the power of remission at a means enquiry under s. 44 does not apply to excise penalties (see p. 516) nor to orders for payment of back duty.

With regard to imprisonment, any person under twenty-one or an adult who has not previously been sent to prison must not be sent to prison or given a suspended sentence unless no other method of dealing with him is appropriate and, in deciding on appropriate-ness, the court must get and consider information about the circum-stances and shall take into account information relevant to the offender's character and physical and mental condition (Powers of Criminal Courts Act, 1973, ss. 19, 20). Persons who have been committed to prison for contempt and persons who have been given a suspended prison sentence which has not been put into operation have not " previously been sent to prison " within the meaning of s. 20. These provisions do not apply to detention. The obligation of the court under the Act is merely a duty to think twice before passing a prison sentence on a first offender and, provided that the court consider the requirements of the Act, they may justifiably pass a prison sentence if the deliberate nature of the offence and the need to protect the public justify it (*Vassall* v. *Harris* [1964] Crim.L.R. 322; *Morris* v. *The Crown Office* [1970] 1 All E.R. 1079).

Juveniles (under seventeen) can be sentenced to detention in a detention centre, committed to care or ordered to attend at an attendance centre only for offences punishable in adults with imprisonment. Consecutive terms of imprisonment exceeding six months in the aggregate cannot be passed at one time by magistrates on any person for road traffic offences save taking conveyances, for which consecutive sentences not exceeding twelve months in the aggregate may be passed. No person under the age of seventeen may be sentenced to prison by any court, nor may any person aged seventeen or above but under twenty-one be sentenced to prison for a road traffic offence by any court for more than six months, with exceptions for such persons who are convicted of causing death by dangerous driving or who are already in prison or who have previously been to borstal or served a term of six months' imprisonment or more (Criminal Justice Act, 1961, s. 3).

A sentence of detention in a detention centre may be passed by a magistrates' or juvenile court on an offender who has attained the age of fourteen and is under the age of seventeen for an offence carrying imprisonment; the period of detention shall be three months, neither more nor less, even if the maximum term of imprisonment on an adult is less or more than this period. A magistrates' court may pass a sentence of detention for not less than three nor more than six months on a person who has attained the age of seventeen and is under twenty-one provided that the offence carries imprisonment for more than three months, i.e., dangerous and drunken driving, drink " above the limit " offences and taking conveyances; otherwise the sentence is one of three months, e.g., for driving while disqualified. By s. 4 (4) an offender who has already been to borstal or served a term of six or more months' imprisonment shall not be sent to detention unless there are special circumstances and a report from the Prison Department has been received. Section 7 relates to consecutive terms of detention for persons of seventeen and above. A sentence of detention cannot be suspended, but a prison sentence which has been suspended may be ordered to be served in a detention centre if the offender at the time it is put into operation is under twenty-one.

A person who is not legally represented shall not be sentenced to imprisonment, borstal training or detention unless he has been offered and he has refused legal aid or the court have refused his application on the grounds that his means were such that he did not require legal aid (Powers of Criminal Courts Act, 1973, s. 21).

A person convicted of an offence carrying imprisonment may, instead of being imprisoned, be detained for not more than four days in police cells approved by the Home Secretary (Magistrates' Courts Act, 1952, s. 109) or detained in the court-house or at any police station up to eight p.m. on the day of the order (*ibid.*, s. 110).

Suspended Sentences

Sentences of imprisonment for all the offences dealt with in this book of two years or less may be suspended for a minimum period of one year and a maximum of two years (Powers of Criminal Courts Act, 1973, s. 22 (1)). A court shall not impose a suspended sentence unless the court are of the opinion that a sentence of immediate imprisonment would have been appropriate in the absence of any power to suspend it (s. 22 (2)). A suspended sentence should not be passed if a probation order for another offence is made on the same occasion, nor should one be passed on the same occasion as one of immediate imprisonment is passed for another offence, nor should the period of a suspended sentence be made consecutive to a term which the accused is already serving. Where, however, the suspended sentence for a single offence is for more than six months, the court may make a suspended sentence supervision order for a period not exceeding the period for which the sentence of imprisonment is suspended (Powers of Criminal Courts Act, 1973, s. 26). If the offender is convicted of an offence in Great Britain punishable with imprisonment during the operational period of his suspended sentence, it must be put into effect for the full term unless it would be unjust to do so in view of all the circumstances which have arisen since the suspended sentence was passed including the facts of the subsequent offence in which case the court may pass a shorter term than that originally suspended or extend the operational period or make no order (s. 23). If the offence is punishable by fine *or* imprisonment the punishment must be either a fine or sentence of imprisonment, but where the offence is punishable by fine or imprisonment or both, both may be imposed. This applies also in the case of a suspended sentence of imprisonment and fine (*R.* v. *Leigh* (1969), 113 S.J. 897). (Note, however, that the offences of dangerous and drunken driving and driving with blood/alcohol above the limit are all punishable with a fine *or* with imprisonment, not both.)

Magistrates have power to mitigate a pecuniary penalty for any road traffic offence, including excise licence ones, however many the previous convictions (Magistrates' Courts Act, 1952, s. 27), unless the statute otherwise provides.

As to the fixed penalty procedure for certain offences under s. 80 of the Road Traffic Regulation Act, 1967, see that section, as amended by s. 131 of the Transport Act, 1968, and s. 203 of the Road Traffic Act, 1972, and the Fixed Penalty (Procedure) (No. 2) Regulations, 1974 (S.I. 1974, No. 1475) (see also, where a fixed penalty is not paid, " Vehicle Owner Liability ", pp. 584–593).

When a defendant is conditionally discharged under the Powers of Criminal Courts Act, 1973, s. 7, no condition can legally be imposed other than that he commits no further offence within the specified period of up to three years.

Where a penalty in excess of the permitted maximum is imposed, the High Court need not quash the penalty altogether but may substitute the proper penalty (Administration of Justice Act, 1960, s. 16).

Deferment of Sentence

Section 1 of the Powers of Criminal Courts Act, 1973, allows a court to defer sentence for a period of up to six months for the purpose of enabling the court in determining the sentence to have regard to the defendant's conduct during the period of deferment, including the making of reparation for his offence. The court can only defer sentence if the defendant consents (s. 1 (3)) (the consent must be obtained from the defendant personally (*R*. v. *Gilbey, infra*)); moreover the court must be satisfied, having regard to the nature of the offence and the character and circumstances of the offender, that it would be in the interests of justice to defer sentence. It would not seem normally appropriate for a court to defer sentence of an obligatorily disqualifiable offence, because the main penalty, that of disqualification, could not be altered after any deferment; the disqualification is mandatory unless " special reasons " exist and such special reasons are limited to the offence and cannot include " the character and circumstances of the defendant " or " his conduct during the period of deferment " (see s. 1).

Once sentence has been deferred, justices no longer have the power to commit the defendant to the Crown Court for sentence (*R*. v. *Gilbey* [1975] Crim.L.R. 352; a substituted custodial sentence is not appropriate after deferment where the report on the conduct and circumstances of the defendant during the period of deferment was not unfavourable (*ibid.*).

It is bad practice and contrary to the statute to impose an order of disqualification and then defer sentence (*R*. v. *Fairhead* [1975] Crim.L.R. 351).

Compensation

Compensation (of up to £400 by a magistrates' court, unlimited for a Crown Court) may be ordered under s. 35 of the Powers of Criminal Courts Act, 1973, to be paid by any person convicted of an offence. Compensation is not limited to any damage which has been incurred but includes compensation for any personal injury, loss or damage resulting from the offence for which the offender was convicted or any other offence taken into consideration by the court. In deciding how much compensation to award, the court are required to have regard to the defendant's means. No application for compensation need be made by the loser to the court; the court may award compensation on its own motion. In the case of an offence under the Theft Act, 1968, where the property in question is recovered, any damage which occurred while it was out of the owner's possession shall be treated as having resulted from the offence, howsoever and by whomsoever the damage was caused (s. 35 (2)).

No compensation may be ordered in respect of loss suffered by the dependants of a person in consequence of his death, nor may compensation be ordered in respect of " injury, loss or damage due to an accident arising out of the presence of a motor vehicle on a road " (s. 35 (3)). Compensation may be awarded, notwithstanding s. 35 (3), where the offence is under the Theft Act. The effect is that if a vehicle has been taken without the owner's consent or has been stolen, the thief or person convicted under s. 12 may be ordered to pay compensation in respect of any damage to the owner's vehicle, including damage that has occurred in respect of a road accident before the vehicle was recovered.

Although compensation can legally be awarded to the Department of the Environment in respect of excise offences, it is submitted that courts should not use their discretionary power to award compensation under s. 1 for such regulatory offences (see pp. 505–506).

Compensation can be ordered to be paid jointly and severally by co-defendants, but in view of the difficulties which ensue as to accountability and enforcement, such an order should not be made (*R.* v. *Grundy* [1974] 1 All E.R. 292). Nor should compensation be ordered unless the claim is simple and straightforward (*R.* v. *Daly* [1974] 1 All E.R. 290), nor if the amount ordered would take a number of years to repay (*ibid.*). Compensation should not be ordered in respect of costs for a parallel civil claim (*Hammertons Cars, Ltd.* v. *Redbridge L.B.C.* [1974] Crim.L.R. 241).

The effect of a compensation order on a subsequent award in civil proceedings is dealt with in s. 38. A compensation order made by magistrates is suspended until the time has elapsed for notice of appeal (twenty-one days) and if notice of appeal is given until the appeal is determined (s. 36 (1)).

Magistrates may not order compensation on committing a person to the Crown Court for sentence (*R.* v. *Blackpool JJ.*, *ex parte Charlson* [1972] 3 All E.R. 854; *R.* v. *Brogan* (1975), *The Times*, 6th February).

Costs

Costs can be awarded against the defendant, when he has been found guilty, or against the prosecutor, when the case has been dismissed, on conclusion of a trial in a magistrates' court (Costs in Criminal Cases Act, 1973, s. 2). The amount must be specified by the court and, where the defendant is under seventeen, the amount of costs awarded against him must not exceed the amount of the fine (*ibid.*). By s. 1, examining justices who discharge a defendant instead of committing him for trial may give him his costs out of central funds but may award costs against the prosecutor himself, on refusal to commit for trial, only if of opinion that the charge was not made in good faith (s. 2 (4)). The prosecutor may appeal if ordered to pay more than £25 under s. 2 (4) (s. 2 (5)). A magistrates' court dealing summarily with an indictable offence (e.g., taking a motor vehicle) may order payment of the prosecution's costs out of central funds and should normally do so in the absence of a special reason to the contrary. A defendant may be ordered to pay the whole or part of the prosecution's costs and a certificate for payment of the costs may be granted either for the balance or, if the defendant is given time to pay them, pending payment by the defendant. Witnesses' costs as ascertained by the justices' clerk will also be paid out of central funds, but there is no power to order payment of witnesses' costs out of central funds in respect of summary cases. In summary cases, costs may only be ordered to be paid by a convicted defendant to the prosecutor or by the prosecutor to an acquitted defendant (s. 2), although if an interpreter is needed because of the defendant's lack of knowledge of English, the interpreter's costs must be paid out of central funds even if the defendant is convicted (Administration of Justice Act, 1973, s. 17).

Costs may be ordered to be paid by the prosecutor to a defendant where proceedings are withdrawn (s. 12) and the prosecutor has no right of appeal against an order under s. 12 (*R.* v. *The Crown Court at Lewes, ex parte Rogers* [1974] 1 All E.R. 589). Where an order is made for costs out of central funds, the amount should be ascertained out of court by the justices' clerk (*R.* v. *Chertsey JJ.* [1974] 1 All E.R. 156) and, it is submitted, once a court has decided to make an award of costs, there is no further discretion to award part of the costs only (see *R.* v. *Bow Street Magistrate, ex parte Palmer* (1969), 113 S.J. 735). A defendant acquitted in respect of an indictable offence tried summarily should normally be entitled to have his costs paid out of central funds unless (*a*) the prosecution has acted spitefully or without reasonable cause (in which case the prosecution should be ordered to pay the defendant's costs); (*b*) the defendant's own conduct has misled the prosecution into thinking the case was stronger than it really was; (*c*) there is ample evidence to secure a conviction but the defendant is entitled to be acquitted because of a procedural irregularity; or (*d*) the defendant is convicted on one charge and acquitted on another. In (*b*) and (*c*) above, the defendant should pay his own costs and in (*d*) the court should make such order as is just, depending on the relative importance of the two charges and the defendant's conduct generally (Practice Note [1973] 2 All E.R. 592). In *R.* v. *Burt* [1960] 1 All E.R. 424, an award of two guineas to the prosecution on conviction was upheld, although there had been no legal representation and a constable, who lost no pay, was the witness and prosecutor. In *Palastanga* v. *Salmon* [1962] Crim.L.R. 334, it was said, *obiter*, that a party who brings about an adjourned hearing for a technical point should pay the costs, but it is submitted that this can only be ordered if he loses the case, since s. 2 contains no provision for awarding costs against a successful party.

The power to award costs against a defendant is restricted to the costs of his prosecution and conviction; he cannot be ordered to pay costs relating to the trial of his co-accused (*R.* v. *Gould* [1965] Crim.L.R. 547).

Any criminal court may order a legally aided defendant to pay all or part of the prosecutor's costs, if convicted. A legally aided defendant may be ordered either to pay the whole of the cost of his legal aid or to make a contribution to the cost in accordance with his means, whether or not he is convicted of the offence.

Save where a point of law allowing appeal to the High Court arises or s. 2 (5) (*supra*) applies, there is no appeal against a magistrates' order for costs alone by either party but, in view of the power of the Crown Court to vary a sentence on appeal by a defendant, an appeal against a sentence, not being an order for probation or conditional discharge, might result in the costs ordered being reduced (Magistrates' Courts Act, 1952, s. 83). See pp. 698 and 700 as to costs on appeal.

Costs no longer have to be contained in the particulars of a conviction endorsed on a person's licence (Magistrates' Courts Rules, 1968, r. 28, as amended).

Endorsement and Disqualification Summarised

It is worth summarising the principles of endorsement and disqualification formerly contained in the Act of 1962 before discussing their detailed application. A lack of knowledge or awareness of these basic rules has led many courts into making errors which could otherwise have been avoided. The principles or rules may be summarised as follows:—

(1) Unless an offence is one which is contained in Sched. 4 to the Act of 1972 and shown thereby to involve " obligatory endorsement ", a court has no power to order endorsement or disqualification (other than the Crown Court where a vehicle has been used for criminal purposes: see p. 641).

(2) All offences involving obligatory endorsement either involve obligatory or discretionary disqualification.

(3) Unless the order is suspended pending appeal, all orders

of disqualification (except for " totting up "), whether obligatory or discretionary, *must* commence from the moment the order of disqualification is imposed. Thus, orders of disqualification cannot be made to run consecutively unless they are for " totting up ".

(4) On the other hand if the order is for " totting up " the disqualification *must* run consecutively to any other order of disqualification whether imposed on that or any other occasion. " Totting up " disqualification orders cannot therefore be ordered to run concurrently with each other or any other order of disqualification.

(5) The court may order the motorist to be disqualified until he takes a test for any offence involving obligatory endorsement (see p. 660).

(6) Where the offence involves obligatory endorsement or obligatory disqualification the court may only refrain from endorsing or disqualifying if " special reasons " can be found. (There is a further exception to this rule in respect of certain Construction and Use Regulations offences: see p. 434.)

(7) If a person is convicted and on two separate occasions during the three years prior to the commission of the present offence or offences his licence has been endorsed, he must, unless " mitigating circumstances " are found, be disqualified for at least six months for *each* of the endorsable offences for which he is convicted on the third occasion. (Thus if on the third occasion he has three endorsable offences he must, in the absence of mitigating circumstances, be disqualified for six months on each and the disqualifications must run consecutively, making a total of eighteen months: see p. 633.)

The sole exception to these rules is an order of disqualification imposed by the Crown Court under s. 44 of the Powers of Criminal Courts Act, 1973, in respect of a vehicle used for criminal purposes (see p. 641). Where a person is disqualified under this provision there is no power to endorse the person's licence. For this reason the conviction of the offence for which disqualification was ordered under this provision does not count as a conviction for " totting up " under s. 93.

Endorsement

The Road Traffic Act, 1972, s. 101 (formerly s. 7 of the 1962 Act) contains the law relating to endorsement of driving licences. Endorsement is now obligatory for certain offences, unless there are special reasons; the offences are those against which the word " obligatory " is shown in column 6 of Pt. I of Sched. 4 to the 1972 Act together with those offences listed in Pts. II and III of the same

Schedule. Appropriate extracts from the Schedule are set out on p. 617 and onwards.

Section 101 of the Road Traffic Act, 1972, reads:—

" (1) Subject to subsection (2) below, where a person is convicted of an offence—

(a) under a provision of this Act specified in column 1 of Part I of Schedule 4 to this Act in relation to which there appears in column 6 of that Part the word ' obligatory ' or the word ' obligatory ' qualified by conditions relating to the offence; and

(b) where the said word ' obligatory ' is so qualified, the conditions are satisfied in the case of the offence of which he is convicted;

or where a person is convicted of an offence specified in Part II or Part III of that Schedule (any such offence being in this section referred to as an ' offence involving obligatory endorsement '), the court shall order that particulars of the conviction, and, if the court orders him to be disqualified, particulars of the disqualification, shall be endorsed on any licence held by him; and particulars of any conviction or disqualification so endorsed may be produced as prima facie evidence of the conviction or disqualification.

(2) If the court does not order the said person to be disqualified, the court need not order particulars of the conviction to be endorsed as aforesaid if for special reasons it thinks fit not to do so.

(3) An order that the particulars of a conviction or of a disqualification to which the convicted person has become subject are to be endorsed on any licence held by him shall, whether he is at the time the holder of a licence or not, operate as an order that any licence he may then hold or may subsequently obtain shall be so endorsed until he becomes entitled under subsection (7) below to have a licence issued to him free from the particulars.

(4) A person who is prosecuted for an offence involving obligatory endorsement and who is the holder of a licence, shall either—

(a) cause it to be delivered to the clerk of the court not later than the day before the date appointed for the hearing, or

(b) post it, at such a time that in the ordinary course of post it would be delivered not later than that day, in a letter duly addressed to the clerk and either registered or sent by the recorded delivery service, or

(c) have it with him at the hearing;

and if he is convicted of the offence [the court shall, before making any order under subsection (1) above, require the licence to be produced to it]; and if the offender has not posted the licence or caused it to be delivered as aforesaid and does not produce it as required then, unless he satisfies the court that he has applied for a new licence and has not received it, he shall be guilty of an offence and the licence shall be suspended from the time when its production was required until it is produced to the court and shall, while suspended, be of no effect.

[(4A) Where a person is convicted of an offence involving obligatory endorsement and his licence is produced to the court, then in determining what order to make in pursuance of the conviction the court may take into consideration particulars of any previous conviction or disqualification endorsed on the licence.]

R T O—Z

(5) On the issue of a new licence to a person any particulars ordered to be endorsed on any licence held by him shall be entered on the licence unless he has become entitled under subsection (7) below to have a licence issued to him free from those particulars.

(6) If a person whose licence has been ordered to be endorsed with any particulars and who has not previously become entitled under subsection (7) below to have a licence issued to him free from those particulars applies for or obtains a licence without giving particulars of the order, he shall be guilty of an offence and any licence so obtained shall be of no effect.

(7) Where an order has been made in respect of a person under this section or any previous enactment requiring any licence held by him to be endorsed with any particulars, he shall be entitled [either] on applying for the grant of a licence in pursuance of section 88 (1) (*a*) of this Act and satisfying the other requirements of that subsection [or, subject to the payment of the prescribed fee and the surrender of any subsisting licence, on an application at any time] to have issued to him a new licence free from the particulars, if the application is made not less than three years after the date of the conviction in consequence of which the order was made or, if it was a conviction of an offence under any of the following provisions of this Act, namely section 5 (1), 6 (1) or 9 (3) (where the latter was an offence involving obligatory disqualification), not less than ten years after that conviction.

[(8) Nothing in the provisions of sections 15 (5) and 31 (1) of the Summary Jurisdiction (Scotland) Act 1954 (complaint and previous complaint and previous convictions) shall affect the power of the court under subsection (4A) of this section to take into consideration a previous conviction or disqualification endorsed on the licence of the accused.] "

The words in square brackets in subss. (4) and (7) together with subss. (4A) and (8) above were inserted by the Road Traffic Act, 1974.

Only the offences shown as involving obligatory endorsement in column 6 of Pt. I together with the offences in Pts. II and III of Sched. 4 to the 1972 Act (see p. 617) carry endorsement, and endorsement may not be ordered for any other offences. Those carrying endorsement are manslaughter or, in Scotland, culpable homicide, causing death by dangerous driving, driving or attempted driving or being in charge of a motor vehicle when unfit to drive through drink or drugs or when having in the blood alcohol above the prescribed limit or refusing to give a sample of blood or urine contrary to s. 9 of the Act of 1972, organising or taking part in races on the highway, driving whilst disqualified, dangerous driving, careless driving, exceeding a speed limit, driving when under age, carrying a pillion-passenger otherwise than astride and on a proper seat, disobeying police signals or specified traffic signs under s. 22, leaving a motor vehicle in a dangerous position, certain offences on motorways, pedestrian crossing offences, disobeying school crossing patrols, driving in breach of a street playground order, contravention of Construction and Use Regulations by dangerous parts and accessories or load (p. 433), excessive passengers, defective brakes, steering and tyres or dangerously unsuitable use (see p. 433), not stopping after an accident or not giving particulars or reporting it, driving without a driving licence where none could be granted or not complying with the conditions of a provisional licence, if the driver is only entitled to a provisional licence (see p. 481), using or causing or permitting use without third-party insurance, driving with uncorrected defective eyesight or refusing to submit to a test for it (1972 Act, s. 91), failing to comply with a provisional licence condition, taking or attempting to take a conveyance, being a motor vehicle, or driving or being carried in one knowing it to have been taken without authority (Theft Act, 1968, s. 12), stealing or attempting to steal a motor vehicle under the Theft Act and going equipped for stealing or taking motor vehicles (*ibid.*, s. 25). All such offences must have been committed in respect of a motor vehicle to allow endorsement.

Endorsement should, it is submitted, be ordered when an offender is returned to borstal under the Criminal Justice Act, 1961, s. 12.

The phrasing of s. 101 is such that " any " licence of which the defendant is the holder is required to be endorsed. The court is required to make such an order (in the absence of " special reasons ") whether or not the defendant actually has a licence. A " licence " in the context of s. 101 means a licence issued under Pt. III of the Road Traffic Act, 1972 (s. 110), and a court cannot therefore actually endorse particulars of a conviction on an international driving permit, a foreign licence, a driving permit issued under the Visiting Forces Act, 1952, or a Heavy Goods Vehicle Licence. Nevertheless holders of these driving permits or licences are liable to be disqualified under " totting up " by virtue of s. 93 (3), as this depends, not on whether a licence actually has had endorsed on it particulars of the conviction, but simply on whether orders of endorsement have been made under s. 101. A Northern Ireland driving licence cannot be endorsed by a court in England or Wales.

It used to be thought that a fine or imprisonment or other order should always accompany endorsement. However, in *Bell* v. *Ingham* [1968] 2 All E.R. 333 it was said *obiter* that endorsement can truly be described as " part of the penalty ". This statement, taken with *R.* v. *Bignell,* on p. 635 (that there need be no penalty when disqualification is ordered), suggests that endorsement on its own may be ordered as the sole penalty. While a court on convicting should normally proceed to judgment, it is not clear whether there is precise authority that the " judgment " must include a custodial sentence or a fine or probation or absolute or conditional discharge; convictions followed by recognisances only (which the relevant statutes allowed) were held to be valid in *R.* v. *Miles* (1890), 24 Q.B.D. 423, and *R.* v. *Blaby* [1894] 2 Q.B. 170. It is submitted, however, that endorsement should not be ordered on its own as the sole penalty. As was said in *Bell* v. *Ingham, supra,* it is " part of " the penalty; the court in the absence of special reasons is obliged to order endorsement if it is an obligatorily endorsable offence. Moreover, by r. 28 of the Magistrates' Courts Rules, 1968, particulars of the sentence of the court are required to be included, and it is difficult to regard as a sentence an order under s. 101 that particulars of the conviction, which must include the sentence, are to be endorsed on the licence. It is submitted, to avoid these problems and such circular arguments, that the court should order an absolute discharge where the court considers an endorsement by itself insufficient punishment.

Where a magistrates' court orders endorsement, the particulars to be endorsed shall include the name of the petty sessions area for which the court is acting, the date of the conviction and the date on which sentence is passed (if different), particulars of the offence and its date and particulars of the sentence (including any disqualification) but no longer any order for costs (Magistrates' Courts Rules, 1968, r. 28, as amended). Section 105 (5) of the 1972 Act enables the Secretary of State to determine where a court shall send a notice of endorsement. The form and content of the notice may be similarly determined by the Secretary of State. The court is required to send such a notice even if the defendant does not have a licence, or is driving on an international driving licence or foreign driving permit.

Endorsement Code

The Driving Licences and Vehicle Licences Centre (DVLC) at Swansea is now issuing a new type of computer-based driving licence. These licences will, by November, 1976, replace the existing licences issued by local taxation authorities on behalf of the Secretary of State. Clerks to justices are required to notify the centre at Swansea of all particulars of endorsement in a manner and in the form required by the Secretary of State. To enable the particulars of the conviction to be easily recorded in the computer, particulars of the offence, sentence and disqualification are required to be notified in code form to the computer centre. Similarly particulars of the conviction are endorsed on the new type licences in the same code form. The endorsement code is set out in Appendix II on pp. 874–877.

Attempts

It is submitted that there is no power to endorse for any attempt to commit an endorsable offence save (1) attempting to drive (*a*) when unfit through drink or drug or (*b*) with more than the permitted amount of alcohol in the blood or (*c*) together with refusal of a blood or urine test under s. 9 (3) of the 1972 Act, and (2) attempting to steal or take without authority a motor vehicle; in these excepted cases the statute gives express power to endorse for the attempt. Otherwise, for attempting to drive while disqualified or when under age or attempting to commit any other offence specified in Pts. I, II and III of Sched. 4 to the Road Traffic Act, 1972 (see p. 617), there is no power to endorse (*Bell* v. *Ingham* [1968] 2 All E.R. 333). For a case in which a court disqualified a person convicted of an attempt to take and drive away a motor vehicle prior to s. 12 of the Theft Act, 1968, see *R.* v. *Cockermouth JJ.* [1971] Crim.L.R. 287, where an order of certiorari was granted to quash the original order of disqualification and also another order of disqualification which was made as a result of his conviction for driving during the first period of disqualification.

Where an attempt is endorsable, the endorsement code for the substantive offence is used.

Production of Driving Licence

Section 101 (4) has been amended by the Road Traffic Act, 1974 (paras. 10 (1) and (4) of Sched. 3; the amendments are shown in square brackets on p. 603) to make clear beyond doubt the power of the courts to call for the licence following conviction of an obligatorily disqualifiable offence in order to discover what previous convictions are endorsed on the licence. The position, therefore, is that a person prosecuted for an offence involving obligatory endorsement must deliver his driving licence to the court or send it by registered or recorded delivery post or produce it at the hearing. If he is not convicted of the offence, he commits no offence if he has not sent or produced his licence to the court. If he is convicted of the offence, the court must require the licence to be produced to it. Under the former law in the repealed s. 111 (5) of the 1960 Act, the court could, for offences not involving compulsory endorsement, order production of the licence within five days or more; s. 101 (formerly s. 7 of the 1962 Act), however, appears to allow no suspension of the requirement for production of the licence and, if it has not been sent or is not produced, it is suspended from the time of the making of the order for production. The new subs. (4A) in England and Wales and the new subs. (8)

in Scotland make it clear beyond any doubt that the court is entitled to look at any endorsement on the licence and take it into account in determining sentence. In *Dyson* v. *Ellison* [1975] Crim.L.R. 48 (a case on s. 101 before its amendment by the Act of 1974) it was held that the court should call for the licence after conviction in order to look at the licence to see if any convictions were endorsed upon it. A court is entitled to adjourn after conviction under s. 14 (3) of the Magistrates' Courts Act, 1952, and may quite properly do so for the production of the licence. Where a court does so adjourn it must not be for a period of longer than four weeks at a time (*R.* v. *Talgarth JJ., ex parte Bithell* [1974] R.T.R. 546). Moreover s. 14 (3) requires that the court shall not have sentenced or dealt with the defendant on the first occasion; where the court fined the defendant in his absence and then adjourned under s. 14 (3) and disqualified him on the adjourned hearing, the disqualification was set aside on the ground that the magistrates had acted in excess of their jurisdiction (*ibid.*). If a court is minded to adjourn, it must adjourn the whole question of sentencing and disposal and deal with the whole of the sentencing process at the adjourned hearing (*ibid.*).

On a conviction for an endorsable offence being announced, the court should look at the defendant's licence, if it has been sent to the clerk or the defendant voluntarily produces it, before deciding whether to endorse and disqualify; if the defendant is present and will not produce it voluntarily, an order for production must be pronounced and then an offence arises under s. 101 (4) if it is not produced. If the defendant has not got it with him or is not there and has not sent it, the court may adjourn so that it may be inspected at the adjourned hearing to see if there are previous convictions; in his absence and on non-production, the court should order production and adjourn for not more than four weeks. During this period the police may make enquiries of the Driving Licence Computer Centre at Swansea and may prove previous endorsements under s. 182 of the Act (see pp. 107–109).

The above provisions as to production of a driving licence to the court appear to apply to Northern Irish driving licences (Road Traffic Act, 1972, s. 111 (1)), but not to international or visiting forces' driving permits (Motor Vehicles (International Circulation) Order, 1957, Sched. 3), unless disqualification is ordered.

If the court has not received the offender's driving licence when the order for endorsement is made, he is liable by s. 101 (4) to a fine of £100 and his driving licence is suspended and of no effect until it is produced to the court. An offender who drives a motor vehicle on a road after conviction and prior to the production of the licence appears to offend against s. 84 of the 1972 Act (driving without a licence) in addition to being liable to a fine under s. 101 (4). In any prosecution for disobedience to s. 101 (4) or under s. 84 (as a result of the suspension of the licence for non-production to the court), presumably the prosecution must prove that the defendant was aware that he had been summoned for the offence. In proving that the defendant had had the summons, the Interpretation Act, 1889, s. 26, provides that a properly addressed letter is deemed to have been received, unless the contrary is proved, when it would be delivered in the ordinary course of post, but the late author of this book suggested that posting or personal service should be proved by evidence and not by the certificate endorsed on the back of the duplicate summons. It is submitted that posting may be proved by the certificate endorsed on the duplicate summons. Rule 55 (2) of the Magistrates' Courts Rules, 1968, specifically allows proof of the posting, etc., by such a certificate " in any proceedings before a magistrates' court ". Must the prosecution prove that the defendant had been informed that his licence was required for production? Although most summonses refer to his duty to produce it, the duty does not arise until he is convicted and an order for its production is made, and the prosecutor would be wise to prove that notice to produce it after conviction was duly given to the defendant, though, as disqualification was deemed effective as soon as it was ordered by the court (*Taylor* v. *Kenyon* [1952] 2 All E.R. 726), the making of the order for production alone might suffice where the defendant claimed never to have been told of it. The duty to produce falls on " the holder of a licence " (see s. 101 (4)); if he does not hold one or his licence expired before the conviction without prior production, seemingly he commits no offence of non-production.

If the offender is not at the time of his conviction the holder of a driving licence (*semble*, a current one), he must by s. 101 (6) disclose particulars of the endorsement ordered when he next applies for the grant or renewal of his licence. Further, a licence granted or renewed without such disclosure is of no effect and a person who drives on a licence so obtained offends against s. 84 (driving without a licence) and, if he had never previously held a licence, he may not be covered by a policy of insurance in breach of s. 143. If a defendant charged under s. 101 (6) or s. 84 as mentioned above claims he never received the summons for the original endorsable offence, he may not be guilty but, if he had had the summons but particulars of the order for endorsement had not been sent to him, it may be that the non-sending would not be a defence (*cf. Taylor* v. *Kenyon* [1952] 2 All E.R. 726).

The court cannot require the production of a driving licence to inspect it for endorsements if the offender is convicted of an offence which does not carry endorsement.

Requirement to Endorse

Section 101 (1) of the 1972 Act requires a court to order the defendant's driving licence to be endorsed with particulars of the conviction whenever he is convicted of an offence carrying obligatory endorsement and with particulars of the disqualification also if he is ordered to be disqualified from driving as well, unless:—

(1) There are special reasons justifying non-endorsement (see Chapter VII); or

(2) The Mental Health Act, 1959, s. 60 (2), or the Mental Health (Scotland) Act, 1960, s. 55 (3), applies (see p. 623).

(3) The offence was under reg. 90 (1), (2) or (3) of the Construction and Use Regulations or a regulation as to brakes, steering or tyres and the court finds that he did not know and had no reasonable cause to suspect that the facts were such that an offence would be committed (see p. 434).

Any special reasons under (1) above for not endorsing or disqualifying should be stated in open court and, in the case of a magistrates' court, entered on the court register (Road Traffic Act, 1972, s. 105 (1)); the finding is valid, however, if they are not stated aloud (*Brown* v. *Dyerson* on p. 668).

If the defendant is put on probation or discharged absolutely or conditionally in England or Wales, his licence must be endorsed unless there are special reasons (1972 Act, s. 102 (1), replacing Criminal Justice Act, 1967, s. 51 (1)). In Scotland a court of summary jurisdiction does not proceed to " conviction " on making an order for probation or absolute discharge, so there cannot be an endorsement, it seems (Criminal Justice (Scotland) Act, 1949, ss. 1 and 2).

It is only these offences involving " obligatory " endorsement and listed in Sched. 4 to the Act for which the court is required to endorse. If the offence is not shown in Sched. 4 as involving obligatory endorsement the court has no power to endorse.

Committal for Sentence

Where a person has been committed for sentence to the Crown Court for an offence pursuant to the Vagrancy Act, 1824, the Powers of Criminal Courts Act, 1973, s. 8 (6) (commission of further offence during probation or conditional discharge), the Magistrates' Courts Act, 1952, ss. 28 and 29 (see p. 636), the Powers of

Criminal Courts Act, 1973, s. 24 (2) (putting into effect suspended sentences) or the Criminal Justice Act, 1967, s. 62 (6) (offences on parole), as respectively extended by s. 56 of the Criminal Justice Act, 1967, the magistrates should not endorse his licence in respect of any endorsable offence, but the duty to endorse falls on the court to which he is committed for sentence (s. 56 (5) and (6)). The higher court must order endorsement even when he is sent to borstal (s. 56 (6)).

Where magistrates, on committal for sentence, have disqualified a defendant from driving for the period between the date of committal and the date on which the Crown Court deal with him under s. 103 (1) of the 1972 Act, his licence shall not be endorsed with that disqualification (s. 103 (3)). Such temporary disqualification also does not count as one of the previous convictions for totting up, as s. 93 (3) of the 1972 Act applies to endorsed convictions. On making an interim disqualification under s. 103 (1), the magistrates should order him to produce to them his British or Northern Irish driving licence (under penalty of £100) and the magistrates' clerk then sends it to the clerk of the higher court (s. 103 (2)). The magistrates should not endorse his licence on making an interim disqualification under s. 103 (1) but should send notice of the interim disqualification to the Department of the Environment; if it is a Northern Irish licence, such particulars should also go to the Department of the Environment (s. 103 (3)). If the higher court does not disqualify him, notice of their decision should be sent to the Department. By s. 103 (4), where no interim disqualification is ordered by the committing magistrates, s. 101 (1) and (4) of the 1972 Act (see above) apply to the defendant; as he will usually be in prison, other means of getting his licence will in fact be required.

Breach of Probation, etc.

It is submitted that, where an offender is brought back for breach of probation or for committing a further offence during a period of probation or conditional discharge under the Powers of Criminal Courts Act, 1973, s. 6 or s. 8, and endorsement was not ordered originally, it may be ordered on the second appearance (see p. 646). The court may still endorse at its discretion even if there were special reasons originally.

Deferment of Sentence

Particularly having regard to the amendment of s. 101 of the Road Traffic Act, 1972, by the Road Traffic Act, 1974, it is submitted that where sentence is deferred in respect of an obligatorily endorsable offence, the endorsement can only be ordered when the sentence is imposed following the deferment; it should not be ordered at the time of conviction; any order of endorsement must include particulars of the sentence as well as particulars of conviction. An order of deferment is not a sentence, it is an order that sentence be deferred. For this reason, if sentence is deferred in respect of a second offence which would otherwise be relevant under s. 93 (3) for " totting up " when the defendant commits a third offence, s. 93 (3) will not operate if the third offence was committed during the period of deferment, since the defendant will not have had his licence endorsed in respect of the second offence. The effect, therefore, is that liability under s. 93 (3) for " totting up " on the commission of a third offence is avoided until the defendant is sentenced in respect of a second offence for which sentence was deferred.

Omission to Order Endorsement

If the chairman omits to say " licence endorsed " on a conviction where there are no special reasons, the prosecutor can seek mandamus or a certiorari from the High Court to require endorsement. See p. 92, *supra*, suggesting that a decision once announced cannot be altered, but a distinction should be drawn between altering a decision after it has been pronounced and omitting to pronounce an order which the court is under a duty to make. Moreover if the magistrates' court does not make an order of endorsement it is required to state its reasons for not doing so in open court (s. 105 (1)). If the omission is caused by a slip of the tongue there can be no doubt, it is submitted, that the court may repair the omission (see for example *R. v. Newcastle-upon-Tyne JJ., ex parte Swales* [1972] R.T.R. 57). Section 41 (1) of the Criminal Justice Act, 1972, allows a magistrates' court to vary a sentence or other order made by it when dealing with an offender. This power seems sufficiently wide to include the power to order endorsement which was originally omitted and which the court were obliged to make by virtue of s. 101. An order under s. 41 (1) must, however, be made within fourteen days beginning with the day on which the sentence was imposed or order made and must be made by a court constituted in the same manner as the original court (or where the court consisted of three or more justices by a majority of those justices) (s. 41 (3)).

Endorsement as Evidence

Particulars of any conviction or disqualification endorsed on a driving licence may be produced as *prima facie* evidence of the conviction or disqualification (s. 101 (1)). Endorsement of a licence is especially important now as it is only convictions ordered to be endorsed that count as the "qualifying" ones leading to compulsory disqualification for six months under s. 93 (3) (see p. 616). A court after conviction are bound to require its production (see s. 101 (4), as amended, on p. 603) and are entitled to take into consideration particulars of any convictions endorsed upon it (see s. 101 (4A), on p. 603).

Notification of Endorsement

By s. 105 (2) of the 1972 Act, the court ordering endorsement must notify the Secretary of State or licensing authority who issued the licence. From 1st March, 1973, licences began to be issued not by local authorities but by the Secretary of State from his computerised central licensing department at Swansea. Local authority licences will gradually be replaced by such "centralised" driving licences until November, 1976, when the process will be complete. During this interim period the notification will be either to the local authority or to Swansea depending on the type of licence issued. The notification to the central licensing department is in code form and the endorsement of the new type licences issued from Swansea is in the same code (see p. 606, and for the endorsement code see Appendix II on p. 878). If disqualification is ordered, the court retains the driving licence and sends it to the licensing authority. See p. 615 as to driving licences issued in Northern Ireland or abroad. Courts are also required to notify licensing authorities of the motorist's sex and date of birth, in addition to the other particulars prescribed. The court when making an order of endorsement is required to order the defendant to state in writing his sex and date of birth, if not already known. If a person knowingly fails to comply with such an order he is guilty of a summary offence punishable with a fine not exceeding £50 (s. 104 (4)). Where a person has stated his date of birth to a court, the Secretary of State can require him to produce evidence to verify that date of birth, and where he has changed his name, his name at the date of his birth. Non-compliance with the Minister's order is similarly punishable (s. 104 (5)). (It may be remarked that the subsection places adopted persons in a difficulty. An adopted person usually knows only the names given to him on adoption. He cannot find out his original name without obtaining an order of the court. Presumably the Secretary of State would be content with production of the adoption certificate.)

Aiders and Abettors

A person convicted of aiding, abetting, counselling and procuring an offence is by the Magistrates' Courts Act, 1952, s. 35, "guilty of the like offence " and is presumably liable to the same penalties as the principal offender. Section 35 does not relate to persons specifically charged with "incitement". It is suggested that an aider and abettor's licence should be endorsed in the same circumstances as those under which the principal offender's licence should be (*cf. Bradley* v. *McGivern* [1963] N.I. 11), though it is arguable that s. 101, by its reference to the "person convicted" of the relevant offence, means only the principal offender and that this view gains support from the specific provision as to disqualification of aiders and abettors in s. 93 (6), whereas s. 101 makes no mention of them in relation to endorsement.

If endorsement of the driving licence of an aider and abettor is required, then it may be avoided if "special reasons" are found (see Chapter VII) or the provisions as to certain offences under the Construction and Use Regulations apply (see p. 434).

The endorsement code (see p. 876) provides that an aider and abettor of an endorsable offence is distinguished in that the last numeral " 0 " of the code is replaced by " 2 ". For a person convicted of inciting an offence, the zero is changed to " 6 ". Thus a conviction of taking a conveyance without authority is shown as UT 40, one of aiding and abetting such an offence as UT 42 and one of inciting such an offence as UT 46.

The zero is changed to " 4 " in respect of a person convicted of " causing or permitting ".

Appeal against Endorsement and Removal of Endorsement

The Magistrates' Courts Act, 1952, s. 83, confers a right of appeal to the Crown Court by a defendant against his " sentence " and that term is defined as including any order made on conviction by a magistrates' court. Endorsement is by " order "; there are several references to an " order " in s. 101, but s. 83 (3) (*d*) provides that there is no appeal to the Crown Court in respect of an " order made in pursuance of any enactment under which the court has no discretion as to the making of the order or its terms." It is submitted that an order of endorsement falls within this definition and that there is thus no right of appeal to the Crown Court. If, however, a defendant appeals against sentence generally to the Crown Court, it would appear that the Crown Court is entitled to consider when deciding whether or not to vary the sentence any question as to endorsement (see further on p. 697). See Chapter VIII as to appeals. On the other hand either side may appeal by case stated on a point of law against an endorsement or refusal to endorse. If an appeal against endorsement or against a conviction requiring endorsement succeeds, the appellate court notifies the licensing authority (s. 105 (3)). See p. 702 as to endorsements ordered by the Crown Court.

The view is advanced at 112 J.P.Jo. 284 that endorsement should be carried out immediately on conviction even though an appeal is pending. There is certainly no statutory provision allowing endorsement to be suspended pending an appeal as there is with a disqualification; nor is there any power for the court to remove an endorsement after lapse of time. The Secretary of State was advised in 1905 that where an endorsement had been ordered under the Motor Car Act, 1903, " it is open to justices to refuse to defer endorsement on the ground that the defendant announces an intention to appeal." By s. 101 (7), the endorsement remains on the licence for not less than three years after the date of the conviction (ten years if the conviction was for offences under ss. 5 (1), 6 (1) or 9 (3): unfitness, over the 80 mg. limit or refusing a laboratory specimen) and there is now no distinction between endorsements for speeding and those for other offences. In reckoning the period of three or ten years, the period during which the defendant was disqualified is now included, as the proviso to s. 111 (9) of the 1960 Act (excluding such period) has been repealed. *Semble*, the date of the conviction stated in the endorsement, where there has been an appeal against conviction, should be that in the magistrates' court, not that of a decision of the Crown Court or High Court upholding the conviction. See p. 625. The period of three or ten years applies to convictions before and after the 1972 Act came into operation (see the reference to " any previous enactment " in s. 101 (7)). By para. 10 (3) of Sched. 3 to the 1974 Act the period of three or ten years is increased to one of four or eleven years, respectively. At present this provision is not yet in force. Paragraph 10 (3) is defective in that it says " on . . . the day appointed under s. 22 of this Act ". This is clearly a mistake on the part of Parliament and the paragraph should be read as if it referred to s. 24, which is the commencement section of the Act; otherwise the paragraph is nonsensical. Parliament, like Homer, may nod, and it is submitted that this is clearly a typographical error and would be recognised as such by the courts.

On the expiry of three years from the date of the conviction, a new licence without the relevant endorsement will not be automatically issued; the holder must apply for it and pay any appropriate fee.

Licences Issued outside Great Britain

If the holder of a Northern Irish driving licence is convicted in Great Britain and the court orders endorsement of his driving licence, the court must send particulars of the conviction to the Department of the Environment, Swansea, but may not enter the particulars on the licence. If the court orders endorsement of a foreign driving permit, the court should send particulars of the conviction to the Department of Environment and may not enter particulars of it on the permit (Motor Vehicles (International Circulation) Order, 1957, Sched. 3). This provision applies to visiting forces.

Disqualification

The Road Traffic Act, 1962, s. 5, enacted the present provisions as to offences carrying compulsory and optional disqualification. Section 5 has now been re-enacted as s. 93 of the Act of 1972, which reads:—

" (1) Where a person is convicted of an offence—

(a) under a provision of this Act specified in column 1 of Part I of Schedule 4 to this Act in relation to which there appears in column 5 of that Part the word ' obligatory ' or the word ' obligatory ' qualified by conditions or circumstances relating to the offence; and

(b) where the said word ' obligatory ' is so qualified, the conditions or circumstances are satisfied or obtain in the case of the offence of which he is convicted;

or where a person is convicted of the offence specified in Part II of that Schedule (any such offence being in this Part of this Act referred to as an ' offence involving obligatory disqualification ') the court shall order him to be disqualified for such period not less than twelve months as the court thinks fit unless the court for special reasons thinks fit to order him to be disqualified for a shorter period or not to order him to be disqualified.

(2) Where a person is convicted of an offence—

(a) under a provision of this Act specified in column 1 of Part I of Schedule 4 to this Act in relation to which there appears in column 5 of that Part the word ' discretionary ' or the word ' discretionary ' qualified by conditions or circumstances relating to the offence; and

(b) where the said word ' discretionary ' is so qualified, the conditions or circumstances are satisfied or obtain in the case of the offence of which he is convicted;

or where a person is convicted of an offence specified in Part III of that Schedule (any such offence being in this Part of this Act referred to as an ' offence involving discretionary disqualification '), the court may order him to be disqualified for such period as the court thinks fit.

(3) Where a person convicted of an offence involving obligatory or discretionary disqualification has within the three years immediately preceding the commission of the offence been convicted on not less than two occasions of any such offence and particulars of the convictions have been

ordered to be endorsed in accordance with section 101 of this Act, the court shall order him to be disqualified for such period not less than six months as the court thinks fit, unless the court is satisfied, having regard to all the circumstances, that there are grounds for mitigating the normal consequences of the conviction and thinks fit to order him to be disqualified for a shorter period or not to order him to be disqualified.

(4) Where a person convicted of an offence under any of the following provisions of this Act, namely sections 5 (1), 6 (1) or 9 (3) (where the latter is an offence involving obligatory disqualification), has within the ten years immediately preceding the commission of the offence been convicted of any such offence, subsection (1) above shall apply in relation to him with the substitution of three years for twelve months.

(5) The period of any disqualification imposed under subsection (3) above shall be in addition to any other period of disqualification imposed (whether previously or on the same occasion) under this section or section 5 of the Road Traffic Act 1962 or under the Road Traffic Act 1960 or an enactment repealed by that Act or under the Motor Car Act 1903.

(6) The foregoing provisions of this section shall apply in relation to a conviction of an offence committed by aiding, abetting, counselling or procuring, or inciting to the commission of an offence involving obligatory disqualification as if the offence were an offence involving discretionary disqualification.

(7) Where a person is convicted of an offence involving obligatory or discretionary disqualification the court may, whether or not he has previously passed the test of competence to drive prescribed under this Act, and whether or not the court makes an order under the foregoing provisions of this section, order him to be disqualified until he has, since the date of the order, passed that test; and a disqualification by virtue of an order under this subsection shall be deemed to have expired on production to the Secretary of State of evidence, in such form as may be prescribed by regulations under section 107 of this Act, that the person disqualified has, since the order was made, passed that test."

Offences Involving Obligatory Disqualification and Endorsement

The former provisions of the 1962 Act repealed by the Act of 1972 have been incorporated in tabular form in Sched. 4 to that Act. Those offences which involve obligatory disqualification are shown by the word " obligatory " in column 5 in Pt. I of the Schedule. These are as follows:—

1. Causing death by reckless or dangerous driving (s. 1).
2. Reckless and dangerous driving if committed within three years after a previous conviction of an offence either under s. 1 or s. 2 (s. 2).
3. Driving or attempting to drive when unfit to drive through drink or drugs (s. 5 (1)).
4. Driving or attempting to drive with blood/alcohol concentration above the prescribed limit (s. 6 (1)).
5. Failing to provide a specimen of blood or urine for a laboratory test where at the *relevant time* the offender was driving or

attempting to drive a motor vehicle on a road or other public place (s. 9 (3)). "Relevant time" is defined by Pt. V of the Schedule as:—

  (a) in relation to a person required under s. 8 (1) to provide a specimen of breath for a breath test, the time when he was so required;

  (b) in relation to a person required under s. 8 (2) to provide such a specimen, the time of the accident;

  (c) in relation to a person arrested under s. 5 (5), the time of his arrest.

6. Motor racing and speed trials on highways (s. 14). In addition Pt. II of Sched. 4 lists as an offence involving obligatory disqualification, manslaughter or, in Scotland, culpable homicide, by the driver of a motor vehicle.

Offences Involving Discretionary Disqualification and Obligatory Endorsement

The offences for which a court may disqualify are those offences in Pt. I of Sched. 4, as amended by the Act of 1974, which have the word " discretionary " in column 5 together with all the offences contrary to other Acts contained in Pt. III of the Schedule. The offences involving discretionary disqualification are as follows:—

1. Dangerous driving (s. 2) if committed otherwise than within three years after a previous conviction of an offence under s. 1 or s. 2.

2. Careless and inconsiderate driving (s. 3).

3. Driving under age (s. 4 (4)).

4. Being *in charge* of a motor vehicle when unfit to drive through drink or drugs (s. 5 (2)).

5. Being *in charge* of a motor vehicle with excess blood/alcohol concentration (s. 6 (2)).

6. Failing to provide a specimen of blood or urine when at the relevant time (see Pt. V of Sched. 4, *supra*) it was not shown that he was driving or attempting to drive.

7. Carrying passenger on motor cycle contrary to s. 16.

8. Failing to comply with traffic directions (s. 22) by a constable or an indication given by a sign specified in regulations (these are " Stop " signs, traffic lights, " double " white lines, " Phone for permission to cross " at automatic level crossings and census signs) (see p. 315).

9. Leaving a motor vehicle in a dangerous position (s. 24).

10. Failing to stop after accident and give particulars or report accident (s. 25 (4)).

11. Except where the offender proves that he did not know and had no reasonable cause to suspect that the facts of the case were such that the offence would be committed, contravention of Construction and Use Regulations if committed by using, or causing or permitting the use of, any motor vehicle or trailer (a) so as to cause, or to be likely to cause, danger by the condition of the vehicle or its parts or accessories, the number of passengers carried by it, or the weight, distribution, packing or adjustment of its load; or (b) in breach of a construction and use requirement as to brakes, steering-gear, or tyres; or (c) in the case of an offence by a goods vehicle, for the carrying of a load which by reason of its insecurity or position is likely to cause danger; or (d) for any purpose for which the vehicle is so unsuitable as to cause or to be likely to cause danger.

12. Driving without a licence (s. 84 (1)) if " the offence is committed by driving a motor vehicle in a case where either no licence authorising the driving of that vehicle could have been granted to the offender or, if a provisional (but no other) licence to drive it could have been granted to him, the driving would not have complied with the conditions thereof."

13. Failing to comply with conditions prescribed for a provisional licence or a full licence treated as a provisional licence (s. 88 (6)).

14. Driving with uncorrected defective eyesight (s. 91 (1)).

15. Refusing to submit to test of eyesight (s. 91 (2)).

16. Driving whilst disqualified (s. 99 (b)).

17. Using a motor vehicle whilst uninsured (s. 143).

18. Taking a motor vehicle in Scotland without authority, etc. (s. 175).

Part III of Sched. 4, which lists offences contrary to Acts other than the Road Traffic Act, 1972, involving discretionary disqualification, reads as follows:—

" 1. Stealing or attempting to steal a motor vehicle.

2. An offence, or attempt to commit an offence, in respect of a motor vehicle under section 12 of the Theft Act, 1968 (taking conveyance without consent of owner, etc., or, knowing it has been so taken, driving it or allowing oneself to be carried in it).

3. An offence under section 25 of the Theft Act, 1968 (going equipped for stealing, etc.) committed with reference to the theft or taking of motor vehicles.

4. An offence under section 13 (4) of the Road Traffic Regulation Act, 1967 (contravention of traffic regulations on special roads) committed in respect of a motor vehicle otherwise than by unlawfully stopping or

allowing the vehicle to remain at rest on a part of a special road on which vehicles are in certain circumstances permitted to remain at rest.

5. An offence under section 23 (5) of the Road Traffic Regulation Act, 1967 (contravention of pedestrian crossing regulations) committed in respect of a motor vehicle.

6. An offence under section 25 (2) of the Road Traffic Regulation Act, 1967 (failure to obey sign exhibited by school crossing patrol) committed in respect of a motor vehicle.

7. An offence under section 26 (6) or 26A (5) of the Road Traffic Regulation Act, 1967 (contravention of order prohibiting or restricting use of street playground by vehicles) committed in respect of a motor vehicle.

8. An offence punishable by virtue of section 78A of the Road Traffic Regulation Act, 1967 (speeding offences under that and other Acts)."

The only alteration since the last edition of this book is the inclusion of two additional categories of offence under the Construction and Use Regulations as obligatorily endorsable offences (see (c) and (d) in para. 11, above, and also pp. 433–434).

It will be noted that para. 1 of Pt. III of Sched. 4 requires the convicting court to order endorsement for " stealing or attempting to steal a motor vehicle ". It is submitted that the omission of any reference to any particular section of the Theft Act is deliberate and that an offender may be disqualified and is required to have his licence endorsed if he is convicted of burglary or robbery involving the stealing or attempted stealing of a motor vehicle.

Paragraph 3 of Pt. III of Sched. 4 allows disqualification and requires endorsement if a person, when not at his place of abode, has with him any article for use in the course of or in connection with any theft or taking of motor vehicles, e.g., a set of duplicate ignition keys. The power to disqualify and endorse seems to be confined to cases where the offender was equipped to steal or take a motor vehicle itself and not to extend to cases where he was equipped only to steal from the car. *Semble*, evidence as to his intentions should be sought after he has been found guilty, if not otherwise apparent.

It may also be noted that this offence, like the other offences in the Theft Act involving obligatory endorsement, contains no requirement that the offence was committed on a road or highway. Section 12 makes it an offence to " take " the motor vehicle; there is no requirement that it be driven away. Theft of a motor vehicle merely requires a dishonest appropriation; the offence of theft under the Theft Act no longer requires asportation, although the offence under s. 12 of taking does (see p. 352).

Second Conviction for Drink/Driving, etc., Offences

A previous conviction in the ten years preceding the commission of a second such offence for driving or attempted driving when unfit through drink or drugs, for driving or attempted driving with blood/alcohol concentration above the prescribed limit or for refusing to give a specimen of blood or urine for a laboratory test when the accused had been driving or attempting to drive at the relevant time brings a three-year compulsory disqualification (unless there are " special reasons ") on subsequent conviction for any one of those three offences (Road Traffic Act, 1972, s. 93 (4)). Consequently a person convicted in 1972 of driving with excess blood/alcohol content must be disqualified for three years if within the ten years prior to the date of the commission of the offence for which he was convicted in 1972 he had been *convicted* of driving a motor vehicle contrary to s. 6 of the Road Traffic Act, 1960 (driving whilst unfit), or s. 1 of the Road Safety Act, 1967 (excess blood/alcohol content), or refusing to supply a specimen of blood or urine when at the relevant time he was driving a motor vehicle. It should be noted that the ten-year period is calculated from the date of *commission* of the second offence back to the date of *conviction* of the earlier offence. An offender just within the ten-year period cannot therefore avoid his liability to a three-year disqualification by obtaining an adjournment. These provisions do not apply where the conviction is for being in charge or refusing to supply a laboratory specimen while in charge at the relevant time. By s. 102 (2) of the 1972 Act, replacing s. 51 (2) of the Criminal Justice Act, 1967, a conviction for which disqualification or endorsement was ordered, but on which an order for probation or absolute or conditional discharge was made in England or Wales, shall be taken into account in determining liability to punishment and disqualification for any offence involving obligatory or discretionary disqualification committed subsequently. Thus, if *A* is put on probation in 1974 for driving when unfit, his licence being endorsed, and in 1975 again commits that offence or one of driving with more than 80 mg. or of refusing a blood or urine specimen after driving, he is liable to the three years' compulsory disqualification. The minimum three-year period arises under s. 93 (4) as soon as the offender commits another offence after having been *convicted* of a previous offence. There is no requirement in s. 93 (4) that he should have been disqualified or his licence endorsed for the previous offence. It would, therefore, seem that even if he escaped disqualification for the first offence on the ground of special reasons, he is nevertheless liable to three years' minimum disqualification for a subsequent similar offence. Likewise s. 93 (4) operates where a person commits another offence after he has been convicted of a previous offence, even if he has not been sentenced for that previous offence because sentence had been adjourned or deferred.

Attempts

Unless the statute allows it, there is no power to disqualify or endorse for an attempt to commit an offence involving obligatory or discretionary disqualification (*Bell* v. *Ingham* [1968] 2 All E.R. 333; *R.* v. *Cockermouth JJ.* [1971] Crim.L.R. 287). There is specific statutory authority, as p. 619 shows, to disqualify for attempted driving of a motor vehicle when unfit through drink or drugs, attempted driving with a blood/alcohol concentration above the prescribed limit, refusal of a blood or urine specimen contrary to s. 9 (3) when caught attempting to drive, attempted theft and attempted taking without authority of a motor vehicle. Otherwise there is no power to disqualify for an attempt to commit an offence, e.g., attempting to drive while disqualified or when under age or with uncorrected defective eyesight. For this reason there is no special endorsement code for attempts; only for aiders or abettors and inciters and causers or permitters (see p. 613). Where a person is convicted of an attempt for which there is specific statutory authority for disqualification and endorsement, e.g., attempting to drive with excess blood/alcohol, this will be shown as DR 10 in the same way as the substantive offence.

Offences Involving Obligatory Disqualification

On conviction for an offence involving obligatory disqualification (see *supra*), the offender must (save as mentioned below) be disqualified for holding or obtaining a licence to drive a motor vehicle for not less than twelve months (1972 Act, s. 93 (1)). See *supra* as to the three-year compulsory disqualification for committing within ten years of the previous conviction a second offence of driving or attempted driving when unfit or with more than 80 mg. of alcohol or refusing a blood/urine specimen. The requirements of s. 93 (1) of the 1972 Act apply on first or subsequent conviction, save that for dangerous driving under s. 2 it applies only on commission of a second or subsequent offence if the date of the offence (not conviction) is within three years after the date of a previous conviction under s. 1 or s. 2; the date of the first conviction is excluded in computing the three years. *Semble*, under s. 102 (2) of the 1972 Act, if a defendant in England or Wales was put on probation or absolutely or conditionally discharged, this counts as a conviction, if it was endorsed; see discussion on p. 620 as to the three-year disqualification for " drink " offences. See *infra* as to Scotland.

There cannot be a disqualification in the defendant's absence unless the case has been adjourned to give him an opportunity to be present and he has been warned in the notice of adjournment of the probable intention to disqualify; see para. (2) on p. 630.

The court may only refrain from imposing the twelve-month or three-year disqualification for any offence involving obligatory disqualification or impose a shorter period of disqualification:—

- (i) if there are special reasons (see Chapter VII)—then the court may either not disqualify at all or disqualify for less than twelve months (s. 93 (1)) (or for less than three years on a second " drink " conviction);
- (ii) if the offenders are aiders and abettors, counsellors or procurers of an obligatory disqualifiable offence—when they need not be disqualified (s. 93 (6));
- (iii) where, under the Mental Health Act, 1959, s. 60 (2), or the Mental Health (Scotland) Act, 1960, s. 55 (3), the court is satisfied of the defendant's guilt and makes a guardianship or hospital order " without convicting him " —presumably there can be no disqualification or endorsement at all as there is no " conviction ".

In Scotland where the defendant is absolutely discharged or put on probation, he cannot be disqualified at all (Criminal Justice (Scotland) Act, 1949, ss. 1, 2 (1) and 9 (2)). In England and Wales, he must be disqualified, unless there are special reasons, on the making of an order for probation or absolute or conditional discharge for an offence for which disqualification is obligatory (Road Traffic Act, 1972, s. 102 (1); *Owen* v. *Imes* [1972] R.T.R. 489).

The disqualification imposed under s. 93 (1) must be imposed even if the court is obliged to impose an additional six-month period under s. 93 (3), but it may be logical and proper in such a case for there to be only one order totalling the period required and imposed under s. 93 (3), in place of one order under s. 93 (1) and another under s. 93 (3) (see (12) on p. 629).

The court may at its discretion disqualify for a longer period than the obligatory period of twelve months or three years.

Any order of disqualification, whether it be discretionary under s. 91 (2) or obligatory under s. 91 (1), must commence to run from the moment it is pronounced (*R.* v. *Higgins* [1973] R.T.R. 216; *R.* v. *Bain* [1973] R.T.R. 213). Thus where a defendant was disqualified for two and a half years on one count of causing death by dangerous driving and two and a half years on another count of driving with excess blood/alcohol, the order of the trial judge that the two periods of disqualification should run consecutively was set aside by the Court of Appeal, who ordered them to run concurrently (*R.* v. *Meese* [1973] R.T.R. 400). The only order of disqualification which can run consecutively is an order under s. 93 (3) for totting up, *infra*.

Formerly, if the conviction was for driving whilst disqualified, the twelve-month period of disqualification ordered under s. 5 (1) of the 1962 Act was required to be additional and consecutive to any other period then or previously imposed (1962 Act, s. 5 (5)). The offence, as a result of the Road Traffic (Disqualification) Act, 1970, now no longer involves obligatory disqualification and if a period of disqualification for the offence is ordered it commences from the date upon which it is pronounced (unless suspended on an appeal) (*R.* v. *Bain, supra*).

Where the court does not disqualify in a case under s. 93 (1) or disqualifies for a shorter period, the grounds must be stated in open court and entered in the register (1972 Act, s. 101), but failure to state them aloud does not invalidate the decision (*Brown* v. *Dyerson* [1968] 3 All E.R. 39).

Compulsory Disqualification under s. 93 (3)—" Totting up "

Section 93 (3), formerly s. 5 (3) of the Act of 1962, is often called the " totting up " provision.

The effect of s. 93 (3) is that, when a defendant is convicted of an offence carrying obligatory endorsement and he has two endorsed previous convictions for such offences within the three years immediately preceding the commission of the offence, he must be disqualified for at least six months additional to any period imposed previously or on the same occasion, unless the court is satisfied having regard to all the circumstances that there are grounds for mitigating the normal consequences of the conviction (see p. 688). Note the following:—

(1) There must have been two previous " convictions " for an endorsable offence; as the Road Traffic Acts apply throughout Great Britain, convictions in England and Wales count in Scotland and vice versa. In Scotland, courts of summary jurisdiction do not proceed to " conviction " on making an order for probation or absolute discharge (Criminal Justice (Scotland) Act, 1949, ss. 1 and 2 (1)). In England and Wales, endorsements ordered on making an order for probation or absolute or conditional discharge are to be taken into account in determining liability to disqualification for an offence involving obligatory or discretionary disqualification (Road Traffic Act, 1972, s. 102 (2)); consequently any such order counts as a previous conviction. There is no conviction if a court has acted under the Mental Health Act, 1959, s. 60 (2), or the Mental Health (Scotland) Act, 1960, s. 55 (3), nor, in Scotland, where an order for

probation or absolute discharge has been made by a higher court (Criminal Justice (Scotland) Act, 1949, s. 9 (1) and (2)). It was a matter for argument whether courts in England or Wales could lawfully endorse when making orders for absolute or conditional discharge prior to 1st October, 1967 (see fifth edition of this book, pp. 332–333).

(2) The previously-convicting courts must have ordered those convictions to be endorsed. Production of an unendorsed licence *prima facie* shows that endorsement was not ordered but this presumption could be rebutted by evidence of those courts' orders, for the defendant might have neglected to produce his licence to them, have failed to disclose his endorsements when applying for his licence, or have been driving on a domestic driving permit. There is no power to endorse interim disqualifications ordered on committal for sentence (s. 103 (1)).

(3) The dates of the two previous convictions (not the dates of the offences) must have been as follows:—

(a) The previous convictions must have taken place within the three years immediately preceding the commission of the third offence (not conviction for it); *semble*, this means the day of the third offence, which day is excluded in computing the three years (see cases on pp. 68–69, so that a conviction on or after 10th January, 1972, counts under s. 93 (3) for an offence committed on 10th January, 1975. The third offence must have been committed after the second conviction to qualify under s. 93 (3) (*R.* v. *Hollier* [1973] R.T.R. 395). Again, there is no requirement to disqualify under s. 93 (3) where the conviction for the second offence was after the date of the commission of the third offence (*Maynard* v. *Andrews* [1973] R.T.R. 398).

Defending advocates should watch that an endorsement ordered by the Crown Court at a date just within the three-year period is not in respect of an appeal from a conviction by magistrates outside the period; in such a case it is submitted that the date of the conviction should be that of the magistrates' decision, so that s. 93 (3) may not apply. Where the first offence was near the start of the three-year period, the defence should make sure that the date of conviction and not the date when the case was finally dealt with has been given, e.g., an offence on 1st January, 1975, a previous conviction in 1974 and another said to have been on 4th January, 1972.   If the latter was an adjourned sentence from December, 1971, and the conviction was in that December, s. 93 (3) does not apply.

[While the day is excluded in computing the three years, *supra*, it is nevertheless submitted that where a person who has been previously convicted on two separate occasions commits the third offence on the same day immediately after he was convicted of the second offence he is liable to disqualification under s. 93 (3).   It is submitted that the words " immediately preceding " in s. 93 (3) (see p. 616) should bear their ordinary meaning.   Moreover, although the law normally takes no notice of fractions of a day, where it is necessary to show which was the first of two acts the court is at liberty to consider fractions of a day (*Campbell* v. *Strangeways* (1877), 3 C.P.D. 105).]

(*b*) The previous convictions must also have taken place on two or more separate occasions, i.e., at different courts or on different days.   Convictions by one court for several offences, whether committed separately or together, count under s. 93 (3) as one conviction only, if all the convictions were on the same day (*R.* v. *Rogers* [1953] 1 All E.R. 206, a case on the Criminal Justice Act, 1948, s. 21, where the term " two previous occasions " is used; *R.* v. *Sixsmith, ex parte Morris* [1966] 3 All E.R., at p. 475, letter H); *semble*, if there are convictions on different days on different charges arising out of the same incident, e.g., for dangerous driving and disobeying a traffic sign, they would not necessarily count as one occasion but this fact would be a ground for mitigating the compulsory disqualification under s. 93 (3).   See generally Jo.Crim.L. (1964) 66, and pp. 693–694, *post*.

[Some examples may help.   *X* is convicted on 1st April, 1975, of careless driving committed on 15th March, 1975; he was convicted of careless driving in November, 1974, and of speeding on 20th March, 1972.   This last-mentioned conviction is within three years of his offence on 15th March, 1975, and therefore counts under s. 93 (3), although the conviction in 1975 is more than three years after that 1972 conviction.   But if *X*'s first conviction had been on 12th March, 1972, s. 93 (3) would not apply, because the first conviction is more than three years from the third offence, although the court could still disqualify at its discretion on conviction for the third offence for any period of, or more or less than six months. If a person were convicted of an offence in 1976, a conviction in 1972 would not count, as it would be outside the three-year period.]

(4) By s. 93 (5), the six-month period of disqualification imposed under s. 93 (3) is additional and consecutive to any period imposed previously or on the same occasion for any offence for which the offender can or could previously be disqualified. The court cannot order a disqualification under s. 93 (3) to be served concurrently with another period of disqualification (*R.* v. *Jones* [1970] 3 All E.R. 815). An order under s. 93 (3) must run consecutively to any other order of disqualification (s. 93 (5)), even if the court register does not state that it is consecutive (*R.* v. *Bowsher* [1973] R.T.R. 202). Thus, if *X* is convicted of driving under the influence of drink and has two previous endorsed convictions at separate hearings for, say, speeding within the previous three years, he must be disqualified under s. 93 (1) for twelve months for the drunken-driving offence and for a further six months consecutive under s. 93 (3) and (5)— eighteen months in all (but it may be " logical and proper " in such circumstances for the period of twelve months under s. 93 (1) and the six months period under s. 93 (3) to be imposed in the form of one period of eighteen months under para. (12) below). Also, if he was disqualified for an earlier conviction, the six-month period under s. 93 (3) does not start to run until the earlier period ordered expires. Again, if *X* has the two endorsements specified above and appears on the third occasion for two or more endorsable offences, e.g., careless driving and no insurance, he must be disqualified under s. 93 (3) for six months on each charge consecutive, twelve months in all (eighteen months if there were three charges), unless (5) below applies. See further under " Concurrent and Consecutive Disqualifications " on p. 631.

(5) The court need not disqualify pursuant to s. 93 (3) or may impose a shorter period of disqualification than six months if the court is satisfied that, having regard to all the circumstances, there are grounds for mitigating the normal consequences of the conviction. See p. 688 as to this provision. Endorsement must also be ordered for the third offence unless there are special reasons.

(6) An aider and abettor of an offence whether it involves obligatory or discretionary endorsement must, it seems, be

disqualified for six months under s. 93 (3) if he has two previous convictions within the relevant period and their endorsement has been ordered: see s. 93 (6). Likewise, previous convictions as aider and abettor count under s. 93 (3) if the court ordered them to be endorsed. Cf. *Bradley* v. *McGivern* [1963] N.I. 11.

(7) There can be no disqualification under s. 93 (3) if in Scotland the defendant is put on probation or absolutely discharged (Criminal Justice (Scotland) Act, 1949, ss. 1, 2 (1) and 9 (2)) or if, in England, Wales or Scotland under the Mental Health Act, 1959, s. 60 (2), or the Mental Health (Scotland) Act, 1960, s. 55 (3), the court does not convict. In England and Wales there can be disqualification on the making of an order for absolute or conditional discharge or probation (Road Traffic Act, 1972, s. 102), and if it is obligatory to disqualify because of the nature of the offence the court must do so (*Owen* v. *Imes* [1972] R.T.R. 489); similarly if s. 93 (3) applies, unless mitigating circumstances are found (see p. 688).

(8) If the defendant is convicted on the third occasion of an offence in contravention of a construction and use requirement of causing danger by the unsuitable use of a vehicle, the insecurity of its load, the condition of the vehicle or its parts or accessories, the number of passengers carried, or the weight, distribution, packing or adjustment of its load, or in breach of a requirement as to brakes, steering gear or tyres, he should not be disqualified nor should his licence be endorsed under s. 93 (3) or at all if he did not know and had no reasonable cause to suspect that the facts of the case were such that that offence would be committed (column 5 shown against these offences under s. 40 (5) in Pt. I of Sched. 4 to the 1972 Act). See p. 434.

(9) A defendant who has already had a compulsory " totting up " disqualification remains liable to have a further such disqualification if he makes a fourth court appearance for an offence committed at a time when there were two endorsements from separate court hearings within the three years preceding the fourth offence and so with a fifth and subsequent appearance; liability under s. 93 (3) does not disappear when it has once been incurred, but continues (*Fearon* v. *Sydney* [1966] 2 All E.R. 694).

(10) In addition to the period imposed for totting up the court shall impose the obligatory period for an obligatorily disqualifiable offence under s. 93 (1) and for other offences a

discretionary disqualification under s. 93 (2) (but see (12) below).

(11) A defendant may not be disqualified, even under s. 93 (3), in his absence unless the case has been adjourned to give him the opportunity of attending (see para. (2), overleaf).

(12) Where there are no mitigating circumstances justifying a reduction in the six months' period and the court considers the offence or the offender's record either requires or justifies an order of disqualification under s. 93 (1) (obligatory disqualification) or s. 93 (2) (discretionary disqualification) it may be " logical and proper " for the court to make one order for the total period of disqualification under s. 93 (3) rather than two orders, one under s. 93 (1) or s. 93 (2) and the other under s. 93 (3) (*R.* v. *Middlesex Area Quarter Sessions, ex parte Bull* [1972] R.T.R. 205).

(13) An order of disqualification under s. 44 of the Powers of Criminal Courts Act, 1973 (motor vehicle used for criminal purposes) cannot count as a conviction for " totting up " as there is no power to endorse when making such an order (see p. 641).

(14) A court may not fine or otherwise sentence on one occasion and on another occasion subsequently disqualify. The court should impose the whole of the sentence including the ancillary power of disqualification at the same time (*R.* v. *Talgarth JJ., ex parte Bithell* [1973] R.T.R. 546).

Where the court does not disqualify under s. 93 (3) or does so for a shorter period, the grounds must be stated in open court and entered in the register (1972 Act, s. 105 (1)), but the non-disqualification remains valid although the court does not state them aloud (*Brown* v. *Dyerson* [1968] 3 All E.R. 39).

If a magistrates' court convicts and sentences a defendant who produced a duplicate licence free from endorsements, the court cannot re-open the matter and disqualify under s. 93 (3) when it is discovered that the duplicate licence should have had endorsements of two previous convictions within the three-year period (*R.* v. *Northampton JJ., ex parte Nicholson* [1974] R.T.R. 97). *Semble*, a magistrates' court also cannot do so if it sentenced without having had a licence produced to it.

Discretionary Disqualification

Column 5 in Pt. I together with Pt. III of Sched. 4 to the 1972 Act indicate the offences for which disqualification may at the court's discretion be ordered, subject to s. 93 (3), *supra*. It should be noted that the offences for which the court has a discretionary power of disqualification under s. 93 (2) are all those offences for which endorsement is obligatory but which do not involve obligatory disqualification under s. 93 (1). Note the limitations on the power to disqualify for certain traffic sign offences (see p. 315), and for certain driving licence offences (see pp. 481–482). It is entirely a matter for the court whether or not to order disqualification, and, if so, for how long in a case where the court has a discretion to disqualify, subject to these qualifications:—

(1) Disqualification may not be ordered in Scotland for an offence for which the offender is absolutely discharged or put on probation (Criminal Justice (Scotland) Act, 1949, ss. 1, 2 (1) and 9 (2)), although, if he is charged with two disqualifiable offences, he can be put on probation for one and convicted and disqualified for the other. See p. 646 as to breaches of probation. In England and Wales he may be disqualified at the court's discretion on making an order for probation or absolute or conditional discharge (Road Traffic Act, 1972, s. 102).

(2) A person who has pleaded guilty in writing under the Magistrates' Courts Act, 1957, may not be disqualified in his absence unless he has been given the opportunity of attending at an adjourned hearing (see s. 1 (2), proviso (iii), of the 1957 Act and p. 99). The notification of the adjourned hearing shall indicate the reason for the adjournment, e.g., that the magistrates are considering disqualification (*R.* v. *Mason* [1965] 2 All E.R. 308). Disqualification may be ordered in his absence if he has been duly notified and does not attend. The same rule applies in " totting up " cases under s. 93 (3) (*R.* v. *Llandrindod Wells JJ., ex parte Gibson* (1968), 112 S.J. 218).

Where the procedure of the 1957 Act has not been used for the first hearing but the defendant has been summoned and fails to attend he may not be disqualified in his absence at that first hearing, but the case should be adjourned to give him the opportunity of attending and the notice of adjournment to him should give the reason for the adjournment (Criminal Justice Act, 1967, s. 26 (2) and (3); *R.* v. *Bishop's Stortford JJ., ex parte Shields* (1968), 113 S.J. 124). If he fails to attend at the adjourned hearing he may then be disqualified. An absent defendant represented by counsel or solicitor is deemed not to be absent (Magistrates' Courts Act, 1952, s. 99).

(3) An aider and abettor of an offence involving obligatory or

discretionary disqualification may be disqualified at the court's discretion (s. 93 (6)).

(4) Where the Mental Health Act, 1959, s. 60 (2), or the Mental Health (Scotland) Act, 1960, s. 55 (3), applies, disqualification may not be ordered.

(5) Where the defendant has been convicted of a Construction and Use Regulations offence as to dangerous condition, dangerously unsuitable use, insecure load, or brakes, steering or tyres (see p. 434), he may not be disqualified if he did not know and had no reasonable cause to suspect that the facts of the case were such that that offence would be committed (1972 Act, Sched. 4, Pt. I, offences contrary to s. 40 (5), column 5).

(6) The whole of the sentence, including any order of disqualification, should be imposed on the same occasion (*R*. v. *Talgarth JJ.*, *ex parte Bithell* [1973] R.T.R. 546; *R*. v. *Fairhead* [1975] Crim.L.R. 351).

Concurrent and Consecutive Disqualifications

Disqualification, save where s. 93 (5) applies (see p. 632) starts to run as soon as it is ordered (*Taylor* v. *Kenyon* [1952] 2 All E.R. 726; *R*. v. *Graham* [1955] Crim.L.R. 319; *R*. v. *Phillips* (1955), 119 J.P. 499). Except for a " totting up " disqualification (see p. 624), a disqualification, whether it be obligatory or discretionary, cannot be ordered to run consecutively to any other order of disqualification or, for example, to commence at the end of a sentence of imprisonment (*R*. v. *Meese* [1973] R.T.R. 400; *R*. v. *Bain* [1973] R.T.R. 213; *R*. v. *Bowsher* [1973] R.T.R. 202; *R*. v. *Higgins* [1973] R.T.R. 216). The disqualification runs from the moment it is pronounced, and s. 94 (4) provides that, in determining the expiration of the period for which a person was disqualified by an order made in consequence of a conviction, any time after the conviction during which he was not disqualified or the disqualification was suspended shall be disregarded. Consequently, if a defendant is convicted on 1st June and the case is then adjourned to 14th June and he is disqualified for a year on that later day, the year will start to run on 14th June. It is thus accurate to say that disqualification runs from the date of the sentence of disqualification if that date is different from the date upon which he is convicted. The dates are frequently dissimilar, particularly in " totting up " cases because in a large number of such cases the defendant will initially have been convicted in his absence under the procedure of the Magistrates' Courts Act, 1957, and the court will have had to adjourn to give the defendant an opportunity to ask not to be disqualified.

Save where "totting up" applies, disqualifications run concurrently both with those ordered by the same court at the same hearing and with those previously ordered by the same or another court on another occasion. Thus, if a defendant who is not subject to "totting up" appears before a court for several offences, whether they involve discretionary or obligatory disqualification, all the disqualifications then ordered will run concurrently (*R.* v. *Higgins* [1964] 3 All E.R. 714N.; *Williamson* v. *MacMillan* [1962] S.L.T. 63; cf. *Jones* v. *Powell* [1965] 1 All E.R. 674; *R.* v. *Camfield* [1971] R.T.R. 449). Consequently, if such a defendant is convicted of driving when unfit through drink, no insurance and failing to stop after an accident at one court hearing and is disqualified for one year on each charge, his period of disqualification lasts for one year only and the periods cannot be made consecutive; if the court wants him to be off the road for three years, there must be a disqualification for three years ordered on at least one of the charges. Similarly, save where the disqualification is for "totting up", disqualifications ordered by one court cannot be made to run consecutively to periods ordered previously at other court hearings; a court which wishes to increase the period of disqualification which a defendant is serving from another court must make its own period of disqualification long enough to continue for some time after the first period expires.

Where, however, the defendant is subject to "totting up", having had convictions endorsed on two previous occasions, and is convicted of an offence carrying optional or compulsory disqualification, disqualifications then imposed must, by s. 93 (5), be in addition to any other period of disqualification imposed on the same occasion or previously. The magistrates' court register should state that an order under s. 93 (3) runs consecutively, but if it does not do so, such an order is nevertheless consecutive by virtue of s. 93 (5) (*R.* v. *Bowsher* [1973] R.T.R. 202). Consequently, if the defendant is subject to "totting up" and appears on several charges for disqualifiable offences, he must be disqualified for at least six months consecutive on each charge, unless there are grounds for mitigating the normal consequences of the conviction, so that such a defendant appearing on two charges must be disqualified for a total of twelve months at least or, if on four charges, for a total of twenty-four months at least (6+6+6+6), each period of six months running consecutively (*R.* v. *McNulty* [1964] 3 All E.R. 713; *R.* v. *Sixsmith, ex parte Morris* [1966] 3 All E.R. 473; *R.* v. *Camfield, supra*). If he had previously been disqualified and that previous disqualification was still running at the time of the third conviction, no period of further disqualification then ordered under s. 93 (3) would start to run until that previous period of disqualification had expired.

It was said in *R.* v. *Sixsmith, supra,* that, where s. 93 (3) applied, the court should first determine the disqualifications to be imposed apart from the application of s. 93 (3) and (5) and then determine the period of disqualification to be imposed under s. 93 (3) for each offence to which it applied. This ruling is plainly correct but it is submitted that, so long as magistrates (where there are no mitigating circumstances) disqualify for at least six months on each charge, it suffices if they determine in advance for how long the defendant is to be disqualified; periods of disqualification amounting to that length of time may be imposed without necessarily insisting on two periods of disqualification on one or more of the charges. Thus, if *A*, being subject to " totting up ", is convicted of two offences and the magistrates want him off the road for eighteen months, they may disqualify for twelve months (rather than 6+6) on the first and for a further six months consecutive on the second. They certainly do not have to disqualify him for eighteen months on the first charge and then for a further six months on the same charge and for a further six months on the second charge.

Although consecutive disqualifications are complicated, it is submitted that it may be undesirable that the court should put the whole of the consecutive disqualification periods into one and impose that aggregate on one offence only and simply endorse for the others; for example, if *A*, being subject to totting up, is convicted on the third occasion of four disqualifiable offences, he is liable to an aggregate disqualification of two years (i.e., six months on each) if there are no grounds for mitigating the normal consequences of the convictions. The court, however, should not content itself with disqualifying for two years on the first charge only and endorsing on the other three but should give six months consecutive on each of the four charges, because, if two years were given only on one charge and nothing on the others, a successful appeal against conviction or disqualification on that charge would result in the defendant not being disqualified at all, assuming that he had not appealed on the other charges. *Semble,* though, in such a case the High Court could at its discretion direct mandamus to the magistrates to disqualify on the other charges when the appeal on the first had succeeded.

Where a defendant is subject to " totting up " and his third offence merits discretionary disqualification or is an obligatorily disqualifiable offence, it was said to be " logical and proper " for the total period to be imposed by one order under s. 93 (3) rather than one under s. 93 (1) or 93 (2) and one under s. 93 (3) (*R.* v. *Middlesex Area Quarter Sessions, ex parte Bull* [1972] R.T.R. 205).

Examples of Concurrent and Consecutive Disqualifications

It will be assumed in these examples that there are no special reasons under s. 93 (1) and no grounds for mitigating the normal consequences of the conviction under s. 93 (3).

(1) *A*, who has no previous convictions, is convicted on 1st July, 1975, of drunken driving, dangerous driving and no insurance. He is disqualified for one year for each offence; these will be concurrent disqualifications starting on 1st July, 1975 and will expire on 30th June, 1976, at 11.59 p.m.   They cannot be made consecutive.

(2) *B* was disqualified on 1st December, 1974, for one year. On 4th April, 1975, he is convicted of driving with excess blood/alcohol, driving whilst disqualified and driving whilst uninsured. He is subject to " totting up " disqualification because of a conviction for speeding on 1st November, 1974.   The court is required to disqualify him for twelve months for the excess blood/alcohol. This disqualification will commence on 4th April, 1975, and expire one year later.   The court is, however, required also to impose an additional six months' disqualification for each of the offences for " totting up ", *viz.* six months for excess blood/alcohol, six months for driving whilst disqualified, and six months for not being insured.   These latter disqualifications are required to be consecutive and additional.   *B's* disqualification is therefore from 4th April, 1975, for one year (excess blood/alcohol) plus six months (" totting up ") plus six months (" totting up "—driving while disqualified) plus six months (" totting up "—uninsured use), i.e., until 4th October, 1977.   Although he is currently disqualified until 1st December, 1975, this period runs concurrently with the excess blood/alcohol disqualification, which expires in April, 1976.

(3) *C* is subject to " totting up " but has not been disqualified. He appears on 1st July, 1975, for careless driving and no insurance. He must be disqualified for six months on each charge consecutive, the first six-month period starting on 1st July, 1975, and the second on 1st January, 1976; he may not drive again till 1st July, 1976.

(4) *D* is subject to " totting up " and to a disqualification expiring at 11.59 p.m. on 31st December, 1975.   On his third appearance in June, 1975, he is charged with (*a*) driving while disqualified and (*b*) no insurance.   He is liable to a six months' consecutive period for " totting up " for (*a*) and an additional six months' period consecutive to the latter for " totting up " for (*b*).   He will thus be disqualified till 11.59 p.m. on 31st December, 1976.   Driving while disqualified no longer involves obligatory disqualification.

Disqualification Generally

Where the special reasons under s. 93 (1) or the mitigating circumstances under s. 93 (3) are somewhat tenuous, the power to disqualify for a lesser period than the maximum may be a satisfactory compromise in fact, though not in strict law.

A person may be disqualified without any other sentence, such as a fine, being passed on him for the offence (*R.* v. *Bignell* (1968), 52 Cr.App.R. 10), but Brian Harris in The Criminal Jurisdiction of Magistrates, 4th ed., p. 141, states that an order of disqualification is not a sentence but merely an order ancillary to sentence, his argument being expanded in an article at 131 J.P.Jo. 677. *R.* v. *Surrey Quarter Sessions, ex parte Commissioner of Police* [1963] 1 Q.B. 990, which is to the contrary, was not cited to the court in *Bignell* but it is nevertheless considered that unless and until *Bignell* is reconsidered by the Court of Appeal it may be relied on. It is, however, submitted that if a court does not wish to impose any penalty other than disqualification, it is proper to make an order of absolute discharge under s. 7 of the Powers of Criminal Courts Act, 1973.

A person who holds a foreign driving licence is, if disqualified by a court in Great Britain, forbidden to drive on roads in Great Britain even though his foreign licence is still valid (Motor Vehicles (International Circulation) Order, 1957 (S.I. 1957 No. 1074), art. 2 (4)); moreover s. 99 (*b*) forbids a person to drive when disqualified for holding or obtaining a licence issued under the Road Traffic Act, 1972.

The effect of a disqualification is that the defendant may not drive in Great Britain a motor vehicle of any type (see p. 2) on a road which is a highway or to which the public have access (see p. 26) during the period of a disqualification, but he may drive on private land or on places which are not " roads ". If a disqualified farmer drives straight across the highway on a tractor from one field to another he commits an offence, though the brevity of the journey and lack of any other vehicles when he crosses might possibly be a " special reason " (see *Coombs* v. *Kehoe* and other cases on p. 673). A British disqualification does not forbid driving abroad but the driver must comply with the foreign law as to licences, etc.

Disqualification may or, as the case may be, must be ordered where a defendant is returned to borstal, on committing an offence, pursuant to the Criminal Justice Act, 1961, s. 12.

The court should decide on the period of disqualification which is appropriate to the facts of the case; it is wrong of the court in pronouncing sentence to advert to the fact that the defendant, after the appropriate period, can apply for the restoration of his licence under s. 95 (*R.* v. *Lobley* [1974] R.T.R. 550).

Disqualification on Committal

By s. 56 of the Criminal Justice Act, 1967, where a magistrates' court commits an offender to the Crown Court for sentence under s. 28 or s. 29 of the Magistrates' Courts Act, 1952, the Crown Court may or shall disqualify him and shall order endorsement of his licence, as required, whether or not he is sent to borstal (see s. 56 (5) and (6)). By s. 103 (1) of the 1972 Act, a magistrates' court committing for sentence, in custody or on bail, may order the defendant to be disqualified, if he has been convicted of an offence carrying disqualification, till the Crown Court has dealt with him; by s. 103 (5) any period of disqualification imposed by the Crown Court on any such person committed for sentence shall be treated as reduced by any period he was disqualified by reason only of an order made under s. 103 (1), but such latter period shall not be taken into account for the purpose of reducing more than one other period of disqualification. Thus, if *A* is disqualified, on committal on bail for sentence under s. 28 or s. 29 till the Crown Court deals with him, and the Crown Court does deal with him a month later and imposes a single two-year disqualification, the latter will expire one year and eleven months from the date on which the Crown Court ordered it. If, however, he was disqualified for two periods each of two years concurrent, only one of them is shortened and the other runs for the full two years. *Semble*, the period for removal of the disqualification ordered by the Crown Court runs from the date on which the Crown Court ordered that disqualification. If, however, the magistrates ordered a temporary disqualification on committal for all charges, all disqualifications ordered by the Crown Court would be correspondingly reduced.

The provisions above and in the next paragraph extend to offences occurring during the currency of a probation or conditional discharge order, to those to which s. 62 (offences during parole) of the Criminal Justice Act, 1967, or s. 24 (suspended sentences) of the Powers of Criminal Courts Act, 1973, apply, and to offenders committed for sentence under the Vagrancy Act, 1824. They do not extend to offenders committed under the Mental Health Act, 1959, s. 67; *semble*, the magistrates should endorse and disqualify in s. 67 cases.

Committal of Summary Offences to the Crown Court

By s. 56 (1), where a magistrates' court has convicted a person of an offence or offences which carry compulsory or optional disqualification, whether a summary offence or one triable summarily or on indictment, and is committing him to the Crown Court for another offence under s. 28 or s. 29 of the Magistrates' Courts Act or under the powers mentioned in the last paragraph, the magistrates may commit him in respect of the first-mentioned offences also, notwithstanding that they are not triable on indictment. By s. 56 (5), the Crown Court may deal with him for such offence or offences in any way in which the magistrates could have dealt with him and, in particular, may disqualify and endorse for them. Thus, if *A* is convicted by magistrates of stealing a car, driving it carelessly and using it without insurance and the magistrates commit him for sentence for the first of those offences under s. 29 of the Magistrates' Courts Act, they may also, by s. 56 (1), commit him to the Crown Court for the other two offences also, so that the Crown Court may fix the total amount of disqualification and will not be hampered by any decision of the magistrates, whose views as to the period of his disqualification may be more severe than those of the Crown Court. The fine for those two offences should generally be left to the Crown Court also. This power of committal of summary, etc., offences, which anyhow arises only after the magistrates have convicted, does not extend to committals *for trial*; if a person is charged with causing death by dangerous driving and with not stopping after an accident, the magistrates should commit for trial on the first charge and either not hear and convict on the second one till the Crown Court has dealt with the other, or convict, fine and, if they are so minded, disqualify on it notwithstanding that the Crown Court has not dealt with the first charge. It is submitted that it is better that in such a case the magistrates should delay trying the lesser charge till the trial at the Crown Court is finished.

Magistrates may by s. 103 (1) of the 1972 Act disqualify for a summary offence so committed for sentence until it is dealt with by the Crown Court. See above as to the deduction of the period of their disqualification from the period ordered by the Crown Court.

The powers under s. 56 (1) of the Criminal Justice Act, 1967, of committing summary, etc., offences for sentence when committal of another offence for sentence is being done extend to summary, etc., offences punishable with imprisonment as well as to those for which disqualification may or must be ordered.

Trams and Trolley Buses

The driver of a tram operated under statutory powers cannot be disqualified and a person disqualified from driving motor vehicles may drive a tram so operated; trolley bus drivers may be disqualified and no disqualified person may drive a trolley bus (Road Traffic Act, 1972, s. 198 (4)).

Period and Commencement of Disqualification

Unless it is for " totting up " an order of disqualification must commence from the moment the order is pronounced; it cannot be ordered to run consecutively; whether consecutively to any other order of disqualification or to an order of imprisonment (*R.* v. *Meese* [1974] R.T.R. 400; *R.* v. *Higgins* [1974] R.T.R. 216; *R.* v. *Bain* [1974] R.T.R. 213; *R.* v. *Graham, infra*).

In all cases disqualification should be for a specified period and not for an indefinite one (*R.* v. *Fowler* [1937] 2 All E.R. 380). Offences for which disqualification is a proper penalty should not be taken into consideration when sentence is being passed for a different offence (*R.* v. *Collins* [1947] 1 All E.R. 147), but it is permissible to take into consideration another offence of a similar kind (*R.* v. *Jones* [1970] 3 All E.R. 815). Disqualification is effective as soon as it is ordered by the court (*Taylor* v. *Kenyon* [1952] 2 All E.R. 726) and a disqualification expressed to run from the day of release from prison is void (*R.* v. *Graham* [1955] Crim.L.R. 319). When it is imposed along with imprisonment, the period of disqualification should not be so short that most of it will have expired on release from prison (*R.* v. *Phillips* (1955), 119 J.P. 499) (but see also *R.* v. *Pashley* on p. 654). Unless its minimum period be limited by statute, the disqualification can be for such period, long or short, as the court orders. If a period less than the statutory minimum is imposed, the High Court may substitute the period allowed by law (Administration of Justice Act, 1960, s. 16). The court should decide on the period of disqualification which is appropriate to the facts of the case; it is wrong for the court in pronouncing sentence to advert to the fact that the defendant after the appropriate period can apply for restoration of his licence under s. 95 (*R.* v. *Lobley* [1974] R.T.R. 550). Disqualification for life was upheld in *R.* v. *Wallace* [1955] N.I. 137 and in *R.* v. *Tunde-Olarinde* [1967] 2 All E.R. 491, but the policy of the Court of Appeal is increasingly to discourage disqualification for life or for very long periods, particularly where the offender is young. Thus in *R.* v. *Ward* [1971] Crim.L.R. 665, a " bad case of dangerous driving " by a person sentenced to borstal, disqualification was varied from life to five years. Likewise in *R.* v. *Lee* [1971] Crim.L.R. 177 a disqualification for another young man sentenced to borstal was reduced from ten to three years. Indeed in *R.* v. *North* [1971] R.T.R. 366 (applied in *R.* v. *Ward, supra*) it was said that " unless there were unusual circumstances a disqualification for life is wrong in principle ". The danger of imposing long consecutive periods of disqualification was, of course, recognised by Parliament itself when enacting the Road Traffic (Disqualification) Act, 1970 (now repealed by and incorporated in the Road Traffic Act, 1972: see in particular para. 7 of Sched. 10 to the Act), which removed the offence of driving while disqualified from the list of offences involving obligatory disqualification and allowed persons who had been disqualified for " additional " periods for that offence to apply for their removal (see p. 655).

Disqualification starts to run on the day on which the order of disqualification is made, even though that day is later than the day of conviction, e.g., because there has been an adjournment. See p. 631. The day on which the order is made counts as one full day of the period of disqualification and the defendant may not drive from the moment when the court pronounces the order; someone else must drive his vehicle away from the court unless notice of appeal in writing is given and the court suspends the disqualification. Thus, a disqualification for twelve months imposed on the afternoon of 1st January will expire at 11.59 p.m. on 31st December. If an unlawful period of disqualification has been imposed and the High Court substitutes the correct period, that runs from the date of the magistrates' original decision, unless the High Court otherwise orders (Administration of Justice Act, 1960, s. 16). Time during which the disqualification was suspended is disregarded (Road Traffic Act, 1972, s. 94 (4)). There is no power to disqualify pedal cyclists or tricyclists or indeed from the driving of any type of vehicle other than a motor vehicle or trolley vehicle.

No Power to Limit Disqualification

There is now no power to limit disqualification to the type of vehicle in use at the time of the offence. If disqualification is imposed, the defendant is disqualified from driving all types of motor vehicles and for all purposes.

" Disqualified " in a policy was held to mean " disqualified by order of the court " and not to cover the case of a person who had been refused renewal of his driving licence because of mental deficiency (*Edwards* v. *Griffiths* [1953] 2 All E.R. 874). But a person is " disqualified " if he is prohibited by the Road Traffic Act, 1960, s. 97 (now s. 96 of the 1972 Act) from driving because he is under age (*Mumford* v. *Hardy* [1956] 1 All E.R. 337) and it is in order to prosecute a person under age for driving while disqualified under s. 99 rather than for driving under age contrary to s. 4 despite the heavier penalty and compulsory disqualification under s. 99 (*R.* v. *Saddleworth JJ., ex parte Staples* [1968] 1 All E.R. 1189). Similarly, if a person is disqualified until he passes a test under s. 93 (7) he may be prosecuted for driving while disqualified under s. 99 (*b*) if after having obtained a provisional licence he fails to comply with a provisional licence condition (*Scott* v. *Jelfe* [1974] R.T.R. 256). It is submitted at 122 J.P. Jo. 780 that a person whose licence is suspended because of its non-production for endorsement under s. 7 of the 1962 Act (now s. 101 of the 1972 Act) is not " disqualified "; he merely commits the offence of driving without a driving licence if he drives prior to its due production.

Undertaking Not to Drive

Sometimes a defendant will give an undertaking to the court that he will not drive again, and the court may refrain from disqualifying in reliance on this undertaking. Should he then drive again, vows, etc., deriding, the books on criminal law do not mention such a breach as being the crime of contempt but breaches of an undertaking to the courts in general are mentioned in 8 Halsbury, 3rd ed., p. 29, as being contempts. It is suggested that, in such a case, the matter should be reported to the Director of Public Prosecutions.

If the defendant has surrendered his licence, after having given such an undertaking, he may be prosecuted for driving without a licence because, having given up his licence to the Department of the Environment, he is no longer the holder of it.

Vehicles Used for Crime

The Criminal Justice Act, 1972, introduced two new orders where motor vehicles are used for criminal purposes, first, an order of disqualification for holding or obtaining a driving licence if a vehicle was used in the course of a crime or for its facilitation, and secondly an order depriving an offender of property used for criminal purposes. The powers were contained in ss. 23 and 24 of the Act and have now been repealed and re-enacted in ss. 43 and 44 of the Powers of Criminal Courts Act, 1973.

Sections 43 and 44 read as follows:—

" **43.**—(1) Where a person is convicted of an offence punishable on indictment with imprisonment for a term of two years or more and the court by or before which he is convicted is satisfied that any property which was in his possession or under his control at the time of his apprehension—

    (*a*) has been used for the purpose of committing, or facilitating the commission of, any offence; or
    (*b*) was intended by him to be used for that purpose;

the court may make an order under this section in respect of that property.

(2) Facilitating the commission of an offence shall be taken for the purposes of this section and section 44 of this Act to include the taking of any steps after it has been committed for the purpose of disposing of any property to which it relates or of avoiding apprehension or detection,

and references in this or that section to an offence punishable with imprisonment shall be construed without regard to any prohibition or restriction imposed by or under any enactment on the imprisonment of young offenders.

(3), (4) and (5) (*Application of the Police (Property) Act, 1897, and effect of the order on the offender's rights to the property.*)

44.—(1) This section applies where a person is convicted before the Crown Court of an offence punishable on indictment with imprisonment for a term of two years or more or, having been convicted by a magistrates' court of such an offence, is committed under section 29 of the Magistrates' Courts Act 1952 to the Crown Court for sentence.

(2) If in a case to which this section applies the Crown Court is satisfied that a motor vehicle was used (by the person convicted or by anyone else) for the purpose of committing, or facilitating the commission of, the offence in question (within the meaning of section 43 of this Act), the court may order the person convicted to be disqualified, for such period as the court thinks fit, for holding or obtaining a licence to drive a motor vehicle granted under Part III of the Road Traffic Act 1972.

(3) (*Court to require production of driving licence and application of ss.* 95 *and* 101 (4) *of the Road Traffic Act,* 1972.)

(1) *Disqualification for use of a vehicle for criminal purposes.*— It will be noted that the motor vehicle does not have to be actually used in the course of the crime; it merely has to have been used for the purposes of committing or facilitating the offence. Note also the very wide definition of " facilitating " in s. 43 (2). Moreover the offender does not have to be the person driving the vehicle; the only requirement is that the person is convicted of the offence in respect of which the motor vehicle was used.

An offender allowed himself to be carried as a passenger in a motor vehicle to ten separate banks, at each of which he drew £30 on a stolen cheque. While he was in the bank, an accomplice in the car prepared a duplicate cheque-book for use at the next bank to be visited. It was held that the motor vehicle was used by the defendant for the purpose of facilitating the commission of offences (*R. v. Mathews* [1975] R.T.R. 32). The power may only be exercised by the Crown Court either when the defendant is convicted by the Crown Court or when he is committed for sentence to the Crown Court under s. 29 of the Magistrates' Courts Act, 1952. The offence must be punishable on indictment with imprisonment of at least two years. " Motor vehicle " is not defined in the Powers of Criminal Courts Act, 1973, and the wide definition in the Road Traffic Act, 1972, does not seem to be applicable.

Although the section is in very wide terms, the provision seems primarily designed to enable the courts to disqualify " the motor man ", the driver of the getaway car, in a serious crime such as a wages snatch or bank robbery. In *Mathews, supra,* the Court of

Appeal, although holding that the trial judge was legally entitled to disqualify the offender, allowed his appeal against the sentence of disqualification, since the vehicle was not used as a getaway car. Moreover, as the offender was sentenced to prison for five years, it was unnecessary and undesirable that he should have the additional penalty of disqualification when he was released, which could hinder him in earning an honest living. On the other hand, where an offender was paid £50 to drive a vehicle containing carpets worth £33,000 stolen from a warehouse, his disqualification for 2½ years, together with an order under s. 43 depriving him of the car, were upheld (*R.* v. *Brown* (*Edward*) [1975] R.T.R. 36*n*). In *R.* v. *Thomas* (*Derek*) [1975] R.T.R. 38*n* a disqualification of six years was reduced to five; the defendant was sent to prison for five years for driving another man to a car park to steal jewellery worth £20,000 from the boot of a parked car belonging to a jeweller.

The court are under a duty to require the person disqualified to produce his licence to the court. If he does not do so he commits an offence under s. 101 (4) of the Road Traffic Act, 1972 (see p. 608), of failing to produce a licence (s. 44 (3)). An order of disqualification under the section may be removed, like any other disqualification, under s. 95 of the Road Traffic Act, 1972 (s. 44 (3); for s. 95 see p. 646). It would seem that an order under s. 44 may be suspended pending the hearing of an appeal under s. 94 (2) of the Road Traffic Act, 1972, as s. 94 (2) does not seem to be limited to an order of disqualification made under the Road Traffic Act. However, an appellate court cannot suspend the disqualification under s. 94A or s. 94B, as these sections are specifically limited to offences " involving obligatory or discretionary disqualification " and these words seemingly refer to s. 93 (1) and (2) of the Road Traffic Act.

The court cannot order the licence to be endorsed, because the power of endorsement only applies to the offences referred to in s. 101 (1) of the Road Traffic Act, 1972. For this reason a conviction of an offence for which the defendant is disqualified under s. 44 does not count as a conviction for the purpose of " totting up " under s. 93 (3). (*Aliter*, it would seem, if the offence is an obligatorily endorsable offence referred to in s. 101 (1), e.g., the theft or taking of a motor vehicle contrary to s. 1 or s. 12 of the Theft Act; also, it is submitted, robbery or burglary where a motor vehicle is stolen in the course of the robbery or burglary (see p. 620).)

The court are obliged to send notice of the disqualification to the Department of the Environment (s. 105 of the Road Traffic Act, 1972).

(2) *Deprivation of property used for criminal purposes.*—The power of deprivation of property under s. 43 (see p. 640) may be used in respect of motor vehicles used for criminal purposes, since " property " must clearly include a motor vehicle. In *R*. v. *Brown (Edward)*, *supra*, the offender was not only disqualified but also deprived under this section of the motor vehicle which he drove. Where an order is made under s. 43 the offender is deprived of all right to the property and it is required to be taken into police possession (if not already in their possession) (s. 43 (3)). By s. 43 (4) and (5) a person claiming ownership may apply under the Police (Property) Act, 1897, within six months of the order but cannot succeed in his application unless he satisfies the magistrates' court that he did not consent to the offender having possession or did not know and had no reason to suspect that it would be used for criminal purposes.

It should be noted that, unlike s. 44, a magistrates' court has power to make an order under s. 43. The offence merely has to be one for which a person if convicted on indictment is punishable with two years' or more imprisonment. This definition in s. 43 (1) appears to include virtually all indictable offences triable summarily under s. 19 of the Magistrates' Courts Act, 1952, and also many " hybrid " offences under s. 18 of that Act as well.

Appeal and Suspensions

By the Road Traffic Act, 1972, s. 94 (3), a person who by virtue of an order of a magistrates' court is disqualified from driving may appeal against the order in the same way as against a conviction, and the court may, if it thinks fit, pending the appeal, suspend the operation of the order. The wording suggests that the disqualification may be suspended only if there is an appeal against the order of disqualification; a defendant wishing to appeal against his conviction should presumably include an appeal against the order of disqualification also in his notice of appeal and later abandon it if he fears that the Crown Court may increase the period of disqualification. The time for appealing to the Crown Court is twenty-one days, extendable with the leave of the Crown Court (see p. 696). Although the time-limit for giving notice of application to appeal to the Crown Court was altered from fourteen to twenty-one days by the Courts Act, 1971, or rules made thereunder, s. 87 (2) of the Magistrates' Courts Act, 1952, which prescribes a time-limit of fourteen days for making an application to a magistrates' court to state a case, has been left unaltered. Appeal on law would be by case stated or by application for certiorari to the High Court. Appeal on facts from magistrates will be to the

Crown Court (see p. 696, particularly as to cases where a defendant has been committed to a Crown Court other than the one to which he would normally appeal).   The court here seems to mean any court acting for the same place and, *semble*, a single magistrate for the same court may hear the application for suspension pending the hearing of the appeal.   This power extends to automatic disqualifications, e.g., for drunken driving, on the grounds that there were " special reasons ".   It is submitted that, as the Magistrates' Courts Act, 1952, ss. 84 and 87, require written notice of appeal (see rr. 63 and 65 of the Magistrates' Courts Rules, 1968), the court should not suspend a disqualification until the written notice is received.

There is an appeal, with the leave of the Court of Appeal, Criminal Division, to that court against an order of disqualification imposed by a Crown Court whether on conviction on indictment there or on dealing with a person committed for sentence (Criminal Appeal Act, 1968, ss. 9, 10 (3), 11 (1) and 50 (1), as amended by the Courts Act, 1971).   The relevant Crown Court may, by the Road Traffic Act, 1972, s. 94 (3), suspend the disqualification pending an appeal against the order; presumably it should not be suspended till notice of appeal against the disqualification has been duly given.   The time for appealing is twenty-eight days but it may be extended with the Court of Appeal's leave.   The Criminal Appeal Rules, 1968, contain no provision automatically suspending a disqualification pending an appeal, as the revoked 1908 Rules did (but see below).

In Scotland, there is an appeal against a disqualification ordered by any court and the latter court may suspend it pending the appeal.

Until 1975 only the court which disqualified the offender could suspend the disqualification, but now appellate courts can suspend an order of disqualification imposed by the court of first instance by virtue of ss. 94A and 94B of the Road Traffic Act, 1972   These sections are inserted in the 1972 Act by Sched. 3 to the 1974 Act and enable all appellate courts other than the House of Lords to suspend an order of disqualification pending appeal.   A Crown Court may suspend an order of disqualification pending the hearing of an appeal from a magistrates' court (s. 94A (2)), the Court of Appeal may do so on appeal or application for leave to appeal (s. 94A (2)), the High Court may do so on appeal by way of case stated from a magistrates' court or Crown Court (s. 94A (4)) or on application for certiorari or for leave to make such an application (s. 94A (5)).   Similar powers apply to Scottish appellate courts (s. 94B).   The Court of Appeal or the Divisional Court may suspend an order of disqualification on appeal, or after application has been made for leave to appeal, to the House of Lords (s. 94A (3)).

Disqualification must be endorsed on any licence held or to be held by the defendant (Road Traffic Act, 1972, s. 101). Disqualification is not suspended by notice of appeal alone (*Kidner* v. *Daniels* (1910), 74 J.P. 127); there must be an application to suspend it. There seems to be no appeal against refusal to suspend but if the court of first instance has refused to suspend, application may be made to the appellate court and, seemingly, *vice versa*. A power to suspend also exists where the appeal is from the magistrates to the High Court. On suspending an order of disqualification pending appeal, the court suspending the order must notify the Department of the Environment (ss. 94 (3A, 94A (7) and 94B (3) of the Act of 1972 as amended by Scheds. 3 and 6 to the Act of 1974). The power to suspend an order of disqualification pending appeal applies to an order of disqualification for use of a vehicle for crime but the appellate courts cannot do so (see p. 642).

For the reasons given on p. 649 under " Effect and Removal of Consecutive Disqualifications ", it is submitted that the order of a court imposing consecutive disqualifications should declare that each commences on the expiration of the one or ones to which it is added and that no dates should be given in the order, although there would be no objection to explaining the order, with its dates, to the defendant.

By the Road Traffic Act, 1972, s. 94 (4), in calculating the period for which a person is disqualified, by conviction or order, any time after conviction during which the disqualification was suspended or he was not disqualified shall be disregarded. Thus, if Jehu is convicted of driving under the influence of drink on 1st July, 1975 and disqualified from driving for a year but immediately appeals and has the disqualification suspended the same day till the appeal is heard, the period of disqualification will run from the hearing of the appeal. If the Crown Court affirm the disqualification on 1st October, 1975, he will be disqualified from then until the first moment of 1st October, 1976. Again, if Toad is convicted of a like offence on 1st August, 1975, and the magistrates omit to disqualify and the High Court, on appeal by the prosecutor, directs on 4th December, 1975, that he be disqualified for a year, his disqualification will run from then till the first moment of 4th December, 1976. Days during which disqualification runs prior to suspension should be subtracted from the period running from the date of the appeal. And see *R.* v. *Lambeth Metropolitan Magistrate* on p. 649.

It is submitted that, where a defendant has been put on probation or conditionally discharged and not disqualified and he commits a breach of the conditions of his probation or an offence during his period of probation or discharge, the court then sentencing him for the original offence under s. 6 or s. 8 of the Powers of Criminal Courts Act, 1973, may disqualify him; the court is empowered to " deal with him " as if he had just been convicted and the reference in s. 13 (3) to the non-imposition of a disqualification relates to a person who " is " placed on probation or discharged, not one who " has been ". See further 128 J.P.Jo. 670 and 705 and 129 J.P.Jo. 70 and argument on p. 353 of the 5th edition of this book. The Road Traffic Act, 1972, s. 102 (1), relates to the occasion when a person is put on probation or conditionally discharged and not to subsequent proceedings for breach.

Removal of Disqualification

Disqualification prior to 29th May, 1963

It is now possible to make an application for removal of any order of disqualification which has not yet expired and which was imposed prior to the 29th May, 1963, when the Road Traffic Act, 1962, came into force (s. 6 (2) of the Road Traffic Act, 1962, preserved by para. 2 of Sched. 10 to the 1972 Act).

Disqualification on or after 29th May, 1963

By the Road Traffic Act, 1972, s. 95 (re-enacting s. 106 of the 1960 Act as amended by s. 6 of the Road Traffic Act, 1962) a person disqualified on or after 29th May, 1963, may apply for removal of his disqualification—

(a) if the disqualification is for less than four years, when two years from the date on which it was imposed have expired;

(b) if the disqualification is for less than ten years but not less than four years, when half the period of disqualification has expired;

(c) in any other cases, i.e., ten years or more or for " life ", when five years have expired from the date of disqualification.

Thus, a person disqualified on or after 29th May, 1963, for two years or less cannot apply at all for removal of his disqualification; his only course is to appeal to the Crown Court in the hope of a reduction of the period. This limitation is modified, however, in respect of " additional " periods of disqualification imposed for the offence of driving while disqualified (see p. 655).

An order of disqualification under s. 24 of the Criminal Justice Act, 1972, or s. 44 of the Powers of Criminal Courts Act, 1973 (disqualification for using a vehicle for criminal purposes (see p. 641)) may be removed under s. 95 (but is, of course, subject to the time limits set out above).

There is no power to remove a disqualification under s. 93 (7) of the 1972 Act, i.e., a disqualification until a driving test is passed (see p. 660). Section 95, *supra*, does not apply to such a disqualification (s. 95 (5)). In *R.* v. *Nuttall* [1971] Crim.L.R. 485 the applicant was disqualified for five years for the offence of causing death by dangerous driving and also disqualified until he passed a test of competence to drive. In view of s. 95 (6) some doubt had been expressed whether the five years' disqualification could be removed in view of the additional order of disqualification pending a test. Bridge J., in hearing the case, considered the matter, held that he had power to do so and granted the application on its merits.

Procedure

If removal is refused, the applicant may again apply and continue to apply at intervals of not less than three months thereafter. The court may, if it thinks proper, having regard to the applicant's character and his conduct subsequent to his conviction, the nature of the offence and any other circumstances of the case, remove the disqualification from that day or any later day named. The magistrates' clerk notifies the appropriate licensing authority of the removal of disqualification. Where the disqualification was imposed by a Crown Court, the application should be made to the location of the Crown Court where it was originally made, or, if it was made by assizes or quarter sessions, to the location of the Crown Court which is most convenient to the place where the order was made (Directions given by the Lord Chief Justice with the concurrence of the Lord Chancellor under ss. 4 (5) and 5 (4) of the Courts Act, 1971). Where it was imposed by a magistrates' court, application is made to a magistrate for the same court by complaint for issue of a summons, which is heard in that court at a later date; a precedent for such complaint is in Oke's Magisterial Formulist, 18th ed., pp. 922–923. The appropriate senior police officer is notified by summons of the application and may, if he wishes, oppose it (Magistrates' Courts Rules, 1968, r. 84). Where the disqualification was imposed by assizes or quarter sessions or by the Crown Court, the applicant should get in touch with the Crown Court offices at the location specified in the Directions of the Lord Chief Justice (see above). It is said at 111 J.P.Jo. 699

that, where a juvenile court has disqualified a young person, any application to remove the disqualification should be made to the juvenile court, although the defendant may have since become an adult.

If a disqualification is " for life ", it is submitted that five years must elapse before the first application to remove can be made.

It is submitted that a magistrate or justices' clerk cannot refuse to issue a summons for removal of a disqualification, whatever they may think of the applicant's chances, provided the application is not less than three months after any previous one and not before the expiry of the period after which he may first apply (see *supra*); the reason for this view is that r. 84 says that the magistrate " shall " issue a summons to the police, thus taking away the normal discretion whether or not to issue one.

The application need not be heard by the same judge or justices as imposed disqualification, so long as the same court hears it, but, where a disqualification period is varied on appeal to quarter sessions or the Crown Court, it seems that the magistrates' court can hear an application to remove (*The Times*, 4th February, 1931; [1956] Crim.L.R. 41; for a contrary view see [1955] Crim. L.R. 767 and [1956] Crim.L.R. 110). It is submitted that the correct view is that given at 121 J.P.Jo. 819, viz., that in view of the latter part of s. 86 of the Magistrates' Courts Act, 1952, declaring that a decision of quarter sessions on appeal has effect as if it is made by the magistrates' court, it is the latter court which hears an application to remove a disqualification imposed or confirmed by quarter sessions on appeal. The Courts Act, 1971, has made no difference to the legal position, it is submitted, save to substitute the Crown Court for quarter sessions. However, in *Sherrard* v. *Woods* [1958] N.I. 13, where a like Northern Irish statute was under consideration, it was said that, while the magistrates' court was the proper tribunal to remove a disqualification imposed there and upheld by sessions on appeal without alteration, it might be otherwise if the magistrates' order had been varied or sessions had imposed a disqualification and the magistrates had not. No doubt the magistrates can obtain leave by letter from the Crown Court to deal with the application if in doubt as to their powers; see generally 120 J.P.Jo. 294 and 374. There is no appeal from a refusal to remove the disqualification or against a removal save in either case to the High Court on a point of law. The applicant may be ordered to pay costs, whether successful or not (s. 95 (4)), and by the Magistrates' Courts Act, 1952, s. 55, the person opposing removal may be ordered to pay costs if the disqualification is removed (see the Magistrates' Courts Rules, 1968, r. 84, declaring such applications to be by complaint and making the police, in effect, the respondent).

By s. 94 (4), in computing the time after which a person may apply for removal of a disqualification, any time after the conviction during which it was suspended or he was not disqualified shall be disregarded. See also p. 639.

It seems that the court must either remove the disqualification altogether or refuse the application altogether; a disqualification cannot be varied under s. 95 (*R.* v. *Cottrell* (*No.* 2) [1956] 1 All E.R. 751), but a court may remove the disqualification " from such date as may be specified in the order " (s. 95 (1)). There seems nothing to prevent a court, therefore, granting the application for removal to come into effect—say—in one year's time from the date of the hearing of the application. A person was disqualified in April, 1954, for three years. In May, 1955, the court removed the disqualification as from April, 1956. He applied in August, 1955, for its immediate removal. It was held that the magistrates were not estopped by their May decision from hearing the August application (*R.* v. *Manchester JJ.*, *ex parte Gaynor* [1956] 1 All E.R. 610).

Where a licence is restored under s. 95 the court is required to endorse particulars of the order on any licence previously held by the applicant (s. 94 (4)), except where the order of disqualification which is removed is an order under s. 24 of the Criminal Justice Act, 1972, or s. 44 of the Powers of Criminal Courts Act, 1973 (disqualification for using a vehicle for criminal purposes: see p. 641). The court is obliged to notify the licensing authority of an order under s. 95 (whether it is an ordinary order of disqualification or one under s. 24 or s. 44, above).

Effect and Removal of Consecutive Disqualifications

Where a person has been subjected to a second period of disqualification consecutive to a first, he cannot apply to remove the second period until two years (or the longer applicable term if the second period is for more than four years) of that second period have elapsed; the second period does not start to run until the first has expired or been earlier determined and so with third and subsequent consecutive disqualifications (*R.* v. *Lambeth Metropolitan Magistrate,* *ex parte Everett* [1967] 3 All E.R. 648, where it was held that a defendant who had been disqualified for three years plus three years consecutive on the same day and applied for removal of the second disqualification three and one quarter years after it had been imposed and when it had been effective for only three months, must wait till two years had elapsed from the date on which the second disqualification began to run, viz., five years from the date it was imposed).   Section 106 (2) (now s. 95 (4) of the 1972 Act) should be read as saying that " time after the conviction during which the disqualification was suspended or he was not disqualified *by virtue of that order* shall be disregarded "; " suspended " means " suspended pending an appeal under s. 105 (1) " (now s. 94 (1) and (2)).

If the subsequent consecutive orders have been imposed as a result of an incorrect original order of disqualification, the court will normally remove all the orders of disqualification either by certiorari or allowing an appeal out of time.   Thus in *R.* v. *Middleton, &c., JJ., ex parte Collins* [1970] 1 Q.B. 216 in excess of jurisdiction a defendant was initially disqualified for a year.   He drove during that first year, for which he was disqualified for a further five years.   He again drove and was disqualified for yet another five years.   All the convictions and disqualifications were set aside.

Similarly in *R.* v. *Lambert* [1974] R.T.R. 244 the Court of Appeal quashed a conviction for driving while disqualified in respect of periods of disqualification which were wrongly ordered to run consecutively; the court also refused to apply s. 11 (3) of the Criminal Appeal Act, 1968, to quash the unlawful consecutive orders of disqualification and substitute lawful orders of disqualification disqualifying him for the same period.

Driving while Disqualified

The offence of driving while disqualified or obtaining a driving licence while disqualified is dealt with by the Road Traffic Act, 1972, s. 99, which reads:—

" If a person disqualified for holding or obtaining a licence—
  (a) obtains a licence while he is so disqualified, or
  (b) while he is so disqualified drives on a road a motor vehicle, or
      if the disqualification is limited to the driving of a motor vehicle
      of a particular class, a motor vehicle of that class,
he shall be guilty of an offence."

Section 99 of the 1972 Act replaces s. 110 of the Act of 1960, as amended by the Act of 1962 and the Vehicle and Driving Licences Act, 1969.   This last Act repealed the offence of applying for a licence while disqualified.   Presumably the reason was to allow a disqualified person, or a person under age, to make his application shortly before his disqualification ends or he becomes of age so that he can be sent the licence as soon as he is entitled to it.   A disqualified person who applies for a licence to be issued whilst disqualified can presumably be charged with attempting to obtain a licence whilst disqualified. Moreover an offence under s. 170 of the 1972 Act of knowingly making a false declaration to obtain a driving licence would almost certainly be committed.

By s. 180, proceedings for an offence under s. 99 may be brought within a period of six months from the date on which sufficient evidence of the commission of the alleged offence came to the knowledge of the prosecutor, provided that no proceedings may be brought more than three years after the commission of the offence. Section 180 applies to summary proceedings; proceedings for an offence under s. 99 (b) may, it seems, be tried on indictment at any time but those under s. 99 (a) must be within the limits specified in s. 180 because offences under s. 99 (a) may only be tried summarily (for text of s. 180 see p. 69).

A constable in uniform may arrest at any time a person driving or attempting to drive a motor vehicle whom he has reasonable cause to suspect of being disqualified (s. 100).

The power of arrest by a police constable is limited to a person " driving or attempting to drive " whom the constable has reasonable cause to suspect of being disqualified. These words, " driving or attempting to drive " in s. 30 of the Road Safety Act, 1967 (now s. 100 of the 1972 Act), are identical with the words in s. 2 (1) of the Road Safety Act which were considered in *Pinner* v. *Everett* (see p. 184). This fact was referred to by Lord Morris in his dissenting judgment in *Pinner* v. *Everett* when he said: " It would be irrational to suppose that an arrest under that section had to be while the car was in motion." It is also clear from the judgment of the Court of Appeal in *R.* v. *Jones* (*E. J. M.*) that the doctrine of " fresh pursuit " (see p. 191) applies to an arrest under this section as it does to an arrest under s. 2 (now s. 8 of the 1972 Act).

Two points may be made. First, should s. 100 come to be construed by the High Court, the words may not necessarily be construed in the same fashion as the majority judgments in *Pinner* v. *Everett* because there is no alternative offence of being " in charge " of a vehicle while a disqualified driver. Secondly, even assuming that the words " driving or attempting to drive " are held to bear the same meaning as in s. 8 (1), a wrongful arrest cannot, it is submitted, affect a conviction for driving whilst disqualified contrary to s. 99. An arrest is not an essential part of an offence under s. 99 and the principle of *Scott* v. *Baker* [1968] 2 All E.R. 993 cannot apply.

The defendant no longer has any right to elect trial by jury under s. 99 (a), as the offence is a purely summary offence and the Road Traffic Act, 1974, has removed the power of imprisonment. For an offence under s. 99 (b) the prosecutor can apply for trial on indictment under s. 18 of the Magistrates' Courts Act, 1952, but the defendant can no longer elect trial by jury under s. 25 of that Act, as the maximum period of imprisonment has been reduced to three months by the Road Traffic Act, 1974 (for a short discussion on the right of trial by jury under s. 18, see p. 80).   A person may not be committed for sentence to the Crown Court for an offence under s. 18 unless the proceedings commenced as committal proceedings under s. 18 (1) (*R.* v. *South Greenhoe JJ.*, *ex parte D.P.P.* [1950] 2 All E.R. 42).   The defendant may be committed to the Crown Court under s. 28 of the 1952 Act with a view to a sentence of borstal training.   He may also be committed to the Crown Court under s. 56 of the Criminal Justice Act, 1967, if committed for sentence in respect of another offence.

Offences under s. 99 include driving when the defendant has been ordered by a court to take a driving test and fails to comply with a provisional licence condition (*Scott* v. *Jelfe, infra*).

In s. 99 (and in all other sections of Pt. III), " licence " means a licence to drive a motor vehicle granted under Pt. III of the Road Traffic Act, 1972.

It will be noted that " driving ", as discussed on p. 21, must be proved.   If the defendant is merely in charge, without any attempt at driving, there is no offence.   If he has attempted to drive whilst disqualified (see p. 655 for an example of attempted driving), he may be tried summarily with his consent pursuant to the Magistrates' Courts Act, 1952, s. 19, and may be committed for sentence under s. 29 of that Act, if appropriate.

A person who drives when under age can be charged under s. 99 as well as under s. 4 of the 1972 Act (though he should not be punished for both offences), as he is deemed to be disqualified (*R.* v. *Saddleworth JJ.*, *ex parte Staples* [1968] 1 All E.R. 1189).   A person disqualified under s. 93 (7) until he passes a test commits an offence under s. 99 if after taking out a provisional licence he fails to comply with a provisional licence condition (*Scott* v. *Jelfe* [1974] R.T.R. 256).   A person from abroad who is disqualified under s. 93 of the 1972 Act by a court in Great Britain may not drive here though he may hold a driving licence or permit of his own country; s. 99 forbids driving while disqualified for holding or obtaining a " licence " (which means a licence issued under Pt. III of the 1972 Act).

Allowing a person who is known to be disqualified to drive can amount to aiding and abetting this offence (*Pope* v. *Minton* [1954] Crim.L.R. 711), but it is otherwise where the car-owner allows a disqualified person to drive in ignorance of the disqualification and after making enquiries which a reasonable man should make

(*Bateman* v. *Evans* (1964), 108 S.J. 522). Proof of the order of disqualification may be by the endorsement (s. 101 (1)), by a certified statement under s. 182 or by certificate of conviction or extract from the magistrates' court register, with identification of the defendant (*Stone* v. *Bastick* [1965] 3 All E.R. 713, where there was a certificate of quarter sessions to which the defendant had been committed for sentence and which had disqualified him, after conviction by magistrates). Only the offence for which he was disqualified should appear in the certificate or extract; if he was disqualified for more than one offence, it seems that only a conviction involving one of the current disqualifications should be shown (*ibid.*). *Semble*, if there were consecutive disqualifications, it might be necessary to show more than one. If the defence are not disputing the disqualification, an admission under s. 10 of the Criminal Justice Act, 1967, can be used to avoid the magistrates or jury having to look at a certificate or extract which shows more than is necessary. It would also be possible to prove an order of disqualification by certificate under s. 182 of the Act of 1972 (see p. 107).

Driving while disqualified is an offence of strict liability. The defendant commits the offence if he drives when disqualified even if he neither knew nor ought to have known of the disqualification. A defendant was disqualified for six months on 19th November, 1970, and on 2nd February, 1971, a different court disqualified him for a further six months under s. 93 (3) for " totting up ". The licensing authority, not realising that the order in February was, by virtue of s. 93 (5), consecutive to the six months imposed in November, returned the licence to the defendant in August and he then resumed driving. His conviction for driving while disqualified was upheld (*R.* v. *Bowsher* [1973] R.T.R. 202, following and applying *Taylor* v. *Kenyon* [1952] 2 All E.R. 726).

A disqualified person may not, in Great Britain, drive on a road any motor vehicle (including a trolley vehicle) even though he may have joined H.M. Forces and have been issued with a service driving licence.

A charge of driving while disqualified should not normally be tried along with another road traffic offence in view of the possible prejudice to the defendant (*R.* v. *Pomeroy* (1935), 25 Cr.App.R. 147, as qualified on p. 77).

Penalty, Endorsement and Disqualification for Driving whilst Disqualified

The penalty for obtaining a licence while disqualified (s. 99 (*a*)) is £100 for a first or subsequent offence. The penalty for driving while disqualified (s. 99 (*b*)) is three months' imprisonment or

£400 or both if tried summarily. When tried on indictment it is twelve months' imprisonment or a fine of unlimited amount or both.

Endorsement of driving licences to be held by the offender must be ordered for the offence of driving whilst disqualified, unless there are special reasons. A driving test may be ordered for that offence (s. 93 (7)).

Endorsement, disqualification and a driving test cannot be ordered for the offence of obtaining a licence whilst disqualified. The endorsement code for an offence under s. 99 (b) is BA 10 (see p. 874).

Disqualification

It was said in R. v. Phillips (1955), 119 J.P. 499, that when disqualification and imprisonment are imposed together, the period of disqualification should be sufficiently long to ensure that the greater part of it will not have expired by the time the defendant is released from gaol, but it is suggested that regard should also be had to the danger of imposing long periods of disqualification, particularly if it is likely to cause the offender to drive while disqualified or is likely to hinder him in leading an honest life. A defendant sentenced to twelve months' imprisonment and disqualified for three years had the disqualification reduced to twelve months by the Court of Appeal on the ground that the period of imprisonment was the deterrent and he would face financial difficulties when leaving prison, strengthening the temptation to drive while disqualified (R. v. Pashley [1973] R.T.R. 149).

Formerly the offence involved obligatory disqualification of at least twelve months and, like " totting up " disqualifications, was required to be additional to any other period of disqualification whether imposed on that or any other occasion. This had the effect that a significant number of young men who ignored the law and persistently drove while disqualified in a short space of time found themselves disqualified for a considerable number of years. Moreover, as the periods of disqualification, although lengthy in total, were mostly of two years or less, it was not possible to apply for their removal (see R. v. Lambeth Metropolitan Magistrate on p. 649). For this reason and following judicial criticism (see for example R. v. Shirley (1969), 113 S.J. 721), the Road Traffic (Disqualification) Act, 1970, was enacted. The Act came into force on 15th July, 1970, and applied to any person sentenced on or after that date, whether or not the offence of driving while disqualified was committed before or after that date. Section 1 (1) of the Act removed the offence of driving while disqualified from the category of offences involving obligatory disqualification to the category of offences involving discretionary disqualification only. Section 1 (2) amended s. 5 (5) of the Act of 1962 by deleting the reference to s. 110 offences. The effect of the amendment was to make any disqualification imposed for the offence of driving while disqualified no longer " additional ". The amendments made by s. 1 (1) and (2) have been incorporated in the provisions as to disqualification contained in the Road Traffic Act, 1972. The effect, therefore, is that a court is no longer obliged to impose any disqualification on conviction of the offence of driving while disqualified. Any disqualification that is imposed cannot be made to run consecutively, but must commence at the moment the order of disqualification is pronounced by the court. The court may order an offender to be disqualified until he passes a test of competence to drive under s. 93 (7) of the 1972 Act.

Section 93 (3) of the 1972 Act, however, still applies, so that a person convicted under s. 99 (b) who has within the three years immediately preceding the commission of the offence been convicted on not less than two occasions of an endorsed disqualifiable offence must be disqualified for at least six months additional and consecutive to any period then or previously imposed, unless the court is satisfied having regard to all the circumstances that there are grounds for mitigating the normal consequences of the conviction. See p. 688 and onwards.

Attempts

There is no power to disqualify or endorse for attempting to drive while disqualified (*Bell* v. *Ingham* [1968] 2 All E.R. 333) nor for attempting to drive when under age.

A disqualified motor cyclist pushed a motor cycle on a car park six yards to the entrance on to a public road, where he was about to ride it; although he could not be convicted of driving while disqualified, since the car park was not a road, he could be convicted of attempting to drive while disqualified (*Shaw* v. *Knill* [1973] R.T.R. 142).

Removal of Disqualifications for Driving while Disqualified (for orders made before 15th July, 1970)

Section 2 of the Road Traffic (Disqualification) Act, 1970, allowed persons disqualified for " additional " periods of disqualification for the offence of driving while disqualified to apply for their removal. Section 2 has been repealed and replaced by para. 7 of Sched. 10 to the 1972 Act. It reads as follows:—

" (1) Without prejudice to section 95 of this Act, any person who by an order of a court made before 15th July, 1970, was, in pursuance of section 5 (5) of the Road Traffic Act, 1962, disqualified for holding or obtaining a licence to drive a motor vehicle granted under Part II of the Road Traffic Act, 1960, for an additional period in consequence of a conviction of an offence under section 110 (b) of the said Act of 1960 may apply for the removal of the disqualification to the court by which the order was made or, if there are in force two or more such orders disqualifying him for an additional period, he may apply for the removal of the disqualification to the court which made the last of the orders to expire; and on any such application the court may, as it thinks proper, either by order remove the disqualification or all or any of the disqualifications as from such date as may be specified in the order or refuse the application.

(2) If under this paragraph a court orders a disqualification to be removed, the court shall cause particulars of the order to be endorsed on any licence to drive a motor vehicle granted to the applicant under Part II of the Road Traffic Act, 1960, and the court shall, in any case, have power to order the applicant to pay the whole or any part of the costs of the application."

The court has a complete discretion as to whether to grant an application for removal. It may refuse the application or remove the whole or part of the disqualification from such date as it thinks fit. No restriction appears to be placed on the number of applications for removal or on the frequency with which such applications are made. The only sanction against frivolous applications is that the court, whether or not the application is granted, has power to order the applicant to pay the whole or any part of the costs of the application. It is submitted that a court when considering applications in the absence of special circumstances may wish to have regard to the purpose of the Act, namely the rehabilitation of young men who after a period of " car mad " adolescence wish to settle down and earn an honest living, and to whom the possession of a driving licence will be a help in doing so. In *R. v. Muncaster* [1974] Crim.L.R. 320, the defendant had been disqualified for two years in February, 1961 for driving uninsured. Two months later he was disqualified for twenty years for driving while disqualified and in 1965, 1969 and 1971 received further terms of disqualification for driving while disqualified, so that he became disqualified until 1986. The Court of Appeal in directing his release expressed regret that the court had no jurisdiction to remove the twenty-year disqualification and expressed the view that they could not understand why application had not been made for its removal.

It will be noted that for a disqualification to be removable it must be " additional " and imposed in consequence of a conviction under s. 110 (b) of the Road Traffic Act, 1960. In *R. v. Bradfield and Sonning JJ., ex parte Holdsworth* [1971] 3 All E.R. 755 the applicant drove while disqualified and was convicted of the offence after his original period of disqualification had expired. He was also liable for " totting up ". On his conviction he was disqualified for twelve months for the offence of driving while disqualified and was additionally disqualified for six months for " totting up " under s. 5 (3) of the 1962 Act. The justices granted his application for the removal of both orders of disqualification. The Divisional Court reversed the justices' decision, holding that the twelve months' disqualification was not " additional " because his original dis-qualification had expired by the time he was convicted and, there-fore, it commenced running at the moment the court made the order. The six months' disqualification for " totting up " was also reimposed by the Divisional Court as this disqualification was not imposed as a consequence of his conviction under s. 110 (*b*) but because of s. 5 (3) of the 1962 Act (now s. 93 (3) of the 1972 Act).

It will be noted that application has to be made to the court that imposed the last " additional " order of disqualification and that that court may review all the orders of disqualification, whether imposed by that or any other court. Thus if the last court which disqualified the applicant is a magistrates' court, and the previous disqualification was imposed by quarter sessions or assizes, the magistrates' court nevertheless can deal not only with its own order but with that of the superior court also. Rule 84 of the Magistrates' Courts Rules, 1968, has been amended so as to apply the provisions of the rule to applications for removal of disquali-fication under s. 2 of the 1970 Act (now para. 7 of Sched. 10 to the 1972 Act). The rule requires a summons to be issued to the chief of police for the area requiring him to appear at the hearing of the application to show cause why an order should not be made. Application to the Crown Court for removal of disqualification will be to the Crown Court at the location of the Crown Court which is most convenient to the place where the order of quarter sessions or assizes was made (Directions made by the Lord Chief Justice). The Magistrates' Courts Rules do not apply to applications to the Crown Court but presumably the appropriate Crown Court officers will notify the police of the application in order that they may be represented. Although the magistrates' court, if it is the last court that made an order of disqualification, may review an order of disqualification made by a court of assize or quarter sessions, there appears to be nothing to prevent the clerk to the justices seeking the views of the appropriate Crown Court before his justices con-sider the application.

The fact that there is no power under para. 7 of Sched. 10 to the 1972 Act to remove " totting up " disqualifications can lead to complications where the applicant has been subject to a number of orders of disqualification both for the offence of driving while disqualified and for " totting up ". In addition it can often happen that the police and licensing authorities' records differ as to whether or what orders of disqualification were made for what offence. Where the situation is of any complexity, the applicant or his solicitor will be wise to apply to each of the courts by which he has been disqualified for a certified extract from the court register or, where an order was imposed by quarter sessions or assizes, to the appropriate Crown Court officer having custody of the records of those courts. Despite this precaution it will often be found difficult to work out for how long a young man who has persistently defied the law is disqualified. If the wording of the court register or certificate of conviction does not make it clear whether an order of disqualification is concurrent or consecutive, regard must be had to the requirements of the Road Traffic Act, 1972, and in particular to s. 93 (5), viz.—

(a) an order of disqualification for " totting-up " and any order of disqualification for the offence of driving while disqualified imposed before 15th July, 1970, *must* be additional to any other order of disqualification, whether imposed on that or any other occasion, even if the court register does not state it to be consecutive (*R.* v. *Bowsher* [1973] R.T.R. 202); and

(b) any other type of order of disqualification *must* begin to run at the moment it is pronounced and cannot be consecutive to any other order (*R.* v. *Meese* [1973] R.T.R. 400).

It may help to set out an example of the effect of para. 7 of Sched. 10 to the Act (as interpreted in *R.* v. *Bradfield and Sonning JJ.*, *supra*).

1. On 1st April, 1968, *A* was disqualified for six months for " totting up " and twelve months for no insurance.

2. On 1st January, 1969, he was disqualified for twelve months for driving while disqualified, and six months for " totting up ", together with another six months for " totting up " for an offence of no insurance.

3. On 1st September, 1969, he was disqualified for three years for driving while disqualified, plus six months " totting up ". On the same occasion he was disqualified for six months for the offence of taking a motor vehicle without the owner's consent, plus six months for " totting up " for that offence. Another six months " totting up " was imposed for no insurance.

4. On 1st January, 1970, he was disqualified for five years for driving while disqualified, plus six months for " totting up ", plus another six months " totting-up " for taking a vehicle without the owner's consent, plus a further six months " totting up " for using the vehicle without insurance.

In this example it will be seen that A is disqualified for a total of fourteen and a half years, i.e., until 1st October, 1982. At his first court appearance he was disqualified for eighteen months in total, at his second appearance two years in total, at his third appearance four and a half years in total (for the *offence* of taking a vehicle without consent, the order of disqualification is concurrent and does not add to the total as it does not postpone the disqualification he is already serving), and at his fourth appearance for a total of six and a half years.

If on 1st January, 1975, A applies for the removal of the orders of disqualification imposed for driving while disqualified, he will have completed the eighteen months' disqualification imposed on the first occasion together with the total of two years imposed on 1st January, 1969, which began running on 1st October, 1969. He has also served the three years' disqualification imposed on 1st September, 1969, which began running on 1st October, 1971, and is at present serving the first six-month disqualification order imposed on that occasion, 1st September, 1969. The court (which must be the court which imposed the orders of disqualification on 1st January, 1970) may remove the five-year period imposed on 1st January, 1970. If these applications are granted on 1st January, 1975, A must still serve the remaining three months of his first " totting up " imposed on 1st September, 1969, the two other six-month periods also imposed on that occasion and, finally, the eighteen months for the three periods of " totting up " imposed on 1st January, 1970. He thus remains disqualified until 1st October, 1977.

The example given is by no means exceptional, and the only solution suggested is that A should apply to the appropriate Crown Court for leave to appeal out of time against the remaining orders for " totting up ". This, however, may be of little use unless mitigating circumstances can be found (see *R.* v. *Sixsmith* on p. 632). Paragraph 7 (1) enables a court to remove a disqualification " as from such date as may be specified in the order ". Can a court remove a disqualification from a date earlier than the court hearing? It is submitted that it cannot do so; alternatively if it can do so it has no effect on any other order of disqualification.

It may also be difficult to work out which periods of disqualification the applicant has served and which he has not. It will obviously be of great advantage for him to be able to argue that he has served the " totting up " disqualification which cannot be removed and that he has not served the " driving while disqualified " disqualifications which can be removed. It has been suggested that the court, when considering an application to remove the " driving while disqualified " disqualifications, can rule that the " totting up " disqualifications are deemed to have been served first in order to enable the applicant to obtain a driving licence earlier. It is submitted that there is no statutory authority for a court to do this and that the order in which successive orders of disqualification are served depends on the dates upon which the orders were made and, where any were made by a court on the same day, the order in which they appear in the court register.

Driving Tests

By the Road Traffic Act, 1972, s. 93 (7), the court convicting the driver of a motor vehicle of an offence involving discretionary or obligatory disqualification (listed on pp. 617–620) may order him to be disqualified until he passes a driving test, whether or not he has previously passed one. Such an order cannot be made for any other road traffic offence. The order may take effect immediately or on the expiration of a period of complete disqualification if the court orders the latter. The court under s. 93 (7) can order him to be disqualified until he has passed the test, but by s. 98 (3) he may hold a provisional licence. By s. 85 (3) a magistrates' court may determine whether a driving test (whether of a new driver or of a person convicted and ordered to undergo a test under s. 93 (7)) was properly conducted in accordance with the Regulations and, if it finds in favour of the person tested, he may undergo another test in less than a month without further fee. The court is limited to inquiring whether the test was properly conducted and cannot inquire into the findings of the examiner (*Geraghty* v. *Morris* [1939] 2 All E.R. 269) and an appeal should not succeed if there is no evidence of malice, oppression or unfair conduct by the examiner which deprived the learner of a reasonable opportunity to show his skill (*Corrigan* v. *Fox* [1966] S.L.T.(Sh.) 79). There seems to be no appeal on facts from the court's finding. *Semble,* the examiner should be made respondent to the summons. By s. 90 (2) of the Act of 1972 the magistrates' court (without prejudice to the appeal under s. 85 (3), *supra*) cannot entertain any question whether the applicant passed the test if the examiner declares he failed it. A precedent for a complaint is in Oke's Magisterial Formulist, 18th ed., p. 921.

Section 93 (7) is not a punitive section. An order of disqualification until the passing of a test should not be imposed as part of the penalty for the offence. It should be used where the offender is aged, infirm or inexperienced and where the circumstances of the offence or the offender are such that it is in the public interest that there should be a driving test before the offender again drives on a full licence. It should also be used where the offender is inexperienced and the length of ordinary disqualification is such that he should be required to pass a test before he obtains a full licence. In general, the less experience the driver has had and the longer the period of the disqualification, the more important it is that an order under s. 93 (7) should also be made.

In *R*. v. *Donelly* [1975] R.T.R. 243 the defendant, aged fifty-two, pleaded guilty to driving with 229 mg. of alcohol in 100 ml. of blood. An order under s. 93 (7) was removed on appeal, as such an order should not be imposed as a punishment and there was no reason to question the defendant's driving competence. The Court of Appeal approved the reasoning of quarter sessions in *Ashworth* v. *Johnson; Charlesworth* v. *Johnson* [1959] Crim.L.R. 735, where it was said that the powers of a court under s. 6 (3) of the 1934 Act (now s. 93 (7)) should be used in respect of persons who are growing old or infirm or who show in the circumstances of the offence some kind of incompetence which requires looking into. In *R*. v. *Guilfoyle* [1973] R.T.R. 272 a nineteen-year-old lorry-driver was disqualified for three years and also disqualified until he passed a test, for causing death by dangerous driving. The Court of Appeal reduced the disqualification to twelve months but upheld the order that he should pass a test before obtaining a full licence. An interruption of twelve months in his driving career was substantial for one of his length of experience. In general the longer the period of disqualification the more important it is that there should be a driving test before the driver obtains a full licence (*ibid.*). In *R*. v. *Lobley* [1974] R.T.R. 550 a nineteen-year-old driver who pleaded guilty to causing death by dangerous driving had his disqualification of four years reduced to two, but the Court of Appeal upheld the order that he should pass a test before driving on a full licence. The facts of the case were such that the court had doubts as to his ability and qualifications for driving.

The disqualification until the test is passed cannot be removed under s. 95 of the 1972 Act; the person must pass the test (s. 95 (5)). Section 95 (5) does not prevent a person who was disqualified for five years and who was also disqualified until he passes a test from applying for the removal of the five-year disqualification (*R*. v. *Nuttall* [1971] Crim.L.R. 485). The two orders are separable.

When the term of disqualification expires or is removed under s. 95 or para. 7 of Sched. 10, the applicant may then take out a provisional licence and on passing the test may obtain a full licence.

Where a person is considered to be a danger on the road because of some disease or disability, the licensing authority should be asked to revoke his licence (see p. 477) under the Road Traffic Act, 1972, s. 87 (5), and by s. 92 of the 1972 Act, if in any proceedings for an offence committed in respect of a motor vehicle it appears to the court that the accused may be suffering from any disease or disability likely to cause his driving to be a source of danger to the public, the licensing authority must be notified by the court. The court's duty arises whether there is a conviction or not, it is submitted (see p. 479).

A notice sent by a court to the licensing authority shall be sent in such manner and to such address and contain such particulars as the Secretary of State may determine.

A person who has been disqualified from driving until he has passed the test offends against s. 99, *supra* (driving while disqualified), if he drives after having taken out a provisional licence and fails to comply with a provisional licence condition (e.g., not displaying L plates, driving while not accompanied by a qualified driver, etc.: see p. 652) (*Scott* v. *Jelfe* [1974] R.T.R. 256); but the law is different in Northern Ireland (*McGimpsey* v. *Carlin*, Jo.Crim.L. (1968) 221, showing the resident magistrate's decision to have been upheld by the Court of Appeal). Such a disqualification expires as soon as evidence of passing the test is produced to the licensing authority (s. 93 (7)).

The effect of the above provisions is that, if Jehu is disqualified from driving for twelve months on 1st July, 1975, and ordered to take a driving test, he is disqualified from that moment and may not drive at all until 1st July, 1976. On and from 1st July, 1976, he may drive only as a learner-driver, i.e., with L plates and accompanied in a car by a duly qualified person, until he passes the test.

Pedal cyclists and tricyclists cannot be ordered to take a test.

Endorsement and Sentence Codes

No endorsement code is prescribed for an order under s. 93 (7). Instead the court notify the computer licensing centre on form D 20. Where a court imposes imprisonment for an offence this is shown by the letter A, a suspended prison sentence by the letter C, conditional discharge E, binding over F, probation order G, absolute discharge J, attendance centre order K, detention centre order L, care order W, borstal R, hospital/guardianship order T, and, in Scotland, admonition U and young offenders institution V.

Sentences are coded in a 4 character form of which the first and last are letters and the middle two numerals to show the period of any such order, e.g.: A 01Y (imprisonment for 1 year)

A 21D (imprisonment for 21 days)

G 18M (probation for 18 days).

Where there is no period three zeros are shown, e.g.: J 000 (absolute discharge).

Where a suspended prison sentence is ordered two codes are needed, with the letter Z prefixing the period of suspension, e.g.: C 06M ⌠6 months' imprisonment⌡

Z 02Y ⌡suspended 2 years   ⌠.

A period of disqualification is similarly shown, e.g.: 01M (1 month)

14D (14 days)

03Y (3 years).

Where the disqualification is under s. 93 (3) a further entry XX99 is required to show that it is consecutive.

Where a person is disqualified because a vehicle was used for criminal purposes the licence is not endorsed (see p. 641).

The Endorsement and Sentence codes are set out in part II of the Appendix on pp. 874–877.

CHAPTER VII

SPECIAL REASONS AND MITIGATING CIRCUMSTANCES

A COURT is required to disqualify if the offence carries obligatory disqualification (for list of offences see p. 617) unless the court is able to find " special reasons " either for disqualifying the defendant for a shorter period or for not ordering him to be disqualified (Road Traffic Act, 1972, s. 93 (1)). Similarly if an offender is convicted of an offence carrying obligatory endorsement (for a list of offences see pp. 617–620) the court is required to find " special reasons " before the court can refrain from ordering endorsement.

A special reason is one special to the facts of the particular case, i.e., special to the facts which constitute the offence, and a circumstance peculiar to the offender as distinguished from the offence is not a special reason. A " special reason " therefore bears a very restricted meaning and should be contrasted with " mitigating circumstances " for refraining from disqualifying for " totting up " under s. 93 (3) of the Act of 1972. While a " special reason " is a mitigating or extenuating circumstance limited to the facts of the offence, " mitigating circumstances " for refraining from disqualifying for " totting up " are not so limited and an advocate should be careful to distinguish between the two. " Mitigating circumstances " for refraining from disqualifying for " totting-up " are discussed separately in the second half of this chapter (see p. 688 onwards).

If the court considers that an absolute, conditional discharge or probation order is the appropriate method of dealing with the offender, an English or Welsh court must still disqualify or endorse if the offence is an obligatorily disqualifiable offence or an obligatorily endorseable offence (Road Traffic Act, 1972, s. 102; *Owen* v. *Imes* [1972] R.T.R. 489).

Special Reasons

" Special reasons " and " special circumstances " have the same meaning (*Lines* v. *Hersom* [1951] 2 All E.R. 650). The term " special circumstances " is now no longer in the Road Traffic Act but cases on it may still be of relevance in regard to special reasons.

A circumstance peculiar to the offender as distinguished from the offence is not a special reason (*Whittall* v. *Kirby* [1946] 2 All E.R. 552).

Whether facts amount to "special reasons" is a matter of law (*Knowler* v. *Rennison* [1947] K.B. 488) but it was said in *Taylor* v. *Rajan* [1974] R.T.R. 304, at p. 309, that the mere fact that the facts disclose a special reason does not mean that the disqualification should not be imposed; there is still a very serious burden on the court as to whether to exercise their discretion; and in *R.* v. *Newton* [1974] R.T.R. 451, Lord Widgery, C.J., at p. 455, stated that the problem should be considered by the court in two stages. First, the court should decide whether the facts as found on a balance of probabilities amount to a "special reason" in law. If the facts do not amount to a special reason, then the court must impose any obligatory disqualification and endorsement, but if a special reason is found the court must then go on to decide whether it is right in all the circumstances of the case, having regard also to the driver's conduct, to exercise the discretion not to disqualify.

The onus of proof to establish "special reasons" is on the defendant (*Jones* v. *English* [1951] 2 All E.R. 853), on the balance of probabilities (*Pugsley* v. *Hunter* [1973] R.T.R. 284).

In *R.* v. *Wickens* (1958), 42 Cr.App.R. 236, four criteria were laid down for a reason to be judged a "special reason":—

(*a*) it must be a mitigating or extenuating circumstance;

(*b*) it must not amount in law to a defence to the charge;

(*c*) it must be directly connected with the commission of the offence;

(*d*) the matter must be one which the court ought properly to take into consideration when imposing punishment.

In Scotland and Northern Ireland the same rule appears to prevail (*R.* v. *Crossen* [1939] N.I. 106; *Adair* v. *Munn* [1940] S.C.(J.) 69).

R. v. *Wickens* must now be read subject to *Delaroy-Hall* v. *Tadman, Watson* v. *Last, Earl* v. *Lloyd* [1969] 2 Q.B. 208, in relation to offences of excess blood/alcohol level contrary to s. 6 of the Act of 1972, where it was pointed out that if the four criteria in *R.* v. *Wickens* were satisfied it did not necessarily follow that the court was then required to exercise its discretion (as was also said in *R.* v. *Agnew* (1968), *infra*, and *R.* v. *Newton, supra*). There might be some overriding reason precluding a court from exercising its discretion and the fact that Parliament laid down in the Road Safety Act (now s. 6 of the 1972 Act) a statutory limit of alcohol in the blood which must not be exceeded was such an overriding reason. If, therefore, the defendant's blood/alcohol was only slightly in excess of the limit this could not be a special reason—a special reason must be something other than the commission of the offence itself (*Delaroy-Hall* v. *Tadman, supra*; *Nicholson* v. *Brown, infra*). There are other instances where what were held to be " special reasons " in cases of driving under the influence of drink are not " special reasons " in offences of excess blood/alcohol under the Road Safety Act or s. 6 of the Act of 1972 (see p. 671).

Special reasons can no longer be found in the triviality of the offence in dangerous and careless driving cases (*Nicholson* v. *Brown*, *infra*), but may be found in the triviality of the offence because of the shortness of the distance driven (see *James* v. *Hall*, *infra*, under " Driving under Influence of Drink ", and *Reay* v. *Young*, *infra*, under " Insurance "), in the fact that the defendant was misled by the action of another person when committing it (see *infra*, under " Insurance "), that he was acting in an emergency (see *infra*, under " Driving whilst Disqualified ", *R.* v. *Lundt-Smith*, *infra*, under " Dangerous and Careless Driving " and *R.* v. *Baines*, *infra*, under " Driving with Excess Blood/Alcohol "), that he was genuinely unaware that a non-negligent action by him would lead to the commission of an offence (see *R.* v. *Wickens* and *Chapman* v. *O'Hagan*, *infra*, and *Brewer* v. *Metropolitan Police Commissioner*, *infra*, under " Driving under Influence of Drink "), or that the actual offender was another person, for whose actions the defendant is legally responsible, and the defendant is morally blameless (see *Kerr* v. *McNeill* and *Blows* v. *Chapman*, *infra*, under " Insurance "), in a misunderstanding not due to the defendant's carelessness (cf. *Boss* v. *Kingston*, *infra*, under " Insurance "), in the fact that the defendant's drink was laced (see *R.* v. *Shippam*, and other cases *infra*, under " Driving with Excess Blood/Alcohol "), that he was only just above the limit and deprived of an independent analysis of the sample (see *R.* v. *Anderson*, *infra*, under " Driving with Excess Blood/Alcohol ", but see also in this context *Harding* v. *Oliver*, on p. 678), or that he was speeding in order to avoid delaying the business of quarter sessions (see *Police Prosecutor* v. *Humphreys*, *infra*, under " Speed Limits ").

Advocates should always bear in mind when representing defendants charged with a breach of the Construction and Use Regulations that endorsement and disqualification cannot be ordered if the defendant proves that he did not know and had no reasonable cause to suspect that the facts of the case were such that an offence would be committed (for a discussion of this statutory provision see p. 434).

Special reasons are not found in the defendant's good character, nor the fact that it is his first offence or that he has driven for very many years without complaint, nor the personal or financial hardship which would result from disqualifying him, nor the inconvenience to the public generally or to his business which would so result, nor the fact that disqualification might result in his losing his job, nor the severity of the fine, nor the unlikelihood of his offending again, nor the fact, in an excess blood/alcohol case, that his driving ability was unimpaired or that the amount of drink taken was only a little over the statutory limit. Nor may they be found where he has knowingly committed an offence which is not trivial, nor where it was a condition of bail on committal for trial that he did not drive, nor where, on a charge of driving with excess blood/alcohol, the defendant's excess has been in part due to a liver condition whereby alcohol was retained longer than normally, or he was a small man consuming alcohol on an empty stomach.

It was suggested in the sixth edition that the question whether the defendant's good character could be a special reason is still open, as s. 11 (3) of the Road Traffic Act, 1930 (re-enacted in a different form in para. 4 of Sched. 11 to the 1960 Act), referred to a court refraining from disqualifying " having regard to the lapse of time since the date of the previous or last previous conviction or for any *other* special reason ". The use of the word " other " can suggest that a lapse of time since a previous conviction and, *a fortiori*, a lack of previous offences are themselves special reasons. This provision does not seem to have been brought to the attention of the High Court in the cases defining special reasons. The argument is developed at [1964] Crim.L.R. 349–351. However, it was said in *R.* v. *Steel* (1968), 52 Cr.App.R. 510, that it is much too late now to challenge the decision in *Whittall* v. *Kirby, supra*. Although *Whittall* v. *Kirby* has never been considered in a case going to the House of Lords Parliament when re-enacting " special reasons " in ss. 5 and 7 of the Act of 1962 presumably intended these words to bear the meaning as interpreted by *Whittall* v. *Kirby*. This view is reinforced by the fact that in the Bill which became the Road Traffic Act, 1962, the clause creating obligatory disqualification for " totting up " originally allowed the court to refrain from disqualifying only if special reasons existed and the phrase was altered in the committee stage of the Bill to the present formula. In *R.* v. *Anderson* [1972] Crim.L.R. 245 the Court of Appeal declined to redefine " special reasons " and stated that *Whittall* v. *Kirby* remained good law and should be followed.

Special reasons, where urged, should be supported by evidence and the court should not merely accept statements by advocates (*Jones* v. *English* [1951] 2 All E.R. 853; *Brown* v. *Dyerson* [1968] 3 All E.R. 39; *R.* v. *Lundt-Smith* [1964] 2 Q.B. 147; *MacLean* v. *Cork* [1968] Crim.L.R. 507, applying *Jones* v. *English* to Road Safety Act cases). It was suggested in *Brown* v. *Dyerson* that a formal admission by the prosecutor of facts which amount to special reasons under the Criminal Justice Act, 1967, s. 10, might suffice in lieu of evidence, but it is submitted that the court is still entitled to insist on sworn evidence if the prosecutor makes the admission in order to be obliging and without actual knowledge of the facts admitted. Not only must the court insist on hearing evidence, but such evidence must be admissible evidence and not hearsay (*Flewitt* v. *Horvath* (1972), 136 J.P.Jo. 164, where a case was sent back to the justices for rehearing, after the justices had accepted the defendant's evidence that he had been told that his Guinness had been laced with vodka). Special reasons must be found where the court disqualifies the offender for a lesser period than the obligatory period (s. 93 (1)) (*MacLean* v. *Cork, supra*).

Where a court has found special reasons for not disqualifying for the period laid down by s. 93 (1), (3) or (4) or for not disqualifying at all or for not endorsing, the reasons must be stated in open court and entered in the register (Road Traffic Act, 1972, s. 105). This requirement is directory, not mandatory, and failure to comply with s. 105 is not a ground of appeal by the prosecutor against a non-disqualification (*Brown* v. *Dyerson* [1968] 3 All E.R. 39).

The cases on special reasons and special circumstances are reviewed below. The principles will generally be applicable to disqualification and endorsement for offences other than that to which the case relates. The court can still, however, order endorsement, if thought fit, even if special reasons exist for not disqualifying; the magistrates in *Brown* v. *Dyerson, supra*, had purported to find special reasons for not disqualifying the defendant but, notwithstanding such finding, had ordered endorsement, and the High Court did not comment on this. Even where facts amounting to a " special reason " exist in law, the court should then go on to consider whether in all the circumstances of the case, including the conduct of the defendant, the court should exercise its discretion not to disqualify (*R.* v. *Newton* [1974] R.T.R. 451; *Taylor* v. *Rajan* [1974] R.T.R. 304, at p. 309; *R.* v. *Agnew* (1969), 113 Sol.J. 58), save, one adds, in cases under the Construction and Use Regulations (see p. 434). There is, of course, an obvious difference between the consequences of a disqualification and those of an endorsement. It may be very undesirable in the view of a driver to have an endorsement or two endorsements on his licence because of the likelihood of a compulsory disqualification under s. 93 (3) if he offends for a third time, but there is a very simple remedy open to him to avoid that consequence, viz., not to commit that third offence. He suffers no hardship from the mere fact of endorsement, except that possibly in times of heavy unemployment applicants with un-endorsed licences might be preferred for driving jobs.

Condition of Bail Not to Drive

A magistrates' court, when bailing a defendant either to another sitting of the magistrates' court or to the Crown Court for trial or sentence, may impose a special condition of bail under s. 21 of the Criminal Justice Act, 1967. It is lawful to impose a condition that the defendant does not drive while on bail, and if such a condition is imposed it is not a special reason for reducing the obligatory period of disqualification when sentence is given by the Crown Court (*R.* v. *Kwame* [1975] R.T.R. 106), but magistrates when considering such a condition should understand that its imposition may sometimes have unexpected or unjust results (*ibid.*). The court did not specify the unjust or unexpected results of the imposition of such a condition, but clearly the imposition would be unjust if there was a possibility of the defendant's not being disqualified by the Crown Court, either on the ground of " special reasons " or because of his acquittal. Moreover, where the Crown Court is likely to impose only the minimum obligatory period of disqualification, a condition not to drive while on bail has the effect of adding to that period, as the period of disqualification imposed by the Crown Court can only begin to run when the defendant is sentenced.

A person may apply to a High Court judge in chambers for a variation in conditions of bail (Criminal Justice Act, 1967, s. 22 (1)). The procedure is regulated by Rules of the Supreme Court, Ord. 79, r. 9.

Review of Decisions

Dangerous and Careless Driving

Absolute or conditional discharge should never be given for an offence of dangerous driving save in the most exceptional circumstances (*Whittall* v. *Kirby*, *supra*). Such circumstances were found as special reasons in *R.* v. *Lundt-Smith* [1964] 3 All E.R. 225, where an ambulance-driver conveying an urgent case to hospital at night crossed against red traffic lights, with his bell sounding and after looking both ways and seeing no traffic. A motor cyclist coming on the green light was killed in the ensuing collision; there was some evidence that his front lamp was poor. An absolute discharge was granted and the compulsory year's disqualification was not inflicted. (See also *R.* v. *O'Toole* (1971), 55 Cr.App.R. 206.)

Special reasons were found on conviction for careless driving in *Smith* v. *Henderson* [1950] S.C.(J.) 48 on the ground that the carelessness was so slight. The facts were that the defendant had stopped his car at the halt line before entering a main road and, when he started, his attention was distracted by a car entering his side road and he collided with a vehicle in the main road. This case has long been relied on by advocates in England and Wales in urging magistrates not to endorse in respect of comparatively trivial careless driving offences, but in *Nicholson* v. *Brown* [1974] R.T.R. 177 the Divisional Court declined to follow *Smith* v. *Henderson*, holding that *Smith* v. *Henderson* could not be distinguished from *Delaroy-Hall* v. *Tadman* [1969] 2 Q.B. 208 and that the later decision should be followed. In *Delaroy-Hall* it was held that if the offence was only a relatively minor one (e.g. 2 mg. over the prescribed blood/alcohol limit) this could not amount to a special reason; similarly in *Nicholson* v. *Brown* the Divisional Court held that a slight degree of blameworthiness was not a special reason for not endorsing. Either the degree of blameworthiness is so slight that the defendant should not be convicted, or if it is such that he is guilty of the offence, in the absence of some special reason properly to be treated as such, endorsement must follow (*ibid.*). It will be noted that this reasoning of the Divisional Court is similar to the reasoning adopted in laboratory test refusal cases, viz. either there is a reasonable excuse for refusing, in which case the defendant is entitled to be acquitted, or if there is no reasonable excuse, there is no special reason not to disqualify (see p. 235). It was said by Lord Parker, C.J., in *Delaroy-Hall* v. *Tadman* [1969] 2 Q.B. 208, at p. 216B, that the real reasons for not endorsing the licence in *Smith* v. *Henderson* related to the circumstances of the offence and not the blameworthiness of the offender, but in *Nicholson* v. *Brown* the Divisional Court disagreed with this dictum of Lord Parker.

It is not a special reason that a person convicted of careless driving has been driving for many years without a conviction (*Muir* v. *Sutherland* [1940] S.C.(J.) 66).

Driving under Influence of Drink and Driving with Excess Blood/Alcohol

Circumstances which have been held to be special reasons for not disqualifying a defendant charged under the former law of driving while unfit to drive through drink or drugs contrary to s. 6 of the 1960 Act (now s. 5 of the 1972 Act) will frequently not amount to special reasons for not disqualifying if the offender has been convicted on a charge of excess blood/alcohol under s. 1 of the Road Safety Act, 1967 (now s. 6 of the 1972 Act).

Special reasons were found (with reluctance) in *Chapman* v. *O'Hagan* [1949] 2 All E.R. 690, where the defendant took a drug to soothe the pain from his injured leg, not knowing that this would make him more susceptible to the effects of drink; he then took his normal amount of drink and became unfit to drive but did so. They were found again in *R.* v. *Wickens* (1958), 42 Cr.App.R. 236, where a diabetic took some beer which, but for his illness, would not have affected his driving; he did not know at the time that he was a diabetic. In *R*. v. *Holt* [1962] Crim.L.R. 565, all the members of the full Court of Criminal Appeal were of opinion that special reasons could be found where a driver took Amytal tablets prescribed by his doctor and then drank two small gins and his doctor had failed to warn him of the danger of taking even a small amount of drink after taking the tablets.

Special reasons not found.—The circumstances outlined in the above three cases of *Chapman* v. *O'Hagan*, *R*. v. *Wickens* and *R*. v. *Holt* will, it is submitted, now not amount to special reasons for not disqualifying if the offence is excess blood/alcohol under s. 1 of the Road Safety Act, 1967 (now s. 6 of the 1972 Act). In *Goldsmith* v. *Laver* (1970), 134 J.P.Jo. 310, the defendant (as in *R*. v. *Wickens*), unknown to himself was suffering from diabetes. It was held, distinguishing *R*. v. *Wickens*, that as the offence was under s. 1 of the Road Safety Act, 1967, the fact that he did not know he was suffering from a disease which made the effect of alcohol on him greater was irrelevant to the charge. Similarly in *R*. v. *Scott* [1969] 2 All E.R. 450 the fact that the motorist did not know that the sleeping pills which had been prescribed for her produced a more violent reaction in terms of her ability to drive than if she had taken the drink alone was held not to be a special reason when she was convicted under s. 1 of the Road Safety Act, 1967. In *Taylor* v. *Austin* [1969] 1 W.L.R. 264 it was held that the fact that the defendant's driving ability was not impaired could amount to a mitigating circumstance but could not amount to a special reason for not disqualifying under the Road Safety Act. *Taylor* v. *Austin* was applied in *R*. v. *Jackson* [1969] 2 All E.R. 453, where, following a review of many of the cases, it was held that in a charge of excess blood/alcohol it is not a special reason that the defendant's driving ability might be unimpaired. It was held that the purpose of the Road Safety Act, 1967, was to create an offence for which evidence of impairment of driving ability was irrelevant and for which disqualification was mandatory. Nor is it a special reason that the defendant suffers from a liver complaint and thus retains alcohol longer than a man with normal physique (*R*. v. *Jackson, supra*; *Goldsmith* v. *Laver, supra*). Any general state of health of an offender or bodily defect can only be peculiar to the offender and not to the offence, and a court cannot conduct an investigation of the condition of the defendant's bodily organs (*R*. v. *Jackson, supra*). The Road Safety Act, s. 1, refers to " his " blood, i.e., the defendant's blood/alcohol level; it does not refer to the blood/alcohol of the normal individual or the man on a Clapham omnibus.

Nor is it a special reason that at the time of driving the blood/
alcohol level could have been below the limit (*Ferriby* v. *Sharman*
[1971] Crim.L.R. 288). Normally the fact that the sample for
analysis is taken some little time after the motorist has driven is
to his advantage because the blood/alcohol level usually declines.
It is not open to the prosecution to argue back to show a higher
alcohol content; equally it is not open to the defence to argue back
to show a lower alcohol content at the time of driving (*Ferriby* v.
Sharman). It was held in *Newnham* v. *Trigg, infra*, that the fact that
the sample was taken long after the last consumption of alcohol
was not a special reason. Nor is it a special reason that it was the
defendant's wedding day, on which he had drunk frugally but was
still affected by heavy drinking the night before (*Punshon* v. *Rose*
(1968), 113 S.J. 39); nor the fact that as soon as he realised he was
affected by drink he stopped driving (*Duck* v. *Peacock* [1949] 1 All
E.R. 318). Nor is it a special reason that the defendant was a
small man and had imbibed alcohol on an empty stomach and
therefore might have a higher blood/alcohol level (*Knight* v. *Baxter*
(1971), 115 S.J. 350, applying *Archer* v. *Woodward* [1959] Crim.L.R.
461, where it was held that a lack of food contributing to the defendant's unfitness to drive was not a special reason). It is not a
special reason that the analysis of the blood/alcohol level shows it
to be only 2 mg. above the limit (*Delaroy-Hall* v. *Tadman* [1969]
2 Q.B. 208) or that the defendant's sample of the blood specimen
was lost (*Harding* v. *Oliver* [1973] R.T.R. 497). Previous good
character, hardship, the severity of the fine and the unlikelihood
of the defendant offending again are not special reasons (*Whittall* v.
Kirby, supra; *R.* v. *Steel* (1968), 52 Cr.App.R. 510) nor the fact
that he is a disabled driver and would suffer hardship (*R.* v. *Hart*
[1969] 2 All E.R. 453) even if the hardship to the disabled driver
is " appalling " and he would have to be maintained out of public
funds if disqualified (*R.* v. *Mullarkey* [1970] Crim.L.R. 406), nor
that he is a married man with four children who would lose his
livelihood if disqualified and that he was only 3 mg. over the limit
(*Glendinning* v. *Batty* [1973] R.T.R. 405). Nor is it a special reason
that the defendant was breath-tested following an accident for
which he was not to blame (*Taylor* v. *Austin, supra*), or following
an accident in which only the defendant was involved and which
he himself had reported to the police, asking for their attendance
(*Kerr* v. *Armstrong* [1974] R.T.R. 141). The prejudice to the public
interest which would arise from disqualifying an officer who super-
vised the organisation of the Territorial Army throughout a county
is not a special reason (*M'Fadyean* v. *Burton* [1954] S.C. (1) 18) nor
is it a special reason that the defendant is an Army driver in Northern

Ireland: the state of emergency is insufficient special reason (*Gordon* v. *Smith* [1971] Crim.L.R. 173; *Hopgood* v. *Chapman* [1975] Crim.L.R. 397), nor that the defendant is a National Health Service doctor in general practice in an under-doctored area (*Holroyd* v. *Berry* [1973] R.T.R. 145). It is not a special reason that the defendant was an export merchant obliged to entertain overseas business associates (*MacLean* v. *Cork* [1968] Crim.L.R. 507). It is not a special reason in respect of a charge under s. 5 of unfit through drugs that the defendant took the drugs because he intended to kill himself or that he was not in control of his actions when he drove because of the drugs (*Bullen* v. *Keay* [1974] R.T.R. 559); the first reason was special to the offender and not special to the offence (*ibid.*) and the second reason could not be advanced on a plea of guilty (*ibid.*). (" This produces the perverse argument that if a man drinks so much that he cannot understand what he is doing, he can then go on the road and not be at the risk of having his licence taken away under a breach of the Road Traffic Act ": *per* Lord Widgery, C.J., at p. 563B.) Other examples can be cited but it is submitted that the above cases show that, no matter how peculiar the facts relating to the offender or how appalling the hardship, the facts must be special to the offence and not the offender. In prosecutions under the Road Safety Act, 1967 (now s. 6 of the 1972 Act) it is not a special reason that the offender was above the limit through reasons of personal physical idiosyncrasy or that his driving was unimpaired. Magistrates who strain the law on special reasons out of compassion to a defendant are in fact doing him a disservice by doing so (*per* Lord Widgery, C.J., in *Glendinning* v. *Batty* [1973] R.T.R. 405, at p. 408H).

Shortness of distance driven.—In *James* v. *Hall* [1968] Crim.L.R. 507 it was held to be a special reason that the defendant only intended to drive his car a few yards from the road into a friend's driveway. Likewise in *R.* v. *Agnew* [1969] Crim.L.R. 152 a passenger who was asked by the owner to drive the car a distance of six feet was not disqualified. Moving a vehicle ten yards at the request of a constable was found to be a special reason for not further disqualifying a disqualified driver (*Ambrose* v. *Jamieson*; see p. 687). In *R.* v. *Mullarkey* [1970] Crim.L.R. 406 the mere fact of driving 400 yards after midnight in winter where there was little traffic about could not itself amount to a special reason, nor is the fact that the road was straight and no other road user put at risk a special reason for imposing six months' disqualification only (*Milliner* v. *Thorne* [1972] Crim.L.R. 245). In *Coombs* v. *Kehoe* [1972] R.T.R. 224 it was held that *James* v. *Hall, supra,* should be restricted to its special circumstances and the justices were directed to disqualify a lorry driver who had driven through busy streets to park his lorry in a space 200 yards away, colliding with cars at either end of the space.

It is submitted, following *R.* v. *Mullarkey* and *Coombes* v. *Kehoe* (*per* Lord Widgery, C.J.), that special reasons on the grounds of the shortness of the distance driven may only be found where the distance and circumstances are such that the defendant is unlikely to be brought into contact with other road users and in which this, if it did happen, would be unlikely to produce a source of danger. In *R.* v. *Shaw* (*Charles*) [1974] R.T.R. 225, the Crown Court refused to refrain from disqualifying for an offence of driving with 223 mg. of alcohol in 100 ml. of blood " a short distance " along a private council road used by the public. The Court of Appeal held that it could not be said that any discretion had been wrongly exercised by the Crown Court.

Medical or other emergency.—In *Brown* v. *Dyerson* [1969] 1 Q.B. 45 the defendant was convicted of a charge under s. 1 of the Road Safety Act, 1967, and it was said by the court that a sudden medical emergency was capable of amounting to a special reason. A public medical emergency was also a special reason for not disqualifying an ambulance driver on a charge under s. 1 of the Road Traffic Act, 1960, for causing death by dangerous driving (*R.* v. *Lundt-Smith* [1964] 3 All E.R. 225) and a public emergency was held to be a special reason for not disqualifying on a charge for driving while disqualified in *Aichroth* v. *Cottee* (see p. 687). But before a court can find a medical emergency, it must have proper evidence to show that it was an emergency. It is not sufficient for the defendant to give unsupported evidence of that fact (*Brown* v. *Dyerson, supra*); the evidence must be admissible and not hearsay (*Flewitt* v. *Horvath* (1972), 136 J.P.Jo. 164). It is also necessary for the defendant to show that he had no alternative other than to drive. Thus in *R.* v. *Baines* [1970] Crim.L.R. 590 special reasons were not found. Although the defendant could show that there was a medical emergency in that he had been asked to rescue his partner's frail, ailing and elderly mother, who was stranded at night in a fairly remote spot in a car which had run out of petrol, he was not able to show that it was necesary for him to drive. If he had shown that he had explored other possibilities, such as telephoning a garage, contacting the A.A. or R.A.C. or asking the police if they could help, before he went out to drive, he might have been able to establish special reasons (*ibid.*).

A sudden emergency requiring a motorist to drive in circumstances when he never expected to have to drive can be a " special reason " special to the offence and not the offender (*Jacobs* v. *Read* [1974] R.T.R. 81—father drinking at international airport while changing planes, telephoned by wife that daughter for second time has failed to turn up at school, wife upset, cancels flight to Paris to drive home without considering alternative means of transport: held, he had not established " special reasons "); the onus is on the defendant to show by evidence " special reasons " and the test in such circumstances is an objective one (*ibid.*). In *Taylor* v. *Rajan, Fraser* v. *Barton* [1974] R.T.R. 304, the " emergency " situation was again considered, and it was again held, following *Jacobs*, that the test is not a subjective one; the emergency must be a compelling emergency; the court should consider the nature and degree of the crisis, whether there were alternative methods of dealing with it or alternative means of transport, and the manner in which the defendant drove (speeding or careless driving should be held against him). If a special reason exists, the court should then consider whether to exercise its discretion not to disqualify; if the alcohol exceeds 100 mg. in 100 ml. of blood the discretion should rarely if ever be exercised in the defendant's favour in such " emergency " cases (*ibid.*). It is more difficult to find "special reasons " when the defendant is found driving away after the emergency has been dealt with (*ibid.*).

Ignorance of amount of alcohol.—In *Brewer* v. *Metropolitan Police Commissioner* [1969] 1 All E.R. 513 special reasons were found by the Divisional Court in a case under s. 6 of the 1960 Act where the defendant had absorbed fumes from a vat which made him unfit to drive if he drank a small amount of alcohol afterwards. Even though quarter sessions had found that he ought to have known that he had absorbed fumes from the vat, the Divisional Court were able to find special reasons because in fact he did not know. In *Newnham* v. *Trigg* [1970] R.T.R. 107 it was held that ignorance of the exact *quantity* is not a special reason, although ignorance of the *quality* of the drink could amount to a special reason. The defendant had been given whisky in bed by his wife the night before the offence because of a cold; special reasons were not found because the defendant knew he had been drinking whisky even though because of his cold he did not know how much he had been given. In that case Lord Parker (following similar remarks made by him in *Brewer* v. *Metropolitan Police Commissioner, supra*) said that it might be a special reason " where a man thinking he is drinking ginger ale has, unknown to him, strong drink put into it behind his back ". The situation of lacing the defendant's drink arose directly in *R.* v. *Shippam* [1971] Crim.L.R. 434 and in *Williams* v. *Neale* [1971] Crim.L.R. 598. In the former case the defendant pleaded guilty to a charge under s. 1 of the Road Safety Act, 1967, and the certificate of analysis showed his blood/alcohol level to be only 4 mg. above the limit.   The evidence of himself and his friend showed that one of his drinks of lager and lime had been laced with vodka as a practical joke.   [Such practical jokers render themselves liable to prosecution.   In *Attorney-General's Reference No. 1 of 1975* (1975), *The Times*, 25th April, it was held that a person who surreptitiously laces a motorist's drink knowing that he would drive and that because of the lacing his blood/alcohol would exceed the prescribed limit is guilty of procuring the motorist's offence under s. 6 (1).] The Divisional Court found that special reasons existed because he did not know that his drink had been laced *and the added vodka accounted for his being over the limit.*   In *Williams* v. *Neale* the defendant pleaded guilty to a charge of being unfit to drive through drink.   The justices found that the " fiuit cup " which the defendant had been drinking had been laced with brandy without his knowing.   The justices' finding of special reasons was upheld.   The analysis showed 216 mg. of alcohol per 100 ml. of blood.   It should be noted that the charge in *Williams* v. *Neale* was driving whilst unfit to drive and not excess blood/alcohol. It is usually easier to show that lacing may have caused impairment than that lacing accounted for the excess in the blood/alcohol level, particularly if the amount of the excess is large.   In *Flewitt* v. *Horvath, supra,* magistrates found special reasons after the defendant gave evidence that he had afterwards been told that someone had added vodka to his Guinness;   the case was remitted to the justices for reconsideration;   special reasons could not be found on evidence which was hearsay and thus inadmissible.   In *R.* v. *Messom* [1973] R.T.R. 140, special reasons were found by the Court of Appeal where a defendant, thinking he was drinking a large ginger ale topped up with a small whisky, in fact drank a large measure of brandy topped up with a small ginger ale.   The alcohol level of the defendant in *Messom* was 132 mg. of alcohol in 100 ml. of blood.   It is difficult to reconcile this case with *Pugsley* v. *Hunter* [1973] R.T.R. 284 and also with *R.* v. *Newton (David)* [1974] R.T.R. 451, in which *Pugsley* v. *Hunter* but not *Messom* was considered.   In *Pugsley* v. *Hunter* it was held that it was for the defendant to show on a balance of probabilities that the added alcohol with which his drink was laced accounted for the amount by which his blood/alcohol level exceeded the prescribed limit; unless it is really obvious to a layman that the added liquor explains the excess, the only way in which the defendant can discharge the onus is by calling medical or scientific evidence.   The case was remitted back to the stipendiary magistrate to reconsider whether special reasons existed in accordance with the opinions expressed by the High Court.   (It is understood that the defendant was then disqualified; the defendant's blood/alcohol was 161 mg. and his drink had been laced with two double vodkas.) It was also said that where the defence propose to prove facts or call medical opinion to prove special reasons, sufficient notice should be given to the prosecution. In *R.* v. *Newton* (*David*) the Court of Appeal refused to disturb a disqualification of eighteen months where the defendant's blood/alcohol level was 127 mg. The Court of Appeal held that even where special reasons existed, a court should then go on to consider whether it was right in all the circumstances of the case to exercise the discretion in the defendant's favour, regard being had particularly to the defendant's own conduct; a driver who mixed drink with driving had a very heavy and important duty not to exceed the limit; moreover, the court were unable to accept that with 127 mg. of alcohol in 100 ml., the applicant did not really feel any effect of drink. Following *Pugsley* v. *Hunter* it was again held in *Weatherson* v. *Connop* [1975] Crim.L.R. 239 that the onus is on the defendant to prove that the lacing accounted for the defendant's being above the prescribed limit.

Summary

It is suggested that before special reasons may be found evidence must be given which is admissible and not hearsay to show on the balance of probabilities, the onus being on the defendant:—

(*a*) that the defendant did not know his drink was laced or did not know that his drink contained alcohol or, in a charge under s. 5 of the 1972 Act, did not know that the drug increased the effect of alcohol;

(*b*) if the charge is excess blood/alcohol, that, but for the lacing of his drink or the absorption of alcoholic fumes, he would not have been above the limit (unless it would be really obvious to a non-medical man that the lacing would account for the excess, medical evidence is required to be adduced to show this);

(*c*) if the charge is of being unfit to drive under s. 5 of the 1972 Act (formerly s. 6 of the 1960 Act), that the lacing of the drink or the taking of drugs caused the impairment of his driving;

(*d*) having found special reasons, the court should then consider whether it is right to exercise their discretion not to disqualify, regard being had to all the circumstances of the case, particularly the defendant's own conduct and degree of responsibility.

It can hardly be a special reason that a defendant did not realise the quantity of drink he had taken, nor could it be a special reason that he did not realise how strong Guinness is; such reasons are special to the offender and not the offence, but it can be a special reason that the offender did not know that diabetic lager was twice as strong as ordinary (*Alexander* v. *Latter* [1972] Crim.L.R. 646), but *Alexander* v. *Latter* was distinguished in *Adams* v. *Bradley* [1975] Crim. L.R. 168. The former case was explained as amounting to special reasons because the defendant had been misled by the barman as to the strength of the lager he was drinking; in *Adams* the defendant had made no enquiries as to the strength of the lager he was drinking.

Deprivation of possible defence.—In *R.* v. *Anderson* [1972] Crim.L.R. 245 the defendant was told that he would not be prosecuted. For this reason he destroyed his sample of the blood taken from him for analysis. The official analysis showed 81 mg. of alcohol in 100 ml. of blood. The Court of Appeal agreed with *Delaroy-Hall* v. *Tadman* (see p. 670), holding that an excess of 1 mg. could not on the principle of *de minimis* amount to a special reason, but held that the facts that he was told he would not be prosecuted and, as a consequence, destroyed his sample, thus losing an opportunity of independently testing the official analysis which was only one milligramme over the limit, were facts which must be regarded as special to the offence. The Court of Appeal added that it was difficult for their lordships' conclusion to be a precedent in another case, and in *Harding* v. *Oliver* [1973] R.T.R. 497 it was held that loss of the defendant's part blood specimen given to him for independent analysis could not amount to a special reason.

See also under " General Considerations ", p. 688, *infra*.

Refusing to Supply Specimen of Blood or Urine for Analysis.—This is now an offence contrary to s. 9 of the 1972 Act and replaces s. 3 (3) of the Road Safety Act, 1967, which provided that a person who refused without reasonable excuse to supply a specimen for laboratory analysis should be liable to be proceeded against and punished as if he were guilty of an offence either under s. 1 (1) or s. 1 (2) of the 1967 Act. The 1972 Act, although a consolidating enactment, now makes a refusal to supply a specimen for laboratory analysis a separate offence contrary to s. 9 of that Act.

In *R.* v. *Hart* [1969] 2 All E.R. 453 it was said that it was not easy to think of a special reason for not disqualifying where the charge arose because the defendant had refused to supply a specimen of blood or urine. The offence can only be committed if the defendant has no reasonable excuse for refusing both blood and urine. In *Scobie* v. *Graham* [1970] Crim.L.R. 589 the justices found the defendant guilty but refrained from disqualifying on the ground that the defendant was in hospital in a certain amount of pain and had received a blow on the head which might have affected

him. In *Hockin* v. *Weston* (1971), 115 S.J. 675, the justices accepted
the defendant's plea of guilty but did not disqualify him on the
ground that the defendant was physically and mentally incapable
of thinking clearly and was in great emotional stress, believing his
wife was about to die. In both cases the Divisional Court reversed
the justices' decisions not to disqualify and held that the justices
were confused between " reasonable excuse " and " special
reasons ". While great physical or emotional stress might amount
to a " reasonable excuse " for refusing, as the magistrates had either
convicted the defendant or accepted his plea of guilty, it followed
that the magistrates had come to the conclusion in each case that
the defendant had no reasonable excuse for refusing. Therefore,
as he had no reasonable excuse for refusing, he could not put the
circumstances of his refusal before the court as a special reason for
not disqualifying. It is not a reasonable excuse for refusing that
the defendant before consenting wished to speak to a solicitor (*Law*
v. *Stephens* (1971), 115 S.J. 369), nor, if the defendant is an Australian, that he wished to speak on the telephone to someone from
the High Commissioner's office (*R.* v. *Seaman* (1971), 115 S.J. 742).
In the latter case it was also held that his wish to consult the High
Commissioner was not a special reason for not disqualifying. It
was held in *Hosein* v. *Edmunds* (1969), 113 S.J. 759, that it was not
a special reason for not disqualifying that the defendant wished to
speak to a solicitor after he had refused to supply a specimen.
Neither would it be a special reason, it would seem, following *R.*
v. *Seaman* and *R.* v. *Hart*, if the motorist had wished to consult a
solicitor *before* refusing, but in *R.* v. *Reid* (*Philip*) [1973] R.T.R. 536
the Court of Appeal held that the trial judge was " absolutely
right " in finding special reasons not to disqualify when there was
no indication that the defendant had taken very much to drink
and he had refused to provide breath and laboratory samples because he thought he was justified in doing so in law, had before
leaving the police station consulted a senior police officer and
immediately consented to supply a sample for laboratory testing,
but was nevertheless prosecuted for refusing even though a sample
could have been obtained.

Other cases on " reasonable excuse " will be found on pp. 231–
234, notably *R.* v. *Lennard*, at p. 233, *R.* v. *Harding*, at p. 232, and
R. v. *John*, at p. 234.

It is difficult, if not impossible, to argue (except in such a special
case as *R.* v. *Reid*, *supra*) that special reasons exist on a charge of
refusing on the ground that the defendant has had little if any
alcohol, because he only had to consent to supply a laboratory
specimen for analysis to have shown that this was true.

Traffic Signs, Pedestrian Crossings and School Crossings

The triviality of an offence of disobeying a traffic sign, e.g., going past a stop sign at 5 m.p.h. in the early hours of the morning when there was no traffic on the major road, might amount to a special reason.   Normally, however, if an offence of any seriousness has been deliberately committed, special reasons should not be found (*Taylor* v. *Saycell* [1950] 2 All E.R. 887).   Special reasons might also be found where, because of bad weather or other unusual circumstances, it was extremely difficult for a driver driving carefully to see the sign or the pedestrian on a crossing (cf. the facts in *Leicester* v. *Pearson* [1952] 2 All E.R. 71).   Or they might be found where the driver had been misled by the actions of a pedestrian or school crossing patrol, or where pedestrians went on a crossing when a car was close (see *Scott* v. *Clint*, on p. 450) or where the defendant is charged with overtaking on the approach to a pedestrian crossing in circumstances where the High Court have suggested it might be unjust to prosecute (see p. 454).   It should, however, be remembered that the triviality of the offence has been held not to be a special reason in careless driving and excess alcohol offences and it is submitted that the mere fact that the offence is slight or that no one is endangered cannot easily be said to be a special reason.

Speed Limits

It might be a special reason if a driver exceeded the speed limit because he had suddenly been called to attend a dying relative or because he was a doctor going to an urgent call (*per* Lord Goddard, C.J., in *Whittall* v. *Kirby*, *supra*; 123 J.P.Jo. 723).   Other such cases will be found in *R.* v. *Lundt-Smith* on p. 669 and under " Driving whilst Disqualified", *infra*.   Magistrates have held it to be a special reason for a defendant employed on emergency services by an Electricity Board to speed in order to deal with a breakdown in electricity supplies covering a large area.   It is submitted that special reasons could similarly be found where other emergency services are forced to speed because of the urgency of the emergency, e.g., gas leaks and bursting of water mains causing flooding.   A solicitor's articled clerk persuaded magistrates not to endorse his licence on the ground that he had been delayed in getting to quarter sessions to instruct counsel and if he had not exceeded a speed limit the whole business of quarter sessions would have been held up.   The prosecution appealed to the Divisional Court, contending that this was not a special reason.   The Divisional Court dismissed the appeal (*Police Prosecutor* v. *Humphreys* [1970] Crim.L.R. 234), stating that the justices had not erred in law.   Exceeding a speed limit by 50 per cent. normally would not amount to a special reason even where there was no danger (*Baker* v. *Cole* on p. 691).

Reporting Accidents

Special reasons, it is submitted, might be found where the defendant has been misled by the actions of others into thinking that there was no need for him to stop and wait at the scene or to report the accident or where the damage or injury was apparently so trivial as to excuse compliance with s. 25 and the other person concerned thought the same. Or where the defendant, being on urgent business, e.g., an ambulance driver, failed to stop but reported the incident as soon as possible. It can be argued, too, that a bus driver in a place where his company's buses are well known might urge special reasons if he failed to stop during rush hours for an incident which was not serious and which he reported very soon.

Insurance

Before the 1956 Act, disqualification was compulsory for use without insurance or causing or permitting such use and there are several decisions on the question of special reasons.

While it is the obvious duty of people to make themselves acquainted with their policies and, if they do not understand them, to take advice, a garage proprietor, who had applied for full cover and had been issued with a named-driver policy without having the difference pointed out by the insurance company, was held to have been misled by the company and this constituted a special reason (*Labrum* v. *Williamson* [1947] 1 All E.R. 824). Special reasons were found where the defendant owned a fleet of cars one of which was taken off the road temporarily, cover being suspended for it; his manager had forgotten to tell the insurance company that it had come back on risk when it was driven again, but the company was willing to accept liability (*Pilbury* v. *Brazier* [1950] 2 All E.R. 835). Special reasons were found where a car had been advertised for sale as " taxed and insured " and the seller had undertaken to transfer the policy to the buyer (defendant) immediately; the buyer, a few days later, drove it, honestly but wrongly assuming that he was covered accordingly (*Quelch* v. *Collett* [1948] 1 All E.R. 252). Again, they were found when after a lorry had been repaired at a garage, the owner (defendant) requested the garage proprietor to drive it to his premises, wrongly assuming that, according to ordinary commercial experience, the garage proprietor would be covered in so driving it (*Lyons* v. *May* [1948] 2 All E.R. 1062). They were found where an employer told an unlicensed servant to get a licence—the policy forbidding unlicensed drivers to drive—and gave him the licence money; a few days later, without enquiring whether he had the licence and so assuming, the employer (defendant) permitted him to drive (*Kerr* v. *McNeill* [1949] N.I. 19).   The headnote reads:—

" The owner of a motor tractor was convicted under s. 6 of the Motor Vehicles and Road Traffic Act (Northern Ireland), 1930, of causing or permitting his employee to use the tractor on the highway without there being in force in relation to such user such policy of insurance or such security in respect of third-party risks as complied with the requirements of Part II of the Act.   The policy of insurance held by the defendant excluded from its cover any driver who did not at the time of driving hold a licence to drive and the employee had no such licence.   It was found that the defendant when engaging the employee a fortnight previously had learned that he had no licence, that he thereupon instructed him to obtain a licence and gave him time off and money for this purpose, that he never enquired whether the employee had obtained a licence, but that when he gave the employee instructions to drive the tractor on the occasion in question he believed that a licence had been obtained and that accordingly there was in force a policy of insurance covering the tractor while being driven by the employee, and that in these circumstances the defendant was not guilty of carelessness.

Held, by the Court of Appeal (Andrews, L.C.J., and Porter, L.J.; Babington, L.J., dissenting) that these facts disclosed a ' special reason ' for which the trial court could properly exercise its discretion under s. 6 (2) of the Act not to disqualify the defendant for holding or obtaining a licence."

Special reasons were found where an unlicensed person drove for only 150 yards on a lonely moorland road under the supervision of a competent driver (*Reay* v. *Young* [1949] 1 All E.R. 1102; *Reay* v. *Young* was said to be a special case in *Milliner* v. *Thorne* [1972] Crim. L.R. 245, and contrast *Gott* v. *Chisholm* (1950), 114 J.P.Jo. 212, *infra*, and *James* v. *Hall* and *Coombs* v. *Kehoe* on p. 673).   They were found where an employee (defendant) was told by his master to take a vehicle on the road; it was reasonable for the defendant to assume without question that such use was covered by insurance (*Blows* v. *Chapman* [1947] 2 All E.R. 576).   The servant would now have a defence to the charge under s. 143 (2) of the 1972 Act (see p. 378). Quarter sessions found special reasons where an inexperienced driver owned a car which was insured for owner-driver only and was driving it with an experienced driver as passenger.   Darkness fell and the owner, not wishing to drive in the dark, asked his friend to drive.   His friend (defendant) asked if the car's insurance covered his driving and the owner said that it did.   It was held that defendant was entitled to rely on the owner's word and should not be expected to ask to see the certificate of insurance as well.   See also under " General Considerations ", p. 688, *infra*, as to the liability of partners.   It may be that merely leaving an uninsured vehicle on the road, in the absence of a garage for it, would be a sufficiently trivial offence to justify special reasons. Special reasons would seemingly be findable where perusal of the policy by a layman would suggest he was covered (*Boss* v. *Kingston* [1963] 1 All E.R. 177). In *Carlton* v. *Garrity* [1964] Crim.L.R. 146, the defendant, a youth, had studied his insurance policy and asked his father and work-mates if it allowed another person to ride his machine; they all said it did. He allowed another to ride it, believing honestly and on proper grounds that such use was covered by the policy. In fact, it was not but it was held that special reasons were properly found. It would be the same if he had received wrong advice from an insurance agent.

Forgetfulness or carelessness in renewing the policy, previous good character and hardship to the defendant are not special reasons (*Whittall* v. *Kirby*, *supra*). Nor is a mistaken belief that the policy covers the risk, for it is defendant's duty to acquaint himself with its terms; *aliter*, where his belief is based on reasonable grounds (see *Boss* v. *Kingston* and *Carlton* v. *Garrity*, *supra*) and where he has been misled by the insurance company (*Rennison* v. *Knowler* [1947] 1 All E.R. 302). Nor is the shortness of the defendant's journey where, being an unskilled driver, he has caused an accident in a shopping street while driving without supervision (*Gott* v. *Chisholm* (1950), 114 J.P.Jo. 212). Where a defendant has driven knowing he is uninsured, he should never be absolutely or conditionally discharged (*Gardner* v. *James* [1948] 2 All E.R. 1069; *Taylor* v. *Saycell* [1950] 2 All E.R. 887), save in special circum-stances such as in *Reay* v. *Young*, *supra*, the lonely road case. A long lapse of time between the offence and the conviction and the defendant's injuries are not special reasons (*Pollard* v. *Light* (1950), 48 L.G.R. 447). The defendant's ignorance of the require-ments of the law as to insurance is not a special reason (*Swell* v. *McKechnie* [1956] Crim.L.R. 423). Nor are the facts that he had made several attempts to get a policy, that he was not very con-versant with insurance practice and that he had not deliberately or intentionally tried to evade the law (*Surtees* v. *Benewith* [1954] 3 All E.R. 261). The fact that a member of the army or of the R.A.F. had already been dealt with and punished by court-martial or by his commanding officer for the offence was not a special reason for not disqualifying him but a nominal fine might properly be inflicted having regard to the previous punishment (*Dennis* v. *Tame* (1954), 118 J.P. 358). The statutes mentioned on pp. 61 and 58 now restrict a civil court in trying servicemen of Great Britain and visiting forces who have already been dealt with by their own service tribunals but the principles of *Dennis* v. *Tame* presumably apply where the defendant has already been dealt with by some domestic tribunal.

The Motor Vehicles (Construction and Use) Regulations

Where a disqualification or endorsement is compulsory for an offence under the Motor Vehicles (Construction and Use) Regulations (see p. 433 as to the offences for which it is inflictable), special reasons may, it is submitted, generally be found where the offender has unknowingly and without negligence committed an offence of " using " under the Regulations, although he may be absolutely liable in law for it. In addition, the Road Traffic (Amendment) Act, 1967, s. 7 (infra) (now contained in the 1972 Act, Sched. IV, Pt. I, entry relating to s. 40 (5), cols. 5 and 6), applies to the offences. In *Kerr* v. *McNeill* [1949] N.I. 19, an insurance case, a master had told his servant to get a driving licence and given him the money for it; a few days later, without enquiry as to whether the servant had done so, the master permitted him to drive. It was held that there were special reasons shown in respect of the employer. In *Blows* v. *Chapman* [1947] 2 All E.R. 576, a servant was ordered to drive his master's vehicle and it was held that, as it was reasonable for the servant to assume that his master would have made certain that the vehicle was insured, this was a special reason for not disqualifying the servant. In *Hart* v. *Bex* [1957] Crim.L.R. 622, a defect in the brakes of a vehicle arose suddenly and unexpectedly, the driver not being under a duty to inspect them; he was prosecuted for using with defective brakes and the High Court said that he should be given an absolute discharge.

It is submitted that these cases show that special reasons can properly be found where a master or a servant has been prosecuted for an offence for which, though liable in law, he is in fact morally blameless because, without intent or negligence on his part, the commission of the offence was due to the action of his servant or his partner (in a master's case) or to that of his master or a superior employee (in a servant's case) or, in either case, to that of some person whose action he could not control, or to some natural cause beyond his control. Thus, on the facts of *Austin (Leyton), Ltd.* v. *East* on p. 34, the High Court seems to have suggested that an absolute discharge could be given (partner in firm convicted of causing use of vehicle away from depot with latent defect in mechanism). Again, such a discharge might be given or special reasons found, it is suggested, in circumstances not unlike those in *Green* v. *Burnett* on p. 43 (master convicted of using vehicle with defective brakes; vehicle away from depot when defect developed but master had given instructions to driver to take vehicle to an engineer whenever maintenance needed or defect observed). In that case, there was in fact some evidence of negligence by the master, so special reasons could not, it seems, properly have been found in the particular circumstances but, had there been no negligence, it is submitted that they could have been if the master had proved a proper system of maintenance and full instructions to drivers out on the road.   Quarter sessions found special reasons where the owner of a lorry in a defective condition proved that there was no negligence on his part and that he had a reasonably sound system of regular inspection; his licence was not endorsed (*Johnstone* v. *Dearsley* [1966] C.L.Y. 10539).   Again, special reasons might be found in a case like *Gifford* v. *Whittaker*, on p. 42 (driver convicted of using vehicle with insecure load; crates had been loaded on it by experienced draymen of another firm, who also rode on the vehicle, and driver took no part in loading), and quarter sessions found special reasons where the defective state of a lorry's tyres and its improper loading were due to the action or inaction of others than the defendant-driver (*R.* v. *Hurst* [1966] Crim.L.R. 683).   Obviously, it is unfair to endorse a licence, having regard to the consequences of " totting up," where the offender himself has been quite guiltless of any negligence or has had to rely on his superiors; in the case of an employer especially, he might find himself liable to disqualification under " totting up " for offences committed by his employees when he himself might not have driven on the road for months.   The owner of several vehicles which are driven by his employees on his business should consider turning his business into a limited company.   But in all such cases, if there is any evidence of negligence by the defendant, generally it would not be right to find special reasons, e.g., a master failing to give sufficient instructions or assistance to his driver or not having an adequate system of vehicle-maintenance or allowing his vehicles to remain out on the road without inspection by mechanics for a long time, or, again, a driver continuing to drive after a latent defect has begun to develop or driving when he knew that his lorry had been loaded by inexperienced people or failing to inspect the security of his load after a long journey.   However, having regard to *Crawford* v. *Haughton* and *Carmichael & Sons* v. *Cottle* (see p. 45), the conviction of an employer for unknowingly " causing " or " permitting " the use of a vehicle contravening a Construction and Use Regulation will be rare, as the conviction for " causing " or " permitting " will generally only be possible where the prosecution have been able to show that the employer knew or should have known of the defect.   If he knew or should have known of the defect, he will not have a special reason for non-endorsement.

The Road Traffic (Amendment) Act, 1967, s. 7 (re-enacted in the 1972 Act, Sched. IV, Pt. I, entry relating to s. 40 (5), cols. 5 and 6), provides that where a person is convicted of an offence under the Motor Vehicles (Construction and Use) Regulations or the like Regulations for track-laying vehicles, being an offence for which disqualification and endorsement may or must be ordered (see p. 434), endorsement, disqualification and driving test cannot be ordered if he proves that he did not know and had no reasonable cause to suspect that the facts of the case were such that that offence would be committed. The defendant is not exempted from conviction, fine or absolute or conditional discharge for such an offence but is exempted from endorsement and disqualification (including " totting up ") on such proof, even if the magistrates wish to disqualify because of his age. The standard of proof is presumably on balance of probabilities, and sworn evidence by the defence or admissions by the prosecution would be required. The section obviously applies where the facts amount to special reasons, as in the cases and examples given above, but it is doubtful if it goes beyond them, as the defendant must show not only that he did not know of the defect, etc., but also that he had no reasonable cause to suspect it. It would seem to extend to members of a motorist's family who take a car reasonably assuming that its brakes, tyres and steering are in order and who, while driving, still have no reason to assume otherwise and clearly extends to persons who believe that recent servicing at a garage has obviated defects.

Driving Licence Offences

Special reasons could generally be found for offences by persons not qualified to drive or by learner drivers only in the triviality of the offence (cf. *Reay* v. *Young* under " Insurance " on p. 682) or because of an emergency (see under " Driving whilst Disqualified ", *infra*). They could, it is submitted, also be found where a person who holds or is entitled to hold a provisional licence is driving under the supervision of a person who is fully entitled to be his supervisor but for the fact that the supervisor's licence, though properly renewable on demand, has in fact expired. Again, the fact that a defendant has been misled by a person on whom he is entitled to rely as to what vehicles his licence allows him to drive might be a special reason.

Driving whilst Disqualified

Formerly the offence of driving while disqualified involved obligatory disqualification for at least twelve months unless " special reasons " were found. The offence no longer involves obligatory disqualification but the cases discussed below may be of relevance in respect of other offences involving obligatory disqualification.

An emergency can be special reasons and they were found in *Aichroth* v. *Cottee* [1954] 2 All E.R. 856 (defendant who had been disqualified drove a baker's van in the early morning, when no taxis or other drivers were available, to his bakery to deal with an unexpected breakdown in the machinery; if he had not gone there, a large number of loaves would have been spoilt and thousands of people would have been deprived of their bread). If a disqualified driver drives to fetch a doctor because of a sudden illness of his wife or child, this might be a special circumstance if no other means of transport were available to cope with the emergency (*R.* v. *Phillips* (1955), 119 J.P. 499). A defendant's ignorance of the law, the return to him, in error, of his licence by the magistrates' clerk soon after the disqualification and his consequent belief, from inquiry among other motorists, that he was not disqualified were held by a Metropolitan magistrate to be special circumstances (Jo.Crim.L. (1955) 100). Special circumstances were found by another Metropolitan magistrate where the defendant had been disqualified for a month but had his licence back from the court after three weeks with no mention of disqualification in the endorsement and he had been told by a constable that he must consequently have been confused over the length of his period of disqualification (Jo.Crim.L. (1959) 100). A stipendiary magistrate has held that, where the defendant's solicitors had told him that they would get the disqualification suspended pending the hearing of an appeal against it, his reliance on their statements constituted special circumstances. *Semble*, on the analogy of the insurance cases, *supra*, a defendant could plead special circumstances where he had been misled as to the effect or period of his disqualification by a person whom he could reasonably regard as competent to advise him, if the period had not been made plain by the court or court documents. Special reasons were found when a disqualified driver moved an obstructing vehicle for ten yards on a constable's request (*Ambrose* v. *Jamieson* [1967] Crim.L.R. 114).

It might be deemed to be special reasons where a disqualified person was only pushing a vehicle on a level road, without danger to anyone, assuming it to be " driving " (see p. 21), provided his intended journey was a short one and he was not wrongly taking the vehicle without the owner's consent.

It is not a special reason that a period of disqualification of one year had only four weeks to run when the defendant drove; whether the driving takes place on the first or last day of the period has no effect on the gravity of the offence (*Gosling* v. *Paul* [1961]

Crim.L.R. 318). Nor is it a special reason that conviction and imprisonment (under the old law) might lead to a student's expulsion from the university (*Carnegie* v. *Clark* [1947] S.C.(J.) 74).

It may or may not be a special reason that the defendant did not know he was disqualified at the time he committed the offence of driving while disqualified (*R.* v. *Lynn* [1971] Crim.L.R. 429). In fact no special reason was found because the defendant had means of finding out whether he was disqualified and the circumstances of the case were such that he ought to have made inquiry and discovered his driving status (*ibid.*).

General Considerations

It is obviously impossible to forecast all the circumstances which might constitute special reasons but some general examples can be given. As indicated particularly under the part of this chapter relating to the Construction and Use Regulations, the moral guilt of partners may vary very much between one another and it is submitted that, where one partner in a firm is in practice responsible for the transport side of the business, an absolute discharge or finding of special reasons would generally be justifiable for any other partners summoned, in the absence of any blameworthy conduct by them. Again, doctors, volunteer firemen, ambulance drivers, gas and electrical engineers and like persons concerned with public emergencies are liable to be called upon to drive at any time and a call to such a person, however much of an emergency it may be for the patient or the public in general, would be routine for him rather than emergency. He must expect to be called upon to drive at a moment's notice and should regulate his drinking accordingly; if he does drink too much and is then called to an emergency, this will, it is submitted, not justify finding special reasons. But where a doctor has no reasonable expectation of being called out suddenly (e.g., because the doctor's partner has agreed to answer all the emergency calls that night) and takes more drink than usual, it might be a special reason if he had to drive to an urgent case because his partner was engaged on another urgent case and no chauffeur or taxi was available (see the emergency cases on p. 674). Like considerations would apply to firemen and the other types of people mentioned.

Circumstances Justifying Non-Disqualification on " Totting Up "

The Road Traffic Act, 1972, s. 93 (3), provides that where a person convicted of a disqualifiable offence has within the three years immediately preceding the offence been convicted on at least

two occasions of endorsed disqualifiable offences, he must be disqualified for at least six months for the third offence *unless the court is
satisfied, having regard to all the circumstances, that there are grounds for
mitigating the normal consequences of the conviction,* in which case the
court may, at its option, not disqualify or may impose a period less
than six months. It will be noted that the court can have regard
to " all the circumstances " and not merely to " all the circumstances of the case ".

In *Lambie* v. *Woodage* [1972] 2 All E.R. 462 the House of Lords
held that the purpose of s. 93 (3) was to deal with the man who does
not commit serious offences and that the subsection is aimed at the
person who commits comparatively trivial offences frequently.
Disqualification for serious offences can be dealt with under s. 93
(2) of the Act. Evidence that the previous convictions were for
trivial offences is admissible for a defendant caught within the
provisions of s. 93 (3), but such evidence, although not necessarily
immaterial, is unlikely to be of much, if any, weight. The House
of Lords specifically approved the *dictum* of Lord Parker in *Baker*
v. *Cole* [1971] 3 All E.R., at p. 681, " I would like to observe that
the justices, in considering matters such as the offence being committed on the open road, should give little if any weight to such a
consideration, bearing in mind that the mischief aimed at by this
subsection is the man who commits maybe a series of offences
all comparatively trivial in themselves."

The facts of *Lambie* v. *Woodage* were that the motorist was convicted on the third occasion of driving at 50 m.p.h. in a 30 m.p.h.
speed limit and was allowed to give evidence, in face of objection by
the prosecution, that his two previous convictions (which were both
for exceeding 30 m.p.h.) were for speeds of 34 and 37 m.p.h. respectively. The House of Lords refused to quash the decision of the
magistrates in allowing him to give evidence to that effect. The
fact that evidence may be of little weight does not render it inadmissible. Their lordships were careful to confine their speeches to this
narrow question of admissibility and were careful not to give the
impression that they would have upheld the justices if the question
had been whether they approved of the manner in which the justices
had exercised the discretion given to them under s. 93 (3). Viscount
Dilhorne, at p. 465, observed that their decision might have been
different if the question for decision had been whether there were
in fact mitigating circumstances. Lord Cross of Chelsea, at p. 468,
doubted whether the bare fact that three offences of speeding were
relatively trivial could amount to a reason for not disqualifying,
and Lord Salmon, at p. 470, emphasised that the sole and narrow
question for consideration was whether the evidence was admissible.

It was said in *Baker* v. *Cole* [1971] 3 All E.R. 680*n.*, that anything which amounts to a special reason can be taken into account by the court and so can reasons special to the offender as well as those special to the offence, for the wording is intended to catch circumstances wider than those which constitute special reasons. Some of these can be considered now:—

(1) *Good character*.—This is, in theory, relevant but in fact the defendant will always have two previous convictions within the three years prior to the commission of the instant offence. It will be relevant, it is suggested, where there is more than three years between the dates of the offences but because of the delay before the defendant was convicted of the first of the offences the defendant comes within the ambit of the section. For example *A* committed an offence on 1st January, 1972, but was not convicted until 1st October, 1972; he committed another offence on 1st January, 1974, and was convicted on 1st February, 1974; and he commits another endorsable offence on 1st July, 1975. Although s. 93 (3) operates in such a case, as he was *convicted* on two previous occasions (1st October, 1972, and 1st February, 1974) within three years before the third offence (1st July, 1975) it is suggested that *A*'s character is not that of the persistent traffic offender usually caught within s. 93 (3), as three and a half years separate the first offence (1st January, 1972) and the third offence (1st July, 1975).

It is submitted that a court when hearing evidence as to the circumstances of the two previous offences, should be cautious before concluding that the previous courts' decisions were too severe. Three reasons are suggested. First, the court will only usually be able to hear the evidence of the defendant; it is unlikely that the prosecutor will be in a position to put before the court the facts of the previous prosecutions. Secondly, the court will not wish to be thought to be acting as a court of appeal on the previous court. If the earlier court's decision had been harsh or oppressive the defendant could have appealed against sentence. Thirdly, the previous convictions may have taken place on written pleas of guilty under the Magistrates' Courts Act, 1957, and if this is the case the defendant cannot say what in fact occurred at the previous court as he was not there. It was said in *Woodage* v. *Lambie* by the Divisional Court ([1971] 3 All E.R. 674) that such facts as the court may consider relevant may be obtained simply from the particulars endorsed on the driver's licence, and although the House of Lords ([1972] 2 All E.R. 462) held that evidence as to the circumstances of the previous offences was technically *admissible* their lordships equally made it plain that very little *weight* could normally be given to it.

(2) *Hardship.*—Hardship to the defendant would be a circumstance which can properly be taken into account under s. 93 (3). In *Baker* v. *Cole,* noted at [1971] 3 All E.R. 680, the High Court held that, in all circumstances of the case, the magistrates were entitled not to disqualify on the third conviction, where " totting up " applied, where the defendant was a craftsman whose type of work was not readily available in the town where he lived, he had to be at his work at times when public transport was not running, he could not cycle because of an injury, his place of work was too far away for walking, and if he could not use a motor vehicle to get to work, this would be equivalent to dismissal.   It was said that any special reasons also, as defined on p. 664, could be mitigating circumstances under s. 93 (3).   It was held in the same case that the fact that the defendant drove at 45 m.p.h. on a broad suburban highway subject to a 30 m.p.h. limit, without showing lack of care towards other road-users and without there being any element of special danger, was not a mitigating circumstance.   The fact that the third offence is one of the less serious ones in the Schedule is not a ground for refraining from disqualifying or for disqualifying for less than six months.   The court can treat circumstances pertaining to the offender as mitigating circumstances under s. 93 (3).

In *R.* v. *Sixsmith, ex parte Morris* [1966] 3 All E.R. 473, it was held that, where a person is convicted at the third hearing of a number of offences, particularly if they arise out of the same driving or user of the vehicle, each resulting in a requirement to disqualify under s. 93 (3), the court can have regard to that, together with all the other circumstances, as a ground for mitigating the normal consequences of the conviction and imposing a shorter disqualification (or not disqualifying at all) under s. 93 (3) in respect of one, or some, of the offences.   It is submitted that this judgment shows that the fact that several offences arise out of one incident is a mitigating circumstance, if taken with all the other circumstances, and the fact alone that the defendant has committed several offences will not of itself justify non-disqualification but the aggregate of periods of disqualification, if all were imposed, could often amount to hardship to him, especially if he depended on driving for his living, thus justifying non-disqualification (or for less than six months) on some of the charges.

If a defendant who depends very much on driving appears before a court and is liable to " totting up ", it is suggested that the court should carefully examine his personal circumstances; if he drives for a living, e.g., he is a bus or lorry driver, or a commercial traveller, and would lose or could not do his job if he were disqualified, that could be a ground for not disqualifying under the "totting up" provision, though it would never be a special reason for not disqualifying for a "drink-driving" offence (see for example *Glendinning* v. *Batty,* on p. 672). But it is suggested that the court should be satisfied that he will in fact lose his job and not be given an inside one during his period of disqualification, so long as the pay for the inside job is not so much less as to cause financial hardship. Again, for the traveller the court should be satisfied that he cannot do his rounds by public transport as adequately even if not so comfortably. In *Baker* v. *Cole, supra,* the decision might have been different had the defendant been able to ride a bicycle or use buses to get to work. The hardship could be not only financial hardship, such as loss of a job, but also personal, e.g., where the defendant has a disability which makes the use of public transport for him very difficult or he lives in a place where a car is the only method of transport and it is impracticable for anyone else to drive him. Hardship to the public, e.g., by the disqualification of the village doctor, can also, it is suggested, be a matter which can properly be regarded (although it is not a "special reason" for not disqualifying: *Holroyd* v. *Berry,* on p. 673). The court should presumably in all cases consider the general circumstances before refraining from disqualifying, e.g., a person in a town who says he needs a car to get to work should be asked about the public transport and other facilities available.

It is submitted that where hardship is advanced as a mitigating circumstance the court should primarily have regard to the degree of hardship which would be caused by disqualifying the offender. Disqualification almost invariably involves hardship to every driver but Parliament can hardly have intended that all persons who can show hardship should not be disqualified, because this would mean that s. 93 (3) entitles almost every offender to avoid disqualification. Parliament no doubt did not intend that all lorry drivers, for example, should not be disqualified but disqualification will be a greater hardship to a lorry driver than to the average driver as a lorry driver depends on a licence to earn a living. It is submitted that the degree of hardship, if this is the only mitigating circumstance, must be out of the ordinary. It is also suggested that the court should have special regard to whether hardship will be caused to persons other than the offender himself. If hardship will be caused to his family, or, if he is a doctor, to his patients, this might be regarded as a strong mitigating circumstance. Even where great hardship would undoubtedly be caused if the defendant were disqualified for the full six months, this will not necessarily be sufficient "mitigating circumstances" to justify total relief from disqualification. If the defendant is entitled to immediate leave or if his employer is prepared to employ him on non-driving duties for a period, the court would seem to be under an obligation to impose disqualification for the period of leave or the period for which he can be employed on non-driving duties without risk of dismissal causing hardship.

(3) *Offence not serious.*—Triviality of the offence in itself may not be a special reason (see *Nicholson* v. *Brown* on p. 670) but, even where the offence is not trivial, there might be circumstances which would justify non-disqualification under s. 93 (3), e.g., the fact that although he was not insured, the insurance company agreed to accept that he was covered or that a driver who went past a " stop " sign did so at a slow pace and with adequate precautions after satisfying himself that the light would not change. Again, not reporting an accident to the police might be excusable under s. 93 (3) if the defendant shows that he had been in touch with the other person involved and the latter was likely to be fully indemnified for any loss caused by the accident. So might an offence under the Pedestrian Crossings Regulations where the driver was absolutely liable and had not been negligent causing hardship. But see *Baker* v. *Cole* and *Lambie* v. *Woodage, supra.*

(4) *Other circumstances.*—Carelessness by a defendant in reading the policy or his relying on someone else to renew it for him or on someone else's interpretation of it might justify non-disqualification under s. 93 (3). So might the serious results of an accident to him, e.g., being off work for some months because of his injuries in an accident arising from his own careless driving or even the heavy bill he had to pay because of the damage to his car. The present editor would not consider that loss of a " no-claim " bonus would be within the exception of s. 93 (3) but doubtless some advocates will be heard to urge it.

It is submitted that it would not be proper to exempt an offender from the disqualification under s. 93 (3) merely because the court had fined him much more heavily than other comparable offenders for that very exempting purpose; the High Court does not like heavy fines on rich offenders when a poorer person who could not pay such a fine would have to go to prison or suffer the disqualification. On the other hand, if the court finds that mitigating circumstances exist and does not disqualify, it is submitted that it would be perfectly proper to increase the financial penalty on the ground that the defendant is a persistent offender.

Where the defendant proves that, although his licence shows convictions on different days, all these convictions arose from one incident and that they were recorded on different days because of necessary adjournments, the court acting under s. 93 (3) might properly refrain from disqualifying if satisfied that, but for the adjournments, the defendant would have been convicted on one occasion only and consequently not have been liable to " totting up ".

The fact that an interval exceeding three years had occurred between the commission of the instant offence and the earlier of the two previous offences might be a mitigating circumstance (see p. 626). The section is designed (see *Baker* v. *Cole*) to deal with the relatively persistent traffic offender. As the three-year period is the three years from the date of the third *offence* back to the date of the earliest *conviction* it can easily happen that the offender is caught by s. 93 (3) although the period between the dates of the respective offences is well outside a period of three years.

It is sometimes suggested that the fact that the defendant drives an exceptional mileage each year is a mitigating circumstance in that it increases the chance of his being convicted of traffic offences. It is doubtful how far this argument has validity. Section 93 (3) lays down a period of time within which offences must not be repeated, not a set mileage. A person who is constantly driving on the road should, if anything, set a higher standard than that of an average road user.

All the circumstances mentioned above are speculation, however, and it may be that the High Court will interpret s. 93 (3) in a narrower or wider sense. On the other side, it is suggested that the compulsory disqualification required by s. 93 (3) is not merely punitive but is in the interests of road safety also in that it is meant to keep bad and irresponsible drivers off the road, so that the court should, in considering whether or not to operate s. 93 (3), always give weight to the question of the public interest in banning such people from driving.

It is suggested that the requirement that a court should insist on properly admissible sworn evidence before special reasons can be found (see *Jones* v. *English*, *Brown* v. *Dyerson*, etc., on p. 667) applies also to where a court finds there are mitigating circumstances under s. 93 (3). What an advocate is instructed by a defendant in the comfort of a solicitor's office to say may well differ from what the defendant is prepared to say on oath in open court in a witness box. One of the grounds for allowing sworn evidence of the circumstances of the previous offences to be admissible is that the defendant's evidence can—in time—be checked by the prosecution (*per* Lord Cross in *Lambie* v. *Woodage* [1972] 2 All E.R., at p. 467).

Statement of Reasons for Not Disqualifying

Where the court does not disqualify under s. 93 (3) or does so for a shorter period than six months, the grounds must be stated in open court and entered in the register (1972 Act, s. 105) but the prosecutor cannot appeal against a non-disqualification on the ground that the court omitted to do this (see *Brown* v. *Dyerson*, on p. 668).

CHAPTER VIII

APPEALS

APPEALS from magistrates' courts lie to the Crown Court by the defendant against conviction or sentence or both and to the High Court by the defendant or prosecutor against conviction or dismissal and, to a limited extent, sentence. The appeal to the High Court will be heard by a Divisional Court of the Queen's Bench Division.

Crown Court

The matter is now regulated by the Summary Jurisdiction (Appeals) Act, 1933, as amended, the Magistrates' Courts Act, 1952, Pt. V, the Courts Act, 1971, the Crown Court Rules, 1971, and the Magistrates' Courts Rules, 1968, rr. 62 to 64. Appeal lies against conviction only if the defendant did not plead guilty before the justices; the Courts Act, 1971, and the Crown Court Rules substitute the Crown Court as the appellate court in place of quarter sessions and extend the time for giving notice of appeal from fourteen to twenty-one days. The notice of appeal must be in writing and has to be given to the magistrates' clerk and to the other party. It has to be given within twenty-one days of the day on which the court's decision was given; s. 84 (2) of the Magistrates' Courts Act, 1952, provides that such day shall, where there was an adjournment after conviction, be the day on which the court sentences or otherwise deals with the offender (but see 115 J.P.Jo. 805 where a defendant wishing to appeal is kept in custody for inquiries). Such day is excluded in computing the twenty-one days. The Crown Court may extend the time for appealing (Magistrates' Courts Act, 1952, s. 84 (3)). A form of notice of appeal is in Stone (1975), p. 5090; the magistrates' clerk notifies the Crown Court of it.

Appeal also lies against sentence only; " sentence " includes any order made on conviction by the magistrates, not being a probation order, an order of conditional discharge, an order for payment of costs or " an order made in pursuance of any enactment under which the court has no discretion as to the making of the order or as to its terms " (s. 83 (3) (d)). An obligatory disqualification under the Road Traffic Act, 1972, s. 93 (1) or (3), it is submitted, comes within this definition and it is for this reason that s. 94 (1) of the 1972 Act specifically allows an appeal to be made against such orders in the same manner as against a conviction. A discretionary order of disqualification under s. 93 (2) is appealable (*R.* v. *Surrey Quarter Sessions, ex parte Commissioner of Police of the Metropolis* [1962] 126 J.P. 269) but, it is submitted, neither an endorsement nor an order for the payment of back duty under s. 9 of the Vehicles (Excise) Act, 1971, may be appealable as both types of order appear to come within the definition under s. 83 (3) (*d*), above. However, if appeal is lodged against sentence generally, it would seem to be open to the Crown Court in considering sentence to review an order of endorsement or as to back duty. Whether or not the appeal is against the whole of the decision, the Crown Court may increase or lessen the sentence provided the punishment is one which the magistrates' court might have awarded (Courts Act, 1971, s. 9 (4), (5)). The same period of notice applies whether the appeal is against conviction, sentence or other order, and the other side and the magistrates' clerk must be notified. The notices may be sent in all cases by registered letter or recorded delivery. A notice of appeal arising out of a conviction must state whether the appeal is against sentence or conviction or both (Crown Court Rules, r. 7 (3)). Where the appellant is in custody, the magistrates' court may fix the amount of the recognisance, with or without sureties, for his appearance at the appeal and such recognisances may be entered into before any magistrates, magistrates' clerk or officer in charge of a police station, or the prison governor. On this being done, he should be released. Appeal lies to the High Court against refusal to admit to bail and against a condition of bail (see p. 669) (Criminal Justice Act, 1948, s. 37; Criminal Justice Act, 1967, s. 22), but s. 13 (4) of the Courts Act, 1971, now gives power to the Crown Court to grant bail to any person who has appealed to the Crown Court.

It is the duty of the magistrates' clerk to send to the Crown Court the notice of appeal, a statement of the decision from which the appeal is brought, and notification of the last or usual place of abode of the parties. Most justices' clerks will supply a copy of any notes taken to either side on request.

No recognisance is required for the appellant to prosecute an appeal to the Crown Court. There is no appeal by the prosecutor in road traffic prosecutions, unless there be one in an excise prosecution (Customs and Excise Act, 1952, s. 283 (4): see p. 490, *supra*).

An appeal against conviction is a rehearing, and either side may call additional witnesses or refrain from calling witnesses called before the justices. The Crown Court may confirm, reverse or vary the justices' decision or remit it to them with their opinion, and exercise any power which the magistrates could have exercised. The Crown Court may not have regard to evidence given before the magistrates but not before it (*Bishop* v. *Hosier* (1962), *The Guardian*, 11th October). The Crown Court has no power to amend an information on appeal (*Garfield* v. *Maddocks* [1973] 2 All E.R. 303). The prosecution call their evidence first and then the defence theirs.

Where a person convicted or sentenced by a magistrates' court desires to appeal to the Crown Court, either court may order that legal aid be given to him and to the other party (Legal Aid Act, 1974, s. 28 (5)). A legal aid order for proceedings before a magistrates' court automatically confers authority on the solicitor to advise the defendant whether there are reasonable grounds for appeal either to the Crown Court or to the High Court by way of case stated (Legal Aid Act, 1974, s. 30 (5)). It is submitted that if he wishes to appeal, it is proper for the court considering an application for legal aid to cover the costs of his appeal to enquire from the solicitor who acted before the magistrates' court as to whether he advised that there were reasonable grounds for appeal.

Costs may be awarded against the unsuccessful party to the appeal; the amount may either be fixed by the appellate court or ascertained by taxation. But on a successful appeal against sentence costs should not be awarded against the police unless the original case was so trivial that it should never have been brought or the police have taken a part in the appeal beyond laying the facts before the Crown Court (*David* v. *Commissioner of Police of the Metropolis* [1962] 1 All E.R. 491).

Where the appeal is against conviction or sentence the Crown Court may increase or lessen the sentence, provided that the punishment is one which the magistrates' court might have awarded (Courts Act, 1971, s. 9 (4)). The powers of the Crown Court contained in s. 9 apply whether or not the appeal is against the whole of the magistrates' court's decision (s. 9 (5)).

Either party to the appeal to the Crown Court may, if dissatisfied with the determination of the court as being erroneous in point of law, apply to have a case stated by the Crown Court for the opinion of the Divisional Court (Courts Act, 1971, s. 10). The application must be made in writing to the Crown Court within fourteen days of the decision but the Crown Court may extend the time for making application to state a case (Crown Court Rules, 1971, r. 21). Legal aid will be available to either side under Pt. I of the Legal Aid Act, 1974. Appeal will lie from the Divisional Court, with leave, to the House of Lords (Administration of Justice Act, 1960, s. 1), provided that the Divisional Court certifies that a point of law of general public importance is involved.

Once notice of appeal has been given the appellate court now, as well as the court of first instance, may suspend an order of disqualification pending appeal.

Cases Stated

Either side in a road traffic prosecution may appeal to the High Court from a decision of a magistrates' court on the ground that it is wrong in law or in excess of jurisdiction (Magistrates' Courts Act, 1952, s. 87; Magistrates' Courts Rules, rr. 65 to 68; R.S.C., Ords. 56, 57). Note that written notice has to be given to the magistrates' clerk within *fourteen* days from, and excluding the day on which the justices finally disposed of the matter. Note also that not only is the time limit only fourteen days but this time limit cannot be extended; failure to comply with it is fatal. Sundays are included in computation of the fourteen days (*Peacock* v. *R.* (1858), 22 J.P. 403).

Rules 65–68 of the Magistrates' Courts Rules, 1968, have been replaced by the Magistrates' Courts (Amendment) (No. 2) Rules, 1975 (S.I. 1975 No. 518 (L.8)). The main object of the new rules is to reduce the delays in cases reaching the Divisional Court. The new r. 65 (1) places on the justices' clerk the responsibility for delivering the first draft of the case to the parties concerned. The intention is thereby to place on the justices' clerk the responsibility for preparing the initial draft unless the justices wish to assume the responsibility themselves. A detailed timetable is prescribed by the new rules. A period of twenty-one days is allowed for delivering by the justices' clerk of the first draft to the parties, a further period of twenty-one days is allowed for the parties to make representations after receiving the case and a final period of twenty-one days for the case to be settled by the court after having received the parties' observations. Rule 67 enables those time limits to be extended but if there is a delay a written statement of the reasons for it must accompany the final case. The new r. 65 (1) requires the applicant to identify the point of law upon which the opinion of the High Court is sought or, where the point of law is that there was insufficient evidence to support the decision, the application must identify the particular finding of fact which cannot be supported by the evidence (r. 65 (2)). The case may now be signed by the clerk to the justices on their behalf.

Hitherto the High Court have not been prepared to hear argument on any point not raised before the magistrates' court. As the point of law is now required to be stated in the application, it may well be that the High Court will not be prepared to hear or consider any argument on any other point of law (other than a point of jurisdiction) unless it arises on the face of the facts stated in the case or upon a point of law which no evidence could alter. It was said in *Whitehead* v. *Haines* [1964] 2 All E.R. 530 that on an appeal by case stated the High Court should entertain and determine a point of pure law open, on the facts found in the case, to an appellant convicted on a criminal charge, if that point of law was one which, if sound, might afford him a defence, notwithstanding that the point was not raised prior to his conviction.

Generally, the appellant must argue his point on the facts as found by the justices and indicated in their case. But the decisions of magistrates that certain facts did amount to obstruction and that other facts did not amount to dangerous driving were upset by the High Court in *Gill* v. *Carson* (1917), 81 J.P. 250, and *Bracegirdle* v. *Oxley* [1947] 1 All E.R. 126, respectively. The High Court can confirm, reverse or vary the magistrates' determination and can send back the case for further hearing with the High Court's ruling. The Divisional Court will not usually interfere with findings of fact by magistrates unless there was no evidence to support those findings or they were such that no reasonable magistrates, giving themselves proper directions and applying the proper considerations, could reach them. *Bracegirdle's* case, *supra*, was an example of a successful appeal by the prosecutor against the dismissal of a dangerous driving charge.

An appellant in custody has the same right to apply for bail and to appeal against its refusal as he has on an appeal to the Crown Court (see *supra*). The appellant, whether prosecutor or defendant, is usually required to enter into a recognisance to prosecute the appeal before the High Court and to submit to judgment.

Appeals by the prosecution against sentence on a point of law are sometimes brought where an order of conditional discharge, for example, has been made and it is considered there has been an improper exercise of that power in view of the seriousness of the charge (*Gardner* v. *James* [1948] 2 All E.R. 1069). They are frequently brought by prosecutors contesting a finding of special reasons. Costs may be, but are not always, awarded against an unsuccessful respondent (Summary Jurisdiction Act, 1857, s. 6); they can include the appellant's costs before the magistrates (*Turner* v. *Owen* [1955] 3 All E.R. 565).

Where the appellant abandons his appeal by way of case stated, there appears to be no statutory provision enabling the other party to obtain the costs incurred as a result. If, however, he has entered into a recognisance to prosecute his appeal, such recognisance can be forfeited. Although a forfeited recognisance is payable to the

Crown and not to the respondent, it may be wise for a respondent, if he suspects that a case stated may be withdrawn by the appellant, to insist on a recognisance being entered into by the appellant. If this is done it is suggested that if the appellant wishes to withdraw his appeal the respondent should be able to request payment of his reasonable costs by the appellant or forfeit his recognisance. The conditions of an appellant's recognisance under s. 90 of the Magistrates' Courts Act, 1952, are that he should prosecute his appeal without delay, to submit to the judgment of the High Court and pay any costs that the court may award.

Legal aid may be granted to either side, as with other High Court proceedings, under the Legal Aid Act, 1974, Pt. I.

A legal aid order for proceedings before a magistrates' court includes the cost of a solicitor's assistance in making application for a case to be stated within fourteen days (Legal Aid Act, 1974, s. 30 (5)).

Examining justices have no power to state a case (*Dewing* v. *Cummings* [1971] R.T.R. 295, where the defendant elected trial on indictment on a charge under s. 1 (1) of the Road Safety Act, 1967 (now s. 6 of the 1972 Act), and the justices found that there was no case to commit for trial). In the event of an unreasonable refusal to commit for trial, the prosecution can, if the facts warrant, apply to a judge of the High Court for leave to prefer an indictment under the Administration of Justice (Miscellaneous Provisions) Act, 1933, s. 2.

Appeal by either side will lie from the Divisional Court, with leave, to the House of Lords (Administration of Justice Act, 1960, s. 1), provided the Divisional Court certifies that a point of law of general public importance is involved.

The Divisional Court may suspend on order of disqualification pending hearing of an appeal by way of case stated, or on application for leave to apply for a writ of certiorari (see p. 644).

In accordance with the Practice Note ([1974] 3 All E.R. 528) an " expedited hearing list " is maintained of prerogative writs and appeals by way of case stated which involve sentences of imprisonment, disqualification for driving or possession of property. The main purpose is to dispose of short and simple cases quickly. Any party may apply to be placed on the list and the court of its own motion may place a case on the list.

Appeals Generally

See generally as to appeals to the Crown Court and to the High Court, Brian Harris, Criminal Jurisdiction of Magistrates, Chap.

24. A defendant's advisers should carefully consider the position where he wishes to appeal against conviction. If his case is strong on law and facts, the case will end completely if the Crown Court allows his appeal on the facts. If, however, the Crown Court decides the appeal in his favour on a point of law only, this gives to the prosecution the right to appeal to the High Court from the decision of the Crown Court, with consequent delay and further expense. Also, though a defendant can on an appeal to the Crown Court call additional witnesses or refrain from calling witnesses who were unhelpful before the magistrates, the prosecution can do the same in order to bolster up weaknesses in their own case. *Quaere* if an appellant may appeal to the Crown Court and seek certiorari simultaneously.

An article at 118 J.P.Jo. 116 discusses whether withdrawal of an application to state a case revives the right of appeal to the Crown Court.

If the defendant's case rests on law only, appeal by case stated would generally be the better course. Where the possible success of the appeal will depend largely on the facts as found by the magistrates, the appeal can always be abandoned if, when the case is sent to the appellant, the facts as stated leave little room for argument on a point of law. The clerk's fee for drawing the case is fifty new pence for the first 450 words and then five new pence for every ninety words. However, if a recognisance to prosecute the appeal to the High Court has been entered into, there is danger of its forfeiture.

The textbooks will show the occasions for which certiorari, mandamus and prohibition are the appropriate remedies (see Stone (1975), pp. 538–542; Brian Harris, Criminal Jurisdiction of Magistrates, Chap. 24). The powers of the High Court are extended by the Administration of Justice Act, 1960, s. 16. Costs on certiorari to remedy a mistake made by the magistrates should not be granted against them unless they have been guilty of deliberate misconduct (*R.* v. *Amersham JJ.* (1964), 108 S.J. 841; *R.* v. *Leeds JJ.* (1966), 110 S.J. 92). R.S.C., Ord. 53, applies to these proceedings.

A person convicted on indictment may appeal against the conviction on a question of law alone and, with the Court of Appeal's leave, on fact or mixed fact and law or other grounds; the trial judge may also give leave to appeal as indicated in s. 1 (2) of the Criminal Appeal Act, 1968. By s. 7 re-trial may be ordered as therein stated. By ss. 9, 10 and 11 there is an appeal, with leave of the Court of Appeal, against sentence. The term "sentence" includes, by s. 50 (1), an order of disqualification and, *semble*, of endorsement where there are special reasons for not endorsing. The right of appeal against sentence may be exercised whether the offender was convicted on indictment or sentenced on committal for sentence but it is arguable that, in view of the express mention of disqualification in s. 10 (3) and the omission of any reference in s. 10 to endorsement, there is no appeal against an endorsement ordered on committal for sentence. The Court of Appeal, in altering a sentence, must not deal with the appellant more severely than the court of trial dealt with him (s. 11 (3)). The time for appealing is twenty-eight days from the day of conviction, or, in the case of a sentence, from the day it was passed or the day the order was made (s. 18), but the Court of Appeal may extend that time. A person sentenced by the Crown Court on committal for sentence may, by s. 10 (3), appeal against a sentence of borstal training as the magistrates cannot pass such a sentence (but not an order of recall to borstal: *R. v. Bebbington* [1969] 1 W.L.R. 1348) and against imprisonment for six months or more or against consecutive terms aggregating six months or more but not against detention (*R. v. Moore* [1968] 1 All E.R. 790). Procedure is regulated by the Criminal Appeal Rules, 1968.

It sometimes happens that a defendant is convicted of an offence and afterwards a decision of the High Court in another case shows that his conviction was wrong. In such circumstances he should be advised to apply to the Home Office for a Royal Pardon. If the defendant pleaded guilty on a mistake of fact (believing, for example, that he was uninsured as his own policy did not cover him but subsequently finding that the car owner's policy covers him) he can apply to the Home Office for a *Remission* under the Sovereign's Royal Prerogative. This has the effect of commanding the magistrates to remit the penalty imposed (Remission of Penalties Act, 1859, s. 1).

APPENDIX I

REGULATIONS AND ORDERS

S.I. 1959 No. 1147

THE MOTORWAYS TRAFFIC REGULATIONS, 1959, AS AMENDED BY
S.I. 1966 No. 530

[NOTE: These Regulations do not apply in Scotland: see the Motorways Traffic (Scotland) Regulations, 1964 (S.I. 1964 No. 1002).]

*   *   *   *   *

Interpretation

3.—(1) In these Regulations, unless the context otherwise requires, the following expressions have the meanings hereby respectively assigned to them, that is to say—

(a) " carriageway " means that part of a motorway which is constructed with a surface suitable for the regular passage of vehicular motor traffic along the motorway and is distinguishable from the other parts of the motorway by the fact that on each side that part of the motorway either consists of a marginal strip or is contiguous to a raised kerb, but the said expression does not include any part of a central reservation;

(b) " central reservation " means that part of a motorway which separates two carriageways running along that motorway parallel or approximately parallel to each other and which is contiguous on one side to one of those carriageways and on the other side to the other of those carriageways;

(c) " excluded traffic " means traffic which is not traffic of Classes I or II;

(d) " marginal strip " means a continuous narrow strip of the surface of a carriageway which is at the side of that carriageway and is distinguishable from the rest of that surface by having a colour which is different from the colour of the rest of that surface;

(e) " the Minister " means the Minister of Transport and Civil Aviation;

(f) " motorway " means any road or part of a road to which these Regulations apply by virtue of Regulation 4;

(g) " traffic sign " has the meaning assigned thereto by subsection (1) of section 35 of the Road Traffic Act, 1956;

(h) " verge " means any part of a motorway which is not a carriageway or a central reservation.

(2) A vehicle shall be treated for the purposes of any provision of these Regulations as being on any part of a motorway specified in that provision if any part of the vehicle (whether it is at rest or not) is on the part of the motorway so specified.

(3) Any provision of these Regulations containing any prohibition or restriction relating to the driving, moving or stopping of a vehicle, or to its remaining at rest, shall be construed as a provision that no person shall use a motorway by driving, moving or stopping the vehicle or by causing or permitting it to be driven or moved, or to stop or remain at rest, in contravention of that prohibition or restriction.

(4) In these Regulations references to numbered classes of traffic are references to the classes of traffic of those numbers set out in the Second Schedule to the Special Roads Act, 1949, or, on the coming into operation of the Highways Act, 1959, in the Fourth Schedule to that Act, as for the time being varied or amended by virtue of any order made by the Minister under section 2 of the Special Roads Act, 1949, or section 12 of the Highways Act, 1959.

(5) The Interpretation Act, 1889, shall apply for the interpretation of these Regulations as it applies for the interpretation of an Act of Parliament and as if for the purposes of section 38 of that Act these Regulations were an Act of Parliament and the Regulations revoked by Regulation 2 were Acts of Parliament thereby repealed.

The Motorways

4.—(1) These Regulations apply—

(*a*) to every special road or part of a special road provided in pursuance of a scheme made or confirmed by the Minister under section 1 of the Special Roads Act, 1949, or section 11 of the Highways Act, 1959, being a road or, as the case may be, a part of a road which (save as otherwise provided by or under regulations made under section 12 of the Special Roads Act, 1949) can only be used by traffic of Classes I or II, and

(*b*) to any trunk road or part of a trunk road to which the provisions of the said section 12 apply by virtue of section 15 of the Special Roads Act, 1949, or of section 19 of the Highways Act, 1959, being a road or, as the case may be, a part of a road which (save as aforesaid) can only be used by traffic of Classes I or II:

Provided that these Regulations shall not apply to any part of any such road until such date as may be declared in accordance with subsection (8) of section 12 of the Special Roads Act, 1949, to be the date on which it is open for use as a special road.

(2) Nothing in these Regulations applies to any road in Scotland.

Vehicles to be driven on the carriageways only

5. Subject to the following provisions of these Regulations, no vehicle shall be driven on any part of a motorway which is not a carriageway.

Direction of driving

6.—(1) Where there is a traffic sign indicating that there is no entry to a carriageway at a particular place, no vehicle shall be driven or moved on to that carriageway at that place.

(2) Where there is a traffic sign indicating that there is no left or right turn into a carriageway at a particular place, no vehicle shall be so driven or moved as to cause it to turn to the left or (as the case may be) to the right into that carriageway at that place.

(3) Every vehicle on a length of carriageway which is contiguous to a

central reservation shall be driven in such a direction only that that reservation is at all times on the right-hand or offside of the vehicle.

(4) Where traffic signs are so placed that there is a length of carriageway (being a length which is not contiguous to a central reservation) which can be entered at one end only by vehicles driven in conformity with paragraph (1) of this Regulation, every vehicle on that length of carriageway shall be driven in such a direction only as to cause it to proceed away from that end of that length of carriageway towards the other end thereof.

(5) Without prejudice to the foregoing provisions of this Regulation, no vehicle which—

    (a) is on a length of carriageway on which vehicles are required by any of the foregoing provisions of this Regulation to be driven in one direction only and is proceeding in or facing that direction, or

    (b) is on any other length of carriageway and is proceeding in or facing one direction,

shall be driven or moved so as to cause it to turn and proceed in or face the opposite direction.

Restrictions on stopping

7.—(1) Subject to the following provisions of this Regulation, no vehicle shall stop or remain at rest on a carriageway.

(2) Where it is necessary for a vehicle which is being driven on a carriageway to be stopped while it is on a motorway—

    (a) by reason of a breakdown or mechanical defect or lack of fuel, oil or water required for the vehicle; or

    (b) by reason of any accident, illness or other emergency; or

    (c) to permit any person carried in or on the vehicle to recover or move any object which has fallen on a motorway; or

    (d) to permit any person carried in or on the vehicle to give help which is required by any other person in any of the circumstances specified in the foregoing provisions of this paragraph,

the vehicle shall, as soon and in so far as is reasonably practicable, be driven or moved off the carriageway on to, and may stop and remain at rest on, the verge which lies on the left-hand or near side of that vehicle while it is proceeding along that carriageway in accordance with the provisions of Regulation 6.

(3) A vehicle which is at rest on a verge in any of the circumstances specified in paragraph (2) of this Regulation—

    (a) shall so far as is reasonably practicable be allowed to remain at rest on that verge in such a position only that no part of it or of the load carried thereby shall obstruct or be a cause of danger to vehicles using the carriageway, and

    (b) shall not remain at rest on that verge for longer than is necessary in those circumstances.

(4) Nothing in the foregoing provisions of this Regulation shall preclude a vehicle from stopping or remaining at rest on a carriageway while it is prevented from proceeding along that carriageway by the presence of any other vehicle or any person or object.

Restrictions on reversing

8. No vehicle on a carriageway shall be driven or moved backwards except in so far as it is necessary to back the vehicle to enable it to proceed forwards along the carriageway or to be connected to any other vehicle.

Restrictions on use of verges

9. No vehicle shall be driven or moved or stop or remain at rest on any verge except in accordance with paragraphs (2) and (3) of Regulation 7.

Vehicles not to use the central reservation

10. No vehicle shall be driven or moved or stop or remain at rest on a central reservation.

Vehicles not to be driven by learner drivers

11. No motor vehicle shall be driven on a motorway by a person who is authorised under the Road Traffic Acts, 1930 to 1956, to drive that vehicle on a road by virtue only of his being the holder of a provisional licence granted to him under subsection (3) of section 5 of the Road Traffic Act, 1930:

Provided that this Regulation shall not apply to a vehicle which is being driven on a motorway by a person authorised as aforesaid if that person has, since the date of coming into force of the said provisional licence, passed a test prescribed under the Road Traffic Acts, 1930 to 1956, sufficient to entitle him to be granted under those Acts a licence, other than a provisional licence, authorising him to drive that vehicle on a road.

Restriction on use of right-hand or off side lane

11A.—(1) This Regulation applies to:—

(*a*) a motor vehicle other than—

(i) a motor car with an unladen weight not exceeding 3 tons;
(ii) a heavy motor car constructed solely for the carriage of passengers and their effects and not adapted or used for any other purpose; or
(iii) a motor cycle; and

(*b*) a motor vehicle drawing a trailer.

(2) No vehicle to which this Regulation applies shall be driven, or moved or stop or remain at rest on the right-hand or off side lane of any length of carriageway which has three traffic lanes at any place where all three lanes are open for use by traffic proceeding in the same direction:

Provided that this prohibition shall not apply to any vehicle while it is being driven on the right-hand or off side lane in order to pass another vehicle which is carrying or drawing a load of such exceptional width that that vehicle can pass it only if it is driven on the right-hand or off side lane.

Restrictions affecting persons on foot on a motorway

12. No person shall at any time while on foot go or remain on any part of a motorway other than a verge except in so far as it is necessary for him to do so to get to a verge or to secure compliance with any of these Regulations or to recover or move any object which has fallen on a motorway or to give help which is required by any other person in any of the circumstances specified in paragraph (2) of Regulation 7.

Restrictions affecting animals carried in vehicles

13. The person in charge of any animal which is carried by a vehicle using a motorway shall, so far as is practicable, secure that—

    (*a*) the animal shall not be removed from or permitted to leave the vehicle while the vehicle is on the motorway, and

    (*b*) if it escapes from, or it is necessary for it to be removed from, or permitted to leave, the vehicle—

        (i) it shall not go or remain on any part of a motorway other than a verge, and

        (ii) it shall whilst it is not on or in the vehicle be held on a lead or otherwise kept under proper control.

Use of motorway by excluded traffic

14.—(1) Excluded traffic is hereby authorised to use a motorway on the occasions or in the emergencies and to the extent specified in the following provisions of this paragraph, that is to say—

    (*a*) traffic of Classes III or IV may use a motorway for the maintenance, repair, cleaning or clearance of any part of a motorway or for the erection, laying, placing, maintenance, testing, alteration, repair or removal of any structure, works or apparatus in, on, under or over any part of a motorway;

    (*b*) pedestrians may use a motorway—

        (i) when it is necessary for them to do so as a result of an accident or emergency or of a vehicle being at rest on a motorway in any of the circumstances specified in paragraph (2) of Regulation 7, or

        (ii) in any of the circumstances specified in sub-paragraphs (*b*), (*d*), (*e*) or (*f*) of paragraph (1) of Regulation 15.

(2) Without prejudice to the foregoing provisions of this Regulation, the Minister may authorise the use of a motorway by any excluded traffic on occasion or in emergency or for the purpose of enabling such traffic to cross a motorway or to secure access to premises abutting on or adjacent to a motorway.

(3) Without prejudice to the foregoing provisions of this Regulation, where by reason of any emergency the use of any road (not being a motorway) by any excluded traffic is rendered impossible or unsuitable the Chief Officer of Police of the police area in which a motorway or any part of a motorway is situated, or any officer of or above the rank of superintendent authorised in that behalf by that Chief Officer, may—

    (*a*) authorise any excluded traffic to use that motorway or that part of a motorway as an alternative road for the period during which the use of the other road by such traffic continues to be impossible or unsuitable, and

    (*b*) relax any prohibition or restriction imposed by these Regulations in so far as he considers it necessary to do so in connection with the use of that motorway or that part of a motorway by excluded traffic in pursuance of any such authorisation as aforesaid.

Exceptions and relaxations

15.—(1) Nothing in the foregoing provisions of these Regulations shall preclude any person from using a motorway otherwise than in accordance with those provisions in any of the following circumstances, that is to say—

(*a*) where he does so in accordance with any direction or permission given by a constable in uniform or with the indication given by a traffic sign;

(*b*) where he does so in accordance with any permission given by a constable and for the purpose of investigating any accident which has occurred on or near a motorway;

(*c*) where—

(i) it is necessary for him to do so to avoid or prevent an accident or to obtain or give help required as the result of an accident or emergency, and

(ii) he does so in such manner as to cause as little danger or inconvenience as possible to other traffic on a motorway;

(*d*) where he does so in the exercise of his duty as a constable or as a member of a fire brigade or of an ambulance service;

(*e*) where it is necessary for him to do so to carry out in an efficient manner—

(i) the maintenance, repair, cleaning, clearance, alteration or improvement of any part of a motorway, or

(ii) the removal of any vehicle from any part of a motorway, or

(iii) the erection, laying, placing, maintenance, testing, alteration, repair or removal of any structure, works or apparatus in, on, under or over any part of a motorway; or

(*f*) where it is necessary for him to do so in connection with any inspection, survey, investigation or census which relates to a motorway or any part thereof and which is carried out in accordance with any general or special authority granted by the Minister.

(2) Without prejudice to the foregoing provisions of these Regulations, the Minister may relax any prohibition or restriction imposed by these Regulations.

S.I. 1964 No. 1857

The Traffic Signs Regulations and General Directions, 1964 (as amended by S.I. 1964 No. 2069, S.I. 1966 Nos. 489 and 490, S.I. 1969 No. 1269, S.I. 1970 Nos. 468 and 1972, and S.I. 1971 No. 2095.)

Part I

Traffic Signs Regulations

*   *   *   *   *

Section II

Miscellaneous General Provisions

Authorisations by the Minister or the Secretary of State

6. Nothing in these Regulations shall be taken to limit the powers of the Minister or the Secretary of State, as the case may be, under section 51 of the Road Traffic Act, 1960, to authorise the erection or retention of traffic signs of a character not prescribed by these Regulations.

Application of s. 14 *of the Road Traffic Act* 1960, *to signs*

7. Section 14 of the Road Traffic Act 1960 shall apply—

(a) to signs of the type shown in any of the diagrams 601, 602, 603, 605, 606, 610, 616 and 649;

(b) to the red signal when shown by the light signals prescribed by Regulation 31, by Regulation 31 as varied by Regulation 32, or by Regulation 33;

(c) to the road marking shown in diagram 1013 in so far as that marking conveys the requirements specified in Regulation 23 (2).

Variation in dimensions

8.—(1) Any variation in a dimension (other than as to the height of a letter) specified in any of the diagrams in Schedule 1, Schedule 3 or Schedule 4 shall be treated as permitted by these Regulations if the variation—

(a) in the case of a dimension so specified as 12 inches or as over 12 inches, does not exceed $2\frac{1}{2}\%$ of that dimension;

(b) in the case of a dimension so specified as 2 inches or as over 2 inches but as under 12 inches, does not exceed 5% of that dimension; or

(c) in the case of a dimension so specified as under 2 inches, does not exceed 10% of that dimension.

(2) Any variation in a dimension as to the height of a letter specified in any of the diagrams in Schedule 1 shall be treated as permitted by these Regulations if the variation—

(a) in the case of a dimension so specified as 4 inches or as over 4 inches, does not exceed $2\frac{1}{2}\%$ of that dimension; or

(b) in the case of a dimension so specified as under 4 inches, does not exceed 5% of that dimension.

(3) Any variation in a dimension specified in any of the diagrams in Schedule 2 shall be treated as permitted by these Regulations if the variation—

(a) in the case of a dimension so specified as 10 feet or as over 10 feet, does not exceed 15% of that dimension;

(b) in the case of a dimension so specified as 1 foot or as over 1 foot but under 10 feet, does not exceed 20% of that dimension; or

(c) in the case of a dimension so specified as under 1 foot, where the actual dimension exceeds the dimension so specified, does not exceed 30% of the dimension so specified, and where the actual dimension is less than the dimension so specified, does not exceed 10% of the dimension so specified.

(4) Any variation in a dimension as to the angle of hatching specified in any of the said diagrams shall be treated as permitted by these Regulations if the variation does not exceed 5 degrees.

SECTION III

Traffic Signs shown in Schedule 1

Signs to be of the sizes, colours and types shown in diagrams

9. Subject to the provisions of these Regulations, a traffic sign for conveying—

(*a*) to vehicular traffic on roads a warning of the description specified in or under a diagram in Part I of Schedule 1 shall be of the size, colour and type shown in the diagram relating to that warning;

(*b*) to vehicular traffic on roads a requirement, prohibition or restriction specified in or under a diagram in Part II of Schedule 1 (other than a requirement shown in diagram 601 or 602) shall be of the size, colour and type shown in the diagram relating to that requirement, prohibition or restriction;

(*c*) to traffic on a road other than a motorway information of a directional nature of the description specified in or under a diagram in Part III of Schedule 1 shall be of the size, colour and type shown in the diagram relating to that information;

(*d*) to traffic on roads information of the description specified in or under a diagram in Part IV of Schedule 1 shall be of the size, colour and type shown in the diagram relating to that information;

(*e*) to traffic on a motorway information of a directional or other nature specified in or under a diagram set out in Part V of Schedule 1 shall be of the size, colour and type shown in the diagram relating to that information.

Signs shown in diagrams 601 and 602

10. Subject to the provisions of these Regulations, a traffic sign for conveying to vehicular traffic on roads the requirements specified in paragraph (2) of the next succeeding Regulation shall be of the size, colour and type shown in diagram 601 and a traffic sign for conveying to such vehicular traffic the requirement specified in paragraph (3) of the said Regulation shall be of the size, colour and type shown in diagram 602.

Significance of signs shown in diagrams 601 and 602

11.—(1) for the purposes of this Regulation—
" minor road " means a road at a road junction on which road is placed the sign shown in diagram 601 or 602;
" major road " means the road at a road junction into which road emerges vehicular traffic from a minor road.

(2) The requirements conveyed by the sign shown in diagram 601 shall be that—

(*a*) every vehicle shall before entering the major road stop at the transverse lines shown in diagram 1002 or, if they are not for the time being visible, at the major road; and

(*b*) no vehicle shall proceed past such one of the said transverse lines as is nearest to the major road into that road, or if those lines are not for the time being visible shall enter into the major road, in such a manner or at such a time as is likely to cause danger to the driver of any other vehicle on the major road or as to necessitate the driver of any such other vehicle to change its speed or course in order to avoid an accident with the first-mentioned vehicle.

(3) The requirement conveyed by the sign shown in diagram 602 shall be that no vehicle shall proceed past such one of the transverse

lines shown in diagram 1003 as is nearest to the major road into that road, or if those lines are not for the time being visible shall enter into the major road, in such a manner or at such a time as is likely to cause danger to the driver of any other vehicle on the major road or as to necessitate the driver of any such other vehicle to change its speed or course in order to avoid an accident with the first-mentioned vehicle.

Significance of sign shown in diagram 649

11A.—(1) For the purposes of this Regulation—

" automatic half-barrier level crossing " means a level crossing where a road is crossed by a railway and where barriers are installed to descend automatically across part of the road when a train approaches;

" vehicle combination " means a combination of vehicles made up of one or more motor vehicles and one or more trailers all of which are linked together when travelling;

" abnormal transport unit " means—

(*a*) a motor vehicle or a vehicle combination—

  (i) the overall length of which, inclusive of the load (if any) on the vehicle or the combination, exceeds 55 feet;

  (ii) the overall width of which, inclusive of the load (if any) on the vehicle or the combination, exceeds 9 feet 6 inches; or

  (iii) the weight of which, inclusive of the load (if any) on the vehicle or the combination, exceeds 32 tons; or

(*b*) a motor vehicle, or a vehicle combination, which in either case is incapable of proceeding, or is unlikely to proceed, over an automatic half-barrier level crossing at a speed exceeding 5 miles per hour; and

" driver ", in relation to an abnormal transport unit, means where that unit is a single motor vehicle the driver of that vehicle and, where that unit is a vehicle combination the driver of the only or the foremost motor vehicle forming part of that combination.

(2) The requirement conveyed by the sign shown in diagram 649 shall be that no abnormal transport unit shall proceed on to or over an automatic half-barrier level crossing unless:—

(*a*) the driver thereof has himself before the unit so proceeds used a telephone at the said sign or the one at the crossing for the purpose of obtaining from a person duly authorised by the railway authority permission for that unit so to proceed;

(*b*) such permission has been obtained before the unit so proceeds; and

(*c*) the unit so proceeds only in accordance with the terms of that permission:

Provided that conditions (*b*) and (*c*) above shall not apply if—

  (i) on the use by the driver of the telephone placed at the crossing he receives an indication for not less than two minutes that the telephone at the other end of the telephone line is being called but no duly authorised person answers it; and

  (ii) the driver then drives the unit on to the crossing with the reasonable expectation of crossing it within times specified in a railway notice at that telephone as being times between which trains do not normally travel over that crossing.

*   *   *   *   *

Dimensions

13.—(1) Where as respects any diagram in Schedule 1 a dimension for the sign shown in the diagram is indicated in one or more sets of brackets against a dimension not indicated in brackets, any dimension indicated in a set of brackets may be treated as an alternative to the dimension not so indicated.

(1A) Where a sign shown in any of the diagrams 606 to 614, 616 or 636 to 645 is placed only temporarily on a road by a police constable or a person acting under the instructions (whether general or specific) of the chief officer of police for the purposes of a temporary statutory provision, any dimension for the sign specified in such a diagram may be reduced, subject to any dimension shown in the diagram horizontally as opposed to vertically not being reduced to less than 8 inches.

(2) A sign shown in a diagram in Part III of Schedule 1 other than in diagrams 717, 726 and 746 and a sign shown in a diagram in Part V of that Schedule other than in any of the diagrams 901, 902, 910 and 912 to 920 shall be of such dimensions having regard to the character of the road and the speed of the vehicular traffic generally using it as are necessary to accommodate any place name, route symbol, route number, arrow, any indication of distance, or any other indication which in accordance with these Regulations may be shown therein and it is appropriate to show for the purpose for which the sign is place on a road.

Proportions and form of letters and numerals

14.—(1) Subject to the provisions of paragraphs (2) and (3) of this Regulation, all letters incorporated in the signs shown in the diagrams in Schedule 1 other than in diagram 742 shall have the proportions and form shown in either Part I, Part II, Part V or Part VI of Schedule 5, all numerals incorporated in the signs shown in the diagrams in Schedule 1 shall have the proportions and form shown in Part III or Part VII of Schedule 5 and all other characters incorporated in the signs shown in the diagrams in Schedule 1 shall have the proportions and form shown in Part IV or Part VIII of Schedule 5.

(2) Letters and numerals used for the purposes of indicating a route number on the sign shown in diagram 738 and on any sign shown in a diagram in Part V of Schedule 1 shall have the proportions and form shown in Part IX of Schedule 5.

(3) Any arrow to be used in a sign shown in diagram 908 and any other sign of a directional nature shown in a diagram in Schedule 1 which is mounted over the carriageway shall have the proportion and form of the arrow secondly shown in Part IV or Part VIII in Schedule 5.

Illumination of signs by lighting

15.—(1) The provisions of the following paragraphs of this Regulation in their application to the signs shown in diagrams 521, 606, 609, 612 to 614, 616 and 809 are subject to the provisions of Regulation 16.

(2) The signs shown in diagrams 612 to 614—

    (*a*) when fixed to light signals as prescribed by Regulation 31 or by Regulation 31 as varied by Regulation 32 shall be illuminated at all times by a means of internal lighting, and (*b*) when not so fixed shall be illuminated throughout the hours of darkness by a means of internal or external lighting unless the signs are placed only temporarily on a road for the purposes of a temporary statutory provision or by reason of the execution of works or any obstruction on a road or some emergency.

  (3) The sign shown in diagram 606—

    (*a*) when fixed to light signals mentioned in the last paragraph shall be illuminated at all times by a means of internal lighting,

    (*b*) when mounted in a bollard shall be illuminated throughout the hours of darkness by a means of internal or external lighting, and

    (*c*) when not fixed or mounted as aforesaid, but when erected on a road within 50 yards of a street lamp lit by electricity shall be illuminated throughout the hours of darkness by a means of internal or external lighting unless the sign is placed only temporarily on the road for the purposes of a temporary statutory provision or by reason of the execution of works or any obstruction on a road or some emergency.

  (4) The signs shown in diagrams 609 to 611, and 616—

    (*a*) when mounted in a bollard shall be illuminated throughout the hours of darkness by a means of internal or external lighting, and

    (*b*) when not mounted as aforesaid, but when erected on a road within 50 yards of a street lamp lit by electricity shall be illuminated throughout the hours of darkness by a means of internal or external lighting unless the signs are placed only temporarily on the road for the purposes of a temporary statutory provision or by reason of the execution of works or any obstruction on a road or some emergency.

  (5) The signs shown in diagrams 521 and 809 when erected on a road within 50 yards of a street lamp lit by electricity shall be illuminated throughout the hours of darkness by a means of internal or external lighting unless in the case of the sign shown in diagram 521 it is placed only temporarily on the road for the purposes of a temporary statutory provision or by reason of the execution of works or any obstruction on a road or some emergency.

  (6) The sign shown in diagram 814 shall be illuminated throughout the hours of darkness by a means of internal or external lighting.

  (7) The sign shown in diagram 828 shall be illuminated by a means of internal lighting only during such times as it is necessary that the sign shall be illuminated for the purpose of indicating the information shown in the diagram relating to that sign.

  (8) The signs shown in diagrams 560 and 561 shall not be illuminated by the fitting of a means of internal or external lighting.

  (9) Subject to the foregoing paragraphs of this Regulation and to Regulation 19 every sign shown—

    (*a*) in a diagram in Part I and Part II of Schedule 1 other than the signs shown in diagrams 515, 536, 539 to 542, 545, 548 to 552, 554, 557 to 559, 562, 564 to 569, 603 to 605, 615, 617 (when used in combination with the sign shown in diagram 618), 624 and 633 to 644, and

    (*b*) in diagrams 701 to 712, 718 to 723, 727 and 729 to 731, when erected on a road within 50 yards of a street lamp lit by electricity shall be illuminated throughout the hours of darkness by a means of internal or external lighting unless the sign is placed only temporarily on the road for the purposes of a temporary statutory provision or by reason of the execution of works or any obstruction on a road or some emergency.

(10) Subject to the foregoing paragraphs of this Regulation and to the provisions of Regulation 19, any sign shown in a diagram in Schedule 1 may be illuminated by a means of internal or external lighting.

(11) Subject to the provisions of Regulation 19, where any sign shown in a diagram in Schedule 1 is to be illuminated by a means of external lighting, that means shall be either fitted to the sign or to the structure on which it is mounted or otherwise specially provided.

16. Where a sign shown in any of the diagrams 521, 606, 609, 612 to 614, 616 and 809 is placed on a road in connection with a statutory prohibition, restriction or requirement relating to vehicular traffic which does not apply at all times, the sign shall be illuminated by a means of internal or external lighting only during such times that it is necessary for the purposes of that prohibition restriction or requirement that the sign shall be visible from a reasonable distance to drivers of approaching motor vehicles.

*   *   *   *   *

Illumination of signs by reflecting material

18.—(1) Nothing in this Regulation shall apply to the signs shown in diagrams 536, 560 and 561.

(2) Subject to the provisions of the last and the next paragraph and of Regulation 19, every sign shown in a diagram in Schedule 1 shall be illuminated by the use of reflecting material in accordance with the provisions of paragraphs (5) and (6) of this Regulation unless the sign is at all times or at particular times illuminated by lighting in accordance with the provisions of Regulation 15 or 16.

(3) The requirements of the last preceding paragraph shall not apply to the signs shown in diagrams 624, 637 to 641, 643, 644, 739, . . . 742, 826, 833 to 836 and 841 to 843, and shall not apply to any signs shown in diagrams 636, 642, 734 to 736, 743 to 746, 801 to 808, 810, 812, 813, 815 to 820, 827, 829 to 832 and 840 if any such sign is so illuminated by street lighting throughout the hours of darkness as to be legible from a reasonable distance by drivers of approaching motor vehicles.

(4) Subject to the foregoing paragraphs of this Regulation and to Regulation 19, any sign shown in a diagram in Schedule 1 other than those shown in diagrams 637 to 641 may be illuminated by the use of reflecting material in accordance with the following provisions of this Regulation.

(5) Subject to paragraph (6) of this Regulation, where reflecting material is used on any sign shown in a diagram in Schedule 1 it shall be of the same colour as that of, and extend throughout, that part of the sign to which it is applied:

Provided that

(a) no reflecting material shall be applied to any part of a sign coloured black, (*b*) no reflecting material shall be applied to that part of any sign shown in Part III of Schedule 1 which is coloured green, **and**

(*c*) no reflecting material shall be applied to that part of any sign shown in diagrams 711, 721, 738 and 837 to 839, or to that part of any sign shown in Part V of Schedule 1, which is coloured blue.

(6) Where in accordance with the last paragraph, different colours of reflecting material are used immediately adjacent to one another on the same sign, a gap of not more than ¾ of an inch in width nor less than ¼ of an inch in width may be left between the different colours of reflecting material.

*   *   *   *   *

Section IV

Traffic Signs shown in Schedule 2

Road markings

20.—(1) Subject to the provisions of these Regulations, a traffic sign consisting of a line or mark on a road (in these Regulations referred to as a " road marking ") for conveying to traffic on roads a warning, a requirement or information of the description specified under a diagram (other than diagrams 1003 and 1013) in Schedule 2 shall be of the size and type shown in the diagram relating to that warning, requirement or information:

(2) In diagrams 1001, 1004, 1009, 1010, 1013, 1019 to 1022, 1024, 1038 and 1039 the dimensions indicated in brackets against dimensions not so indicated may be treated as an alternative to the last mentioned dimensions.

Particular road markings

21. A road marking for conveying to vehicular traffic the requirement specified in paragraph (2) of the next succeeding Regulation shall be of the size and type shown in diagram 1003.

22.—(1) For the purposes of this Regulation—

" minor road " means a road at a road junction on which road are placed the transverse lines shown in diagram 1003;

" major road " means the road at a road junction into which road emerges vehicular traffic from a minor road.

(2) The requirement conveyed by the said transverse lines, whether or not they are used in conjunction with the sign shown in diagram 602, shall be that no vehicle shall proceed past such one of those lines as is nearest to the major road into that road in such a manner or at such a time as is likely to cause danger to the driver of any other vehicle on the major road or as to necessitate the driver of any such other vehicle to change its speed or course in order to avoid an accident with the first-mentioned vehicle.

23.—(1) A road marking for conveying the requirements specified in the next succeeding paragraph and the warning specified in paragraph (5) of this Regulation shall be of the size and type shown in diagram 1013.

(2) The requirements conveyed by the road marking mentioned in the last preceding paragraph shall be that—

    (*a*) subject to the provisions of paragraph (3) of this Regulation, no vehicle shall stop on any length of road along which the marking has been placed at any point between the two ends of the marking; and

    (*b*) subject to the provisions of paragraph (4) of this Regulation every vehicle proceeding on any length of road along which the marking has been so placed that, as viewed in the direction of travel of the vehicle, the continuous line is on the left of a dotted line or a continuous line shall be so driven as to keep the first-mentioned continuous line on the right hand or off side of the vehicle.

(3) Nothing in sub-paragraph (*a*) of the last preceding paragraph shall apply—

    (*a*) so as to prevent a vehicle stopping on any length of road so long as may be necessary—

        (i) to enable a person to board or alight from the vehicle,

        (ii) to enable goods to be loaded on to or to be unloaded from the vehicle, or

        (iii) to enable the vehicle, if it cannot be used for such purpose without stopping on that length of road, to be used in connection with any building operation or demolition, the removal of any obstruction to traffic, the maintenance, improvement or reconstruction of that length of road, or the laying, erection, alteration or repair in or near to that length of road of any sewer or of any main, pipe or apparatus for the supply of gas, water or electricity, or of any telegraphic line as defined in the Telegraph Act, 1878,

    so, however, that no vehicle shall be enabled by virtue of this sub-paragraph to stop for any of the purposes at (i), (ii) or (iii) above on a part of that length of road, not being a lay-by or a road verge, if it is reasonably practicable to stop the vehicle for that purpose on a part of that length of road, being a lay-by or a road verge;

    (*b*) to a vehicle used for fire brigade, ambulance or police purposes;

    (*c*) to a pedal bicycle not having a sidecar attached thereto, whether additional means of propulsion by mechanical power are attached to the bicycle or not;

    (*d*) to a vehicle stopping in any case where the person in control of the vehicle is required by law to stop, or is obliged to do so in order to avoid an accident, or is prevented from proceeding by circumstances outside his control; or

    (*e*) to anything done with the permission of a police constable in uniform.

(4) Nothing in sub-paragraph (*b*) of paragraph (2) of this Regulation shall apply so as to prevent a vehicle crossing or straddling the continuous line first mentioned in that sub-paragraph for the purpose of obtaining access to any other road joining the length of road along which the line is placed or to land or premises situated on or adjacent to the said length of road or if it is necessary to do so—

(*a*) in order to pass a stationary vehicle, or owing to circumstances
outside the control of the driver or in order to avoid an accident, or

(*b*) for the purpose of complying with any direction of a police constable in uniform.

(5) The warning conveyed by the road marking mentioned in paragraph (1) of this Regulation shall be that no vehicle while travelling
next to a dotted line placed on the left, as viewed in the direction of travel
of the vehicle, of a continuous line should cross or straddle the first mentioned line unless it is seen by the driver of the vehicle to be safe to do so.

Colour of road markings

24.—(1) Subject to the provisions of this Regulation, the road markings
shown in the diagrams in Schedule 2 shall be white.

(2) Road markings shown in diagrams 1015 to 1021 shall be yellow.

(3) Road markings shown in diagrams 1030 and 1031 when consisting
of studs may be silver instead of white.

Use of reflecting material and studs with reflectors on road markings

25.—(1) The road markings shown in diagrams 1011 to 1014 shall
be illuminated with reflecting material and along the length of and between the two lines constituting the marking shown in diagram 1013
there may be fitted studs incorporating reflectors:

Provided that—

(*a*) until the 31st December 1967 it shall not be necessary for the
road markings shown in the diagrams 1013 and 1014 to be illuminated with reflecting material; and

(*b*) until the 31st December 1973 studs incorporating reflectors may
be fitted either to the marking shown in diagram 1013 or along
the length of or between the two lines constituting the marking.

(2) Subject to the foregoing provisions of this Regulation, any road
marking may be illuminated with reflecting material and studs incorporating reflectors may be fitted to the markings shown in diagrams 1004
to 1007, 1010 to 1012.

(3) Reflectors incorporated in studs shall be white except that in the
case of the reflectors fitted to the markings shown in diagrams 1010 to
1012 they may be red where the near side of the carriageway is indicated
to drivers of approaching motor vehicles.

*   *   *   *   *

SECTION V

Miscellaneous Traffic Signs

Certain temporary signs

27.—(1) Notwithstanding the provisions of Regulation 9 and subject
to the succeeding paragraphs of this Regulation, signs placed temporarily
on or near a road—

(*a*) for conveying to traffic—

(i) information as respects deviations of, or alternative traffic
routes,

(ii) information as respects the route which may conveniently be followed on the occasion of a sports meeting, exhibition or other public gathering, in each case attracting a considerable volume of traffic, or

(iii) a warning of works being executed on or near a road or any obstruction on a road;

(*b*) for conveying to vehicular traffic any prohibition, restriction or requirement of a description required for the purposes of a temporary statutory provision; or

(*c*) pending the erection of any permanent sign prescribed by these Regulations, for conveying to traffic the indication which such a permanent sign indicates,

may be of such size, colour and type as is specified in the following provisions of this Regulation.

(2) Every such sign placed as aforesaid (hereinafter referred to as a " temporary sign ") shall be of a shape which—

(*a*) is rectangular;

(*b*) is rectangular, but with the corners rounded; or

(*c*) is rectangular, but with one end pointed.

(3) Every temporary sign shall be of such size as is necessary to accommodate the wording, numerals and arrows or chevrons appropriate to the purpose for which it is placed as aforesaid and any arms, badge, device, words or letters incorporated in the sign in accordance with the provisions of paragraph (6) of this Regulation.

(4) Every letter and numeral incorporated in a temporary sign other than any letter incorporated in the sign in accordance with the provisions of paragraph (6) of this Regulation shall be not less than $1\frac{1}{2}$ inches nor more than 10 inches in height, and every arrow so incorporated shall be not less than 10 inches nor more than 20 inches in length except that where an arrow is incorporated in the index part of a sign with a pointed end such arrow shall be not less than 4 inches nor more than 8 inches in length.

(5) Every letter, numeral, arrow or chevron incorporated in a temporary sign shall be—

(*a*) black on a background of white, silver or yellow; or

(*b*) white or silver on a blue background.

(6) There may be incorporated in or attached to a temporary sign the arms, badge or other device of a highway authority, police authority or the Royal Automobile Club, the Royal Scottish Automobile Club or the Automobile Association or words or letters indicating the highway authority or that the sign is a police sign.

(7) No sign shall after the 31st December 1967 by virtue of this Regulation convey to traffic any warning, requirement, restriction or prohibition of a description which can be so conveyed either by a sign shown in a diagram in Part I or Part II of Schedule I or by a sign so shown used in combination with or in conjunction with another sign shown in such a diagram.

*   *   *   *   *

Light signals for vehicular traffic

31.—(1) Light signals may be used for the control of vehicular traffic
and shall be of the size, colour and type prescribed either by paragraph
(2) or by paragraph (3) or by paragraph (3A) of this Regulation.

(2) The size, colour and type of light signals prescribed by this paragraph
shall be as follows:—

    (*a*) three lights shall be used, one red, one amber and one green;

    (*b*) the lamps showing the coloured lights aforesaid shall be arranged
vertically, the lamp showing a red light being the uppermost
and that showing a green light the lowermost;

    (*c*) each lamp shall be separately illuminated and the effective
diameter of the lens thereof shall be not less than 8 inches nor
more than 8⅝ inches;

    (*d*) the height of the centre of the amber lens from the surface of
the carriageway in the immediate vicinity shall be in the case
of signals placed at the side of the carriageway or on a street
refuge not less than 7 feet 9 inches nor more than 13 feet and
in the case of signals placed elsewhere and over the carriageway not less than 17 feet 9 inches nore more than 29 feet;

    (*e*) the centres of the lenses shall be not more than 14 inches apart;

    (*f*) the word "STOP" in black lettering may be placed upon
the lens of the lamp showing a red light and no other lettering
shall be used upon the lenses or in connection with a light signal;

    (*g*) the sequence of the signal lights shown for the purpose of con-
trolling vehicular traffic shall be as follows:—

        (i) red,
        (ii) amber and red together,
        (iii) green,
        (iv) amber.

(3) The size, colour and type of light signals prescribed by this paragraph shall be as follows:—

    (*a*) two lamps each showing an intermittent red light shall be used;

    (*b*) the lamps shall be arranged horizontally so that there is a distance
of not less than 1 foot 9 inches nor more than 2 feet 3 inches
between the centres of the lenses of the lamps;

    (*c*) each lamp shall be separately illuminated and the effective
diameter of the lens thereof shall be not less than 8 inches nor
more than 8¼ inches;

    (*d*) when the signal is operated, each lamp shall show its intermittent
red light at a rate of flashing of not less than 54 nor more than
66 flashes per minute or of not less than 70 nor more than 90
flashes per minute, and in such a manner that the light of one
lamp is always shown at a time when the light of the other lamp
is not shown;

    (*e*) the height of the centre of each lens from the surface of the car-
riageway in the immediate vicinity shall be in the case of signals
placed at the side of the carriageway or on a street refuge not
less than 7 feet nor more than 11 feet 6 inches and in the case of
signals placed elsewhere and over the carriageway not less than
17 feet nor more than 20 feet;

    (*f*) the word "STOP", in black lettering, may be placed upon the
lens of each lamp and no other lettering shall be used upon the lens.

(3A) The size, colour and type of light signals prescribed by this paragraph shall be as follows:—

(a) two lamps each showing an intermittent red light and one lamp showing a steady amber light shall be used;

(b) the lamps showing an intermittent red light shall be arranged horizontally so that there is a distance of not less than 22 inches nor more than 26 inches between the centres of the lenses of the lamps;

(c) the lamp showing the amber light shall be placed below the red lenses in such a position that a vertical line passing through the centre of that lamp is horizontally equidistant from a vertical line passing through the centre of each red lens and that the vertical distance between a horizontal line passing through the centre of that lamp and a horizontal line passing through the centres of the red lenses is not less than 9 inches nor more than 10⅝ inches;

(d) each lamp shall be separately illuminated and the effective diameter of the lens thereof shall be not less than 8 inches nor more than 8¼ inches;

(e) when the lamps showing an intermittent red light are operated, each such lamp shall show a red light at a rate of flashing of not less than 70 nor more than 90 flashes per minute or of not less than 54 nor more than 66 flashes per minute, and in such a manner that the light of one lamp is always shown at a time when the light of the other lamp is not shown;

(f) the height of the centres of the red lenses from the surface of the carriageway in the immediate vicinity shall be in the case of signals placed at the side of the carriageway or on a street refuge not less than 8 feet 9 inches nor more than 13 feet and in the case of signals placed elsewhere and over the carriageway not less than 19 feet nor more than 22 feet;

(g) the lenses shall be provided with a rectangular backing board having an overall width of not less than 52 inches and extending not less than 12 inches above the centre of each of the red lenses and not less than 12 inches below the centre of the amber lens, which board shall be coloured black on both sides, save for a white border having a width of not less than 3¼ inches nor more than 3⅞ inches on the side from which the lamps show;

(h) the sequence of the signal lights prescribed by this paragraph shown for the purpose of controlling vehicular traffic shall be amber followed by red.

(i) the word " STOP ", in black lettering, may be placed upon the red lenses but no other lettering shall be used thereon.

(4) Light signals prescribed by either of the last two paragraphs may be surmounted by a cross of the size, colour and type shown in diagram 542.

32.—(1) Subject to the next following paragraph of this Regulation, a lens or lenses of the size and colour shown in diagram 1 in Schedule 3, which, when illuminated, shows a green arrow—

(a) may be substituted for the lens showing the green light in the light signals referred to in Regulation 31 (2) in any of the methods shown in diagrams 3, 5, 6 and 7 in the said Schedule;

(b) may be affixed to the light signals referred to in Regulation 31 (2) or to those signals as altered in accordance with the preceding sub-paragraph in any of the methods shown in diagram 2 and diagrams 4 to 9 in the said Schedule; or

(c) may be affixed below the light signals referred to in Regulation 31 (2) or below those signals when altered in accordance with sub-paragraph (a) of this paragraph by the substitution of a green arrow for the lens showing the green light in the method shown in diagram 3 in the said Schedule.

(2) A lens which is, without prejudice to the provisions of Regulation 8, such as is shown in diagram 1 in Schedule 3 except only that the size thereof has been increased by 5000 as to each and every dimension specified in the said diagram 1, shall be treated for the purposes of and subject to these Regulations as a lens of the size shown in the said diagram 1 notwithstanding that the size has been so increased as aforesaid.

(3) When a lens is, or lenses are, so affixed as provided in sub-paragraph (b) or (c) of paragraph (1) of this Regulation and any one lens so affixed is of the increased size permitted by the preceding paragraph, the distance between the centre of that lens and the centre of any other lens affixed next in position immediately above, below or to the side of that first mentioned lens shall be not more than 17¼ inches.

(4) The direction in which the arrow shown in diagram 3 in the said Schedule points may be varied so as to be—

(a) a direction which lies straight upright, or

(b) a direction which lies at any angle between 90 degrees either to the left or to the right of the said upright direction.

(5) The direction in which any arrow shown in any of the diagrams 2 and 4 to 7 in the said Schedule points may be varied so as to be—

(a) a direction which lies straight upright, or

(b) a direction which lies between the direction shown in the diagram showing that arrow and the said upright direction.

(6) Any arrow shown on a lens provided in accordance with paragraph (1) (c) of this Regulation may point in a direction which lies straight upright or at any angle between 90 degrees either to the left or to the right of the said upright direction.

Portable light signals for vehicular traffic

33.—(1) Portable light signals may be used for the control of vehicular traffic—

(a) where, owing to roadworks being in progress or for some other reason, the width of the carriageway is temporarily restricted so that it will carry only one line of traffic, or

(b) during the progress of temporary schemes of traffic control, if the signals are in the control of the police.

(2) Subject to the provisions of paragraph (4) of this Regulation, such light signals shall comply either—

(a) with the provisions of sub-paragraphs (a), (b), (c), (e), (f) and (g) of paragraph (2) of Regulation 31 and sub-paragraph (d) of paragraph (3) of this Regulation, or

(b) with all the provisions of the said paragraph (3).

(3) (a) Two lights shall be used, one red and the other green;

    (b) the lamps showing the coloured lights aforesaid shall be arranged vertically, the lamp showing a red light being uppermost;

    (c) each lamp shall be separately illuminated and the effective diameter of the lens thereof shall be not less than 8 inches nor more than 8¼ inches;

    (d) the height of the centre of the green lens from the surface of the carriageway in the immediate vicinity shall be not less than 5 feet nor more than 11 feet 6 inches;

    (e) the centres of the lenses shall be not more than 28 inches apart;

    (f) the word " STOP " in black lettering shall be placed upon the lens of the lamp showing a red light and where the signals are in the control of the police appropriate words indicating that the signals are police signals may be used; and

    (g) the red and green lights shall not be shown together and one shall follow the other without any appreciable interval of time.

(4) On and after the 31st December 1969 the alternative provision made by sub-paragraph (b) of paragraph (2) of this Regulation shall cease to have effect.

Significance of light signals

34.—(1) The significance of the light signals prescribed by paragraph (2) of Regulation 31 or by Regulation 33 shall be as follows:—

    (a) the red signal shall convey the prohibition that vehicular traffic shall not proceed beyond the stop line on the carriageway provided in conjunction with the signals or, if that line is not for the time being visible or there is no stop line, beyond the signals;

    (b) the amber-with-red signal (where an amber signal is provided) shall be taken to denote an impending change in the indication given by the signals from red to green but shall not alter the prohibition conveyed by the red signal;

    (c) the green signal shall indicate that vehicular traffic may pass the signals and proceed straight on or to the left or to the right;

    (d) the amber signal (when provided) shall, when shown alone, convey the prohibition that vehicular traffic shall not proceed beyond the stop line or, if that line is not for the time being visible or there is no stop line, beyond the signals, except in the case of any vehicle which when the signal first appears is so close to the said line or signals that it cannot safely be stopped before passing the line or signals.

(2) The significance of the light signals prescribed by paragraph (2) of Regulation 31, as varied in accordance with the provisions of Regulation 32, shall be as follows:—

    (a) subject as provided in sub-paragraph (d) of this paragraph, the red signal shall convey the prohibition that vehicular traffic shall not proceed beyond the stop line on the carriageway provided in conjunction with the signals or if the stop line is not for the time being visible, beyond the signals;

    (b) subject as provided in sub-paragraph (d) of this paragraph, the amber-with-red signal shall denote an impending change in the indication given by the signals from red to green (where a green signal is provided) or from red to a green arrow or arrows but shall not alter the prohibition conveyed by the red signal;

(c) the green signal (where a green signal is provided) shall indicate that vehicular traffic may pass the signals and proceed straight on or to the left or to the right;

(d) any green arrow during such time as it is illuminated shall indicate that vehicular traffic may pass the signals and proceed in the direction indicated by the arrow notwithstanding any other indication given by the signals;

(e) the amber signal shall, when shown alone, convey the prohibition that vehicular traffic shall not proceed beyond the stop line, or, if the stop line is not for the time being visible, beyond the signals, except in the case of any vehicle which when the signal first appears is so close to the said line or signals that it cannot safely be stopped before passing the line or signals.

(3) Vehicular traffic passing any light signals in accordance with the foregoing provisions of this Regulation shall proceed with due regard to the safety of other users of the road and subject to the direction of any police constable in uniform or other duly authorised person who may be engaged in the regulation of traffic.

(4) The significance of the light signals prescribed by paragraph (3) of Regulation 31 shall be that the intermittent red lights convey the prohibition that vehicular traffic shall not proceed beyond the stop line on the carriageway provided in conjunction with the signals or, if the stop line is not for the time being visible, beyond the signals, except in the case of any vehicle which, when the lights first begin to flash, is so close to the line or signals that it cannot safely be stopped before passing the line or signals.

(4A) The significance of the light signals prescribed by paragraph (3A) of Regulation 31 shall be as follows:—

(a) the amber signal shall convey the prohibition that vehicular traffic shall not proceed beyond the stop line on the carriageway provided in conjunction with the signals or, if that line is not for the time being visible or there is no stop line, beyond the signals, except in the case of any vehicle which when the signal first appears is so close to the said line or signals that it cannot safely be stopped before passing the line or signals; and

(b) the intermittent red signals shall convey the prohibition that vehicular traffic shall not proceed beyond the stop line on the carriageway provided in conjunction with the signals or, if that line is not for the time being visible or there is no stop line, beyond the signals.

(5) For the purposes of this Regulation the expression " stop line " means the traffic sign shown either in diagram 1001 or, until the 31st December 1967, in diagram No. RM1 mentioned in Regulation 3 (1).

*   *   *   *   *

Part II

General Directions

*　　*　　*　　*　　*

5. Signs shown in diagrams 502, 511, 543 (except when used in connection with the execution of road works), 544 (when erected on or near a road on which a speed limit of 40 miles per hour or less on the driving of motor vehicles is in force), 545 (when not erected in conjunction with the sign shown in diagram 546 or 547), 548 to 551, 601, 615 (except when used in connection with the execution of road works), 837 to 839 (when used on primary routes) and 1026 may be placed only at sites approved in writing by or on behalf of the Minister or the Secretary of State, as the case may be.

5A. After 16th May 1966 road markings shown in diagram 1013 which are not fitted with studs incorporating reflectors in accordance with the Regulations may be placed for the first time at a site only if the site is approved in writing by or on behalf of the Minister or the Secretary of State, as the case may be.

6. Signs shown in diagrams 606 (except when erected on the central island of a roundabout or when used in combination with a plate of the type shown in diagram 608), 607, 609 (except when used in combination with a plate of the type shown in diagram 608), 612 to 614, 616 (except when placed at a site which has been approved in writing by or on behalf of the Minister or the Secretary of State, as the case may be), 617 to 632, 636 to 645, 712, 806 to 810, 819, 1015 to 1021, 1028 (when varied to read " Solo motor cycles only," " Solo motor cycles," " Motor cycles " or " Solo m/c's "), 1029, 1032 to 1034, 1036 and 1037 may be placed on or near a road only to indicate the effect of an Order, Regulation, Bye-law or Notice which prohibits or restricts the use of the road by vehicular traffic.

*　　*　　*　　*　　*

10. The sign shown in diagram 601 may be used on a road only in conjunction with the road marking shown in diagram 1002 and the road marking shown in diagram 1022, and the sign shown in diagram 602 may be used on a road only in conjunction with the road marking shown in diagram 1003 and the road marking shown in diagram 1023:

Provided that the provisions of this paragraph requiring the use of the signs shown in diagrams 601 and 602 in conjunction with a road marking shall not apply during the execution of works on a road in the vicinity of the place where the sign shown in diagram 601 or in diagram 602 is erected, if those works necessitate the temporary removal of that marking, and shall not apply if the said signs are erected only temporarily in connection with the execution of works on a road.

11.—(1) The sign shown in diagram 501 may be used only either in combination with a plate of the type shown in diagram 502 and in conjunction with the sign shown in diagram 601 or in combination with a plate of the type shown in diagram 503 and in conjunction with the sign shown in diagram 602.

(2) The sign shown in diagram 533 may be used only in combination with a plate of the type shown in diagram 534 or 535.

(3) The sign shown in diagram 562 may be used only in combination with a plate of the type shown in diagram 563.

(4) The sign shown in diagram 617 may be used only in combination with a plate of the type shown in diagram 618.

(5) The sign shown in diagram 622 may be used only in combination with a plate of the type shown in diagram 623.

(6) The sign shown in diagram 630 may be used only in combination with a plate of the type shown in diagram 631.

12. A plate of the type shown in diagrams 502, 503, 511, 518, 519, 525 to 527, 534, 535, 546, 547, 553, 563, 570 to 573, 607, 608, 618, 620, 623, 627, 631, 643 to 645, 802 to 805 and 807 may be used only in combination with the signs which are specified beneath the diagram showing the plate.

*   *   *   *   *

18.—(1) Signs shown in diagrams 603 and 604 may be used only where one-way working is necessary owing to a temporary closure to vehicular traffic of a width of the carriageway of a road.

(2) The signs shown in diagrams 615 and 811 may only be used in conjunction with one another and shall not be used in conjunction with the signs shown in diagrams 603 or 604.

19. The sign shown in diagram 605 shall be used only by a person duly authorised by a highway authority for the purposes of section 224 of the Road Traffic Act, 1960 (which relates to the weighing of motor vehicles), and may not be used during the hours of darkness.

20. Signs shown in diagrams 830 to 832 may be used only—

(a) in connection with a traffic census the taking of which on a road has been approved by the highway authority for that road, by the chief officer of police of the police area in which the road is situate, and by or on behalf of the Minister or the Secretary of State, as the case may be; and

(b) in the vicinity of the traffic census points appointed by or on behalf of the Minister or the Secretary of State, as the case may be.

*   *   *   *   *

24. The road marking shown in diagram 1001 may be placed on a road only in conjunction with the light signals prescribed by Regulation 31 or those light signals as varied in accordance with Regulation 32 of the Regulations or at a site where vehicular traffic is from time to time controlled by the police.

25. The road markings shown in diagrams 1002 and 1022 may be placed on a road only in conjunction with the sign shown in diagram 601.

*   *   *   *   *

32. No sign, beacon, cone or portable traffic light signals used in accordance with the provisions of Regulation 27, 28, 29 or 33 respectively of the Regulations may be retained at any place after the expiration of six months from the date on which the sign, beacon, cone or signals were erected at that place or such longer time as may be approved in writing by or on behalf of the Minister or the Secretary of State, as the case may be, or in any case after the termination of the need for such sign, beacon, cone or signals.

*　　*　　*　　*　　*

34.—(1) Light signals for the control of vehicular traffic as prescribed by the Regulations may be placed on or near a road only—

(a) so that they face the stream of traffic which the signals are intended to control; and

(b) at sites approved in writing by or on behalf of the Minister or the Secretary of State, as the case may be, after consideration of such plans for the sites, particulars of the apparatus to be used and information as to the volume and character of the traffic affected as he may require; and

(c) in the case of light signals prescribed by paragraph (3) of Regulation 31 of the Regulations, if the mechanism by means of which the signals are capable of complying with the provisions of sub-paragraph (d) of the said paragraph (3) is of a type which has been approved in writing by or on behalf of the Minister or the Secretary of State, as the case may be.

(2) Sub-paragraph (1) (b) of this paragraph shall not apply—

(a) in the case of such light signals as are prescribed by paragraph (3) of Regulation 31 of the Regulations, being signals provided at or near to any level crossing in pursuance of an Order made by the Minister under section 66 of the British Transport Commission Act, 1957 (which empowers the Minister to authorise special arrangements at public level crossings);

(b) in the case of such portable light signals as are prescribed by Regulation 33 of the Regulations; or

(c) in the case of any other light signals where the Minister or Secretary of State, as the case may be, has agreed to contribute, either wholly or in part, towards the cost of the installation of those signals.

(3) The light signals mentioned in sub-paragraph (1) of this paragraph may be used only in conjunction with the road marking shown in diagram 1001 or, until the 31st December 1967, with the traffic sign shown in diagram No. RM1 mentioned in Regulation 3 (1) of the Regulations.

(4) Sub-paragraph (3) of this paragraph shall not apply in the case at (b) in sub-paragraph (2) of this paragraph or during the execution of works on a road in the vicinity of the place where the light signals are erected if those works necessitate the temporary removal of the road marking or sign therein mentioned.

(5) In the case of the light signals mentioned in sub-paragraph (1) of this paragraph the head of the signals enclosing the lamps shall be coloured black or black and white in alternative horizontal bands and the post, if any, on which it is mounted shall, in so far as it extends above ground level, be coloured black and white in alternate horizontal bands, the lowest band visible to approaching traffic being coloured black and not less than 11 inches nor more than 3 feet 3 inches in width and, except in the case of

the band which coincides with the lower edge of the lowest lamp supported by the post, each other band being not less than 11 inches nor more than 13 inches in width:

Provided that on and after the 31st December 1966 this sub-paragraph shall apply as respects the head of the signals as if the words " or black and white in alternate horizontal bands " were omitted.

(S.I. 1969 No. 1270)

TRAFFIC SIGNS (DISQUALIFICATION FOR OFFENCES) REGULATIONS 1969

1.—(1) These Regulations shall come into operation on the 16th September 1969 and may be cited as the Traffic Signs (Disqualification for Offences) Regulations 1969.

(2) The Traffic Signs (Disqualification for Offences) Regulations 1964 and the Traffic Signs (Disqualification for Offences) (Amendment) Regulations 1966 are hereby revoked.

(3) The Interpretation Act 1889 shall apply for the interpretation of these Regulations as it applies for the interpretation of an Act of Parliament, and as if for the purposes of section 38 of that Act these Regulations were an Act of Parliament and the Regulations revoked by paragraph (2) of this Regulation were Acts of Parliament thereby repealed.

2. The signs specified for the purposes of paragraph 13 of Schedule 1 to the Road Traffic Act 1962 are:—

(a) the sign shown in the diagram numbered 601 in Schedule 1 to the Traffic Signs Regulations 1964 as amended;

(b) the sign shown in the diagram numbered 649 in the said Schedule;

(c) the light signals prescribed by Regulation 31, by Regulation 31 as varied by Regulation 32 or by Regulation 33 of the said Regulations;

(d) the road markings shown in the diagram numbered 1013 in Schedule 2 to the said Regulations.

S.I. 1973 No. 180

MOTOR CYCLES (WEARING OF HELMETS) REGULATIONS 1973

*　　　*　　　*　　　*　　　*

Interpretation

2.—(1) In these Regulations the following expressions have the meanings hereby assigned to them:—

" motor bicycle " means a two wheeled motor cycle, whether having a side-car attached thereto or not, and for the purposes of this definition any wheels of a motor cycle shall, if the distance between the centres of the areas of contact between such wheels and the road surface is less than 460 millimetres, be counted as one wheel;

" protective headgear " means headgear which—

(a) is either—

(i) a helmet bearing a marking applied by the manufacturer indicating compliance with the specification contained in British Standard 2001 published on 25th October

1956, or British Standard 1869 published on 20th April, 1960, or British Standard 2495 published on 20th April, 1960; or

(ii) a helmet which by virtue of its shape, material and construction could reasonably be expected to afford to persons on motor bicycles a degree of protection from injury in the event of an accident similar to or greater than that provided by a helmet of a type complying with one of the specifications referred to in the preceding sub-paragraph; and

(b) is securely fastened to the head of the wearer by means of the straps or other fastening provided on the headgear for that purpose.

(2) The Interpretation Act 1889 shall apply for the interpretation of these Regulations as it applies for the interpretation of an Act of Parliament.

Wearing of protective headgear

3.—(1) Save as provided in paragraph (2) of this Regulation, every person driving or riding (otherwise than in a side-car) on a motor bicycle when on a road shall wear protective headgear.

(2) Nothing in paragraph (1) of this Regulation shall apply to any person driving or riding on a motor bicycle if—

(a) it is a mowing machine; or
(b) it is for the time being propelled by a person on foot.

THE 60 MILES PER HOUR AND 50 MILES PER HOUR
(TEMPORARY SPEED LIMIT) ORDER 1974

2.—(1) Subject to paragraph (2) of this Article, no person shall, during the period commencing at midnight on Saturday 14th December, 1974, and ending at midnight on Sunday 30th November, 1975, drive a motor vehicle—

(a) at a speed exceeding 60 miles per hour on any dual carriageway road;
(b) at a speed exceeding 50 miles per hour on any road which is not a dual carriageway road.

(2) Nothing in this Order shall prohibit a person from driving a motor vehicle on a road at a speed exceeding that which would apply to the road under paragraph (1) of this Article in a case where a higher speed limit is after the coming into operation of this Order prescribed in relation to that road by means of an Order under section 74 of the Road Traffic Regulation Act 1967.

S.I. 1963 No. 1172

THE VARIOUS TRUNK ROADS (PROHIBITION OF WAITING)
(CLEARWAYS) ORDER 1963

*   *   *   *   *

Interpretation

3.—(1) In this Order the following expressions have the meanings hereby
respectively assigned to them:—

" the Act of 1960 " means the Road Traffic Act, 1960;

" main carriageway," in relation to a trunk road, means any carriageway of that road used primarily by through traffic and excludes
any lay-by;

" lay-by," in relation to a main carriageway of a trunk road, means
any area intended for use for the waiting of vehicles, lying at a
side of the road and bounded partly by a traffic sign consisting
of a yellow dotted line on the road, or of a white dotted line and
the words " lay-by " on the road, authorised by the Minister
under subsection (2) of section 51 of the Act of 1960, and partly
by the outer edge of that carriageway on the same side of the road
as that on which the sign is placed;

" verge " means any part of a road which is not a carriageway.

(2) The Interpretation Act 1889 shall apply for the interpretation of
this Order as it applies for the interpretation of an Act of Parliament and
as if for the purposes of section 38 of that Act this Order were an Act of
Parliament and the Orders revoked by Article 2 were Acts of Parliament
thereby repealed.

Prohibition of waiting on main carriageways

4. Save as provided in Article 5 of this Order no person shall, except upon
the direction or with the permission of a police constable in uniform, cause
or permit any vehicle to wait on any of those main carriageways forming
part of trunk roads which are specified in Schedule 1 to this Order.

Exceptions to Article 4

5. Nothing in Article 4 of this Order shall apply—

(*a*) so as to prevent a vehicle waiting on any main carriageway
specified in Schedule 1 to this Order for so long as may be necessary
to enable the vehicle, if it cannot be used for such purpose without
waiting on that carriageway, to be used in connection with any
building operation or demolition, the removal of any obstruction
or potential obstruction to traffic, the maintenance, improvement
or reconstruction of the road comprising that carriageway, or the
erection, laying, placing, maintenance, testing, alteration, repair
or removal of any structure, works, or apparatus in, on, under or
over that road;

(*b*) to a vehicle being used for fire brigade, ambulance or police
purposes;

(*c*) to a vehicle being used for the purposes of delivering or collecting
postal packets as defined in section 87 of the Post Office Act, 1953;

(*d*) so as to prevent a vehicle being used by or on behalf of a local
authority from waiting on any main carriageway specified in
Schedule 1 to this Order for so long as may be necessary to en-

able the vehicle, if it cannot be used for such a purpose without waiting on that carriageway to be used for the purpose of the collection of household refuse from, or the clearing of cesspools at, premises situated on or adjacent to the road comprising that carriageway;

(e) to a vehicle waiting on any main carriageway specified in Schedule 1 to this Order while any gate or other barrier at the entrance to premises to which the vehicle requires access or from which it has emerged is opened or closed, if it is not reasonably practicable for the vehicle to wait otherwise than on that carriageway while such gate or barrier is being opened or closed;

(f) to a vehicle waiting in any case where the person in control of the vehicle:—

(i) is required by law to stop;

(ii) is obliged to do so in order to avoid accident: or

(iii) is prevented from proceeding by circumstances outside his control and it is not reasonably practicable for him to drive or move the vehicle to a place not on any main carriageway specified in Schedule 1 to this Order.

Restriction of waiting on verges, etc.

6. No person shall cause or permit any vehicle to wait on any verge or lay-by immediately adjacent to a main carriageway specified in Schedule 1 to this Order for the purpose of selling goods from that vehicle unless the goods are immediately delivered at or taken into premises adjacent to the vehicle from which sale is effected.

S.I. 1971 No. 694

The Road Vehicles Lighting Regulations, 1971
as amended by S.I. 1973 No. 1006 and S.I. 1975 No. 239

Part I

*   *   *   *   *

Interpretation

3.—(1) In these Regulations, except where the context otherwise requires, the following expressions have the meanings hereby respectively assigned to them—

" the Act " means the Road Transport Lighting Act 1957;

" the Construction and Use Regulations " means the Motor Vehicles (Construction and Use) Regulations 1969, as amended;

" agricultural implement " means an agricultural implement or an agricultural machine, being in either case a vehicle;

" appropriate authority ", in relation to home forces' vehicles or to vehicles in the service of a visiting force, means any such person as is designated opposite such description of vehicles in column 2 of Schedule 3;

" authorising officer ", in relation to home forces' vehicles or to vehicles in the service of a visiting force, means any such person as is designated opposite such description of vehicles in column 2 of Schedule 4;

" Chief Officer of Police " and " police area ", in relation to England and Wales, have the same meanings as in the Police Act 1964, and in relation to Scotland, have the same meanings as in the Police (Scotland) Act 1967;

" cycle " means a pedal bicycle or pedal tricycle, not being in either case propelled by mechanical power;

" dipped beam " means a beam of light emitted by a headlamp, being a beam which is deflected downwards or both downwards and to the left to such an extent that it is at all times incapable of dazzling any person who is on the same horizontal plane as the vehicle at a greater distance than 25 feet from the lamp and whose eye-level is not less than 3 feet 6 inches above that plane;

" direction indicator " means a device fitted to a motor vehicle or trailer for the purpose of intimating the intention of the driver to change the direction of the vehicle to the right or to the left;

" dual-purpose lamp " means a lamp combining with an obligatory front lamp an obligatory rear lamp, both the obligatory front lamp and the obligatory rear lamp satisfying the requirements of these Regulations relating to obligatory front lamps and obligatory rear lamps respectively except in so far as such requirements are modified by Regulation 7;

" dual-purpose vehicle " has the same meaning as in paragraph 14 of Schedule 1 to the Road Traffic Act 1960;

" engineering plant " means movable plant or equipment being a mechanically propelled vehicle or trailer designed and constructed for the special purposes of engineering operations, which when proceeding on a road does not carry any load other than such as is necessary for its propulsion or equipment;

" equipment ", in relation to a vehicle or sidecar, does not include a driving mirror or a direction indicator;

" existing ", in relation to a vehicle, means that the vehicle is not a new vehicle;

" extreme rear " means the rearmost point for the time being of a vehicle or a sidecar, inclusive of any luggage carrier and inclusive of any tailboard or other adjustable part except when the tailboard or adjustable part is extended whilst the vehicle is stationary and being loaded or unloaded;

" fog lamp " means a lamp, on a motor vehicle, which is fitted to be used primarily in conditions of fog or whilst snow is falling;

" front corner marker lamp ", in relation to a trailer, means a lamp showing a white light to the side and front of the trailer through an arc extending ninety degrees forward from a line at right angles to the longitudinal axis of the trailer and complying with the provisions of Regulations 48 and 49;

" goods-carrying trailer " means a trailer constructed or adapted for use for the carriage of goods or burden of any description which is either:—

    (a) a trailer part of which is superimposed on the drawing vehicle; or

    (b) any other trailer with four or more wheels drawn by a goods vehicle, locomotive or tractor;

" goods vehicle " means any mechanically propelled vehicle the unladen weight of which exceeds thirty hundredweight and which is constructed or adapted for use for the carriage of goods or burden of any description;

" gritting machine " means a vehicle designed and constructed for use and used for gritting roads;

" headlamp " means a lamp on a vehicle which is designed, when lit, to illuminate the road in front of the vehicle, and which is not a fog lamp;

" home forces " means the naval, military or air forces of Her Majesty raised in the United Kingdom;

" home forces' vehicles " means vehicles owned by or in the service of the home forces and used for naval, military or air force purposes;

" horse-drawn ", in relation to a vehicle, means that the vehicle is drawn by a horse or other animal;

" kerbside weight " means—

> (a) in relation to a motor vehicle, the weight of the vehicle when it carries—

>> (i) no person thereon;

>> (ii) a full supply of fuel in its tank, an adequate supply of other liquids incidental to its propulsion and no load other than the loose tools and equipment with which the vehicle is normally equipped; and

> (b) in relation to a trailer, the weight of the trailer when it carries no person thereon and it is otherwise unladen;

" large passenger vehicle " means a mechanically propelled vehicle (including a trolley vehicle) designed and constructed for use and used for carrying passengers whether for hire or reward or not other than a mechanically propelled vehicle adapted to carry less than eight passengers exclusive of the driver;

" local authority's vehicle " means a vehicle designed and constructed for use and used by a local authority or by any other person solely in connection with the repairing, cleansing or watering of roads, the collection or disposal of refuse or the collection or disposal of the contents of gullies or cesspools;

" locomotive " means a heavy locomotive or a light locomotive;

" matched pair of headlamps ", in relation to a vehicle, means a pair of headlamps, one on each side of the vertical plane passing through the longitudinal axis of the vehicle (disregarding, for the purpose of ascertaining such axis, any sidecar attached thereto) in respect of which the following conditions are satisfied, namely:—

> (a) each lamp in the pair is at the same height above the ground; and

> (b) the distances between the centre of each lamp in the pair and the said vertical plane passing through the longitudinal axis of the vehicle do not vary by more than 25 millimetres;

" matched pair of obligatory headlamps ", in relation to a vehicle, means a matched pair of headlamps required to be carried by the vehicle by virtue of Regulation 15 or 16;

" main beam " means a beam of light emitted by a headlamp, being a beam which is not a dipped beam;

" moped " means a motor bicycle whereof the cylinder capacity of the engine does not exceed 50 cubic centimetres, being a bicycle equipped with pedals by means whereof it is capable of being propelled;

" motor bicycle " means a bicycle propelled by mechanical power;

" motor vehicle " has the same meaning as in section 253 of the Road Traffic Act 1960;

" moveable platform " means a platform which is attached to, and may be moved by means of, an extensible boom;

" new ", in relation to a vehicle, means that—

> (a) in the case of a mechanically propelled vehicle not required to be registered under the Vehicles (Excise) Act 1971 the vehicle is supplied by its manufacturer to the Crown or any person on or after 1st October 1954;
>
> (b) in the case of any other mechanically propelled vehicle, the vehicle is first registered under the Vehicles (Excise) Act 1949, the Vehicles (Excise) Act 1962 or the Vehicles (Excise) Act 1971 on or after the said date; and
>
> (c) in the case of any vehicle not mechanically propelled, the vehicle is supplied by its manufacturer to the Crown or any person on or after the said date;

" obligatory front lamp " means a lamp showing to the front a white light which is required to be carried under section 1 of the Act and these Regulations;

" obligatory headlamp " means any headlamp required to be carried by a vehicle by Regulation 15 or 16 of these Regulations;

" obligatory rear lamp " means a lamp showing to the rear a red light which is required to be carried under section 1 of the Act and these Regulations;

" obligatory reflector " means a red reflector which is required to be carried under section 1 of the Act and these Regulations;

" outermost part ", in relation to a vehicle, does not include a door, hinged side or other adjustable part of the vehicle when opened or extended or a driving mirror or a direction indicator;

" public service vehicle " shall be construed in accordance with sections 117 and 118 of the Road Traffic Act 1960;

" rear lamp " means a lamp showing to the rear a red light visible from a reasonable distance;

" registered " means—

> (a) in the case of a vehicle which was registered at any time under the Roads Act 1920 the date on which it was first so registered, and
>
> (b) in the case of any other vehicle the date on which it was first registered under the Vehicles (Excise) Act 1949 or the Vehicles (Excise) Act 1962 or the Vehicles (Excise) Act 1971;

" reversing lamp " means a lamp which is carried by a vehicle and shows a white light to the rear for the purpose of reversing;

" road clearance vehicle " means a mechanically propelled vehicle used for dealing with frost, ice or snow on roads;

" sealed beam lamp " means a lamp unit comprising a reflector system, a lens system and one or more electrical filaments, which has been sealed in the course of manufacture and which cannot be dismantled without rendering the unit unusable as a lamp;

" side marker lamp ", in relation to a vehicle, means a lamp showing a white light to the side of the vehicle through an arc extending a minimum of seventy degrees forward from a line at right angles to the longitudinal axis of the vehicle and a red light to the side through an arc extending a minimum of seventy degrees rearward from that line and complying with the provisions of Regulations 48 and 49;

" special equipment," in relation to a vehicle fitted with a movable platform, means the movable platform, the apparatus for moving the platform and any jacks fitted to the vehicle for stabilising it while the movable platform is in use;

"special trailer " means a trailer the use of which on roads is by order authorised by the Secretary of State under section 64 (4) of the Road Traffic Act 1960;

" stop lamp " means a lamp fitted to a motor vehicle, or to a trailer drawn by a motor vehicle, for the purpose of warning other road users, when the lamp is lit, that the brakes of the motor vehicle or, in the case of a trailer, the brakes of the drawing vehicle or of the combination of vehicles, are being applied;

" supplementary main beam " means a main beam which is emitted by an obligatory headlamp which can also emit a dipped beam and which can only be used in conjunction with a main beam from another obligatory headlamp on the same side of the vertical plane passing through the longitudinal axis of the vehicle;

" tractor " means a motor tractor and " heavy tractor " means a tractor the unladen weight of which exceeds fifty hundred-weight;

" trailer " means a vehicle constructed or adapted so as to be drawn by another vehicle;

" vehicle in the service of a visiting force or of a headquarters " has the same meaning as in Article 8 (6) of the Visiting Forces and International Headquarters (Application of Law) Order 1965;

" works trailer " means a trailer designed for use in private premises and used on a road only in delivering goods from or to such premises to or from a vehicle on a road in the immediate neighbourhood, or in passing from one part of any such premises to another or to other private premises in the immediate neighbourhood or in connection with road works while at or in the immediate neighbourhood of the site of such works;

" works truck " means a motor vehicle (other than a motor vehicle constructed to straddle and lift its load for the purpose of transportation) designed for use in private premises and used on a road only in delivering goods from or to such premises to or from a vehicle on a road in the immediate neighbourhood, or in passing from one part of any such premises to another or to other private premises in the immediate neighbourhood or in connection with road works while at or in the immediate neighbourhood of the site of such works;

" heavy locomotive", " light locomotive " and " motor tractor " have the meanings respectively assigned to them in section 253 of the Road Traffic Act 1960;

" agricultural trailer ", " industrial tractor ", " land implement ", " land locomotive ", " land tractor ", " overall length ", " overall width ", " pedestrian controlled vehicle ", " towing implement " and " wheeled " have the meanings respectively assigned to them in Regulation 3 (1) of the Construction and Use Regulations.

(2) For the purposes of these Regulations, in determining when a motor vehicle is first used, the date of such first use shall be taken to be the date which is prescribed as the date of first use by Regulation 3 (2) of the Construction and Use Regulations for the purposes of those Regulations.

(3) Any reference in these Regulations to a vehicle having any number of wheels is a reference to a vehicle having that number of wheels the tyres or rims of which are in contact with the ground when the vehicle is in motion on a road, and any two such wheels shall be treated as one wheel if the distance between the centres of the areas of contact between them and the road surface is less than 18 inches.

(4) For the purposes of these Regulations a vehicle so constructed that it can be divided into two parts both of which are vehicles and one of which is a motor vehicle shall (when not so divided) be treated as that motor vehicle with the other part attached as a trailer.

(5) For the purposes of these Regulations the unladen weight of a motor vehicle shall be calculated in accordance with section 255 of the Road Traffic Act 1960.

(6) For the purposes of these Regulations, any measurement expressed in relation to height from the ground of any part of a vehicle or of a lamp, reflector or direction indicator (or any part thereof) fixed or otherwise fitted to a vehicle shall be taken to be a measurement from the ground when the vehicle is at its kerbside weight and when each tyre, with which the vehicle is fitted, is inflated to the pressure recommended by the manufacturer of the vehicle.

(7) Any reference in these Regulations to any enactment or instrument shall be construed, unless the context otherwise requires, as a reference to that enactment or instrument as amended by any subsequent enactment or instrument.

(8) Any reference in these Regulations to a numbered Regulation or Schedule is a reference to the Regulation or Schedule bearing that number in these Regulations except where otherwise expressly provided.

(9) The Interpretation Act 1889 shall apply for the interpretation of these Regulations as it applies for the interpretation of an Act of Parliament, and as if for the purposes of section 38 of that Act these Regulations were an Act of Parliament and the Regulations revoked by Regulation 2 were Acts of Parliament thereby repealed.

PART II

REGULATIONS GOVERNING FRONT LAMPS ON VEHICLES

Position of obligatory front lamps

4. Subject to the provisions of Regulations 7 and 8, every obligatory front lamp shall:—

(a) except in the case of a large passenger vehicle or of a mechanically propelled vehicle while being used to propel in front thereof a snow plough, be so fixed that the centre of the lamp is at a height not exceeding 5 feet from the ground, provided that in the case of a horse-drawn vehicle the lamp may be fixed so that the centre of the lamp is at a height not exceeding 5 feet 9 inches from the ground and in the case of a land tractor, an agricultural tractor, an industrial tractor, an agricultural implement or engineering plant the lamp may be so fixed that the centre of the lamp is at a height not exceeding 6 feet 3 inches from the ground;

(b) except in the case of a tower wagon or of a bicycle (whether propelled by mechanical power or not), be so fixed that no part of the vehicle or its equipment extends laterally on the same side as the lamp more than 12 inches beyond the centre of the lamp; and

(c) in the case of a horse-drawn vehicle, be so fixed that the centre of the lamp is not—

(i) where such a vehicle has only one axle, behind the axle of the vehicle, or

(ii) where such a vehicle has more than one axle, more than 1 foot 6 inches behind the front axle when in its central position.

5. Where two obligatory front lamps are carried on any vehicle they shall be fixed on opposite sides of the vehicle and, except in the case of a bicycle having a sidecar attached thereto whether propelled by mechanical power or not, shall be fixed at the same height from the ground.

6. Where only one obligatory front lamp is carried on any vehicle that lamp shall (except in the case of a bicycle whether propelled by mechanical power or not) be fixed on the off side of the vehicle.

Position of dual-purpose lamps

7. Where there is carried on a sidecar, attached to a motor bicycle or on a land tractor, agricultural tractor, horse-drawn vehicle or vehicle drawn or propelled by hand a dual-purpose lamp, such lamp may be so fixed that no part (including equipment) of the sidecar, tractor, horse-drawn vehicle or vehicle drawn or propelled by hand, as the case may be, extends laterally on the same side as the lamp more than 16 inches from the nearest part of the illuminated area of the obligatory front lamp combined in the dual-purpose lamp.

Additional provisions as to position on mechanically propelled vehicles of front lamps

8.—(1) Save as provided in paragraph (2) of this Regulation, every lamp carried on a mechanically propelled vehicle and showing a light to the front to which the provisions of Regulation 9 of these Regulations apply shall be so fixed that the centre of the lamp is:—

(a) except in the case of a mechanically propelled vehicle while being used to propel in front thereof a snow plough, a mechanically propelled vehicle being an aerodrome fire tender, an aerodrome runway sweeper, a land tractor, an agricultural tractor, an industrial tractor, an agricultural implement or engineering plant, not more than 3 feet 6 inches from the ground; and

(b) except in the case of a lamp which is used only in conditions of fog or whilst snow is falling, not less than 2 feet from the ground.

(2) This Regulation shall not apply in the case of—

    (*a*) a vehicle first used before 1st January 1952;

    (*b*) a vehicle owned by the Secretary of State for Defence, the Secretary of State for Trade and Industry or the Minister of Aviation Supply and constructed or adapted for actual combative purposes or for engineering operations in combat areas if its construction or nature is such as to render impracticable compliance with the provisions of this Regulation; or

    (*c*) any other vehicle so owned, used for naval, military, air force or development or inspection purposes and supplied by its manufacturer at any time before 1st January 1956.

Character of front lamps

9.—(1) This Regulation shall apply to every lamp showing a light to the front which is derived from an acetylene burner or an electric bulb or a sealed beam lamp:

Provided that it shall not apply to—

    (*a*) a lamp normally used as a direction indicator;

    (*b*) a lamp fitted with an electric bulb or bulbs, if the rated wattage of any bulb or the total rated wattage of all the bulbs which are capable of being illuminated at the same time does not exceed 7 watts and the lamp is fitted with frosted glass or other material which has the effect of diffusing the light; or

    (*c*) a lamp carried on a vehicle in accordance with the provisions of Regulation 64 or 65 or a lamp carried on a four-wheeled pedal cycle, not propelled by mechanical power.

(2) No lamp to which this Regulation applies shall be used on any vehicle other than a cycle unless such lamp is so constructed, fitted and maintained that the beam of light emitted therefrom:—

    (*a*) is permanently deflected downwards to such an extent that it is at all times incapable of dazzling any person standing on the same horizontal plane as the vehicle at a greater distance than 25 feet from the lamp and whose eye-level is not less than 3 feet 6 inches above that plane; or

    (*b*) can be deflected downwards or both downwards and to the left at the will of the driver in such manner as to render it incapable of dazzling any such person in the circumstances aforesaid; or

    (*c*) can be extinguished by the operation of a device which at the same time causes a beam of light to be emitted from the lamp which complies with sub-paragraph (*a*) of this paragraph; or

    (*d*) can be extinguished by the operation of a device which at the same time either deflects the beam of light from another lamp downwards or both downwards and to the left in such manner as to render it incapable of dazzling any such person in the circumstances aforesaid, or brings into or leaves in operation a lamp or lamps (other than the obligatory front lamps) which complies or comply with sub-paragraph (*a*) of this paragraph:

Provided that a lamp (unless it is used only in conditions of fog or whilst snow is falling) shall not be held to comply with sub-paragraph (*a*) of this paragraph unless it is also so fixed that its centre is not less than 2 feet from the ground.

Side deflection of front lamps

10. The beam of light emitted from not more than two lamps showing a light to the front (other than the obligatory front lamps) fitted to any vehicle may be deflected to either side by the movement of, although not necessarily through the same angle as, the front wheels of the vehicle when turned for the purpose of steering the vehicle, provided that the centre of any such lamp is not more than 3 feet 6 inches from the ground.

Markings of electric bulbs in front lamps and of front sealed beam lamps

11. Every electric bulb used in a lamp, and every sealed beam lamp, being in either case a lamp showing a light to the front fitted to any mechanically propelled vehicle, shall be indelibly marked with the rated wattage thereof in a readily legible manner.

Additional markings for obligatory front lamps

12.—(1) In this Regulation, " approval mark " means a marking designated as an approval mark by Regulation 2 (2) of the Motor Vehicles (Designation of Approval Marks) Regulations 1968.

(2) Every obligatory front lamp to which this paragraph applies shall be marked with an approval mark and with the symbol " A " enclosed in a square above such mark and in relation to such a lamp so marked the last preceding Regulation shall not apply.

(3) The obligatory front lamps to which the last preceding paragraph applies are obligatory front lamps carried on every mechanically propelled vehicle (other than a motor bicycle) first used on or after 1st January 1972.

(4) Nothing in this Regulation shall be taken to authorise any person to apply an approval mark or the said symbol " A " to any obligatory front lamp in contravention of the Trade Descriptions Act 1968.

Extinguishment of front lamps on stationary vehicles

13. No electric bulb or bulbs of a rated wattage or of a combined rated wattage, as the case may be, exceeding 7 watts in any lamp and no sealed beam lamp having a rated wattage exceeding 7 watts, being in either case a lamp showing a light to the front fitted to any vehicle, shall be kept illuminated while such vehicle is stationary on a road:

Provided that this Regulation shall not apply to:

(*a*) lamps used—

(i) on any vehicle during an enforced stoppage of the vehicle;

(ii) on any large passenger vehicle when stopping to pick up or set down passengers;

(iii) for the interior illumination of any vehicle;

(iv) on a break-down vehicle for the purpose of illuminating the scene of an accident or break-down;

(v) on a tower wagon when in use for the special purpose for which it is intended;

(vi) as direction indicators; or

(vii) on a vehicle in accordance with Regulation 64 of these Regulations;

(*b*) searchlights or other special lamps fitted to any vehicle used for naval, military, air force, police or fire brigade purposes; or

(*c*) searchlights or other special lamps fitted to any vehicle used for the purpose of carrying out emergency repairs to any road, to any sewer, to any main, pipe, cable or other apparatus for the supply of gas, water, or electricity, or to any telegraphic line as defined in the Telegraph Act 1878 whilst such repairs are actually being carried out.

PART III

REGULATIONS GOVERNING HEADLAMPS ON VEHICLES

Application and exemptions

14.—(1) Except as provided by paragraph (2) of this Regulation, this Part of these Regulations applies to every motor vehicle—

(a) which is a wheeled vehicle;
(b) the obligatory front lamp or lamps of which are electrically operated; and
(c) which is on a road.

(2) This Part of these Regulations does not apply—

(a) to a vehicle first used before 1st January 1931; or
(b) to a pedestrian controlled vehicle; or
(c) to an agricultural implement, a land locomotive, a land tractor, a works truck, or a road roller; or
(d) to a vehicle which is so constructed as to be incapable of exeeding a speed of 6 miles per hour on the level; or
(e) to a vehicle brought temporarily into Great Britain by a person resident outside the United Kingdom provided that it complies in every respect with the requirements as to lighting equipment and reflectors relating thereto contained in Part II of Annex 6 to the Convention on Road Traffic concluded at Geneva on 19th September 1949; or
(f) to a vehicle manufactured in Great Britain which has been purchased by a person who is temporarily in Great Britain and is or is about to be resident abroad and in respect of which—

(a) relief from purchase tax has been afforded by virtue of section 23 of the Purchase Tax Act 1963, or
(b) there is no liability to pay purchase tax,

for a period—

(i) in the case at (a), not exceeding one year during which relief from purchase tax continues to be afforded in respect of that vehicle, and
(ii) in the case at (b), not exceeding one year from the date it was purchased by such a person as a new vehicle from a manufacturer of or dealer in mechanically propelled vehicles, provided the vehicle complies in every respect with the requirements specified in sub-paragraph (e) above of this Regulation and contained in the Convention of 1949 therein referred to as if the vehicle had been brought temporarily into Great Britain; or
(ff) to a vehicle manufactured in Great Britain, the supply of which has been zero rated under Regulation 44 or 45 of the Value

Added Tax (General) Regulations 1972 (S.I. 1972 No. 1147); or

(g) to a vehicle owned by or in the service of the naval, military or air forces of Her Majesty raised in the United Kingdom and used for naval, military or air force purposes; or

(h) to a vehicle in the service of a visiting force or of a headquarters; or

(i)   (i) to an electrically propelled goods vehicle which is so constructed as to be incapable of exceeding a speed of 15 miles per hour on the level; or

(ii) until 1st January 1974 to an electrically propelled goods vehicle which has two or three wheels, which is first used before 1st January 1972 and which is so constructed as to be capable of exceeding a speed of 15 miles per hour on the level; or

(iii) until 1st October 1971 to an electrically propelled goods vehicle which has four or more wheels, which is first used before 1st October 1969 and which is so constructed as to be capable of exceeding a speed of 15 miles per hour on the level.

Headlamps to be carried by vehicles with two wheels and some vehicles with three wheels

15.—(1) This Regulation applies to a motor vehicle to which this Part of these Regulations applies and which—

(a) has two wheels; or
(b) has three wheels and is first used before 1st January 1972; or
(c) has three wheels, is first used on or after 1st January 1972 and except in the case of a motor bicycle with a sidecar attached thereto has an unladen weight of not more than 400 kilogrammes and an overall width of not more than 1.30 metres.

(2) Every vehicle to which this Regulation applies shall carry—

(a) one headlamp in the vertical plane passing through the longitudinal axis of the vehicle (disregarding, for the purpose of ascertaining such axis, any sidecar attached thereto) which either—

(i) in the case of a moped with or without a sidecar attached thereto and first used before 1st January 1972 or in the case of any vehicle which is so constructed as to be incapable of exceeding a speed of 25 miles per hour on the level, can only emit a dipped beam; or

(ii) in the case of any vehicle, is wired to a device the operation of which at the will of the driver can cause to be emitted from it either a main beam or a dipped beam; or

(b) a matched pair of headlamps both headlamps in the pair being wired to a device, the operation of which at the will of the driver can cause to be emitted from them at the same time either—

(i) in the case of any vehicle which is so constructed as to be incapable of exceeding a speed of 25 miles per hour on the level, only dipped beams; or

(ii) in the case of any vehicle, either main beams or dipped beams.

(3) Every beam emitted by any lamp required to be carried by this Regulation shall be derived from the filament or filaments of an electric bulb or bulbs, or from the filament or filaments of a sealed beam lamp, the rating of such filament or at least one of such filaments not being less than—

(a) 10 watts in the case of a main or dipped beam emitted by a lamp carried by a moped with or without a sidecar attached thereto which is first used before 1st January 1972 and which is so constructed as to be incapable of exceeding a speed of 25 miles per hour on the level;

(b) 15 watts in the case of a main or dipped beam emitted by a lamp carried by—

(i) a moped with or without a sidecar attached thereto which is first used on or after 1st January 1972 and which is so constructed as to be incapable of exceeding a speed of 25 miles per hour on the level; or

(ii) a moped with or without a sidecar attached thereto which is first used before 1st January 1972 and which is so constructed as to be capable of exceeding a speed of 25 miles per hour on the level; or

(iii) a motor bicycle (not being a moped) with or without a sidecar attached thereto, which is first used before 1st January 1972 and whereof the cylinder capacity of the engine is not more than 250 cubic centimetres;

(c) 18 watts in the case of a main or dipped beam emitted by a lamp carried by—

(i) a moped with or without a sidecar attached thereto which is first used on or after 1st January 1972 and which is so constructed as to be capable of exceeding a speed of 25 miles per hour on the level; or

(ii) a motor bicycle (not being a moped) with or without a sidecar attached thereto, which is first used on or after 1st January 1972, and whereof the cylinder capacity of the engine is not more than 250 cubic centimetres;

(d) 24 watts in the case of a dipped beam emitted by a lamp carried by any other vehicle; and

(e) 30 watts in the case of a main beam emitted by a lamp carried by any other vehicle.

(4) Where any vehicle carries a matched pair of headlamps in accordance with the requirements of this Regulation, each of the lamps in the pair shall, except in the case of lamps carried by a vehicle which is engineering plant, an industrial tractor or a motor bicycle with or without a sidecar attached thereto, be so positioned on one side of the vehicle that no part of its illuminated area is less than 300 millimetres from any part of the illuminated area of the other lamp in the pair.

Headlamps to be carried by some vehicles with three wheels and by vehicles with four or more wheels

16.—(1) This Regulation applies to a motor vehicle to which this Part of these Regulations applies and which—

(*a*) has three wheels, is not a motor bicycle with a sidecar attached thereto, is first used on or after 1st January 1972 and has an unladen weight of more than 400 kilogrammes or an overall width of more than 1.30 metres;   or

(*b*) has four or more wheels.

(2) Every vehicle to which this Regulation applies shall carry—

(*a*) a matched pair of headlamps, both headlamps in the pair being wired to a device the operation of which at the will of the driver can cause to be emitted from them at the same time either—

(i) in the case of any vehicle which is so constructed as to be incapable of exceeding a speed of 25 miles per hour on the level, only dipped beams;   or

(ii) in the case of any vehicle, either main beams or dipped beams;   or

(*b*) two or more matched pairs of headlamps, the headlamps being arranged so that—

(i) they form two groups of headlamps, one on each side of the vertical plane passing through the longitudinal axis of the vehicle;

(ii) the headlamps in one of the matched pairs, which are at least as far away from the vertical plane passing through the longitudinal axis of the vehicle as any other headlamps in another matched pair of headlamps, can each emit a dipped beam without at the same time emitting a main beam, and so that every other headlamp can emit a main beam;   and

(iii) all the headlamps in both groups are wired to a device the operation of which at the will of the driver can at the same time extinguish every main beam emitted by every headlamp in both groups, and cause either to be emitted or to continue to be emitted the dipped beams from the two headlamps in the matched pair which are at least as far away from the vertical plane passing through the longitudinal axis of the vehicle as any other headlamps in another matched pair of headlamps:

Provided that in the case of a public service vehicle used before 1st October 1969 it shall be a sufficient compliance with the requirements of this paragraph if the vehicle carries a matched pair of headlamps one of which can emit a dipped beam without either lamp at the same time emitting a main beam.

(3) Every main or dipped beam emitted by any lamp required to be carried by this Regulation shall be derived from the filament or filaments of an electric bulb or bulbs or from the filament or filaments of a sealed beam lamp the rating of such filament or at least one of such filaments not being less than 30 watts.

(4) Every headlamp which emits a dipped beam carried by a vehicle in accordance with the requirements of this Regulation shall, except in the case of a lamp carried by a vehicle which is engineering plant or an industrial tractor, be so positioned on one side of the vehicle that—

(*a*) no part of its illuminated area is, in the case of a vehicle first used before 1st October 1969, less than 350 millimetres, or, in the case of a vehicle first used on or after that date, less than 600 millimetres, from any part of the illuminated area of any such lamp on the other side;   and (*b*) in the case of a vehicle first used on or after 1st January 1972 the outermost part of the illuminated area of the lamp is not more than 400 millimetres from the outermost part of the vehicle on the side on which the lamp is placed.

Single units for side and head lamps

17.—(1) In the case of a vehicle which carries one obligatory side lamp and one obligatory headlamp, such lamps may be combined so as to form a single unit.

(2) In the case of a motor bicycle with a sidecar attached thereto, being a vehicle which carries two obligatory side lamps and one obligatory headlamp, one of the obligatory side lamps may be combined with the obligatory headlamp so as to form a single unit.

(3) In the case of a vehicle which carries two obligatory side lamps they may be combined—

(*a*) in the case of a vehicle which has only two obligatory headlamps, with such lamps, or

(*b*) with the two obligatory headlamps in the matched pair which are at least as far away from the vertical plane passing through the longitudinal axis of the vehicle as any other obligatory headlamps in another matched pair of obligatory headlamps,

so as to form two single units each comprising an obligatory headlamp and an obligatory side lamp.

Requirements for every obligatory headlamp

18. Every obligatory headlamp carried by any vehicle shall comply with the following conditions, namely—

(1) it shall be securely fixed to the vehicle;

(2) it shall be so constructed and maintained that the direction of the beam of light emitted therefrom can be adjusted whilst the vehicle is stationary so that the lamp when lit emits the type of beam which it is required to be capable of emitting by this Part of these Regulations; and

(3) it shall be kept in a clean and efficient condition.

Requirements for every matched pair of obligatory headlamps

19. Every matched pair of obligatory headlamps carried on any vehicle to which this Part of these Regulations applies shall comply with the following conditions, namely:—

(1) both lamps in the pair shall, except in the case of lamps carried by a public service vehicle first used before 1st October 1969, have the same area and shape when illuminated;

(2) both lamps in the pair shall, except in the case of lamps carried by a public service vehicle first used before 1st October 1969, have their wiring arranged so that—

(*a*) if they can emit either main beams or dipped beams, the beams which they can emit can only be switched on or off together;

(*b*) if they can emit both main and dipped beams, the dipped beams can only be switched on or off together and the main beams can only be switched on or off together;

(c) if they can emit supplementary main beams, such beams can only be switched on or off together with the main beams emitted by another pair of obligatory headlamps; and

(3) both lamps in the pair shall, when lit, emit beams of the same colour light.

Colour of headlamp beams

20. Every main or dipped beam emitted by any headlamp or fog lamp carried on any vehicle to which this Part of these Regulations applies shall be a beam of white or yellow light.

Requirements as to use of headlamps

21.—(1) This Regulation applies to every motor vehicle to which this Part of these Regulations applies and which has four or more wheels.

(2) This Regulation applies to every length of road, except that it does not apply to a length of road—

(a) on which there is provided a system of street lighting furnished by means of lamps placed not more than two hundred yards apart, and

(b) while such lamps are lit.

(3) When any motor vehicle to which this Regulation applies is in motion during the hours of darkness on a length of road to which this Regulation applies a matched pair of obligatory headlamps carried by the vehicle shall be kept lit:

Provided that this paragraph shall not apply—

(i) in conditions of fog or whilst snow is falling to a vehicle which carries two permitted lamps, if both such permitted lamps are kept lit;

(ii) to a public service vehicle first used before 1st October 1969 if one obligatory headlamp carried by the vehicle is kept lit, or, in conditions of fog or whilst snow is falling, and if the vehicle carries a fog lamp, if that lamp is kept lit;

(iii) to a vehicle being drawn by another vehicle; or

(iv) to a vehicle while being used to propel in front thereof a snow plough.

(4) In this Regulation " two permitted lamps " means two fog lamps or one fog lamp and one headlamp (not being an obligatory headlamp), being lamps which comply with the following conditions, namely:—

(a) the two lamps shall be fixed one on each side of the vertical plane passing through the longitudinal axis of the vehicle;

(b) the centres of both lamps shall be at the same height above the ground;

(c) the distances between the centre of each lamp and the vertical plane passing through the longitudinal axis of the vehicle shall be the same; and

(d) each lamp shall be so positioned that—

(i) in the case of a vehicle first used before 1st January 1971 no part of the illuminated area of one lamp is less than 350 millimetres from any part of the illuminated area of the other lamp; and

(ii) in the case of a vehicle first used on or after 1st January 1971 the outermost part of the illuminated area of either lamp

is not more than 400 millimetres from the outermost part
of the vehicle on the side on which the lamp is placed.

22.—(1) This Regulation applies to every motor vehicle to which this
Part of these Regulations applies and which has two or three wheels.

(2) This Regulation applies to every length of road, except that it
does not apply to a length of road—

(a) on which there is provided a system of street lighting furnished
by means of lamps placed not more than two hundred yards apart,
and

(b) while such lamps are lit.

(3) When any motor vehicle to which this Regulation applies is in
motion during the hours of darkness on a length of road to which this
Regulation applies an obligatory headlamp or, as the case may be, a
matched pair of obligatory headlamps carried by the vehicle shall be kept
lit:

Provided that this paragraph shall not apply—

(i) in conditions of fog or whilst snow is falling to a vehicle which
carries one obligatory headlamp and either one fog lamp or
two permitted lamps, if (in the case where one fog lamp is carried)
that lamp is kept lit or (in the case of a vehicle which has three
wheels and which carries two permitted lamps) both such permitted lamps are kept lit or (in the case of a vehicle which has
two wheels and which carries two permitted lamps) one only
of such permitted lamps is kept lit;

(ii) in such conditions as aforesaid to a vehicle which carries a
matched pair of obligatory headlamps and two permitted lamps,
if (in the case of a vehicle which has three wheels) both such
permitted lamps are kept lit or (in the case of a vehicle which
has two wheels) one only of such permitted lamps is kept lit;
or

(iii) to a vehicle being drawn by another vehicle.

(4) In this Regulation, " two permitted lamps " means two fog lamps
or one fog lamp and one headlamp (not being an obligatory headlamp),
being lamps which comply with the following conditions, namely:—

(a) the two lamps shall be fixed one on each side of the vertical plane
passing through the longitudinal axis of the vehicle;

(b) the centres of both lamps shall be at the same height above the
ground;

(c) the distances between the centre of each lamp and the vertical
plane passing through the longitudinal axis of the vehicle shall
be the same; and

(d) each lamp shall be so positioned that—

(i) in the case of a vehicle to which Regulation 15 of these
Regulations applies and which has three wheels, no part
of the illuminated area of one lamp is less than 300 millimetres
from any part of the illuminated area of the other lamp; and

(ii) in the case of a vehicle to which Regulation 16 of these
Regulations applies and which has three wheels, the outermost
part of the illuminated area of either lamp is not more than
400 millimetres from the outermost part of the vehicle on the
side on which the lamp is placed.

PART IV

REGULATIONS GOVERNING OBLIGATORY REAR LAMPS ON VEHICLES

Position of obligatory rear lamps

23. In the case of a vehicle of a description specified in column 1 of Schedule 1, the number of obligatory rear lamps specified in column 2 of the said Schedule in relation to that description of vehicle shall be fixed on the vehicle in accordance with the requirements with respect to the lateral and longitudinal position of the said lamps, their maximum and minimum height from the ground and otherwise, which are specified in relation to that description of vehicle in columns 3, 4, 5, 6 and 7 of the said Schedule.

Character of obligatory rear lamps

24.—(1) This Regulation shall not apply in the case of obligatory rear lamps carried on existing large passenger vehicles and any reference in this Regulation to any obligatory rear lamp shall be construed accordingly.

(2) Except as provided in paragraphs (3) and (4) of this Regulation and in Regulation 25 (6) and (9), every obligatory rear lamp shall, if circular, have an illuminated area not less than 2 inches in diameter or, if not circular, have an illuminated area not less than the area of a circle of 2 inches in diameter and of such a shape that a circle of 1 inch in diameter may be inscribed therein.

(3) Except as provided in paragraph (4) of this Regulation, every obligatory rear lamp carried on—

(a) a cycle, a four-wheeled pedal cycle not propelled by mechanical power, a motor bicycle of which the cylinder capacity of the engine does not exceed 250 cubic centimentres or a sidecar attached thereto, a horse-drawn vehicle, a vehicle drawn or propelled by hand, a trailer fire pump or an agricultural implement, or

(b) a motor bicycle of which the cylinder capacity of the engine exceeds 250 cubic centimetres or a sidecar attached thereto

shall, if circular, have an illuminated area of not less than 1½ inches in diameter or, if not circular, have an illuminated area of not less than the area of a circle of 1½ inches in diameter and of such a shape that a circle of 1 inch in diameter may be inscribed therein.

(4) Nothing in paragraphs (2) and (3) of this Regulation shall apply in respect of a mechanically propelled vehicle or a trailer manufactured in Italy (not being a mechanically propelled vehicle or a trailer brought temporarily into Great Britain by a person resident outside the United Kingdom) carrying obligatory rear lamps in accordance with Regulation 23, such lamps bearing a marking approved by the Italian Ministry of Transport, namely, one including two separate groups of letters consisting of the letters " IGM " and " LP ".

(5) Except as provided in Regulation 25 (10), every electric bulb used in an obligatory rear lamp carried on a vehicle other than a vehicle of a description specified in sub-paragraph (a) of paragraph (3) of this Regulation shall have a rated wattage of not less than 5 watts and the rated wattage thereof shall be indelibly marked upon the glass or the metal cap thereof in a readily legible manner.

(6) When two obligatory rear lamps are carried on a vehicle, both

lamps shall have the same appearance, when illuminated, and the same illuminated area and if such lamps are electrically operated, the wiring shall be so arranged that in the event of any failure of a bulb in either of the lamps the other lamp shall not thereby be extinguished.

(7) In this Regulation the expression " illuminated area " means, in relation to a lamp, the area of the orthogonal projection on a vertical plane at right angles to the longitudinal axis of the vehicle of that part of the lamp through which light is emitted.

25.—(1) In this Regulation " approval mark " means a marking designated as an approval mark by Regulation 2 (2) of the Motor Vehicles (Designation of Approval Marks) Regulations 1968 and " motor bicycle " means a motor bicycle with or without a sidecar attached thereto.

(2) Save as provided in paragraphs (8) and (9) of this Regulation, every obligatory rear lamp fitted with an electric bulb and carried on—

(a) every mechanically propelled vehicle registered on or after 1st April 1959 but before 1st September 1964,

(b) every mechanically propelled vehicle not required to be registered under the Vehicles (Excise) Act 1971 and supplied by its manufacturer to the Crown or any person on or after 1st April 1959 but before 1st September 1964,

(c) every trailer supplied as aforesaid,

shall be marked—

(i) with the specification number of the British Standard for Tail Lights for Vehicles, namely, B.S.2516,

(ii) with the grade " Grade 1 " or " Grade 2 "; and

(iii) with the name, trade mark or other means of identification of the manufacturer of the lamp.

(3) Every obligatory rear lamp fitted with an electric bulb and carried on a cycle or any other vehicle not mechanically propelled and not a trailer shall be marked—

(a) with the specification number of the British Standard for Cycle Rear Lamps, namely, B.S.3648 and

(b) with the name, trade mark or other means of identification o the manufacturer of the lamp.

(4) Save as provided in paragraphs (8) and (9) of this Regulation, every obligatory rear lamp fitted with an electric bulb and carried on a vehicle to which this paragraph applies shall be marked—

(a) with the particulars specified in sub-paragraphs (i) and (iii) of paragraph (2) of this Regulation, and

(b) with the grade " Grade 1 ".

(5) The last preceding paragraph applies to the following vehicles—

(a) every motor bicycle registered on or after 1st September 1964;

(b) every mechanically propelled vehicle (other than a motor bicyle) registered on or after 1st September 1964 and before 1st January 1974;

(c) every mechanically propelled vehicle (other than a motor bicycle) registered on or after 1st January 1974 if manufactured before 1st August 1973;

(d) every mechanically propelled vehicle (other than a motor) registered under the Vehicles (Excise) Act 1971 and every trailer, in each case supplied by its manufacturer to the Crown or any person—

> (i) on or after 1st September 1964 and before 1st January 1974, or
> (ii) on or after 1st January 1974, if manufactured before 1st August 1973.

(6) Every obligatory rear lamp fitted with an electric bulb and carried on a vehicle to which this paragraph applies shall be marked with an approval mark and—

> (a) in the case of a rear lamp not combined with a stop lamp, the symbol " R " enclosed in a square above such mark, or
> (b) in the case of a rear lamp combined with a stop lamp the symbol " R-S1 " or " R-S2 " enclosed in a rectangle above such mark;

and when a rear lamp is marked as provided by this paragraph nothing in Regulation 24 (2) shall apply to it.

(7) The last preceding paragraph applies to the following vehicles—

> (a) every mechanically propelled vehicle (other than a motor bicycle) manufactured on or after 1st August 1973 and registered on or after 1st January 1974;
> (b) every mechanically propelled vehicle (other than a motor bicycle) not required to be registered under the Vehicles (Excise) Act 1971, manufactured on or after 1st August 1973 and supplied by its manufacturer to the Crown or any person on or after 1st January 1974;
> (c) every trailer manufactured on or after 1st August 1973 and supplied as aforesaid.

(8) Nothing in paragraph (2) or (4) of this Regulation shall require an obligatory rear lamp to be marked as provided in that paragraph, if it is carried on such a mechanically propelled vehicle or trailer as is mentioned in Regulation 24 (4) of these Regulations.

(9) Nothing in paragraph (2) or (4) of this Regulation shall require an obligatory rear lamp to be marked as provided in that paragraph if, in the case of a rear lamp carried on a vehicle other than a motor bicycle, it is marked with an approval mark and—

> (i) in the case of a rear lamp not combined with a stop lamp, the symbol " R " enclosed in a square above such mark, or
> (ii) in the case of a rear lamp combined with a stop lamp, the symbol " R-S1 " or " R-S2 " enclosed in a rectangle above such mark;

and when a rear lamp is marked as provided by this paragraph nothing in Regulation 24 (2) shall apply to it.

(10) The provisions of Regulation 24 (5) shall not apply to any obligatory rear lamp to which paragraph (2), (3), (4) or (6) of this Regulation applies or to any such lamp marked as provided in paragraph (9) of this Regulation.

(11) Nothing in this Regulation shall be taken to authorise any person to apply the said specification number B.S.2516, the said specification number B.S.3648, an approval mark, the said symbol " R ", the said symbol " R-S1 " or the said symbol " R-S2 " to any obligatory rear lamp in contravention of the Trade Descriptions Act 1968.

Part V

Regulations Governing Reversing Lamps on Vehicles

Reversing lamps

26. No vehicle shall carry more than two reversing lamps.

27. Every reversing lamp shall comply with the following conditions:—

(a) it shall be illuminated by electricity;

(b) it shall be so constructed that it cannot be switched on otherwise than either:—

    (i) automatically by the selection of the reverse gear of the vehicle; or

    (ii) by the operation of a switch by the driver of the vehicle, being a switch which, except in the case of a mechanically propelled vehicle first used before 1st July 1954, serves no other purpose;

(c) the rated wattage of the electric bulb or the total rated wattage of all such bulbs with which it is fitted or the rated wattage of the sealed beam lamp with which it is fitted shall not exceed 24 watts; and

(d) it shall be so constructed, fitted and maintained that the light emitted thereby is at all times incapable of dazzling any person who is standing on the same horizontal plane as the vehicle at a greater distance than 25 feet from the lamp and whose eye-level is not less than 3 feet 6 inches above that plane.

28. Except in the case of a mechanically propelled vehicle first used before 1st July 1954, where a reversing lamp is so constructed and fitted that it can be switched on by the operation of a switch by the driver of the vehicle, the vehicle shall be equipped with a device so fitted as to be readily visible to the driver at all times when in his seat and so designed as to indicate when the reversing lamp is illuminated.

29. No reversing lamp constructed and fitted as provided in the last preceding Regulation shall be illuminated except in so far as is necessary for the purpose of reversing the vehicle.

Part VI

Regulations Governing Obligatory Reflectors on Vehicles

Position of obligatory reflectors

30. In the case of a vehicle of a description specified in column 1 of Schedule 2, the number of obligatory reflectors specified in column 2 of the said Schedule in relation to that description of vehicle shall be fixed on the vehicle in accordance with the requirements with respect to the lateral and longitudinal position of the said reflectors, their maximum and minimum height from the ground and otherwise, which are specified in relation to that description of vehicle in columns 3, 4, 5, 6 and 7 of the said Schedule.

Character of reflectors and markings thereon

31.—(1) In this Regulation and in the following Regulations in this Part of these Regulations, the expression " approval mark " means a marking designated as an approval mark by the Motor Vehicles (Designation of Approval Marks) (No. 2) Regulations 1964.

(2) Every obligatory reflector shall comply in all respects with the following conditions:—

(a) except as provided in the following paragraph, the reflecting area shall, if circular, be not less than $1\frac{1}{2}$ inches in diameter or, if not circular, be of not less than the area of a circle of $1\frac{1}{2}$ inches in diameter and of such a shape that a circle of 1 inch in diameter may be inscribed therein;

(b) except as provided in the following paragraph, the reflecting area shall be of such a shape as to be capable of lying wholly within a circle of 6 inches in diameter;

(c) the reflector shall be so fixed to the vehicle that the reflecting area of the reflector is in a vertical position and facing squarely to the rear; and

(d) the reflector shall be kept clean and shall be plainly visible from the rear.

(3) Nothing in sub-paragraphs (a) and (b) of paragraph (2) of this Regulation shall apply—

(a) in respect of a mechanically propelled vehicle or a trailer manufactured in Italy (not being a mechanically propelled vehicle or a trailer brought temporarily into Great Britain by a person resident outside the United Kingdom) carrying obligatory reflectors in accordance with Regulation 30, such reflectors bearing a marking approved by the Italian Ministry of Transport, namely, one including two separate groups of symbols consisting of " IGM " and " C.1." or " C.2."; or

(b) to an obligatory reflector marked with an approval mark incorporating the roman numeral I, II or III or with the specification number of the British Standard for Reflex Reflectors for Vehicles, namely, AU40 followed by a marking " L I ", " L IA ", " L III " or " L IIIA ".

(4) In this Regulation the expression " reflecting area " means, in relation to a reflector, the area of the orthogonal projection on a vertical plane at right angles to the longitudinal axis of the vehicle of that part of the reflector designed to reflect light.

32.—(1) Subject to Regulation 33, every obligatory reflector to which this Regulation applies shall be marked—

(a) with the specification number of the British Standard for Reflex Reflectors for Vehicles, namely, B.S.2515, and " Grade 1 " or " Grade 2 " and with the name, trade mark or other means of identification of the manufacturer of the reflector, or

(b) with the specification number of the British Standard for Reflex Reflectors for Vehicles, namely, AU40 followed by a marking " L I " or " L IA " and with the registered trade name or trade mark of the manufacturer of the reflector, or

(c) with an approval mark incorporating the roman numeral I or II:

Provided that nothing in this paragraph shall require a reflector to be marked as aforesaid if it is carried on such a mechanically propelled vehicle as is mentioned in Regulation 31 (3) (a).

(2) The obligatory reflectors to which this Regulation applies are reflectors carried on every vehicle which is not a trailer.

(3) Nothing in this Regulation shall be taken to authorise any person to apply the said specification number B.S.2515 or AU40 or the said approval mark to any obligatory reflector to which this Regulation applies in contravention of the Trade Descriptions Act 1968.

33. Nothing in Regulation 32 shall be taken as permitting an obligatory reflector to which that Regulation applies to be marked in accordance with paragraph (1) (a) of that Regulation or with an approval mark incorporating the roman numeral II in accordance with paragraph (1) (c) of that Regulation if it is carried on—

    (a) a mechanically propelled vehicle first registered under the Vehicles (Excise) Act 1962 or the Vehicles (Excise) Act 1971 on or after 1st July 1970;

    (b) a mechanically propelled vehicle not required to be registered under the last mentioned Act and supplied by its manufacturer to the Crown or any person on or after the said date, or

    (c) any other vehicle (not being a trailer) supplied as aforesaid.

34.—(1) Subject to Regulation 35 every obligatory reflector to which this Regulation applies shall be marked—

    (a) with the specification number of the British Standard for Reflex Reflectors for Vehicles, namely, B.S.2515 and " Grade 1 " or " Grade 2 " and with the name, trade mark or other means of identification of the manufacturer of the reflector, or

    (b) with the specification number of the British Standard for Reflex Reflectors for Vehicles, namely, AU40 followed by a marking " L III " or " L IIIA " and with the registered trade name or trade mark of the manufacturer of the reflector, or

    (c) with an approval mark incorporating the roman numeral III:

Provided that nothing in this paragraph shall require a reflector to be marked as aforesaid if it is carried on such a trailer as is mentioned in Regulation 31 (3) (a).

(2) The obligatory reflectors to which this Regulation applies are reflectors carried on every trailer other than a trailer which is a broken down motor vehicle.

(3) Nothing in this Regulation shall be taken to authorise any person to apply the said specification number B.S.2515 or AU40 or the said approval mark to any obligatory reflector to which this Regulation applies in contravention of the Trade Descriptions Act 1968.

35.—(1) Nothing in Regulation 34 shall be taken as permitting an obligatory reflector to which that Regulation applies to be marked in accordance with paragraph (1) (a) of that Regulation if it is carried on a trailer supplied by its manufacturer to the Crown or any person on or after 1st July, 1970.

(2) Without prejudice to paragraph (1) of this Regulation, on and after 1st July, 1972 nothing in the said Regulation 34 shall be taken as permitting an obligatory reflector to which that Regulation applies to be marked in accordance with paragraph (1) (a) of that Regulation.

Part VII

Regulations Governing Lamps Indicating Overhanging or Projecting Loads on Vehicles

Part VIII

Regulations Governing Additional Lamps on Long Vehicles and Trailers

Part IX

Regulations Governing Additional Reflectors on Long Vehicles and Trailers

Part X

Exemptions from and Variations of Requirements of the Road Transport Lighting Act 1957

Vehicles of the Home Forces and of Visiting Forces

57. The visiting forces to which Regulations 58 and 59 of these Regulations apply are those visiting forces specified in column 1 of Schedule 3 and, subject as aforesaid, in those Regulations the expression " vehicle in the service of a visiting force " has the same meaning as it has in Article 8 (6) of the Visiting Forces and International Headquarters (Application of Law) Order 1965.

58. In the case of home forces' vehicles and vehicles in the service of a visiting force the following exemptions from and variations of the requirements of the Act shall apply:—

(*a*) every such vehicle shall be exempted from all the requirements of the Act whilst being used in connection with training which is certified in writing for the purposes of this Regulation by the appropriate authority to be training on a special occasion provided that not less than 48 hours' notice of such training is given by that authority to the Chief Officer of Police of every police area in which the place selected for the purposes of the training is wholly or partly situate;

(*b*) every such vehicle shall be exempted from all the requirements of the Act whilst being used on manœuvres within such limits and during such period as may from time to time be specified by Order in Council under the Manœuvres Act 1958;

(*c*) where not less than six nor more than twelve such vehicles are proceeding together in convoy on tactical or driving exercises and the interval between any two vehicles in such convoy does not exceed twenty yards—

(i) paragraph (*a*) of subsection (1) of section 1 of the Act shall have effect in relation to every vehicle in the convoy other than the leading vehicle as though the words " visible from a reasonable distance " were omitted therefrom; and

(ii) except in the case of the rearmost vehicle every vehicle in the convoy shall be exempted from the requirements of paragraph (*b*) of the said subsection (1) provided that the vehicle carries a white light under the vehicle illuminating either a part of the vehicle or anything attached to the vehicle or the road surface beneath the vehicle, in such manner that the presence of the vehicle can be detected from the rear.

In this paragraph the expression " tactical or driving exercises " means tactical or driving exercises which are authorised in writing by the authorising officer and of which not less than 48 hours' notice in writing has been given to the Chief Officer of Police of every police area through which it is intended that the convoy shall pass; and

(*d*) in relation to every such vehicle section 3 of the Act shall have effect as though the words " or a searchlight " were inserted immediately after the words " a dipping headlight ".

59.—(1) The provisions of subsections (1) (*b*) and (2) of section 1 and of section 8 (2) of the Act shall not apply in relation to any home forces' vehicle or any vehicle in the service of a visiting force, which in either case is constructed or adapted for actual combative purposes and the construction or nature of which is such as to render impracticable compliance with those provisions, if it carries two lamps each showing to the rear a red light and two red reflectors, being lamps and reflectors which satisfy the relevant requirements.

(2) For the purposes of paragraph (1) of this Regulation the relevant requirements in the case of the two lamps each showing to the rear a red light shall be that each lamp complies with the relevant provisions of Regulations 24 and 25 as to obligatory rear lamps and that they are so fixed to the vehicle that—

(*a*) one lamp is on each side of the longitudinal axis of the vehicle;

(*b*) no part of the vehicle or its equipment on the same side of the longitudinal axis of the vehicle as a lamp extends laterally on that side beyond the nearest part of the illuminated area of that lamp for a distance of—

(i) more than 16 inches, or

(ii) more than such greater distance as may be necessary, having regard to the construction or nature of the vehicle, to enable the lamp to be fixed to the vehicle;

(*c*) the highest part of the illuminated area of each lamp is—

(i) in the case of a vehicle supplied by its manufacturer before 1st January 1959, not more than 5 feet 6 inches from the ground, and

(ii) in the case of a vehicle so supplied on or after that date not more than 5 feet from the ground

and at the same height from the ground; and

(*d*) no part of the vehicle, its equipment or its load (if any) projects at any time to the rear more than 3 feet 6 inches measured horizontally beyond such lamps or the rearmost of such lamps, unless an additional lamp showing to the rear a red light is carried not more than 20 inches from the rearmost point of the vehicle (including its load, if any).

(3) For the purposes of paragraph (1) of this Regulation, the relevant requirements in the case of the two reflectors shall be that each reflector complies with the relevant provisions of Regulations 31 to 35 as to obligatory reflectors and that they are so fixed to the vehicle that—

(a) one reflector is on each side of the longitudinal axis of the vehicle;

(b) no part of the vehicle or its equipment on the same side of the longitudinal axis of the vehicle as a reflector extends laterally on that side beyond the nearest part of the reflecting area of that reflector for a distance of—

   (i) more than 16 inches, or
   (ii) more than such greater distance as may be necessary, having regard to the construction or nature of the vehicle, to enable the reflector to be fixed to the vehicle; and

(c) the highest part of the reflecting area of each reflector is—

   (i) in the case of a vehicle supplied by its manufacturer before 1st January 1959 not more than 5 feet 6 inches from the ground, and
   (ii) in the case of a vehicle so supplied on or after that date not more than 5 feet from the ground

and at the same height from the ground.

60. The provisions of the Act in so far as they require compliance in the case of mechanically propelled vehicles or trailers with Parts II, IV and VI of these Regulations shall not apply in the case of a vehicle in the service of a visiting force or of a headquarters, if such a vehicle complies in every respect with the requirements as to lighting equipment and reflectors relating thereto contained in Part II of Annex 6 to the Convention on Road Traffic concluded at Geneva on 19th September 1949.

Vehicles drawn or propelled by hand

61.—(1) If a vehicle drawn or propelled by hand is, together with its load (if any), not more than 2 feet 6 inches in greatest width, not more than 6 feet in greatest length and not more than 4 feet 6 inches in greatest height, it shall not be necessary for such vehicle to show any lights or to carry any reflector provided that it is kept when in use on a road during the hours of darkness as near as possible to the near or left-hand edge of the carriageway.

(2) In the case of a vehicle drawn or propelled by hand which, together with its load (if any), exceeds any of the dimensions set out in the preceding paragraph of this Regulation but does not exceed 4 feet in greatest width, it shall be necessary for such vehicle to carry—

(a) only one obligatory front lamp; and

(b) only either one obligatory reflector or one obligatory rear lamp.

(3) In the case of a vehicle drawn or propelled by hand which, together with its load (if any), exceeds 4 feet in greatest width, it shall be necessary for such vehicle to carry, in addition to the two obligatory front lamps, only either one obligatory reflector or one obligatory rear lamp.

(4) Every obligatory reflector carried on a vehicle in pursuance of the provisions of paragraph (2) or (3) of this Regulation shall be so fixed that—

(*a*) no part of the vehicle or its equipment extends laterally on the off side more than 16 inches from the nearest part of the reflecting area of the reflector; and

(*b*) no part of such reflecting area is more than 3 feet 6 inches, or less than 15 inches, from the ground.

(5) Every obligatory rear lamp carried on a vehicle in pursuance of the provisions of paragraph (2) or (3) of this Regulation shall be so fixed that—

(*a*) no part of the vehicle or its equipment extends laterally on the off side more than 16 inches from the nearest part of the illuminated area of the lamp; and

(*b*) no part of such illuminated area is more than 3 feet 6 inches, or less than 15 inches, from the ground.

(6) Every obligatory rear lamp or obligatory reflector carried on a vehicle in pursuance of the preceding provisions of this Regulation shall be so fixed that no part of the vehicle projects to the rear more than 3 feet 6 inches measured horizontally beyond any such lamp or reflector.

Vehicles carrying loads obscuring rear lamps etc.

62.—(1) The requirements of section 1 of the Act and of Regulation 23 as to the position of lamps showing to the rear a red light which are to be carried attached to vehicles shall not apply to any mechanically propelled vehicle or trailer which—

(*a*) is constructed or adapted for use for the carriage of goods or burden of any description; and

(*b*) is being used to carry a load projecting to the rear in such manner that if any such lamp were carried attached to the vehicle in accordance with the said requirements the light therefrom would not be visible from a reasonable distance.

but instead the following requirements as to the position of the said lamps shall apply in the case of any such vehicle or trailer, that is to say, the said lamps shall be carried attached to the load in positions which would satisfy such of the requirements specified in Schedule 1 as are applicable to such a vehicle or trailer but as if any reference in column 4 of that Schedule to the extreme rear of the vehicle were a reference to the extreme rear of the load.

(2) The requirements of section 1 of the Act and of Regulation 30 as to the position of red reflectors which are to be carried attached to vehicles shall not apply to any mechanically propelled vehicle or trailer which—

(*a*) is constructed or adapted for use for the carriage of goods or burden of any description; and

(*b*) is being used to carry a load projecting to the rear in such manner that if any such reflector were carried attached to the vehicle in accordance with the said requirements the reflector would be obscured,

but instead the following requirements as to the position of the said reflectors shall apply in the case of any such vehicle or trailer, that is to say, the said reflectors shall be carried attached to the load in positions which would satisfy such of the requirements specified in Schedule 2 as are applicable to such a vehicle or trailer but as if any reference in column 4 of that Schedule to the extreme rear of the vehicle were a reference to the extreme rear of the load.

(3) Save as otherwise provided in the foregoing provisions of this Regulation, the requirements of section 1 of the Act and of Parts IV and VI of these Regulations shall apply to lamps and reflectors carried by any such vehicle or trailer as is mentioned in this Regulation.

Vehicles brought temporarily into Great Britain

63.—(1) The requirements of section 1 of the Act in so far as they relate to the carrying of red reflectors and the provisions of the Act in so far as they require compliance with Parts II, IV and V of these Regulations shall not apply to any mechanically propelled vehicle brought temporarily into Great Britain by a person resident outside the United Kingdom or any trailer brought as aforesaid and drawn by the mechanically propelled vehicle, if there is issued in respect of the mechanically propelled vehicle an International Certificate for Motor Vehicles under Article 4 of the International Convention relative to Motor Traffic concluded at Paris on 24th April 1926, and the mechanically propelled vehicle and trailer comply in every respect with the requirements as to lighting equipment relating thereto contained in paragraphs IV, V, VI and VII in Article 3 of the said Convention.

(2) The provisions of the Act in so far as they require compliance with Parts II, IV, V and VI of these Regulations shall not apply to any mechanically propelled vehicle or trailer (not being one in respect of which the provisions contained in the last paragraph apply) brought temporarily into Great Britain by a person resident outside the United Kingdom provided that it complies in every respect with the requirements as to lighting equipment and reflectors relating thereto contained in Part II of Annex 6 to the Convention on Road Traffic concluded at Geneva on 19th September 1949.

Distinctive lamps on certain vehicles

64.—(1) The provisions of section 2 (1) (*b*) of the Act shall be varied so as to permit—

(*a*) one or more lamps showing a blue light to be carried on—

(i) motor vehicles used for fire brigade, ambulance, or police purposes,

(ii) motor vehicles owned by a body formed primarily for the purposes of fire salvage and used for those or similar purposes,

(iii) motor vehicles owned by the Forestry Commission or by local authorities and used from time to time for the purposes of fighting fires,

(iv) motor vehicles owned by the Secretary of State for Defence and used for the purposes of the disposal of bombs or explosives,

(v) motor vehicles owned by the Secretary of State for Defence and used by the Naval Emergency Monitoring Organisation for the purposes of a nuclear accident or incident involving radio-activity,

(vi) motor vehicles primarily used for the purposes of the Blood Transfusion Service under Part II of the National Health Service Act 1946 or under Part II of the National Health Service (Scotland) Act 1947,

(vii) motor vehicles used by Her Majesty's Coastguard or the Coastguard Auxiliary Service to aid persons in danger or vessels in distress on or near the coast, and

(viii) motor vehicles owned by the National Coal Board and used for the purposes of rescue operations at mines, and

(ix) motor vehicles owned by the Secretary of State for Defence and used by the Royal Air Force Mountain Rescue Service for the purposes of rescue operations in connection with crashed aircraft or any other emergencies;

(x) motor vehicles owned by the Royal National Lifeboat Institution and used for launching lifeboats; and

(b) one or more lamps showing an amber light to be carried on—

(i) road clearance vehicles,

(ii) break-down vehicles,

(iii) vehicles used for the purposes of testing, maintaining, improving, cleansing or watering roads, or for any purpose incidental to any operation as aforesaid,

(iv) vehicles used for the purposes of inspecting, cleansing, maintaining, adjusting, renewing or installing any apparatus which is in, on, under or over a road or for any purpose incidental to any operation as aforesaid,

(v) vehicles used for or in connection with any purpose for which they are authorised to be used on roads by an Order under subsection (4) of section 64 of the Road Traffic Act 1960, being an Order authorising those vehicles to be so used notwithstanding that they do not comply with the requirements prescribed under the said section 64 or with such of the said requirements as are specified in the said Order.

(2) Each lamp carried in pursuance of this Regulation shall be so fixed to the vehicle that the centre of the lamp is at a height not less than 5 feet from the ground and that it is on or near as practicable to the longitudinal axis of the vehicle.

(3) The shape and size of each such lamp shall be such that the area of the orthogonal projection on to any vertical plane of that part of the lamp through which light is emitted shall be capable of lying wholly within a rectangle having sides 9 inches in length.

(4) Where only one lamp is carried in pursuance of this Regulation the light shown by it shall be visible from a point on any part of a circle drawn in a horizontal plane with the lamp at the centre, and where more than one lamp is so carried the light shown by all such lamps together shall be visible from a point on any part of a circle drawn in a horizontal plane and having as its centre a point on the longitudinal axis of the vehicle.

(5) When observed from any point on a circle drawn as aforesaid the light shown by any one such lamp shall be visible not less than 60 nor more than 150 equal times per minute, and the intervals between each display of light towards that point shall be constant.

(6) The light shown by each lamp carried in pursuance of this Regulation shall be in the form of a concentrated beam or beams rotating in a substantially horizontal plane.

(7) In the case of such a lamp showing a blue light the rated wattage of the electric bulb or the total rated wattage of all the bulbs with which it is fitted shall not exceed 55 watts, and in the case of such a lamp showing

an amber light the rated wattage of the electric bulb or the total rated wattage of all the bulbs with which it is fitted shall not exceed 36 watts.

(8) No break-down vehicle shall carry a lamp showing an amber light in pursuance of this Regulation except while it is being used in connection with, and is in the immediate vicinity of, an accident or break-down, or while it is being used to draw a broken down vehicle, and no other vehicle shall carry a lamp showing an amber or blue light in pursuance of this Regulation except when the vehicle is being used for the relevant purposes specified in paragraph (1) of this Regulation and it is necessary or desirable to do so either to indicate to other road users the urgency of the purposes for which the vehicle is being used, or to warn other road users of the presence of the vehicle on the road.

(9) No vehicle, other than a vehicle specified in paragraph (1) (a) of this Regulation, shall carry a lamp similar to a lamp which, when it is showing a blue light, may be carried by a vehicle so specified by virtue of this Regulation.

Special lights on break-down vehicles

65.—(1) The provisions of section 2 (1) (b) of the Act shall be varied so as to permit break-down vehicles to carry one or more lamps showing a white light which comply with paragraph (2) of this Regulation for the purposes of illuminating the scene of an accident or break-down.

(2) Each lamp shall be so constructed, fitted and maintained that no part of its illuminated area is less than 5 feet from the ground.

(3) No person shall illuminate any lamp carried by a break-down vehicle by virtue of this Regulation except while the vehicle is in the immediate vicinity of an accident or break-down and there is illuminated a lamp or lamps showing an amber light carried on the vehicle in accordance with the last preceding Regulation.

(4) Any person using a lamp carried on a break-down vehicle by virtue of this Regulation shall ensure that it is so directed that no person who is driving a vehicle is dazzled by the light emitted therefrom.

(5) The light shown by a lamp carried on a break-down vehicle by virtue of this Regulation may be moved by swivelling, deflecting or otherwise while the vehicle is in motion in the immediate vicinity of the accident or break-down.

Rearward facing amber surfaces on certain vehicles

66. The provisions of section 2 (1) (b) of the Act shall be varied so as to permit road clearance vehicles to carry an amber reflecting surface facing to the rear of the vehicle.

Vehicles fitted with movable platforms

67.—(1) Where a vehicle fitted with a movable platform, being a vehicle used for the purpose of facilitating overhead working, is being used on a road during the hours of darkness and jacks with which the vehicle is fitted for the purpose of stabilising it while the movable platform is in use project from the sides of the vehicle, the vehicle shall carry on or near each such jack a lamp to indicate the position of the jack showing a white light to the front and a red light to the rear, each light being visible from a reasonable distance.

(2) Each lamp carried on or near a jack in pursuance of this Regulation shall be fitted—

(*a*) with an electric bulb not exceeding 7 watts and frosted glass or
     other material which has the effect of diffusing the light,

(*b*) so that no part of the jack projects more than 12 inches beyond
     a vertical line through the centre of the lamp, and

(*c*) so that it is not more than 2 feet in front of or behind the jack
     and the centre of the lamp is at a height of not more than 3 feet
     6 inches and not less than 15 inches from the ground.

PART XI

REGULATIONS GOVERNING DIRECTION INDICATORS
AND STOP LAMPS ON VEHICLES

Application of Part XI

68.—(1) Except as provided by paragraph (2) of this Regulation,
this Part of these Regulations applies to wheeled vehicles.

(2) This Part of these Regulations does not apply to a vehicle falling
within Regulation 4 (3), (6), (6A), (7) and (8) of the Construction and
Use Regulations or to any towing implement within the meaning of
those Regulations.

Provision as to direction indicators when fitted

69.—(1) Every motor vehicle (other than a two-wheeled motor cycle with
or without a sidecar attached) first used on or after 1st January 1936 and
before 1st September 1965 which is fitted with a direction indicator shall—

(*a*) if it is a vehicle fitted with electric lighting equipment, comply
     with the provisions relating to direction indicators contained in
     either Part I or Part II or Part III of Schedule 5; or

(*b*) if it is a vehicle not fitted with such equipment, comply with
     the provisions relating to direction indicators contained in Part V
     of the said Schedule.

(2) Every two-wheeled motor cycle with or without a sidecar attached
first used on or after 1st January 1936 which is fitted with a direction
indicator shall comply with the provisions relating to direction indicators
contained in either Part I or Part II or Part V of the said Schedule.

(3) Save as provided in paragraph (4) of this Regulation, every trailer
manufactured after 1st July 1955 and before 1st January 1971 which is
fitted with a direction indicator shall comply with the provisions relating
to direction indicators contained in either Part III or Part VI of Schedule 5.

(4) Every motor vehicle (other than a two-wheeled motor cycle with
or without a sidecar attached) first used on or after 1st September 1965
and before 1st January 1971 which is fitted with a direction indicator
shall comply with the provisions relating to direction indicators contained
in Part III of Schedule 5, and any trailer drawn by such a motor vehicle,
or by a motor vehicle first used before 1st September 1965 and fitted
with direction indicators in accordance with those provisions, shall be
fitted with direction indicators in accordance with those provisions.

Requirements for direction indicators to be fitted

70.—(1) Save as provided in paragraph (2) of this Regulation—

(*a*) every motor vehicle first used before 1st September 1965 shall

be fitted with direction indicators in accordance with the provisions of either Part I, Part II or Part III of Schedule 5, and

(b) every motor vehicle (except a motor vehicle to which sub-paragraph (a) of this paragraph applies) which was manufactured
before 1st August 1973 or first used before 1st January 1974
shall be fitted with direction indicators in accordance with the
provisions of Part III of Schedule 5;

(c) every trailer manufactured after 1st July 1955 and before 1st
July 1974 shall be fitted with direction indicators in accordance
with the provisions of either Part III or Part VI of Schedule 5,
except that if it is drawn by a motor vehicle fitted with direction
indicators in accordance with Part III of the said Schedule it
shall be fitted with direction indicators in accordance with that
Part.

(2) Nothing in this Regulation shall apply to—

(a) a motor vehicle—

(i) which is a two-wheeled motor cycle with or without a
sidecar attached;

(ii) which is an industrial tractor, a land locomotive, a
land tractor, a works truck or a pedestrian controlled vehicle;

(iii) which carries lamps for the purposes of section 1 of
the Act which are not electrically operated or which carries
no lamps for such purposes;

(iv) first used before 1st January 1936;

(v) which it is unlawful at all times to drive at a speed
exceeding 15 miles per hour; or

(vi) which is incapable by reason of its construction of
exceeding a speed of 15 miles per hour on the level under its
own power; or

(vii) which is a public service vehicle first used before 1st
January 1960, until 1st July 1971;

(b) to a trailer—

(i) which is a land implement, a works trailer or an agricultural trailer;

(ii) which carries lamps for the purposes of section 1 of the
Act which are not electrically operated or which carries no
lamps for such purposes;

(iii) which is drawn by a motor vehicle not required to be
fitted with direction indicators in accordance with this Regulation;

(iv) which forms part of an articulated vehicle and was
manufactured before 1st September 1965;

(v) the dimensions of which are such that when the longitudinal axis of the trailer lies in the same vertical plane as the
longitudinal axis of the drawing vehicle both rear or both side
direction indicators on that vehicle are visible to an observer
in that vertical plane, from a point 6 metres behind the rear
of the trailer whether it is loaded or not; or

(vi) which is a broken down motor vehicle or forms part
of a broken down articulated vehicle or which draws another
trailer behind it.

71.—(1) In this Regulation, " excepted motor vehicle " means a motor vehicle mentioned in Regulation 70 (2) (*a*) and " excepted trailer " means a trailer mentioned in Regulation 70 (2) (*b*).

(2) Except as provided in paragraph (3) of this Regulation, this Regulation applies to the following vehicles, namely—

(*a*) every motor vehicle (other than an excepted motor vehicle) first used on or after 1st January 1974;

(*b*) every trailer (other than an excepted trailer) manufactured on or after the said date;

(*c*) every excepted motor vehicle (other than a two-wheeled motor cycle with or without a sidecar attached) first used on or after the said date which is fitted with a direction indicator;

(*d*) every excepted trailer manufactured on or after the said date which is fitted with a direction indicator.

(3) This Regulation does not apply to a motor vehicle manufactured before 1st August 1973.

(4) Every vehicle to which this Regulation applies shall be fitted with direction indicators in accordance with the provisions of Part III of Schedule 5.

(5) Every direction indicator fitted to a vehicle in accordance with the last preceding paragraph shall be marked with an approval mark and—

(*a*) in the case of a front indicator, the number " 1 " above such mark, or

(*b*) in the case of a rear indicator, the number " 2b " above such mark, or

(*c*) in the case of a side indicator, the number " 2a " or " 3 " above such mark, or

(*d*) in the case of a shoulder indicator, the number " 4 " above such mark, or

(*e*) in the case of a flank indicator, the number " 5 " above such mark.

(6) Where a rear direction indicator fitted to a vehicle in accordance with paragraph (4) of this Regulation is capable of being operated on either of the two levels of illumination it shall be wired in such a way that, when the obligatory front and obligatory rear lamps of the motor vehicle on which the indicator is fitted, or of the motor vehicle which is drawing the trailer on which the indicator is fitted, are switched off, the indicator when operated is lit at the higher level of illumination, and when the obligatory front and obligatory rear lamps of the motor vehicle are switched on, the indicator when operated is lit at the lower level of illumination, so, however, that the foregoing provisions shall not preclude each rear direction indicator and the obligatory front and obligatory rear lamps of the motor vehicle being wired in such a way that, when such lamps are switched on and any fog lamp on that motor vehicle is switched on, the indicator when operated is lit at the higher level of illumination, and when such obligatory lamps are switched on but no fog lamp is switched on, the indicator when operated is lit at the lower level of illumination:

Provided that nothing in this paragraph shall apply to a rear direction indicator fitted to a trailer mentioned in Regulation 70 (2) (*b*) (iii) or which is being drawn by a motor vehicle which is equipped with rear direction indicators not marked with the number " 2b " above an approval mark.

(7) Nothing in this Regulation shall be taken to authorise any person to apply an approved mark or the said numbers " 1 ", " 2a, " " 2b ", " 3 ", " 4 " or " 5 " to any direction indicator in contravention of the Trade Descriptions Act 1968.

(8) In this Regulation

" approval mark " means a marking designated as an approval mark by Regulation 2 (2) of the Motor Vehicles (Designation of Approval Marks) Regulations 1968.

Provision as to stop lamps when fitted

72.—(1) Every stop lamp fitted to a motor vehicle first used on or after 1st January 1936 and before 1st January 1971 or to a trailer manufactured before the last mentioned date shall be fitted at the rear of the vehicle and not to the left of the centre thereof and when in operation shall show a red light:

Provided that nothing in this paragraph shall prevent the fitting of a duplicate stop lamp on the left or nearside of the vehicle which (except when the stop lamp fitted on the right or offside of the vehicle is showing a flashing light as a direction indicator) comes into operation at the same time as the stop lamp fitted at the centre or on the right or offside of the vehicle.

(2) Every light shown by a stop lamp shall be diffused by means of frosted glass or other adequate means and shall be a steady light.

Requirements for stop lamps to be fitted

73.—(1) Save as provided in paragraph (2) of this Regulation, every motor vehicle first used before 1st January 1971 and every trailer manufactured before that date shall be fitted with a stop lamp and in relation to that lamp the provisions of the last preceding Regulation shall apply as they apply to a stop lamp mentioned in that Regulation.

(2) Nothing in paragraph (1) of this Regulation shall require any vehicle specified in Part I of Schedule 6 to be fitted with any stop lamp.

74.—(1) Save as provided in paragraph (2) of this Regulation, every two-wheeled motor cycle with or without a sidecar attached and every invalid carriage first used on or after 1st January 1971 shall be fitted with one stop lamp, and every other motor vehicle first used on or after that date and every trailer manufactured on or after that date shall be fitted with two stop lamps.

(2) Nothing in paragraph (1) of this Regulation shall require any vehicle specified in Part I of Schedule 6 to be fitted with any stop lamp.

(3) Every stop lamp fitted to any motor vehicle or trailer mentioned in paragraph (1) of this Regulation (whether or not in pursuance of the said paragraph (1)) shall comply with the conditions set out in Part II of Schedule 6.

75.—(1) Save as provided in paragraph (2) of this Regulation, every stop lamp fitted to a motor vehicle first used on or after 1st January 1974 or to a trailer manufactured on or after that date shall, in addition to complying with the conditions set out in Part II of Schedule 6, comply with the conditions set out in Part III of that Schedule.

(2) Nothing in paragraph (1) of this Regulation shall in so far as it requires compliance by a stop lamp with Part III of Schedule 6 apply to any stop lamp fitted—

(a) to any motor vehicle manufactured before 1st August 1973; or

(b) to any two-wheeled motor cycle with or without a sidecar attached thereto, or

(c) [. . .]

(d) to any vehicle mentioned in paragraph 5 of Part I of Schedule 6.

Maintenance of direction indicators and stop lamps

76. Every direction indicator and every stop lamp fitted to a motor vehicle or trailer shall at all times while the vehicle is used on a road be maintained in a clean condition and in good and efficient working order.

Use of direction indicators as a hazard warning

77.—(1) In this Regulation " appropriate device " means a device which—

(a) is fitted to a motor vehicle so as to operate simultaneously—

    (i) one or more direction indicators on both sides of the motor vehicle, or

    (ii) those indicators and one or more direction indicators on both sides of any trailer being drawn by the motor vehicle;

(b) includes a warning light capable of indicating to the driver of the motor vehicle when the device is being operated;

(c) is actuated by a switch controlling only that device or, in the case of a public service vehicle, only that device and an audible warning instrument fitted pursuant to the Construction and Use Regulations.

(2) An appropriate device may only be used—

(a) when the motor vehicle is stationary on a road, for the purpose of warning other road users by the simultaneous illumination of the indicators, of a temporary obstruction on the carriageway of a road, or

(b) if the motor vehicle is a public service vehicle (whether stationary or in motion), for the purpose of summoning assistance for the driver, the conductor or an inspector.

(3) No device other than an appropriate device shall be fitted to a motor vehicle for the purpose of operating direction indicators as provided in sub-paragraph (1) (a) of this Regulation.

S.I. 1975 No. 245

THE ROAD VEHICLES (USE OF LIGHTS DURING DAYTIME) REGULATIONS 1975

1.—(1) . . .

(2) In these Regulations the following expressions have the meaning hereby respectively assigned to them:—

    " daytime hours" means the time between half-an-hour before sunrise and half-an-hour after sunset;

    " the driver of the vehicle ", in relation to a trailer, means the driver of the vehicle drawing the trailer;

    " obligatory lamps ", in relation to a vehicle, means such of the obligatory front lamps, obligatory headlamps and obligatory rear lamps as the vehicle is required, by virtue of sections 68 to 82 of the Road Traffic Act 1972 and the regulations made, or having effect as if made, under any of these sections, to carry when on a road during the hours of darkness (as defined in section 82 of the said Act of 1972);

" poor visibility conditions ", in relation to a vehicle used on a road during daytime hours, means such conditions adversely affecting visibility (whether consisting of, or including, fog, smoke, heavy rain or spray, snow, dense cloud, or any similar condition) as seriously reduce the ability of the driver (after the appropriate use by him of any windscreen wiper and washer) to see other vehicles or persons on the road, or the ability of other users of the road to see the vehicle;

and any other expressions which are used in these Regulations and are defined in Regulation 3 of the Road Vehicles Lighting Regulations 1971 have in these Regulations the meaning given to those expressions in that Regulation.

(3) Any reference in these Regulations to any enactment or instrument shall be construed as a reference to that enactment or instrument as amended by or under any subsequent enactment or instrument.

(4) The Interpretation Act 1889 shall apply for the interpretation of these Regulations as it applies for the interpretation of an Act of Parliament.

Use of lights on vehicles

2.—(1) Where a vehicle, which carries the obligatory lamps, is used on a road during daytime hours, those lamps shall, subject to paragraph (3) of this Regulation, be kept lit while the vehicle is in motion during any period when poor visibility conditions prevail on that road.

(2) The lighting, in the circumstances mentioned in paragraph (1) of this Regulation, of a headlamp which is capable of emitting both a main beam and a dipped beam shall be effected by causing the lamp to emit either beam.

(3) Where under Regulation 21 (use of headlamps by vehicles having four or more wheels) or Regulation 22 (use of headlamps by vehicles having two or three wheels) of the Road Vehicles Lighting Regulations 1971 the illumination of one headlamp or one fog lamp or one or both of two per-mitted lamps (as defined in paragraph (4) of either of those Regulations) is permitted by either of those Regulations in relation to a vehicle when in conditions of fog or whilst snow is falling the vehicle is in motion during the hours of darkness (as defined in section 82 of the Road Traffic Act 1972) on a road to which those Regulations apply, the same illumination of such lamp or lamps on that vehicle shall in the circumstances mentioned in paragraph (1) of this Regulation be a sufficient compliance with the requirements of that paragraph with respect to keeping the obligatory headlamps lit.

S.I. 1973 No. 24

The Motor Vehicles (Construction and Use) Regulations 1973
as amended by S.I. 1973 Nos. 756, 1347, 1706 and 1864, S.I. 1974 Nos.
64, 765 and 973, S.I. 1975 Nos. 186, 238 and 641

Part I

Preliminary

* * * * *

Interpretation

3.—(1) In these Regulations, unless the context otherwise requires,
the following expressions have the meanings hereby assigned to them
respectively, that is to say—

" the 1960 Act " means the Road Traffic Act 1960;

" the 1972 Act " means the Road Traffic Act 1972;

" agricultural trailer " means a trailer the property of a person engaged
in agriculture which is not used on a road for the conveyance
of any goods or burden other than agricultural produce or articles
required for the purposes of agriculture;

" articulated vehicle " means a heavy motor car or motor car with a
trailer so attached to the drawing vehicle that part of the trailer
is superimposed upon the drawing vehicle, and when the trailer
is uniformly loaded not less than 20 per cent. of the weight of
its load is borne by the drawing vehicle;

" braking efficiency ", in relation to the application of brakes to a
motor vehicle at any time, means the maximum braking force
capable of being developed by the application of those brakes,
expressed as a percentage of the weight of the vehicle including
any persons (not being fare paying or other travelling passengers)
or load carried in the vehicle at that time;

" close-coupled ", in relation to a trailer, means that the wheels on the
same side of the trailer are so fitted that at all times while it is in
motion they remain parallel to the longitudinal axis of the trailer,
and that the distance between the centres of their respective areas
of contact with the road surface does not exceed 840 millimetres;

" deck " means a floor or platform upon which seats are provided for
the accommodation of passengers;

" direction indicator " means a device fitted to a motor vehicle or
trailer for the purpose of intimating the intention of the driver
to change the direction of the vehicle to the right or to the left;

" double-decked vehicle " means a vehicle having two decks one of
which is wholly or partly above the other and each deck of which
is provided with a gangway serving seats on that deck only;

" dual-purpose vehicle " means a vehicle constructed or adapted for
the carriage both of passengers and of goods or burden of any
description, being a vehicle of which the unladen weight does
not exceed 2040 kilograms, and which either—

(i) is so constructed or adapted that the driving power of
the engine is, or by the appropriate use of the controls of the
vehicle can be, transmitted to all the wheels of the vehicle, or

(ii) satisfies the following conditions as to construction, namely:—

(a) the vehicle must be permanently fitted with a rigid roof, with or without a sliding panel;

(b) the area of the vehicle to the rear of the driver's seat must—

(i) be permanently fitted with at least one row of transverse seats (fixed or folding) for two or more passengers and those seats must be properly sprung or cushioned and provided with upholstered back-rests, attached either to the seats or to a side or the floor of the vehicle; and

(ii) be lit on each side and at the rear by a window or windows of glass or other transparent material having an area or aggregate area of not less than 1850 square centimetres on each side and not less than 770 square centimetres at the rear;

(c) the distance between the rearmost part of the steering wheel and the back-rests of the row of transverse seats satisfying the requirements specified in head (i) of the foregoing sub-paragraph (b) (or, if there is more than one such row of seats, the distance between the rearmost part of the steering wheel and the back-rests of the rearmost such row) must, when the seats are ready for use, be not less than one-third of the distance between the rearmost part of the steering wheel and the rearmost part of the floor of the vehicle;

" engineering plant " means—

(a) movable plant or equipment being a motor vehicle or trailer specially designed and constructed for the special purposes of engineering operations, and which cannot, owing to the requirements of those purposes, comply in all respects with the requirements of these Regulations and which is not constructed primarily to carry a load other than a load being either excavated materials raised from ground by apparatus on the motor vehicle or trailer or materials which the vehicle or trailer is specially designed to treat while carried thereon, or

(b) a mobile crane which does not comply in all respects with the requirements of these Regulations;

" exhaust brake " means a device with which a vehicle is fitted as a means of using cylinder pressure or exhaust back pressure so as to provide for the vehicle a retarding force greater than would ordinarily result for a vehicle not so fitted;

" gangway " means the space provided for obtaining access from any entrance to the passengers' seats or from any such seat to an exit other than an emergency exit but does not include a staircase or any space in front of a seat which is required only for the use of passengers occupying that seat or that row of seats;

" gas " means any fuel that is wholly gaseous at 16·7°C under a pressure of 760 millimetres of mercury;

" gas equipment " means a container or containers for holding, or plant and materials for producing, gas;

" gas trailer " means a trailer used solely for the carriage of gas equipment for the purpose of the propulsion of the drawing vehicle;

" goods vehicle " means a motor vehicle constructed or adapted for use for the carriage of goods, or a trailer so constructed or adapted;

" half-decked vehicle " means any vehicle not being a single-decked vehicle or a double-decked vehicle;

" hours of darkness " means the time between half-an-hour after sunset and half-an-hour before sunrise;

" indivisible load " means a load which cannot without undue expense or risk of damage be divided into two or more loads for the purpose of conveyance on a road;

" industrial tractor " means a tractor, not being a land tractor, which—

(a) has an unladen weight not exceeding 7370 kilograms,

(b) is designed and used primarily for work off roads, or for work on roads in connection only with road construction or maintenance (including any such tractor when fitted with an implement or implements designed primarily for use in connection with such work, whether or not any such implement is of itself designed to carry a load), and

(c) is so constructed as to be incapable of exceeding a speed of 20 miles per hour on the level under its own power;

" land implement " means any implement or machinery used with a land locomotive or a land tractor in connection with agriculture, grass cutting, forestry, land levelling, dredging or similar operations and includes a living van and any trailer which for the time being carries only the necessary gear or equipment of the land locomotive or land tractor which draws it;

" land implement conveyor " means a trailer, having an unladen weight not exceeding 510 kilograms, which is specially designed and constructed for the conveyance of not more than one land implement and which is marked with its unladen weight, has each of its wheels fitted with a pneumatic tyre and is drawn by a land locomotive or a land tractor;

" land locomotive " means a locomotive designed and used primarily for work on the land in connection with agriculture, forestry, land levelling, dredging or similar operations, which is driven on a road only when proceeding to and from the site of such work and which when so driven hauls nothing other than land implements or land implement conveyors;

" land tractor " means a tractor, having an unladen weight not exceeding 7370 kilograms, designed and used primarily for work on the land in connection with agriculture, grass cutting, forestry, land levelling, dredging or similar operations, which is—

(a) the property of a person engaged in agriculture or forestry or of a contractor engaged in the business of carrying out on farms or forestry estates any such operations as aforesaid; and

(b) not constructed or adapted for the conveyance of a load other than—

(i) water, fuel, accumulators and other equipment used for the purpose of propulsion, loose tools and loose equipment,

(ii) a load (consisting of goods or burden of a description referred to in paragraph 7 (3) of Schedule 4 to the Vehicle's (Excise) Act 1971) in or on any appliance which satisfies the conditions whereby the vehicle to which the said appliance is fitted does not, by virtue of the said paragraph 7 and of any regulations made from time to time under paragraph 8 of the said Schedule 4, become chargeable with duty as a goods vehicle, and

(iii) an implement fitted to the tractor and used for work on the land on farms or forestry estates in connection with any such operations as aforesaid;

" locomotive " means a heavy locomotive or a light locomotive;

" multi-pull means of operation ", in relation to a braking system, means a device which causes the muscular energy of the driver to apply the brakes of that system progressively as a result of successive applications of that device by the driver;

" overall length " means the length of a vehicle measured between vertical planes at right angles to the longitudinal axis of the vehicle and passing through the extreme projecting points thereof exclusive of—

(a) any driving mirror;

(b) any starting handle;

(c) any hood when down;

(d) any expanding or extensible contrivance forming part of a turntable fire escape fixed to a vehicle;

(e) any telescopic fog lamp when extended;

(f) any snow-plough fixed in front of a vehicle;

(g) any post office letter box the length of which measured parallel to the longitudinal axis of the vehicle does not exceed 305 millimetres; and

(h) any container specially designed to hold and keep secure a seal issued for the purposes of custom's clearance,

and, except for the purposes of Regulation 130, exclusive of any front corner marker lamp or side marker lamp within the meaning of the Road Vehicles Lighting Regulations 1971, carried on the vehicle in accordance with those Regulations.

In ascertaining the extreme projecting points of a vehicle account shall be taken of any device or any receptacle on or attached to the vehicle which increases the carrying capacity of the vehicle unless—

(i) it is a tailboard which is let down while the vehicle is stationary in order to facilitate its loading or unloading,

(ii) it is a tailboard which is let down in order to facilitate the carriage of, but which is not essential for the support of, loads which are in themselves so long as to extend at least as far as the tailboard when in the upright position, or

(iii) it is a receptacle which is constructed or adapted for the purpose of being lifted on or off vehicles with goods or burden contained therein and is from time to time actually used for that purpose in the ordinary course of business;

" overall width " means the width of a vehicle measured between vertical planes parallel to the longitudinal axis of the vehicle and passing through the extreme projecting points thereof exclusive of—

(a) any driving mirror;

(b) any direction indicator;

(c) any snow-plough fixed in front of the vehicle;

(*d*) so much of the distortion of any tyre as is caused by the weight of the vehicle;

(*e*) in the case of vehicles registered before 2nd January 1939, so much of a swivelling window designed to allow the driver to give hand signals as projects when opened not more than 105 millimetres beyond the side of the vehicle; and

(*f*) any container specially designed to hold and keep secure a seal issued for the purposes of custom's clearance,

and, except for the purposes of Regulation 130 exclusively of any such front corner marker lamp or side marker lamp as aforesaid.

In ascertaining the extreme projecting points of a vehicle account shall be taken of any device or any receptacle on or attached to the vehicle which increases the carrying capacity of the vehicle unless—

(i) it is a sideboard which is let down while the vehicle is stationary in order to facilitate its loading or unloading, or

(ii) it is a receptacle which is constructed or adapted for the purpose of being lifted on or off vehicles with goods or burden contained therein and is from time to time actually used for that purpose in the ordinary course of business;

"overhang" means the distance measured horizontally and parallel to the longitudinal axis of a vehicle between two vertical planes at right angles to that axis passing through the two points respectively specified in paragraphs (*a*) and (*b*) of this definition,

(*a*) the rearmost point of the vehicle exclusive of—

(i) any hood when down;

(ii) any post office letter box the length of which measured parallel to the longitudinal axis of the vehicle does not exceed 305 millimetres;

(iii) any expanding or extensible contrivance forming part of a turntable fire escape fixed to a vehicle;

(iv) in the case of a motor car constructed solely for the carriage of passengers and their effects and adapted to carry not more than seven passengers exclusive of the driver, any luggage carrier fitted to the vehicle; and

(v) in the case of a public service vehicle constructed to draw a trailer, any part of the vehicle designed primarily for use as a means of attaching the trailer and any fitting designed for use in connection with such part, being a part and fitting the total length of which measured parallel to the longitudinal axis of the vehicle does not exceed 305 millimetres; and

(*b*) (i) in the case of a motor vehicle having not more than three axles of which only one is not a steering axle, through the centre point of that axle;

(ii) in the case of a motor vehicle having three axles of which the front axle is the only steering axle and of a motor vehicle having four axles of which the two foremost are the only steering axles, through a point 110 millimetres in rear of the centre of a straight line joining the centre points of the two rearmost axles; and

(iii) in any other case through a point situated on the longitudinal axis of the vehicle and such that a line drawn from it at right angles to that axis will pass through the centre of the minimum turning circle of the vehicle;

" passenger vehicle " means a vehicle constructed solely for the carriage of passengers and their effects;

" pedestrian controlled vehicle " means a motor vehicle which is controlled by a pedestrian and not constructed or adapted for use or used for the carriage of a driver or passenger;

" plating certificate ", in relation to a vehicle, means a plating certificate issued or having effect as if issued, for that vehicle under the plating and testing regulations, and which shows therein the following particulars, namely, the gross weight for the vehicle, the axle weight for each axle of the vehicle and in the case of a motor vehicle constructed or adapted to form part of an articulated vehicle, the train weight for that motor vehicle;

" pneumatic tyre " means a tyre which complies in all respects with the following requirements:—

(a) it shall be provided with, or together with the wheel upon which it is mounted shall form, a continuous closed chamber inflated to a pressure substantially exceeding atmospheric pressure when the tyre is in the condition in which it is normally used, but is not subjected to any load;

(b) it shall be capable of being inflated and deflated without removal from the wheel or vehicle;

(c) it shall be such that, when it is deflated and is subjected to a normal load, the sides of the tyre collapse;

" registered " means—

(a) in the case of a vehicle which was registered at any time under the Roads Act 1920, the date on which it was first so registered;   and

(b) in the case of any other vehicle, the date on which it was first registered under the Vehicles (Excise) Act 1949, the Vehicles (Excise) Act, 1962 or the Vehicles (Excise) Act 1971;

" recut pneumatic tyre " means any pneumatic tyre in which an existing tread pattern has been cut or burnt deeper or a new tread pattern has been cut or burnt except where the pattern is cut entirely in additional material added to the tyre for the purpose;

" rigid vehicle " means a motor vehicle which is not constructed or adapted to form part of an articulated vehicle;

" safety glass " means glass so constructed or treated that if fractured it does not fly into fragments likely to cause severe cuts;

" single-decked vehicle " means a vehicle upon which no part of a deck or gangway is vertically above another deck or gangway;

" split braking system ", in relation to a motor vehicle, means a braking system so designed and constructed that—

(a) it comprises two independent sections of mechanism capable of developing braking force such that, excluding the means of operation, a failure of any part (other than a fixed member or a brake shoe anchor pin) of one of the said sections shall not cause a decrease in the braking force capable of being developed by the other section;

(b) the said two sections are operated by a means of operation which is common to both sections;

(c) the braking efficiency of either of the said two sections can be readily checked;

" stored energy ", in relation to a braking system of a vehicle, means energy (other than the muscular energy of the driver or the mechanical energy of a spring) stored in a reservoir for the purpose of applying the brakes under the control of the driver, either directly or as a supplement to his muscular energy;

" straddle carrier " means a motor vehicle constructed to straddle and lift its load for the purpose of transportation;

" statutory power of removal " means a power conferred by or under any enactment to remove or move a vehicle from any road or from any part of a road;

" towing implement " means any device on wheels designed for the purpose of enabling a motor vehicle to draw another vehicle by the attachment of that device to that other vehicle in such a manner that part of that other vehicle is secured to and either rests on or is suspended from the device and some but not all of the wheels on which that other vehicle normally runs are raised off the ground;

" the plating and testing regulations " means the Goods Vehicles (Plating and Testing) Regulations 1971 as amended;

" track laying ", in relation to a vehicle, means that the vehicle is so designed and constructed that the weight thereof is transmitted to the road surface either by means of continuous tracks or by a combination of wheels and continuous tracks in such circumstances that the weight transmitted to the road surface by the tracks is not less than half the weight of the vehicle;

" two-tone horn " means an instrument or apparatus which, when operated, automatically produces a sound which alternates at regular intervals between two fixed notes;

" vehicle in the service of a visiting force or of a headquarters " has the same meaning as in Article 8 (6) of the Visiting Forces and International Headquarters (Application of Law) Order 1965;

" wheel " in the case of a motor vehicle or trailer means a wheel the tyre or rim of which when the vehicle is in motion on a road is in contact with the ground;

" wheeled " in relation to a vehicle means that the whole weight of the vehicle is transmitted to the road surface by means of wheels;

" wide tyre " means a pneumatic tyre as respects which its area of contact with the road surface is not less than 300 millimetres in width when measured at right angles to the longitudinal axis of the vehicle;

" works trailer " means a trailer designed for use in private premises and used on a road only in delivering goods from or to such premises to or from a vehicle on a road in the immediate neighbourhood, or in passing from one part of any such premises to another or to other private premises in the immediate neighbourhood or in connection with road works while at or in the immediate neighbourhood of the site of such works;

" works truck " means a motor vehicle (other than a straddle carrier) designed for use in private premises and used on a road only in delivering goods from or to such premises to or from a vehicle on a road in the immediate neighbourhood, or in passing from one part of any such premises to another or to other private premises in the immediate neighbourhood or in connection with road works while at or in the immediate neighbourhood of the site of such works.

(2) For the purpose of these Regulations, in determining when a motor vehicle is first used, the date of such first use shall be taken to be such date as is the earliest of the undermentioned relevant dates applicable to that vehicle:—

(a) in the case of a vehicle registered under the Roads Act 1920, the Vehicles (Excise) Act 1949, or the Vehicles (Excise) Act 1962, or the Vehicles (Excise) Act 1971 the relevant date is the date on which it was first so registered; and

(b) in each of the following cases—

(i) in the case of a vehicle which is being or has been used under a trade licence as defined in section 16 of the Vehicles (Excise) Act 1971 (otherwise than for the purposes of demonstration or testing or of being delivered from premises of the manufacturer by whom it was made, or of a distributor of vehicles or dealer in vehicles to premises of a distributor of vehicles, dealer in vehicles or purchaser thereof, or to premises of a person obtaining possession thereof under a hiring agreement or hire purchase agreement);

(ii) in the case of a vehicle belonging, or which has belonged, to the Crown which is or was used or appropriated for use for naval, military or air force purposes;

(iii) in the case of a vehicle belonging, or which has belonged, to a visiting force or a headquarters or defence organisation to which in each case the Visiting Forces and International Headquarters (Application of Law) Order 1965, applies;

(iv) in the case of a vehicle, being a vehicle which has been used on roads outside Great Britain and which has been imported into Great Britain, and

(v) in the case of a vehicle, being a vehicle which has been used otherwise than on roads after being sold or supplied by retail and before being registered;

the relevant date is the date of manufacture of the vehicle.

In sub-sub-paragraph (v) of this paragraph " sold or supplied by retail " means sold or supplied otherwise than to a person acquiring solely for the purpose of resale or re-supply for a valuable consideration.

(3) Except where otherwise provided in these Regulations a tyre shall not be deemed to be of soft or elastic material unless the said material is either—

(a) continuous round the circumference of the wheel; or

(b) fitted in sections so that so far as reasonably practicable no space is left between the ends thereof,

and is of such thickness and design as to minimise, so far as reasonably possible, vibration when the vehicle is in motion and so constructed as to be free from any defect which might in any way cause damage to the surface of a road.

(4) For the purpose of these Regulations a brake drum shall be deemed to form part of the wheel and not of the braking system.

(5) For the purpose of these Regulations any two wheels of a motor vehicle or trailer shall be regarded as one wheel if the distance between the centres of the areas of contact between such wheels and the road surface is less than 460 millimetres.

(6) For the purpose of these Regulations, other than Regulations 83 to 87 and Schedule 7, in counting the number of axles of and in determining the sum of the weights transmitted to the road surface by any one axle of a vehicle, where the centres of the areas of contact between all the wheels and the road surface can be included between any two vertical planes at right angles to the longitudinal axis of the vehicle less than 1.02 metres apart, those wheels shall be treated as constituting one axle.

(7) Any reference in these Regulations to any enactment shall be construed as a reference to that enactment as amended by any subsequent enactment.

(8) Any reference in these Regulations to a numbered Regulation or Schedule is a reference to the Regulation or Schedule bearing that number in these Regulations except where otherwise expressly provided.

(9) The Interpretation Act 1889, shall apply for the interpretation of these Regulations as it applies for the interpretation of an Act of Parliament, and as if for the purpose of section 38 of that Act these Regulations were an Act of Parliament and the Regulations revoked by Regulation 2 were Acts of Parliament thereby repealed.

(10) In so far as any consent, notice, direction or dispensation given, Ministry plate issued or any other thing done under a provision of the Regulations revoked by these Regulations could have been given or done under a corresponding provision of these Regulations it shall not be invalidated by the revocation effected by Regulation 2 but shall have effect as if given or done under that corresponding provision.

Application and Exemptions

4.—(1) Except where the context otherwise requires these Regulations shall apply to wheeled vehicles only.

(2) Regulations 11, 12, 23, 27, 44, 45 and 51 shall not apply to road rollers.

(3) Regulations 9 to 12 inclusive, 14 to 21 inclusive, 23, 24, 28 to 74 inclusive and 91 shall not apply to vehicles proceeding to a port for export.

(4) Regulations 12, 49, 58, 60, 61 and 64 shall not apply to any pedestrian controlled vehicle.

(5) Regulations 11, 12, 20, 45, 51, 55, 60, 71, 72, 74 and 76 to 88 inclusive shall apply only to motor vehicles and trailers used on highways.

(6) Every motor vehicle registered before the expiration of one year from the making of any Regulation hereof (other than Regulation 89 and other than a regulation contained in Part V of these Regulations) by which the requirements as regards the construction or weight of any class of vehicles are varied shall be exempt from the requirements of that Regulation for a period of five years from the making thereof provided that it complies with the requirements of the Regulations to which it would have been subject immediately prior to the making of that Regulation.

(7) Part II of these Regulations, except Regulations 9, 42 to 44 inclusive, 48, 52, 57, 65, 68 and 69 shall not apply to any motor vehicle or trailer at any time brought temporarily into Great Britain by a person

resident abroad, provided that such motor vehicle or trailer respectively complies in every respect with the requirements relating to motor vehicles or trailers contained in:—

(a) Article 21 and paragraph (1) of Article 22 of the Convention on Road Traffic concluded at Geneva on 19th September 1949, and Part I, Part II (so far as it relates to direction indicators and stop lights) and Part III of Annex 6 to that Convention; or

(b) paragraphs I, III and VIII of Article 3 of the International Convention relative to Motor Traffic concluded at Paris on 24th April 1926.

(8) Part II of these Regulations, except Regulations 9, 42 to 44 inclusive, 48, 52, 57 and 65, shall not apply to any motor vehicle manufactured in Great Britain which—

(1) has been purchased by a person who is temporarily in Great Britain and is or is about to be resident abroad and in respect of which—

(a) relief from purchase tax has been afforded by virtue of section 23 of the Purchase Tax Act 1963, or

(b) there is no liability to pay purchase tax,

for a period—

(i) in the case at (a), not exceeding one year during which relief from purchase tax continues to be afforded in respect of that vehicle; and

(ii) in the case at (b), not exceeding one year from the date it was purchased by such a person as a new vehicle from a manufacturer of or dealer in mechanically propelled vehicles,

provided the vehicle complies in every respect with the requirements specified in the last preceding paragraph of this Regulation and contained in the Conventions of 1949 and 1926 therein referred to as if the vehicle had been brought temporarily into Great Britain; or

(2) has been zero rated under Regulation 44 or 45 of the Value Added Tax (General) Regulations 1972.

(9) Regulations 9 to 12 inclusive, 14 to 20 inclusive, 22 to 30 inclusive, 33A, 34, 36 to 88 inclusive, and 130 shall not apply to any vehicle in the service of a visiting force or of a headquarters.

(10) Part II of these Regulations and Regulations 74 to 106 inclusive and Regulation 132 shall not apply to—

(a) a motor vehicle which has been submitted for an examination under section 43 of the 1972 Act while it is being used on a road in connection with the carrying out of that examination and is being so used by a person who is empowered under the said section 43 to carry out that examination, or by a person acting under the direction of a person so empowered: or

(b) a motor vehicle or trailer which has been submitted for an examination either under regulations under section 45 of the 1972 Act or under section 45 (3) or (4) of that Act while it is being used on a road in connection with the carrying out of that examination and is being used so by a person who is empowered under the said regulations to carry out that examination, or by a person acting under the direction of a person so empowered.

(11) Regulations 18, 20, 27 (4), 61, 64 and 110 (2) shall not apply to any motor car or motor cycle in respect of which a certificate has been issued by the Officer in Charge of the National Collections of Road Transport, the Science Museum, London, S.W. 7, that it was designed before 1st January 1905 and constructed before 31st December 1905, and paragraphs (1) to (3), (5) to (7), (9) to (11) and (13) to (15) of Regulation 59 shall not apply to any such motor car if it complies with the provisions of paragraph (8) of the said Regulation 59 as though it were a vehicle first registered under the Motor Car Act 1903 before 1st January 1915 and paragraphs (1), (2), (5) and (6) of Regulation 62 shall not apply to any such motor cycle if it complies with the provisions of paragraph (4) of the said Regulation 62 as though it were a motor cycle first registered under the Motor Car Act 1903 or the Roads Act 1920 before 1st January 1927.

(12) The provisions of these Regulations applicable to trailers contained in Part II (except paragraph (2) of Regulation 8) and Regulations 75 and 118 shall not apply—

(a) to any towing implement which is being drawn by a motor vehicle while it is not attached to any vehicle except the one drawing it if the following conditions are satisfied, that is to say,—

(i) the towing implement is not being so drawn during the hours of darkness, and

(ii) the vehicle by which it is being so drawn is not driven at a speed exceeding 20 miles per hour; or

(b) to any vehicle which is being drawn by a motor vehicle in the exercise of a statutory power of removal.

(13) Any reference in these Regulations to a vehicle which is being drawn by a motor vehicle in the exercise of a statutory power of removal or to a broken down vehicle shall include a reference to any towing implement which is being used for the drawing of any such vehicle.

4A.—(1) This Regulation applies to a motor vehicle or trailer in respect of which—

(a) a type approval certificate has been issued by the Secretary of State under Regulation 5 of the Motor Vehicles (Type Approval) Regulations 1973 (which provides for the issue of such a certificate in respect of a vehicle which is approved as a type vehicle where it conforms to certain requirements as to design, construction, equipment and marking) or by the competent authority of any member State other than the United Kingdom under a provision of the law of that State which corresponds to the said Regulation 5; or

(b) a certificate of conformity has been issued by the manufacturer of the vehicle under Regulation 6 of those Regulations (which provides for the issue of such a certificate in respect of a vehicle where it is manufactured so as to conform with a type vehicle in respect of such of the said requirements as apply in relation to that vehicle) or under a provision of the law of any member State other than the United Kingdom which corresponds to the said Regulation 6.

(2) Where in the case of any motor vehicle or trailer to which this Regulation applies the type approval certificate or, as the case may be, the certificate of conformity in question has been issued by reason of the vehicle's conforming to the requirements of a Community Directive specified in column 1 of the Table set out below (the Directives there specified being the Council Directives which are referred to in Schedule 2 to the said Regulations of 1973 and which contain requirements with respect to the design, construction, equipment and marking of vehicles or their components) and the vehicle is first used on or after the date specified opposite to that Directive in column 2 of the said table, then that one or more (as the case may be) of these Regulations which are specified opposite to that Directive in column 3 of the said table shall not apply to that vehicle.

(3) In paragraph (1) above " member State " has the same meaning as in Regulation 3 (1) of the said Regulations of 1973.

TABLE

The Community Directives to whose requirements the vehicle must conform	Date on or after which the vehicle is first used	Regulations from which the vehicle is then exempted
Council Directive 71/320/EEC of 26th July 1971 (relating to the braking devices of certain categories of motor vehicles and their trailers)	1st July 1973	13, 14, 47, 50, 54, 59, 66 and 70
Council Directive 70/387/EEC of 27th July 1970 (relating to the doors of motor vehicles and their trailers)	1st July 1973	15
Council Directive 74/297/EEC of 4th June 1974 relating to the interior fittings of motor vehicles (the behaviour of the steering mechanism in the event of an impact).	4th December 1975	16
Council Directive 70/221/EEC of 20th March 1970 (relating to the liquid fuel tanks and rear protective devices for motor vehicles and their trailers)	1st July 1973	19
Council Directive 71/127/EEC of 1st March 1971 (relating to the rear-view mirrors of motor vehicles)	1st July 1973	23 (3)
Council Directive 70/388/EEC of 27th July 1970 (relating to the audible warning devices for motor vehicles)	1st July 1973	27 (2)
Council Directive 70/157/EEC of 6th February 1970 (relating to the permissible sound level and exhaust system of motor vehicles)	1st July 1973	29

The Community Directives to whose requirements the vehicle must conform	Date on or after which the vehicle is first used	Regulations from which the vehicle is then exempted
Council Directive 70/157/EEC of 6th February 1970, as amended by Commission Directive 73/350/EEC of 7th November 1973 (relating to the permissible sound level and exhaust system of motor vehicles)	1st March 1974	29
Council Directive 72/245/EEC of 20th June 1972 (relating to the suppression of radio interference produced by spark-ignition engines fitted to motor vehicles)	1st April 1974	30
Council Directive 70/220/EEC of 20th March 1970 (relating to the measures to be taken against air pollution by gases from positive-ignition engines of motor vehicles)	10th November 1973	33A
Council Directive 70/220/EEC of 20th March 1970, as amended by Council Directive 74/290/EEC of 28th May 1974 (relating to the measures to be taken against air pollution by gases from positive ignition engines of motor vehicles).	1st January 1975	33A
Council Directive 72/306/EEC of 2nd August 1972 relating to the measures to be taken against the emission of pollutants from diesel engines for use in vehicles.	2nd February 1974	34

4B. Any reference in these Regulations to any Community Directive shall be construed as a reference to that Directive as amended by the Act of Accession.

5.—(1) In relation to a land tractor which complies with the conditions specified in paragraph (3) of this Regulation—

  (a) Regulations 12, 18, 27 and 52 to 61 inclusive shall not apply; and
  (b) Regulation 74 shall not apply if its unladen weight does not exceed 3050 kilograms.

(2) Regulations 48 to 51 inclusive shall apply in relation to a land tractor which is a heavy motor car or motor car as they apply in relation to a land tractor which is a motor tractor.

(3) The conditions referred to in paragraph (1) of this Regulation are that while a land tractor is used on a road—

  (a) it does not haul any object except—

      (i) a land implement which is being hauled to or from the site of agricultural, grass cutting, forestry, land levelling, dredging or similar operations or from one part of a farm or forestry estate to another part of that farm or forestry estate,

    (ii) a land implement conveyor which is being hauled as aforesaid, or

    (iii) an agricultural trailer;

(b) it does not carry any load except any such load as it is constructed or adapted to carry;

(c) if it is a three-wheeled vehicle fitted with a removable appliance, it does not carry any load;

(d) if it is a land tractor fitted with a removable appliance in or on which any such load as aforesaid could be carried, it does not carry any load in or on such appliance unless there is a distance of at least 1.22 metres between the centre of the area of contact with the road surface of—

    (i) a rear wheel, in a case where only one appliance is being used for the carriage of a load, and is fitted to the back of the vehicle,

    (ii) any wheel on one side of the vehicle, in any other case, and that of the nearest wheel on the other side;

(e) if it is a land tractor carrying a load in or on a removable appliance in conformity with the foregoing conditions, it does not draw a trailer and not more than one such appliance is fitted to it at any one time or, in a case where one such appliance is a specified appliance for the purposes of paragraph 8 (2) of Schedule 4 to the Vehicles (Excise) Act 1971, not more than two of such appliances, fitted at opposite ends of the land tractor;   and

(f) it is not driven at a speed exceeding 20 miles per hour.

Special application of certain Regulations

6. The Secretary of State is satisfied—

(a) that it is requisite that the provisions of Regulations 34 (1), 40 (1) and 41 (1) (being provisions which vary the requirements as regards the construction of the vehicles specified in each of those Regulations) shall apply at 1st April 1973 to such of the vehicles respectively so specified as are registered under the Vehicles (Excise) Act 1971 before the expiration of one year from the making of these Regulations;   and

(b) that notwithstanding that the said provisions will then apply to those vehicles no undue hardship or inconvenience will be caused thereby.

(2) Nothing in Regulation 4 (6) shall be taken to affect the application of the said Regulations 34 (1), 40 (1) and 41 (1).

Provision as respects Trade Descriptions Act 1968

7. Where by a provision of any Regulation hereof any vehicle or any of its parts or equipment is required to be marked with a specification number or the registered certification trade mark of the British Standards Institution or with an approval mark, nothing in that provision shall be taken to authorise any person to apply any such number or mark to the vehicle, part or equipment in contravention of the Trade Descriptions Act 1968.

PART II

REGULATIONS GOVERNING THE CONSTRUCTION, WEIGHT AND EQUIPMENT OF MOTOR VEHICLES AND TRAILERS

A.—GENERAL

Construction

8.—(1) Every motor cycle and invalid carriage shall be so constructed that it is a wheeled vehicle.

(2) Save as aforesaid every motor vehicle and trailer shall be so constructed that it is either a wheeled vehicle or a track laying vehicle.

Overall length

9.—(1) The overall length of an articulated vehicle shall not exceed 15 metres.

Provided that this paragraph shall not apply in the case of an articulated vehicle constructed and normally used for the conveyance of indivisible loads of exceptional length—

    (i) if each wheel of the vehicle is fitted with a pneumatic tyre, or

    (ii) if each wheel of the vehicle is not so fitted but the vehicle is not driven at a speed exceeding 12 miles per hour.

(2) The overall length of a public service vehicle or a vehicle which is constructed or adapted for use as such a vehicle or a chassis which is constructed for such a vehicle shall not exceed 12 metres.

(3) The overall length of a motor vehicle other than one falling within either of the two foregoing paragraphs shall not exceed 11 metres.

Overall height of public service vehicles

10. The overall height of a public service vehicle shall not exceed 4.57 metres.

Variation of wheel load

11. Every motor vehicle or trailer with more than four wheels and every trailer having more than two wheels being part of an articulated vehicle shall be provided with such compensating arrangement as will ensure that all the wheels will remain in contact with the road surface and under the most adverse conditions will not be subject to abnormal variations of load:

Provided that this Regulation shall not apply to any steerable wheel of a motor vehicle if the load on such wheel does not exceed 3560 kilograms.

Springs

12. Every motor vehicle and every trailer drawn thereby shall be equipped with suitable and sufficient springs between each wheel and the frame of the vehicle:

Provided that this Regulation shall not apply—

    (*a*) to any vehicle first used on or before 1st January 1932;

    (*b*) to any motor tractor not exceeding 4070 kilograms in weight unladen if each unsprung wheel of the vehicle is fitted with a pneumatic tyre;

(c) to any land locomotive, land implement, land implement conveyor, agricultural trailer or trailer used solely for the haulage of felled trees;

(d) to any motor tractor not exceeding 4070 kilograms in weight unladen used in connection with railway shunting operations which is only used on a road when passing from one portion of the railway track to another for the purpose of such operations;

(e) to motor cycles;

(f) to mobile cranes;

(g) to works trucks and works trailers;

(h) to any vehicle not exceeding 4070 kilograms in weight unladen specially designed for and mainly used in operations which necessitate working on rough ground or unmade roads if each wheel of the vehicle is fitted with a pneumatic tyre and if the vehicle is not driven or drawn at a speed exceeding 20 miles per hour;

(i) to any vehicle not exceeding 4070 kilograms in weight unladen, constructed or adapted for use and used solely for road sweeping if each wheel of the vehicle is fitted with a pneumatic tyre or a tyre of soft or elastic material and if the vehicle is not driven or drawn at a speed exceeding 20 miles per hour;

(j) to any pedestrian controlled vehicle, all the wheels of which are equipped with pneumatic tyres;   or

(k) to any broken down vehicle which is being drawn by a motor vehicle in consequence of the breakdown.

Parking brake

13.—(1) Save as provided in paragraph (3) of this Regulation, every motor vehicle first used before the 1st January 1968, shall be equipped with a braking system (which may be one of the braking systems prescribed in Regulation 46, 47, 50, 54 (other than paragraph 2), and 59 (other than paragraph 2)) so designed and constructed that it can at all times be set so as effectually to prevent two at least, or in the case of vehicles with only three wheels one, of the wheels from revolving when the vehicle is not being driven or is left unattended.

(2) Save as provided in paragraph (3) of this Regulation, every motor vehicle first used on or after the 1st January 1968, shall be equipped with a braking system so designed and constructed that—

(a) its means of operation, whether being a multi-pull means of operation or not, is independent of the means of operation of any braking system required by Regulation 54 (5) or, as the case may be, Regulation 59 (5) to have a total braking efficiency of not less than 50 per cent.;

(b) its braking force, when the vehicle is not being driven or is left unattended—

(i) can at all times be maintained in operation by direct mechanical action without the intervention of any hydraulic, electric or pneumatic device;   and

(ii) when so maintained in operation by direct mechanical action, is capable of holding the vehicle stationary on a gradient of at least 1 in 6.25 without the assistance of stored energy.

(3) Nothing in paragraphs (1) and (2) of this Regulation shall apply to—

(a) a two-wheeled motor cycle with or without a sidecar attached;

(b) an invalid carriage; or

(c) a land locomotive first used on or before 1st January 1932.

[*Regulation 14 provides for a warning device to be fitted on certain vehicles equipped with vacuum or pressure braking systems.*]

[*Regulation 15 provides for approved side door latches and hinges.*]

[*Regulation 16 provides for protective steering mechanisms to be fitted to certain three-or-more-wheeled vehicles first used on or after 1st July 1972.*]

Seat belts and anchorage points

17.—(1) Except as provided by paragraph (2) of this Regulation, this Regulation applies to—

(a) every motor car registered on or after 1st January 1965; and

(b) every three-wheeled motor cycle, the unladen weight of which exceeds 255 kilograms, first used on or after 1st September 1970.

(2) This Regulation does not apply:—

(a) to a goods vehicle (other than a dual-purpose vehicle), being a motor car, unless it was manufactured on or after 1st September 1966, is registered on or after 1st April 1967, and has an unladen weight not exceeding 1525 kilograms;

(b) to a three-wheeled motor cycle manufactured before 1st March 1970 or a two-wheeled motor cycle with a side-car attached thereto;

(c) to a passenger vehicle or a dual-purpose vehicle being in either case a vehicle adapted to carry more than twelve passengers exclusive of the driver;

(d) to a land tractor;

(e) to a works truck;

(f) to an electrically propelled goods vehicle;

(g) to a pedestrian controlled vehicle;

(h) to a vehicle in respect of which, under section 23 of the Purchase Tax Act 1963, any tax has been remitted and has not subsequently become payable or which has been zero rated under Regulation 44 or 45 of the Value Added Tax (General) Regulations 1972;

(i) to a motor car manufactured before 30th June 1964; or

(j) to a vehicle which has been used on roads outside Great Britain and has been imported into Great Britain, whilst it is being driven after its importation into Great Britain on the journey from the place where it has arrived in Great Britain to a place of residence of the owner or driver of the vehicle, and on the journey from any such place to a place where, by a previous arrangement, the vehicle will be provided with such anchorage points and seat belts as will comply with the requirements of this Regulation.

(3) Every vehicle to which this Regulation applies shall be provided with anchorage points designed to hold body-restraining seat belts securely in position on the vehicle for—

(a) the driver's seat; and

(b) the specified passenger's seat (if any):

Provided that this paragraph shall not apply so as to require anchorage points to be provided for any seat which is a seat with integral seat belt anchorages.

(4) Every vehicle to which this Regulation applies shall be provided with—

(a) a body-restraining seat belt designed for use by an adult for the driver's seat;   and

(b) a body-restraining seat belt for the specified passenger's seat (if any):

Provided that this paragraph shall not apply to a vehicle—

(a) while it is being used under a trade licence within the meaning of the Vehicles (Excise) Act 1971;   or

(b) while it is being driven from premises of the manufacturer by whom it was made, or of a distributor of vehicles or dealer in vehicles—

(i) to premises of a distributor of vehicles, dealer in vehicles or purchaser thereof, or

(ii) to premises of a person obtaining possession thereof under a hiring agreement or hire-purchase agreement.

(5) Every seat belt provided in pursuance of this Regulation shall, if the seat for which it is provided is a seat with integral seat belt anchorages, be properly secured to the integral seat belt anchorage points forming part thereof, or, if the seat for which it is provided is not such a seat, be properly secured to the structure of the vehicle by the anchorage points provided for it under paragraph (3) of this Regulation and to any other anchorage points provided in the seat for it.

(6) Subject to the next succeeding paragraph, where a seat belt, other than a restraining device for a young person or a seat belt comprising a lap belt and shoulder straps, is provided in pursuance of this Regulation for a motor car or a motor cycle first used on or after 1st April 1973, and in either case manufactured on or after 1st October 1972, the following additional conditions shall apply as respects that seat belt—

(a) the belt shall be so arranged that a person can, when sitting in the seat for which the belt is provided and with the belt previously adjusted to fit him, remove the belt from the device required by sub-paragraph (c) of this paragraph and by using one hand, or by taking the belt with one hand and transferring it from one hand to the other, put the belt on;

(b) the fastenings by means of which the belt is secured on the wearer shall be so designed that they can be engaged with a single movement of one hand in one direction and released with such a movement in one direction;

(c) an efficient device, unlikely to become dislodged in normal use, for retaining the belt in position when stowed away shall be provided and the centre of this device shall be located not more than 75 millimetres behind a point which is in the same horizontal plane and is positioned on the rear side of the door aperture provided for access to the front seat:

For the purpose of determining the position of the aforesaid point the door and any rubber, felt or other soft trimming or sealing material around the door aperture shall be disregarded;

(d) the said device shall be at a sufficient height from the floor of the vehicle to ensure that, so far as is practicable, any part of the belt that would come in contact with the clothing of a person wearing the belt in normal circumstances does not lie on the floor when the belt is in the stowed position;

(e) it shall be possible to stow away the belt for retention on the device mentioned in sub-paragraph (c) of this paragraph without employing any manual device for adjusting the belt to fit the wearer; and

(f) the belt, after being put on by the wearer, shall either adjust automatically to fit him or be such that the said manual device shall be convenient to use and capable of being operated with one hand.

(7) The last preceding paragraph shall not apply to:—

(a) a seat belt fitted to the specified passenger's seat which is treated as such by virtue of sub-paragraph (b) of paragraph (9) of this Regulation; or

(b) a seat belt fitted to the specified passenger's seat of a goods vehicle which has an unladen weight of more than 915 kilograms and has more than one forward facing front seat for a passenger alongside the driver's seat any such seats for passengers being joined together in a single structure.

(8) (a) Every motor car manufactured on or after 1st September 1966, and registered on or after 1st April 1967, and every three-wheeled motor cycle manufactured on or after 1st April 1972, and first used on or after 1st October 1972, which is provided with seat belt anchorage points in pursuance of paragraph (3) of this Regulation shall be legibly and permanently marked with the specification number of the British Standard for seat belt anchorage points, namely either B.S. AU 48: 1965: or B.S. AU 48a.

(b) where in the case of any motor car to which this Regulation applies and which was registered on or after 1st April 1967, or in the case of any motor cycle to which this Regulation applies and which is first used on or after 1st October 1972, the driver's seat or the specified passenger's seat is a seat with integral seat belt anchorages, such seat shall be legibly and permanently marked with the specification number of the British Standard for Seats with Integral Seat Belt Anchorages followed by the suffix " 1 ", namely, either B.S. AU 140/1: 1967 or B.S. AU 140a/1.

(c) if any seat with integral seat belt anchorages is provided on or after 1st January 1969, for a motor car to which this Regulation applies and which was manufactured on or after 1st September 1966, and registered on or after 1st April 1967, or is provided on or after 1st July 1971, for a motor cycle to which this Regulation applies and which is manufactured on or after 1st January 1971, and first used on or after 1st July 1971, the vehicle for which it is so provided shall be legibly and permanently marked with the specification number, namely, either B.S. AU 140: 1967: or B.S. AU 140a.

(d) each seat belt provided for any person in any vehicle to which this Regulation applies shall be legibly and permanently marked with the specification number of the British Standard for Seat Belt Assemblies for Motor Vehicles, namely, either B.S. 3254: 1960 or, except in the case of a restraining device for a young person, B.S. AU 160a, and with the registered certification trade mark of the British Standards Institution.

(9) In this Regulation—

" body-restraining seat belt " means a seat belt designed to provide restraint for both the upper and lower parts of the trunk of the wearer in the event of an accident to the vehicle;

" seat belt " means a belt intended to be worn by a person in a vehicle and designed to prevent or lessen injury to its wearer in the event of an accident to the vehicle and includes, in the case of a restraining device for a young person, any special chair to which the belt is attached;

" seat with integral seat belt anchorages " means a seat which is fitted with all the anchorage points required for use in connection with the seat belt provided for that seat, and

" specified passenger's seat " means—

(a) in the case of a vehicle which has one forward-facing front seat alongside the driver's seat, such seat, and in the case of a vehicle which has more than one such seat, the one furthest from the driver's seat; or

(b) if the vehicle normally has no seat which is the specified passenger's seat under the last preceding sub-paragraph, the forward-facing front seat for a passenger which is foremost in the vehicle and furthest from the driver's seat, unless there is a fixed partition separating such seat from the space in front of it alongside the driver's seat.

Speedometer

18. To every motor vehicle first used on or after 1st October 1937, there shall be fitted an instrument so constructed and in such a position as at all times readily to indicate to the driver of the vehicle the speed thereof within a margin of accuracy of plus or minus 10 per cent. if and when he is driving at a speed in excess of 10 miles per hour:

Provided that this Regulation shall not apply—

(a) to an invalid carriage;

(b) to a motor cycle, the cylinder capacity of the engine of which does not exceed 100 c.c.;

(c) to a motor cycle neither constructed or adapted for use nor used for the carriage of a driver or passenger;

(d) to a vehicle which it is at all times unlawful to drive at a speed exceeding 12 miles per hour;

(e) to a vehicle which is incapable by reason of its construction of exceeding a speed of 12 miles per hour on the level under its own power; or

(f) to a works truck.

Construction of petrol tank

19. Every motor vehicle first used on or after 1st July 1973, and not manufactured before 1st February 1973, shall be so constructed that—

(a) any tank, in which petroleum-spirit as defined in section 23 of the Petroleum (Consolidation) Act 1928 used either for the propulsion of the vehicle or for the driving of any ancillary engine or equipment forming part of the vehicle is contained, is made only of metal;

(b) the said tank is fixed on the vehicle in such a position that it is reasonably secure against its being damaged; and

(c) the leakage of any liquid or vapour from the said tank is adequately prevented so, however, that nothing in this paragraph shall be taken to preclude the tank being fitted with a device which by the intake of air or the emission of vapour relieves changes in pressure in the tank.

Diameter of wheels

20. All wheels of a motor vehicle and all wheels of a trailer which are fitted with tyres other than pneumatic tyres shall have a rim diameter of not less than 670 mm.:

Provided that this Regulation shall not apply—

(a) to any motor vehicle first used on or before 2nd January 1933;
(b) to any trailer manufactured before 1st January 1933;
(c) to any wheel fitted to a motor car first used on or before 1st July 1936, if the diameter of the wheel inclusive of the tyre is not less than 670 mm.;
(d) to any works truck or works trailer;
(e) to any motor vehicle or trailer designed for use and used solely in connection with street cleansing, the collection or disposal of refuse or the collection or disposal of the contents of gullies or cesspools;
(f) to any pedestrian controlled vehicle;
(g) to any mobile crane;
(h) to any land implement;
(i) to any broken down vehicle which is being drawn by a motor vehicle in consequence of the breakdown; or
(j) to any electrically propelled goods vehicle the unladen weight of which does not exceed 1270 kilograms.

Reversing

21. Every motor vehicle which exceeds 410 kilograms in weight unladen shall be capable of being so worked that it may travel either forwards or backwards.

View to the front

22. Every motor vehicle shall be so designed and constructed that the driver thereof while controlling the vehicle can at all times have a full view of the road and traffic ahead of the motor vehicle.

Mirrors

23.—(1) Save as provided in paragraph (2) of this Regulation—

(a) the following motor vehicles, that is to say, every passenger vehicle adapted to carry more than seven passengers exclusive of the driver and every goods vehicle, including every dual-purpose vehicle, but excluding locomotives and motor tractors, shall be equipped with at least two mirrors one of which shall be fitted externally on the off-side of the vehicle and the other either internally or on the nearside externally and the mirrors shall be so constructed and fitted to the motor vehicle as to assist the driver, if he so desires, to become aware of traffic to the rear and on both sides rearwards; and

(b) every land tractor shall be equipped with a mirror fitted externally on the off-side of the tractor and so constructed and fitted to the tractor as to assist the driver, if he so desires, to become aware of traffic on that side rearwards, unless he can easily obtain a clear view of traffic to the rear (including traffic to the rear of any trailer being drawn) without having any mirror fitted to the tractor; and

(c) subject to the provisions of the foregoing sub-paragraphs every motor vehicle shall be equipped either internally or externally with a mirror so constructed and fitted to the motor vehicle as to assist the driver, if he so desires, to become aware of traffic to the rear of the vehicle.

(2) Paragraph (1) of this Regulation shall not apply—

(a) to a two-wheeled motor cycle with or without a sidecar attached;

(b) to a land locomotive;

(c) to a motor vehicle when drawing a trailer if a person is carried on the trailer in a position which affords an uninterrupted view to the rear and such a person is provided with efficient means of communicating to the driver the effect of signals given by the drivers of other vehicles to the rear thereof;

(d) to a works truck if the driver can easily obtain a clear view of traffic to the rear; or

(e) to a pedestrian controlled vehicle.

(3) In the case of a motor vehicle first used on or after 1st April 1969, the edges of any mirror fitted internally to the vehicle to assist any person, if he so desires, to become aware of traffic to the rear of the vehicle shall be surrounded by some material such as will render those edges and that material unlikely to cause severe cuts in the event of the mirror or that material being struck by any occupant of the vehicle.

Safety glass

24.—(1) In the case of motor vehicles first used on or after 1st January 1959—

(a) being passenger vehicles or dual-purpose vehicles, the glass of windscreens and all windows on the outside,

(b) being goods vehicles, other than dual-purpose vehicles, and locomotives and motor tractors, the glass of windscreens and all windows in front and on either side of the driver's seat,

shall be safety glass.

(2) Save as provided in the foregoing paragraph, the glass of windscreens and windows facing to the front on the outside of any motor vehicle, except glass fitted to the upper deck of a double-decked vehicle, shall be safety glass.

For the purposes of this paragraph any windscreen or window at the front of the vehicle the inner surface of which is at an angle exceeding 30 degrees to the longitudinal axis of the vehicle shall be deemed to face to the front.

Windscreen wipers

25.—(1) In the case of a vehicle which is fitted with a windscreen, the vehicle shall be fitted with one or more efficient automatic windscreen wipers, unless the driver can obtain an adequate view to the front of the vehicle without looking through windscreen, for example by opening the windscreen or looking over it.

(2) The windscreen wipers required by the last preceding paragraph shall be capable of clearing the windscreen so that the driver has an adequate view of the road in front of the near and off sides of the vehicle in addition to an adequate view to the front of the vehicle.

Windscreen washers

26.—(1) Subject to the following paragraph every motor vehicle, which is required to be fitted with one or more efficient automatic windscreen wipers by virtue of the last preceding Regulation, shall be fitted with a windscreen washer capable of clearing, in conjunction with those windscreen wipers, the area of the windscreen swept by those windscreen wipers of mud or other similar deposit.

(2) This Regulation shall not apply to land tractors, vehicles which are incapable by reason of their construction of exceeding 20 miles per hour on the level under their own power or vehicles being used for the time being as stage carriages or on any journey incidental to such use.

Audible warning instrument

27.—(1) Subject to the provisions of this Regulation, every motor vehicle shall be fitted with an instrument capable of giving audible and sufficient warning of its approach or position.

(2) The sound emitted by any instrument of the kind described in the preceding paragraph fitted to a motor vehicle, being a motor vehicle first used on or after 1st August 1973, shall be continuous and uniform and not strident.

(3) Paragraph (1) of this Regulation shall not apply to a works truck or a pedestrian controlled vehicle.

(4) Except as provided in paragraphs (5) and (6) of this Regulation, no motor vehicle shall be fitted with a gong, bell, siren or two-tone horn.

(5) The following vehicles may be fitted with a gong, bell, siren or two-tone horn—

(*a*) motor vehicles used for fire brigade, ambulance or police purposes;

(*b*) motor vehicles owned by a body formed primarily for the purposes of fire salvage and used for those or similar purposes;

(*c*) motor vehicles owned by the Forestry Commission or by local authorities and used from time to time for the purposes of fighting fires;

(*d*) motor vehicles owned by the Secretary of State for Defence and used for the purposes of the disposal of bombs or explosives;

(*e*) motor vehicles used for the purposes of the Blood Transfusion Service under Part II of the National Health Service Act 1946, or under Part II of the National Health Service (Scotland) Act 1947;

(*f*) motor vehicles used by Her Majesty's Coastguards or the Coastguard Auxiliary Service to aid persons in danger or vessels in distress on or near the coast, and

(*g*) motor vehicles owned by the National Coal Board and used for the purposes of rescue operations at mines.

(6) A motor vehicle used for the conveyance of goods for sale from the vehicle may, if it is also fitted with an instrument or apparatus for the purpose of complying with paragraph (1) of this Regulation, be fitted

with an instrument or apparatus other than a two-tone horn designed to emit a sound for the purpose of informing members of the public that goods are on the vehicle for sale.

(7) References in paragraphs (4) and (5) of this Regulation to a gong, bell or siren include references to any instrument or apparatus capable of emitting a sound similar to that emitted by a gong, bell or siren.

Silencer

28. Every vehicle propelled by an internal combustion engine shall be fitted with a silencer, expansion chamber or other contrivance suitable and sufficient for reducing as far as may be reasonable the noise caused by the escape of the exhaust gases from the engine.

Noise

29.—(1) Except as provided in the next following paragraph of this Regulation, every motor vehicle first used after 1st April 1970, shall be so constructed that, at a time when the noise emitted by it is measured under the specified conditions by an apparatus of the kind prescribed by paragraph (3) of this Regulation, the sound level (A weighting) in decibels indicated by that apparatus in relation to the said noise so measured does not exceed the sound level which appears in Column 2 of Schedule 9 as the maximum sound level (A weighting) in decibels permitted for the relevant class or description of vehicle shown against that sound level in Column 1 of that Schedule.

(2) This Regulation shall not apply—

> (*a*) to a motor vehicle proceeding to a place where, by previous arrangement—
>
>> (i) noise emitted by it is about to be measured for the purpose of ascertaining whether or not that vehicle complies with this Regulation, or
>>
>> (ii) the vehicle is about to be mechanically adjusted, modified or equipped for the purpose of securing that it so complies, or
>
> (*b*) to a motor vehicle returning from such a place immediately after the noise has been so measured, or the vehicle has been so adjusted, modified or equipped, or
>
> (*c*) to a road roller.

(3) The apparatus prescribed for the purposes of paragraph (1) of this Regulation shall be a noise meter—

> (*a*) which, at the time when it is used for those purposes, is in good working order and complies with the requirements laid down by the British Standards Institution for vehicle noise meters in Part I of the British Standard Specification for Sound Level Meters published on 7th September 1962, under the number B.S. 3539: 1962, as amended by Amendment Slip No. 1 numbered AMD22 and published on 1st July 1968, and
>
> (*b*) which has, not more than 12 months before the date of the measurement made in accordance with the said paragraph (1), undergone all the tests for checking calibration applicable in accordance with the Appendix to the said British Standard Specification, and
>
> (*c*) in respect of which there has been issued by the National Physical Laboratory, the British Standards Institution or the Secretary of State a certificate recording the date on which as a result of those

tests the meter was found to comply with the requirements of clauses 8 and 9 of the said British Standard Specification.

(4) In this Regulation, " the specified conditions " means the method of measuring the noise emitted by motor vehicles (excluding signalling devices) which is described by the British Standard Method for the Measurement of Noise Emitted by Motor Vehicles published on 24th June 1966, under the number B.S. 3425: 1966.

(5) The definition of sound level (A weighting) in decibels contained in clause 2 of the British Standard numbered B.S. 3539: 1962, as amended by the said Amendment Slip No. 1, shall apply for the purposes of this Regulation and Schedule 9.

Radio Interference Suppression

30.—(1) This Regulation applies to every motor vehicle first used on or after 1st April 1974, and not manufactured before 1st October 1973, which is propelled by a spark ignition engine.

(2) Every motor vehicle to which this Regulation applies shall be legibly and indelibly marked in a conspicuous and readily accessible position with the marking designated as an approval mark by Regulation 2 (1) of the Motor Vehicles (Designation of Approval Marks) (No. 2) Regulations 1969 (which designates an approval mark that may be applied to a vehicle to indicate that the vehicle is fitted with certain parts consisting of radio interference suppression equipment).

Emission of smoke or vapour

31. Every motor vehicle shall be so constructed that no avoidable smoke or visible vapour is emitted therefrom.

32.—(1) This Regulation shall apply to every motor vehicle (other than a works truck) propelled by a compression ignition engine.

(2) Where a motor vehicle to which this Regulation applies is equipped with a device designed to facilitate the starting of the engine by causing it to be supplied with excess fuel the device and any apparatus by means of which it is operated shall be fitted in such a position, or such other provision shall be made, as to ensure that the device cannot readily be operated by a person while he is being carried by the vehicle:

Provided that this Regulation shall not apply in the case of a vehicle fitted with such a device as aforesaid if the device is so designed that—

    (i) its use after the engine has been started cannot cause the engine to be supplied with excess fuel, or

    (ii) it does not cause any increase in the smoke or visible vapour emitted from the vehicle.

33.—(1) This Regulation shall apply to every motor vehicle first used on or after 1st January 1972, and propelled by a spark ignition engine (not being a two-stroke engine) other than—

    (*a*) a vehicle manufactured before 1st July 1971; and

    (*b*) a two-wheeled motor cycle with or without a side-car attached, and

    (*c*) a vehicle to which Regulation 33A applies.

(2) The engine of every motor vehicle to which this Regulation applies shall be equipped with means sufficient to ensure that, while the engine is

running, any vapours or gases in the engine crank case or in any other part of the engine to which vapours or gases may pass from the said crank case are prevented, so far as is reasonably practicable, from escaping into the atmosphere otherwise than through the combustion chamber of the engine.

33A. (1) Except as provided by paragraph (2) below, this Regulation applies to every motor vehicle which is propelled by a spark ignition engine and which—

(a) in the case of any vehicle other than a vehicle described in paragraph (1A), (1B) or (1C) below, is first used on or after 10th November 1973;

(b) in the case of any of the vehicles described in the said paragraph (1A), is first used on or after 1st March 1974;

(c) in the case of any of the vehicles described in the said paragraph (1B), is first used on or after 1st November 1974; and

(d) in the case of the vehicles described in sub-paragraph (a) in the said paragraph (1C), is first used on or after 1st December 1975, and in the case of any of the other vehicles described in the said paragraph (1C), is first used on or after 1st December 1974.

(1A) The vehicles referred to in paragraph (1) (b) above are vehicles—

(a) manufactured by the Reliant Motor Company Limited, known as the Rebel Saloon, Estate or Van, allocated the Vehicle Identification number FW4B or FW4BE2, or

(b) manufactured by Chrysler (UK) Limited, known as—

(i) the Imp SC or DL S/C, or

(ii) the Imp Super S/C or Sport T/C, or

(iii) the Commer Semi-Forward Control vehicles allocated the Vehicle Identification number KC-25, KC-30 or KC-40, or

(iv) the Karrier Forward Control Light Commercial Truck allocated the Vehicle Identification number FB3, or

(v) the Commer Forward Control Light Commercial and Passenger Vehicles allocated the Vehicle Identification number PB 1500, PB 2000 or PB 2500.

(1B) The vehicles referred to in paragraph (1) (c) above are vehicles manufactured by British Leyland (U.K.) Limited, known as—

(a) the Mini 850 Saloon (automatic and manual), allocated the Vehicle Identification number XA2SI, or

(b) the Mini 850 Van (manual), allocated the Vehicle Identification number XAV1, or

(c) the Mini 850 Pick-up (manual), allocated the Vehicle Identification number XAU1, or

(d) the Mini 1000 Saloon (manual and automatic), allocated the Vehicle Identification number XA2SIN, or

(e) the Mini 1000 Van (manual), allocated the Vehicle Identification number XAV1, or

(f) the Mini 1000 Pick-up (manual), allocated the Vehicle Identification number XAU1, or

(g) the Mini Clubman Saloon (manual and automatic), allocated the Vehicle Identification number XA2S2, or

(h) the Mini Clubman Estate (manual and automatic), allocated the Vehicle Identification number XA2W2, or (*i*) the Mini 1275 GT (manual) allocated the Vehicle Identification number XAD2, or

    (*j*) the Austin 1300 Countryman (manual and automatic), allocated the Vehicle Identification number AAWA, or

    (*jj*) the Austin 1300 (manual and automatic), allocated the Vehicle Identification numbers AASAS and AAHDA or

    (*k*) the Vanden Plas Princess 1300 (manual and automatic), allocated the Vehicle Identification number VAS2, or

    (*l*) the Austin-Morris 180/200 J4 Petrol-engined Van, Pick-up, Chassis cab and chassis front end, allocated the Vehicle Identification number 180 J4 or 200 J4, or

    (*m*) the Austin-Morris 250 JU Petrol-engined Van, Pick-up, Chassis cab and Minibus, allocated the Vehicle Identification number 250 JU, or

    (*n*) the Austin 2200 (manual and automatic), allocated the Vehicle Identification number AB4 SE, or

    (*o*) the Morris 2200 (manual and automatic), allocated the Vehicle Identification number MB4 SE, or

    (*p*) the Wolseley 6 (manual and automatic), allocated the Vehicle Identification number WB4 SE, or

    (*q*) the MG-B-GT V8, allocated the Vehicle Identification number GD 2D1.

(1C) The vehicles referred to in paragraph (1) (*d*) above are vehicles—

    (*a*) being ambulances manufactured by British Leyland (UK) Limited, allocated the Vehicle Identification number 350 FG; or

    (*b*) manufactured by VEB Autommobilwerk Eisenach, known as the Wartburg Knight Saloon or the Wartburg Knight Estate, allocated the Vehicle Identification numbers 353-005 and 353-903 respectively; or

    (*c*) manufactured by Chrysler (UK) Limited, known as—

        (i) the Sunbeam/Hillman Hunter GLS (manual), allocated the Vehicle Identification number 040-Q-2, or

        (ii) the Sunbeam/Hillman Hunter GLS (overdrive), allocated the Vehicle Identification number 040-Q-3, or

        (iii) the Sunbeam Rapier H120, allocated the Vehicle Identification number 120-Q-3; or

    (*d*) manufactured by the Ford Motor Company Limited, known as the 2·0 litre V4 Capri, allocated the Vehicle Identification number ECJ; or

    (*e*) manufactured by Bristol Cars, known as the Bristol Model 411 Series IV.

(2) This Regulation does not apply to:

    (*a*) a vehicle manufactured before 20th September 1973;

    (*b*) a vehicle described in paragraph (1A) of this Regulation manufactured before 1st January 1974;

    (*c*) a vehicle described in paragraph (1B) of this Regulation manufactured before 20th September 1974;

    (*d*) a vehicle described in sub-paragraph (*a*) of paragraph (1C) of this Regulation manufactured before 20th September, 1975, and any other vehicle described in the said paragrph (1C) manufactured before 20th September 1974;

    (*e*) a vehicle with less than four wheels, if—

      (i) its weight, whether laden or unladen, does not exceed 400 kilograms; or

      (ii) it is not so constructed as to be capable of exceeding a speed of 30 miles per hour on the level under its own power; or

  (*f*) a vehicle, the weight of which whether laden or unladen exceeds 3500 kilograms.

(3) Every vehicle to which this Regulation applies and which is manufactured before 1st October, 1976, or first used before 1st April 1977, shall be legibly and indelibly marked in a conspicuous and readily accessible position—

      (i) with the marking designated as an approval mark by Regulation 2 (3) of the Motor Vehicles (Designation of Approval Marks) (No. 2) Regulations 1972, or

      (ii) with the marking designated as an approval mark by Regulation 2 of the Motor Vehicles (Designation of Approval Marks) Regulations 1975

(which respectively designate approval marks that may be applied to a vehicle to indicate that the vehicle meets certain requirements concerning the emission of gaseous pollutants by the engine thereof).

(4) Every vehicle to which this Regulation applies and which is manufactured on or after 1st October, 1976, and first used on or after 1st April, 1977, shall be legibly and indelibly marked in a conspicuous and readily accessible position with the marking designated as an approval mark by Regulation 2 of the said Motor Vehicles (Designation of Approval Marks) Regulations 1975.

Vehicles propelled by a compression ignition engine to meet certain requirements as to emission of smoke

34.—(1) Subject to the provisions of paragraph (3) of this Regulation, every motor vehicle first used on or after 1st April 1973, and not manufactured before 1st October 1972, which is propelled by a compression ignition engine, shall be so constructed that the engine thereof is of a type for which there has been issued by a person authorised by the Secretary of State a type test certificate in accordance with the British Standard Specification for the Performance of Diesel Engines for Road Vehicles published on the 19th May 1971, under the number BS AU 141a: 1971, the said certificate indicating that that type of engine does not, as respects the emission of smoke, exceed the acceptable upper limits of exhaust gas opacity as laid down in clause 7 of the said Specification.

(2) In the application of the provisions of the preceding paragraph to a motor vehicle which is a land tractor, industrial tractor, works truck or engineering plant, for the purposes of the measurements laid down in the said specification of exhaust gas opacity of the engine of any such vehicle leading to the issue of a type test certificate mentioned in that paragraph, those measurements shall be made with the engine running at 80 per cent. of its full load over the speed range from maximum speed down to the speed at which maximum torque occurs as declared by the manufacturer of the engine for the said purposes.

(3) This Regulation shall not apply to:—

  (*a*) a land tractor, land locomotive, industrial tractor, works truck or engineering plant which is propelled by a compression ignition engine having not more than 2 cylinders; or (*b*) a motor vehicle propelled by a compression ignition engine, known as the Perkins 6·354 engine, being a vehicle manufactured before 1st April 1973.

Emission of sparks or grit

35. Every motor vehicle using solid fuel shall be fitted—

(*a*) with an efficient appliance for the purpose of preventing the emission of sparks or grit; and

(*b*) with a tray or shield to prevent ashes and cinders from falling on to the road.

Closets, urinals, lavatory basins and sinks

36. No motor vehicle first used on or after 15th January 1931, or trailer shall be equipped with any closet, urinal, lavatory basin or sink, unless the following requirements are complied with, that is to say—

(*a*) no vehicle shall be equipped with a closet or urinal the contents of which can be discharged directly on to a road and, except in the case of a living van, every closet pan or urinal pan shall empty into a tank carried by the vehicle, such tank being efficiently ventilated by means of a pipe the outlet of which is outside the vehicle;

(*b*) every tank into which a closet pan or urinal pan empties and, where no such tank is fitted, every closet and urinal, shall contain non-inflammable and non-irritant chemicals of such character and in such quantity as to form at all times an efficient deodorant and germicide in respect of the contents of the tank, closet or urinal as the case may be; and

(*c*) no lavatory basin or sink shall drain into any closet or urinal or into any tank into which a closet or urinal empties.

[*Regulation 37 provides for the maximum seating capacity of half-decked vehicles.*]

Lighting equipment and reflectors

38.—(1) Every motor vehicle shall be equipped with such lighting equipment and reflectors as to render the vehicle capable of being driven on a road during the hours of darkness without contravention of any of the statutory provisions relating to obligatory lamps or reflectors which are applicable to that vehicle:

Provided that this paragraph shall not apply to a motor vehicle which is not provided with any front lamp or rear lamp.

(2) Where a motor vehicle is provided with a headlamp that lamp shall be so constructed and fitted to the vehicle that if that lamp were to be used to show a light to the front while the vehicle was driven on a road during the hours of darkness such use would not be in contravention of the provisions of Regulation 9 of the Road Vehicles Lighting Regulations 1971.

(3) For the purposes of the foregoing provisions of this Regulation, a vehicle shall not be treated as provided with any such lamp as is mentioned in those provisions by reason of its carrying such a lamp if—

(*a*) that lamp is so painted over or fitted with a mask that it is not capable of being immediately used, or readily put to use, to show, in the case of a front lamp, a light to the front or, in the case of a rear lamp, a light to the rear; or

(b) where the lamp is a lamp constructed to show a light derived from an electric bulb or bulbs, the vehicle is not provided with any system of wiring by means of which that lamp is, or can readily be, connected with a source of electricity.

(4) In this Regulation—

(a) the expressions " front lamp " and " rear lamp " in relation to a vehicle, mean respectively—

(i) a lamp carried by that vehicle which faces, or is capable of being readily moved so as to face, to the front, and

(ii) a lamp carried by that vehicle which faces, or is capable of being readily moved so as to face, to the rear,

whether (in either case) that lamp does or does not contain a burner or an electric bulb by means of which it can be used to show a light:

Provided that neither of the said expressions shall include any lamp carried by a vehicle for any one or more of the following purposes only, that is to say,—

(i) for use as, or to illuminate, a direction indicator,

(ii) for intimating the intention of the driver of the vehicle to stop or slow down,

(iii) for showing a light to the rear when reversing the vehicle, and

(iv) for the internal illumination of the vehicle,

or any lamp carried by a vehicle which is a land locomotive, a land tractor, a mobile crane, a straddle carrier, a works truck or a vehicle which is movable plant or equipment specially designed or constructed for the purposes of engineering operations, if the lamp is carried by the vehicle for the purpose of providing illumination so as to enable the vehicle to be used at night otherwise than on a road for the particular operations for which it is designed or constructed;

(b) the expression " statutory provisions relating to obligatory lamps or reflectors " means the provisions contained in sections 68 to 73 and 76 to 79 of the Road Traffic Act 1972, or in any regulations made or having effect as if made under those sections with respect to the lamps or reflectors which are thereby required to be carried on vehicles while they are on a road during the hours of darkness, not being provisions which apply to such vehicles only when they are carrying a load overhanging laterally or projecting to the rear or are drawing or being drawn by another vehicle, or are over a length prescribed by the regulations; and

(c) the expression " headlamp ", in relation to a vehicle, means a front lamp fitted to that vehicle and constructed for the purpose of showing a light derived from an acetylene burner or from an electric bulb the rated wattage of which, or from electric bulbs the total rated wattage of which, exceeds 7 watts, whether the lamp does or does not contain any such burner or any such bulb or bulbs.

Certain vehicles to be equipped with plates

39.—(1) This Regulation applies to:—

   (*a*) every heavy motor car and motor car first used on or after 1st January 1968, not being a passenger vehicle, a dual purpose vehicle, a land tractor, a works truck, or a pedestrian controlled vehicle; and

   (*b*) every locomotive and motor tractor first used on or after 1st April 1973, not being—

   (i) a land locomotive;
   (ii) a land tractor;
   (iii) an industrial tractor;
   (iv) a works truck;
   (v) engineering plant;
   (vi) a pedestrian controlled vehicle; or
   (vii) a vehicle manufactured before 1st October 1972; and

   (*c*) every trailer manufactured on or after 1st January 1968, which exceeds 1020 kilograms in weight unladen and is other than:—

   (i) a trailer not constructed or adapted to carry any load, other than plant or special appliance or apparatus which is a permanent or essentially permanent fixture, and not exceeding 2290 kilograms in total weight;
   (ii) a living van not exceeding 2040 kilograms in weight unladen and fitted with pneumatic tyres;
   (iii) a works trailer;
   (iv) a trailer mentioned in Regulation 70 (3); or
   (v) a trailer which was manufactured and used outside Great Britain before it was first used in Great Britain.

(2) Every vehicle to which this Regulation applies shall be equipped with a plate securely affixed to the vehicle in a conspicuous and readily accessible position and the said plate shall contain in the case of a heavy motor car, motor car, locomotive or motor tractor the particulars required by Part I of Schedule 2 and in the case of a trailer the particulars required by Part II of that Schedule, the said particulars being completed in accordance with Part III of that Schedule and the plate otherwise complying with the provisions contained in that Part.

Certain vehicles to satisfy a minimum power to weight ratio

40.—(1) Subject to the provisions of paragraph (2) of this Regulation—

   (*a*) every heavy motor car and motor car first used on or after 1st April, 1973, and not manufactured before 1st October 1972, and otherwise falling within Regulation 39 (1) (*a*), and

   (*b*) every locomotive and motor tractor falling within Regulation 39 (1) (*b*);

which is propelled by a compression ignition engine, shall be so constructed that the number indicating the power of the engine at item 3 on the plate with which the vehicle is equipped in accordance with paragraph (2) of Regulation 39 is such that it indicates that the engine produces at least 4·4 kilowatts for every 1000 kilograms of the relevant weight.

In this paragraph " relevant weight " means the maximum train weight of the vehicle shown at item 8 on the said plate or, if no such weight is so shown, the maximum gross weight of the vehicle shown at item 7 on the said plate.

(2) Nothing in the preceding paragraph shall apply in the case of a vehicle propelled by a compression ignition engine, known as the Perkins 6·354 engine, being a vehicle manufactured before 1st April 1973.

41.—(1) Every motor vehicle to which Regulation 40 applies shall, where it is fitted with ancillary equipment designed for use or likely to be used when the vehicle is in motion on a road at a speed in excess of 5 miles per hour and the power absorbed by that equipment is provided by the engine propelling the vehicle, be so constructed that, when the said ancillary equipment is being used, the power of the engine remaining available to drive the vehicle is at least 4·4 kilowatts for every 1000 kilograms of the relevant weight.

(2) For the purposes of this Regulation " ancillary equipment " means machinery or apparatus forming part of the vehicle or mounted thereon, used for purposes not connected with the driving of the vehicle and " relevant weight " has the meaning given in the last preceding Regulation.

[*Regulation 42 and Sched. 3 relate to the requirements for gas containers for vehicles propelled by gas.*]

C.—LOCOMOTIVES

Overall width

43. The overall width of a locomotive shall not exceed 2·75 metres.

Distribution of weight

44.—(1) This Regulation shall apply to every locomotive having not more than four wheels and first used before 1st June 1955.

(2) Not more than three-quarters of the total weight of a locomotive to which this Regulation applies shall be transmitted to the road surface by any two wheels.

Tyres

45.—(1) Save as provided in paragraph (2) of this Regulation, every wheel of a locomotive shall be fitted with a pneumatic tyre or a tyre of soft or elastic material which either—

(*a*) extends continuously round the circumference of the wheel; or
(*b*) is fitted in sections in such manner that—

(i) at no point is any section separated by more than 20 millimetres from any adjacent section, and
(ii) the aggregate extent of all spaces between the sections measured along any line taken round the outer surface of the tyre and parallel to its edge does not exceed 150 millimetres.

(2) Paragraph (1) of this Regulation shall not apply to a land locomotive if—

(*a*) the tyre of every steering wheel is smooth-soled and where the tyre touches the surface of the road it is not less than 125 millimetres in width, and
(*b*) the tyre of every driving wheel is not less than 300 millimetres in width and is either—

(i) smooth-soled,

(ii) shod with diagonal cross bars of not less than 76 millimetres in width nor more than 20 millimetres in thickness, extending the full breadth of the tyre and so arranged that the space intervening between adjacent cross bars is not more than 76 millimetres, or

(iii) shod with diagonal cross bars of soft or elastic material of not less than 60 millimetres in width, extending the full breadth of the tyre and so arranged that the space between adjacent cross bars is not more than 76 millimetres.

Brakes

46. Every locomotive first used before 1st June 1955, shall be equipped with an efficient braking system, the brakes of which act upon all the wheels of the vehicle other than the steering wheels, and so designed and constructed that the application of the brakes will bring the vehicle to rest within a reasonable distance:

Provided that this Regulation shall not apply to a locomotive first used on or before 2nd January 1933, if the locomotive is propelled by steam and the engine thereof is capable of being reversed.

47.—(1) This Regulation shall apply to every locomotive first used on or after 1st June 1955.

(2) Every locomotive to which this Regulation applies shall be equipped with an efficient braking system or efficient braking systems in either case having two means of operation, so designed and constructed that notwithstanding the failure of any part (other than a fixed member or a brake shoe anchor pin) through or by means of which the force necessary to apply the brakes is transmitted, there shall still be available for application by the driver to not less than half the number of the wheels of the vehicle brakes sufficient under the most adverse conditions to bring the vehicle to rest within a reasonable distance:

Provided that this paragraph shall not apply in the case of a road roller if the vehicle is equipped with one braking system with one means of operation.

(3) The application of one means of operation shall not affect or operate the pedal or hand lever of the other means of operation.

(4) No braking system shall be rendered ineffective by the non-rotation of the engine.

(5) All the brakes which are operated by one of the means of operation shall be capable of being applied by direct mechanical action without the intervention of any hydraulic, electric or pneumatic device.

(6) Where any brake shoe is capable of being applied by more than one means of operation, all the wheels of a locomotive to which this Regulation applies shall be fitted with brakes all of which are operated by one of the means of operation:

Provided that—

(a) where a vehicle has more than six wheels, at least four of which are steering wheels, it shall be a sufficient compliance with this paragraph if brakes are fitted to all the wheels, other than two steering wheels which are situated on opposite sides of the vehicle, and if all such brakes are operated by one of the means of operation;

(b) where a vehicle has more than four wheels and the drive is transmitted to all wheels other than the steering wheels without the interposition of a differential driving gear or similar mechanism between the axles carrying the driving wheels, it shall be deemed to be a sufficient compliance with this paragraph if one means of operation operates the brakes on two driving wheels situated on opposite sides of the vehicle and the other means of operation operates brakes on all the other wheels required to be fitted with brakes by this paragraph; and

(c) where means of operation are provided in addition to those prescribed by this Regulation such additional means of operation may be disregarded for the purposes of this paragraph.

(7) One at least of the means of operation shall be capable of causing brakes to be applied directly, and not through the transmission gear, to not less than half the number of the wheels of the vehicle:

Provided that where a locomotive to which this Regulation applies has more than four wheels and the drive is transmitted to all wheels other than the steering wheels without the interposition of a differential driving gear or similar mechanism between the axles carrying the driving wheels, it shall be deemed to be a sufficient compliance with this paragraph if the brakes applied by one means of operation act directly on two driving wheels on opposite sides of the vehicle and the brakes applied by the other means of operation act directly on all other driving wheels.

(8) For the purpose of this Regulation—

(a) not more than one front wheel shall be included in half the number of the wheels of the vehicle for the purposes aforesaid except that this provision shall not apply to a locomotive with more than three wheels, whether or not any brake shoe is capable of being applied by more than one means of operation, if as respects the fitting of its wheels with brakes and the operation of those brakes the provisions of paragraph (6) of this Regulation relating to such matters are complied with; and

(b) every moving shaft to which any part of a braking system or any means of operation thereof is connected or by which it is supported shall be deemed to be part of that system.

D.—Motor Tractors

Overall width

48. The overall width of a motor tractor shall not exceed 2·5 metres.

Overhang

49. The overhang of a motor tractor shall not exceed 1·83 metres.

Brakes

50.—(1) Every motor tractor shall be equipped with an efficient braking system or efficient braking systems in either case having two means of operation, so designed and constructed that, notwithstanding the failure of any part (other than a fixed member or a brake shoe anchor pin) through or by means of which the force necessary to apply the brakes is transmitted, there shall still be available for application by the driver to not less than half the number of the wheels of the vehicle brakes sufficient under the most adverse conditions to bring the vehicle to rest within a reasonable distance:

Provided that this paragraph shall not apply in the case of a road roller or a land tractor, not propelled by steam, if the vehicle is equipped with one braking system with one means of operation.

(2) The application of one means of operation shall not affect or operate the pedal or hand lever of the other means of operation.

(3) In the case of vehicles first used on or after 1st April 1938, no braking system shall be rendered ineffective by the non-rotation of the engine:

Provided that this paragraph shall not apply in the case of any vehicle referred to in sub-paragraph (b) of paragraph (7) of this Regulation.

(4) In the case of a motor tractor first used on or after 1st April 1938, all the brakes which are operated by one of the means of operation shall be capable of being applied by direct mechanical action without the intervention of any hydraulic, electric or pneumatic device.

(5) Where any brake shoe is capable of being applied by more than one means of operation, all the wheels of the motor tractor shall be fitted with brakes all of which are operated by one of the means of operation:

Provided that where means of operation are provided in addition to those prescribed by this Regulation such additional means of operation may be disregarded for the purposes of this paragraph.

(6) In the case of a motor tractor first used after 14th January 1931, other than a land tractor, one at least of the means of operation shall be capable of causing brakes to be applied directly, and not through the transmission gear, to not less than half the number of the wheels of the vehicle:

Provided that where a motor tractor has more than four wheels and the drive is transmitted to all wheels other than the steering wheels without the interposition of a differential driving gear or similar mechanism between the axles carrying the driving wheels, it shall be deemed to be a sufficient compliance with this paragraph if the brakes applied by one means of operation act directly on two driving wheels on opposite sides of the vehicle and the brakes applied by the other means of operation act directly on all other driving wheels.

(7) For the purpose of this Regulation—

(a) in the case of a motor tractor first used on or after 1st October 1938—

(i) not more than one front wheel shall be included in half the number of the wheels of the vehicle for the purposes aforesaid except that this provision shall not apply to a motor tractor with more than three wheels, whether or not any brake shoe is capable of being applied by more than one means of operation, if as respects the fitting of its wheels with brakes and the operation of those brakes the provisions of paragraph (5) of this Regulation relating to such matters are complied with, and

(ii) every moving shaft to which any part of a braking system or any means of operation thereof is connected or by which it is supported shall be deemed to be part of that system; and

(b) in the case of a motor tractor propelled by steam the engine shall be deemed to be an efficient braking system with one means of operation if the engine is capable of being reversed and, in the case of a motor tractor first used on or after 1st October 1943, is incapable of being disconnected from any of the driving wheels of the vehicle except by the sustained effort of the driver.

Tyres

51.—(1) Save as provided in paragraph (3) of this Regulation, every wheel of a motor tractor shall be fitted with a pneumatic tyre or a tyre of soft or elastic material.

(2) Recut pneumatic tyres shall not be fitted to any wheel of a motor tractor the weight of which unladen is less than 2540 kilograms unless the rim diameter of the wheel is 405 millimetres or more.

(3) Paragraph (1) of this Regulation shall not apply to a land tractor if—

(*a*) the tyre of every steering wheel is smooth-soled and where the tyre touches the surface of the road it is not less than 60 millimetres in width; and

(*b*) the tyre of every driving wheel, in the case of vehicles exceeding 3050 kilograms in weight unladen, is not less than 150 millimetres in width and, in the case of vehicles not exceeding 3050 kilograms in weight unladen, is not less than 76 millimetres in width and is either—

(i) smooth-soled,

(ii) shod with diagonal cross bars of not less than 76 millimetres in width nor more than 20 millimetres in thickness, extending the full breadth of the tyre and so arranged that the space between adjacent cross bars is not more than 76 millimetres, or

(iii) shod with diagonal cross bars of soft or elastic material of not less than 60 millimetres in width, extending the full breadth of the tyre and so arranged that the space between adjacent cross bars is not more than 76 millimetres.

E.—HEAVY MOTOR CARS

Overall width

52. The overall width of a heavy motor car shall not exceed 2·5 metres.

Overhang

53. The overhang of a heavy motor car shall not exceed 60 per cent. of the distance between the plane perpendicular to the longitudinal axis of the vehicle which passes through the centre or centres of the front wheel or wheels and the foremost vertical plane from which the overhang is to be measured as defined in Regulation 3:

Provided that—

(*a*) in the case of a vehicle designed for use and mainly used for the purpose of heating a road or other like surface in the process of construction, repair or maintenance, no part of the heating plant shall be taken into account when calculating the overhang; and

(*b*) this Regulation shall not apply in the case of—

(i) a heavy motor car first used before 15th August 1928,

(ii) a heavy motor car designed for use and used solely in connection with street cleansing, the collection or disposal of refuse or the collection or disposal of the contents of gullies or cesspools,

(iii) a works truck, or

(iv) a heavy motor car designed so that it can dispose of its load by tipping to the rear, if the overhang does not exceed 1·15 metres.

Brakes

54.—(1) Save as provided in paragraph (2) of this Regulation, every heavy motor car shall be equipped either with an efficient braking system having two means of operation or with two efficient braking systems each having a separate means of operation:

Provided that for the purpose of this paragraph no account shall be taken in the case of a heavy motor car first used on or after 1st January, 1968, of a multi-pull means of operation, unless that means, at the first application, operates an hydraulic, electric or pneumatic device which causes brakes to be applied sufficient to have a total braking efficiency of not less than the total braking efficiency required by paragraph (5) (*b*) of this Regulation in relation to brakes as applied by a second independent means of operation.

(2) Nothing in the paragraph (1) or (3) of this Regulation shall apply in the case of a heavy motor car, if the said vehicle is equipped with one efficient braking system with one means of operation and the said system is a split braking system.

(3) Save as provided in paragraph (2) of this Regulation, the braking system or braking systems of every heavy motor car first used after 15th August 1928, shall be so designed and constructed that, notwithstanding the failure of any part (other than a fixed member or a brake shoe anchor pin) through or by means of which the force necessary to apply the brakes is transmitted, there shall still be available for application by the driver to not less than half the number of the wheels of the vehicle brakes sufficient under the most adverse conditions to bring the vehicle to rest within a reasonable distance.

(4) The braking system or braking systems of every heavy motor car to which Schedule 4 applies and first used before 1st January 1968, shall comply with the requirements of that Schedule relating to the efficiency of the brakes of such heavy motor cars.

(5) The braking system or braking systems of every heavy motor car first used on or after 1st January 1968, which is not a works truck or a pedestrian controlled vehicle, shall—

(*a*) have brakes acting on all the wheels of the vehicle which as applied by one means of operation have a total braking efficiency of not less than 50 per cent.;

(*b*) except in the case mentioned in the following sub-paragraph (*c*), have brakes which as applied by a second independent means of operation have a total braking efficiency of not less than 25 per cent.;

(*c*) in the case of a heavy motor car equipped with a split braking system in accordance with paragraph (2) of this Regulation, have brakes which in the event of a failure of any part (other than a fixed member or a brake shoe anchor pin) of one of the independent sections comprised in the split braking system are such that there remain brakes applied by the other section sufficient to have a total braking efficiency of not less than 25 per cent.

(6) The braking system or braking systems of every heavy motor car first used after 15th August 1928, and before 1st January 1968, and

which is a goods vehicle other than a pedestrian controlled vehicle or a works truck and is a rigid vehicle with two axles shall—

(a) have brakes which as applied by one means of operation have a total braking efficiency of not less than 45 per cent.;

(b) except in the case mentioned in the following sub-paragraph (c), have brakes which as applied by a second independent means of operation have a total braking efficiency of not less than 20 per cent.;

(c) in the case of a heavy motor car equipped with a split braking system in accordance with paragraph (2) of this Regulation, have brakes which in the event of a failure of any part (other than a fixed member or a brake shoe anchor pin) of one of the independent sections comprised in the split braking system are such that there remain brakes applied by the other section sufficient to have a total braking efficiency of not less than 20 per cent.

(7) The braking system or braking systems of every heavy motor car first used after 15th August 1928, and before 1st January 1968, and which is a goods vehicle other than a pedestrian controlled vehicle or a works truck and is a rigid vehicle with more than two axles or is constructed or adapted to form part of an articulated vehicle shall—

(a) have brakes which as applied by one means of operation have a total braking efficiency of not less than 40 per cent.;

(b) except in the case mentioned in the following sub-paragraph (c), have brakes which as applied by a second independent means of operation have a total braking efficiency of not less than 15 per cent.;

(c) in the case of a heavy motor car equipped with a split braking system in accordance with paragraph (2) of this Regulation, have brakes which in the event of a failure of any part (other than a fixed member or a brake shoe anchor pin) of one of the independent sections comprised in the split braking system are such that there remain brakes applied by the other section sufficient to have a total braking efficiency of not less than 15 per cent.

(8) The braking system or braking systems of every heavy motor car first used on or before 15th August 1928, not being a heavy motor car to which the said Schedule 4 applies, shall be sufficient under the most adverse conditions to bring the vehicle to rest within a reasonable distance.

(9) Paragraphs (1) and (3) of this Regulation shall not apply in the case of a works truck if it is equipped with one braking system having one means of operation.

(10) The application of one means of operation shall not affect or operate the pedal or hand lever of the other means of operation.

(11) In the case of vehicles first used on or after 1st April 1938, no braking system shall be rendered ineffective by the non-rotation of the engine:

Provided that this paragraph shall not apply in the case of any vehicle referred to in paragraph (16) (b) of this Regulation.

(12) All the brakes of a heavy motor car which are operated by one means of operation shall be capable of being applied by direct mechanical action without the intervention of any hydraulic, electric or pneumatic device:

Provided that this paragraph shall not apply to a heavy motor car which satisfies the requirements of Regulation 13 (2) of these Regulations.

(13) In the case of a heavy motor car first used before 1st January 1968, where any brake shoe is capable of being applied by more than one means of operation all the wheels of the heavy motor car shall be fitted with brakes all of which are operated by one of the means of operation:

Provided that—

(a) where a heavy motor car has more than six wheels, at least four of which are steering wheels, it shall be a sufficient compliance with this paragraph if brakes are fitted to all the wheels, other than two steering wheels which are situated on opposite sides of the vehicle, and all such brakes are operated by one of the means of operation;

(b) where a heavy motor car has more than four wheels and the drive is transmitted to all wheels other than the steering wheels without the interposition of a differential driving gear or similar mechanism between the axles carrying the driving wheels, it shall be deemed to be a sufficient compliance with this paragraph if one means of operation operates the brakes on two driving wheels situated on opposite sides of the vehicle and the other means of operation operates brakes on all the other wheels required to be fitted with brakes by this paragraph; and

(c) where means of operation are provided in addition to those prescribed by this Regulation such additional means of operation may be disregarded for the purposes of this paragraph.

(14) One at least of the means of operation shall be capable of causing brakes to be applied directly, and not through the transmission gear, to not less than half the number of the wheels of the vehicle:

Provided that—

(a) in the case of a heavy motor car having brakes acting on all the wheels of the vehicle and capable of being applied by one means of operation, any shaft leading from any differential driving gear of an axle to a driving wheel shall be deemed not to form part of the transmission gear;

(b) where in the case of any other heavy motor car it has more than four wheels and the drive is transmitted to all wheels other than the steering wheels without the interposition of a differential driving gear or similar mechanism between the axles carrying the driving wheels, it shall be deemed to be a sufficient compliance with this paragraph if the brakes applied by one means of operation act directly on two driving wheels on opposite sides of the vehicle and the brakes applied by the other means of operation act directly on all other driving wheels.

(15) Paragraphs (10) to (14) inclusive of this Regulation shall not apply to a heavy motor car first used on or before 15th August 1928.

(16) For the purposes of this Regulation—

(a) in the case of any motor vehicle—

(i) not more than one front wheel shall be included in half the number of the wheels of the vehicle for the purposes aforesaid except that this provision shall not apply either to a heavy motor car with more than three wheels, whether or not any brake shoe is capable of being applied by more than one means of operation, if as respects the fitting of its wheels with brakes and the operation of those brakes the provisions of paragraph (13) of this Regulation relating to such matters are complied with, or to a works truck, and

(ii) every moving shaft to which any part of a braking system or any means of operation thereof is connected or by which it is supported shall be deemed to be part of that system; and

(b) in the case of a heavy motor car propelled by steam and not used as a public service vehicle the engine shall be deemed to be an efficient braking system with one means of operation if the engine is capable of being reversed and, in the case of a heavy motor car first used on or after 1st January 1927, is incapable of being disconnected from any of the driving wheels of the vehicle except by the sustained effort of the driver.

Tyres

55.—(1) Save as provided in paragraph (2) of this Regulation, every wheel of a heavy motor car shall be fitted with a pneumatic tyre.

(2) In the case of any of the following vehicles every wheel shall be fitted with a pneumatic tyre or a tyre of soft or elastic material:—

(a) heavy motor cars first used on or before 2nd January 1933;

(b) heavy motor cars exceeding 4070 kilograms in weight unladen mainly used in operations which necessitate working on rough ground or unmade roads;

(c) vehicles designed for use and used solely in connection with street cleansing, the collection or disposal of refuse or the collection or disposal of the contents of gullies or cesspools;

(d) turntable fire escapes;

(e) tower wagons; and

(f) works trucks.

Wings

56. A heavy motor car shall be equipped with wings or other similar fittings to catch, so far as practicable, mud or water thrown up by the rotation of the wheels, unless adequate protection is afforded by the body of the vehicle:

Provided that this Regulation shall not apply—

(a) in relation to the rear wheels of any heavy motor car for the time being forming part of an articulated vehicle if the trailer forming the remaining part of the articulated vehicle is used only for or, when empty, in connection with the carriage of round timber;

(b) in the case of a vehicle in an unfinished condition proceeding to a works for completion; or

(c) in the case of a works truck.

F.—MOTOR CARS

Overall width

57. The overall width of a motor car shall not exceed 2·5 metres.

Overhang

58. The overhang of a motor car shall not exceed 60 per cent. of the distance between the plane perpendicular to the longitudinal axis of the vehicle which passes through the centre or centres of the front wheel or wheels and the foremost vertical plane from which the overhang is to be measured as defined in Regulation 3:

Provided that—

    (*a*) in the case of a motor car first used before 1st January 1966, the overhang may be increased by not more than 76 millimetres, if the distance between the foremost and rearmost axles does not exceed 2·29 metres and

    (*b*) this Regulation shall not apply in the case of—

        (i) a motor car first used on or before 2nd January 1933,

        (ii) a motor car designed for use and used solely in connection with street cleansing, the collection or disposal of refuse or the collection or disposal of the contents of gullies or cesspools or as an ambulance, or

        (iii) a works truck.

Brakes

59.—(1) Save as provided in paragraph (2) of this Regulation, every motor car shall be equipped either with an efficient braking system having two means of operation or with two efficient braking systems each having a separate means of operation:

Provided that for the purpose of this paragraph no account shall be taken in the case of a motor car first used on or after 1st January 1968, of a multi-pull means of operation, unless that means, at the first application, operates an hydraulic, electric or pneumatic device which causes brakes to be applied sufficient to have a total braking efficiency of not less than the total braking efficiency required by paragraph (5) (*b*) of this Regulation in relation to brakes as applied by a second independent means of operation.

(2) Nothing in paragraph (1) or (3) shall apply in the case of a motor car if the said vehicle is equipped with one efficient braking system with one means of operation and the said system is a split braking system.

(3) Save as provided in paragraph (2) of this Regulation, the braking system or braking systems of every motor car shall be so designed and constructed that notwithstanding the failure of any part (other than a fixed member or a brake shoe anchor pin) through or by means of which the force necessary to apply the brakes is transmitted there shall still be available for application by the driver to not less than half the number of the wheels of the vehicle brakes sufficient under the most adverse conditions to bring the vehicle to rest within a reasonable distance:

Provided that in the event of such failure as aforesaid it shall not be necessary for brakes to be available for application by the driver—

    (*a*) in the case of a motor car first used before 1st October 1938, to more than two wheels;

    (*b*) in the case of a vehicle having less than four wheels, to more than one wheel.

(4) The braking system or braking systems of every motor car to which Schedule 4 applies and first used before 1st January 1968 shall comply with the requirements of that Schedule relating to the efficiency of the brakes of such motor cars.

(5) The braking system or braking systems of every motor car first used on or after 1st January 1968, which is not a works truck or a pedestrian controlled vehicle, shall—

    (a) have brakes acting on all the wheels of the vehicle which as applied by one means of operation have a total braking efficiency of not less than 50 per cent.;

    (b) except in the case mentioned in the following sub-paragraph (c), have brakes which as applied by a second independent means of operation have a total braking efficiency of not less than 25 per cent.;

    (c) in the case of a motor car equipped with a split braking system in accordance with paragraph (2) of this Regulation, have brakes which in the event of a failure of any part (other than a fixed member or a brake shoe anchor pin) of one of the independent sections comprised in the split braking system are such that there remain brakes applied by the other section sufficient to have a total braking efficiency of not less than 25 per cent.

(6) The braking system or braking systems of every motor car first used after 1st January 1915 and before 1st January 1968, and which is a goods vehicle exceeding 1525 kilograms in unladen weight other than a dual-purpose vehicle, a pedestrian controlled vehicle or a works truck and is a rigid vehicle with two axles shall—

    (a) have brakes which as applied by one means of operation have a total braking efficiency of not less than 45 per cent.;

    (b) except in the case mentioned in the following sub-paragraph (c), have brakes which as applied by a second independent means of operation have a total braking efficiency of not less than 20 per cent.;

    (c) in the case of a motor car equipped with a split braking system in accordance with paragraph (2) of this Regulation, have brakes which in the event of a failure of any part (other than a fixed member or a brake shoe anchor pin) of one of the independent sections comprised in the split braking system are such that there remain brakes applied by the other section sufficient to have a total braking efficiency of not less than 20 per cent.

(7) The braking system or braking systems of every motor car first used after 1st January 1915, and before 1st January 1968, and which is a goods vehicle exceeding 1525 kilograms in unladen weight other than a dual-purpose vehicle, a pedestrian controlled vehicle or a works truck and is a rigid vehicle with more than two axles or is constructed or adapted to form part of an articulated vehicle shall—

    (a) have brakes which as applied by one means of operation have a total braking efficiency of not less than 40 per cent.;

    (b) except in the case mentioned in the following sub-paragraph (c), have brakes which as applied by a second independent means of operation have a total braking efficiency of not less than 15 per cent.;

    (c) in the case of a motor car equipped with a split braking system in accordance with paragraph (2) of this Regulation, have brakes which in the event of a failure of any part (other than a fixed member or a brake shoe anchor pin) of one of the independent sections comprised in the split braking system are such that there remain brakes applied by the other section sufficient to have a total braking efficiency of not less than 15 per cent.

(8) Paragraphs (1) and (3) of this Regulation shall not apply in the case of a motor car first registered under the Motor Car Act 1903, before 1st January 1915, but—

    (a) such a motor car shall be equipped with an efficient braking system;

    (b) that system shall be so designed and constructed that brakes shall be available for application by the driver, in the case of a vehicle with not less than four wheels, to two wheels of the vehicle, and in the case of a vehicle with less than four wheels, to one wheel of the vehicle; and

    (c) if such a motor car is not one to which the said Schedule 4 applies, the brakes required by the foregoing sub-paragraph to be available for application shall be brakes sufficient under the most adverse conditions to bring the vehicle to rest within a reasonable distance.

(9) The foregoing paragraphs of this Regulation shall not apply in the case of a works truck if it is equipped with one braking system with one means of operation.

(10) The application of one means of operation shall not affect or operate the pedal or hand lever of the other means of operation.

(11) In the case of vehicles first used on or after 1st April 1938, no braking system shall be rendered ineffective by the non-rotation of the engine:

Provided that this paragraph shall not apply in the case of any vehicle referred to in paragraph (15) (b) of this Regulation.

(12) All the brakes of a motor car which are operated by one of the means of operation shall be capable of being applied by direct mechanical action without the intervention of any hydraulic, electric or pneumatic device:

Provided that this paragraph shall not apply to a motor car which satisfies the requirements of Regulation 13 (2).

(13) In the case of a motor car first used before 1st January 1968, with more than three wheels where any brake shoe is capable of being applied by more than one means of operation all the wheels shall be fitted with brakes all of which are operated by one of the means of operation:

Provided that—

    (a) where a motor car has more than six wheels, at least four of which are steering wheels, it shall be a sufficient compliance with this paragraph if brakes are fitted to all the wheels, other than two steering wheels which are situated on opposite sides of the vehicle, and all such brakes are operated by one of the means of operation;

    (b) where a motor car has more than four wheels and the drive is transmitted to all wheels other than the steering wheels without the interposition of a differential driving gear or similar mechanism between the axles carrying the driving wheels, it shall be deemed to be a sufficient compliance with this paragraph if one means of operation operates the brakes on two driving wheels situated on opposite sides of the vehicle and the other means of operation operates brakes on all the other wheels required to be fitted with brakes by this paragraph;

(c) where means of operation are provided in addition to those prescribed by this Regulation such additional means of operation may be disregarded for the purposes of this paragraph;

(d) this paragraph shall not apply to a pedestrian controlled vehicle not exceeding 410 kilograms in weight unladen;   and

(e) in the case of a motor car the unladen weight of which does not exceed 2040 kilograms or which is constructed solely for the carriage of passengers and their effects and adapted to carry not more than seven passengers exclusive of the driver, it shall be deemed to be a sufficient compliance with this paragraph if one means of operation operates brakes fitted to all but two of the wheels and, as respects each of those two wheels, operates a brake on the shaft leading thereto and no gearing is interposed between the brake and the wheel.

(14) One at least of the means of operation shall be capable of causing brakes to be applied directly and not through the transmission gear to not less than half the number of the wheels of the vehicle:
Provided that—

(a) in the case of a motor car having brakes acting on all the wheels of the vehicle and capable of being applied by one means of operation, any shaft leading from any differential driving gear of an axle to a driving wheel shall be deemed not to form part of the transmission gear;

(b) in the case of a motor car having more than four wheels and first used before 1st October 1938, it shall be deemed to be sufficient compliance with this paragraph if one of the means of operation applies brakes directly and not through the transmission gear to not less than two of the wheels of the vehicle;   and

(c) where a motor car has more than four wheels and the drive is transmitted to all wheels other than the steering wheels without the interposition of a differential driving gear or similar mechanism between the axles carrying the driving wheels, it shall be deemed to be a sufficient compliance with this paragraph if the brakes applied by one means of operation act directly on two driving wheels on opposite sides of the vehicle and the brakes applied by the other means of operation act directly on all other driving wheels.

(15) For the purpose of this Regulation—

(a) in the case of a motor car first used on or after 1st October 1938—

(i) not more than one front wheel shall be included in half the number of the wheels of the vehicle for the purposes aforesaid:

Provided that this provision shall not apply—

(1) to a motor car the unladen weight of which does not exceed 1020 kilograms,

(2) to a motor car which is a passenger vehicle constructed or adapted to carry not more than seven passengers exclusive of the driver,

(3) to a works truck, or

(4) to a motor car with more than three wheels, whether or not any brake shoe is capable of being applied by more than one means of operation, if as respects the fitting of its wheels with brakes and the operation of those brakes the provisions of paragraph (13) of this Regulation relating to such matters are complied with, and

(ii) every moving shaft to which any part of a braking system or any means of operation thereof is connected or by which it is supported shall be deemed to be part of that system; and

(b) in the case of a motor car propelled by steam and not used as a public service vehicle, the engine shall be deemed to be an efficient braking system with one means of operation if the engine is capable of being reversed and is incapable of being disconnected from any of the driving wheels of the vehicle except by the sustained effort of the driver.

Tyres

60.—(1) Save as provided in paragraph (3) of this Regulation, every wheel of a motor car shall be fitted with a pneumatic tyre.

(2) Recut pneumatic tyres shall not be fitted to any wheel of a motor car except—

(a) where the motor car is a goods vehicle the weight of which unladen is 2540 kilograms or more and the rim diameter of the wheel is 405 millimetres or more; or

(b) in the case of an electrically propelled goods vehicle.

(3) In the case of any of the following descriptions of vehicles every wheel may, subject to the provisions of paragraph (2) of this Regulation, be fitted with a pneumatic tyre, or a tyre of soft or elastic material:—

(a) motor cars the weight of which unladen does not exceed 1020 kilograms;

(b) works trucks;

(c) motor cars first used on or before 2nd January 1933;

(d) motor cars designed for use and used solely in connection with street cleansing, the collection or disposal of refuse or the collection or the disposal of the contents of gullies or cesspools; and

(e) electrically propelled goods vehicles the weight of which unladen does not exceed 1270 kilograms.

Wings

61. A motor car shall be equipped with wings or other similar fittings to catch, so far as practicable, mud or water thrown up by the rotation of the wheels unless adequate protection is afforded by the body of the vehicle:

Provided that this Regulation shall not apply—

(a) in relation to the rear wheels of any motor car for the time being forming part of an articulated vehicle if the trailer forming the remaining part of the articulated vehicle is used only for or, when empty, in connection with the carriage of round timber;

(b) in the case of a vehicle in an unfinished condition proceeding to a works for completion; or

(c) in the case of a works truck.

G.—Motor Cycles

Brakes

62.—(1) Every motor cycle shall be equipped either with an efficient braking system having two means of operation or with two efficient braking systems each having a separate means of operation.

(2) The braking system or braking systems with which a motor cycle is required to be equipped shall be so designed and constructed that notwithstanding the failure of any part (other than a fixed member or a brake shoe anchor pin) through or by means of which the force necessary to apply the brakes is transmitted there shall still be available for application by the driver to at least one wheel of the vehicle brakes sufficient under the most adverse conditions to bring the vehicle to rest within a reasonable distance.

(3) The braking system or braking systems of every motor cycle to which Schedule 4 applies shall comply with the requirements of that Schedule relating to the efficiency of the brakes of such motor cycles.

(4) Paragraphs (1) and (2) of this Regulation shall not apply in the case of a motor cycle first registered under the Motor Car Act 1903, or the Roads Act 1920, before 1st January 1927, but—

   (a) such a motor cycle shall be equipped with an efficient braking system, and

   (b) that system shall be so designed and constructed that brakes shall be available for application by the driver to at least one wheel of the vehicle.

(5) The foregoing paragraphs of this Regulation shall not apply in the case of a works truck if it is equipped with one braking system having one means of operation.

(6) In the case of a motor cycle required to have two means of operating brakes, the application of one means of operation shall not affect or operate the pedal or hand lever of the other means of operation.

Tyres

63. Every wheel of a motor cycle shall be fitted with a pneumatic tyre, other than a recut pneumatic tyre;

Provided that this Regulation shall not apply to a works truck or a pedestrian controlled vehicle if, in either case, every wheel of the vehicle is fitted with a tyre of soft or elastic material.

Wings

64. Every motor cycle other than a works truck shall be equipped with wings or other similar fittings to catch, so far as practicable, mud or water thrown up by the rotation of the wheels.

H.—Invalid Carriages

Width

65. The overall width of an invalid carriage shall not exceed 2·2 metres.

Brakes

66. Every invalid carriage shall be equipped with an efficient braking system, the brakes of which act on at least two wheels of the vehicle, so designed and constructed that the application of the brakes shall bring the vehicle to rest within a reasonable distance.

Wings

67. Every invalid carriage shall be equipped with wings or other similar fittings to catch, so far as practicable, mud or water thrown up by the rotation of the wheels.

I.—TRAILERS

Overall length

68.—(1) Save as provided in paragraph (2) of this Regulation, the overall length of a trailer shall not exceed 7 metres:

Provided that the said maximum length may be 12 metres in the case of a trailer which—

(*a*) has not less than 4 wheels and where the distance between the centres of the respective areas of contact with the road of the foremost and the rearmost wheels on the same side of the trailer is not less than three-fifths of its overall length;   and

(*b*) is drawn by a motor vehicle having an unladen weight of 2030 kilograms or more.

(2) This Regulation shall not apply—

(*a*) to a trailer constructed and normally used for the conveyance of indivisible loads of exceptional length;

(*b*) to a land implement;

(*c*) to a trailer forming part of an articulated vehicle;

(*d*) to any broken down vehicle which is being drawn by a motor vehicle in consequence of the breakdown;

(*e*) to a trailer which is a trolley vehicle in course of construction or delivery;   or

(*f*) to any trailer which is drying or mixing plant designed for the production of asphalt or of bituminous or tar macadam and used mainly for the construction, repair or maintenance of roads or which is a road planing machine used as aforesaid if, in any such case, the overall length of the trailer together with that of the motor vehicle by which it is drawn does not exceed 18·3 metres.

(3) For the purposes of this Regulation, the overall length of a trailer shall be treated as excluding any part of the trailer designed primarily for use as a means of attaching it to another vehicle and any fitting designed for use in connection with any such part.

Overall width

69.—(1) Save as provided in paragraph (3) of this Regulation, the overall width of a trailer shall not exceed 2·3 metres;

Provided that the said width may be—

(*a*) 2·5 metres in the case of a trailer in relation to which the conditions mentioned in paragraph (2) of this Regulation are complied with;

(*b*) exceeded by not more than 380 millimetres in the case of a trailer which is in use by a travelling showman in connection with his business and was in such use before 15th January 1931;   and

(c) exceeded by not more than 150 millimetres in the case of a trailer manufactured before 1st January 1933, which has been converted from use with solid tyres to use with pneumatic tyres if the width of no part of the vehicle exceeds 2·3 metres except in so far as such increase is rendered necessary by the conversion.

(2) The conditions referred to in paragraph (1) of this Regulation are that:—

(a) every wheel of the trailer is fitted with a pneumatic tyre;

(b) the trailer is drawn by a locomotive, a motor tractor or a heavy motor car or, where the trailer forms part of an articulated vehicle the other part of which is a motor car, the motor car exceeds 2030 kilograms in weight unladen;

(c) every wheel of the vehicle (not being a locomotive) by which the trailer is drawn is fitted with a pneumatic tyre;   and

(d) the outermost part of the trailer comprised in its overall width and on either side of the trailer does not extend more than 305 millimetres outwards beyond the outermost part comprised in the overall width of the vehicle by which it is being drawn on the same side, when the longitudinal axis of that vehicle and the longitudinal axis of the trailer lie in parallel vertical planes.

(3) This Regulation shall not apply to a land implement, to a trailer which is a trolley vehicle in course of construction or delivery or to a broken down vehicle which is being drawn by a motor vehicle in consequence of the breakdown.

Brakes

70.—(1) Save as provided in paragraph (3) of this Regulation, every trailer manufactured before the 1st January 1968, and every agricultural trailer whenever manufactured which in either case exceeds 102 kilograms in weight unladen shall be equipped with an efficient braking system the brakes of which are capable of being applied when it is being drawn—

(a) to at least two wheels in the case of a trailer having not more than four wheels;

(b) to at least four wheels in the case of a trailer having more than four wheels;   and

(c) in the case of trailers manufactured after 1st April 1938, to at least half the number of wheels of the trailer,

and so constructed that—

(i) the brakes can be applied either by the driver of the drawing vehicle or by some other person on such vehicle or the trailer,

(ii) in the case of a trailer forming part of an articulated vehicle and being permanently attached to the drawing vehicle, the brakes are capable of being set so as effectively to prevent two at least of the wheels from revolving when the trailer is not being drawn, and

(iii) in the case of any other trailer, the brakes are capable of being set so as effectively to prevent two at least of the wheels from revolving when the trailer, whether it is attached to the drawing vehicle or not, is not being drawn:

Provided that the provisions of item (i) of this paragraph shall not apply in the case of a trailer if the brakes of the trailer automatically come into operation on the overrun of the trailer.

In this paragraph the expression " permanently attached " means that the trailer can only be detached from the drawing vehicle by an operation involving the use of facilities which are normally found only in a workshop.

(2) Save as provided in paragraph (3) of this Regulation, every trailer manufactured on or after 1st January 1968, except an agricultural trailer, and which exceeds 102 kilogrammes in weight unladen shall be equipped with an efficient braking system so designed and constructed that—

(a) when the trailer is being drawn, the brakes of that braking system are capable of being applied to all the wheels of the trailer by the driver of the drawing vehicle using the means of operation applying those of the brakes of the drawing vehicle which were designed and constructed to have the highest braking efficiency of any of the brakes of any braking system with which the drawing vehicle is equipped;

(b) when the trailer is being drawn, in the event of a failure of any part (other than a fixed member or a brake shoe anchor pin) of the braking system with which the drawing vehicle is equipped (excluding the means of operation of a split braking system) or of any part (other than as aforesaid) of the braking system with which the trailer is equipped, brakes shall still be capable of being applied to at least two wheels of the trailer or, in the case of a two-wheeled trailer, to one wheel in the manner indicated in the last preceding sub-paragraph or by the driver using any other means of operation of a braking system with which the drawing vehicle is by these Regulations required to be equipped;

(c) when the trailer is stationary—

(i) the brakes of that system can also be applied to at least two wheels of the trailer and released by a person standing on the ground by a means of operation fitted to the trailer;

(ii) the braking force of that system can, when applied in the manner indicated in sub-paragraph (a) or (c) (i) of this paragraph, at all times be maintained in operation by direct mechanical action without the intervention of any hydraulic, electric or pneumatic device; and

(iii) such braking force, when so applied and so maintained in operation by direct mechanical action, is capable of holding the trailer stationary on a gradient of at least 1 in 6·25 without the assistance of stored energy:

Provided that the provisions of sub-paragraphs (a) and (b) of this paragraph shall not apply in the case of a trailer if the brakes of the trailer automatically come into operation on the overrun of the trailer.

(3) Paragraphs (1) and (2) of this Regulation shall not apply—

(a) to any land implement or land implement conveyor drawn by a motor vehicle;

(b) to any trailer designed for use and used for street cleansing which does not carry any load other than its necessary gear and equipment;

(c) to any broken down vehicle which is being drawn by a motor vehicle in consequence of the breakdown;

(d) to any agricultural trailer manufactured before 1st July 1947, when drawn by a motor tractor or a land tractor which is not a motor tractor if—

      (i) its laden weight does not exceed 4070 kilograms,

      (ii) it is the only trailer so drawn, and

      (iii) it is not drawn at a speed exceeding 10 miles per hour; or

(e) to any trailer used only for the carriage of plant and materials for producing gas for the propulsion of the drawing vehicle if the drawing vehicle is either a goods vehicle weighing not less than 2030 kilograms in weight unladen or a public service vehicle.

(4) In the case of trailers manufactured on or after 1st April 1938, the braking system shall be so constructed that it is not rendered ineffective by the non-rotation of the engine of the drawing vehicle.

Tyres

71. Subject to the provisions of Regulation 72, every wheel of a trailer when the trailer is being drawn on a road shall be fitted with a pneumatic tyre or a tyre of soft or elastic material:

Provided that this Regulation shall not apply—

(a) to any land implement or agricultural trailer;

(b) to any trailer manufactured before 15th January 1931, which is specially designed for the conveyance of horses and cattle and is used either for that purpose or for some other purpose connected with agriculture;

(c) to any trailer manufactured before 15th January 1931, which is specially designed and used for the conveyance of furniture and other similar household effects; or

(d) to any trailer used for the purpose of carrying water for a road roller which is being used in connection with the construction, maintenance or repair of roads.

72.—(1) Save as provided in paragraph (3) of this Regulation, every wheel of a trailer manufactured after 1st January 1933, when drawn by a heavy motor car or a motor car shall be fitted with a pneumatic tyre.

(2) Save as provided in paragraph (3) of this Regulation, where trailers of the following descriptions manufactured after 1st January 1933, are drawn by a heavy motor car or motor car every wheel of such trailers shall be fitted with a pneumatic tyre, other than a recut pneumatic tyre:—

(a) a trailer which does not exceed 1020 kilograms in weight unladen;

(b) a trailer which is not constructed or adapted to carry any load other than plant or other special appliance or apparatus which is a permanent or essentially permanent fixture and which does not exceed 2290 kilograms in total weight; or

(c) a trailer which is a living van which does not exceed 2040 kilograms in weight unladen.

(3) Paragraphs (1) and (2) of this Regulation shall not apply to any trailer:—

(a) which is a works trailer;

(b) which is designed for use and used solely in connection with street

cleansing, the collection or disposal of refuse or the collection or
disposal of the contents of gullies or cesspools;

(c) when drawn by a heavy motor car every wheel of which is not
required to be fitted with a pneumatic tyre;

(d) when used for the purpose of carrying water for a road roller
which is being used in connection with the construction, maintenance or repair of roads;

(e) which is a land implement or an agricultural trailer drawn by a
land tractor; or

(f) which is a broken down vehicle and is being drawn by a motor
vehicle in consequence of the breakdown.

Wings

73. The rear wheels of every trailer or, in the case of a two-wheeled
trailer both its wheels, shall be equipped with wings or other similar fittings
to catch, so far as practicable, mud or water thrown up by the rotation
of the wheels, unless adequate protection is afforded by the body of the
trailer:

Provided that this Regulation shall not apply—

(a) to trailers in an unfinished condition proceeding to a works for
completion;

(b) to land implements;

(c) to land implement conveyors;

(d) to living vans;

(e) to watercarts;

(f) to trailers used only for or, when empty, in connection with the
carriage of round timber;

(g) to trailer pumps used for fire brigade purposes;

(h) to trailers drawn by a vehicle the maximum speed of which is
restricted by virtue of the provisions of Schedule 5 to the Road
Traffic Regulation Act 1967, to 12 miles per hour or less; or

(i) to any broken down vehicle which is being drawn in consequence
of the breakdown.

Part III

Regulations Governing the Use on Roads of Motor Vehicles and Trailers

Markings on locomotives, tractors and heavy motor cars

74. The owner of a locomotive, motor tractor or heavy motor car
shall cause the unladen weight of the vehicle to be painted or otherwise
plainly marked upon some conspicuous place on the left or near side of
the vehicle:

Provided that this Regulation shall not apply to a heavy motor car
not registered under the Roads Act 1920, the Vehicles (Excise) Act 1949,
or the Vehicles (Excise) Act 1962 or the Vehicles (Excise) Act 1971.

Trailer plate

75.—(1) Save as provided in paragraph (4) of this Regulation, when
a motor vehicle is drawing a trailer or trailers on a road there shall be
exhibited in a conspicuous position on the back of the trailer (or when

more than one trailer is being drawn on the back of the rearmost trailer) a distinguishing mark in the form and complying with the provisions set out in the diagram contained in Schedule 5.

(2) The reflex lenses indicated in the said diagram shall be not less than 19 mm. in diameter and the colour thereof shall be red.

(3) The mark shall be so fixed to the trailer that—

(a) it is vertical and easily distinguishable from behind the trailer;
(b) it is either on the centre line or to the offside of the trailer; and
(c) no part of it is at a height exceeding 1·22 metres from the ground, and in all cases it shall be kept clean and unobscured.

(4) This Regulation shall not apply—

(a) to any trailer forming part of an articulated vehicle;
(b) to any broken down vehicle while being drawn in consequence of the breakdown;
(c) to any trailer drawn by a motor cycle being a passenger vehicle or by a motor car being either a passenger vehicle or a dual-purpose vehicle and in each case adapted to carry not more than seven passengers exclusive of the driver;
(d) to any trailer specially constructed for the carriage of round timber;
(e) to any land implement (other than a living van) or any land implement conveyor or any agricultural trailer;
(f) to any water cart drawn by, and used for carrying water for, a road roller; or
(g) to any trailer carrying two obligatory reflectors in accordance with the Road Vehicles Lighting Regulations 1971, as amended, such reflectors being marked either " AU40L III " or " AU40L IIIA " or with an approval mark incorporating the roman numeral III by virtue of Regulation 23 of those Regulations and being either mounted on a white background forming part of the reflector or surrounded by a white border at least 12 millimetres in width.

Laden weight of locomotive

76.—(1) Save as provided in paragraph (2) of this Regulation, the laden weight of a locomotive shall not exceed 20,830 kilograms.

(2) The laden weight of a locomotive which is equipped with suitable and sufficient springs between each wheel and the frame of the vehicle and every wheel of which is fitted with a pneumatic tyre or a tyre of soft or elastic material shall not exceed—

(a) in the case of a vehicle with less than six wheels, 2236 kilograms;
(b) in the case of a vehicle with six wheels, 26,420 kilograms; or
(c) in the case of a vehicle with more than six wheels, 30,490 kilograms.

(3) The total weight transmitted to the road surface by any two wheels of a locomotive in line transversely shall not exceed 11,180 kilograms:
Provided that this paragraph shall not apply to a road roller or to a vehicle with not more than four wheels first used before 1st June 1955.

Weight of trailers drawn by a locomotive

77. The maximum total weight of all trailers, whether wheeled or track laying and whether laden or unladen, drawn by a locomotive whether wheeled or track laying shall not exceed 40,650 kilograms.

Laden weight of heavy motor car or motor car

78.—(1) Save as provided in paragraph (2) of this Regulation, in the case of a heavy motor car which is a public service vehicle the total weight transmitted to the road surface by any two wheels in line transversely shall not exceed 9150 kilograms and the sum of the weights so transmitted by all the wheels shall not exceed 14,230 kilograms.

(2) In the case a heavy motor car or motor car having brakes which as applied by one means of operation have a total braking efficiency of not less than 50 per cent. and which as applied by a second independent means of operation or as applied on a failure in the case of a split braking system have a total braking efficiency of not less than 25 per cent. the following provisions shall apply—

(i) the total weight transmitted to the road surface by any two wheels in line transversely may amount to but shall not exceed 10,170 kilograms, if each such wheel is fitted with either two pneumatic tyres having the centres of their areas of contact with the road surface not less than 300 millimetres apart measured at right angles to the longitudinal axis of the vehicle or with a wide tyre; and

(ii) the sum of the weights transmitted to the road surface by all the wheels of the vehicle may amount to but not exceed, where the distance between the front and rear axles is at least 3·25 metres but less than 3·65 metres, 15,250 kilograms, and where the dis-ance between the front and the rear axles is at least 3·65 metres, 16,260 kilograms.

For the purpose of this sub-paragraph the distances between any two axles shall be obtained in the same manner as is provided in paragraph 1 of Schedule 6.

(3) For the purpose of this Regulation the weight transmitted to the road surface by a vehicle shall be taken to be the weight so transmitted by the vehicle when it is complete and fully equipped for service with a full supply of water, oil and fuel and loaded with weights of 63·5 kilograms per person placed in the correct relative positions for each passenger for whom a seat is provided and for the driver and conductor (if carried) and, in the case of a public service vehicle registered after 31st December 1954, in which by or under any enactment more than eight standing passengers may be carried, with additional weights of 63·5 kilograms per person for each standing passenger in excess of eight reasonably distributed in the space in which any such passengers may be so carried.

79.—(1) Save as provided in paragraph (2) of this Regulation, in the case of a heavy motor car or motor car which is not a public service vehicle, the weight transmitted to the road surface by any one wheel where no other wheel is in the same line transversely shall not exceed 4580 kilo-grams, the total weight so transmitted by any two wheels in line trans-versely shall not exceed 9150 kilograms, and the sum of the weights so transmitted by all the wheels shall not exceed—

(a) in the case of a vehicle with not more than four wheels, 14,230 kilograms;

(b) in the case of a vehicle with more than four wheels but not more than six wheels, 20,330 kilograms; and

(c) in the case of a vehicle with more than six wheels, 24,390 kilograms,

so, however, that in relation to a vehicle first used on or after 1st June 1973, not being a vehicle to which Regulation 83 applies and in so far as it is a vehicle to which either of sub-paragraphs (*b*) and (*c*) of this paragraph applies, for the weight limits of 20,330 kilograms and 24,390 kilograms specified in those sub-paragraphs there shall be substituted respectively weight limits of 16,260 kilograms and 18,290 kilograms.

(2) In the case of a prior 1968 vehicle, a post 1968 vehicle or a temporarily imported vehicle the following provisions shall apply—

(i) the weight transmitted to the road surface by any one wheel where no other wheel is in the same line transversely may amount to but not exceed 5090 kilograms and the total weight so transmitted by any two wheels in line transversely may amount to but shall not exceed 10,170 kilograms, if each such wheel is fitted with either two pneumatic tyres having the centres of their areas of contact with the road surface not less than 300 millimetres apart measured at right angles to the longitudinal axis of the vehicle or with a wide tyre; and

(ii) if it is fitted with a number of axles specified in column 1 of paragraph 2 of Schedule 6 as respects which the measurements apply as so specified, the sum of the weights transmitted to the road surface by all the wheels of the vehicle may amount to but shall not exceed the weight specified in relation to that vehicle in column 2 of the said paragraph:

Provided that the provisions of sub-paragraph (ii) of this paragraph shall not apply to a motor vehicle when drawing a trailer other than a trailer to which Regulation 80 (3) applies.

(3) For the purpose of this Regulation the following expressions have the meanings hereby respectively assigned to them:—

" a prior 1968 vehicle " means a heavy motor car or motor car (other than a public service vehicle)—

(*a*) first used before 1st January 1968;

(*b*) equipped with a plate complying with the requirements of paragraph (2) of Regulation 39, whether that paragraph applies to that vehicle or not; and

(*c*) having brakes which as applied by means of one operation have a total braking efficiency of not less than 50 per cent. and which as applied by a second independent means of operation or as applied on a failure in the case of a split braking system have a total braking efficiency of not less than 25 per cent.;

" a post 1968 vehicle " means a heavy motor car or motor car (other than a public service vehicle) first used on or after 1st January 1968;

" a temporarily imported vehicle " means a heavy motor car or motor car (other than a public service vehicle) brought temporarily into Great Britain by a person resident abroad which—

(*a*) is not registered under the Vehicles (Excise) Act 1971;

(*b*) complies with the requirements mentioned in Regulation 4 (7);

(*c*) carries a plate securely affixed to it in a conspicuous and readily accessible position issued by the competent authority in the country where it is registered indicating the permissible maximum weight for the vehicle in that country; and

(*d*) has brakes which as applied by one means of operation have a total braking efficiency of not less than 50 per cent.

and which as applied by a second independent means of operation or as applied on a failure in the case of a split braking system have a total braking efficiency of not less than 25 per cent.

Laden weight of trailer

80.—(1) Save as provided in paragraph (3) of this Regulation, the total weight transmitted to the road surface by any two wheels of a trailer in line transversely shall not exceed 9150 kilograms.

(2) Save as provided in paragraph (3) of this Regulation, the total laden weight of a trailer with less than six wheels and not forming part of an articulated vehicle shall not exceed 14,230 kilograms.

(3) In the case of—

(*a*) a trailer equipped with a plate complying with the rquirements of paragraph (2) of Regulation 39, whether that paragraph applies to that trailer or not; or

(*b*) a temporarily imported trailer;

which in either case is drawn by a prior 1968 vehicle, a post 1968 vehicle or a temporarily imported motor vehicle the following provisions shall apply—

(i) the weight transmitted to the road surface by any two wheels of the trailer in line transversely may amount to, but shall not exceed 10,170 kilograms, if each wheel is fitted with either two pneumatic tyres having the centres of their areas of contact with the road surface not less than 300 millimetres apart measured at right angles to the longitudinal axis of the vehicle or with a wide tyre, and

(ii) if it is fitted with a number of axles specified in column 1 of paragraph 2 of Schedule 6 as respects which the measurements apply as so specified, the sum of the weights transmitted to the road surface by all the wheels of the trailer may amount to but not exceed the weight specified in relation to that trailer in column 2 of the said paragraph.

(4) The total laden weight of a trailer which has no other brakes than a parking brake, and brakes which automatically come into operation on the overrun of the trailer, shall not exceed 3560 kilograms.

(5) For the purpose of this Regulation the following expressions have the meanings hereby respectively assigned to them:—

" a prior 1968 vehicle " means a motor tractor, heavy motor car or motor car—

(*a*) first used before 1st January 1968;

(*b*) equipped with a plate complying with the requirements of paragraph (2) of Regulation 39, whether that paragraph applies to the vehicle or not; and

(*c*) which while drawing a trailer mentioned in paragraph (3) of this Regulation has brakes which (whether assisted by the brakes on the trailer or not) as applied by one means of operation have a total braking efficiency of not less than 50 per cent. and as applied by a second independent means of operation or as applied on a failure in the case of a split braking system have a total braking efficiency of not less than 25 per cent.;

" a post 1968 vehicle " means a heavy motor car or motor car—

(*a*) first used on or after 1st January 1968, or a motor tractor first used on or after the said date which complies with the requirements of paragraph (2) of Regulation 39 and paragraph (5) of Regulation 54, notwithstanding that those paragraphs do not apply to the said motor tractor;   and

(*b*) which in each case while drawing a trailer mentioned in paragraph (3) of this Regulation has brakes which (whether assisted by the brakes on the trailer or not) as applied by one means of operation have a total braking efficiency of not less than 50 per cent. and as applied by a second independent means of operation or as applied on a failure in the case of a split braking system have a total braking efficiency of not less than 25 per cent.;

" a temporarily imported motor vehicle " means a motor tractor, heavy motor car or motor car brought temporarily into Great Britain by a person resident abroad which—

(*a*) is not registered under the Vehicles (Excise) Act 1971;

(*b*) complies with the requirements mentioned in Regulation 4 (7);

(*c*) carries a plate securely affixed to it in a conspicuous and readily accessible position issued by the competent authority in the country where it is registered indicating the permissible maximum weight for the vehicle in that country;   and

(*d*) while drawing a trailer mentioned in paragraph (3) of this Regulation has brakes which (whether assisted by the brakes of the trailer or not) as applied by one means of operation have a total braking efficiency of not less than 50 per cent. and as applied by a second independent means of operation or as applied on a failure in the case of a split braking system have a total braking efficiency of not less than 25 per cent.;

" a temporarily imported trailer " means a trailer whenever manufactured brought temporarily into Great Britain by a person resident abroad which—

(*a*) complies with the requirements mentioned in Regulation 4 (7);   and

(*b*) carries a plate securely affixed to it in a conspicuous and readily accessible position issued by the competent authority in a country outside Great Britain indicating the permissible maximum weight for the trailer in that country.

Laden weight of vehicle and trailer

81.—(1) The total laden weight of a trailer, whether wheeled or track laying, together with that of any motor tractor, heavy motor car or motor car drawing such trailer, in each case whether wheeled or track laying, shall not exceed 22,360 kilograms.

Provided that

(*a*) in the case of a wheeled trailer drawn by a wheeled motor tractor, wheeled heavy motor car or wheeled motor car, the total laden weight of the trailer together with that of the drawing vehicle may equal, but shall not exceed, 24,390 kilograms;   and

(b) where the trailer is fitted with power-assisted brakes which can be operated by the driver of the drawing vehicle and are not rendered ineffective by the non-rotation of the engine of the drawing vehicle, the total laden weight of the trailer together with that of the drawing vehicle, if the drawing vehicle is equipped with a warning device so placed as to be readily visible to the driver when in the driving seat in order to indicate an impending failure or deficiency in the vacuum or pressure system, may equal, but not exceed, 32,520 kilograms.

(2) This Regulation shall not apply to any trailer forming part of an articulated vehicle.

Laden weight of articulated vehicle

82.—(1) Save as provided in paragraph (2) of this Regulation, the total laden weight of an articulated vehicle shall not exceed—

    (a) if the trailer has less than four wheels, 20,330 kilograms; and
    (b) if the trailer has four wheels or more, 24,390 kilograms.

(2) In the case of an articulated vehicle formed by—

    (a) a trailer equipped with a plate complying with the requirements of paragraph (2) of Regulation 39, whether that paragraph applies to the trailer or not, or a temporarily imported trailer; and
    (b) a prior 1968 vehicle, a post 1968 vehicle or a temporarily imported motor vehicle,

where the articulated vehicle is fitted with a number of axles specified in column 1 of paragraph 3 of Schedule 6 as respects which the measurements apply as so specified, the sum of the weights transmitted to the road surface by all the wheels of the articulated vehicle may amount to but shall not exceed the weight specified in relation to that vehicle in column 2 of the said paragraph.

(3) For the purpose of this Regulation, " a temporarily imported trailer " has the same meaning as in Regulation 80 (5) and " a prior 1968 vehicle ", " a post 1968 vehicle " and " a temporarily imported motor vehicle " have the same meanings as in the definitions of those terms in that Regulation subject, however, to any reference to a motor tractor in those definitions being omitted.

Laden weight of certain vehicles not part of articulated vehicles

83.—(1) This Regulation applies to the following vehicles, namely,—

    (a) a heavy motor car or motor car—

        (i) equipped with a plate complying with the requirements of Regulation 39 (2);
        (ii) having brakes which as applied by one means of operation have a total braking efficiency of not less than 50 per cent. and which as applied by a second independent means of operation or as applied on a failure in the case of a split braking system have a total braking efficiency of not less than 25 per cent.;
        (iii) not forming part of an articulated vehicle;

    (b) a temporarily imported vehicle as defined in Regulation 79 (3)—

(i) if the plate which it carries indicates a permissible maximum weight for each axle thereof;

(ii) not forming part of an articulated vehicle;

(c) a trailer—

(i) equipped with a plate complying with the requirements of Regulation 39 (2);

(ii) drawn by a motor tractor, heavy motor car or motor car which in each case whilst drawing the trailer has brakes which (whether assisted by the brakes on the trailer or not) as applied by one means of operation have a total braking efficiency of not less than 50 per cent. and as applied by a second independent means of operation or as applied on a failure in the case of a split braking system have a total braking efficiency of not less than 25 per cent.;

(iii) not forming part of an articulated vehicle;

(d) a temporarily imported trailer as defined in Regulation 80 (5)—

(i) if the plate which it carries indicates a permissible maximum weight for each axle thereof;

(ii) drawn by a motor tractor, heavy motor or motor car which in each case whilst drawing the trailer has brakes which comply with the provisions of sub-paragraph (c) (ii) above;

(iii) not forming part of an articulated vehicle.

(2) Nothing in Regulation 79 and Regulation 80 (other than paragraph (4) of that Regulation) shall apply to a vehicle to which this Regulation applies.

(3) In the case of a vehicle to which this Regulation applies, the sum of the weights transmitted to the road surface by all the wheels of the vehicle may, subject to the provisions of Regulation 80 (4), amount to but shall not exceed such weight as is specified in Part I of Schedule 7 and is relevant to the class of vehicle in column 1 of that Part in which it falls:

Provided that nothing in this paragraph shall apply so as to require a vehicle first used before 1st June 1973, to be used on a road at a weight below that at which it could have been used under Regulation 79 (1) (b) and (c).

Laden weight of certain motor vehicles forming part of articulated vehicles

84.—(1) This Regulation applies to—

(a) a heavy motor car or motor car complying with the provisions of sub-paragraphs (i) and (ii) of paragraph (1) (a) of Regulation 83 and forming part of an articulated vehicle;

(b) a temporarily imported vehicle as defined in Regulation 79 (3) complying with the provisions of sub-paragraph (i) of paragraph (1) (b) of Regulation 83 and forming part of an articulated vehicle.

(2) Nothing in Regulation 79 shall apply to a vehicle to which this Regulation applies.

(3) In the case of a vehicle to which this Regulation applies, the sum of the weights transmitted to the road surface by all the wheels of the vehicle may amount to but shall not exceed such weight as is specified in Part II of Schedule 7 and is relevant to the class of vehicle in column 1 of that Part in which it falls:

Provided that nothing in this paragraph shall apply so as to require a vehicle first used before 1st June 1973, to be used on a road at a weight below that at which it could have been used under Regulation 79 (1) (*b*) and (*c*).

Laden weight of certain articulated vehicles

85.—(1) This Regulation applies to an articulated vehicle formed by—

(*a*) a heavy motor car or motor car to which Regulation 84 (1) (*a*) applies or a temporarily imported vehicle as defined in Regulation 84 (1) (*b*), and

(*b*) a trailer which—

(i) is equipped with a plate complying with the requirements of Regulation 39 (2); or

(ii) is a temporarily imported trailer as defined in Regulation 80 (5),

the said heavy motor car or motor car in each case whilst drawing the trailer having brakes which (whether assisted by the brakes on the trailer or not) as applied by one means of operation have a total braking efficiency of not less than 50 per cent. and as applied by a second independent means of operation or as applied on a failure in the case of a split braking system have a total braking efficiency of not less than 25 per cent.

(2) Nothing in Regulation 82 shall apply to an articulated vehicle to which this Regulation applies.

(3) In the case of an articulated vehicle to which this Regulation applies, the sum of the weights transmitted to the road surface by all the wheels of the vehicle may amount to but shall not exceed the weight specified in column 3 of Part III of Schedule 7 in relation to the class of vehicle in column 1 of that Part and to the axle spacing in column 2 of that Part to which it conforms.

Total weights for certain closely spaced axles etc.

86.—(1) This Regulation applies to—

(*a*) a heavy motor car or motor car to which Regulation 83 (1) (*a*) (i) and (ii) or Regulation 83 (1) (*b*) (i) applies; and

(*b*) a trailer to which Regulation 83 (1) (*c*) (i) and (ii) or Regulation 83 (1) (*d*) (i) and (ii) applies,

whether or not any such heavy motor car or motor car or trailer forms part of an articulated vehicle.

(2) Except as provided in paragraph (3) below, where two closely spaced axles of a vehicle to which this Regulation applies are spaced at such distance apart as is specified in column 1 of Part IV of Schedule 7, the total weight transmitted to the road surface by all the wheels of those axles may amount to but shall not exceed the weight specified in column 2 of that Part in relation to those axles at the distance specified in the said column 1:

Provided that nothing in this paragraph shall apply so as to require a vehicle first used before 1st June 1973, to be used on a road at a weight as respects the wheels of those axles below that at which it could have been used under Regulation 88.

(3) Where two closely spaced axles of a vehicle to which this Regulation applies are spaced at such distance apart as is specified in column 1 of the said Part IV, the total weight transmitted to the road surface by all the wheels of those axles may amount to but shall not exceed the higher

permitted weight not being greater than the weight shown in column 3 of that Schedule in relation to those axles at the distance specified in the said column 1.

In this paragraph " higher permitted weight " means the sum of the plated weights for each of the axles in question, if neither of those plated weights exceeds one half of the weight shown in the said column 3.

(4) Where the outer axles of three closely spaced axles of a vehicle to which this Regulation applies are spaced at such distance apart as is specified in column 1 of Part V of Schedule 7, the total weight transmitted to the road surface by all the wheels of each of those closely spaced axles may amount to but shall not exceed the weight shown in column 2 of that Part in relation to the case where the outer axles are at the distance specified in the said column 1:

Provided that nothing in this paragraph shall apply so as to require a vehicle first used before 1st June 1973, to be used on a road at a weight as respects the wheels of those closely spaced axles below that at which it could have been used under Regulation 88.

(5) Where the plated weight of any one of three adjacent axles of a vehicle to which this Regulation applies, being a trailer forming part of an articulated vehicle, exceeds 7630 kilograms, the total weight transmitted to the road surface by all the wheels of those axles may amount to but shall not exceed such weight as is specified in Part VI of Schedule 7 and is relevant to those axles by virtue of the provision made in that Part:

Provided that nothing in this paragraph shall apply so as to require a vehicle first used before 1st June 1973, to be used on a road at a weight as respects the wheels of any of those axles below that at which it could have been used under Regulation 88.

(6) In this Regulation—

" closely spaced " means—

    (a) in the case of two axles they are spaced at a distance apart of 2·5 metres or less; and

    (b) in the case of three axles the outermost axles are spaced at a distance apart of 3·25 metres or less and no one of those three axles has a plated weight more than 7630 kilograms:

" plated weight," in relation to an axle, means the weight for that axle shown in column 2 of a Ministry plate as defined in Regulation 138 and carried on the vehicle or, if no such plate is carried on the vehicle, the maximum weight in Great Britain shown for that axle in the plate complying with the requirements of Regulation 39 (2) or the weight shown for that axle in the foreign plate with which the vehicle is equipped;

" foreign plate " means the plate mentioned in Regulation 83 (1) (b) (i) or 83 (1) (d) (i).

(7) Nothing in Regulation 88 shall apply to a vehicle to which this Regulation applies.

Wheel and axle weights for certain vehicles

87.—(1) This Regulation applies to the same vehicles to which Regulation 86 applied.

(2) Save as provided in paragraphs (3) and (4) of this Regulation, in the case of a vehicle to which this Regulation applies the weight transmitted to the road surface by any one wheel where no other wheel is in

the same line transversely shall not exceed 4580 kilograms and the total weight so transmitted by any two wheels in line transversely shall not exceed 9150 kilograms.

(3) In the case of a vehicle to which this Regulation applies, the weight transmitted to the road surface by any one wheel where no other wheel is in the same line transversely may amount to but not exceed 5090 kilograms and the total weight so transmitted by any two wheels in line transversely may amount to but shall not exceed 10,170 kilograms, if each such wheel is fitted with either two pneumatic tyres having the centres of their areas of contact with the road surface not less than 300 millimetres apart measured at right angles to the longitudinal axis of the vehicle or with a wide tyre.

(4) In the case of a vehicle to which this Regulation applies, having more than two wheels in line transversely, the total weight transmitted to the road surface by those wheels may amount to but shall not exceed 11,180 kilograms, so, however, that the total weight so transmitted shall not exceed 10,170 kilograms in the case of the wheels of any one of two closely spaced axles within the meaning of Regulation 86 (6) or in the case of the wheels of any one of three adjacent axles mentioned in Regulation 86 (5).

(5) Nothing in Regulation 88 shall apply to a vehicle to which this Regulation applies.

Distribution of weight

88. In the case of a heavy motor car, motor car or trailer, whether laden or unladen, the weight transmitted by more than two wheels to any strip of the road surface upon which the vehicle rests contained between any two parallel lines drawn on that surface at right angles to the longitudinal axis of the vehicle—

  (a) less than 1·02 metres apart shall not exceed 11,180 kilograms;
  (b) less than 1·22 metres apart but 1·02 metres or more apart shall not exceed 16,260 kilograms; and
  (c) less than 2·13 metres but 1·22 metres or more apart shall not exceed 18,290 kilograms.

Additional weight restrictions

89.—(1) In this Regulation " plate ", in relation to a vehicle, means the plate with which it is required to be equipped by Regulation 39.

(2) Paragraph (4) of this Regulation applies to a goods vehicle, being a heavy motor car or motor car to which Regulation 39 (1) applies, and for which no plating certificate has been issued.

(3) As from 1st April 1973, paragraph (4) of this Regulation shall also apply to a locomotive or motor tractor to which Regulation 39 (1) (b) applies.

(4) As respects a motor vehicle to which this paragraph applies, whether or not drawing or being drawn by another vehicle, the following provisions of this paragraph shall apply—

  (a) the maximum gross weight shown in its plate shall not be exceeded;
  (b) the maximum axle weight for each axle shown in its plate shall not be exceeded:
      Provided that this sub-paragraph shall not apply in the case of any axle being one of two or more axles to which the following sub-paragraph applies;

(c) where any two or more axles are fitted with a compensating arrangement in accordance with Regulation 11, the sum of the maximum axle weights for those axles so fitted shown in its plate shall not be exceeded;

(d) the maximum train weight (if any) shown in its plate shall not be exceeded.

(5) Paragraph (6) of this Regulation applies to a goods vehicle, being a trailer to which Regulation 39 (1) applies, and for which no plating certificate has been issued.

(6) As respects a trailer to which this paragraph applies, the following provisions of this paragraph shall apply as from 1st February 1970—

(a) the maximum gross weight shown in its plate shall not be exceeded;

(b) the maximum axle weight for each axle shown in its plate shall not be exceeded:
    Provided that this sub-paragraph shall not apply in the case of any axle being one of two or more axles to which the following sub-paragraph applies;

(c) where any two or more axles are fitted with a compensating arrangement in accordance with Regulation 11, the sum of the maximum axle weights for those axles so fitted shown in its plate shall not be exceeded.

(7) Nothing in any of the following Regulations, namely, Regulations 76 and 79 to 88 shall be taken to permit any such weight as is mentioned in the preceding provisions of this Regulation to be exceeded and nothing in this Regulation shall be taken to permit any weight mentioned in any of the said Regulations 79 to 88 which is applicable to the vehicle in question to be exceeded.

Special provisions as to display of particulars by certain trailers and drawing vehicles

89A.—(1) When—

(a) a motor vehicle is drawing a trailer on a road, which is not a special road, in circumstances where the speed limit prescribed by Schedule 5 to the Road Traffic Regulation Act 1967 (as varied) for the drawing vehicle is 50 miles per hour, or

(b) a motor vehicle, having an unladen weight not exceeding 30 hundredweight, is drawing a trailer on a special road in circumstances where the speed limit prescribed by Schedule 5 to the said Act (as varied) for the drawing vehicle is 50 miles per hour;

then appropriate weights shall be displayed as follows:—

(i) in the case of the drawing vehicle, its kerbside weight shall be legibly marked in a conspicuous and readily accessible position—

(A) inside the vehicle, or
(B) outside the vehicle and on its left or near side, and

(ii) in the case of the trailer being a living van, or being neither a living van nor a load-carrying trailer, its maximum gross weight shall be legibly marked in a conspicuous and readily accessible position on the left or near side of, and on the outside of, the trailer.

(2) The appropriate weights referred to in paragraph (1) above may be stated in imperial units or in metric units but the same units shall be

employed for both the drawing vehicle and the trailer, and if metric units are employed the weights shall be stated in kilograms.

(3) No trailer when being drawn on a road in circumstances where the speed limit for the drawing vehicle prescribed by Schedule 5 to the Road Traffic Regulation Act 1967 (as varied) is less than 50 miles per hour shall display the plate referred to in paragraph 25 of that Schedule.

(4) In this Regulation—

" kerbside weight " means, in relation to a motor vehicle, the weight of the vehicle (inclusive of any towing bracket with which it is normally equipped) when it carries—

(i) no person thereon, and
(ii) a full supply of fuel in its tank, an adequate supply of other liquids incidental to its propulsion and no load other than the loose tools and equipment with which the vehicle is normally equipped;

" maximum gross weight " means, in relation to a trailer, the weight which it is designed or adapted not to exceed when in use and travelling on a road laden.

Maintenance and use of vehicle so as not to be a danger

90.—(1) A motor vehicle, every trailer drawn thereby and all parts and accessories of such vehicle and trailer shall at all times be in such condition, and the number of passengers carried by such vehicle or trailer, the manner in which any passengers are carried in or on such vehicle or trailer, and the weight, distribution, packing and adjustment of the load of such vehicle or trailer shall at all times be such that no danger is caused or is likely to be caused to any person in or on the vehicle or trailer or on a road:

Provided that in the case of a public service vehicle the provisions of this Regulation with regard to the number of passengers carried shall be deemed to be complied with if the number does not exceed that for the time being permitted by regulations made or having effect as if made under section 148 of the 1960 Act with regard to the carrying capacity of public service vehicles.

(2) The load carried by a motor vehicle or trailer shall at all times be so secured or be in such a position that danger is not likely to be caused to any person by reason of the load or any part thereof falling from the vehicle or by reason of any other movement of the load or any part thereof in relation to the vehicle.

(3) No motor vehicle or trailer shall be used for any purpose for which it is so unsuitable as to cause or be likely to cause danger to any person in or on the vehicle or trailer or on a road.

Maintenance of speedometer

91. Every instrument for indicating speed fitted in compliance with the requirements of Regulation 18 shall—

(a) at all material times be maintained in good working order; and
(b) be kept free from any obstruction which might prevent its being easily read:

Provided that it shall be a good defence to proceedings taken in respect of a contravention of paragraph (a) of this Regulation to prove that—

(i) the defect occurred in the course of the journey during which the contravention was detected, or

(ii) at the time when the contravention was detected steps had already been taken to have the defect remedied with all reasonable expedition.

Maintenance of power to weight ratio

92.—(1) On and after 1st April 1973, no person shall use or cause or permit to be used any ancillary equipment on a motor vehicle to which Regulation 40 applies, while the vehicle is in motion on a road at a speed in excess of 5 miles per hour, unless the number of brake horse power of the engine remaining available to drive the vehicle is at least 4·4 kilowatts for every 1000 kilograms of the relevant weight.

(2) For the purposes of this Regulation " ancillary equipment " means machinery or apparatus forming part of the vehicle or mounted thereon, used for purposes not connected with the driving of the vehicle and " relevant weight " has the meaning given in Regulation 40.

Maintenance of glass

93. All glass or other transparent material fitted to motor vehicles shall be maintained in such condition that it does not obscure the vision of the driver while the vehicle is being driven on a road.

Maintenance of brakes

94.—(1) Every part of every braking system and of the means of operation thereof fitted to a motor vehicle or trailer shall at all times while the vehicle or trailer is used on a road—

(a) be maintained in good and efficient working order and be properly adjusted;

(b) in the case of motor vehicles to which Schedule 4 applies and first used before the 1st January 1968, be so maintained that the brakes forming part of the system comply with the requirements as to the efficiency of brakes which are applicable to such a vehicle by virtue of the provisions contained in Regulation 54 (4), Regulation 59 (4) and Regulation 62 (3);

(c) in the case of motor vehicles to which paragraph (5) of either Regulation 54 or Regulation 59 applies, where such a vehicle is not being used while drawing a trailer, be so maintained that the brakes forming part of the system comply with the requirements as to the efficiency of brakes which are applicable to such a vehicle by virtue of the provisions contained in either of such paragraphs;

(d) in the case of motor vehicles to which paragraph (6) or (7) of either Regulation 54 or Regulation 59 applies, where such a vehicle is not being used while drawing a trailer, be so maintained that the brakes forming part of the system comply with the requirements as to the efficiency of brakes which are applicable to such a vehicle by virtue of the provisions contained in any of such paragraphs; and

(e) in the case of motor vehicles or trailers to which paragraph (2) of Regulation 13 or, as the case may be, paragraph (2) of Regulation 70 applies, be so maintained that the system complies with the requirements as to its braking force which are applicable to such a vehicle by virtue of sub-paragraph (*b*) (ii) of Regulation 13 (2) or by virtue of sub-paragraph (*c*) (iii) of Regulation 70 (2);

(*f*) in the case of motor vehicles or trailers to which Regulation 4A (1) applies, being vehicles to which that Regulation applies by virtue of the vehicles' conforming to the requirements of Council Directive (EEC) No. 71/320 of 26th July 1971 (which relates to the braking devices of certain categories of motor vehicles and their trailers), be so maintained that the braking devices forming part of the system comply with the requirements as to the performance and characteristics of those devices which are applicable thereto by virtue of the requirements of the said Directive.

(2) Where a motor vehicle to which paragraph (5) of either Regulation 54 or Regulation 59 applies is being used while drawing a trailer manufactured on or after 1st January 1968 (other than a trailer not required by these Regulations to be equipped with a braking system), whether or not that motor vehicle and trailer together form an articulated vehicle, then every part of every braking system with which that motor vehicle is equipped and every part of every braking system with which the trailer is equipped shall be so maintained that, when the brakes of any braking system of that motor vehicle (being a system to which the said paragraph (5) applies) are applied by their means of operation and the brakes of any braking system of that trailer applied by that same means of operation are applied, those brakes together produce the same total braking efficiencies as would be required of the brakes of such a motor vehicle when applied by that means of operation if that motor vehicle were not drawing a trailer.

(3) Where a motor vehicle to which paragraph (5) of either Regulation 54 or Regulation 59 applies being a goods vehicle, is being used while drawing a trailer manufactured before 1st January 1968 (other than a trailer not required by these Regulations to be equipped with a braking system), whether or not that motor vehicle and trailer together form an articulated vehicle, then every part of every braking system with which that motor vehicle is equipped and every part of every braking system with which the trailer is equipped shall be so maintained that, when the brakes of any braking system of the motor vehicle (being a system to which the said paragraph (5) applies) are applied by their means of operation they produce (whether assisted by the brakes on the trailer or not) the same total braking efficiencies as would be required of the brakes of such a motor vehicle when applied by that means of operation if that motor vehicle were not drawing a trailer and if it were treated as being a motor vehicle first used before 1st January 1968, and as having to comply with paragraph (7) of either Regulation 54 or Regulation 59 notwithstanding that the said paragraph does not apply to that motor vehicle.

(4) Where a motor vehicle to which paragraphs (6) or (7) of either Regulation 54 or Regulation 59 applies is being used while drawing a trailer (whenever manufactured) other than a trailer not required by these Regulations to be equipped with a braking system, whether or not that motor vehicle and trailer together form an articulated vehicle, then every part of every braking system with which that motor vehicle is equipped and every part of every braking system with which the trailer is equipped shall be so maintained that, when the brakes of any braking system with which the motor vehicle is equipped are applied by their means of operation, they produce (whether assisted by the brakes on the trailer or not) the same

total braking efficiencies as would be required of the brakes of such a motor vehicle when applied by that means of operation if that motor vehicle were not drawing a trailer, and if, in the case of a motor vehicle to which the said paragraph (6) applies, it were treated as being a motor vehicle having to comply with paragraph (7) of either Regulation 54 or Regulation 59.

(5) Where a motor vehicle to which Regulation 13 (2) applies is attached to a trailer manufactured on or after 1st January 1968 (other than a trailer not required by these Regulations to be equipped with a braking system), whether or not that motor vehicle and trailer together form an articulated vehicle, and the combination of those vehicles is stationary, then every part of every braking system with which that motor vehicle is equipped and every part of every braking system with which the trailer is equipped shall be so maintained that the brakes of those systems as applied by the means of operation specified in the said paragraph (2) can together produce a braking force sufficient to hold the combination of vehicles stationary on a gradient of at least 1 in 6·25 without the assistance of stored energy.

Maintenace of steering gear and windscreen wiper

95.—(1) All steering gear fitted to a motor vehicle shall at all times while the vehicle is used on a road be maintained in good and efficient working order and be properly adjusted.

(2) Every windscreen wiper required by these Regulations to be fitted to a motor vehicle shall at all times while the vehicle is used on a road be maintained in good and efficient working order and be properly adjusted.

Maintenance of petrol tank

96.—Every motor vehicle shall at all times be so maintained that—

(a) any tank, in which petroleum-spirit as defined in section 23 of the Petroleum (Consolidation) Act 1928 used either for the propulsion of the vehicle or for the driving of any ancillary engine or equipment forming part of the vehicle is contained, is reasonably secure against its being damaged, and

(b) the leakage of any liquid or vapour from the said tank is adequately prevented so, however, that nothing in this paragraph shall be taken to preclude the tank being fitted with a device which by the intake of air or the emission of vapour relieves changes in pressure in the tank.

Maintenance of lighting equipment and reflectors

97.—(1) Subject to the following provisions of this Regulation, every lamp and reflector and all other equipment with which a motor vehicle is required by Regulation 38 (1) to be equipped shall at all times while the vehicle is used on a road be maintained in such a condition as to render the vehicle capable of being driven on a road during the hours of darkness without contravention of any of the statutory provisions relating to obligatory lamps or reflectors which are applicable to that vehicle.

(2) Subject to the following provisions of this Regulation, every head lamp carried by a vehicle which, by virtue of paragraph (2) of Regulation 38, is required to be constructed and fitted to that vehicle in accordance with the provisions of the said paragraph (2) shall at all times while the vehicle is used on a road be maintained in such a condition that if that lamp were to be used to show a light to the front while the vehicle was driven on a road during the hours of darkness such use would not be in

contravention of the provisions of Regulation 9 of the Road Vehicles Lighting Regulations 1971.

(3) Where a person is charged with a contravention of any provision of this Regulation in respect of the use of a vehicle on a road otherwise than during the hours of darkness, it shall be a defence for that person to prove—

    (a) that the contravention arose from a defect in the lighting equipment of, or in a reflector carried by, the vehicle which occurred in the course of the journey during which the contravention occurred; or

    (b) that the contravention arose from a defect in the lighting equipment of, or in a reflector carried by, the vehicle and that before the contravention occurred steps had been taken to have the defect remedied with all reasonable expedition.

(4) In this Regulation, the expressions " statutory provisions relating to obligatory lamps or reflectors " and " headlamp " have the same meanings as in Regulation 38.

Use and maintenance of silencer

98.—(1) No person shall use or cause or permit to be used on a road any vehicle propelled by an internal combustion engine so that the exhaust gases from the engine escape into the atmosphere without first passing through the silencer, expansion chamber or other contrivance required by these Regulations to be fitted.

(2) Every such silencer, expansion chamber or other contrivance shall at all times while the vehicle is used on a road be maintained in good and efficient working order and shall not have been altered in such a way that the noise caused by the escape of the exhaust gases is made greater by the alteration.

Condition and maintenance of tyres

99.—(1) Save as provided in paragraph (1A) and (2) of this Regulation, no person shall use or cause or permit to be used on a road any motor vehicle or trailer a wheel of which is fitted with a pneumatic tyre, if—

    (a) the tyre is unsuitable having regard to the use to which the motor vehicle or trailer is being put or to the types of tyres fitted to its other wheels;

    (b) the tyre is not so inflated as to make it fit for the use to which the motor vehicle or trailer is being put;

    (c) the tyre has a break in its fabric, or has a cut in excess of 25 millimetres or 10 per cent. of the section width of the tyre, whichever is the greater, measured in any direction on the outside of the tyre and deep enough to reach the body cords;

    (d) the tyre has any lump or bulge caused by separation or partial failure of its structure;

    (e) the tyre has any portion of the ply or cord structure exposed; or

    (f) where the tyre is fitted to a wheel of a motor vehicle, being a motor cycle whereof the cylinder capacity of the engine does not exceed 50 cubic centimetres, the tread of the tyre does not show throughout at least three quarters of the breadth of the tread and round the entire outer circumference of the tyre a pattern the relief of which is clearly visible, or where the tyre is fitted to the wheel of any other motor vehicle or any trailer, the tread pattern (excluding any tie-bar) of the tyre does not have a depth of at least 1 mm. throughout at least three-quarters of the breadth of the tread and round the entire outer circumference of the tyre:

Provided that this sub-paragraph shall not apply in the case of a motor cycle having three wheels, the unladen weight of which does not exceed 102 kilograms and which is incapable of exceeding a speed of 12 miles per hour on the level under its own power or in the case of a pedestrian controlled vehicle being a works truck.

(1A) Paragraph (1) of this Regulation shall not prohibit the use on a road of a motor vehicle or trailer by reason only of the fact that a wheel of the vehicle or trailer is fitted with a tyre which is deflated or not fully inflated and which has any of the defects described in sub-paragraph (c), (d) or (e) of paragraph (1) of this Regulation, if the tyre and the wheel to which it is fitted are so constructed as to make the tyre in that condition fit for the use to which the motor vehicle or trailer is being put and the outer sides of the wall of the tyre are so marked as to enable the tyre to be identified as having been constructed to comply with the requirements of this paragraph.

(2) Nothing in paragraph (1) of this Regulation shall apply to a land locomotive, land tractor, land implement or land implement conveyor, or to an agricultural trailer when the trailer is being drawn by a land tractor and nothing in that paragraph or in the next succeeding paragraph shall apply to a broken down vehicle or to a vehicle proceeding to a place where it is to be broken up, in either case being drawn by a motor vehicle at a speed not exceeding 20 miles per hour.

(3) No person shall use or cause or permit to be used on a road any motor vehicle or trailer a wheel of which is fitted with a recut pneumatic tyre the fabric of which has been cut or exposed by the recutting process.

(4) Without prejudice to paragraphs (1) and (3) of this Regulation, all the tyres of a motor vehicle or trailer shall at all times while the vehicle or trailer is used on a road be maintained in such condition as to be fit for the use to which the vehicle or trailer is being put, and as to be free from any defect which might in any way cause damage to the surface of the road or danger to persons on or in the vehicle or to other persons using the road.

100.—(1) No person shall use or cause or permit to be used on a road a vehicle to which this paragraph applies, if pneumatic tyres of different types of structure are fitted to the same axle of the vehicle.

(2) Paragraph (1) of this Regulation applies to a passenger car, a dual-purpose vehicle, a goods vehicle (other than a dual-purpose vehicle) the unladen weight of which does not exceed 1525 kilograms and to a trailer drawn by any such vehicle.

(3) No person shall use or cause or permit to be used on a road a vehicle to which this paragraph applies, if—

(a) a diagonal-ply tyre or a bias-belted tyre is fitted on the rear axle of the vehicle and that vehicle has a radial-ply tyre fitted on the front axle thereof; or

(b) a diagonal-ply tyre is fitted on the rear axle of the vehicle and that vehicle has a bias-belted tyre fitted on the front axle thereof.

(4) Paragraph (3) of this Regulation applies to a passenger car, a dual-purpose vehicle, and a goods vehicle (other than a dual-purpose vehicle) the unladen weight of which does not exceed 1525 kilograms.

(5) For the purposes of this Regulation—

" a diagonal-ply tyre " means a pneumatic tyre, the structure of which is such that the ply cords extend to the bead so as to be laid at alternate angles of substantially less than 90° to the peripheral line of the tread, but not being a bias-belted tyre;

" a bias-belted tyre " means a pneumatic tyre, the structure of which is such that the ply cords extend to the bead so as to be laid at alternate angles of substantially less than 90° to the peripheral line of the tread, and are constrained by a circumferential belt comprising two or more layers of substantially inextensible cord material laid at alternate angles smaller than those of the ply cord structure;

" a radial-ply tyre " means a pneumatic tyre, the structure of which is such that the ply cords extend to the bead so as to be laid at an angle of substantially 90° to the peripheral line of the tread, the ply cord structure being stabilised by a substantially inextensible circumferential belt;

" type of structure ", in relation to a tyre, means a type of structure of a tyre of a kind defined in the foregoing provisions of this paragraph; and

" passenger car " means a passenger vehicle with three or more wheels and not constructed to carry more than seven passengers exclusive of the driver, but does not include a two-wheeled motor cycle with a sidecar attached.

Maintenance and use of vehicles so as not to emit smoke, etc.

101. No person shall use or cause or permit to be used on a road any motor vehicle from which any smoke, visible vapour, grit, sparks, ashes, cinders, or oily substance is emitted if the emission thereof causes or is likely to cause damage to any property or injury to any person who is actually at the time or who reasonably may be expected on the road, or is likely to cause danger to any such person as aforesaid.

102.—On and after 1st April 1973, no person shall use or cause or permit to be used on a road a motor vehicle to which Regulation 34 or a motor vehicle to which Regulation 4A (1) applies by virtue of the vehicle's conforming to the requirements of Council Directive 72/306/EEC of 2nd August 1972 (which relates to the measures to be taken against the emission of pollutants from diesel engines for use in vehicles), applies, if the fuel injection equipment, the engine speed governor or any other parts of the engine by which it is propelled have in any way been altered or adjusted so as to increase by such alteration or adjustment the emission of smoke from that vehicle.

103. Where a motor vehicle, being a vehicle propelled by a compression ignition engine, is fitted with a device to facilitate the starting of the engine by causing it to be supplied with excess fuel—

(*a*) the device shall be maintained in such a condition that it does not cause the engine to be supplied with excess fuel while the vehicle is in motion on a road; and

(*b*) no person shall use the device or cause, or permit it to be used, so as to cause it to supply the engine with excess fuel while the vehicle is in motion on a road:

Provided that paragraph (b) of this Regulation shall not apply as respects a device such as is mentioned in sub-paragraph (ii) of the proviso to Regulation 32 (2).

104. The engine of every motor vehicle to which Regulation 33 applies shall at all times while the vehicle is used on a road be so maintained that the means by which (in compliance with that Regulation) vapours or gases in the engine crank case or in other parts of the engine are prevented from escaping into the atmosphere are in good and efficient working order.

Contents of lavatories, etc.

105. No person shall cause or permit the contents of any closet, urinal, lavatory basin or sink carried by a motor vehicle or trailer or of any tank into which such closet, urinal, lavatory basin or sink drains to be discharged or to leak on to a road.

Excessive noise

106. No person shall use or cause or permit to be used on a road any motor vehicle or trailer which causes any excessive noise:

Provided that it shall be a good defence to proceedings taken in respect of a contravention of this Regulation—

   (i) to prove that the noise or continuance of the noise in respect of which the proceedings are taken was due to some temporary or accidental cause and could not have been prevented by the exercise of due diligence and care on the part of the owner or driver of the motor vehicle, or

   (ii) in the case of proceedings against the driver or person in charge of the motor vehicle who is not the owner thereof, to prove that the noise arose through a defect in design or construction of the motor vehicle or trailer or through the negligence or fault of some other person whose duty it was to keep the motor vehicle or trailer in proper condition or in a proper state of repair or adjustment or properly to pack or adjust the load of such motor vehicle or trailer as the case may be and could not have been prevented by the exercise of reasonable diligence and care on the part of such driver or other person in charge of the motor vehicle.

107. No motor vehicle shall be used on a road in such manner as to cause any excessive noise which could have been avoided by the exercise of reasonable care on the part of the driver.

Limitation of noise by measurement

108.—(1) Except as provided in paragraph (4) of this Regulation, this Regulation applies to any vehicle which is a motor vehicle first used on or after 1st January 1931, or which is a trailer.

(2) Subject to the following provisions of this Regulation, no person shall use or cause or permit to be used on a road any vehicle to which this Regulation applies if—

   (a) at a time when the noise emitted by that vehicle is measured under the conditions set out in Schedule 10 by an apparatus of the kind prescribed by paragraph (5) of this Regulation, there is indicated by that apparatus in relation to the said noise so measured a sound level (A weighting) in decibels which exceeds the maximum sound level permitted in relation to that vehicle by the next following paragraph, and

(b) the sound level of such noise as is described in paragraph 4 of Schedule 10 when measured in accordance with the provisions of that paragraph is found to be at least 10 decibels (A weighting) below the sound level indicated as hereinbefore provided by the said apparatus in relation to the noise emitted by the vehicle.

(3) The maximum permitted sound level for the purposes of the last preceding paragraph shall be—

(a) if the vehicle to which this Regulation applies is a motor vehicle first used before 1st November 1970, the sound level (A weighting) in decibels which appears in Column 3 of Schedule 9 as the maximum sound level permitted for the relevant class or description of vehicle shown against that sound level in Column 1 of that Schedule, and

(b) if the vehicle to which this Regulation applies is a motor vehicle first used on or after 1st November 1970, the sound level (A weighting) in decibels which appears in Column 4 of Schedule 9 as the maximum sound level permitted for the relevant class or description of vehicle shown against that sound level in Column 1 of that Schedule.

(4) This Regulation shall not apply—

(a) to a motor vehicle proceeding to a place where, by previous arrangement—

(i) noise emitted by it is about to be measured for the purpose of ascertaining whether or not that vehicle complies with Regulation 29, or

(ii) the vehicle is about to be mechanically adjusted, modified or equipped for the purpose of securing that it so complies, or

(b) to a motor vehicle returning from such a place immediately after the noise has been so measured, or the vehicle has been so adjusted, modified or equipped, or

(c) to a vehicle at a time when it is stationary otherwise than through enforced stoppage owing to the necessities of traffic and at the same time Regulation 109, by virtue of the proviso thereto, does not apply in relation to that vehicle, or

(d) to a motor vehicle first used before the date mentioned in paragraph (3) (a) of this Regulation at a time when an exhaust brake with which that vehicle is fitted is in operation, or

(e) to a road roller.

(5) The apparatus prescribed for the purposes of paragraph (2) of this Regulation shall be a noise meter of the same kind as that prescribed for the purposes of paragraph (1) of Regulation 29 and paragraph (3) of that Regulation shall have effect in relation to this Regulation as if any references therein to paragraph (1) of Regulation 29 were references to paragraph (2) of this Regulation.

(6) It shall be a good defence to proceedings taken in respect of the use of a vehicle which does not comply with this Regulation to prove the matters which would, by virtue of either proviso (i) or proviso (ii) to Regulation 106, constitute a good defence to proceedings taken in respect of the use of a motor vehicle which does not comply with that Regulation.

(7) The definition of sound level (A weighting) in decibels specified in Regulation 29 (5) shall apply for the purposes of this Regulation and Schedules 9 and 10.

(8) In this Regulation and Schedule 10, any reference to noise emitted by a vehicle shall be construed as including a reference to noise howsoever arising which is attributable to any load, burden or goods carried on or by the vehicle or to anything (other than an audible warning instrument fitted in accordance with Regulation 27 (1) or an instrument or apparatus fitted in accordance with Regulation 27 (6)) fitted to it, or attributable to the manner in which the vehicle is loaded or fitted.

(9) Where any motor vehicle to which this Regulation applies is drawing a trailer, this Regulation and Schedules 9 and 10 shall have effect in relation to that motor vehicle as if any reference to it were a reference both to the motor vehicle and to the trailer drawn thereby.

(10) Where any motor vehicle to which this Regulation applies is also a vehicle to which Regulation 4A (1) applies by virtue of the vehicle's conforming to the requirements of Council Directive (EEC) No. 70/157 of 6th February 1970 (which relates to the permissible sound level and exhaust system of motor vehicles), and is a vehicle of which the power of the engine is not less than 200 HP DIN, the maximum permitted sound level for the purposes of paragraph (2) above shall, instead of that specified in paragraph (3) above, be 94 decibels (A weighting).

Stopping of engine when stationary

109. The driver of every motor vehicle shall, when the vehicle is stationary otherwise than through enforced stoppage owing to the necessities of traffic, stop the action of any machinery attached to or forming part of such vehicle so far as may be necessary for the prevention of noise:

Provided that this Regulation shall not apply—

    (a) so as to prevent the examination or working of the machinery attached to or forming part of a motor vehicle where any such examination or working is rendered necessary by any failure or derangement of the said machinery or where the machinery attached to or forming part of the vehicle is required to be worked for some ancillary purpose; or

    (b) in the case of a motor vehicle which is propelled by gas produced in plant carried on the vehicle or on a trailer drawn by the vehicle.

Use of audible warning instruments

110.—(1) Subject to the provisions of this Regulation, no person shall—

    (a) in the case of a vehicle which is stationary on a road, at any time, other than at times of danger due to another motor vehicle on or near the road; or

    (b) in the case of a vehicle which is in motion on a restricted road, between the hours of 23.30 hours in the evening and 07.00 hours in the following morning.

sound or cause or permit to be sounded any instrument or apparatus fitted to or otherwise carried on the vehicle, being an instrument or apparatus capable of giving audible and sufficient warning of its approach or position.

(2) Subject to the provisions of this Regulation and without prejudice to the provisions of the foregoing paragraph, no person shall sound or

cause or permit to be sounded a gong, bell, siren, any instrument or apparatus capable of making a sound similar to that emitted by a gong, bell or siren, or a two-tone horn, fitted to or otherwise carried on a vehicle (whether it is stationary or not).

(3) Nothing in paragraph (1) or (2) of this Regulation shall have effect to prevent the sounding of an instrument or apparatus fitted to, or otherwise carried on, a vehicle at a time when the vehicle is being used for one of the relevant purposes specified in Regulation 27 (5) and it is necessary or desirable to do so either to indicate to other road users the urgency of the purposes for which the vehicle is being used, or to warn other road users of the presence of the vehicle on the road.

(4) Nothing in paragraph (1) of this Regulation shall have effect to prevent the driver of a vehicle or some other authorised person sounding or causing or permitting to be sounded an instrument or apparatus fitted to or otherwise carried on the vehicle if it is sounded for the purpose of raising an alarm as to the theft or attempted theft of the vehicle or its contents

> (a) if it is sounded for the purpose of raising an alarm as to the theft or attempted theft of the vehicle or its contents, or
>
> (b) if the vehicle is a public service vehicle as defined by sections 117 and 118 of the Road Traffic Act 1960 and the instrument or apparatus is sounded for the purpose of summoning assistance for the driver, the conductor or an inspector.

(5) Subject to the provisions of section 2 (1) and (3) of the Noise Abatement Act 1960, and notwithstanding the provisions of paragraph (2) of this Regulation, a person may sound or cause or permit to be sounded an instrument or apparatus other than a two-tone horn fitted to or otherwise carried on a vehicle, being an instrument or apparatus designed to emit a sound for the purpose of informing members of the public that the vehicle is conveying goods for sale, if—

> (a) when the instrument is sounded, it is sounded only for that purpose; and
>
> (b) in a case where a vehicle is on a restricted road, the instrument is sounded otherwise than between the hours of 23.30 hours in the evening and 07.00 hours in the following morning.

(6) In this Regulation:—
" restricted road " means a length of road—

> > (a) on which there is provided a system of street lighting furnished by means of lamps placed not more than 200 metres apart, or
> >
> > (b) as respects which there is in force a direction under section 72 (3) of the Road Traffic Regulation Act 1967, that the said length shall become a restricted road for the purposes of section 71 of that Act or a direction under section 1 (4) of the Road Traffic Act 1934, which, by virtue of paragraphs 1 and 10 of Schedule 8 to the said Act of 1967, has effect under that Act as such a direction as aforesaid.

Duties relating to driving and stopping

111. No person while actually driving a motor vehicle on a road shall be in such a position that he cannot have proper control of that vehicle or that he cannot retain a full view of the road and traffic ahead and no person shall cause or permit any other person while actually driving a motor vehicle on a road to be in such a position as aforesaid.

112. No person shall cause or permit a motor vehicle to travel backwards for a greater distance or time than may be requisite for the safety or reasonable convenience of the occupants of that vehicle or of other traffic on the road:

Provided that this Regulation shall not apply in the case of a road roller or other road plant while actually engaged in the construction maintenance or repair of roads.

113. The driver of every vehicle propelled by steam (other than a motor car) shall, unless two persons are carried on it for the purpose of driving or attending to the vehicle, stop the vehicle whenever it is necessary to attend to the furnace.

114. No person in charge of a motor vehicle or trailer shall cause or permit the motor vehicle or trailer to stand on a road so as to cause any unnecessary obstruction thereof.

115.—(1) Save as provided in paragraph (2) of this Regulation, no person shall, except with the permission of a police officer in uniform, cause or permit any motor vehicle to stand on any road during the hours of darkness otherwise than with the left or near side of the vehicle as close as may be to the edge of the carriageway.

(2) This Regulation shall not apply—

(*a*) to any motor vehicle when it is being used for fire brigade, ambulance or police purposes or for defence purposes (including civil defence purposes) if compliance with this Regulation would hinder or be likely to hinder the use of the vehicle for the purpose for which it is being used on that occasion;

(*b*) to any motor vehicle standing on a part of a road specially set aside for the parking of vehicles or as a stand for hackney carriages or as a stand for public service vehicles or as a place at which such vehicles may stop for a longer time than is necessary for the taking up and setting down of passengers where compliance with this Regulation would conflict with the provisions of any order, regulations or byelaws governing the use of such part of a road for that purpose;

(*c*) to any motor vehicle waiting to set down or pick up passengers in accordance with regulations made or directions given by a chief officer of police in regard to such setting down or picking up;

(*d*) to any motor vehicle on any road in which vehicles are allowed to proceed in one direction only; or

(*e*) to any motor vehicle whilst it is being used in connection with—

(i) any building operation or demolition,

(ii) the repair of any other vehicle,

(iii) the removal of any obstruction to traffic,

(iv) the maintenance, repair or reconstruction of any road, or

(v) the laying, erection, alteration or repair in or near to any road of any sewer, of any main, pipe or apparatus for the supply of gas, water or electricity, of any telegraph or telephone wires, cables, posts or supports or of the apparatus of any electric transport undertaking if, in any such case, compliance with this Regulation would hinder or be likely to hinder the use of the vehicle for the purpose for which it is being used on that occasion.

116. No person shall cause or permit to be on a road any motor vehicle which is not attended by a person duly licensed to drive it unless the engine is stopped and the relevant parking brake is effectively set:

Provided that the requirements of this Regulation as to the stopping of the engine shall not apply in the case of—

(a) a fire brigade vehicle the engine of which is being used for any fire brigade purpose;

(b) a vehicle which is propelled by gas produced in plant carried on the vehicle or on a trailer drawn by the vehicle;

(c) a vehicle when it is being used for police or ambulance purposes; or

(d) a vehicle engaged in operations which require its engine to be used—

(i) to drive special machinery or apparatus forming part of the vehicle or mounted thereon, such machinery or apparatus being that used for purposes other than in connection with the driving of the vehicle; or

(ii) to maintain the electrical power in the batteries of the vehicle at a level required for the driving of such machinery or apparatus,

so, however, that paragraph (d) of this proviso shall not have effect in the case of a vehicle which is stationary on a road in such a position or in such condition or in such circumstances (including the gradient of the road) as to be likely to cause danger to any person or property.

In this Regulation, " relevant parking brake " means—

(a) in the case of a motor vehicle to which Regulation 4A (1) applies, being a vehicle to which that Regulation applies by virtue of the vehicle's conforming to the requirements of Council Directive (EEC) No. 71/320 of 26th July 1971, the parking brake provided in accordance with those requirements; and

(b) in the case of any other motor vehicle, the parking brake provided in accordance with Regulation 13.

Opening of doors

117. No person shall open or cause or permit to be opened any door of a motor vehicle or trailer on a road so as to cause injury or danger to any person.

Application of brakes of trailers

118. Where a trailer is drawn by a motor vehicle whether wheeled or track laying the driver (or in the case of a locomotive one of the persons employed in driving or tending the locomotive) shall be in a position readily to operate any brakes required to be fitted to the trailer as well as the brakes of the motor vehicle unless a person other than the driver is in a position and competent efficiently to apply the brakes of the trailer:

Provided that this Regulation shall not apply in the case of trailers which, in compliance with these Regulations, are fitted with brakes which automatically come into operation on the overrun of the trailer or where a motor vehicle is drawing a broken down vehicle, whether or not in consequence of a breakdown, in such a manner that the broken down vehicle cannot be steered by its own steering gear.

In this Regulation, the reference to the brakes required to be fitted to a trailer means—

(a) in the case of a trailer to which Regulation 4A (1) applies, being a trailer to which that Regulation applies by virtue of the trailer's conforming to the requirements of Council Directive (EEC) No. 71/320 of 26th July 1971 the brakes fitted in accordance with those requirements; and

(b) in the case of any other trailer, the brakes fitted in accordance with the requirements of these Regulations.

119. No person in charge of a motor vehicle, whether wheeled or track laying, or trailer drawn thereby shall cause or permit such trailer to stand when detached from the drawing vehicle unless one at least of the wheels of the trailer is prevented from revolving by the setting of the brake or the use of a chain.

Restriction on distance between motor vehicles and trailers and marking of trailer connections

120.—(1) Where a motor vehicle is drawing a trailer solely by means of a rope or chain or, in a case where more than one trailer is being drawn, where a trailer is attached to another trailer solely by such means, the length of the rope or chain shall be such that the distance between the nearest points of the trailer and the vehicle to which it is so attached cannot exceed 4·5 metres.

(2) Where a motor vehicle is drawing a trailer or trailers and the distance between the nearest points of the trailer or, as the case may be, of any trailer so drawn and the vehicle to which it is attached exceeds 1·5 metres, steps shall be taken to render the means whereby that trailer is attached to that vehicle clearly visible to other persons using the road within a reasonable distance from either side of either vehicle.

(3) For the purposes of this Regulation, in determining the nearest points of two vehicles any part of either vehicle designed primarily for use as a means of attaching the one vehicle to the other and of any fitting designed for use in connection with any such part shall be disregarded.

Restrictions on the use of vehicles to draw trailers and of trailers drawn

121. Every sidecar fitted to a motor cycle shall be so attached that the wheel thereof is not wholly outside perpendicular planes at right angles to the longitudinal axis of the motor cycle passing through the extreme projecting points in the front and in the rear of the motor cycle.

122. A motor cycle with not more than two wheels and without a sidecar shall not draw a trailer:

Provided that this Regulation shall not apply to prevent the towing of a broken down motor cycle which is being drawn by another motor cycle in consequence of the breakdown.

123. No motor cycle shall draw a trailer exceeding 254 kilograms in weight unladen or 1·5 metres in overall width.

124. No straddle carrier or invalid carriage shall draw a trailer.

125. No trailer shall be used for the conveyance of passengers for hire or reward:

Provided that this Regulation shall not apply to a trailer, being either a broken down motor vehicle or a trailer carrying a broken down motor vehicle, while being drawn in consequence of a breakdown of the said motor vehicle if the following conditions are fulfilled—

(a) the trailer is not drawn at a speed in excess of 30 miles per hour; and

(b) where the trailer is, or is carrying, a broken down motor vehicle constructed or adapted to carry more than 7 passengers exclusive of the driver or any other broken down motor vehicle carrying more than 8 persons, it is attached to the drawing vehicle by means of a rigid draw bar.

126. No trailer, which is a living van and either has less than 4 wheels or is a four-wheeled trailer having two close-coupled wheels on each side, shall be used for the carriage of any passenger:

Provided that this Regulation shall not apply to a trailer while it is being tested by the manufacturer by whom it was made, or by the repairer by whom it is being or has been repaired, or by a distributor of trailers or a dealer in trailers.

127. No trailer shall be drawn by a public service vehicle:

Provided that this Regulation shall not apply—

(1) to the drawing of one empty public service vehicle by another empty public service vehicle in case of emergency:

(2) to the drawing of a gas trailer, or

(3) to the drawing of a trailer if—

(a) the public service vehicle is being used—

(i) under, or for the purposes of providing a road service under, a road service licence a condition of which is that trailers may be used, or

(ii) on a London bus service within the meaning of the Transport (London) Act 1969; and

(b) a certifying officer has approved the drawing of the trailer by the public service vehicle and the means of attachment.

128.—(1) Where a motor vehicle is drawing only one trailer the overall length of the combination of vehicles shall not exceed 18 metres, except that this paragraph shall not apply where the trailer being drawn is constructed and normally used for the conveyance of indivisible loads of exceptional length or in the case of a broken down vehicle being drawn by a motor vehicle in consequence of the breakdown.

(2) Where a motor vehicle is drawing two or more trailers or only one trailer constructed and normally used for the conveyance of indivisible loads of exceptional length, the overall length of the motor vehicle shall not exceed 9·2 metres and unless the conditions specified in paragraphs 1

and 2 of Schedule 8 have been complied with, the overall length of the combination of vehicles shall not exceed 25·9 metres.

(3) Where a motor vehicle is drawing two trailers only one such trailer may exceed 7 metres in overall length, and, where a motor vehicle is drawing three trailers, no trailer in the combination of vehicles shall exceed 7 metres in overall length.

(4) For the purposes of this Regulation the reference to the combination of vehicles shall be construed in the same manner as provided in sub-paragraph (*g*) of Regulation 130 (1) for the purposes of Regulation 131 and the overall length of such a combination shall be measured in the manner provided in sub-paragraph (*h*) of the said Regulation 130 (1).

Passengers on motor bicycles

129. If any person in addition to the driver is carried astride any two-wheeled motor cycle (whether a sidecar is attached thereto or not) suitable supports or rests for the feet shall be available on such cycle for that person.

Restrictions on use of vehicles carrying wide or long loads or having fixed appliances or apparatus

130.—(1) For the purposes of this and the following Regulation and of Schedule 8—

(*a*) the expression " lateral projection ", in relation to a load carried by a vehicle, means that part of the load which extends beyond a side of the vehicle;

(*b*) the width of any lateral projection shall be measured between vertical planes parallel to the longitudinal axis of the vehicle and passing through the extreme projecting point of the vehicle on that side on which the projection lies and that part of the projection furthest from that point;

(*c*) references to a special appliance or apparatus, in relation to a vehicle, are references to any crane or other special appliance or apparatus fitted to the vehicle which is a permanent or essentially permanent fixture;

(*d*) the expressions " forward projection " and " rearward projection "—

(i) in relation to a load carried in such a manner that its weight rests on only one vehicle, mean respectively that part of the load which extends beyond the foremost point of the vehicle and that part which extends beyond the rearmost point of the vehicle,

(ii) in relation to a load carried in such a manner that part of its weight rests on more than one vehicle, mean respectively that part of the load which extends beyond the foremost point of the foremost vehicle by which the load is carried except where the context otherwise requires and that part of the load which extends beyond the rearmost point of the rearmost vehicle by which the load is carried, and

(iii) in relation to any special appliance or apparatus, mean respectively that part of the appliance or apparatus which, if it were deemed to be a load carried by the vehicle, would be a part of a load extending beyond the foremost point of the vehicle and that part which would be a part of a load extending beyond the rearmost point of the vehicle, and references in the following Regulation and in Schedule 8 to a forward projection or to a rearward projection in relation to a vehicle shall be construed accordingly;

(e) the length of any forward projection or of any rearward projection shall be measured between vertical planes at right angles to the longitudinal axis of the vehicle and passing—

(i) in the case of a forward projection, through the foremost point of the vehicle and that part of the projection furthest from that point, and

(ii) in the case of a rearward projection, through the rearmost point of the vehicle and that part of the projection furthest from that point.

In this and the foregoing sub-paragraph the expression " vehicle " shall not include any special appliance or apparatus or any part thereof which is a forward projection or a rearward projection within the meaning of this Regulation;

(f) references to the distance between vehicles, in relation to vehicles carrying a load, are references to the distance between the nearest points of any two adjacent vehicles by which the load is carried, measured when the longitudinal axis of each vehicle lies in the same vertical plane.

For the purposes of this sub-paragraph, in determining the nearest point of two vehicles any part of either vehicle designed primarily for use as a means of attaching the one vehicle to the other and of any fitting designed for use in connection with any such part shall be disregarded;

(g) references to a combination of vehicles, in relation to a motor vehicle which is drawing one or more trailers, are references to the motor vehicle and the trailer or trailers drawn thereby, including any other motor vehicle which is used for the purpose of assisting in the propulsion of the trailer or the trailers on the road;

(h) the overall length of a combination of vehicles shall be taken as the distance between the foremost point of the drawing vehicle comprised in the combination and the rearmost point of the rearmost vehicle comprised therein, measured when the longitudinal axis of each vehicle comprised in the combination lies in the same vertical plane;

(i) the extreme projecting point of a vehicle shall be taken as excluding any part of, or part of the equipment of, a vehicle which, by virtue of sub-paragraphs (a) to (f) of the definition of the overall width of a vehicle contained in Regulation 3 (1) falls to be excluded in determining that overall width; and

(j) the foremost or, as the case may be, the rearmost points of a vehicle shall be taken as excluding any part of, or part of the equipment of, a vehicle which, by virtue of sub-paragraphs (a) to (h) of the definition of the overall length of a vehicle contained in Regulation 3 (1) falls to be excluded in determining that overall length.

131.—(1) No load shall be carried on a vehicle where the overall width of the vehicle together with the width of any lateral projection or projections of its load exceeds 4·3 metres.

(2) Subject to the following provisions of this Regulation, no load shall be carried on a vehicle—

(a) where the load has a lateral projection exceeding 305 millimetres in width; or

(b) where the overall width of the vehicle together with the width of any lateral projection or projections of its load exceeds 2·9 metres:

Provided that this paragraph shall not apply—

(i) to the carriage of an indivisible load if—

(a) it is not reasonably practicable to comply with the requirements of the said paragraph, and

(b) the conditions specified in paragraph 1 of Schedule 8 have been complied with, and

(c) where the overall width of the vehicle together with the width of any lateral projection or projections of its load exceeds 3·5 metres, the conditions specified in paragraph 2 of Schedule 8 have been complied with; or

(ii) to the carriage of loose agricultural produce not baled or crated.

(3) Where a load is carried in such a manner that its weight rests—

(a) on one vehicle being a heavy motor car or a trailer the overall length of the heavy motor car or, as the case may be, of the trailer together with the length of any forward and of any rearward projection of the load shall not exceed 27·4 metres; or

(b) on more than one vehicle being—

(i) a motor vehicle drawing one trailer whether forming part of an articulated vehicle or not, or

(ii) any other combination of vehicles,

then, in the case at (i) above, the overall length of the trailer together with the length of any forward projection of the load extending beyond the foremost point of the trailer and of any rearward projection of the load shall not exceed 27·4 metres and, in the case at (ii) above, the overall length of the vehicles together with the distance between vehicles and the length of any forward and of any rearward projection of the load shall not exceed 27·4 metres.

(4) Subject to the following provisions of this Regulation—

(a) no load shall be carried on a vehicle where the overall length of the vehicle together with the length of any forward projection and of any rearward projection of the load exceeds 18·3 metres, and as respects a motor vehicle which is drawing a trailer or trailers, no load shall be carried in such a manner that its weight rests on more than one of the vehicles being—

(i) the motor vehicle and one trailer whether forming part of an articulated vehicle or not, or

(ii) any other combination of vehicles,

if, in the case at (i) above, the overall length of the trailer together with the length of any forward projection of the load extending beyond the foremost point of the trailer and of any rearward projection of the load exceeds 18·3 metres and, in the case at (ii) above the overall length of the vehicle together with the distance between vehicles and the length of any forward and of any rearward projection of the load exceeds 18·3 metres; and

(b) without prejudice to the foregoing sub-paragraph, no load shall be carried on a trailer drawn by a motor vehicle or in such a manner that part of its weight rests on more than one trailer so drawn where the overall length of the combination of vehicles together with the length of any forward projection of the load extending beyond the foremost point of the drawing vehicle comprised in the combination and the length of any rearward projection of load extending beyond the rearmost point of the rearmost vehicle comprised therein exceeds 25·9 metres,

unless the conditions specified in paragraphs 1 and 2 of Schedule 8 have been complied with.

(5) Subject to the following provisions of this Regulation, no vehicle having a special appliance or apparatus which—

(*a*) has a forward projection exceeding 1·83 metres in length but not exceeding 3·05 metres in length, shall be used on a road unless the conditions specified in paragraphs 2 and 3 of Schedule 8 have been complied with;

(*b*) has a rearward projection exceeding 1·07 metres in length but not exceeding 1·83 metres in length, shall be used on a road unless the condition specified in paragraph 4 of the said Schedule has been complied with;

(*c*) has a rearward projection exceeding 1·83 metres in length but not exceeding 3·05 metres in length, shall be used on a road unless the condition specified in paragraph 3 of the said Schedule has been complied with;

(*d*) has a forward or a rearward projection exceeding 3·05 metres in length, shall be used on a road unless the conditions specified in paragraphs 1, 2 and 3 of the said Schedule have been complied with.

(6) Subject to the following provisions of this Regulation, no load shall be carried on a vehicle—

(*a*) where the load has a forward projection exceeding 1·83 metres in length but not exceeding 3·05 metres in length, unless the conditions specified in paragraphs 2 and 3 of Schedule 8 have been complied with;

(*b*) where the load has a rearward projection exceeding 1·07 metres in length but not exceeding 1·83 metres in length, unless the condition specified in paragraph 4 of the said Schedule has been complied with;

(*c*) where the load has a rearward projection exceeding 1·83 metres in length but not exceeding 3·05 metres in length, unless the condition specified in paragraph 3 of the said Schedule has been complied with;

(*d*) where the load has a forward or a rearward projection exceeding 3·05 metres in length, unless the conditions specified in paragraphs 1, 2 and 3 of the said Schedule have been complied with;

(*e*) where the load is carried on an articulated vehicle not exceeding 15 metres in overall length and which is not constructed and normally used for the conveyance of indivisible loads of exceptional length and where the overall length of the articulated vehicle together with any forward or rearward projections of the load exceeds 16·8 metres, unless the condition specified in paragraph 1 of the said Schedule has been complied with:

Provided that—

(a) this paragraph shall not apply—

   (i) to the carriage of a load which consists, whether wholly or partly, of a boat used for racing and propelled solely by oars if any provision of this paragraph would otherwise apply by reason only of the boat being so carried that it has a forward projection or, as the case may be, a rearward projection, or

   (ii) to the carriage of a load by a straddle carrier; and

(b) notwithstanding that sub-paragraphs (c) and (d) of this paragraph provide for the condition specified in paragraph 3 of Schedule 8 to be complied with as respects a load which has a rearward projection specified in either of such sub-paragraphs, that condition in relation to the exhibition of the end projection surface on that rearward projection need not be complied with in the case of such a load which carries a rear marking in accordance with the Motor Vehicles (Rear Markings) Regulations 1970, as amended.

(7) Subject to the following provisions of this Regulation, where the load or part of the load carried by a vehicle consists, whether wholly or partly, of a boat used for racing and propelled solely by oars, the boat shall not be so carried that it has a forward projection or a rearward projection—

   (a) exceeding 1·07 metres in length unless the condition specified in paragraph 4 of Schedule 8 has been complied with; or

   (b) exceeding 3·05 metres in length unless the conditions specified in paragraphs 1 and 4 of the said Schedule have been complied with.

(8) Subject to the following provisions of this Regulation, no load shall be carried on a straddle carrier where the load has a rearward projection exceeding 1·07 metres in length unless the condition specified in paragraph 4 of Schedule 8 has been complied with:

Provided that this paragraph shall not apply in the case of a vehicle used in passing from one part of any private premises to any other part thereof or to other private premises in the immediate neighbourhood.

(9) Subject to the following provisions of this Regulation, no load shall be carried on a straddle carrier—

   (a) where the load has a forward projection exceeding 1·83 metres;

   (b) where the load has a rearward projection exceeding 3·05 metres in length;

   (c) where the overall length of the vehicle together with the length of any forward projection and of any rearward projection of its load exceeds 12·2 metres;

      Provided that this paragraph shall not apply in the case of a vehicle used in passing from one part of any private premises to any other part thereof or to other private premises in the immediate neighbourhood if—

         (i) the vehicle is not driven at a speed exceeding 12 miles per hour, and

         (ii) where the overall length of the vehicle together with the length of any forward projection and of any rearward projection of its load exceeds 12·2 metres, the conditions specified in paragraphs 1 and 2 of Schedule 8 have been complied with.

(10) In a case where a vehicle has a special appliance or apparatus or is

carrying a load or a boat used for racing as mentioned in paragraph (7) of this Regulation and the appliance or apparatus, the load or the said boat has, in relation to the vehicle, a forward projection or a rearward projection, and another vehicle is attached to that end of the vehicle from which the appliance or apparatus or, as the case may be, the load or the said boat projects and is attached to that vehicle in such manner that—

    (*a*) in the case where there is a forward projection, the foremost point of that other vehicle extends beyond the foremost part of the projection or, in the case where there is a rearward projection, the rearmost point of that other vehicle extends beyond the rearmost part of the projection; or

    (*b*) in the case where there is a forward projection, the foremost part of the projection extends beyond the foremost point of that other vehicle or, in the case where there is a rearward projection, the rearmost part of the projection extends beyond the rearmost point of that other vehicle, then—

        (i) in either of the cases mentioned in sub-paragraph (*a*) of this paragraph, the provisions of paragraphs (5), (6) and (7) of this Regulation, in so far as they provide for compliance with paragraphs 3 or 4 of Schedule 8, shall not apply as respects any such projection, and

        (ii) in either of the cases mentioned in sub-paragraph (*b*) of this paragraph, the provisions of the said paragraphs (5), (6) and (7), in so far as they provide for compliance with the said paragraph 3 or 4, shall apply as if each of the references in the said paragraphs (5), (6) and (7) to a forward projection and to a rearward projection were treated respectively as a reference to so much of a forward projection as extends beyond the foremost point of that other vehicle and to so much of a rearward projection as extends beyond the rearmost point of that other vehicle measured, in either case, when the longitudinal axis of each vehicle lies in the same vertical plane between vertical planes at right angles to the said longitudinal axis and passing, in the case of a forward projection, through the foremost point of the said other vehicle and that part of the projection furthest from that point or, in the case of a rearward projection, through the rearmost point of the said other vehicle and that part of the projection furthest from that point.

    (11) This Regulation shall not apply to any motor vehicle or trailer being used—

    (*a*) for fire brigade, ambulance or police purposes or for defence purposes (including civil defence purposes); or

    (*b*) in connection with the removal of any obstruction to traffic

if, in any such case, compliance with any provision of this Regulation would hinder or be likely to hinder the use of the vehicle for the purpose for which it is being used on that occasion.

Mascots

132. No mascot shall be carried by a motor vehicle first used on or after 1st October 1937, in any position where it is likely to strike any person with whom the vehicle may collide unless the mascot is not liable to cause injury to such person by reason of any projection thereon.

Television sets

133.—(1) No person shall use or install for use in a motor vehicle a television receiving apparatus if the screen thereof is partly or wholly, and whether directly or in any reflection, visible to the driver whilst in the driving seat, or if the controls thereof, other than the sound volume control and the main switch, are within reach of the driver whilst in the driving seat.

(2) No person shall use a television receiving apparatus in a motor vehicle under circumstances and in a position such that it might cause distraction to the driver of any other vehicle on the road.

Implements suspended from lifting appliances

134. Where a vehicle is fitted with any apparatus or appliance designed for lifting and part of the apparatus or appliance consists of an implement to facilitate lifting which is suspended from the apparatus or appliance, the implement shall at all times while the vehicle is in motion on a road and when the implement is not attached to any load supported by the appliance or apparatus be so secured either to the appliance or apparatus or to some part of the vehicle that no danger is caused or is likely to be caused to any person on the vehicle or on the road.

Attendants on trailers and certain other vehicles

135.—(1) The requirements of section 34 of the 1972 Act with regard to the employment of drivers and attendants shall not apply in the following cases, that is to say—

(*a*) in the case of any articulated vehicle;

(*b*) where a land implement or land implement conveyor is drawn by a land locomotive or land tractor or where an agricultural trailer is drawn by a land tractor;

(*c*) where a trailer with not more than two wheels is drawn by a motor car or a motor cycle or where a four-wheeled trailer having two close-coupled wheels on each side is drawn by a motor car;

(*d*) where a motor tractor is drawing—

(i) any closed trailer specially constructed and used for the conveyance of meat between docks and railway stations or between wholesale markets and docks or railway stations,

(ii) any machine or implement used for the purpose of the maintenance, repair or cleansing of roads, or

(iii) any trailer designed for use and used solely in connection with street cleansing, the collection or disposal of refuse or the collection or disposal of the contents of gullies or cesspools;

(*e*) where a works truck is drawing any works trailer and the weight unladen of each vehicle does not exceed 1525 kilograms;

(*f*) where a gas trailer is drawn by a heavy motor car or a motor car;

(*g*) where a motor vehicle is drawing a trailer which has no other brakes other than a parking brake, and brakes which automatically come into operation on the overrun of the trailer;

(*h*) in the case of any road roller;

(*i*) where a motor vehicle belonging to the Secretary of State for Defence and being used for naval, military or air force purposes is drawing a trailer fitted with brakes which can be applied by the driver of the drawing vehicle;

(*j*) where a motor vehicle is drawing a broken down vehicle, whether or not in consequence of a breakdown, in such a manner that the broken down vehicle cannot be steered by its own steering gear;

(*k*) where a vehicle is being drawn by a motor vehicle in the exercise of a statutory power of removal in such manner that the vehicle being so drawn cannot be steered by its own steering gear;

(*l*) where a towing implement is being drawn by a motor vehicle while it is not attached to any vehicle except the one drawing it; or

(*m*) where a motor vehicle is drawing a trailer or trailers and every such trailer is fitted with power assisted or power operated brakes which can be operated by the driver of the drawing vehicle and are not rendered ineffective by the non-rotation of the engine of the drawing vehicle—

    (i) where one such trailer is drawn; or

    (ii) where two or more such trailers are drawn, if one attendant is carried either on the drawing vehicle or a trailer for the purpose of attending to the trailers.

(1A) The requirements of the said section 34 with regard to the employment of persons to drive or attend a locomotive whilst being driven on a highway shall not apply in the case of a locomotive propelled by the combustion of liquid fuel or by electrical power, whether or not the locomotive is drawing a trailer or trailers.

(2) The provisions of this Regulation shall not be treated as prejudicing the operation of any provision of Regulation 131 in so far as it provides, in relation to the use of a vehicle on a road, for compliance with the conditions specified in paragraph 2 of Schedule 8 (which relates to the employment of persons in attending to vehicles and their load).

Restriction on number of trailers drawn

136.—(1) Subject to paragraph (2) below, the number of trailers which may be drawn by a motor vehicle on a road shall not exceed—

    (*a*) in the case of a locomotive, three;

    (*b*) in the case of a motor tractor, one, if laden, or two, if unladen;

    (*c*) in the case of a motor car or heavy motor car, one.

(2) A motor car or a heavy motor car may draw two trailers on a road in a case where one of the trailers being drawn is a towing implement and the other is a vehicle, part of which is secured to and either rests on, or is suspended from, the towing implement.

(3) For the purposes of this Regulation—

    (*a*) the expression " trailer " does not include a vehicle used solely for carrying water for the purposes of the drawing vehicle or an agricultural vehicle not constructed to carry a load; and

    (*b*) an articulated vehicle, when being drawn by another motor vehicle because the articulated vehicle has broken down, shall, if the articulated vehicle is unladen, be treated in relation to the drawing vehicle as a single trailer.

PART IV

TESTING AND INSPECTION OF BRAKES, SILENCERS, STEERING GEAR, TYRES,
LIGHTING EQUIPMENT AND REFLECTORS

Testing of brakes, etc.

137.—(1) Any police constable in uniform and any person for the
time being appointed by the Secretary of State as a certifying officer or
public service vehicle examiner under Part III of the 1960 Act or as
an examiner appointed under Part IV of that Act or under section 56 (1)
of the 1972 Act or appointed by the Commissioner of Police of the Metropolis to examine and inspect public carriages for the purposes of the
Metropolitan Public Carriage Act 1869, or appointed by the police
authority for a police area to act, under the directions of the Chief Officer
of Police, for the purposes of section 53 of the 1972 Act, who shall produce
his authority if required, is hereby empowered to test and inspect the brakes,
silencers, steering gear, tyres, lighting equipment and reflectors of any
motor vehicle or trailer on any premises where that motor vehicle or trailer
is, subject however to the consent of the owner of the premises.

(2) The power conferred by this Regulation to test and inspect the brakes,
silencers, steering gear, tyres, lighting equipment and reflectors of a vehicle
on any premises where the vehicle is shall not be exercised unless either
the owner of the vehicle consents or notice of the date and time at which
it is proposed to carry out the test and inspection has been given to him
in accordance with the provisions of the following paragraph.

(3) The said notice shall be given to the owner of the vehicle personally
or left at his address not less than 48 hours before the time of the proposed test and inspection or shall be sent to him not less than 72 hours
before that time by recorded delivery service at his address.

(4) The provisions of paragraph (2) of this Regulation shall not apply
in the case of a test and inspection made within 48 hours of an accident
to which section 25 of the 1972 Act applies and in which the vehicle has
been involved.

(5) For the purposes of this Regulation, the owner of the vehicle shall
be deemed to be—

(a) in the case of a vehicle which is for the time being registered under
the Vehicles (Excise) Act 1971, and is not being used under a
trade licence under that Act the person appearing as the owner
of the vehicle in the register kept by the Secretary of State under
that Act;

(b) in the case of a vehicle used under a trade licence, the holder of
the licence; and

(c) in the case of a vehicle exempt from excise duty by virtue of the
Motor Vehicles (International Circulation) Order 1957 as
amended the person resident outside the United Kingdom who
has brought the vehicle into Great Britain,

and in cases (a) and (b) the address of the owner as shown on the said
register or, as the case may be, on the licence may be treated as his address.

PART V

PARTICULAR REGULATIONS RELATING TO VEHICLES FOR WHICH PLATING
CERTIFICATES HAVE BEEN ISSUED

Interpretation

138. In this Part of these Regulations, unless the context otherwise requires, the following expressions have the meanings hereby assigned to them respectively, that is to say—

" axle weight ", in relation to each axle of a motor vehicle or trailer, means the sum of the weights transmitted to the road surface by all the wheels of that axle;

" design gross weight ", in relation to a vehicle, means the gross weight of the vehicle at or below which in the opinion of the Secretary of State or of a person authorised in that behalf by the Secretary of State the vehicle could safely be driven on roads;

" design ", in relation to the gross weight, each axle weight or the train weight of a motor vehicle or trailer, means any such weight is one at or below which in the opinion of the Secretary of State or of a person authorised in that behalf by the Secretary of State the vehicle could safely be driven on roads;

" gross weight ", in relation to a motor vehicle, means the sum of the weights transmitted to the road surface by all the wheels of the vehicle;

" gross weight ", in relation to a trailer, means the sum of the weights transmitted to the road surface by all the wheels of the trailer and includes any weight of the trailer imposed on the drawing vehicle;

" Ministry plate " means a plate issued, or having effect as if issued by the Secretary of State, for a goods vehicle following the issue or amendment of a plating certificate and in the form in, and containing the particulars required by, Schedule 11, the said particulars being those shown in the plating certificate for the vehicle;

" Ministry test date disc " means a plate issued by the Secretary of State for a goods vehicle, being a trailer, following the issue of a goods vehicle test certificate for that trailer under the plating and testing regulations and containing the following particulars, namely:—

(*a*) the identification mark allotted to that trailer and shown in that certificate;

(*b*) the date until which that certificate is valid;

(*c*) the number of the vehicle testing station shown in the said certificate;

" operative date " means the date on which these Regulations come into operation;

" train weight ", in relation to a motor vehicle which may draw a trailer, means the maximum laden weight for the motor vehicle together with any trailer which may be drawn by it.

Application of Part V

139. This Part of these Regulations applies to goods vehicles, being goods vehicles of a class to which the plating and testing regulations apply, for which a plating certificate has been issued.

Ministry plates for goods vehicles

140. Every goods vehicle to which this Part of the Regulations applies shall as from the relevant date as defined in section 46 (1) of the 1972 Act or the operative date, whichever date is the later, be equipped with a Ministry plate securely affixed to the vehicle in the cab thereof in a conspicuous and readily accessible position or, if the vehicle is constructed without a cab, in a conspicuous and readily accessible position elsewhere on the vehicle, and the said plate shall at all times be legible.

141. Every goods vehicle to which this Part of these Regulations applies, being a trailer, for which a goods vehicle test certificate is issued under the plating and testing regulations, shall as from each date such a certificate is issued or the operative date, whichever date is the later, carry in the relevant position and in legible condition a Ministry test date disc issued for that trailer following the issue of that test certificate until the date of expiry of that test certificate or the date of issue of a further test certificate for that trailer, whichever date is the earlier, and shall not display that disc after that one of such dates as is the earlier.

In this Regulation "relevant position" means a conspicuous and readily accessible position, being such that the disc is clearly visible by daylight from the nearside of the road.

Weight restrictions

142.—(1) As respects a goods vehicle to which this Part of the Regulations applies, whether laden or unladen and whether or not drawing or being drawn by another vehicle, the following provisions of this Regulation shall apply as from the said relevant date, namely mentioned in Regulation 140 or the operative date, whichever date is the later,

  (a) the gross weight shown in column (2) of the plating certificate for that vehicle shall not be exceeded;

  (b) the axle weight for each axle shown in column (2) of the plating certificate for that vehicle shall not be exceeded:

    Provided that this sub-paragraph shall not apply in the case of any axle being one of two or more axles to which the following sub-paragraph applies;

  (c) where any two or more axles are fitted with a compensating arrangement in accordance with Regulation 11, the sum of the axle weights for all the axles so fitted shall not exceed the sum of such weights for those axles as are shown in column (2) of the said plating certificate.

(2) As respects a goods vehicle to which this Part of these Regulations applies, being a motor vehicle, the train weight if any shown in column (2) of the plating certificate for that vehicle shall not be exceeded.

(3) Nothing in any plate mentioned in Regulation 39 with which a goods vehicle to which this Part of the Regulations applies is equipped or in Regulations 79 to 88 shall be taken to permit any such weight as is mentioned in the preceding provisions of this Regulation to be exceeded and nothing in paragraph (1) or (2) of this Regulation shall be taken to permit any weight mentioned in any of the said Regulations 79 to 88 which is applicable to the vehicle in question to be exceeded.

Additional markings

143.—(1) Without prejudice to the provision of Regulation 140, any weight which by virtue of Regulation 142 may not be exceeded in the case of a goods vehicle to which this Part of the Regulations applies may be marked on the near side of the vehicle, the off side of the vehicle or on both sides thereof.

(2) Where at any time by virtue of any provisions containing in Regulation 79, 80, 83 or 84 a goods vehicle to which this Part of these Regulations applies may not be used in excess of a weight, being a weight equal to the sum of the weights transmitted to the road surface by all the wheels of the vehicle and less than the gross weight which may not be exceeded by that vehicle by virtue of Regulation 142, the first mentioned weight may be marked on the near side of the vehicle, the off side of the vehicle or on both sides thereof.

(3) Where at any time by virtue of any provision contained in Regulation 81, 82 or 85 a goods vehicle to which this Part of these Regulations applies is drawing, or being drawn by, another vehicle and those vehicles may not be used together in excess of a laden weight applicable to those vehicles by virtue of any such provision, that weight may be marked on the near side of that goods vehicle, the off side of that vehicle or on both sides thereof.

Alteration of braking requirements

144. In relation to a goods vehicle, being a motor vehicle to which this Part of these Regulations applies and to which paragraph (5), (6) or (7) of either Regulation 54 or Regulation 59 applies, each such paragraph shall as from the date a plating certificate issued for the vehicle or the operative date, whichever date is the later, have effect as though there were added at the end of that paragraph the following provision:—

" In the application of this paragraph to a motor vehicle, being a vehicle for which a plating certificate has been issued, the aforesaid requirements as to total braking efficiencies shall not be treated as being complied with unless such efficiencies are capable of being produced when the sum of the weights transmitted to the road surface by all the wheels of the vehicle is either equal to the design gross weight shown in that plating certificate or, if no such weight is so shown, equal to the gross weight shown in column (2) of that certificate."

Additional provisions as to breaking requirements

145.—(1) In this Regulation " original braking requirements " means the requirements of Regulations 54 (5), 54 (6), 54 (7), 59 (5), 59 (6) and (7), as read prior to their amendment by Regulation 144, and with Regulation 94 (1) (c) and (d).

(2) Notwithstanding the said amendment, no person shall use or cause or permit to be used on a road a goods vehicle, being a motor vehicle to which this Part of these Regulations applies, as from the date a plating certificate is issued for the vehicle or the operative date, whichever date is the later, if it does not also comply with the original braking requirements.

Tyres

146. Each axle of every goods vehicle to which this Part of these Regulations applies shall as from the date a plating certificate is issued for the vehicle or the operative date, whichever date is the later, be equipped with tyres which, as respects strength, are designed and maintained adequately to support the axle weight shown in column (2) of that certificate for that axle.

SCHEDULE 1

[REGULATIONS REVOKED]

SCHEDULE 2

(See Regulations 39, 40, 79, 80, 82, 83, 85 and 88)

PART I

Particulars to be shown on plate for motor vehicles (including motor vehicles forming part of articulated vehicles)

1. Manufacturer's name.
2. Vehicle type.
3. Engine type and power (*a*).
4. Chassis or serial number.
5. Number of axles.
6. Maximum axle weight for each axle (*b*).
7. Maximum gross weight (*c*).
8. Maximum train weight (*d*).
9. Maximum weight in Great Britain for each axle (*b*) (*e*).
10. Maximum gross weight in Great Britain (*c*) (*e*).

(*a*) The power need not be shown in the case of a motor vehicle manufactured before 1st October 1972 (hereinafter in this Schedule referred to as " an excepted vehicle ") and shall not be shown in the case of any motor vehicle which is propelled otherwise than by a compression ignition engine.

(*b*) This weight as respects each axle is the sum of the weights to be transmitted to the road surface by all the wheels of that axle.

(*c*) This weight is the sum of the weights to be transmitted to the road surface by all the wheels of the motor vehicle (including any load imposed by a trailer, whether forming part of an articulated vehicle or not, on the motor vehicle).

(*d*) This weight is the sum of the weights to be transmitted to the road surface by all the wheels of the motor vehicle and of any trailer drawn, but this item need not be completed where the motor vehicle is not constructed to draw a trailer.

(*b*), (*c*), (*d*) References to the weights to be transmitted to the road surface by all or any of the wheels of the vehicle or of any trailer drawn are references to the weights so to be transmitted both of the vehicle or trailer and of any load or persons carried by it.

(*e*) This item need not be completed in the case of an excepted vehicle or in the case of a vehicle which is a locomotive or motor tractor.

Part II

Particulars to be shown on plate for trailers (including trailers forming part of articulated vehicles)

1. Manufacturer's name.
2. Chassis or serial number.
3. Number of axles.
4. Maximum weight for each axle (*a*).
5. Maximum load imposed on drawing vehicle (*b*).
6. Maximum gross weight (*c*).
7. Maximum weight in Great Britain for each axle (*a*) (*e*).
8. Maximum gross weight in Great Britain (*c*) (*f*).
9. Year of manufacture (*d*).

(*a*) This weight as respects each axle is the sum of the weights to be transmitted to the road surface by all the wheels of that axle.

(*b*) Only for trailers forming part of articulated vehicles or where some of the weight of the trailer or its load is to be imposed on the drawing vehicle.

(*c*) This weight is the sum of the weights to be transmitted to the road surface by all the wheels of the trailer, including any weight of the trailer to be imposed on the drawing vehicle.

(*a*), (*b*), (*c*) References to the weights to be transmitted to the road surface by all or any of the wheels of the trailer are references to the weight so to be transmitted both of the trailer and of any load or persons carried by it and references to the weights to be imposed on the drawing vehicle are references to the weights so to be imposed both of the trailer and of any load or persons carried by it except where only the load of the trailer is imposed on the drawing vehicle.

(*d*) This item need not be completed in the case of a trailer manufactured before 1st April 1970.

(*e*) This item need not be completed in the case of a trailer manufactured before 1st October 1972.

(*f*) This item need not be completed in the case of a trailer manufactured before 1st October 1972 or which forms part of an articulated vehicle.

Part III

1. The power of the engine, which is only to be shown in the case of a compression ignition engine on the plate in respect of item 3 in Part I of this Schedule, shall be the amount of kilowatts equivalent in accordance with the British Standard Specification for the Performance of Diesel Engines for Road Vehicles published on the 19th May 1971 under the number BS AU 141a: 1971 to the installed power output shown in a type test certificate issued under that Specification by a person authorised by the Secretary of State for the type of engine to which the engine in question conforms.

2 (*a*) The weights to be shown on the plate in respect of items 6, 7 and 8 in Part I of this Schedule and of items 4, 5 and 6 in Part II thereof shall be those, which the manufacturer of the vehicle or a person duly authorised

on behalf of the manufacturer, considers to represent the weight limits at or below which the vehicle is fit for use, having regard to its design, construction and equipment and the stresses to which it is likely to be subject in use:

Provided that, where alterations are made to a vehicle which may render the vehicle fit for use at weights which exceed those referred to above in this paragraph and shown on the plate—

(i) there may be shown on the plate in place of any of those weights, such new weights as the manufacturer of the vehicle or any person carrying on business as a manufacturer of motor vehicles or trailers (or a person duly authorised on behalf of that manufacturer or any such person) or a person authorised by the Secretary of State considers to represent the weight limits at or below which the vehicle will then be fit for use, having regard to its design, construction and equipment and to those alterations and to the stresses to which it is likely to be subject in use,

(ii) where the new weights shown on the plate have been determined

(a) by or on behalf of a person carrying on business as aforesaid or

(b) by a person authorised by the Secretary of State, the name of that person shall be shown in the plate as having made that determination, and in the case (b) the appointment of the person in question shall be shown.

(b) In relation to a vehicle manufactured on or after 1st October 1972, in the foregoing paragraph—

(i) the reference to equipment shall not be treated as including a reference to the type of tyres with which the vehicle is equipped; and

(ii) for the words " weight limits at or below " in both places where they occur there shall be substituted the words " maximum weights at ".

3. The weights to be shown on the plate—

(a) in respect of item 9 in Part I of this Schedule shall be the weights shown at item 6 in that Part and in respect of item 7 in Part II of this Schedule shall be the weights shown at item 4 in that Part, in each case reduced so far as necessary to indicate the maximum weight applicable to each axle of the vehicle, if the vehicle is not to be used in contravention of Regulations 11, 83, 84, 86 or 87 and if the tyres with which the vehicle is equipped are not, as respects strength, to be inadequate to support the weight to be so shown at item 9 and item 7,

(b) in respect of item 10 in the said Part I shall be the weight shown at item 7 in that Part and in respect of item 8 in the said Part II shall be the weight shown at item 6 in that Part, in the first case reduced so far as necessary to indicate the maximum permissible weight applicable if the vehicle is not to be used in contravention of Regulation 83 or 84 and in the second case reduced so far as necessary to indicate the maximum permissible weight applicable to the vehicle if the vehicle is not to be used in contravention of Regulation 83 and in each such case reduced so far as necessary to indicate the maximum permissible weight applicable to the vehicle if the tyres with which the vehicle is equipped are not, as respects strength, to be inadequate to support the weights to be so shown at item 10 and item 8.

4.—(1) Subject to sub-paragraph (2) of this paragraph weights on plates first affixed to a vehicle on or after 1st April 1973 shall be shown in kilograms, weights on plates first so affixed before that date but on or after 1st October 1972 shall be shown in tons and decimals thereof together with the equivalent weight in kilograms and weights on plates first so affixed before the last-mentioned date shall be shown in tons and decimals thereof.

(2) Where a new weight is first shown on a plate by virtue of the proviso to paragraph 2 (1) above the weight shall be shown as if it was on a plate first affixed to a vehicle on the date it was first shown.

5. All letters and figures shown on the plate shall not be less than 6 millimetres in height.

6. In this Schedule references to the manufacturer of a motor vehicle or trailer are—

    (a) in relation to a motor vehicle or a trailer constructed with a chassis which has not previously formed part of another vehicle, references to the person by whom that chassis was made,

    (b) in relation to any other motor vehicle or trailer references to the person by whom that vehicle was constructed.

SCHEDULE 3 (See Regulation 42)
[Gas Containers]

SCHEDULE 4 (See Regulations 54, 59, 62 and 94)

Requirements with Respect to the Efficiency of the Brakes of Certain Motor Vehicles

1. This Schedule applies to a motor vehicle which is a heavy motor car, a motor car or a motor cycle and is not—

    (a) a goods vehicle the unladen weight of which exceeds 1525 kilograms;

    (b) a public service vehicle adapted to carry 8 or more passengers;

    (c) an articulated vehicle or a vehicle constructed or adapted for the purpose of forming part of an articulated vehicle;

    (d) a works truck; or

    (e) a pedestrian controlled vehicle;

and references to a motor vehicle in the following provisions of this Schedule shall be construed accordingly.

In this paragraph " goods vehicle " does not include a dual purpose-vehicle.

2. For the purposes of this Schedule a two-wheeled motor cycle shall not, by reason that a sidecar is attached thereto, be treated as three-wheeled.

3. In the case of a motor vehicle having at least four wheels and required to have two means of operating brakes—

    (a) if each means of operation applies brakes to at least four wheels, the brakes as applied by one of the means shall have a total braking efficiency of not less than 50 per cent. and the brakes as applied by the other means shall have a total braking efficiency of not less than 25 per cent.;

(b) if only one of the means of operation applies brakes to at least four wheels, the brakes as applied by that means shall have a total braking efficiency of not less than 50 per cent. and the brakes as applied by the other means shall have a total braking efficiency of not less than 25 per cent.;   and

(c) if neither means of operation applies brakes to at least four wheels, the brakes as applied by one of the means shall have a total braking efficiency of not less than 30 per cent. and the brakes as applied by the other means shall have a total braking efficiency of not less than 25 per cent.

4. In the case of a three-wheeled motor vehicle required to have two means of operating brakes—

(a) if each means of operation applies brakes to all three wheels, the brakes as applied by one of the means shall have a total braking efficiency of not less than 40 per cent. and the brakes as applied by the other means shall have a total braking efficiency of not less than 25 per cent.;

(b) if only one of the means of operation applies brakes to all three wheels, the brakes as applied by that means shall have a total braking efficiency of not less than 40 per cent. and the brakes as applied by the other means shall have a total braking efficiency of not less than 25 per cent.;   and

(c) if neither means of operation applies brakes to all three wheels, the brakes as applied by one of the means shall have a total braking efficiency of not less than 30 per cent. and the brakes as applied by the other means shall have a total braking efficiency of not less than 25 per cent.

5. In the case of a motor vehicle, being a two-wheeled motor cycle, required to have more than one means of operating brakes, the brakes as applied by one of the means shall have a total braking efficiency of not less than 30 per cent. and the brakes as applied by the other means shall have a total braking efficiency of not less than 25 per cent.

6. In the case of a motor vehicle not required to have two means of operating brakes—

(a) if the vehicle has at least four wheels and one or more means of operation applying brakes to at least four wheels, the brakes as applied by that means or one of those means shall have a total braking efficiency of not less than 50 per cent.

(b) if the vehicle has at least four wheels and no means of operation applying brakes to at least four wheels, the brakes as applied by the means or one of the means of operation shall have a total braking efficiency of not less than 30 per cent.;

(c) if the vehicle is three-wheeled and has one or more means of operation applying brakes to all three wheels, the brakes as applied by that means or one of those means shall have a total braking efficiency of not less than 40 per cent.;

(d) if the vehicle is three-wheeled and has no means of operation applying brakes to all three wheels, the brakes as applied by the means or one of the means of operation shall have a total braking efficiency of not less than 30 per cent.;   and

(e) if the vehicle is two-wheeled, the brakes as applied by the means or one of the means of operation shall have a total braking efficiency of not less than 30 per cent.

SCHEDULE 5

[DIAGRAM OF TRAILER PLATE (see Regulation 75)]

SCHEDULE 6

(see Regulations 79, 80 and 82)

PERMISSIBLE MAXIMUM WEIGHTS

1. For the purposes of this Schedule the distance between any two axles shall be obtained by measuring the shortest distance between the line joining the centres of the points of contact with the road surface of the wheels of one axle and the line joining the centres of the points of contact with the road surface of the wheels of the other axle.

Column 1 Class of vehicle	Column 2 Kilo- grams

2. Heavy motor cars, motor cars and trailers in each case not forming part of an articulated vehicle.

(a) in the case of a vehicle with two axles—

(i) where the distance between the axles is at least 3·25 metres but less than 3·65 metres 15,250

(ii) where the distance between the axles is at least 3·65 metres 16,260

(b) in the case of a vehicle with three axles, where the distance between the foremost and rearmost axles is at least 5·48 metres 22,360

(c) in the case of a vehicle with more than three axles—

(i) where the distance between the foremost and rearmost axles is at least 7·01 metres but less than 7·92 metres 26,420

(ii) where the distance between the foremost and rearmost axles is at least 7·92 metres 28,450

3. Articulated vehicles:—

(a) in the case of an articulated vehicle with three axles—

(i) where the distance between the foremost and rearmost axles is less than 5·48 metres 20,330

(ii) where the distance between the foremost and rearmost axles is at least 5·48 metres 24,390

(b) in the case of an articulated vehicle with four axles—

(i) where the distance between the foremost and rearmost axle is less than 7·01 metres 24,390

(ii) where the distance between the foremost and rearmost axles is at least 7·01 metres but less than 7·92 metres 26,420

(iii) where the distance between the foremost and rearmost axles is at least 7·92 metres but less than 9·75 metres 28,450

(iv) where the distance between the foremost and rearmost axles is at least 9·75 metres but less than 11·58 metres 30,490

(v) where the distance between the foremost and rearmost axles is at least 11·58 metres 32,520

Column 1	Column 2
Class of vehicle	Kilo-grams

(c) in the case of an articulated vehicle with more than four axles—

    (i) where the distance between the foremost and rear-most axles is less than 7·01 metres   24,390

    (ii) where the distance between the foremost and rear-most axles is at least 7·01 metres but less than 7·92 metres   26,420

    (iii) where the distance between the foremost and rear-most axles is at least 7·92 metres but less than 8·99 metres   28,450

    (iv) where the distance between the foremost and rear-most axles is at least 8·99 metres but less than 9·75 metres   30,490

    (v) where the distance between the foremost and rear-most axles is at least 9·75 metres   32,520

SCHEDULE 7

(See Regulations 83 to 86)

Permissible Maximum Weights, etc.

For the purposes of this Schedule—

(1) the distance between any two axles shall be obtained by measuring the shortest distance between the line joining the centres of the areas of contact with the road surface of the wheels of one axle and the line joining the centres of the areas of contact with the road surface of the wheels of the other axle;

(2) where by virtue of any provision made in Part I, II or III of this Schedule, two or more maximum weights specified in any such Part are applicable to any vehicle the highest of such maximum weights shall be treated as being the weight which the vehicle must not exceed and where by virtue of any provision made in Part IV, V or VI of this Schedule two or more maximum weights are applicable to the axles of a vehicle, the highest of such maximum weights shall be treated as being the weight which those axles must not exceed.

Part I (See Regulation 83)

Maximum permissible weights for heavy motor cars and motor cars and trailers in each case not forming part of an articulated vehicle

For the purposes of this Part of this Schedule—

" maximum axle weight " means the highest weight shown for any axle in column 2 of a Ministry plate as defined in Regulation 138 and carried on the vehicle or, if no such plate is carried on the vehicle, the highest maximum weight in Great Britain shown for any axle in the plate complying with the requirements of Regulation 39 (2) or the highest weight shown for any axle in the foreign plate with which the vehicle is equipped;

" foreign plate " means the plate mentioned in Regulation 83 (1) (b) (i) or 83 (1) (d) (i).

Column 1
Class of vehicle

(a) Two axled vehicles

    (i) where the distance between the axles is less than 2·65
metres   14,230
    (ii) where the distance between the axles is at least 2·65
metres   16,260

(b) Three axled vehicles

  Their weight shall not exceed 16,260 kilograms except in a case
below, where the weight opposite that case shall apply—

    (i) where the distance between the foremost and rear-
most axle is at least 3 metres   18,290
    (ii) where the distance between the foremost and rearmost
axle is at least 3·2 metres and the maximum axle weight is
not more than 8130 kilograms   20,330
    (iii) where the distance between the foremost and rear-
most axle is at least 3·9 metres and the maximum weight
is more than 8130 kilograms   20,330
    (iv) where the distance between the foremost and rear-
most axle is at least 3·9 metres and the maximum axle weight
is not more than 8640 kilograms   22,360
    (v) where the distance between the foremost and rear-
most axle is at least 4·6 metres and the maximum axle weight
is more than 8640 kilograms   22,360
    (vi) where the distance between the foremost and rear-
most axle is at least 4·9 metres and the maximum axle
weight is not more than 9400 kilograms   24,390
    (vii) where the distance between the foremost and rear-
most axle is at least 5·1 metres and the maximum axle
weight is more than 9400 kilograms..   24,390

(c) Vehicles with four or more axles

  Their weight shall not exceed 18,290 kilograms except in a case
below, where the weight opposite that case shall apply—

    (i) where the distance between the foremost and rear-
most axle is at least 3·7 metres and the maximum weight
is not more than 8640 kilograms   20,330
    (ii) where the distance between the foremost and rear-
most axle is at least 4·6 metres and the maximum axle
weight is not more than 8640 kilograms   22,360
    (iii) where the distance between the foremost and rear-
most axles is at least 4·7 metres and the maximum axle
weight is not more than 8640 kilograms   24,390
    (iv) where the distance between the foremost and rear-
most axle is at least 5 metres and the maximum axle weight
is not more than 9150 kilograms   24,390
    (v) where the distance between the foremost and rear-
most axle is at least 5·6 metres and the maximum axle
weight is not more than 9150 kilograms   26,420
    (vi) where the distance between the foremost and rear-
most axle is at least 6 metres and the maximum axle weight
is not more than 9660 kilograms   26,420
    (vii) where the distance between the foremost and rear-
most axle is at least 5·9 metres and the maximum axle
weight is not more than 9150 kilograms   28,450
    (viii) where the distance between the foremost and rear-
most axle is at least 6·3 metres and the maximum axle

Column 1 Class of vehicle	Column 2 Kilo- grams
weight is not more than 9660 kilograms	28,450
(ix) where the distance between the foremost and rear-most axle is at least 6·3 metres and the maximum weight is not more than 9400 kilograms	30,490
(x) where the distance between the foremost and rear-most axle is at least 6·5 metres and the maximum axle weight is not more than 9660 kilograms	30,490

PART II (See Regulation 84)

Maximum permissible weights for heavy motor cars and motor cars in each case forming part of an articulated vehicle

For the purposes of this Part of this Schedule—

" intermediate axle weight " means the highest weight shown for any axle in column 2 of a Ministry plate as defined in Regulation 138 and carried on the vehicle or, if no such plate is carried on the vehicle, the highest maximum weight in Great Britain shown for any axle in the plate complying with the requirements of Regulation 39 (2) or the highest weight shown for any axle in the foreign plate with which the vehicle is equipped, any such axle not being the foremost or rearmost;

" foreign plate " means the plate mentioned in Regulation 83 (1) (b) (i).

Column 1 Class of vehicle	Column 2 Kilo- grams
(a) Two axle motor vehicles—	
(i) where the distance between the axles is less than 2·4 metres	14,230
(ii) where the distance between the axles is at least 2·4 metres	16,260
(b) Three or more axled motor vehicles—	

Their weights shall not exceed 18,290 kilograms except in a case below, where the weight specified opposite that case shall apply—

(i) where the distance between the foremost and rear-most axle is at least 3 metres and the intermediate axle weight is not more than 8385 kilograms	20,330
(ii) where the distance between the foremost and rear-most axle is at least 3·8 metres and the intermediate axle weight is not more than 8640 kilograms	22,360
(iii) where the distance between the foremost and rear-most axle is at least 4·3 metres and the intermediate axle weight is not more than 9150 kilograms	24,390

PART III (See Regulation 85)

For the purposes of this Part of this Schedule " inner axle spacing " means the distance between the rearmost axle of the motor vehicle and the foremost axle of the trailer.

Column 1	Column 2		Column 3
Class of articulated vehicle	Inner axle spacing		Gross train weight
		Metres	Kilograms

Two axled motor vehicle with—

(a)	1 axled trailer	less than	2·1	20,330
(b)	1 axled trailer	at least	2·1	22,360
(c)	1 axled trailer	at least	3·1	24,390
(d)	2 or more axled trailer	less than	2·9	24,390
(e)	2 or more axled trailer	at least	2·9	26,420
(f)	2 or more axled trailer	at least	3·1	28,450
(g)	2 or more axled trailer	at least	3·6	30,490
(h)	2 or more axled trailer	at least	4·2	32,520

Three or more axled motor vehicle with—

(a)	1 axled trailer	less than	2	22,360
(b)	1 axled trailer	at least	2	24,390
(c)	1 axled trailer	at least	2·7	26,420
(d)	1 axled trailer	at least	3	28,450
(e)	1 axled trailer	at least	4	30,490
(f)	1 axled trailer	at least	4·4	32,520
(g)	2 or more axled trailer	less than	2	24,390
(h)	2 or more axled trailer	at least	2	26,420
(i)	2 or more axled trailer	at least	2·3	28,450
(j)	2 or more axled trailer	at least	3·2	30,490
(k)	2 or more axled trailer	at least	4	32,520

PART IV (See Regulation 86 (2) and (3))

Maximum weights for two closely spaced axles

Column 1		Column 2	Column 3
Distance between axles		Total weight	Total weight
	Metres	Kilograms	Kilograms
less than	1·02	11,180	11,180
at least	1·02	12,200	16,260
at least	1·05	15,250	17,280
at least	1·2	16,260	18,290
at least	1·35	17,280	18,800
at least	1·5	18,290	19,310
at least	1·85	19,310	20,330

PART V (See Regulation 86 (4))

Maximum weights for three closely spaced axles

Column 1		Column 2
Distance between outer axles		Axle weight
	Metres	Kilograms
less than	1·4	3720
at least	1·4	4070
at least	1·5	6100
at least	2	6610
at least	2·55	7120
at least	3·15	7630

PART VI (See Regulation 86 (5)

Maximum weights for three adjacent axles

For the purposes of this Part of this Schedule—

" intermediate axle weight " means the weight shown for the axle, being the middle axle of three adjacent axles, in column 2 of a Ministry plate as defined in Regulation 138 and carried on the vehicle or, if no such plate is carried on the vehicle, the maximum weight in Great Britain shown for that axle in the plate complying with the requirements of Regulation 39 (2) or the weight shown for that axle in the foreign plate with which the vehicle is equipped;

" foreign plate " means the plate mentioned in Regulation 83 (1) (*b*) (i) or 83 (1) (*d*) (i).

The total weight transmitted to the road surface by the wheels of three adjacent axles shall not exceed 1829 kilograms except in a case below, where the weight opposite that case shall apply—

		Kilograms
(i)	where the distance between the foremost and rearmost axle is at least 3 metres and the intermediate axle weight is not more than 8385 kilograms	20,330
(ii)	where the distance between the foremost and rearmost axle is at least 3·8 metres and the intermediate axle weight is not more than 8640 kilograms	22,360
(iii)	where the distance between the foremost and rearmost axle is at least 4·6 metres and the intermediate axle weight is not more than 9150 kilograms	24,390

SCHEDULE 8

(see Regulations 128 and 131)

CONDITIONS TO BE COMPLIED WITH IN RELATION TO THE USE OF VEHICLES CARRYING WIDE OR LONG LOADS OR VEHICLES CARRYING LOADS OR HAVING FIXED APPLIANCES OR APPARATUS WHICH PROJECT

PART I

1. The conditions referred to in Regulation 128 and in paragraphs (2), (4), (6), (7) and (9) of Regulation 131 as the conditions specified in paragraph 1 of this Schedule are as follows:—

(*a*) save in so far as the chief officer of police of any police area in which it is proposed that the vehicle or vehicles in question will be used dispenses, as respects the use of the vehicle or vehicles in that area, with any of the requirements contained in this and in the following sub-paragraph as to length of notice or particulars to be given, the owner of the vehicle or vehicles shall, before using the vehicle or, as the case may be, the vehicles on a road, give at least two clear days' notice of the intended use (excluding Sundays, any bank holiday, Christmas Day or Good Friday) to the chief officer of police of any such area as aforesaid.

In this sub-paragraph—

(i) " chief officer of police ", and " police area ", in relation to England and Wales, have respectively the same meanings as in the Police Act 1964, and, in relation to Scotland, have respectively the same meanings as in the Police (Scotland) Act 1967 and

(ii) the expression "bank holiday", in relation to notice of the intended use of a vehicle on a road, means a day which is, or is to be observed as, a bank holiday, or a holiday, under the Bank Holidays Act 1871, or the Holidays Extension Act 1875, either generally or in the locality in which that road is situated;

(b) the notice referred to in the foregoing sub-paragraph shall contain particulars of the time, date and route of the journey and—

(i) in a case where this paragraph applies by virtue of paragraph (2) of Regulation 131 particulars of the overall length and overall width of the vehicle by which the load is to be carried and of the width of any lateral projection or projections of its load,

(ii) in a case where this paragraph applies by virtue of paragraph (4) (a) of Regulation 131 particulars of the overall length and overall width of each vehicle by which the load is to be carried and of the length of any forward projection and of any rearward projection of the load and, where the load is to be carried by more than one vehicle, of the distance between vehicles,

(iii) in a case where this paragraph applies by virtue of Regulation 128 or paragraph (4) (b) of Regulation 131, particulars of the overall length of the combination of vehicles to be used and, in the second-mentioned case, particulars of the length of any forward projection and of any rearward projection of the load, being the projection or projections thereof as mentioned in the said paragraph (4) (b), and

(iv) in a case where this paragraph applies by virtue of paragraphs (5), (6), (7) or (9) of Regulation 131, particulars of the overall length of the vehicle to be used and of the length of any forward projection and of any rearward projection of its special appliance or apparatus or, as the case may be, of its load;   and

(c) subject to any variations in the time, date or route of the journey which the owner of the vehicle or vehicles may be directed to make by any such chief officer of police as aforesaid and subject to any delay which may be occasioned by reason of a direction given by a police constable, in the interests of road safety or to avoid undue traffic congestion, to the driver of a vehicle to halt it in a place on or adjacent to the road on which the vehicle is travelling, the vehicle or, as the case may be, the vehicles shall be used only in circumstances which accord with the particulars given in compliance with the foregoing sub-paragraph as to the time date and route of the journey and only if any dimension or measurement relating to the vehicle or the vehicles (including that relating to a combination of vehicles), to a special appliance or apparatus or to a load, being a dimension or measurement of which particulars have been given as aforesaid, is not exceeded.

For the purposes of this sub-paragraph and of item (iv) of the foregoing sub-paragraph, the reference to a load shall, in a case where this paragraph applies by virtue of paragraph (7) of Regulation 131, be treated as a reference to a boat used for racing as mentioned in the said paragraph (7).

2. The conditions referred to in Regulation 128 and in paragraphs (2), (4), (5), (6) and (9) of Regulation 131 as the conditions specified in paragraph 2 of this Schedule are that at least one person in addition to the person or persons employed in driving the motor vehicle in question shall be employed in attending to that vehicle and its load and any other vehicle or vehicles drawn by that vehicle and the load or loads carried on the vehicle or vehicles so drawn and to give warning to the driver of the said motor vehicle and to any other person of any danger likely to be caused to any such other person by reason of the presence of the said vehicle or vehicles on the road:

Provided that, where three or more motor vehicles as respects which the conditions in this paragraph are applicable are travelling together in convoy, it shall be a sufficient compliance with this paragraph if only the foremost and rearmost vehicles in the convoy are attended in the manner prescribed in this paragraph.

For the purpose of this paragraph—

    (a) in a case where a motor vehicle is drawing a trailer or trailers any person employed in pursuance of section 34 of the 1972 Act in attending that vehicle or any such trailer shall be treated as being an attendant required by this paragraph so long as he is also employed to discharge the duties mentioned in this paragraph, and

    (b) in a case where a motor vehicle is drawing a trailer or trailers and another motor vehicle is used for the purpose of assisting in their propulsion on the road, the person or persons employed in driving that other motor vehicle shall not be treated as a person or persons employed in attending to the first-mentioned vehicle or any vehicle or vehicles drawn thereby.

3. The conditions referred to in paragraphs (5) and (6) of Regulation 131 as the conditions specified in paragraph 3 of this Schedule are as follows:—

    (a) there shall be exhibited on every relevant projection such a number of plane unbroken surfaces as are required by the following provisions of this paragraph, the said surfaces to be of the size, shape and colour specified in those provisions and to be situated in accordance therewith.

        In this sub-paragraph the expression " relevant projection " means any such forward or rearward projection as is mentioned in sub-paragraph (a), (c) or (d) of the said paragraph (5) or of the said paragraph (6);

    (b) subject to the provisions of sub-paragraph (e) of this paragraph, three surfaces shall be exhibited of which one (hereafter referred to as " the end projection surface ") shall be of the shape and colour shown in the diagram first set out in Part II of this Schedule and shall conform with the dimensions there shown in relation to the size and colouring of that surface, and the other two, and any surface additional to those two required by the said sub-paragraph (e), (each hereafter referred to as a " side projection surface ") shall be of the shape and colour shown in the diagram secondly set out in the said Part II and shall conform with the dimensions there shown in relation to the size and colouring of that surface;

(c) the end projection surface shall be exhibited so that it may be seen, in the case of a forward projection, from the front thereof or, in the case of a rearward projection, from the rear thereof and shall be situated—

(i) so that it lies, as near as practicable, in a vertical plane at right angles to the longitudinal axis of the vehicle and passing through a point not more than 0·6 metres from the extreme end of the projection,

(ii) so that the vertical distance between the carriageway of the road and the nearest point on the surface does not exceed 2·5 metres.

(iii) so that the surface and any object or device by means of which it is exhibited impedes, as little as possible, the view of the driver to the front or, as the case may be, to the rear of the vehicle, and

(iv) so that every part of the surface is clearly visible to other persons using the road within a reasonable distance from that end of the projection from which the surface may be seen as provided by the foregoing provisions of this sub-paragraph;

(d) the two side projection surfaces shall be exhibited so that one may be seen from one side of the projection and the other may be seen from the other side thereof and each surface shall be situated—

(i) so that it lies, as near as practicable, in a vertical plane parallel to the longitudinal axis of the vehicle,

(ii) so that no part of it extends beyond the end of the projection,

(iii) so that the horizontal distance between it and the end projection surface or a rear marking carried in accordance with the Motor Vehicles (Rear Markings) Regulations, 1970, as amended, does not exceed 0·9 metres,

(iv) so that the vertical distance between the carriageway of the road and any point on at least one side of the surface does not exceed 2·5 metres, and

(v) so that every part of the surface is clearly visible to other persons using the road within a reasonable distance from that side of the projection from which the surface may be seen as provided by the foregoing provisions of this sub-paragraph;

(e) in the case of a forward projection exceeding 4·5 metres in length or a rearward projection exceeding 5·1 metres in length such a number of side projection surfaces additional to the two side projection surfaces required by sub-paragraph (b) of this paragraph shall be exhibited on each side of the projection, as to ensure that the horizontal distance between the foremost or, as the case may be, the rearmost point of the vehicle and that part of any side projection surface exhibited on the same side nearest that point, or between the nearest points of adjacent side projection surfaces exhibited on the same side, does not exceed, in the case of such surfaces exhibited on a forward projection, 2·4 metres or, in the case of such surfaces exhibited on a rearward projection, 3·6 metres.

For the purposes of this sub-paragraph the expression "the vehicle" shall not include any special appliance or apparatus or any part thereof which is a forward projection or a rearward projection within the meaning of Regulation 130;

(*f*) the provisions of items (i), (iv) and (v) of sub-paragraph (*d*) of this paragraph shall apply in relation to the additional side projection surfaces exhibited in accordance with the foregoing sub-paragraph as they apply in relation to the side projection surfaces referred to in the said sub-paragraph (*d*); and

(*g*) every surface exhibited in compliance with the foregoing provisions of this paragraph shall be kept clean and unobscured and during the hours of darkness shall be illuminated by means of lamps sufficient to render the surface readily distinguishable from a reasonable distance and so shielded that only light reflected from the surface is visible to other persons using the road.

Provided that the conditions in sub-paragraph (*b*) so far as it relates to side projection surfaces and the condition in sub-paragraph (*d*) shall not apply by reason only that a vehicle has a special appliance or apparatus, or is carrying a load, which has a rearward projection exceeding 1·8 metres in length but not exceeding 3 metres in length.

4. The conditions referred to in paragraphs (5), (6), (7) and (8) of Regulation 131 as the condition specified in paragraph 4 of this Schedule is that steps shall have been taken to render the relevant projection clearly visible to other persons using the road within a reasonable distance, in the case of a forward projection, from the front thereof or, in the case of a rearward projection, from the rear thereof and, in either case, from either side thereof.

In this paragraph the expression "relevant projection" means any such forward or rearward projection as is mentioned in sub-paragraph (*b*) of the said paragraph (5) or of the said paragraph (6) or in the said paragraph (7) or the said paragraph (8).

PART II

[Diagrams of Projection Markers; see paragraph 3 (*b*)]

SCHEDULE 9

Maximum Sound Levels (A weighting) in Decibels (dBA)

Column 1 Class or description of vehicle	Column 2 Regulation 29 Maximum (dBA)	Column 3 Regulation 108 (3) (*a*) Maximum (dBA)	Column 4 Regulation 108 (3) (*b*) Maximum (dBA)
1. Motor cycle of which the cylinder capacity of the engine does not exceed 50 cubic centimetres	77	80	80

Column 1 Class or description of vehicle	Column 2 Regulation 29 Maximum (dBA)	Column 3 Regulation 108 (3) (a) Maximum (dBA)	Column 4 Regulation 108 (3) (b) Maximum (dBA)
2. Motor cycle of which the said cylinder capacity exceeds 125 cubic centimetres	86	90	89
3. Any other motor cycle	82	90	85
4. Goods vehicle to which Regulation 39 applies and which is equipped with a plate complying with the requirements of paragraph (2) of that Regulation and showing particulars of a maximum gross weight of more than 3560 kilograms	89	92	92
5. Goods vehicle first used before 1st January 1968, which complies with the requirements of Regulation 79 (3) (c) and is equipped with such a plate as aforesaid notwithstanding that Regulation 39 does not apply to that vehicle by reason only that it was so first used		92	
6. Motor tractor	89	92	92
7. Locomotive	89	92	92
8. Land tractor	89	92	92
9. Works truck	89	92	92
10. Engineering plant	89	92	92
11. Passenger vehicle constructed for the carriage of more than 12 passengers exclusive of the driver	89	92	92

Column 1 Class or description of vehicle	Column 2 Regulation 29 Maximum (dbA)	Column 3 Regulation 108 (3) (a) Maximum (dbA)	Column 4 Regulation 108 (3) (b) Maximum (dBA)
12. Any other passenger vehicle	84	87	87
13. Motor car within the meaning of section 190 (2) (b) of the 1972 Act not being a goods vehicle of either of the kinds described in paragraphs 4 and 5 of this Column	85	88	88
14. Any other vehicle not elsewhere classified or described in this Column	85	92	88

SCHEDULE 10

Conditions mentioned in Regulation 108 (2)

1. At the time when the noise emitted by the vehicle is measured, the microphone of the apparatus shall be so placed that the top of the microphone is set at a height of 1·2 metres ± 0·1 metres above a point at ground level which is not less than 5·2 metres away from the nearest part of the carriageway on which the vehicle is being used.

2.—(1) For the purposes of this paragraph, the area in the vicinity of the microphone shall be treated as comprising areas the situation and extent of which shall be determined by reference to a line joining a point at ground level above which the microphone is placed to the said nearest part of the carriageway and in accordance with the diagram at the end of this Schedule including the directions contained therein; and the said areas shown marked I, II, III or IV on the said diagram are hereafter in this Schedule respectively referred to as the areas so marked.

(2) At the time when the noise is measured there shall not be:—

    (a) in the area marked I, any physical object higher than 610 millimetres above ground level;

    (b) in the area marked II, any physical object higher than 920 millimetres above ground level; and

    (c) in the areas marked III or IV, any physical object higher than 1525 millimetres above ground level:

Provided that the requirements at (c) above shall not apply in relation to the following objects or to any of them, that is to say:—

    (i) to plants, shrubs, trees or any other kind of vegetation, or

    (ii) to any physical object, of which a continuous surface less than 305 millimetres wide or all its height would be visible in daylight, to a person looking at it from the point above which the microphone is placed and whose eye level is at the height of the microphone.

(3) For the purpose of sub-paragraph (2) of this paragraph, neither the vehicle nor any part thereof, nor any person nor thing in or on the vehicle, nor the apparatus nor any part thereof, nor any persons being less than 3 in number attending the apparatus, shall be taken into account.

3. At the time when the noise emitted by the vehicle is measured, the vehicle shall be wholly or partly on a part of the road which falls within the area marked IV on the said diagram.

4. As soon as the vehicle has left the area marked IV on the said diagram the apparatus shall be used to measure the sound level (A weighting) in decibels of such noise as is then capable of affecting the sound level indicators of the apparatus, such measurement being carried out in the manner in which the measurement of the sound emitted by the vehicle was carried out and under the conditions applicable under the foregoing provisions of this Schedule, excluding paragraphs 2 (2) (c) and 3.

DIAGRAM

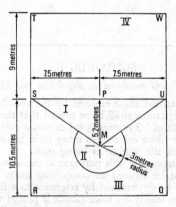

DIAGRAM DIRECTIONS (including Key and Dimensions)

M = a point at ground level above which the microphone is placed.
P = the nearest part of the carriageway to the microphone.
The area marked I consists of the triangle MSU.
The area marked II consists of so much of the circle of radius 3 metres with centre at M as does not enclose any part of the area marked I.
The area marked III consists of so much of the rectangle RSUQ as does not enclose any parts of the areas marked I or II.
The area marked IV consists of the rectangle STWU.

DIMENSIONS

The distance MP is not less than 5·2 metres.
The lengths of SR and UQ are each 10·5 metres.
The lengths of TW, SU and RQ are each 15 metres.
The lengths of SP and PU are each 7·5 metres.
The lengths of TS and WU are each 9 metres.

SCHEDULE 11

MINISTRY PLATE

PLATE	DEPARTMENT OF THE ENVIRONMENT Road Traffic Act 1972, Sections 40 and 45 Examination of Goods Vehicles	Serial No.

REGISTRATION/IDENTIFICATION MARK (where applicable)	CHASSIS/SERIAL NO. (where marked on vehicle)	YEAR OF ORIGINAL REGISTRATION (where applicable)	YEAR OF MANUFACTURE	MAKE	MODEL (where applicable)

(1) DESCRIPTION OF WEIGHTS APPLICABLE TO VEHICLE	(2) WEIGHTS NOT TO BE EXCEEDED IN GREAT BRITAIN KILOGRAMS	(3) DESIGN WEIGHTS (if higher than shown in col. (2)) KILOGRAMS	Space for Authenticating Stamp
AXLE WEIGHT (numbered from front to rear) AXLE 1			
AXLE 2			
AXLE 3			
AXLE 4			
GROSS WEIGHT (see warning opposite)			DATE OF ISSUE OF PLATING CERTIFICATE
TRAIN WEIGHT (see warning opposite)			

WARNING

1. A reduced gross weight may apply in certain cases to a vehicle towing or being towed by another.
2. A reduced train weight may apply depending on the type of trailer drawn.
3. All weights shown are subject to fitting of correct tyres.

Notes: 1. A Ministry Plate may contain the words "MINISTRY OF TRANSPORT" instead of the words "DEPARTMENT OF THE ENVIRONMENT" and may contain the words "Road Safety Act 1967, Sections 8 and 9" instead of the words "Road Traffic Act 1972, Sections 40 and 45". It may also contain additional columns in Columns (2) and (3) showing the weights in tons.
2. Entries in respect of train weight are required only in the case of motor vehicles constructed or adapted to form part of an articulated vehicle.
3. A Ministry Plate may, in a space provided for the purpose, show the DOE (Department of the Environment) reference number for the particular type of vehicle. Where provision is made for this number, the spaces for the make and model of the vehicle may be combined.

APPENDIX II

ENDORSEMENT AND SENTENCE CODES

I. ENDORSEMENT CODE

(The codes marked * are included primarily for use by Scottish Courts)

Code	Offences
	Offences in relation to Accidents
AC 10	Failing to stop and/or give particulars after an accident
AC 20	Failing to report an accident within 24 hours
	Offence of Driving while Disqualified
BA 10	Driving while disqualified
	Careless Driving Offences
CD 10	Driving without due care and attention ⎫ NOT
CD 20	Driving without reasonable consideration for ⎬ APPLICABLE other road users ⎭ TO SCOTLAND
*CD 30	Driving without due care and attention or without reasonable consideration for other road users
	Construction and Use Offences (Vehicles or Parts Dangerous)
CU 10	Using a vehicle with defective brakes
CU 20	Causing or likely to cause danger by reason of use of unsuitable vehicle or using a vehicle with parts or accessories (excluding brakes, steering or tyres) in a dangerous condition
CU 30	Using a vehicle with defective tyres
CU 40	Using a vehicle with defective steering
CU 50	Causing or likely to cause danger by reason of load or passengers
	Dangerous Driving, etc. Offences
DD 10	Driving in a dangerous manner ⎫ NOT
DD 20	Driving at a dangerous speed ⎬ APPLICABLE
DD 30	Reckless driving ⎭ TO SCOTLAND
*DD 40	Driving in a dangerous manner, at a dangerous speed, or recklessly
DD 50	Causing death by dangerous driving
DD 60	Manslaughter or, in Scotland, culpable homicide by driver of a motor vehicle
	Drink or Drugs Offences
DR 10	Driving or attempting to drive with blood/alcohol concentration above limit
DR 20	Driving or attempting to drive when unfit through drink or drugs
DR 30	Driving or attempting to drive then failing to provide a specimen of blood or urine for laboratory testing
DR 40	In charge of a vehicle with blood/alcohol concentration above limit

Code	Offences
DR 50	In charge of a vehicle when unfit through drink or drugs
DR 60	In charge of a vehicle then failing to provide a specimen of blood or urine for laboratory testing
	Insurance Offences
IN 10	Using a vehicle uninsured against third-party risks
	Licence Offences
LC 10	Driving without a licence
LC 20	Driving under age
	Miscellaneous Offences
MS 10	Leaving vehicle in a dangerous position
MS 20	Unlawful pillion riding
MS 30	Playstreet offence
MS 40	Driving with uncorrected defective eyesight or refusing to submit to a test of eyesight
MS 50	Motor racing on the highway
	Motorway Offences
MW 10	Contravention of special roads regulations (excluding speed limits)
	Non-Endorsable Offence
NE 99	A disqualification under s. 24 of the Criminal Justice Act 1972 (now s. 44 of the Powers of Criminal Courts Act 1973)
	Pedestrian Crossing Offences
*PC 10	Undefined contravention of pedestrian crossing regulations
PC 20	Contravention of pedestrian crossing regulations with moving vehicle
PC 30	Contravention of pedestrian crossing regulations with stationary vehicle
	Provisional Licence Offences
PL 10	Driving without L-plates
PL 20	Not accompanied by a qualified person
PL 30	Carrying a person not qualified
PL 40	Drawing an unauthorised trailer
	Speed Limits Offences
SP 10	Exceeding goods vehicle speed limit
SP 20	Exceeding speed limit for type of vehicle (excluding goods/passenger vehicles)
SP 30	Exceeding statutory speed limit on a public road
SP 40	Exceeding passenger vehicle speed limit
SP 50	Exceeding speed limit on a motorway
	Traffic Directions and Signs Offences
TS 10	Failing to comply with traffic light signals
TS 20	Failing to comply with double white lines
TS 30	Failing to comply with a " Stop " sign
TS 40	Failing to comply with directions of a traffic constable
TS 50	Failing to comply with a traffic sign (excluding " Stop " signs, traffic lights or double white lines)
TS 60	Failure to comply with a school crossing patrol sign

Code	Offences

Offences of Theft or Unauthorised Taking
*UT 10 Taking and driving away a vehicle without consent or an attempt thereat (in England and Wales prior to Theft Act, 1968, only)
UT 20 Stealing or attempting to steal a motor vehicle
UT 30 Going equipped for stealing or taking a motor vehicle
UT 40 Taking or attempting to take a vehicle without consent. Driving or attempting to drive a vehicle knowing it to have been taken without consent. Allowing oneself to be carried in or on a vehicle knowing it to have been taken without consent

Special Code
XX 99 To signify a disqualification under the " totting up " procedure

Aiding and/or Abetting and/or Counselling and/or Procuring
Offences as coded above but with zero changed to " 2 ", e.g., UT 10 becomes UT 12

Causing or Permitting
Offences as coded above but with zero changed to " 4 ", e.g., LC 20 becomes LC 24

Inciting
Offences as coded above but with zero changed to " 6 ", e.g., DD 30 becomes DD 36

II. SENTENCE CODE

1. Sentences are to be coded in a four-character form of which the first and last characters are letters and the middle two numbers. The first letter indicates the type of sentence; the two figures indicate the length of the sentence; and the last letter shows whether the figures are in hours, days, months or years (H, D, M or Y). There are no codes for fines or disqualification.

2. The first letter is allocated as follows:—

A Imprisonment
B Detention in a place approved by the Secretary of State
C Suspended sentence of imprisonment
E Conditional discharge
F Bound over
G Probation
J Absolute discharge
K Attendance Centre
L Detention Centre
P Approved School
R Borstal
T Hospital/Guardianship Order
U* Admonition
V* Young Offenders' institution
W Care of fit person order
Z Period of suspension of sentence of imprisonment

* Scottish Courts only

[It will be noted that the sentence code is out of date, e.g., there is no code for a care order, which replaced fit person and approved school orders (P and W, above).   No up-to-date code has yet (July, 1975) been pre-scribed.—*Ed.*]

3. The following examples show how the code works:—

   (i) A 01 Y   Imprisonment for 1 year

  (ii) G 18 M Probation for 18 months

 (iii) L 03 M   Detention Centre for 3 months

 (iv) A 14 D   Imprisonment for 14 days

  (v) C 02 Y⎫ 2-year prison sentence suspended for 1 year
       Z 01 Y⎭ (Two codes are needed here, as shown, one written beneath the other)

 (vi) J 000   Absolute discharge (here no time period can be shown, but the three 0's should be inserted)

APPENDIX III

SUGGESTIONS FOR ASSESSING PENALTIES FOR MAIN MOTORING OFFENCES

[Published by the Magistrates' Association, April, 1975]

To avoid misunderstandings please read this

IMPORTANT EXPLANATION

1. This is an attempt to be fair to all road traffic offenders. As far as possible their penalties should be consistent (not uniform: see 6 below). Yet responsibility for sentencing rests solely on the court which tries each case on its merits, and these vary between cases and offenders.

2. It follows that greater consistency can be achieved only by Benches voluntarily adopting a similar framework which they accept as just and reasonable. These suggestions are not a tariff of set penalties but " starting points " for discussion by courts in their assessment of penalties. The suggested figures should not be followed slavishly but increased (even to the maximum penalty) or decreased (even to an absolute discharge) whenever this is just in all the circumstances.

3. The circumstances include the gravity of the particular offence, and sometimes its prevalence; the record of the offender; the means of the offender (as required by Statute); the number of convictions arising from the same incident; and the different impact of disqualification on different offenders.

4. Many road traffic offences are more dangerous on motorways where speeds are higher and this should be reflected in the penalties imposed.

5. This folder is approved in principle by the Lord Chancellor and the Lord Chief Justice. The figures, suggested after consulting every Branch, represent a broad consensus of view on appropriate penalties for " average " offences committed by first offenders of average means.

6. There may be good reasons for local variations. Average rates of pay are much higher in some areas than in others, so it is consistent that average fines should vary too. A column [omitted in this book] has been left for the Bench " norm " which it is hoped each Bench will review after consulting neighbouring Benches and giving full weight to these considered suggestions.

7. Maximum fines have been greatly increased for road traffic offences committed after 1st January 1975. This means that normal fines should go up. There is, however, a danger that this may bring road traffic fines out of proportion to other fines, which should also be reviewed, especially since inflation represents about 30% increase since the last edition of this folder in May 1973.

A. JOSEPH BRAYSHAW
Secretary.

SUGGESTIONS FOR ASSESSING PENALTIES FOR MAIN MOTORING OFFENCES
[Subject to the important explanation above]
Unless there are special reasons the following offences carry at least 12 months' compulsory disqualification (from date of conviction), compulsory endorsement, optional driving test:—

Offence	Maximum Penalty		Suggested Penalty
1a. Drunken driving or driving with excess alcohol	£400 or 4 months	Must disqualify at least 12 months.	£80 and 12 months disqualification (longer if over 120 mg. in blood)
1b. Refusing urine or blood specimen (when driving)	£400	(3 years if previous conviction in last 10 years)	£80 and 12 months disqualification (longer for bad case)

The following offences carry optional disqualification, optional driving test, compulsory endorsement (unless there are special reasons) save where otherwise stated:—

Offence	Maximum Penalty	Suggested Penalty
2. Driving while disqualified	£400 and/or 3 months	£100 and consider disqualification for longer than existing disqualification; or detention centre or prison
3. Dangerous or reckless driving or dangerous speed	£400 or 4 months	£100 and 6 months disqualification
4. In charge drunk or with excess alcohol or refusing urine or blood specimen	£200	£50 and consider disqualification
5. Careless or inconsiderate driving	£200	£50 and consider disqualification
6. Learner driver: (a) Unsupervised in car		£25
(b) M/cyclist with unqualified passenger	£100	£15 and consider disqualification
(c) No L-plates		£15
7. Speeding	£100	£1·50 per mph over any limit. More for heavy vehicles. Consider disqualification particularly if 30 mph over limit
8. Parking offences: (a) Dangerous position		£25
(b) On zigzags by pedestrian crossing	£100	£20
(c) Obstruction	£100*	£8 minimum
9. No insurance (or permitting)	£200	£50 and consider disqualification

Footnotes:
Maximum penalty means on summary conviction.
Periods in months mean imprisonment unless otherwise stated.
* indicates no power to disqualify, endorse or test.

Offence	Maximum Penalty	Suggested Penalty		
10. Taking vehicle without consent	£400 and/or 6 months	£60 and 12 months disqualification or consider detention centre or prison		
11. Carried in taken vehicle	£400 and/or 6 months	£50 and 6 months disqualification		
12. Failing to stop after accident	£100	£25 if later reported: otherwise £45 and consider disqualification		
13. Failing to report accident	£100	£25		
14. Failing to comply with police or traffic signs (except traffic lights or double white lines)	£100 (power to disqualify, endorse, test, in some cases only)	£20		
15. Traffic lights or double white lines	£100	£25 and consider disqualification		
16. Pedestrian or school crossing offences (other than parking)	£100	£25 and consider disqualification		
17. Construction and Use Regulations:			Goods Vehicle	
(a) Offences re brakes, steering, tyres,† number of passengers, dangerous condition of vehicle, weight distribution, packing and adjustment of load	£100: but for goods vehicles £400	Driver £25	Owner £50	
(b) Overloading commercial vehicle or exceeding maximum axle weight¶	£400*	£30	£100	More on motorways
(c) Insecure load	£100: but for goods vehicles £400	£30	£100	
(d) Goods vehicle, dangerously unsuitable use	£400	£30	£100	
(e) Other offences	£100*	£10	£25	
18. No driving licence	£100	£30 if endorsable: otherwise £5		

Footnotes:
Maximum penalty means on summary conviction.
Period in months mean imprisonment unless otherwise stated.
* indicates no power to disqualify, endorse or test.
† penalty refers to each tyre.
¶ suggested penalty refers to conviction on each charge.

The following offences do not carry disqualification, endorsement or driving test:—

Offence	Maximum Penalty	Suggested Penalty	
		lit road	unlit road
19. Driving without lights	⎫	£10	£20
20. Driving without matched headlights on unlit road	⎬ £100	—	£15
21. Parking during darkness on wrong side	⎭	£8	£15
22. No test certificate	£100	£8 (more if over 3 months overdue)	
23. No excise licence	£50 or 5 times annual duty	Actual duty lost plus fine of approximately twice that amount (minimum £25)	
24. Failing to produce documents	£50	£3 per document	
25. No crash helmet	£50	£10	

The law requires " Totting up " disqualifications to run consecutively to any other order of disqualification (whether imposed on that or any other occasion).   All other disqualifications *must* commence from the moment they are pronounced and cannot be ordered to run consecutively.

If disqualified for a lengthy period, or if driving skill suspect, disqualify until test passed.

[CONTINUED

MOTORWAY OFFENCES

The following offences carry optional disqualification, optional driving test, compulsory endorsement (unless there are special reasons):—

Offence	Maximum Penalty	Suggested Penalty
26. Driving off carriage-way	£100	On central reservation £60; On hard shoulder or verge £20
27. Driving on slip road against "No entry" sign	£100	£30
28. Driving in wrong direction	£100	On main motorway £75 and 3 months disqualification; On sliproad £30
29. Making U-turn	£100	£75 and 3 months disqualification
30. Driving in reverse	£100	On main motorway £60 and 3 months disqualification; On sliproad £30
31. Learner driver or excluded vehicle	£100	£30
32. Vehicle over 3 tons or drawing trailer in third lane	£100	£45

The following offences do not carry disqualification, endorsement or driving test:—

Offence	Maximum Penalty	Suggested Penalty
33. Stopping on hard shoulder	£100	On main motorway £20; On sliproad £10
34. Walking on motorway	£100	On main motorway or slip-road £20; On hard shoulder or verge £10

[CONTINUED]

INDEX

ABANDONED VEHICLES—
    regulations as to, 396, 397
ABROAD—
    drivers from, 63, 64
            driving licence, 480, 481
    servicemen committing offence, 60, 61
    witnesses, 105, 106
ABSENCE, *see* DEFENDANT
ABSOLUTE DISCHARGE—
    disqualification where defendant given, 630
ABSOLUTE LIABILITY—
    imposition of, 41, 49, 50
ACCESS—
    public, definition, 27–29
ACCESSORY—
    causing or permitting offence, 50
    company as, 46
    may be convicted as principal, 47
ACCIDENT—
    additional alcohol consumed after, 168
    breath test may be required following, 148, 152, 195–197
    certificate of insurance, duty to produce after, 341
    damage to other vehicle, duty to stop, 342, 347
    definition of, 130, 131, 148, 348
    driver for purpose of reporting, 26
    duty to exchange names and addresses after, 342, 345–347
            remain at scene, 347
            stop after, 342 *et seq.*, 347
    failure to report, special reasons for not disqualifying, 681
            stop after or report, may be manslaughter, 254
    knowledge of, driver must have, 344
    notice of intended prosecution not required where there is, 130–132
    penalties for failure to report, 348, 349
            stop after, 348, 349
    personal injury, involving, duty to stop, 342 *et seq.*
ADAPTED VEHICLES—
    meaning of, 333, 334
ADJOURNMENT—
    defendant's right to, 89
ADMISSIONS—
    committal proceedings, at, 82
    employees, by, 121
    evidence, as, 120
AERODROMES—
    roads within, 30
AFFIRMATION—
    instead of oath, 102
AGE—
    day of attaining particular, 58
    driving, for, heavy goods vehicles, 484
            motor car, 482
                cycle, 482
AGENT—
    driving motor vehicle, 367

AGRICULTURAL VEHICLES—
    excise duty, 493
    farmers' goods vehicles, 498, 499
    regulations affecting, 51, 52
    trailer, 13, 51, 766
AIDING AND ABETTING—
    causing offence, 52
    company, by, 46
    court having jurisdiction, 66
    dangerous driving, 276, 277
    death by dangerous driving, 257, 260, 277
    defences to, 52 *et seq.*
    disqualification for, 623, 627, 631
    disqualified driver, 54
    drivers' hours, offences relating to, 559
    driving instructor, by, 53, 277
            while disqualified, offence of, 652
    drunken driving, 53, 165, 252, 475
    elements of, 52
    employer, 49, 50, 52, 53, 54
    endorsement of licence for, 613, 614
    juvenile, 57
    knowledge as element of offence, 52, 54
    loan of vehicle, in case of, 43, 54
    notice of intended prosecution, 129
    passenger, by, 47, 55
    principal, by, 47, 55
    use of motor vehicle, 46, 50, 52–55
    venue, provisions as to, 66
    what amounts to, 52–55
AMBULANCE—
    dangerous or careless driving of, 268
    excise duty, not subject to, 500
    speed limit exemption, 338
ANIMAL—
    motorways, on, restrictions on, 708
APPEAL—
    case stated, by, 699–701
    Crown Court, to, 696–699
    disqualification, against, 643
    endorsement, against, 614, 615
    generally, 701
    prosecution, by, 697, 700
ARMED FORCES, *see* SERVICEMEN
ARREST—
    drink or drug offences, in case of, 148, 163, 206, 208–212, 236
    driving or attempting to drive motor vehicle with excess blood/alcohol, 208–212
            while disqualified, 651
    obstruction of highway, 394
    power of, for careless or dangerous driving, 263, 469
    taking conveyance without authority, 354
ARTICULATED VEHICLE—
    definition, 10 *et seq.*, 329, 766
    excise duty on, 11, 12
    speed limit, 11, 336
    weight of, 822, 823, 824, 860, 861
ATTEMPTS—
    disqualification for, 622

ATTEMPTS—*continued*
  driving while disqualified, 652
  endorsement, when permitted, 607, 622
AUDIBLE WARNING SYSTEM—
  requirements as to use of, 788, 837
AUTOMATIC LEVEL CROSSING—
  half-barrier, definition, 712
  requirements as to telephoning at, 308, 309, 712
  traffic signs at, 309, 712
AUTOMATISM—
  defence of, 24, 269
AUTREFOIS ACQUIT, 92–94
AUTREFOIS CONVICT, 93, 94, 339

BAIL—
  arrest for failing breath test, after, 163
  condition of, not to drive, 669
BEES—
  driver attacked by, 269
BICYCLE, *see also* CYCLE; CYCLIST
  lights on, 406, 407
BLACK-OUT—
  driver, by, 269, 270
BLOOD—
  specimen of, *see* DRINK or DRUG OFFENCES
BORSTAL—
  disqualification of offender returned to, 635
BRAKES—
  braking efficiency, definition of, 766
                    regulations as to, 858
  Construction and Use Regulations, 415–418
  heavy motor car, 802
  invalid carriages, 811
  locomotive, requirement as to, 329, 798
  maintenance of, absolute duty, 416
  motor car, 806
      cycle, 811
      tractor, requirement as to, 329, 799
  parking, regulations as to, 781
  split braking system, 771
  stored energy, 772
  testing of, 851
  trailer, requirement as to, 329, 813
  vehicles having plating certificate, 854
BREAKDOWN VEHICLES—
  lights on, 406, 759
BREATH TEST—
  accident, following, 148, 152, 195–197
  Alcotest, *see* device, *below*
  being in charge of motor vehicle, no power to require, 164
  breathalyser, *see* device, *below*
  constable may require, 147
  cyclist, in case of, 158, 159
  device, approval of, 200
      correct use of, 202
      incorrectly assembled, 203, 204, 207
      instructions for use, 200
      storage of, 203
  drink prior to, 191
  driving off road, effect of, 191

BREATH TEST—*continued*
    failure to supply specimen of breath for, 150, 152, 204–208, 227–229
    general requirements as to, 147, 148
    grounds for requiring, 184 *et seq.*
    hospital patients, by, 223, 228
    lawful administration of, 200
    manufacturer's instructions as to, 148, 200
    meaning of, 155
    must be administered "as soon as reasonably practicable", 147, 198, 199
                        "there or nearby", 147, 197, 198
    person in charge of motor vehicle, of, 164
    police constable in uniform, must be required by, 199
    positive, blood or urine specimen may be required after, 213
              liability to arrest, 148, 164, 204
    power to require, 147, 184 *et seq.*
    reasonable grounds for refusing, 208, 227–229
    refusal to take, 150, 204 *et seq.*, 227–229
              arrest for, 206
              penalties for, 228
              summary offence, 160
    second, at police station, 148, 149, 212–214
    smoking prior to, 202, 203
    statutory provisions, 152, 153
    "there or nearby", must be administered, 147, 197, 198
    who may require, 199
BRIDGE—
    highway, as, 26
BRIDLEWAY—
    driving on, 397 *et seq.*
    road, as, 32, 44
BUILDERS' SKIPS—
    highway, on, 399
BUSES, *see* PASSENGER VEHICLES; PUBLIC SERVICE VEHICLES

CAR DOOR—
    negligent opening of, 399–401
    opening of, in breach of Construction and Use Regulations, 840
CARELESS CYCLING, *see* CYCLIST
CARELESS DRIVING—
    additional charge to, 290
    aiding and abetting, 277
    alternative charges, 265, 266
    ambulance, of, 268
    arrest without warrant for, 263
    black-out by driver, 269, 270
    civil cases, 280 *et seq.*
    common danger, driving to, 292
    Crown servants, by, 263
    dangerous driving charge heard together with, 267
                     distinguished from, 278, 279
                     prosecution after acquittal for, 264
    decided cases on, 282 *et seq.*
    disqualification for, 294
    drink or drugs, evidence as to taking of, 274
    driving test may be ordered after conviction for, 294
    due care and attention, driving without, 263
                        obligation to show, 284
    endorsement for, 294
    evidence as to, 268 *et seq.*
                 res ipsa loquitur, 271

CARELESS DRIVING—*continued*
    examples of, 269 *et seq*, 282–286
    falling asleep, caused by, 273
    fire engine, of, 268
    hand signals, failure to give, 288
    Highway Code, breach of, 286, 287
    insect enters car, 288
    learner driver, by, 277
    magistrates, must be tried by, 265
    mechanical defects, 277, 278
    misleading signals, by giving, 283
    penalties for, 293, 294
    plea to, where there is charge of dangerous driving, 76
    police, by, 268
    proceeding with, after acquittal for dangerous driving, 264
    proof of, 123
    public emergency, in, 268
    reasonable consideration, driving without, 263
        failure to show, 283, 284
    reduction of dangerous driving to, 266 *et seq.*
    reversing when road not clear, 289
    serviceman, by, whilst abroad, 265
    special reasons for not disqualifying, 669
    standard of care, 269 *et seq.*
    state of traffic, evidence as to, 275
    two separate offences, includes, 266
    white line, disobedience of, 311
        disregard of, 285
CAR HIRE—
    liability of firms for parking penalties, 586, 587
    statutory statement of hiring, 587, 592, 593
CAR PARK—
    highway, as, 29, 30
    public place, as, 173
CARRIAGEWAY—
    definition of, 437, 704
CARRIER—
    licence, failing to comply with, 68
CARTS—
    vehicles, as, 9
CAUSING—
    company, by, 33, 34
    control and direction relevant, 34
    definition of, 33
    generally, 32, 33
    use contrary to Construction and Use Regulations, 412
CAUTION—
    necessity for, 117, 118
CENSUS—
    requirement to stop for, 309, 310
CENTRAL RESERVATION—
    meaning of, 437
    parking on, 395, 396
CERTIFICATE—
    driving licence records proved by, 107–111
    insurance, of, *see* INSURANCE
    registration particulars proved by, 107 *et seq.*
CERTIFICATE OF ANALYSIS—
    admissibility in evidence, 147
    error in, 178

CERTIFICATE OF ANALYSIS—*continued*
    proof by means of, 176 *et seq.*
    service of, 179
CERTIORARI—
    omission to order endorsement, in case of, 612
CHARACTER—
    evidence as to, 94–97
CHILD—
    maximum fine in respect of, 594
    sworn evidence by, 101–103
CLEARWAYS, 394, 395
    regulations as to, 730
CO-DEFENDANTS—
    trial of, together, 266
COMMITTAL PROCEEDINGS—
    admissions at, 82
    defendant, evidence by, 82
        must be present, 98
    depositions, 81, 82
    disqualification at, 636, 637
    speeches at, 82 *et seq.*
    submission of no case to answer, 82 *et seq.*
    under s. 1 of the Criminal Justice Act, 1967, 82
COMMON DANGER—
    driving to, offence of, 292
COMMON LAND—
    driving on, 397 *et seq.*
COMPANY, *see also* CORPORATION
    aiding and abetting dangerous driving, 257, 277
    causing or permitting offence, 35, 36, 37
    pleading guilty in writing, 99
    using motor vehicle, 45
COMPENSATION—
    power to award, 598, 599
    taking vehicle without consent, 361
CONDUCTOR—
    public service vehicles, of, duties, 578–580
CONSENT—
    separate charges being heard together, to, 74
CONSPIRACY—
    time limit for offence, 71
CONSTABLE—
    power of, in relation to traffic survey, 295, 296
        to arrest for driving offences, 263
            direct traffic, 304–306
            require breath test, 147
            stop vehicle, 147
CONSTRUCTION AND USE REGULATIONS—
    abroad, car brought from, 63
    agricultural trailer, 13, 766
    application of, 774
    audible warning system, 788
        use of, 837
    brakes, requirements as to, 415–418, 829, *see also* BRAKES
        testing of, 851
    Crown vehicles, application to, 413
    dangerous load, 418 *et seq.*
        vehicle, 418 *et seq.*
    definitions, 410 *et seq.*, 766–773

CONSTRUCTION AND USE REGULATIONS—*continued*
    duties relating to driving and stopping, 838
    E.E.C. directives to which vehicles must conform, 778, 779
    exemptions, 410, 411, 774
    glass, maintenance of, 829
    grit, emission of, 794, 834
    heavy motor car, requirements as to, *see* MOTOR CAR
    height, requirements as to, 780
    implements suspended from lifting appliances, 849
    invalid carriages, requirements as to, *see* INVALID CARRIAGE
    land implements, application to, 413
    leaving vehicle unattended, 421
    length, requirements as to, 413, 414, 780
    lights on vehicles, 404, 794, 831
    locomotives, requirements as to, *see* LOCOMOTIVE
    long load, restrictions on use of vehicles carrying, 843
    maintenance, requirements as to, 828
    mascots, restrictions on, 422, 848
    mirrors, requirements as to, 786, 787
    motor car, requirements as to, *see* MOTOR CAR
        cycle, requirements as to, *see* MOTOR CYCLE
        tractors, requirements as to, *see* MOTOR TRACTOR
    noise, measurement of, 424, 835
        requirements as to, 789, 835
    obstruction under, 383
    offences, special reasons for not disqualifying, 684
    oil, emission of, 424
    overall length, definition, 769
        width, definition, 769
    overhang, definition of, 770
        requirements as to, 413, 414
    parking brakes, 781
    penalties for failure to comply with, 432–436
    permitting use in breach of, 40
    petrol tanks, requirements as to, 424, 785, 831
    plated vehicles, relating to, 852 *et seq.*
    plates, vehicles to be equipped with, 796
    power to weight ratio, requirements as to, 796, 829
    quitting vehicle, offence of, 421
    radio interference suppression, 790
    rear markings, requirements as to, 415
    reflectors, provision and maintenance of, 404, 794, 831
    reversing, requirements as to, 786
    safety glass, requirements as to, 787
    seat belts, requirements as to, 423, 782
    silencer, requirements as to, 789, 832
    smoke or vapour, emission of, 790, 834
    sparks, emission of, 794, 834
    special types of vehicle, provisions as to, 430
    speedometer, 415, 785, 828
    springs, provision of, 780
    steering gear, maintenance of, 831
    stopping of engine when stationary, 837
    summons under, should specify defect, 421
    testing of vehicles, 426 *et seq.*, 851
    text of, 766 *et seq.*
    toilet facilities, as to, 794, 835
    trailer, requirements as to, *see* TRAILER
    tyres, requirements as to, 423, 424, 832
    unladen weight, 18

CONSTRUCTION AND USE REGULATIONS—*continued*
    unroadworthy vehicles, prohibition on sale, 424 *et seq.*
    using in breach of, 46, 47
    view to front, 786
    weight, reference to, 16, 17, 18
    wheel, diameter of, 786
        load, variation of, 780
    wide loads, restrictions in respect of, 843
    windscreen washers, requirements as to, 788
        wipers, requirements as to, 787, 831

CONTAINER—
    suitable, for blood or urine specimen, 220

CONVEYANCE—
    definition of, 351
    taking without authority, 351 *et seq.*
        arrestable offence, 354
        attempts, 358
        compensation for, 361
        consent obtained by intimidation, 355
        defences to, 354–356
        disqualification and endorsement for, 620
        employee, position of, 358–360
        hirer, position of, 358–360
        in Scotland, 363
        insurance of, 374
        juvenile offender, 361
        passenger may be liable for, 356–358
        penalties for, 360–363
        prima facie evidence, 122, 123
        procedure for trial, 353

CONVICTION—
    announcement of, after "no case" submission, 84
    cross examination as to previous, 96, 97
    disclosure of previous, 91
    duty to inform defendant's solicitor of, 119
    proof of, 94–96

CORPORATION, *see also* COMPANY
    admissions by, 122
    service of summons on, 72

CORROBORATION—
    child's evidence, of, 102
    defendant's statement, of, 126
    evidence as to speeding, of, 318
    need for, 102

COSTS—
    appeal against order for, 600, 601
    award of, 599–601
    central funds, payment out of, 600
    defendant, against, 601
    indictable offence tried summarily, 600
    prosecution, against, 599, 600, 601

COURTS MARTIAL—
    dangerous and careless driving triable at, 265
    notice of intended prosecution, 133

CRIME—
    vehicle used for, 640 *et seq.*

CRIMINAL DAMAGE—
    committal for sentence, 79
    driving, whilst, 364, 365

CROSS EXAMINATION—
    character, as to, 96, 97
    failure to subject witness to, 125, 126
    joint defendants, where there are, 75, 76
CROWN—
    Construction and Use Regulations, application to, 413
    lighting provisions, application to, 406
    obstruction by vehicles of, 383
    offence affecting, summary trial, 81
    proceedings against, 60–63
    roads, 30, 31, 63
    servants, dangerous or careless driving by, 263
        occasions when exempted from liability, 61, 62
    vehicles, insurance of, 369
CROWN COURT—
    appeal to, 696–699
    committal to, 78 et seq., see also COMMITTAL PROCEEDINGS
                    juvenile, of, 57
                    summary offences, of, 637
CYCLE—
    auto-assisted, 291
    definition of, 292
    drink or drug offences, 158, 159, 247, 252
    motor, see MOTOR CYCLE
    pedal, brakes on, 417 et seq.
            lights on, 407
            taking without owner's consent, 353
CYCLIST—
    breath test, 158, 159
    careless riding, 291, 292
                    penalties for, 293
    dangerous riding by, 291, 292
                    penalties for, 293
    drink or drug offences, 158, 159, 247, 252
                    penalties for, 247
    traffic signs, must comply with, 299
    unfit to ride through drink or drugs, 158

DAMAGE—
    caused by driving, 364, 365
DANGEROUS CONDITION—
    vehicle or load in, 418 et seq.
DANGEROUS CYCLING, see CYCLIST
DANGEROUS DRIVING—
    absolute prohibition on, 269
    acquittal, proceeding with lesser charge in case of, 264
    aiding and abetting, 276, 277
    alternative charges, 265, 266
    ambulance, of, 268
    arrest without warrant for, 263
    black-out by driver, 269, 270
    careless driving distinguished from 278, 279
    charge reduced to careless driving, 266 et seq.
    civil cases, 280 et seq.
    common danger, driving to, 292
    Crown servants, by, 263
    dangerous manner and speed, 275, 276
    death caused by, 253–262
                    aiding and abetting, 257, 260, 277
                    alternative conviction possible, 254

DANGEROUS DRIVING—*continued*
    death caused by, defective vehicle, knowingly driving, 257
                direction to jury, 255 *et seq.*
                evidence of blood/alcohol in case of, 256
                      drunken driving admissible at trial, 256
                inquest, 258
                mens rea, 257
                notice of intended prosecution not required, 133
                penalties for, 260 *et seq.*
                vehicles racing each other, 260
    decided cases on, 281 *et seq.*
    defendant charged with careless and, 76
    disqualification for, 293
    drink or drugs, evidence as to taking of, 274
    driving test may be ordered after conviction for, 294
    endorsement for, 293
    evidence of, 268
            res ipsa loquitur, 271
    examples of, 269
    falling asleep, caused by, 273
    fire engine, of, 268
    intention need not be proved, 280
    mechanical defects, 277, 278
    mens rea, 280
    notice of intended prosecution, 128
    Offences Against The Person Act, 1861, under, 258, 259
    overtaking on inside lane of motorway, 270
    penalties for, 292
    plea to careless driving, 76
    police, by, 268
    previous driving, evidence as to, 276
    procedure, 76, 79
            for trial, 264, 265
    proof of, 123
    public emergencies, in, 268
    reckless driving, includes, 262
    serviceman, by, whilst abroad, 265
    special reasons for not disqualifying, 669
    standard of danger, 269 *et seq.*
    state of traffic, evidence as to, 275
    time limit for bringing proceedings, 268
    trial by jury, election for, 264
DANGEROUS POSITION—
    vehicles in, 401, 402
            notice of intended prosecution, 129, 131
DANGEROUS SPEEDING—
    notice of intended prosecution, 128
    penalties for, 293, 294
DATE OF BIRTH—
    defendant may be required to give, 613
    police may require, 466
DEATH—
    dangerous or reckless driving, caused by, *see* DANGEROUS DRIVING
    offences causing, notice of intended prosecution, 133
    witness, of, 105
DEFENCE—
    automatism, of, 24, 269
DEFENDANT—
    absence of, 72, 73, 78, 81, 98, 99, 630

DEFENDANT—*continued*
  evidence by, at committal proceedings, 82
  joint, *see* JOINT DEFENDANTS
  statement of, admissibility of, 117–120
  two or more persons, separate trials, 74 *et seq.*
  witness for prosecution, as, 124
DEFINITIONS—
  abnormal transport unit, 712
  accident, 130, 131, 148, 348
  accord precedence, 451
  adapted, 333, 334
  agricultural machine, 51
              produce, 51
  agriculture, 495
  articulated combination, 540
              vehicle, 10 *et seq.*, 329, 766
  authorised examiner, 427
              vehicle, 540
  automatic half-barrier level crossing, 712
  braked trailer, 331
  braking efficiency, 766
  breath test, 155
  business purpose, 521
  carriage of goods, 540
  carriageway, 437, 704
  causing, 33
  central reservation, 437, 704
  close-coupled, 766
  contract carriage, 567
  conveyance, 351
  cycle, 292
  dock road, 30, 31
  drink, 241
  drive, 21
  driver, 21–26, 540, 585, 591
  driving away, 24, 25
              or attempting to drive, 24
  drug, 241
  dual-carriageway road, 437
              purpose vehicle, 328
  fog lamp, 732
  foreign vehicle, 331, 332
  give-way line, 437, 444
  goods-carrying trailer, 732
              vehicles, 495, 496, 540, 544, 733
  hackney carriage, 492
  hauling vehicle, 536
  heavy commercial vehicle, 395
              locomotive, 3
              motor car, 3
  hours of darkness, 404
  industrial tractor, 768
  invalid carriage, 3
  kerbside weight, 332, 733, 828
  land implements, 413
              tractor, 768
  lay-by, 730
  light locomotive, 3
  load-carrying trailer, 328
  loose equipment, 15, 16

DEFINITIONS—*continued*
  magistrates' court, 1
  main carriageway, 730
  major road, 711, 716
  marginal strip, 704
  maximum gross weight, 332
  mechanically propelled, 6, 7
  minor road, 711, 716
  motor car, 2
      cycle, 3, 349, 728
      tractor, 3
      trader, 520
      vehicle, 2 *et seq.*
  motorway, 704
  one-way street, 437
  overall length, 769
          width, 769
  overhang, 770
  owner, 55, 56, 351
  pallet, 536
  passenger car, 834
              vehicle, 771
  pedestrian controlled vehicle, 771
  pneumatic tyre, 771
  protective headgear, 349, 728
  public access, 27–29
  recovery vehicle, 521, 525, 526
  relevant time, 618
  restricted road, 838
  rigid vehicle, 771
  road, 26, 27, 31
  safety glass, 771
  single-decked vehicle, 771
  split braking system, 771
  stradle carrier, 772
  stud, 437
  sunset, 403
  tower wagon, 497
  towing implement, 772
  track laying, 772
  traffic direction, 296
          signs, 296
  trailer, 9 *et seq.*, 497, 498
  uncontrolled zebra crossing, 438
  urban roads, 395
  use, 375
  vehicle, 4, 5, 343
          combination, 540, 712
          tester, 520
  verge, 395, 704
  wheel, 772
  wheeled, 772
  wide tyre, 772
  working day, 559
          week, 559
  works trailer, 772
          truck, 772
  zebra controlled area, 437
          crossing, 438

DEPOSITION—
    use of, at trial, 103
DETENTION CENTRE—
    juveniles, for, 595, 596
DIABETIC—
    dangerous or careless driving by, 269
DIPLOMATIC PRIVILEGE—
    provisions as to, 59, 60
DIRECTION INDICATOR, *see* LIGHTS ON VEHICLES
DIRECTOR OF PUBLIC PROSECUTIONS—
    prosecution by, 81
DISABILITY—
    court's duty to inform licensing authority of, 479
DISQUALIFICATION—
    absence of defendant, in, 630
    absolute discharge, in case of, 630
    aiding and abetting, for, 623, 627, 631
    appeal against, 643
    attempted offences, for, 622
    borstal offender, of, 635
    careless driving, for, 294
    certificate of conviction to prove, 94
    commencement of, 601, 602, 623, 631, 639
    committal for sentence, on, 611, 636
    concurrently, running, 623, 631
    consecutively, running, 623, 627, 631
                removal of, 649
    Construction and Use Regulations, failure to comply with, 435, 436
    criminal purposes, vehicle used for, 641
    dangerous driving, for, 293
                load, using vehicle with, 420
    death by dangerous driving, 260 *et seq.*
    defective eyesight, driving with, 291
    defendant must be present, 622
    discretionary, 629, 630
                offences involving, 618–620
    drink or drug offences, for, 156, 157, 247 *et seq.*
                        aiders and abettors, 252
                        compulsory, 248
                        optional, 251
                        periods of, 247
                        second conviction, 620, 621
    driving licence offences, 481–483
                    retained by court after, 613
            test, pending, 617, 647, 660
            while disqualified, 650 *et seq.*
                        aiding and abetting, 652
                        arrest, powers of, 651
                        attempted, 652, 655
                        committal for sentence, 652
                        initial disqualification in excess of jurisdiction, 650
                        other charges not to be heard with, 77
                        penalties for, 653
                        proof of disqualification, 653
                        removal of, 655 *et seq.*
                        special reasons for not disqualifying, 686
                        strict liability, 653
                        trial by jury, right to, 651
effect of, 635

DISQUALIFICATION—*continued*
    failure to report accident, 348, 349
        stop and/or give particulars after accident, 349,
    foreign driver, of, 481, 635
    imprisonment imposed in addition to, 654
    insurance offences, for, 380
    interim order of, 79
        on committal for sentence, 611, 636
    leaving vehicle in dangerous position, 401
    life, for, 638
        application to remove, 648
    manslaughter, for, 260
    motorway offences, for, 583
    obligatory, offences involving, 617, 618, 622–624
    period of, 624, 638, 645
    plea of guilty in writing, after, 630
    prejudice of jury knowing of, 77
    principles, summary of, 601, 602
    probation is imposed, where, 630
        order, for breach of, 646
    proof of, 94
    removal of, 646 *et seq.*
        consecutive disqualifications, 649
        driving while disqualified, 655 *et seq.*
        procedure, 647–649
    re-opening of matter to impose, 629
    right of further address as to, 85
    school crossing patrol, failing to stop at, 460, 461
    sole penalty, as, 635
    special reasons for not ordering, *see* SPECIAL REASONS
    speed limit, for exceeding, 339, 340
    statutory provisions, 616 *et seq.*
    suspension of, by appellate courts, 644
        pending appeal, 643
    taking vehicle without authority, 360–363
    temporary, on committal for sentence, 611, 636
    theft, going equipped for, 620
    totting-up, 624 *et seq.*
        aiders and abettors, in case of, 627
        consecutive disqualification in case of, 627
    traffic signs, failure to comply with, 314–316, 728
    tram driver, of, 637
    trolley bus driver, of, 637
    undertaking not to drive, 640
    zebra crossing regulations, for breach of, 455, 456
DOCTOR—
    speed limit applicable to, 338
DOCUMENTS—
    admissibility of, 111
    production of, 101, 106 *et seq.*
DOOR—
    opening of, contrary to Construction and Use Regulations, 840
        negligent, 399–401
DRINK OR DRUG OFFENCES—
    aiding or abetting, 53, 165, 252, 475
    alcohol in blood or urine over prescribed limits—
        accident, in case of, 195 *et seq.*
        additional alcohol consumed before specimen taken, 168, 182

DRINK OR DRUG OFFENCES—*continued*
   alcohol in blood or urine over prescribed limit—
      analysis, proof of, 176 *et seq.*
      arrest for driving while unfit, 236
         in case of, 208 *et seq.*
            essential for conviction, 209
            where more than one charge, 209, 210
      attempting to drive with, 146–149, 151, 163, 171, 184
      being in charge with, 149, 150, 151, 163 *et seq.*
      certificate of analysis, 147, 177 *et seq.*
            error in, 178
            service of, 179
      cyclists, in case of, 158, 159, 247, 252
      detention, powers of, 155, 222
      disqualification for, 247
      driving with, 146–149, 151, 171, 175, 184
      endorsement for, 247
      evidence as to, 175 *et seq.*, 216, 241
         ancillary provisions, 154, 155
      hospital patients, tests in case of, 222 *et seq.*
      laboratory tests, 153, 154, 155
          results of, 175–183
      offences, 156, 157
      penalties, 156, 157, 243 *et seq.*
      reasonable cause to suspect, 192–195
      special reasons for not disqualifying, 670 *et seq.*
      specimen—
         adequacy of, 220
         contamination of, 180
         defendant requiring analysis of, 220
         failure to provide, 150, 152, 153, 214, 229 *et seq.*
            penalties for, 247
            reasonable excuse, 231 *et seq.*
            warning as to, 162, 214
         general provisions as to, 148, 149
         hospital patients, 222 *et seq.*
         medical practitioner must take, 215
         method of analysis, 219
        * more than one, 217, 219
         offer of, from finger, 216
         part of body may not be specified by defendant, 216
         power to require, 148, 153, 183, 213
         quantity and quality of, 220
         supply of, to defendant, 217
            in suitable container, 220
         taking of, 215
         thrown away, 217, 219
      summary of offences, 145, 156, 157
      suspicion of, 192 *et seq.*
      trial by jury, 80, 145, 159–161
         court and procedure, 159–163
   arrest in case of, 148, 163, 206, 208–212, 236
   attempting to drive under influence of drink or drugs, 146–149, 151, 163, 171, 184 *et seq.*
   being in charge of motor vehicle, defences to, 168 *et seq.*
               driving instructor, 164, 165
               meaning of, 163 *et seq.*
               question of fact, 164
               under influence of drink or drugs, 149, 150, 163 *et seq.*, 237

DRINK OR DRUG OFFENCES—*continued*
 breath test, *see* BREATH TEST
 carriage, drunk in charge of, 252
 cattle, drunk in charge of, 252
 certificate of analysis, of, *see* CERTIFICATE OF ANALYSIS
 constable, power to stop vehicle, 147
 cyclists, by, 158, 159, 247, 252
 defences to, standard of proof, 169, 170
 detention, police powers of, 155, 222
 disqualification for, 247 *et seq.*
                         second conviction, 620, 621
 driving instructor, by, 164, 172
     under influence of drink or drugs, 146–149, 151, 163, 171, 184 *et seq.*
                         service of summons, 135, 136

 drug, meaning of, 241
 election for trial, 145, 159–161
 endorsement for, 247
 evidence, by non-expert witness, 241
         of, in dangerous or careless driving proceedings, 274, 275
 horse, drunk in charge of, 252
 "hybrid offences", 80, 160
 impaired by alcohol, meaning, 236
 laboratory tests, 153, 154, 155, 175–183
 learner driver, 164
 magistrates' powers of sentencing, 145, 243 *et seq.*
 penalties for, 156, 157, 243, *et seq.*
 public place, in, 173
 relevant time, for purposes of, 617, 618
 road or other public place, may be committed on, 173 *et seq.*
 second conviction for, 620, 621
 servicemen abroad, committed by, 60, 61
 special reasons for not disqualifying, 670 *et seq.*, 675
 specimen, failure to provide, 150, 153, 214, 229 *et seq.*
                         special reasons for not disqualifying, 678
         laboratory tests on, 153, 154, 214 *et seq.*
         requirement of, 148, 149, 214–227
 summary of law, 145 *et seq.*
         statutory provisions and penalties, 156, 157
         trial of, 161
 supervisor, liability of, 164, 172
 traffic offence, power to require breath test, 192, 195
 trial by jury, 80, 145, 159–161
     procedure at, 159–161
 unfitness to drive through drink or drugs, arrest for, procedure after, 236
                         breath test in case of, 236
                         evidence as to, 242
                         impaired by alcohol, meaning of,
                         237–239
 vehicles other than motor vehicles, relating to, 252
DRIVER—
 abroad, from, provisions as to, 63, 64
 automatism, defence of, 24
 definition of, 21–26, 540, 585, 591
 hit and run, 254
 hours of driving, *see* GOODS VEHICLES; PUBLIC SERVICE VEHICLES
 information as to, duty to give, 461–467
 knowledge of, relating to accident, 344
 production of insurance certificate by, 380, 381
 proof as to who was, 50, 107, 121
 public service vehicles, offences by, 579, 580

DRIVER—*continued*
    records, duty to keep, *see* GOODS VEHICLES
    steersman of towed vehicle, 23
    time limit for prosecuting, 68–70
DRIVING—
    automatism, 24
    bridleways, on, 397 *et seq.*
    careless, *see* CARELESS DRIVING
    committing damage whilst, 364, 365
    common land, on, 397 *et seq.*
    dangerous manner, in, 275, *see also* DANGEROUS DRIVING
    defective eyesight, with uncorrected, 290, 291
    definition of, 21, 22
    footpath, on, 397 *et seq.*
    furious, causing bodily harm by, 258, 259
    pushing as, 25, 26
    whilst disqualified, *see* DISQUALIFICATION
    without reasonable consideration, 283, 284
DRIVING EXAMINER, *see* EXAMINER
DRIVING INSTRUCTOR—
    aiding and abetting offence, 53, 277, 475
    drunken, 172
    registration of, requirements as to, 473
    supervising drunken learner, 164, 475
DRIVING LICENCE—
    age limits, 482
    automatic transmission cars, for, 467, 468
    defendant must prove he has, 123
    employer absolutely liable for employee without, 468
    endorsement of, *see* ENDORSEMENT
    expiry of, 468–473
    failure to sign, 481
    false answer on application for, 480
    foreign, 480, 481
        disqualification of holder of, 635
        visitor's need for, 63, 64
    fraudulent use of, 480
    heavy goods vehicle, 483–485
                statutory provisions, 467
    H.M. forces, 467, 468
    learner drivers, 473–477
    offences, penalities for, 481–483
        special reasons for not disqualifying, 686
    power to seize, 480
    production of, 468–473
        power of court to order, 607–610
    provisional, duties of holder, 474 *et seq.*
        "full" licences may be used as, 468
    public service vehicles, statutory provisions, 467
    records, evidence by certificate as to, 107–111
    refusal of, 477–480
        appeal against, 478, 479
    restoration of, 649
    revocation of, 477–480
        appeal against, 479
    statutory provisions, 467, 468
    surrender of, power to require, 472, 473
    use of, with intent to deceive, 480
DRIVING PERMITS—
    issued to armed forces, 468

DRIVING TEST—
    disqualification pending, 660
    examiners, position of, 277
    grounds for ordering, 661
    order of, offence involving obligatory endorsement, 602
    power to order, after conviction for dangerous or careless driving, 294
    traffic signs, may be ordered after failure to comply with, 316
DRUG OFFENCES—see DRINK AND DRUG OFFENCES
DUAL CARRIAGEWAY—
    definition of, 437
DUAL-PURPOSE VEHICLE—
    definition of, 328
DYING DECLARATION
    admissible as evidence, 253, 255

E.E.C.—
    common transport policy, 555
    directives to which vehicles must conform, 778
    regulations, application of, 63, 64
                drivers' hours, 555
                goods vehicles, installation and operation of recording equipment,
                565
EIRE—
    resident, licence of, 64
ELECTION—
    prosecution, of, 79
    trial by jury, for, 78
                dangerous driving, 264
                drink or drug offences, 145, 159–161
EMPLOYEE—
    admissions by, 121
    disobedience of, no defence, 38
    driving licence, without, employer's liability, 468
    insurance required for, 367, 378
    taking conveyance without consent, 358–360
    uninsured use of vehicle by, 378
EMPLOYER—
    absolutely liable for employee without licence, 468
    admission by employee, 121
    aiding and abetting offence, 52, 53, 54
    causing offence, 35
    duty to preserve drivers' records, 548
    permitting offence, 36–39
    procuring or inciting speeding, 321
    using motor vehicle, 45 et seq.
ENDORSEMENT—
    aiding and abetting, for, 613, 614
    appeal against, 614, 615
    attempt at endorsable offences, for, 607, 622
    borstal recall order made, where, 605
    breach of probation, in case of, 611
    careless driving, for, 294
    codes, 606, 874
    committal for sentence, in case of, 610, 611
    Construction and Use Regulations, for failure to comply with, 433 et seq.
    court may take, into consideration, 95, 96
    dangerous driving, for, 293
                load, using vehicle with, 420
    death by dangerous driving, 260

ENDORSEMENT—*continued*
  defective eyesight, for driving with, 291
  deferred sentence, in case of, 611
  drink or drug offences, for, 247
  driving licence offences, 481–483
          production for, 607
      while disqualified, for, 654
      without provisional licence, 477
  duty to disclose, when applying for licence, 609
  evidence, as, 612, 613
      of, 95
  failure to report accident, 349
          stop and/or give particulars after accident, 348, 349
  foreign licence, of, 605, 615, 616
  insurance offences, for, 380
  international driving permit, of, 605
  leaving vehicle in dangerous position, 401
  manslaughter, for, 260
  motorway offences, for, 583
  Northern Irish licence, of, 605, 615
  notification of, to licensing authority, 613
  obligatory, 601, 602, 603, 610
      offences involving, 604, 605, 610, 617–620
  omission to order, 612
  particulars to be endorsed, 606
  principles, summary of, 601, 602
  proof of previous, 608
  removal of, 615
  school crossing patrol, failing to stop at, 460
  sole penalty, as, 605
  speed limit, exceeding, 339, 340
  taking vehicle without authority, 360–363
  theft, going equipped for, 620
  totting-up, 602
  traffic signs, failure to comply with, 314–316
  zebra crossing regulations, for breach of, 455, 456
EVIDENCE—
  admissions as, 82, 120
  affirmation, 102
  careless driving, of, 268 *et seq.*
  certificate, by, 107 *et seq.*
      of analysis as, 147
  character, as to, 94–97
  child, by, 101–103
  corroborative, need for, 102
  dangerous driving, of, 268 *et seq.*
  dead witness, 105
  documentary, 101, 106 *et seq.*
  drink or drugs, as to taking of, 274, 275
          offences, in, 175 *et seq.*, 216, 241
  drivers' records admissible as, 553, 562
  driving licence records, as to, 107 *et seq.*
  drunken driving, of, in proceedings for careless or dangerous driving, 274, 275
  dying declaration, 105, 253, 255
  endorsement as, 612, 613
      of, 95
  false, production of, 263
  further, admitting, 124
  illegally obtained, 126
  inspection of vehicle, 115

EVIDENCE—*continued*
    insurance, of, 379
    joint defendants, by, 75
    leading questions, 125
    locus in quo, view of, 125
    manufacturers' records as, 111, 112
    maps as, 114, 321
    oath, on, 101–103
    operator's licence offences, 538
    opinion of speed, 321
    photographs as, 115
    plans as, 113–115
    plea of guilty by post, where, 99
    presumptions, *see* PRESUMPTION
    previous convictions, of, *see* CONVICTION
    refreshing memory, 112, 113, 319
    registration particulars, as to, 112, 113
    re-opening case to admit further, 86 *et seq.*
    second trial, at, by sick witness, 104
    sick witnesses, of, 103, 104
    sketches as, 114
    speeding, of, 318–321
    spouses, by, 115–117
    statements by defendant as, 117–120
    sworn, 101–103
    tape-recording as, 126
    timetable as, 111, 321
    weight ticket as, 111
    witnesses, enforcing attendance of, 101
EXAMINER—
    Ministry of Transport, is not supervisor, 476
EXCISE DUTY—
    agricultural vehicles, 493
    articulated vehicle, on, 11, 12
    authorisation of proceedings in respect of, 488
    back-duty, payment of, 509, 510
    construction vehicles, 493, 494
    dishonoured cheque used for payment of, 491, 506
    dual-purpose vehicles, 496
    exemptions, 500
    failure to display licence, 502–504
                        defences to, 517
                    transfer licence, effect of, 509
    false declarations in respect of, 502
    farmers' goods vehicles, 498, 499
    fraudulent use or alteration of registration book, 514
    goods vehicles, 495–499
    hackney carriages, 491, 492
    hired car, on, 492
    liability for, vehicle must be kept on public road, 486, 487
    licence, effect of failure to transfer, 509
          failure to display, 502–504, 517
          false declaration for purpose of, 502
    motor cycle, 491
          vehicle, when chargeable, 45
    non-payment of, penalties for, 506–513
    offences, burden of proof, 514, 515
            mitigated penalties, 501, 502
            prosecution for, 486–490
            remission of penalty, 516, 517

EXCISE DUTY—*continued*
    private cars, 499, 500
                kept on road, 10, 45
    registration marks, 513, 514, 518
    regulations as to, 517, 518
    remission of fine or penalty, 516, 517
    statutory provisions, 485, 486
    three wheeled vehicle, on, 491
    time limit for proceedings, 70, 490, 505
    tower wagons, 497
    tractors, 493, 494
    trade licences, 519 *et seq.*
    trailers, 497, 498
    underpayment of, 504–506
    weight of vehicle for purpose of, 16, 515, 516
    works truck, 492
EYESIGHT—
    defective, driving with, 290, 291
    test, police may require, 291

FINES—
    enforcement of payment of, 594
    maximum, for children, 594
            for young persons, 594
    remission of, 516, 517
    vehicle owner's liability for, 584 *et seq.*
FIRE ENGINE—
    dangerous and careless driving of, 268
    excise duty, not subject to, 500
    speed limit exemption, 338
FOG LAMP, *see* LIGHTS ON VEHICLES
FOOTPATH—
    driving on, 397 *et seq.*
    parking on, 395, 396
    public, obstruction of, 383
FORECOURTS—
    highways, as, 29, 30, 114
FORGERY—
    insurance certificate, of, 381, 382

GIVE WAY SIGNS, *see* TRAFFIC SIGNS
GLASS—
    maintenance of, 829
    safety, requirements as to, 787
GO-KART—
    motor vehicle, as, 7
GOODS VEHICLES—
    adaptation of passenger vehicles, 497
    adapted, 334
    braking requirements, 858
            alteration of, 854
    definition of, 495, 496, 540, 544
    drivers' hours, 555 *et seq.*
                emergency, exemption in case of, 559
                evidence that driver has exceeded, 562
                exemptions, 559
                light vans, 559
                penalties for offences, 558, 566
                recording equipment, 565
                rest periods, employer's liability, 561

GOODS VEHICLES—*continued*
    drivers' hours, unavoidable delay, what amounts to, 560, 561
                working day or week, 559
           records, *see* records, *below*
    E.E.C. vehicles, 554, 555
    excise duty, 495–499
    farmers', 498, 499
    foreign, 430, 554, 555
    heavy, age limit for drivers, 484
          driving licence provisions, 483–485
    hire or reward, provisions as to, 542–544
    large, consignment notes, duty to carry, 538
        penalties for unauthorised journeys, 537
        special authorisation for long journeys, 534
    light vans, hours of driving, 559
    Ministry plates for, 853
    operator's licence, 527 *et seq.*
                authorised vehicles, 540
                evidence as to offences, 538
                licensing authority, 539
                statutory provisions, 527–541
                transport manager, provisions as to, 531–534
    plating certificate, having, 852 *et seq.*
    recording equipment, installation and operation of, 565
    records, admissible as evidence, 553, 562
        duty to keep, penalties for not doing so, 546
                statutory provisions, 544 *et seq.*
        employer's liability for staff defaults, 553
        penalties for keeping false, 549
        power to inspect and seize, 548, 549
        register of, 548
    speed limits, 326, 333–335, 337
    test certificate, requirement of, 427
    transport managers' licences, 539
    tyres, where plating certificate issued, 855
    unloading in no waiting area, 391 *et seq.*
GUILTY—
    plea of, *see* PLEA

HACKNEY CARRIAGES—
    excise duty provisions, 491, 492
    meaning of, 492
    registration marks, 513, 518
HAND SIGNALS—
    failure to give, 288
HEADLIGHTS—
    colour of, 745
    definition of, 733
    dipped beam, 732
    driver blinded by, 288, 290
                driving without reasonable consideration, 405, 406
    regulations relating to, 289, 290, 409, 740 *et seq.*
    use of, 289, 409, 745
        for signalling, 289
HEAVY GOODS VEHICLES, *see* GOODS VEHICLES
HEAVY LOCOMOTIVE, *see* LOCOMOTIVE
HEAVY MOTOR CAR, *see* MOTOR CAR
HIGHWAY, *see also* ROAD
    builders' skips deposited on, 399
    car park as part of, 29, 30

INDEX

HIGHWAY—continued
forecourt as part of, 29, 30, 114
mud on, 402
obstruction of, see OBSTRUCTION
roped off, 31
HIGHWAY CODE—
non-observance of, 286, 287
reliance upon, 125, 286, 287
breaking distances contained in, 287
HIRE AGREEMENT—
owner in case of, 55
HIRED CAR—
excise duty on, 492
statutory statement of hiring, 587, 592, 593
vehicle owner liability, 586
HIRE-PURCHASE AGREEMENT—
owner in case of, 55
taking vehicle subject to, without consent of owner, 360
HIRER—
liability of, fixed parking penalties, 587
motor vehicle, of, liability, 43, 50
taking vehicle without consent of owner, 360
HIT AND RUN DRIVERS—
charge against, 254
HORN—
requirements as to, 424, 788
three-toned, 424
two-toned, definition of, 772
HORSE RIDERS—
failing to comply with traffic signs, 299
police signals, not bound to observe, 306
HOSPITAL PATIENTS—
blood or urine tests by, 222, 224
breath test by, 223
HOURS OF DARKNESS—
meaning of, 404
HOURS OF DRIVING, see GOODS VEHICLES
HOVERCRAFT—
definition of, 3, 4
motor vehicle, as, 4
HYBRID OFFENCES—
trial by jury, 80
venue for, 65, 66

IDENTITY—
driver, of, information required as to, 107
police may request, 461 et seq.
evidence as to, 120–123
IMPRISONMENT—
legal representation, offer of, prior to sentence of, 596
matters to be considered before imposing, 595
maximum term of, 595
suspended sentences of, 596, 597
INDICTABLE OFFENCES—
limitation of time, 68, 69
tried summarily, change over to committal, 81
INDICTMENT—
addition of counts to, 80
death by dangerous driving, 255

INFORMATION—
    driver, as to, refusal to give, 461 *et seq.*
        refusing to give, 342, 345
    laying of, necessity for, 56
        time for, 268
INQUEST—
    death arising from motor accident, 258
INSPECTION—
    vehicle, of, 115
INSURANCE—
    agent, vehicle driven by, 367
    associated company, of, 369
    certificate, forgery of, 381, 382
        production of, 380, 381
            after accident, 341
    cover-note, 373
    Crown vehicles, of, 369
    driving without, proof of, 123
    employee using vehicle without, 378
    evidence as to policy of, 379
    fraudulent application for, 381, 382
    invalid carriages, 369
    liability, general conditions of, 372–377
    misrepresentation, policy obtained by, 376
    offences, 365 *et seq.*
        absolute liability, 377, 378
        limitation of time, 379
        penalties for, 380
        permitting, 38
        special reasons for not disqualifying, 681
    onus on defendant to prove he has, 379
    passenger aware of uninsured use, 374
        unaware of uninsured use, 378
    permitting use without, 377, 378
    policy of, production of, 379
        overrides certificate, 372
    provisional licence holder, of, 368
    public authorities, of, 369
    servant, vehicle driven by, 367
    social and business purposes, 366, 367
    third party, permitting use without, 38
        using without, 41, 42, 44
    trailers, covering use of, 371, 372
    using vehicle without, 375, 376
        absolute liability, 377 *et seq.*
        time limit, 70
    vehicles of visiting forces, 369
    void conditions, 370, 371
INVALID CARRIAGE—
    brakes, 811
    Construction and Use Regulations, 811
    definition, 3
    insurance of, 369
    motor car, as, 4
    cycle, as, 4
    non-disabled driver, 4
    passenger carried in, 4
    use of footpath by, 4
    width, 811
    wings, requirements as to, 812

JOINT DEFENDANTS—
 cross-examination of each other, 75
 evidence of, 124
JUDGES' RULES—
 compliance with, 117, 118
JURISDICTION—
 magistrates' court, of, 65 *et seq.*
JURY, *see also* TRIAL; ELECTION
 advantages of trial by, 81
 inspection of vehicle by, 115
JUVENILES—
 aiding and abetting, 57
 committal of, to Crown Court, 57
 detention centre order, 595, 596
 evidence on oath by, 101, 102
 jurisdiction of magistrates' court, 57, 58
 pleading guilty by post, not possible, 58, 99
 proceedings against, 57, 58
 taking conveyance without authority, 360

KEEP LEFT SIGNS, *see* TRAFFIC SIGNS

LAND IMPLEMENTS—
 Construction and Use Regulations, 413
 definition of, 768
LAND LOCOMOTIVE, *see* LOCOMOTIVE
LAND TRACTOR, *see* TRACTOR
LAY-BY—
 definition of, 730
LEADING QUESTIONS—
 use of, 125, 126
LEARNER DRIVER—
 aiding and abetting, 53, 277
 definition of, 21
 duties of, 474 *et seq.*
 motorway regulations as to, 707
 provisional licence, driving without, 477
    failing to comply with conditions of, 481, 482
 supervisor's duties, 475 *et seq.*
LEGAL AID—
 provisions as to, 100
LENGTH—
 Construction and Use Regulations, 413
 overall, definition of, 769
 permitted, combination of vehicles, 13
LEVEL CROSSING—
 automatic half-barrier, definition, 712
    requirements as to telephoning at, 308, 309, 712
    traffic signs at, 309, 712
LICENCE—
 driving, *see* DRIVING LICENCE
 vehicle excise, *see* EXCISE DUTY
LIFTING APPLIANCES—
 safety provisions, 849
LIGHT LOCOMOTIVE, *see* LOCOMOTIVE
LIGHTS ON VEHICLES—
 amber flashing, 406
 blue flashing, 406
 breakdown vehicles, 406, 759
 brought temporarily into U.K., 757

LIGHTS ON VEHICLES—*continued*
    Construction and Use Regulations, 404
    Crown, belonging to, 406
    definitions as to, 731–735
    direction indicators, 409, 410
            definition of, 732
            regulations governing, 760
    display during daylight hours, 403
    exempted vehicles, regulations as to, 753 *et seq.*
    fog lamp, 409
          definition of, 732
    front lamps, regulations governing, 736
          stationary vehicles, 739
    general requirements as to, 406 *et seq.*
    hand-propelled vehicles, 755
    hazard warning, 409
            regulations as to, 764
    headlights, colour of, 745
          definition of, 733
          dipped beam, 732
          driver blinded by, 288, 290, 405, 406
          regulations relating to, 289, 290, 409, 740
          requirements as to use of, 745
    hours of darkness, 404
    maintenance of, 408, 831
    matched pair of headlamps, 733
    motor cycles, 406, 407
    movable platforms, with, 759
    multi-purpose lamps, 407
    number of, 406
    number plates, illumination of, 408, 518
    obligatory, 734
    offences as to, 403 *et seq.*
           defences, 405 *et seq.*
           penalties, 410
           strict liability, 405
    parked vehicles, 408, 409
    poor visibility conditions, duty to display, 403
    position of, 406
    rear, 407
        load obscuring, 756
        regulations governing, 747
    reflectors, 404, 405, 406
           regulations governing, 750 *et seq.*
    regulations as to, 731 *et seq.*
    reversing lamps, 407
          definition of, 734
          regulations governing, 750
    sale of vehicle not complying with requirements as to, 407, 408
    spotlights, 406
    stop lights, 409, 410
          definition of, 735
          regulations governing, 760
    testing of, 851
LIMITATION OF TIME—
    continuing offences, 70
    driving licence, offences relating to, 480
    excise duty offences, 490, 505
    indictable offences, 68, 69

LIMITATION OF TIME—*continued*
    insurance offences, 379
    summary offences, 68, 69

LOAD—
    dangerous condition, in, 418–421
    improperly secured, 42
    indivisible, definition of, 768
    long, conditions applying to, 865
    projecting beyond permitted distance, 413
    wide, conditions applying to, 865

LOCOMOTIVE—
    braking system, requirement of, 329, 798, 799
    Construction and Use Regulations, 797
    heavy, definition, 3
        speed limit, 327
    land, definition of, 768
    light, definition, 3
        speed limit, 327
    markings on, 816
    trailer drawn by, weight of, 817
    tyres, 797
    weight, distribution of, 797
        laden, 817
    width, overall, 797

LONG LOAD—
    regulations applying to, 865

LORRY—
    crate falling off of, 418

MAGISTRATES' COURT—
    appeal from, chances of success, 81
    careless driving offences must be heard in, 265
    committal proceedings, *see* COMMITTAL PROCEEDINGS
    definition, 1
    irregularity in proceedings at, 91, 92
    jurisdiction of, 65 *et seq.*
    juveniles, jurisdiction over, 57, 58
    rectification of mistake by, 73
    venue for proceedings, for, 65–67

MANDAMUS—
    omission to order endorsement, 612
    refusal to issue summons, 56

MANSLAUGHTER—
    arrest on suspicion of, 253
    conviction for lesser offence on charge for, 253
    disqualification and endorsement for, 260
    dying declaration, admissibility of, 253
    hit and run drivers, 254
    inquest, provisions as to, 258
    negligence, standard of, 253
    notice of intended prosecution not required, 133
    penalties for, 260 *et seq.*
    spouse is competent witness, 253

MAPS—
    evidence, as, 114, 321

MASCOTS—
    restrictions on, 422, 848

MECHANICAL DEFECT—
    dangerous or careless driving, defence to, 277, 278

MECHANICALLY PROPELLED—
  definition of, 6, 7
MENS REA—
  causing to be used, 34
  dangerous driving, 280
  death caused by dangerous driving, 257
  evidence of, not necessary, 123
  permitting use, in case of, 34, 38, 41
  using motor vehicle, 43, 48
MIRRORS—
  Construction and Use Regulations, 786
MISTAKE—
  rectification of, by magistrates, 73
MITIGATION—
  plea in, 100
MOTOR BICYCLE, *see* MOTOR CYCLE
MOTOR CAR—
  brakes, requirements as to, 806
  Construction and Use Regulations, 806
  definition of, 22
  engine removed from, 6
  flat battery, with, 7
  heavy, brakes, requirements as to, 802
      Construction and Use Regulations, 801
      definition, 3
      markings on, 816
      maximum weight of, 818
      overall width of, 801
      overhang, 801
      plated weights, 18, 19
      tyres, requirements as to, 805
      weight of, 860
      wings, requirements as to, 805
  invalid carriage as, 4
  overhang, 806
  private, excise duty of, 499, 500
  tyres, requirements as to, 810
  weight of, 860
          maximum, 818
  width, overall, 806
  wings, requirements as to, 810
MOTOR CYCLE—
  age limit for driving, 477
  brakes, requirements as to, 811
  carrying goods, speed limit, 335
  Construction and Use Regulations, 811
  definition of, 3, 349, 728
  excise duty, 491
  invalid carriage as, 4
  lights on, 406, 407
  motorway, use on, 580, 581
  passengers on, 843
  penalties for not wearing protective helmets, 351
          selling sub-standard protective helmets, 350
  protective headgear, definition of, 728
          regulations requiring wearing of, 349, 728
  sidecar, attachment of, 841
          is part of, 13
  trailer, must not draw, 12, 841

MOTOR CYCLE—*continued*
>tyres, requirements as to, 811
>wings, requirements as to, 811
MOTOR MOWER—
>definition of, 8
MOTOR SCOOTER—
>brakes on, 417
MOTOR TRACTOR—
>braking system, requirement of, 329, 799
>Construction and Use Regulations, 799
>definition, 3
>markings on, 816
>overhang, 799
>speed limit, 327
>tyres, requirements as to, 801
>weight of, imposition of speed limit, 327, 329
>width, overall, 799
MOTOR TRADER—
>definition, 520
MOTOR VEHICLE, *see also* VEHICLE
>abandoned, 396, 397
>adapted for use on road, 7, 8
>brakes, *see* BRAKES
>change of use, 4, 5
>Construction and Use Regulations, 816 *et seq.*
>definition, 2 *et seq.*
>getting on, without lawful authority, 363, 364
>hovercraft as, 3, 4
>intended for use on road, 7, 8
>length of, *see* LENGTH
>lights on, *see* LIGHTS ON VEHICLES
>loan of, 43, 44, 50
>maintenance, 828
>motorway, use on, 580, 581
>plate for, particulars to be shown, 855
>private, excise duty on, 499, 500
>roadside test on, 427
>speed limits, 324 *et seq.*
>taking without authority, *see* CONVEYANCE
>tampering with mechanism of, 363, 364
>towed, being, 10
>trailer, as, 10
>using, *see* USING MOTOR VEHICLE
>weight of, *see* WEIGHT
MOTORWAY—
>animals carried in vehicles, restrictions affecting, 708
>carriageway, definition of, 704
>central reservation, definition of, 704
>>prohibition on use of, 707
>classes of vehicle permitted to use, 580, 581
>definition of, 704
>direction of driving, 705, 706
>excluded traffic, use of motorway by, 708
>learner drivers, prohibition on, 707
>marginal strip, definition of, 704
>offences, penalties for, 583
>off-side lane, restriction on use of, 707
>pedestrians on, 707
>regulations, 581, 582, 704 *et seq.*

MOTORWAY—*continued*
    restrictions on reversing, 706, 707
                stopping, 582, 706
                use of verges, 707
    speed limits, 336–338, 581
    statutory provisions, 580–584
    stopping on, 582, 706
    verge, definition of, 704
MOWER, *see* MOTOR MOWER
MUD—
    highway, on, 402

NEGLIGENCE—
    civil cases as to, 284
    opening of car door as, 400
    standard of, in manslaughter cases, 253
NO CASE TO ANSWER—
    submission of, 82 *et seq.*
                dangerous driving, 264
NOISE—
    Construction and Use Regulations, 424, 789
    maximum sound levels, 869
NOTICE OF INTENDED PROSECUTION—
    accident, not required where there is, 130–132
    change in charge, failure to serve, 141, 142
    error in, 142
    form of, 136–140
    offences for which required, 128, 129
    oral warning at time of offence, 133, 134
    presumption that requirements as to, have been complied with, 132, 133
    provisions as to, 127–143
    receipt of, presumed, 132, 133
    service of, 136 *et seq.*
                reasonable diligence, 140, 141
    traffic signs, failure to comply with, 300
    waiver of, 130
NO WAITING, *see also* CLEARWAYS; OBSTRUCTION; PARKING
    order, 390 *et seq.*
                buses unaffected by, 393
                unloading in street subject to, 391
    signs, 298, 299, 393, 394
NUMBER PLATES—
    illumination of, 408, 518

OATH—
    evidence on, 101–103
OBSTRUCTION—
    arrest for, 394
    broken-down vehicle, by, 390
    builders' skips deposited on highway, 399
    clearways, 394, 395
    Construction and Use Regulations, under, 383
    loading and unloading, 391
    mud on highways, 402
    negligent opening of car doors, 399–401
    no waiting street, 390 *et seq.*
    penalties for, 402
    person left in charge of vehicle, 389
    proceedings for, 383
    public footpath, of, 383

OBSTRUCTION—*continued*
    Scotland, in, 388
    slow vehicles, by, 388, 389
    vehicle left in dangerous position, 401, 402
    what amounts to, 385 *et seq.*
OIL—
    emission of, 424
OPERATOR'S LICENCE—
    carriage of goods, for, *see* GOODS VEHICLES
OVERHANG—
    Construction and Use Regulations, 413
    definition of, 770
OVERTAKING—
    zebra crossing, at, 439, 454, 455
OWNER—
    definition of, 55, 351
    liability of, for excess motor charges and fixed penalties, 584 *et seq.*
    vehicle, of, presumption as to use by, 50, 120, 121, 585
OWNERSHIP—
    failing to notify change of, time limit for prosecution, 70

PARKING, *see also* OBSTRUCTION
    central reservations, on, 395, 396
    clearways, 394, 395
    excess charges, vehicle owner's liability for, 589
    fixed penalty, meaning of, 591
            owner's liability for, 584 *et seq.*
    lighting requirements, 408, 409
    removal of vehicles, 396
    urban roads, on, 395, 396
    verges, on, 395, 396
    zebra crossing, on, 439, 440, 441
PARKING METER—
    offences, 384, 385
    regulations, 384
PASSENGER—
    aiding and abetting, 47, 55
    car used without insurance, of, 374, 378
    motor cycle, on, 843
    taking vehicle without consent, may be liable for, 356–358
    trade licence used for purpose of carrying, 524
    trailer carrying, 842
    using own motor vehicle, 47
PASSENGER VEHICLES, *see also* PUBLIC SERVICE VEHICLES
    adapted, 333
    drivers' hours, 555 *et seq.*, 563
    speed limit, 325, 326, 332, 333
PEDESTRIAN—
    police signal, failure to comply with, 314
    precedence of, at zebra crossings, 439
PEDESTRIAN CROSSINGS—*see* PELICAN CROSSINGS; ZEBRA CROSSINGS
PELICAN CROSSINGS—
    definition of, 445
PENALTIES—
    disqualification, *see* DISQUALIFICATION
    endorsement, *see* ENDORSEMENT
    fines, *see* FINES
    fixed, owner's liability for, 584 *et seq.*
        procedure, 597
    imposition of, in excess of permitted maximum, 597

PENALTIES—*continued*
    imprisonment, *see* IMPRISONMENT
    suggested by Magistrates' Association, 594, 878 *et seq.*
PERMITTING—
    definition of, 35
    knowledge essential element, 37
    use contrary to Construction and Use Regulations, 412
    what constitutes, 41
PETROL TANK—
    Construction and Use Regulations, 424, 785, 831
PHOTOGRAPHS—
    evidence, as, 115
PLANS—
    evidence, as, 113–115
PLATE—
    Ministry of Transport, regulations relating to, 852 *et seq.*
    motor vehicle, for, particulars to be shown on, 855
PLEA—
    change of, 92
    guilty of, admissibility at subsequent trial of, 92
            by corporation, 73, 99
            by juvenile, 58, 99
            in writing, 58, 98, 99
                    disqualification after, 630
            on behalf of client, 73
POLICE—
    careless or dangerous driving by, 268
    constable, powers of, *see* CONSTABLE
    signal, failure to comply with, 304–306
        pedestrian failing to comply with, 314
        penalty for failing to comply with, 314
    vehicles, speed limit exemption, 338, 339
PRESS, *see* REPORTING
PRESUMPTION—
    conformity, of, traffic signs, 300
    notice of intended prosecution, as to, 132, 133
    user of vehicle, as to, 50, 120, 121, 585
PROBATION—
    disqualification for breach of, 646
            where defendant put on, 630
PROCEEDINGS—
    commencement of, 56–65
    committal, 81 *et seq.*
    Crown, against, 60–63
    hearing of charges together, 74–78
    irregularity in, 91, 92
    juveniles, against, 57, 58
    servicemen, against, 58, 59, 60, 61
    service of summons must be proved, 72
    venue for, 65–68
    who may commence, 56
PROOF—
    requirements as to, 120–126
PROSECUTION—
    appeal by, 697
    authority necessary for, 56, 57
    commencement of proceedings, 56 *et seq.*
    costs against, 599, 600
    notice of intended, *see* NOTICE OF INTENDED PROSECUTION
    re-opening of case by, 86 *et seq.*

PROSECUTION—*continued*
time limit for, 68–71
warning of possible, 133–135
PROTECTIVE HELMET—
defective, proceedings relating to, 78
regulations requiring wearing of, 349, 728
PUBLIC ACCESS—
relevance of, 27–29
PUBLIC ROAD, *see* ROAD
PUBLIC SERVICE VEHICLES—
adapted, 567
boarding between stops, 578
classification of, conditions affecting, 568
conduct on, 577 *et seq.*
conductor, duties of, 578, 579
contract carriage, definition, 567
driver, offences by, 579, 580
E.E.C. authorisation, 570
express carriages, road service licence, 574
fares, non-payment of, 578
foreign, 570
height of, regulations as to, 780
hire and reward, carrying passengers for, 567
hours of driving, 555 *et seq.*, 563
                    duty to keep record, 545
international journeys, 570
licence, requirement of, 567
offences, penalties for, 577, 579, 580
                    proceedings in respect of, 572–574
overseas visitors, parties of, 569
passengers, four or less, 568
                    inclusion of driver in number of, 570
road service licence, requirement as to, 567, 574
special occasion, use for, 576, 577
speed limit, 333
stage carriages, road service licence, 574
statutory provisions, 566–570
trailer may not be drawn by, 842

RACING—
death caused by vehicles, 260
RADAR SPEED METER—
evidence of reading from, 319, 320
REAR MARKINGS—
Construction and Use Regulations, 415
RECKLESS DRIVING, *see* DANGEROUS DRIVING
RECORD—
causing, to be kept, 35
criminal, evidence as to, 94–97
drivers' hours, of, *see* GOODS VEHICLES
manufacturers', as evidence, 111, 112
RECOVERY VEHICLE—
definition, 521, 525, 526
REFLECTORS—
regulations governing, 750, 794, 831
requirements as to, 404, 405, 406
REFRESHING MEMORY—
witnesses, 112, 113, 126, 319
REGISTRATION—
evidence by certificate as to, 107–111

REGISTRATION MARKS—
    exhibition of, 513, 514, 518
RE-OPENING—
    case, of, 86–88
                to impose disqualification, 629
REPORTING—
    restrictions on, 82
REVERSING—
    Construction and Use Regulations, 786
    motorway, on, 706, 707
ROAD, see also HIGHWAY
    Crown, 30, 31
    definition of, 26, 27, 31, 173
    dock, definition of, 30, 31
    dual-carriageway, meaning of, 437
    major, definition of, 711, 716
    markings, see TRAFFIC SIGNS
    minor, definition of, 711, 716
    private drive may be, 28, 29
    public, 31
                access, 27–29
    restricted, 321–324
                definition of, 838
    urban, 395
ROADSIDE TESTING—
    meaning of, 427 et seq.

SAFETY GLASS—
    requirement as to, 787
SCHOOL BUSES—
    licensing exemptions as to, 568
SCHOOL CROSSING PATROLS—
    children must be going to or from school, 459
    Crown servants ignoring, 61, 62
    duty to stop, absolute liability, 458
    penalties for failing to comply with, 460, 461
    regulations as to, 456–460
    signs to be used, 458
    traffic wardens as, 460
    uniform of, 458, 459
SEAT BELTS—
    Construction and Use Regulations, 782
    requirements as to, 423
SENTENCE, see also PENALTIES
    codes, 876
    committal for, 79
    deferment of, 598
                endorsable offence, 611
    entire, should be imposed on one occasion, 629
    imprisonment, of, see IMPRISONMENT
SEPARATE TRIALS—
    right to, 74 et seq.
SERVANT—
    driving motor vehicle, 367
SERVICEMEN—
    proceedings against, 58, 59, 60, 61, 265
SIGNAL—
    police, see POLICE
SILENCER—
    Construction and Use Regulations, 789, 832

SKETCHES—
    evidence, as, 114
SKIPS, *see* BUILDERS' SKIPS
SMOKE—
    emission of, 790
SOLDIER—
    abroad, offence committed by, 60, 61
SOLICITOR—
    plea of guilty by, on behalf of client, 73
SPECIAL REASONS—
    for imposing lesser period of disqualification, 668
    for not disqualifying, burden of proving, 665
                careless driving, 669, 670
                circumstances peculiar to offender are not, 664 *et seq.*
                Construction and Use Regulation offences, 684
                dangerous driving, 669, 670
                decisions as to, review of, 669
                drink or drug offences, 670 *et seq.*
                            ignorance of amount of alcohol,
                            675
                driving licence offences, 686
                            while disqualified, 686
                evidence must be called, 667
                failure to report accident, 681
                financial hardship as, 667
                good character as, 666, 667
                insurance offences, 681
                laced drinks, 675, 676
                medical or other emergency, 674, 675
                pedestrian crossing offences, 680
                refusing to supply specimen, 678
                school crossing offences, 680
                shortness of distance driven, 673
                speed limit offences, 680
                totting-up cases, 688 *et seq.*
                traffic sign offences, 680
                triviality of offence, 666, 670, 672
SPECIMEN—
    blood or urine, of, *see* DRINK OR DRUG OFFENCES
SPEECHES—
    order of, at committal proceedings, 82 *et seq.*
SPEEDING—
    dangerous, *see* DANGEROUS DRIVING; DANGEROUS SPEEDING
    notice of intended prosecution, 129, 130
SPEED LIMIT—
    articulated vehicle, 11, 336
    derestriction signs, absence of, 322
    dual-purpose vehicle, 335, 336
    exceeding, evidence of, 318–321
            four possible offences, 316
            opinion evidence that driver is, 321
            warning of intended prosecution, 317
    exemption from, 338, 339
    goods vehicles, 326, 333–335
    heavy locomotives, 327
    light locomotives, 327
    minimum, 324
    motor tractor, 327
    motorway, 336–338, 581
    offences, special reasons for not disqualifying, 680

SPEED LIMIT—*continued*
    passenger vehicles, 325, 326, 332, 333
    penalties for not observing, 324, 339, 340
    Port of London Authority area, 316
    radar speed meter, 319, 320
    restricted roads, 321 *et seq.*
    restriction signs, 323
            illumination of, 323
            necessity for, 322
    Royal Parks, in, 316
    signs, presence of, 321
    statutory provisions imposing, 317
    temporary order, defendant must show inapplicable, 319
            regulations imposing, 316, 317
            statutory instrument, 729
    track-laying vehicle, 327, 328
    trailers, 326, 329, 331, 336
    vascar, proof of speeding by use of, 320
    vehicles of certain classes, of, 324 *et seq.*
SPEEDOMETER—
    Construction and Use Regulations, 415, 785, 828
    evidence as to accuracy, 318
SPOUSE—
    witness, as, 115–117, 253
SPRINGS—
    requirements as to, 780
STAGE CARRIAGE, *see* PUBLIC SERVICE VEHICLES
STATEMENT—
    defendant, of, admissibility of, 117–120
    in presence of defendant, 117–120
STATUTE—
    interpretation of, 39
    taxation, interpretation of, 47
STEERING GEAR—
    Construction and Use Regulations, *see* CONSTRUCTION AND USE REGULATIONS
STOP LIGHTS, *see* LIGHTS ON VEHICLES
STOP SIGNS—
    major roads, at, 306
STREET LIGHTING—
    system of, makes road restricted, 321
SUBMISSIONS—
    no case to answer, 82 *et seq.*
            dangerous driving, 264
SUMMARY OFFENCES—
    committal of, to Crown Court, 636, 637
    limitation of time, 68, 69
    venue for trial of, 66–68
SUMMONS—
    amendment of, 88–91
    Construction and Use Regulations, under, 421
    contents of, 65
    death of justice does not effect, 69
    defect in, 88
            right to object to, 64, 65
    duplicity in, 91
    form of, 65
    further or alternative charge, for, may be waived, 64
    irregularity in, 65
    refusal to issue, 56

SUMMONS—*continued*
    right to, 64
    service of, 72, 73, 135, 136
                on Sunday, 138
    waiving, 64, 65, 90
    withdrawal of, does not bar subsequent proceedings, 92, 93
    witness, 101
SUNSET—
    definition of, 403
SUPERVISION ORDER—
    suspended sentence imposed, where, 597

TAKING CONVEYANCES, *see* CONVEYANCE
TAMPERING—
    motor vehicle, with, 363, 364
TAPE-RECORDING—
    evidence, as, 126
    use of, to refresh memory, 113, 126
TELEVISION SETS—
    Construction and Use Regulations, 849
TEST CERTIFICATE—
    penalty for not having, 429
    requirement of, 426
THREE WHEELED VEHICLE—
    excise duty on, 491
TIMETABLE—
    evidence, as, 111, 321
TOTTING-UP—
    absolute discharge, in case of, 628
    aiders and abettors, applies to, 627, 628
    circumstances justifying non-disqualification on, 688 *et seq.*
    compulsory disqualification, 624 *et seq.*
    consecutive disqualification in case of, 251, 623, 627, 631 *et seq.*
    date of offence not relevant, 625
                previous convictions, 625, 626
    driving while disqualified, 655
                        removal of disqualification, 657 *et seq.*
    endorsement ordered at Crown Court, 625
    further conviction following disqualification for, 628
    general requirements as to, 602, 624 *et seq.*
    period of disqualification, 624, 627, 629
    previous convictions, dates of, 625, 626
                        requirements as to, 624–626
    probation imposed, where, 628
    reasons for not disqualifying must be stated, 695
    traffic signs, failure to comply with, 316
    triviality of offences, 693
    vehicle used for criminal purposes, 602, 629, 642
TRACK-LAYING VEHICLE—
    speed limits, 327, 328
TRACTOR—
    industrial, definition of, 768
    land, definition of, 768
    motor, *see* MOTOR TRACTOR
TRADE LICENCE—
    business purpose, must be used for, 521
    carriage of goods, restriction on, 523
                passengers, restriction on, 524
    offences in connection with, penalties for, 527

TRADE LICENCE—*continued*
    recovery vehicles, *see* RECOVERY VEHICLE
    renewal of, 527
    restriction on use of, 521 *et seq.*
    statutory provisions, 519–525
TRADE PLATES, *see also* TRADE LICENCE
    employer's liability for illegal use of, 526
    restriction on use of, 521
TRAFFIC—
    state of, evidence as to, 275
TRAFFIC CENSUS, *see* CENSUS
TRAFFIC LIGHTS—
    dimensions of, 303, 720, 721
    disregard of, by emergency services, 301, 302
    general provisions as to, 301 *et seq.*
    penalties for failure to comply with, 314–316
    portable, 302, 722
    regulations, 301, 302, 303, 720 *et seq.*
    sequence of, 720
    significance of, 723
    stuck at red, 302
    vehicular traffic, for, 720
TRAFFIC SIGNS—
    application of, to vehicles other than motor vehicles, 299, 300
    authorisation of, 294, 709
    automatic level crossing, 309, 712
    cyclist, application to, 299, 300
    damaged, 313
    defendant failing to see, 300
    dimensions of, 710 *et seq.*
    disobeying, notice of intended prosecution, 129
    emergency, 310
    failure to comply with, 295
            conviction for careless or dangerous driving should
                bar proceedings for, 314
            defective vehicle, 301
            driving test may be ordered after, 316
    give way, 307, 311
    illumination of, 301, 713 *et seq.*
    intended prosecution, warning of, 300
    keep left signs and arrows, 307, 308
    meaning of, 296
    motorway, legal position, 298
    non-conforming, 313, 314
    no waiting, 298, 299, 393, 394
    one way traffic, 298
    penalties for failure to comply with, 314–316, 728
    person pushing pram or cycle, liability to obey, 299, 300
    placing of, 296, 297
    portable, 310
    prescribed size, colour and type, 710 *et seq.*
                deemed to be of, 295, 300
    presumption of conformity, 295, 300
    prohibition against right-hand turn, 298, 299
    regulations, 297, 709 *et seq.*
    road markings, 716 *et seq.*
    signs listed as, 297
    special reasons for not imposing disqualification, 680
    speed limit sign incorrectly painted, 314
    stop signs at major roads, 306, 307

TRAFFIC SIGNS—*continued*
 temporary, 297, 718
 white lines, provisions as to, 310 *et seq.*
 zebra crossings, at, 438, 442, 443
TRAFFIC SURVEY, *see also* CENSUS
 police constable's powers, 295, 296
TRAFFIC WARDEN—
 driving documents need not be produced to, 305
 ignoring direction of, 305
 school crossing patrol, as, 460
TRAILER—
 agricultural, definition of, 13, 51
 application of brakes of, 840
 articulated vehicle, as, 10–12
 attendants on, 13, 14, 421, 849
 braked, meaning of, 331
 braking system, requirement of, 329, 813
 Construction and Use Regulations, 421, 812 *et seq.*
 conveyance of passengers in, 842
 definition of, 9 *et seq.*, 497, 498
 distance between motor vehicle and, 841
 excise duty, 497, 498
 goods-carrying, definition of, 732
 gross weight, definition of, 852
 insurance of, 371, 372
 length of, 812
 load-carrying, meaning of, 328
 motor cycle may not draw, 12, 841
   vehicle as, 10
 motorway, use on, 581
 plate, requirements as to, 816
 public service vehicle may not draw, 842
 restriction on drawing a number of, 850
    use of vehicle to draw, 841
 speed limit, 336, 842
 tyres, requirements as to, 815
 vehicle towing number of, 13
 weight of, imposition of speed limit, 326, 329, 331
    maximum, 817, 820, 821, 826, 827
 width of, 812
 wings, requirements as to, 816
TRANSPORT MANAGER—
 liability of, 533, 534
 statutory provisions, 531–534
TRIAL—
 committal for, 78 *et seq.*
 Crown Court, at, *see* CROWN COURT
 election for, *see* ELECTION
 irregularity during, 91, 92
 jury, by, advantages of, 81
TROLLEY BUS—
 disqualification of driver, 637
TURNING TRAFFIC—
 prohibition against, 298, 299
TYRES—
 condition and maintenance of, 832
 diagonal-ply, definition of, 834
 pneumatic, definition of, 771
 radial-ply, definition of, 834

TYRES—*continued*
 requirements as to, 423, 424
 worn, knowingly driving vehicle with, 257

UNLOADING—
 no waiting area, in, 391
UNROADWORTHY—
 sale of vehicle which is, 424 *et seq.*
URINE—
 specimen of, *see* DRINK OR DRUG OFFENCES
USING MOTOR VEHICLE—
 abandoned car, in lay-by, 44
 absolute liability, 41, 49
 aiding and abetting, 46, 50
 company, liability of, 45
 defective brakes, with, 43
 employer's liability, 45 *et seq.*
 excise offences, 44, 45
 hired vehicle, 47
 hirer, position of, 43, 50
 improperly secured load, with, 42
 licence, without, 44
 loan of vehicle, 43, 44
 owner deemed to be, 50
 passenger, as, 47
 stationary vehicle, 44
 third party insurance, without, 41, 42, 44
 towed vehicle, 45

VEHICLE—
 adapted, 333, 334
 combination of, permitted length, 13
 constable's power to stop, 147
 crime, used for, 640
 dangerous condition, in, 418 *et seq.*
 defective, death resulting from knowingly driving, 257
 dual-purpose vehicle, meaning of, 328, 335
         speed limit, 335, 336
 foreign, 331, 332
 goods, *see* GOODS VEHICLES
 half-decked, definition of, 768
 inspection of, 115
 leaving unattended, 421
 lights on, *see* LIGHTS ON VEHICLES
 meaning of, 343
 passenger, *see* PASSENGER VEHICLES
 recovery, *see* RECOVERY VEHICLE
 removal and disposal of, 396, 397
 slow, obstruction by, 388, 389
 speed limits, 324 *et seq.*
 track-laying, *see* TRACK-LAYING VEHICLES
 unroadworthy, sale of, 424 *et seq.*
 wheeled, 768
VEHICLE EXCISE LICENCE, *see* EXCISE DUTY
VEHICLE OWNER—
 parking penalties, liability for, 584 *et seq.*
VEHICLE TESTER—
 definition, 520
VENUE—
 aiding and abetting offence, for, 66

VENUE—*continued*
excise duty offences, for hearing of, 489, 490
hybrid offences, for, 65, 66
proceedings, for, 65 *et seq.*
summary offences, 66–68
VERGE—
parking on, 395, 396
VIEW—
locus in quo, of, 124, 125

WARRANT—
limitations on issue of, 72
WEIGHT—
articulated vehicle, of, 822, 823, 824, 860
ascertainment of, 16–18
axle, definition of, 852
calculation of, 332
display of, 330, 331
distribution of, 826
excise duty, calculation for, 16
purposes, for, 515, 516
goods vehicles, of, speed limit imposed by, 326, 334
heavy motor car, of, 818
kerbside, 331, 332
definition of, 733, 828
locomotive, of, 817
distribution of, 797
loose equipment, of, 15, 16
marking of, 816
maximum gross, 332
definition, 828
permissible, schedule of, 860
motor car, of, 818
tractor, of, imposition of speed limit, 327, 329
vehicles, of, 14–21
plated, 18–21, 331
definition of, 825
prosecutions, defences to, 19–21
removable containers, of, 16
restrictions on plated vehicles, 853
ticket, evidence of, 111
trailer, of, 817, 820, 821, 826, 827
imposition of speed limit, 326, 329, 331
train, definition of, 852
transmitted to road surface, 16, 17
unladen, calculation of, 15
classification by, 15
proof may be required, 15
WHEEL—
definition of, 772
WHITE LINES—
disobedience of, careless driving, 311
double, provisions as to, 311–313
WIDE LOADS—
regulations applying to, 865
WIDTH—
overall, definition of, 769
WINDSCREEN WASHERS—
Construction and Use Regulations, 788

WINDSCREEN WIPERS—
    Construction and Use Regulations, 787, 831
WITNESS, *see also* EVIDENCE
    abroad, 105, 106
    attendance of, enforcing, 101
    child as, *see* CHILD
    dead, evidence of, 105
    failure to cross examine, 125
    inspection of vehicle by, *see* INSPECTION
    interviewing, 119
    presence of, in court, 126
    recall of, 124
    refreshing memory, 112, 113, 126, 319
    sick, evidence of, 103, 104
    spouse as, 115–117
    statements of, supply of, 119
    summons, application for, 101
WORKS VEHICLES—
    excise duty on, 492–494

ZEBRA CONTROLLED AREA—
    definition of, 437
    overtaking in, 454, 455
    regulations, 445
    stopping in, 453, 454
ZEBRA CROSSINGS—
    absolute liability of driver, 449–453
    definitions of, 437
    failure to accord precedence, defences to, 452
                                proceedings for other offences, 447
    give-way lines, 437, 438, 444
    globes, requirements as to, 443, 446
    limits of, 453
    marks and studs, 441, 442
    overtaking at, 439, 440, 454, 455
    pedestrians, precedence of, 439
    penalties for breach of regulations relating to, 455, 456
    precedence, duty to accord, 447 *et seq.*
    proof of conformity of, 445 *et seq.*
    regulations, 436–445
    stopping in areas adjacent to, 440, 453
    stripes, width and extent of, 442, 446
    studs, 437, 441, 442
    traffic signs at, 438, 442, 443
    uncontrolled, 438
    waiting on, prohibition against, 439